# Text and Materials on Housing Law

# OXFORD

## UNIVERSITY PRESS

Great Clarendon Street, Oxford, OX2 6DP

Oxford University Press is a department of the University of Oxford.
It furthers the University's objective of excellence in research, scholarship,
and education by publishing worldwide in

Oxford New York

Auckland Bangkok Buenos Aires Cape Town Chennai
Dar es Salaam Delhi Hong Kong Istanbul Karachi Kolkata
Kuala Lumpur Madrid Melbourne Mexico City Mumbai Nairobi
São Paulo Shanghai Taipei Tokyo Toronto

Oxford is a registered trade mark of Oxford University Press
in the UK and in certain other countries

Published in the United States
by Oxford University Press Inc., New York

© David Hughes, Martin Davis, Veronica Matthew and Alwyn Jones 2005

The moral rights of the author have been asserted

Database right Oxford University Press (maker)

First published 2005

British Library Cataloguing in Publication Data
Data available

Library of Congress Cataloging in Publication Data
Data available

ISBN 0 406 96651 6

1 3 5 7 9 10 8 6 4 2

Typeset in 10/12pt Times New Roman by Kerrypress Ltd, Luton, **www.kerrypress.co.uk**

Printed in Great Britain by Biddles Ltd, King's Lynn

# Text and Materials on Housing Law

**Professor David Hughes**

*Professor of Housing and Planning Law, De Montfort University, Leicester*

**Martin Davis**

*Principal Lecturer in Law, De Montfort University, Leicester*

**Veronica Matthew**

*Principal Lecturer in Law, De Montfort University, Leicester*

**Alwyn Jones**

*Lecturer in Law, De Montfort University, Leicester*

OXFORD
UNIVERSITY PRESS

# Contents

# Acknowledgments

The authors of this work gratefully acknowledge the co-operation of the following publishers in allowing publication of portions of their copyright material.

Crown Copyright is reproduced with the permission of the Controller of Her Majesty's Stationery Office (Crown copyright acknowledged); the Incorporated Council of Law Reporting for England and Wales for extracts from the Law Reports; International Thomson Publishing Services Limited (Sweet & Maxwell) for extracts from the Housing Law Reports and Property and Compensation Law Reports; the Office of Fair Trading for extracts from OFT Bulletin 356.

We also wish to place on record our most grateful thanks to those who have assisted in the task of typing this work: Barbara Goodman, Sheila Brammall and Anne Aarseth.

# Foreword

An earlier version of this book appeared in 2000 under the Blackstone Press imprint. We are grateful to our publishers for having the confidence in us to commission what, we believe, should be regarded as a new work, having only some resemblances to its predecessor. There are, for example, entirely new chapters on housing and human rights (an issue only in its infancy four years ago but now, as will become apparent, a topic of fierce judicial disagreement), on housing procedures, and on the issue of bad practices by landlords. This latter extends not only to harassment and illegal eviction but also to the rapidly burgeoning topic of the impact of fair trading and consumer protection laws on the relationships between landlord and tenant.

The march of legislation, both actual and proposed, has also led to major revisions of our previous work. We have had to respond to initiatives in housing policy from both central government and the Law Commission. In addition, since 2000 Parliament has passed the Homelessness Act 2002 and the Anti-Social Behaviour Act 2003, both of which have major implications for the practices of all social landlords. Currently there are also before Parliament the Civil Partnership Bill 2004, and the Housing Bill initially introduced into Parliament in 2003. Both of these require comment both here and in the main body of this book. The Civil Partnership Bill will bring about radical alterations in the rights and status of those who live in homosexual and lesbian relationships, provided they are willing and able to register their relationships. Some, however, might have wished for a more revolutionary reform whereby the interests and entitlements of heterosexual cohabitants might also have been addressed by the legislation. It is surely more than arguable that the historic marriage discipline whereby society has made a fundamental distinction between those who are married and all others no longer reflects how individuals conduct their lives. Even so, the Civil Partnership Bill is to be welcomed as a civilising and liberalising measure. The Housing Bill is likewise a radical measure in many ways, containing as it does major provisions on, inter alia, housing repairs, licensing of lettings, houses in multiple occupation and the right to buy. This latter topic we touch on very briefly as the right to buy is in reality a right *to cease* to be a tenant. However, the other issues we have dwelt on at some length in the following chapters. The task has not, however, been an easy one as the Housing Bill has grown substantially on its passage through Parliament – a not uncommon event with housing legislation – and was still not on the statute book at the time of submission of our manuscript, in July 2004. This is particularly apparent in **Chapters 12 and 13**, where we have had to give accounts of both the existing and the proposed law. In writing those chapters we have decided that there should be much more by way of 'text' and much less by way of 'materials' as a way of dealing with the law at a time of considerable change and flux. Similarly **Chapters 1 and 2** are primarily textually based, as they did not lend themselves to the reproduction of statutory or judicial material. Elsewhere, however, we have attempted to strike a balance between our own words and those of Parliament and the courts.

Mention of the courts prompts acknowledgment that it is not only Westminster and Whitehall that have been active in modifying our law of housing: there has been a considerable judicial input also, not least with regard to human rights issues. That input continues on a regular basis, and since the submission of the manuscript of this book there are two cases requiring some comment at length.

I

### *Ghaidan v Godin Mendoza* [2004] UKHL 30 [2004] 3 All ER 411

The defendant shared a flat with his same-sex partner from 1972 until that partner's death. That partner had been a Rent Act protected tenant of the flat in which he lived in a stable relationship with the defendant. On the death of the tenant a question arose as to the succession rights of the defendant. Under the decision in *Fitzpatrick v Sterling Housing Association* [1999] 4 All ER 705 he was entitled to succeed to an assured tenancy under para 3(1) of Sch 1 to the Rent Act 1977 (as amended) because he was considered to be a member of the original tenant's 'family'. The issue was, however, whether that was compatible with the defendant's Convention Rights under the Human Rights Act 1998. A number of questions had to be addressed:

- Was the previous interpretation of the law, that persons in same-sex relationships could not succeed to a statutory tenancy as surviving spouses, incompatible with Convention Rights under Arts 8 and 14 of the European Convention on Human Rights?

- If so, was it possible to interpret the 1977 Act in such a way as to render the relevant provision compatible?

- The Court of Appeal (as considered at length in **Chapter 14**) answered 'yes' to both these questions. The House of Lords, despite a strong dissent from Lord Millett who considered that the exercise undertaken by the House transgressed the boundary between interpretation and creativity, affirmed the Court of Appeal's decision.

Lord Nicholls in his judgment pointed out that the defendant's argument was that his right to respect for his home, under Art 8 of the convention, when read together with Art 14 (the prohibition on discrimination with regard to the enjoyment of other Convention Rights) was infringed if he was not allowed to succeed to the tenancy of his deceased partner in the same way and on the same terms as if their union had been one of marriage. In other words the argument was that his rights were being downgraded on the basis of sexual orientation. Lord Nicholls pointed out that it is accepted nowadays that certain distinctions between people do not justify differences in their legal treatment. He identified differences of race, sex, religion and sexual orientation in this context, and relied on the arguments of the European Court of Human Rights in *Fretté v France* [2003] 2 FLR 9, 23:

> 'Unless good reason exists, differences in legal treatment based on grounds such as these are properly stigmatised as discriminatory.'

His Lordship was clearly therefore convinced that both Arts 8 and 14 were engaged in the instant case, though preferring to leave open the issue of the point at which Art 14 comes into play when another Convention right is infringed. Some commentators have argued that even a highly tenuous link is enough, but Lord Nicholls gave no concluded opinion on that point.

Given that he found there was discrimination against the defendant, could Lord Nicholls find justification for that discrimination? It was argued that the legislation had made a historic distinction between heterosexual and same-sex unions in order to provide protection for the 'traditional' family. However, as Lord Nicholls pointed out the traditional concept of the family had been blurred over a long period with both courts and Parliament extending protection under the Rent Act 1977 to heterosexual cohabitants as well as to married couples.

> 'The line drawn by Parliament is no longer drawn by reference to the status of marriage. Nor is parenthood, or the presence of children in the home, a pre condition of security of tenure for the survivor of the original tenant. Nor is procreative potential a prerequisite. The survivor is protected even if, by reason of age or otherwise, there was never any prospect of either member of the couple having a natural child.'

Lord Nicholls could find no reason why the legal protection conferred on a heterosexual couple could not also extend to a same-sex couple who 'share their lives and make their home together'. Lord Nicholls acknowledged that in the area of national housing policy,

> 'Parliament has to hold a fair balance between the competing interests of tenants and landlords, taking into account broad issues of social and economic policy. But, even in such a field, where the alleged violation comprises differential treatment based on grounds such as race or sex or sexual orientation the court will scrutinise with intensity any reasons said to contribute justification. The reasons must be cogent if such differential treatment is to be justified.'

He would find no national housing policy in the Rent Act 1977 nor the amending statute the Housing Act 1988 which could justify treating cohabiting heterosexual couples differently from those in same-sex unions.

Having thus determined that the defendant had been subjected to unjustifiable discrimination, Lord Nicholls proceeded to the issue of whether it was possible to interpret the legislation in such a way as to make it compatible with

Convention Rights. He pointed out that under s 3 of the Human Rights Act 1998 it is the intention of Parliament that all legislation is to be read and given effect so as to be compatible with Convention Rights 'so far as it is possible to do so'. However, he asked, what does 'possible' mean here? It certainly includes resolving ambiguities, so that if a phrase can have two means the compatible one is to be chosen, but does the process go further than that? Lord Nicholls pointed to cases such as *R v A (No 2)* [2001] UKHL 25, [2002] 1 AC 45 as an example of a case which had certainly not involved an ambiguity. He argued:

> 'Section 3 [of the Human Rights Act 1998] may require the court to depart from ... the intention of Parliament ... The question of difficulty is how far, and in what circumstances, Section 3 requires a court to depart from the intention of the enacting Parliament.'

He proceeded to argue that s 3 enables language to be interpreted restrictively or expansively:

> 'But Section 3 goes further than this. It is also apt to require a court to read in words which change the meaning of enacted legislation so as to make it Convention-compliant.'

The limit to this power is that s 3 does not allow a meaning inconsistent with the fundamental features of the legislation in question, in other words 'the meaning imported by application of s 3 must be compatible with the underlying thrust of the legislation construed'. In the instant case, Lord Nicholls concluded, the legislation would be effectively reworded to make it compatible but not in a way which conflicted with the underlying purpose of Parliament which was to confer security of tenure on certain people.

Lord Steyn agreeing with Lord Nicholls argued:

> 'If the core remedial purpose of section 3(1) [of the 1998 Act] is not to be undermined a broader approach [than the purely literal and technical] is required. That is, of course, not to gainsay the obvious proposition that inherent in the use of the word "possible" ... is the idea that there is a Rubicon which courts may not cross. If it is not possible, within the meaning of Section 3, to reach or give effect to legislation in a way which is compatible with Convention rights, the only alternative is to exercise, where appropriate, the power to make a declaration of incompatibility. Usually, such cases should not be too difficult to identify.'

On that basis Lord Steyn felt happy to read the provisions of Sch 1 to the Rent Act 1977 'as his or her wife or husband' as '*as if they were* his wife or husband', and this gave the defendant the ability to succeed as a statutory tenant to his deceased partner's home.

Lord Rodger was also concerned to explore the limit of the courts' interpretive powers. He pointed out that the obligation on the court is twofold, it is 'to read' and 'to give effect to'. These are complementary but distinct obligations. In other words, interpretation is only part of the task of the court which, as a public authority, must ensure that legislation is given effect in those ways which are compatible with Convention rights. There are, as Lord Rodger conceded, limits to this obligation, such as where the clear and unavoidable words of Parliament impose a duty to act in a particular way. However, the key to understanding that limit is to realise that they are cases where the entire substance of the provision is incompatible with the Convention: 'The only cure [there] is to change the provision and that is a matter for Parliament and not for the courts'. Thus s 3 of the 1998 Act does not allow a court to change the substance of a legislative provision completely, eg so as to say something must happen when Parliament has said it must not. The courts are also not to turn legislative schemes inside out, they must not by interpretation create something entirely different from what Parliament has provided. Neither can they negative explicit powers given to Ministers by Parliament. In addition courts must be wary not to cross the boundary line between interpretation and amendment where the result may have important practical repercussions a court may not be equipped to evaluate. In short it is not possible for the process of interpretation to allow a court to do anything inconsistent with the cardinal principles of legislation, for example by introducing something into an Act which was not there in some way before. However, Lord Rodger then went on to say:

> 'this is not to say that, where a provision can be read compatibly with the Convention without contradicting any principle that it enshrines or the principles of the legislation as a whole, such an interpretation is not possible simply because it may involve reading into the provision words which go further than the specific words used by [Parliament]. … the key to what is possible for the courts to imply into legislation without crossing the border from interpretation to amendment does not lie in the number of words that have to be read in. The key lies in a careful consideration of the essential principles and scope of the legislation being interpreted. If the insertion of one word contradicts those principles or goes beyond the scope of the legislation it amounts to impermissible amendment. On the other hand, if the implication of a dozen words leaves the essential principles and scope of the legislation intact but allows it to be read in a way which is compatible with Convention rights, the implication is a legitimate exercise of the powers conferred [by the 1998 Act].'

For those familiar with Gilbert and Sullivan's *Iolanthe,* Lord Rodger's allusion is clear. In that Savoy opera the Fairy Law provides that it is death for a fairy to marry a mortal. By the end of the opera *all* the fairies have married members of the House of Lords, so all have incurred death. The Lord Chancellor neatly solves the problem by inserting a single word: it is death for a fairy *not* to marry a mortal. Such a stroke of Gilbertian logic is not possible under s 3 of the Human Rights Act 1998.

Baroness Hale, agreeing with Lords Nicholls, Steyn and Rodger, based her judgment on the arguments that the law should not reflect stereotypical assumptions about a person, and should not be swayed by irrelevant character-istics of a person, such as race or sex, which the person in question did not choose and could do nothing about. She argued also that the principle of equal treatment is essential in a democratic society, for democracy is based on the principle that each individual has equal value: 'If distinctions are to be drawn, particularly on a group basis, it is an important discipline to look for a rational basis for those distinctions.'

Baroness Hale then pointed to the '*Michalak* questions' ([2003] 1 WLR 617) as useful tools of analysis in cases where alleged discrimination in regard to Convention rights has occurred:

- '• Do the facts fall within the ambit of one or more of the Convention rights?
- • Was there a difference in treatment in respect of that right between the complainant and others put forward for comparison?
- • Were those others in an analogous situation?
- • Was the difference in treatment objectively justifiable? ie did it have a legitimate aim and bear a reasonable relationship of proportionality to that aim?'

She then added a further question: is the difference in treatment based on one or more of the grounds expressly or impliedly prescribed by Art 14?

These questions are not, of course, to be treated as a rigid formula, but they remain as useful means of analysis.

While, Baroness Hale argued, it may be legitimate for a legislature to make laws which have as their object the protection of 'the traditional family', that argument could not apply in the instant case, for Parliament had not restricted protection under the Rent Act 1977 solely to spouses. Protection had been extended to stable heterosexual cohabitation relationships. On that basis she could see no reason why protection should not also extend to equivalent same-sex unions.

> 'What matters most is the essential quality of the relationship, its marriage-like intimacy, stability, and social and financial interdependence. Homosexual relationships can have exactly the same qualities of intimacy, stability and inter-dependence that heterosexual relationships do.'

Furthermore Baroness Hale argued a 'traditional family' is not protected by being granted benefits which are denied to those who cannot or will not become 'traditional'. Had Parliament intended to encourage marriage by means of the Rent Act 1977, she argued, it would surely have stopped short of granting protection to those in cohabiting heterosexual relationships.

There is much powerful language and much exquisite argument in this decision. It is one that clearly shows the House of Lords testing the limits of its powers under s 3 of the 1998 Act. That is particularly apparent in the judgment of Lord Rodger which may well come to be seen as a landmark in laying down guidelines and limits as to what can and cannot be done. However, let it also be remembered that the decision is one that can only affect a very limited number of people who have rights under the 1977 Act. The vast majority of tenants have rights – such as they are – under the Housing Acts of 1985 and 1988 as amended, and for them at the time of writing it is not possible to treat a same-sex union as one equivalent to that of a heterosexual couple.

Under the Civil Partnerships Bill that will change, but even then the question remains why should the law be concerned only with those whose relationship is of a sexual, or apparently sexual, nature? There may be many reasons why people form some sort of stable and lasting relationship in which there is no sexual element, for example as friends or carers, or simply as companions irrespective of any age difference between them. Where such a stable relationship lasts, and it is important to remember that in *Ghaidan v Godin-Mendoza* Baroness Hale, at least, laid great stress on the stability aspect of a relationship, why should it not result in property rights for its members?

## II

### Manchester City Council v Romano, Manchester City Council v Samari [2004] EWCA Civ 834, [2004] All ER (D) 349 (Jun)

This is an important decision on the interface between housing and disability discrimination legislation. Section 22 of the Disability Discrimination Act 1995 Provides, inter alia, that

> 'it is unlawful for a person managing any premises to discriminate against a disabled person occupying those premises ... by evicting the disabled person or subjecting him to any other detriment.'

Section 24 of the Act provides:

> 'a person (A) discriminates against a disabled person if—
>
> (a)  for a reason which relates to the disabled person's disability, he treats him less favourably than he treats or would treat others to whom that reason does not or would not apply; and
>
> (b)  he cannot show that the treatment in question is justified ...
>
> For the purposes of this section, treatment is justified only if—
>
> (a)  in A's opinion one or more of the conditions [mentioned below] are satisfied, and
>
> (b)  it is reasonable in all the circumstances of the case for him to hold that opinion ...
>
> The conditions are that—
>
> (a)  in any case, the treatment is necessary in order not to endanger the health or safety of any person (which may include that of the disabled person) ...'

Both defendants were secure tenants of Manchester City Council. The Council sought possession against them under the 'nuisance' grounds of Sch 2 to the Housing Act 1985. In each case there was evidence of the defendants' mental state and of the nuisance they were causing to their neighbours' detriment. Both defendants appealed against the possession orders granted to the Council.

Brooke LJ began by reviewing the evidence of nuisance. In the case of Romano this included an alleged assault on a neighbour occasioning actual bodily harm following the throwing of a brick. There were an alleged 60 incidents of anti-social behaviour recorded on the part of both Ms Romano and her son, including the playing of loud music at inappropriate times, foul and abusive language, rowdy and abusive behaviour by visitors and loud noise during the early hours as a result of 'DIY' activity. There was also a history of rent arrears. There was evidence from Ms Romano's GP that Ms Romano might have outbursts which she could not clearly recall and that she might be unable to deliver on promises to amend her behaviour.

In Ms Samari's case there were allegations of nuisance and annoyance and harassment of neighbours. A next-door neighbour claimed to have become suicidal as a result of the conduct of Ms Samari and her children, and it was found that Ms Samari had been abusive and threatening in conduct and language to her neighbours and their children.

Brooke LJ then reviewed the law which made it clear that in deciding whether the making of a possession order is 'reasonable', account must be take of any mental disorders from which the defendant is suffering, see *Croydon London Borough Council v Moody* (1998) 31 HLR 738. However, this has to be balanced against the obligations a landlord has to its other tenants, see Woking *Borough Council v Bistram* (1993) 27 HLR 1. What then is the effect of the Disability Discrimination Act on these principles? This was a matter which had come before the High Court in *North Devon Houses Ltd v Brazier* [2003] EWHC 574, [2003] HLR 59 (p 905). Brooke LJ pointed out, however, that that case was markedly different from the present cases. The tenant there had engaged in allegedly anti-social behaviour, but this arose because she was suffering from paranoid psychosis. That case turned upon the failure of the landlord to show justification for seeking to evict Ms Brazier. There was no evidence of any actual physical risk to a neighbour.

Brooke LJ then proceeded to consider the scheme of the 1995 Act. Disability, he pointed out, can include physical or mental impairments which have a substantial and long-term adverse effect on a person's ability to carry out normal day-to-day activities. 'Mental impairment' includes impairments result- ing from or consisting of mental illnesses but only where those illnesses are clinically recognised. Regulations made under the 1995 Act have laid down that certain conditions are *not* to be regarded as 'impairments'; these are: a tendency to set fires; a tendency to steal; a tendency to the physical or sexual abuse of others; exhibitionism and voyeurism. Similarly alcoholism and drug depend- ency are generally excluded from the definition of impairment. Impairments must also satisfy a 'long-term' test; in general this means that an impairment must have a duration of 12 months, and furthermore the impairment must be one affecting 'day-to-day' the memory or an ability to concentrate, learn or understand, or the perception of the risk of physical danger. It was accepted that these 'impairments' were relevant to the instant case. Guidance issued under the 1995 Act points out, inter alia, that

> 'Account should be taken of the person's ability to remember, organise his/her thoughts, plan a course of action and carry it out, take in new knowledge, or understand spoken or written instructions.'

The Guidance also counsels that a person suffering from a mental impairment may underestimate dangers to others, for example as a result of neglecting basic functions such as eating, drinking, sleeping, keeping warm, personal hygiene, or reckless behaviour which puts another person at risk. This guidance has to be taken into account in relevant cases by a court under s 53A of the 1995 Act.

Having reviewed the general background of the 1995 Act and its application in employment cases, Brooke LJ then turned to the specific provisions relating to accommodation. It was accepted on both sides that by seeking possession orders, the local authority could be caught by the provision which forbids discrimination against a disabled person by evicting him/her or subjecting the person to some other detriment. With regard to the provision of accommodation Brooke LJ turned once more to the statutory guidance issued under the 1995 Act which points out that 'disabilities' may not be apparent, but which goes on to state that the prohibition on discrimination

> 'does not prevent the eviction of a disabled tenant where the law allows it, for example where he or she is in arrears of rent or has breached other terms of the tenancy, and where the reason for the eviction is not related to disability.'

Brooke LJ commented:

> 'if the landlord wishes to obtain possession for a breach of tenancy agreement that has been committed for reasons relating to a disabled tenant's disability, he will have to show that his action is justified on one of the grounds identified [in the 1995 Act].'

The issue thus became one of the justifiability of the local authority's opinion and action. There was a twofold test: (a) did the authority actually hold the belief that eviction was necessary in order not to endanger the health and safety of neighbours, and (b) was it reasonable for the authority to hold that opinion? In relation to this test the statutory guidance indicates landlords need to take into account all relevant circumstances, including any information which is available, any advice it would be reasonable to seek *and* the opinion of the disabled person in question. It is stressed that the lawfulness of the landlord's actions will be judged by what the landlord knew or reasonably should have known, and why it acted as it did at the time of the alleged discriminatory action. This, Brooke LJ argued, adopting arguments in the Scottish case of *Rose v Bouchet* [1999] IRLR 463, means:

- There must be an objective assessment of all relevant circumstances.
- What is 'relevant' will not mean everything which might come out in the course of litigation, but it will extend to what might emerge in a proper dialogue with the disabled person.
- The landlord's actions must be tested on the basis of the facts reasonably known (or as they should have been known) at the time of the action complained of.
- It may vary from case to case whether or not a more extended investigation is needed to determine more facts.

Brooke LJ then went on to argue that where the justifiability of a landlord's actions is called into question on the basis of an alleged infringement of the 1995 Act, the issue should be raised as one in which the reasonableness of making a possession order is questioned. In this Brooke LJ may have been making an implicit allusion to the decision of David Steel J in *North Devon Homes Ltd v Brazier* in which he said that where an 'eviction' is not justified under the terms of the 1995 Act and is thus unlawful, that is a 'highly relevant consideration in the exercise of the discretion' under the Housing Acts 1985 and 1988 to grant possession. This seems to suggest that there *might* be a case in which, despite unlawfulness under the 1995 Act, a court could grant possession under the Acts of 1985 and 1988. Brooke LJ then went on to examine the complex and difficult relationship between the Housing Acts and the Disability Discrimination Act. The latter had not specifically amended the former, hence it had to be accepted that Parliament had intended the general scheme of possessory powers to remain in place subject only to some modification to accommodate the 1995 Act. However, he argued, following the Brazier case alluded to earlier, the courts could be faced with a multiplicity of actions in which all sorts of disability defences could be envisaged in possession actions – for example that the reason for rent arrears was a tenant's inability to manage finances consequent on some form of mental incapacity.

In an attempt to head off too much litigation Brooke LJ argued:

> 'All that the 1995 Act has done is to state that if an tenant is disabled and the reason why the landlord is seeking possession relates to the tenant's disability, then the landlord must believe that he is justified in taking this action on section 24(3) grounds and his justification can arise if the landlord reasonably believes that a failure to act will result in danger to someone's health or safety.'

In this context Brooke LJ adopted the World Health Organisation definition of 'health' as a state of complete physical, mental and social wellbeing. Thus impairment of sleep, disturbance of peace, deprivation of rest, subjection to stress may all amount to endangering health. Furthermore, Brooke LJ opined, the Human Rights Act 1998 is relevant in that endangering a person's health may well amount to an infringement of their Convention Rights under Art 8 of the European Convention on Human Rights, see *Hatton v United Kingdom* (2003) 37 EHRR 28 and *Ashworth v United Kingdom* (*Application No 39561/98*) (20 January 2004, unreported). In these circumstances the court's powers under s 3 of the 1998 Act would require the court to interpret the 1995 Act as follows:

> '• Did the landlord hold the opinion that it was necessary to serve a notice seeking possession and/or to bring possession proceedings in order that the health of A (an identified person or persons) would not be put at risk?
> • Was that opinion objectively justified?'

Applying those tests to the facts before him, Brooke LJ examined the medical history first of Ms Romano and read the evidence of a Dr Bhatt who had treated Ms Romano that she was suffering from a recurrent depressive disorder 'recognised by the ICD 10 and DSM IV classification of mental disease'. This disorder apparently affected normal day-to-day activities and produced irritability of mood and paranoid ideation which led to a misreading of other people's intentions and to hostile and anti-social behaviour. However, it further appeared that while her mental condition might go some way to explain some of her behaviour, it could not explain all of it, for example playing loud music or indulging in 'DIY' activities. Nor could it explain the anti-social acts of her sons who lived with her. The authority had further obtained its own report on Ms Romano from a consultant psychiatrist which again concluded that Ms Romano's condition could not explain all her anti-social activities, nor the activities of her sons and her friends. However, because of certain procedural issues in the case neither of the medical experts had been invited specifically to comment on the issues raised by the 1995 Act. Even so, Brooke LJ considered that the making of a possession order could be justified because there was ample evidence from one of Ms Romano's neighbours that his health (as widely interpreted) had been endangered. It would thus be objectively reasonable under the 1998 Act for the local authority to seek possession.

In the case of Ms Samari there was medical evidence that she suffered from a borderline personality disorder. It appeared from the evidence of a consultant psychiatrist who treated her initially suggested that her aggressive behaviour 'pertained more to her underlying personality problems than to mental illness per se'. However, a subsequent report from the same consultant stated that Ms Samari was suffering from a mental impairment which had a substantial and long-term effect on her ability to carry out normal day to day activities within the meaning of the 1995 Act. It appeared Ms Samari was unable to learn how to cope with stressful situations and to react accordingly. However, Brooke LJ stressed even though that may be the conclusion of the expert reports, it is still for the court to determine the attribution of legal consequences to activities, and furthermore the interests of persons other than the tenant have to be taken into account. There was ample evidence that the health of Ms Samari's neighbours had been endangered, and indeed one of them had been forced to take anti-depressive medication herself. Brooke LJ concluded the evidence objectively supported the reasonableness of the authority's possession proceedings and of the county count in granting a possession order.

Brooke LJ then went on to make other general observations.

- What is the impact of s 218A of the Housing Act 1996 (as inserted by the Anti-social Behaviour Act 2003) on the Disability Discrimination Act 1995, bearing in mind that it requires all social landlords to have a policy on and procedures to deal with anti-social behaviour? He pointed out:

  'difficulties might arise from the fact that if a landlord obtains an injunction restraining a mentally disabled tenant from anti-social behaviour it will not be able to enforce that injunction by committal proceedings unless it can establish to the criminal standard of proof that it held an opinion on one of the matters specified in section 24(3) of the [1995] Act, and that it was reasonable in all the circumstances of the case for it to hold that opinion.'

In other words there has to be an element of danger to the health of a person before proceedings will be possible.

- What of cases where there is no such danger to health? Brooke LJ gave the following warning:

  > 'if complaints by a former council tenant of robust temperaments who has bought his property under the "right-to-buy" scheme have induced the local housing authority to seek and obtain an injunction against his neighbour in the council house next door restraining his anti-social behaviour, the council as the person managing the tenant's premises may not subsequently embark on enforcement proceedings unless it can establish statutory justification to the requisite standard of proof. In other words the owner-occupier whose health or safety is not endangered by his next door neighbour's breach of a court order will have to watch the value of his property deteriorating because the injunction cannot in those circumstances be enforced by his neighbour's landlord through the court.'

In the instant case the anti-social behaviour was directed against *next door neighbours* who were prepared to give convincing testimony of the impairment their health had undergone, but what of cases where a next door neighbour may be too frightened to give such evidence, or of those cases where a tenant's anti-social behaviour affects a wider area but only to the level of annoyance amongst those who suffer it? It must be doubtful in cases such as these whether a landlord would meet the requirements of the 1995 Act before taking action by way of possession proceedings or an application for an injunction. In this context it should be remembered that the 1995 Act outlaws 'discriminatory eviction'. An injunction which forbade a person the use of his/her home could thus amount to an eviction, even though it is not a possessory action.

What then is the current position?

- It is unlawful for a landlord to discriminate against a disabled person by evicting that person for a reason which related to that person's disability unless that action can be shown to be justified.

- This prohibition relates not only to those who suffer from physical impairments, but also those who suffer from mental disabilities, though in each case the impairment must be substantial and have long term adverse effects on the sufferer's ability to carry out day-to-day activities.

- In the context of mental disabilities only clinically recognised illnesses count as impairments, and certain pathological conditions such as tendencies to set fires or to steal, physical and sexual abuse of others, exhibitionism and voyeurism are excluded from the definition of 'impairment'.

- Where a landlord encounters a tenant whose behaviour is causing problems it will be necessary to inquire whether the tenant *is or might be mentally impaired*, for ignorance of the tenant's mental condition will not avail the landlord in subsequent proceedings, as Brooke LJ was at pains to point out.

- This inquiry must take place before possessory or injunctive proceedings are commenced. This may well require early consultation with Health and Social Service Authorities.

- It would appear that sending a warning letter to a tenant whose behaviour is causing problems is not within the prohibitions imposed by the 1995 Act.

- However, any action of a possessory nature and some of an injunctive nature would require the landlord to show that in good faith it held the reasonable and objectively justified opinion that such action is necessary in order to prevent the health or safety of a person from being at risk.

- 'Health' in this context is quite widely interpreted and would extend to fears a person had for his or her safety, but would not cover merely trivial risks to health, for example annoyance or, perhaps, an occasional headache.

- Landlords may well require the assistance of experts to ensure they come to the appropriate opinion, and that, of course, will involve expense.

- It will be, however, for the court determine on the basis of all the evidence whether a landlord's opinion was both reasonable and appropriate, and the Court of Appeal will be generally unwilling to interfere with a county court decision on such a matter, nor to require a county court judge to adhere to the opinion of one medical expert as against that of another. In this context it must be remembered there may be conflicts of expert evidence as to both the question whether the tenant is labouring under a mental impairment, *and* whether that impairment was the cause of the behaviour in question. Where a person is disabled within the terms of the 1995 Act as a result of mental impairment but that disability did not cause the behaviour in respect of which possession is sought, a possession order may be granted. See *Servite House v Perry* (March 2004, as yet unreported) where a person suffered from temporal lobe epilepsy which gave rise to complex seizures, and who took anti-convulsant medicine, but whose acts of harassment, nuisance and annoyance were not attributable to her condition.

- Much will depend on the nature of the risks to which a person's neighbours are being put before action can be taken against that person. The timing, nature and duration of anti-social incidents will have to be carefully considered as must the degree of severity of affliction of the health of others and the likely progress of that affliction. This may be particularly relevant where a landlord wishes to take early action against an anti-social tenant.

Mental illness and mental disability – the two should not be confused – afflict many in our society. It is argued by some commentators that as many as one in four people suffers from some form of mental illness during their lives, and for some that illness may be prolonged. Mental disability on the other hand may be a severe life-long affliction for a person. Government policy has for many years been based on the notion that those who labour under mental illness or mental disabilities should wherever possible take their proper place in the community and should not be excluded. The consequences of that for providers of social accommodation are considerable as many of those who have some form of mental impairment may well be unable to buy their own homes. Striking an acceptable balance between the protection of the interests of those with mental impairments and those of their neighbours is not an easy task. The state of the current law which has grown piecemeal over the years with little apparent thought being given to connection and consequences does not help, and Brooke LJ's invitation to Parliament to reconsider the 1995 Act and the regulations and guidance issued under it must be applauded and supported. Even so until such a review comes about – if ever – landlords may well find it prudent to assess the mental state of any tenant who appears to be the cause or source of anti-social activity at the outset of considering an appropriate course of remedial action. Somewhat ominously, as Brooke LJ opined, such an exercise may also be necessary where the tenant's activities consist of non-payment of rent or breach of some other tenancy obligation. Dario Fo's well known play, 'Can't Pay, Won't Pay' (a phrase which has entered general circulation) might well become 'can't pay because my mental state is such that I don't know how to pay'.

## III

### The interrelationship of Possession Proceedings, Injunctions, Demoted Tenancies and Anti-social Behaviour Orders[1]

The new injunctive powers available to landlords (both local authorities and registered social landlords) under ss 153A–D of the Housing Act 1996, as inserted by the Anti-social Behaviour Act 2003, are being generally welcomed, as are the provisions enabling courts to make orders demoting assured tenancies granted by registered social landlords to 'demoted assured shorthold tenancies' and local authority secure tenancies to 'demoted tenancies'. However, there are points of distinction between the powers available. The package of changes introduced under the 2003 Act in many ways enables the county court to be seen as a 'one stop shop' in relation to housing matters in that possession, injunction, and demotion proceedings may be taken there, as, of course, in effect, may Anti-social Behaviour Order proceedings once other relevant proceedings are before the court. Even so there may be points of distinction between procedures which should be borne in mind. Thus a demotion order can only be made where it is reasonable to do so, and the tenant or a person residing in or visiting the dwelling house has engaged or threatened to engage in conduct amounting to anti-social behaviour, or where there is use of the premises for an unlawful purpose. These are the same conditions for the award of an injunction in respect of anti-social behaviour under s 153A etc of the Housing Act 1996. While, however, it is contemplated that a demotion order may be sought as an alternative to a possession proceedings for acts of nuisance or annoyance, it appears that there may be procedural problems. The basis for a demotion order is an act of anti-social behaviour or unlawful use of premises as defined in s 153A of the 1996 Act. This in not precisely the same wording as that in the Housing Acts 1985 and 1988 relating to the grounds for seeking possession in respect of *nuisance or annoyance* to persons residing, visiting or otherwise engaging in lawful activities in the locality, or using premises for *immoral or illegal purposes*. 'Anti-social behaviour' under s 153A is more widely defined than it is in the 1985 and 1988 Acts, while the 'unlawful' use of premises is rather narrower than immoral or

---

[1]    Indebtedness is gratefully acknowledged to Gail Sykes of Greenwoods Solicitors LLP who raised and elucidated these issues at a presentation at De Montfort University on 7 July 2004.

illegal use. It appears that using premises for the purpose of prostitution (which is immoral) is a ground for seeking possession, while it would not be for the purposes of seeking a demotion order, *nor* an injunction under s 153B of the 1996 Act. There are also differences in the time limits for seeking demotion orders and those where possession is sought on the basis of nuisance or annoyance, etc. In the former case at least two weeks' notice of intention to pursue demotion proceedings has to be given to the tenant. Thus while the new court forms issued to take account of the recent changes in the law contemplate proceedings being pursued in the alternative, the technical differences will still need to be borne in mind.

Commenting on those new procedures Gail Sykes has stated:

> 'It will be interesting to see how the court deals with Applications for Demotion Orders. In particular landlords will have to consider whether it is appropriate to seek an Outright Possession Order, a Suspended Order or a Demotion Order. It can be argued that Demotion Orders are far easier to enforce than Suspended Possession Orders which will allow the tenant to apply to suspend any warrant issued by the landlord. On the other hand a Demotion Order will not be [an] "Order for Possession" as such and it can be argued that the tenant is being given a "second chance" …'

While it is the landlord's prerogative to decide which type of remedy to pursue, it *may* be that there could be attempts on behalf of tenants to raise disproportionality arguments with regard to particular proceedings on the basis that a remedy which does not immediately put the continued occupation of premises at risk (eg a demotion order or an injunction) is preferable to one, such as a possession order, which does.

Note also the Demoted Tenancies (Review of Decisions) (England) Regulations SI 2004/1679 of 1 July 2004. Once a tenancy has been granted by a local authority or registered social landlord it may be 'demoted', however, in either case before demotion can be sought the landlord *must* serve notice of this on the tenant, see s 6A of the Housing Act 1988 and s 83 of the Housing Act 1985 as amended. Once demoted should the opportunity 'for amendment of life' by the tenant not be taken the landlord may end the tenancy by applying to the court for a possession order. Before doing this the landlord must, under the 2004 Regulations, serve notice of its intent on the tenant, setting out the reasons for its decision, and informing the tenant of his/her right to seek an internal review. That review must be carried out by a person not involved in the original decision to seek possession, and where that decision was made by an officer, the reviewer must be senior in rank. Not less than five clear days' notice of the review must be given, and the tenant has the right to require an oral hearing, provided the request is made within 14 days of the date of service of the notice seeking possession. In *any* case the tenant may make written representations, provided these are received two clear days before the review. Where there is an oral hearing the tenant may have representation, and evidence may be called and questioned. Hearings may be postponed or adjourned, but where the tenant fails to appear at a hearing (having been given due notice), the person holding the review may continue with it.

To end on a financial note, it appears to be the view of practitioners that the 'new' injunctive remedies will be generally cheaper and easier to obtain than ASBOs, though the latter have to be used where a 'minor' is concerned as the courts are unwilling to issue an injunction against a child, see *G v Harrow London Borough Council* [2004] EWHC 237 (Admin), while, of course, if an ASBO is made against a person under the age of 16 a parenting order should also be made in order to 'draw in' the parent(s) of the child to the supervisory regime.

# Preface

The authors of this book have been teaching housing law at undergraduate and postgraduate level for many years, and have been providing continuing professional development in the housing field for lawyers, housing managers and advice centre workers.

Those who study and practise housing law need to be conversant with both case law and legislation in order to determine what exactly the law is on a given point. The statutory language is often opaque, and so are many of the judgments. Students of housing law therefore need to use the original sources and it is often not easy for them to have access to a properly stocked law library. This book gives extensive quotations from case and statute law; there are also comments and questions, to enable students to consider whether the law is logical or just.

We are grateful to our publishers for their patience while we produced this book. We would especially like to thank Alison Mather for dealing with the complex manuscript cheerfully and efficiently.

# Table of Statutes

References in this Table to *Statutes* are to *Halsbury's Statutes of England* (Fourth Edition) showing the volume number and page at which the annotated text of the Act will be found. Page numbers in **bold** type indicate where the legislation is set out in part or in full.

# Table of Cases

PARA

PARA

PARA

PARA

# CHAPTER 1

# Introduction to the Study of the History and Policy Background of Housing Law

The title of this book presupposes that there is such a subject as 'the law of housing'. Certainly from a teaching point of view, in many universities and colleges there is a subject labelled 'housing law' which is taught, perhaps at undergraduate and/or postgraduate level, perhaps as a 'stand alone' module or double module, as part of a 'welfare law' course or for courses for the Chartered Institute of Housing's qualifications. That in itself is a sufficient reason for the authors of the present volume to produce a collection of those cases and materials which, in their experience, are most germane to the needs of teachers and students on such courses. The aims of such a collection must be to inform and stimulate study by the provision of a comprehensive selection of material from both Parliament and the courts, coupled with textual matter that elucidates, analyses, informs and challenges the reader. Within the confines of these covers we hope that we have achieved those aims.

Nevertheless, we return to the presupposition with which we began. Though it is clear that there is in educational terms a subject known as 'housing law', there is amongst academics much less certainty and agreement than the curricula of universities and colleges would tend to suggest. While not pretending to be able to settle the various debates about whether there is in reality any such subject – and if there is, what its content should be – it would be contrary to our stated aims of elucidation and stimulation if we did not address some of the issues involved.

## HOUSING LAW AS THE PRODUCT OF HISTORY

Housing law is primarily a subspecies of the law of landlord and tenant, which results in it being firmly based on property law principles, and the law of contract. Thus many of the concepts which will be encountered in this book are shared in common with that general body of law, for example notions such as covenants, weekly and monthly tenancies, and bedrock issues such as whether an individual is a tenant with a legal interest in land, or a mere licensee with only a personal permission to be present on land. What differentiates housing law from landlord and tenant law in general, however, is that, first, it deals only with residential accommodation and, secondly, by long-standing conventional understanding it also deals with housing conditions, houses in multiple occupation and standards not just in rented property but in virtually all residential accommodation, and with the promotion of the interests of those who have no residential property at all, ie the homeless.

More recently a considerable element of the law relating to crime and disorder has been infused into the already eclectic body of housing law in the form of Anti-social Behaviour Orders and strategies.

Many strands of 'public' and 'private' law thus intertwine to create the fabric of housing law. To understand this complex growth it is necessary to know something of the background history of housing provision in this nation.

With the industrial revolution of the mid- to late-18th century came a considerable change in the pattern of population distribution. The United Kingdom gradually ceased to be a rural nation: indeed, the year 1850 marked the point at which the urban and rural populations were even, ever since which we have been an increasingly urban nation. As the people moved from the countryside into the towns they increased in number, and the nature of their legal interests in land and accommodation changed.

It should never be thought that in pre-industrial Britain there was a kind of rural paradise in which everyone was well housed. William Blake's 'Jerusalem' does us all something of a disservice by talking about 'dark, satanic mills', for many may be led to suppose that before their creation people worked and lived in healthy and happy surroundings: they did not. The average rural labourer lived in appalling conditions – cave dwelling, for example, did not fully disappear until the early years of the 20th century, and most of the attractive country cottages we see today are either the product of 19th-century building, or of even more recent combinations of smaller, older dwellings into acceptable units. It was not uncommon for rural dwellers to live in tiny, cramped 'one up–one down' houses, with access to the upper floor by ladder, and the cattle and domestic animals living in adjacent rooms. The poor – and most people were poor – lived badly, and their legal entitlements to the land they occupied were frequently determined by local manorial custom, often dating from medieval times[1].

Those moving from the countryside to the towns thus did not expect high standards of accommodation; nor did they find them. Though in London, from the 18th century onwards, there were some attempts to impose certain standards on the building of properties, such legislation did not exist elsewhere. Moreover, the great majority of dwellings were available, irrespective of the social class of the tenant, on a leasehold basis only, and their condition thus deteriorated where lessors were concerned only to receive rent and not to take effective steps to ensure that repairs were carried out and property maintained. The influx of people from the country-side led to more overcrowding of existing properties and, where new accommodation was built, to the provision of filthy, insanitary slums. As many houses as possible per acre were squeezed in; these were often built on a 'back-to-back' basis, so that the only entrance was via the front of the house, and no natural light or ventilation reached the rear rooms of dwellings. An alternative was the court system, with dwellings built around a common courtyard – often back-to-back and

---

[1]   See Gauldie, E, *Cruel Habitations. A History of Working-Class Housing 1780–1918* (1974) George Allen & Unwin.

court housing were combined. Such dwellings were available on weekly lettings, which thus became the standard tenure for the poorer classes of society[2].

In the early years of the 19th century, to propose any alleviation of these poor conditions was seen as running against two basic legal principles which had almost the status of constitutional fundamentals – freedom of contract and freedom of property. Freedom of contract depended on the notion that all persons are of equal bargaining power, and thus if a tenant wished to secure better conditions on his home he should negotiate these freely with his landlord. The vast disparity of economic power between landlords and tenants was utterly ignored by the law[3]. That is not to say that tenants had absolutely no remedy – they could, in some cases, simply get out and find other accommodation; something which could often be done in larger towns with an abundance of landlords in competition with one another. Very often tenants would depart without paying rent owed – the famous 'moonlight flit' celebrated in the old music hall song 'My Old Man':

> 'We had to move away,
> for the rent we couldn't pay.
> The moving van came round right after dark.
> There was me and my old man
> piling things inside the van,
> which we've often done before, let me remark.'

Indeed, from time to time so prevalent was this habit that landlords complained they could not make an economic return on their property. However, for most of the 19th century the 'whip hand' lay with landlords, and they were largely able to dictate the rent and conditions of letting of property on a 'take it or leave it' basis. Freedom of property drew much of its intellectual justification from what was seen as a most important issue in the Constitutional struggle between 1642 and 1688 – namely, the right of freeborn Englishmen to enjoy their property without interference by the state. Furthermore, if a man had property it was seen as a mark of divine favour – the just reward for thrift, hard work, self-denial and assiduous attention to business.

What led to a gradual, and bitterly contested, erosion of these principles was the clear evidence of ill health and suffering caused by the insanitary living conditions of the urban poor. These were first systematically investigated by Edwin Chadwick in 1845, and were then unmistakably manifested to the whole nation in the great cholera epidemics of the 1850s. Infant mortality ran at an appallingly high level, and for those children who survived infancy life expectancy was low. In the mid-19th century in Leicester, it has been calculated that the average life expectancy of a working class woman was about 20 years, of a middle class woman about 30 years and of an upper class woman 40 years. A combination then of genuine social concern for suffering, and fear on the part of those anxious lest disease should yet further spread, led to legislation to deal with nuisances, though the effect of this in practice took a long time to produce positive results.

What may be called the first substratum of the modern law of housing was thus concerned with the eradication of public health hazards and the removal of

[2]    See Burnett, J, *A Social History of Housing 1815–1985* (2nd edn, 1986) Methuen, esp. Chapter 2.
[3]    See Denning, Sir Alfred, *Freedom Under the Law* (1949) Stevens, esp. Chapter 3.

'nuisances' such as foul water courses and piles of rotting human and animal waste. Local Boards of Health and Sanitary Authorities – the ancestors of our modern local authorities – were given a series of powers to deal with conditions that were prejudicial to health, from the 1840s onwards. However, it was not until 1875 that they were given power under the Public Health Act to prescribe minimum building standards for new houses. What they were not given was power to build new homes, and early slum clearances, coupled with the building of railways into town centres and their voracious demands for land, often led to the poor being forced from one area into another which was just as bad, often with increased overcrowding.

The other substratum of housing law, namely the provision of housing on a non-speculative, non profit-making basis, did not begin to emerge until the end of the 19th century, and is in reality a 20th-century phenomenon.

There has been since the Middle Ages a tradition of philanthropic housing provision in England and Wales, as the survival of almshouses shows. In the 19th century this was continued by a number of charitable trusts such as the Guinness, Peabody and Sutton foundations. At the same time a number of employers, both rural and urban, built 'model' dwellings for their employees, as witness, for example, Saltaire, Swindon, Eastleigh, Crewe, Wolverton, and a little later Bourneville and Port Sunlight. However, such provision did little to help the vast mass of the unskilled, urban labouring poor. To meet their housing needs accommodation had to be provided that was available for rent on a non profit-making basis, and the capital cost of construction of which was subsidised.

Though a hesitant start was made on the creation of publicly-provided housing towards the end of the 19th century, the legal strands of which were consolidated in the first recognisable modern 'Housing Act' – the Housing of the Working Classes Act 1890 – it was not until after the end of the First World War, when social pressures made it clear that there was a need to build 'a land fit for heroes' (as the then Prime Minister David Lloyd-George put it in an electoral address in Wolverhampton), that on a nationwide basis major programmes of subsidised housing got under way, with central funding from the Exchequer under the Housing Act of 1923.

It was not the voluntary and philanthropic sectors which undertook the building of subsidised housing, however, for they were not willing to take on the task, but local authorities. Thus there came together local oversight of housing conditions and local housing provision[4].

## HOUSING LAW AS THE PRODUCT OF POLICY

What the local authorities faced in the early 1920s was a housing market in which the vast majority of homes were still owned by private landlords – they accounted for 90 per cent of the housing provision at the turn of the century. Much of that housing was of very poor quality and little new housing for rent was being built. Moreover, in an effort to defuse public unrest over rising rent levels during the First

---

[4]  See generally Hughes, D and Lowe, S, *Public Sector Housing Law* (3rd edn, 2000) Butterworths, Chapter 1.

World War, in 1915 the Government had introduced rent controls, and these were to remain a generally important feature of the private rented sector until 1988. There was at the same time a small, but growing, owner-occupied sector which was fostered by generally rising levels of income, making it possible for an increasing number of people to own their own homes with assistance from the burgeoning building society movement, and the encouragement of builders more than ready to build for sale as opposed to renting.

It was at this point that the confused nature of what we call the 'Law of Housing' emerged. All housing, irrespective of who owns it or how it is occupied, is a matter of social concern, for everyone needs shelter and the health and the cohesion of society is affected when that need is not met for a number of its members. Therefore a truly 'social' system of housing law would be concerned with both those who rent and those who own, and would deal with their rights, the financing and the upkeep and maintenance of their homes in a comprehensive and coherent fashion. While it is possible to trace themes and issues of this sort on a cross-sectoral basis, it has to be admitted that for the vast majority of those who teach and study the Law of Housing it is not how they proceed.

On the continental mainland of Europe where housing provision by local authorities is uncommon, and the basis of landlord and tenant law is more likely to be considered to be contract or consumer law, a different attitude to these issues is to be found. Thus in France there are affinities between the law of residential lettings and contracts of employment. In the UK, however, we retain our eclecticism, with a land law substratum, a contractual super structure – heavily influenced by central governmental interference – and a great deal of local authority provision and regulation. All of this is compounded by a *social* distinction between 'owner occupiers' (legally freeholders and long leaseholders) and 'tenants' (legally those who rent on a periodic basis from landlords, public or private.)

Thus the law relating to owner-occupation is treated by most housing lawyers as part of the law relating to conveyancing and town and country planning – the former to deal with acquisition and transfer, the latter to govern location and siting. 'Housing law' thus has come to be the law of rented housing in both the public and private sectors, but with the addition of the law relating to housing conditions on a cross-sectoral basis – though the worst housing conditions are still to be found in rentals. A further addition which most housing practitioners need to know is that portion of family law relating to the occupation and transfer of rented dwellings.

When pressed then to give a description of 'housing law', many teachers and practitioners would identify the 'core' as the various housing and homelessness functions of local housing authorities. In England these are the London Borough Councils (eg, Camden), the Metropolitan District Councils (eg, Birmingham), the Shire District Councils (eg, Cambridge) and, where they exist, Unitary Authorities (eg, Leicester); and in Wales the single-tier County Councils (predominantly in rural areas) and County Boroughs (predominantly in urban areas). Around this core most people would place the law of the private rented sector and the law of other 'registered social landlords', of which more below, together with some Family Law as described above.

That is a description, not a definition, of housing law, because a satisfactory definition remains elusive. What is studied, and what is dealt with in this book, is, frankly, a somewhat eclectic set of rules and principles. There is, however, one generally unifying feature bringing together these various elements, and that is the social welfare issue, or (to be blunt) the issue of poverty.

Looking back from the beginning of the 21st century, one could be forgiven for thinking that local authorities would inevitably take on a 'welfare' role in relation to housing given their combination of powers to demolish unfit properties and provide new dwellings. However, in the 1920s this was far from clear. The first great council building programmes were designed to provide accommodation, which, while subsidised, was still intended for the class of skilled workers. Thus in the 1920s local authorities built housing that was spacious and architecturally attractive – but at a price. It was only in the 1930s that Government policy changed and authorities were encouraged to build larger numbers of cheaper homes primarily to rehouse those displaced from demolished slum dwellings.

The Second World War interrupted that process, and public house building did not truly recommence until after the passing of the Housing Act 1949 which enabled authorities to build for all social groups, not just the working classes – an indication that in post-1945 Britain the public sector was to supersede the private landlord as a provider of rented accommodation. However, under the Conservative Government from 1951 to 1964 there was a return to building properties largely to rehouse slum dwellers, while a totally independent body – the Commission for the New Towns – oversaw the creation of 'New Town Corporations' in places as far apart as Harlow, Crawley, Washington and Skelmersdale, to house people identified as 'over-spill' from overcrowded industrial centres.

'New Towns' continued to be established throughout the 1960s, with the final phase being the massive expansion of existing towns such as Peterborough and Northampton, though by then much of the new housing was built for sale, not rent. At the same time local authorities were encouraged, particularly via central subsidy arrangements, to continue building replacements for slum housing, increasingly on a 'high-rise-system built' basis, largely because it was thought that that was the only way to provide sufficient 'units of accommodation' to meet the needs of an increasing population, and to replace all the unfit properties still standing. The council slum clearance and new building programmes continued into the mid-1970s. What was built, however, was often inner urban housing of a most unlovely and unloved variety – tower blocks and medium rise 'deck-access' housing. Shortly thereafter, in 1977, local housing authorities were also placed under legal duties to house homeless persons whose increasing numbers throughout the 1960s became a cause for social concern and led to the creation of the charity 'Shelter'.

By this time it was becoming clear that Britain was polarising socially according to housing tenure. Owner-occupation developed rapidly as the major housing tenure as real incomes continued to rise. Those who could afford to bought their own homes. Indeed, it is arguable that many who could barely afford to buy were encouraged to do so by various means, including tax relief on mortgage payments and the extremely generous discounts for tenants under the 'right to buy' policy introduced under the Housing Act 1980, which will be dealt with below. Council housing became increasingly the place for the less well-off, those with insecure or no employment and, of course, the homeless. At the same time the private rented sector continued a seemingly inexorable decline. There arose calls for a 'third arm' in housing, something midway between local authority and owner-occupied housing. In an attempt to answer that call, the Labour Government in 1974 sought to foster the philanthropic and voluntary non profit-making sector by boosting housing associations with public funding provided by a central body, the Housing Corporation, set up by the Housing Act 1964. A housing association is a group of people who band together to provide housing on a non profit-making, grant-aided basis. Though some such bodies had been created in the early years of the century, it was only after the 1974 Act, when these associations were prepared to register with – and thus be subject to control by – the Housing Corporation, that this sector in housing began to grow.

Alongside the emergence of housing associations there was also a growing questioning of the role of local authorities as landlords and of the way in which they discharged their functions – particularly with regard to the rights of the tenants which, as a matter of law, hardly existed at all. The idea that tenants of both authorities and associations should enjoy a new legal status and a package of associated rights – the 'secure tenancy' – was initially enshrined in the Labour Government's Housing Bill of 1979. However, with the election to power of the Conservatives in 1979 this Bill was radically transformed into the Housing Act 1980, where the principal right given to secure tenants was the 'right to buy', ie a right to cease to be a tenant and to become an owner-occupier at a heavily discounted price. Under this popular policy over 1 million local authority dwellings have been sold to their occupiers, very often leaving authorities with the least attractive stock. Before 1980 local authorities had had a discretionary power to sell their homes, but whether or not this was used depended very often on the political control of individual councils. Labour-controlled authorities were less inclined to sell than Conservative ones. The radical change made by the 1980 Act was that authorities lost the ability to decline to sell.

The right to buy, however, was only the first in a number of policy initiatives which sought to take away from local authorities their role as housing providers, and to give that function, in a way limited by the amount of public money available for grants in aid of new construction, to housing associations. In 1988, under the Housing Act of that year, the Conservative Government introduced the policies of 'tenants' choice' and 'the Housing Action Trust'. The former was designed to enable the transfer of council estates to new landlords, ostensibly at the wish of tenants but in reality at the initiative of those new landlords; the latter was an initiative designed to regenerate whole sections of run-down council housing in inner urban areas by transferring their ownership to new appointed bodies who would improve them, and at the same time seek to enhance employment prospects for their occupiers, with a view to their transfer to the private sector. Neither policy succeeded: 'tenants' choice' floundered when there was a dearth of bodies willing to become new landlords; while the Housing Action Trusts (HATs) were resisted by tenants who regarded them as an imposition. Only a limited number of HATs were created following assurances by ministers, and appropriate modifications of the law, enabling tenants to return to local authority ownership after a HAT had done its work. Much more successful as a means of reducing the local authority stock was the Large Scale Voluntary Transfer (LSVT) developed by authorities themselves where they were ideologically opposed to being landlords, or saw the scheme as a way of raising money for much needed repairs of stock. Using their general powers to dispose of housing and land, a number of authorities began to dispose of their housing either to existing housing associations or to purposely created new ones. Beginning in the mid-1980s, by the late 1990s there had been 64 LSVTs involving the transfer of 260,000 homes. On the whole, however, it was the stock of rural and suburban authorities which was transferred, leaving the large urban authorities with less attractive, often 'hard-to-let' stock, and thus further reinforcing the negative perception of council housing as welfare property available for the poor and the socially deprived.

## THE POSITION AT THE END OF THE TWENTIETH CENTURY

The start of the 1990s saw the stock of local authority dwellings continuing to erode as a result of right to buy sales and large-scale voluntary transfers, the stock of housing associations slowly increasing (albeit from a small base compared with that of local authorities), the beginnings of a slight revival in the fortunes of private landlords consequent on the removal of rent controls over new lettings under the Housing Act 1988, and the continued consolidation of the owner-occupier sector as the dominant tenure in housing. The increase in the number of properties rented from private landlords was also partly attributable to difficulties experienced by some owner-occupiers in the early years of the decade as economic recession led to job losses and a consequent inability of some owner-occupiers to meet mortgage commitments. Of the stock held by local authorities, much was in the form of urban estates suffering from multiple deprivation in the form of a lack of educational, health, welfare, social and employment opportunities, and often so afflicted by crime and vandalism that people grew unwilling to live in them, thus rendering such stock 'hard-to-let'. Some of these estates were to be found in inner-urban areas, others were in peripheral locations away from easy access to central facilities such as hospitals and shopping areas. Furthermore, there was evidence on a nationwide basis that entry into council housing was increasingly less available to general applicants as authorities used their available stock to accommodate the homeless – in the Greater London area over 60 per cent of allocations being generally made each year to homeless applicants. These figures should be treated with a degree of reserve, in that many so called 'homeless' applicants might well have qualified for being housed anyway under general allocation rules. However, the seeming bias in the figures led to apparently radical changes in the law in the Housing Act 1996. These, though, did nothing to reserve the generally held view amongst concerned professionals that housing had become a welfare service, that social housing was welfare housing and that the Law of Housing, far from relating to the residentially occupied built environment generally, had become an aspect of Welfare Law concerned with the problems, rights and aspirations of one part of the community only.

What the 1996 Act did achieve was to bring a legislative end to what had become, in many places, an effective right to a council house for homeless people. It also created a new concept in social housing, that of the 'registered social landlord'. Most members of this new class of bodies were already in existence as housing associations. However, the idea behind the legislation was yet further to vary the ownership of public rented housing by creating 'local housing companies' to whom transfers of houses could be made. These would operate at a distance from local authorities, though their management structures would include local authority representatives, tenant representatives and other people prominent in the local business and social community. Such bodies would be able to seek funding for new construction outside the very strict public finance borrowing limits otherwise imposed on local authorities.

## Back to the future?

The ink was hardly dry on the 1996 Act when the Labour Party returned to power in May 1997. One of the first tasks of the Blair Government was to initiate a Comprehensive Public Spending Review. The implications of this for public sector housing were that:

(a)   there would be no major public sector building programme because there was no willingness to devote public resources to a major new wave of public sector housebuilding, and the official argument was that only about 17,000 new units per annum were needed, while those unable to work needed 24,000 new tenancies per annum, and many of those would be available in the existing stock of public dwellings;

(b)   most public investment in housing would be devoted to renovating local authority stock, with authorities thus being favoured in preference to housing associations;

(c)   in return for increased funding authorities would be expected to produce the 'best practice' value for money results obtained by the most efficient and effective councils;

(d)   it might take up to 20 years to remedy the most run-down, inner-urban areas, though as a start, in September 1998 the Government announced new public investment of £800m – the 'New Deal' – with £12m being initially available for 17 'pathfinder' areas in which local partnerships of local authorities, voluntary groups and community organisations would identify ways of regenerating areas not just by undertaking work on houses but also by improving shopping, recreational, health and education facilities;

(e)   there would, however, be a competitive element in the regeneration process, for the regeneration 'packages' would be submitted in the form of 'bids' for funding and only those considered successful would be financed.

What was clear, however, was that, as the Government's Social Exclusion Unit had shown in its reports, there is a sector of our society which does not participate in the generally comfortable style of life enjoyed by most people. The majority who live in their own homes are, overall, comfortably off. That is not to say that there are no problems in the owner-occupied sector. There are problems in relation to those owner-occupiers who, having been encouraged to buy, now find that their employment is insecure and that they cannot meet their mortgage commitments. There are problems for those who, being encouraged to believe that house prices must inexorably always climb, find from time to time that prices fall and that their homes are worth less than the sums for which they are mortgaged – the so-called 'negative equity' effect. There are problems for those owner-occupiers who have purchased older houses – and a very large proportion of our housing stock dates from before 1919 – and who have made no long-term provision to fund the expensive capital repairs, such as new roofs and damp proof courses, such properties are already needing. Even so, the overall picture of the owner-occupied sector is one of reasonable comfort.

It is also true that in the public sector all is not gloom. Not all council tenants live in poverty and social deprivation – far from it in fact. But what is true is that for much of this century, and increasingly since the 1970s, council accommodation has been a refuge for those who are the most vulnerable in our society. That may not have been the intention of the framers of housing policy and law in the 1920s, but it is a fate that has increasingly overtaken council housing since the 1930s, though down to the 1950s and 1960s a substantial number of council tenants would have been in secure, well-paid employment. Of course it has been the better-off tenants who have largely exercised the right to buy. Council accommodation has now become the place where those in insecure accommodation, elderly non owner-occupiers, single parents, the jobless, and the disabled look to find a home. That of itself does not, of course, produce urban decay: to follow that line of argument would indeed be to blame victims for their own misfortune. What does appear to be the case, however, is that where vulnerable persons are congregated together in housing from which they have little chance to move, because more desirable properties have been disposed of and no new property is being built, and they then suffer the 'double (or more) whammy' of poor educational and employment opportunities, their areas begin to decline still further. Those who can move out do so, and what is left is decaying houses, many of which are empty, in areas prone to crime and social disorder. Furthermore, in earnings terms the gap between the poorest 10 per cent of the population and those on average earnings is now wider than at any time since the 19th century.

It is a sad reflection on a society which has seen such a general improvement in the living conditions of most of its citizens throughout the 20th century that pockets of relative deprivation continue to exist. No one should suppose that even in the most run-down estates living conditions are as vile as those that existed in pre-industrial rural England, or those that developed as the pace of urbanisation grew throughout the 19th century. But that is little comfort to those who currently live in the stigmatised hard-to-let estates, or who have nowhere to live at all. For it should be remembered that while the official estimate is that only 17,000 new units are needed per annum, other estimates, for example those of Shelter, are that there is a hidden, unmet need for decent, healthy accommodation which requires the building of 100,000–130,000 units per annum.

More recent developments in housing policy and related issues in housing are dealt with in Chapter 2, but first some general word is needed on the tasks of housing law and those who study it.

## The role of law

Housing law, it was argued earlier, is the product of housing policy, and housing policy has come increasingly to be an aspect of social welfare policy, or, to be more frank, policy about those who are the less well-off and most insecure in our society. The reality is that housing law has little to say about owner-occupation. For better or worse, housing law is largely concerned with the poor and the vulnerable – and they are largely found in rented accommodation, much of it, rented from social landlords such as local authorities and housing associations. That being so, what is the role of the law?

No one should suppose that bad housing conditions can be eradicated by law. The role of the law from the mid-19th century onwards has been to declare unacceptable certain types and conditions of housing, and then to provide frameworks and procedures within which by the deployment of public resources that unacceptable housing could be demolished, and, in time, replaced. However, the key element in this has not been the law but the willingness to devote public finances to the eradication of bad housing and the creation of better conditions. In more recent years the law has been developed so as to recognise the rights and entitlements of those who live in the units of accommodation provided. This was a rather belated development which came about in response to a slow recognition that the vast majority of tenants suffered in terms of status when compared to owner-occupiers who enjoyed numerous rights consequent on their status as freeholders.

The law is still concerned with eradicating poor housing conditions, even though the desire to fund major new public housing programmes no longer seems to exist. It is also concerned to protect the interests of individual tenants, and to improve general social conditions by eradicating anti-social behaviour, though this, it must be stressed is not confined to areas of housing owned by either local authorities or registered social landlords. Given the poor conditions found on many estates, however, there is a new realisation that it is not enough to protect the individual rights of tenants, such as security of tenure and succession. What is now needed are provisions to ensure the collective safety of tenants – 'security' in the non-legal sense. Urban squalor and decay do not just mean poor housing conditions, they also bring with them crime, prostitution, vandalism, noise, drug dealing and general bad behaviour. Much attention in housing law is now directed to how these problems may be most appropriately tackled.

The law of Human Rights has also had some limited impact on housing law, and the final chapter of this work is dedicated to a detailed examination of this issue. Other appropriate references will be found in various chapters.

What follows in this book is primarily concerned with the issues that have been identified in the previous two paragraphs. That is, housing law as it has come to be. But students of housing law must never forget that all the statutes ever passed and all the judgments ever made have not by themselves ensured that a single house has ever been built or improved – that process demands in addition finance and political will. Without those elements the law remains a somewhat sterile intellectual exercise – a forum within which arguments take place over the allocation of increasingly scarce resources.

## FURTHER READING

Burnett, J, *A Social History of Housing 1815–1985* (1986) Methuen.

Holmans, A, *Housing Policy in Britain: A History* (1987) Croom Helm.

Lowe, S and Hughes, D (eds), *A New Century of Social Housing* (1991) Leicester University Press.

Merrett, S, *Housing in Britain* (1979) Routledge & Kegan Paul.

Swenarton, M, *Homes Fit for Heroes* (1981) Heinemann.

# CHAPTER 2

# The Future Shape of Housing Law and Policy

## INTRODUCTION

The eclectic history of housing law, considered in Chapter 1 above, has led to a number of serious problems, which collectively can be generally characterised as complexity and confusion. It must be remembered that the current law is an amalgam of common law and statute, and the latter relates to both the public (or social) and private (or commercial) sectors in housing. In addition, other areas of law have impinged upon and indeed have become embedded in housing law, for example public health law and the law relating to relationship breakdown. Then it has to be remembered that the law's development has been greatly affected (arguably it has been distorted) by political and policy changes throughout the 20th century – changes which continue into the 21st century.

Amongst the forces which have been of most impact has been the tension created by the continuing need to strike a balance between the fact that a rented *house* is also someone's *home*. Finding an acceptable balance between the interests of the 'home owner' – the landlord – and the home occupier – the tenant – has proved elusive. The tension is inherent in the land law based nature of a tenancy. Both landlord and tenant have legal estates in the land on which the residence stands. Such legal estates are the source of both rights and responsibilities; in the case of landlords historically, primarily the former. State intervention in the form of legislation either to dispossess landlords of housing unfit for human habitation or to modify the terms of the relationship between landlords and their tenants does not displace the fundamental character of the relationship. Neither does the fact that the relationship is also contractual, for the contract is based on the existence of legal estates in land. It is thus not possible in this country to treat contracts of lettings as simple commercial ventures which can be governed by some form of uniform commercial code, which, though this is a generalisation, is the preferred approach of many continental European nations. This is not to say that the law of residential lettings has escaped some of the consumer-based thinking which now informs much of the present day law of contract, a matter to which we shall return later; rather it is to accept that there are powerful historical forces centred on landlords' possession of the freeholds of their properties, and that these colour attitudes towards tenants and property management.

The problem is exacerbated by issues arising from questions concerning the sectoral location of any given property. Thus whereas the late 20th century saw, admittedly in very general terms, a slow retreat from the high degree of protection once afforded to tenants in the private rented sector (with a more rapid retreat from 1988 onwards), the same century saw a slow and grudging advance in the degree of protection afforded to public sector tenants. It has to be remembered, however, that whatever the outward form of the law, the reality experienced by tenants has frequently been very different from what the law might suggest. The notorious activities of landlords such as Peter Rachman in London in the early 1960s gave the lie to notions that tenants in the private rented sector actually 'enjoyed', in the fullest sense of that word, security within their homes. At the same time council tenants, who were effectively without statutory protection, as a matter of fact generally could expect, while they paid their rents, to live in their homes without interference, and indeed, in practice, for their children to be able to succeed them. Thus the search for a balance between the polar notions of a house being the landlord's property, and therefore an economic asset, while at the same time being the tenant's home, and therefore a social asset and a key requirement for meaningful participation in civil society, was never realised in practice. The issue became even more confused when the need to recognise occupancy interests other than those of the tenant, eg those of the tenant's spouse, became recognised.

It is further of interest that the interests of tenants in the privately rented sector were most fully protected in law while that sector seemingly declined inexorably in size. It would be tempting to see here a correlation: landlords sought to escape from renting because of the onerous burden of the obligations they had imposed on them by law. Such a conclusion would be, however, simplistic. The private rented sector shrank in size for a variety of reasons. Slum clearance drives before 1939 and throughout the 1950s, 1960s and into the 1970s did a great deal to remove from the market a considerable amount of rented property. In addition the increasing ease with which it was possible to finance house purchase, particularly after the middle of the 20th century, meant that many of those who at one time would have rented could now purchase. Indeed it is well documented that after the relaxation of controls over rented property under the Rent Act 1957, many landlords used their new freedom to leave the market: their wealth could at that time be better invested in other forms elsewhere. The revival, albeit modest, in the size of the private rented sector at the end of the 20th century may have much less to do with the relaxing of legal controls over that sector than with the emergence of a new constituency for renting, namely younger people, largely in the 18–25 age range. It may also be asked whether this new constituency for renting is looking to the traditional small private landlord for accommodation. Though a number of individuals have been persuaded to take up the landlord role by the availability of mortgage finance on a 'buy-to-let' basis, the press is not short of instances where the returns such investors have received have been less than expected – much less, in some cases. Furthermore amongst certain younger renters, students and 'key workers' such as health service employees for example, many are now looking for accommodation from major new commercial providers.

By way of contrast, the rights of tenants in the public sector of housing, particularly those who are tenants of local authorities, have on paper at least, apparently increased while that sector has declined in size. That decline is, again, attributable to a variety of factors. The Right to Buy policy for council tenants introduced under the Housing Act 1980 has seen the transfer into private hands of over a million dwellings. Within the social sector of housing as a whole, ie local authorities and registered social landlords, the stock owned by authorities has also declined because of transfers to other social landlords. It must also be remembered that the amount of finance made available for new development by social landlords has, for at least the last 25 years, been severely restricted, with a consequent dampening effect on their activities.

There have thus been internal stresses within the law of housing arising from regular changes brought about in the balance between the interests of landlords and of tenants by changes of governmental policy, and external stresses imposed by social and economic forces. It is hardly to be wondered that what we find today is the law in a state of complexity and confusion.

## Quality and Choice

It is against this background that recent initiatives in both policy and law have to be set. The first in time was the April 2000 Housing Green Paper, 'Quality and Choice: A Decent Home for All', which was arguably the widest-ranging review of housing policy in a quarter of a century. It adopted a holistic view of housing, extending its ambit to cover the owner-occupied sector, and the condition of its stock, as well as the conveyancing process, in addition to more traditional areas of concern such as rented housing. It also set housing policy within a wider framework of social inclusion and cohesion, arguing that: 'People who are decently housed have a stronger sense of security and place'. The paper acknowledged the continuing existence of housing problems, such as the £19bn needed simply to upgrade the worst quality council stock to modern standards, a lack of energy efficiency in many homes, poor quality of council estates, a lack of choice for those in the public sector of housing, where 'The most disadvantaged have often been concentrated in the poorest housing'. The paper further accepted the problems some homeowners have in maintaining their homes, the inability of those on modest incomes in some parts of the country to even rent, let alone buy, a home, the continuing problems of homelessness and of the complexities of the housing benefits system.

The key proposal of the Green Paper were therefore:
- enhancing the housing role of local authorities, particularly by encouraging them to take a strategic view of housing provision and to work in partnership with their local communities, local organisations and registered social land-lords, particularly with a view to linking housing and planning policies;
- promoting 'sustainable home ownership' by enabling the provision of afford-able housing by key workers in areas of high housing costs, eg police, health and education workers, and enabling local authorities to target resources for housing improvement and renovation in a more strategic fashion;
- raising management standards in the private rented sector, inter alia, by promoting 'voluntary accreditation and lettings schemes and best practice guidance' and by exploring the use of landlord licensing on a discretionary

basis by local authorities in areas where housing is in poor condition and there is evidence of exploitation by bad landlords;

- improving the quality of social housing and its management by further encouraging the transfer of existing stock from local authorities to registered social landlords at a rate of 200,000 pa, provided this is supported by tenants, by promoting the establishment of new local companies operating 'at arm's length' from the local authority to take on housing management functions, and by promoting tenant participation in housing management of the stock of both authorities and registered social landlords;
- improving the delivery of affordable housing by, inter alia, new schemes of funding to be operated by the Housing Corporation for registered social landlords, together with more use of mixed tenure housing developments to create sustainable communities and by using planning powers to encourage the provision of affordable housing;
- reforming lettings policies to promote choice based lettings systems and more local flexibility in lettings policies;
- enhancing the protection given by the law to the homeless;
- reviewing the entire system of tenure within all parts of the rented sector;
- maintaining rent levels in the social housing sector at affordable sub market levels, though with some increases to reflect improvements in quality as a result of extra investment and other changes to remove unjustifiable differences between rents charged for homes owned by registered social landlords and local authorities;
- restricting rents in the social sector so that while they remain fair they also reflect 'more closely the size, quality and location of homes, taking account of property values so that tenants would pay a comparable rent for a comparable home', nevertheless also bearing in mind regional variations in incomes and running costs, and taking into the account the need to phase in any increases over time subject to weekly increase limits, with specific protection for vulnerable groups such as pensioners;
- restructuring housing benefits and introducing a simple claims procedure, with better information-sharing between the Department of Social Security and local authorities, less complex entitlement rules and, inter alia, a national housing benefit fraud 'hotline' service.

What emerges from these proposals is a policy framework in which the promotion of affordable housing is encouraged, but whereunder it appears the cost to individuals – or to certain groups of individuals – of that housing is likely to increase, albeit only within limits and over time. It is also clear that the long-term central policy of encouraging local authorities to be strategic enablers as opposed to direct providers of social housing is continued. The role of registered social landlords is enhanced. The programme of approved transfers from local authorities to registered social landlords for 2002/2003 was announced in March 2002, and related primarily to transfers by smaller authorities though some of the larger metropolitan authorities were also enabled to transfer some stock. Quite how this policy may develop in the future is open to some doubt, however. For instance, in April 2002, council tenants in Birmingham voted to reject a transfer proposal. Fears over rent increases may have prompted the large rejection vote. Even so it remains central policy that within a decade, local authorities should only control a small proportion of the housing stock. A much greater degree of integration between housing and planning policies is also foreshadowed, with the aim of promoting the development of affordable housing. The search for a balance between the interests of landlords and of tenants in the social rented sector is also continued under the Green Paper consultative proposals. However, here, as with so many of the other proposals, the emphasis remains firmly on recommendation and exhortation, rather than on highly specific requirements and commandments. The notion of tenants having enhanced legal rights of management and control over their homes on a collective basis is not a specific policy proposal, though this is a matter to be returned to below.

## The Way Forward for Housing

On 13 December 2000 the Government issued its *Housing Policy Statement: The Way Forward for Housing*. This stated that the Green Paper proposals had been generally welcomed, and, in particular, it restated the need for local authorities to be strategic role-players in 'meeting needs across all types of housing and integrating housing policy with wider social, economic and environmental policies'. Four specific policy measures were then identified in connection with this role:

- increasing resources available to local authorities and allowing them greater flexibility to pursue policies that meet the needs of communities across all housing types;
- via the provision of guidance, enabling authorities to carry out proper needs assessments and stock condition surveys to ensure proper underpinning of housing strategies;
- developing relationships between the Housing Corporation and local authorities, particularly to ensure that investment in new social housing meets local priorities;
- encouraging co-operation between local authorities in particular areas to ensure that housing problems are tackled effectively, and not shifted from place to place.

Particular mention was also made of reforms within the private rented sector and the following were identified as 'key measures':

- assisting well-intentioned landlords to improve managerial expertise via voluntary accreditation schemes and other best practice initiatives;
- introducing a compulsory licensing system for Houses in Multiple Occupation and selective licensing of private landlords in areas of low demand (here, see the Housing Bill 2003 and Chapter 13);
- introducing a new health and safety rating scale for assessing housing conditions in all sectors (here, see the Housing Bill 2003 and Chapter 12).

In this connection the 2001 results from the English House Condition Survey (EHCS) are relevant. These estimated that there were 700,000 private landlords in England providing some 2.2m dwellings, or about 10 per cent of the housing stock – it is generally thought such landlords provided 80 per cent of the stock 100 years previously. While much of the poorest quality housing is still found in the private sector, there has been a recent influx of better quality property, some of it newly built. The ECHS reported that 65 per cent of privately rented dwellings are still owned by private individuals, while only 7 per cent appear to be owned by residential property companies. Lettings to those on housing benefit comprise 18 per cent of lettings, and landlords who rent in this sub-sector of the market would generally prefer not to do so. Management practices appear now to favour more formal arrangements than have hitherto been found in the private rented sector, while 58 per cent of all rented dwellings are let and managed by agents. Significantly, these appear to be better managed and in better repair than those managed directly by landlords. Those landlords who do manage directly have few resources to assist them and have little information about how to manage, also having little contact with local authorities. Interestingly, neither landlords nor agents considered they had sufficient information to enable them to comply with safety and good management standards.

From a financial point of view there was evidence of over-confidence with regard to the costs of keeping property in good condition, yet landlords were not generally making a high rental return on their investments (disregarding possible increased capital values), with a net rental return of only 5.5 per cent per annum. Even so most landlords expected to re-let properties falling vacant and landlords of one in five dwellings expected to increase their holdings within two years.

The Policy Statement contained further commitments with regard to raising the quality of social housing, and the provision of new affordable housing. It also promised to take forward the Green Paper proposals on widening choice in the letting of social housing and with regard to homelessness. These latter undertakings have resulted in the passage of the Homelessness Act 2002.

The Housing Green Paper set out the government's strategy to improve the quality of social housing and made a commitment to bring all social housing up to a decent standard within ten years.

With regard to this latter initiative the Government undertook to:
- bring all social housing up to a decent standard by 2010;
- ensure that local authorities adopt a more business-like approach to housing management and investment, including a Major Repairs Allowance of £1.6 billion from 2001/02 in respect of maintaining council housing in sound condition;
- support the transfer of up to 200,000 homes annually from authorities to registered social landlords, where such proposals are supported by tenants;
- encourage the creation of new arm's-length management arrangements for local authority housing;
- ensure consistent and rigorous application of Best Value and Tenant Participation Compact principles across all social housing.

An undertaking was also given to reform the tenurial system for the rented sector. This has resulted in initiatives from the Law Commission which will be considered further below.

The Office of the Deputy Prime Minister also issued proposals in the early part of 2003 which were concerned with alleged abuses in the Right to Buy scheme.

These proposals outlined the existing scheme, whereby under Part V of the Housing Act 1985, secure tenants may buy their homes from their local authority landlord at a discount which starts (after a two-year qualifying period) at 32 per cent for houses (44 per cent for flats), rising by 1 per cent per year (2 per cent for flats) to a maximum of 60 per cent for houses (70 per cent for flats), subject to a cap which varies between regions. Thus under the Housing (Right to Buy) (Limits on Discount) (Amendment) Order 2003 SI 2003/498 the maximum discount in parts of the Eastern, London and South East regions was fixed at a modest £16,000. The Government's consultation proposals, however, went much further with regard to restricting Right to Buy sales, with a view to conserving the existing stock of affordable housing, and to tackling the issue of profiteering whereby some who have purchased have then made substantial sums on re-sale. The proposals would:

- extend the initial qualification period from two years to five years;
- extend the period after sale during which landlords are able to require repayment of some or all of the discount on early resale, from three years to five years;
- clarify the position on the discretion to waive repayment;
- change the basis of repayment to a percentage of the re-sale value of the property, as opposed to the current flat rate basis.

(On these issues see now the Housing Bill 2003.)

With regard to rent levels for Social Housing, the 2000 Housing Policy Statement reiterated the following key elements of rent policy:
- keeping social rents below market levels and based on size, relative property values and local earnings;
- ensuring that no tenant's rent increases by more than £2 per week per year above the normal inflation-linked increases;
- overall rent increases for registered social landlords should be no more than ½ per cent above inflation in any year from 2002/03; and
- achieving a coherent structure for social rents within ten years, but giving social landlords some flexibility over detailed implementation.

## POLICY DEVELOPMENTS SINCE THE GREEN PAPER AND POLICY STATEMENT

Some of the policy proposals have achieved legal status, notably those on homelessness and choice in housing allocation under the Homelessness Act 2002. This contains extensive measures to promote the interests of the homeless and to reverse many of the changes introduced by the John Major Government under the Housing Act 1996. However, it is open to question whether the somewhat anodyne and vague provisions on tenants' choice with regard to housing allocation really amount to a great deal in practice, even though in March 2001 the former DTLR announced funding for 27 pilot schemes to test and evaluate choice-based systems. The 2002 provisions appear overall to promote the discretionary powers of authorities with regard to allocation which inevitably enhances the powers of landlords and reduces the opportunities for individuals to make choices at the allocation stage, see further Chapter 7 below.

## Policy developments

Many current developments have their roots in initiatives announced before the Green Paper proposals.

The issue here concerns the development of collective rights in the social rented sector, and some explanation of this term is needed. Any right conferred on members of a group so that each can vindicate it for him/herself, may be categorised as a 'collective right'. Security of tenure in this sense is a collective right. Security of tenure, however, is something which is enjoyed individually; it radically alters the nature of the relationship between an individual tenant and their landlord, so it is perhaps better to categorise it as an 'individual right'. Likewise, a right to sue a landlord for failure to do repairs, or to effect an exchange of dwellings is an 'individual right', because it affects the performance or the very nature of the landlord/tenant relationship, that relationship being grounded in the contract between persons. The use of the term 'collective rights' is here restricted to those rights which relate to the overall functioning of a particular landlord with regard to the landlord's tenants. Even though the rights are exercised by individual tenants, it is the *sum total* of those exercises that is significant for the landlord. A right to be consulted is a clear example. In theory local authorities have had extensive *powers* to involve tenants by consultation in housing management for many years. In *practice* these powers have been variously implemented and restricted by the interpretation of the courts as to their ambit and application.

Section 105 of the Housing Act 1985 requires that authorities shall maintain such arrangements *as they consider appropriate*, to enable secure tenants who are likely to be substantially affected by matters of housing management to be informed of proposed changes and developments, and also to ensure that such persons are able to make their views known to the authority within a specified time. Matters of 'housing management' are defined by s 105 to include matters which, *in the opinion of the authority*, relate to management, maintenance, improvement, or demolition of municipal dwellings, or are connected with provision of services or amenities to such dwelling, *and* which represent new programmes of maintenance, improvement or demolition, or some change in the practice or policy of the authority, *and* which are likely to affect substantially all an authority's secure tenants or a group of them. A 'group' is defined as tenants forming a distinct social group, or those who occupy dwelling-houses which constitute a distinct class, whether by reference to the kind of dwelling, or the housing estate or larger area in which they are situated. However, in *Short v Tower Hamlets London Borough Council*[1] the Court of Appeal held that a decision taken 'in principle' to market the sale of certain council properties was not a matter of 'housing management' requiring consultation. Neither is the identity of a possible purchaser a consultative issue at such a stage[2]. The obligation to consult arises where there is a real question of *implementing* a change.

A matter is *not* one of housing management in so far as it relates to rent payable or to any charge for services or facilities provided by the authority. It is the duty of an

---

[1]   (1985) 18 HLR 171.
[2]   *R v Hammersmith and Fulham London Borough Council, ex p Beddowes* [1987] QB 1050, [1987] 1 All ER 369.

authority to *consider* (though not, of course, necessarily to act in compliance with) any representation made by secure tenants before making any decisions on a matter of housing management. Authorities must publish details of their consultation arrangements. A copy of any published material must be made available for free public inspection at their principal offices during reasonable hours. Copies must also be available for sale at reasonable charges. 'Landlord authorities' for the purposes of this provision *include* district and London borough councils.

Duties to consult tenants and licensees generally may arise outside the context of s 105 where the law considers it would be procedurally unfair to allow an authority to proceed with a proposal without taking into account the view of occupiers likely to be affected by it – such instances are likely to be rare[3].

Practice has varied greatly as to the involvement of tenants in management. Some authorities set up joint estate management committees (JEMS) to transfer a measure of power to tenants, or created area or district committees of tenants, members and officers to discuss relevant housing issues. Consultation rights and procedures may or may not have been mentioned in tenancy agreements or tenants' handbooks.

## A NEW APPROACH UNDER 'NEW LABOUR'?

Since spring 2000, English and Welsh authorities have been subject to a duty to achieve 'Best Value' in the performance of their functions – including housing management – under the Local Government Act 1999. Under s 3 of the 1999 Act the duty, which is not exhaustively defined in the legislation, requires authorities to make a continuous improvement in the performance of management functions by taking into account the principles of economy, efficiency and effectiveness, and in this context to consult, inter alia, representatives of persons likely to use the service in question – ie tenants. Guidance has been issued centrally on this consultative duty, including the persons to be consulted and the form, timing and content of consultations. The Secretary of State also has powers, under s 4, to specify 'performance indicators' according to which authorities' performance in exercising their functions can be measured, and 'performance standards' which they will be required to meet. In discharging this function the Secretary of State will be advised by the Audit Commission (which functions under the aegis of the Audit Commission Act 1998), which will analyse data on performance from relevant authorities.

Authorities are further required, by s 5, to conduct Best Value reviews of their functional performance at prescribed intervals. Factors to be considered in the review are centrally prescribed and include the level at which a function should be performed – eg is there a need for more than basic provision of a service – and the extent to which a service is meeting performance indicators and targets. From these reviews emerge action plans and targets, under s 6, which will feed into yearly Best Value Performance Plans (BVPPs) required of each authority, and these form the basis for local accountability on the provision of services. This is achieved by requiring plans to provide local people with: a summary of the extent to which their

---

3   *R v Devon County Council, ex p Baker*, Times, 20 October (1992); *R v Durham County Council, ex p Curtis & Broxson* [1995] 1 All ER 73.

authority was successful in meeting the previous year's targets and objectives and a comparison of its performance with other relevant authorities; a statement of targets to be set for the following and future years; a statement of the outcome of any review carried out, for example by way of a revision of targets and the programme for achieving them. The Secretary of State is also able to prescribe the content of BVPPs. BVPPs are subject to local audit under s 7 as to their accuracy and with a view to recommending remedial action. The initial audit is carried out by each authority's own auditor, but may give rise to later action undertaken by a central inspectorate or the Secretary of State. In response to an auditor's report on its BVPP each authority is obliged by s 9 of the 1999 Act to respond where the circumstances are that the report has identified serious deficiencies in the BVPP *and* the auditor has recommended that the Secretary of State should intervene. The response must be made as soon as practicable and must state what action the authority proposes to take and the proposed timetable for action. This response must be forwarded to the Secretary of State and be incorporated in the next edition of the BVPP.

The legislation gives to the Audit Commission powers under ss 10 and 11 to inspect authorities with a view to check how they are complying with Best Value policy, for example to check whether authorities have reviewed their performance as required and whether they have set sufficiently challenging performance targets to obtain Best Value in future years. Such inspections will be carried out on a programmed basis; but provision is also made for non programmed ad-hoc or 'spot check' inspections where an authority's performance is considered to be falling well below required levels and the authority in question have no immediate plans to review the function in question. The Secretary of State has power, under s 10(2)–(4) to issue guidance to the Audit Commission in this connection, and may direct them to carry out an inspection of an individual authority. In carrying out inspections the Commission has extensive powers to obtain papers and other relevant information.

Following an inspection the Commission will issue a report to the authority concerned. If the conclusion is that the authority is failing in its functions, but not sufficiently seriously for referral to the Secretary of State, the authority will be required to record its failure and the action taken to remedy the situation within the next BVPP: see s 15.

Where serious failures are detected the Commission will also send its report to the Secretary of State. This will be one potential 'trigger' for the Secretary of State to utilise enforcement powers under s 15 to require an authority to prepare or amend a BVPP, or to follow specified procedures with regard to such a plan, to carry out a review of the performance of specified functions, or to take such other action as is considered requisite by the Secretary of State to meet Best Value criteria. The Secretary of State may further hold a local inquiry into the performance of specified functions of an authority, and may further, after giving the relevant authority an opportunity to be heard on the issue, direct that a specified function shall be taken over by him or by some other nominated person, for a specified period, or for so long as he considers appropriate.

Serious mismanagement of an authority's housing stock could thus lead to the authority losing housing functions to commissioners appointed by the Secretary of State. This is a very considerable extension of central powers with regard to local government. In 1999 35 English and three Welsh authorities had been initially identified to undertake pilot Best Value schemes to run for a period of three years from 1998.

## BEST VALUE – THE CURRENT POLICY

Responsibility for implementing Best Value policy now lies with the Office of the Deputy Prime Minister (ODPM) which inherited responsibility for housing issues in July 2002 from the former Department of Transport Local Government and the Regions. The ODPM website makes the following statements about Best Value with specific regard to housing.

### 'What is Best Value?

Best Value is a new duty which means that councils must review all the services they provide for local people and improve them by the best means available. This must be done in consultation with the people who use the services and the wider local community.

Under Best Value councils will be required to consult local people on all their services.

### Best Value in housing

Our homes can influence our well-being, our sense of worth and our ties to our families, the local community and work. Housing is a very important part of a council's work, and the Government wants to see it improve year on year. All tenants and residents have a role to play in helping their local council bring this about.'

Having pointed out that Best Value requirements apply to all housing functions operated by local authorities, irrespective of whether they have transferred the ownership or management of their housing, the website information outlines what local authorities have to do.

'They will need to draw up a plan for the whole community showing what they are trying to do, why and how. This will be the "community strategy". They will then have to agree a programme for reviewing all council services, including housing, within a five year cycle and publish the programme in a Best Value performance plan. The first plans must be published no later than 31 March 2000 and then every year to the same deadline. Each local council will send a copy of its plan, or a summary of it, to local households and to other places of residence in the council's area.

In carrying out reviews of their services councils will have to consider four elements which are often referred to as the "four Cs":
* **challenge**: why, how and by whom the service is being provided;
* **compare**: how well they are doing in comparison with other councils and organisations;

- **consult**: people who use the service and other local people to see what they think of it and how they think it could be improved;
- **competition**: consider if using fair and open competition can provide the best solution.

Councils' Best Value performance plans will also have to show their perform-ance against nationally set (that is set by the Government) and locally set (that is set by the council) performance indicators and targets for improvement.'

It is further declared that, as outlined above, authorities are subject to monitoring on Best Value, and it is further made clear that the principles of Best Value policy will also apply to the functions of registered social landlords, see below. A key feature of achieving Best Value is the use of Tenant Participation Compacts which were introduced in April 2000 and are local agreements enabling the tenants of social landlords to be involved in decisions on 'housing matters' – a phrase which *may* be given an extended meaning in practice to cover issues such as neighbourhood nuisance and street cleaning. There is thus room here for variation in practice. However, to prevent over wide variation, central government has issued a 'National Framework for Tenant Participation Compacts'. Subsequent policy statements have stated that it is policy that compacts should:

- enable tenants to be involved in 'planning, improving and monitoring housing services' and dealing with issues affecting localities;
- allow tenants a choice as to how to be involved generally and in relation to particular issues;
- develop in a sustainable way and at a pace suited to tenant involvement;
- reflect local circumstances and meet local needs and priorities.

Thus a compact might relate to district wide or neighbourhood wide issues.

Compacts should further:
- ensure tenants receive information in a clear and accessible form on all aspects of housing services;
- make tenants aware of issues such as tenant management schemes and their benefits;
- enable tenants' views to be taken into account on housing issues so they may influence final decisions;
- make it clear how tenant involvement can lead to improved services;
- make it clear how an authority promotes tenant participation;
- explain how accessible training is available for tenants to enable effective participation;
- make available financial assistance to enable participation;
- facilitate the formation of new tenant groups and foster the working of existing ones by provision of office facilities;

- explain how decision making on housing becomes open and accountable;

- ensure that equal opportunities policies are made to work properly.

Specific funding is made available to encourage participation either through the normal Housing Investment Programme of funding from central to local govern-ment, or under the 1999 Act's 'Tenant Empowerment Grant Programme'.

In parallel with compact schemes for local authority tenants the Housing Corporation, which oversees the functioning of Registered Social Landlords, has introduced performance standards to ensure that their tenants also have participatory programmes made available to them. Registered Social Landlords are subject not only to s 105 of the Housing Act 1985, but must also comply with the 2002 Regulatory Code of the Housing Corporation. This not only encourages regular consultation with tenants but also promotes the inclusion of tenant representatives on the governing bodies of their landlord. Indeed since 2000 it has been Housing Corporation policy that resident and community control of housing should be encouraged by giving residents opportunities to take control of their homes on a collective and local basis provided this is what they wish and the transfer of control is otherwise appropriate.

All of the above remains central policy. Further guidance has also been issued by the ODPM on training programmes for tenants, and on using Compacts as a means of solving disputes between council landlords and their tenants.

Compacts are, however, primarily consultative arrangements – an exercise in representative, as opposed to responsible, democratic government of housing by those who occupy it.

Though they represent an advance in the concept of giving collective rights to tenants, a fully responsible system of governance would require the transfer of management powers to tenants.

## TRANSFER OF POWERS TO TENANTS

It has been possible since 1975 to transfer authority housing management powers to housing co-operatives, but little use was made of this power, so that by 1993 there were only 62 estates under tenant management organisations. Section 27 of the Housing Act 1985, as amended, allows authorities to transfer specified management functions over specified properties to 'another person', subject to ministerial consent. Such devolutions are made by 'management agreements' which must contain any provisions specified in regulations made by the Secretary of State. Ministerial approval is needed for such devolutions of power.

The history of the law here is tortuous, with the basic management provisions of the Housing Act 1985 being overlain and amended by a variety of subsequent ones. Section 27 of the 1985 Act, inter alia, permitted authorities to make agreements with what were known as 'housing co-operatives', which in practice meant a management co-operative, whereby management responsibilities could be transferred[4].

### Transfer arrangements

As the law stood from 1993 where an authority proposed to make a management agreement under s 27 it had to follow the procedure laid down in s 27AA which

---

[4]    Arden, A, *Housing Act 1985*, (1986) Sweet & Maxwell, paras 68–40 to 68–41.

required consultation with tenants as to the proposal. This was replaced in 1996 with new provisions contained in s 27AB of the 1985 Act. This empowered the Secretary of State to make regulations to require authorities to consult tenants generally – or to consider tenant representations – with regard to the exercise of their housing management functions. This provision has a clear applicability to proposals to transfer management functions, for the regulations may require consultation in relation to, inter alia, specifications of functions proposed for exercise by an authority or 'another person' the authority proposes to invite to bid for the exercise of management functions; standards of service to be achieved by any such persons; proposals to enforce standards of service under management agreements. Provision may be made as to the identity of consultees, the means by which consultation is to take place, arrangements for making representations, and the action to be taken when representations from tenants are received. They supersede the provisions of s 105 where relevant.

Where consultation with tenants is required, the prime responsibility for conducting it lies with the authority, and the Secretary of State may only intervene where that consultation process is flawed[5].

## Proactive tenant management

Though s 27 of the 1985 Act permitted delegation of housing management functions, authorities were for many years apparently reluctant to transfer functions to tenants – even though a tenants' organisation could clearly fall within the concept of 'another person' in the Act. Thus, as already stated, by 1993 a transfer of management had taken place on only 62 estates. Changes to the law were introduced in 1993 to force the pace of change.

Section 27AB of the 1985 Act, as inserted in 1993, empowers the Secretary of State to make regulations requiring authorities to take steps to respond where any tenant management organisation (TMO) serves written notice proposing that the authority should enter into a management agreement with the TMO. Those regulations were the Housing (Right to Manage) Regulations 1994, SI 1994/627 (see also DoE Circular 6/94). These regulations supersede any other consultation requirements under ss 27AB or 105. Under these a TMO may serve a right to manage notice (RMN) on an authority where it is a representative and accountable body, eg it must be open to any tenant of a relevant dwelling to join the TMO and the TMO must pursue an equal opportunity policy. It must serve a defined geographical area and have a membership of at least 20 per cent of *both* secure tenants and of *all* tenants of houses, flats, hostels etc belonging to the authority within the designated area. The TMO must take a democratic decision to serve a RMN by delivering a copy to each affected dwelling, and authorities are able, inter alia, to refuse a RMN relating to fewer than 25 dwellings let on secure tenancies. Only members of the TMO can vote, and a majority of members must back the proposal. If a notice is accepted the TMO will select a training agency and the authority is expected to support the TMO with accommodation and office facilities, and the TMO will select a training agency

---

[5]    *R v Secretary of State for the Environment, ex p Harrow London Borough Council* (1996) 29 HLR 1.

(an 'approved person') from a list maintained by central government and a feasibility study funded by a grant under s 429A of the 1985 Act by the Secretary of State will be undertaken. This study will be in two parts: the full study can only proceed if the initial study indicates to the approved person it is reasonable to proceed, and at that point the authority will arrange for a ballot or poll of *all* affected tenants. (It is not reasonable to proceed where it is concluded a TMO is unlikely to progress towards full tenant management, or where it appears TMO is not representative of its community and will not reform itself.) If the ballot is in favour by a majority of all tenants and a majority of all secure tenants, the full study proceeds. A further training agency *then* selected by the TMO from the centrally maintained list will proceed to develop a programme of management skills for the TMO by reference to the range of functions the TMO wishes to assume: a training programme – *Preparing to Manage* – has been developed for this purpose. Seventy five per cent of these development costs will be met by s 429A grants, the rest will come from authorities (see also the TMO Modular Management Agreement, HMSO 1994).

If, however, the training agency concludes that the development programme is unlikely to result in the TMO assuming a range of management functions, a timely report should be made to the TMO, the authority and the Secretary of State, and if the TMO accepts the conclusion its proposal is deemed withdrawn and no further similar proposal can be put forward for two years. But when a programme is successful the TMO will need registration as a company or an industrial or provident society so as to provide a legal 'person' with whom the management agreement can be made. Only when the training agency certifies a TMO has reached the requisite level of competency for the functions it wishes to discharge can matters proceed. If the agency decides against the TMO on this point, the TMO may submit the issue to arbitration. If, however, the TMO is certified to proceed then within two months the authority must inform affected tenants of the terms of the proposed management agreement with the TMO, and a ballot will then be held in prescribed form: all tenants of affected dwellings must be given the chance to vote and a vote must be given to each tenant. If the TMO gains a majority vote from all tenants, including a majority of secure tenants, the proposed management agreements must be entered into; a failure to obtain a majority result is the deemed withdrawal of the proposal and a moratorium of two years on similar proposals.

Note, however, that it is also possible for authorities to enter into management agreement with TMOs voluntarily, provided the Secretary of State approves the form of the agreement and the requirements of s 27 are complied with. It is also possible for a TMO to invite an authority to nominate one or more people to be directors/officers of the TMO where the authority have entered into or propose to enter a management agreement with the TMO.

Individual TMO agreement were, by April 1994, in place for 11 estates with a further 67 well advanced. It was then government policy that authorities should divest themselves of direct housing management by 1996 and it was considered likely that large-scale voluntary transfer of management (LSVT) to associations or TMO transfers would be the preferred means for authorities to achieve this.

As so often happens with housing policy, however, the reality was different from the expectation. In the first place TMOs have taken on a variety of forms. Some are Tenant Management Co-ops (TMCs) with a management committee elected by tenants which have delegated management tasks; some are Estate Management Boards (EMBs) with a mixture of elected tenant representatives and authority nominees, again having delegated responsibilities for a particular estate; some (a few) are Par Value Co-ops (PVCs) which were effectively registered as housing associations totally controlled as co-operatives by their members, and which have provided new housing.

The Price Waterhouse study for the former Department of the Environment, 'Tenants in Control: an Evaluation of Tenant led Housing Management organisations'[6] concluded that TMOs in general have flourished where groups of tenants have perceived a need to safeguard and sustain improved housing conditions on their estates, and where an incentive has existed to obtain the finance needed to carry out improvement and modernisation of housing. It was found that each form of TMO outlined above could be effective in securing improved conditions and management for tenants, but those which were most successful were: small in scale; driven by the desire of residents for improved management services and greater control over their delivery; characterised by continuing high levels of resident involvement; effectively controlling their budgets; able to call upon specialised outside agencies for particular services; supported by their authorities with practical and financial help. TMOs are best suited to areas where they can be 'mission driven', and will enjoy a high level of tenant involvement with consequent autonomy for residents over how their homes are managed. They are generally unsuitable for large areas of housing having no common focus, or where they will be tightly constrained as to budgetary or policy changes, or where the tenants are disadvantaged in terms of low income, poor employment or lack of amenities. The conclusion of the Price Waterhouse study was thus that small-scale community-based TMOs are best able to deliver superior value for money in management terms.

A central 'Modular Management Agreement for Tenant Management Co-operatives' has existed for some time. Extensive guidance on this issue is available via the ODPM website.

## Further research evidence

Two recent studies cast light on the implementation of tenant participation issues generally.

'Tenant Participation and Housing Management'[7] argued that between 1998 and 2000 many authorities had made substantial progress on tenant participation. They had created agendas for action and had made improvements to accessing information on tenants' views, while many had consulted tenants through mechanisms such

---

[6]   (1995) HMSO.
[7]   ODPM, 'Analysis of 1999 HIP Data on Best Value, Tenant Participation and Housing Management', Housing Research Summary No 112, 2000.

as panels, forums, and focus groups. Others stated they had published (or were in process of publishing) participation policies. There were higher levels of participation by tenants in strategic policy making but lower, although improved, levels of evaluation with regard to the effectiveness of tenant participation strategies.

The content of tenant participation policies, however, was very diverse. Some focused on processes, some on outputs, some involved specific groups, others had community-wide development, some promoted tenant management, some supported new tenants' groups. TMOs were seen as important in the larger metropolitan and urban areas but enthusiasm amongst local authorities for this form of participation appeared to be waning, and estate agreements appeared to be regarded as a more popular alternative. In areas of housing management, such as environmental improvement and regeneration, there was evidence of broad tenant participation, including standard setting and performance evaluation, at both operational and strategic levels.

With regard to budgetary decision-making, participation was generally 'top down'. Tenants were more likely to participate in standard setting and contract monitoring with respect to capital investment decisions, though even here tenant input into strategic capital decision-making and in assessments of policy effectiveness was atypical, while there was little involvement in decisions about rents. Participation typically consisted of a one-day event where tenants could chose between previously prepared rent level options. One-day events typified the approach taken to participation in housing strategy decisions in general.

The identification of tenant training needs was largely ad hoc, and even in those authorities which systematically addressed the issue, many of these were supply-led rather than demand-led. Some authorities carried out training needs analyses and skills audits, though these authorities tended to be metropolitan or London-based.

Several authorities reported that 'the same few tenants were involved in everything'. Few authorities had determined to use different mechanisms and structures (and people) for different issues. With regard to the recognition of tenants' associations, most authorities used a model constitution but there was doubt about the monitoring of compliance with recognition criteria, while a number of authorities confused monitoring tenant association activity with evaluating tenant participation policy.

That research would tend to suggest that, in 1999, only limited headway was being made with developing truly effective tenant participation on a wide scale. One particular problem is that for participation to become more than a cosmetic exercise, large numbers of people need to be actively involved, otherwise the collective right nature of the process is fundamentally undermined. However, there was evidence that only a few tenants were becoming actively involved.

'Implementing Best Value in Housing and Tenant Participation Complaints – the first year'[8] reported, however, 'significant process impacts … resulting from the introduction of BVH [Best Value in Housing] and TPCs [Tenant Participation Compacts]. Both policy interventions have caused the large majority of social housing landlords to review and rethink the way they delivery their housing

---

[8]    ODPM, Housing Research Summary No 156, 2002.

services'. However, this optimistic assessment must be read subject to the other key findings of the research which were that the implementation, by authorities and, where applicable, housing associations, of both BVH and TPCs was still at an early stage. Most social housing landlords were only applying the processes and procedures involved in implementing the policies and had not made changes to services. Those who had were still at an early stage in doing so.

Social housing landlords, however, considered that BVH and TPCs had affected their practices, including:
- changing the ways they engaged with tenants;
- changing organisational cultures;
- changing the ways in which they undertook business planning; and
- improving service delivery.

However the report added:

> 'There are indications however that for some organisations the implementation of BVH involves doing simply what is necessary to conform rather than fully embracing the principles and spirit of the policies.'

Even so, there was some progress to report in that nearly all those authorities surveyed which had not undergone large-scale voluntary transfer of their housing stock to a registered social landlord either had a TPC in place or planned to produce one within the year. Even so, while many social landlords reported that they had undertaken extensive training for staff, members and tenants, evaluation of the effectiveness of that training was needed. Some interviewees in the survey were unsure whether they had received training on BVH or TPCs, while some were unsure what the training was about.

The majority of organisations surveyed had selected the weakest areas of service first for review, normally on the basis of officers' perceptions or as a result of making comparisons with national performance indicators.

So far as the views of 'customers' were concerned, the report stated:
- '*Involvement in the development of TPCs tends to be limited to formal tenant groups.*
- *Evidence from the focus groups with tenants*, and the Omnibus Survey with tenants and residents, *suggests that generally most have not heard of either BV or TPCs* – however they believe the principles for both initiatives are sound.
- *Tenants and residents have yet to see the benefits of these policies by way of improved service delivery.*
- Views from the focus groups suggest that tenants, on the whole, are wary of performance data supplied by their landlord – they feel it either doesn't match their experiences of the services provided, or that it is too global and not relevant to their estate or area.
- The results from the focus groups suggest that the development of neighbourhood Compacts would be welcomed by tenants.' (Emphasis provided.)

Intriguingly, it was younger tenants who argued that formal tenant groups held no interest for them, feeling that such groups served the interests and concerns of older tenants. The report concluded that 'landlords will need to continue to develop a range of consultation mechanisms to ensure that the views of all tenants are being incorporated'.

This latest survey evidence points to the same conclusion reached by its predecessor considered above. The road to achieving tenant participation in housing management decisions will be a long one. While landlords, or at least some of them, may be ready to embrace a participatory style of management, questions remain as to whether tenants are. Some appear to be willing to become involved but questions arise as to whether these are self-selecting groups representing only sectional interests, for example older long-term tenants on estates. If these conclusions are true with regard to participation generally then how many more questions must hang over the more advanced concept of tenant management of estates? Though there are currently some 300 TMOs, most of these exist with regard to local authority housing, and there appear to be few in the registered social landlord sector. Though TMOs are to be found throughout most of the metropolitan areas of England, with a few in smaller settlements, the overwhelming majority are located in London, and appear to be highly localised there.

In 2002 the Government commenced a further consultation exercise on the future of s 27 of the Housing Act 1985 with a view to introducing changes which would enable more flexible transfers of management functions so that subcontracting of certain functions would be allowable. The justification for this was claimed to be the need to inject 'Best Value' principles into management transfers so that those who contract to take on management functions could bring in specialist subcontractors for particular issues which would ensure maximum value for money. Such changes could not affect the legal, consultative or tenurial position of secure tenants, though they would apply to any TMO entering into a new management agreement.

The procedures relating to transfer of management powers are complex and it is no surprise that, nationwide, so little use has been made of them by TMOs. Collective rights to function well have to be collectively desired and collectively exercised. People may be reasonably well acquainted with the notion of having and exercising individual rights with regard to their homes, they appear to be much less familiar with collective rights notions. However, if the search for an acceptable balance between the interests of landlords and tenants is to be fruitful then progress has to be made with both collective and individual rights notions.

## TENANT INVOLVEMENT AT THE NATIONAL LEVEL

The above material considers the legal requirements concerning tenant involvement at a local level. There is no similar framework with regard to national policy making. That is not to say that this does not happen as a matter of practice, however. The Office of the Deputy Prime Minister (ODPM) has a strong record with regard to consulting tenants' organisations, though largely on a single issue basis as topics of concern have arisen. A more recent development has been the creation of the Tenant Sounding Board to provide a permanent forum within which there could be ongoing dialogue between tenants, ministers and officials. The Board has 12 tenants who are experienced in participation issues, and also with regard to housing policy and practice. One represents TAROE (the national tenants' association) while the rest are independently selected on the basis of their skills, knowledge and experience. Some members are employed in housing, some come from minority groups and disabled groups, and there is a balance between male and female members. The effectiveness of this body was considered in 2003, when it was argued that:

- Clarification needs to be provided as to whether and how the Board can influence housing policy and policy making, especially with regard to disseminating information about the policy making process and the various actors in it.
- Improved feedback on the views expressed by Board members to ministers and officials needs to be given, a merely formal response is not enough, the Board needs to know what, if any, use has been made of its suggestions and comments.
- The Board needs to be consulted earlier in the policy making process than is currently the case if its contributions are to be truly effective.
- The Board itself needs to develop ongoing contacts with policy makers to improve mutual understanding and trust.
- The work of the Board needs to be publicised by ODPM, and the work of Board members needs to be properly valued.
- The Board needs to take on board the importance of housing policy making at a regional level, and should be slightly increased in size.

It has to be said that the Board is hardly a major player in the area of housing policy making; however, its existence is a significant development with regard to enhancing the status and role of tenants.

## THE DEPUTY PRIME MINISTER'S JULY 2002 PARLIAMENTARY STATEMENT

Following the 2002 Comprehensive Public Spending Review the Deputy Prime Minister (DPM) made a statement in the House of Commons on housing and planning policy which explored some of the issues already considered. That statement recognised that housing provision continues to fall short of housing need. The demand for housing grows as people live longer and also tend to live in much smaller family units than historically was the case. However by the beginning of the twenty-first century in the UK 150,000 fewer dwellings were being constructed per annum than was the case 30 years previously. One consequence of this in areas of high demand has been rapidly rising house prices, which has a further consequence that housing costs for some 'key workers' in the public sector, such as teachers and nurses, make it hard, if not impossible in places, to either rent or buy a home. Problems of this sort can, so the DPM argued, only be met by a 'step change' in policy which must be reflected in both housing and planning terms.

So far as planning control is concerned Regional Planning Guidance Note No 9 issued in 2000 indicated a need for planning authorities to consent to the building of 23,000 dwellings pa in London and 39,000 pa in the wider South Eastern Region.

These targets have not been met and the shortfall over two years is some 10,000 dwellings. The DPM insisted that targets must be met and threatened to take intervention action using his powers in the Town and Country Planning Act 1990 in the case of any local planning authority not meeting target figures. Many of the tens of thousands of new dwellings which are needed will have to be built to a much higher density than has been the case for some time. This means greater use of flat and maisonette developments and terraced housing, as opposed to semi-detached and detached properties. Currently 60 per cent of new dwellings are being built on 'brownfield' (ie previously developed) sites. This target, initially set in 1998 for 2006, has already been achieved. However, the DPM made it clear that even greater use must be made of such sites as part of an overall reduction in 'land take' for new housing developments. The DPM therefore announced his intention to use his interventionist planning powers in respect of any planning application for new housing involving a density of less than 30 dwellings per hectare.

Turning then to housing policies the DPM stated that 20,000 new 'affordable' homes pa are to be built, ie dwellings for sale or rent at subsidised prices. Currently £1.2bn of public funding is used for this purpose. That will be increased, in particular to provide dwellings for nurses, teachers and other key public sector workers. Such affordable housing may be provided as a result of partnership arrangements with employers and via both public and private landlords. The DPM also laid particular stress on continuing the improvement and upgrading of all current local authority housing to acceptable modern standards by 2010, with one-third of those in the worst condition (some 550,000 properties) improved by 2004. A new 'single housing inspectorate' was announced to take over at some future time the housing improvement monitoring functions of the Housing Corporation and the Audit Commission. Furthermore, new legislation was promised to tackle abuses on the part of 'unscrupulous landlords' in the private sector and also in respect of poor housing conditions there. (See now the Housing Bill 2003, and Chapters 12 and 13 below.)

To the policy initiatives already examined above, the DPM then added further commitments made possible by the release of extra public funding over a number of years. It must, however, be remembered that this funding is dependent on tax revenue. Should those revenues decline, for example because companies make smaller taxable profits or because fewer people are in taxable employment, then either the promises will have to be broken or taxes otherwise will have to increase to meet undertakings given.

## LEGAL DEVELOPMENTS

Reference has already been made to legislative and other changes necessary to carry into effect the above policy programme. Some of the necessary legal measures will appear from Parliament. Some already have, in the form of the Homelessness Act 2002. However, much more remains to be done by way of sorting through and generally clearing out much of the existing confused tangle of statutory and common law rules relating to housing. In March 2001 The Law Commission published 'Reform of Housing Law: A Scoping Paper'. This pointed to a need for a fundamental reappraisal of the whole law of housing as opposed to piecemeal responses to individual problems as they have arisen. It may here, however, be argued that a such fundamental reappraisal may well need an agreed base in principle, ie a set of underlying concepts which command general acceptance. If that is not the case then changes made are likely to be over taken by the same fate that has befallen other housing measure over the last century or more, namely that they too will be seen as isolated responses to a perceived historical problem.

The Law Commission did make some rather general statements of principle which they identified as 'legal' and 'broader policy' objectives.

'The legal objectives include:
(1)   Regulation of relations between landlords and tenants during the lives of tenancies to ensure a proper balance between the interests of both groups;
(2)   Regulation of relationships between local authorities and those affected by their social welfare and enforcement functions connected with housing; and
(3)   Provision of a cheap, straightforward and stable framework for the resolution of disputes.

The broader social objectives include:
(1)   Ensuring adequate supplies of accommodation for those who intend to rent at a price that they could afford;
(2)   Increasing the degree of choice available to tenants and prospective tenants;
(3)   Facilitating the mobility of the labour market, and providing improved housing opportunities for key groups of workers;
(4)   Providing suitable accommodation for different social groups, particularly those in vulnerable social groups;
(5)   Meeting the housing needs of other groups who are not necessarily at the forefront of social welfare concern, such as the single and students;
(6)   Ensuring that the accommodation which is available is of an appropriate quality. ...

Although we are clear that there must be an appropriate (statutory) regulatory framework relating to the housing market, we want the many initiatives that have occurred in both the public and private rented sectors to set standards and develop Codes of Good Practice to continue to be encouraged. This is a particular challenge for the private sector of the market since ... it is characterised by having a very large number of suppliers of rented accommodation each providing only one or a very small number of properties.'

It may, however, be asked whether these principles in themselves are sufficient to provide a broadly acceptable base for the law.

It is submitted that such underlying principles should in general be as follows.
●      Recognition of the need to recognise that while the property in question is the landlord's *house* it is actually primarily the tenant's *home*, and that in the balancing exercise between the interests of both parties primacy should be

given to the recognition and protection of home rights, as indeed is consistent with the basic principles of the European Convention on Human Rights.
- Acceptance that tenants may well need both individual and collective rights with respect to their landlords. The problems of creating effective systems of collective rights have been referred to above but these difficulties should not be allowed to prevent the task from proceeding.
- The need to ensure that there are effective external regulators to ensure compliance with the law by all parties. More than one such regulator is needed given the nature and complexity of housing. Such a regulator already exists with regard to Registered Social Landlords in the form of the Housing Corporation, but where is there any regulator for the private rented sector?
- The need to ensure that tenants are not made subject to over regulation simply by virtue of the fact that they are tenants. It can be argued that local authority tenants can be subject to a variety of forms of control, for example with regard to anti-social behaviour, which are inapplicable to owner occupiers. This arises because their landlords have extensive powers under housing legislation to deal with bad behaviour as a repossession issue.

It will be noted that these statements go somewhat beyond what the Law Commission proposed.

However, leaving aside debate on principle, the Law Commission was surely correct to argue that reform of the current law is also needed on the grounds of its sheer bulk (they pointed to the size of the current *Encyclopaedia of Housing Law* at six volumes, weighing over 10 kilos and taking up to 22 inches of shelf space) – its complexity which is disproportionate to the needs of many landlords and their tenants, and its cost when litigation does result. They pointed in particular to the fact that there are currently at least 13 different residential statuses in the rented housing sector, with three separate codes of security.

The Commission argued for a comprehensive reform and codification of the law of housing which should be undertaken in phases. Phase 1 would deal with the basic issue of housing status, with the aim of reducing the various existing statuses to two. The second phase would consider issues such as harassment, unlawful eviction and succession. It was also accepted that further independent reform studies of issues such as repairing obligations would need to integrated into the overall task of reform at some future stage.

This initial scoping proposal was succeeded a few months later by 'Renting Homes 1: Status and Security', Law Commission Consultation Paper no 162. It will be seen from the following extract from the basic proposals that the Commission proposed a radical revision of the law, but one which is still predicated on a fundamental distinction between the rights of those in the social or public sector of housing and those who look to private or commercial landlords for accommodation. Even so, the Commission stated that: 'Four basic principles underpin our proposals'. These were

'(1)  The state should continue to guarantee security of tenure in appropriate circumstances.
(2)  Repossession of homes should only follow due process.
(3)  Housing law should adopt a more consumer perspective.

(4)   Our proposals must reflect the impact of the European Convention on Human Rights.'

Immediate issue could, however, be taken with these statements. First of all, what was meant by 'appropriate circumstances? The phrase was vague, to say the least. Secondly, it would be asked quite what was meant by a 'more consumer perspective?' From other portions of the Commission's work it was made rather more clear that, in line with overall central government thinking on housing policy, a reference was being made to consumerist notions whereby bargains must not only be legally made to be binding, they must also be fair. This 'consumerist' approach to housing law moves UK thinking on the issue rather closer to Continental European notions referred to above. In itself this is not really new. Ann Stewart in *Rethinking Housing Law*[9] pointed out the construction of the housing consumer can be traced back to the Major Government of 1991 and its emphasis on Citizen's Charter approaches with regard to the delivery of services, including housing. Housing consumerism thus owes something to the market-based thinking of right wing political parties. It also draws sustenance from EC requirements.

The Unfair Terms in Consumer Contracts Regulations 1999, SI 1999/2083 were made to comply with European Community obligations. We shall return to them in detail in Chapter 5; suffice it to say here that terms in contracts of letting are unfair if they are contrary to a requirement of good faith (ie an obligation lies on the landlord to deal fairly and openly with the tenant) and cause a significant imbalance in the rights and obligations of the parties to the tenant's detriment. Terms which are 'unfair' in this sense are not binding. In November 2001 The Office of Fair Trading (OFT) which is the enforcing agency for the regulations issued guidance for landlords and tenants with regard to fair contract terms, with particular reference to the private rented sector in which 1.4 million tenancy agreements worth an aggregate £5,700m are made each year. In May 2003 the OFT announced that a number of trade organisations representing landlords, such as the Association of Residential Letting Agents, the Residential Landlords Association and the Royal Institution of Chartered Surveyors had agreed with the OFT to produce fairer and clear standard tenancy agreements. This is but one example of how consumerist thinking is already affecting one area of housing law.

The thinking of the Blair Government on the provision of accommodation has also stressed a need for this to be seen as a form of service provision and that not just in the public/social sector. The problem here is that there is a long history of housing provision being seen as a form of property management, and, arguably, of late with much emphasis on the control of anti-social behaviour, housing provision may be seen as a form of social control and people management. To then argue that it should be seen as the provision of a service requires changes of attitude on the part of landlords. Maybe social landlords might find the concept of service provision as one reasonably easy with which to come to terms, though in the present writer's experience there is a degree of ambivalence across the sector in this regard. However, it is by no means certain that private landlords would be able to accept such a notion. The reasons why such landlords rent out property are multifarious,

---

[9]   (1996) Sweet & Maxwell, at pp 258–275.

and *include* making money (though rarely a total living) and making use of property acquired in some way, for example by inheritance. It may be asked whether such a diverse body of people as private landlords undoubtedly are could accept a 'service' notion of housing provision. In addition it may be asked whether a consumerist philosophy of housing provision can be effective unless it is coupled with adequate means of vindicating and enforcing rights on both sides of the bargain. Historically it was accepted that the only effective way to protect the interests of tenants in this respect has been to grant them security of tenure. That position was abandoned so far as the private rented sector is concerned with the Housing Act 1988 and the introduction of assured shortholds. The abandonment was confirmed when the Housing Act 1996 made the essentially insecure assured shorthold tenancy the norm for private lettings. It may be argued that the renascent private rented sector is growing – albeit none too quickly and from a very low base – because of the removal of security of tenure. On the contrary, however, it may be growing largely because there is a constituency looking to rent, and that group in society is largely the young aged from 18 to 25 plus. Some might think young people in that age range are able to look after themselves. Others would not agree and would point to the existence of vulnerable groups within the age range such as students and the unemployed who might well find it hard to vindicate consumer rights.

These are issues to be borne in mind when the Law Commission's final proposals are examined. These were contained in 'Renting Homes'[10].

The Law Commission's 2003 document continued its earlier commitment to a consumer approach to housing law. This has the consequences that:
- both sides to a contract of letting should know their rights and duties from the terms of their agreement;
- such agreements should be in writing;
- all terms should be fair and transparent;
- the agreement should be written in plain language;
- the agreement should be structured in a user friendly fashion;
- model agreements will be needed, which will be contained in regulations issued under proposed legislation, and landlords would be encouraged to use such forms, with particular changes to meet their special circumstances as appropriate.

The core proposals are that there should be Type I and Type II occupation agreements, the former with a high degree of statutory security, the latter with security largely determined by the individual agreement. Social landlords would in general be *required* to use Type I agreements, save in limited legislatively listed exceptions, while it is expected that private landlords would normally utilise Type II. As a consequence of this the historic distinction between leases and licences will cease to be important for all occupation agreements would fall within the new scheme. The all embracing nature of the scheme has further consequences in that the current rule which prevents a court from ordering possession to be given up during the initial six months of an assured shorthold tenancy would be abolished, which would enable service tenancies and tenancies of student accommodation

---

[10]  Law Com No 284, Law Commission, 2003.

provided by universities to be brought within the purview of the scheme. Only a few tenancy types in the residential sector would be left outside the scheme, eg agricultural lettings, mobile homes, holiday lettings and lettings where accommodation is shared with the landlord. Existing tenancies would generally also be modified retrospectively to fall within the new scheme, save for those covered by the Rent Act 1977 and the Rent (Agriculture) Act 1976.

## THE AGREEMENT

While an agreement could be made orally, the proposal is that the landlord should be under an obligation to provide a written statement of the terms subsequently, and failure to do that would result in penalties, such as, in the case of a Type I tenancy a financial penalty related to rent payable.

The agreement would contain:
- key terms – information about the parties, the property and the rent;
- compulsory minimum terms – the circumstances in which possession may be sought, and statutory obligations such as repairing terms, such terms would only be enhanced in favour of the occupier and would not be subject to contracting-out;
- special terms – eg those relating to the suppression of anti-social behaviour;
- other terms – some of these would be supplied on a default basis by the model agreements alluded to above, which would apply unless displaced by the parties;
- provision for variation of agreements made;
- local authority tenants would retain their 'right to repair' and consultative rights under separate statutory provisions.

## TERMINATION

No termination by the landlord without due process of law would be a key feature of the scheme, and such process could only be initiated after notice of intention to seek possession, save that in case of anti-social behaviour the proceedings would be commenced at the same time as the notice. Possession under Type I would only be available in respect of stated grounds at the discretion of the court, but mandatory grounds would also exist with regard to Type II, such as serious rent arrears. The Type I grounds would include an ability for landlords to seek possession on an estate management basis, though only where suitable alternative accommodation is to be provided. Where a discretionary ground is relied on the court would be required to take into account the interests of the occupier, the landlord, other occupiers and neighbours. In addition where a public body – a phrase sadly left undefined by the Law Commission – seeks possession in respect of one of the few exceptional situations where a social landlord is able to utilise a Type II agreement, the county court would have power to review the matter applying judicial review principles. this would, inter alia, allow the county court to continue to deal with cases where a local authority has granted a tenancy in respect of interim homeless obligations, see currently s 204A of the Housing Act 1996 and Chapter 10 below.

In relation to fixed term agreements the Law Commission proposals are that where such an agreement ends through effluxion of time, the occupier would continue on a periodic basis under a Type II agreement.

Occupiers under periodic agreements would have the right to terminate by giving one month's notice, but occupation thereafter would be on the basis that the former occupier has become a trespasser. In relation to Type II agreements a notice of intention to terminate by the occupier would enable the landlord to treat that notice as a landlord's notice of intention to seek possession, thus enabling the landlord to seek a possession in court.

In relation to the vexed issue of notice of termination given only by one of two or more joint tenants (see further Chapter 11 below), notice given by all would end the tenancy for all, notice given by one would have the effect of ending the interest only of that one, without prejudice to the other(s). Where a property is abandoned a new measure is proposed to enable the landlord to recover possession following service of an 'abandonment notice', which would be open to challenge in court where the occupier alleges he/she has not actually abandoned the dwelling.

## VARYING AGREEMENTS

### Joint occupation

There is no proposal to end the basic rule that where a property is jointly occupied the liabilities of the occupiers are on a joint and several basis, eg each is liable for all the rent, etc. However, occupation in reality may often be on a 'fluid' basis. Hence it is proposed:

- An occupier (or occupiers) will in general be able to add new parties to the agreement, subject to the consent of the landlord, who would be able to determine the age and general characteristics of new occupants, *and* subject to the general law on overcrowding.
- A joint occupier should be able to leave an agreement by giving notice, the remaining occupier(s) being liable for rent, etc, and where a joint occupier leaves without giving notice, that should enable the landlord to serve an abandonment notice.
- Where there are non-contractual occupants in a dwelling affected by possession proceedings, they should, under the Civil Procedure Rules, be notified of those proceedings.
- Type I occupiers should be able to take in lodgers without their landlord's consent, but Type II would need such consent, while lodgers themselves would have no entitlement to a written agreement, neither would their presence bind the head landlord.
- Where sub-occupation takes place this should be subject to the landlord's veto, but where consent is given, it should result in the sub-occupier having only a periodic Type II agreement.

## Transfers

Landlords should have a general right to veto a transfer of property from the original contacting party to a third party, save:

- where there is a mutual right of exchange, such as that currently enjoyed by local authority secure tenants (which should be extended to all Type I tenants) subject to the landlord's consent;
- where there is a potential successor tenant to a Type I agreement, again subject to the landlord's consent;
- where the property (no matter what the tenancy type) is transferred by a court acting under the Family jurisdiction, which should extend to enable transfers of *all* occupation agreements.

## Death

- The current principle of survivorship to a joint tenancy should continue to apply to a case of joint occupation.
- Where an occupier dies leaving no joint occupier or other successor any periodic agreement should be deemed to end after a defined date.
- There should be succession rights for spouses and partners (including same-sex partners who have cohabited together), other members of the deceased's family and unpaid carers, though people in the last two groups would have had to have lived in the home, or resided with the deceased for 12 months before the death in order to succeed. Where more than one person is entitled to succeed (subject to priority always being given to a spouse/partner) joint succession would be available, but in general there should only be a single succession right, two successions being possible only where a surviving spouse/partner succeeds and, following the death of that person, there is a member of the family or carer also qualifying to succeed.

A number of the Law Commission's proposals (especially those with regard to anti-social behaviour and succession rights for same sex couples) have been taken up by the Government and are reflected in the provisions of the Anti Social Behaviour Act 2003 and the Housing Bill 2003, however, the legislation needed to introduce the proposals on Type I and Type II tenancies would be quite extensive in bulk and would lead to the replacement of much of the current corpus of housing statutes. The question is whether Parliamentary time will be found for such a major revision of the law.

The basic proposals overall are welcome in that they seek to provide a simple and robust basis for the law. It is certainly desirable that there should be commonalty of rights between local authority and registered social landlords' tenants. Where concern arises is with regard to the assumption – and the assumption harks back to the 19th century – that there is effectively equality of arms between landlords and tenants, albeit that a certain amount of consumerist 'tweaking' needs to be applied. But in the present writer's experience there rarely is such equality between the parties in either the private rented or social rented sectors at any time during the course of a tenancy. Even where the law does give protection to tenants they are frequently unaware of their rights or are unwilling or unable to pursue remedies –

for a whole variety of reasons. There may therefore actually be an argument for enhanced rights for all tenants *and* enhanced external regulation, particularly with regard to vulnerable groups of tenants. On the other hand it has to be remembered that extensive regulation in the private sector may lead landlords to withdraw from housing provision on the basis of a reluctance to put up with external 'interference'. There is also the need to bear in mind that enhanced regulation *not* coupled with effective enforcement would lead to the law falling into disrepute and a collapse of tenant confidence in legal protection.

We need here to heed the warning sounded by Alder and Handy in *Housing Association: Law and Practice*[11]. They pointed out that consumerist philosophy is predicated on the basis that consumers have options both to voice their complaints and also to 'exit' from a service, both being means to affect the behaviour of the service provider. The 'voice' option may be seen reflected in the provision of services charters, consultation and grievance mechanisms. The 'exit' option is reflected in the ability of tenants to acquire their own homes, either by the Right to Buy, or by other forms of purchase, in an ability to move to another provider, or to bring about a change in the identity of the service provider. Alder and Handy quite rightly question these assumptions:

'... the width of the discretionary powers exercised by local authorities, housing associations and the Housing Corporation make this perspective unreal. Housing association residents have few determinate legal rights, a position that is unlikely to be affected by the Human Rights Act 1998. Moreover, lack of resources means that "exit" rights are not available to the most vulnerable residents, except in areas of low demand, and in any case there are no corresponding "entry" rights to social housing.'

The present author would agree with that statement and considers it applicable within the local authority and private rented sectors. Indeed we may go somewhat further than this and inquire further into the nature of the consumerist approach to the issue. It appears to derive, as Ann Stewart has pointed out in *Rethinking Housing Law*, from an argument that neither central or local government can become over involved in the minutiae of the delivery of services. Instead there should be competing service providers between whom consumers may choose. This argument, in the context of housing, is reinforced by evidence that the current regulatory based system does not work well because of its inherent complexity, the ignorance of both landlords (social as well as private) and tenants of their rights and obligations, and the unwillingness of both sides to utilise legal remedies. 'Consumerism' in this context would seek to cohere the various provisions on housing with a view to ensuring good standards of service for all recipients who would be protected by standards applicable across the entire housing sector with Codes of Practice being overseen by an external body such as the Office of Fair Trading. Indeed this approach underlies both the Law Commission's Proposals and the Unfair Terms in Consumer Contracts Regulations referred to above. A similar philosophy also underlies central government thinking on 'The Tenant's Charter' in the local authority sector and the Regulatory Code for registered social landlords issued by the Housing Corporation.

---

[11] (2003) Sweet & Maxwell, para 5.04a.

Where housing 'consumers' are able either to voice complaints about standards of service effective, or where they have the – much less likely – ability to 'exit' from the service and seek something better, such a consumerist approach undoubtedly has attractions. However, as we have seen Alder and Handy argue, it is also subject to drawbacks. In the rented housing sector generally those who 'consume' or receive the 'housing service' are generally in an unequal position compared to the provider, either because they have no real choices open to them, or lack the economic means to access choices, or are dependent on the expertise of the landlord – particularly in the 'social housing sector'. Such 'consumers' are vulnerable because of a variety of factors such as age, income, employment, health, poor formal education, single parenthood, ethnic or national origin, and they tend to be concentrated in rented housing, especially in the social rented sector. For such vulnerable consumers, as we have seen Alder and Handy argue, the 'exit' choice is not a viable option. Indeed many in this group may have spent considerable time waiting to access their housing, so they will be unwilling to give it up. This does not, however, prevent complaints being made about the service received. About one-third of tenants in the social housing sector express dissatisfaction with their homes, with repair issues being a considerable cause of complaint.

Can consumerist approaches deal with the issues outlined above? In particular can they apply within the social sector where we have seen Alder and Handy point to the wide discretionary powers of landlords and question the applicability of a contract based consumerist approach. Despite the views of the Law Commission, the latest proposals from central government which we shall examine in detail below (see Chapter 13) appear to favour selective licensing of landlords, a decidedly *regulatory* rather than a consumerist approach. It is indeed hard to conceive how a system based solely on contract could deal with circumstances in which social landlords have to decide on priorities with regard to, for example, repairs. If every tenant has an absolutely equal right to a high standard of repairs – which is undoubtedly desirable – how could a landlord determine whose home should receive attention first, and the issue would be massively compounded if addressed on the basis of 'which housing estate is to have priority?' Furthermore it is hard to see how a purely contractual approach to housing issues could deal with the issue of those who have no contract, ie those who seek access to housing and the homeless.

It has to be said in fairness to the Law Commission that the proposals they put forward in 2002 were only an initial set and particular issues, especially those relating to repairs, were expressly stated to be the subject of work to be undertaken at a later date. Even so the incursion of the Commission into the area of housing law took them into a politically controversial and highly divided area of thinking and debate. Though the injection of a dose of consumerist thinking *may* be both welcome and overdue, it is hard to see how the Law of Housing can easily move from its present eclectic mix of land law, contract and regulatory provision.

It thus seems likely that both housing law and policy in this country will continue for the foreseeable future to be this eclectic mix of provisions and initiatives with no very clearly definable philosophical base, particularly with regard to the rented sector.

## FURTHER READING

Alder, J and Handy, C, *Housing Associations: Law and Practice* (2003) Sweet & Maxwell.

Bright, S, 'Of Estates and Interests: A Tale of Ownership and Property Rights' in Bright, S and Dewar, J (eds) *Land Law: Themes and Perspectives* (1998) OUP.

Davis, M, and Hughes, D, 'An End of the Affair – Social Housing, Relationship Breakdown and the Human Rights Act 1998' [2004] 68 Conv 19.

Gray, K and Gray, S, 'Private Property and Public Property' in McLean, J (ed) *Property and Constitution* (1999) Hart Publishing.

Gray, K and Gray, S, 'The Idea of Property in Land' in Bright, S and Dewar, J (eds) *Land Law: Themes and Perspectives* (1998) OUP.

Grear, A, 'A tale of the land, the insider, the outsider and human rights (an exploration of some problems and possibilities in the relationship between the English Common Law property concepts, human rights law and discourses of exclusion and inclusion' (2003) 23(1) Legal Studies 33–65.

Karn, V, Lickiss, R and Hughes, D, *Tenants' Complaints and The Reform of Housing Management* (1997) Gower.

King, P, 'Housing as a Freedom Right' (2003) 18(5) Housing Studies 661.

Miles, J, 'Property Law v Family Law: resolving the problems of family property'. (2003) 23(4) Legal Studies 624.

Millward, L, and Richardson, J, *Review of the Tenant Sounding Board* (2003) Centre for Comparative Housing Research, De Montfort University, Leicester.

Stewart, A, *Rethinking Housing Law* (1996) Sweet & Maxwell.

# CHAPTER 3

# The Categories of Occupation and the Status of Occupants

## INTRODUCTION

As explained in Chapter 1, housing law, although potentially a subject of enormous width, normally (and for the purposes of this book) is confined to the rights and duties, statutory and common law, of landlords of residential premises and their tenants. However, for reasons to be explored later, even if owner-occupation is excluded, it is not always self-evident that a landlord and tenant relationship has come into being, or whether (instead) some 'lesser' occupational status has been created. In general, occupiers without tenant status are in a worse position legally than those who possess such status.

Aside from owner-occupation and tenancy, the main forms of occupational status are trespass (if this can be termed a 'status'), tolerated trespassers[1] and licensees. In addition, apart from specific statutory forms of tenancy, such as the assured tenant or the secure tenant, the common law recognises a number of variants on the standard tenancy 'model', most obviously joint tenancies and sub-tenancies. This chapter is concerned with the way in which such occupational categories are determined.

Whether such complexity is necessary or desirable is, of course, another matter. The Law Commission in its recent consultation paper (see Chapter 2) generally felt that significant simplification would be desirable.[2] In paragraph 9.40 it states: 'We see no reason why any distinction should be drawn between a contract which comprises a lease and a contract which comprises a licence. This distinction is essential where the proprietary consequences of the contract are concurred, and should remain so, but it should not affect the statutory regulation of the contract as between the contracting parties themselves.' However, the fate of the Law Commission's proposals remains unclear, and, even if adopted, the proposals would only minimise the significance of the 'lease-licence' distinction, rather than eliminating the distinction altogether.

---

[1] Bright, 'The Concept of the Tolerated Trespasser: An Analysis' 119 LQR 495; Cafferkey, 'Tolerated Trespass – what does this mean for the former landlord and tenant?' [1998] 62 Conv 39.

[2] Law Commission Consultation Paper No 162, *Renting Homes 1: Status and Security*.

## TRESPASSERS

A trespasser is someone who occupies premises without any permission to do so. The popular term for occupational trespass today is 'squatting' – although some people who initially 'squat' are later given permission to remain and so cease to be trespassers[3]. The legal position of squatters has been steadily weakened over the past 25 years, through a combination of simplified possession procedures to evict them[4], and increasing criminalisation of their entry into and continued occupation of residential premises[5]. In very limited situations a trespasser may acquire rights effectively if no action is taken to remove him/her after the expiry of 12 years. For this purpose the limitation period begins to run when the trespasser takes 'adverse possession' of the land[6]. In order to be 'adverse'. a trespasser must have factual possession of the land and an intention to exclude others from it, including (as appropriate) the legal owner. However, it is not necessary for the same group of persons to be in 'adverse possession' for the whole 12-year period – the adverse possession of successive trespassers may be added together[7].

## TOLERATED TRESPASSERS

The 'tolerated trespasser' has been described as 'a recent, somewhat bizarre, addition to the *dramatis personae* of the law'[8]. It is far from uncommon for a possession order to be obtained against a tenant, but not enforced. In the 'classic' case the possession order is an 'outright' one bringing the tenancy to an end, yet the ex-tenant remains in occupation, probably paying rent (or at least a charge for the occupation of property) to the landlord[9]. This is particularly likely in relation to public sector tenancies[10]. In some cases this may be simply a matter of sloppy housing management. In other, however, it simply indicates the pressures public landlords are under – if eviction takes place the result may simply be a homeless family on their hands and it may be easier to stick with the 'status quo'. On conventional analysis, there is a serious risk that the voluntary acceptance of rent would result in a new tenancy being created, and certainly the apparent permission for the occupants to remain in the property would prevent them being trespassers. However, as regards public landlords in particular, the courts are aware of the pressures they are under and of the serious difficulties finding a new tenancy relationship could cause them. Matters came to a head in 1996 in the case of *Burrows v Brent London Borough Council*[11]. Here, in August 1984, Brent granted a joint tenancy of a flat to Burrows and her husband. In January 1986 the husband left the premises. Burrows fell into serious arrears with her rent (£2,313 by the time of

---

3    *Greater London Council v Jenkins* [1975] 1 All ER 354; *Camden London Borough Council v Shortlife Community Housing* (1992) 25 HLR 330; *Bruton v London and Quadrant Housing Trust* [2000] 1 AC 406.
4    CPR 1998 r 55 and Sch 1, RSC 1965 Ord 113, and CCR 1981 Ord 24.
5    Criminal Law Act 1977 Pt II as amended by ss 72–76 Criminal Justice and Public Order Act 1994.
6    Limitation Act 1980 s 15(6) and Sch 1.
7    *Pye (JA) (Oxford) Ltd v Graham* [2002] UK HL 30, [2003] 1 AC 419; *Lambeth London Borough Council v Bigden* (2000) 33 HLR 478.
8    Clarke LJ *Pemberton v Southwark London Borough Council* [2000] 1 WLR 1672 at 1683.
9    What has sometimes been called a 'use and occupation' charge, or in old parlance mesne profits.
10   A survey by ROOF, Jan/Feb 2002 p 22 indicates that only 59% of local authority possession orders result in eviction.
11   [1996] 4 All ER 577.

the possession order) and on 29 January 1992 Brent obtained a 14-day outright possession order against Burrows and her estranged husband (effective from 12 February). However, on 5 February the council made a written 'arrangement' with Burrows under which they undertook not to evict her, provided she paid future rent on time plus a sum of £3 per week off the arrears. Burrows did not comply with this agreement and in May 1994 the council issued a warrant for possession, informing her that she would be evicted on 8 June. In fact she moved out of the flat on 7 June. The order was executed and when Burrows returned to the flat on 8 June she found herself locked out, and the premises boarded up. Subsequently she brought an action seeking a declaration that she remained a tenant, a mandatory injunction to be allowed back into the premises and damages for unlawful eviction. The county court found in her favour and the Court of Appeal dismissed the council's appeal. However, the House of Lords unanimously reversed the Court of Appeal finding that no new tenancy had come into being – rather Burrows had acquired nothing more than a 'tolerated trespasser' status. In the words of Lord Browne-Wilkinson:

> 'One factor which weighed heavily with the Court of Appeal in *Regan's* case (to which I also attach importance) is the practical effect of the decision under appeal, ie any consensual variation of an order for possession produces a new secure tenancy or licence. Local authorities and other public housing authorities try to conduct their housing functions as humane and reasonable landlords. In so doing they frequently need to grant indulgences to their tenants to reflect changes in the tenants' circumstances. When applying for possession orders for non-payment of rent local authorities agree to the order being suspended upon the payment of arrears, the rate of payment being adjusted to meet the means of the tenant at the date of the order. If the tenant subsequently loses his job, the landlord will often be willing to reduce the rate of payment of arrears. Why should this not be done by agreement? Yet the effect of the local authority agreeing to such a reduction will be that the tenant, whilst keeping up his payments at the agreed reduced rate, will be in breach of the conditions specified by the order at the higher rate. If so his old tenancy will be terminated. On the view of the law adopted by the Court of Appeal in the present case, a new secure tenancy requiring a new order will come into existence. Similarly where, as with Miss Burrows, the court makes an immediate order for possession but the landlord grants an indulgence by agreeing not to execute the order immediately: if the Court of Appeal decision is correct, the effect of granting the indulgence is to create a new tenancy or licence and the local authority will have to obtain a new possession order. The practical result therefore will be either that the local authority will be reluctant to make reasonable and humane concessions by agreement or in every case will have to make an application to the court to vary the existing order so as to ensure that the old tenancy is not brought to an end. I find it impossible to believe that Parliament intended to produce such an unreasonable regime, penalising sensible agreements out of court and requiring repeated applications to an already overstretched court system.
>
> What, then, is the correct legal analysis? I start from the proposition that were a former tenant is by agreement allowed to remain in possession of the demised property after the termination of the tenancy, the question in each

case is *quo animo* the parties have so acted: depending upon the circumstances, their conduct may give rise to a new tenancy, a licence or some other arrangement. In the present case, on 5 February 1992 the parties plainly did not intend to create a new tenancy or licence but only to defer the execution of the order so long as Miss Burrows complied with the agreed conditions. It cannot be right to impute to the parties an intention to create a legal relationship such as a secure tenancy or licence unless the legal structures within which they made their agreement force that conclusion.

A secure tenancy protected by Part IV of the Act of 1985 is not like an ordinary tenancy. It can only be terminated by an order of the court ordering possession to be given on a particular date or in a particular event. But even determination by order of the court is not final. Until the possession order is executed, the court can by variation of its order change the date on which possession is to be given and thereby revise a secure tenancy which has already been terminated. During the period between the date specified by the order for the giving of possession and the date on which the order is executed there is a period of limbo: the old tenancy has gone but may yet be revived by a further order of the court varying the date of possession. If the parties reach an agreement as to the continued occupation of the premises by the tenant during that limbo period, what intention is to be imputed to them?

In my judgment little guidance is to be obtained from the cases where a tenant holds over after the termination of an ordinary tenancy where there is no possibility that the expired tenancy can revise. The position in relation to secure tenancies is *sui generis*. In my judgment, the agreement can and should take effect in the way the parties intend, ie it is an agreement by the landlords that, upon the tenant complying with the agreed conditions, the landlords will forbear from executing the order, ie from taking the step which would finally put an end to the tenant's right to apply to the court for an order reviving the tenancy. There is no need to impute to the parties an intention to create a new tenancy or licence: the retention of possession and the payment of rent relate to occupation under the old tenancy which is in limbo but which may be revived. In these circumstances I think it is fair to characterise the former tenant as a trespasser whom the landlord has agreed not to evict – a "tolerated trespasser" – pending either the revival of the old tenancy or the breach of the agreed conditions.'

Since *Burrows v Brent* there has been a steady stream of cases further clarifying the nature of 'tolerated trespasser' status[12]. It is clear, for example, that none of the covenants in the former tenancy (for example repair covenants) are enforceable by landlord or tenant – although the courts has an inherent power to 'revive' a secure tenancy, thereby re-establishing the rights and duties which previously existed[13]. Equally if there is clear evidence of an intention to re-establish a new legal relationship, for example by provision of a new tenancy agreement coupled perhaps

---

[12] *Lambeth London Borough Council v Rogers* (1999) 32 HLR 361; *Marshall v Bradford Metropolitan District Council* [2001] EWCA Civ 594, [2002] HLR 428; *Stirling v Leadenhall Residential 2 Ltd* [2001] EWCA Civ 1011, [2002] HLR 19, *Dunn v Bradford Metropolitan District Council* [2002] EWCA Civ 1137; [2003] HLR 154, and *Swindon Borough Council v Aston* [2002] EWCA Civ 1850, [2003] HLR 610.
[13] Housing Act 1985 s 35(2)(b).

with an increase in weekly payments, courts are likely to infer that a new tenancy has come into being. The convenient 'fiction' of 'tolerated trespasser' status can only be taken so far.

Perhaps the key issue is whether 'tolerated trespasser' status is applicable only to public sector tenants, perhaps only to secure tenants. Certainly the case law overwhelmingly concerns such tenants and the concept derived from a desire to ease acknowledged housing management pressures on council landlords. A private landlord who allows a tenant to 'hold over' at the end of an existing tenancy and continues to accept payment for the continued use of the property is much more likely to find that a new tenancy is inferred[14]. However, it is simply that a finding that a person is merely a 'tolerated trespasser' is *more* likely in relation to the public sector, or that it is *exclusively applicable* on policy grounds to the public sector?

The recent case of *Stirling v Leadenhall Residential 2 Ltd*[15] suggests the former. Stirling was a private sector tenant under an assured tenancy. The nature of assured tenancies is discussed in the next chapter but broadly they are the current form of private sector tenancy which give the most legal protection as well as being the standard form of tenancy used by housing associations. Stirling fell into serious rent arrears (£2,832 at the time of the possession hearing). His landlord obtained an outright possession order. Approximately two weeks before this order was to take effect, Stirling wrote to his landlord offering to pay the arrears at the rate of £100 per month. This offer was accepted. However, when some three years later he had again fallen significantly into arrears, his landlord sought possession. A possession order was made and the Court of Appeal subsequently dismissed Stirling's appeal. It was accepted that a new tenancy had come into being, but this had only occurred in March 1998 when the rent was formally increased and so (for reasons discussed in the next chapter) this tenancy was an assured shorthold tenancy not giving legal security. In the period from July 1996 when the agreement over arrears was made, until March 1998 Stirling only occupied the property as a 'tolerated trespasser'. Equally, it is reasonably clear from the case that such findings are far less likely to be made in private sector cases and, in particular, if Leadenhall had given Stirling the kind of assurance about future occupational rights which Brent gave to Burrows it is likely that a new tenancy would have come into being. In the words of Lloyd J:

> 'The first question is whether what was said in July 1996 was intended to alter the relations between the parties so that they should be governed by a new agreement rather than by the order. No new or different terms were come to, as regards the terms on which Mr Stirling was to remain in occupation. He was to go on paying for his occupation at the same rate. The only point dealt with expressly was the rate at which he would pay off the arrears. I can see the force of Mr Luba's criticisms of Judge Coningsby's approach. If there was a new contractual arrangement under which, after July 19, 1996, Mr Stirling had the benefit of exclusive possession of the property for an indefinite period in return for payment, it would be hard to categorise that as anything other than tenancy, in the light of *Street v Mountford*. However, I am impressed by

---

[14] It is of course a question of fact in every case, see *Clarke v Grant* [1950] 1 KB 104 and *Vaughan-Armitrading v Sarsah* (1995) 27 HLR 631.

[15] [2001] EWCA Civ 1011, [2002] HLR 19.

Mr Morgan's submission as to the artificiality of distinguishing what happened in the present case from a case where the landlord does nothing except to accept payments from the former tenant by way of mesne profits, at the rate set out in the order, and towards the arrears, and refrains from enforcing the order. The content of the suggested new contract in the present case is very much more limited than the express agreement entered into in the *Burrows* case. In my judgment, this is a quite different case from *Burrows* on the facts. In agreement with the deputy district judge, I consider the correct analysis of the relevant events to be that the exchange of letters of July 4 and July 8, 1996 was not intended to, and did not, affect the legal relations between the parties which were then, and continued to be, governed by the terms of the order. That remained so until Leadenhall took a position inconsistent with the order, by seeking from Mr Stirling, and obtaining, an increase in the monthly payment for use and occupation. The increased payment could not be justified by reference to the order, and therefore had to be analysed on a different legal basis. It is not disputed and could not be, that this created a new tenancy. From then on, the legal relations between the parties were affected. In my judgment, until then they were not.'

## LICENSEES

In traditional terms a *licensee* is someone who has a right or permission to be on the premises (so that no issue of trespass arises) but whose right is a *personal* rather than a *proprietary* one so that no legal interest in the land is acquired. A licensee's rights are primarily contractual, stemming from the licence agreement. The classic definition of a licence was given as long ago as 1673 in the case of *Thomas v Sorrell*[16], in which it was stated that 'A dispensation or licence properly posseth no interest, nor alters or transfers property in anything but only makes an action lawful, which, without it, had been unlawful.'

In a number of respects a licensee is at a disadvantage in terms of residential status and rights; most importantly, in relation to a lack of statutory rent controls and effective statutory security of tenure (these issues are discussed further in Chapter 4). Correspondingly, the legal position of a licensor 'landlord' is significantly stronger. If the matter was to be seen by the courts as merely one of drafting, of contract 'construction', then few well-advised landlords would fail to avail themselves of the licence loophole. Prior to the key decision of *Street v Mountford*, the law was in danger of accommodating landlords in just this way. However, Lord Templeman, in giving the unanimous judgment of the House of Lords in *Street*, was at pains to emphasise that merely calling something a licence did not necessarily make it one. Instead, the 'reality' of what had been agreed had to be discerned. Above all, what distinguished a tenancy from a licence was that in reality a tenant enjoyed exclusive possession of the property occupied (the right to exclude others from the property for the duration of the term granted), whereas a licensee did not.

---

[16]   *Thomas v Sorrell* (1673) Vaugh 330.

*Street v Mountford*[17] concerned an agreement made in March 1983 by which Street (a solicitor in Bournemouth as well as a landlord) granted Mountford a right to occupy two furnished rooms subject to termination by 14 days' written notice. The agreement was stated to be a licence not a tenancy, and contained some clauses more consistent with a licence arrangement (for example, an absolute right for Street to enter the property and inspect it at any time). When Mountford applied for a fair rent (see Chapter 4), Street opposed this on the grounds that she was just a licensee. The Court of Appeal agreed, but the House of Lords did not. The reasons are stated clearly in the following extract from Lord Templeman's judgment:

> 'In the case of residential accommodation there is no difficulty in deciding whether the grant confers exclusive possession. An occupier of residential accommodation at a rent for a term is either a lodger or a tenant. The occupier is a lodger if the landlord provides attendance or services which require the landlord or his servants to exercise unrestricted access to and use of the premises. A lodger is entitled to live in the premises but cannot call the place his own. In *Allan v Liverpool Overseers* (1874) LR 9 QB 180, 191–192 Blackburn J said:
>
> > "A lodger in a house, although he had the exclusive use of rooms in the house, in the sense that nobody else is to be there, and though his goods are stowed there, yet he is not in exclusive occupation in that sense, because the landlord is there for the purpose of being able, as landlords commonly do in the case of lodgings, to have his own servants to look after the house and the furniture, and has retained to himself the occupation, though he has agreed to give the exclusive enjoyment of the occupation to the lodger."
>
> If on the other hand residential accommodation is granted for a term at a rent with exclusive possession, the landlord providing neither attendance nor services, the grant is a tenancy; any express reservation to the landlord of limited rights to enter and view the state of the premises and to repair and maintain the premises only serves to emphasise the fact that the grantee is entitled to exclusive possession and is a tenant. In the present case it is conceded that Mrs Mountford is entitled to exclusive possession and is not a lodger. Mr Street provided neither attendance nor services and only reserved the limited rights of inspection and maintenance and the like set forth in clause 3 of the agreement. On the traditional view of the matter, Mrs Mountford not being a lodger must be a tenant.
>
> There can be no tenancy unless the occupier enjoys exclusive possession; but an occupier who enjoys exclusive possession is not necessarily a tenant. He may be owner in fee simple, a trespasser, a mortgagee in possession, an object of charity or a service occupier. To constitute a tenancy the occupier must be granted exclusive possession for a fixed or periodic term certain in consideration of a premium or periodical payments. The grant may be express, or may be inferred where the owner accepts weekly or other periodical payments from the occupier. ...
>
> In the present case, the agreement dated 7 March 1983 professed an intention by both parties to create a licence and their belief that they had in fact created

[17]   *Street v Mountford* [1985] AC 809, [1985] 2 All ER 289.

a licence. It was submitted on behalf of Mr Street that the court cannot in these circumstances decide that the agreement created a tenancy without interfering with the freedom of contract enjoyed by both parties. My Lords, Mr Street enjoyed freedom to offer Mrs Mountford the right to occupy the rooms comprised in the agreement on such lawful terms as Mr Street pleased. Mrs Mountford enjoyed freedom to negotiate with Mr Street to obtain different terms. Both parties enjoyed freedom to contract or not to contract and both parties exercised that freedom by contracting on the terms set forth in the written agreement and on no other terms. But the consequences in law of the agreement, once concluded, can only be determined by consideration of the effect of the agreement. If the agreement satisfied all the requirements of a tenancy, then the agreement produced a tenancy and the parties cannot alter the effect of the agreement by insisting that they only created a licence. The manufacture of a five pronged implement for manual digging results in a fork even if the manufacturer, unfamiliar with the English language, insists that he intended to make and has made a spade.

It was also submitted that in deciding whether the agreement created a tenancy or a licence, the court should ignore the Rent Acts. If Mr Street has succeeded, where owners have failed these past 70 years, in driving a coach and horses through the Rent Acts, he must be left to enjoy the benefit of his ingenuity unless and until Parliament intervenes. I accept that the Rent Acts are irrelevant to the problem of determining the legal effect of the rights granted by the agreement. Like the professed intention of the parties, the Rent Acts cannot alter the effect of the agreement. ...

Exclusive possession is of first importance in considering whether an occupier is a tenant; exclusive possession is not decisive because an occupier who enjoys exclusive possession is not necessarily a tenant. The occupier may be a lodger or service occupier or fall within the other exceptional categories mentioned by Denning LJ in *Errington v Errington and Woods* [1952] 1 KB 290.

In *Isaac v Hotel de Paris Ltd* [1960] 1 WLR 239 an employee who managed a night bar in a hotel for his employer company which held a lease of the hotel negotiated "subject to contract" to complete the purchase of shares in the company and to be allowed to run the nightclub for his own benefit if he paid the head rent payable by the company for the hotel. In the expectation that the negotiations "subject to contract" would ripen into a binding agreement, the employee was allowed to run the nightclub and he paid the company's rent. When negotiations broke down the employee claimed unsuccessfully to be a tenant of the hotel company. The circumstances in which the employee was allowed to occupy the premises showed that the hotel company never intended to accept him as a tenant and that he was fully aware of that fact. This was a case, consistent with the authorities cited by Lord Denning in giving the advice of the Judicial Committee of the Privy Council, in which the parties did not intend to enter into contractual relationships unless and until the negotiations "subject to contract" were replaced by a binding contract.

In *Abbeyfield (Harpenden) Society Ltd v Woods* [1968] 1 WLR 374 the occupier of a room in an old people's home was held to be a licensee and not a tenant. Lord Denning MR said, at p. 376:

"The modern cases show that a man may be a licensee even though he has exclusive possession, even though the word 'rent' is used, and even though the word 'tenancy' is used. The court must look at the agreement as a whole and see whether a tenancy really was intended. In this case there is, besides the one room, the provision of services, meals, a resident house-keeper, and such like. The whole arrangement was so personal in nature that the proper inference is that he was a licensee."

As I understand the decision in the *Abbeyfield* case the court came to the conclusion that the occupier was a lodger and was therefore a licensee, not a tenant.

In *Shell-Mex and BP Ltd v Manchester Garages Ltd* [1971] 1 WLR 612 the Court of Appeal after carefully examining an agreement whereby the defendant was allowed to use a petrol company's filling station for the purposes of selling petrol, came to the conclusion that the agreement did not grant exclusive possession to the defendant who was therefore a licensee. At p. 615 Lord Denning MR in considering whether the transaction was a licence or a tenancy said:

"Broadly speaking, we have to see whether it is a personal privilege given to a person (in which case it is a licence), or whether it grants an interest in land (in which case it is a tenancy). At one time it used to be thought that exclusive possession was a decisive factor. But that is not so. It depends on broader considerations altogether. Primarily on whether it is personal in its nature or not: see *Errington v Errington and Woods* [1952] 1 KB 290."

In my opinion the agreement was only "personal in its nature" and created "a personal privilege" if the agreement did not confer the right to exclusive possession of the filling station. No other test for distinguishing between a contractual tenancy and a contractual licence appears to be understandable or workable.

*Heslop v Burns* [1974] 1 WLR 1241 was another case in which the owner of a cottage allowed a family to live in the cottage rent free and it was held that no tenancy at will had been created on the ground that the parties did not intend any legal relationship. Scarman LJ cited with approval, at p. 1252, the statement by Denning LJ in *Facchini v Bryson* [1952] 1 TLR 1386, 1389:

"In all the cases where an occupier has been held to be a licensee there has been something in the circumstances, such as a family arrangement, an act of friendship or generosity, or such like, to negative any intention to create a tenancy."

In *Marchant v Charters* [1977] 1 WLR 1181 a bedsitting room was occupied on terms that the landlord cleaned the rooms daily and provided clean linen each week. It was held by the Court of Appeal that the occupier was a licensee and not a tenant. The decision in the case is sustainable on the grounds that the occupier was a lodger and did not enjoy exclusive possession. But Lord Denning MR said, at p. 1185:

"What is the test to see whether the occupier of one room in a house is a tenant or a licensee? It does not depend on whether he or she has exclusive possession or not. It does not depend on whether the room is furnished or not. It does not depend on whether the occupation is permanent or temporary. It does not depend on the label which the parties put upon it. All these are factors which may influence the decision but none of them is conclusive. All the circumstances have to be worked out. Eventually the answer depends on the nature and quality of the occupancy. Was it intended that the occupier should have a stake in the room or did he have only permission for himself personally to occupy the room, whether under a contract or not? In which case he is a licensee."

But in my opinion in order to ascertain the nature and quality of the occupancy and to see whether the occupier has or has not a stake in the room or only permission for himself personally to occupy, the court must decide whether upon its true construction the agreement confers on the occupier exclusive possession. If exclusive possession at a rent for a term does not constitute a tenancy then the distinction between a contractual tenancy and a contractual licence of land becomes wholly unidentifiable. ...

In the present case the Court of Appeal, 49 P & CR 461 held that the agreement dated 7 March 1983 only created a licence. Slade LJ, at p. 329 accepted that the agreement and in particular clause 3 of the agreement "shows that the right to occupy the premises conferred on the defendant was intended as an exclusive right of occupation, in that it was thought necessary to give a special and express power to the plaintiff to enter ..." Before your Lordships it was conceded that the agreement conferred the right of exclusive possession on Mrs Mountford. Even without clause 3 the result would have been the same. By the agreement Mrs Mountford was granted the right to occupy residential accommodation. The landlord did not provide any services or attendance. It was plain that Mrs Mountford was not a lodger. Slade LJ proceeded to analyse all the provisions of the agreement to the category of terms which he thought are usually to be found in a tenancy agreement and of assigning other provisions to the category of terms which he thought are usually to be found in a licence. Slade LJ may or may not have been right that in a letting of a furnished room it was "most unusual to find a provision in a tenancy agreement obliging the tenant to keep his rooms in a 'tidy condition'" (p. 329). If Slade LJ was right about this and other provisions there is still no logical method of evaluating the results of his survey. Slade LJ reached the conclusion that "the agreement bears all the hallmarks of a licence rather than a tenancy save for the one important feature of exclusive occupation": p. 329. But in addition to the hallmark of exclusive occupation of residential accommodation there were the hallmarks of weekly payments for a periodical term. Unless these three hallmarks are decisive, it really becomes impossible to distinguish a contractual tenancy from a contractual licence save by reference to the professed intention of the parties or by the judge awarding marks for drafting. Slade LJ was finally impressed by the statement at the foot of the agreement by Mrs Mountford "I understand and accept that a licence in the above form does not and is not intended to give me a tenancy protected under the Rent Acts." Slade LJ said, at p. 330:

"it seems to me that, if the defendant is to displace the express statement of intention embodied in the declaration, she must show that the declaration was either a deliberate sham or at least an inaccurate statement of what was the true substance of the real transaction agreed between the parties; ..."

My Lords, the only intention which is relevant is the intention demonstrated by the agreement to grant exclusive possession for a term at a rent. Sometimes it may be difficult to discover whether, on the true construction of an agreement, exclusive possession is conferred. Sometimes it may appear from the surrounding circumstances that there was no intention to create legal relationships. Sometimes it may appear from the surrounding circumstances that the right to exclusive possession is referable to a legal relationship other than a tenancy. Legal relationships to which the grant of exclusive possession might be referable and which would or might negative the grant of an estate or interest in the land include occupancy under a contract for the sale of the land, occupancy pursuant to a contract of employment or occupancy referable to the holding of an office. But where as in the present case the only circumstances are that residential accommodation is offered and accepted with exclusive possession for a term at a rent, the result is a tenancy.

The position was well summarised by Windeyer J sitting in the High Court of Australia in *Radaich v Smith* (1959) 101 CLR 209, 222, where he said:

"What then is the fundamental right which a tenant has that distinguishes his position from that of a licensee? It is an interest in land as distinct from a personal permission to enter the land and use it for some stipulated purpose or purposes. And how is it to be ascertained whether such an interest in land has been given? By seeing whether the grantee was given a legal right of exclusive possession of the land for a term or from year to year or for a life or lives. If he was, he is a tenant. And he cannot be other than a tenant, because a legal right of exclusive possession is a tenancy and the creation of such a right is a demise. To say that a man who has, by agreement with a landlord, a right of exclusive possession of land for a term is not a tenant is simply to contradict the first proposition by the second. A right of exclusive possession is secured by the right of a lessee to maintain ejectment and, after his entry, trespass. A reservation to the landlord, either by contract or statute, of a limited right of entry, as for example to view or repair is, of course, not inconsistent with the grant of exclusive possession. Subject to such reservations, a tenant for a term or from year to year or for a life or lives can exclude his landlord as well as strangers from the demised premises. All this is long established law: see *Cole on Ejectment* (1857) pp. 72, 73, 287, 458."

My Lords, I gratefully adopt the logic and the language of Windeyer J. Henceforth the courts which deal with these problems will, save in exceptional circumstances, only be concerned to inquire whether as a result of an agreement relating to residential accommodation the occupier is a lodger or a tenant. In the present case I am satisfied that Mrs Mountford is a tenant, that the appeal should be allowed, that the order of the Court of Appeal should be set aside and that the respondent should be ordered to pay the costs of the appellant here and below.'

The impact of *Street v Mountford* was immediate and profound[18]. Presumptively in all cases where a grant of 'exclusive possession' was made and some kind of term/rent provision existed, there would be a tenancy unless exceptional circumstances applied. No longer would the simple device of terming something to be a licence be sufficient. Lord Templeman does not attempt to delineate in detail what such exceptional circumstances might be. However, a close reading of his judgment, particularly his reference to 'informal acts of friendship', 'lodgers' and 'service occupiers' suggests that the following would be typical instances:

* informal arrangements between family members and friends, particularly in relation to cohabitants, or where it is clearly intended to be a loose short-term arrangement[19];
* retirement and nursing homes where there is a need for continual supervision and care requiring constant access[20];
* genuine hostel arrangements, particularly where the occupier may be required to move out to accommodate new entrants;
* accommodation like a hotel or bed and breakfast establishment where the provision of meals and/or significant services where room cleaning is central to the arrangement;
* accommodation which 'comes with the job', and where it is a condition of the employment that the person lives in the accommodation for the better performance of their employment obligations[21].

However, a moment's reflection indicates that these categories are far from watertight; for example, it is certainly not the case that simply calling something a hotel is enough to legitimise a claim that merely licences have been created. Likewise, simply because one family member makes an arrangement with another to allow them to occupy a property owned by the first does not preclude a finding of tenancy if the arrangement is a relatively formal one[22]. In similar vein courts will be quick to detect the sham of purely notional services attaching to an otherwise clear-cut landlord and tenant arrangement[23]. In all the above cases the key seems to be exclusive possession. If this exists, it will be normal to see a tenancy. If it does not exist (either because the landlord needs constant access, or because of the informal nature of the arrangement), then the arrangement is likely to be viewed as a licence.

It is possible that Lord Templeman could have been even more explicit in *Street v Mountford*. Certainly he might have avoided the occasional confusion between 'exclusive occupation', which even many licensees will possess, and 'exclusive possession'. Nevertheless, the lack of consistency in a number of subsequent Court of Appeal decisions was surprising[24].

---

[18] Academic comment was substantial, see for example Anderson, 'Licences: Traditional Law Revived' 48 MCR 712; Bridge, '*Street v Mountford* No Hiding Place?' (1986) 50 The Conveyancer 344 and Street, 'Coach and Horses Cancelled? Rent Act Avoidance After *Street v Mountford*' (1985) 49 The Conveyancer 328.

[19] *Monmouth Borough Council v Marlog* (1995) 27 HLR 30.

[20] *Abbeyfield (Harpenden) Society v Woods* [1968] 1 All ER 352n.

[21] *Norris v Checksfield* [1991] 4 All ER 327.

[22] *Ward v Warnke* (1990) 22 HLR 496.

[23] *Aslan v Murphy (No 2)* [1989] 3 All ER 130 and *Duke v Wynne* [1989] 3 All ER 130.

[24] In particular, the clear inconsistency in approach manifested in *AG Securities v Vaughan* [1988] 2 All ER 173 and *Antoniades v Villiers* [1990] 1 AC 417, [1988] 2 All ER 309.

In some cases a wide 'policy orientated' view of *Street* was taken. In other cases the landlord's continuing right to 'contract out' of protective legislation was underlined. Finally, the House of Lords returned to the issue again in the linked cases of *AG Securities v Vaughan* and *Antoniades v Villiers*[25]. These two appeals were heard together by the House of Lords. In *Vaughan*, AG Securities owned a block of flats in north London. One flat comprised six living rooms as well as a kitchen and bathroom. Two of the living rooms were for the common use of the occupants of the flat, the other four were bedrooms. Each of the occupants had their own bedroom and had made separate agreements with AG Securities which were stated to be licence agreements. The four occupants had never operated as a group, indeed they had occupied the property at separate dates between 1982 and 1985. Despite this the Court of Appeal had found that a joint tenancy existed. In *Villiers*, the occupants, Villiers and Bridger, were a couple cohabiting in an attic flat in south London owned by Antoniades. The flat comprised a bedroom, a small living room and a kitchen and bathroom. Villiers and Bridger had signed separate licence agreements which in theory allowed others to occupy the flat with them, although this had never happened in practice. The Court of Appeal construed the arrangement as consisting of two separate licences.

The House of Lords reversed both Court of Appeal decisions and took the opportunity to restate the law even more explicitly than in *Street*. Lord Templeman again delivered the leading judgment:

'Parties to an agreement cannot contract out of the Rent Acts; if they were able to do so the Acts would be a dead letter because in a state of housing shortage a person seeking residential accommodation may agree to anything to obtain shelter. The Rent Acts protect a tenant but they do not protect a licensee. Since parties to an agreement cannot contract out of the Rent Acts, a document which expressed the intention, genuine or bogus, of both parties or of one party to create a licence will nevertheless create a tenancy if the rights and obligations enjoyed and imposed satisfy the legal requirements of a tenancy. A person seeking residential accommodation may concur in any expression of intention in order to obtain shelter. Since parties to an agreement cannot contract out of the Rent Acts, a document expressed in the language of a licence must nevertheless be examined and construed by the court in order to decide whether the rights and obligations enjoyed and imposed create a licence or a tenancy. A person seeking residential accommodation may sign a document couched in any language in order to obtain shelter. Since parties to an agreement cannot contract out of the Rent Acts, the grant of a tenancy to two persons jointly cannot be concealed, accidentally or by design, by the creation of two documents in the form of licences. Two persons seeking residential accommodation may sign any number of documents in order to obtain joint shelter. In considering one or more documents for the purpose of deciding whether a tenancy has been created, the court must consider the surrounding circumstances including any relationship between the prospective occupiers, the course of negotiations and the nature and extent of the accommodation and the intended and actual mode of

25   [1990] 1 AC 417, [1988] 3 All ER 1058.

occupation of the accommodation. If the owner of a one-bedroomed flat granted a licence to a husband to occupy that flat provided he share the flat with his wife and nobody else and granted a similar licence to the wife provided she shared the flat with the husband and nobody else, the court would be bound to consider the effect of both documents together. If the licence to the husband required him to pay a licence fee of £50 per month and the licence to the wife required her to pay a further licence fee of £50 per month, the two documents read together in the light of the property to be occupied and the obvious intended mode of occupation would confer exclusive occupation on the husband and wife jointly and a tenancy at the rent of £100.

Landlords dislike the Rent Acts and wish to enjoy the benefits of letting property without the burden of the restrictions imposed by the Acts. Landlords believe that the Rent Acts unfairly interfere with freedom of contract and exacerbate the housing shortage. Tenants on the other hand believe that the Acts are a necessary protection against the exploitation of people who do not own the freehold or long leases of their homes. The court lacks the knowledge and the power to form any judgment on these arguments which fall to be considered and determined by Parliament. The duty of the court is to enforce the Acts and in so doing to observe one principle which is inherent in the Acts and has been long recognised, the principle that parties cannot contract out of the Acts.

The enjoyment of exclusive occupation for a term in consideration of periodical payments creates a tenancy, save in exceptional circumstances not relevant to these appeals: see *Street v Mountford* [1985] AC 809, 826–827. The grant of one room with exclusive occupation in consideration of a periodic payment creates a tenancy, although if the room is not a dwelling, the tenant is not protected by the Rent Acts: see *Curl v Angelo* [1948] 2 All ER 189. The grant of one room with exclusive occupation as a dwelling creates a tenancy but if a tenant shares some other essential living premises such as a kitchen with his landlord or other persons, the room is not let as a separate dwelling within the meaning of section 1 of the Rent Act 1977: see *Neale v Del Soto* [1945] KB 144 and *Cole v Harris* [1945] KB 474. Section 21 of the Act of 1977 confers some rights on a tenant who shares essential living premises with his landlord, and section 22 confers protection on a tenant who shares some essential living premises with persons other than the landlord.

If, under an agreement, the owner of residential accommodation provides services or attendance and retains possession for that purpose the occupier is a lodger and the agreement creates a licence. Under an agreement for the exclusive occupation of a room or rooms consisting of a dwelling for periodic payments then, save in the exceptional circumstances mentioned in *Street v Mountford* [1985] AC 809, 826–827, a single occupier, if he is not a lodger, must be a tenant. The agreement may provide expressly or by implication, power for the owner to enter the dwelling to inspect or repair but if the occupier is entitled to the use and enjoyment of the dwelling and is not a lodger he is in exclusive occupation and the agreement creates a tenancy.

Where residential accommodation is occupied by two or more persons the occupiers may be licensees or tenants of the whole or each occupier may be a separate tenant of part. In the present appeals the only question raised is whether the occupiers are licensees or tenants of the whole. ...

In the first appeal the four agreements were independent of one another. In the second appeal the two agreements were interdependent. Both would have been signed or neither. The two agreements must therefore be read together. Mr Villiers and Miss Bridger applied to rent the flat jointly and sought and enjoyed joint and exclusive occupation of the whole of the flat. They shared the rights and the obligations imposed by the terms of their occupation. They acquired joint and exclusive occupation of the flat in consideration of periodical payments and they therefore acquired a tenancy jointly. Mr Antoniades required each of them. Mr Villiers and Miss Bridger, to agree to pay one half of each aggregate periodical payment, but this circumstance cannot convert a tenancy into a licence. A tenancy remains a tenancy even though the landlord may choose to require each of two joint tenants to agree expressly to pay one half of the rent. The tenancy conferred on Mr Villiers and Miss Bridger the right to occupy the whole flat as their dwelling. Clause 16 reserved to Mr Antoniades the power at any time to go into occupation of the flat jointly with Mr Villiers and Miss Bridger. The exercise of that power would at common law put an end to the exclusive occupation of the flat by Mr Villiers and Miss Bridger, terminate the tenancy of Mr Villiers and Miss Bridger, and convert Mr Villiers and Miss Bridger into licensees. But the powers reserved to Mr Antoniades by clause 16 cannot be lawfully exercised because they are inconsistent with the provisions of the Rent Acts.

When Mr Antoniades entered into the agreements dated 9 February 1985 with Mr Villiers and Miss Bridger and when Mr Antoniades allowed Mr Villiers and Miss Bridger to occupy the flat, it is clear from the negotiations which had taken place, from the surrounding circumstances, and from subsequent events, that Mr Antoniades did not intend in February 1985, immediately or contemporaneously, to share occupation or to authorise any other person to deprive Mr Villiers and Miss Bridger of exclusive occupation of the flat. Clause 16, if genuine, was a reservation by a landlord of a power at some time during the currency of the tenancy to share occupation with the tenant. The exclusive occupation of the tenant coupled with the payment of rent created a tenancy which at common law could be terminated and converted into a licence as soon as the landlord exercised his power to share occupation. But under the Rent Acts, if a contractual tenancy is terminated, the Acts protect the occupiers from eviction. ...

In *Street v Mountford* [1985] AC 809, 825, I said:

> "Although the Rent Acts must not be allowed to alter or influence the construction of an agreement, the court should, in my opinion, be astute to detect and frustrate sham devices and artificial transactions whose only object is to disguise the grant of a tenancy and to evade the Rent Acts."

It would have been more accurate and less liable to give rise to misunderstandings if I had substituted the word "pretence" for the references to "sham devices" and "artificial transactions". *Street v Mountford* was not a case which involved a pretence concerning exclusive possession. The agreement did not mention exclusive possession and the owner conceded that the occupier enjoyed exclusive possession. In *Somma v Hazelhurst* [1978] 1 WLR 1014 and other cases considered in *Street v Mountford*, the owner wished to let residential accommodation but to avoid the Rent Acts. The occupiers wished to take a letting of residential accommodation. The owner stipulated for the execution of agreements which pretended that exclusive possession was not to be enjoyed by the occupiers. The occupiers were obliged to acquiesce with this pretence in order to obtain the accommodation. In my opinion the occupiers either did not understand the language of the agreements or assumed, justifiably, that in practice the owner would not violate their privacy. The owner's real intention was to rely on the language of the agreement to escape the Rent Acts. The owner allowed the occupiers to enjoy jointly exclusive occupation and accepted rent. A tenancy was created. *Street v Mountford* reasserted three principles. First, parties to an agreement cannot contract out of the Rent Acts. Secondly, in the absence of special circumstances, not here relevant, the enjoyment of exclusive occupation for a term in consideration of periodic payments creates a tenancy. Thirdly, where the language of licence contradicts the reality of lease, the facts must prevail. The facts must prevail over the language in order that the parties may not contract out of the Rent Acts. In the present case clause 16 was a pretence.

The fact that clause 16 was a pretence appears from its terms and from the negotiations. Clause 16 in terms conferred on Mr Antoniades and other persons the right to share the bedroom occupied by Mr Villiers and Miss Bridger. Clause 16 conferred power on Mr Antoniades to convert the sitting-room occupied by Mr Villiers and Miss Bridger into a bedroom which could be jointly occupied by Mr Villiers, Miss Bridger, Mr Antoniades and any person or person nominated by Mr Antoniades. The facilities in the flat were not suitable for sharing between strangers. If clause 16 had been genuine there would have been some discussion between Mr Antoniades, Mr Villiers and Miss Bridger as to how clause 16 might be operated in practice and in whose favour it was likely to be operated. The addendum imposed on Mr Villiers and Miss Bridger sought to add plausibility to the pretence of sharing by forfeiting the right of Mr Villiers and Miss Bridger to continue to occupy the flat if their double-bedded romance blossomed into wedding bells. Finally and significantly, Mr Antoniades never made any attempt to obtain increased income from the flat by exercising the powers which clause 16 purported to reserve to him. Clause 16 was only designed to disguise the grant of a tenancy and to contract out of the Rent Acts. In this case in the Court of Appeal [1988] 3 WLR 139, 148, Bingham LJ said:

> "The written agreements cannot possibly be construed as giving the occupants, jointly or severally, exclusive possession of the flat or any part of it. They stipulate with reiterated emphasis that the occupants shall not have exclusive possession."

My Lords, in *Street v Mountford* [1985] AC 809, this House stipulated with reiterated emphasis that an express statement of intention is not decisive and that the court must pay attention to the facts and surrounding circumstances and to what people do as well as to what people say.'

The above decision(s) go some way to resolving the questions left unanswered by *Street v Mountford*. Above all, convert 'contracting out' of the Rent Act and other 'protective' legislation via the use of purported licences is not to be allowed. Lord Templeman's judgment is probably the clearest on this point (at p 458):

> 'Parties to an agreement cannot contract out of the Rent Acts; if they were able to do so the Acts would be a dead letter because in a state of housing shortage a person seeking residential accommodation may agree to anything to obtain shelter. ... Since parties ... cannot contract out of the Rent Acts, a document which expresses the intention, genuine or bogus, of both parties or of one party to create a licence will nevertheless create a tenancy if the rights and obligations enjoyed and imposed satisfy the legal requirements of a tenancy.'

However, Lord Oliver is almost as clear, and Lords Ackner and Bridge agreed with Lords Oliver and Templeman. Secondly, it is clear that although the form of the agreement cannot be ignored, it must give way to the 'substance and reality' of the agreement. In coming to a decision as to the 'substance' of the agreement, evidence as to how it was likely to work and indeed did work in practice is of particular importance. Lord Oliver is particularly clear on this (in relation to *Antoniades v Villiers*)

> 'There is equally no question but that the premises are not suitable for occupation by more than one couple save on a very temporary basis ... the size of the accommodation and the facilities available clearly do not make the flat suitable for multiple occupation ... There is an air of total unreality about the documents read as separate and individual licences in the light of the circumstance that the appellants were together seeking a flat as a quasi matrimonial home.'

The decisions also give further indication as to situations where the normal approach might not apply, or as to where an agreement is likely to be seen as a licence, even if the normal approach is followed. For example, in overturning the majority ruling in *AG Securities v Vaughan* that a joint tenancy had been created, the House of Lords were at pains to point out that it was not solely a policy issue with which they were concerned, there had to be a realistic claim that (sole or joint) exclusive possession had been created/granted. As Lord Oliver stated:

> 'The facts in this appeal are startlingly different from those in the case of *Antoniades*. To begin with, the appeal concerns a substantial flat in a mansion block consisting of four bedrooms, a lounge, a sitting-room and usual offices. ... There is no question but that the agreements with which the appeal is concerned reflect the true bargain between the parties. It is the purpose and intention of both parties to each agreement that it should confer an individual right on the licensee named, that he should be liable only for the payment which he had undertaken, and that his agreement should be capable of termination without reference to the agreements with other persons occupying the flat. ... I agree with the dissenting judgment of Sir George Waller in finding no unity of interest, no unity of title, certainly no unity of time and, as I think, no unity of possession. I find it impossible to say that the agreements

entered into with the respondents created either individually or collectively a single tenancy either of the entire flat or of any part of it.'

It is clear from this that there must be some credibility in the claim that either sole or joint exclusive possession was granted; and that where there is a 'shifting population' owing little affinity to one another, such a claim will be harder to sustain. For further exemplification of this point, see *Stribling v Wickham*[26] and *Nicolaou v Pitt*[27]. In *Stribling*, a county court finding of a joint tenancy was overturned where a flat, originally occupied by three friends, was at the time of legal proceedings occupied by only one of the original three plus two others. In the words of Parker LJ:

'The flat was suitable for use by a multiple but shifting population, and was so used. ... Each licensee had a specific obligation to pay the amount reserved by his agreement only. In my judgment there is no process of "legal alchemy" by which the agreement can be placed into the mould of a tenancy.'

In *Nicolaou*, a county court finding of a tenancy was upheld where a small flat (two rooms, bathroom and kitchen) was at the time of the legal proceedings occupied by the ex-husband of one of the original three occupants (none of whom was any longer in occupation). The Court of Appeal felt that there was ample justification for the judges finding that *de facto* exclusive possession had been granted to the husband and wife, of which the husband was the 'successor'.

It might be thought that the easiest way to bolster a 'licence' argument would be to demonstrate that services were provided or rights over the property were retained, so as to undermine any wholly 'exclusive' possession in the occupants – perhaps by retaining a key for this purpose. However, while the provision of substantial services is likely to convert an occupant into a lodger (and so a licensee), the court will be vigilant to detect pretences and shams aimed solely at undermining tenancy status. This is demonstrated by *Aslan v Murphy (Nos 1 and 2)*[28] and *Duke v Wynne*[29].

In *Aslan,* Murphy occupied a small single room under a claimed licence agreement. The licence agreement reserved the right of the 'landlord' to use the room between midnight and 10.30 am and noon and midnight each day. Various services, such as rubbish collection, laundering of bed linen and window cleaning were promised. In practice, the landlord never used the property and very few services were provided. The Court of Appeal had little difficulty in finding the arrangement to be a tenancy and to dismiss provisions to the contrary in the agreement as shams. Lord Donaldson MR was very clear:

'The judge was, of course, quite right to approach the matter on the basis that it is not a crime, nor is it contrary to public policy, for a property owner to license occupiers to occupy a property on terms which do not give rise to a tenancy. Where he went wrong was in considering whether the whole agreement was a sham and, having concluded that it was not, giving effect to

---

[26]  (1989) 21 HLR 381.
[27]  (1989) 21 HLR 487.
[28]  [1990] 1 WLR 766.
[29]  [1989] 3 All ER 130.

its terms, *ie* taking it throughout at face value. What he should have done, and I am sure would have done if he had known of the House of Lords approach to the problem, was to consider whether the whole agreement was a sham and, if it was not, whether in the light of the factual situation the provisions for sharing the room and those depriving Mr Murphy of the right to occupy it for 90 minutes out of each 24 hours were part of the true bargain between the parties or were pretences. Both provisions were wholly unrealistic and were clearly pretences.

In this court an attempt to uphold the judge's decision was made upon a different basis, namely, the landlord's right to retain the keys. The provisions relevant to this aspect of the agreement are as follows:

> "1. ... The licensor will retain the keys to the room and his absolute right of entry at all times for the purpose of exercising such control and (without prejudice to the generality of the foregoing) for the purpose of effecting any repairs or cleaning to the room or building or for the purpose of providing the attendance mentioned in Clause 4 hereof or for the purpose of removing or substituting such articles of furniture from the room as the licensor might see fit. The said right of entry is exerciseable by the licensor or his servants or agents with or without any other persons (including prospective future licensees of the room).
>
> ...
>
> 4. The licensor will provide the following attendance for the licensee:
>
> (1)  housekeeping
>
> (2)  lighting of common parts
>
> (3)  cleaning of common parts
>
> (4)  window cleaning
>
> (5)  intercom
>
> (6)  telephone coin box
>
> (7)  cleaning of room
>
> (8)  collection of rubbish
>
> (9)  provision and laundering of bed linen
>
> (10) hot water
>
> (11) provision of household supplies."

Provisions as to keys are often relied upon in support of the contention that an occupier is a lodger rather than a tenant. Thus in *Duke v Wynne*, to which we turn next, the agreement required the occupier "not to interfere with or change the locks on any part of the premises, [or] give the key to any other than an authorised occupier of the premises." Provisions as to keys, if not a pretence which they often are, do not have any magic in themselves. It is not a requirement of a tenancy that the occupier shall have exclusive possession of the keys to the property. What matters is what underlies the provisions as to keys. Why does the owner want a key, want to prevent keys being issued to the friends of the occupier or want to prevent the lock being changed?

A landlord may well need a key, in order that he may be able to enter quickly in the event of emergency: fire, burst pipes or whatever. He may need a key to enable him or those authorised by him to read meters or to do repairs which are his responsibility. None of these underlying reasons would of themselves indicate that the true bargain between the parties was such that the occupier was in law a lodger. On the other hand, if the true bargain is that the owner will provide genuine services which can only be provided by having keys, such as frequent cleaning, daily bed-making, the provision of clean linen at regular intervals and the like, there are materials from which it is possible to infer that the occupier is a lodger rather than a tenant. But the inference arises not from the provisions as to keys, but from the reason why those provisions formed part of the bargain.

On the facts of this case, the argument based upon the provisions as to keys must and does fail for the judge found that "during the currency of the present agreement virtually 'no services' had been provided." These provisions may or may not have been pretences, but they are without significance in the context of the question which we had to decide.'

Since the restatement of the *Street v Mountford* principle in *Antoniades v Villiers* and *AG Securities v Vaughan* the legal framework concerning private sector landlords and the use of licences seems reasonably clear. Private sector landlords cannot evade protective legislation by spurious claims to have created a licence. As long as there is legal intent to enter into a contractual relationship, such a relationship will be a landlord and tenant one (assuming that the occupier has exclusive possession *in practice*) save for exceptional cases. Claims that no exclusive possession was granted will be tested against the reality of how the agreement functions in practice.

Paradoxically, this somewhat belated judicial embrace of the policy underlying protective legislation[30] came at almost the precise moment that it was legislatively undermined. As will be discussed in the following chapters, the Housing Act 1988 Part I[31] replaced the protective regime of fair rents and generalised security of tenure with a 'market oriented' regime of limited security and little or no statutory rent control. So, it became much more difficult for private landlords to create licences at almost the same moment as it became far less likely that they would see any need to do so! Of course, if a valid licence can be created it further limits any legal rights which an occupier has[32] so that the limits of the permissible exceptions to the general rule remains a pertinent issue. Nevertheless the significance of the distinction between tenancy and licence is much reduced. However, as the issue lessened in importance in the private sector it assumed somewhat greater importance in the public sector.

---

[30] In particular the security of tenure and fair rent provisions of the Rent Act 1977.
[31] In force 15 January 1989. The move to a market oriented regime was taken further by Housing Act 1996 Part III, Chapter II, in force 28 February 1997.
[32] For example security reduced from the six-month minimum prescribed by Housing Acts 1988 and 1996 to the period prescribed in the contract (subject to Protection from Eviction Act 1977, s 5), the loss of the protection of the covenant of 'quiet enjoyment', and the absence of protection against disrepair provided by Landlord and Tenant Act 1987, s 11.

As will be explained in Chapter 8, since 1980, most occupiers of council accommodation have enjoyed 'secure' status (see now the Housing Act 1985, Pt IV). Such tenants have the benefit of security of tenure in their homes and a catalogue of rights (commonly known as the 'tenants charter'), ranging from the right to buy to rights of succession. Many local authorities originally expressed concern that this development would lead to them having diminished control over occupiers they wished to house only temporarily (for example, some homeless persons, the temporary occupiers of accommodation pending works and the occupiers of short life properties). Moreover, most local authorities were (initially at least) concerned, where possible, to protect their housing stock from erosion by the right to buy.

Quite apart from statutory exceptions to secure status which cover some of the above categories[33], councils have often been attracted to the device of granting licences rather than tenancies. However, two difficulties appeared to bar the way to the successful use of licences in most situations by public sector landlords. First, *Street v Mountford* applied in principle as much to public sector landlords as to private sector ones, so that (particularly after *Antoniades v Villiers*) most occupants paying rent with *de facto* exclusive possession will be tenants whatever the form of the agreement they have signed. This appeared to be confirmed by the Court of Appeal in *Family Housing Association v Jones*[34]. Secondly, in any event, s 79(3) of the Housing Act 1985 states that 'The provisions of this Part apply in relation to a licence to occupy a dwelling house ... as they apply in relation to a tenancy' – the part referred to being the key Pt IV of the Act. This appeared to suggest that even if the occupier was a licensee, he or she still enjoyed the benefits of the 'tenants charter' and security of tenure.

However, both the above assumptions were significantly undermined by the House of Lords' decision in *Westminster City Council v Clarke*[35]. Here, Clarke occupied one of the 31 single rooms in a hostel operated by Westminster Council. Each of the rooms had a bed and limited cooking facilities. The hostel was for single vulnerable homeless men, most of whom were suffering from physical or psychological disabilities. There was a resident warden in the hostel, supported by a 'resettlement' team of social workers. All residents, including Clarke, signed a 'licence to occupy' agreement before moving in. The licence was stated to be terminable by seven days' notice in writing, or 'forthwith' if an occupant broke the terms of the licence. The council served notice on Clarke because his 'erratic' behaviour was causing nuisance and annoyance to the other occupants of the hostel. Subsequently they sought and (initially) obtained a possession order against him[36]. However, the Court of Appeal reversed this, holding that Clarke was a secure tenant. In turn, the House of Lords reversed the Court of Appeal. Lord Templeman delivered the unanimous judgment of the House:

---

33   See Housing Act 1985 Sch 1.
34   [1990] 1 All ER 385.
35   [1992] 2 AC 288, [1992] 1 All ER 695.
36   Arguably if the licence was effective, no possession order was needed and theoretically Clarke would have to leave at the expiry of the notice period, as many licences to occupy council hostel accommodation are 'excluded' licences under the Housing Act 1988, s 31(8), removing the requirement of a court order to evict. The point, however, depends on the interpretation of a further statutory provision (s 622 Housing Act 1985) so that it was probably pragmatic to seek a possession order.

'Mr Clarke occupies room E at his only home. If room E is a separate dwelling house occupied under a tenancy or licence by Mr Clarke as his only home, then Mr Clarke is a secure tenant. The exceptions set forth in Schedule 1 do not apply.

If Mr Clarke is a secure tenant the council cannot obtain possession unless they first serve a notice prescribed by regulations made under section 83 of the Act of 1985 and institute proceedings within the time-limit prescribed by that section. By section 84, as applied to the present case, the court will then only be able to make an order for possession if Mr Clarke has been guilty of conduct which is a nuisance or annoyance to neighbours and if the court considers that it is reasonable to make the order. If therefore Mr Clarke is a secure tenant, the council may not be able to obtain possession of room E and cannot speedily obtain possession of any of the hostel rooms. If Mr Clarke is not a secure tenant then he has no defence to the council's present action for possession. ...

Mr Clarke is a secure tenant of Room E if he enjoys exclusive possession of room E. In order to determine whether Mr Clarke enjoys exclusive possession of room E, the rights conferred on Mr Clarke and the rights reserved to the council by the licence to occupy must be considered and evaluated.

Mr Sedley, who appeared on behalf of Mr Clarke, submitted that Mr Clarke was a secure tenant even if he was not granted exclusive possession of room E. Section 79(3), he said, applied to any licence to occupy a dwelling house. This submission would confer security of tenure on a lodger and on a variety of licensees and is contrary to the language of section 79(3) which applies the provisions of Part IV of the Act to a licence "as they apply in relation to a tenancy". Part IV only applies to a tenancy of a dwelling house let as a separate dwelling, namely with exclusive possession. Part IV therefore applies to a licence which has the same characteristics. A tenant or licensee can only claim to be a secure tenant if he has been granted exclusive possession of a separate dwelling house.

The predecessor of section 79(3) of the Act of 1985 was section 48 of the Housing Act 1980 which provided that where under a licence

"the circumstances are such that, if the licence were a tenancy, it would be a secure tenancy then ... this Part of this Act applies to the licence as it applies to a secure tenancy."

The result of section 48 of the Act of 1980 was that, whether the occupier was a tenant or a licensee, he must be granted exclusive possession in order to become a secure tenant. The Court of Appeal so held in *Family Housing Association v Miah* (1982) 5 HLR 94 and *Kensington and Chelsea Royal Borough Council v Hayden* (1984) 17 HLR 114.

The Rent Acts do not apply to a licence and section 48 of the Act of 1980 was enacted at a time when some private landlords were granting exclusive possession of residential accommodation at a rent but in the form of a licence. Section 48 of the Act of 1980 made clear that such a licence created a secure tenancy. Subsequently in *Street v Mountford* [1985] AC 809 this House reaffirmed the general principle that a grant of exclusive possession of residential accommodation at a rent created a tenancy protected by the Rent

Acts notwithstanding that the parties intended to grant and expressed themselves as having granted a licence and not a tenancy. The decision of this House in *Street v Mountford* [1985] AC 809 was published on 2 May 1985. The Act of 1985 received the Royal Assent on 30 October 1985. In *Family Housing Association v Jones* [1990] 1 WLR 779, 790 Balcombe LJ held that in these circumstances section 79(3) of the Act of 1985 must have been intended to alter the law and to confer the status of a secure tenant on a licensee who did not enjoy exclusive possession. The Court of Appeal in the instant case, 89 LGR 917, felt bound to follow its decision in *Family Housing Association v Jones* though Dillon LJ doubted the soundness of that decision so far as it construed section 79(3) and Balcombe LJ to some extent resiled from his earlier views. In my opinion section 79(3) did not alter the law. The Act of 1985 was an enactment which consolidated various statutes including the Act of 1980 and gave effect to certain recommendations of the Law Commission. Those recommendations did not relate to section 48 of the Act of 1980. Therefore section 79(3) was a consolidating measure and in redrafting section 48 of the Act of 1980 in the form of section 79(3) of the Act of 1985 the draftsman had no power to alter the law. In my opinion, on the true construction of section 48 of the Act of 1980 and on the true construction of section 79(3) of the Act of 1985, whether those sections be considered together or separately a licence can only create a secure tenancy if it confers exclusive possession of a dwelling house.

So the question is whether the "licence to occupy" followed by the allocation of room E and the payment of rent conferred on Mr Clarke exclusive possession of room E. In *Street v Mountford* the landlord agreed to grant a licence of residential accommodation for a weekly fee. The agreement was designated a licence and contained a declaration that the licence did not create and was not intended to create a tenancy protected by the Rent Acts. Nevertheless the licensee enjoyed exclusive possession; a third party could not lawfully interfere with that possession and the landlord only reserved limited power to enter to protect his own interests as a landlord. The licence created a tenancy. ...

The question is whether upon the true construction of the licence to occupy and in the circumstances in which Mr Clarke was allowed to occupy room E, there was a grant by the council to Mr Clarke of exclusive possession of room E.

From the point of view of the council the grant of exclusive possession would be inconsistent with the purposes for which the council granted the accommodation at Cambridge Street. It was in the interests of Mr Clarke and each of the occupiers of the hostel that the council should retain possession of each room. If one room became uninhabitable another room could be shared between two occupiers. If one room became unsuitable for an occupier he could be moved elsewhere. If the occupier of one room became a nuisance he could be compelled to move to another room where his actions might be less troublesome to his neighbours. If the occupier of a room had exclusive possession he could prevent the council from entering the room save for the purpose of protecting the council's interests and not for the purpose of supervising and controlling the conduct of the occupier in his interests. If the occupier of a room had exclusive possession he could not be obliged to comply with the terms and the conditions of occupation. Mr Clarke could not, for example, be obliged to comply with the directions of the warden or to exclude visitors or to comply with any of the other conditions of occupation which are designed to help Mr Clarke and the other occupiers of the hostel and to enable the hostel to be conducted in an efficient and harmonious manner. The only remedy of the council for breaches of the conditions of occupation would be the lengthy and uncertain procedure required by the Act of 1985 to be operated for the purpose of obtaining possession from a secure tenant. In the circumstances of the present case I consider that the council legitimately and effectively retained for themselves possession of room E and that Mr Clarke was only a licensee with the rights corresponding to the rights of a lodger. In reaching this conclusion I take into account the object of the council, namely the provision of accommodation for vulnerable homeless persons, the necessity for the council to retain possession of all the rooms in order to make and administer arrangements for the suitable accommodation of all the occupiers and the need for the council to retain possession of every room not only in the interests of the council as the owners of the terrace but also for the purpose of providing for the occupiers supervision and assistance. For many obvious reasons it was highly undesirable for the council to grant to any occupier of a room exclusive possession which obstructed the use by the council of all the rooms of the hostel in the interests of every occupier. By the terms of the licence to occupy Mr Clarke was not entitled to any particular room, he could be required to share with any other person as required by the council and he was only entitled to "occupy accommodation in common with the council whose representative may enter the accommodation at any time." It is accepted that these provisions of the licence to occupy were inserted to enable the council to discharge its responsibilities to the vulnerable persons accommodated at the Cambridge Street terrace and were not inserted for the purpose of enabling the council to avoid the creation of a secure tenancy. The conditions of occupancy support the view that Mr Clarke was not in exclusive occupation of room E. He was expressly limited in his enjoyment of any accommodation provided for him. He was forbidden to entertain visitors without the approval of the council staff and was bound to comply with the council's warden or other staff in charge of the hostel. These limitations confirmed that the council retained possession of all the rooms of the hostel in order to supervise and control the activities of the occupiers, including Mr Clarke. Although Mr Clarke physically occupied room E he did not enjoy possession exclusively of the council.

This is a very special case which depends on the peculiar nature of the hostel maintained by the council, the use of the hostel by the council, the totality, immediacy and objectives of the powers exercisable by the council and the restrictions imposed on Mr Clarke. The decision in this case will not allow a landlord, private or public, to free himself from the Rent Acts or from the restrictions of a secure tenancy merely by adopting or adapting the language of the licence to occupy. The provisions of the licence to occupy and the circumstances in which that licence was granted and continued lead to the conclusion that Mr Clarke has never enjoyed that exclusive possession which he claims. I would therefore allow the appeal and restore the order for possession made by the trial judge.'

Lord Templeman stated that this was 'a very special case', which should not encourage landlords (public or private) to think that by calling something a licence, or by purporting to deny exclusive possession they would thereby avoid protective legislation. Indeed, it is hard to see how the House of Lords *could* have countenanced such a development only four years after explicitly rejecting it in *Antoniades/Vaughan*. However, it is not clear that the situation in *Clarke*, though distinct, was necessarily 'very special'. Indeed, it seems typical of a significant number of hostels operated by local authorities. The difficulty lies in knowing where the line should be drawn: at one extreme is the type of hostel where it would be absurd to suggest that any form of 'exclusivity' was granted (for example, a refuge where there is no guarantee of a particular room, or indeed of any room, being available on a particular day); at the other is something which is a 'hostel' in name only, where the occupier does not receive social service care requiring constant access, and is able to live in an independent and self-contained manner. *Clarke*, whatever Lord Templeman's views, appears to be somewhere in the middle, and the court appears to approach the *realities* of exclusive possession in a somewhat 'cavalier' manner (for example, is it ever asked whether the clause allowing occupants to be moved, the so-called 'mobility clause', was operated in practice?).

'Policy' considerations clearly underpin the judgment, as indicated by the constant references by Lord Templeman to the considerable inconvenience which an opposite finding would cause to the local authority concerned. No doubt the House was aware that none of the exceptions to security that are set out in Sch 1 to the Housing Act 1985 specifically excludes hostel accommodation from protection. However, did the House overstate the difficulties in such cases for public sector landlords? It is *possible* for a landlord to obtain an expedited hearing for a possession claim, and injunctions may be available where an occupant breaks the terms of an agreement.

Moreover, in seeking to protect the position of the public landlord, it is also possible to argue that the House of Lords made a nonsense of s 79(3) of the 1985 Act referred to above. This subsection appears to state that a licensee fulfilling the conditions for a secure tenancy would gain equivalent protection to a secure tenant, ie it creates the concept of the *secure licence*.

Many hostel dwellers will fail to attain this status because they do not occupy a 'separate dwelling' as required by s 79(1) of the Act, most typically because they share kitchen facilities with other residents of the hostel (see *Central YMCA Housing Association Ltd v Saunders*[37]). This is a quite separate concept to that of exclusive possession, focusing on whether essential living accommodation is in practice shared with others, rather than on whether there is a legal right to exclude others from the separate accommodation undoubtedly occupied. By accident, or design, Lord Templeman conflates the two notions 'Part IV only applies to a tenancy of a dwelling house let as a separate dwelling, *namely* with exclusive

---

[37]   (1990) 23 HLR 212.

possession' (emphasis added). This interpretation seems to leave s 79(3) largely without content, since if there is exclusive possession there will normally be a tenancy in any case. Moreover, it might be thought that licensees who do share kitchens and bathrooms are exactly those whom local authorities most need to 'manage' and control, whereas where there is relatively separate living this need is much reduced.

Since *Clarke* the 'licence' issue has come before the Court of Appeal in a number of further cases concerning hostels. For example, in *Brennan v Lambeth London Borough Council*[38], a homeless applicant was provided with accommodation, with his 14-year-old son, at a hostel while his application was considered. The hostel consisted of seven large Victorian houses, converted into shared units (kitchen, bathrooms, and toilets were all shared). Hostel officers had an office in one of the houses. Residents of the hostel were responsible for cleaning their own rooms, but common parts were cleaned by council staff. In agreeing with the county court, that no court order was required to secure the applicant's removal from the hostel, the Court of Appeal held that his occupational status in the hostel was that of licensee. *Clarke* was referred to, but not analysed in any detail. Brooks LJ clearly felt that the applicant's status was beyond argument. Potter LJ emphasised, again, how significant a role is played by policy in this area:

> '... it is necessary to keep an eye on ... the problems which face a Local Authority in the management of hostels ... [even where] the residents may require a lower level of care ... [since] the need to reconcile the interests of short term occupants, plainly call for an effective power and genuine need to remove tenants from room to room during their occupancy ...'

In *Mohamed v Manek and Royal Borough of Kensington and Chelsea*[39], another homeless applicant was placed in temporary (private sector) bed and breakfast accommodation. This consisted of a room on the fourth floor of a hotel, with its own bathroom/toilet plus shared use of a kitchen (along with 35 other occupiers of the hotel!). In allowing the authority's appeal from the county court's granting of an injunction preventing the applicant's eviction, the Court of Appeal held that not only did the applicant merely have a licence (this point was barely discussed), but that s 3 of the Protection from Eviction Act 1977 did not apply so as to require a court order. Section 3(2B) applies the normal requirement of a court order to licences as well as to tenancies, so long as they are not 'excluded licences' and so long as the premises involved are 'occupied as a dwelling'. Hostels of the *Brennan* type, operated by authorities themselves, are often excluded from s 3 if licences are involved (see s 3A(8)[40]). In *Manek* this exclusion could not apply, but the court found that temporary occupation of the hotel room by a homeless applicant did not amount to occupying 'a dwelling'. In the words of Nourse LJ 'Without some element of more than transient occupation, premises cannot properly be called a dwelling'.

The trend of the post-*Clarke* case law has generally been to protect public sector landlords from the full impact of *Street v Mountford* and its offspring. In similar

---

[38]  (1997) 30 HLR 481.
[39]  (1995) 27 HLR 439.
[40]  Added by Housing Act 1988 s 31(8); see n 33, above.

vein, cases such as *Camden London Borough Council v Shortlife Community Housing*[41] were concerned to avoid conferring the status of tenant on the occupiers of flats and houses under 'short life' housing schemes. Indeed, such decisions, although clearly coloured by policy considerations, seemed to flow reasonably naturally from the reasoning in *Street v Mountford*. In a typical arrangement, the local authority licensed the properties to a housing cooperative, or other community housing organisation, which either lacked the legal personality to acquire a secure tenancy, or in any event was not granted exclusive possession. The cooperative then purported to license the properties to the individual occupiers. Even if these occupiers initially appeared to have exclusive possession, quite apart from the policy context, it seemed impossible for them to acquire tenancies. Briefly, because their immediate landlord (the cooperative) had no legal estate themselves, they could not pass one on to the occupiers. The words of Denning LJ in *Lewisham Metropolitan Borough v Roberts*[42] seemed to sum matters up clearly '[The Crown] ... cannot grant a lease or create any legal interest in the land in favour of any other person, because it has itself no estate in the land out of which to carve any interest.' However, the House of Lords decision in *Bruton v London and Quadrant Housing Trust*[43] has thrown all the above into doubt, and in so doing has raised fundamental doubts about the very nature of a 'tenancy' itself[44].

In 1975 the London Borough of Lambeth acquired a block of flats, intending to demolish it and build new flats on the site. However, financial and other considerations delayed this scheme, and on 27 March 1986 an agreement was made between the authority and Quadrant Housing Trust that the latter should have a 'licence' to use the property for their charitable housing purposes, including short-term housing for the homeless. It was further agreed that no legal estate or proprietary interest passed to the Trust. On 31 January 1989 Bruton agreed with the Trust that he would occupy a flat in the block. His agreement stated that the property was 'short life' that the Trust itself only held a licence, that he was to occupy on a weekly licence, and that he must vacate the flat on being given 'reasonable' notice by the Trust (normally four weeks). Subsequently the authority abandoned its redevelopment scheme and the flat fell into disrepair. Were the Trust in breach of the implied covenant to repair in s 11, Landlord and Tenant Act 1985 (see further Chapter 12)? Aside from other considerations this section would only apply if a relationship of landlord and tenant existed between Bruton and the Trust. Bruton sought to enforce the repairing covenant and the Trust then served notice to quit on him, and sought a declaration that he was merely a licensee. In the County Court and the Court of Appeal[45] Bruton was found to be merely a licensee. However, the House of Lords overturned this, unanimously. The leading judgment is that of Lord Hoffmann, with which the majority of the remainder of the House expressly agreed.

'Did this agreement create a "lease" or "tenancy" within the meaning of the Landlord and Tenant Act 1985 or any other legislation which refers to a lease

---

[41]   (1992) 25 HLR 330, and see n 3, above.
[42]   [1949] 2 KB 608, at 622.
[43]   [2000] 1 AC 406, [1995] 3 All ER 481.
[44]   Academic comment on *Bruton*, was considerable, see for example, Dixon, 'The Non-Proprietary Lease: The Rise of the Feudal Phoenix? [2000] Cambridge Law Journal 25; Routley, 'Tenancies and Estoppel' 63 MLR 424; Rook, 'Whether a Licence Agreement is a Lease' [1999] Vol 63 The Conveyancer, 517; Bright, 'Leases, Exclusive Possession and Estates' LQR 116, 7.
[45]   [1998] QB 834, [1997] 4 All ER 970.

or tenancy? The decision of this House in *Street v Mountford* [1985] 2 All ER 289 [1985] AC 809 is authority for the proposition that a "lease" or "tenancy" is a contractually binding agreement, nor referable to any other relationship between the parties, by which one person gives another the right to exclusive occupation of land for a fixed or renewable period or periods of time, usually in return for a periodic payment in money. An agreement having these characteristics creates a relationship of landlord and tenant to which the common law or statute may then attach various incidents. The fact that the parties use language more appropriate to a different kind of agreement, such as a licence, is irrelevant if upon its true construction it has the identifying characteristics of a lease. The meaning of the agreement, for example, as to the extent of the possession which it grants, depend upon the intention of the parties, objectively ascertained by reference to the language and relevant background. The decision of your Lordships' House in *Westminster City Council v Clarke* [1992] 1 All ER 695 [1992] 2 AC 288 is a good example of the importance of background in deciding whether the agreement grants exclusive possession or not. But the classification of the agreement as a lease does not depend upon any intention additional to that expressed in the choice of terms. It is simply a question of characterising the terms which the parties have agreed. This is a question of law.

In this case it seems to me that the agreement, construed against the relevant background, plainly gave Mr Bruton a right to exclusive possession. There is nothing to suggest that he was to share possession with the trust, the council or anyone else. The trust did not retain such control over the premises as was inconsistent with Mr Bruton having exclusive possession, as was the case in *Westminster City Council v Clarke*. The only rights which it reserved were for itself and the council to enter at certain times and for limited purposes. As Lord Templeman said in *Street v Mountford* [1985] 2 All ER 289 at 293 [1985] AC 809 at 818 such an express reservation "only serves to emphasise the fact that the grantee is entitled to exclusive possession and is a tenant". Nor was there any other relationship between the parties to which Mr Bruton's exclusive possession could be referable.

Mr Henderson, who appeared for the trust, submitted that there were "special circumstances" in this case which enabled one to construe the agreement as a licence despite the presence of all the characteristics identified in *Street v Mountford* [1985] 2 All ER 289 [1985] AC 809. These circumstances were that the trust was a responsible landlord performing socially valuable functions, it had agreed with the council not to grant tenancies, Mr Bruton had agreed that he was not to have a tenancy and the trust had no estate out of which it could grant one.

In my opinion none of these circumstances can make an agreement to grant exclusive possession something other than a tenancy. The character of the landlord is irrelevant because although the Rents Acts and other Landlord and Tenant Acts do make distinctions between different kinds of landlords, it is not by saying that what would be a tenancy if granted by one landlord will be something else if granted by another. The alleged breach of the Trust's licence is irrelevant because there is no suggestion that the grant of a tenancy would have been ultra vires either the trust or the council: see section 32(3) of the

Housing Act 1985. If it was a breach of a term of the licence from the council, that would have been because it was a tenancy. The licence could not have turned it into something else. Mr Bruton's agreement is irrelevant because one cannot contract out of the statute. The trust's lack of title is also irrelevant, but I shall consider this point at a later stage. In *Family Housing Association v Jones* [1990] 1 All ER 385 [1990] 1 WLR 779, where the facts were very similar to those in the present case, the Court of Appeal construed the "licence" as a tenancy. Slade LJ gave careful consideration to whether any exceptional ground existed for making an exception to the principle in *Street v Mountford* [1985] 2 All ER 289 [1985] AC 809 and came to the conclusion that there was not. I respectfully agree. For these reasons I consider that the agreement between the trust and Mr Bruton was a lease within the meaning of section 11 of the Landlord and Tenant Act 1985.

My Lords, in my opinion, that is the end of the matter. But the Court of Appeal did not stop at that point. In the leading majority judgment, Millett LJ said [1997] 4 All ER 970, at 979 [1998] QB 834 at 845 that an agreement could not be a lease unless it had a further characteristic, namely that it created a legal estate in the land which "binds the whole world". If, as in this case, the grantor had no legal estate, the agreement could not create one and therefore did not qualify as a lease. The only exception was the case in which the grantor was estopped from denying that he could not create a legal estate. In that case, a "tenancy by estoppel" came into existence. But an estoppel depended upon the grantor having purported to grant a lease and in this case the trust had not done so. It had made it clear that it was only purporting to grant a licence.

My Lords, I hope that this summary does justice to the closely reasoned judgment of Millett LJ but I fear that I must respectfully differ at three critical steps in the argument.

First, the term "lease" or "tenancy" describes a relationship between two parties who are designated landlord and tenant. It is not concerned with the question of whether the agreement creates an estate or other proprietary interest which may be binding upon third parties. A lease may, and usually does, create a proprietary interest called a leasehold estate or, technically, a "term of years absolute". This will depend upon whether the landlord had an interest out of which he could grant it. Nemo dat quod non habet. but it is the fact that the agreement is a lease which creates the proprietary interest. It is putting the cart before the horse to say that whether the agreement is a lease depends upon whether it creates a proprietary interest.

Thirdly, I cannot agree that there is no inconsistency between what the trust purported to do and its denial of the existence of a tenancy. This seems to me to fly in the face of *Street v Mountford* [1985] 2 All ER 289 [1985] AC 809. In my opinion, the trust plainly did purport to grant a tenancy. It entered into an agreement on terms which constituted a tenancy. It may have agreed with Mr Bruton to say that it was not a tenancy. But the parties cannot contract out of the Rent Acts or other landlord and tenant statutes by such devices. Nor in my view can they be used by a landlord to avoid being estopped from denying that he entered into the agreement he actually made.

'For these reasons I would allow the appeal and declare that Mr Bruton was a tenant. I should add that I express no view on whether he was a secure tenant or on the rights of the council to recover possession of the flat.'

The implications of this decision are, potentially, enormously wide-ranging, although considerable uncertainty will still attach to it until it is considered further by the courts.

- On its immediate facts it demonstrates that 'short life' agreements are now generally at risk of being classified as tenancies, and not licences. Certainly the simple facts that the 'intermediate' landlord lacks an estate in land, is forbidden to grant tenancies and specifically alludes to these facts in the purported licence(s) with the property occupiers, appear unable to alter the position as all these points were present, and were dismissed, in Bruton itself. In principle there could be situations where 'short life' occupiers lacked exclusive possession (perhaps because they were occupying something akin to a hostel) and so no tenancy would be created.

  However, in the typical case, a tenancy seems the likely result. This seems to sit very uneasily with *Clarke* and the general trend of post-Clarke case law concerned to facilitate local authority flexibility in matters of housing management. The impact of *Bruton* would appear to hamper the freedom of authorities and charitable bodies to use 'short life' agreements to assist the homeless.

- The *extent* to which local authority freedom *is* curbed depends on issues left somewhat uncertain in *Bruton*. As regards the relationship between the trust and Bruton a tenancy clearly existed. However, what kind of tenancy was this? The House of Lords leaves the matter open; Lord Hoffmann states 'I should add that I express no view on whether (Mr Bruton) was a secure tenant, or on the rights of the council to recover possession of the flat', whereas Lord Jauncey cites Slade LJ in *Family Housing Association v Jones*[46] to the effect that 'whatever their wishes or intentions, it may at least be difficult for bodies charged with responsibilities for the housing of the homeless to enter into any arrangement pursuant to section 65(2) of the Housing Act 1985 under which the person housed is to enjoy exclusive occupation of premises, however temporarily, without conferring on that person security of tenure by virtue of the Act'. *These* views (echoed by Lord Slynn) *suggest* (but no more) that a secure tenancy might have come into being in *Jones*, which was possible, when that case was decided, as Housing Associations before 1989 could grant such tenancies. The approving references to *Family Housing Association v Jones* are particularly confusing, since the case appeared to have been substantially overruled in *Clarke*. In the case of Bruton the prima facie conclusion as to his status is that he acquired an assured tenancy under the Housing Act 1988.

- What *is* clear is that by (however inadvertently) creating a tenancy the trust was in breach of its obligations to the authority, and most of their lordships in *Bruton* are at pains to point out that a tenancy *not* constituting an estate in land would not necessarily bind third parties. Does this mean that occupiers

---

46   [1990] 1 All ER 385, at 396.

such as *Bruton* have only common law tenancies, or that their rights as secure or assured tenants could be determined by the authority terminating their immediate landlord's interest for breach of *their* licence terms (in either scenario the occupiers would have no long-term security in the property. In the latter case because the sub-agreements would come to an end at the same time as the head licence ends)? These are murky waters which the judgments in *Bruton* do nothing to clear.

*However*

- Worrying though the above uncertainties are, they are of much less significance than the startling new proposition which lies at the heart of Lord Hoffmann's judgment, in effect that although a typical consequence of a tenancy is the creation of an estate in land, this is not invariable, and that 'it is putting the cart before the horse to say that whether the agreement is a lease depends upon whether it creates a proprietary interest.' As Lords Hope, Slynn and Hobhouse all expressly agreed with Lord Hoffmann's reasoning this proposition must clearly be taken to represent the courts collective view. The view can perhaps, most easily be characterised as exemplifying Maitland's famous dictum of the move from 'status to contract' – above all a tenancy is seen as a species of contractual relationship. Of course there has always been a tension between the proprietary and contractual attributes of a tenancy; a tension which has caused the courts considerable difficulty in recent years, in areas as diverse as the applicability of contractual doctrines such as frustration and repudiatory breach to tenancies (see *National Carriers v Panalpina (Northern) Ltd*[47] and *Hussein v Mehlman*[48], and the capacity of one joint tenant to determine the interests of another by the service of a notice to quit. In a key decision on the later issue, *Hammersmith and Fulham London Borough Council v Monk*[49], Lord Bridge stated 'As a matter of principle I see no reason why this question should receive any different answer in the context of the contractual relationship of landlord and tenant than that which it would receive in any other contractual context', although Lord Browne-Wilkinson, more cautiously noted that 'instinctive reactions' to the correct analysis could be 'diametrically' opposed dependent on whether a contract or property perspective were adopted[50]. He continued 'The contract of tenancy confers on the tenant a legal estate in the land: such legal estate gives rise to rights and duties incapable of being founded in contract alone'. It is a very large step from such cautious analysis to the sweeping certainties of Lord Hoffmann. It is one thing to advert to the tension between the contractual and proprietary attributes of a tenancy, but quite another to deny that a tenancy need have any proprietary attributes at all (even Lord Bridge in *Monk* refers to a tenancy as an 'estate' without there seeming to be any dispute on the point). Lord Hoffmann's heterodoxy, which seems to have 'carried the day' did not balk at a highly partial reading of *Lewisham* ('cannot create a lease' is rendered as

---

[47]   [1981] AC 675.
[48]   [1992] 2 EGLR 87.
[49]   [1992] 1 All ER 1, at 3.
[50]   [1992] 1 All ER 1, at 10.

'cannot bind third parties'!) nor at the fact that throughout Lord Templeman's definitive judgment in *Street v Mountford* it is, at least, assumed that a tenancy is an interest in land.

The dilemma which subsequent courts will face is very clear; if a tenancy is not (of necessity) an interest in land, what is it? There is no assistance in *Bruton* on this point. To put it even more simply: if a tenancy need not be an interest in land, how is it, at root, conceptually different from a licence? The traditional position is well summarised by Windeyer J in *Radaich v Smith*[51], cited with approval by Lord Templeman in *Street v Mountford*:

> 'what then is the fundamental right which a tenant has that distinguishes his position from that of a licensee? It is an interest in land as distinct from a personal permission to enter the land, and use it for some stipulated purpose, or purposes. And how is it to be ascertained whether such an interest in land has been given? By seeing whether the grantee was given a legal right of exclusive possession of the land for a term. ... If he was, he is a tenant. And he cannot be other than a tenant, because a legal right of exclusive possession is a tenancy, and the creation of such a right is a demise ... a tenant for a term ... can exclude his landlord as well as strangers from the demised premises. All this is long established law.'

In other words, it is the reality of exclusive possession which inevitably creates a leasehold estate, with its accompanying right to exclude others. The two are interwoven, indeed inextricable and so there can be no question of 'putting the cart before the horse' (Lord Hoffmann in *Bruton*). It seems likely that the House of Lords has 'boxed itself in' by failing to clearly distinguish between exclusive *possession* and (mere) exclusive *occupation* of premises (a tendency which can be traced back to Lord Templeman in *Street v Mountford*). Exclusive *occupation* characterises many licences. Sole *occupation in fact* is often the preserve of contractual licensees such as residents in a hotel, or persons living in a retirement home. Exclusive *possession* is, of course, not merely about sole occupation, but overall *control* of the premises, entailing crucially the right to *exclude*. By blurring this, the House of Lords, in *Bruton* has raised the spectre that 'licensees' with sole occupation rights, but no overall control of the premises they occupy will now be able to argue that they have some form of tenancy.

Very recently, in *Kay v Lambeth London Borough Council and London and Quadrant Housing Trust*[52], the Court of Appeal has confirmed that the possessor of a '*Bruton*' tenancy did not possess rights good against the 'whole world', but only rights vis-à-vis their immediate landlord(s). Specifically, once the local authority had brought the head licence to an end the *Bruton* tenancy fell as well, leaving the occupiers as trespassers. There could be no question of the *Bruton* tenant 'rising up' to become a secure tenant of the local authority, thereby guaranteeing them long-term legal protection (see Chapter 8). The tenants' contention that LQHT had been acting as agents for Lambeth so as to bring into being a direct landlord and tenant relationship between Lambeth and themselves was decisively rejected.

[51]  (1959) 101 CLR 209, at 222.
[52]  [2004] EWCA Civ 926.

This, of course, removes many of the concerns which authorities had about the *Bruton* decision, but raises yet more questions about the reasons which led the House of Lords in *Bruton* to deviate from orthodoxy in the way they did.

## SUB-TENANTS

The previous section focused on the crucial distinction between licensees and tenants. However, even if the prerequisites for a tenancy do exist[53], not all tenancies carry the same implications. There are numerous statutory forms of tenancy, such as assured tenancies and secure tenancies, which carry specific statutory implications as will be discussed in the following chapters. In structural terms there are, at common law, two principal forms of tenancy: periodic tenancies and fixed-term tenancies. A periodic tenancy is one which does not have a fixed predetermined length, but 'runs on' from period to period (eg week to week or month to month) [54]. A fixed-term tenancy is one granted for a specific period of time, for example six months, or a year. At common law the distinction between these two basic forms of tenancy was profound enough, particularly when it came to how they were to be brought to an end[55]. However, as will be seen, statute has built in further implications.

Perhaps the most important distinction in terms of status is between a person who holds their tenancy directly from the owner of the property, and one who holds their tenancy from another tenant. In such cases the middle or intermediate tenant is usually termed the 'mesne' tenant, and the lower tenant is usually termed the sub-tenant. Broadly, so long as the mesne tenancy continues to exist, the sub-tenant has much the same status as any other tenant – albeit their rights will be as much, if not more, affected by the status of their immediate landlord (the mesne tenant) than that of the ultimate owner of the property. However, once the mesne tenant's interest comes to an end, it has to be determined whether the sub-tenant has any right to remain in occupation against the head landlord. In part this issue is affected by the nature of the original sub-tenancy and will be discussed as relevant in subsequent chapters. However, in addition the sub-tenant's rights are heavily dependent upon whether the sub-tenancy was legal or illegal. A sub-tenancy will be illegal if the terms of the mesne tenancy prohibit sub-letting, either absolutely or without the consent of the landlord[56]. In the latter case, the law implies a covenant then consent will not be unreasonably withheld and if unreasonably withheld shall be treated as given[57]. Generally, illegal sub-tenants lack any security and their interest in the property will come to an end on the determination of the mesne tenancy. However, if the mesne tenant surrenders their tenancy (ie voluntarily relinquishes it) and the

[53] In terms of *Street v Mountford* this means exclusive possession, an identifiable term and an identifiable rent. It would be usual to add to this identifiable 'premises', although in this context 'premises' may be no more than a single room.
[54] As stated in Blackstone's *Commentaries* (1766) they are 'tenancies from year to year so long as both parties please'. Blackstone might have added 'or from month to month or week to week'.
[55] Whether by notice to quit (periodic), forfeiture (fixed-term), or surrender (both).
[56] Although an absolute prohibition on sub-letting is generally not permissible in relation to secure tenancies, Housing Act 1985, s 93(1)(b) in conjunction with s 94.
[57] Save where the covenant is implied by Housing Act 1988, s 15.

landlord accepts the surrender any sub-tenant becomes a tenant of the landlord regardless of whether the sub-tenancy was illegal[58].

## JOINT TENANTS

A joint tenancy occurs wherever more than one person in a dwelling shares a tenancy. Joint tenants do not possess separate parts of the property, they are all equally entitled to joint exclusive possession of the whole of it. Joint tenants, collectively, possess one tenancy. Of course, not all those living under one roof do so as joint tenants; they may hold separate tenancies from the same landlord; they may hold separate non-exclusive licences; one may be the tenant and the other(s) sub-tenant(s) of that person (or perhaps sub-licensees of that person). Perhaps the clearest recent discussions of these issues is to be found in *AG Securities v Vaughan*[59] and in *Hammersmith and Fulham London Borough Council v Monk*[60].

In *Vaughan* the House of Lords unanimously ruled that the separate occupiers of the flat lacked all the ingredients necessary for the creation of a joint tenancy; their interests started on different days, in different documents and were for different periods. In the words of Lord Bridge:

'The four respondents acquired their contractual rights to occupy the flat in question, and undertook their relevant obligations by separate agreements ... made at different times and on different terms. These rights and obligations having initially been several, I do not understand by what legal alchemy they could ever become joint.'

The 'joint and several' nature of a joint tenancy means that each joint tenant is liable for the actions of the others and, in particular, each is liable for the whole rent of the premises. Therefore a 'surviving' joint tenant can be held accountable for all the arrears which have accrued in relation to the tenancy.

All landlords, public or private, have the power to grant joint tenancies, whether the tenancies in question are protected, assured or secure. Private sector landlords seem increasingly to favour joint tenancies, not least because of the control it gives them over rent in particular. In the public sector, as Annex C to the Code of Guidance on Parts VI and VII, Housing Act 1996 advises local authorities 'normally' to grant a joint tenancy where the members of a household have a long-term commitment to the home, whether as married couples, as friends, in other relationships or even as live-in carers. Moreover, the authority should inform applicants in writing of their reasons if they refuse to grant a joint tenancy.

Generally, joint tenants have collective responsibilities, and must act together. Therefore, if joint tenants wish to surrender a fixed-term lease they must all act together to do so. As Somervell LJ stated in *Leek and Moorlands Building Society v Clark*[61]: 'They all have the right to the full term, and all must concur if this right is to be abandoned'. However, it now seems that is *not* the case concerning the service

---

[58] *Parker v Jones* [1910] 2 KB 32.
[59] [1990] 1 AC 417, [1988] 3 All ER 1058.
[60] [1992] 1 AC 478, [1992] 1 All ER 1.
[61] [1952] 2 QB 788 at 794.

of notices to quit, and in the context of local authority tenancies in particular, this has proved to be a point of considerable importance in recent years – an issue discussed at length in Chapter 11.

Joint tenancies throw into sharp relief the conflict between contract, property law and statute which was discussed earlier in this chapter in relation to the *Bruton*[62] case. Some of the ensuing difficulties were discussed by the House of Lords in *Burton v Camden London Borough Counci*[63]. Burton and her partner, Hannawin, were granted a joint weekly tenancy of a three-bedroom flat owned by Camden. The two of them occupied with Hannawin's son, who at the time of the grant of the tenancy in February 1994 was aged six. In July 1996, Hannawin bought a property elsewhere, and moved out. This was likely to cause Burton financial difficulties in that, as one of a pair of joint tenants, it seemed likely that she would continue to receive housing benefit in respect of only half the rent of the flat, even though in practice Hannawin would make no further payments of rent after she left the flat, because there was a severe shortage of larger 'units' to house families waiting in temporary accommodation. A simple assignment (transfer) of Hannawin's interest to Burton was probably legally ineffective[64]. Instead, Burton signed a so-called 'deed of release' under which Hannawin simply relinquished her interest in the property and, in turn, Burton accepted it. Was this effective in law? The Court of Appeal said 'yes', but the House of Lords (4:1) said 'no'.

Lord Nicholls delivered the main judgment for the majority:

> 'The foundation of her case is that where property is held by joint tenants, each of them has an identical interest in the whole of the property. If one joint tenant wishes to vest the entire interest in the property as the other, the appropriate mode is by way of release, not assignment. As a matter of conveyancing formality the property may now be conveyed by joint tenants to one of themselves, pursuant to the Law of Property Act 1925, s 72(4), but the right of one joint tenant to release his interest to the other is preserved by s 16(2).
> I cannot accept the conclusion for which Miss Burton contended. The difference between a release and an assignment is familiar to property lawyers, although less so than formerly. The difference was important at a time when use of appropriate words of limitation could be crucial. As your Lordships were reminded, the distinction can be traced at least as far back as the days of *Coke on Littleton*. But this ancient distinction does not provide the answer to the issue before your Lordships' House. The legal concept relied upon for Miss Burton is that a joint tenant, as distinct from a tenant in common, has nothing to transfer to the other tenant, because each already owns the whole. I have to say that this esoteric concept is remote from the realities of life. It should be handled with care, and applied with caution. In the present case the transaction sought to be carried through was that the tenancy should become vested in Miss Burton alone, and that Miss Hannawin

---

[62] See nn. 44–47.
[63] [2000] 2 AC 399, [2000] 1 All ER 943.
[64] Because of Housing Act 1985 s 91(1) which states that a periodic secure tenancy cannot be assigned save in the secure special circumstances outlined in s 91(3) – see further Chapter 8.

should give up to Miss Burton her right to live in the flat. Whatever precise form of words was chosen, this transaction would ordinarily be regarded as a transfer of Miss Hannawin's rights in the flat to Miss Burton. Miss Hannawin was passing over her interest to Miss Burton. As a matter of conveyancing this transfer could be achieved by one of two means: either by a deed of assignment ("Miss Burton and Miss Hannawin hereby assign the tenancy to Miss Burton") or by a deed of release ("Miss Hannawin hereby releases her estate and interest in the property to Miss Burton"). Each would achieve the same result. In each case the legal state in the tenancy, formerly held by the two of them, would become vested in one of them. It cannot be that section 91(1) bites or not according to which of these two conveyancing modes is used. That would make no sense.

Against this background I approach the matter as follows. The issue before your Lordships is whether the deed of release was effectual to vest the tenancy in Miss Burton alone. More precisely, before the execution of the deed of release the legal estate in the tenancy was held by Miss Burton and Miss Hannawin in trust for themselves as joint tenants: see s 36(1) of the Law of Property Act 1925, as amended. The issue is whether the deed of release was effectual to vest this legal estate in Miss Burton alone. This was the object she sought to achieve. Anything less would not assist her.

Having in mind that this is the issue, I turn to the non-assignability provision in section 91. In the context of a lease, assign normally connotes the transfer of the lease from one person to another. The simplest example is a transfer of a lease from A to B. Another example is a transfer of a lease from A to A and B. The present case is different because the transaction under consideration did not involve the introduction of a new tenant. The present case concerned a transfer of the legal estate from A and B to A alone. What was involved was that one of the existing tenants should cease to be a tenant. This difference is not material. Here also, as a matter of ordinary usage, such a transfer of a lease, changing the identity of the tenants, would be regarded as an assignment.

… I can see nothing in the statutory context to indicate that assign in s 91 should be given a more limited meaning and not apply where one joint tenant drops out.

… Accordingly, the deed of release was ineffectual to achieve its object of vesting the tenancy in Miss Burton alone.'

Lord Millett's dissenting speech is powerful, centring on the perception that although the word 'assignment' is not a 'term of art', at its heart is one essential notion – the transfer or disposition of property from one party to another. In the case of joint tenants the concept of 'assignment' could not work because each of the joint tenants is already the owner of the whole. Since Hannawin was not 'assigning' her interest to Burton the 'deed of release' did not fall foul of Housing Act 1985, s 91(1).

It has been pointed out[65] that if a 'release' and an 'assignment' amount to the same thing, then the nature of a joint tenancy is not as previously conceived to be.

---

[65] Bridge, 'Assignment Under Attack' [2000] 64 Conv 474.

Specifically, for there to be an 'assignment' of Hannawin's interest, one would have expected it to be necessary for Hannawin and Burton to have to jointly agree to transfer the tenancy interest to Burton in her own name.

The decision of the majority was, of course, largely determined by policy considerations[66]. Just as in the *Bruton*[67] case, the House of Lords was prepared to override orthodox and traditional analysis in pursuit of an end result seen to be desirable.

---

[66]   Centring on the perceived consequences of an effective 'release' being to end Hannawin's liability to pay rent concerning the property and manoeuvre the housing benefit scheme to Burton's advantage. Bridge queries both these assumptions.

[67]   *Bruton v London and Quadrant Housing Trust* [2000] 1 AC 406, [1999] 3 All ER 481.

# CHAPTER 4

# Private Sector Tenancies

## PRIVATE SECTOR TENANCIES: CLASSIFICATION AND STATUS

### Introduction

At the end of the previous chapter reference was made to the removal of substantial amounts of tenant protection by recent legislation (more specifically, Pt I of the Housing Act 1988). The form that these changes take renders the structure of this area of the law particularly complex. In general, Pt I of the Housing Act 1988 is not retrospective in effect so that two distinct legislative codes stand side by side: first, the Rent Act 1977 and associated legislation; and, secondly, the Housing Act 1988. In general, a tenancy entered into before 15 January 1989 is governed by the Rent Act, and a tenancy entered into from 15 January 1989 onwards by the Housing Act. Each code has a distinct set of categories into which a tenancy might fall: in the case of the Rent Act, protected tenancies, statutory tenancies and restricted contracts; in the case of the Housing Act, assured tenancies statutory periodic tenancies and assured shorthold tenancies. Such classification has fundamental implications for the rights attaching to landlords and tenants under the tenancies in question. The Housing Act 1988 has now been, in its turn, amended by the Housing Act 1996, as explained below.

Legislative involvement in the private sector dates back to the Increase of Rent and Mortgage Interest (War Restrictions) Act 1915[1]. As its name suggests, this was intended as a temporary measure, aimed at curbing excessive rent increases during wartime. It was envisaged that 'normal service' would be resumed after the war, and indeed, the Hunter Committee of 1918 broadly recommended this. However, the reality was a continuation of a system of rent control based on rateable values which lasted until the introduction of the more flexible 'fair rent' scheme in the Rent Act 1965. Over the intervening years there were numerous calls by those supporting landlords' interests for wholesale 'decontrol' of the market, but this never occurred (although the provisions in the Housing Act 1957 to 'decontrol' all properties with rateable values over £30 (£40 in London) came close). The Rent Act 1965 introduced a less rigid system focusing on individual 'fair rent' evaluations by rent

---

[1]  For a good general survey of the history of legislative involvement in the private rented sector, see S Lowe and D Hughes, 'The New Private Rented Sector' in (S Lowe and D Hughes eds), *The Private Rented Sector in a New Century*. (Polity Press, 2002).

officers. However, any 'creeping decontrol' implicit in the Housing Act 1957 was sharply reversed, the new measures applying to most private sector tenancies (even, from 1974 onwards, to furnished ones)[2]. The Rent Act 1977, Pts III and IV now contain the relevant 'fair rent' legislation for those tenancies still governed by the Act.

As the titles of most of the relevant legislation suggest, the main purpose of the above measures was rent control. However, it was acknowledged from the outset (see s 1(3) of the 1915 Act) that unless this was coupled with security of tenure (ie security from eviction save on specified grounds) it was likely to be ineffective. All legislation from 1915 to 1977 centred on the two basic issues of rent control and security of tenure.

As to so many other areas, the Conservative Government in power from 1979, broke up the consensus which had emerged in favour of substantial market intervention and regulation in the private rented sector. All legislation introduced from 1979 to 1988 had the effect of reducing the scope of full Rent Act controls (most obviously by the introduction of the protected shorthold tenancy). However, not until 1988 was a direct assault made on the general framework of protection and rent control. Prior to the legislation, a White Paper[3] had indicated the depth of the Government's opposition to the existing system:

> '1.3 Too much preoccupation since the War with controls in the private rented sector ... has resulted in substantial numbers of rented houses and flats which are badly ... maintained and which fail to provide decent homes. The return to private sector landlords has been inadequate to persuade them to stay in the market, or to keep their property in repair ...
> 1.8 Rent controls have prevented property owners from getting an adequate return on their investment. People who might have been prepared to grant a temporary letting have also been deterred by laws on security of tenure which made it impossible to regain their property when necessary. These factors have contributed to shortages of supply and poor maintenance.'

The 1988 Act swept away all rent control in the traditional sense and reintroduced the primacy of the market. Security of tenure was provided for (albeit on a more limited basis) through the concept of the assured tenancy; but the significance of this was substantially undermined by the facility for landlords to create assured shorthold tenancies, to which no true security of tenure attached. Indeed, s 96 of the Housing Act 1996 (inserting a new s 19A into the 1988 Act) went further in introducing a presumption that all 'new' tenancies were to be as assured shorthold tenancies unless the agreement provided to the contrary, or one of the other (limited) exceptions in the (new) Sch 2A applied.

Despite initially fierce opposition to the 'deregulation' in the Housing Act 1988 Part I[4], the approach of 'New Labour' in power has been to accept the changes without any hint that the clock will be turned back and, in particular, assured

---

[2]   As a result of s 1 Rent Act 1974.
[3]   *Housing: The Government's Proposals* (1987) Cm 214.
[4]   For example, see Clive Soley the acting Labour housing spokesman in *Hansard* Vl 123, column 632, 30 November 1987: 'The Government's policy in the Bill is deregulation of the private sector ... the Government tried this crazy idea in 1957 and again in 1980. In 1957 a new word entered the English language – "Rachmanism" ...'.

shorthold tenancies now dominate the market. For example, in 1990, the first full year of the 1988 reforms, assured shortholds accounted for only 8 per cent of the overall private rented sector, whereas by 2000/2001 they comprised 56 per cent. Correspondingly whereas Rent Act regulated tenancies accounted for 59 per cent of the market in 1988, by 2000/2001 they had declined to 6 per cent (a decrease from 1.1 million to only 122,000). The jury is still out, however, on the overall success of deregulation as a prime stimulus of reviving the private rented sector. Between 1989 and 1996/7 the size of the sector as a percentage of all households increased from 8.6 per cent to 10.2 per cent. However, since then there has been no further progress – indeed in percentage terms the sector has seen a small decline (down to 9.7 per cent of all households in 2000/2001)[5].

As the overwhelming majority of private sector tenancies are now governed by the Housing Act 1988, attention is first given to the provisions in the 1988 Act. Following this, the distinct provisions in the Rent Act 1977 are (briefly) considered.

## HOUSING ACT 1988 TENANCIES

### Assured tenancies

Despite the predominance in practice of the assured shorthold tenancy, the starting point has to be the concept of the assured tenancy. Indeed, the definition of an assured shorthold tenancy initially requires that the tenancy fulfils the definition of an assured tenancy (Housing Act 1988, s 20(1)).

The basic definition is contained in s 1 of the Housing Act 1988, which provides (in part):

(1) A tenancy under which a dwelling-house is let as a separate dwelling is for the purposes of this Act an assured tenancy if and so long as—

(a)   the tenant or, as the case may be, each of the joint tenants is an individual; and
(b)   the tenant or, as the case may be, at least one of the joint tenants occupies the dwelling-house as his only or principal home; and
(c)   the tenancy is not one which, by virtue of subsection (2) or subsection (6) below, cannot be an assured tenancy.

(2) Subject to subsection (3) below, if and so long as a tenancy falls within any paragraph in Part I of Schedule 1 to this Act, it cannot be an assured tenancy; and in that Schedule—

(a)   'tenancy' means a tenancy under which a dwelling-house is let as a separate dwelling;

The key concepts in the above all derive from previous legislation, principally the Rent Act 1977 and its predecessors or the (public sector) Housing Act 1985. There is, therefore, a considerable amount of case law to draw on. For example:

### *'Dwelling-house'*

Section 45(1) states clearly that a 'dwelling-house' may be a 'house or part of a house' (echoing s 1 of the Rent Act 1977). It is clear that a flat or even a room can

---

[5]   All figures from Bates M, Joy S, Perry J, Swales K and Thurnby M, *Housing in England* 2000/1 (DETR 2002).

constitute (for this purpose at least) a 'dwelling-house' (although whether a room constitutes a separate dwelling is another matter). This is supported by 'Rent Act' cases such as *Curl v Angelo*[6], *Langford Property Co v Goldrich*[7] and more recently the key Housing Act 1988 case of *Uratemp Ventures Ltd v Collins*[8]. Equally two distinct properties, can, for this purpose, constitute one 'dwelling-house'[9].

### 'Is let'

This of course raises the tenancy or licence question discussed in the previous chapter. True licences are outside the scope of assured tenancy protection.

### 'As a separate dwelling'

Although this compound phrase needs, ultimately, to be read as a whole, each word also carries an individual significance requiring individual comment.

### 'As'

The word 'as' in the above phrase indicates that the key is the purpose for which the property was originally let and not any subsequent use that may have taken place. The leading case, consistently referred to in the subsequent authorities, is *Wolfe v Hogan*[10]. (It was applied by the Court of Appeal specifically in relation to s 1 of the Housing Act 1988 in *Andrews v Brewer*[11].)

In August 1939, Noller, a tenant of a property in Chelsea, sub-let to Hogan (the 'tenant') a large room on the ground floor, divided by means of two folding doors and, behind that, a small brick-built edifice attached to the larger room. The large room, when let, contained a number of articles of furniture and junk, Noller being a dealer in such articles. It was plain that Hogan's intention was to carry on the business of an antique and junk dealer at this shop. No water was laid on to these rooms and there was no toilet. Noller arranged with his other tenants upstairs that Hogan could have the use of their toilet and bathroom, which was on a halfway floor. It was found by the trial judge that there was no express covenant by the tenant that she would not use the premises as a dwelling-house, but that the whole of the negotiations proceeded on the footing that the tenant was taking this composite room to use it as an antique shop.

Later, when London was exposed to air bombing, the tenant asked Noller whether he would have any objection to her sleeping on the premises, and he, feeling that she might well be in difficulty in going home in air raids, agreed. In 1942, the freeholders parted with the freehold, Noller's lease came to an end and the tenant's sub-tenancy died with it, but she remained in occupation as a tenant of the freeholder. Wolfe was now the freeholder and the landlord of Hogan.

6   [1948] 2 All ER 189.
7   [1949] 1 KB 511.
8   [2001] UKHL 43, [2002] 1 AC 301, [2002] 1 All ER 46.
9   [1950] 2 KB 32.
10  [1949] 1 All ER 570.
11  (1997) 30 HLR 203.

Wolfe, having given due notice to terminate the tenancy, brought an action claiming possession. The tenant resisted the claim, contending that her rooms were let to her 'as a separate dwelling', within the meaning of the (then) s 12(2), of the Rent and Mortgage Interest (Restrictions) Act, 1920. It was proved that for some time, Hogan lived in the rooms as well as conducting her business there. Noller and Wolfe denied that they knew that she was living there, but this was contested.

Stable J found that there was merely a letting of premises described as a shop and held that there should be implied in the contract a covenant against the use of the premises otherwise that as a shop. He gave judgment for possession.

The Court of Appeal unanimously upheld the first instance decision, ruling that the premises had been originally let as a 'lock-up' shop, and that nothing subsequently had occurred to change this.

Denning LJ (as he then was) summed up the approach of the Court of Appeal clearly:

'In determining whether a house or part of a house is "let as a dwelling" within the meaning of the Rent Restriction Acts, it is necessary to look at the purpose of the letting. If the lease contains an express provision as to the purpose of the letting, it is not necessary to look further. But, if there is no express provision, it is open to the court to look at the circumstances of the letting. If the house is constructed for use as a dwelling-house, it is reasonable to infer the purpose was to let it as a dwelling. But if, on the other hand, it is constructed for the purpose of being used as a lock-up shop, the reasonable inference is that it was let for business purposes. If the position were neutral, then it would be proper to look at the actual user. It is not a question of implied terms. It is a question of the purpose for which the premises were let. These premises were let in 1939 by the head lessee to Miss Hogan. On the facts, there was ample material on which the judge could find that the purpose of the letting was for use as a shop. At the beginning of the tenancy, therefore, the premises were not within the Act. But the point that has arisen in the course of argument is this: What is the effect of the tenant changing the use she made of the premises? She changed its use from one for business purposes to one partly for business and partly for dwelling purposes. During the air-raids in 1940 she started to sleep on the premises and continued to sleep there. She has thereafter continued to use a part for dwelling purposes. Indeed, when the notice to quit was given in 1947, she was for all practical purposes permanently residing in the back part of the room. Moreover, there is ground for supposing that the landlord accepted rent, knowing of the change of user: because, in 1942, after the original letting to the head lessee under the lease had come to an end, the head landlord became the immediate landlord of Miss Hogan and, knowing the position of affairs in the house, accepted rent from her.
What is the effect of that? In my opinion, it does not give the tenant the protection of the Act. A house or a part of a house originally let for business purposes does not become let for dwelling purposes, unless it can be inferred from the acceptance of rent that the landlord has affirmatively consented to the change of user.'

## 'A'

The Court of Appeal twice ruled in the 1970s that the phrase 'let as *a* dwelling' could only be interpreted in the singular (notwithstanding the Interpretation Act). So, a house let as *several* dwellings fell outside Rent Act protection, and will equally fall outside the Housing Act 1988. The cases were *Horford Investments Ltd v Lambert*[12] and *St Catherine's College v Dorling*[13].

## 'SEPARATE'

The word 'separate' is a key concept which involves the idea that the accommodation occupied is (relatively) 'self-contained'. Therefore any sharing of essential living accommodation (other than with other joint tenants) will result in the accommodation falling outside protection. The case law suggests that 'living accommodation' involves living rooms, bedrooms and kitchens, but not bathrooms or toilets. For example in *Cole v Harris*[14] Mackinnon LJ said: '… a dwelling-house is that in which a person dwells or lives, and it seems reasonable that a separate dwelling should be one containing essential living rooms. A WC may be essential in modern days, but I do not think it is a living room, whereas a kitchen, I think is.' Some of the cases have concerned the difficulties caused by the sharing (with the landlord or other tenant) of facilities which would normally be seen as 'essential'[15].

## 'DWELLING'

Even if none of the living accommodation is shared with others, the accommodation may fall outside protection if it is not 'the "home" of anybody'. So, if one of the essential features of 'normal living' is carried on elsewhere, and never in the accommodation, then the accommodation may not (for this purpose) be a 'dwelling'. Into the category of 'essential features' would come sleeping and eating. As a general approach it would be realistic to say that if a person rarely if ever sleeps or eats in the accommodation it is not a 'dwelling'; but, of course, any case may have features so that this norm will not be applied.

The key division on this point, and, indeed on s 1 Housing Act 1988 generally is *Uratemp Ventures Ltd v Collins*[16]. Collins was a long-term resident of one of the 58 rooms in a private hotel in West London. He first took up occupation of a room in the hotel in January 1985. The room contained a bed, plus a separate toilet and wash basin. Collins subsequently changed rooms three times, but all the rooms were much the same; in particular no cooking facilities were provided in any of the rooms, although each of them contained at least one power point. Collins acquired basic cooking equipment such as a toasted sandwich maker, a warming plate and a kettle (he was not prohibited by the terms of his occupation from bringing such equipment into his room). He also took takeaway meals into his room and ate them there. In 1993, the hotel published rules (claiming to be on safety grounds) which prohibited cooking in rooms. However, Collins never 'signed up' to the new rules. In April 1998 Uratemp served a notice terminating what they claimed was Collins's

---

[12]  [1974] 1 All ER 131.
[13]  [1979] 3 All ER 250.
[14]  [1945] 2 All ER 146, at 148.
[15]  For example, *Neale v Del Soto* [1945] 1 All ER 191.
[16]  [2001] UKHL 43, [2002] 1 AC 30, [2002] 1 All ER 46.

'licence' to occupy the room and brought possession proceedings. In the county court it was held that the claim failed because Collins occupied the room as an assured tenant. The Court of Appeal reversed the county court finding that the absence of cooking facilities precluded a finding that the room was a 'dwelling' under s 1. However, the House of Lords, in turn, reversed this and restored the judgment of the county court (the 'lease/licence' issue was thought by the Court of Appeal to have been inadequately explored by the county court, and, on this point, they would have remitted the matter to the county court for more factual findings on the issue. In the event it was not explored further, because Collins and Uratemp reached an 'understanding' – indeed Uratemp took no part in the appeal to the House of Lords. All the discussion in the House *assumes* that Collins occupied the room as a tenant and not as a licensee).

The leading judgment in the House of Lords is that of Lord Millett, with which the rest of the House agreed. Lord Millett stated:

'The words "dwell" and "dwelling" are not terms of art with a specialised legal meaning. They are ordinary English words, even if they are perhaps no longer in common use. They mean the same as "inhabit" and "habitation" or more precisely "abide" and "abode", and refer to the place where one lives and makes one's home. They suggest a greater degree of settled occupation than "reside" and "residence", connoting the place where the occupier habitually sleeps and usually eats, but the idea that he must also cook his meals there is found only in the law reports. It finds no support in English literature. According to the Book of Common Prayer, "the fir trees are a dwelling for the storks" (Psalm 104); while W S Gilbert condemned the billiard sharp "to dwell in a dungeon cell" (where it will be remembered he plays with a twisted cue on a cloth untrue with elliptical billiard balls): *The Mikado*, Act II. It is hardly necessary to observe that Victorian prison cells did not possess cooking facilities. Of course, the word "dwell" may owe its presence to the exigencies of the rhyme, but it does not strike the listener as incongruous. If faintly humorous, it is because the occupation of a prison cell is involuntary, not because of the absence of cooking facilities. As I shall show hereafter, Gilbert, who had qualified at the Bar, had got his law right. An earlier and greater poet wrote of Lucifer being hurled "to bottomless perdition, there to dwell in adamantine chaos and penal fire": (*Paradise Lost*, Book I, L $_{47}$).

In both ordinary and literary usage, residential accommodation is "a dwelling" if it is the occupier's home (or one of his homes). It is the place where he lives and to which he returns and which forms the centre of his existence. Just what use he makes of it when living there, however, depends on his mode of life. No doubt he will sleep there and usually eat there; he will often prepare at least some of his meals there. But his home is not the less his home because he does not cook there but prefers to eat out or bring in ready-cooked meals. It has never been a legislative requirement that cooking facilities must be available for a premises to qualify as a dwelling. Nor is it at all evident what policy considerations dictate that a tenant who prepares his meals at home should enjoy security of tenure while a tenant who brings in all his meals ready-cooked should not.

In my opinion the position is relatively straightforward. The first step is to identify the subject matter of the tenancy agreement. If this is a house or part of a house of which the tenant has exclusive possession with no element of sharing, the only question is whether, at the date when the proceedings were brought, it was the tenant's home. If so, it was his dwelling. (He must also occupy it as his only or principal home, but that is a separate requirement). If the tenancy agreement grants, in addition, the right to the shared use of other rooms, the question is whether the room or rooms of which he as exclusive possession are his dwelling place or only part of it. This depends on the nature and extent of the right and the character of the other rooms. The right to occupy a living room in common with and at the same time as the landlord is such an invasion of his privacy that Parliament cannot be taken to have intended that the tenant should enjoy security of tenure. For this purpose a kitchen is a living room, at least if it is possible to occupy it and not merely cook and wash up in it; so that a right to occupy a kitchen (as distinct from a right to make some limited use of its facilities) in common with the landlord will take the tenancy out of the Acts. The presence or absence of cooking facilities in the part of the premises of which the tenant has exclusive occupation is not relevant.'

It may be that the significance of *Uratemp* is relatively limited[17], in that, since the Housing Act 1996 in particular, the assured shorthold dominates the private rented sector and the legal protection attaching to assured shorthold tenants is not significantly greater than for wholly non-assured tenants[18]. Nevertheless the approach of the House of Lords is clear, and easy to apply. At its simplest once a person has exclusive possession, uncluttered by sharing, of something that can be called his/her 'dwelling', then s 1 is satisfied. A 'dwelling' is, quite simply, where a person lives and, in the words of Lord Steyn, 'A bed-sitting room which a tenant occupies as his home may be a dwelling even if he brings in all his meals, or goes out for all his meals'.

### 'Individual'

The word 'individual' in s 1(1)(a) indicates that the letting must be to a natural person and not to a company, or other form of 'artificial' person. If the courts are not astute to detect 'shams' there is considerable scope here for avoidance of the legislation by landlords via the drafting ploy of the letting being to a company, albeit that the only member of that company is the occupant of the premises. This issue was discussed in *Hilton v Plustitle Ltd*[19].

Hilton, the owner of the property, was in the business of reconstructing premises so as to create 'upmarket' flats. He advertised the flats as only available through a company which would normally be (in effect) 'set up' by him. In the event the ultimate tenant in this case, a Ms Rose, bought an 'off the peg' company called Plustitle Ltd herself (she was the only director and shareholder). Hilton then contracted with Plustitle for the company to let one of his flats, and the company in

---

[17] See P F Smith, 'Fir Trees and Dwellings' (2002) 66 Conv 285.
[18] Although there are differences, for example, a minimum initial six months' security of tenure.
[19] [1988] 3 All ER 1051.

turn (in accordance with this agreement) nominated Rose as the occupier. Initially the let was for a fixed term of six months. This was later extended for a further three months, but, after a rent dispute, Hilton sought possession. The county court granted the order sought, and its judgment was upheld in the Court of Appeal. The Court of Appeal rejected arguments based on the approach taken by the House of Lords in *Street v Mountford*[20]. that the 'company let' was a 'sham' disguising the true nature of the transaction – a letting to Ms Rose.

However, two further points should be noted. Firstly, the significance of such 'avoidance devices' is now much less, in that Housing Act 1988 tenancies (particularly assured shortholds) are far more in tune with landlords' interests than the Rent Act 1977 tenancies which were at issue in *Hilton v Plustitle*. Indeed it is likely, now, to be rare for such elaborate schemes to be set up.

Secondly, the approach of the Court of Appeal in *Hilton v Plustitle* is somewhat suspect. The distinction drawn in the case between attempts to evade protective legislation (which were clearly illegitimate) and the construction schemes to avoid the implications of such legislation (which were acceptable) may not be inconsistent with *Street v Mountford*, but sits uncomfortably with it. Moreover, the Court of Appeal places much reliance on the approach of the Court of Appeal in *Antoniades v Villiers* which (shortly after) was to be overruled in the House of Lords.

### 'Only or principal home'

The requirement in s 1(1)(b) that the tenant must occupy the dwelling-house as his only or principal home is *not* one with a long legislative pedigree in the private sector. The equivalent Rent Act formula is broader in scope – 'as his residence' (s 2(1)(a), Rent Act 1977) – but narrower in application (affecting only the 'secondary' definition of a statutory tenancy). There is, however, a directly equivalent provision to be found in s 81 of the Housing Act 1985 as part of the statutory definition of a (public sector) secure tenant. Relevant case law is, therefore, dealt with in Chapter 8[21].

As already noted several times in this chapter, the advantages of being classified as an assured tenant are fewer than being classified as a Rent Act protected or statutory tenant. Meaningful rent control does not attach to such tenancies, and even security of tenure is less substantial. It is likely, therefore, that although many of the basic criteria involved in the process of classification as an assured tenant are carried over from the Rent Acts, there will be far fewer contested cases on s 1 of the Housing Act 1988 than was true under s 1 of the Rent Act 1977 and its predecessors (this is certainly reflected in the small number of relevant reported cases in the period 1989 to 2003). However, to be outside even assured or assured shorthold status eliminates security altogether (leaving only the procedural controls in the Protection from Eviction Act 1977) and leaves rent as a wholly 'market' issue.

Two further points should be noted.

---

[20] See Chapter 3.
[21] The most recent case on s 1(1)(b) itself, *Sumeghova v McMahon* [2002] EWCA Civ 1581, [2003] HLR 349 adopted the same approach as that taken by the courts in the various 'public sector' cases.

Firstly, when considering cases such as *St Catherine's College v Dorling*[22] it must be remembered that sub-letting by a tenant will not, of itself, take the dwelling outside the Housing Act 1988, Pt I. (Although sub-letting without landlord permission is a breach of an implied term of the tenancy (s 15(1)(b), Housing Act 1988), and sub-letting the whole premises de facto precludes them being the tenant's only or principal home.) The key is how the property was let in the first place – as one property or a number of dwellings under one roof. In *St Catherine's College v Dorling*, the letting was seen to be of a number of dwellings from the beginning.

Secondly, the requirement of 'separateness' of the dwelling can throw up difficult cases, particularly where the premises are shared. At one extreme, the premises occupied are shared in all respects with others – living rooms; kitchens; bathroom; even bedrooms. In such a case the lack of any distinct 'separate' accommodation would not only preclude an assured tenancy arising, but would lead to the conclusion that no tenancy exists at all but merely a licence (in effect this was the aim of the 'non-exclusive occupation' agreements discussed in the previous chapter). Of course such 'separateness' is not required if a joint tenancy exists between the various parties, the sole requirement then being that the joint tenancy 'unit' itself occupies separate accommodation. At the other extreme all that is 'shared' is 'facilities' – toilets/bathrooms, etc. – rather than 'living' accommodation. In such a case assured tenancy status should not normally be affected. On the other hand, prima facie, the sharing of (say) a living room *would* undermine such status, the requirement of complete 'separateness' (or 'self-containedness') being breached. Such was indeed the position at first under the Rents Acts (see *Curl v Angelo*[23]. However, the matter was eventually dealt with by a specific section in the Rent Act (s 22 in the 1977 Act) and there is an equivalent provision in s 3 of the Housing Act 1988:

3. (1) Where a tenant has the exclusive occupation of any accommodation (in this section referred to as 'the separate accommodation') and—

    (a)  the terms as between the tenant and his landlord on which he holds the separate accommodation include the use of the other accommodation (in this section referred to as 'the shared accommodation') in common with another person or other persons, not being or including the landlord, and

    (b)  by reason only of the circumstances mentioned in paragraph (a) above, the separate accommodation would not, apart from this section, be a dwelling-house let on an assured tenancy,

the separate accommodation shall be deemed to be a dwelling-house let on an assured tenancy. ...

The key is, therefore, whether the tenant has exclusive use of at least one room (the 'separate' accommodation), even if this is not wholly self-contained. Implicit in all the above is the fact that the sharing is with persons other than the landlord of the property. Sharing with the landlord complicates matters considerably. First, s 3 does not apply (see s 3(1)(a) above) so that any sharing of essential living accommodation with the landlord prevents an assured tenancy arising (this is quite apart from the specific exclusions concerning 'resident landlords' contained in Sch 1 para 10 of

22  [1980] 1 WLR 66.
23  [1948] 2 All ER 189.

the 1988 Act – see below). However, the position is even less favourable for a tenant when ss 31 and 32 of the Housing Act 1988 are considered. As relevant, these read as follows:

31.   After section 3 of the 1977 Act there shall be inserted the following section—

## '3A.   Excluded tenancies and licences

(1) Any reference in this Act to an excluded tenancy or an excluded licence is a reference to a tenancy or licence which is excluded by virtue of any of the following provisions of this section.

(2) A tenancy or licence is excluded if—

(a)   under its terms the occupier shares any accommodation with the landlord or licensor; and

(b)   immediately before the tenancy or licence was granted and also at the time it comes to an end, the landlord or licensor occupied as his only or principal home premises of which the whole or part of the shared accommodation formed part.

(3) A tenancy or licence is also excluded if—

(a)   under its terms the occupier shares any accommodation with a member of the family of the landlord of licensor;

(b)   immediately before the tenancy or licence was granted and also at the time it comes to an end, the member of the family of the landlord or licensor occupied as his only or principal home premises of which the whole or part of the shared accommodation formed part; and

(c)   immediately before the tenancy or licence was granted and also at the time it comes to an end, the landlord or licensor occupied as his only or principal home premises in the same building as the shared accommodation and that building is not a purpose-built block of flats.

(4) For the purposes of subsections (2) and (3) above, an occupier shares accommodation with another person if he has the use of it in common with that person (whether or not also in common with others) and any reference in those subsections to shared accommodation shall be construed accordingly, and if, in relation to any tenancy or licence, there is at any time more than one person which is the landlord or licensor, any reference in those subsections to the landlord or licensor shall be construed as a reference to any one of those persons.

(5) In subsections (2) and (4) above—

(a)   'accommodation' includes neither an area used for storage nor a staircase, passage, corridor or other means of access;

(b)   'occupier' means, in relation to a tenancy, the tenant and, in relation to a licence, the licensee; and

(c)   'purpose-built block of flats' has the same meaning as in Part III of Schedule 1 to the Housing Act 1988;

and section 113 of the Housing Act 1985 shall apply to determine whether a person is for the purposes of subsection (3) above a member of another's family as it applies for the purposes of Part IV of that Act.'

   …

32.   (1) In section 5 of the 1977 Act (validity of notices to quit) at the beginning of subsection (1) there shall be inserted the words 'Subject to subsection (1B) below'.

(2) After subsection (1) of that section there shall be inserted the following subsections—

'(1A) Subject to subsection (1B) below, no notice by a licensor or a licensee to determine a periodic licence to occupy premises as a dwelling (whether the licence was granted before or after the passing of this Act) shall be valid unless—

(a) it is in writing and contains such information as may be prescribed, and

(b) it is given not less that 4 weeks before the date on which it is to take effect.

(1B) Nothing in subsection (1) or subsection (1A) above applies to—

(a) premises let on an excluded tenancy which is entered into on or after the date on which the Housing Act 1988 came into force unless it is entered into pursuant to a contract made before that date.'

The '1977 Act' amended (see s 32(1)) is the Protection from Eviction Act 1977. In effect, these amendments mean that a landlord who has been sharing *any* 'accommodation' (subject to s 3A(5)(a)) with a tenant is not even hindered by the procedural hurdles of statutory notices to quit and court orders if possession is sought against the tenant. These matters are explored further later in this chapter, and in Chapter 5.

## Non-assured tenancies

Subsequent sections will serve to indicate how limited in *practice* remaining tenant protection is, given the increasing predominance and ease of creation of the assured shorthold tenancy. Nevertheless, a tenant's rights are still fewer and a landlord's position is still stronger if the tenancy falls outside the scheme of statutory regulation altogether. The most obvious instance of a contract falling outside protection is, of course, where it creates a licence not a tenancy, but the significance of this has been much diminished (at least in the private sector!) since *Antoniades v Villiers* (Chapter 3). Secondly, if the provisions in s 1 of the Housing Act 1988 are not complied with then the tenancy cannot be an assured one. A decision like *Hilton v Plustitle Ltd* (above), if followed, effectively allows a landlord to 'contract out' of the legislation. However, in addition, Sch 1 of the 1988 Act provides for a disparate group of tenancies which 'cannot be assured tenancies' (it is not entirely clear what they should be called instead, but 'non-assured' should suffice). Many of these replicate equivalent provisions in the Rent Act 1977 and bear (at least) a resemblance to the list of 'non-secure' tenancies in the Housing Act 1985. The key exceptions are itemised here.

In addition Sch 1 para 2 concerns properties with high rateable values, Sch 1 para 5 concerns premises licensed for the 'on-site' sale of alcohol, Sch 1 paras 6 and 7 concern tenancies of agricultural land, and Sch 1 para 11 concerns tenancies where the Crown is the landlord. Of the remainder, many of the provisions are reasonably self-explanatory and require little further comment. Of those that do require comment, para 10 is the most complex and interesting.

# SCHEDULE 1
# TENANCIES WHICH CANNOT BE
# ASSURED TENANCIES

## PART 1
## THE TENANCIES

*Tenancies entered into before commencement*

1. A tenancy which is entered into before, or pursuant to a contract made before the commencement of this Act. ...

*Tenancies at a low rent*

3. A tenancy under which for the time being no rent is payable.

3A. A tenancy—

(a) which is entered into on or after 1st April 1990 (otherwise than, where the dwelling-house had a rateable value of 31st March 1990, in pursuance of a contract made before 1st April 1990), and

(b) under which the rent payable for the time being is payable at a rate of, if the dwelling-house is in Greater London, £1,000 or less a year and, if it is elsewhere, £250 or less a year.

3B. A tenancy—

(a) which was entered into before 1st April 1990 or, where the dwelling-house had a rateable value on the 31st March 1990, on or after 1st April 1990 in pursuance of a contract made before that date, and

(b) under which the rent for the time being payable is less than two-thirds of the rateable value of the dwelling-house on 31 March 1990.

3C. Paragraph 2(2) above applies for the purposes of paragraphs 3, 3A and 3B as it applies for the purposes of paragraph 2(1).

*Business tenancies*

4. A tenancy to which Part II of the Landlord and Tenant Act 1954 applies (business tenancies). ...

*Lettings to students*

8.—(1) A tenancy which is granted to a person who is pursuing, or intends to pursue, a course of study provided by a specified educational institution and is so granted either by that institution or by another specified institution or body of persons.

(2) In sub-paragraph (1) above 'specified' means specified, or of a class specified, for the purposes of this paragraph by regulations made by the Secretary of State by statutory instrument.

(3) A statutory instrument made in the exercise of the power conferred by sub-paragraph (2) above shall be subject to annulment in pursuance of a resolution of either House of Parliament.

*Holiday lettings*

9. A tenancy the purpose of which is to confer on the tenant the right to occupy the dwelling-house for a holiday.

*Resident landlords*

10.—(1) A tenancy in respect of which the following conditions are fulfilled—

(a) that the dwelling-house forms part only of a building and, except in a case where the dwelling-house also forms part of a flat, the building is not a purpose-built block of flats; and

(b) that, subject to Part III of this Schedule, the tenancy was granted by an individual who, at the time when the tenancy was granted, occupied as his only or principal home another dwelling-house which—

(i) in the case mentioned in paragraph (a) above, also forms part of the flat;

or

(ii) in any other case, also forms part of the building; and

(c) that, subject to Part III of this Schedule, at all times since the tenancy was granted the interest of the landlord under the tenancy has belonged to an individual who, at the time he owned that interest, occupied as his only or principal home another dwelling-house which—

   (i)   in the case mentioned in paragraph (a) above,

also formed part of the flat; or

   (ii)  in any other case, also formed part of the building; and

(d) that the tenancy is not one which is excluded from this sub-paragraph by sub-paragraph (3) below.

(2) If a tenancy was granted by two or more persons jointly, the reference in sub-paragraph (1)(b) above to an individual is a reference to any one of those persons and if the interest of the landlord is for the time being held by two or more persons jointly, the reference in sub-paragraph (1)(c) above to an individual is a reference to any one of those persons.

(3) A tenancy (in this sub-paragraph referred to as 'the new tenancy') is excluded from sub-paragraph (1) above if—

(a) it is granted to a person (alone, or jointly with others) who, immediately before it was granted, was a tenant under an assured tenancy (in this sub-paragraph referred to as 'the former tenancy') of the same dwelling-house or of another dwelling-house which forms part of the building in question; and

(b) the landlord under the new tenancy and under the former tenancy is the same person or, if either of those tenancies is or was granted by two or more persons jointly, the same person is the landlord or one of the landlords under each tenancy.

…

*Local authority tenancies etc.*

12.—(1) A tenancy under which the interest of the landlord belongs to—

(a) a local authority, as defined in sub-paragraph (2) below;
(b) the Commission for the New Towns;
(c) the Development Board for Rural Wales;
(d) an urban development corporation established by an order under section 135 of the Local Government, Planning and Land Act 1980;
(e) a development corporation, within the meaning of the New Towns Act 1981;
(f) an authority established under section 10 of the Local Government Act 1985 (waste disposal authorities);
(g) a residuary body, within the meaning of the Local Government Act 1985;
[(gg)the Residuary Body for Wales (Corff Gweddiolliol Cymru);]
(h) a fully mutual housing association; or
(i) a housing action trust established under Part III of this Act.

Paragraph 4 seems clear enough at first glance. The main difficulty is that there is no requirement that the premises should have been *originally* let *as a business*. This is because s 23(1) of the Landlord and Tenant Act 1954 applies 'to any tenancy where the property comprised in the tenancy is or includes premises which are occupied for the purpose of a business carried on by him or for those and other purposes'. Therefore the essence is the purpose for which the premises are *occupied* rather than the purpose for which they were originally *let* (quite contrary to the 'original purpose' requirement under s 1 – see *Wolfe v Hogan*[24]). The provision has

---

[24]  [1949] 1 All ER 570.

a long pedigree, given the transparent need to exclude true 'business lets' from the scope of protective residential legislation. Probably the clearest analysis is to be found in Lord Denning MR's judgment in *Cheryl Investments v Saldanha* and *Royal Life Saving Society v Page*[25]:

'Here we have a topsy-turvy situation. Two landlords contend that their tenants are "business tenants" and entitled to have their tenancies continued under the statute in that behalf: whereas the tenants contend that they are not so entitled at all. The reason for this oddity is because, if the tenants are not "business tenants", their tenancies are "regulated tenancies" and they are protected by the Rent Acts. The protection under the Rent Acts is much better for the tenants than the protection under the business statute. So the landlords seek to chase them out of the Rent Acts and put them into the business Acts.

…

### The application of the statute

There was much discussion before us as to the meaning of the Business Tenancy Act 1954 (I use those words because I think "Landlord and Tenant Act 1954" is a little confusing), especially the word "purposes" in section 23(1) and the time or times at which those "purposes" had to exist: and the effect of a change by the tenant in the use to which he put the property. Could he take himself in or out of the Act at his option? …

*First*, take the case where a professional man is the tenant of two premises: one his office where he works, the other his flat, conveniently near, where he has his home. He has then a "business tenancy" of his office and a "regulated tenancy" of his home. This remains the situation even though he takes papers home and works on them at evenings or weekends and occasionally sees a client at home. He cannot in such a case be said to be occupying his flat "for the purpose of" his profession. He is occupying it for the purpose of his home, even though he incidentally does some work there: see *Sweet v Parsley* [1969] 1 All ER 347, at 355; [1970] AC 132, at 155 *per* Lord Morris of Borth-y-Gest.

*Second*, take the case where a professional man takes a tenancy of one house for the very purpose of carrying on his profession in one room and of residing in the rest of the house with his family, like the doctor who has a consulting room in his house. He has not then a "regulated tenancy" at all. His tenancy is a "business tenancy" and nothing else. He is clearly occupying part of the house "for the purpose of" his profession, as one purpose; and the other part for the purpose of his dwelling as *another* purpose. Each purpose is significant. Neither is merely incidental to the other.

*Third*, suppose now that the first man decides to give up his office and do all his work from his home: there being nothing in the tenancy of his home to prevent him doing it. In that case he becomes in the same position as the second man. He ceases to have a "regulated tenancy" of his home. He has only a "business tenancy" of it.

[25]  [1979] 1 All ER 5.

*Fourth*, suppose now that the second man decides to give up his office at home and to take a tenancy of an office elsewhere so as to carry on his profession elsewhere. He then has a "business tenancy" of his new premises. But he does not get a "regulated tenancy" of his original home, even though he occupies is now only as his home, because it was never let to him as a separate dwelling: unless the landlord agrees to the change.

Those illustrations point to the solution of the present two cases.

### *Royal Life Saving Society v Page*

No. 14, Devonshire Street is a house with four floors. It is owned by the Howard de Walden Marylebone Estate. In 1945 they let it on a long lease to the Royal Life Saving Society for 64½ years. That society occupy most of the house themselves: but in 1960 they let the top two floors as a maisonette to a Mr Gut for 14 years at a rent of £600 a year. There was no restriction on the use which the tenant made of the premises. But it would appear that the maisonette was constructed for use as a separate dwelling: and that the letting was "as a separate dwelling" within the tests laid down in *Wolfe v Hogan* [1949] 2 KB 194, 204–205.

In 1963 Mr Gut made arrangements to assign the lease to the present tenant, Dr Page. He was a medical practitioner who had his consulting rooms at no. 52, Harley Street. … Dr Page took the maisonette in Devonshire Street so that he could live there as his home. But he thought that in the future he might possibly want to use it occasionally to see patients there. So, when he took the assignment, he asked for consent to do so. Such consent was readily given by the Royal Life Saving Society (his immediate landlords) and by the Howard de Walden Estate (the head landlords). It was a consent for Dr Page to carry on his profession in the maisonette. After the assignment he moved in and occupied it as his home. He put both addresses (Harley Street and Devonshire Street) in the medical directory. He had separate notepaper for each address and put both telephone numbers on each. This was, of course, so that anyone who wished to telephone him could get him at one or other place. But he did very little professional work at the maisonette. Over the whole period of the tenancy he had only seen about one patient a year there. The last patient was in distress 18 months ago. He summarised the position in one sentence: "Harley Street is my professional address, and the other is my home."

On those facts it is quite clear that no. 14, Devonshire Street was let as a separate dwelling and occupied by Dr Page as a separate dwelling. There was only one significant purpose for which he occupied it. It was for his home. He carried on his profession elsewhere in Harley Street. His purpose is evidenced by his actual use of it. Such user as he made in Devonshire Street for his profession was not a significant user. It was only incidental to his use of it as his home. He comes within my first illustration. He is, therefore, protected by the Rent Acts as a "regulated tenancy" …

### *Cheryl Investments Ltd v Saldanha*

46/47 Beaufort Gardens have been turned into 25 separate apartments. These are owned by a property company called Cheryl Investments Ltd. In December 1975 the company advertised the apartments in the "Evening Standard" in these words: "Knightsbridge. Essex House, near Harrods, serviced flat and flatlets. Doubles from 20 guineas, Flats from 27 guineas. Short-long lets."

Mr Roland Saldanha answered the advertisement. ... He was shown one of the flats which he liked. It had a large double room with twin beds in it, a bathroom and a toilet. It had no separate kitchen, but there was an entrance hall with a cooker in it which could be used as a kitchen. The landlords provided the furniture and service in the shape of a maid to clean it and change the towels etc. It took her half an hour a day. The charge was £36.75 a week, plus five per cent surcharge.

Mr Saldanha's stay there turned out to be very unhappy with quarrels between him and the landlords. Eventually on February 9, 1977, the landlords gave him notice to quit on March 26, 1977. He claimed the protection of the Rent Acts. He said: "I am a fully fledged tenant entitled to full protection under the Rent Acts." The landlords took proceedings in the county court claiming that he was not a tenant but a licensee. ... But the judge held that he was a tenant.
...

But ... the landlords amended their particulars of claim so as to assert that Mr Saldanha occupied the flat for business purposes and was, therefore, not entitled to the protection of the Rent Acts; and they sought a declaration accordingly. The judge rejected this claim. It is from this decision that the landlords appeal to this court.

On this point the evidence was that Mr Saldanha is an accountant by profession and a partner in a firm called Best Marine Enterprises. They carry on the business of importing sea foods from India and processing them in Scotland. The firm has no trade premises. The two partners carry on the business from their own homes. The other partner works at his home in Basildon. Mr Saldanha works at the flat in Beaufort Gardens; and goes from there out to visit clients. ... He had notepaper printed: "Best Marine Enterprises. Importers of Quality Sea-foods. Telephone 589 0232" – that is the number I have just mentioned – "PO Box 211, Knightsbridge, London, SW3". He issued business statements on that very notepaper. A copy of one was found by the maid in a wastepaper basket showing that the firm had imported goods at a total cost of £49,903.30 and sold them for £58,152.35. The maid (whose evidence the judge explicitly accepted in preference to Mr Saldanha's) said: "I presumed Mr Saldanha conducted business there".

On that evidence I should have thought it plain that Mr Saldanha was occupying the flat, not only as his dwelling, but also for the purposes of a business carried on by him in partnership with another. When he took the flat it was, no doubt, let to him as a separate dwelling. No one can doubt that it was constructed for use as a dwelling and let to him as such within the test in *Wolfe v Hogan* [1949] 1 All ER 570, at 575; [1949] 2 KB 194 at 204–205. But as soon as he equipped it for the purposes of his business of importing sea foods – with telephone, table and printed notepaper – and afterwards used it by receiving business calls there, see customers there and issuing business statements from there – it is plain that he was occupying it "for the purposes of a business carried on by him". This was a significant purpose for which he was occupying the flat, as well as a dwelling. It was his only home, and he was carrying on his business from it. It comes within my second illustration.'

As regards para 8 (lettings to students), the list of specified institutions is to be found in the Assured and Protected Tenancies (Lettings to Students) Regulations 1998 (SI 1998/1967). A wide variety of universities and colleges are included, thereby taking the (increasingly common) situation of the university or college sub-letting to its own students (often called 'head tenancy' schemes) outside true statutory regulation[26].

The equivalent provision to para 9 (holiday lettings) proved contentious under the Rent Acts (see s 9, Rent Act 1977), for if the courts were not 'astute' to detect shams, the provision would obviously be attractive to landlords anxious to avoid protective legislation (this is particularly likely when it is borne in mind that most true holiday 'lets' will be construed as merely conferring licences in any event – see Chapter 3). The extent to which the courts were mindful of this is open to debate (the number of reported decisions is, in any event, small). In *Buchmann v May*[27], a tenancy agreement for a term of three months contained the following clause: 'It is mutually agreed and declared that the letting hereby made is solely for the purpose of the tenant's holiday in the London area'. The Court of Appeal held that the clause was, prima facie, conclusive as to the partiers' intentions, and added that 'The court would be astute to detect a sham when it appeared in the context of the Rent Acts, but the burden was on the tenant to prove it, not on the landlord to show that the agreement was correct'. (Sir John Pennycuick, at p 998.)

On the other hand, the tenant (a New Zealand national) did lack permanent residence status in this country, giving some credibility to the stated 'holiday' purpose of the agreement, and in the later case of *R v Rent Officer for London Borough of Camden, ex p Plant*[28] a markedly different approach was taken by the court. Again, the tenancy agreement stated that the accommodation was occupied 'for a holiday', despite the landlord knowing that the prospective tenants were students! As Glidewell J (as he then was) stated (at p 718):

> 'Prima facie this agreement … was to occupy and use this flat for a holiday … but … both parties knew perfectly well that [the tenants] were going to occupy it for the purpose of their work as students. I so find, and that seems to me to be conclusive of the matter … I find that there is clear evidence that the purpose expressed in the tenancy agreement was not the true purpose of that agreement.'

This approach is far more in line with that adopted in the most recent lease/licence cases discussed in Chapter 3. (*Buchmann* of course pre-dates even *Street v Mountford* by some seven years.)

In any event, although prior to the Housing Act 1988 the use of (claimed) 'holiday lets' was fairly widespread (particularly in London), the same is not true under the 1988 Act given the availability of the assured shorthold tenancy.

Paragraph 10 *is* of considerable significance still. Unlike many of the other exceptions its pedigree is relatively short, dating originally from the 1974 Rent Act.

---

[26] In fact the validity of the reference in para 8 to 'specified body of persons' does allow for regulation to 'specify' bodies as exempt other than those which would normally be thought to come within para 8 – see D Hughes and M Davis, 'Student Housing: a cautionary tale of one city' JSWFL 24(2), 135.
[27] [1978] 2 All ER 993.
[28] (1980) 257 EG 713.

Paragraph 10 and its ancillary paragraphs have much in common with the Rent Act provisions (now s 12, Rent Act 1977), but there are significant differences. The principal paragraph is supplemented by paras 17–22, the key elements of which are reproduced below.

# PART III
# PROVISIONS FOR DETERMINING APPLICATION OF PARA-GRAPH 10 (RESIDENT LANDLORDS)

17.—(1) In determining whether the condition in paragraph 10(1)(c) above is at any time fulfilled with respect to a tenancy, there shall be disregarded—

(a) any period of not more than twenty-eight days, beginning with the date on which the interest of the landlord under the tenancy becomes vested at law and in equity in an individual who, during that period, does not occupy as his only or principal home another dwelling-house which forms part of the building or, as the case may be, flat concerned;

(b) if, within a period falling within paragraph (a) above, the individual concerned notifies the tenant in writing of his intention to occupy as his only or principal home another dwelling-house in the building or, as the case may be, flat concerned, the period beginning with the date on which the interest of the landlord under the tenancy becomes vested in that individual as mentioned in that paragraph and ending—

(i) at the expiry of the period of six months beginning on that date, or

(ii) on the date on which that interest ceases to be so vested, or

(iii) on the date on which that interest becomes again vested in such an individual as is mentioned in paragraph 10(1)(c) or the condition in that paragraph becomes deemed to be fulfilled by virtue of paragraph 18(1) or paragraph 20 below, whichever is the earlier …

(2) Where the interest of the landlord under a tenancy becomes vested at law and in equity in two or more persons jointly, of whom at least one was an individual, sub-paragraph (1) above shall have effect subject to the following modifications—

(a) in paragraph (a) for the words from 'an individual' to 'occupy' there shall be substituted 'the joint landlords if, during that period none of them occupies'; and

(b) in paragraph (b) for the words 'the individual concerned' there shall be substituted 'any of the joint landlords who is an individual'; and for the words 'that individual' there shall be substituted 'the joint landlords'.

(2) If a period during which the condition in paragraph 10(1)(c) is deemed to be fulfilled by virtue of sub-paragraph (1) above comes to an end on the death of a person who was in occupation of a dwelling-house as mentioned in paragraph (b) of that sub-paragraph, then, in determining whether that condition is at any time thereafter fulfilled, there shall be disregarded any period—

(a) which begins on the date of the death;

(b) during which the interest of the landlord remains vested as mentioned in sub-paragraph (1)(a) above; and

(c) which ends at the expiry of the period of two years beginning on the date of the death, or on any earlier date on which the condition in paragraph 10(1)(c) becomes again deemed to be fulfilled by virtue of sub-paragraph (i) above.

…

22. For the purposes of paragraph 10 above, a building is a purpose-built block of flats if as constructed it contained, and it contains, two or more flats; and for this purpose 'flat' means a dwelling-house which—

(a)  forms part only of a building; and

(b)  is separated horizontally from another dwelling-house which forms part of the same building.

Although the degree of 'permanence' attaching to an assured tenancy is significantly less than that attaching to a Rent Act protected tenancy, the observation of J. T. Farrand and A. Arden (commenting on the Rent Act 1977, s 12)[29] that 'This resident landlord exception rests on the elementary idea of allowing an owner-occupier to let off a spare room or two without creating any awkwardly permanent protected tenancies' still has pertinence. Indeed, it is, at least, arguable that para 10 is more obviously focused on the *true* owner-occupier than s 12.

The main features of para 10 are:

(a)  The dwelling-house in question must be part only of a building.

(b)  The building must not be a purpose-built block of flats (see para 22, above).

(c)  The tenancy in question was granted by an individual who occupied as his/her *only or principal home* another dwelling-house also part of the building.

The concept of 'only or principal home' is also to be found in the definition of 'assured tenant' and has been discussed earlier. It is clear that landlords can no longer claim to take advantage of this statutory exception, except in respect of dwellings which form (at least) their *main* residence. The key concept not fully defined in paras 10 and 17 is that of 'building'. Obvious questions to ask are: Is a pair of semi-detached houses *one* building? Is a terrace of eight houses *one* building? What of a flat structurally 'tied in' to another building but with its own access? The permutations are endless! *Some* help is provided by the case of *Bardrick v Heycock*[30] particularly in the judgment of Scarman LJ (on this point the Rent Act definition is the same as the Housing Act one).

A house, originally built as a family house in one occupation, was converted into six self-contained flats. The freeholder subsequently demolished a garage, which was structurally an extension of the house, and built in its place a two-storey residential extension. The extension was tied structurally into the main house, but there were no internal communications between it and the main house, and it had its own front door. The freeholder let out the self-contained flats in the main house, and lived himself in the extension. The three flats in question in the present action were let furnished to various of the defendants. In actions by the freeholder for possession of the flats it was common ground that each flat formed part only of a building and that the building was not a purpose-built block of flats. The judge held that the question whether the freeholder occupied as his residence a dwelling-house which also formed part of the building was one of fact and he concluded that the extension occupied by the freeholder did not form part of the same building as the defendants' flats. He accordingly held that the freeholder did not bring himself within the exemption in s 5A(1) of the Rent Act 1968 and that accordingly the defendants were entitled to the protection of the Act, and he refused the orders for possession sought.

The freeholder appealed, contending that the judge had erred in law and that as a matter of statutory interpretation he should have held that the freeholder's extension and the defendants' flats were all part of the same building.

---

[29]  J T Farrand and A Arden, *Rent Acts and Regulations* (Sweet & Maxwell, 1981).

[30]  (1976) 31 P & CR 420.

The Court of Appeal dismissed the appeal, holding that 'building' was an ordinary English word and could not be given a defined or precise meaning as a matter of law; and that the question whether the defendants' flats were part of the same building as the freeholder's extension was one of fact for the judge; and that he had been entitled to conclude that the freeholder's extension was not part of the same building. Lord Justice Scarman stated:

'The point to which this court has to direct its attention is whether on a proper construction of section 5A of the Act of 1968 the question which we are considering has been left as one of fact for the judge. I think that it has. The judge must, of course, direct himself in law correctly, and he must, therefore, pay attention to the context of section 5A, occurring as it does within the code of the Rent Act 1968.

The English word "building" covers an immense range of all sorts of structures. It is an ordinary English word, and its meaning must therefore be a question of fact, always assuming that the court directs itself correctly as to the intention and meaning of the statute which uses it. As a matter of law, to give a defined or precise meaning to the word "building" is an impossibility. It is beyond the capacity of even the most consummate master of the English language to do so. This itself is, in my judgment, an indication that Parliament is leaving the question of fact to the judge. One must, moreover, remember that the county court judge is likely to be in the best possible position to determine within the area of his jurisdiction what are the housing circumstances, what is the local situation, and the way in which he should approach an answer to this question of fact.'

## Assured shorthold tenancies

The 'jewel in the crown' of the Housing Act 1988 is undoubtedly the assured shorthold tenancy, which gives landlords maximum flexibility over the long-term future of the property, while providing for only limited controls on the rents which can be charged. In short, as originally conceived in the 1988 Act an assured shorthold tenancy is a short (the minimum period is six months) fixed-term tenancy which satisfies the requirements of an assured tenancy but in relation to which a statutory notice has been served indicating that it is merely to be an assured shorthold. In its original form, the key section (s 20) reads as follows.

20. (1) Subject to subsection (3) below, an assured shorthold tenancy is an assured tenancy—

(a) which is a fixed term tenancy granted for a term certain of not less than six months; and

(b) in respect of which there is no power for the landlord to determine the tenancy at any time earlier than six months from the beginning of the tenancy; and

(c) in respect of which a notice is served as mentioned in subsection (2) below.

(2) The notice referred to in subsection (1)(c) above is one which—

(a) is in such form as may be prescribed;

(b) is served before the assured tenancy is entered into;

(c) is served by the person who is to be the landlord under the assured tenancy on the person who is to be the tenant under that tenancy; and

(d)   states that the assured tenancy to which it relates is to be a shorthold tenancy.

(3) Notwithstanding anything in subsection (1) above, where—

(a)   immediately before a tenancy (in this subsection referred to as 'the new tenancy') is granted, the person to whom it is granted or, as the case may be, at least one of the persons to whom it is granted was a tenant under an assured tenancy which was not a shorthold tenancy, and

(b)   the new tenancy is granted by the person who, immediately before the beginning of the tenancy, was the landlord under the assured tenancy referred to in paragraph (a) above,

the new tenancy cannot be assured shorthold tenancy.

(4) Subject to subsection (5) below, if, on the coming to an end of an assured shorthold tenancy (including a tenancy which was an assured shorthold but ceased to be assured before it came to an end), a new tenancy of the same or substantially the same premises comes into being under which the landlord and the tenant are the same as at the coming to an end of the earlier tenancy, then, if and so long as the new tenancy is an assured tenancy, it shall be an assured shorthold tenancy, whether or not it fulfils the conditions in paragraph (a) to (c) of subsection (1) above.

(5) Subsection (4) above does not apply if, before the new tenancy is entered into (or, in the case of a statutory periodic tenancy, takes effect in possession), the landlord serves notice on the tenant that the new tenancy is not to be a shorthold tenancy.

As its name (and s 20(1)) indicates, an assured shorthold tenancy is a sub-species of assured tenancy, so that for a valid assured shorthold to exist the tenancy must fulfil all the requirements of a valid assured tenancy, and not (for example) be within one of the Sch 1 exceptions (although if wholly non-assured a tenant's rights are even fewer than under an assured shorthold). The key to an assured shorthold in its original form was that a statutory notice (s 20(2) and Assured Tenancies (etc) (Forms) Regulations 1988 (SI 1988/2203)) had to be served on the tenant prior to the tenancy being entered into, indicating that the tenancy was to be an assured shorthold. There was to be no power to dispense with the strict requirements relating to the service of this notice, although the regulations (reg 2) do state that 'a form substantially to the same effect' as the specified form (Form 7) will suffice. Indeed the procedural safeguard of the notice appeared fundamental to the concept of the assured shorthold in that at least, by this mechanism a prospective tenant would have an inkling of the restricted nature of the agreement. Most of the case law on s 20 (and assured shortholds in general) has been generated by disputes over the validity of such notices.

For example, see *Panayi & Pyrkos v Roberts*[31]. On 6 November 1990, the plaintiffs granted the defendant a tenancy of a flat for a term of 12 months from 7 November. Prior to the grant, she was served with notice of an assured shorthold tenancy which described the term of the tenancy as being 'from November 7, 1990, to May 6, 1991', ie for six months.

On 4 November 1991, a further tenancy for six months was granted to the defendant. On 16 March 1992 a notice requiring possession on 25 May 1992 was served on the defendant by the plaintiffs in accordance with s 21 of the Housing Act 1988. The defendant appealed on the grounds that:

---

[31]   (1993) 25 HLR 421.

(1)   The notice of assured shorthold tenancy served in November 1991 was defective in that it described a different term for the tenancy than the tenancy agreement itself.
(2)   The notice of 16 March 1992 was defective in that it did not comply with s 8 of the 1988 Act.

The Court of Appeal held that:
(1)   The prescribed form for creation of an assured shorthold tenancy requires for its completion the specification of a date of termination and must therefore predicate the insertion of the correct date for the tenancy 'in respect of which a notice is served';
(2)   A notice with an incorrect date is not substantially to the same effect as a notice with the correct date and in this case the mistake was not obvious; accordingly the appellant was not granted an assured shorthold tenancy because there was no proper prefatory notice.
(3)   Although unnecessary to decide the point, no legislative purpose would be served by subjecting a notice under s 21 to the requirements of s 8

As Mann LJ stated:

'The issue can be narrowed. There is a statutory precondition that a notice should have been served in the prescribed form. The prescribed form requires for completion a specification of the date on which the tenancy in respect of which a notice is served both commences and ends. The narrow issue is whether a notice which gives a wrong date (here a termination) is "substantially to the same effect" as one which gives the correct date. Authority and an evident error apart, I would exclude a quality of obtuseness as being extraordinary. The writing of "1793" for "1993" would be an evident error. The writing in this case of "May" rather than "November" in my judgment would be a perplexity rather than an evident error to an ordinary recipient proposing and taking a tenancy of 64, Granville Road.
We were referred to *Tegerdine v Brooks* (1977) 36 P & CR 261 and *Morrow v Nadeem* [1986] 1 WLR 1381, which are both decisions of this court in regard to whether particular notices served under section 25 of the Landlord and Tenant Act 1954 were in sufficient compliance with a statutory requirement to serve a notice in the prescribed form or in one substantially to the like effect. In the earlier decision Roskill LJ (as he then was) said (at page 266):

"If, as Bridge LJ said during the argument, a notice is incomplete or inaccurate in a relevant respect, then it does not matter that the tenant has not been misled by that inaccuracy. If, however, the omission or inaccuracy is wholly irrelevant, as was the omission here of notices 4, 5 and 7, then *a fortiori* there can be no question of the tenant being misled and I see no reason why we should hold here that this was a bad notice."

In this case there is no evidence as to whether or not the appellant was actually misled. In the light of Roskill LJ's endorsement of the observation of Bridge LJ (as he then was) I would have regarded any such evidence as irrelevant had it been tendered.

In *Morrow v Nadeem* the document which had been served failed correctly to identify the landlord. Nicholls LJ (as he then was) said of the prescribed form (at page 1386B):

> "That form predicates that the blank spaces preceding the phrase 'landlord of the above-mentioned premises' will be duly completed with the name and address of the person who is correctly so described."

Later he said (at page 1387G):

> "There might perhaps be an exceptional case in which, notwithstanding the inadvertent mis-statement or omission of the name of the landlord, any reasonable tenant would have known that that was a mistake and known clearly what was intended."

Neill LJ (at page 1391F) spoke of an "exceptional case" and Slade LJ agreed with both of the preceding judgments.

Those observations confirm the view which I independently formed. Form No. 7 requires for its completion the specification of a date of termination and must therefore predicate the insertion of the correct date for the tenancy "in respect of which a notice is served". A notice with an incorrect date is not substantially to the same effect as a notice with the correct date and in this case the mistake was not obvious. The short answer to Mr Shah's submission is that although the legislative purpose of the primary legislation could perhaps be met without a specification of date, the legislative requirement of the secondary legislation is that there should be a date, and a correct one, in respect of the tenancy granted.

I wish to give no encouragement to arguments which are based on what were described to us as 'slips of the pen' and which I have exemplified as "1793" for "1993". However, an insistence on accuracy seems to me likely to simplify the task of the county court and more importantly to enable tenants to know with certainty of their status. I would thus allow this appeal on the ground that the appellant was not granted an assured shorthold tenancy because there was no proper prefatory notice. The consequences must be that the appellant is an assured tenant enjoying the protection appropriate to that status. ...'

However, the courts have equally been concerned not to allow minor inaccuracies or deficiencies to invalidate a s 20 notice and (therefore) an assured shorthold.

For example, in *Bedding v McCarthy*[32], an agreement was expressed to be for a fixed term from 18 December 1990 until 17 June 1991 (ie six months) and was stated to be an assured shorthold tenancy. On the morning of 18 December the prospective tenant was handed a s 20 notice which he signed and returned to the landlord. Later that morning the tenancy agreement was signed, and the defendant took possession of the house in the afternoon. Subsequently (in 1993) the landlord sought possession of the property. The tenant contended that, since the agreement was not entered into until some hours into 18 December it did not confer a tenancy for at least six months. Alternatively, the tenant argued that if the agreement took

---

[32]   (1994) 27 HLR 103.

effect from the beginning of 18 December, the s 20 notice was not served before the tenancy was entered into. In both the county court, and the Court of Appeal these arguments failed, the Court of Appeal finding:

(1)   That tenancy agreements dealt with years, months, weeks and even days, but not with hours, minutes or seconds. Therefore a fixed term for a minimum six-month period was wholly consistent with the description in the notice of the tenancy running from 18 December 1990 to 17 June 1991.

(2)   It was a question of fact whether the s 20 notice was, or was not, served before the tenancy was entered into and the judge at first instance had been entirely satisfied that the documents were not signed/served contemporaneously but that the notice *did* precede the agreement.

As Nolan LJ (as he then was) stated:

'The respondent landlords in their skeleton argument referred us to *Halsbury's Laws* (4th ed.), Vol. 45, para. 1143. In that paragraph we find quoted what is described as the general rule relating to fractions of a day, and I need only read the first two sentences:

"In computing a period of time, at any rate when counted in years or months, no regard is, as a general rule, paid to fractions of a day, in the sense that the period is regarded as complete although it is short to the extent of a fraction of a day. In cases in which the day of the date of an instrument of lease is included in the term it is immaterial that the tenant's enjoyment cannot begin with the beginning of that day."

This proposition which is supported by copious and ancient authority in the notes to the text of *Halsbury*, appears to me to dispose completely of the initial argument put forward by the appellant/defendant. It is, of course, a commonplace that tenancy agreements and leases deal with years, months and weeks and sometimes days, but not with hours, minutes or seconds, so the lease in the present case is described as a tenancy agreement for a period of six months. That is, in my judgment, perfectly consistent with the description of the proposed tenancy in the notice as one running from 18 December 1990 to 17 June 1991. That is precisely how it would be construed and understood in the ordinary law of landlord and tenant, and I can see no reason why one different standard or approach should be adopted for the purposes of the Housing Act 1988. The remarks of Russell LJ were directed solely to the common form of tenancy agreement dealing with, in that case, years and months,. They were not directed or supportive of the proposition that the term of the tenancy should be measured by reference for something less than a whole day.

Mr Naish says if that is so, and if it be the case that the tenancy agreement signed during the morning of 18 December dates back to the beginning of that day, then the landlords fail to satisfy the condition specified in section 20(2)(b), namely the condition that the notice must be served before the tenancy is entered into. This seems to me to confuse the time when the tenancy is entered into with the time when, as a matter of law, it is deemed to commence. It would seem to me clear that the tenancy was entered into when the agreement was signed. It is not the less clear that it was entered into at that point in time because it was deemed to commence some hours earlier.

We come to the question which appears to me to be a pure question of fact: was the notice served before the tenancy was entered into? Mr Naish says it is not consistent for that purpose to look at the fractions of a day. If you are going to ignore fractions of a day, you must do so consistently. But again, I think that is wrong. In paragraph 1144 of *Halsbury's Laws* it is stated:

> "The general rule that fractions of a day are to be disregarded does not apply where the object of the statute would be defeated unless the precise hour of an occurrence were noted, or where conflicting claims depend upon the question which of two events was first in order of time, for then the particular hour when the events occurred may become material."

It seems to me the question posed by section 20(2)(b) falls within that category. It is a pure question of fact whether the notice was or was not served before the tenancy was entered into, and the agreed statement of facts on its natural reading establishes that it was served before the tenancy was entered into. In terms, the agreed statement of facts states, "The defendant signed document 5", that is the notice, "and returned it, and then all parties signed document 4," that is the tenancy agreement. Mr Naish argued that these should be regarded essentially as contemporaneous events. He submitted that on their most favourable reading there can only have been a short time between the two events, and it is not therefore to be assumed that the purpose of the Act was fulfilled because this, he submitted, must contemplate a reasonable period of time being given to the proposed tenant to study the document and determine what it is that he is entering into. The difficulty here is that the Act says nothing to suggest that there must be any particular minimum time.'

Subsequently a number of further decisions have reinforced this approach. For example, in *Andrews v Brewer*[33], an error in a s 20 notice which provided that a tenancy would begin on 29 May 1993 and end on 28 May 1993 was held, by the Court of Appeal *not* to have invalidated the notice. In the words of Auld LJ (at p 210) it was 'an obvious clerical error … [which] does not in any way detract from the effect of the notice'. In *York v Casey*[34], the Court of Appeal held that in considering s 20 notices, the court should adopt the same principles which the House of Lords applied to contractual notices in *Mannai Investment Co Ltd v Star Life Assurance Co Ltd*[35]; broadly this meant first considering whether the error in the notice was obvious or evident and secondly whether, despite the error, the notice was still sufficiently clear to leave a reasonable recipient in no reasonable doubt as to its terms. This approach was applied by the Court of Appeal in *Clickex Ltd v McCann*[36] and the three appeals *Ravenseft Properties Ltd v Hall, White v Chubb* and *Freeman v Kasseer*, heard together by the Court of Appeal in 2001[37]. Ultimately, these decisions turn on their own facts but, as an indicative comparison,

---

[33]    (1997) 30 HLR 203.
[34]    (1998) 31 HLR 209.
[35]    [1997] AC 749.
[36]    (1999) 32 HLR 324.
[37]    [2001] EWCA 2034, [2002] HLR 624.

in *York v Casey* the s 20 notice stated that the tenancy term was to be from 28 September 1996 to 6 September 1996 (rather than 1997). The notice was still held to be valid, whereas in another Court of Appeal decision, *Manel v Memon*[38], a notice which omitted reference to the need to seek legal advice and the fact that the giving of the notice by the landlord did not commit the tenant to take the tenancy was held to be invalid.

From the above it seems clear that, even as originally drafted, the foundations required for the creation of an assured shorthold tenancy were not unduly burdensome, and that those foundations which did exist could be seen as necessary safeguards to (at least) ensure that tenants were sufficiently forewarned. However, government thinking was clearly that even this did not go far enough; errors in notices and 'slips' (such as letting a tenant into possession prior to the service of a s 20 notice) could result in the inadvertent creation of an assured tenancy. The (apparent) undesirability of this has led to the significant amendments contained in ss 96–99 of the Housing Act 1996. Although s 20 (as above) will continue to contain the relevant law for tenancies entered into prior to 28 February 1997 (the commencement date of the amendments), all tenancies claimed to be assured shortholds which are entered into on or after that date are to be governed by the new law.

Section 96 and Sch 7 of the 1996 Act provide (by inserting s 19A and Sch 2A into the 1988 Act) that any assured tenancy coming into force on or after the commencement date is to be an assured shorthold unless it falls within certain parameters (the majority of which are contained in Sch 7).

*Assured shorthold tenancies*

96. (1) In Chapter II of Part I of the Housing Act 1988 (assured shorthold tenancies) there shall be inserted at the beginning—

'19A. **Assured shorthold tenancies: post-Housing Act 1996 tenancies**

An assured tenancy which—

(a) is entered into on or after the day on which section 96 of the Housing Act 1996 comes into force (otherwise than pursuant to a contract made before that day), or

(b) comes into being by virtue of section 5 above on the coming to an end of an assured tenancy within paragraph (a) above,

is an assured shorthold tenancy unless it falls within any paragraph in Schedule 2A to this Act.'

(2) After Schedule 2 to that Act there shall be inserted the Schedule set out in Schedule 7 to this Act. …

---

[38] (2000) 624 HLR 235.

# SCHEDULE 7
# ASSURED TENANCIES: SCHEDULE INSERTED AFTER SCHEDULE 2 TO THE HOUSING ACT 1988

# 'SCHEDULE 2A
# ASSURED TENANCIES: NON-SHORTHOLDS

*Tenancies excluded by notice*

1.—(1) An assured tenancy in respect of which a notice is served as mentioned in sub-paragraph (2) below.

(2) The notice referred to in sub-paragraph (1) above is one which—

(a) is served before the assured tenancy is entered into,

(b) is served by the person who is to be the landlord under the assured tenancy on the person who is to be the tenant under that tenancy, and

(c) states that the assured tenancy to which it relates is not to be an assured shorthold tenancy.

2.—(1) An assured tenancy in respect of which a notice is served as mentioned in sub-paragraph (2) below.

(2) The notice referred to in sub-paragraph (1) above is one which—

(a) is served after the assured tenancy has been entered into,

(b) is served by the landlord under the assured tenancy on the tenant under that tenancy, and

(c) states that the assured tenancy to which it relates is no longer an assured shorthold tenancy.

*Tenancies containing exclusionary provision*

3. An assured tenancy which contains a provision to the effect that the tenancy is not an assured shorthold tenancy.

*Tenancies under section 39*

4. An assured tenancy arising by virtue of section 39 above, other than one to which subsection (7) of that section applies.

*Former secure tenancies*

5. An assured tenancy which became an assured tenancy on ceasing to be a secure tenancy.

*Tenancies under Schedule 10 to the Local Government and Housing Act 1989*

6. An assured tenancy arising by virtue of Schedule 10 to the Local Government and Housing Act 1989 (security of tenure on ending of long residential tenancies).

*Tenancies replacing non-shortholds*

7.—(1) An assured tenancy which—

(a) is granted to a person (alone or jointly with others) who, immediately before the tenancy was granted, was the tenant (or, in the case of joint tenants, one of the tenants) under an assured tenancy other than a shorthold tenancy ('the old tenancy'),

(b)   is granted (alone or jointly with others) by a person who was at that time the landlord (or one of the joint landlords) under the old tenancy, and

(c)   is not one in respect of which a notice is served as mentioned in sub-paragraph (2) below.

(2) The notice referred to in sub-paragraph (1)(c) above is one which—

(a)   is in such form as may be prescribed,

(b)   is served before the assured tenancy is entered into,

(c)   is served by the person who is to be the tenant under the assured tenancy on the person who is to be the landlord under that tenancy (or, in the case of joint landlords, on at least one of the persons who are to be joint landlords), and

(d)   states that the assured tenancy to which it relates is to be a shorthold tenancy.

8. An assured tenancy which comes into being by virtue of section 5 above on the coming to an end of an assured tenancy which is not a shorthold tenancy.

...'

The commentary in the original Bill simply observed that these changes made 'it possible to create an assured shorthold tenancy without serving a prior notice'. This is, of course, grossly misleading – the law prior to 28 February 1997 is that a tenancy is *assured* unless a valid s 20 notice is served, whereas from 28 February all this is reversed so that all tenancies will be assured shortholds (assuming they fulfil 'assured' requirements) unless declared to be assured or falling within one of the other exceptions. This even applies to periodic tenancies as well as to fixed-term ones. Indeed the only 'assurance' most private sector tenants will continue to have is that a normal assured shorthold possession order cannot take effect until six months have elapsed from the beginning of the tenancy (s 99, Housing Act 1996). It should, however, also be noted that s 97 adds a new s 20A to the 1988 Act which does, at least, enable a tenant to receive a written notice of the basic terms of the tenancy (though application must be made by the tenant before the duty to provide such information arises).

97.   After section 20 of the Housing Act 1988 there shall be inserted—

**'20A.   Post-Housing Act 1996 tenancies: duty of landlord to provide statement as to terms of tenancy**

(1) Subject to subsection (3) below, a tenant under an assured shorthold tenancy to which section 19A above applies may, by notice in writing, require the landlord under that tenancy to provide him with a written statement of any term of the tenancy which—

(a)   falls within subsection (2) below, and

(b)   is not evidenced in writing.

(2) The following terms of a tenancy fall within this subsection, namely—

(a)   the date on which the tenancy began or, if it is a statutory periodic tenancy or a tenancy to which section 39(7) below applies, the date on which the tenancy came into being,

(b)   the rent payable under the tenancy and the dates on which that rent is payable,

(c)   any term providing for a review of the rent payable under the tenancy, and

(d)   in the case of a fixed term tenancy, the length of the fixed term.

(3) No notice may be given under subsection (1) above in relation to a term of the tenancy if—

(a)   the landlord under the tenancy has provided a statement of that term in response to an earlier notice under that subsection given by the tenant under the tenancy, and

(b)   the term has not been varied since the provision of the statement referred to in paragraph (a) above.

(4) A landlord who fails, without reasonable excuse, to comply with a notice under subsection (1) above within the period of 28 days beginning with the date on which he received the notice is liable on summary conviction to a fine not exceeding level 4 on the standard scale.

(5) A statement provided for the purposes of subsection (1) above shall not be regarded as conclusive evidence of what was agreed by the parties to the tenancy in question.

...'

The attractiveness of assured shortholds to landlords could well lead less scrupulous ones to 'winkle out' their existing tenants to replace them with those holding under an assured shorthold. In part such deviousness is deterred by the provisions on unlawful eviction and harassment contained in ss 27 and 28 of the Housing Act 1988. However, other landlords may use persuasion rather than pressure or threats to achieve the desired result; for example, an offer of a new contract on superficially improved terms could be attractive to (say) a Rent Act tenant unaware that the proposed new contract was on an assured shorthold basis. Section 34(1)(b) of the 1988 Act attempts to deal with such 'ploys' by providing that:

(1) A tenancy which is entered into on or after the commencement of this Act cannot be a protected tenancy, unless—

...

(b)   it is granted to a person (alone or jointly with others) who, immediately before the tenancy was granted, was a protected or statutory tenant and is so granted by the person who at that time was the landlord (or one of the joint landlords) under the protected or statutory tenancy; ...

The drafting deficiencies in this are obvious enough; above all, the section does not state that such a tenancy *cannot* be an assured shorthold, but merely that it *can* be a protected tenancy. This could leave the way open for the argument that the protected tenant had voluntarily and expressly relinquished his or her existing rights. In practice, however, it is likely that the courts will give the section a fairly broad reading and block most attempts at the conversion of protected tenancies into assured shortholds. On the other hand, if the landlord transfers his or her interest so that the assured shorthold is under the aegis of a new landlord, the section appears not to apply. Similar provisions apply under the new 'regime' to curb the attempted transfer of assured tenants into assured shorthold tenants (Sch 7, para 7, above).

Another limitation on the creation of assured shortholds is that (under s 20(3) of the 1988 Act) once a tenancy *is* an assured tenancy it cannot subsequently become an assured shorthold, whether a s 20 notice is served on it or not. It is likely that certain well-publicised cases of landlords 'inadvertently' letting prospective tenants into possession and accepting rent prior to a service of s 20 notice – thereby *arguably* creating an assured tenancy and precluding an assured shorthold – were significant factors in the Housing Act 1996 'reforms'.

From 28 February 1997, a periodic tenancy can as readily be an assured shorthold as a fixed-term tenancy. Under the original provisions, for the initial creation of an assured shorthold, the tenancy had to be fixed-term (see s 20(1)(a)). However, even under the original provisions (s 20(4)) 'continuation' tenancies (whether by new grant or simply by allowing the tenant to continue in possession and carry on paying rent) would be assured shortholds even if periodic. In such cases there may be differences in the form of a notice required by the landlord (in advance of possession proceedings) and the length of notice required (although the minimum two-month notice requirement still applies.

In *Lower Street Properties Ltd v Jones*[39] the plaintiffs granted the defendant's partner an assured shorthold tenancy of a house for a term of six months. The defendant lived there with the tenant. After the initial term expired, the plaintiffs allowed the tenant to stay for another three months. Subsequently, further three-month and six-month 'concessions' were granted. After the expiry of the last of these (January 1991) the tenant and the defendant continued to live in the property. In February 1992 the tenant died, and the defendant continued to occupy the property alone. In June 1994, the plaintiffs served the defendant with a two-month notice requiring possession of the property, and subsequently sued for possession (for further details on possession procedures and assured shortholds see elsewhere in this chapter). The defendant counterclaimed for a declaration that she was an assured tenant by succession. The county court dismissed the claim for possession because the plaintiffs had commenced proceedings one day before the notice had expired (!), but equally dismissed the counterclaim – s 20(4) of the 1988 Act could operate not only on the first tenancy consequent upon the initial assured shorthold, but on any number of subsequent agreements. The tenant succeeded to an assured shorthold periodic tenancy. The Court of Appeal upheld the county court on both points. On the s 20(4) point, see Kennedy LJ (at p 881):

'In the context of the present case the effect of section 20(4) is to make it clear that Mr van Praag was an assured shorthold tenant until 27 December 1989. What happened then? It is the case for the appellant that section 20(4) can only operate once, at the end of an assured shorthold tenancy created pursuant to section 20(1), so that in December 1989 Mr van Praag became, by virtue of section 5 of the Act, a tenant under an assured tenancy which was not a shorthold tenancy. If she is right, or if at any time before he died Mr van Praag became an assured shorthold tenant, no further assured shorthold tenancy could have come into existence because section 20(3) prevents the grant of an assured shorthold tenancy to an assured tenant. But, for the plaintiff/respondents Mr James contends that section 20(4) can operate again and again, and is intended if necessary so to operate until either the tenant vacates or the landlord brings the situation to an end by serving notice pursuant to section 20(5). The whole purpose of Chapter II of the 1988 Act was to prevent stagnation in the property market by, amongst other things, preventing a tenant who entered as an assured shorthold tenant acquiring the rights of an assured tenant without the consent of the landlord.

...

In my judgment Mr van Praag became an assured shorthold tenant, pursuant to section 20(4), for the second time in late 1989 and the process was repeated thereafter at intervals until his death. Sometimes he had a periodic tenancy, sometimes the tenancy was for a fixed term, but always it was an assured

---

[39]   (1996) 28 HLR 877.

shorthold tenancy and always, as it seems to me, the tenancy took effect pursuant to section 20(4) because the two attempts to create an assured shorthold tenancy pursuant to section 20(1) in April 1990 and July 1990 were ineffective. The result was that when Mr van Praag died the tenancy which vested in the defendant was an assured shorthold tenancy.'

## RENT ACT 1977 TENANCIES

As indicated in the introduction to this chapter, the last two decades have seen a steady erosion of the substantial degree of tenant security and rent control provided for under the Rent Acts (most recently the Rent Act 1977). In particular, the Housing Acts 1988 and 1996 have largely replaced a 'regime' based on long-term tenant security and rent control, with one based on short-term contracts and market rents (see further Chapter 3). However, quite apart from the fact that, as already noted, many Rent Act concepts have been carried forward into the new law, the 1977 Act still continues to govern most tenancies entered into prior to 15 January 1989 and a significant number of tenancies acquired by succession after that date.

Acquiring full rights under the Rent Act 1977 involves possessing the status of either a contractual protected tenant, or a statutory tenant – and it is to these two key concepts that attention is first paid.

### Full Rent Act protection: protected and statutory tenancies

The starting point in determining Rent Act status is s 1 of the Rent Act 1977, which states:

> Subject to this Part of this Act, a tenancy under which a dwelling-house (which may be a house or part of a house) is let as a separate dwelling is a protected tenancy for the purposes of this Act.

The requirement of a 'dwelling house ... let as a separate dwelling' is also at the foundation of the definition of an assured tenancy and has already been discussed. The principal definitional difference between s 1 of Rent Act 1977 and s 1 Housing Act 1988 is that there is no requirement in the Rent Act for the 'dwelling-house' to be the 'only or principal home' of the tenant(s) concerned. Indeed, there appears to be no need (as far as s 1 is concerned) for the tenant to occupy the property at all! As Scarman LJ stated in *Horford Investments Ltd v Lambert*[40]:

> 'A house (or part of a house) must be let as *a* dwelling, that is to say, as a single dwelling, for the tenancy to be protected for the purposes of the Act. If it is let as a single dwelling, the fact that the tenant does not himself live there, or that he carries on a business as well as a living there, or that he sub-lets part or the whole, or that he uses only part of the premises for habitation does not put the letting outside the Act – unless what is done either modifies the terms of the letting, or brings the house within some specific exclusion stated in the Act.'

---

[40]  [1976] Ch 39, at 54.

Further, there is no requirement in s 1 of the Rent Act 1977 that the tenant should be an individual, so that a tenancy granted to a company can still, in principle, be a protected tenancy.

However, the significance of this is minimised by the fact that tenant residence *is* a key element in the linked concept of the *statutory tenancy*. Broadly, any contractual protected tenancy may be brought to an end by the service of a notice to quit (so long as the formalities of s 5 of the Protection from Eviction Act 1977 are complied with – see further elsewhere in this chapter and Chapter 5).Continued tenant security is maintained by the device of the statutory tenancy, a highly idiosyncratic 'animal' which confers a 'status of irremoveability' (Stephenson LJ in *Jessamine Investment Co v Schwarz*[41]) rather than a property right. As relevant, s 2 of the 1977 Rent Act provides as follows (emphasis added):

2.  (1) Subject to this Part of this Act—

(a)  after the termination of a protected tenancy of a dwelling-house the person who, immediately before that termination, was the protected tenant of the dwelling-house shall, *if and so long as he occupies the dwelling-house as his residence*, be the statutory tenant of it: …

Unlike, however, the requirement for assured tenancies that the dwelling-house must be the tenant's 'only or principal home' (s 1(1)(b), 1988 Act), s 2 only requires that the dwelling-house be a residence of the tenant. From this it is clear that a tenant can live elsewhere part or even most of the time and yet still maintain a statutory tenancy of the property in dispute.

As to what in law *is* a residence (as against a mere convenience), it is necessary to turn to case law, the Rent Act being empty of further definition. Similar provisos have existed for many years, and the case law is equivalently extensive. Two cases, *Brown v Brash* and *Brickfield v Hughes*, perhaps best illustrate the issues involved.

In *Brown v Brash*[42] in 1941 the freeholder of a dwelling-house, café, and petrol pump station let the premises to the plaintiff on a quarterly tenancy. On 20 September 1945, he served on the claimant a three months' notice to quit. The claimant continued in possession after that date, remaining as a statutory tenant under the Rent Restriction Acts. Shortly after the notice had been given the plaintiff had been sentenced to two years' imprisonment, leaving in physical possession of the premises his cohabitee of seven years, and two children. On 11 January 1946, the freeholder sold the freehold of the premises. On 9 March 1946 the claimant's cohabitee left the premises taking with her a substantial part of the furniture and leaving the two children elsewhere with the claimant's mother. There was evidence that only three articles of domestic furniture remained in the house.

In July 1946, the new owners brought an action in the county court against the claimant, claiming possession of the premises on the ground amongst others that he had abandoned possession of them. On 12 September 1946, judgment was given for the tenant, the judge basing his decision on findings that the tenant had not abandoned possession of the premises and that, although he had failed in some of his obligations under the tenancy, it was not reasonable to make an order for possession against him. Between September and late in December 1946, relations of

---

[41]   [1977] 2 WLR 145, at 147.
[42]   [1948] 2 KB 247.

the plaintiff spent two or three hours two or three times a week cleaning the premises. On 9 December 1946, the freehold was sold to the present defendants under a contract which provided that the purchasers might at their own risk take immediate possession on paying a deposit of £500. Brash, the first defendant, entered into possession of the premises. A few days later on 24 January 1947, the claimant was released from prison and sought to repossess the premises but Brash refused to leave and continued in possession of them. On 14 April 1947, the plaintiff brought this action in the county court claiming possession of the premises and damages for trespass. The defendants, although in possession, counterclaimed (inter alia) for possession. The county court judge upheld the claim for possession, awarded £100 damages for trespass and rejected the defendants' counterclaim for possession. The defendants appealed. The Court of Appeal allowed the appeal, finding that the claimant had lost his status as a statutory tenant.

Asquith LJ stated:

> 'We are of opinion that a "non-occupying" tenant prima facie forfeits his status as a statutory tenant. But what is meant by "non-occupying"? The term clearly cannot cover every tenant who, for however short a time, or however necessary a purpose, or with whatever intention as regards returning, absents himself from the demised premises. To retain possession or occupation for the purpose of retaining protection the tenant cannot be compelled to spend twenty-four hours in all weathers under his own roof for three hundred and sixty-five days in the year. Clearly, for instance, the tenant of a London house who spends his week-ends in the country or his long vacation in Scotland does not necessarily cease to be in occupation. Nevertheless, absence may be sufficiently prolonged or uninterrupted to compel the inference, prima facie, of a cesser of possession or occupation. The question is one of fact and of degree. Assume an absence sufficiently prolonged to have this effect: The legal result seems to us to be as follows: (1.) The onus is then on the tenant to repel the presumption that his possession has ceased. (2.) In order to repel it he must at all events establish a de facto intention on his part to return after his absence. (3.) But we are of opinion that neither in principle nor on the authorities can this be enough. To suppose that he can absent himself for five or ten years or more and retain possession and his protected status simply by proving an inward intention to return after so protracted an absence would be to frustrate the spirit and policy of the Acts … Notwithstanding an absence so protracted the authorities suggest that its effect may be averted if he couples and clothes his inward intention with some formal, outward, and visible sign of it; that is, installs in the premises some caretaker or representative, be it a relative or not with the status of a licensee and with the function of preserving the premises for his own ultimate home-coming. There will then, at all events, be someone to profit by the housing accommodation involved, which will not stand empty. It may be that the same result can be secured by leaving on the premises, as a deliberate symbol of continued occupation, furniture; … Apart from authority, in principle, possession in fact (for it is with possession in fact and not with possession in law that we are here concerned) requires not merely an "animus possidendi" but a "corpus possessionis", namely, some visible state of affairs in which the animus possidendi finds expression. (5.) If

the caretaker (to use that term for short) leaves or the furniture is removed from the premises, otherwise than quite temporarily, we are of opinion that the protection, artificially prolonged by their presence, ceases, whether the tenant wills or desires such removal or not. A man's possession of a wild bird, which he keeps in a cage, ceases if it escapes, notwithstanding that his desire to retain possession of it continues and that its escape is contrary thereto. We do not think in this connection that it is open to the plaintiff to rely on the fact of his imprisonment as preventing him from taking steps to assert possession by visible action. The plaintiff, it is true, had not intended to go to prison; he committed intentionally the felonious act which in the events which have happened, landed him there; and thereby put it out of his power to assert possession by visible acts after March 9, 1946. He cannot, in these circumstances, we feel, be in a better position than if his absence and inaction had been voluntary.'

In *Brickfield v Hughes*[43] the defendant tenant was aged 74. In 1968 he had become the statutory tenant of a flat in London, on the expiry of a seven-year lease. In 1970 his wife had inherited a cottage in Lancashire. It had been used initially as a holiday home, but from 1978 the tenant and his wife remained there permanently. Between that time and March 1987 the defendant had not returned to the flat in London at all and his wife made only three visits.

Their adult children had remained in the flat after their departure, and at the time of the trial it was occupied by three of them and the defendant's son-in-law. The defendant and his wife also left furniture and books in the property. The landlord sought possession of the flat, on the basis that the defendant no longer occupied it as his residence. At the trial, evidence was given that the defendant intended to return to London if his wife, who was 71 and in poor health, predeceased him, or if they were unable to manage on their own in Lancashire, which he thought might occur in about five years' time. His daughter gave evidence that she thought that they might well not be able to manage very soon and would not last another winter in the cottage.

The judge found that the defendant had a sufficient intention to return and refused to grant possession. The landlord appealed.

The Court of Appeal dismissed the appeal. Although they clearly felt that it was a marginal case, Neil and Ralph Gibson LJJ did not feel that the finding of the county court judge was so clearly wrong that it should be disturbed. As Neil LJ stated:

'(1) Where the tenant's absence is more prolonged than is to be explained by holiday or ordinary business reasons and is unintermittent, the onus lies on the tenant of establishing an intention to return if he seeks the protection of the Act.
(2) An inward intention, however, is not enough. It must be accompanied by some outward and visible sign of the tenant's intention. The continued occupation by a caretaker or relative or the continued presence of furniture

---

[43] (1987) 20 HLR 108.

may be sufficient, but in each case the question is whether or not the person or furniture can be regarded as a genuine symbol of his intention to return "home".

(3) In addition the tenant must show that there is a "practical possibility" … or a "real possibility" … of the fulfilment of that intention within a reasonable time. What is a reasonable time depends on the circumstances …

(4) The protection of the Act can be claimed even though the tenant has another home or residence – the two words appear to be synonymous in this context … but the court will look with particular care at two-home cases.

The arguments concerning Mr Hughes' intention, however, are more diffi-cult … The question which the judge had to consider was whether, on the facts there was a real possibility that Mr Hughes' intention to return would be fulfilled in a reasonable time. As to this the judge was clearly impressed by the daughter's evidence that she did not think that they could last another winter in the cottage. It seems to me that, though the prospect of Mr Hughes coming back because his wife had predeceased him might well have failed the test of a real possibility, the judge was entitled to infer and did infer that there was a real possibility that with advancing years they will both have to come back to the flat quite soon. As the judge put it "The time cannot be far away." '

## Excepted tenancies

Even if the conditions in s 1 or s 2 of the 1977 Act are fulfilled, a tenancy will not acquire full legal protection if it falls within one of the exceptions contained in ss 4–26 of the Act. (This is the significance of the phrase 'Subject to this Part of this Act' which begins both s 1 and s 2.) The majority of these exceptions are the same as, or very similar to, those contained in Sch 1 to the Housing Act 1988 and have already been discussed. The most significant exception to have no direct equivalent in the Housing Act 1988 relates to lettings involving payments for board and attendance (s 7). To come within the exception the board and attendance 'linkage' must be bona fide (see *Palser v Grinling*[44]). 'Board' implies service as well as the provision of food (see *Otter v Norman*[45]). Under the Rent Acts this provided a convenient (if controversial) loophole for landlords who wished to minimise their long-term obligations and retain letting control and rent flexibility. However, as the vast majority of such lettings were on a short-term basis and/or attached to transient tenants, it is unlikely that much significance still attaches to this exception more than 15 years after the demise of (most) new Rent Act lettings!

Perhaps of most remaining interest is the exception contained in s 12, concerning resident landlords – particularly in the contrast it provides with the resident landlord exception contained in Sch 1, para 10 of the Housing Act 1988. Whereas Sch 1, para 10 requires that the landlord occupy another dwelling-house in the same building as the tenant as his or her *only or principal home*, s 12 merely requires that it is 'occupied as his residence'. This parallels s 2 discussed above, and clearly suggests that a landlord can live relatively irregularly in the dwelling-house and still

---

[44]   [1948] AC 291.
[45]   [1989] AC 129.

come within the exception (although there must be more than merely 'token' or 'convenience' occupation, assuming equivalence of interpretation of s 2 and s 12).

The question arose relatively recently in the following case: *Palmer v McNamara*[46]. In 1987, the defendant was granted a tenancy of the front room of a flat with a kitchen-diner at the rear end of the room. The landlord occupied and kept his belongings in a back room of the flat, including a fridge and a kettle. The bathroom was to be shared.

Although the landlord spent each day in his room, he had no cooker as he was unable to cook. If he wished to eat there he bought food that did not need to be cooked, or hot take-away meals. Also as a result of a medical condition which prevented him from dressing or undressing himself, the plaintiff did not sleep in his room but went each night to stay with a friend.

The landlord sought possession against the defendant on the basis that he was a resident landlord. He succeeded at first instance and the defendant appealed.

The appeal was dismissed. As Dillon LJ stated:

'Does he then occupy the dwelling-house as his residence? He used to beyond any question. Indeed in this field of law the terms used, which have now been part of the jurisprudence on the subject for 70 years, are very well understood – residence, dwelling-house, occupied as his residence – and so the cases that come before the courts tend to be cases where the facts are unusual. To that generality the present case is no exception. Apart from his inability to cook, which has had the result that he does not have a cooker in the room, the plaintiff suffers from ailments as a result of which he has not slept in the room since before the tenancy was granted to the defendant. The plaintiff's evidence is that he has diabetes, but more seriously he has a three-inch shortening of his left leg and osteo-arthritis in his left hip which has caused serious deterioration. That is supported by a doctor's certificate which refers to it as "long-standing hip joint disease". The effect of that, particularly if the climate is damp, is that he needs help to dress and undress himself. Therefore since 1987 he has spent his night in the spare room of the house of a very old friend, a Miss Ducker, who lives about a mile or mile-and-a-half away from Drakefield Road. The plaintiff has a car and can travel between the two houses. He uses her spare room and keeps a change of clothes there. He probably now has baths there, because of the difficulty in dressing and undressing, and sometimes has his evening meal or Sunday lunch with Miss Ducker at her home. He may keep the odd book there, but he does not keep his other possessions there. The furniture in the spare room is Miss Ducker's furniture.

It is said that because he sleeps at Miss Ducker's home he does not use his room at 84 Drakefield Road as his residence. He does not use Miss Ducker's spare room as a residence either, and he is therefore in the position, which is not impossible but perhaps unusual, of a man with accommodation but no residence. He spends his days at 84 Drakefield Road. He does his writing and

---

[46] (1990) 23 HLR 168.

reading there. He watches television and video and has meals that he brings in. But it is said that because he does not sleep there he does not occupy it as his residence.

The question whether a dwelling-house is occupied as a residence is commonly paraphrased as "does he occupy it as his home?" ...

Applying that test, which raises a question of fact and degree to be determined by applying ordinary commonsense, I have no doubt that the judge was entitled, and indeed right, to take the view that the plaintiff occupied his back room as his home. That is enough to determine this appeal.

We were referred to authorities which are concerned with the question, whether, if a person has ceased, for whatever reason, to occupy a dwelling-house as his home, he can nonetheless save the position for the purposes of the Rent Act if he has an intention or desire to return to the dwelling-house, and we had argument on whether it was relevant that at one stage the plaintiff had had it in mind to sell 84 Drakefield Road. But this does not to my mind arise as a question for decision if I am right in the view, which the judge also took, that he is currently occupying the room as his residence or home. I would dismiss this appeal.'

The approach of the Court of Appeal in *Palmer v McNamara* prefigures that of the House of Lords in *Uratemp Ventures Ltd v Collins*[47], albeit on a differently worded statutory provision.

## Restricted contracts

Section 19 of the Rent Act 1977 creates a class of 'restricted' tenancy agreements which fall midway between full legal protection and lacking any protection save procedural controls under the Protection from Eviction Act 1977. Initially the main protection attaching to restricted contracts was the right to seek six-month 'stays of execution' once a landlord sought to repossess, but this right was effectively removed by the Housing Act 1980. The power in rent tribunals to fix 'reasonable' rents concerning such tenancies remained. The key to the existence of a restricted contract is that the rent includes payment for the use of furniture, or for services (s 79(2)) (save in relation to resident landlord cases, where no payment for furniture or services is required (ss 20 and 21)), and the tenancy does not fall within one of the 'exceptions' seen to be wholly unprotected (most obviously holiday lets). Restricted contracts are being swiftly phased out, s 36(1) of the 1988 Act providing that there can be no new restricted contracts from the commencement of the 1988 Act.

## SECURITY OF TENURE

The previous section examined in detail the criteria determining tenancy status in the private sector. The status of the tenancy – protected, statutory, assured, assured shorthold and so on – largely determines the rights of the parties on such key matters as security of tenure, rent control and rights of succession (although the

---

47  [2001] UKHL 43, [2002] 1 AC 301, [2002] 1 All ER 46.

tenancy agreement itself may still provide the legal basis for matters on which the legislation is silent). Correspondingly, this section of the chapter is concerned with the detailed examination of these various rights, dependent on the prior classification of the tenancy.

In general the trend over the past 20 years has been to strip away the curbs on landlord freedom which Rent Act legislation provides, and in so doing to curtail tenants' rights. The culmination of this process is the assured shorthold tenancy, which, despite its name, gives few 'assurances' other than an initially guaranteed six-month right of occupancy.

The following material is organised around the three issues mentioned above, ie security of tenure, rent control and succession, examined in turn with reference to assured tenancies, assured shorthold tenancies, protected and statutory tenancies and common law tenancies.

## Assured tenancies

The Department of the Environment White Paper (1987), *Housing: The Government's Proposals*[48], recognised that the abolition of all tenant security was questionable:

> 'It is reasonable that, when entering a tenancy, the tenant should expect to have to pay the market rent for the property, with suitable adjustments over time. But once a tenant has a market rent tenancy and is occupying a property as his or her home it is right that he or she should have a reasonable degree of security of tenure. This will continue to require some degree of statutory backing.'

Assured tenancies *do* provide for such partial security (although equally clearly assured shortholds do not). The starting point is s 5 of the Housing Act 1988, which provides (in part) as follows:

5. **Security of tenure**

(1) An assured tenancy cannot be brought to an end by the landlord except by obtaining an order of the court in accordance with the following provisions of this Chapter or Chapter II below or, in the case of a fixed term tenancy which contains power for the landlord to determine the tenancy in certain circumstances, by the exercise of that power and, accordingly, the service by the landlord of a notice to quit shall be of no effect in relation to a periodic assured tenancy.

(2) If an assured tenancy which is a fixed term tenancy comes to an end otherwise than by virtue of—

(a)   an order of the court, or
(b)   a surrender or other action on the part of the tenant,

then, subject to section 7 and Chapter II below, the tenant shall be entitled to remain in possession of the dwelling-house let under that tenancy and, subject to subsection (4) below, his right to possession shall depend upon a periodic tenancy arising by virtue of this section.

(3) The periodic tenancy referred to in subsection (2) above is one—

---

[48]   Cmnd 214, para. 39.

(a)   taking effect in possession immediately on the coming to an end of the fixed term tenancy;

(b)   deemed to have been granted by the person who was the landlord under the fixed term tenancy immediately before it came to an end to the person who was then the tenant under that tenancy;

(c)   under which the premises which are let are the same dwelling-house as was let under the fixed term tenancy;

(d)   under which the periods of the tenancy are the same as those for which rent was last payable under the fixed term tenancy; and

(e)   under which, subject to the following provisions of this Part of this Act, the other terms are the same as those of the fixed term tenancy immediately before it came to an end, except that any term which makes provision for determination by the landlord or the tenant shall not have effect while the tenancy remains an assured tenancy.

The principal 'provisions' referred to in s 5(1) are contained in ss 7–9 of the 1988 Act. As relevant, these state as follows:

### 7.   Orders for possession

(1) The court shall not make an order for possession of a dwelling-house let on an assured tenancy except on one or more of the grounds set out in Schedule 2 to this Act; but nothing in this Part of this Act relates to proceedings for possession of such a dwelling-house which are brought by a mortgagee, within the meaning of the Law of Property Act 1925, who has lent money on the security of the assured tenancy.

(2) The following provisions of this section have effect, subject to section 8 below, in relation to proceedings for the recovery of possession of a dwelling-house let on an assured tenancy.

(3) If the court is satisfied that any of the grounds in Part I of Schedule 2 to this Act is established then, subject to subsection ... (6) below, the court shall make an order for possession.

(4) If the court is satisfied that any of the grounds in Part II of Schedule 2 to this Act is established, then, subject to subsection (6) below, the court may make an order for possession if it considers it reasonable to do so.

(5) Part III of Schedule 2 to this Act shall have effect for supplementing Ground 9 in that Schedule and Part IV of that Schedule shall have effect in relation to notices given as mentioned in Grounds 1 to 5 of that Schedule.

...

(6) The court shall not make an order for possession of a dwelling-house to take effect at a time when it is let on an assured fixed term tenancy unless—

(a)   the ground for possession is Ground 2 or Ground 8 in Part I of Schedule 2 to this Act or any of the grounds in Part II of that Schedule, other than Ground 9 or Ground 16; and

(b)   the terms of the tenancy make provision for it to be brought to an end on the ground in question (whether that provision takes the form of a provision for re-entry, for forfeiture, for determination by notice or otherwise).

(7) Subject to the preceding provisions of this section, the court may make an order for possession of a dwelling-house on grounds relating to a fixed term tenancy which has come to an end; and where an order is made in such circumstances, any statutory periodic tenancy which has arisen on the ending of the fixed term tenancy shall end (without any notice and regardless of the period) on the day on which the order takes effect.

8.   **Notice of proceedings for possession [as amended by Housing Act 1996]**

(1) The court shall not entertain proceedings for possession of a dwelling-house let on an assured tenancy unless—

(a)   the landlord or, in the case of joint landlords, at least one of them has served on the tenant a notice in accordance with this section and the proceedings are begun within the time limits stated in the notice in accordance with subsections (3) to (4B) below; or

(b)   the court considers it just and equitable to dispense with the requirement of such a notice.

(2) The court shall not make an order for possession on any of the grounds in Schedule 2 to this Act unless that ground and particulars of it are specified in the notice under this section; but the grounds specified in such a notice may be altered or added to with the leave of the court.

(3) A notice under this section is one in the prescribed form informing the tenant that—

(a)   the landlord intends to begin proceedings for possession of the dwelling-house on one or more of the grounds specified in the notice; and

(b)   those proceedings will not begin earlier than a date specified in the notice in accordance with subsections (4) to (4B) below; and

(c)   those proceedings will not begin later than twelve months from the date of service of the notice.

(4) If a notice under this section specifies in accordance with subsection (3)(a) above Ground 14 in Schedule 2 to this Act (whether with or without other grounds), the date specified in the notice as mentioned in subsection (3)(b) above shall not be earlier than the date of the service of the notice.

(4A) If a notice under this section specifies in accordance with subsection (3)(a) above, any of Grounds 1, 2, 5 to 7, 9 and 16 in Schedule 2 to this Act (whether without other grounds or with any ground other than Ground 14), the date specified in the notice as mentioned in subsection (3)(b) above shall not be earlier than—

(a)   two months from the date of service of the notice; and

(b)   if the tenancy is a periodic tenancy, the earliest date on which, apart from section 5(1) above, the tenancy could be brought to an end by a notice to quit given by the landlord on the same date as the date of service of the notice under this section.

(4B) In any case, the date specified in the notice as mentioned in subsection (3)(b) above shall not be earlier than the expiry of the period of two weeks from the date of the service of the notice.

(5) The court may not exercise the power conferred by subsection (1)(b) above if the landlord seeks to recover possession on Ground 8 in Schedule 2 to this Act.

(6) Where a notice under this section—

(a)   is served at a time when the dwelling-house is let on a fixed term tenancy, or

(b)   is served after a fixed term tenancy has come to an end but relates (in whole or in part) to events occurring during that tenancy,

the notice shall have effect notwithstanding that the tenant becomes or has become tenant under a statutory periodic tenancy arising on the coming to an end of the fixed term tenancy.

8A.   **Additional notice requirements: ground of domestic violence**

(1) Where the ground specified in a notice under section 8 (whether with or without other grounds) is Ground 14A in Schedule 2 to this Act and the partner who has left the

dwelling-house as mentioned in that ground is not a tenant of the dwelling-house, the court shall not entertain proceedings for possession of the dwelling-house unless—

   (a)   the landlord or, in the case of joint landlords, at least one of them has served on the partner who has left a copy of the notice or has taken all reasonable steps to serve a copy of the notice on that partner, or

   (b)   the court considers it just and equitable to dispense with such requirements as to service.

(2) Where Ground 14A in Schedule 2 to this Act is added to a notice under section 8 with the leave of the court after proceedings for possession are begun and the partner who has left the dwelling-house as mentioned in that ground is not a party to the proceedings, the court shall not continue to entertain the proceedings unless—

   (a)   the landlord or, in the case of joint landlords, at least one of them has served a notice under subsection (3) below on the partner who has left or has taken all reasonable steps to serve such a notice on that partner, or

   (b)   the court considers it just and equitable to dispense with the requirement of such a notice.

(3) A notice under this subsection shall—

   (a)   state that proceedings for the possession of the dwelling-house have begun,

   (b)   specify the ground or grounds on which possession is being sought, and

   (c)   give particulars of the ground or grounds.

## 9.   Extended discretion of court in possession claims

(1) Subject to subsection (6) below, the court may adjourn for such period or periods as it thinks fit proceedings for possession of a dwelling-house let on an assured tenancy.

(2) On the making of an order for possession of a dwelling-house let on an assured tenancy or at any time before the execution of such an order, the court, subject to subsection (6) below, may—

   (a)   stay or suspend execution of the order, or

   (b)   postpone the date of possession,

for such period or periods as the court thinks just.

(3) On any such adjournment as is referred to in subsection (1) above or on any such stay, suspension or postponement as is referred to in subsection (2) above, the court, unless it considers that to do so would cause exceptional hardship to the tenant or would otherwise be unreasonable, shall impose conditions with regard to payment by the tenant of arrears of rent (if any) and rent or payments in respect of occupation after the termination of the tenancy (mesne profits) and may impose such other conditions as it thinks fit.

(4) If any such conditions as are referred to in subsection (3) above are complied with, the court may, if it thinks fit, discharge or rescind any such order as is referred to in subsection (2) above.

In effect, these provisions require that an appropriate notice (normally referred to as a Notice of Possession Proceedings (NOPP) or 's 8' notice) is served on an assured tenant, or (in the case of fixed-term assured tenancies) an appropriate contractual 'break' clause is triggered. In the latter case, s 5(2) and s 5(3) clearly indicate that a periodic assured tenancy will normally then arise. The principal exception is where the fixed-term in question is an assured shorthold tenancy or (following amendments contained in s 96 of the Housing Act 1996, adding a new s 19A to the Housing Act 1988) where it stems from a contract entered into on or after 28 February 1997 (the commencement date of the relevant parts of Housing Act 1996). A 's 8' notice should:

(a)  be in the prescribed statutory form (see Assured Tenancy and Agricultural Occupancies (Forms) Regulations 1988 (SI 1988 No. 2203));
(b)  contain the ground on which possession is sought and particulars of that ground; and
(c)  give prescribed minimum periods of notice (s 8(3)–(4B) above).

The Housing Act 1996 has amended s 8 so as to, in particular, allow possession proceedings to be commenced virtually simultaneously with the service of the statutory notice in cases of nuisance/illegal conduct by tenants; and in the case of the new 'domestic violence' ground for possession, so as to require reasonable steps to be taken to serve notice on partners.

A 's 8' notice remains in force for 12 months from the date of service (s 8(3)(c)).

The importance of compliance by landlords with these formalities has led to s 8 coming under close judicial scrutiny.

For example, in *Mountain v Hastings*[49] the plaintiff granted the defendant an assured tenancy of a flat in June 1990, at a monthly rent of £160. On 30 July 1992 the defendant was served with a notice of proceedings for possession which was allegedly in accordance with s 8 of the Housing Act 1988. The notice specified that the plaintiff intended to seek possession on Grounds 8, 10, 11, 12, 13 and 14 of Sch 2 to the Act. In response to the note on Form 3 that he should give the full text of each ground being relied upon, the plaintiff gave summaries of the statutory text. In respect of Ground 8 he wrote: 'At least three months rent is unpaid'. Later in the form, under the heading 'particulars,' the plaintiff stated: 'The monthly rent is £160. No payment has been received since November 2, 1991. The total arrears due and payable amount to £1,280'. In reliance on the notice, the plaintiff took possession proceedings.

On the first date for hearing, the defendant sought an adjournment to allow her to serve a defence and counterclaim. She admitted that no rent had been paid since November 1991, but alleged that this was because of difficulties with housing benefit. The plaintiff contended that since Ground 8 gave a mandatory right to possession he was entitled to an immediate order for possession. The judge accepted the plaintiff's submission and made an order for possession in 28 days. The defendant appealed on the basis that the s 8 notice was invalid.

It was held, allowing the appeal, that:
(i)  The ground in Sch 2 to the Housing Act 1988 may validly be specified in the notice in words different from those in which the ground is set out in the Schedule, provided that the words used set out fully the substance of the ground so that the notice is adequate to achieve the legislative purpose of the provision; that purpose is to give to the tenant the information which the provision requires to be given in the notice to enable the tenant to consider what she should do and, with or without advice, to do that which is in her power and which will best protect her against the loss of her home; but that
(ii)  The notice was defective because the words 'At least three months rent is unpaid' did not specify Ground 8; the omitted information was that the ground which must be proved included the requirement that 'both at the date

49  (1993) 25 HLR 427.

of the service of the notice ... and at the date of the hearing ... at least ... three months' rent is unpaid and ... "rent" means rent lawfully due from the tenant'; without the omitted words, the description of Ground 8 was not substantially to the like effect; the provision of full information as to the terms in which Ground 8 is expressed in the Schedule is part of that which must be stated if the ground is to be specified and if the notice is to be substantially to the like effect as the notice in the prescribed form.

As Ralph Gibson LJ stated:

'As to the submission that the notice was defective because Ground 8 was not specified by the full text of that ground as set out in Schedule 2, I do not decide this issue upon that basis. I prefer the view that the ground in Schedule 2 may validly be "specified in the notice" as required by Parliament, in words different from those in which the ground is set out in the schedule, provided that the words used set out fully the substance of the ground so that the notice is adequate to achieve the legislative purpose of the provision. That purpose, in my judgment, is to give to the tenant the information which the provision requires to be given in the notice to enable the tenant to consider what she should do and, with or without advice, to do that which is in her power and which will best protect her against the loss of her home.

Thus, in *Torridge District Council v Jones* (1985) 18 HLR 107, with reference to section 33 of the Housing Act 1980 (later section 83 of the Housing Act 1985 which contains a similar provision), the issue related not to the words in which the ground was specified but to the sufficiency of the particulars of the ground given in the notice. Oliver LJ said at p. 113:

"... as it seems to me, in the case of the instant statute, we are really concerned with quite a different type of notice. This is a warning shot across the bows of the tenant and the object of it is to warn him that unless he repairs what is stated as the ground on which possession is going to be sought, he is going to be liable to court proceedings. It seems to me as plain as a pikestaff that the object of the notice is to bring to the tenant's notice the defect of which complaint is made to enable him to make a proper restitution before proceedings are commenced and to deal with them."

Later, at p. 114, he said:

"It seems to me that it is plain that this subsection does require a specification sufficient to tell the tenant what it is he has to do to put matters right before the proceedings are commenced. In my judgment, therefore, the notice which was served upon the appellant in this case was not a proper notice that complied with section 33(3). Accordingly ... the notice not complying with the subsection, the court was then prohibited from entertaining the proceedings at all."

If, with reference to the specification of the ground upon which the landlord intends to begin proceedings for possession, the ground is specified in words which give to the tenant every piece of information which Parliament has said that he shall have and in words which are clear, then, as it seems to me, the legislative purpose of the provision would be satisfied and there would be no effective requirement of the ground to be specified in the very words set out in Schedule 2 unless Parliament has made that requirement.

The word "specified" takes its particular meaning from the context in which it is used and from the matter to which it is applied. The Shorter Oxford Dictionary gives the first meaning of the word as: "to speak or make relation of some matter fully or in detail."

The requirement in section 8(2) is to specify the ground: it is not that the ground be set out as in Schedule 2. I would add that it is also not merely to identify the ground. If the ground is specified in the notice in terms which set out all the necessary information, ie the substance of the ground, it seems to me that the requirement that the ground be specified would be met. I would add that it is difficult to think of any good reason why a person, given the task of settling a form of notice, should choose to use words different from those in which the ground is stated in the schedule.

The notice must also be in the prescribed form. The regulation by which the form is prescribed requires the form used to be in the form there set out or "substantially to the same effect." If the form served is to be completed fully in accordance with the form, it will set out the text of the ground as it appears in Schedule 2 because the form in paragraph 3 says: "the landlord intends to seek possession on ground(s) … in Schedule 2 *which reads*" and Note (3) in the margin says: "give the full text of each ground which is being relied on."

The regulation, however, expressly permits the notice to be effective in the prescribed form if it is "substantially to the same effect" which I take to mean to be showing no difference in substance having regard to the legislative purpose of the provisions as a whole. I, therefore, am not persuaded that there is a statutory requirement that the ground be set out verbatim from the schedule. I am troubled by the risk that, if the tenant is faced with a set of words which effectively set out the substance of a ground but in markedly different words, the tenant may, if he has access to the words of Schedule 2, be puzzled and troubled by the difference. There is something to be said in favour of the use of the words in which the ground was enacted by Parliament. I do not decide this point, however, because the case can be, and I think should be, decided on the ground that the plaintiff's notice was not "substantially to the same effect" as that required by the Act and regulations …

I would hold this notice to be defective because, in my judgment, it did not specify Ground 8 by the words: "at least three months rent is unpaid". The omitted information is that the ground which must be proved includes the requirement that "both at the date of the service of the notice … and the date of a hearing … at least … three months rent is unpaid and … 'rent' means rent lawfully due from the tenant." '

Section 8(1)(a) allows a court to 'dispense' with the requirement of a notice where it is 'just and equitable' to do so. An interesting application of this can be seen in

*North British Housing Association Ltd v Sheridan*[50]. Clause 4(2) of the standard form agreement of the housing association, which Sheridan had signed in August 1994, stated that the association would not give less than four weeks' notice of its intention to seek a possession order. After Sheridan had been convicted (in June 1998) under the Protection from Harassment Act 1997 of harassing his daughter who lived on the same estate, the Association sought a possession order against him, relying on Ground 14 of Sch 2 to the Housing Act 1988. Prior to 28 February 1997, the relevant 's 8' notice period applicable to Ground 14 was still two weeks, but under amendments contained in the Housing Act 1996, from 28 February 1997 possession proceedings in such cases could be commenced from the date of service of the notice. The Court of Appeal held unanimously that the standard tenancy terms were not meant to last for ever, irrespective of changes in the general legal framework and, in any event, did not override the court's general discretion to disperse with notice under s 8(1)(a).

May LJ stated:

'The gloss to which I referred relates to the Association's agreement "that it will not give less than four weeks' notice of its intention to seek a Possession Order". I have already given my reasons why this does not refer to a notice bringing to an end the contractual tenancy. By virtue of section 5 of the 1988 Act there was no need for the plaintiffs to give – and no use in giving – such a notice. In its context, this is in my view reference to a notice of the kind prescribed by section 8 of the 1988 Act. It is an agreement by the plaintiffs that they will operate section 8 with the substitution of four weeks for any shorter period that would otherwise apply. But because the notice is of this kind, it is an agreement which leaves intact the plaintiffs' ability to ask the court to dispense with the requirement of notice under section 8(1)(b) if the court considers it just and equitable to do so. The judge in this case was not asked to consider this question because he decided in the plaintiffs' favour on a basis which did not reach that consideration. This court has all the powers of the judge. In my judgment, in the light of my reasons for considering that the plaintiffs were entitled to seek a possession order on Ground 14 as amended by the 1996 Act, this court should entertain an application for dispensation and conclude that it was just and equitable to grant it. I reach this conclusion because (a) Parliament has decided that landlords should be enabled to bring immediate proceedings for possession on amended Ground 14; (b) the judge decided on very strong factual grounds that it was reasonable to make a possession order; and (c) since the defendant's conduct provided a ground for possession which was not remediable, the defendant would have suffered no prejudice from not having been given four weeks' notice of the plaintiffs' intention to seek a possession order'.

And Brooke LJ noted:

'The answer to the present appeal must depend on an interpretation of the parties' intentions when they entered into this agreement in 1994. Did they intend that if Parliament altered the statutory grounds on which an assured

---

[50] (1999) 32 HLR 346; and see also *Kelsey Housing Association v King* (1995) 28 HLR 270.

tenancy might be terminated, any such amendment would have any effect in relation to clause 4(2) of their agreement?

I have already observed that the Association intended to give their tenants a more generous (four week) notice of intention to seek a Possession Order than the minimum two week notice prescribed by statute for assured tenants in most situations (see the 1988 Act, s 8(3)(b)). In my judgment, there is nothing in the relevant legislation to prevent the landlord from binding itself by contract to give a more generous period of notice, subject always to the court's overriding discretion in section 8(1)(b) of the 1988 Act to dispense with the requirements of such notice if it considers it just and equitable to do so. I am satisfied that the parties must be held to have intended the court to retain this overriding discretionary power, since they expressly agreed that the status of the tenancy was an assured tenancy in accordance with the provisions of the 1988 Act.

The reason why I am of this opinion is that the notice will continue to be a notice required by section 8(1)(a) of the Act. As such, it must inform the tenant of the matters specified in section 8(3), including the fact that the landlord's proceedings will not begin earlier than the date specified in the notice. The fact that the landlord has bound itself by contract to give slightly longer notice of the date when intended proceedings will start than the minimum period of two weeks mentioned, in some contexts, in section 8 does not alter the status of the notice from being a notice served in accordance with that section (section 8(1)(a)), over which the court has a general dispensing power if it considers it just and equitable to exercise it (section 8(1)(b)).'

A possession order will be granted against an assured tenant (once the matter is validly before the courts) only if (at least) one of the grounds listed in the Housing Act 1988, Sch 2 is made out (s 7(1)). These grounds are of two general types: Part I grounds, where the court must make an order if the provisions of the ground are satisfied (often termed *mandatory grounds*); and Part II grounds, where, in addition to being satisfied that a ground has been made out, a court should order possession if it considers it *reasonable* to do so (often termed *discretionary grounds*). On this, see s 7(3) and (4).

## Mandatory grounds for possession

The following grounds are as amended by the Housing Act 1996.

# HOUSING ACT 1988
## SCHEDULE 2

# GROUNDS FOR POSSESSION OF DWELLING-HOUSES LET ON ASSURED TENANCIES

## PART I
## GROUNDS ON WHICH COURT MUST ORDER POSSESSION

### *Ground 1*

Not later than the beginning of the tenancy the landlord gave notice in writing to the tenant that possession might be recovered on this ground or the court is of the opinion that it is just and equitable to dispense with the requirement of notice and (in either case)—

(a)   at some time before the beginning of the tenancy, the landlord who is seeking possession or, in the case of joint landlords seeking possession, at least one of them occupied the dwelling-house as his only or principal home; or

(b)   the landlord who is seeking possession or, in the case of joint landlords seeking possession, at least one of them requires the dwelling-house as his or his spouse's only or principal home and neither the landlord (or in the case of joint landlords, any one of them) nor any other person who, as landlord, derived title under the landlord who gave the notice mentioned above acquired the reversion on the tenancy for money or money's worth.

### *Ground 2*

The dwelling house is subject to a mortgage granted before the beginning of the tenancy and—

(a)   the mortgagee is entitled to exercise a power of sale conferred on him by the mortgage or by section 101 of the Law of Property Act 1925; and

(b)   the mortgagee requires possession of the dwelling-house for the purpose of disposing of it with vacant possession in exercise of that power; and

(c)   either notice was given as mentioned in Ground 1 above or the court is satisfied that it is just and equitable to dispense with the requirement of notice;

and for the purposes of this ground 'mortgage' includes a charge and 'mortgagee' shall be construed accordingly.

### *Ground 3*

The tenancy is a fixed term tenancy for a term not exceeding eight months and—

(a)   not later than the beginning of the tenancy the landlord gave notice in writing to the tenant that possession might be recovered on this ground; and

(b)   at some time within the period of twelve months ending with the beginning of the tenancy, the dwelling-house was occupied under a right to occupy it for a holiday.

### *Ground 4*

The tenancy is a fixed term tenancy for a term not exceeding twelve months and—

(a)   not later than the beginning of the tenancy the landlord gave notice in writing to the tenant that possession might be recovered on this ground; and

(b)   at some time within the period of twelve months ending with the beginning of the tenancy, the dwelling-house was let on a tenancy falling within paragraph 8 of Schedule 1 to this Act.

...

### Ground 6

The landlord who is seeking possession or, if that landlord is a registered housing association or charitable housing trust, a superior landlord intends to demolish or reconstruct the whole or a substantial part of the dwelling-house or to carry out substantial works on the dwelling-house or any part thereof or any building of which it forms part and the following conditions are fulfilled—

(a)   the intended work cannot reasonably be carried out without the tenant giving up possession of the dwelling-house because—
  (i)   the tenant is not willing to agree to such a variation of the terms of the tenancy as would give such access and other facilities as would permit the intended work to be carried out, or
  (ii)   the nature of the intended work is such that no such variation is practicable, or
  (iii)   the tenant is not willing to accept an assured tenancy of such part only of the dwelling-house (in this sub-paragraph referred to as 'the reduced part') as would leave in the possession of his landlord so much of the dwelling-house as would be reasonable to enable the intended work to be carried out and, where appropriate, as would give such access and other facilities over the reduced part as would permit the intended work to be carried out, or
  (iv)   the nature of the intended work is such that such a tenancy is not practicable; and

(b)   either the landlord seeking possession acquired his interest in the dwelling-house before the grant of the tenancy or that interest was in existence at the time of that grant and neither that landlord (or, in the case of joint landlords, any of them) nor any other person who, alone or jointly with others, has acquired that interest since that time acquired it for money or money's worth: and

(c)   the assured tenancy on which the dwelling-house is let did not come into being by virtue of any provision of Schedule 1 to the Rent Act 1977, as amended by Part I of Schedule 4 to this Act or, as the case may be, section 4 of the Rent (Agriculture) Act 1976, as amended by Part II of that Schedule.

For the purposes of this ground, if, immediately before the grant of the tenancy, the tenant to whom it was granted or, if it was granted to joint tenants, any of them was the tenant or one of the joint tenants of the dwelling-house concerned under an earlier assured tenancy ..., any reference to paragraph (b) above to the grant of the tenancy is a reference to the grant of that earlier assured tenancy ...

### Ground 7

The tenancy is a periodic tenancy (including a statutory periodic tenancy) which has devolved under the will or intestacy of the former tenant and the proceedings for the recovery of possession are begun not later than twelve months after the death of the former tenant or, if the court so directs, after the date on which, in the opinion of the court, the landlord or, in the case of joint landlords, any one of them became aware of the former tenant's death.

For the purposes of this ground, the acceptance by the landlord of rent from a new tenant after the death of the former tenant shall not be regarded as creating a new periodic tenancy, unless the landlord agrees in writing to a charge (as compared with the tenancy before the death) in the amount of the rent, the period of the tenancy, the premises which are let or any other term of the tenancy.

### Ground 8

Both at the date of the service of the notice under section 8 of this Act relating to the proceedings for possession and at the date of the hearing—

(a)  if rent is payable weekly or fortnightly, at least eight weeks' rent is unpaid;
(b)  if rent is payable monthly, at least two months' rent is unpaid;
(c)  if rent is payable quarterly, at least one quarter's rent is more than three months in arrears; and
(d)  if rent is payable yearly, at least three months' rent is more than three months in arrears;

and for the purpose of this ground 'rent' means rent lawfully due from the tenant.

Many of the above grounds are either self-explanatory, or duplicate those in the Rent Act discussed below. However, on a general level it is highly significant that in the 1988 Act (unlike the 1977 Act) the mandatory grounds come first (at the very least of psychological significance!). Moreover, any legislative amendments to these grounds seem likely to tighten them up, rather than to liberalise them. (See the comments on Ground 8 below.)

The relationship between Grounds 1 and 2 is not unproblematic. It *appears* that the type of notice envisaged in Ground 2 is one served by a 'Ground 1' landlord, ie a past or future 'owner-occupier'. The idea seems to be that to facilitate repossession by a mortgagee the tenant should first have been put on guard by the landlord indicating his or her occupational interest in the property (no doubt a well-advised mortgagee would normally insist on the mortgagor creating an assured shorthold, but it has been suggested that even lets as long as six months might sometimes prove inconvenient to a mortgagor ideally wishing to sell the property and desiring to create a (very) short-term let, often to tide him or her over temporary financial difficulties. An alternative justification could be the (perceived) general social benefit in encouraging 'absentee' property owners to let empty properties until a sale is agreed. Ground 1, in itself, seems to be an amalgam of the 1977 Act cases 9, 11 and 12 (below), all adjusted to make things easier for landlords. In particular, there is no need for the landlord to demonstrate that he or she was a former owner-occupier *and* now wishes to reoccupy, merely that one *or* the other is the case (admittedly it must have been or be intended to be 'genuine' owner-occupation, ie as the landlord's 'only or principal home').

The court has a general discretion to 'waive' the need for the usual Ground 1 notice. In *Boyle v Verrall*[51] and *Mustafa v Ruddock*,[52] the Court of Appeal held that the following matters were relevant to the exercise of the discretion to dispense with the statutory notice:

(a)  whether hardship would (thereby) be caused to the defendant, or not;
(b)  whether hardship would (thereby) be caused to the landlord, if the notice requirement was not 'waived';

---

[51]  (1996) 29 HLR 436.
[52]  (1997) 30 HLR 495.

(c)    whether the tenancy agreement itself indicated that security of tenure was to be limited; and

(d)    whether other written (or oral) indications had been given to the tenant concerning limited security.

Ground 6 has no counterpart in the Rent Acts, and is both of considerable interest and some difficulty. Broadly equivalent provisions are to be found in Ground 10 of Sch 2 to the Housing Act 1985 (concerning public sector residential tenants) and in s 30(1)(f) of the business tenancy 'code' in the Landlord and Tenant Act 1954. There is fairly extensive case law on the 1954 Act, concerning issues such as the genuineness of the landlord's intention to demolish or reconstruct (it has been pointed out that this 'intention' need exist only up to the date possession has been obtained!).

As a curb on the pure 'speculator', it is not possible to use the ground if the landlord acquired the freehold *after* the tenancy was created. Also, if the ground is invoked the tenant is entitled to reasonable removal expenses (s 11, 1988 Act). Overall, the objective of the ground is both clear and instructive as to the general philosophy underlying the 1988 Act; the right of a freeholder to develop and improve his property should not be curbed even if this is at the expense of removing the occupational security of the tenant. Prior to the Act, the only way that such a freeholder could secure the necessary repossession was if he or she was prepared to offer the tenant 'suitable alternative accommodation' (Rent Act 1977 s 98(1)(a) and Sch 15, Part IV – below).

A typical business sector case is *Fisher v Taylors Furnishing Stores Ltd*,[53] in which Denning LJ (as he was then) stated:

> 'The court must be satisfied that the intention to reconstruct is genuine … that it is a firm and settled intention … that the reconstruction is of a substantial part of the premises, indeed so substantial that it cannot be thought a device to get possession: that the work is so extensive that it is necessary to get possession of the holding in order to do it; and that it is intended to do the work at once, and not after a time.'

Ground 7 is required because, whereas a statutory tenancy under the Rent Acts is personal to a tenant and prima facie terminates automatically on that tenant's death, an assured tenancy can, in principle, 'devolve' by will or on intestacy. More generally, in the 1988 Act rights of succession are limited to spouses or cohabitees (s 17, below).

Ground 7 refers to the need for 'proceedings for possession' to be commenced no later than twelve months after the death of the former tenant. In *Shepping v Osada*[54] it was held that this meant the issue of court proceedings, and not the service of a s 8 notice. The court drew analogies between the wording of Ground 7 and the wording of s 8 and Ground 10 (below). Ground 10 seemed particularly instructive in that when the legislature wished to refer to a 's 8' notice it did so explicitly, and not by ambiguous references to 'proceedings for possession'.

---

[53]    [1956] 2 QB 78, at 84.
[54]    (2000) 33 HLR 146.

As will be seen shortly, Grounds 10 and 11 of Sch 2 provide for discretionary grounds of possession in rent arrears cases. Ground 8 is mandatory and must be strictly construed given the fact that there is no in-built flexibility for a court to grant suspended orders (or adjourn proceedings) conditional on an agreed arrears schedule. Above all, the arrears must still exist *both* at the date of service of the s 8 notice *and* at the date of the hearing. The severity of Ground 8 has recently been increased by amendments contained in s 101 of the Housing Act 1996 which reduce the period of arrears in Ground 8(a) from 13 weeks to eight weeks, and in the case of Ground 8(b) from three months to two months. Given that Ground 8 is mandatory, mitigating circumstances (for example that housing benefit is late being paid – and it has been estimated that up to one-third of all local authorities fail to pay housing benefit on time[55]) appear irrelevant.

### Discretionary grounds for possession

As indicated above, a prerequisite for the invocation of one of these grounds is that, in addition to a relevant ground being made out, it is seen by the court(s) as *reasonable* to grant a possession order (s 7(4), above). Numerous judicial formulations exist concerning the approach to be adopted in adjudicating on 'reasonableness' (a concept with a long Rent Act 'pedigree'). Perhaps the most succinct is that of Lord Greene MR in *Cumming v Danson*[56].

> 'The duty of the judge is to take into account all relevant circumstances as they exist at the date of the hearing. That he must do in what I venture to call a broad, common sense way as a man of the world, and come to the conclusion giving such weight as he thinks right to the various factors in the situation. Some factors may have little or no weight, others may be decisive, but it is quite wrong for him to exclude from his consideration matters which he ought to take into account.'

What *is* clear is that the interests/needs/circumstances of both the landlord *and* the tenant should be considered, and that unless the first instance judge has plainly misdirected himself or herself (as was indeed the case in *Cumming v Danson*) it will be unusual for an appeal court to disturb a preliminary finding on 'reasonableness'. Equally, the court has a very wide discretion to adjourn the proceedings, or suspend any possession order actually granted. In such cases conditions as to payment of (any) rent arrears *will* normally be imposed, and other conditions *may* be imposed (generally see s 9 above and Chapter 5).

The grounds themselves are predominantly similar to those to be found in the Rent Act 1977 and the Housing Act 1985, centring on tenant 'default', in such cases as nuisance, non-payment of rent and deterioration of the property. They have been significantly amended by the Housing Act 1996.

---

[55]   See, for example *Hansard* HL Deb (1996) Vol 572 col 613.
[56]   [1942] 2 All ER 653, at 655.

# PART II
# GROUNDS ON WHICH COURT MAY ORDER POSSESSION

### *Ground 9*

Suitable alternative accommodation is available for the tenant or will be available for him when the order for possession takes effect.

### *Ground 10*

Some rent lawfully due from the tenant—

(a)  is unpaid on the date on which the proceedings for possession are begun; and
(b)  except where subsection (1)(b) of section 8 of this Act applies, was in arrears at the date of the service of the notice under that section relating to those proceedings.

### *Ground 11*

Whether or not any rent is in arrears on the date on which proceedings for possession are begun, the tenant has persistently delayed paying rent which has become lawfully due.

### *Ground 12*

Any obligation of the tenancy (other than one related to the payment of rent) has been broken or not performed.

### *Ground 13*

The condition of the dwelling-house or any of the common parts has deteriorated owing to acts of waste by, or the neglect or default of, the tenant or any other person residing in the dwelling-house and, in the case of an act of waste by, or the neglect or default of, a person lodging with the tenant or a sub-tenant of his, the tenant has not taken such steps as he ought reasonably to have taken for the removal of the lodger or sub-tenant.

For the purposes of this ground, 'common parts' means any part of a building comprising the dwelling-house and any other premises which the tenant is entitled under the terms of the tenancy to use in common with the occupiers of other dwelling-houses in which the landlord has an estate or interest.

### *Ground 14*

The tenant or a person residing in or visiting the dwelling-house—

(a)  has been guilty of conduct causing or likely to cause a nuisance or annoyance to a person residing, visiting or otherwise engaging in a lawful activity in the locality, or
(b)  has been convicted of—
  (i)  using the dwelling-house or allowing it to be used for immoral or illegal purposes, or
  (ii)  an arrestable offence committed in, or in the locality of, the dwelling-house.

### *Ground 14A*

The dwelling-house was occupied (whether alone or with others) by a married couple or a couple living together as husband and wife and—

(a)  one or both of the partners is a tenant of the dwelling-house,
(b)  the landlord who is seeking possession is a registered social landlord or a charitable housing trust,

(c)   one partner has left the dwelling-house because of violence or threats of violence by the other towards—

    (i)   that partner, or

    (ii)   a member of the family of that partner who was residing with that partner immediately before the partner left, and

(d)   the court is satisfied that the partner who has left is unlikely to return.

   ...

### Ground 15

The condition of any furniture provided for use under the tenancy has, in the opinion of the court, deteriorated owing to ill-treatment by the tenant or any other person residing in the dwelling-house and, in the case of ill-treatment by a person lodging with the tenant or by a sub-tenant of his, the tenant has not taken such steps as he ought reasonably to have taken for the removal of the lodger or sub-tenant.

### Ground 16

The dwelling-house was let to the tenant in consequence of his employment by the landlord seeking possession or a previous landlord under the tenancy and the tenant has ceased to be in that employment.

### Ground 17

The tenant is the person, or one of the persons, to whom the tenancy was granted and the landlord was induced to grant the tenancy by a false statement made knowingly or recklessly by—

(a)   the tenant, or

(b)   a person acting at the tenant's instigation.

As under s 98(1)(a) of the Rent Act 1977 (below), but unlike the position under the Housing Act 1985, the offering of *suitable alternative accommodation* by the landlord is an independent ground for possession (Ground 9). It remains a discretionary ground despite calls from many landlords for it to become mandatory in order to facilitate tenant transfer and enhance the scope for property redevelopment (as indeed was the case, in the Housing Bill as originally drafted). However, in the light of the mandatory Ground 6 (above), it is debatable how significant this point remains. 'Suitability' is defined by Pt III of Sch 2 to the 1988 Act. Much of the structure and content of Pt III is similar to that in the Rent Act 1977, Sch 15, Pt IV discussed below – the main difference lying in the (fairly obvious) substitution of 'assured tenancy' for 'protected tenancy' in relation to alternatives deemed to be suitable (assured shortholds excepted). Under s 11(1) of the 1988 Act, a landlord must pay a tenant's reasonable removal expenses. Again, in the original Housing Bill, Ground 11 was to be a mandatory ground – no doubt better to deter the '11th hour' payer. As now enacted, it still provides a useful tool for landlords frustrated by a tenant who consistently heads off legal proceedings by paying off all arrears prior to the service of the possession summons. The main uncertainty is the scope of 'persistent'. It appears to encompass both the 'persistent' late payer and a particular sum 'persistently' remaining in arrears.

Ground 14 has been considerably widened and strengthened by the Housing Act 1996 (s 148) in terms now identical to those in the Housing Act 1985 (Sch 2, Ground 2 as amended). As will be discussed in relation to the 1985 Act, the aim is to arm the courts with clearer and more effective powers to deal with 'anti-social' tenants. It is likely that some of the main landlord users of this new provision will be housing associations. Indeed almost all of the reported cases on the amended s 14 have concerned housing associations. For example, in *North British Housing Association Ltd v Sheridan*[57], noted above, it was also held the strengthening of landlords' powers to seek possession because of 'anti-social' behaviour which the amended Ground 14 represents was not to be undermined by a clause in a standard assured tenancy agreement which pre-dated the 1996 Act and had been drafted largely to reflect the 'old' law. On the other hand, in *Pollards Hill Housing Association v Marsh*[58], a clause in an assured tenancy agreement post-dating the 1996 Act amendment was held binding on the housing association, despite being narrower in scope than the amended Ground 14.

The clause in question (as relevant) stated that 'you or anyone living in or visiting the premises have been guilty of conduct causing or likely to cause a nuisance or annoyance to others ...in the locality, or you have been convicted of ... an arrestable offence carried out at, or in the locality of the premises'. The Court of Appeal held that the 'you' in relation to the arrestable offence proviso applied only to the tenant, and did not include any other person. Moreover the association's right to claim possession was thereby limited to cases where the tenant had been convicted of the offence, even though the amended Ground 14 also applied to any person 'residing in, or visiting the dwelling house'. Therefore, in the instant case possession could not be granted merely on the basis that the tenant's cohabitant had been convicted of a drug dealing offence centring on the tenanted premises.

Kay LJ stated:

'Clause 4.7 would in my judgment clearly lead to the conclusion that there was an intention to restrict the rights to apply for possession under Ground 14. Nor do I accept that it is a restriction which makes no sort of sense at all. To cause somebody to have to leave their premises because of the actions of somebody else living in or visiting the premises is a harsh course to take. There may be a justification for it, and Parliament clearly saw that in giving Ground 14 its wider ambit. But equally, one could see that a party to a contract of this kind might take the view that it was wider than was necessary and be prepared to limit the use that it could make of that ground. In particular, it has to be borne in mind that if the commission of an arrestable offence in the premises or in the locality of the premises by someone other than the tenant caused nuisance or annoyance to anybody residing locally, visiting or otherwise engaging in lawful activity locally, that would engage Ground 14(a), which is clearly within clause 4.7. Accordingly, I find it impossible to say that the meaning suggested on behalf of the defendant is not one that this clause could sensibly or commercially have and on the clear wording of the clause I am satisfied that anybody reading the clause as it is set out would come to the conclusion that the claimant had imposed a restriction upon its right to make use of the second limb of Ground 14.'

[57]  (1999) 32 HLR 346.
[58]  [2002] EWCA Civ 199, [2002] HLR 662.

Again, Ground 14A (inserted by s 149 of the 1996 Act) mirrors the new public sector provision, now in Ground 2A of Sch 2 to the 1985 Act. The definition of 'domestic' violence required to 'trigger' the new ground is somewhat narrow (significantly narrower than the new concept of 'associated person' which correspondingly triggers 'domestic violence' provisions in relation to homelessness – see the Housing Act 1996, s 178). Gay couples and others sharing a common household, but not married or cohabiting, are, in particular, not covered. Ground 17 is also new, and also mirrors Housing Act 1985 provisions, although in this case Ground 5 in Sch 2 to the Housing Act 1985 is *not* a new provision. It seems clear that the measure is designed to put housing associations and other registered social landlords (Pt I of the 1996 Act) in the same position as local authorities as regards those 'jumping the queue' by deceit.

## Assured shorthold tenancies

As discussed earlier in this chapter, the centrepiece of the Housing Act 1988 is the assured shorthold, a form of tenancy giving landlords maximum letting flexibility, both in terms of the rent that can be charged (subject to a few minor caveats – see below) and the ability to recover possession of the property. An assured shorthold tenant (despite a somewhat contradictory impression conveyed by the name) has no *legal* security of tenure past the first six months of the tenancy. Even during the initial six months, such a tenant is vulnerable to repossession on the same bases as any assured tenant (above). In relation to assured shortholds in fixed-term form (pre- or post-Housing Act 1996), this means Grounds 2, 8, 10–15 and 17 (1988 Act, s 7(6)(b)). In relation to periodic (s 19A) assured shortholds, any ground seems theoretically available.

More significantly, at the end of the original minimum six-month fixed term ('old' assured shortholds: s 20(1) and s 21(1), 1988 Act) or after six months have passed from the commencement of the tenancy ('new' assured shortholds: s 21(5), 1988 Act as amended) a landlord has an absolute right to obtain possession without any ground for possession having to be shown at all. Two months' notice of the intention to repossess must be given by the landlord (s 21(1)(b)); or in the case of continuation periodic assured shortholds, a period equal to a tenancy period if this is longer than two months (s 21(4)(a)). However, it seems implicit that a notice can be served so as to expire on the last day of the original six months of the tenancy. No particular form is required for a s 21 notice, although it must now be in writing (since the 1996 Act, s 98).

21.   **Recovery of possession on expiry or termination of assured shorthold tenancy**

   (1) Without prejudice to any right of the landlord under an assured shorthold tenancy to recover possession of the dwelling-house let on the tenancy in accordance with Chapter I above, on or after the coming to an end of an assured shorthold tenancy which was a fixed term tenancy, a court shall make an order for possession of the dwelling-house if it is satisfied—

      (a)   that the assured shorthold tenancy has come to an end and no further assured tenancy (whether shorthold or not) is for the time being in existence, other than an assured shorthold periodic tenancy (whether statutory or not); and

(b)  the landlord or, in the case of joint landlords, at least one of them has given to the tenant not less than two months' notice in writing stating that he requires possession of the dwelling-house.

(2) A notice under paragraph (b) of subsection (1) above may be given before or on the day on which the tenancy comes to an end; and that subsection shall have effect notwithstanding that on the coming to an end of the fixed term tenancy a statutory periodic tenancy arises.

(3) Where a court makes an order for possession of a dwelling-house by virtue of subsection (1) above, any statutory periodic tenancy which has arisen on the coming to an end of the assured shorthold tenancy shall end (without further notice and regardless of the period) on the day on which the order takes effect.

(4) Without prejudice to any such right as is referred to in subsection (1) above, a court shall make an order for possession of a dwelling-house let on an assured shorthold tenancy which is a periodic tenancy if the court is satisfied—

(a)  that the landlord or, in the case of joint landlords, at least one of them has given to the tenant a notice in writing stating that, after a date specified in the notice, being the last day of a period of the tenancy and not earlier than two months after the date the notice was given, possession of the dwelling-house is required by virtue of this section; and

(b)  that the date specified in the notice under paragraph (a) above is not earlier than the earliest day on which, apart from section 5(1) above, the tenancy could be brought to an end by a notice to quit given by the landlord on the same date as the notice under paragraph (a) above.

(5) Where an order for possession under subsection (1) or (4) above is made in relation to a dwelling-house let on a tenancy to which section 19A above applies, the order may not be made so as to take effect earlier than—

(a)  in the case of a tenancy which is not a replacement tenancy, six months after the beginning of the tenancy, and

(b)  in the case of a replacement tenancy, six months after the beginning of the original tenancy.

(6) In subsection (5)(b) above, the reference to the original tenancy is—

(a)  where the replacement tenancy came into being on the coming to an end of a tenancy which was not a replacement tenancy, to the immediately preceding tenancy, and

(b)  where there have been successive replacement tenancies, to the tenancy immediately preceding the first in the succession of replacement tenancies

(7) For the purposes of this section, a replacement tenancy is a tenancy—

(a)  which comes into being on the coming to an end of an assured shorthold tenancy, and

(b)  under which, on its coming into being—

(i)  the landlord and tenant are the same as under the earlier tenancy as at its coming to an end, and

(ii)  the premises let are the same or substantially the same as those let under the earlier tenancy as at that time.

Unsurprisingly, under the shorthold 'regime', a court has no power to adjourn proceedings, suspend an order for possession, or postpone the date of possession (s 9(6)(b)). Indeed, an 'accelerated' possession procedure is available to landlords seeking repossession of assured shortholds (and also assured tenancies under Grounds 1, 3, 4, and 5). In outline, no hearing is necessarily required – a district judge can make a possession order without a hearing if satisfied by the landlord's written application that the necessary legal requirements have been made out (ss 19A and 20, plus s 21 as appropriate). The landlord's original application (supported by affidavit) is sent to the tenant who has 14 days to reply. On receipt of the tenant's reply (or failure to reply in the time allowed) the court must decide whether to grant possession or fix a hearing date. In the former case the tenant has to vacate the dwelling-house within 14 days of the order (the courts can extend this up to six weeks if there is 'exceptional hardship'). On all this see CCR Ord 49, r 6A(3) and (9) and see further Chapter 6.

However, in serving a 's 21' notice a landlord must, at least, make sure that he or she does not attempt to commence possession proceedings before the notice expires. In *Lower Street Properties Ltd v Jones*[59], Kennedy LJ stated: '... from the point of view of the tenant, I regard it as objectionable that having been given a period in which to leave, legal proceedings to obtain possession should be instituted ... before that period has expired'.

Much of s 21 seems moderately straightforward, but s 21(4) has generated some controversy, in particular, the wording of s 21(4)(a). Must it be interpreted literally, so that if a 's 21' notice is expressed so as to expire other than on the last day of a 'period' of the tenancy, it is invalid? Recently, in *McDonald v Fernandez*[60], the Court of Appeal has answered 'yes' to this question. Tenants had obtained an assured shorthold tenancy of a house in Leicester. Initially, the tenancy was to run for six months (4 September 1999 to 3 March 2000). However, on the expiry of the original fixed term they stayed on as statutory periodic tenants[61], paying rent monthly (the new periodic tenancy ran from the fourth of each month to the third of the following month). On 24 October 2002 the landlord served them with a notice referring to s 21(4)(a) and requiring possession on 4 January 2003.

The Court of Appeal (allowing the tenants' appeal) found that this notice was invalid, s 21(4)(c) clearly stating that the date specified in a notice had to be '... the last day of a period of the tenancy' and there was no requirement to interpret such plain words other than literally. Moreover there was no 'saving formula' in s 21 such as that a notice 'substantially to the same effect' would suffice[62]. It was not difficult for a landlord to comply with such a strict requirement or (indeed) subsequently to cure any defect. One purpose of s 21 was 'to give the courts a clear and simple set of criteria which trigger their mandatory duty to order possession' (Hale LJ).

It has been suggested[63] that the current relationship of landlord and tenant (typically now via assured shortholds) could be made fairer via one 'simple' reform; this would be to repeal (or amend) s 89 Housing Act 1980 which (currently) requires that a possession order must take effect within 14 days, or (if exceptional hardship is proved) within six weeks. Instead, the courts could be given the discretion to fix an appropriate date for possession, taking into account any hardship that an early possession date would cause. However, there seems little immediate prospect of (any) such reform.

---

[59]   (1996) 28 HLR 877, at 883.
[60]   [2003] EWCA Civ 1219, [2004] HLR 189
[61]   Housing Act 1988, s 5(7).
[62]   See, for example, Assured Tenancies (Forms) Regulations 1988 No. 2 (SI 1988/2203) (as amended by SI 1990/1532 which (in relation to s 20 Housing Act 1988 notice) talks of a form 'substantially to the same effect' sufficing).
[63]   R. Campbell, *Roof,* July 1 August 1997, at p 15.

## Rent Act tenancies

Rent Act tenants, a declining but still surviving 'breed', continue to enjoy full security of tenure. This security is the result of substantive hurdles imposed by the Rent Act 1977 (s 98 and Sch 15 in particular), and procedural hurdles imposed by the Protection from Eviction Act 1977 (in particular ss 3 and 5).

As relevant, s 98 of the Rent Act 1977 and ss 3 and 5 of the Protection from Eviction Act 1977 provide as follows:

# RENT ACT 1977

### Grounds for possession of certain dwelling-houses

98.  (1) Subject to this Part of this Act, a court shall not make an order for possession of a dwelling-house which is for the time being let on a protected tenancy or subject to a statutory tenancy unless the court considers it reasonable to make such an order and either—

(a)  the court is satisfied that suitable alternative accommodation is available for the tenant or will be available for him when the order in question takes effect, or

(b)  the circumstances are as specified in any of the Cases in Part I of Schedule 15 to this Act.

(2) If, apart from subsection (1) above, the landlord would be entitled to recover possession of a dwelling-house which is for the time being let on or subject to a regulated tenancy, the court shall make an order for possession if the circumstances of the case are as specified in any of the Cases in Part II of Schedule 15.

(3) Part III of Schedule 15 shall have effect in relation to Case 9 in that Schedule and for determining the relevant date for the purposes of the Cases in Part II of that Schedule.

(4) Part IV of Schedule 15 shall have effect for determining whether, for the purposes of subsection (1)(a) above, suitable alternative accommodation is or will be available for a tenant.

# PROTECTION FROM EVICTION ACT 1977

### Prohibition of eviction without due process of law

3.  (1) Where any premises have been let as a dwelling under a tenancy which is neither a statutorily protected tenancy nor an excluded tenancy and—

(a)  the tenancy (in this section referred to as the former tenancy) has come to an end, but

(b)  the occupier continues to reside in the premises or part of them,

it shall not be lawful for the owner to enforce against the occupier, otherwise than by proceedings in the court, his right to recover possession of the premises.

(2) In this section 'the occupier', in relation to any premises, means any person lawfully residing in the premises or part of them at the termination of the former tenancy.

(2A) Subsections (1) and (2) above apply in relation to any restricted contract (within the meaning of the Rent Act 1977) which—

(a)  creates a licence; and

(b)  is entered into after the commencement of section 69 of the Housing Act 1980;

as they apply in relation to a restricted contract which creates a tenancy.

(2B) Subsections (1) and (2) above apply in relation to any premises occupied as a dwelling under a licence, other than an excluded licence, as they apply in relation to premises let as a dwelling under a tenancy, and in those subsections the expressions 'let' and 'tenancy' shall be construed accordingly.

(2C) References in the preceding provisions of this section and section 4(2A) below to an excluded tenancy do not apply to—

(a)   a tenancy entered into before the date on which the Housing Act 1988 came into force, or

(b)   a tenancy entered into on or after that date but pursuant to a contract made before that date,

but, subject to that, 'excluded tenancy' and 'excluded licence' shall be construed in accordance with section 3A below.

(3) This section shall, with the necessary modifications, apply where the owner's right to recover possession arises on the death of the tenant under a statutory tenancy within the meaning of the Rent Act 1977 or the Rent (Agriculture) Act 1976.

## Excluded tenancies and licences

3A.   (1) Any reference in this Act to an excluded tenancy or an excluded licence is a reference to a tenancy or licence which is excluded by virtue of any of the following provisions of this section.

(2) A tenancy or licence is excluded if—

(a)   under its terms the occupier shares any accommodation with the landlord or licensor; and

(b)   immediately before the tenancy or licence was granted and also at the time it comes to an end, the landlord or licensor occupied as his only or principal home premises of which the whole or part of the shared accommodation formed part.

(3) A tenancy or licence is also excluded if—

(a)   under its terms the occupier shares any accommodation with a member of the family of the landlord or licensor;

(b)   immediately before the tenancy or licence was granted and also at the time it comes to an end, the member of the family of the landlord or licensor occupied as his only or principal home premises of which the whole or part of the shared accommodation formed part; and

(c)   immediately before the tenancy or licence was granted and also at the time it comes to end, the landlord or licensor occupied as his only or principal home premises in the same building as the shared accommodation and that building is not a purpose-built block of flats.

(4) For the purposes of subsections (2) and (3) above, an occupier shares accommodation with another person if he has the use of it in common with that person (whether or not also in common with others) and any reference in those subsections to shared accommodation shall be construed accordingly, and if, in relation to any tenancy or licence, there is at any time more than one person who is the landlord or licensor, any reference in those subsections to the landlord or licensor shall be construed as a reference to any one of those persons.

(5) In subsections (2) to (4) above—

(a)   'accommodation' includes neither an area used for storage nor a staircase, passage, corridor or other means of access;

(b)   'occupier' means, in relation to a tenancy, the tenant and, in relation to a licence, the licensee; and

(c) 'purpose-built block of flats' has the same meaning as in Part III of Schedule 1 to the Housing Act 1988;

(6) A tenancy or licence is excluded if it was granted as a temporary expedient to a person who entered the premises in question or any other premises as a trespasser (whether or not, before the beginning of that tenancy or licence, another tenancy or licence to occupy the premises or any other premises had been granted to him).

(7) A tenancy or licence is excluded if—

(a) it confers on the tenant or licensee the right to occupy the premises for a holiday only, or

(b) it is granted otherwise than for money or money's worth.

### Validity of notices to quit

5. (1) Subject to subsection (1B) below no notice by a landlord or a tenant to quit any premises let (whether before or after the commencement of this Act) as a dwelling shall be valid unless—

(a) it is in writing and contains such information as may be prescribed, and

(b) it is given not less than four weeks before the date on which it is to take effect.

(1A) Subject to subsection (1B) below, no notice by a licensor or a licensee to determine a periodic licence to occupy premises as a dwelling (whether the licence was granted before or after the passing of this Act) shall be valid unless—

(a) it is in writing and contains such information as may be prescribed, and

(b) it is given not less than four weeks before the date on which it is to take effect.

(1B) Nothing in subsection (1) or subsection (1A) above applies to—

(a) premises let on excluded tenancy which is entered into on or after the date on which the Housing Act 1988 came into force unless it is entered into pursuant to a contract made before that date; or

(b) premises occupied under an excluded licence.

The 'prescribed information' referred to in s 5 is contained in the Notices to Quit, etc. (Prescribed Information) Regulations 1988 (SI 1988/2201), which provide:

1. If the tenant or licensee does not leave the dwelling, the landlord or licensor must get an order for possession from the court before the tenant or licensee can lawfully be evicted. The landlord or licensor cannot apply for such an order before the notice to quit or notice to determine has run out.

2. A tenant or licensee who does not know if he has any right to remain in possession after a notice to quit or a notice to determine runs out can obtain advice from a solicitor. Help with all or part of the cost of legal advice and assistance may be available under the Legal Aid Scheme. He should also be able to obtain information from a Citizens' Advice Bureau, a Housing Aid Centre or a rent officer.

Failure to provide this information renders the notice invalid.

Notices to quit, unlike 's 8' notices under the 1988 Act have the effect of bringing the contractual tenancy to an end, continued security being dependent on the tenant satisfying the Rent Act s 2 conditions for a statutory tenancy (above). Aside from that, the Protection from Eviction Act 1977 adds to the inherent common law requirement of a notice to quit to bring a contractual tenancy to an end (below) the further requirements of a *minimum* four-week notice period, and the provision of information designed to alert tenants to their legal rights. Additionally (and of crucial importance) s 3 requires court proceedings before *any* right to possess of a landlord can be exercised. Indeed the 'unlawfulness' of any attempt to repossess other than by court proceedings (s 3(1)) is reinforced by s 1(2) of the Act, which makes it a criminal offence so to do unless the person concerned proves that he believed, and had reasonable cause to believe, that the occupier had ceased to reside in the premises.

Of particular interest are the amendments introduced by the Housing Act 1988 to both ss 3 and 5 (and so only applicable to tenancies created *on* or after 15 January 1989). In simple terms, the procedural requirements of a court order and a statutory notice to quit (although presumably not the common law requirement of a notice to quit) are inapplicable to a range of *excluded* tenancies and licences. Perhaps the most significant of these are the 'holiday lets' (s 3A(7)) and cases where landlords share accommodation with their tenants (s 3A(2)–(5)). In the latter case the sharing even of a toilet or bathroom with the tenant (s 3A(5)) obviates the need for a statutory notice to quit or a court order to obtain possession.

Section 98 of the Rent Act 1977 (in conjunction with Sch 15) introduces the substantive framework for security of tenure, in terms reasonably similar to those already discussed in relation to assured tenancies (although the emphasis in the Rent Act is considerably more towards tenant protection). Structurally the grounds for possession divide into suitable alternative accommodation, other 'discretionary' grounds and the mandatory grounds (considerably more limited than in the 1988 Act).

*Suitable alternative accommodation*

## RENT ACT 1977

## SCHEDULE 15

# GROUNDS FOR POSSESSION OF DWELLING-HOUSES LET ON OR SUBJECT TO PROTECTED OR STATUTORY TENANCIES

## PART IV
## SUITABLE ALTERNATIVE ACCOMMODATION

3. For the purposes of section 98(1)(a) of this Act, a certificate of the housing authority for the district in which the dwelling-house in question is situated, certifying that the authority will provide suitable alternative accommodation for the tenant by a date specified in the certificate, shall be conclusive evidence that suitable alternative accommodation will be available for him by that date.

4. Where no such certificate as is mentioned in paragraph 3 above is produced to the court, accommodation shall be deemed to be suitable for the purposes of section 98(1)(a) of this Act if it consists of either—

(a) premises which are to be let as a separate dwelling such that they will then be let on a protected tenancy other than one under which the landlord might recover possession of the dwelling-house under one of the cases in part II of this Schedule, or

(b)   premises to be let as a separate dwelling on terms which will, in the opinion of the court, afford to the tenant security of tenure reasonably equivalent to the security afforded by Part VII of this Act in the case of a protected tenancy of a kind mentioned in paragraph (a) above,

and in the opinion of the court, the accommodation fulfils the relevant conditions as defined in paragraph 5 below.

5.—(1) For the purposes of paragraph 4 above, the relevant conditions are that the accommodation is reasonably suitable to the needs of the tenant and his family as regards proximity to place of work, and either—

(a)   similar as regards rental and extent to the accommodation afforded by dwelling-houses provided in the neighbourhood by any housing authority for persons whose needs as regards extent are, in the opinion of the court, similar to those of the tenant and of his family; or

(b)   reasonably suitable to the means of the tenant and to the needs of the tenant and his family as regards extent and character; and

that if any furniture was provided for use under the protected or statutory tenancy in question, furniture is provided for use in the accommodation which is either similar to that so provided or is reasonably suitable to the needs of the tenant and his family.

(2) For the purposes of sub-paragraph (1)(a) above, a certificate of a housing authority stating—

(a)   the extent of the accommodation afforded by dwelling-houses provided by the authority to meet the needs of tenants with families of such number as may be specified in the certificate, and

(b)   the amount of the rent charged by the authority for dwelling-houses affording accommodation of that extent,

shall be conclusive evidence of the facts so stated.

6. Accommodation shall not be deemed to be suitable to the needs of the tenant and his family if the result of their occupation of the accommodation would be that it would be an overcrowded dwelling-house for the purposes of Part X of the Housing Act 1985.

As noted above, the Housing Act 1988 (with necessary amendments) adopts much of the structure of this in Pt III of Sch 2, and case law under the Rent Act will remain relevant for Housing Act purposes. There is indeed a considerable body of case law on Sch 15, Pt IV and some of the key decisions are discussed below.

Perhaps the two most important points are, first, that the question is whether the premises offered are a *suitable alternative* not (per se) whether they are as good as the existing premises and, secondly, that there is considerable uncertainty about the precise meaning of the notion of 'character' (para. 5(1)(b) above).

In *Hill v Rochard*[64], an elderly married couple held a statutory tenancy of a period country house in which they had resided for many years. The premises contained many spacious rooms, a staff flat, outbuildings, a stable, and one and a half acres of land, including a paddock, where the tenants kept a pony. The landlords wished to obtain possession of the house and offered the tenants a modern, detached, four-bedroomed house as alternative accommodation. The house was situated in a cul-de-sac on a housing estate in a nearby country village. The garden covered one eighth of an acre and there was no stable or paddock. The tenants refused the offer

---

[64]   [1983] 2 All ER 21.

and the landlords sought an order for possession in the county court on the ground that the modern house was reasonably suitable to the needs of the tenant as regards extent and character within the meaning of Sch 15, Pt IV, para 5(1)(b) to the Rent Act 1977 and constituted suitable alternative accommodation for the purposes of s 98(1) of the Act. The judge found that the tenants were not ordinary tenants and for the past 15 years had not been ordinarily housed. Adopting the test whether the accommodation which was offered met the standard of the needs of an ordinary and reasonable tenant, she found that the alternative accommodation satisfied that test as regards extent and character and it would permit the tenants to live reasonably comfortably in the style of life which they liked to lead, in a reasonably similar way to that permitted by their present accommodation. She held that suitable alternative accommodation was available to the tenants, that it was reasonable to make an order for possession and, accordingly, granted the landlords an order for possession.

The tenants' appeal was dismissed by the Court of Appeal. As Dunn LJ stated,

> 'It is said [that] the test ... is not whether the accommodation offered meets the standard of needs of an ordinary and reasonable tenant: the test is whether the accommodation meets the standard of needs of these particular tenants. In considering that question regard may be had to the lifestyle of the tenants in their present accommodation, and if that lifestyle cannot be continued in the alternative accommodation offered, then that alternative accommodation is not suitable to the needs of the tenant ...

> Mr Gordon submits that ... in considering the suitability of needs, the court is not simply confined to the provision of suitable habitation but can also have regard to other amenities enjoyed by the tenant in his present accommodation.

> He referred us to *Redspring Ltd v Francis* [1973] 1 All ER 640, which he said established the point. In that case the tenant, who occupied a flat in a quiet residential road, was offered alternative accommodation in a flat which, unlike the first flat, had no garden and was in a busy traffic thoroughfare with a fried fish shop next door. The county court judge made the order for possession and this court allowed the appeal, holding that what a tenant needed was somewhere where he could live in reasonably comfortable conditions suitable to the style of life which he led. Mr Gordon relied particularly on a passage in the judgment of Buckley LJ when, after referring to a concession which had been made by counsel for the landlord, he said, at p. 643:

>> "That concession was, in my judgment, properly made, for if a tenant who occupies accommodation in a residential area is offered other accommodation which may be physically as good as or better than the accommodation which he is required to vacate but is situated in an area which is offensive as the result of some industrial activity in the neighbourhood, which perhaps creates offensive smells or noises, or which is extremely noisy as a result of a great deal of traffic passing by, or in some other respect is clearly much less well endowed with amenities than the accommodation which the tenant is required to vacate, then it seems to me that it would be most unreal to say that the alternative accommodation is such as to satisfy the needs of the tenant with regard to its character. What he needs is

somewhere where he can live in reasonably comfortable conditions suitable to the style of life which he leads, and environmental matters must inevitably affect the suitability of offered accommodation to provide him with the sort of conditions in which it is reasonable that he should live."

Sachs LJ said, at p. 645:

"In each case it is a question of fact having regard to the needs of the tenant in the circumstances as a whole. The view which I have just expressed coincides with the tenor of those sparsely reported decisions of the court (for example, in the 'Estates Gazette') to which reference has already been made. Any other view of the meaning of the relevant words would, indeed, produce astonishing results, some of which were canvassed in the course of argument. It would result in accommodation on the third floor of premises facing on to the Edgware Road being necessarily held to be equivalent in character to a quiet third floor flat in nearby Montague Square. Another example was put in argument of a cottage in a quiet country lane which has one character and that of a cottage of identical construction which finds itself implanted in or entangled with a new motorway."

Mr Gordon submitted that those two cases supported his proposition to which I have referred. He submitted, that the two cases of *MacDonnell v Daly* and *Redspring Ltd v Francis* show that the court is not concerned, as might appear from *Christie v Macfarlane*, with the needs of the ordinary tenant, but is concerned with the needs of the tenant in question, and those needs include the ability of the particular tenant, in his new accommodation, to follow the lifestyle which he had enjoyed in the old accommodation.

For myself I prefer to go first to the relevant statutory provisions before considering how they have been construed. [His lordship here referred to s 98(1) of the Rent Act 1977.]

…

It has not been seriously suggested, in this appeal, that 2, Chestermaster Close is not suitable as regards extent. A four-bedroomed house with two living rooms is perfectly extensive enough for an elderly couple living alone, as these tenants are.

The argument in this court has revolved around the word "character." The sub-paragraph does not provide, and it is not necessary, that the character of the alternative accommodation should be similar to that of the existing premises. Indeed, there are, in this case, certain obvious differences between the character of The Grange and the character of 2, Chestermaster Close. 2, Chestermaster Close is a modern house and not a period house. It stands in a housing estate and does not stand alone. But the question is whether 2, Chestermaster Close is reasonably suitable to the tenants' housing needs as regards its character. In considering those needs the cases to which I have referred show that it is permissible for the court to look at the environment to which the tenants have become accustomed in their present accommodation, and to see how far the new environment differs from that. The new house is on the outskirts of a village, and the tenants will, in ordinary parlance, still be living in the country. It is not as if they have been offered accommodation on a housing estate in a town. In so far as their style of life is relevant they will still be able to enjoy the amenities of country life. Indeed, looked at from the point of view of reasonable suitability, as this court is required to do by the paragraph, many people would say that a modern house in a country village is more suitable to the needs of people of the ages of these tenants than a large isolated country house such as The Grange.

In my view the judge was right to say that these tenants were not ordinary tenants. By that I take her to mean that, accommodation aside, the present tenancy enables them to enjoy the use of certain amenities, including the paddock and outbuildings, so that they could keep their animals. Even on a liberal construction of the statutory provisions I do not think that the Rent Acts were intended to protect incidental advantages of that kind. The Rent Acts are concerned with the provision of housing and accommodation.'

A particularly controversial 'line' on the 'character' question was taken in the later case of *Siddiqui v Rashid*[65]. Here, the tenant, a Muslim, occupied a room in a house in London under a protected tenancy and worked in Luton. The landlords of the house were the trustees of an Islamic mission. They wished to sell the house with vacant possession in order to buy a larger property for their charitable work, and accordingly offered the tenant alternative accommodation in Luton which was reasonably suitable to the needs of the tenant as regards rental and extent and to his means and which was closer to his work. The tenant refused to move and the landlords brought proceedings in the county court for possession. The county court judge granted a possession order on the ground that the Luton premises constituted 'suitable alternative accommodation' for the purposes of s 98(1)(a) of the Rent Act 1977 since it fulfilled the conditions as to suitability set out in para 5 of Sch 15 to that Act. The tenant appealed, contending that the alternative accommodation was not suitable to his needs as regards 'character' within para 5(1)(b) because it would take him away from his friends and his local mosque and cultural centre in London.

In dismissing the tenant's appeal, the Court of Appeal held that in determining for the purposes of para 5(1)(b) of Sch 15 to the 1977 Act whether alternative accommodation offered to a tenant was suitable to his needs as regards 'character', environmental or peripheral matters could be taken into account only in so far as they related to the character of the property itself, since the term 'character' did not extend to such matters as the society of friends or cultural interests. On that basis, the alternative accommodation offered was suitable to the tenant's needs, and, having regard to the necessity for the landlords to sell the house for their charitable work, it satisfied the statutory requirements. As Stephenson LJ stated,

'No question arises as to this room in Luton being reasonably suitable to the needs of the tenant as regards proximity to place of work. Equally no dispute arises as to the suitability of this room as regards rental and extent; and no question arises as to its reasonable suitability to the defendant's means. But

---

[65] [1980] 3 All ER 184.

what is in dispute is whether this room would be reasonably suitable to the needs of the defendant and his family as regards character. The judge, as I said, made an order for possession and was satisfied that it was reasonably suitable accommodation as regards character to the needs of the tenant, and he has found that it was reasonable for him to make the order …

We are bound by authority not to give a very narrow construction to the word "character" in para 5(1)(b) of Sch 15 to the 1977 Act. The wording of the relevant statutory provisions which this court had to consider in *Redspring v Francis* was the same, and in that case this court rejected the argument that the character to which the court must have regard did not include what the county court judge in that case had called 'environmental aspects or peripheral amenities'. That was a case which in some respects resembled this. Buckley LJ, in the leading judgment, said at p 642:

> "So we have to consider whether in the present case the accommodation offered at 108 Fleet Road is reasonably suitable to the needs of the tenant as regards extent and character. No point arises in this case in relation to proximity to the place of work or the means of the tenant. We are concerned only with the question whether the accommodation is reasonably suitable to her needs as regards extent and character. Extent, as I have already stated, is conceded. So the question is whether the accommodation is reasonably suited to her needs in respect of its character."

That was exactly the same position as in this case. There the judge had made an order for possession, because he took the view that equally good accommodation next to a smelly fish and chip shop and a good deal of motor traffic and noise was suitable alternative accommodation to similar premises in a quiet street not far off which Mr Francis had been occupying for 30 years. He was able to take that view because of the narrow view which he took on the meaning of the word character. In his judgment, quoted by Buckley LJ at p. 642 he had said:

> "The 'needs' contemplated by the paragraph 3(1)(b) of Part IV of Sch 3 to the Rent Act 1968, cited in argument, are not the same as tastes and inclinations: they are needs of an urgent, compelling nature – space, transport, a bathroom etc. Peripheral amenities are of a different category; by this I am not saying that Mr Francis's objections are fanciful but I find that her needs are met, apart from the environmental aspect. One must look at the whole of the picture, and I have not forgotten the hospital, the fish and chip shop, the public house and the cinema."

This court held that in spite of that last sentence the judge really had forgotten, or, at any rate, put out of the picture, the hospital, the fish and chip shop, the public house and the cinema and the smells and the noises that all that the proximity of a busy road provide; and was wrong in excluding from his consideration the question whether the accommodation offered was reasonably suited to Mr Francis's needs in respect of its character. Buckley LJ lists "environmental matters" at, pp 643–644.

"… environmental matters such as the smell from the fish and chip shop, the noise from the public house, noise perhaps from vehicles going to and from the hospital and matters of that kind. In so doing, with respect to the judge I think he misdirected himself. Those, I think, are all matters properly to be taken into consideration in connection with the making of such an order as was sought in this case."

… As was pointed out in the course of the argument, the statutory provisions say nothing of difference in character, but Mr Morgan has submitted that it was only if there could be shown to be some difference in character between the two premises that this question of unsuitability of alternative accommodation to the needs of the tenant as regards character could arise. What he submits and he did not appear in the county court, but it was submitted in the county court is that the court must look at environmental aspects, and that means the respective locations of the two premises, and see whether the tenant's needs are satisfied as regards the new location. Those needs are not merely physical needs, it was submitted, but such needs as were given in evidence here; need for a devout Muslim to keep in touch with his local mosque and cultural centre (in this case the mosque and cultural centre in Regent's Park) and need to enjoy the company of friends whom he had made in the course of his many years' residence in London. The judge was not wholly satisfied, according to a note which he made in the course of his notes of the evidence, with the defendant's evidence as to his attendances and need to attend at the Regent's Park mosque, but he ruled that the need of the defendant's to visit that mosque and the cultural centre there, and to keep in touch with his London friends, did not relate to the character of the property, as environmental aspects had to relate if they were to be a relevant consideration to the question of the suitability of the alternative accommodation.

The 1977 Act does not say that the alternative accommodation must be reasonably suitable to the needs of the tenant as regards location or, of course, as regards environment, and for my part I would regard the judge as right in this case in confining "character" to the "character of the property". I find nothing in the judgment of this court in *Redspring v Francis* to indicate that that is wrong, or to extend the meaning of "character" beyond character of the property. The character of the property was directly affected by the environmental matters which were the subject of Mr Francis's objection to her move. I have read them from Buckley LJ's judgment; noise and smell were matters which would directly affect the tenant in the enjoyment of her property, so they could well be said to relate to the character of the property. I cannot think that Parliament intended to include such matters as the society of friends, or cultural interests, in using the language that it did in the particular word "character". Nor can I accept that Buckley LJ had any such considerations in mind when he referred, in the passages which the county court quoted from his judgment, to the needs of the tenant to have "somewhere where [the tenant] could live in reasonably comfortable conditions suitable to the style of life which he leads …", and referred to the accommodation providing him with the sort of conditions in which it is reasonable that he should live. To extend the character of the property to cover the two matters on which the defendant relies, namely his friends in London and his mosque and cultural centre would, in my judgment, be unwarranted. The defendant said he did not want to leave London or to live in Luton, although he worked there, but it is clear that his preference for London and objection to Luton was based on those two considerations.

In my judgment it would be impossible to say that the room in Luton was not one in which he could live in reasonably comfortable conditions suitable to the style of life which he was leading in London, or that it did not provide him with the sort of conditions in which it was reasonable that he should live.'

In *Macdonnell v Daly*[66] it was held that the offer (by a landlord) of part of the tenant's existing accommodation was not *on the facts* 'suitable alternative accommodation', but that does not rule out the possibility of such an offer being 'suitable' on other facts, particularly where the extra rooms are not used or are used mostly for storage. However, even if 'suitable' accommodation is offered, it must still be seen as 'reasonable' by the court to order possession (in this case – inevitably – outright possession): s 98(1)) The general question of 'reasonableness' and discretionary grounds for possession has already been addressed in relation to *Cumming v Danson*[67] and is equally applicable to the other Rent Act discretionary grounds (Rent Act 1977, Sch 15, Pt I). However, the issue is particularly acute in 'suitable alternative accommodation' cases where no issue of tenant 'default' arises, and where the ground exists largely to cater for landlords' convenience.

The issues are demonstrated well in the case of *Battlespring v Gates*[68]. Gates had resided in an unmodernised maisonette for 35 years. She had brought her family up there, and lived there with her husband, who had died. There was only one other flat in the same house, which was empty. The landlords had recently purchased the property, with the intention of renovating the premises for reselling with vacant possession. They offered the tenant accommodation at a pleasanter end of the same road, in a modernised flat at a lower rent.

The tenant refused to move, and the county court declined to make an order for possession, on the grounds that it would not be reasonable to do so, taking into account both the time she had lived there and the fact that the landlords had only bought the property one year beforehand, with the intention of obtaining vacant possession and reselling. The landlords appealed, on the principal grounds that the court should not have taken their intentions, and the recent character of their purchase, into account, or placed so much weight on the tenant's objections to moving.

The Court of Appeal dismissed the appeal holding that there was no basis for saying that the lower court had erred. Both types of questions were proper to be taken into account. As Watkins LJ stated:

'The learned and experienced county court judge in the present case seems to me to have had that guidance well in mind in coming to the conclusion which he did. He expressed his reasons for arriving at his decision finally in this lucid and brief way:

---

[66] [1969] 3 All ER 851.
[67] [1942] 2 All ER 653.
[68] *Battlespring v Gates* (1983) 11 HLR 6.

"I have decided not to make the order and I base my decision on the fact that here is a tenant who has occupied the accommodation for a very long time and a landlord who has only bought the property less than one year ago, and bought it, on the evidence, with the intention of obtaining vacant possession and re-selling it. Subject to any authorities which might have been pointed out to me, I feel that that would be an unreasonable order to make."

He had earlier referred to the personal situation and feelings of the defendant, for whom he obviously felt a great deal of sympathy.

I ask myself whether it is possible to say that the judge misdirected himself in the exercise of his discretion. In reviewing the exercise of a judge's discretion in this context, it is well to bear in mind what was said by Singleton LJ in the *Cresswell* case

"When there has been an appeal to this court on that question of reasonableness it has to be said time and time again that it is really a question of fact, and that unless the appellant can show that the judge has misdirected himself in some measure, this court cannot interfere, for the decision on that question is for the county court judge. It is for him to consider whether he thinks it reasonable to make an order."

Mr Acton-Davies submits that the judge in this case did not exercise his discretion properly; in the first place he took into account the fact that the plaintiffs were new landlords, whose only object was to make a quick profit upon the property in which the defendant now lives. That, he says, was wholly irrelevant and should not have been allowed to have influenced the judge's mind at all. If allowed to influence it, it was a factor to be used in favour of the plaintiffs, rather than against them.

Secondly, he contends that this really was a decision founded almost exclusively upon a sympathetic consideration of the defendant's objection to moving from a place which she had occupied for a very long time – the prospect of going to another and superior place notwithstanding.

Lastly he maintained that to make reference, as the judge did, to the fact that this was a recent acquisition by the plaintiffs of the relevant property, was yet another instance of his taking into account factors which should not have been allowed to influence him.

I regard the decision of the judge as the product of the exercise of a discretion which I cannot possibly fault. What in fact he did was, on the one hand, to consider the position of the plaintiffs, and properly to find that they were landlord who were simply interested in the property for the purpose of gain. There is, as he said, nothing wrong in that motive whatsoever, but that was precisely their position. It was quite unlike the situation of other landlords who seek orders for possession on the basis that they have either nowhere to live, or that the dwelling which they have at the moment is over-crowded.

Balanced against that was the personal position of this elderly defendant, which was among other things that she had occupied these premises for thirty-five years. It seems always to have been her home – all her memories are still there. I do not consider that a factor of that kind should not be allowed to influence the judge in coming to a conclusion as to whether or no it would be reasonable to turn her out – even though alternative, and suitable alternative accommodation (as he found) was available to her.'

## Grounds for possession

Many of the Rent Act grounds for possession (or 'cases' as they are referred to in the legislation) mirror those in the Housing Act 1988, and they will not be reproduced in full here. Again, the grounds divide into discretionary ones and mandatory ones, with the same implications already discussed. However, the different emphasis in the Rent Act 1977 is well demonstrated by the fact that the mandatory grounds *follow* the discretionary ones and are much more limited in scope than under the Housing Act 1988. In particular, there is no equivalent to Ground 8 (two months'; rent arrears) or Ground 6 (landlord redevelopment 'needs') in the Rent Act 1977. If a detailed examination of the Rent Act grounds is required, Sch 15 to the 1977 Act should be consulted; attention is given here only to those Rent Act grounds which differ significantly from their Housing Act counterparts.

### CASE 2: NUISANCE OR IMMORAL OR ILLEGAL PURPOSE

*Case 2*

Where the tenant or any person residing or lodging with him or any sub-tenant of his has been guilty of conduct which is a nuisance or annoyance to adjoining occupiers, or has been convicted of using the dwelling-house or allowing the dwelling-house to be used for immoral or illegal purposes.

This discretionary ground is considerably narrower in scope than the newly amended Ground 14 in the Housing Act 1988. The nuisance 'limb' extends only to 'adjoining occupiers' rather than to persons generally affected in the 'locality'. The illegality 'limb' does not extend to arrestable offences committed *in* the locality, nor even to arrestable offences per se, but only the use of the property for illegal purposes.

Indeed, the limitation of those relevantly affected by the nuisance to 'adjoining occupiers' might, on one construction, exclude even near neighbours whose property did not physically 'abut' or attach to the tenants'. Such a construction would severely limit the influence of the ground, and could lead to illogical results, such as that a person (say) 'next door but one' who was routinely 'abused' by the tenant could not in this context make his complaints felt. A wider interpretation of the phrase was, however, given in the Court of Appeal case of *Cobstone Investments Ltd v Maxim.*[69] In the words of Dunn LJ:

'This point has never previously been decided by the Court of Appeal. It is possible that that is because of a short passage in the present Vice-Chancellor's classic work, *Megarry The Rent Acts* 10th ed., (1967) p. 271,

---

[69]  [1984] 2 All ER 635.

although, as we know from the judgment of Judge Harold Brown in *Metropolitan Railway Land Corp v Burfitt* [1960] CLY 2749, it was certainly in the 8th edition which was published in 1955 and very likely earlier still. The passage states:

> "The word 'adjoining' has been construed as meaning 'contiguous', so that the occupants of a second floor flat have been held not to be 'adjoining occupiers' to the ground floor flat beneath them."

Then he cites the *Trustees of Marquess of Northampton Estate v Bond* (1949) 155 EG 412 continues:

> "But this seems too strict a view; for one meaning of the word is 'neighbouring' and all that the context seems to require is that the premises of the adjoining occupiers should be near enough to be affected by the tenant's conduct on the demised premises."

I accept that statement as an accurate statement of the law. The premises here, which were occupied by the complainants, were in the same building as that occupied by the defendant. They were sharing the common parts, including the common entrance, with the defendant, and in my judgment they were near enough to be affected by her conduct on the premises. And that was the view that was taken by the assistant recorder, who did not have the advantage of the citations from authority which we have had, but did have various textbooks cited to him; and he expressed the view: not only the occupiers within no. 12 upstairs, be they tenants or other persons lawfully on the premises, were adjoining within the meaning and spirit of Case 2 of Schedule 15 to the Rent Act 1977 but also the occupiers of flat 3 in no. 11 were adjoining.'

The difficulties posed by the need (concerning the illegality 'limb') to establish that the *dwelling-house* had been *used* for an illegal purpose were dealt with in the case of *Abrahams v Wilson*[70] where a tenant who had been convicted of possession of cannabis found on the premises she rented had later been sued for possession by her landlord. The county court judge refused to grant possession, and in this was supported by the Court of Appeal. In rejecting the landlord's appeal the court found that there must be a close causal relationship between the criminal conviction and a *use* of the premises involved (applying *S Schneiders Ltd v Abrahams*[71]) Edmund Davies LJ stated (at p. 1116):

> 'But, having said that the certificate of conviction itself makes no reference to any particular premises, it emerges from a series of cases that this fact does not prevent the circumstances which led to the conviction from being adduced in evidence. The matter was dealt with at length by this court in *S Schneiders and Sons Ltd v Abrahams*, which was a case where a tenant had been convicted under the Larceny Act of receiving at the demised premises certain property, well knowing it to have been stolen. The place where the act of receiving occurs is in general of no materiality in law; but there it was held that the tenant, having made use of the premises in order to commit that

[70] [1971] 2 All ER 1114.
[71] [1925] 1 KB 301.

crime, must be regarded as having been convicted of 'using' the premises for an illegal purpose within the meaning of the statutory provision then applicable, namely, section 4 of the Rent and Mortgage Interest Restrictions Act 1923. But there must be some link between the criminal conviction and the premises which are the subject-matter of the proceedings for possession, and the test applied by Bankes LJ is one which I would respectfully adopt for the purposes of the present case. Bankes LJ said at p. 306:

> "I reject the argument that the section includes only offences in which use of the premises is an essential element. But I think it is necessary to show that the tenant has taken advantage of his tenancy of the premises and of the opportunity they afford for committing the offence. In this view the tenant who uses the demised premises as a coiner's den, or as a deposit for stolen goods, and is convicted of counterfeiting coin or receiving goods, would be 'convicted of using the premises for an … illegal purpose' within the meaning of section 4."

Scrutton LJ applied this test, at p. 309;

> "Were the words meant to have their strict meaning or were they meant to cover all cases where a tenant is convicted of a crime and had used the premises to facilitate the commission of it?"

He later said, at p. 310:

> "Giving the case the best consideration I can, I come to the conclusion that the conviction need not be for using the premises for one or another immoral or illegal purpose, and that it is enough if there is a conviction of a crime which has been committed on the premises and for the purpose of committing which the premises have been used; but that it is not enough that the tenant has been convicted of a crime with which the premises have nothing to do beyond merely being the scene of its commission."

Applying that test to the present case, I for my part would put it in this way: In proper and clear circumstances – which must be established, of course, by the landlord – a conviction of using premises for an illegal purpose, within the meaning of Case 2, can be established by proof that in the demised premises a quantity of cannabis resin was found. One must, however, look at the circumstances very carefully before an isolated finding on a single occasion is held to constitute proof of such user. The evidence produced in the civil proceedings was very unsatisfactory regarding what transpired at the criminal trial and I am not prepared to hold that user was established. But, even if it were, my conclusion in relation to Case 2 must ultimately turn upon the overriding requirement, imposed by section 10 of the Act, that no order for possession may be made by the court (even though the circumstances are such as to bring the matter clearly within any other of the Cases set out in Part I of Schedule 3) 'unless the court considers it reasonable to make the order.'

## CASE 9: LANDLORD REQUIRES THE PROPERTY AS A RESIDENCE

*Case 9*

Where the dwelling-house is reasonably required by the landlord for occupation as a residence for—

(a)  himself, or
(b)  any son or daughter of his over 18 years of age, or
(c)  his father or mother, or
(d)  if the dwelling-house is let on or subject to a regulated tenancy, the father or mother of his wife or husband,

and the landlord did not become landlord by purchasing the dwelling-house or any interest therein after [certain specified dates].

This needs to be seen in the light of Sch 15, Pt III, para 1, which states:

'A court shall not make an order for possession of a dwelling-house by reason only that the circumstances of the case fall within Case 9 in Part I of this Schedule if the court is satisfied that, having regard to all the circumstances of the case, including the question whether other accommodation is available for the landlord or the tenant, greater hardship would be caused by granting the order than by refusing to grant it.'

This ground (unlike Ground 1(b) of Sch 2, the nearest Housing Act equivalent) is discretionary, but quite apart from the consequent *general* landlord need to demonstrate that is 'reasonable' to grant possession, Pt III of Sch 15 contains a specific 'balance of inconvenience' test. This inevitably requires a court to engage in difficult (and delicate) 'balancing acts' between the claims of parties both of which may be meritorious. It seems likely that in a marginal case a court will tend to come down in a landlord's favour and the breadth of the discretion vested in a court of first instance indicates that future appeals will only rarely succeed. As Croom-Johnson LJ stated in *Manaton v Edwards*[72].

'When one comes to consider the issue of greater hardship, this court cannot merely upset the decision of the county court judge or recorder simply because it might have come to a different conclusion itself.'

However the case is, in itself, one of those unusual instances where the first instance decision *was* overturned, primarily because the recorder had failed to recognise that there was in such cases a primary evidential burden on the tenant to establish a significant degree of hardship should possession be granted.

### CASE 11: RETURNING OWNER-OCCUPIER

*Case 11*

Where a person (in this Case referred to as 'the owner-occupier') who let the dwelling-house on a regulated tenancy had, at any time before the letting, occupied it as his residence and—

(a)  not later than the relevant date the landlord gave notice in writing to the tenant that possession might be recovered under this Case, and
(b)  the dwelling-house has not [since certain specified dates] been let by the owner-occupier on a protected tenancy with respect to which the condition mentioned in paragraph (a) above was not satisfied, and
(c)  the court is of the opinion that of the conditions set out in Part V of this Schedule one of those in paragraphs (a) and (c) to (f) is satisfied.

---

[72]  (1985) 18 HLR 116 at 121.

The conditions mentioned in (c) above are:

(a)    that the dwelling-house is required as a residence for the owner or any member of his family who resided with him when he last occupied it as a residence; or

(b)    the owner has retired from regular employment and requires the dwelling-house as a residence;

(c)    that the owner has died and the dwelling-house is required as a residence for a member of his family who was residing with him at the time of his death; or

(d)    that the owner has died and the dwelling-house is required by a successor in title as his residence or for the purpose of sale with vacant possession; or

(e)    the dwelling-house is subject to a mortgage, made by deed and granted before the tenancy, and the mortgagee:

(i) is entitled to exercise a power of sale conferred on him by s 101 of the Law of Property Act 1925, and

(ii) requires the dwelling-house for the purpose of disposing of it with vacant possession in exercise of that power; and

(f)    the dwelling-house is not reasonably suitable to the needs of the owner, having regard to his place of work, and he requires it for the purpose of disposing of it with vacant possession and of using the proceeds of that disposal in acquiring, as his residence, a dwelling-house which is more suitable to those needs.

In the 1988 Act, Ground 1(a) of Sch 2 also protects the position of an owner-occupier. The crucial difference is that the landlord in such a case need give no reason(s) for seeking possession – his or her previous occupancy already limits the long-term security of the tenant. Again, the apparent requirement of prior notice for Case 11 to be effective is limited in practice by the power of the court to ignore both the relevant dates and the requirement of prior notice if it is deemed 'just and equitable' for possession to be granted. The history of Case 11 has not been free of difficulty. For example, in *Pocock v Steel*[73], the Court of Appeal ruled that the case could not operate unless the landlord had been in occupation immediately prior to the letting in question (not easy to achieve where absentee owners let through agents). This decision was swiftly reversed in the Rent (Amendment) Act 1985.

## Common law tenancies

Tenancies falling outside the statutory schemes of the Housing Act 1988 and the Rent Act 1977 do not provide for security of tenure. However, the Protection from Eviction Act 1977 does at least allow for a measure of procedural protection, requiring landlords seeking possession to serve notices to quit in specified forms, containing specified information and of specified duration. Moreover, court orders are generally required before repossession by a landlord can be obtained (even if no grounds for possession as such need to be shown). The relevant provisions (ss 3 and 5) of the 1977 Act have already been cited. Tenancies coming into force on or after the commencement date of Pt I of the Housing Act 1988 (15 January 1989) are excluded from the above protection in a number of prescribed circumstances, most

---

[73]    [1985] 1 WLR 229.

importantly holiday lets and where the tenant shares any accommodation with the landlord (s 3A). However, a well-advised landlord should still have in mind the inherent *common law* need to serve a notice to quit to terminate a periodic tenancy (the length of which should correspond to the period of the tenancy), and that even if not legally required to go through the courts in order to recover possession it may be advisable to obtain an order given the risks attached to forcible eviction.

In *Haniff v Robinson*[74], Woolf LJ (as he then was) stated that the object of s 3 was to provide protection for a tenant until execution of a warrant for possession by court bailiffs. Therefore, even after a possession order has been granted a landlord had no right to resort to self-help to recover possession.

## RENT CONTROL

It is here that the differences between the 1977 and the 1988 Acts are at their most stark. The guiding principle of the 1977 Rent Act is rent *control* via a system of rent officer investigation and regulation. The perception that this had had the effect of 'choking off' the supply of private rented accommodation was a principal driving force behind the 1988 Act. Little direct rent control exists for assured and assured shorthold tenancies, although residual regulation by Rent Assessment Committees does survive. Common law tenancies are, of course, wholly market driven as regards rents.

## Assured tenancies

The relevant sections of the 1988 Act are ss 13 and 14.

*Rent and other terms*

**13.    Increases of rent under assured periodic tenancies**

(1) This section applies to—

(a) a statutory periodic tenancy other than one which, by virtue of paragraph 11 or paragraph 12 in Part I of Schedule 1 to this Act, cannot for the time being be an assured tenancy; and

(b) any other periodic tenancy which is an assured tenancy, other than one in relation to which there is a provision, for the time being binding on the tenant, under which the rent for a particular period of the tenancy will or may be greater than the rent for an earlier period.

(2) For the purpose of securing an increase in the rent under a tenancy to which this section applies, the landlord may serve on the tenant a notice in the prescribed form proposing a new rent to take effect at the beginning of a new period of the tenancy specified in the notice, being a period beginning not earlier than—

(a) the minimum period after the date of the service of the notice; and

(b) except in the case of a statutory periodic tenancy, the first anniversary of the date on which the first period of the tenancy began; and

(c) if the rent under the tenancy has previously been increased by virtue of a notice

---

[74]   (1992) 26 HLR 386.

under this subsection or a determination under section 14 below, the first anniversary of the date on which the increased rent took effect.

(3) The minimum period referred to in subsection (2) above is—

(a)  in the case of a yearly tenancy, six months;
(b)  in the case of a tenancy where the period is less than a month, one month; and
(c)  in any other case, a period equal to the period of the tenancy.

(4) Where a notice is served under subsection (2) above, a new rent specified in the notice shall take effect as mentioned in the notice unless, before the beginning of the new period specified in the notice,—

(a)  the tenant by an application in the prescribed form refers the notice to a rent assessment committee; or
(b)  the landlord and the tenant agree on a variation of the rent which is different from that proposed in the notice or agree that the rent should not be varied.

(5) Nothing in this section (or in section 14 below) affects the right of the landlord and the tenant under an assured tenancy to vary by agreement any term of the tenancy (including a term relating to rent).

## 14.   Determination of rent by rent assessment committee

(1) Where, under subsection 4(a) of section 13 above, a tenant refers to a rent assessment committee a notice under subsection (2) of that section, the committee shall determine the rent at which, subject to subsections (2) and (4) below, the committee consider that the dwelling-house concerned might reasonably be expected to be let in the open market by a willing landlord under an assured tenancy—

(a)  which is a periodic tenancy having the same periods as those of the tenancy to which the notice relates;
(b)  which begins at the beginning of the new period specified in the notice;
(c)  the terms of which (other than relating to the amount of the rent) are the same as those of the tenancy to which the notice relates; and
(d)  in respect of which the same notices, if any, have been given under any of Grounds 1 to 5 of Schedule 2 to this Act, as have been given (or have effect as if given) in relation to the tenancy to which the notice relates.

(2) In making a determination under this section, there shall be disregarded—

(a)  any effect on the rent attributable to the granting of a tenancy to a sitting tenant;
(b)  any increase in the value of the dwelling-house attributable to a relevant improvement carried out by a person who at the time it was carried out was the tenant, if the improvement—
    (i)  was carried out otherwise than in pursuance of an obligation to his immediate landlord, or
    (ii) was carried out pursuant to an obligation to his immediate landlord being an obligation which did not relate to the specific improvement concerned but arose by reference to consent given to the carrying out of that improvement; and
(c)  any reduction in the value of the dwelling-house attributable to a failure by the tenant to comply with any terms of the tenancy.

   …

Section 13 (broadly) governs the mechanisms underlying rent increases under assured tenancies. Section 14 (broadly) governs the degree to which rent increases can be 'pegged' and/or rents reduced. In reality, the Rent Assessment Committee's (RAC's) powers are very limited; even if they do have power to intervene, they are confined to bringing the rent into line with the market if it is self-evidently excessive (s 14(1)). However, it is doubtful whether most assured tenancy agreements will let the RAC 'in'. Section 13(1)(b) exempts from scrutiny any assured tenancy containing a 'rent review' clause. It can be assumed that most will contain such a clause. Further, even where no such clause exists a landlord and tenant may subsequently agree that the rent shall be increased completely outside the complex scheme of notice of rent increases and RAC scrutiny apparently provided for by s 13. Lastly, it is clear that any powers the RAC may have apply only to proposed rent increases – the original contract rent is not open to external alteration.

However, the Court of Appeal held in *Bankway Properties Ltd v Penfold-Dunsford and Leech*[75] that a clause allowing for grossly excessive rent increases could be ruled invalid as unfair.

In February 1994 the claimant's predecessor in title granted the defendants an assured tenancy of a flat – initially for a 12-month fixed term (15 February 1994 to 16 February 1995) at a rent of £4,680 a year. Clause 8(b) of the tenancy agreement allowed for rent to be increased initially (from 15 February 1995) by 10 per cent but then from 11 February 1996 to £25,000 a year (!). This term was drawn to the defendant's attention by the landlord before they took up occupation, although they later claimed that they had signed without properly reading it, or seeking legal advice. In fact the rent was not increased in February 1995 or 1996, but in January 1997 clause 8(b) was varied, so as to allow rent to be increased to £25,000 at five weeks' notice. In June 1998, the claimants acquired the landlord's interest in the flat, and in March 2000 served notice on the defendants that rent would be increased to £25,000 a year. The defendants, unsurprisingly, were unable to pay this, and in May 2000 the claimants commenced proceedings for possession based on rent arrears.

Overturning the decision at first instance, the Court of Appeal held that clause 8(b) was a transparent device to enable landlords to avoid the statutory restrictions on repossession against assured tenants and amounted to an unlawful 'contracting out' of the statutory scheme. It would, therefore, not be given legal effect.

Arden LJ stated:

> 'Miss Padley for the respondent submits that this was not a case of contracting out of the Act of 1988. The appellants here have the protection of an assured tenancy. She distinguishes *Street v Mountford* [1985] 1 AC 809. Miss Padley submits that the parties are not limited in their freedom to agree rents. Section 13 of the Act of 1988 is excluded where parties had contracted for a particular rent. Because clause 8(b)(iii) limited the rent to £25,000, the relevant provisions of the Act of 1988 applied. Assured tenancies could cease to be such if the rent went above £25,000, or if for some other reason they cease to qualify under the Act of 1988.
>
> Miss Padley submits that clause 8(b)(iii) was not a pretence. This was not a lease pretending to be licence. It was not the intention of both parties to enter into a transaction to mislead a third party, as required by the test of "sham" to be found in *Snook*. An example of a lease which was a sham on this basis and of no effect was the lease in *Bhopal v Walia* (1999) L & TR 460, where the

---

[75]  [2001] EWCA Civ 528, [2002] HLR 795.

landlord and tenant (acting at the landlord's request) entered into a written tenancy agreement which had been backdated and falsely showed the rent to be more than it in fact was. The reason why the agreement was executed was to enable the landlord to show it to his bank. By contrast the agreement in this case was a genuine agreement.

If, however, clause 8(b)(iii) is not in substance or reality a provision for the fixing of rent, but a provision to enable the landlord to recover possession otherwise than in accordance with the mandatory scheme, either because the tenant voluntarily surrenders possession when asked to pay a sum purporting to be but not in fact rent or because it facilitates the landlord relying on a mandatory ground for possession when in truth he is not entitled to do so, then, in my judgment, the provision amounts to a contracting out of the statutory scheme for assured tenancies and is not enforceable. The statutory scheme does not provide a mandatory ground for a possession order for non-payment of rent unless the rent is properly due as such.

The question whether a document is a sham or a pretence or in substance an unlawful contracting out or evasion of an Act of Parliament is a pure question of fact. As regards the evidence, the judge in effect confined himself to the agreement and did not consider the surrounding circumstances, including subsequent conduct. In this regard in my judgment he fell into error for, as I have explained, all such evidence is relevant to the question of sham, pretence or whether in substance there was an unlawful contracting out of the Act of 1988. I must therefore consider whether, in the light of the evidence as to the surrounding circumstances, the appropriate conclusion which the judge should have reached was that the agreement was in substance an unlawful contracting out of the Act of 1988.

As I see it, the effect of the Act of 1988 is that where a tenant is in a position to pay the sum genuinely reserved as rent at the time provided in the tenancy agreement or at such later date as Parliament allows, he should be free to do so and not lose possession. In my judgment the effect of this agreement is that the tenant is prevented from paying the genuine rent by a provision for payment of a sum which was never expected to be paid and which is not on its true analysis rent at all. That provision in my judgment offends against the mandatory scheme of the Act of 1988 and is unenforceable. I differ from the judge in that in my judgment this device (as he fairly called it) is not permissible.'

Pill LJ approached the matter slightly differently, whilst coming to the same conclusion:

'I do have difficulty with the concept, which has featured in the proceedings, that there was an unlawful contracting out of the 1988 Act when the parties were free to contract out of it. They could have entered into a shorthold assured tenancy, which did not confer security of tenure, without contravening the Act. They were free to agree the level of rent. The scheme of the Act, as I understand it, was not a mandatory scheme for tenancies such as gave rise to the concept of unlawful contracting out in its usual form.

[However] the intention of clause 8(b)(iii) is in my judgment inconsistent with the statutory purpose which it was the main object of the agreement to achieve. In *Glynn* at page 357 Lord Halsbury stated:

> "Looking at the whole of the instrument, and seeing what one must regard,… as its main purpose, one must reject words, indeed whole provisions, if they are inconsistent with what one assumes to be the main purpose of the contract."

In *Antoniades* Lord Bridge, at page 454, also acknowledged the concept of a clause in a lease being rejected as "repugnant to the true purpose of the agreement", though he did so in the context of what he regarded as an attempt to deceive by making a lease appear to be a licence.

A clause purporting to allow for an increase of rent to £25,000 is inconsistent with and repugnant to the statutory purpose which, in the circumstances, in incorporated into the agreement. To permit the enforcement of clause 8(b)(iii) would be to defeat the main purpose of the agreement. The landlords cannot defeat that purpose by reliance on clause 8(b)(iii). The clause is inconsistent with the "main object and intent of the agreement and must be ignored".'

Another approach to such a clause which might be adopted in future cases is to view the clause as an unfair contract term[76].

## Assured shorthold tenancies

Prior to the implementation of the 1988 Act much was made of the 'choice' supposedly existing for landlords and tenants between assured tenancies (which provided for a measure of security of tenure, but at market rents) and assured shorthold tenancies (which gave no long-term security but were subject to a measure of rent control). The reality is that while assured shorthold tenancies do contain a little more in the way of real rent review than do assured tenancies, the degree of regulation falls far short of genuine rent control. Moreover, tenant insecurity means that the likelihood of most assured shorthold tenants challenging their rents is small. The relevant 1988 Act provision is s 22.

**22. Reference of excessive rents to rent assessment committee**

(1) Subject to section 23 and subsection (2) below, the tenant under an assured shorthold tenancy in respect of which a notice was served as mentioned in section 20(2) above may make an application in the prescribed form to a rent assessment committee for a determination of the rent which, in the committee's opinion, the landlord might reasonably be expected to obtain under the assured shorthold tenancy.

(2) No application may be made under this section if—

(a)   the rent payable under the tenancy is a rent previously determined under this section; or

(aa) the tenancy is one to which section 19A above applied and more than six months

---

[76] Particularly in relation to the Unfair Terms in Consumer Contracts Regulations SI 1999/2083. In *Bankway* there was some doubt about whether the 1994 version of these regulations applied because of the tenancy agreement having been entered into prior to 1 July 1995.

have elapsed since the beginning of the tenancy or, in the case of a replacement tenancy, since the beginning of the original tenancy; or

(b) the tenancy is an assured shorthold tenancy falling within subsection (4) of section 20 above (and, accordingly, is one in respect of which notice need not have been served as mentioned in subsection (2) of that section).

(3) Where an application is made to a rent assessment committee under subsection (1) above with respect to the rent under an assured shorthold tenancy, the committee shall not make such a determination as is referred to in that subsection unless they consider—

(a) that there is a sufficient number of similar dwelling-houses in the locality let on assured tenancies (whether shorthold or not); and

(b) that the rent payable under the assured shorthold tenancy in question is significantly higher than the rent which the landlord might reasonably be expected to be able to obtain under the tenancy, having regard to the level of rents payable under the tenancies referred to in paragraph (a) above.

(4) Where, on an application under this section, a rent assessment committee make a determination of a rent for an assured shorthold tenancy—

(a) the determination shall have effect from such date as the committee may direct, not being earlier than the date of the application;

(b) if, at any time on or after the determination takes effect, the rent which, apart from this paragraph, would be payable under the tenancy exceeds the rent so determined, the excess shall be irrecoverable from the tenant; and

(c) no notice may be served under section 13(2) above with respect to a tenancy of the dwelling-house in question until after the first anniversary of the date on which the determination takes effect.

(5) Subsections (4), (5) and (8) of section 14 above apply in relation to a determination of rent under this section as they apply in relation to a determination under that section and, accordingly, where subsection (5) of that section applies, any reference in subsection (4)(b) above to rent is a reference to rent exclusive of the amount attributable to rates.

Unlike the position concerning assured tenancies, the tenant can make direct application to the RAC contending that the rent is 'excessive'. However, the RAC's powers are confined (in effect) to determining whether the rent in question significantly exceeds the local market 'norm' (s 22(3)(b)). Issues as to whether rent levels generally in the area are 'excessive' are outside the RAC's powers. Moreover, such an application can be made only once by the tenant (s 22(2)(a)), and can be made only during the initial fixed term of the tenancy (s 22(2)(b)). In the (likely to be rare) instance of an RAC reducing an assured shorthold tenancy's rent they have a wide discretion to decide the date from which the new rent commences, and consequently what degree of 'overpayment' by the tenant there has been (s 22(4)). Lastly, if the tenant leaves, the 'assured' rent ceases to bind the landlord who can agree such new rent as he chooses with the incoming tenant (unlike the position under the Rent Acts – below).

For assured shortholds coming into force after 28 February 1997, in line with the new s 19A, ss 22 is amended by s 100 of the Housing Act 1996 as follows:

100. (1) Section 22 of the Housing Act 1988 (reference of excessive rents to rent assessment committee) shall be amended as follows.

(2) In subsection (2) (circumstances in which no application under the section may be made) after paragraph (a) there shall be inserted—

'(aa) the tenancy is one to which section 19A above applies and more than six months have elapsed since the beginning of the tenancy or, in the case of a replacement tenancy, since the beginning of the original tenancy; or'.

(3) At the end there shall be inserted—

'(6) In subsection (2)(aa) above, the references to the original tenancy and to a replacement tenancy shall be construed in accordance with subsections (6) and (7) respectively of section 21 above.'

In part this is a 'tidying up' provision made necessary by the fact that assured shortholds (post-28 February 1997) can be periodic as well as fixed-term. However, given that many fixed-term assured shortholds were for periods longer than the six month minimum, it further restricts tenants' rights to apply to RACs by confining such rights to six months, rather than the period of the original fixed term.

## Rent Act tenancies

As their name would suggest, here true rent control is to be found. Either party to a protected or statutory tenancy can apply to a rent officer for a fair rent to be registered on the property. The rent ultimately registered by the rent officer binds not just the parties themselves, but future tenants within the registration period (typically two years unless both parties otherwise agree or there has been a change in the condition of the premises (ss 67(3) and (4), Rent Act 1977).

As to how a 'fair rent' is to be assessed, much discretion is left to the rent officer, under s 70 of the 1977 Act.

70.   **Determination of fair rent**

(1) In determining, for the purposes of this Part of this Act, what rent is or would be a fair rent under a regulated tenancy of a dwelling-house, regard shall be had to all the circumstances (other than personal circumstances) and in particular to—

(a)   the age, character, locality and state of repair of the dwelling-house, and
(b)   if any furniture is provided for use under the tenancy, the quantity, quality and condition of the furniture, and
(c)   any premium or sum in the nature of a premium which has been or may be lawfully required or received on the grant, renewal, continuance or assignment of the tenancy.

(2) For the purposes of the determination it shall be assumed that the number of persons seeking to become tenants of similar dwelling-houses in the locality on the terms (other than those relating to rent) of the regulated tenancy is not substantially greater than the number of such dwelling-houses in the locality which are available for letting on such terms.

Some points are clear – primarily that it is the particular property, good or bad, that should be considered, even if assistance is derived from other rents in the locality (s 70(1)). However, the 'essence' of the section is s 70(2) which instructs the rent officer to ignore 'scarcity value'. Traditionally this had the effect of driving down fair rent determinations to significantly below typical 'market' rents in the locality. However, more recently there has been pressure from landlords to persuade rent officers to refocus their approach, based on the fact that most new rents would be market rents, and the (supposed) fact that scarcity conditions now no longer apply in most parts of the country. The issues have been authoritatively considered by the House of Lords in *R v Secretary of State for the Environment, Transport and the Regions, ex p Spath Holme Ltd*[77].

What might be termed the '*Spath Holme* saga' had a long history. Initially the property company challenged RAC determinations on a number of flats they owned and let, primarily on the basis that the committee had erred in law in failing to take the 'going rate' for assured tenancies into the equation. In essence the Court of Appeal agreed with Spath Holme[78], and stated explicitly that in the absence of any quantifiable scarcity of housing to rent, a 'fair' rent fixed by the rent officer under the Rent Act 1977 should equal a market rent. Subsequently, in *Curtis v London Rent Assessment Committee*[79] the Court of Appeal went further and ruled that, in a deregulated market, the best evidence of a fair rent would normally be rent obtained under assured and assured shorthold tenancies[80]. Subsequently legislation was introduced with the clear intention of curbing the impact of the potentially substantial fair rent increases which adoption of the above approach might produce[81]. In essence the relevant order limits the maximum rent increase to RPI plus 10 per cent on a first re-registration and limits subsequent increase to RPI plus 5 per cent. Spath Holme then brought an action claiming that the new order was ultra vires in that the legislative source of the power to make the order, s 31 of the Landlord and Tenant Act 1985, was limited to measures aimed at controlling inflation.

The Court of Appeal agreed, but the House of Lords reversed the Court of Appeal and confirmed the vires of the order. In doing so extensive comment was made on the history and scope of the relevant Rent Act provisions as well.

Lord Bingham stated:

'During the last century England and Wales suffered from a persistent shortage of housing. The demand, in particular for private rented accommodation, was greater than the supply. This enabled some private landlords to exploit the scarcity of what they had to let by exacting exorbitant rents and letting on terms disadvantageous to the tenant. A series of statutes, beginning in 1915, sought to address this problem, by controlling the rents which could be charged and affording security of tenure to tenants. This control, beneficial though it was in many ways, tended by its very effectiveness to exacerbate the problem: the financial return to the landlord was at times so modest that there was very little incentive to let accommodation to private tenants, with the result that the supply of accommodation available for private letting tended to shrink. Thus statutes were passed with the object of giving landlords a return sufficient to induce them to make accommodation available.

The Rent Act 1965 was intended to revitalise the market in privately rented accommodation by introducing a new regime of what were called fair rents.

---

[77]  (2001) 33 HLR 301.
[78]  *Spath Holme Ltd v Chairman of the Greater Manchester and Lancashire Rent Assessment Committee* (1995) 28 HLR 107. This decision was discussed extensively in the previous edition of this book.
[79]  [1997] 4 All ER 842.
[80]  On all the above see C Rogers, 'Fair Rents and the Market: Judicial Approaches to Rent Control Legislation' [1999] 63 Conv 201.
[81]  Rent Acts (Maximum Fair Rent) Order 1999 (SI 1999/6).

These provisions were consolidated in the Rent Act 1968, extended in the Rent Act 1974 and consolidated in the Rent Act 1977, which remains in force. Section 70 of that Act governs the assessment of fair rents, which are to be open market rents adjusted to discount for scarcity and to disregard certain matters specified in section 70(3). While the statute does not in terms refer to open market rents, that has been held by the Court of Appeal to be the proper starting point in the process of assessing and registering a fair rent under the 1977 Act: see *Spath Holme Ltd v Chairman of the Greater Manchester and Lancashire Rent Assessment Committee* (1995) 28 HLR 107, *Curtis v London Rent Assessment Committee,* above.

In giving effect to this statutory regime, rent officers and rent assessment committees faced the practical difficulty that there was no open market in unregulated privately-rented property with which comparison could be made. The years following 1965 were also years of very high inflation. The result was that rents set by rent officers and rent assessment committees did not keep up with inflation, to the benefit of tenants but to the obvious disadvantage of landlords. So the problem which Parliament had sought to address in 1965 once more became acute, and the market in privately-rented accommodation declined. By the Housing Act 1988 it was again sought to stimulate a free market in such accommodation by providing for assured and assured shorthold tenancies, which (subject to a limited safeguard for some tenants) provided for rents to be negotiated and agreed between landlord and tenant. Regulated tenancies under the Rent Act 1977 continued to exist, but no new regulated tenancies were to come into existence.

The 1988 Act had its desired effect of tempting private landlords back into the market. But it also had another effect, important for present purposes, of giving rise to rents negotiated between landlord and tenant in the market. Whereas rent officers and rent assessment committees had previously relied on other registered fair rents as the basis of comparison when setting new fair rents, there was now available a range of comparators, drawn from the market, on which they could rely (subject to making the adjustments required by statute) instead of the less factual basis of previously registered fair rents. In most areas, rent officers and rent assessment committees took advantage of this new basis of comparison in undertaking their statutory task, but in some areas (notably London and the North West) they were reluctant to do so. In these areas the gap between registered fair rents and open market rents increased, to the point where the former were at a level about half the latter, even in the absence of scarcity. In the two judgments already mentioned the Court of Appeal clearly laid down the correct approach to the assessing of fair rents, and at last even the rent officers and rent assessment committees who had previously been reluctant to do so gave effect to the basis of assessment prescribed by the 1977 Act. This had the unfortunate side-effect that tenants whose rents had previously been registered at levels well below the adjusted open market level at which they should have been set suffered very sharp and unexpected increases in the rent payable.

...

The 1985 Act did not itself repeal any earlier statutory provision. It was, however, one of three consolidating statutes passed in that year in the housing field, and the repeals, consequential amendments, transitional matters and savings in connection with each of the three were contained in a fourth Act, the Housing (Consequential Provisions) Act 1985, which provided for repeal of the whole of the Housing Rents and Subsidies Act 1975 ("the 1975 Act"). While the propriety of referring to the provision consolidated in section 31 was in issue between the parties to this appeal, it was accepted that the provision which section 31 consolidated was section 11 of the 1975 Act. This section was preceded by a heading "Rent – general power" and carried a sidenote "Reserve power to limit rents". It provided in full:

"(1) An order may provide for restricting or preventing increases of rent for dwellings which would otherwise take place, or for restricting the amount of rent which would otherwise be payable on new lettings of dwellings.

(2) The supplemental and incidental provisions that may be made by an order under this section may include provisions excluding, adapting or modifying any provision contained in or having effect under any Act which relates to rent (including this Act and any Act passed after it), and in particular provisions for the recovery of overpaid rent.

(3) An order under this section shall be subject to annulment in pursuance of a resolution of either House of Parliament.

(4) Upon the coming into force of this subsection, the power to make orders under section 11 of the Counter-Inflation Act 1973 (general power to make orders restricting or preventing increases of rent) shall cease to include power to make orders relating to rent for dwellings; but the coming into force of this subsection shall not affect the validity of anything done, whether before or after the coming into force of this subsection, by virtue of any order under the said section 11.

(5) The Counter-Inflation (Private Sector Residential Rents) (England and Wales) Order 1974 and the Counter-Inflation (Private Sector Residential Rents) (England and Wales) No 2 Order 1974 are revoked, and the standstill period under the first order (which was extended by Article 3 of the second order) shall terminate on the coming into force of this subsection."

This section, as its terms made plain, replaced the power previously conferred by section 11 of the Counter-Inflation Act 1973, which itself replaced the power conferred by section 2(4) of the Counter-Inflation (Temporary Provisions) Act 1972. This context, as Mr Bonney submitted and the Court of Appeal accepted, showed that the power in section 11 of the 1975 Act, and therefore section 31 of the 1985 Act, was conferred, and conferred only, to enable the minister to restrict rents where such represented a significant cause of general inflation. This was the foundation of Mr Bonney's central argument that the Order was ultra vires, since the ministers in making it were not seeking to curb general inflation in the national economy.

It is a matter of historical record that in the early and mid-1970s excessive inflation in the national economy was recognised as a major threat to the economic health and social cohesion of the nation. The Acts of 1972 and 1973 to which I have referred were passed to counter that threat, and I think it plain from the terms of section 11 of the 1975 Act that it conferred a power to restrict rents where such represented a significant cause of general inflation. The more difficult, and for present purposes more crucial, question is whether that was the only purpose for which the section 11 power could be lawfully exercised. A number of considerations lead me to conclude that the power could in appropriate circumstances be used for other purposes as well: ...'

All this raises the question of whether a substantive distinction between a fair rent and a market rent is likely to disappear, or, indeed, is in the process of disappearing. The recent DETR (Department of the Environment, Transport, and the Regions) Consultation Paper (May 1998) shows that between April and September 1997 increases made by rent officers were more than five percentage points higher than the increase in the retail price index (RPI) in over 86 per cent of cases. Where cases were appealed to RACs, over half of the rents were further increased, by an average of 18 per cent. It is highly significant that most of the recent landlord appeals against fair rent registrations have been in London, where (broadly) the private rented sector is thriving and scarcity levels are relatively low. The DETR in the 1998 Consultation Paper recognised that most tenants could never have anticipated increases of the magnitude currently taking place under the fair rent system. The Paper proposed using a power contained in s 31 of the Landlord and Tenant Act 1985 to limit fair rent increases, by linking increases to the increase in the retail price index (the RPI then functioning as an index of 'affordability'). Specifically, for the first re-registration the maximum rent increase should be limited to RPI plus 10 per cent, and subsequently should be no more than RPI plus 5 per cent. This proposal was implemented by the Rent Acts (Maximum Fair Rent) Order 1999 discussed above. The effect of the 1999 Order is, of course, to limit the impact of an approach based on assured and assured shorthold tenancy 'comparables'. However, the inherent approach taken by the Court of Appeal in the earlier *Spath Holme* case and in *Curtis* was approved by the House of Lords in the later *Spath Holme* decision and it seems inevitable that over the next few years the gap between the diminishing number of 'fair' rents and post-1989 'market' rents will steadily diminish.

Although a detailed treatment of housing benefit is outside the scope of this book, it should be noted that the maximum rent payable (or 'eligible rent') is pegged to a rent ceiling based partly on size but also on maximum rent criteria (Housing Benefit (General) Regulations 1987 (SI 1987/1071), reg 11, as amended. In general it can be assumed that unless the size criteria are exceeded a fair rent, even a substantially increased fair rent, will be under the appropriate 'local reference rent' ceiling. Indeed, since all such rent determinations for housing benefit purposes are themselves made by rent officers, any other result would seem wholly anomalous (for rent officer powers and duties, see Housing Benefit (General) Regulations 1987, reg 12A and the Rent Officer (Additional Functions) Order 1995). If the tenant has been claiming housing benefit since before 1 January 1996, the unamended form of reg 11 specifically provides for registered (fair) rents being recoverable unless size criteria are exceeded. Nevertheless, a tenant who is in receipt of maximum housing benefit because he or she is unemployed may find it difficult to afford the rent (given current levels of fair rent increases) if he or she finds *some* work with consequent reduction in, or loss of, housing benefit.

## SUCCESSION

In 1982, Honoré wrote[82] that protective legislation attempted to 'provide those who cannot afford to buy their own homes with a substitute for home ownership, a right to remain in occupation for at least a lifetime, and often more'. Certainly the Rent Acts, at that time, provided that statutory tenancies passed, on death, to spouses or other 'family' members and that this right to 'succeed' could apply, in many cases, even on the death of the first 'successor'. In effect this injected into the private rented sector the concept of the 'family home', providing security equivalent to the tenant's for members of the tenant's family at the time they were most vulnerable (after the tenant's death). However, even then the extent to which this wholly equated with 'home ownership' is debatable. For example, as discussed above, a statutory tenancy is maintained only *during* the tenant's lifetime if the tenant occupies the property as his or her residence (Rent Act 1977, s 2(1)(a)). So, however understandable the desire of a statutory tenant to assign his or her statutory tenancy to one or more of the members of his or her family during the tenant's lifetime, this was not, per se, allowed for in the legislation (although the sub-text of a case like *Brickfield v Hughes* is perhaps of a court's liberality in practice to such a desire). Secondly, although a statutory tenant has security of tenure vis-à-vis his or her landlord, this does not necessarily mean security of tenure vis-à-vis the particular property, since s 98(1)(a) of the Rent Act 1977 provides that a landlord *may* be able to recover possession of property A, if willing to offer a suitable alternative property B to the tenant. Of course the longer the property had been the tenant's home the more unreasonable it *might* seem to seek eviction (see *Battle-spring v Gates*, above).

Whatever the original status of a Rent Act statutory tenancy as a true 'home' of the tenant and his or her family, the Housing Act 1988 significantly eroded it for many Rent Act tenants and substituted a much more limited right of succession in relation to statutory tenancies.

### Assured tenancies

The 'core' provision is s 17 of the Housing Act 1988:

17.  **Succession to assured periodic tenancy by spouse**

(1) In any case where—

(a)  the sole tenant under an assured periodic tenancy dies, and

(b)  immediately before the death, the tenant's spouse was occupying the dwelling-house as his or her only or principal home, and

(c)  the tenant was not himself a successor, as defined in subsection (2) or subsection (3) below,

---

[82]  *The Quest for Security: Employees, tenants, wives* (1982) Stevens, p. 37.

then, on the death, the tenancy vests by virtue of this section in the spouse (and, accordingly, does not devolve under the tenant's will or intestacy).

(2) For the purposes of this section, a tenant is a successor in relation to a tenancy if—

(a) the tenancy became vested in him either by virtue of this section or under the will or intestacy of a previous tenant; or

(b) at some time before the tenant's death the tenancy was a joint tenancy held by himself and one or more other persons and, prior to his death, he became the sole tenant by survivorship; or

(c) he became entitled to the tenancy as mentioned in section 39(5) below.

(3) For the purposes of this section, a tenant is also a successor in relation to a tenancy (in this subsection referred to as 'the new tenancy') which was granted to him (alone or jointly with others) if—

(a) at some time before the grant of the new tenancy, he was, by virtue of subsection (2) above, a successor in relation to an earlier tenancy of the same or substantially the same dwelling-house as is let under the new tenancy; and

(b) at all times since he became such a successor he has been a tenant (alone or jointly with others) of the dwelling-house which is let under the new tenancy or of a dwelling-house which is substantially the same as that dwelling-house.

(4) For the purposes of this section, a person who was living with the tenant as his or her wife or husband shall be treated as the tenant's spouse.

(5) If, on the death of the tenant, there is, by virtue of subsection (4) above, more than one person who fulfils the condition in subsection (1)(b) above, such one of them as may be decided by agreement or, in default of agreement, by the county court shall be treated as the tenant's spouse for the purposes of this section.

The s 17 right of 'succession' applies only to periodic tenancies (not including statutory periodic tenancies), and so prior to the Housing Act 1996 could have no application to initial assured shorthold tenancies (although it could apply to 'follow on' periodic assured shortholds[83]). Assured shortholds under the 1996 Act 'regime' could in principle come within s 17 if periodic, but given the extremely limited security they provide long-term this seems a largely theoretical point.

Fixed-term assured tenancies (including pre-Housing Act 1996 assured shortholds) devolve, if at all, to 'successors' only by will or via intestacy law. Interestingly, the absence of a concept equivalent to the statutory tenancy in the Housing Act 1988 (a statutory tenancy conferring only rights personal to the statutory tenant) would have meant that all assured tenancies could be 'left' in a tenant's will, in addition to any s 17 rights that might exist. However, so long as the landlord acts relatively swiftly to seek possession, Sch 1 Ground 7 largely blocks this particular 'loophole'.[84]

Controversially, succession under s 17 is limited to spouses and cohabitees and does not extend to other members of the tenant's family. This, of course, substantially undermines any concept of an assured tenancy representing a family home. The 'policy' and other issues surrounding it are discussed in Chapter 11.

## Rent Act tenancies

Prior to the Housing Act 1988, all Rent Act tenancies were governed by the same regime in s 2(1)(b) and Sch 1, Pt I of the 1977 Act. These provided for spouses to

---

[83] See, for example, *Lower Street Properties Ltd v Jones* (1996) 28 HLR 877.
[84] For an interesting recent discussion on Ground 7, see *Shepping v Osada* (2000) 33 HLR 13.

succeed to statutory tenancies and for other 'family' members (undefined) who had lived with the deceased tenant for six months or more also to succeed to statutory tenancies. Two 'successions' were possible. The relevant provisions were significantly amended by Sch 4 of the Housing Act 1988 for the majority of cases still relevant today (the original rules survived where the tenant died prior to 15 January 1989).

The amended versions of s 2(1)(b) and Sch 1 of the 1977 Rent Act provide as follows:

2.   **Statutory tenants and tenancies**

(1) …

(b)   Part I of Schedule 1 to this Act shall have effect for determining what person (if any) is the statutory tenant of a dwelling-house [or, as the case may be, is entitled to an assured tenancy of a dwelling-house by succession] at any time after the death of a person who, immediately before his death, was either a protected tenant of the dwelling-house or the statutory tenant of it by virtue of paragraph (a) above.

# STATUTORY TENANCIES SCHEDULE 1

## PART I
## STATUTORY TENANTS BY SUCCESSION

1. Paragraph 2 … below shall have effect, subject to section 2(3) of this Act, for the purpose of determining who is the statutory tenant of a dwelling-house by succession after the death of the person (in this Part of this Schedule referred to as 'the original tenant') who, immediately before his death, was a protected tenant of the dwelling-house or the statutory tenant of it by virtue of his previous protected tenancy.

2. If—

(1)   the survivor's spouse (if any) of the original tenant, is residing in the dwelling-house immediately before the death of the original tenant, shall, after the death, be the statutory tenant if, and so long, as he or she occupies the dwelling-house or his or her residence.

(2)   for the purpose of this paragraph a person who was living with the original tenant or his or her wife or husband shall be treated as the spouse of the original tenant.

(3)   if immediately after the death of the original tenant, there is, by virtue of sub-paragraph (2) above, more than one person who fulfills the conditions in sub-paragraph (1) above, such one of them as may be decided by agreement or, in default of agreement, by the county court, shall be treated as the surviving spouse for the purpose of this paragraph.

3. Where paragraph 2 above does not apply, but a person who was a member of the original tenant's family was residing with him in the dwelling-house at the time of and for the period of 2 years immediately before his death then, after his death, that person or if there is more than one such person such one of them as may be decided by agreement, or in default of agreement by the county court, shall be entitled to an assured tenancy of the dwelling-house by succession. …

4. A person who becomes the statutory tenant of a dwelling-house by virtue of paragraph 2 above is in this Part of this Schedule referred to as 'the first successor'.

5. If, immediately before his death, the first successor was still a statutory tenant, paragraph 6 below shall have effect, for the purpose of determining who is the statutory tenant after the death of the first successor.

6.—(1) Where a person who—

(a) was a member of the original tenant's family immediately before that tenant's death, and

(b) was a member of the first successor's family immediately before the first successor's death,

was residing in the dwelling-house with the first successor at the time of, and for the period of 2 years immediately before, the first successor's death, that person or, if there is more than one such person, such one of them as may be decided by agreement or, in default of agreement, by the county court shall be entitled to an assured tenancy of the dwelling-house by succession.

In the amended version of Sch 1 where the original tenant dies a surviving *spouse* can succeed to a *statutory* tenancy if resident with the tenant immediately prior to the death (cohabitees are aligned with spouses for this purpose). Other 'family' members only succeed to *assured* tenancies, and then only if they have lived with the tenant for at least two years prior to the death. On the death of the first successor, very limited succession rights apply – such a successor must have been a statutory tenant, and any 'claimant' to a further succession must have been a member *both* of the original tenant's family *and* of the first successor's family, and also must have been resident in the dwelling-house for two years, up to and including the first successor's death. Even then, only succession to an assured tenancy is possible. Again in the severe diminution of the rights of non-cohabitee 'family' members via the Housing Act 1988 amendments is highly controversial.

In all the above there is much controversy over the width of the concept of 'member of the tenant's family'. Originally, the debate centred on the status of cohabitees. More recently it has turned on the status of 'platonic' and 'gay' relationships[85].

## FURTHER READING

Cowan, D, *Housing Law and Policy* (1999) Macmillan, Chapter 2.

*Housing: The Government's Proposals* (1987), Cm 214.

Lowe, S, and Hughes, D (eds) *The Private Rented Sector in a New Century* (2002) Polity Press.

---

[85]   See, for example [1997] 4 All ER 991, [2002] EWCA Civ 1533, [2003] HLR 505; and [2002] EWCA Civ 271, [2002] 4 All ER 1136.

# CHAPTER 5

# Unlawful and Unfair Practices by Landlords

## INTRODUCTION

A central part of this chapter is concerned with issues relating to harassment and unlawful eviction by landlords. The ability of a landlord to forcibly remove an occupier from their home or harass them into leaving is, in many ways, the paradigm for the potential abuse of power which may follow from inequalities in the relative positions of the parties. However, inequality of bargaining power can lead to other manifestations of unfairness: one-sided termination rights, excessive deposits, unduly restrictive occupational terms and so on. Two relatively recent developments have brought all this into sharp focus: the implementation of Directive 93/13/EEC, ie the Unfairness Terms in Consumer Contracts Regulations[1] and the Law Commission Report, *Renting Homes*[2].

## RENTING HOMES

As discussed in Chapter 2, the Law Commission, in November 2003, published *Renting Homes*, its final report on a proposed new legal framework for renting accommodation. A cornerstone of the approach underpinning the Law Commission's recommendation is what the Commission terms 'the consumer approach'[3]. The Commission has stated that[4]:

'This approach has a number of practical implications:
(1) The regulatory framework governing the relationship between landlord and occupier will apply wherever there is a contractual agreement … for the occupation of a dwelling as a home.
(2) The principles underlying the Unfair Terms in Consumer Contract [sic][5] Regulations (UTCCR) will extend to all landlords and occupiers; and all terms save key terms that are also core terms will be subject to the UTCCR principles of fairness and transparency.

---

[1] Originally introduced with effect from 1 July 1995 (SI 1994/3159), but now in an amended 'second edition' as from 1 October 1999 (SI 1999/2083).
[2] Law Com No. 284 Cm 6018 (November 2003).
[3] This is outlined in Part III of the Report and discussed in detail in Parts IV and VIII.
[4] *Renting Homes* para 3.4.
[5] They are, in fact, the Unfair Terms in Consumer Contracts Regulations.

(3)  The language of occupation agreements should be as comprehensible as possible; and the structure of agreements should be as clear and user-friendly as possible.'

Subsequently, in Part IV the Commission stated that[6]:

'In the past, housing legislation attempted to protect tenants against the weakness of their bargaining position under unregulated principles of land law and contract by overlaying separate statutory rules on top of the tenancy agreement. Our proposed scheme seeks to create the appropriate levels of protection directly though the terms of the agreement, by subjecting the terms themselves to statutory regulation.'

More specifically, the Commission has recommended[7]:

1.  The focus of occupational rights should be on the contractual agreement. It would not matter whether, in traditional terms an estate in land was created. The distinction between a lease and a licence (see Chapter 3) would cease, in this context at least, to have any practical relevance.

2.  There should be legislatively prescribed model agreements which would be fair and transparent. Such agreements would presumptively be UTCCR compliant[8].

3.  There should be a number of modifications to the normal UTCCR regime to reflect distinct features of housing law, for example that the regulations should apply to individually negotiated terms[9] (although self-evidently the freer any such negotiation the more likely the term is to be seen as fair in any event), that no exemption to the regulations concerning 'core terms' should exist, save where such terms are included in the 'model' contract and that all landlords and occupiers should be specifically brought within the regulations irrespective of any issues which might otherwise exist with the concept of 'seller', 'supplier' or 'consumer'[10].

In Pt VIII the Commission elaborates on its proposals for 'model' agreements. In outline there would be four categories of terms, which the Commission refers to as *key terms, compulsory-minimum terms, special terms* and *other terms* – default or specifically agreed on by the parties[11]:

•  *Key terms* would include the name of the landlord and the occupier, a description of the property, the date on which the occupier could enter into possession, and whether the contract is indefinite or due to end on a fixed date and the nature/amount of the consideration.[12]

•  *Compulsory-minimum terms* – these represent what the Commission refers to as a 'floor of rights and obligations'. Any variation would need to be in favour of the occupier. There would be terms relating to security of tenure, terms

---

6   *Renting Homes* para 4.2.
7   Ibid paras 4.8–4.25.
8   SI 1999/2083, r 4(2)(a) of which provides that the regulations do not apply to contractual terms which reflect mandatory statutory as regulatory provisions.
9   In itself a recommendation made by the Commission in relation to its general proposal re 'unfair' terms in contract – see Consultation Paper 166 paras 4.42–4.54.
10  See below in this chapter.
11  For the detail, see *Renting Homes* 8.11–8.88.
12  Or as we are more used to referring to these matters – whether the agreement is fixed-term, or periodic and the nature/amount of the rent or other charge payable!

relating to the 'operation of the agreement' (including issues like lodgers and succession rights), and terms relating to issues implied by statute or common law. In the last category would be terms relating to repairs and fitness, quiet enjoyment and consultation and information.

- *Special terms* – these would deal with what the Commission refers to as 'social policy concerns'. Specifically they would concern anti-social behaviour, domestic violence and giving false information when applying for an occupation agreement.
- *Other terms* – either as 'default' clauses, or where specifically agreed on by the parties[13].

As discussed in Chapter 2, it is not yet clear what the ultimate fate of the Law Commission's proposals is likely to be. If implemented they would undoubtedly represent a significant simplification of the current law. This chapter alone serves to demonstrate the complex patchwork of 'state' regulation and private rights, of civil law and criminal law, of tort and contract which the current legal framework represents. The extent to which a 'consumer' perspective perfectly 'fits' as a model for housing occupational rights is more debateable. The Commission only addresses this issue fleetingly and seems to take it as axiomatic that a 'consumer' approach does provide the ideal working basis for their new proposed framework of occupational rights[14]. Indeed, this is not a new notion – as long ago as 1981 David Tiplady wrote that[15]:

> 'The modern city dweller ... buys a package of goods and services, not an interest in land. He is essentially a consumer, and the law must protect his legitimate expectations here, just as in the analogous situations of sale or consumer credit.'

Moreover recent cases such *as Bruton v London and Quadrant Housing Trust*[16] (discussed in Chapter 3) demonstrate a contractual analysis of residential landlord and tenant relationships triumphing over one based on requiring an estate in land. The importance of the UTCCR in relation to redressing potential unfairness in tenancy agreements is stressed in the next section of this chapter[17]; however, it is not self-evident that providing legal protection by way of contract is more coherent and satisfactory than providing it by way of direct statutory regulation. In itself it accepts that 'freeing up' the market for rented accommodation and protecting the interests of often vulnerable occupiers are issues capable of ready harmonisation via a somewhat 'light touch' regime of model contracts backed up by Office of Fair Trading supervision.

---

[13] Any such additional terms would need to be in writing. *Renting Homes* para 8.83.
[14] *Renting Homes* paras 4.4–4.8.
[15] Tiplady, D, 'Recent Developments in the Law of Landlord and Tenant' (1981) 44 Modern Law Review 129.
[16] [2000] 1 AC 406.
[17] Either to supplement statutory protection in the case of secure and assured tenancies, or to provide much of the remaining legal protection for tenants in a largely unregulated private rented sector.

## UNFAIR TERMS IN CONSUMER CONTRACTS REGULATIONS (UTCCR)

The first general attempt to control the abuse of unfair contractual terms in England, Wales and Northern Ireland was made by the Unfair Contract Terms Act 1977[18] – popularly known as UCTA. However, UCTA only applies to *some* unfair contractual terms (primarily exclusion and limitation clauses) and in Sch 1(b) it is stated that many of its more significant provisions do not apply to 'any contract so far as it relates to the creation or transfer of an interest in land, or to the termination of such an interest, whether by extinction, merger, surrender, forfeiture or otherwise'[19].

In 1994 the Unfair Terms in Consumer Contracts Regulations[20] were introduced. These regulations incorporated into our law (with little significant drafting amendment) Directive 93/13 EEC. The Directive had as its central aim a limited harmonisation of domestic laws around the community in relation to terms in standard form[21] consumer contracts. Initially, there was much academic debate as to whether the UTCCR covered contracts for the sale or disposition of interests in land (whether by way of sale or lease). Some commentators[22] took the view that as the 1994 regulations only applied to the sale of goods or the provision of services, they were inappropriate to cover transfers of interests in land. In effect, the argument ran that real property could not properly be described as 'goods', given the crucial distinction in English law between real and personal property. Others[23] took the opposite view, pointing out that the original (French) version of the Directive simply referred to 'biens', which in French law can encompass land. It would seem that the 1999 regulations[24] largely side-step this issue by stating that the regulations simply apply 'in relation to unfair terms in contracts, concluded between a seller or a supplier and a consumer'[25]. Recently the Court of Appeal has confirmed that a local authority is a 'seller or supplier', and a tenant (or indeed a prospective tenant) is a 'consumer' under the 1999 regulations[26]. The specific issues raised in *Khatun* are discussed later in this section, but the Court of Appeal's general approach to the relevance of the regulations to 'land' transactions is worth noting now. Laws LJ states that[27]:

'[53] The Directive was adopted pursuant to Article 100a of the Treaty (now Article 95). In light of some aspects of the argument, it is necessary to cite Article 100a to this following extent:

"1. … The Council shall … adopt the measures for the approximation of

---

[18] In force 1 February 1978.
[19] Although UCTA could apply to attempts to exclude/limit liability in relation to misleading information (for example by an agent) which induces a tenancy agreement – see *Walker v Boyle* [1982] 1 WLR 495.
[20] SI 1994/3159. In force 1 July 1995.
[21] Defined by the regulations as terms which have not been 'individually negotiated' (see now SI 1999/2083.
[22] For example, Treitel, GH, *Law of Contract* 10th ed.
[23] For example the Office of Fair Trading, and the Consumers' Association.
[24] Unfair Terms in Consumer Contracts Regulations 1999, SI 1999/2083 – in force 1 October 1999.
[25] Ibid reg 4(1).
[26] *R (on the application of Khatun) v Newham London Borough Council* [2004] EWCA Civ 55, [2004] 3 WLR 417.
[27] Ibid at para 53 onwards.

the provisions laid down by law, regulation or administrative action in Member States which have as their object the establishment and functioning of the internal market.

2.   Paragraph 1 shall not apply to fiscal provisions, to those relating to the free movement of persons nor to those relating to the rights and interests of employed persons.

3.   The Commission, in its proposals envisaged in paragraph 1 concerning health, safety, environmental protection and consumer protection, will take as a base a high level of protection, taking account in particular of any new development based on scientific facts. Within their respective powers, the European Parliament and the Council will also seek to achieve this objective."

[54] Much reference was made in the course of argument to the recitals in the Directive's preamble. It is a theme of Mr Underwood's submissions for the Council that phrases such as "goods and services" and "sellers of goods and supplies of services" (used in the Directive and, as I shall show, elsewhere) suggest a legislative intention to exclude transactions in land from the regime in hand. I will come later to the significance of these expressions, not least the repeated references to "goods and services". It is enough for the purpose of introducing the Directive to indicate that this form of words frequently appears in the recitals; I need not cite examples merely to demonstrate the fact. At this stage I will set out only the following excerpts from the recitals (to which I have attributed numbers for convenience):

"(8) Whereas the two Community programmes for a consumer protection and information policy underlined the importance of safeguarding consumers in the matter of unfair terms of contract.

(9)   Whereas in accordance with the principle laid down under the heading 'Protection of the economic interests of the consumers', as stated in those programmes: 'acquirers of goods and services should be protected against the abuse of power by the seller or supplier, in particular against one-sided standard contracts and the unfair exclusion of essential rights in contracts';

(10) Whereas more effective protection of the consumer can be achieved by adopting uniform rules of law in the matter of unfair terms; whereas those rules should apply to all contracts concluded between sellers or suppliers and consumers; whereas as a result inter alia contracts relating to employment, contracts relating to succession rights, contracts relating to rights under family law and contracts relating to the incorporation and organisation of companies or partnership agreements must be excluded from this Directive."

…

## (2) The Regulations

[56] The only *vires* cited in the preamble to the Regulations is s 2(2) of the European Communities Act 1972. Thus the Regulations purport to do no

more nor less than constitute the transposition of the Directive's requirements into the law of the United Kingdom. Accordingly their scope is to be determined by reference to the scope of the Directive. So much, I understand, is uncontentious.

...

[68] It is elementary that all the languages in which EU texts are officially published are equally authoritative for the purpose of the texts' interpretation. Here, Mr Green points in particular to the use of the French "biens" for what in the English versions are referred to as "goods" in the expression "goods and services" (or "goods or services"). "Biens", say Mr Green, in French includes or may include immovables. So much is demonstrated by art 516 of the French Civil Code and is not, I think, sought to be contradicted by Mr Underwood. The same is true of "beni", "bienes", and "bens" respectively appearing in the Italian, Spanish and Portuguese texts. Mr Green says also that where a French text makes reference specifically to the free movement of goods (which obviously excludes land) the word "merchandises" is used, and again there are analogues in the Italian, Spanish and Portuguese texts.

[69] I should notice that where the English text of the Explanatory Memorandum has on p.2, in a passage which I have already cited, "to buy goods or services, or to invest or acquire property in other Member States", the French text (helpfully supplied by the Treasury Solicitor since the hearing) has "pour acheter des biens ou des services, ou pour investir ou acquerir une propriete", which might suggest a distinction between "biens" (goods) and "propriete" (a piece of land). But in my judgment no such distinction can have been intended. The reference to the acquisition of property appears in the Commission's general explanation of the reasons for the Directive, and thus lends significant support to the view that land transactions are included. The choice of words in which to express that very reference cannot sensibly be held to point in the opposite direction.

...

## (10) Conclusions on the Second Issue: (A) Do The Directive and the Regulations Apply to Contracts Relating to Land?

[77] The starting-point for the resolution of this question is in my judgment the nature of the Directive's dominant purpose: as I have already said, that of consumer protection. In particular I have in mind the terms of art 100a(3) of the Treaty, "[t]he Commission ...will take as a base a high level of protection". It is plainly to be assumed that in framing the Directive the Community legislator intended to carry this purpose into effect. On this basis, one would expect transactions in land to fall within the Directive's scope. Some tenants or prospective tenants are especially vulnerable people. For most consumers the acquisition of a home, rent or buy, is a key event in their lives. If the home is bought rather than rented it will most likely be the biggest purchase the buyer has so far ever made. I recognise of course that sales of private houses are most often effected between consumers, rather than between a consumer

and a trader. But not all are. And it is commonplace that tenancies are let by landlords who are in business as such. In consequence I am unable to perceive any rationale for the exclusion of land transactions from the Directive's scope. Such an exclusion would cut across the grain of the legislation's aim to provide "a high level of protection". I agree with Mr Green that one would expect to find such an exclusion expressly provided for; and it is not to be found.

[78] As for the bite of the various materials I have cited, I consider that the OFT had the better of the argument. First, Mr Underwood's seemingly strong point on the language – that "goods and services" does not include land – is effectively demolished by the impact of the other language texts. "Biens" and its cognates in Italian, Spanish and Portuguese refer to immovables as readily as movables. This alone undercuts a good deal of what Mr Underwood had to say. But more than this: I think, with respect to Mr Underwood, that other aspects of his submissions on this part of the case place an implicit but illegitimate reliance on the large divide in the law of England between real and personal property. He submitted that the Directive should be interpreted as only applying to "contracts for goods and services as an English lawyer would understand those terms". There is plainly no general principle to support such a proposition. Quite the contrary: European legislation has to be read as a single corpus of law binding across the Member States. And the proposition leads to absurdity. A licence of land, which transfers no estate, might be covered by the Directive (as the provision of a service), but a lease or tenancy would not. The sale of a fixture, which by English law is treated as part of the land, would be excluded, but the sale of an identical object – say a statue – which was not fixed to the land would be included. In our domestic law these distinctions have a long history and a present utility. In the context of a Europe-wide scheme of consumer protection, they could be nothing but an embarrassing eccentricity.

[79] In fairness Mr Underwood did not at all suggest that his putative conformity between the scope of the Directive and the law of England relating to goods and services was supported by any general principle whatever. But in that case, if his approach is to be made good, it must find some positive support in the text of the Directive or other relevant materials.

[80] In my judgment, once one discounts Mr Underwood's argument from language, no such support is to be found and such indications as there are in fact favour the inclusion of land transactions. In particular there are features in the travaux which suggest that the Community legislator attached no significance to the difference between land and other transactions, and proceeded on the basis that the Directive would apply to both. I have already set out art 1 of the draft directive and the statement in the Explanatory Memorandum (pp. 2–3) that the Article defines the measure's scope as including every contract between a consumer and a party acting in the course of his trade. I draw attention also to the reference to investment and the acquisition of property at p.2 of the Memorandum. Taken together these references powerfully suggest that the proposal was to cover all consumer contracts whatever their subject-matter; if there were to be exclusions, they would be specifically provided for.

(And that, in my judgment, is precisely what was done in the Doorstep Selling and Distance Selling Directives: I would reject Mr Underwood's submission that the provisions there contained which I have set out do other than evince a legislative intention to exclude land transactions).

[81] There is then the absence from the Explanatory Memorandum of any reference either to the *exclusion* of land transactions from the British consumer protection legislation, or to their *inclusion* in the German legislation. That, as it seems to me, sits alongside the fact that in para 2.2.2 of the ECOSOC Opinion the laws of Germany and the United Kingdom (and seven other Member States) are, if I may use the phrase, lumped together for all the world as if there were no significant differences between them; and in my judgment, from the perspective of the Community legislator there were not.

[82] Once it is appreciated that any difference between transactions in land on the one hand, and goods and services (as those terms are understood in this jurisdiction on the other, simply raised no issue for the Directive's drafters, there is nothing left in the text of the *travaux* to assist Mr Underwood. Nor in the other materials to which I have referred. And while there is plainly no authority, domestic or European, which binds this court to conclude in Mr Green's favour, the learning such as it is points in that direction ...'

## Substantive matters

The structure of the regulations is clear enough. Any term in a consumer contract which has not been 'individually negotiated' is not binding on a consumer if it is 'unfair'. Such a term will be 'unfair' if:

- it is contrary to the requirement of 'good faith';
- it causes a 'significant imbalance' in the parties' rights and obligations;
- it acts to the detriment of the consumer.

The 'burden of proof' concerning fairness/unfairness is on the seller/supplier[28]. In addition to these general provisions, the regulations provide[29] a so-called 'indicative and non-exhaustive' list of terms which 'may be regarded' as unfair. The precise status of this list is open to debate – it is certainly not a black-list of automatically unfair terms but seems at least to operate as an indication of terms which would normally be seen as unfair unless the person seeking to rely on them brings forward evidence of their appropriateness on the facts of the particular case.

The key substantive provisions of the regulations are as follows.

### 4.   Terms to which these Regulations apply

(1) These Regulations apply in relation to unfair terms in contracts concluded between a seller or a supplier and a consumer.

(2) These Regulations do not apply to contractual terms which reflect—

---

[28]   On the above, see UTCCR (respectively) regs 5(1), 5(4) and 8.
[29]   Ibid Sch 2.

(a)  mandatory statutory or regulatory provisions (including such provisions under the law of any Member State or in Community legislation having effect in the United Kingdom without further enactment);

(b)  the provisions or principles of international conventions to which the Member States or the Community are party.

## 5.  Unfair Terms

(1) A contractual term which has not been individually negotiated shall be regarded as unfair if, contrary to the requirement of good faith, it causes a significant imbalance in the parties' rights and obligations arising under the contract, to the detriment of the consumer.

(2) A term shall always be regarded as not having been individually negotiated where it has been drafted in advance and the consumer has therefore not been able to influence the substance of the term.

(3) Notwithstanding that a specific term or certain aspects of it in a contract has been individually negotiated, these Regulations shall apply to the rest of a contract if an overall assessment of it indicates that it is a pre-formulated standard contract.

(4) It shall be for any seller or supplier who claims that a term was individually negotiated to show that it was.

(5) Schedule 2 to these Regulations contains an indicative and non-exhaustive list of the terms which may be regarded as unfair.

## 6.  Assessment of unfair terms

(1) Without prejudice to regulation 12, the unfairness of a contractual term shall be assessed, taking into account the nature of the goods or services for which the contract was concluded and by referring, at the time of conclusion of the contract, to all the circumstances attending the conclusion of the contract and to all the other terms of the contract or of another contract on which it is dependent.

(2) Insofar as it is in plain intelligible language, the assessment of fairness of a term shall not relate—

(a)  to the definition of the main subject matter of the contract, or

(b)  to the adequacy of the price or remuneration, as against the goods or services supplied in exchange.

## 7.  Written contracts

(1) A seller or supplier shall ensure that any written term of a contract is expressed in plain, intelligible language.

(2) If there is doubt about the meaning of a written term, the interpretation which is most favourable to the consumer shall prevail but this rule shall not apply in proceedings brought under regulation 12.

## 8.  Effect of unfair term

(1) An unfair term in a contract concluded with a consumer by a seller or supplier shall not be binding on the consumer.

(2) The contract shall continue to bind the parties if it is capable of continuing in existence without the unfair term.

...

# SCHEDULE 2

## REGULATION 5(5)

*INDICATIVE AND NON-EXHAUSTIVE LIST OF TERMS WHICH MAY BE REGARDED AS UNFAIR*

1. Terms which have the object or effect of—

(a) excluding or limiting the legal liability of a seller or supplier in the event of the death of a consumer or personal injury to the latter resulting from an act or omission of that seller or supplier;

(b) inappropriately excluding or limiting the legal rights of the consumer vis-à-vis the seller or supplier or another party in the event of total or partial non-performance or inadequate performance by the seller or supplier of any of the contractual obligations, including the option of offsetting a debt owed to the seller or supplier against any claim which the consumer may have against him;

(c) making an agreement binding on the consumer whereas provision of services by the seller or supplier is subject to a condition whose realisation depends on his own will alone;

(d) permitting the seller or supplier to retain sums paid by the consumer where the latter decides not to conclude or perform the contract, without providing for the consumer to receive compensation of an equivalent amount from the seller or supplier where the latter is the party cancelling the contract;

(e) requiring any consumer who fails to fulfil his obligation to pay a disproportionately high sum in compensation;

(f) authorising the seller or supplier to dissolve the contract on a discretionary basis where the same facility is not granted to the consumer, or permitting the seller or supplier to retain the sums paid for services not yet supplied by him where it is the seller or supplier himself who dissolves the contract;

(g) enabling the seller or supplier to terminate a contract of indeterminate duration without reasonable notice except where there are serious grounds for doing so;

(h) automatically extending a contract of fixed duration where the consumer does not indicate otherwise, when the deadline fixed for the consumer to express his desire not to extend the contract is unreasonably early;

(i) irrevocably binding the consumer to terms with which he had no real opportunity of becoming acquainted before the conclusion of the contract;

(j) enabling the seller or supplier to alter the terms of the contract unilaterally without a valid reason which is specified in the contract;

(k) enabling the seller or supplier to alter unilaterally without a valid reason any characteristics of the product or service to be provided;

(l) providing for the price of goods to be determined at the time of delivery or allowing a seller of goods or supplier of services to increase their price without in both cases giving the consumer the corresponding right to cancel the contract if the final price is too high in relation to the price agreed when the contract was concluded;

(m) giving the seller or supplier the right to determine whether the goods or services supplied are in conformity with the contract, or giving him the exclusive right to interpret any term of the contract;

(n) limiting the seller's or supplier's obligation to respect commitments undertaken by his agents or making his commitments subject to compliance with a particular formality;

(o) obliging the consumer to fulfil all his obligations where the seller or supplier does not perform his;

(p) giving the seller or supplier the possibility of transferring his rights and obligations under the contract, where this may serve to reduce the guarantees for the consumer, without the latter's agreement;

(q) excluding or hindering the consumer's right to take legal action or exercise any other legal remedy, particularly by requiring the consumer to take disputes exclusively to arbitration not covered by legal provisions, unduly restricting the evidence available to him or imposing on him a burden of proof which, according to the applicable law, should lie with another party to the contract.

Aside from the status of Sch 2, the main area of difficulty/uncertainty concerns the exclusion of so-called 'core terms' from the ambit of the regulations (see reg 6(2)(a)) and the meaning of 'good faith' in reg 4(1).

Regulation 6(2) does not refer to 'core terms' per se but (rather) to terms which '[define] the main subject matter of the contract'. For this 'exclusion' to apply, the terms need to be in 'plain intelligible language', but assuming this 'plain English' requirement is fulfilled, the sense of reg 6(2)(a) seems to be that there are terms at the heart of the contract – which go to the very essence of what the contract is – which are unchallengeable. In a housing context this would obviously refer to terms which define the nature of the tenancy agreement, such as that it is fixed term or periodic and (if fixed term) the length of the term[30]. More difficult would be clauses which state whether a fixed term contract is renewable and (if so) on what basis, or what degree of notice can be given (by landlord or tenant), or the circumstances under which rent can be reviewed. If these were seen as core terms the usefulness of the regulations would be seriously diminished. Arguably, there-fore, interpreting the regulations purposively[31] a narrow view should be taken of reg 6(2)(a) and such clauses *should* be subject to the general test of fairness[32]. The Law Commission in *Renting Homes*[33] recommended that in relation to residential occupational agreements, the 'core terms' exclusion should only apply if one of the legislatively prescribed 'model tenancies' has been used.

As regards reg 4(1) the issues of 'significant imbalance' and consumer 'detriment' seem largely matters of fact, to be decided case by case. 'Good faith' is a more elusive concept – it is borrowed from many of the European civil codes and seems broadly to be about incorporating flexibility, humanity and justice to what might otherwise be a rather schematic and technical legal framework[34]. So, even in a (now) market-driven private rented sector (see Chapter 4), landlords, even if primarily driven by profit-oriented self-interest, will also need to have the best interests of their tenants at heart when formulating their tenancy agreements. The concept of 'good faith' was lucidly analysed by Bingham LJ (as he then was) in *Interfoto Picture Library Ltd v Stiletto Visual Programmes Ltd*[35]:

'In many civil law systems, and perhaps in most legal systems outside the common law world, the law of obligations recognises and enforces an

---

[30]  Likewise a clause stating the level of rent payable seems excluded by reg 6(2)(b).
[31]  This certainly seems the broad approach of the House of Lords in *Director General of Fair Trading v First National Bank plc* [2002] 1 AC 481 – see below.
[32]  Of course, a 'rent review' clause legitimised/underpinned by Housing Act 1988 ss 13 and 14 would seem to be excluded from the fairness test by virtue of reg 4(2).
[33]  See nn 6 and 7 above.
[34]  So, in the broadest sense, playing a similar role to that of equity in relation to the common law.
[35]  [1989] QB 433, at p 439.

overriding principle that, in making and carrying out contracts, parties should act in good faith. This does not simply mean that they should not deceive each other, a principle which any legal system must recognise; its effect is perhaps most aptly conveyed by such metaphorical colloquialisms as "playing fair", "coming clean" or "putting one's cards face upwards on the table". It is, in essence, a principle of fair and open dealing.'

Case law on the regulations is very limited, for reasons discussed below. However, there is interesting comment on many of the above provisions in *Director General of Fair Trading v First National Bank plc*[36] (the facts of the case are not particularly helpful in a housing context).

Lord Bingham[37] states that:

'17. The test laid down by regulation 4(1), deriving as it does from article 3(1) of the Directive, has understandably attracted much discussion in academic and professional circles and helpful submissions were made to the House on it. It is plain from the recitals to the Directive that one of its objectives was partially to harmonise the law in this important field among all member states of the European Union. The member states have no common concept of fairness or good faith, and the Directive does not purport to state the law of any single member state. It lays down a test to be applied, whatever their pre-existing law, by all member states. If the meaning of the test were doubtful, or vulnerable to the possibility of differing interpretations in differing member states, it might be desirable or necessary to seek a ruling from the European Court of Justice on its interpretation. But the language used in expressing the test, so far as applicable in this case, is in my opinion clear and not reasonably capable of differing interpretations. A term falling within the scope of the Regulations is unfair if it causes a significant imbalance in the parties' rights and obligations under the contract to the detriment of the consumer in a manner or to an extent which is contrary to the requirement of good faith. The requirement of significant imbalance is met if a term is so weighted in favour of the supplier as to tilt the parties' rights and obligations under the contract significantly in his favour. This may be by the granting to the supplier of a beneficial option or discretion or power, or by the imposing on the consumer of a disadvantageous burden or risk or duty. The illustrative terms set out in Schedule 3 to the Regulations provide very good examples of terms which may be regarded as unfair; whether a given term is or is not to be so regarded depends on whether it causes a significant imbalance in the parties' rights and obligations under the contract. This involves looking at the contract as a whole. But the imbalance must be to the detriment of the consumer; a significant imbalance to the detriment of the supplier, assumed to be the stronger party, is not a mischief which the Regulations seek to address. The requirement of good faith in this context is one of fair and open dealing. Openness requires that the terms should be expressed fully, clearly and legibly, containing no concealed pitfalls or traps. Appropriate prominence should be given to terms which might operate

---

[36]  [2002] 1 AC 481.
[37]  Ibid at p 494.

disadvantageously to the customer. Fair dealing requires that a supplier should not, whether deliberately or unconsciously, take advantage of the consumer's necessity, indigence, lack of experience, unfamiliarity with the subject matter of the contract, weak bargaining position or any other factor listed in or analogous to those listed in Schedule 2 to the Regulations. Good faith in this context is not an artificial or technical concept; nor, since Lord Mansfield was its champion, is it a concept wholly unfamiliar to British lawyers. It looks to good standards of commercial morality and practice. Regulation 4(1) lays down a composite test, covering both the making and the substance of the contract, and must be applied bearing clearly in mind the objective which the Regulations are designed to promote.'

Lord Steyn[38] states that:

'There are three independent requirements. But the element of detriment to the consumer may not add much. But it serves to make clear that the Directive is aimed at significant imbalance against a consumer, rather than the seller or supplier. The twin requirements of good faith and significant imbalance will in practice be determinative. Schedule 2 to the Regulations, which explains the concept of good faith, provides that regard must be had, amongst other things, to the extent to which the seller or supplier has dealt fairly and equitably with the consumer. It is an objective criterion.

…

the commentary to *Lando & Beale, Principles of European Contract Law, Parts I and II* (combined and revised 2000), p 113 prepared by the Commission of European Contract Law, explains that the purpose of the provision of good faith and fair dealing is "to enforce community standards of decency, fairness and reasonableness in commercial transactions"; a fortiori that is true of consumer transactions. Schedule 3 to the Regulations (which corresponds to the annex to the Directive) is best regarded as a check list of terms which must be regarded as potentially vulnerable. The examples given in Schedule 3 convincingly demonstrate that the argument of the bank that good faith is predominantly concerned with procedural defects in negotiating procedures cannot be sustained. Any purely procedural or even predominantly procedural interpretation of the requirement of good faith must be rejected.

37. That brings me to the element of significant imbalance. It has been pointed out by Hugh Collins that the test "of a significant imbalance of the obligations obviously directs attention to the substantive unfairness of the contract": "Good Faith in European Contract Law" (1994) 14 Oxford Journal of Legal Studies 229, 249. It is, however, also right to say that there is a large area of overlap between the concepts of good faith and significant imbalance.'

## Enforcement issues

As mentioned above, reported case law on the regulations is very limited. In part, this is because most actions brought will not proceed beyond the county court (most

---

[38] Ibid at p 499.

likely via the small claims track). However, even more significant is the fact that specific methods of 'public' regulation of unfair terms is provided for by regs 10–16 and Sch 1. The 'lead' regulator[39] is the Office of Fair Trading (OFT) and the capacity of the OFT to negotiate modifications to standard terms perceived by them to be unfair is of key significance in the practical operation of the regulations. The OFT also publishes regular bulletins which provide a ready made 'data base' of terms seen by them to be unfair and details of how such terms were modified or removed. An OFT press release of 7 May 2003 gives a flavour of their general approach. It quotes John Vickers, OFT 'chairman', as stating[40]:

> 'Tenancy agreements need to be clear and fair. Fairer and clearer standard contracts are now widely available for landlords and tenants. We urge letting agents and landlords to review their tenancy agreements to ensure that they meet required standards of fairness.'

The press release adds a number of organisations have reviewed and revised their tenancy standard terms in consultation with the OFT, including the Association of Residential Letting Agents, the Residential Landlords Association, the RICS and Oyez Forms Publishing.

All the above standard terms relate to assured shortholds as used by private landlords. In the light of the limited statutory control over assured shortholds[41] it might be thought that the need for OFT intervention was at its strongest here. However, an examination of OFT bulletins indicates that the UTCCR can and will be invoked in relation to 'excluded' tenancies such as lets by educational institutions to students, to housing association assured tenancies[42], and to local authority secure tenancies. For example, Leeds City Council[43] agreed to 12 modifications or deletions to its standard secure tenancy terms, including deleting an obligation to require tenants to sweep chimneys(!) and making it clear that any required consents to sublets and the carrying out of improvements would not be 'unreasonably withheld'[44]. Later in the same bulletin[45] it is reported that the University of the West of England agreed to over 40(!) modifications or deletions in relation to its standard student tenancy terms, including:

- deleting a term prohibiting the causing of nuisance or annoyance to the university (as to which the university seemed to have an unrestricted interpretive discretion);
- deleting a term prohibiting a student from holding parties in the accommodation without the prior permission of the university;
- deleting references to 'immorality' in relation to a student being in breach of the tenancy agreement;

---

[39]   Others include the Consumers Association, the Rail Regulator, the Financial Services Authority and local authority trading standards departments.
[40]   See www.oft.gov.uk/News/Press & releases/2003.
[41]   See Chapter 4.
[42]   Indeed the Housing Corporation has issued two circulars, R3–27/95 and R5–29 in relation to the regulations.
[43]   See OFT Bulletin 24/25, p 77.
[44]   As, indeed, is required in any event by the Housing Act 1985, see Chapter 8.
[45]   At p 131.

- revising a term imposing collective liability on students for damage in the accommodation to provide that students only paid a 'fair proportion' of the damage and had a right of appeal;
- deleting a term permitting a university to withhold tuition and access to the university's facilities in the event of a breach of tenancy terms and conditions.

In *Khatun*[46] the local authority had argued that even if the UTCCR applied to land transactions, they should not apply to public authorities. This was decisively rejected by the Court of Appeal. Laws LJ stated[47]:

'[88] It is to my mind plain beyond doubt that the Council is not taken out of the Directive's scope by reason only of the fact that it is a public or governmental body. Such a conclusion is not only strongly suggested by the *Hofner* line of reasoning in the competition cases. It is also I think lent force by the two further recitals from the Directive's preamble which I have set out, and, for good measure, the expression "whether publicly owned or privately owned" in art 2(c). The true question here is analogous to that arising in *Bettercare* relating to "economic activity": do the Council's Part VII functions fall within the meaning of "trade, business or profession" in art 2(c)?

[89] I have no doubt but that the answer to this question is Yes. The Part VII functions centrally involve the grant of a tenancy for rent. This is obviously "an activity which could … be carried on by a private undertaking in order to make profits". It is so carried on by private undertakings every day.

[90] In the course of his reply Mr Underwood sought to make something of the fact that the Council does not act under considerations of commercial choice but is obliged to provide accommodation to applicants if the conditions prescribed by statute are met. That is plainly so. However the nature of the activity which the Part VII function produces – the grant of a tenancy for rent – remains one which could be (and is, all the time) carried on by private undertakings in order to make profits. But there is a deeper point. Mr Underwood might be on firm ground if he were able to show that the public interest in the integrity of the domestic statutory scheme in question would be undermined by the application of the Directive's discipline. A like consideration was, as I understand it, the focus of the decision in *Poucet and Pistre* in the competition field. In that case the public interest in the social welfare scheme's "national solidarity" was not compatible with the rigours of the competition regime. But in this case, there is no such point to be made. How could the Part VII function be undermined by an insistence on fair contractual terms? It could not. Fair contractual terms run with, not across, the grain of good administration in this field. In my judgment therefore Mr Underwood is not supported by the circumstance that the Council is obliged to provide accommodation to applicants where the conditions prescribed by Part VII of the 1996 Act, notably s.193, are met.'

---

[46] *R (on the application of Khatun) v Newham London Borough Council* [2004] EWCA Civ 55, [2004] 3 WLR 417.
[47] Ibid para 88.

## Office of Fair Trading – Guidance on Unfair Terms in Tenancy Agreements

Although the OFT bulletins provide instructive indicators as to terms likely to be seen as unfair, the most systematic approach to the question of fairness can be obtained by reference to their published guidance on unfair terms[48]. The guidance is a detailed analysis of over 100 contract terms in assured and assured shorthold tenancy agreements under 19 types of contract terms which may be considered to be unfair. For example, Group 1 terms include exclusion and limitation clauses, Group 4 terms include those unfairly allowing a landlord to hold on to prepayments in the event of tenant cancellation and Group 10 terms include wholly one-sided contractual variation clauses (ie allowing the landlord to vary the contract whilst giving no equivalent right to a tenant). The Guidance is much too detailed to allow reproduction in full here (running to some 57 pages). However, the following extracts give an indication of the OFT's approach.

> '2.1.5 State of repair. Ideally, the parties to a tenancy agreement should clearly agree the condition of the property when let. In practice, a prospective tenant is unlikely to know whether a statement declaring a certain state of repair is correct, or to employ a surveyor. Standard terms about the structural state of the property at the time of letting may be potentially unfair if the tenant is required to accept them without question. However, these objections do not apply to terms that reflect agreement about obvious conditions that the tenant could confirm by looking round the property.
>
> …
>
> 4.5 Some tenancy agreements include a financial penalty that applies equally to either party who pulls out of the contract. Such a provision may not be effectively balanced, despite appearances, or fair. It may, for example, grant no real benefit to the tenant, compared with that gained by the agent or landlord. Terms governing the tenant's right to recover prepayments can be made fair by limiting them to the ordinary legal position. Where cancellation is the fault of the tenant, the landlord is entitled to hold back from any refund of prepayments a reasonable sum to cover *either* the net costs *or* the net loss of profit resulting directly from the default. Tenants would be at fault if, for instance, they gave false or misleading information, but not merely because the landlord thought their references were not sufficiently good (see paragraph 6.2.3.). The landlord is not entitled to keep any money that could reasonably be saved by finding another tenant, for example.
>
> 4.6 The alternative is to set a pre-contract deposit that reflects only the ordinary expenses necessarily incurred by the landlord. Such a genuine "deposit" can legitimately be kept in full, since it would be a reservation fee rather than an advance payment. But such a deposit will not normally be more than a very small percentage of the price. Otherwise it is liable to be seen as a disguised penalty, even if it is expressed as a payment for a service (see paragraph 5.11).

---

[48]   OFT 356, November 2001 (see OFT press release 44/01).

...

5.6 Security deposits. Similar points apply to terms that require the forfeit of the whole of a tenant's security deposit if the property is left in a damaged state at the end of the tenancy. A landlord can fairly say that he will deduct the reasonable costs caused directly and foreseeably by the tenant's failure to take reasonable care of the property. However he should not be able to profit from the term. If it could give him an unfair windfall, for example when disrepair is minor and easily rectified, the OFT is likely to challenge it.

...

6.1.1 Misleading termination clauses. Tenants with assured and assured shorthold fixed term tenancy agreements are legally protected against eviction before the fixed term expires. A landlord cannot terminate an agreement early, against a tenant's wishes, just because he wants to recover the property. However, this does not mean that unenforceable terms dealing with terminations of tenancies are fair because they are ineffective. A term stating or implying that the tenant could be evicted at the landlord's discretion would be seriously misleading and open to challenge on that basis.

...

**Examples of Potentially Unreasonable Prohibitions:**
- *Against having guests overnight.* Terms that ban overnight guests may be seen as producing an unnecessary and unreasonable restriction on normal and harmless use and enjoyment of the property. This term could also cause hardship and suffering, for example, if a tenant's daytime visitor falls ill.
- *Against keeping pets.* Such a term has been considered unfair under comparable legislation in another EU state because it could prevent a tenant keeping a goldfish. A term prohibiting the keeping of pets that could harm the property or be a nuisance to other residents would be unlikely to meet the same objection.

...

18.8.6 In appropriate cases (such as the examples above, and terms such as those banning the hanging of pictures), it may be possible for prohibitions to be considered fair if the conduct is allowed only "with the landlord's consent, which will not be unreasonably withheld".'

## HARASSMENT AND UNLAWFUL EVICTION[49]

The first legislative provisions to deal specifically with harassment and unlawful eviction were contained in s 2 of the Protection from Eviction Act 1954, soon after consolidated into and extended by Pt III of the Rent Act 1965. As already

---

[49] For an extensive treatment of this area see Arden et al, *Quiet Enjoyment* 6th ed (2002) Legal Action Group.

mentioned[50], the partial deregulation of the private rented sector in the 1957 Rent Act led to well-recorded instances of undue pressure and threats from landlords aimed at inducing sitting tenants to leave[51].

The form of deregulation adopted by the 1957 Rent Act provided an incentive for landlords to act in this way, since the rents of less expensive properties[52] only became decontrolled when the sitting tenant left. This, of course, gave landlords an incentive to try to remove sitting tenants and replace them with tenants paying higher rents[53]. The incoming Labour government had made a pledge in opposition[54] not only to reintroduce regulation over rents, but also to curb such landlord abuses.

The provisions in Pt III Rent Act 1965 are now to be found in Pt I Protection from Eviction Act 1977. They provide that landlords who are guilty of unlawful eviction and/or harassment of their tenants commit criminal offences. It was not until ss 27 and 28 of the Housing Act 1988 were introduced that unlawful eviction and harassment became specific civil 'wrongs' (in effect, statutory torts). However, even before this, the civil law did penalise landlords, most typically for breach of the implied covenant of quiet enjoyment. Most recently the ambit of the criminal offence of harassment has been extended by the Protection from Harassment Act 1997.

## Part I Protection from Eviction Act 1977

The general aim of the Protection from Eviction Act (PEA) 1977 is to protect 'residential occupiers' from being harassed or unlawfully evicted. The legislation creates three distinct criminal offences:

- unlawful eviction[55]
- harassment by landlords or their agents[56]
- harassment by others[57].

## PROTECTION FROM EVICTION ACT 1977

## PART 1 UNLAWFUL EVICTION AND HARASSMENT

### 1   Damages from unlawful eviction

(1) In this section 'residential occupier', in relation to any premises, means a person occupying the premises as a residence, whether under a contract or by virtue of any

---

[50] See Chapter 4.
[51] Practices sometimes referred to as 'winkling'. These shady practices are notoriously associated with the slum landlord Peter Rachman.
[52] At the time fixed at those with a rateable value of up to £40.00 in London, or up to £30.00 elsewhere.
[53] All too reminiscent of the process of 'creeping decontrol' provided for in the Housing Act 1988 Pt I (see Chapter 4).
[54] See Harold Wilson MP *Hansard,* HC Debs, vol 681, cols 1058–59.
[55] PEA 1977 s 1(2).
[56] Ibid s 1(3A).
[57] Ibid s 1(3).

enactment or rule of law giving him the right to remain in occupation or restricting the right of any other person to recover possession of the premises.

(2) If any person unlawfully deprives the residential occupier of any premises of his occupation of the premises or any part thereof, or attempts to do so, he shall be guilty of an offence unless he proves that he believed, and had reasonable cause to believe, that the residential occupier had ceased to reside in the premises.

(3) If any person with intent to cause the residential occupier of any premises—

(a)  to give up the occupation of the premises or any part thereof; or

(b)  to refrain from exercising any right or pursuing any remedy in respect of the premises or part thereof;

does acts [likely] to interfere with the peace or comfort of the residential occupier or members of his household, or persistently withdraws or withholds services reasonably required for the occupation of the premises as a residence, he shall be guilty of an offence.

[(3A) Subject to subsection (3B) below, the landlord of a residential occupier or an agent of the landlord shall be guilty of an offence if—

(a)  he does acts likely to interfere with the peace or comfort of the residential occupier or members of his household, or

(b)  he persistently withdraws or withholds services reasonably required for the occupation of the premises in question as a residence,

and (in either case) he knows, or has reasonable cause to believe, that that conduct is likely to cause the residential occupier to give up the occupation of the whole or part of the premises or to refrain from exercising any right or pursuing any remedy in respect of the whole or part of the premises.

(3B) A person shall not be guilty of an offence under subsection (3A) above if he proves that he had reasonable grounds for doing the acts or withdrawing or withholding the services in question.

(3C) In subsection (3A) above 'landlord', in relation to a residential occupier of any premises, means the person who, but for—

(a)  the residential occupier's right to remain in occupation of the premises, or

(b)  a restriction on the person's right to recover possession of the premises,

would be entitled to occupation of the premises and any superior landlord under whom that person derives title].

(4) A person guilty of an offence under this section shall be liable—

(a)  on summary conviction, to a fine not exceeding [the prescribed sum] or to imprisonment for a term not exceeding 6 months or to both;

(b)  on conviction on indictment, to a fine or to imprisonment for a term not exceeding two years or to both.

'Residential occupier' is defined by s 1(1) as including those occupying premises 'as a residence' and doing so by way of a right conferred contractually or statutorily.

In *Schon v Camden London Borough Council*[58] it was held that 'residence' under the PEA had the same meaning as in the Rent Act 1977. This is discussed in detail in Chapter 4 but, in essence, there is no need for constant occupation, so long as there is some evidence of on-going occupation coupled with an intention to return to the premises permanently. If the person is resident they must occupy the premises lawfully – either as tenants (of any type) or licensees. However, some tenants and

---

[58]  (1986) 18 HLR 341.

licensees, known as 'excluded tenants and licensees' are only protected up to the end of their right to occupy – after this they are treated as trespassers and are not protected by PEA. The provisions as to tenancies and 'excluded' licences wee introduced by s 31 of the Housing Act 1988, adding a new s 3A to the PEA. Again this is discussed in Chapter 4 but the main categories of 'excluded' tenancies and licences are:

- those sharing accommodation with their landlord
- holiday occupational agreements
- licensees of local authority hostels.

The offence of unlawful eviction in s 1(2) PEA is committed by anyone who unlawfully deprives 'a residential occupier' of their occupation of premises. The 'unlawfulness' of the 'deprivation' will depend on whether a court order has been obtained[59]. Whether an occupier had been 'deprived' of occupation is largely a question of fact. A good example of the difficulties involved can be seen in *R v Yuthiwatthana*[60].

In this case, the occupier lived in a ground floor bed-sit of a house in which his landlady and her husband also lived. He enjoyed shared use of a kitchen and bathroom[61]. For various reasons the relationship between the parties rapidly deteriorated, various acts of (claimed) harassment took place (see below) and eventually the landlady 'ordered' the tenant out of the house. He left and spent the night in a homeless persons' hostel. The following morning he was readmitted to the premises. The Court of Appeal held that to constitute the 'deprivation' of occupation there had to be something having the 'character' of an eviction. This need not be permanent, but had to be more than transient. 'Locking out' cases should be dealt with (if at all) as cases of harassment. Therefore here the defendant was not guilty of unlawful eviction. Kerr LJ stated[62]:

> 'In that connection Mr Stephenson referred us to a decision of this court which is a long way from the present case but which was concerned with the concept of eviction: *Commissioners of Crown Lands v Page* [1960] 2 QB 274. I need not refer to the facts of that case, but at p 279 Lord Evershed said that the short point raised in the action and the appeal was whether the exercise by the Minister of certain rights of requisition operated as an eviction of the lessee, as that term is properly understood. At p 282, having referred to some of the authorities, he said that to constitute an eviction it "must be of a permanent character"; and that is in substance what Mr Stephenson submits.

> In our view "permanency" goes too far. For instance, if the owner of the premises unlawfully tells the occupier that he must leave the premises for some period, it may be of months or weeks, and then excludes him from the premises, or does anything else with the result that the occupier effectively has to leave the premises and find other accommodation, then it would in our view be open to a jury to convict the owner under subs (2) on he ground that he had unlawfully deprived the occupier of his occupation. On the other hand,

---

[59]　PEA 1977 s 3(1) – again discussed in Chapter 4.
[60]　(1984) 16 HLR 49.
[61]　Today this would, of course, mean he was excluded from protection under the amended s 3A PEA.
[62]　(1984) 16 HLR 49, at p 63.

cases which are more properly described as "locking out" or not admitting the occupier on one or even more isolated occasions, so that in effect he continues to be allowed to occupy the premises but is then unable to enter, seem to us to fall appropriately under subs (3)(a) or (b), which deal with acts of harassment.

In our view, the prosecution case about the events of 28 April fell into this category. They might have been presented in a different way. It might have been alleged that the appellant there and then intended to exclude Mr Nelson permanently, never to allow him to come back, but that there was then a change of mind on her part or that of her husband.

But that was not how the case was put. Having regard to how it was put, the mere exclusion for one night cannot, in our view, properly be regarded as a deprivation of occupation under subs (2).'

There are two separate offences of harassment, one where the defendant is the landlord (or their agent) – the other can be committed by any person. The definition of the type of conduct necessary to establish harassment is common to both offences, the difference lies in the nature of the intent which needs to be proved (it is more rigorous in relation to the specific 'landlord' offences).

The 'harassing conduct' may be one of two acts:
- acts 'likely to interfere with ...peace and comfort'
- persistently 'withdraw[ing] or withhold[ing]' services[63].

Although the PEA does not define either of these concepts their meaning is reasonably clear:
- The former relates to what is now most commonly referred to as 'anti-social behaviour'. Specific instances could include excessive noise, threats of violence, knocking holes in the premises(!) and so on. One possible limitation is that an offence is not committed if a landlord simply fails to act, for example by a landlord discontinuing work in the premises commenced for legitimate reasons and then failing to put things 'right' again[64].
- 'Services' have been held to include the supply of gas, water or electricity[65].

As already mentioned a lesser 'intent' needs to be proved for the specific 'landlord' offence. The 'general' offence requires specific proof that the defendant carried out the acts in question with the intention of causing the 'residential occupier' to leave or refrain from attempting to enforce their rights[66]. The 'landlord' offence merely requires that the landlord knew or had 'reasonable cause to believe' that their actions would have 'harassing' consequences – there is no need to prove a specific intention to bring such consequences about[67].

---

[63]  PEA 1977 s 1(3A).
[64]  See *R v Zafar Ahmad* (1986) 18 HLR 416.
[65]  See *Westminster City Council v Peart* (1968) 19 P & CR 736.
[66]  Although s 29 Housing Act 1988 amended s 1(3) so that the acts only have to be 'likely' to bring out the necessary 'harassing' conduct rather than having to be 'calculated' to do so.
[67]  The 'landlord' offence was introduced by s 29 Housing Act 1988 as it was perceived that the need to prove a specific intent in s 1(3) was a serious practical loophole for landlords.

## Protection from Harassment Act 1997

This legislation is aimed at harassment per se, not merely in relation to housing, but it clearly has implications for tenants and others occupying residential accommodation. The legislation provides for civil remedies as well as criminal sanctions[68]. It clearly provides a further range of sanctions against harassing landlords but also extends to harassment by neighbours, ex-partners, 'flatmates' and so on.

## PROTECTION FROM HARASSMENT ACT 1997

### Prohibition of harassment

1   (1)   A person must not pursue a course of conduct—

(a)   which amounts to harassment of another, and
(b)   which he knows or ought to know amounts to harassment of the other.

(2)   For the purposes of this section, the person whose course of conduct is in question ought to know that it amounts to harassment of another if a reasonable person in possession of the same information would think the course of conduct amounted to harassment of the other.

(3)   Subsection (1) does not apply to a course of conduct if the person who pursued it shows—

(a)   that it was pursued for the purpose of preventing or detecting crime;
(b)   that it was pursued under any enactment or rule of law or to comply with any condition or requirement imposed by any person under any enactment, or
(c)   that in the particular circumstances the pursuit of the course of conduct was reasonable.

### Offence of harassment

2   (1)   A person who pursues a course of conduct in breach of section 1 is guilty of an offence.

(2)   A person guilty of an offence under this section is liable on summary conviction to imprisonment for a term not exceeding six months, or a fine not exceeding level 5 on the standard scale, or both.

### Civil remedy

3   (1)   An actual or apprehended breach of section 1 may be the subject of a claim in civil proceedings by the person who is or may be the victim of the course of conduct in question.

(2)   On such a claim, damages may be awarded for (among other things) any anxiety caused by the harassment and any financial loss resulting from harassment.

(3)   Where—

(a)   in such proceedings the High Court or a county court grants an injunction for the purpose of restraining the defendant from pursuing any conduct which amounts to harassment, and
(b)   the plaintiff considers that the defendant has done anything which he is prohibited from doing by the injunction,

the plaintiff may apply for the issue of a warrant for the arrest of the defendant

---

[68]   Protection from Harassment Act 1997 s 3.

...

## Putting people in fear of violence

4 (1)   A person whose course of conduct causes another to fear, on at least two occasions, that violence will be used against him is guilty of an offence if he knows or ought to know that his course of conduct will cause the other so to fear on each of those occasions.

(2)   For the purposes of this section, the person whose course of conduct is in question ought to know that it will cause another to fear that violence will be used against him on any occasion if a reasonable person in possession of the same information would think the course of conduct would cause the other so to fear on that occasion.

(3)   It is a defence for a person charged with an offence under this section to show that—

(a)   his course of conduct was pursued for the purpose of preventing or detecting crime,

(b)   his course of conduct was pursued under any enactment or rule of law or to comply with any condition or requirement imposed by any person under any enactment, or

(c)   the pursuit of his course of conduct was reasonable for the protection of himself or another or for the protection of his or another's property.

(4)   A person guilty of an offence under this section is liable—

(a)   on conviction on indictment, to imprisonment for a term not exceeding five years, or a fine, or both, or

(b)   on summary conviction, to imprisonment for a term not exceeding six months, or a fine not exceeding the statutory maximum, or both.

A court dealing with an offender under either s 2 or s 4 may make a 'restraining order' prohibiting the offender from further conduct which amounts to harassment or will cause a fear of violence[69].

The definition of 'harassment' in s 1 is very broad and (unlike s 1(3) or (3A) of the 1977 PEA) there is no need to prove any kind of intent it is enough that the conduct amounts to harassment and which the person either knows or 'ought to know' does so.

## Breach of the covenant of quiet enjoyment

In *McCall v Abelesz*[70] it was held that (what is now) s 1(3) PEA 1977 did not create a 'cause of action' for breach of statutory duty, ie did not create direct civil liability for damages. More recently specific statutory torts have been created in relation to various forms of harassment and unlawful eviction[71]. However, it is often forgotten that there may be significant mileage in considering an action for breach of contract – most specifically breach of the implied covenant of quiet enjoyment. All tenants – of whatever type – have a right to relative autonomy and freedom from disturbance by their landlord. Licensees possess no such inherent common law rights, but the courts may be prepared to imply an analogous term to prevent the licensor unduly interfering with the licensee's legitimate use of the premises[72].

---

[69]   Ibid s 5. There is a close affinity here with ASBOs and the other matters mentioned in Chapter 9.

[70]   [1976] QB 585.

[71]   For example, s 27 Housing Act 1988, and s 3 Protection from Harassment Act 1997.

[72]   See, for example, *Smith v Nottinghamshire County Council* (1981) Times, 13 November, where students in a hall of residence owned by Trent Polytechnic were unable to study for their examinations because of noise and other disturbance caused by building works in an adjacent hall.

Quiet enjoyment carries the underlying sense of 'undisturbed' rather than freedom from noise per se (although excessive noise deliberately caused by the landlord no doubt breaches the covenant). Typical instances would include landlords who enter tenanted premises unannounced or who commit classic acts of harassment such as cutting off gas and electricity[73]. The general question of the overall scope of the implied covenant was discussed by the House of Lords in the joint decisions of *Southwark London Borough Council v Tanner and Baxter v Camden London Borough Council (No 2)*[74].

Both cases involved complaints of noise consequent on inadequate design and/or construction standards in local authority accommodation. The cases also involve issues concerning noise nuisance and are further discussed in Chapter 12. However, part of the tenants' claims centred on an argument that in facilitating excessive noise because of inadequate sound insulation, the local authority landlords had breached the implied covenant of quiet enjoyment. The House of Lords held that although regular excessive noise *could* amount to a breach of the covenant, the covenant could not be used concerning noise which was the inevitable result of the condition of the property prior to the commencement of the tenancy.

Lord Hoffmann stated[75]:

> 'The covenant for quiet enjoyment is therefore a covenant that the tenant's lawful possession of the land will not be substantially interfered with by the acts of the lessor or those lawfully claiming under him. For present purposes, two points about the covenant should be noticed. First, there must be a substantial interference with the tenant's possession. This means his ability to use it in an ordinary lawful way. The covenant cannot be elevated into a warranty that the land is fit to be used for some special purpose: see *Dennett v Atherton* (1871–72) LR 7 QB 316. On the other hand, it is a question of fact and degree whether the tenant's ordinary use of the premises has been substantially interfered with. In *Sanderson v Berwick-upon-Tweed Corpn* (1884) 13 QBD 547 the flooding of a substantial area of agricultural land by water discharged from neighbouring land occupied by another tenant of the same landlord was held to be a breach of the covenant. In *Kenny v Preen* [1963] 1 QB 499 a landlord's threats to evict the tenant, accompanied by repeated shouting and knocking on her door, was held to be a breach. It is true that in *Browne v Flower* [1911] 1 Ch 219, 228, Parker J said that:
>
> > "to constitute a breach of such a covenant there must be some physical interference with the enjoyment of the demised premises, and that a mere interference with the comfort of persons using the demised premises by the creation of a personal annoyance such as might arise from noise, invasion of privacy, or otherwise is not enough".
>
> ...
>
> There is however another feature of the covenant which presents the appellants with a much greater difficulty. It is prospective in its nature: see *Norton*

---

[73]   *Perera v Vandiyar* [1953] 1 WLR 672.
[74]   [2001] 1 AC 1.
[75]   Ibid at p 10.

*on Deeds*, 2nd ed (1928), pp 612–613. It is a covenant that the tenant's lawful possession will not be interfered with by the landlord or anyone claiming under him. The covenant does not apply to things done before the grant of the tenancy, even though they may have continuing consequences for the tenant. Thus in *Anderson v Oppenheimer* (1880) 5 QBD 602 a pipe in an office building in the City of London burst and water from a cistern installed by the landlord in the roof flooded the premises of the tenant of the ground floor. The Court of Appeal held that although the escape of water was a consequence of the maintenance of the cistern and water supply by he landlord, it was not a breach of the covenant for quiet enjoyment. It did not constitute an act or omission by the landlord or anyone lawfully claiming through him after the lease had been granted. The water system was there when the tenant took his lease and he had to take the building as he found it. Similarly in *Spoor v Green* (1874) LR 9 Ex 99 the plaintiff bought land and built houses upon it. The houses were damaged by subsidence caused by underground mining which had taken place before the sale. The Court of Exchequer held that there was no breach of the covenant for quiet enjoyment which had been given by the vendor. Cleasby B said, at p.108:

> "it seems to me impossible to say that there is a breach of covenant for quiet enjoyment by reason of the subsidence of the house in consequence of the previous removal of the coal. This subsidence of the house was a necessary consequence of the condition of the property bought by the plaintiff …" '

Later Lord Millett stated[76]:

'The covenant for quiet enjoyment is one of the covenants of title formerly found in a conveyance of land, and the only such covenant found in a lease of land. It has long been understood that the word "quiet" in such a covenant does not refer to the absence of noise. It means without interference. The covenant for quiet enjoyment was originally regarded as a covenant to secure title or possession. It warranted freedom from disturbance by adverse claimants to the property: see *Dennett v Atherton* LR 7 QB 316; *Jenkins v Jackson* 40 Ch D 71; *Hudson v Cripps* [1896] 1 Ch 265. But its scope was extended to cover any substantial interference with the ordinary and lawful enjoyment of the land, although neither the title to the land nor possession of the land was affected: *Sanderson v Berwick-upon-Tweed Corpn* (1884) 13 QBD 547, 551.

Despite this there has lingered a belief that, although there need not be physical irruption into or upon the demised premises, there must be a "direct and physical" interference with the tenant's use and enjoyment of the land.

On this ground the courts have dismissed complaints of the making of noise or the emanation of fumes, of interference with privacy or amenity, and other complaints of a kind commonly forming the subject matter of actions for nuisance. Little harm seems to have been done, since in cases where a remedy was appropriate the tenant has been able to have recourse to the landlord's

---

[76] Ibid at p 22.

implied obligation not to derogate from his grant. But the existence of the limitation has been questioned: (see *Kenny v Preen* [1963] 1 QB 499) or circumvented by the round assertion that it is satisfied in what might be thought somewhat doubtful circumstances: (see *Owen v Gadd* [1956] 2 QB 99), and I think that we should consider whether it is a proper one.

There is nothing in the wording of the conventional covenant that would justify the limitation. I do not know whether it owes its existence to a desire to maintain some connection with the original scope of the covenant as a covenant securing title or possession, or to the mistaken notion that actions for nuisance 'productive of sensible personal discomfort' were actions for causing discomfort to the person rather than for causing injury to the land: see *Hunter v Canary Wharf Ltd* [1997] AC 655, 706. Now that this fallacy has been exposed, however, I can see no sound reason for confining the covenant for quiet enjoyment to cases of direct and physical injury to land.

Accordingly, I agree with the tenants that the covenant for quiet enjoyment is broken if the landlord or someone claiming under him does anything that substantially interferes with the tenant's title to or possession of the demised premises or with his ordinary and lawful enjoyment of the demised premises. The interference need not be direct or physical. Nor, in my opinion, is it a necessary precondition of liability on the covenant that the acts alleged to constitute the breach would support an action in nuisance. I do not doubt that this will usually be a sufficient condition of liability, but there is nothing in the language of the conventional form of the covenant that would justify holding it to be a necessary one.

...

[However] In the present cases the covenants guaranteed "the tenant's right to remain in and to enjoy the quiet occupation of *the dwelling house*" (emphasis added), that is to say the dwelling house comprised in the tenancy. This must be identified at the date when the tenancy was granted. In each case it consisted of a flat in a building constructed or adapted for multiple residential occupation and having inadequate sound insulation. An undesirable feature of the flat was its propensity to admit the sounds of the every day activities of the occupants of adjoining flats. The landlord covenanted not to interfere with the tenant's use and enjoyment of a flat having that feature. It has not done so. It has not derogated from its grant, nor has it interfered with any right of the tenant to make such use and enjoyment of the premises comprised in the tenancy as those premises are capable of providing. To import into the covenant an obligation on the part of the landlord to obtain possession of the adjoining premises and not relet them, or to install sound insulation, would extend the operation of the grant ...'.

If the covenant is breached by a landlord, typical redress would be by way of a claim for damages. The general aim of a damages claim for breach of contract is to put the 'injured' party into the position they would have been in had the contract been carried out as agreed[77].

In the context of a claim for breach of the quiet enjoyment covenant this would typically comprise some combination of:

- 'general' damages for matters like discomfort, loss of enjoyment, mental distress, pain and suffering, physical injury and general inconvenience; and
- 'special' damages concerning specific, identifiable losses, such as damage to the tenant's property, or the cost of alternative accommodation if the tenant is forced out of the premises by the landlord's conduct.

Aggravated and exemplary damages are not available in breach of contract claims[78].

## Other civil law claims

Despite the general rejection of a tort of harassment/unlawful eviction in *McCall v Abelesz*[79] it has always been the case that landlords (and others) who harass/ unlawfully evict their tenants may have committed other torts such as trespass to land, trespass to the person or even nuisance. However, of most significance are the statutory torts provided for by s 27 Housing Act 1988 and s 3 Protection from Harassment Act 1997. There is, as yet, little or no case law on the latter but the former has been extensively litigated.

As discussed earlier[80], the 'creeping decontrol' in the Rent Act 1957 led to significant landlord 'abuse' and (eventually) to the harassment and unlawful eviction provisions in Pt III Rent Act 1965. Similarly the move from a fair rent regime guaranteeing significant tenant security of tenure (in the Rent Act 1977) to a largely market rent regime accompanied by (at best) much reduced tenant security in the Housing Act 1988 Pt I[81] provided a similar temptation for landlords. Therefore the 1988 Act:

- created a new offence of landlord harassment (1977 PEA s 1(3A));
- amended the pre-existing offence of harassment (1977 PEA s 1(3)); and
- provided for new civil law remedies for tenants who had been unlawfully evicted/harassed into leaving.

The amendments to the 1977 PEA s 1(3) have already been discussed. The new civil law rights are contained in ss 27 and 28 of the 1988 Act.

# CHAPTER IV

# PROTECTION FROM EVICTION

### 27.    **Damages from unlawful eviction**

---

[77]  *Robinson v Harman* (1848) 1 Ex 850.
[78]  *Branchett v Beaney* (1992) 24 HLR 348.
[79]  See n 70 above.
[80]  See nn 51–53 above.
[81]  Discussed in more detail in Chapter 4.

(1) This section applies if, at any time after 9th June 1988, a landlord (in this section referred to as 'the landlord in default') or any person acting on behalf of the landlord in default unlawfully deprives the residential occupier of any premises of his occupation of the whole or part of the premises.

(2) This section also applies if, at any time after 9th June 1988, a landlord (in this section referred to as 'the landlord in default') or any person acting on behalf of the landlord in default—

(a) attempts unlawfully to deprive the residential occupier of any premises of his occupation of the whole or part of the premises, or

(b) knowing or having reasonable cause to believe that the conduct is likely to cause the residential occupier of any premises—

    (i) to give up his occupation of the premises or any part thereof, or

    (ii) to refrain from exercising any right or pursuing any remedy in respect of the premises or any part thereof,

does acts likely to interfere with the peace or comfort of the residential occupier or members of his household, or persistently withdraws or withhold services reasonably required for the occupation of the premises as a residence,

and, as a result, the residential occupier gives up his occupation of the premises as a residence.

(3) Subject to the following provisions of this section, where this section applies, the landlord in default shall, by virtue of this section, be liable to pay to the former residential occupier, in respect of his loss of the right to occupy the premises in question as his residence, damages assessed on the basis set out in section 28 below.

(4) Any liability arising by virtue of subsection (3) above—

(a) shall be in the nature of a liability in tort; and

(b) subject to subsection (5) below, shall be in addition to any liability arising apart from this section (whether in tort, contract or otherwise).

...

(6) No liability shall arise by virtue of subsection (3) above if—

(a) before the date on which proceedings to enforce the liability are finally disposed of, the former residential occupier is reinstated in the premises in question in such circumstances that he becomes again the residential occupier of them; or

(b) at the request of the former residential occupier, a court makes an order (whether in the nature of an injunction or otherwise) as a result of which he is reinstated as mentioned in paragraph (a) above;

and, for the purposes of paragraph (a) above, proceedings to enforce a liability are finally disposed of on the earliest date by which the proceedings (including any proceedings on or in consequence of an appeal) have been determined and any time for appealing or further appealing has expired, except that if any appeal is abandoned, the proceedings shall be taken to be disposed of on the date of the abandonment.

(7) If, in proceedings to enforce a liability arising by virtue of subsection (3) above, it appears to the court—

(a) that, prior to the event which gave rise to the liability, the conduct of the former residential occupier or any person living with him in the premises concerned was such that it is reasonable to mitigate the damages for which the landlord in default would otherwise be liable, or

(b) that, before the proceedings were begun, the landlord in default offered to reinstate the former residential occupier in the premises in question and either it was unreasonable of the former residential occupier to refuse that offer or, if he had obtained alternative accommodation before the offer was made, it would have been unreasonable of him to refuse that offer if he had not obtained that accommodation,

the court may reduce the amount of damages which would otherwise be payable by such amount as it thinks appropriate.

(8) In proceedings to enforce a liability arising by virtue of subsection (3) above, it shall be a defence for the defendant to prove that he believed, and had reasonable cause to believe—

(a) that the residential occupier had ceased to reside in the premises in question at the time when he was deprived of occupation as mentioned in subsection (1) above or, as the case may be, when the attempt was made or the acts were done as a result of which he gave up his occupation of those premises; or

(b) that, where the liability would otherwise arise by virtue only of the doing of acts or the withdrawal or withholding of services, he had reasonable grounds for doing the acts or withdrawing or withholding the services in question.

28.  **The measure of damages**

(1) The basis for the assessment of damages referred to in section 27(3) above is the difference in value, determined as at the time immediately before the residential occupier ceased to occupy the premises in question as his residence, between—

(a) the value of the interest of the landlord in default determined on the assumption that the residential occupier continues to have the same right to occupy the premises as before that time; and

(b) the value of that interest determined on the assumption that the residential occupier has ceased to have that right.

(2) In relation to any premises, any reference in this section to the interest of the landlord in default is a reference to his interest in the building in which the premises in question are comprised (whether or not that building contains any other premises) together with its cartilage.

(3) For the purposes of the valuations referred to in subsection (1) above, it shall be assumed—

(a) that the landlord in default is selling his interest on the open market to a willing buyer;

(b) that neither the residential occupier nor any member of his family wishes to buy; and

(c) that it is unlawful to carry out any substantial development of any of the land in which the landlord's interest subsists or to demolish the whole or part of any building on that land.

…

In effect, three substantive defences are made available to the landlord by s 27:

● that the claimant has, in any event, been 'reinstated' in the premises – assuming such 'reinstatement' is genuine and allows true residential occupancy to recommence[82]. In such cases the 'mischief' s 27 is aimed at has been dealt with by other means;

● that the court has ordered 'reinstatement';

● that the landlord believed, and had reasonable cause to believe, that the occupier had ceased to reside in the premises.

---

[82]  See, for example, *Tagro v Cafane and Patel* (1991) 23 HLR 250 where this was *not* the case.

In addition, s 27(7) imposes on the claimant a statutory duty to mitigate her/his loss[83].

Section 28 provides for the way in which 's 27 damages' are to be assessed. Broadly this consists in the difference in value (as at the date when the residential occupier left the premises) between the value of the landlord's interest with a 'sitting' tenant and the value of the landlord's interest without such a tenant.

As should be readily appreciated if the tenant has the 'high security value' of a Rent Act protected or statutory tenant (see Chapter 4), or (to a somewhat lesser extent) a Housing Act 1988 assured tenant, damages are likely to be significant, whereas if they are an assured shorthold tenant they are likely to be low or even non-existent. Likewise the eviction of a tenant who has only a few days of the tenancy remaining is unlikely to lead to a substantial damages claim. Until the mid-1990s a number of instances of very high damages awards under s 27 were reported, but as the numbers of Rent Act tenants have declined *and* as rents even under such tenancies have risen (again see Chapter 4), the size of awards have steeply declined. However, even though not wholly representative of most situations likely to arise today under s 27, *Tagro v Cafane and Patel*[84] still serves to demonstrate well the progress of a 's 27 action' and the interrelationship between 's 27 damages' and other general damages claims.

Tagro suffered numerous acts of harassment from her landlord. Finally she was locked out of her 'bed-sit' room and the locks were changed. Eventually she was readmitted to the premises but found her room in chaos – many of her personal possessions had been broken and others had been stolen. She left the premises and claimed damages. At trial, valuation evidence was given that the landlord's interest with vacant possession was £75,000, and with a sitting tenant, £31,000. The judge awarded £31,000 damages to Tagro under s 27 plus £15,588 in respect of trespass to goods. The Court of Appeal dismissed the appeal.

Lord Donaldson MR stated[85]:

> 'There is no dispute, of course, that Miss Tagro was a residential occupier, and immediately after August 2 she was a former residential occupier.
>
> Mr Carnwath says in relation to subsection (6) that, in the case of Miss Tagro, the court made an order as a result of which she was reinstated as mentioned in paragraph (a), that is to say she was reinstated in the premises in question in such circumstances that she again became the residential occupier of them. He says it cannot seriously be suggested that a tenant who has been unlawfully evicted and whom the landlord is able and willing to reinstate, simply has an option whether to accept reinstatement or not.
>
> There are two quite separate questions there. As to the first – was Miss Tagro actually reinstated? – for my part, I have no doubt or hesitation in saying that she was not and could not be at that stage. Reinstatement does not consist in

---

[83] See, for example, *Regalgrand v Dickerson* (1996) 29 HLR 620 and *Wandsworth London Borough Council v Osei-Bonsu* [1999] 1 WLR 1011.
[84] (1991) 23 HLR 250.
[85] Ibid at p 255.

merely handing the tenant a key to a lock which does not work and inviting her to resume occupation of a room which has been totally wrecked. Therefore, on the facts of this case, that is an argument which simply does not run.

...

Mr Carnwath is therefore reduced to saying that the learned judge can be faulted on the footing that no reasonable judge could have accepted that evidence. That submission he made simply and with force and with slightly more difficulty when Russell LJ said, "Well, what should he have done?" It is true, I suppose, that he could have adjourned the hearing and urged the landlord to call expert evidence. But it is difficult to see how he could have said, "I am not satisfied that any damages are due on this evidence" and, if he is not to say that, then he would have in some way to reduce the surveyor's figure on the basis, I suppose, of what he [the judge] thought were proper values. Had he done so, this could would probably have quashed his decision on the grounds that he was acting not upon evidence and not upon something of which a judge should take judicial knowledge but upon some extraneous view as to a matter of fact.'

## POSTSCRIPT

The previous section would, on paper, suggest that a wide and effective legal armoury exists to combat harassment and unlawful eviction by landlords. However, the regulatory framework has been criticised as more impressive on paper than in practice. Cowan notes[86] that only 143 prosecutions were begun for unlawful eviction and harassment in 1996, of which only 54 ended in conviction. Only four landlords received a custodial sentence. Cowan argues strongly that the small number of prosecutions is a by-product of desire in local authorities, (the normal prosecuting agency) to seek agreement and consensus between landlords and tenants rather than resort to prosecutions save in the most serious cases[87]. He further notes that all previous research[88] indicated that it was small landlords (often resident landlords) who most often fell foul of the legislation, rather than landlords in the image of Rachman[89]: Cowan's general conclusion is that tenants lack sufficient knowledge about their rights and where to find that knowledge, and that the interests of local authorities are commonly against prosecution – particularly as it may be more cost-efficient to mediate[90].

Does any of this cast doubt on the move towards a 'consumer rights' perspective taking over from the entrenched statutory rights which have characterised most

---

[86] Cowan, D, *Harassment and Unlawful Eviction in The Private Sector* [2001] 65 Conv. May/June 249, at p 250.

[87] He cites a Department of the Environment circular, *Housing Act 1988: Protection of Residential Occupiers* Circular 3/89 in support of this.

[88] For example, Nelken, D, *The Limits of the Legal Process: A Study of Landlords, Law and Crime* (1983) Academic Press.

[89] See n 51.

[90] He draws on the results of research he and others conducted for the Department of the Environment, Transport and the Regions (DETR London 2000).

attempts at tenant protection since 1915? If the evidence suggests that, in relation to harassment and unlawful eviction tenants tend not to know their rights and local authorities are reluctant to prosecute might the same not apply to the type of 'regulation' envisaged by the Law Commission? Set against this is the apparent willingness of the OFT to challenge terms in rental agreements and to publicise tenant 'consumer rights' widely. In the end much would appear to depend on the powers likely to be given to the regulatory body involved and whether such a body is imbued with a 'rights enforcement' culture.

## FURTHER READING

Arden, A et al; *Quiet Enjoyment* (6th ed), (2002) Legal Action Group.

Cowan, D, *Housing Law and Policy* (1999) Macmillan, Chapter 15.

Law Commission: *Renting Homes*, Law Com No 284 Cm 6018 (November 2003).

Nelken, D, *The Limits of the Legal Process: A Study of Landlords, Law and Crime* (1983) Academic Press.

Office of Fair Trading: *Guidance on Unfair Terms in Tenancy Agreements*, OFT 356 (November 2001).

# CHAPTER 6

# Housing Law Procedure

## INTRODUCTION

This book is concerned primarily with substantive housing law; the material on related procedural matters in this chapter should not be seen as a substitute for consulting specialist works on housing case procedure[1]. However, housing law and procedure are so interwoven that a full understanding of housing law is not possible without some awareness of procedural issues. Four areas of procedure are examined in this chapter:

- possession claims
- homelessness cases
- disrepair actions
- unlawful eviction.

Taken together, these four areas highlight most 'core' procedural issues, ranging from county court actions, through county courts appellate jurisdictions to judicial review and the High Court. In addition these areas dovetail with distinct chapters, on the related substantive law; 'public' and 'private' security of tenure (Chapters 8 and 4); homelessness (Chapter 10); disrepair and unfitness (Chapter 12) and unfairness in tenancy agreements (Chapter 5).

Before considering these areas in turn, brief consideration is given to relevant procedural terminology and the sources of the main procedural provisions.

## KEY TERMS AND SOURCES

### Terms

An understanding of the basic terminology used in housing cases (and indeed in civil actions generally, in most instances) is important not only in understanding the remainder of this chapter, but also in fully appreciating many of the judgments contained in other chapters of this book. Amongst the more important expressions are the following terms.

---

[1]  For example, R Parmar and M Parry, *Court Procedure and Housing Cases – a practitioner's guide* (2002) Shelter and C Baker, J Manning and J Shepherd, *Housing Law: Pleadings in Practice* (2003) Sweet and Maxwell.

## Acknowledgement of service

A form which is returned to a court by a defendant to acknowledge receipt of the claim form and of the particulars of claim.

## Adjournment

A court order which puts off a court hearing to a specified alternative day or indefinitely. Adjournments may be made on specified terms, for example that a defendant moderates their behaviour – pays current rent plus an amount towards arrears.

## Default judgment (sometimes judgment in default)

If a defendant fails to file an acknowledgement of service – a defence within the time specified, the claimant may obtain a judgment in their favour 'in default'.

## Interim application

An application for a court order, or directions prior to the full hearing of the case.

## Letter before action

A letter written by a potential claimant to put another party on notice of her/his intention to commence proceedings (often written to induce a settlement of the case).

## Statement of case

The 'essentials' of a party's case. Typical examples include: a claim form, particulars (details) of a claim, a defence and a reply to a defence.

## Warrant

An order issued by a court giving court officers (bailiffs) the authority to put into effect the terms of a judgment. In housing cases the two commonest examples are probably:

## Warrant of execution

A warrant entitling a court bailiff to seize goods so that they may be sold to satisfy a judgment debt and court costs.

## Warrant of possession

A warrant used for the execution of a possession order. Under it the bailiff may evict anyone found on the premises.

## Sources

The key sources, as elsewhere in civil law, are the Civil Procedure Rules 1998[2], introduced under the Civil Procedure Act 1997 and related case law. The rules are conventionally abbreviated to CPR. Other housing law statutory and regulatory provisions also play their part. The introduction of the Civil Procedure Rules[3] saw a general standardisation of the forms used in the county court and the High Court. Further, in most instances, the county court now has concurrent jurisdiction with the High Court in housing law[4]. The CPR were the legislative expression of the aims and objectives outlined by Lord Woolf in his report 'Access to Justice'[5]. The guiding principle behind the report was that civil justice should be swifter, cheaper and more accessible. The overriding objective of the rules is to facilitate the above by more effective control by the courts of the process and progress of litigation. Indeed the Civil Procedure Rules begin (1.1(1)) with the words: 'These rules are a new procedural code with the overriding objective of enabling the court to deal with cases justly.'

## POSSESSION CLAIMS

Since 15 October 2001 almost all new possession claims came within Part 55 of the Civil Procedure Rules. More specifically, Part 55 applies to any of the following types of claim, issued after 15 October 2001[6]:
- possession claim brought by landlords
- possession claims against trespassers
- claims by tenants seeking 'relief against forfeiture'.

Section 1 of Part 55 deals with the normal procedure. Section 2 deals with the special procedures to be adopted for accelerated possession claims.

---

[2] CPR 1998 (SI 1998/3132).
[3] On 26 April 1999.
[4] Although judicial review applications remain the exclusive preserve of the High Court, and under CPR 55 PD para 2.1 possession claims can only be brought in the High Court in exceptional circumstances.
[5] Lord Woolf, *Access to Justice – Final Report to the Lord Chancellor on the Civil Justice System in England and Wales* (1996) HMSO.
[6] CPR 55.2.

## Section 1: Normal procedures

### Commencing a possession claim

Claims should normally be commenced in the county court for the district in which the property is situated[7]. The claim is commenced by filling in a claim form (N5 for possession, N5A concerning relief from forfeiture) with accompanying 'particulars of claim'. The latter expand on the nature of the claim outlined in brief on the first page of the claim form[8]. If the claim includes a claim for non-payment of rent, the particulars of claim must also set out the amount due at the start of the proceedings, the dates when arrears of rent arose, the daily rate of any rent and interest, any previous steps taken to recover the arrears of rent and any relevant information about the defendant's circumstances (for example, as to whether they are in receipt of social security benefits)[9].

In relation to the equivalent requirement to provide 'particulars of claim' in s 83(2) Housing Act 1985, it has been stated by the Court of Appeal that[10] '[particulars] require a specification sufficient to tell the tenant what it is he has to do to put matters right'. If that is true concerning a preliminary notice seeking possession, it must surely be even more true at the later stage of the possession claim itself. *Torridge* was concerned with a wholly inadequate specification of claimed rent arrears and here, of course, the Civil Procedure Rules themselves lay down exacting requirements. However, the court's approach is not confined to rent arrears cases but suggests a general need in 'particulars' to give sufficient detail for an adequate defence (where appropriate) to be mounted. On the other hand, exhaustive detail need not be required as the later case of *Dudley Metropolitan Borough Council v Bailey* demonstrates[11]. In this case, Gibson LJ stated[12]: 'the requirement of particulars is satisfied ...if the landlord has stated in summary form the facts which he then intends to prove in support of the stated ground for possession'. Again, this was in relation to a notice seeking possession, but there seems no reason to anticipate that the courts would impose a significantly more exacting requirement under the Civil Procedure Rules.

All possession claims need to identify the land to which the claim relates (in most cases this means the full address of the property), the ground(s) on which possession is sought and details of all occupiers known by the claimant to be in possession of the property[13]. The defendant must be served with the claim form and the particulars of claim not less than 21 days before the hearing date[14].

Where the possession claim relates to trespassers, the particulars of claim must state the claimant's interest in the land, and the circumstances in which the property has

---

[7]   The most obvious exceptions (CPR Practice Direction 55 para 1.3) are where there are important points of law involved, or the risk of public disturbance (eg trespass) so that the case is better dealt with by the High Court.
[8]   CPR 55.4.
[9]   CPR 55 PD 2.2 and 2.3.
[10]  *Torridge District Council v Jones* (1986) 18 HLR 107, at 114 per Oliver LJ.
[11]  *Dudley Metropolitan Borough Council v Bailey* (1990) 22 HLR 424.
[12]  Ibid at 431.
[13]  CPR PD 55 para 2.1.
[14]  CPR 55.5 (3)(b) (On issuing the claim, the court will fix a hearing date – not less than 28 days and normally not more than eight weeks from the date of issue).

been occupied without licence or consent[15]. Here the time period for the issue of the claim form and related particulars is shortened to not less than five days before the hearing date[16]. In some cases involving perceived trespassers, the claimant may not know the name of the occupants. if so, s/he can serve the documents either by attaching copies of them to the main door of the property, or by attaching them (in sealed envelopes) to stakes in the land[17].

## Responding to a possession claim

Normally, a defendant should 'file' a defence to the claim within 14 days of service of the particulars of claim. If s/he does not do so, they can still take part in the hearing but the court is entitled to take their failure into account when ruling on the issue of costs[18]. It is not possible to get judgment 'in default' in a possession claim to which Part 55 applies[19]. In claims against trespassers there is no requirement to file a defence – indicative of the likely short time period between the issue of the claim and the hearing[20].

## The hearing

At the initial hearing (or any adjourned hearing) the court may make a decision on the claim or give directions as to how the case should be dealt with ('case management directions')[21]. Obviously, some cases are sufficiently straightforward to be dealt with there and then, whereas other cases will need more detailed consideration, perhaps involving full legal submissions. In the former instance it is not unknown for county courts, particularly where the cases are undefended to list 40 or more cases for one session – claims often occupying no more than a few minutes of the courts' time. In principle, even in such a necessarily truncated hearing, and even in the absence of the defendant tenant[22], a claimant still has to satisfy the court that a valid notice was served correctly, that the ground(s) for possession are made out and (as appropriate) that it is reasonable for the court to make a possession order. In practice, the absence of written or oral evidence from the defendant will make it difficult for a court to get a full picture of the issues.

Under the post-Woolf procedure in the Civil Procedure Rules, all civil actions are allocated to a 'track' suitable for the value and complexity of the case. In relation to a possession action key issues as to how to allocate will be the amount of any rent arrears[23], the importance to the defendant of keeping possession, and the importance to the claimant of obtaining vacant possession[24]. In most cases possession actions will be allocated to the fast track, designed to ensure that relatively

---

[15]  CPR PD para 2.6.
[16]  CPR 55.5(2).
[17]  CPR 55(6).
[18]  CPR 15.4.
[19]  CPR 55.7(4).
[20]  CPR 55.7(2).
[21]  CPR 55.8.
[22]  And of any legal representative acting on the defendant's behalf.
[23]  CPR 26.
[24]  CPR 55.9 (1).

straightforward cases outside the jurisdiction of the small claims track proceed to trial quickly[25]. A possession case will not be allocated to the small claims track unless all the parties agree to this[26].

The normal rule is that parties should include all the matters they seek to rely on in their statement of case. However, if a claim has been allocated to the fast or multi track it is usually required that witnesses attend court to give oral evidence[27].

If the maker of a witness statement does not attend the hearing, and the defendant disputes evidence material to the case, the court will usually adjourn the proceedings to enable oral evidence to be given[28].

## The Order

If a possession claim succeeds, one of two possible orders can be made: an 'outright' (or absolute) order for possession, or a suspended possession order (often abbreviated to SPO). An outright possession order will require the defendant(s) to give up possession of the property at a specified date. A suspended possession order does not require possession to be given up – instead the order is suspended conditional upon satisfaction of prescribed conditions by the defendant, for example, paying current rent when due (plus a weekly or monthly amount towards the arrears) or refraining from acts of anti-social behaviour.

A breach by the defendant of such terms means that the order takes effect and the tenancy automatically comes to an end (see further Chapters 4 and 8).

A claimant will often seek to enforce a possession order by requesting the court to issue a warrant of possession. The two obvious cases where this will be necessary are where:

- The defendant fails to comply with an outright possession order requiring her/him to leave the property at a specified date.
- The defendant breaches an SPO so that the tenancy comes to an end.

The current rules[29] merely require a claimant to file a request at court for a warrant in the prescribed form, certifying that the possession order has not been complied with. It is not generally necessary for the claimant to give notice of the request to the defendant. This was criticised by the Court of Appeal in *Leicester City Council v Aldwinckle*[30].

Here, Aldwinckle was the secure tenant of a flat owned by Leicester City Council. In 1983 the council obtained an SPO. The terms were that Aldwinckle paid current rent, plus £10 per month towards rent arrears. In 1988 the defendant became ill and fell into further arrears. She was away from her flat for long periods, whilst attending hospital in London. In June 1989 the council housing benefit department

---

[25] CPR 28.
[26] CPR 55.9(2). This will, however, not be appropriate if the trial is likely to take more than one day.
[27] CPR 55.8 (3).
[28] So even though it would be normal practice for a social landlord to file witness statements over matters like the service of notices and the level of arrears, they may have to be prepared for the proceedings to be adjourned if the tenant does attend court and disputes crucial evidence.
[29] CPR Sch 2; County Court Rules Ord 26.
[30] *Leicester City Council v Aldwinckle* (1991) 24 HLR 40.

received an application from Aldwinckle in which she explained her illnesses, gave her London address and an address in the Wirral where she would be convalescing until October 1989. Despite this the council applied and obtained a warrant in July 1989 which was executed in August. When Aldwinckle returned to her flat in November she found that all her furniture and personal possessions had been taken in execution of the warrant. She applied to have the warrant set aside (see further below), but the Court of Appeal upheld the judge's refusal of this application. The council had not been under a duty to give notice to Aldwinckle of their intention to issue a warrant. The Court of Appeal did, however, note that the courts had an inherent power to prevent abuse of proceedings and avoid 'oppression'. As Leggatt LJ stated[31]:

> 'In my judgment it does not follow from the *Fleet Mortgages Ltd* case that where rules of Court do not require notice to be given to a tenant, the court can of its own motion insist on such notice where leave of the court to issue a writ of execution is not necessary. The court undoubtedly has inherent power to prevent abuse of proceedings and void oppression: *cf. Beale v MacGregor* (1886) 2 T.L.R. 311. But in my judgment, even though Miss Aldwinckle was not expecting execution to be levied against her possessions, the use of available process does not of itself constitute abuse nor amount to oppression; and the court would be interfering unjustifiably with the existing policy of Parliament were it to introduce its own requirements as to additional conditions that have to be satisfied before execution may issue.
>
> As a term of art "natural justice" refers to the duty to act fairly breach of which may move the court to intervene by way of judicial review. In that sense "natural justice" is irrelevant here. In the broader sense in which the term was used by Pennycuick V.C. it referred to those principles of fairness which will prompt the exercise of the court of its powers, whether statutory or otherwise. It is true that the Rules of the Supreme Court require notice to be given, and leave of the court obtained, before a warrant of possession is applied for; but the County Court Rules do not. The court cannot write in the missing requirement, because, as Lord Hailsham said in *Pealman v Varty* [1972] 1 W.L.R. 534 at p.540, it is not the function of the courts "to form first a judgment of an Act of Parliament and then to amend or supplement it with new provisions so as to make it conform to that judgment".'

Stocker LJ, and Neill LJ agreed, with some reluctance. In the words of the former[32]:

> 'I agree. I do so with some regret since had the County Court Rules, pursuant to which the warrant for possession and its execution were carried out, contained the same requirements as are contained in the equivalent High Court rule, this unhappy situation might not have arisen. I would also reiterate the hope expressed by my Lord, that in all the circumstances the council might restore the appellant to the occupancy of her flat having regard to the fact that it is standing empty and unlet.'

---

[31]   Ibid, at p 46.
[32]   Ibid, at p 47.

Warrants of possession are executed by court bailiffs, and are initially valid for 12 months, subject to renewal by the court[33].

## Setting aside the order

There are a number of grounds on which a defendant can apply to have a possession order made against her/him set aside. The most common basis for this is that the defendant did not attend the hearing when the order was made against them. Such an application can be made even after the possession order has been executed by a warrant of possession[34]. A court will, typically, look at these factors in such cases:

- whether the defendant acted promptly after finding out that the possession order had been made.
- whether the defendant had a good reason for not attending the trial.
- whether the defendant had a reasonable prospect of success at the trial[35].

As previously discussed (see Chapters 3 and 4; and see Chapter 8 below), a court has wide powers to suspend execution of an order, or to postpone the date of possession[36].

## Staying or suspending the warrant for possession before execution

A court has the power to stay or suspend a warrant at any time before it is executed. The powers largely stem from the same statutory provisions as those already outlined concerning suspending a possession order. However, in addition a county court has a general power to stay execution of court proceedings[37].

## Application to set aside executed warrants

This is, of course, very much the 'last chance saloon' for a defendant. Once a warrant has been executed a defendant is unable to rely on any of the statutory provisions already discussed (although of course a successful application to set aside the possession order itself can still be made at this later stage. If a court sets aside the possession order, the warrant is also set aside)[38].

If the order cannot be set aside, the warrant may only be set aside where it was obtained by fraud, or there has been an abuse of process, or 'oppression' in the execution of the warrant. The issue of 'oppression' has been before the courts on a number of occasions, for example in *London Borough of Hammersmith and Fulham v Hill*[39].

Here, in 1972, the defendant moved into a four-bedroom flat owned by the plaintiff council. In February 1990 the council commenced possession proceedings against

---

[33]  County Court Rules 1981, Ord 26 and r 6.
[34]  *Governors of the Peabody Donation Fund v Hay* (1986) 19 HLR 145.
[35]  CPR 39.3.
[36]  See, for example, s 85(2) Housing Act 1985, and s 9(2) Housing Act 1988.
[37]  S 88 County Courts Act 1984.
[38]  *Governors of the Peabody Donation Fund v Hay* (1986) 19 HLR 145.
[39]  *London Borough of Hammersmith and Fulham v Hill* (1994) 27 HLR 368.

her, alleging rent arrears of £722.62. On 19 April 1990 an order for possession was made against her, suspended on terms that she paid current rent plus arrears of £5.00 per week. The total money judgment was for £1,400. The defendant fell into further arrears. At the beginning of 1993 the council filed a request for a warrant of possession. At that stage the arrears were in excess of £3,000. The warrant was executed and the defendant evicted on 18 February 1993. On 3 March 1993 the defendant applied for the order for possession to be set aside, for leave to file a defence and counterclaim, and for the warrant of possession to be suspended. At the hearing it was accepted that the arrears were in the region of £2,000, the council having credited the defendant with £1,000 in respect of housing benefit. The defendant also swore an affidavit in which she stated that she only learned of the warrant three days before its execution. She said that she was informed by a representative of the council that she would have no chance of suspending the warrant unless she could find £1,000 within 24 hours.

Ultimately the case is inconclusive on the issues as to whether this did amount overall to 'oppression'. However, the Court of Appeal did feel that an arguable case had been made out for the county court to determine. Nourse LJ stated[40]:

'In support of her argument that the evidence in paragraph 19 of the defendant's affidavit discloses an arguable case of oppression, Miss Tagliavini makes the following principal points: first, that the representative of the plaintiffs to whom the defendant spoke was in such a relationship with her as to make it oppressive for him not to inform her of her right to apply to the court under section 85(2); secondly, that he did not inform her of that right; thirdly and alternatively, that if he did, or if she knew about it already, it was oppressive for him to discourage her from exercising it by putting an excessive estimate on what the court would require her to find, especially when the true state of the account between the plaintiffs and herself, as disclosed by the credit given on 1 March, was that she owed approximately £2,000 and not £3,000; fourthly, that in judging whether the estimate was excessive or not it would be pertinent to take into account what terms for a suspension of the warrant the judge himself had regarded as appropriate on 11 March.

Despite Miss Newberry's submissions to the contrary, Miss Tagliavini has persuaded me of the correctness of her second argument. I think that an arguable case on oppression has been disclosed and that it ought to be tried. It is neither necessary nor desirable to say more, although I should of course record that the plaintiffs deny both the factual allegations made by the defendant and their ability to amount to oppression. I have no idea, and I express no view, as to what the result of the trial will be. I am only satisfied that there ought to be one.'

A subsequent case was *Southwark London Borough Council v Sarfo*[41]. Here, on 28 September 1987 the claimant authority had granted the defendant a secure tenancy of a flat. She fell into arrears of rent and on 14 October 1991 the authority

---

[40]   Ibid, at p 372.
[41]   *Southwark London Borough Council v Sarfo* (1999) 32 HLR 602.

obtained an order for the recovery of the flat. At that time the arrears amounted to £5,025.15. The county court gave a money judgment for that amount, together with costs, in addition to making the order for possession. The order for possession was suspended on terms that the appellant paid the current rent and instalments of £2 a week towards the arrears. The arrears continued to grow until the defendant married Mr Sarfo, who made certain payments in respect of the rent and arrears. Warrants for the execution of the order for possession were stayed on terms on three occasions, namely 15 April 1993, 2 March 1994 and 5 July 1994. The arrears as at 2 March 1994 were £5,446.54, and as at 4 July that year, £5,275.15.

The appellant's husband left her in July 1995. On 10 July the arrears stood at £5,133.63, so there had been some reduction in the arrears since March and July of the previous year. On 7 August 1995 the defendant made an application for council tax benefit and housing benefit. The application was unsuccessful. It seems that at that time the Department of Social Security started to pay the defendant income support. On 22 September 1995 the appellant completed a housing benefit and council tax benefit claim form supplied by the respondent. Her file was then lost, and no payments materialised.

Further applications for housing benefit and council tax benefit was made by the defendant to the authority on 2 October 1995. Again, they were not processed. On 5 December 1995 the authority wrote to the defendant warning her that she was in breach of the court order, no payment having been received for the previous 21 weeks. The warning went on that unless the appellant could make up the shortfall of the missing payments, the council would apply to the court for possession of her home. The letter asked the appellant to contact the neighbourhood housing office as a matter of urgency.

That letter was followed by an undated letter headed 'URGENT NOTICE OF EVICTION/RENT ARREARS'. That letter warned the defendant that:

'... preparations are now in hand to send in the Bailiffs to evict you. I would advise you to start looking for another home.

YOU ARE STRONGLY ADVISED TO TAKE THE CONTENTS OF THIS LETTER VERY SERIOUSLY.'

The last sentence was typed in capital letters. The appellant contacted the authority and told them that she had applied for housing benefit.

On that same day an interview report was made ... That was headed in manuscript 'URGENT', with a ring around that word, the word being in capital letters. The form recorded that the appellant had filled in a housing benefit form the previous September, and attached to it was proof that the appellant was in receipt of income support and the date on which income support had started. A copy of that form was sent to the housing benefit team, and was received by them on 22 February. It was noted that the appellant had applied for housing benefit and council tax benefit from 26 September 1995 backdated to February 1995. In capital letters in manuscript at the bottom of the form under the heading 'Advice Given' appeared the words 'STOP COURT PROCEEDINGS – PLEASE'.

By 4 March 1996 the arrears had risen to £7,236.19 and (of course), in the absence of any housing benefit payments, would keep on rising. Eviction took place on 6 March.

In June 1997 the authority demolished the block in which the flat had been situated. In December 1997 the defendant applied to set aside the execution of the warrant on the ground of oppression. The judge found that there had been no oppression. The Court of Appeal refused to use their discretion to set aside the warrant because of the defendant's delay in applying and the fact that, in the interim, the block had been demolished. However, unlike the judge they were clearly of the opinion that 'oppression' had taken place.

Roch LJ stated[42]:

'The Recorder found that the behaviour of the respondent in seeking execution of a warrant for possession was not in the circumstances of this case oppression on the part of the council. I disagree. The eviction of a person from their home, even where there are arrears of rent, is a very grave step. For that reason the respondent rightly has laid down certain procedures which should be followed because those procedures contain certain safeguards for the individual tenants.

In this case the appellant had on no fewer than three occasions completed forms applying for council tax benefit and housing benefit. Had any of those applications been processed properly by the respondent, there is no reason in the papers before us for supposing that the payment of housing benefit and council tax benefit would not have gone back to February 1995 or at least to 10 July 1995 when the appellant's husband left her. Had that happened, there would not have been the enormous increase in arrears on which the respondent relied in seeking its warrant to execute the order for possession. Indeed, it may well be that the appellant would have continued to make modest reductions in the outstanding arrears. Moreover, had the form requesting the eviction been the subject of the respondent's own procedures, it would have been known that the appellant had an outstanding claim for housing benefit, which was outstanding because the respondent had not processed it correctly.

Finally, the pre-eviction letter which should have been sent was not sent, as the housing manager found. Nor was the pre-eviction visit made. Nothing was done to warn the appellant that the bailiffs would evict her on 6 March 1996 until she received a telephone call late on the afternoon of the 5th at a time when it would appear that the court office was either closed or a point had been reached at which nothing could be done that day to stop the bailiffs attending. It would seem that yet another officer of the respondent advised her that there was nothing that could be done, and that she should follow the advice of packing and leaving.

Against that background of maladministration by the respondent, the execution of the warrant depriving the appellant of her home was, in my judgment,

---

[42] Ibid, at p 607.

oppression and an oppressive use of the county court order. To execute the warrant in those circumstances can, in my view, be properly characterised as manifestly unfair.

As Bowen LJ observed in [*McHenry v Lewis* [1882] 22 Ch 397 a passage] which I have already cited, oppression may be very difficult if not impossible to define, but it is not difficult to recognise. It is the insistence by a public authority on its strict rights in circumstances which make that insistence manifestly unfair. The categories of oppression are not closed because no-one can envisage all the sets of circumstances which could make the execution of a warrant for possession oppressive.'

Finally, in *Lambeth London Borough Council v Hughes*[43], the facts were as follows.

The defendant was a secure tenant of the claimant authority. He fell into arrears of rent, which by June 1998 were £1,938. On 10 June 1998 he agreed with the claimant to pay the arrears at the rate of £4.21 per week. He did not keep to the agreement and, on 20 July, the authority commenced possession proceedings. On 8 September, by which time the arrears were £2,173.69, the county court made a possession order suspended on terms that the defendant paid the current rent plus £9.21 per week. The defendant failed to comply with the terms of the order and on 20 September 1998 the authority applied for a warrant of possession.

On 28 September 1999 the authority wrote to the defendant informing him that the warrant would be executed on 28 October 1999 and that he had to pay all the arrears by the day before the eviction if he wanted to avoid being evicted. The applicant went to see his housing officer who confirmed what was said in the authority's letter. She also told him to obtain legal advice but did not tell him of his rights under s 85(2) of the Housing Act 1985 to have a possession order 'stay(ed) or suspended' or that he could apply to the court to suspend the warrant without paying all the arrears.

After unsuccessfully trying to obtain legal advice, the applicant approached the court office. He was told that the warrant had not yet been issued and that although he could apply for a stay, he should not do so until he had received a letter from the bailiffs warning him of the impending eviction. Such a letter was sent on 21 October 1999 by second class post but it did not come to the defendant's attention until 28 October 1999, the day of the eviction.

The defendant then applied unsuccessfully to the county court to have the warrant set aside on the ground of oppression and abuse of process. However, the Court of Appeal allowed the appeal and set the warrant aside. Arden J stated[44]:

'What amounts to oppression must depend on the circumstances. We have been referred by counsel to the dictum of Bowen LJ in *McHenry v Lewis* cited by Brooke LJ in *Camden v Akanni*, and to passages in the judgment of Peter Gibson LJ in *Barking and Dagenham LBC v Sarfo*, but there was no case produced to us which is quite on all fours with this case. It is clear from the authorities that oppression includes oppressive conduct which effectively

43    *Lambeth London Borough Council v Hughes* (2002) 33 HLR 350.
44    Ibid, at p 358.

deprives a tenant of his opportunity to apply for a stay (see the *Hill* case). The position in this case is due to a combination of factors the conduct had that result. There was first the local authority's letter and the conversation with the housing officer, as set out in the judgment of Waller LJ, both of which indicated that payment in full of all arrears was required to avoid eviction. There has already been judicial criticism of the form of letter used by the local authority (see the judgment of HH Judge James in *Johnson*). The letter before us was not materially different from the letter before HH Judge James, and I would emphasise the points made by Waller LJ. In my judgment, it is time that the letter was amended. That should now be done without further delay. Despite the persuasive arguments of Mr Lonergan, I agree with my Lord, Waller LJ, that it was not, on the particular facts of this case, sufficient for the housing officer to tell Mr Hughes that he should take legal advice, although that no doubt was done to be helpful. As the judge pointed out, Mr Hughes was not told what steps he might want to take, with or without legal advice, to forestall Lambeth in seeking to evict him from the property. Complaint had been made at the hearing before the judge about that. Here, however, Mr Hughes was not wholly misled. He went to the legal advice centre, although he did not obtain satisfactory advice from them on this occasion. He also went to the court. He went to the court office where he was given inaccurate information. He was told that eviction papers had not been issued, although that information conflicted with the letter that Mr Hughes had received. He was also told that he should return when he received the warning letter from the bailiffs. It is obviously difficult for the court officials. They are not there to give advice and they were no doubt endeavouring to be helpful to Mr Hughes. It seems likely that they did not foresee that the warning letter to be sent by the bailiffs would be sent a day late and that it would arrive while Mr Hughes was away from the flat. If it had arrived on the 27th and Mr Hughes still had been there, it might have been in time to make an application for a stay. It would have been possible in court hours no doubt to make an emergency application. Rightly or wrongly, applications in this sort of case are also made out of hours to the duty judge in the Chancery Division. However, Mr Hughes says that he did not see the letter in time on the 27th, and it was the combination of all these factors which led to him being deprived of his opportunity to make an application for a stay under section 85(2).'

Waller LJ added[45]:

'The only remaining matter relates to the appropriate form of order. What Mr Lonergan submits is that, even if a case of oppression is made out, the remedy would be a discretionary one, and the discretion should be exercised against Mr Hughes. Mr Lonergan in this context referred to *Southwark LBC v Sarfo*, 19 July 1999, and pointed to the fact that in that case, despite finding oppression, the court exercised its discretion against the tenant. But the circumstances of that case are somewhat different from these. In that case the tenant did not apply for any relief until some 15 months after the eviction. By

---

[45]  Ibid, at p 357.

the time that the application was made the block of flats had been knocked down. The same flat was not available to the tenant. But it is of some interest in the context of Mr Lonergan's submission to note that Roch LJ felt driven to that conclusion, ie that the absence of the flat itself meant that the discretion should be exercised against the tenant, but he did suggest that the respondent authority should take into account the views of this court, thus indicating the way he would have been likely to exercise his discretion if the flat had still been there and despite the lateness of the application of Mr Sarfo. In this instance Mr Hughes applied on the day after the eviction. The grounds for saying that the discretion should be exercised against him are simply that Mr Hughes has been a bad tenant, a bad payer, things have got worse and not better, and thus Mr Hughes has no chance and never did have a chance of persuading any court under section 85(2) to stay or suspend the warrant. It is quite impossible for this court to go into all the details which need to be examined to decide whether a stay should be granted. Mr Luba accepts that his client has an uphill struggle but where, in a case of this sort oppression has been found, and the situation is that the application is made as swiftly as it was here, the appropriate course is to put Mr Hughes back into possession.'

A close examination of the above cases demonstrates clearly that although 'oppression' is incapable of precise definition, matters such as maladministration by the authority will be of paramount significance, particularly if its effect is to mislead the tenant as to her/his legal rights and/or dissuade her/him from applying to the courts before execution of the warrant.

## Section 2: Accelerated Possession Claims[46]

Where a landlord seeks possession of premises held an assured shorthold tenancy[47]. In order to use this procedure, the claim needs to be brought after the expiry of the appropriate period of notice under s 21 Housing Act 1988[48] and[49]:

- the tenancy was entered into on or after 15 January 1989
- the tenancy is the subject of a written agreement, or is a statutory periodic tenancy
- the tenancy did *not* follow on from an assured tenancy
- the relevant conditions for the creation of an assured shorthold tenancy were satisfied
- the only purpose of the claim is to recover possession of the property, and no other clam is made.

A claim is brought by filing a claim form in the prescribed form at court. The form combines a statement of case, plus all evidence in support of the claim (for example including – if appropriate – a copy of the relevant 's 20' notice and a statement of truth).

---

[46]   Generally see Section II CPR 55.
[47]   Before 2 October 2000 this 'special' procedure could also sometimes be used against assured tenants. The relevant 'rule' was revoked by SI 2000/2092.
[48]   See further Chapter 4.
[49]   CPR 55.11.

The defendant is required to put in any defence within 14 days of serve of the claim form. If no defence is filed in time, the claimant may file a written request for possession.

The court will consider the claim and (any) defence and may *in the absence of the parties:*

- make a possession order; or
- fix a hearing date; or
- strike out the claim.

A hearing date will be fixed if there is any doubt about the claimant's right to possession under s 21 Housing Act 1988[50]. In addition a date may be set where the defendant seeks a postponement of possession on the grounds of 'exceptional hardship'[51]. At the hearing, if the court is satisfied that 'exceptional hardship' would be caused by requiring possession to be given at the date of the possession order it may postpone the date by up to six weeks.

Finally, the court may set aside or vary a possession order made under the accelerated possession procedure. Again the maximum postponement is six weeks from the date of the original order. The defendant will need to demonstrate that there are 'exceptional circumstances'[52] – typically, serious procedural flaws.

## HOMELESSNESS CASES

Unlike the other material in this chapter, homelessness procedure is primarily concerned with public law matters. Private law claims in this area are rare, and no particular attention will be paid to them here. Challenging decisions of local housing authorities has, above all, traditionally been concerned with judicial review. Although a significant part of this section is concerned with the use of judicial review in homelessness cases, it will still only be possible to touch on some of the more contentious issues surrounding the scope of judicial review and it may be useful to also consult a specialist text on the subject[53]. Finally, even more than elsewhere in relation to housing issues, law and procedure are inextricably interwoven and a full understanding of homelessness procedure is impossible without an understanding of the substantive law (Chapter 10). This section will focus on three distinct (if linked) areas: internal homelessness reviews; appeals to the county court and judicial review in the High Court.

---

[50] CPR 55.16.
[51] Under s 89(1) Housing Act 1980.
[52] Ibid.
[53] For example Lord Clyde and D Edwards, *Judicial Review* (2000) W A Green; H Southey and A Fulford, *Judicial Review: A Practical Guide* (2004) Jordans; and S Halliday, *Judicial Review and Compliance with Administrative Law* (2003) Hart.

## Internal homelessness reviews

The relevant material here is covered more fully in Chapter 10. However, in outline, all homeless applicants have the right to request the local housing authority to whom they have supplied to review their decision[54]. This right exists in relation to decisions as to:

- eligibility for assistance
- the duties (if any) owed by the authority to the applicant
- notification and referral
- suitability of accommodation.

There is no right to request a review of a review[55]. Any such request must be made within a period of 21 days from the applicant being notified of the authority's decision. If the decision on review is to confirm the original decision the applicant must be notified of the reasons for this[56]. Regulations have been made[57] elaborating on the procedures to be adopted on review. However, these are not particularly prescriptive, leaving much to the discretion of the authority. For example, there is generally no right to an oral hearing[58], but some authorities do have provision for these, either on a preliminary review or on a 'second tier' basis[59]. Broadly the review can be conducted by the authority itself – typically via referral of the case to a person senior to the original decision maker who had not been involved in the original decision[60] or by an independent person or body appointed by the authority[61]. There is a right for the applicant, or their representative, to make representations in writing to the authority[62]. The review should be carried out within a period of eight weeks from the day the authority receives the request for a review, unless the authority and the applicant together agree in writing on a longer period[63].

As noted in Chapter 10, the authority has a power to continue accommodating the applicant whilst the review procedure takes its course. However, unlike the position in relation to appeals to the County Court[64] no appeal lies in relation to an authority's refusal to accommodate at this stage. The homeless applicant can only seek judicial review of that decision[65].

## Appeals to the county court

A homeless applicant who is dissatisfied with the decision on review, or who is not notified of the decision within the prescribed time, may appeal to the county court –

---

[54] S 202 Housing Act 1996.
[55] Ibid s 202(2).
[56] Ibid s 203(4).
[57] Currently the Allocation of Housing and Homelessness (Review Procedures) Regulations 1999, SI 1999/71 issued under a power contained in s 203 Housing Act 1996.
[58] The main exception is where the 'review' identifies a 'deficiency or irregularity' in the original decisions but is still 'minded' to confirm the decision. SI 1999/71, reg 8.
[59] No doubt a more searching internal review procedure is seen as likely to curb the likelihood of appeals to the courts under s 204 Housing Act 1996. The potential conflict of interest which some might see in the review being carried out by another officer of the authority appears not to offend against Art 6 of the European Convention on Human Rights (see Chapters 10 and 14).
[60] SI 1991/71 reg 2.
[61] Ibid reg 7.
[62] Ibid reg 3.
[63] Ibid reg 9. Regs 9(b) and (c) provide for slightly longer periods in a few cases.
[64] S 204A, Housing Act 1996.
[65] *R v Camden London Borough Council ex p Mohammed* (1997) 30 HLR 315.

on any point of law arising from the decision on review (or, if not notified, the original decision)[66]. The appeal must be brought within 21 days of the applicant having been notified of the decision on review (or the date by which s/he should have been notified)[67]. Section 204A of the Housing Act 1996 (added by s 11 of the Homelessness Act 2002) provides a right of appeal to the county court against a refusal, by an authority, to provide 'interim' accommodation pending the outcome of a s 204 appeal. In *Francis v Kensington and Chelsea Royal London Borough Council*[68], the Court of Appeal stated that in hearing such an appeal the process was more akin to judicial review than an appeal in the ordinary sense of the word. This would seem consistent with s 204(6) which states that:

'An order under subsection (5)–
(a)   may only be made if the court is satisfied that failure to exercise the section 204(4) power in accordance with the order would substantially prejudice the applicant's ability to pursue the main appeal ...'

As might be expected, any appeal under s 204A must be brought before the main appeal is heard[69].

Such appeals are governed by the Civil Procedure Rules Part 52 procedure[70]. This procedure is mainly concerned with appeals against decisions of the courts. Broadly, the appeal is commenced by filing a notice plus a skeleton argument, a copy of the decision being appealed and any witness statements, affidavits, or other documents in support of the appeal. Permission to appeal is not required as long as the appeal is brought within the 'normal' 21-day period. If the appeal is out of time the applicant must have good reason for the delay. Time is, of course, of the essence in the appeal being heard – particularly as many applicants may be in highly unsuitable accommodation or be sleeping rough! A request for an expedited hearing is, therefore, normal. In *R v Brighton and Hove Council ex p Nacion*[71], Lord Woolf MR stated:

'While recognising the other problems which confront county courts, it is my hope that in this jurisdiction of homelessness, county courts will do their best to see that points of law which are appropriately brought before them under section 204 are dealt with as promptly as possible.'

If an authority offers to settle the appeal out of court by agreeing to reconsider the case if the appeal is withdrawn it is vital to discover whether this is a mere discretionary reconsideration of the case or a fresh review decision. Only in the latter instance can the 'reconsideration' itself be appealed against[72].

---

[66]  S 204 Housing Act 1996.
[67]  Ibid s 204(2).
[68]  *Francis v Kensington and Chelsea Royal London Borough Council* [2003] HLR 715, discussed more fully in Chapter 10. The county court has power to quash the decision, or order the authority to 'secure' accommodation.
[69]  S 204A(3) Housing Act 1996.
[70]  Specifically CPR r.52.1 and PD 52, paras 17 and 24.2.
[71]  *R v Brighton and Hove Council, ex p Nacion* [1999] 31 HLR 1095 at p 1101.
[72]  *Demetri v Westminster City Council* (1999) 32 HLR 470.

## Judicial review

As already discussed[73], an in-depth examination of the parameters of judicial review is beyond the scope of this book, and if this is required a specialist text should be consulted. Judicial review is, at its broadest, a challenge to the 'legality' of a decision of a public body. In theory a court is properly concerned with whether the decision of that body was arrived at in a procedurally and substantively correct manner and not with the merits of the decision – which is properly a matter for the judgment of the public body itself. Despite this inherent limitation judicial review has proved a potent source of challenge to decisions of local housing authorities in homelessness cases – as Chapter 10 demonstrates. Since the inception of 'modern' homelessness legislation[74] almost all aspects of local authority decision making have been subject to 'judicial review' scrutiny, ranging from who is able to make an application, through key 'status' questions such as homelessness, priority need and intentional homeless to the appropriateness of the accommodation offered. Typical grounds for challenging a decision include; a misdirection of law; taking into account irrelevant considerations (or failing to take account of relevant ones); reaching a decision unsupported by any evidence or deciding an application on the basis of an inflexible rule or policy (often termed 'fettering' one's discretion) and general procedural unfairness.

A primary reason for the widespread use of judicial review in homelessness cases was traditionally the lack of any direct statutory appeal route against adverse decisions. In *O'Rourke v Camden London Borough Council*[75] the House of Lords unequivocally confirmed that proceedings to challenge a statutory homelessness decision[76] had to be by way of judicial review. Lord Hoffmann stated[77]:

> 'The question is whether section 63(1) creates a duty to Mr O'Rourke which is actionable in tort. There is no doubt that, like several other provisions in Part III, it creates a duty which is enforceable by proceedings for judicial review. But whether it gives rise to a cause of action sounding in damages depends upon whether the Act shows a legislative intention to create such a remedy. In *X (minors) v Bedfordshire County Council* [1995] 2 AC 633, 731, the principles were analysed by Lord Browne-Wilkinson in a speech with which the other members of the House agreed. He said that although there was no general rule by reference to which it could be decided that a statute created a private right of action, there were a number of "indicators". The indicator upon which Mr Drabble QC, who appeared for Mr O'Rourke, placed most reliance was the common sense proposition that a statute which appears intended for the protection of a limited class of people but provides no other remedy for breach should ordinarily be construed as intended to create a private right of action. Otherwise, as Lord Simonds said in *Cutler v Wandsworth Stadium Ltd* [1949] AC 398, 407, "the statute would be but a pious aspiration".

---

[73]   See n 53, above.
[74]   On 1 December
[75]   *O'Rourke v Camden London Borough Council* [1998] AC 188.
[76]   Then under the Housing Act 1985, Part III.
[77]   1998] AC 188, at p 192.

Camden, on the other hand, says that although Part III does not expressly enact any remedy for breach, that does not mean that it would be toothless without an action for damages or an injunction in private law. It is enforceable in public law by individual homeless persons who have *locus standi* to bring proceedings for judicial review. Furthermore, there are certain contra-indications which make it unlikely that Parliament intended to create private law rights of action.

The first is that the Act is a scheme of social welfare, intended to confer benefits at the public expense on grounds of public policy. Public money is spent on housing the homeless not merely for the private benefit of people who find themselves homeless but on grounds of general public interest: because, for example, proper housing means that people will be less likely to suffer illness, turn to crime or require the attention of other social services. The expenditure interacts with expenditure on other public services such as education, the National Health Service and even the police. It is not simply a private matter between the claimant and the housing authority. Accordingly, the fact that Parliament has provided for the expenditure of public money on benefits in kind such as housing the homeless does not necessarily mean that it intended cash payments to be made by way of damages to persons who, in breach of the housing authority's statutory duty, have unfortunately not received the benefits which they should have done.

A second contra-indication is that Part III of the 1985 Act makes the existence of the duty to provide accommodation dependent upon a good deal of judgment on the part of the housing authority. The duty to inquire under section 62(1) arises if the housing authority "have reason to believe" that the applicant may be homeless and the inquiries must be such as are "necessary to satisfy themselves" to whether he is homeless, whether he has a priority need and whether he became homeless intentionally. When the investigations are complete, the various duties under section 65 arise only if the authority are "satisfied" that the applicant is homeless and the extent of those duties depends upon whether or not they are "satisfied" as to two other matters, namely that he has a priority need and that he became homeless intentionally. If a duty does arise, the authority has a wide discretion in deciding how to provide accommodation and what kind of accommodation it will provide. The existence of all these discretions makes it unlikely that Parliament intended errors of judgment to give rise to an obligation to make financial reparation. Control by public law remedies would appear much more appropriate: see Lord Browne-Wilkinson in *X (Minors) v Bedfordshire County Council* [1995] 2 AC 633, at pp.747–748.

The question of the appropriate remedy for breach of the duties owed under the 1977 Act was considered by this House in *Cocks v Thanet District Council* [1983] 2 AC 286, which was decided on the same day as *O'Reilly v Mackman* [1983] 2 AC 237. Mr Cocks brought an action in the Thanet County Court, alleging that he was homeless and in priority need but that in breach of duty, the housing authority, Thanet District Council, had refused to house him. He claimed a declaration that the council was in breach of duty, a mandatory injunction and damages. The action was transferred to the Queen's Bench Division and a preliminary issue ordered as to "whether the proceedings were properly brought by action or could only be brought by application for judicial review". In his judgment, Lord Bridge of Harwich described this as a:

> "... procedural issue ... which ... will naturally fall for decision in the light of the principles expounded in the speech of my noble and learned friend, Lord Diplock, in *O'Reilly v Mackman* [1983] 2 AC 237".

This was, if I may say so with respect, a correct description of the way in which the issue was presented to this House. But concealed within it was a substantive question which was not present in *O'Reilly v Mackman* namely, whether the relief sought in the action could be claimed at all. In *O'Reilly v Mackman* all that was claimed was a declaration that an act, undoubtedly operating solely in public law, namely the adjudication of prison visitors, was invalid. The only question was therefore whether such relief could be claimed in an action begun by writ. In *Cocks v Thanet District Council*, on the other hand, the plaintiff claimed a declaration, injunction and damages on the basis that he was owed a private law duty. The first question was therefore whether such a duty existed. If it did, there could be no objection to the plaintiff pursuing a tortuous cause of action by writ. On the other hand, if he did not, then the *O'Reilly v Mackman* question of the procedure by which he could pursue a public law remedy would arise.

Lord Bridge went on, however, to say that a duty in private law would arise once the housing authority had made a decision in the applicant's favour. He said:

> "On the other hand, the housing authority are charged with executive functions. Once a decision has been reached by the housing authority which gives rise to the temporary, the limited or the full housing duty, rights and obligations are immediately created in the field of private law. Each of the duties referred to, once established, is capable of being enforced by injunction and the breach of it will give rise to a liability in damages. But it is inherent in the scheme of the Act that an appropriate public law decision of the housing authority is a condition precedent to the establishment of the private law duty."

My Lords, I must say with all respect that I cannot accept this reasoning. There is no examination of the legislative intent, the various considerations which I have discussed earlier as indicating whether or not a statute was intended to create a duty in private law sounding in damages. The fact that the housing authority is "charged with executive functions" is treated as sufficient to establish a private law duty. No doubt because the question did not have to be decided, Lord Bridge did not undertake a careful examination of the statutory intend such as he afterwards made in *R v Deputy Governor of Parkhurst Prison, ex p Hague* [1992] 1 AC 58, pp. 157–161. I feel sure that if he had, he would have expressed a different opinion. The concept of a duty in private law which arises only when it has been acknowledged to exist is anomalous. It means that a housing authority which accepts that it has a duty to house the applicant but does so inadequately will be liable in damages but an authority which perversely refuses to accept that it has any such duty will not. This seems to me wrong. Of course a private law relationship may arise from the implementation of the housing authority's duty. The applicant may become the authority's tenant or licensee and so bought into a contractual relationship. But there seems to me no need to interpose a statutory duty actionable in tort merely to bridge the gap between the acknowledgement of the duty and its implementation.

Both in principle and on the authority of the actual decision of this House in *Cocks v Thanet District Council* [1983] 2 AC 286 I would therefore hold that the breach of statutory duty of which the plaintiff complains gives rise to no cause of action in private law and I would allow the appeal and restore the order of Judge Tibber striking out the action.'

However, somewhat ironically, at almost the same moment that *O'Rourke* was underscoring the primacy of judicial review in homelessness cases, provisions in the Housing Act 1996 were reducing the significance of judicial review. As already discussed, s 204 Housing Act 1996 provides for a general right of appeal to the county court from local housing authority 'review' decisions. When taken together with the provision for 'internal' review in homelessness cases the scope for the application of judicial review is very significantly reduced. Given the general requirement of judicial review as a remedy that, before bringing such proceedings, a claimant must exhaust all her/his alternative remedies, it seems that it should only be available in situations where there is no right to seek a review and/or appeal to the county court. One important area which still does survive is a challenging to an authority's refusal to continue interim accommodation pending an s 202 review[78]. The courts will only rarely intervene in such cases but they are prepared to do so. In *R v Newham London Borough Council ex p Lumley*[79], Brooke LJ stated:

'I am, however, considering a rather different situation. The homelessness claim has only been considered once at local authority level. There is no question of an early hearing in the county court because no appeal can lie to that court until Mr Clarke completes his review. Regulations permit him a maximum period of eight weeks for his review (unless extended by consent), and his own evidence shows that he has a very heavy caseload.

He is the only appeals officer in the London Borough of Newham. He has an assistant who is able to process administrative tasks but cannot make decisions because of her lack of seniority. On occasion, I was told, he can call for the help of a deputy if he was himself involved in the original decision. Due to the increasingly large number of reviews during the course of 1999, he says that an extension of the review period had to be agreed in many cases. He has produced statistics which show that over a three-month period he was able to complete 108 reviews, a number which was five more than the number of new cases he received during that period, so that he was able to reduce the outstanding backlog from 49 to 44 cases.

[78] There is no right of appeal to the county court concerning such a refusal.
[79] (2000) 33 HLR 124.

...

This is the issue which Latham J addressed in *ex p. Mohammed*. In that case the respondent council had a policy for the provision of interim or temporary accommodation, whereby it would not be considered unless there were exceptional reasons. This, too, was a case in which a review was pending, so that the exercise of discretion under section 188(3) of the Act was in issue.

In that case there were statistics before the court which showed that during a recent three-month period 51 reviews had been dealt with, of which only four had been successful. (There are no similar statistics in the present case). Latham J said that this was a most useful piece of background information, since it indicated that there were very many requests for review of which only very few were found at the end of the day to have been meritorious. It seemed to him that the use by the council of the phrase "exceptional reasons" could properly be understood to reflect that reality. He continued at page 321:

> "The important question is whether, in applying that phrase, it is apparent that the officers of the respondent council have either failed to take into account material considerations, have taken into account immaterial considerations or have otherwise displayed irrationality. The need that I identify as the underlying requirement of the exercise of this discretion is to keep, on the one hand, well in mind the objective of fairness between those who are homeless in circumstances where the local housing authority has in its first decision decided that there is no duty to the particular applicant and, on the other hand, to give proper consideration to the possibility that the applicant may be right, and that to deprive him or her of accommodation could result in a denial of an entitlement.
>
> In carrying out that balancing exercise, it is clear that there are certain matters which will always require consideration. First, the merits of the case itself and the extent to which it can properly be said that the decision was one which was either apparently contrary to the merits of the case or was one which required a very fine balance of judgment which might go either way.
>
> Secondly, it requires consideration of whether there is any new material, information or argument put before the local housing authority which could have a real effect upon the decision under review.
>
> Finally, it requires consideration of the personal circumstances of the applicant and the consequences to him or her of an adverse decision on the exercise of discretion. It may well be that in some cases other considerations may prove to be relevant."

It is Latham J's use of the expression "the merits of the case" which has the potential for giving rise to difficulty. At first blush it would seem to relate to the merits of the case on the facts, once all necessary inquiries have been made. A study of the next page of his judgment (at pages 321–322) shows that he did not intend the expression to be interpreted quite so restrictively.

The reason I say this is that on the facts of the case before him the applicant, who had had to leave her home because of domestic violence, gave inconsistent accounts of her husband's conduct. The council did not invite her to explain these inconsistencies, but simply told her of its decision that she was not homeless because accommodation with her husband was still available. After requesting a review, her solicitors pointed out to the council that she had not been afforded the opportunity to address the inconsistencies in her statements. The council did not respond by giving her that opportunity there and then. Its representative said, however, that she had taken full account of the solicitors' letter and all the matters set out in it before reaching her decision (to refuse temporary accommodation pending the review) based on the entire circumstances of the applicant's case. Latham J commented at page 322:

> "In my judgment, that is an inadequate response to the point that was being made on behalf of this applicant which was, a point of some substance. It follows, that in relation to this particular decision, the respondent council did fall into error in failing to take into account a relevant and material consideration. Further, the original decision was tainted by unfairness; and the refusal to reconsider by bearing the applicant's explanation when the unfairness was identified compounded that unfairness. The consequence is that the decision under challenge must be quashed."

It is therefore clear that in his use of the expression "the merits of the case", Latham J must be taken to have meant "the merits of the applicant's case that the council's original decision was flawed", and I recommend that in any restatement of his guidelines this amendment should be made. In Mrs Mohammed's case he was satisfied that the council's original decision was flawed because it did not comply with its duty, as explained by Simon Brown J in *ex p. Winchester*, to give her an opportunity to explain matters which it was minded to regard as weighing substantially against her. In Mr Lumley's case the council's original decision was even more seriously flawed because it did not pursue proactively any inquiries of its own into his medical condition after being told by Mr Lumley's GP that he suffered from a severe depressive reaction, and did not give him the opportunity of responding to such adverse medical evidence as it did obtain, in the form of Dr Sohail's tick on the tick-box form.

Mr Clark did not take either of these matters into account when he considered the file over the weekend of November 6–7. If he had, he would have realised that it was unfair fro him to make any judgment on the medical evidence he found in the file, since the council had not carried out its duties properly (or indeed, in the relevant respect, at all). If he had realised this, he would in turn have realised that it would be unfair to place Mr Lumley in a worse position, as a result of the council's default, than his position just over five weeks earlier when the council had reason to believe that he might be homeless, eligible for assistance and have a priority need. Under section 188(1) of the Act it was under a duty to provide him with temporary accommodation pending a decision as to the duty (if any) owed to him under Part VII of the

Act. It had clearly not yet made a lawful decision, because of the shortcomings which Mr Woolf conceded. Justice therefore demanded that it should continue to provide him with temporary accommodation until it did.'

The Lord Justice also commented on the continuing relevance of judicial review in homelessness cases, expressing some concern that the numbers of applications appeared to be on the rise, despite the provision for a direct appeal in the Housing Act 1996 s 204 (he did not analyse the basis for these applications).

'The second observation I wish to make is that in 1994 the Law Commission expressed concern about the number of homelessness cases in the Crown Office List in its report on *Judicial Review and Statutory Appeals* (1994) Law Com. No. 226 at paras 2.23 to 2.27: see also Appendix C, paras 6.1 to 6.3, 8.23 and 9.1(2)(ii) and (iv).

There were 152 housing cases among the caseload of the Crown Office List as at the end of July 1994 (see page 176 of the report). That number was very considerably reduced when jurisdiction was transferred to the county court to hear appeals on points of law against certain decisions made under Part VII of the Housing Act 1996 (see s 204(1) of the Act). Parliament did not, however, give the county court jurisdiction over decisions relating to the provision of temporary accommodation under sections 188(3) or 204(4).

I have been told by the head of the Crown Office that following the judgment of the Court of Appeal in *Ali v Westminster City Council* (1998) 31 HLR 349 the number of applications for judicial review in homelessness cases has started to grow again, and that there were nearly 100 such applications in the list last year.

Judicial review applications are expensive and time-consuming, particularly for local authorities and claimants outside London, and even if the House of Lords were to reverse the decision of the Court of Appeal in *Ali*, which is a section 204(4) case concerned with interim protection pending an appeal to the county court, the present case shows that difficulties are much more likely to arise in section 188(3) cases where it is had to see that the county court could possibly be thought to have jurisdiction under the present law.'

In cases where judicial review remains a viable option application can only be made to the High Court[80]. Before bringing proceedings, claimants must comply with the Judicial Review Pre-Action Protocol (save in urgent cases). This generally requires that a detailed letter before claim is sent to the authority, setting out the basis of the challenge to their decision. The authority should generally be given 14 days to respond to this letter. Judicial review proceedings must be commenced promptly, at the latest within three months of the date when the grounds for seeing review first arose (generally the date on which the claimant was informed of the decision)[81]. The claimant must serve the judicial review papers on the authority within seven days of having issued them[82]. The authority then has 21 days to file an 'acknowledgement of service' – setting out whether any part of the claim is to be defended and (if so) a summary of the grounds for defending it.

---

[80]   The judicial review procedure is contained in CPR Pt 54.
[81]   CPR 54.5.
[82]   CPR 54.7.

Permission of the court is required before a judicial review claim can proceed to a final hearing. The permission decision is made 'on the papers' – ie without an oral hearing. If permission is refused the parties will be informed of the reasons for refusal, and the claimant can ask for the decision to be reconsidered at an oral hearing[83]. If s/he is again unsuccessful there is a right of appeal to the Court of Appeal[84]. If permission is granted, the authority has 35 days to submit its detailed defence[85]. At the hearing, most of the time will be occupied by speeches/legal argument by counsel and questions from the judge – there is unlikely to be any oral evidence in most cases.

All judicial review remedies are discretionary. Three orders are available:
- mandatory orders, compelling the performance of a public duty;
- prohibiting orders, preventing a public body from acting illegally, irrationally or improperly (used rarely in homelessness cases);
- quashing orders, 'quashing' an invalid decision.

In addition, the court may make a declaration as to the law and/or the rights of the parties, or issue an Injunction (often granted as a form of interim relief at the 'permission' stage).

## HOUSING DISREPAIR

As discussed in Chapter 12, the courses of action concerning housing conditions and disrepair are complex and wide-ranging, involving contractual and other common law civil rights as well as the criminal law. There is no attempt here to duplicate the discussion of the substantive law dealt with in Chapter 12. Instead, the Civil Procedure Rules applicable to all civil law 'private' disputes is discussed, followed by consideration of the procedure concerning statutory nuisance.

### Procedures under the Civil Procedure Rules

Before a disrepair case comes to court, the claimant or the defendant may choose to make an offer of settlement. This is governed by the CPR Part 36. If the offer is accepted the claim will be stayed on the terms of the offer and the claimant will be entitled to costs up to the service of the acceptance[86]. If the claimant turns down a defendant's 'Part 36' offer s/he will be ordered to pay the defendant's costs incurred after the last date for acceptance of the offer, unless this would be unjust[87].

A disrepair claim will generally be a CPR Part 7 claim and will normally be allocated to the small claims track if the value of the claim is less than £5,000[88]. If the disrepair claim is valued at over £15,000 it will be allocated to the multi-track[89]. If the claim includes a claim for specific performance (and the estimated cost of the

---

[83]  CPR 54.11 and 54.12 .
[84]  CPR 52.15.
[85]  CPR 54.14.
[86]  CPR 36.13 and 36.14.
[87]  CPR 36.20.
[88]  CPR 26.6(3).
[89]  CPR 26.6(4).

necessary work is more than £1,000) or the claim includes an element of personal injury valued at over £1,000 the appropriate route will be the fast-track[90].

Finally, the CPR lay down a number of strict requirements for the use of experts. Broadly, a party requires permission from the court to rely on 'expert' evidence[91]. The court will allow oral evidence from an expert at a fast-track trial only if it is in the interests of justice to do so[92]. The report the expert produces should be addressed to the court, and not to the party from whom the expert has received her/his instructions[93].

## Statutory nuisance

As discussed in Chapter 12, statutory nuisance proceedings under Part III of the Environmental Protection Act 1990 are criminal prosecutions in the magistrates' court rather than civil actions. Any 'person aggrieved' may commence proceedings directly against her/his landlord, whether they are a tenant (private, council, or housing association), licensee or even merely a family member[94]. Proceedings are brought against the person responsible for the nuisance or (if the person responsible cannot be found and the defects are structural) the owner[95].

Section 82 states that proceedings are commenced by a 'complaint' but it is clear that the proceedings are criminal and should be commenced by an 'information'[96]. A complainant is required to give 21 days' notice of her/his intention to bring proceedings[97].

The magistrates' court has a number of options in such cases:
- If satisfied of the existence of a statutory nuisance, it must make a nuisance under requiring 'abatement' of the nuisance.
- If satisfied that the nuisance has been 'abated' but is likely to recur, it must, again, make a nuisance order and can specify any work necessary to prevent its recurrence. It may also, or alternatively, impose a fine.
- If satisfied that the nuisance renders the premises unfit for habitation, it may prohibit their use.
- If any orders are not complied with 'without reasonable excuse', defaulters may be repeatedly fined[98].
- Compensation may also be awarded by the magistrates' court under the court's general power to award compensation for any personal injury, loss or damage resulting from an offence of which a defendant had been convicted[99]. Compensation can relate to all loss suffered including fear and anxiety[100].

---

90   CPR 26.6(1).
91   CPR 35.4.
92   CPR 35.5.
93   CPR 35, para 1.1.
94   S 82(1) Environmental Protection Act 1990.
95   Ibid s 82(4).
96   *R v Newham Justice ex p Hunt* [1976] 1 WLR 420.
97   S 82(6) Environmental Protection Act 1990. This does not apply to noise pollution complaints under s 79(1)(g).
98   As regards all the above see s 82(8) and (9) Environmental Protection Act 1990.
99   S 35 Powers of Criminal Courts Act 1973 (as amended).
100  *Herbert v London Borough of Lambeth* (1991) 24 HLR 299.

However, in general personal injury compensation is inappropriate, being more properly the subject of civil proceedings in the county court[101]. A defendant who had been ordered to pay compensation may appeal to the court of appeal which can vary or annul the order. Appeals against convictions and sentence lie to the crown court. Either party may appeal to the divisional court on a point of law, by way of 'case stated'.

## HARASSMENT AND UNLAWFUL EVICTION

This area (as discussed in Chapter 5) demonstrates almost every legal approach applicable to a housing action. There are possible civil actions deriving from tort, contract and statute and there are potential statutory criminal sanctions. The procedural material (briefly) discussed here is divided into civil remedies and criminal proceedings.

### Civil remedies

These are of two types: injunctions (to facilitate re-entry and restrain repetition of the harassment), and damages. The county court has extended jurisdiction to hear damages claims under ss 27 and 28 of the Housing Act 1988[102]. As regards claims for damages or injunctions at common law for unlawful evidence or harassment, the county court has unlimited jurisdiction[103]. Any such claim commenced in the high court is likely to be transferred to the county court for trial (since it will be unlikely to meet the criteria for allocation to the high court)[104]. All county court claims will be allocated to the fast track or multi track – the small claims track is seen as inappropriate[105].

Injunctions are principally enforced by proceedings for committal for contempt of court[106]. In such cases, a claimant who wishes to enforce the order can issue a claim form[107] or an application notice seeking committal for contempt[108]. A supporting affidavit is required. The claim form or application notice must state prominently the possible consequences (for example, imprisonment) of the court making the committal order[109].

### Criminal proceedings

Proceedings maybe instituted under the Protection from Eviction Act 1977 by local authorities or private individuals. The police do not generally initiate proceedings. Proceedings under s 6 Criminal Law Act 1977 may be initiated by either the police

---

[101] Ibid.
[102] S 40 Housing Act 1988.
[103] S 15 County Courts Act 1984 and High Court and County Courts' Jurisdiction Order 1991 art 2(1)(1).
[104] CPR Pt 7 PD para.2.
[105] CPR 26.7(4).
[106] CPR Sch 2 and County Court Rules Ord 2g.
[107] CPR Pt 7.
[108] CPR Pt 23.
[109] CPR Sch 1.

or a private individual – there is no power for local authorities to initiate prosecutions. Similarly, local authorities have no powers to initiate prosecutions under the Protection from Harassment Act 1997.

Criminal proceedings in the magistrates' courts are commenced either by charge following arrest and appearance in court or by the laying of an information followed by summons or warrant. The information, summons or warrant is sufficient if it describes the offence with which the accused is charged (in ordinary language) and gives such particulars as may be necessary for giving reasonable information of the nature of the charge[110].

## FURTHER READING:

Arden, A, Partington, M, and Hunter, C, *Housing Law*, Sweet & Maxwell, paras 19–102 to 19–109, 19–193 to 19–194, 19–239 to 19–246, 19–268 to 19–270, 19–292 to 19–304.

Baker, C, Manning, J, and Shepherd, J, *Housing Law: Pleadings in Practice* (2003) Sweet & Maxwell.

Driscoll, J, *Housing Law and Precedents*, Sweet & Maxwell, paras 3–273 to 3–301.

Parmar, R and Parry, M, *Court Procedure and Housing Cases – a practitioner's guide* (2002) Shelter.

---

[110] Magistrates' Courts Rules 1981, r 100(1).

# CHAPTER 7

# Social Housing Allocation

## INTRODUCTION

The 'social welfare' aspects of housing are seen at their clearest in the public sector. Local authorities have certain, limited duties to safeguard the interests of the homeless having local connections with their area, to provide priority access programmes to their housing stock for those with particular needs, to supervise the general housing position in their area, and to enforce housing maintenance stand-ards in certain cases.

## LOCAL AUTHORITY TENANTS AND TENANCIES

Paradoxically, the individual welfare of authority tenants was, until comparatively recently, safeguarded by law less than that of the private sector tenant. Perhaps it was felt that public authorities should be 'model landlords', and so until 1980 *legal* security of tenure was very limited, which was anomalous when compared to the private sector from 1919 onwards. A tenant could resist a possession order only by showing that the local authority had acted in a way in which no reasonable authority would act, and that was an effectively impossible burden of proof to discharge[1]. Practical or de facto security was high in most local authority areas, but scope for arbitrariness and high-handedness was great. There were questionable restrictions on matters such as keeping pets, taking in lodgers and redecoration: breach of these had the ultimate sanction of eviction. However, since 1980 a package of public sector tenants' rights has been legislatively provided for, usually termed the 'tenants charter'. These rights are now contained in Pt IV of the Housing Act 1985.

The relationship between an authority and its tenants is more than a simple landlord/tenant one. This chapter will consider some of the facets of this issue. However, at the root of the relationship is still the existence of the tenancy with its contract and property implications, and that should be borne in mind in reading the following text and the accompanying materials which are concerned with the process leading to the creation of that relationship, ie the administrative process known as 'allocation'.

---

[1]  *Cannock Chase District Council v Kelly* [1978] 1 All ER 152, [1978] 1 WLR 1.

# THE ALLOCATION AND TRANSFER OF COUNCIL TENANCIES

Very little new local authority housing has been built for over 20 years and so there is a limited supply available – a supply that has been greatly diminished by the sale of over one million dwellings since 1980 under the 'right to buy' policy. It has therefore become increasingly essential that authorities should have clear and fair rules for allocating this diminishing resource on the basis of need.

## The issue of discretion

Local authority discretion in allocation has historically been very wide. Section 21(1) of the Housing Act 1985 stated that the 'general management, regulation and control of a local authority's houses is vested in and shall be exercised by the authority'. This allowed authorities to 'pick and choose their tenants at their will', see Lord Porter in *Shelley v LCC*[2]. Until recently the courts allowed them considerable latitude as 'model' landlords. This has, however, somewhat altered and it must be remembered that authorities are subject not only to the statutory rules on allocation considered later but also the general principles of Administrative Law which limit their freedom to a degree.

Other measures did somewhat quality the width of the discretionary power. Thus s 22 of the 1985 Act historically stated that in selecting its tenants the authority should give a 'reasonable preference' to those living in overcrowded housing, those with large families, those in unsatisfactory conditions and the homeless. This, however, has now been repealed and replaced by the Housing Act 1996 and the Homelessness Act 2002 (see further below).

The following cases illustrate the general requirements imposed by the courts on authorities with regard to legality, procedural propriety and rationality in the allocation of housing.

In *R v Canterbury City Council, ex p Gillespie*[3] the applicant and her cohabitant lived as joint secure tenants in accommodation owned by Thanet District council. They had two children. After the breakdown of the relationship, the applicant left this accommodation and moved to her mother's home in the respondent authority's area. This accommodation was not adequate and she applied for housing from Canterbury City Council on 11 March 1983. On 25 March 1983 the applicant was awarded custody of her two children.

On 5 April 1983 the applicant was interviewed by an officer of the respondent authority and was informed that she could not be placed upon their waiting list until she relinquished the joint secure tenancy in Thanet. This position was confirmed in a letter to the applicant's solicitors on 15 July 1983 which stated 'It is the policy of my council not to accept on the housing waiting list any person who already has an interest in the title of a council dwelling elsewhere.' The applicant attempted to surrender her interest in the Thanet tenancy but this was refused because there were arrears of rent outstanding. At various points thereafter the respondent authority

[2]   [1949] AC 56.
[3]   (1986) 19 HLR 7.

affirmed its position with regard to the applicant, including a recommendation from the Environmental Health and Housing Policy Committee of 21 May 1985:

'That no applicant registered on the council's housing waiting list be allocated accommodation whilst holding a joint or sole tenancy of another local authority or housing association property unless: (a) a reciprocal arrangement can be agreed with the other landlord or local authority whereby the council may nominate its own tenant or applicant for rehousing or; (b) the case may be considered as a priority within the terms of the Housing (Homeless Persons) Act 1977 or because of violence or a threat of violence the applicant is unable to return to their accommodation in another area.'

On 9 July 1985 the committee met again and considered the applicant's case, resolving as follows:

'That because [the applicant] holds an interest in a secure tenancy with another authority, and paragraphs (a) and (b) of the policy of the council as determined do not apply, no further consideration be given to her application for rehousing for the time being.'

The decision was communicated to the applicant's solicitors by a letter dated 31 July 1985. At that point the applicant sought judicial review.

The applicant was successful and Simon Brown J stated:

'It is plain beyond argument that decisions by a local authority in the exercise of their statutory powers are reviewable by the courts on accepted principles of judicial review. If authority for that proposition were needed, then it is to be found in the Court of Appeal decision of *Bristol District Council v Clark* [1975] 1 WLR 1443. The contrary was not argued before me.
The essential basis upon which the applicant challenges the respondent's continuous stance, as manifested in their various decision letters to which I have referred throughout the long period of this dispute, is that the respondents have fettered their discretion by adopting and implementing a fixed policy which precludes their giving proper individual consideration to such cases as fall within that policy. Putting it slightly differently, the complaint is that the adoption of the policy operates as a rule and precludes the authority taking into consideration all the relevant matters upon any individual application.
...
The relevant law in regard to public authorities holding policies in respect of their exercise of statutory powers, is well known. Mr Watkinson [counsel for the applicant] ... cited the decision of Cooke J in the case of *Stringer v Minister of Housing and Local Government* [1971] 1 All ER 65 as follows:

"It seems to me that the general effect of the many relevant authorities is that a Minister charged with a duty of making individual administrative decision in a fair and impartial manner may nevertheless have a general policy in regard to matters which are relevant to those decisions, provided that the existence of that general policy does not preclude him from fairly judging all the issues which are relevant to each individual case as it comes up for decision."

...

The effect of the council's policy adopted in the instant case is, in my judgment, to exclude from consideration any applicant on the waiting list who has a secure tenancy of the kind referred to in the policy whether with another local authority or a housing association wholly irrespective of the circumstances of that tenancy and in particular of the availability of that tenancy to the applicant, save only where the express exceptions apply.

... [There] is nothing in the documents before me which persuades me that the council have ever applied their mind, as in my judgment they clearly should, to the particular problems which this applicant asserts have faced her in relinquishing [her] interest.

...

In my judgment, this challenge succeeds not essentially because the policy is intrinsically irrational, but rather because it constitutes a rule which requires to be followed slavishly rather than merely a stated general approach which is always subject to an exceptional case and which permits each application to be individually considered.'

Local authorities may not, therefore, fetter their discretion with regard to the allocation of housing. The following case made it clear that their procedures must also be lawful and not dictated by taking into account irrelevant considerations.

In *R v Port Talbot Borough Council, ex p Jones*[4] the respondent was a borough councillor who was divorced and living outside the ward she represented. In July 1984 she applied to the council for a council house. In September the housing tenancy committee resolved that her application should be put on a priority list to be determined on its merits against the merits of others on that list. In the normal course of events the respondent, as a single person, would have been allocated a one- or two-bedroom flat and would have been likely to have had to wait about four years before being rehoused. In April 1986 however, a three-bedroom council house became available in the ward which the respondent represented and under pressure from the chairman of the housing tenancy committee the borough housing officer, to whom the decision was delegated under standing orders, offered the tenancy of the house to the respondent, who accepted it. The chairman's reasons for seeking to influence the decision were that the respondent needed the house rather than a flat because, as a councillor, she would have members of the public visiting her at home and she also needed to return to the ward she represented in time to establish her presence there before the next election. At the time the house was allocated to the respondent the waiting list for council houses was headed by a family with one child who had expressed interest in the house. The applicant, another councillor, sought judicial review of the decision to allocate the house to the respondent.

*Held:* The application would be granted and the decision to allocate the house to the respondent quashed, for the following reasons:

4   [1988] 2 All ER 207.

(1)  Since the dominant role in reaching the decision had been taken by the chairman of the housing tenancy committee when the council's standing orders delegated the decision to the borough housing officer the decision had not been made in an authorised and lawful manner.

(2)  The decision was based on irrelevant considerations, namely the chairman's wish to put the respondent in a better position to fight an election, and was an abuse of power because it was unfair to others on the housing list.

According to Nolan J:

'… Whatever the true explanation or explanations may be, I can find nothing in the housing policy of the council which would justify the giving of priority to Mrs Kingdom's application on the basis of the evidence which is now before me and which was then available. It seems to me unsatisfactory, to put it no higher, that a councillor should be treated as having priority for housing without clear and specific reasons being given for that preferential treatment. …

There are however, in my judgment, other and broader grounds on which [the allocation] should be quashed. The most obvious is that the council's policy is to provide suitable accommodation for those on the waiting list. Mr Hale's duty under the standing orders was to act in accordance with that policy. He clearly did not do so. Counsel for [the tenant] argued that, whatever the normal policy might be, the decision to allocate the house to [the tenant] was authorised by the resolution of September 1984. But that resolution, whatever its other failings, did not authorise the allocation of a three-bedroomed house to [the tenant] in order that she should be the better able to fight an election, without regard to the needs of others who were on the list for housing and against the opinions of the council's officers. There could hardly be a clearer case of a decision which, to adopt one test propounded in *Associated Provincial Picture Houses Ltd v Wednesbury Corp* [1947] 2 All ER 680, [1948] 1 KB 223, was based on irrelevant considerations and ignored relevant considerations. To put it more simply, the decision was unfair to others on the housing list and was an abuse of power.'

This decision was followed by *R v London Borough of Tower Hamlets, ex p Mohib Ali et al*[5]. Here, down to 1986, the respondent authority used a standard lettings criteria (SLC) for rehousing all applicants for housing, including the homeless. Amongst the criteria for letting were: that families with children under 10 years would not be housed above the fourth floor; that families would be provided with one bedroom for every two children of the same sex born within 10 years of each other; and, that the applicant's area of choice would be taken into account where possible. In June 1986, an amended lettings criteria (ALC) was adopted for homeless families, which abandoned the limitation as to floor and allowed smaller properties to be offered. The reason for the change towards homeless families was concern at the time (between two and four years) that the homeless were spending in temporary accommodation.

[5]  (1993) 25 HLR 218.

Concern about the policy was expressed to the respondents in 1986 by the Commission for Racial Equality, and as a result a number of safeguards were introduced. These included monitoring by a panel of members; a right of appeal against an offer; and, automatic entry onto the transfer list for those who were obliged to accept accommodation which did not conform to the SLC criteria. Subsequently, all three safeguards were abandoned, the right of appeal explicitly so in September 1991. Furthermore, the right to two offers to the homeless had been reduced to one in September 1987, despite advice to the contrary from the respondents' director of housing.

Allocation of housing was subsequently devolved to seven neighbourhoods. Within each neighbourhood, the operation of the ALC was not mandatory. Between April and September 1991, 56 per cent of lettings were made under ALC and 44 per cent under SLC. A significantly higher proportion of homeless Asian families were allocated under ALC than homeless white families who were housed. This was due in part to the fact that larger families were nearly all Bangladeshi. The majority of Bangladeshi families were not, however, homeless. Analysis of those being re-housed by the respondents indicated that between 85 and 95 per cent of Bangladeshis being housed were not homeless, while for non-Asians this figure was between 96 and 97 per cent.

The applicant Mohib Ali applied as homeless in July 1987 and a full duty towards him was accepted. He was offered a three-bedroomed maisonette on the fourth and fifth floors of a block for himself, his wife and six children aged between one and 18. He refused on the basis that the maisonette was too small, and appealed against the offer. In February 1990, his appeal was dismissed, and the respondents wrote saying that they had considered that they had discharged their duty.

Mr Ali sought judicial review. It was held as follows.
(1)  Challenge to the policy was not out of time; it is only when a policy affects an individual that he or she can challenge it and it is only then that time starts to run. It should be remembered that the law relating to judicial review requires an applicant to commence action promptly within three months of the illegalities in question arising.
(2)  There is nothing unlawful is seeking to reduce the use of temporary hotel accommodation for homeless persons; the degree of priority accorded to homeless persons by the respondents in their lettings policy was not unlawful, provided that their other policies in relation to the homeless were fair; the decision to adopt the amended lettings criteria was lawful.
(3)  The respondents failed to recognise the two disadvantages occurring from a move under the amended lettings criteria from bed and breakfast, namely that less suitable accommodation might be allocated and that the prospects of a family later being offered suitable permanent accommodation after having once been moved from temporary accommodation are reduced; the subsequent removal of the safeguards of monitoring, appeal and automatic entry on to the transfer list, together with the apparently arbitrary and random way in which the alternate lettings criteria operated in different neighbourhoods demonstrated unfairness and irrationality requiring intervention by the court.

(4)   There was no evidence of direct discrimination under the Race Relations Act 1976; nor did the evidence identify any improper requirement or condition within s 1(1)(b) of the 1976 Act. nor did it show considerable disproportion.

(5)   While authorities are fully entitled in exercising their statutory duties under the Race Relations Act 1976, s 71 to pay regard to what they thought was the best interests of race relations, this did not establish any breach of s 71 in the circumstances of this case. See further below for the provision on discrimination.

Rose LJ:

'It is common ground that the respondents must act rationally ... and must have regard to all relevant considerations ...

...

The allocation of accommodation has been devolved by Tower Hamlets to its seven neighbourhoods. It is not suggested that devolution is improper. But the operation of ALC is not mandatory. It is entirely up to the neighbourhood allocation staff whether or not they apply ALC. Between April and September 1991 there was a range of variation between 49 per cent and 77 per cent in the use made of ALC by different neighbourhoods. For the same period 56 per cent of lettings were made under ALC and 44 per cent under SLC. A significantly higher proportion of homeless Asian families than homeless white families who were housed were allocated under ALC but it is common ground, as we have said, that the larger families are nearly all Bangladeshi. The evidence from Mr Edwards of the CRE in his affidavit of September 15, 1992, paragraph 8, shows that Asian families are disproportionately likely compared with white families to receive lettings amended by area and floor level. It is correct, as Mr Pannick said, that the respondents have not chosen to reply to this on affidavit. Mr Underwood, on the other hand, was entitled, as it seems to us, to point out, as he did, that, excluding, as Mr Edwards does in his calculations, lettings amended *by* size does not accurately reflect lettings amended *because* of size, that is a suitably large property found in a different area would appear statistically as an amendment *by* area but not *because* of area; the true rationale for the amendment will, in fact, be size. Mr Edwards' reliance on figures based on amendments by reference to area and floor level is therefore, as it seems to us, flawed ...

It is clear that, in practice, ALC are applied in relation to Bangladeshis to a much greater extent than in relation to white homeless families. ...

In the light of this material, Mr Pannick's first challenge, based on arbitrariness, is that the respondents have failed to adopt and apply any consistent standards or principles for the allocation of housing for the homeless. Allocation depends on the neighbourhood which makes the allocation. The safeguards which the sub committee thought necessary in 1986 have been abandoned. The respondents have abdicated their responsibility by purporting to adopt a policy which is more honoured in the breach than in the observance. The arbitrary nature of this is particularly shown in Stepney where the policy is regarded as unfair but where it is applied to 71 per cent of lettings.

Mr Pannick's second submission is that the respondents have, arbitrarily, a principle which involves the less favourable treatment of the homeless compared with other persons to whom the respondents must give a reasonable preference in the allocation of accommodation ... and also compared with persons whom the respondents have no duty to house such as those beneficially treated under the sons and daughters scheme. The only proper basis for allocation of accommodation is housing need and it is both arbitrary and irrational for the homeless uniquely not to be placed on the list for transfer to SLC accommodation.

Mr Pannick's third submission is that the treatment of Bangladeshis demonstrates a breach of section 71 of the Race Relations Act in failing to make appropriate arrangements with a view both to eliminating racial discrimination and promoting equality of opportunity and good relations between persons of different racial groups.

Fourth, Mr Pannick submits that the matters to which we have referred demonstrate both direct and indirect discrimination contrary to section 1(1) of the Race Relations Act.

As to direct discrimination, it is common ground that [this] does not depend on intention and motive but simply on whether 'but for' their race, persons would have been more favourably treated (see *R v Birmingham City Council, ex parte Equal Opportunities Commission* [1989] AC 1155 at 1194B *per* Lord Goff). Mr Pannick emphasizes the role played by the CRE in relation to the respondents and stresses that the difficulty of showing discrimination is such that the court should be ready to infer it (see *Baker v Cornwall County Council* (1990) ICR 452 at 459C). He relies on the passage in the affidavit from Mr Edwards to which we have earlier referred.

As to indirect discrimination, he submits that there is a requirement or condition within section 1(1)(b) in that an applicant for housing who wishes to be treated under SLC must not be homeless or he must rely on the discretion of the officer and he referred us to the judgment of Browne-Wilkinson J in *Clarke v Ely* (1983) ICR 165 at 170D to 171D. He submits that a considerably lower proportion of Bangladeshi housing applicants than non-Bangladeshis can in practice comply with this requirement and that the respondents cannot justify their conduct under section 1(1)(b)(ii) in accordance with the test postulated by Balcombe LJ in *Hampson v Department of Education and Science* (1989) ICR 179 at 181F *viz*: "An objective balance between the discriminatory effect of the condition and the reasonable needs of the party who applies the condition." He submits that the practice has a very considerable adverse effect on Bangladeshis, particularly when applied without the safeguards thought necessary in1986 and even though it is criticized both by the CRE and the majority of the neighbourhoods. It is not applied to applicants other than the homeless and an alternative policy would be to provide more housing stock for the homeless as the respondents' officers have suggested. The policy is to the detriment of homeless applicants who cannot comply with it because they are given accommodation less favourable than they would receive if the old lettings policy were applied.

...[It] is pertinent to bear in mind that, as Lord Brightman said in *R v Hillingdon Borough Council, ex parte Puhlhofer* [1986] AC 484 at 518C:

"... it is not ... appropriate that the remedy of judicial review which is a discretionary remedy, should be made use of to monitor the actions of local authorities under the Act save in the exceptional case."

A local authority's resources are limited and they use them as best they can consistent with proper performance of their statutory duties. Accordingly there is nothing unlawful in seeking to reduce the use of temporary hotel accommodation for homeless persons. And the degree of priority accorded to homeless persons by the respondents in their lettings policy was not unlawful, provided that their other policies in relation to the homeless were fair.

In our judgment the reports made to the Housing Sub Committee on June 16, 1986, and October 13, 1986, ... were appropriate. They set out the relevant considerations, including cost, and the particular problems of larger homeless families and the high proportion of Asian families in this group. The consequent disproportionate effect of homelessness on ethnic minorities was recognised in the respondents' published policy document ... They were entitled to take into account the fact that the majority of the Asian applicants for housing were not homeless ... and that, as appears from paragraph 7 of [an officer's] affidavit of June 12, 1992, depending on the basis of the analysis, between 87 per cent and 95 per cent of Bangladeshis and between 96 per cent and 97 per cent of non-Asians were able to comply with the alleged requirement or condition of not being homeless relied on by the applicants as showing indirect discrimination: clearly it cannot be said that there is disproportion, still less considerable disproportion between Asians and non-Asians.

Furthermore, the shortage of units for large families available to the respondents presented a particular and serious problem.'

There then follows the crucial paragraph in Rose LJ's judgment:

'But the need for safeguards in applying the ALC was recognized by the respondents themselves. And their analysis, as a matter of policy and in argument before this court, failed, in our judgment, to recognize the two disadvantages occurring from a move under the ALC from bed and breakfast accommodation, namely that less suitable accommodation might be allocated and that the prospects of a family being later offered suitable permanent accommodation after having once been moved from temporary accommodation are reduced. It is, no doubt, because of these disadvantages that the initial safeguards were introduced. *It seems to us to follow that the removal of those safeguards, together with the apparently arbitrary and random way in which the ALC operate in different neighbourhoods, without any proffered justification, demonstrates unfairness and irrationality requiring intervention by the court.* (Italics supplied.]

With regard to the Race Relations Act, however, we find no evidence of direct discrimination under section 1(1)(a) or section 21: in particular there is nothing to suggest that a large Asian family is treated less favourably than a large white family. As to indirect discrimination, we have already indicated our view that the evidence before us does not identify any improper requirement or condition within section 1(1)(b) or does it show considerable disproportion.

As to section 71 of the Act, it seems to us that the applicants' reliance on *Wheeler v Leicester City Council* [1985] AC 1054 is misconceived. The House of Lords there held that the council had been over-zealous in exercising its section 71 powers. Lord Roskill ... said that the council were fully entitled, in exercising their statutory discretion, to pay regard to what they thought was the best interests of race relations. But this is far from establishing any breach of duty under section 71 in the circumstances with which we are concerned.

Accordingly, the ALC policy as applied to each of these applicants, that is without the safeguards originally envisaged by the respondents, must, in our judgment, be struck down on the one ground which we have indicated.'

*R v Gateshead Metropolitan Borough Council, ex p Lauder*[6] was a further case illustrating the illegality of inflexible policies, when an authority refused to grant points to the applicant under their allocation scheme, on the basis that the scheme contained a policy that:

'Where an applicant moves into a property creating either an overcrowded or medically unsuitable situation, the benefit of the overcrowded, medical and lack of amenity points will be withheld for a period of twelve months.'

Subsequently the authority again considered the applicant's circumstances and the possibility of awarding her the points for overcrowding before the end of the twelve-month period. They decided, however, not to depart from their earlier decision. The applicant applied for judicial review of the authority's two decisions in relation to her application.

Potts J held as follows:

(1)   The respondent authority's policy required the authority to withhold points for a period of twelve months where an applicant moved into overcrowded property; the relevant passage in the policy unlawfully fettered the authority's discretion to consider each case on its merits.

(2)   The authority's initial decision ... was reached because they were satisfied that the applicant came within the terms of the relevant part of their policy; in so doing they had adopted an inflexible approach and the decision was unlawful.

(3)   The [subsequent] decision ... was a decision to which the authority were entitled to come in light of the information available to them and the circumstances in question; it was a decision that they could reasonably have reached.

Potts J:

'Miss Markus's first point is that part of the policy which relates to suspension of points advantage unlawfully fettered the discretion of the respondents to consider cases such as this applicant's on its merits. Miss Markus points to that passage in the policy identified above to the effect that "the benefit of the overcrowded, medical and lack of amenity points *will be* withheld for a period of twelve months" (my emphasis). In essence

[6]   (1996) 29 HLR 360.

Miss Markus submits that the words "will be" are mandatory and require the respondents to withhold overcrowding points whenever "an applicant moves into a property creating an overcrowded situation".

Miss Smart, on behalf of the respondents, submits that this construction cannot be justified. She argues, as I understand it, that because the passage in question requires the respondents to withhold points for a period of 12 months only, the exercise of any power under that passage imports an element of discretion. ...

I accept the applicant's submissions on this point. In my judgment that part of the lettings policy concerned with the suspension of points advantage on its face requires the respondent to withhold points for a period of 12 months where an applicant moves into overcrowded property. On its face that passage fetters the discretion of the respondent to consider each case on its merits as the Housing Act requires. As I observed during argument, and as counsel appeared to accept, the vice in the passage could easily be cured by the insertion of the word "usually" before "will" or by the insertion of the words "in exceptional cases" at some appropriate point. As it is, I am satisfied that the passage in question on its face required the respondents to adopt an inflexible approach. Had I had any doubt about this the terms of the letter of October 2, would have removed it. I am satisfied the terms of that letter indicate that when the respondent initially withheld points they did so because they were satisfied without more that this applicant came within the terms of the passage complained of.

Therefore, I conclude that that part of the policy identified, that is to say that part of the policy relating to suspension of points advantage, was and is unlawful. I am further satisfied that the decision on October 2, was made in direct consequence of that policy.'

Potts J then turned to the authority's decision of 14 November when it appeared all the facts of the situation were available and were considered:

'This court does not sit as a Court of Appeal from the decision of the Chairman, Vice Chairman and Director of Housing. It is not for this court to substitute its own judgment for that of those officers of the respondents. The crucial issue for this court is whether the decision in question was one to which, on all the information identified in the passages above, the respondents were entitled to come to. In my judgment the respondents were entitled to come to this decision on the information available to them and in the circumstances in question. This was a decision taken by the Director of Housing and the Chairman and Vice Chairman of the Housing Committee, gentlemen well equipped to judge questions of housing on South Tyneside, certainly better equipped than this court. Had I been persuaded by any of the arguments advanced by Miss Markus that that decision was unlawful I would have so held. I am not so persuaded. In my judgment it was a decision that the council could reasonably have reached.'

The applicant succeeded in respect of the initial decision of the authority.

In *R v Sutton London Borough Council, ex p Alger*[7] a local authority's allocation rules excluded all owner-occupiers, except elderly persons in medical need, irrespective of housing need. Judicial review was sought of this, but before the case could be heard the authority abolished the restrictive rule. This was followed chronologically by *R v Islington London Borough Council, ex p Aldabbagh.*[8] Here an authority had a policy of refusing to transfer existing tenants to new houses unless they cleared off all arrears of rent. This policy was applied irrespective of urgent medical need evidence. It was held the authority had illegally fettered its discretion.

A number of authorities in the late 1980s introduced revisions to allocation policies to debar those with rates or community charge debts, either by way of non-admission to the waiting list, or by a bar on actual allocation. *R v Forest Heath District Council, ex p West and Lucas*[9] concerned a homeless couple with a young child who were second on the waiting list for council accommodation, but who were believed by the authority to be liable for unpaid community charge (poll tax). They were informed that they would be considered for housing only once their community charge payments were brought up to date. The Court of Appeal indicated this was an abuse of power. The relevant legislation – the Local Government Act 1988 – did not entitle an authority to discriminate against non-payers of the poll tax – in any case, other remedies for non-payment were available. More recently the Court has intervened to grant a remedy against an authority which conceded its policies were illegal but which then did nothing to amend these policies for two years. This was an example of irrationality[10].

The case law is in reality an application of the general principles of administrative law – the 'Wednesbury principles' – which require authorities to stay within the limits of their powers, to behave in a procedurally correct and fair fashion, to base their decisions only on relevant considerations and, overall, to behave reasonably in the discharge of their functions.

The remedy by way of judicial review is (i) discretionary, (ii) theoretically serves only to quash an authority's decision and is not an allocation decision in its own right, and (iii) is available only to someone with a 'sufficient interest' in the matter in question, for example a person actually refused admission to a housing register for some irrelevant reason. Interestingly, in the *Port Talbot* case the applicant was the Leader of the Council whose special position was considered to give him a 'sufficient interest' to challenge a decision taken by his fellow council members.

However, we may ask what it is the courts do when they strike down an allocation decision? They are not substituting their decision for the actual decision of the authority, and indeed the entire administrative process may have to take place again. In making their decision, however, the courts refer to generic values such as 'fairness', 'consistency' and 'impartiality', and it must be asked whether these concepts have an agreed meaning. Subsequently we shall return to judicial decisions on the individual provisions of the allocation legislation, but at this point it may be

---

[7]　[1992] Legal Action, June, p 130.
[8]　(1994) 27 HLR 271.
[9]　(1991) 24 HLR 85.
[10]　*Vatansever v Southwark London Borough Council* [2001] All ER (D) 313 (June).

said that the courts appear to be more willing to intervene in allocation issues than was once the case. Possibly this is because Parliament has enacted more sophisticated allocation legislation which has itself eroded the degree of autonomy once enjoyed by authorities. However, it must always be remembered that the courts will shrink from appearing to make allocation decisions themselves. This is well illustrated by *R (on the application of Bibi) v London Borough of Newham and R (on the application of Al-Nashed) v London Borough of Newham.*[11]

The applicants, who were refugees, had been provided with housing by the local authority since their arrival in the United Kingdom some ten years previously but had never had security of tenure. Although the authority did have the power to provide secure accommodation it had erroneously thought that it had a legal obligation to do and it therefore promised such accommodation to the applicants within 18 months. Following the continued failure of the authority to provide permanent accommodation, the applicants each applied for judicial review based on a legitimate expectation engendered by the local authority. The judge held that both applicants had a legitimate expectation that they would be provided with secure accommodation; that the authority could not renege on its promise; and that it was bound to comply with it. The authority appealed against the judge's decision on the ground that he had developed the concept of legitimate expectation beyond its accepted limits. They contended that although they had made a promise, based on a misunderstanding of the law, the applicants' expectation was not legitimate and it would not be unfair for them to resile from the promise. They further contended that even if that would be unfair there were policy considerations which entitled them so to resile.

The Court of Appeal held that in legitimate expectation cases, it had to be determined whether a public authority's certain action or inaction was an abuse of power and if so, whether the court could come to a substantive decision itself or whether it should send the matter back to the decision taker to decide afresh according to law. Where a local authority, without even considering the fact that they were in breach of a promise which had given rise to a legitimate expectation that it would be honoured, made a decision to adopt a course of action at variance with that promise then the authority was abusing their powers. Once the court had established such an abuse it would not order the authority to honour its promise where to do so would be to assume the powers of the executive, although the court might ask the decision taker to take the legitimate expectation properly into account in the decision-making process. In the instant case, the local authority had generated a legitimate expectation in each applicant that he was to be provided with secure housing in the near future. However, the local authority had made an error of law in their decision-making process in that they had simply not acknowledged that the promises were a relevant consideration in coming to a conclusion as to whether they should be honoured and, if not, what if anything should have been done to assuage the disappointed expectations. The law required that any legitimate expectation be properly taken into account in the decision-making process. It had not been in the instant case and the authority had, accordingly, acted unlawfully. The provision of housing at public expense was, however, a political, not a judicial, decision and the

[11]  (2001) 33 HLR 955.

appropriate body to make the choices as to where priorities lay was the local authority, not the court, although such a decision had to be made in the light of the legitimate expectations. In the circumstances, the judge had gone too far in ordering that the applicants be provided with secure accommodation. It would, therefore, be declared that the local authority was under a duty to consider the applicants' application for suitable housing on the basis that they had a legitimate expectation.

## ANTI-DISCRIMINATION PROVISIONS

Under the Race Relations Act 1976 and the Sex Discrimination Act 1975, the absolute freedom of local authorities in matters of allocation is also limited, and this has not been changed by the Housing Act 1996.

Section 21 of the 1976 Act and s 30 of the 1975 Act prohibit discrimination in relation to entry onto the housing register and allocation from that register. These rules also apply with equal force to the allocation policies of housing associations. Unlawful discrimination may be committed *directly* or *indirectly*. The former involves treating a person less favourably than others on grounds, of race, sex etc, eg, 'No black women'. However, most forms of direct discrimination are more subtle than that, eg allocating the least desirable properties to black people. Such policies need not be *deliberately* or *maliciously* driven – very often they result from unthinking cultural assumptions. Indirect discrimination is the act of applying a condition which, though on its face apparently neutral, has the effect that it is harder for members of minorities (or of one sex) to comply with it than members of the host population (or of the other sex). Indirectly discriminatory practices include allocating 'points' on housing waiting lists to people only according to the number of children actually living with them. This fails to consider the needs of people who have children overseas. There are few housing cases under the anti-discrimination legislation but see *R v London Borough of Tower Hamlets ex p Mohib Ali* (above).

### Discrimination and disability

Sections 22 and 24 of the Disability Discrimination Act 1995 apply the same basic anti-discrimination concepts encountered under the race relations and sex discrimination legislation to the letting of property. Disabled persons under s 1 of the 1995 Act are those having physical or mental impairments which have substantial and long-term adverse effects on their ability to carry out normal day-to-day activities. It is thus unlawful to discriminate against a disabled person by refusing to let to that person, or by virtue of the terms of any letting to such a person, or in relation to any list of persons need of premises of the sort in question. Discrimination arises where a person treats a disabled person less favourably than non-disabled persons for reasons related to that person's disability, and where such treatment cannot be justified. Justification can be shown only where (i) the action results from a reasonable opinion on behalf of the discriminator, and (ii) such an action is necessary in order not to endanger the health or safety of *any* person, *or* the disabled person is incapable of entering into an enforceable agreement or giving an informed consent. Thus a landlord could refuse to let a particular property to a disabled person where either that person's physical disabilities would prevent him/her from using the property safely, or where the person is incapable of understanding the nature and consequences of a tenancy. Note, however, that there is no general duty on a landlord to make reasonable adjustments to a dwelling in order for it to be accessible to a disabled person.

It should also be noted that these anti-discrimination provisions apply to non justifiable evictions of disabled people, see further Chapter 9 below and Foreword II, above. The crucial issue here is the question of justifiability and the 'reasonable' opinion of the landlord. It is clear that landlords will only be 'justified' where the specific grounds mentioned above are satisfied, and where the landlord has gone through an inquiry and evaluation process to enable a 'reasonable' opinion to be formed.

## Recent amendments

The 1976 Race Relations Act was amended by the Race Relations Act 1976 (Amendment) Regulations, SI 2003/1626, which were made to satisfy EC obligations under Council Directive 2000/43EC. The first point of amendment is the enhanced definition of indirect discrimination. Under the former law this consisted of applying to another person a requirement or condition which is applied equally to others not of the same racial group as the victim but which is such that the proportion of persons of the same racial group of the victim who can comply with it is considerably smaller than the proportion of persons not of that group who can, *and* which is not justifiable irrespective of the colour, race, nationality or ethnic or national origins of the victim, *and* which is to the victim's detriment because he/she cannot comply. This is now extended by a new s 1(1A) to cover situations where a person applies to another person a provision, criterion or practice which is applied equally to people not of the same race or ethnic or national origins of the victim, but which puts or would put persons of the same race, etc. as the victim at a particular disadvantage when compared with other people, which also puts the victim at a disadvantage and which cannot be shown to be a proportionate means of achieving a legitimate aim. In addition a new s 3A creates a new wrong of racial harassment which, under reg 20, public bodies who provide services must not commit. Regulations 22 to 24 and 26 also make it unlawful for *persons* concerned with, inter alia, the provision or management of accommodation to subject another to racial harassment. 'Harassment' in this context is defined as subjecting another person to treatment, on grounds of race or ethnic or national origins, by means of unwanted conduct which has the effect (*or* the purpose) of violating that person's dignity, *or* creating an intimidating, hostile, degrading, humiliating or offensive environment for the victim. However, conduct is only to be judged as harassment if, having regard to all the circumstances, *including in particular the perception of the victim*, it should be reasonably considered as having that effect. It further declared illegal either to discriminate against a person by withholding a licence or consent for the disposal of premises to him on racial etc. grounds (which was unlawful under the 1976 Act) or to commit harassment against a person in relation to such a licence or consent, a new departure.

Acts of discrimination have been civil wrongs for many years under s 57 of the Race Relations Act 1976, and a victim may seek redress in the county court. Under s 57ZA the burden of proof in cases of *either* unlawful discrimination *or* harassment is now, however, that where the claimant proves facts from which the court *could* conclude in the absence of an adequate explanation from the respondent that he/she has committed an act of discrimination or harassment, the court *must* uphold the claim unless the respondent proves that he/she did not commit the act.

The enforcement generally of the legislation is a task for the Commission for Racial Equality (CRE), created by the 1976 Act. In particular under s 58 they may issue non-discrimination notices following formal investigations into a person's activities which have led to a finding of unlawful discrimination. Such a notice may require the illegal activity to cease and may also require other changes in practices. Under the changes made in 2003 the CRE's powers here now extend to both discrimination and harassment.

It is clear that the changes made in 2003 will require both housing authorities and other registered social landlords to ensure that not only are their allocation practices generally fair but also that they do not act in ways which are unfairly and disproportionately disadvantageous to people on grounds of race, etc. In addition racially harassing conduct in the provision of housing is now clearly illegal. It is hard – indeed, surely impossible – to conceive of a housing authority or registered social landlord having nowadays blatantly racist notices, such as 'No blacks', in their premises. However, the definition of harassment goes beyond such obvious cases and care must be taken to avoid the creation of hostile or intimidatory practices. Sensitivity and consideration must be the watchwords here.

## THE HISTORIC PRACTICE OF LOCAL AUTHORITIES IN ALLOCATION

Historically, allocation involved the processes of:
(a)  determining who should qualify to apply for housing;
(b)  deciding who should be allocated council housing (normally known as 'selection');
(c)  deciding which particular dwelling any such successful applicant should be offered.

It was common practice to create waiting lists (or 'housing registers') from which all general allocations of council property were made, in accordance with the particular selection scheme used. It was not uncommon for registration on/entry to a waiting list to itself be made subject to the satisfaction of conditions, typically a residential qualification.

Allocation 'off list' (normally termed 'selection') was largely done by housing officers in housing departments, but in many instances detailed policy criteria were laid down by the housing committee which consisted of elected councillors. All but the clearest cases normally entailed not only a written application for housing, but also an interview and/or home visit. Disquiet was sometimes expressed at the effect of inbuilt prejudice in some 'housing visitors', or at the use (perhaps for reasons of time) of crude labelling criteria applied after such visits.

There were three broad types of selection scheme:
(a)  *'Date order' schemes*, ie 'First come, first served'.

(b)   *Points schemes*, ie homes were allocated on the basis of 'points' assessed for satisfying certain stated criteria, eg, so many for size of family or bedrooms needed, so many for length of time on the list, etc.

(c)   *Combined schemes*, a combination of the above.

All this was substantially changed in 1996 as a result of legislation.

## THE STATUTE LAW ON ALLOCATION OF HOUSING ACCOMMODATION

### Part VI of the Housing Act 1996, as amended by the Homelessness Act 2002

159.   **Allocation of housing accommodation**

(1) A local housing authority shall comply with the provisions of this Part in allocating housing accommodation.

(2) For the purposes of this Part a local housing authority allocate housing accommodation when they—

(a)   select a person to be a secure or introductory tenant of housing accommodation held by them,

(b)   nominate a person to be a secure or introductory tenant of housing accommodation held by another person, or

(c)   nominate a person to be an assured tenant of housing accommodation held by a registered social landlord.

(3) The reference in subsection (2)(a) to selecting a person to be a secure tenant includes deciding to exercise any power to notify an existing tenant or licensee that his tenancy or licence is to be a secure tenancy.

(4) The references in subsection (2)(b) and (c) to nominating a person include nominating a person in pursuance of any arrangements (whether legally enforceable or not) to require that housing accommodation, or a specified amount of housing accommodation, is made available to a person or one of a number of persons nominated by the authority.

[(5) The provisions of this Part do not apply to an allocation of housing accommodation to a person who is already a secure or introductory tenant unless the allocation involves a transfer of housing accommodation for that person and is made on his application.]

...

(7) Subject to the provisions of this Part, a local housing authority may allocate housing accommodation in such manner as they consider appropriate.

The 1996 system of housing allocation was based on four principles inherent in the legislation: consistency, fairness, transparency and challengeability. This system of allocation is further based on four positive levels of obligation – MUST, MAY, SHOULD, COULD – and one negative level – CANNOT. Some of these exist under the statute, some under statutory instruments, some under guidance issued by the Secretary of State.

Section 22 of the Housing Act 1985 was repealed, and local housing authorities (LHAs) were placed by s 159 of the 1996 Act under a mandatory obligation to comply with legal requirements in allocating their housing. This 'prime duty' applies:

(a)   when they *select* a person to be a secure tenant of accommodation;

(b)   when they nominate a person to be a secure tenant of accommodation held by some other body (eg another LHA);

(c)   when they nominate a person to be an assured tenant of accommodation held by a 'registered social landlord' (eg a Housing Association);

(d)   where an existing secure or introductory tenant *applies* for a transfer of accommodation, as opposed to a mutual exchange or a decanting move while a tenant's home is under repair.

This is the first of a number of duties, eg legal *requirements*. In full these are:

(a)   to comply with Pt VI of the Act – see s 159(1);

(b)   to allocate only to eligible persons – s 160A (see below);

(c)   to have a 'scheme of allocation' – s 167(1);

(d)   to consult other 'social landlords' before making major policy changes – s 167(7) – though what is 'major' is not defined in the legislation;

(e)   not to allocate save in accordance with the scheme – s 167(8);

(f)   to give out information about the scheme – s 168;

(g)   to have regard to guidance from the Secretary of State – s 169(1).

This is contained in a new Code of Guidance, that is the document which contains the 'shoulds and the coulds' – the foregoing are the 'musts'.[12]

If legal obligations are ignored then mandamus could be obtained to compel compliance with duties, though only by a person with a 'sufficient interest' in the matter. It is arguable that any allocation of accommodation made in breach of a duty could be a nullity and would not confer any interest at all on the purported tenant.

This may appear to be a major extension of the rights of applicants for housing. However, the changes made were already the 'best practice' of the most advanced LHAs.

## Exceptions to the prime duty

There are specific exceptions in s 160 where the mandatory obligation will not apply:

160.   **Cases where provisions about allocation do not apply**

(1) The provisions of this Part about the allocation of housing accommodation do not apply in the following cases.

(2) They do not apply where a secure tenancy—

(a)   vests under section 89 of the Housing Act 1985 (succession to periodic secure tenancy on death of tenant),

(b)   remains a secure tenancy by virtue of section 90 of that Act (devolution of term certain of secure tenancy on death of tenant),

(c)   is assigned under section 92 of that Act (assignment of secure tenancy by way of exchange),

(d)   is assigned to a person who would be qualified to succeed the secure tenant if the secure tenant died immediately before the assignment, or

---

[12]   'Allocation of Accommodation: Code of Guidance for local housing authorities' London, Office of the Deputy Prime Minister, 2002, available on the Website: www.odpm.gov.uk.

(e) vests or is otherwise disposed of in pursuance of an order made under—
   (i) section 24 of the Matrimonial Causes Act 1973 (property adjustment orders in connection with matrimonial proceedings),
   (ii) section 17(1) of the Matrimonial and Family Proceedings Act 1984 (property adjustment orders after overseas divorce, &c.), or
   (iii) paragraph 1 of Schedule 1 to the Children Act 1989 (orders for financial relief against parents).

(3) They do not apply where an introductory tenancy—

(a) becomes a secure tenancy on ceasing to be an introductory tenancy,
(b) vests under section 133(2) (succession to introductory tenancy on death of tenant),
(c) is assigned to a person who would be qualified to succeed the introductory tenant if the introductory tenant died immediately before the assignment, or
(d) vests or is otherwise disposed of in pursuance of an order made under—
   (i) section 24 of the Matrimonial Causes Act 1973 (property adjustment orders in connection with matrimonial proceedings),
   (ii) section 17(1) of the Matrimonial and Family Proceedings Act 1984 (property adjustment orders after overseas divorce, &c.), or
   (iii) paragraph 1 of Schedule 1 to the Children Act 1989 (orders for financial relief against parents).

(4) They do not apply in such other cases as the Secretary of State may prescribe by regulations.

(5) The regulations may be framed so as to make the exclusion of the provisions of this Part about the allocation of housing accommodation subject to such restrictions or conditions as may be specified.

In particular, those provisions may be excluded—

(a) in relation to specified descriptions or persons, or
(b) in relation to housing accommodation of a specified description or a specified proportion of housing accommodation of any specified description.

### 160A   Allocation only to eligible persons

(1) A local housing authority shall not allocate housing accommodation—

(a) to a person from abroad who is ineligible for an allocation of housing accommodation by virtue of subsection (3) or (5);
(b) to a person who the authority have decided is to be treated as ineligible for such an allocation by virtue of subsection (7); or
(c) to two or more persons jointly if any of them is a person mentioned in paragraph (a) or (b).

(2) Except as provided by subsection (12), any person may be allocated housing accommodation by a local housing authority (whether on his application or otherwise).

(3) A person subject to immigration control within the meaning of the Asylum and Immigration Act 1996 (c.49) is (subject to subsection (6)) ineligible for an allocation of housing accommodation by a local housing authority unless he is of a class prescribed by regulations made by the Secretary of State.

(4) No person who is excluded from entitlement to housing benefit by section 115 of the Immigration and Asylum Act 1999 (c.33) (exclusion from benefits) shall be included in any class prescribed under subsection (3).

(5) The Secretary of State may by regulations prescribe other classes of persons from abroad who are (subject to subsection (6)) ineligible for an allocation of housing accommodation, either in relation to local housing authorities generally or any particular local housing authority.

(6) Nothing in subsection (3) or (5) affects the eligibility of a person who is already—

(a)  a secure or introductory tenant;

(b)  an assured tenant of housing accommodation allocated to him by a local housing authority.

(7) A local housing authority may decide that an applicant is to be treated as ineligible for an allocation of housing accommodation by them if they are satisfied that—

(a)  he, or a member of his household, has been guilty of unacceptable behaviour serious enough to make him unsuitable to be a tenant of the authority; and

(b)  in the circumstances at the time his application is considered, he is unsuitable to be a tenant of the authority by reason of that behaviour.

(8) The only behaviour which may be regarded by the authority as unacceptable for the purposes of subsection (7)(a) is—

(a)  behaviour of the person concerned which would (if he were a secure tenant of the authority) entitle the authority to a possession order under section 84 of the Housing Act 1985 (c.68) on any ground mentioned in Part 1 of Schedule 2 to that Act (other than ground 8); or

(b)  behaviour of a member of his household which would (if he were a person residing with a secure tenant of the authority) entitle the authority to such a possession order.

(9) If a local housing authority decide that an applicant for housing accommodation—

(a)  is ineligible for an allocation by them by virtue of subsection (3) or (5); or

(b)  is to be treated as ineligible for such an allocation by virtue of subsection (7), they shall notify the applicant of their decision and the grounds of it.

(10) That notice shall be given in writing and, if not received by the applicant, shall be treated as having been given if it is made available at the authority's office for a reasonable period for collection by him or on his behalf.

(11) A person who is being treated by a local housing authority as ineligible by virtue of subsection (7) may (if he considers that he should no longer be treated as ineligible by the authority) make a fresh application to the authority for an allocation of housing accommodation by them.

# THE ALLOCATION OF HOUSING (ENGLAND) REGULATIONS 2002

SI 2002/3264

## Citation, commencement and application

1.   (1) These Regulations may be cited as the Allocation of Housing (England) Regulations 2002 and shall come into force on 31st January 2003.

(2) These Regulations apply in England only.

## Interpretation

2.   In these Regulations—

'the Act' means the Housing Act 1996;
'the Common Travel Area' means the United Kingdom, the Channel Islands, the Isle of Man and the Republic of Ireland collectively; and
'the immigration rules' means the rules laid down as mentioned in section 3(2) of the Immigration Act 1971 (general provisions for regulation and control).

## Cases where the provisions of Part 6 of the Act do not apply

3.    (1) The provisions of Part 6 of the Act about the allocation of housing accommodation do not apply in the following cases.

(2) They do not apply where a local housing authority secures the provision of suitable alternative accommodation under section 39 of the Land Compensation Act 1973 (duty to rehouse residential occupiers).

(3) They do not apply in relation to the grant of a secure tenancy under sections 554 and 555 of the Housing Act 1985 (grant of tenancy to former owner-occupier or statutory tenant of defective dwelling-house).

## Classes prescribed under section 160A(3) who are eligible persons

4.    The following are classes of persons subject to immigration control prescribed for the purposes of section 160A(3) of the Act (persons prescribed as eligible for an allocation of housing accommodation by a local housing authority)—

(a) Class A – a person recorded by the Secretary of State as a refugee within the definition in Article 1 of the Convention relating to the Status of Refugees done at Geneva on 28th July 1951 as extended by Article 1(2) of the Protocol relating to the Status of Refugees done at New York on 31st January 1967;

(b)    Class B – a person—

(i)    who has been granted by the Secretary of State exceptional leave to enter or remain in the United Kingdom outside the provisions of the immigration rules; and

(ii)    whose leave is not subject to a condition requiring him to maintain and accommodate himself, and any person who is dependent on him, without recourse to public funds;

(c)    Class C – a person who has current leave to enter or remain in the United Kingdom which is not subject to any limitation or condition and who is habitually resident in the Common Travel Area other than a person—

(i)    who has been given leave to enter or remain in the United Kingdom upon an undertaking given by another person (his 'sponsor') in writing in pursuance of the immigration rules to be responsible for his maintenance and accommodation;

(ii)    who has been resident in the United Kingdom for less than five years beginning on the date of entry or the date on which the undertaking was given in respect of him, whichever date is the later; and

(iii)    whose sponsor or, where there is more than one sponsor, at least one of whose sponsors, is still alive;

(d)    Class D – a person who is habitually resident in the Common Travel Area and who—

(i)    is a national of a state which has ratified the European Convention on Social and Medical Assistance [ECSMA] done at Paris on 11th December 1953 or a state which has ratified the European Social Charter [ESC] done at Turin on 18th October 1961 and is lawfully present in the United Kingdom; or

(ii)    before 3rd April 2000 was owed a duty by a housing authority under Part 3 of the Housing Act 1985 (housing the homeless) or Part 7 of the Act (homelessness) which is extant, and who is a national of a state which is a signatory to the European Convention on Social and Medical Assistance done at Paris on 11th December 1953 or a state which is a signatory to the European Social Charter done at Turin on 18th October 1961.

## Classes prescribed under section 160A(5) who are ineligible persons

5.    The following is a class of persons, not being persons subject to immigration control, prescribed for the purposes of section 160A(5) of the Act (persons prescribed as ineligible for an allocation of housing accommodation)—

Class B – a person who is not habitually resident in the Common Travel Area other than—
  (a)   a worker who for the purposes of Council Regulation (EEC) No.1612/68 or (EEC) No.1251/70;
  (b)   a person with a right to reside in the United Kingdom pursuant to the Immigration (European Economic Area) Order 2000 and derived from Council Directive No.68/360/EEC or No.73/148/EEC;
  (c)   a person who left the territory of Montserrat after 1st November 1995 because of the effect on that territory of a volcanic eruption.

### Revocation

6.   The Allocation of Housing (England) Regulations 2000 are revoked.

The scheme of inclusions and exclusions under the allocation provisions as amended in 2002 is complex. There are certain classes of people from abroad who are ineligible *as a class*, while other classes are specifically declared to be eligible. In addition certain *individuals* in the UK may be ineligible because of their conduct. We shall consider the ineligible classes first of all.

- Authorities are *not* to allocate to persons from abroad who are subject to immigration control, *unless* they fall into classes prescribed by the Secretary of State. Those who are subject to immigration control are those who fall under the provisions of the Asylum and Immigration Act 1996.

- Authorities are *not* to allocate to those who are excluded from benefits under s 115 of the Immigration and Asylum Act 1999 because they *cannot* be placed in a 'prescribed class'.

- Authorities are *not* to allocate to persons from abroad who are *not* subject to immigration control if they fall into particular classes prescribed by the Secretary of State. These exclusions do *not* apply to people who already, for whatever reason, hold secure introductory or assured tenancies – eg someone who was allocated such a tenancy, say, in 1990, even though then subject to immigration control.

In rather more detail this means that the following classes are ineligible:
  (i)   those registered with the Home Office as asylum seekers, as opposed to those who have been granted refugee status by the Home Office;
  (ii)   visitors to the UK with limited leave to enter or remain where leave was granted on the basis that the person will have no recourse to public funds;
  (iii)   persons with valid leave to enter or remain in the UK subject to a condition they will have no recourse to public funds;
  (iv)   persons with valid leave to enter or remain in the UK without condition or limitation but who are not habitually resident in the Common Travel Area;
  (v)   those whose entry to the UK has been sponsored and who have been here for less than five years and whose sponsors are still alive;
  (vi)   persons who are nationals of a non EEA nation which has signed either the ECSMA and/or ESC but who have ratified neither;
  (vii)   persons who are nationals of a non EEA nation which has ratified ECSMA and/or/ESC, but who are unlawfully in the UK because, for example, they have entered without leave by evading immigration control, and/or who are *not* habitually resident in the Common Travel Area;
  (viii)   persons who are in the UK illegally, or who have overstayed their leave to be here.

The 'Common Travel Area' for the purpose of the legislative scheme is the UK, the Channel Islands, the Isle of Man and the Republic of Ireland. It should, however, also be noted that 'European workers' under Council Regulation (EEC) No. 1612/68 or (EEC) No. 1251/70, even though they are not habitually resident in the Common Travel Area are eligible, as are those with the Treaty Rights under Directives 68/360/EEC and 73/148/EEC, though British nationals who are not resident in that area are not eligible. It should be noted that, generally, those who are classified as asylum seekers are treated as the responsibility of central government in terms of their accommodation and so fall outside the ambit of this work.

'Habitual residence' implies a degree of permanence of residence and implies an association between person and place, though it is a question largely of fact in each case. Issues such as the length of residence, its continuity, the employment (or employment prospects) of the person, reasons for coming to this country, future intentions, all have to be considered. A person needs to show a period of residence, though this may be broken by, for example holidays, without it ceasing to have effect. Stable long-term employment is an important factor to consider.

## THE EXCLUSION OF INDIVIDUALS

Under the Housing Act 1996, in addition to the various classes of people who were excluded from eligibility for housing by regulations made centrally, other classes of people could be excluded by local authorities themselves. The 1998 Shelter Report 'Access Denied' claimed that some authorities were excluding as a class those believed to be responsible for acts of anti-social behaviour, and certainly 63 per cent of the authorities Shelter surveyed stated they would exclude those who had rent arrears. The 2002 Act took away the power to exclude individuals on such a 'blanket' basis and replaced it with a power which has to be exercised on a case-by-case basis.

An authority *may* (note the discretion, and all that implies in general administrative law terms) decide an applicant is to be *treated as ineligible* where they are satisfied (presumably on objective grounds) that he, or a member of his household, has been guilty of 'unacceptable behaviour serious enough to make him unsuitable to be a tenant of the authority' *and* 'in the circumstances at the time his application is considered, he is unsuitable to be a tenant of the authority by reason of that behaviour'.

Note:
(a) The bad behaviour in question can be that of the applicant or a member of his household.
(b) There are cumulative tests to be satisfied before a person is deemed to be ineligible, ie past bad behaviour, not just in the past, but *which at the time of the application* continues to make the applicant unsuitable.

There are a number of judgments which thus have to be made. First, what is 'unacceptable behaviour'? It is somewhat narrowly defined, and is behaviour which, if the person in question were already a secure tenant, would *entitle* the authority *to a possession order* – eg non payment of rent, acts of nuisance or annoyance against neighbours, etc, and similarly in relation to bad behaviour from a member of the applicant's family. The authority must be satisfied that they would have been able to gain a possession order in the circumstances alleged to make the person 'unsuitable'. In other words, the test is not 'Would we seek a possession order in such circumstances?', but rather 'Would a court be likely to grant an order?' This means the authority must go through the same reasoning process as a court which has to consider the reasonableness of making such an order. This involves considering the interests of all parties, including those of the wider public. The sorts of cases where an order is likely to be awarded, on the basis of case law, are those involving noise problems, domestic violence, nuisance, intimidation, drug dealing, racial harassment and rent arrears, but only where there is good and convincing evidence.

The process here will therefore involve:
(a)  deciding that there is sufficient good evidence of bad behaviour which would justify a court in granting a possession order;
(b)  deciding that the behaviour is serious enough to make the person unsuitable to be a tenant, and here if it is arguable that only a suspended possession order could be obtained, it is unlikely that the seriousness threshold would be passed, eg in cases of rent arrears accruing beyond the person's knowledge or control;
(c)  deciding that the behaviour is serious enough to warrant exclusion at the time of the application; hence past bad behaviour may not automatically justify an 'unsuitability' finding.

Authorities should also generally act reasonably in making such decisions, taking into account all relevant factors including age, health, family circumstances, etc, whilst changes in such circumstances will certainly have to be considered where future applications are made by initially excluded applicants.

Thus there can be *no* blanket exclusions, instead *individuals* may be denied eligibility to seek council housing. Where a person is ineligible or deemed to be ineligible that determination must be notified to the person together with reasons, and the notification must be in writing. Ineligible persons may reapply where they believe the reason for their ineligibility has passed.

Section 167(4A) of the 1996 Act, inserted in 2002, *requires* that schemes must provide for applicants to have the right to request a review of *any* decision affecting their case – including suitability and eligibility issues which have been, or are likely to be, taken into account in an allocation decision. However, in any case where someone is dissatisfied with the outcome of a review their only recourse thereafter is to seek judicial review of the decision with all the complexities and expense that involves.

Furthermore, how are reviews to be conducted, and by whom, and how is their independence to be guaranteed? The Code of Guidance issued by the Office of the Deputy Prime Minister under s 169 of the 1996 Act is singularly silent on these issues; however, the need to ensure fairness and objectivity cannot be ignored. This issue is returned to at the end of this chapter.

Section 166 of the Housing Act (as substituted in 2002) provides as follows.

**166  Applications for housing accommodation**
(1) A local housing authority shall secure that—

(a)  advice and information is available free of charge to persons in their district about the right to make an application for an allocation of housing accommodation; and

(b)  any necessary assistance in making such an application is available free of charge to persons in their district who are likely to have difficulty in doing so without assistance.

(2) A local housing authority shall secure that an applicant for an allocation of housing accommodation is informed that he has the rights mentioned in section 167(4A).

(3) Every application made to a local housing authority for an allocation of housing accommodation shall (if made in accordance with the procedural requirements of the authority's allocation scheme) be considered by the authority.

(4) The fact that a person is an applicant for an allocation of housing accommodation shall not be divulged (without his consent) to any other member of the public.

(5) In this Part 'district' in relation to a local housing authority has the same meaning as in the Housing Act 1985 (c.68).

## Commentary

- Authorities must ensure advice and information is freely available to all in their districts about the right to make applications for housing, and must provide free assistance to those who are likely to have difficulty in making an application.

- Applicants will have to be informed of their rights relation to applications, while authorities will not be able to divulge to the public the fact that a person has applied for housing without that person's consent.

- NB s 166(3). Every application made, provided it is made in due form (so there can be some procedural requirements) has to be considered. This reinforces the 'no blanket exclusions' provisions already considered and the 'case by case' decision process outlined above.

## THE ALLOCATION SCHEME

Section 167 of the Housing Act 1996, as amended in 2002, provides as follows.

### 167.  **Allocation in accordance with allocation scheme**

(1) Every local housing authority shall have a scheme (their 'allocation scheme') for determining priorities, and as to the procedure to be followed, in allocating housing accommodation.

For this purpose 'procedure' includes all aspects of the allocation process, including the persons or descriptions of persons by whom decisions are to be taken.

[(1A) The scheme shall include a statement of the authority's policy on offering people who are to be allocated housing accommodation—

(a)  a choice of housing accommodation; or

(b)  the opportunity to express preferences about the housing accommodation to be allocated to them.

(2) As regards priorities, the scheme shall be framed so as to secure that reasonable preference is given to—

(a)  people who are homeless (within the meaning of Part 7);

(b)  people who are owed a duty by any local housing authority under section 190(2),

193(2) or 195(2) (or under section 65(2) or 68(2) of the Housing Act 1985) or who are occupying accommodation secured by any such authority under section 192(3);

(c)  people occupying unsanitary or overcrowded housing or otherwise living in unsatisfactory housing conditions;

(d)  people who need to move on medical or welfare grounds; and

(e)  people who need to move to a particular locality in the district of the authority, where failure to meet that need would cause hardship (to themselves or to others).

The scheme may also be framed so as to give additional preference to particular descriptions of people within this subsection being descriptions of people with urgent housing needs.

(2A) The scheme may contain provision for determining priorities in allocating housing accommodation to people within subsection (2); and the factors which the scheme may allow to be taken into account include—

(a)  the financial resources available to a person to meet his housing costs;

(b)  any behaviour of a person (or of a member of his household) which affects his suitability to be a tenant;

(c)  any local connection (within the meaning of section 199) which exists between a person and the authority's district.

(2B) Nothing in subsection (2) requires the scheme to provide for any preference to be given to people the authority have decided are people to whom subjection (2C) applies.

(2C) This subsection applies to a person if the authority are satisfied that—

(a)  he, or a member of his household, has been guilty of unacceptable behaviour serious enough to make him unsuitable to be a tenant of the authority; and

(b)  in the circumstances at the time his case is considered, he deserves by reason of that behaviour not to be treated as a member of a group of people who are to be given preference by virtue of subsection (2).

(2D) Subsection (8) of section 160A applies for the purposes of subsection (2C)(a) above as it applies for the purposes of subsection (7)(a) of that section.

(2E) Subject to subsection (2), the scheme may contain provision about the allocation of particular housing accommodation—

(a)  to a person who makes a specific application for that accommodation;

(b)  to persons of a particular description (whether or not they are within subsection (2)).]

(3) The Secretary of State may by regulations—

(a)  specify further descriptions of people to whom preference is to be given as mentioned in subsection (2), or

(b)  amend or repeal any part of subsection (2).

(4) The Secretary of State may by regulations specify factors which a local housing authority shall not take into account in allocating housing accommodation.

[(4A) The scheme shall be framed so as to secure that an applicant for an allocation of housing accommodation—

(a)  has the right to request such general information as will enable him to assess—

(i)  how his application is likely to be treated under the scheme (including in particular whether he is likely to be regarded as a member of a group of people who are to be given preference by virtue of subsection (2)); and

(ii)  whether housing accommodation appropriate to his needs is likely to be made available to him and, if so, how long before such it is likely to be before such accommodation becomes available for allocation to him;

(b)   is notified in writing of any decision that he is a person to whom subsection (2C) applies and the grounds for it;

(c)   has the right to request the authority to inform him of any decision about the facts of his case which is likely to be, or has been, taken into account in considering whether to allocate housing accommodation to him; and

(d)   has the right to request a review of a decision mentioned in paragraph (b) or (c), or in section 160A(9), and to be informed of the decision on the review and the grounds for it.]

(5) As regards the procedure to be followed, the scheme shall be framed in accordance with such principles as the Secretary of State may prescribe by regulations.

(6) Subject to the above provisions, and to any regulations made under them, the authority may decide on what principles the scheme is to be framed.

(7) Before adopting an allocation scheme, or making an alteration to their scheme reflecting a major change of policy, a local housing authority shall—

(a)   send a copy of the draft scheme, or proposed alteration, to every registered social landlord with which they have nomination arrangements, and

(b)   afford those persons a reasonable opportunity to comment on the proposals.

(8) A local housing authority shall not allocate housing accommodation except in accordance with their allocation scheme.

Section 168 (as amended in 2002) provides for information about allocation schemes.

### 168.   Information about allocation scheme

(1) A local housing authority shall publish a summary of their allocation scheme and provide a copy of the summary free of charge to any member of the public who asks for one.

(2) The authority shall make the scheme available for inspection at their principal office and shall provide a copy of the scheme, on payment of a reasonable fee, to any member of the public who asks for one.

(3) When the authority make an alteration to their scheme reflecting a major change of policy, they shall within a reasonable period of time take such steps as they consider reasonable to bring the effect of the allocation to the attention of those likely to be affected by it.

## Commentary

Section 167 of the 1996 Act as amended in 2002 provides new 'reasonable preference categories':

- the homeless;
- people owed homelessness duties;
- people living in unsatisfactory housing conditions – including unsanitary or overcrowded housing;
- people with a particular need to move on medical or welfare grounds;
- people with a particular need to move to avoid hardship to themselves or others (eg to escape violence).

Schemes of allocation may give additional preference to anyone falling within any reasonable preference category, provided they have 'urgent housing needs'. The sort of people contemplated here are those who are homeless in consequence of violence or threatened violence, eg domestic or racial violence, those at risk of intimidation, those in urgent medical need.

Schemes may contain measure for prioritising allocation and may take into account:
- a person's financial resources;
- a person's behaviour affecting suitability to be a tenant (likewise the behaviour of members of his household);
- local connection with the area in question, eg by virtue of residence or employment in an area.

In many cases, of course, there will be applicants under allocation schemes with similar levels of need and some mechanism must be in place for determining priority between them, and these must be clearly set out in the scheme: ad hoc officer discretion is not allowable! It is legitimate to include provisions which reflect the amount of time a person has been on a waiting list.

Whatever provisions are adopted, however, they must strike a balance between the prime importance of the statutory reasonable preference categories, the demands of the law that discretion must never be fettered and the need to take account of local issues and problems, such as the needs of extended families and those of key workers not otherwise in reasonable preference categories such as teachers, nurses and police officers in areas of high housing costs. Whatever scheme is adopted it must, of course, not lead to direct or indirect racial or sexual discrimination, etc.

The Code of Guidance further points out that the involvement of elected members in allocation decisions is limited by the Allocation of Housing (Procedure) Regulations, SI 1997/483, so that a member may not be part of a decision-making body where either the dwelling is in his/her ward or where the applicant is a resident in the member's ward. Members may, however, take decisions in relation to allocations not falling within these classes and may seek information for their constituents and may argue a case for them, provided they do not participate in the actual decision. Members may also be involved in decisions about general housing policies affecting their wards.

Where an authority are satisfied that a person (or a member of his household) has been guilty of 'unacceptable behaviour' (see above) serious enough to make him unsuitable to be a tenant *and* at the time of consideration of his case he does not deserved to be treated as a member of a group which is to be given reasonable preference, then the scheme of allocation *need* not provide any preference for that person. This effectively puts the decision in *R v Wolverhampton Metropolitan Borough Council, ex p Watters*[13] (see below) into a legislative form. the tests to be applied here are exactly the same as for an initial exclusion from eligibility already considered above.

Clearly there has to be a considerable revision of allocation schemes to take account of the 'bad behaviour' provisions now inserted into the 1996 Act. But it needs to be remembered that these have to be framed in such a way that they operate on a case by case basis and not by way of blanket exclusion.

[13] (1997) 29 HLR 931.

## CHOICE-BASED PROVISION

The new s 167(1A) requires authorities to include a policy statement in their scheme on offering people a choice of housing accommodation, or the opportunity to express preferences about the sort of accommodation they would like. This is to enable 'choice-based' schemes of allocation to operate. Of course, much will then depend on how much spare property an authority has – unless there is a great deal of property there cannot be much choice.

This is reinforced by the new s 167(2E), which provides that schemes may contain provisions about allocating particular accommodation to persons who specifically apply for it, or to persons who fall within a particular class or description – even where they fall outside the reasonable preference categories. This is designed to enable authorities to attract as tenants particular groups, classes or individuals where they have housing capacity but not the demand for it.

The types of scheme contemplated by the law are those which resemble 'Harborough Home Search', which has been partnered in Leicestershire by Harborough DC in conjunction with East Midlands HA, De Montfort Housing Society and Leicester HA. The essence of such a scheme is that properties available for social renting are *advertised* by the authority and partner landlords. Potential tenants may then register their interest in a particular property by completing and returning a coupon provided they meet the requirements with which the property has been 'labelled'. The object is to make allocation much more of a self-selection process.

The Harborough scheme was initially drawn up very much as a 'first come first served' basis, though a degree of flexibility was built into it to ensure that the authority did not fetter its discretion. The new law is arguably not over-friendly towards such schemes and the Code of Guidance is not particularly helpful in leading authorities through the new provisions: 'authorities should consider adopting a simplified system of applicant prioritisation in place of a complex points based approach'. In the past, authorities have been singled out as pathfinders when they have created very comprehensive points systems for guiding their discretionary choices. Perhaps there is a distinction between 'complex' and 'comprehensive'. The ODPM favoured approach now seems to be to band applicants into various groups which reflect differing levels of housing need. Prioritisation within groups *may* then take place on the basis of waiting time on lists. It may be asked whether this is a technique that is new. This 'banding' may be accompanied by giving 'time limited priority cards' to those in the most urgent need to enable a fast track into rehousing. On the other hand it may be asked whether the use of such cards is not then undermined when the Code goes on to say: 'It is essential that, where the applicant does not make use of the priority card within the specified time limit, there is a mechanism for reconsidering his housing needs … and for extending the time limit where this is appropriate.' One has to wonder whether this is giving advice to authorities with one hand and taking it away with the other. In any case any choice-based scheme must also ensure that it meets the statutory requirements to give 'reasonable preference' etc to particular groups of people.

The changes made to the law in 2002 mark a step away from the notions of the 1996 Housing Act which were based on the premise that only certain people who 'qualified' for council housing should be assisted. Those who did were placed on a housing register, and thereafter allocation took place to those who were on the register and who satisfied the various preference category criteria. The obligation to maintain a housing register was ended by s 13 of the Homelessness Act 2002, though it is likely that authorities will maintain some form of register for administrative purposes. The elaborate system of appeal measures which the 1996 Act contained to provide mechanisms for those denied registration has also been swept away. The philosophy of the 2002 Act seems to be the promotion of a degree of inclusivity by preventing the blanket exclusion of certain groups of would-be applicants for council housing, and the need for authorities to have a fair system in place to provide for exclusion only on an individual basis. It is thought that in practice allocation schemes will in most cases continue to be based on points systems whereby those in the reasonable preference categories will have their needs measured. 'Choice-based' systems which at one time appeared to be favoured centrally, now have to accommodate the overriding requirements of the reasonable preference categories, and it is hard to see how that can be achieved without some means of 'pointing'.

It has to be stressed, however, that the law only provides a framework within which allocation schemes operate. There is no single national model scheme; nor is there much knowledge of how allocation schemes work in practice and differ from area to area. The operation of schemes will vary according to a mix of factors, for example the amount of housing an authority has, whether some or all of it is in unpopular or stigmatised areas of 'hard to let' properties, whether authorities try to attract a wide range of potential applicants including students and middle income groups. It is not known, for instance, whether access rules are at their most relaxed in areas of low demand with unpopular housing.

The following issues need further investigation:
- Do present systems act as barriers? In some places that may be so, in others there is a virtually open access policy.
- Who are excluded under current systems?
- What are the regional variations, or is there variation between urban and rural areas?
- Is access easiest in areas where demand for council housing is low – in which case, would a further easing of access do anything to stimulate demand?
- If allocation rules were to be relaxed further, would this result in a further influx into council housing of those who are unemployed or currently on benefits, particularly young single males – and what effect might that have on council estates?
- Are there other factors that keep people out of council housing – eg poor location, bad transport, fear of crime, urban depravation, bad schools?[14]
- Are people's housing choices affected particularly by personal factors such as family links and social networks? This is apparently very true in parts of Birmingham with ethnic minority communities.[15]
- Changing allocation policies alone will not result in the provision of more decent, modern, clean, affordable homes. There is a need for more provision

[14]   See Alan Murie, 'Allocation policies: facts and fantasies' (2000) 55(2) axis 6.
[15]   See Emma Hawkey, 'Mixed Messages' (2001) Roof Sept/Oct, p 26.

of good quality social housing in places where people are going to be encouraged to apply for it. Until then many people will continue to prefer being owner occupiers of unsuitable and expensive to maintain housing simply because overall their existing homes are more conveniently sited for them to in terms of support, community, religion, shopping etc.

So far as the law is concerned, however, authorities are required to operate their allocation schemes in a fair and reasonable fashion. While this results in them having still a considerable degree of discretion, that discretion is not without limits.

## Some judicial and departmental guidance on the operation of the 'reasonable preference' categories under the 1996 Act

It has been argued that the categories are 'cumulative', ie if a person figures in more than one of them then those categories *have* to be accumulated together to ensure faster rehousing[16]. Such categoric statements are not, however, supported by the case law. In *R v Islington London Borough Council, ex p Reilly*[17] Richards J considered the categories simply identified need and were not to be treated as separate, and were only *capable* of being cumulative. However, a rather different slant emerged in *R v Westminster London Borough Council, ex p Al-Khorsan*[18] Here an authority had accepted that a person was owed homelessness duties, and they were therefore also in the 'reasonable preference' categories for 'ordinary' allocation. The authority's scheme provided for a quota of available units to be made available to homeless persons, with priority within that group being determined by the date on which a homelessness responsibility had been accepted. The remainder of the available stock was divided amongst the other 'reasonable preference' groups. The applicant argued this ignored other factors relevant to his case, such as medical and welfare factors, and that the scheme should have taken into account whether any of the factors set out in s 167(2)(a)–(f) also applied to him. Latham J agreed: 'insofar as the council's scheme precluded consideration of any of the other categories to which reasonable preference ought to be given under section 167(2) it was unlawful'.

In other words if a person is in a reasonable preference group and has factors affecting him/her which are relevant to other reasonable preference categories, eg a homeless person with medical needs, that person should be considered on the basis of *all* relevant factors. However, Latham J added: 'the extent to which priority should be given within the homeless category to those who fell within the other categories was a matter for the council ... those who had such needs were entitled to have them considered'. In other words an authority cannot say: 'X number of houses for the homeless and Y for the medical needs group and never the twain shall meet'. See further *London Borough of Lambeth v A* and *London Borough of Lambeth v Lindsay*, considered below.

---

[16] See David Cowan, *Housing Law and Policy* p 239.
[17] (1998) 31 HLR 651 at 666.
[18] [2001] 33 HLR 6.

Reference has already been briefly made to *R v Wolverhampton Metropolitan Borough Council, ex p Watters*[19] This was a decision on the former s 22 of the Housing Act 1985 which has now been replaced by the provisions of the 1996 and 2002 Acts considered above. Even under the older law, however, the courts made it clear that a former tenant's bad behaviour could be taken into account by an authority in the allocation of housing. This principle remains true, even though it has been put into a particular statutory form by the 2002 legislation.

Legatt LJ referred to the arguments of council for the applicant, whom he said:

'submitted that because Parliament have ordained that reasonable preference is to be given, a council cannot treat it as reasonable not to grant any preference.'

Legatt LJ then continued:

'For the Council Mr Findlay contended that, once it is conceded that a policy which takes account of rent arrears is not unlawful, a local authority is free to choose which procedure to adopt for determining preferences. Different local authorities adopt different procedures: some award points, whilst others do not allow applicants with particular shortcomings on to the waiting list. ... But reasonable preference means what it says. If two applicants are otherwise equal, but one is within one of the first three categories of section 22, that one will be preferred. It is for the Council to decide what weight to give to relevant factors. Reasonable preference is to be equated with extra weight: it cannot be determined *per se* ... I agree with Mr Findlay's submissions. If section 22 simply required "preference" to be given, Mr Gallivan's argument would be correct. But it does not: it requires "reasonable preference". No preference is to be given except reasonable preference.'

## ALLOCATION OF HOUSING (PROCEDURE) REGULATIONS 1997

SI 1997/483

### Citation and commencement

1.   These Regulations may be cited as the Allocation of Housing (Procedure) Regulations 1997 and shall come into force on 1st April 1997.

### Interpretation

2.   In these Regulations—

'allocation decision' means a decision to allocate housing accommodation;
'authority' means a local housing authority in England;
'decision-making body' means an authority or a committee or sub-committee of an authority.

### Allocation scheme procedure

3.   (1) As regards the procedure to be followed, an authority's allocation scheme shall be framed in accordance with the principle prescribed in this regulation.

---

[19]   (1997) 29 HLR 931.

(2) A member of an authority who has been elected for the electoral division or ward in which—

(a)   the housing accommodation in relation to which an allocation decision falls to be made is situated, or

(b)   the person in relation to whom that decision falls to be made has his sole or main residence,

shall not, at the time the allocation decision is made, be included in the persons constituting the decision-making body.

In Wales similar provision is made by SI 1997/45, which, however, also provides specifically that allocation decisions in Wales may be taken by local authority officers except where the local housing authority determine otherwise.

As a general guiding principle authorities are expected to give priority to those who will need social housing over a long period: thus long-term disability, chronic illness, etc. are more likely to attract rehousing than an acute but temporary housing crisis.

Authorities will, however, still have to determine priority between applicants who fall into the various preference classes. They should act in concert with, and on the advice of, other relevant social agencies, eg, social services and health authorities.

In drawing up a scheme, therefore, authorities are able to take into account a very wide range of factors, but all the allocation criteria must be incorporated into the scheme and made public. The characteristics of tenants may be considered, eg, their suitability for ensuring a good social mix on an estate, or the length of time they have been on the register, so that where there are two households who otherwise qualify for immediate rehousing there is some means of determining priority between them.

Particular guidance has now been on the meaning of s 167 of the 1996 Act by the Court of Appeal in *London Borough of Lambeth v A* and *London Borough of Lambeth v Lindsay*[20]. The scheme of allocation adopted by Lambeth under the 1996 Act contained certain exclusionary categories, so that the authority would not accept for rehousing people having no connection with the borough, or who already had a secure home, or who had got into housing difficulties through their own wrongdoing. The scheme then assessed housing need as follows. Applicants would be placed into one of six allocation groups, and in some cases they would be further classified by determining the area, size and type of property required. In addition applicants' own judgments of their own needs by making choices that would affect how quickly they were housed was also a feature of the scheme. In effect this allowed applicants feeling they had the greatest need to opt for a very wide choice of housing, while those who felt they could wait could be more selective as to which properties for which they put themselves forward. Applicants were also ranked by date order within the various allocation groups. Applicants were given assistance in making statements about their housing needs so that they could make informed choices, and the authority retained a particular discretion to give more priority to certain of its priority groups. When properties became vacant there would be a computer-generated 'match list' of applicants in each of the various allocation groups who had

[20]   [2002] EWCA Civ 1084, [2002] HLR 998.

need for a property of the 'bed size' in question, and who had included the area in which the property was situated in their application. An 'allocating officer' would then decide which 'match list' to offer to in an ordering of the various allocation groups. Within the various allocation groups priority was determined by date order. New applicants were placed at the bottom of the list for their group, for the size of property needed, and in the allocation areas applied for. Thereafter they would moved up the list from time to time and could only be demoted down 'their' list by refusing what the authority considered to be a reasonable offer of a dwelling.

The authority had adopted its scheme because it faced considerable pressure on its housing stock. The amount of stock available had decreased, while the numbers of those seeking assistance from the authority were increasing. Nearly all of those applying for assistance fell into at least one of the reasonable preference categories of s 167 of the Housing Act 1996, many fell into more than one, and only 4 per cent of applicants were entitled to no preference whatsoever. The authority had moved away from a points-based system, considering such schemes to be inflexible, not always capable of identifying real need, and taking no account of applicants' perception of their own need. They also argued that people established as applicants could find themselves effectively 'demoted' if someone assessed as having more 'points' joined the list of applicants. The authority argued that a positive feature of their scheme was to give room for applicants to make informed choices. When an application was made an officer would identify the group into which the applicant should be placed, and also the size of accommodation needed, and the type. An applicant would also be told the 'waiting time' situation in particular areas of the borough. Thus a person could advance his/her chances by opting for consideration for properties in 'hard to let' or otherwise undesirable areas. Even so, the waiting time for those not in the highest category of need was measured in years not months.

The legality of the scheme was attacked as follows.

- The scheme did not provide for the 'reasonable preference' required by s 167 as it covered not only people who fell within the preference categories but those who did not. This, it was argued, did not satisfy the requirement of the statute that allocation schemes have to be 'framed so as to secure that reasonable preference is given' to particular persons.
- The scheme did not enable those who fell into more than one of the reasonable preference categories to achieve a greater degree of priority.

Collins J pointed out, on the basis of the *Watters* case considered above, that no more than 'reasonable preference' to each particular group has to be given. Each authority has to have a scheme which reflects its own situation and problems, and factors other than those specifically mentioned by statute can be taken into account, provided they do not dominate the scheme at the expense of those factors which are statutorily mentioned. Even so positive favour has to be shown to applications which satisfy all or any of the statutory criteria, and then a balancing exercise has to be carried out in making allocation decisions taking into account all the other relevant considerations.

Collins J considered Lambeth's scheme did not meet these legal requirements. It was a date order scheme but its real vice was to include an identified group some of whom did not meet the statutory preference criteria. Admittedly these people constituted only 4 per cent of the applicants, but Collins J argued that the percentage was not a relevant issue. He argued that it must be clear that applicants who are not entitled to preference cannot compete on equal terms with those who are, otherwise the scheme does not meet the statutory requirements. Neither could self-assessment of need meet the need for some people to be given preference since anyone could advance his or her case by being prepared to opt for properties in less desired areas. Collins J pointed out that an authority's scheme does not have to slavishly adhere to the statutory categorisation of preference, but *overall* it must ensure that a 'head start' is always given to those who do fit into those categories.

Collins J then turned to the argument that the way in which the scheme operated rendered it unlawful as it was not possible to consider the various types of need an applicant might have which could have the effect of placing that person in more than one priority need group. He referred initially to decisions in *R v Islington London Borough Council, ex p Reilly* and *R v Westminster City Council, ex p Al-Khorsan* to which earlier reference has been made. Collins J then argued that what is required is that a scheme must have a mechanism for identifying those who have the greatest need and for ensuring that, subject to any countervailing factors such as bad conduct on a person's part, those with the greatest need get due priority. It will not always be the case, he pointed out, that being in more than one priority need group will necessarily equate with being in the greatest degree of need. Everything will depend on particular circumstances. A person who falls into only one preference category *may* be considered to have more need than one who falls into many simply because of the length of time spent waiting for a suitable property to become available. In this respect, he added, any scheme which attempts to assess and balance comparative degrees of need is bound to be imperfect and subjective as it will be based on human judgment. But that does not make the scheme irrational and unlawful.

Lambeth's scheme allowed for much of the allocation decision to be based on individual's perception and assessment of their own need. This he considered led to the scheme operating in an haphazard fashion as individuals would only be concerned with their own situation and could not then supply any element of objectivity.

Pill LJ agreed with Collins J and, along with Judge LJ, argued that it is not for the courts to have to approve in broad terms allocation schemes. The courts can only deal with the *legality* of an individual scheme; the courts must not lay down general criteria of approval and so usurp the functions of authorities. Authorities must draw up their own schemes, and provided these observe the specific requirements of the legislation, then no question of illegality should arise. In the instant case all three judges were agreed that Lambeth's scheme, though well intentioned and designed to deal with an intractable problem, was unlawful because it did not *ensure* that those entitled to preference received it over those who did not, even though 96 per cent of applicants would have had preference anyway under the terms of the scheme. Where there was *some* disagreement between the three judges was as to whether a scheme may be attacked as illegal on the basis that it fails to achieve the principle of the 1996 Act that allocation schemes must be clear and predictable in operation, ie that schemes must be transparent, and capable of showing how preference is accorded, and who qualifies for which groups and who within each group achieves preference. Collins J rejected this argument and argued that a scheme does not have to demonstrate such a degree of precision. The statutory requirement that a scheme must be 'framed to secure' priority does not mean everything has to be set out in precise detail. All that is required is that the scheme should declare all the *aspects* and principles of the allocation process. Pill LJ on the other hand appeared a little more favourable to the argument which Collins J rejected. He accepted that there was a statutory intention that schemes should be as clear and predictable in operation as possible, given the circumstances in which they operate. However, he concluded that over-elaboration may become the enemy of clarity and fairness. Thus:

- The provision of choice within a scheme does not render it unlawful, and under the provisions of the Homelessness Act 2002 *some* provision for choice is needed.
- Authorities must always take account of the central guidance.
- The statutory preference categories must always be complied with and non-preference categories must not be allowed to infiltrate.
- Provided the statutory preference categories are observed, authorities are free to adopt either a points-based or a quota-based system of allocation; even date order may be used, provided it complies with the statutory preference requirements.
- The reasonable preference groups must be reflected in whatever scheme of categorisation is used, and it appears illegal to aggregate all of those entitled to preference in a single undifferentiated group.
- Allocation is a question of reasonable judgment, not a mathematical exercise.

## Challenges to allocation decisions

There are no provisions in the 1996 and 2002 Acts giving jurisdiction to the county court over challenges to allocation decisions, eg where an authority make an allocation not in accordance with their scheme. In such an event it would appear that challenge by way of judicial review would be available to someone with a sufficient interest in the matter – perhaps a person who satisfies the scheme's requirements and who has otherwise had it indicated to him or her that the property would or could be allocated to him or her. Thus the cases on s 22 of the 1985 Act remain relevant to future practice.

## Continuing requirements for legality

There continues to be an overarching requirement to operate an allocation scheme in a lawful fashion, ie without illegality, procedural impropriety or irrationality. Thus there must be no absolute fetters on discretion, such as in *R v Canterbury City Council, ex p Gillespie*[21], or *absolutely automatic* exclusions from the register save as provided for by legislation, eg because an applicant has an arrears history or because of ownership of other property[22]. Certainly houses must not be allocated

---

[21]  (1986) 19 HLR 7.
[22]  See *R v Forest Heath District Council, ex p West and Lucas* (1991) 24 HLR 85 and *R v Bristol City Council, ex p Johns* (1992) 25 HLR 249.

solely for party political reasons[23]. Apart from that, however, the breadth of the residual discretion enjoyed by authorities appears to allow them to consider allocating properties to those under 18, to continue the practice of making numbers of offers of one property only, or to take into account historic factors affecting an applicant such as length of time spent in temporary lets. The Code of Guidance warns, nevertheless, against adopting a formulaic approach, which is reinforced by the *Lindsay* decision. One way of thinking about the system of allocation is to picture it as a three-dimensional matrix where none of the parameters is absolutely determinative. The three principal parameters or groups of parameters in any given situation will be, first, to ask what properties are available and for whom are they suitable; secondly, to determine who are the persons eligible according to scheme criteria and the general law; and then, thirdly, to determine priority as between qualifying groups *and* within groups – date order registration or points totals can be used to help in this determination but must not be used as rigid determinants.

## OTHER ALLOCATIONS

LHAs allocate many of their properties to existing tenants seeking to move home for a variety of reasons – health, employment, family, etc. Such allocations (usually known as 'transfers') used to fall outside the terms of the 1996 Act, though this, as has been stated above was altered under the Homelessness Act 2002, even so, s 106 of the Housing Act 1985, as amended by the Housing Acts 1988 and 1996 and the Local Government (Wales) Act 1994 remains relevant.

Section 106 of the Housing Act 1985 provides as follows.

106.   **Information about housing allocation**

(1) A landlord authority shall publish a summary of its rules—

(a)   for determining priority as between applicants in the allocation of its housing accommodation, and

(b)   governing cases where secure tenants wish to move (whether or not by way of exchange of dwelling-houses) to other dwelling-houses let under secure tenancies by that authority or another body.

(2) A landlord authority shall—

(a)   maintain a set of the rules referred to in subsection (1) and of the rules which it has laid down governing the procedure to be followed in allocating its housing accommodation, and

(b)   make them available at its principal office for inspection at all reasonable hours, without charge, by members of the public.

(3) A landlord authority which is a [registered social landlord] shall, instead of complying with paragraph (b) of subsection (2), send a set of the rules referred to in paragraph (a) of that subsection—

(a)   to the [Corporation], and

(b)   to the council of any district, [Welsh county or county borough] or London borough in which there are dwelling-houses let or to be let by the [landlord authority] under secure tenancies;

---

[23]   *R v Port Talbot Borough Council, ex p Jones* (1987) 20 HLR 265.

and a council to whom a set of rules is sent under this subsection shall make it available at its principal office for inspection at all reasonable hours, without charge, by members of the public.

(4) A copy of the summary published under subsection (1) shall be given without charge, and a copy of the set of rules maintained under subsection (2) shall be given on payment of a reasonable fee, to any member of the public who asks for one.

(5) At the request of a person who has applied to it for housing accommodation, a landlord authority shall make available to him, at all reasonable times and without charge, details of the particulars which he has given to the authority about himself and his family and which the authority has recorded as being relevant to his application for accommodation.

[(6) The provisions of this section do not apply to a landlord authority which is a local housing authority so far as they impose requirements corresponding to those to which such an authority is subject under sections 166 and 168 of the Housing Act 1996 (provision of information about housing registers and allocation schemes).]

The powers of authorities under this provision being discretionary are, of course, subject to the requirements of the general principles of administrative law which have already been considered. However, it should be noted that the section provides no enforcement mechanism, and hence reliance has to be placed on judicial review with all its problems of locus standi and its discretionary nature as a remedy. Case law offers some guidance. Particular note should be taken of the cases which follow.

In *R v London Borough of Tower Hamlets, ex p Spencer*[24] in 1988, the applicant was granted a tenancy of a property owned by the respondent authority. In 1990, following the birth of her son, she applied for a transfer. In January 1994, she underwent an operation for a degenerative condition known as syringomelia. The condition caused her to have difficulties climbing stairs, and walking or standing for long periods of time. She suffered from headaches which could not be relieved by painkillers. At the time, the prognosis was uncertain. The applicant went to convalesce with her parents. She renewed her application for a transfer. Upon her return to the property, she discovered that it had been burgled.

The authority's medical adviser identified the applicant as being in need of a flat served by lifts. In July 1994 their Housing Management Panel placed her in a priority category for management transfer. Before an offer could be made to her, the applicant moved to live in her sister's accommodation (59 Wager Street) and applied to have the tenancy transferred to her. That application was refused.

In November 1994, an occupational therapist completed a report on the applicant which stated that her condition affected both her sensation and muscular power. The report said that although the applicant experienced pain, she had no functional problems. The therapist recommended that the applicant should not be offered a particular property (5 Verity House) which was a ground floor maisonette, which had been specially adapted for the disabled. In December 1994, despite this recommendation, the authority offered the applicant the tenancy of 5 Verity House. The applicant's solicitors wrote to the authority stating that the property was unsuitable and asking that the applicant be granted a tenancy of 59 Wager Street. On 17 January 1995, the authority replied, confirming that the applicant's medical needs would be re-assessed by the respondents' medical adviser.

[24] (1995) 29 HLR 64.

On 29 March 1995, the case was considered by the Housing Management Panel. No medical re-assessment had taken place. The Panel had before them a letter from the consultant who had operated on the applicant, who was of the opinion that the applicant should be able to carry out most everyday activities, although she did experience considerable pain. The Panel also had a report from a housing officer, who explained that 5 Verity House had been offered because it was understood that the applicant's condition would deteriorate and that her longer term needs had to be taken into account. The report concluded by recommending that the applicant be offered a tenancy of her sister's flat.

On 12 April 1995, the Housing Management Panel decided that the applicant should not be offered a tenancy of her sister's property. The Panel decided that the offer would not be made because it would be contrary to the Medical Adviser's recommendation. The applicant sought judicial review of the decision. It was held as follows.

(1) It was procedurally unfair for the Panel to rely on the original medical assessment without giving the applicant an opportunity to make representations as to the inappropriateness of doing so; it was particularly unfair, given that the respondents had represented to the applicant that an updated assessment was being obtained.

(2) In stating that an offer of 59 Wager Street would be contrary to the medical adviser's recommendation, the Panel relied on a recommendation which could not reasonably be relied on in the light of the subsequent evidence from the occupational therapist and the consultant as to the applicant's present, improved condition; the Panel had acted irrationally in relying on these matters as grounds for rejecting the recommendation.

Stephen Richards (*sitting as a Deputy High Court Judge*):

'Mr Luba, for the applicant, advances three grounds for challenging the Panel's decision of April 12: procedural unfairness, failure to give notification and reasons, and irrationality.

In relation to the first ground it is common ground that the council was required to observe "basic administrative law requirements of natural justice and procedural fairness". The case as originally formulated had been that the Panel acted unfairly in reaching its decision on the basis of a new medical assessment that had not been put to the applicant for comment. It was only after service of the council's affidavit that it emerged that there had been no new assessment. The case was then reformulated to the following effect. The applicant had been given legitimately to expect that the Panel would not reach a decision without an updated medical assessment. If the applicant had known that the Panel would proceed on the basis of the original medical assessment and without an undated assessment, she would have asked her medical advisers to comment on the original assessment (to show that it was out of date) and/or would have made representations to be put in front of the Panel as to the inappropriateness of relying on the original assessment.

There is a lot of force in that submission. The original medical assessment of May 1994, with its recommendation that the applicant be given a lifted flat served by two lifts, was based on the evidence that she could not manage stairs and the uncertain prognosis following her operation. Happily, things had improved by the end of the year. The occupational therapist's report of November 1994 stated that the applicant at present had no functional problems. The consultant gave his opinion, in his letter of 31 January 1995, that she should be able to manage stairs and carry out most activities of daily living without significant problems other than pain. The present situation and prognosis were plainly better than they had been at the time of the original assessment.

In my judgment it was procedurally unfair in those circumstances to rely on the original medical assessment without giving the applicant an opportunity to make representations as to the inappropriateness of doing so. Unfairer still to do so after representing to the applicant in categoric terms, until the last letter before the Panel's meeting, that an updated assessment was being obtained. I would quash the Panel's resulting decision on that ground alone.

The approach adopted also goes to the substance of the Panel's decision. The first of the reasons for rejecting the Housing Officer's recommendation that the applicant be offered a tenancy of 59 Wager Street was, "Would be contrary to Medical Adviser's recommendation", presumably on the basis that 59 Wager Street did not meet the description of property recommended in the original assessment. But that recommendation could not reasonably be relied on in the light of the recent evidence from the occupational therapist and the consultant as to the applicant's present condition. Similarly, the third of the reasons for rejecting the Housing Officer's recommendation was "A more suitable offer [had] previously been made and refused", referring no doubt to the offer of 5 Verity House. I am prepared to accept, as Mr Crawford pressed in argument, that there was a sensible rationale behind the offer of 5 Verity House at a time when it was thought that the applicant's condition was likely to deteriorate: it was reasonable to look to the long term. The subsequent evidence about the applicant's condition and prognosis, however, undermined that rationale and flew in the face of the conclusion that premises specially adapted for a person with a much higher level of disability than the applicant were nonetheless suitable for the applicant. I do not see how a reasonable decision-making body, directing itself properly to the issues and the material before it could have relied on these matters as grounds for rejecting the recommendation. I therefore accept the thrust of Mr Luba's submissions on the third ground, irrationality, as well.

It does not follow that the applicant must now be offered 59 Wager Street. The second reason relied on, "Cannot condone a tenant picking properties and queue jumping", might have caused the Panel to reach the same conclusion in any event. That is not a matter for me. But the actual process of reasoning that led to the decision of 12 April was to my mind defective and fresh consideration of the case and a fresh decision are required.'

In *R v Camden London Borough Council, ex p Adair*[25] in 1989 on the breakdown of his marriage, the respondent authority granted the applicant a secure tenancy of a three-bedroomed flat. In 1990, the applicant's girlfriend (Miss Qaddoumi) moved in

---

[25]  (1996) 29 HLR 236.

with him. In February 1992, the secure tenancy was transferred into their joint names. Relations between the couple broke down. On 27 May 1994, Miss Qaddoumi obtained an interim injunction and an ouster order against the applicant requiring him to vacate the flat.

On 23 May 1994, the applicant approached the authority's District Housing Office for accommodation for himself and a new girlfriend. The applicant informed the authority that the had become involved in a dispute between two drug dealers who had made threats against him. The District Housing Office told the applicant that he would not be given temporary accommodation and advised him that he could apply to the Homeless Persons Unit. He was also given an application form for a transfer.

The applicant went to stay with friends in Scotland. Following various letters from the applicant, the authority's District Housing Office wrote to him telling him about a policy operated by the authority to assist those who were in need of re-housing as a result of breakdown in a relationship. On 17 August 1994, the applicant completed a form for consideration under the scheme. He requested a two- or three-bedroomed property for himself, his son, his current partner and her two stepdaughters. He requested housing away from the Kilburn area as he was in fear for his own safety.

On 5 January 1995, the authority wrote to the applicant to notify him of their decision not to consider him for accommodation under the scheme. The reasons given for the decision were that the applicant had applied under similar circumstances on two separate occasions and had on one occasion sublet the property offered to him and returned to live with his partner. The letter reminded the applicant that he could apply to the Homeless Persons Unit.

On 13 January 1995, the applicant was interviewed by the authority's Homeless Persons Unit. The applicant informed the authority that he suffered from anxiety and depression and was being prescribed Diazepam. An attempt was made by the assessment officer to contact the District Housing Office, but this was unsuccessful, and no further inquiries were made. On the same day, the authority decided that the applicant was homeless but was not in priority need. Their decision letter stated that they had taken into account all the evidence and set out that the applicant did not fall within the statutory categories of persons in priority need. No further reasoning or indication of the inquiries which had been made was included.

The applicant applied for judicial review of the authority's decision [amongst other things] not to grant him a transfer for his tenancy under their relationship breakdown policy.

It was held as follows.

(1) The respondent authority had taken into account all the factors relevant to the applicant's application in refusing to offer him a transfer under their discretionary scheme for those who had suffered domestic breakdown; they were entitled to take into account the fact that the applicant had made two previous applications under the authority's discretionary policy to re-house after breakdown of relationship; the system was capable of operating unfairly to other applicants and potential applicants for housing if a person was able to use the relationship breakdown policy as a means of obtaining accommodation for a series of partners; the authority were also

entitled to take into account the fact that the applicant appeared to have sublet property previously let to him by them, the weight to be given to it being a mater for the authority;

(2) The decision letter of 5 January 1995, contained the reasons for the authority's decision; there was nothing in the circumstances of the case to justify the imposition of a legal requirement to give fuller reasoning.

Stephen Richards (*sitting as a Deputy High Court Judge*):

'... The width of the discretion accorded to those responsible for administering ... policy is plain and is not in dispute. The discretion must nevertheless be exercised in accordance with the normal principles of public law. Miss Shelagh MacDonald, on behalf of the applicant, challenges the council's decision on the ground that those principles were infringed in a number of respects, namely failure to take into account relevant considerations, taking into account irrelevant considerations, procedural unfairness and a failure to give reasons.

### Relevant/irrelevant considerations

As regards considerations said to have been wrongly left out of account, Miss MacDonald focused in her submission on the applicant's claim that he could not return to 182 Webheath because of threats of violence from associates of Miss Qaddoumi, *ie* not just from drug dealers. The difficulty about that contention is that, although it is common ground that the applicant referred to the existence of threats against him, the council's evidence is that he did not attribute those threats to Miss Qaddoumi. ...

In his second affidavit, after a detailed account of the incident in which he vouched for the reliability of a cousin's boyfriend and then found himself subjected to threats of violence when the boyfriend disappeared owing money, the applicant does say: "Threats were made about my personal safety by men who I believe were acquaintances of Ms Qaddoumi or were acting on he behalf." This is the nearest he comes to a distinct allegation of threats of violence attributable to Miss Qaddoumi. As a distinct allegation it has little substance to it. But in any event there is nothing to show that it was made in that form to the council. I conclude that the council cannot properly be criticised for a failure to take it into consideration.

... As regards the contention that the council took into account a number of considerations that it should not have taken into account, Miss MacDonald referred first to the council taking into account the fact that the applicant had made two previous applications for transfer. ... In my judgment that is a perfectly proper consideration for the council to take into account in the exercise of a discretionary power relating to the allocation of its limited housing stock. It is plainly a housing related matter, not an extraneous consideration. It is moreover a potentially important consideration. Ms Rutherford's affidavit emphasises that the system is capable of operating unfairly to other applicants and potential applicants for housing if a person is able to use the relationship breakdown policy as a means of obtaining accommodation for a series of partners. Although no deliberate abuse of the system is alleged in the case of this applicant, it was entirely appropriate for the council to have regard to the fact that he had already benefited twice from the policy in the past.

The second allegedly irrelevant consideration was that the applicant wished to transfer because of the threats made against him by drug dealers. This is not mentioned in the decision letter and does not seem to have been given any great weight. In any event, however, I cannot accept that the reasons for wanting a transfer are irrelevant to the decision. They had been put forward by the applicant himself. In so far as it is suggested that Ms Rutherford's note of May 23, 1994 indicates that the council proceeded on the basis that the applicant was actively involved in drugs-related crime or held against him such tangential involvement as he had himself described, neither the note itself nor the affidavit evidence filed on behalf of the council supports the suggestion.

The third matter – though another matter that is not mentioned in the decision letter and does not seem to have been given great weight – was that the applicant appeared to have another family that needed rehousing. The point here was that the applicant was not simply seeking bedsit accommodation for himself as a result of his having to leave is former home following the breakdown of his relationship with Miss Qaddoumi. On his application form, as I have indicated above, he was seeking a two to three bedroom property to house his new partner and that partner's two step-daughters, as well as his own son. It is plain, in my judgment, that the council was entitled to have regard to these matters, and I do not think it necessary to say more about them.

Fourth, the council took into account the fact that the applicant seemed in the past to have sublet, in breach of his tenancy agreement, a previous property rented to him by the council. This is a matter specifically referred to in the council's letter of January 5, 1995. ... Mr McLaughlin observes in his affidavit that, whilst he cannot comment on the nature of the arrangement between the applicant and his friend, the applicant had allowed the friend to stay in the premises for at least a year and the facts as they appeared to the council at the time were sufficiently conclusive for the council to serve a notice to quit on the applicant in 1986. As in the case of the first allegedly irrelevant consideration, I take the view that the council was fully entitled to take into account the previous housing history of the applicant. The weight to be given to it, as with the other factors properly taken into account, was a matter for the council.

Fifthly, the applicant complains about the council taking into account the fact that Miss Qaddoumi had obtained an injunction preventing his entering the property at 182 Webheath, and had apparently done so without his having taken any steps to defend the proceedings. But this, too, was plainly relevant to the council's decision. The applicant had himself referred to the proceedings in his letters of June 27, and July 26, 1994 ... They were relevant to his contention that he could not return to his property at 182 Webheath, and indeed to his invocation of the relationship breakdown policy as a basis for transfer. There is no indication in the evidence that the council, in reliance on these proceedings or other matters, decided against the applicant on the basis of his conduct towards Miss Qaddoumi or more generally on the basis that he was a violent man.

That leads me to the final matter under this head, namely Ms Rutherford's observation, at the end of her note of May 23, 1994, that the applicant was "potentially very violent". It is obscure what prompted that observation. Perhaps one gets some hint of it in the applicant's second affidavit when, in describing the occasion, he denies using, or threatening violence but says "I probably expressed my views fairly forcefully" and "I certainly was very angry at the way I felt that I was being treated and I will not deny that there was an angry exchange of words ..." Be that as it may, Ms Rutherford's observation does not provide a basis upon which the decision can be successfully challenged, since there is no evidence that the council's decision was based on a finding as to the violence or potential violence of the applicant.

[Stephen Richards next considered the issue of alleged procedural unfairness. He found that an authority need only tell an applicant of established facts where they seek to draw inferences from that fact. It is otherwise where an authority comes across facts which would teach them to disbelieve an applicant. Here fairness requires that the matter be put to the applicant[26]. Stephen Richards finally dealt with the issue of whether proper reasons had been given for the local authority's decision:]

Miss MacDonald's propositions of law contained a number of submissions concerning the duty to give reasons, but when it came to the facts there was little to be said under this head in relation to the first decision under challenge.

In *R v London Borough of Newham, ex parte Dawson* (1994) 26 HLR 747 it was held that the nature of the [allocation procedure] was not such as to require reasons to be given in every case, and that reasons were required only if there was something peculiar to the individual decision that called for an explanation (see also *R v Royal London Borough of Kensington & Chelsea, ex parte Grillo* (1995) 28 HLR 94). Miss Macdonald did not seek to take issue with the approach laid down in *ex parte Dawson*. She accepted that the subject-matter of [an allocation decision] was not such as to require reasons to be given as a matter of course, and that it was therefore necessary for her to point to some feature of the particular decision which called for an explanation. To my mind she was wholly unable to point to any such thing. The letter of January 5, 1995 is already a reasoned decision letter, even though it deals only with the principal aspects of the reasoning and not with the totality of the matters taken into account. I cannot find anything in the circumstances of the case that would justify the imposition of a legal requirement to give fuller reasoning.'

In *R v Southwark London Borough Council, ex p Melak*[27] the applicant, a single mother with two children, was in 1989 granted a secure tenancy by the respondent

---

[26]   *R v London Borough of Hackney, ex p Decordova* (1994) 27 HLR 108.
[27]   (1996) 29 HLR 223.

authority of a maisonette consisting of two floors. She had a back complaint which caused her difficulties in negotiating the stairs in the maisonette.

On 6 April 1992, the authority obtained a possession order against the applicant on the ground of rent arrears. The order was suspended on terms that the applicant pay the current rent and £2.15 per week off the arrears. The applicant complied with the terms of the order.

In late 1993, the applicant applied to the authority for a transfer on medical grounds. The authority carried out an assessment of the applicant's condition. The authority awarded her a number of points sufficient to qualify her for a transfer within the authority's allocations policy. On 14 September 1994, an advice centre wrote on the applicant's behalf to the authority requesting information on the progress of the application. On 4 November 1994, the authority replied stating that the application would not be actively considered because the applicant was more than four weeks in arrears of rent. The authority operated a policy under which an applicant for a transfer who owed the authority rent arrears would not be made an offer of accommodation. The policy did, however, provide that some people in a 'priority category' were exempt.

On 28 April 1995, the applicant's solicitors wrote to the authority requesting that her application be considered. The letter expressed the view that the authority's policy was too rigid and represented an unlawful fettering of their discretion. On 28 June 1995, the authority confirmed that – but for the rent arrears – the applicant would have been entitled to a transfer. The applicant applied for judicial review of the authority's refusal to process her application for a transfer.

Sir Louis Blom-Cooper QC, sitting as a Deputy High Court Judge, found that the respondent authority's policy was lawful; if properly applied to the particular features of individual applications it was entirely sound; it was not for the court to adjudicate on the soundness of the authority's housing policy; it was, however, the court's function to ensure that policy matters did not operate to exclude relevant considerations pertaining to the individual applicant; the policy had been rigidly applied by the authority as there was no indication that they had considered the applicant's individual circumstances.

In *R v Lambeth London Borough Council, ex p Ashley*[28] the applicant was the single parent of four children (two girls and two boys) aged between seven and 14. The family lived in a two-bedroomed property owned by the respondent authority. The applicant slept in one bedroom, and the children slept in the other. The applicant applied to the authority for a transfer.

The authority operated a points system for determining priority between applicants on their waiting list. Under the terms of the authority's policy, the condition of an applicant's accommodation was only taken into account in two circumstances. First, where the authority's medical officer had assessed the applicant's circumstances and made specific recommendations, and secondly where the authority's environmental health department had deemed a room in the property to be uninhabitable.

---

[28]   (1996) 29 HLR 385.

The authority's policy also provided that where a person over three years of age had to share a bedroom with a person of the opposite sex over eight years old (the two persons not being partners), a maximum of 20 points would be awarded to the household (without consideration of the number of individuals concerned).

The applicant applied for judicial review of the authority's decisions regarding her application for a transfer on the ground that the authority's policy was unlawfully rigid.

Tucker J held that:

(1) Section 22 of the Housing Act 1985 envisaged that the condition of the property in which an applicant for local authority accommodation resided should be an important factor in making a decision about the allocation of housing; the respondent authority's allocations scheme excluded consideration of the condition of the applicant's housing save in two limited circumstances; the policy unduly restricted the scope of the authority's power in a way which was inconsistent with the criteria set out in s 22;

(2) The limitation on the number of points awarded to a household for the sharing of bedrooms between persons of the opposite sex was illogical; the scheme took no account of the number of persons affected; the scheme was rigid and inflexible and gave no consideration to individual circumstances; it was irrational in the *Wednesbury* sense.

It may be asked how a case such as this would now fare after the changes made by the Homelessness Act 2002 to allocation procedures, see above.

In *R v Wandsworth London Borough Council, ex p Lawrie*[29] both applicants were tenants of the respondent authority. They applied separately to the authority for transfer on medical grounds. The authority's housing transfer scheme provided categories for determining priority for applications, based on a medical assessment by the authority's medical officer. The highest priority was 'Essential Medical'; the next was 'Most Advisable'. The scheme did not provide for priority to be re-assessed in the event of the applicant refusing an offer under the scheme.

In each case, the applicants, having been given Essential Medical priority, refused transfer offers and their priority was downgraded to Most Advisable. Their appeals against this were rejected by the authority.

The applicants sought judicial review of these decisions. The authority did not dispute that, since the original assessment, their housing and medical conditions had not changed but maintained that they were entitled to reconsider the priority afforded in the light of the applicants' refusals of their respective offers.

It was held that the housing transfer scheme did not entitle the authority to say that if a tenant failed to accept an offer, they would no longer regard it as essential that he should be transferred.

Popplewell J pointed out that:

'It is submitted by [counsel for] the applicant, that having regard to the nature of the Housing Transfer Scheme what the respondents have done is contrary

---

[29] (1997) 30 HLR 153.

to the scheme. It is not suggested that it is of itself unlawful if an applicant refuses a proper alternative accommodation to downgrade that person. There has to be some form of sanction against an unreasonable refusal of alternative accommodation given the limited amount of suitable alternative accommodation.'

He then went on to point out, however:

'[There] is nothing in the scheme which indicates that if you refuse an alternative accommodation that that will give grounds for reducing, by way of penalty as it were, the top category to another category. If the borough want to operate a scheme in which they can change you from one category to another, by reason of a refusal, they must say so in their scheme and they do not. All the scheme tends to suggest is that once you have got into the essential medical category you will remain there unless there is some change in your medical condition. This is a very narrow, and I think, not very easy point.'

The principles established under the foregoing cases continued to be applied following the enactment of the Housing Act 1996 and, of course, will also be applicable under the relevant provisions of the Homelessness Act 2002. Thus in *R v Westminster City Council, ex p Hussain*[30], the applicant was assessed by the authority as being in priority need of rehousing for medical reasons and was offered a ground floor bedsit, even though a social services assessment had recommended that he required accommodation with a separate living room. He refused the offer, was automatically suspended from the housing register for two years in line with the authority's normal policy, and he then applied for judicial review. It was held allowing the application, that the authority had failed to give reasons for ignoring the recommendation of social services and the blanket policy by which the applicant was suspended from the register unreasonably fettered the authority's discretion.

In *R v Islington London Borough Council, ex p Reilly*[31] a secure tenant sought a transfer on the basis that her current accommodation was unsuitable. She applied for judicial review of the authority's discretionary system for the allocation of accommodation adopted under the Housing Act 1996 Part VI. This gave points for categories of need by awarding points for the highest relevant category and then a further 100 additional points if a person was eligible under more than one category. The tenant contended, inter alia, that the system was inflexible and resulted in a patently inadequate housing needs assessment, and that the homeless were given undue priority by virtue of the authority's allocation to them of 50 per cent of the available housing stock.

It was held allowing the application, that the allocation scheme was unlawful as being one that no reasonable authority would adopt. The scheme made no allowance for multiple categories of need, nor for the number of people affected in each household. It was too uncertain in operation because applications could be determined according to the residual discretion of the Chief Housing Officer, and particularly so as such a disproportionately large number of points would need to be allocated under that discretion to establish priority in the housing queue. It was not,

---

[30] (1999) 31 HLR 645.
[31] (1998) 31 HLR 651, see also *R v Lambeth London Borough Council, ex p Ashley* (1996) 29 HLR 385, and *R v Tower Hamlets London Borough Council, ex p Uddin* (1999) 32 HLR 391.

however, unreasonable to stipulate a quota for the homeless, especially where, as in the instant case, it was open to discretionary variation. Of course, cases such as this now fall within statutory allocation requirements following the alterations made by the Homelessness Act 2002 considered above.

## Other relevant statutory provisions

it is possible, following a number of recent decisions that the normal allocation provisions may be bypassed by certain applicants who have certain very particular needs and special circumstances. It appears to follow from *R v City of Bristol, ex p Penfold*[32], *R (on the application of Batantu) v London Borough of Islington*[33] and *R v Wigan Metropolitan Borough Council, ex p Tammadge*[34] that there may be cases where authorities are under inescapable *duties* to house by virtue of s 21 of the National Assistance Act 1948, as amended. These authorities were reviewed and applied in *R (on the application of Wahid) v Tower Hamlets London Borough Council*[35].

The claimant (W) suffered from schizophrenia, and had been admitted to hospital for treatment at various times. He had not worked since 1981 and he, his wife and eight children were wholly dependent on social security benefits. All ten of the family lived in a small two-bedroom flat on the ground floor of a large block owned by the defendant housing authority. W was on the authority's waiting list for transfer to larger affordable housing. However, due to the size of the accommodation required, the authority could not say when it could be provided. Upon a request by W's solicitors, the authority carried out an assessment of W's community care needs pursuant to s 47(1) of the National Health Service and Community Care Act 1990. Although that report stated that W and his wife said that overcrowding was their main problem and the only need identified by them, it went on to state that W was mentally stable, was compliant with his medication and was currently monitored by his community mental health nurse, G. An action plan in the report provided for a mental state assessment to be undertaken by G. G's assessment concluded that W's mental stability could only be safely maintained by his transfer into a more congenial and relaxed environment. W applied for judicial review, contending that the absolute duty on an authority to provide accommodation in s 21 of the National Assistance Act 1948 applied in his case. Section 21 provides that an authority, as authorised by the Secretary of State, could make arrangements for providing under s 21(1)(a) 'residential accommodation for persons aged 18 or over who by reason of age, illness disability or any other circumstances are in need of care and attention which is not otherwise available to them'. The Secretary of State had authorised authorities to make arrangements for persons such as W who were in urgent need. W argued that he had a need for accommodation by reason of his schizophrenia and that accommodation was not otherwise available. The authority contended that although W needed accommodation, he was receiving appropriate care and attention and, therefore, as care and attention was otherwise available for

---

[32]   (1998) 1 CCL Rep 315.
[33]   [2000] All ER (D) 1744, (2001) 33 HLR 871.
[34]   (1998) 1 CCL Rep 587.
[35]   [2001] All ER (D) 77 (Aug) (High Court); affd [2002] EWCA Civ 287, [2003] HLR 13.

the purposes of s 21, no other duty under s 21 could arise. An issue also arose as to whether s 21 was applicable to the provision of ordinary residential accommodation.

In the High Court it was held that it was established that if there is a need for care and attention, and the applicant also needs housing accommodation for reasons of illness (or other cause within s 21(1)(a)), and the care, attention and accommodation is not otherwise available, a local authority is under absolute duty to provide that accommodation under s 21 of the 1948 Act. However, on the facts of the instant case, the authority's assessment of W did not find that he was in need of care and attention that was not otherwise available. Accordingly, no duty under s 21 arose. The Court of Appeal affirmed this finding on the basis that there was no *current* need for 'care and attention' arising from the overcrowding. The issue of the extent to which it is possible to bypass the ordinary legislative provisions on allocation thus remains open, though it must be stressed that the number of cases falling within the terms of the 1948 Act will be small.

## ALLOCATION POLICIES: REGISTERED SOCIAL LANDLORDS (RSLS)

Though the constituent documents setting up a RSL such as a housing association may restrict it to housing only certain sorts of people, for example the elderly, the Housing Corporation, under s 36A of the Housing Associations Act 1985, issued HC Circular 36/94 on, inter alia, allocation policies. This continued in force under s 36 of the Housing Act 1996, see HC Circular 36/96, and stressed the general need for allocation policies to be open, fair and based on need. See also s 213 of the Housing Act 1996.

Housing Corporation Circular RI-01/98 stressed the need for such landlords to have fair and accountable allocations policies which, in general, provide access to housing for those in the greatest need (especially those mentioned in s 167(2) of the Housing Act 1996) though allowing for other objects to be given priority where appropriate. Lettings policies are in this way harmonised in general terms, with those of local authorities and the same overall policy objectives are imposed by *administrative* reference to the *statutory* requirements laid on authorities. Thus the lettings policy was required to:

- reflect the landlord's governing instrument;
- be reached, and only varied, after consultation with relevant local authorities and while reflecting any obligations owed to them;
- where possible participate in a 'common housing register' with other relevant landlords, but not to the extent of joining a common allocations policy, save where that would *not* threaten the landlord's aims and objectives;
- be made available in full and in summary form to the public, with a copy sent to the Housing Corporation and relevant local authorities;
- kept under regular review with the aim, inter alia, of creating stable communities and sustainable tenancies;
- provide, where appropriate, for different letting schemes for different types of development.

These requirements are still generally present in the new regulatory regime operated by the Housing Corporation since 2002 and considered further below.

The Housing Corporation indicated it would check compliance with the foregoing by, inter alia, asking relevant local authorities whether they have been consulted on changes to the policies of landlords.

The previous performance standards were, however, superseded by a *Regulatory Code* which came into operation in April 2002. So far as allocations are concerned this requires RSLs to offer choice, while giving reasonable preference to those having priority needs, and to have policies which are fair while also reflecting the diversity of client groups. It is arguable that reasonable preference in this context should have the same meaning as it has under the Housing Act 1996 as amended in 2002. There are further requirements that policies on letting should be flexible, non discriminatory, responsive to demand and designed to promote inclusive and sustainable communities. RSLs should cooperate with authorities in drawing up criteria for accepting or rejecting applicants for housing, while an exclusion on the basis of a person's past anti-social behaviour is possible if the criteria imposed under the Homelessness Act 2002 for authorities are satisfied. Overall letting policies have to be demonstrably fair and effectively controlled. These provisions in the Regulatory Code may go some way to ensuring that RSLs retain some freedom of action, for it is arguable that a sustainable community cannot be created if all those who are accommodated are on low incomes and in insecure employment. However, as will be counter argued at greater length below the independence of RSLs may be much less real than apparent.

With regard to allocation itself landlords should have clear systems indicating who is responsible for making lettings, how applications are received, and prioritised with the greatest preference being given to those in the greatest need. Here RSLs must also comply with the 'Applicants' Charter' issued by the Housing Corporation[36]. In relation to this matter landlords must, of course, comply with the legislation on race, sex and disability discrimination already considered. As a compliance test the Corporation will monitor the percentage of lettings to ethnic minority households in relation to the proportion of such households within relevant local authority districts, and landlords are expected to comply with the Commission for Racial Equality's 1991 Code of Practice for rented accommodated on the elimination of discrimination and the promotion of equal opportunities.

As part of the requirement that landlords should assist wherever possible those in the greatest need, the housing corporation have made it clear they will monitor the average income of new tenants.

Lettings policies are further expected to make provision for transfers and exchanges and to give reasonable preference to those having priority need where this makes the best use of the stock available or contributes to stable communities. Furthermore, in general, landlords are expected to participate in national and local mobility schemes to enable tenants to move from one part of the country to another: the current national scheme is known as HOMES. When a local housing authority makes a request under s 170 of the Housing Act 1996 for co-operation from a landlord the Housing Corporation's understanding is that at least 50 per cent of

---

[36] See further Alder and Handy, *Housing Associations: Law and Practice* (4th ed, 2003), pp 333–336, to which indebtedness is acknowledged.

vacancies (both new and relet) becoming available should be made available to nominees from the authority – this being 'reasonable' co-operation as required by the statute.

It has been forcibly argued by Alder and Handy[37] that 'RSLs are [now] more closely tied to the yoke of local authorities in letting their accommodation', and that, as the Secretary of State has so much power to decide who are eligible for social accommodation, this has a restrictive effect on whom a RSL may house, for example by denying them the ability to assist asylum seekers. This leads to questions as to whether RSLs can truly be considered an independent arm of housing provision. These requirements exist now in addition to the traditional and well-established system whereby local authorities have, by voluntary or contractual arrangements, rights to nominate people from their waiting lists to the vacant dwellings of RSLs. Once again the independence of RSLs can be compromised if they allow too many nomination rights to authorities, even though authorities may be making land available to RSLs for building purposes. This has been recognised by DoE Circular 73/67 and Housing Corporation Circular R3–49/96, and certainly the Housing Corporation policy is to resist authorities having 100 per cent nomination rights. 50 per cent is the more acceptable proportion.

These requirements are monitored by checking the proportion of new lettings going to local authority nominees, and by asking authorities if they are happy with the proportion of a landlords' new tenants who are nominees.

Finally it should be noted that Housing Corporation Circular 36/94 also laid particular stress on: *not* requiring more rent in advance than is due in respect of the initial rental period; no deposits or premiums on the grant of a tenancy – ie a capital payment, nor references from bankers etc; no compliance with residential qualifications, save where inescapable under the constituent rules or a restriction under planning law.

## Summary

The ability of both authorities and RSLs to control the allocation of their stock and the selection of their tenants has been considerably trammelled by legislative intervention, regulation by the Housing Corporation in the case of RSLs, and a greater degree of judicial intervention in the allocation process. So far as authorities are concerned it is clear that the courts are increasingly interested in the way in which allocation and transfer policies are phrased and operated, and, even more importantly, the *content* of those policies. They must be patently flexible in both word and operation. At the same time the courts decline to sit as appellate bodies in relation to housing decisions and will only intervene where an authority is clearly operating an illegally phrased policy or is otherwise behaving unlawfully. The extent to which judicial review is applicable to the decisions of RSLs remains unclear. Historically such bodes being private and voluntary association were not open to judicial review[38]. However, this may be changing following *Poplar Housing*

---

[37] In *Housing Associations: Law and Practice* (4th ed) at p 330.
[38] *Peabody Housing Association Ltd v Green* (1978) 38 P & CR 644.

*and Regeneration Community Association v Donaghue*[39] and Alder and Handy (op cit) argue on the basis of *R (on the application of Painter v Carmarthen County Council*[40] and *R (on the application of Waite) v Hammersmith London Borough Council*[41] that where a RSL *can* be considered as a functional public authority they need to have fair procedures because of the requirements of the Human Rights Act 1998, see further Chapter 14 below.


## ALLOCATIONS AND LETTINGS NOW: THE 2002 REFORM IN PRACTICE

It is quite easily arguable that the history of the law on housing allocation has been in progress from local housing autonomy, a time when authorities enjoyed virtually complete discretion with regard to whom they could allocate, via increasing judicial intervention towards much greater central intervention, with the Homelessness Act 2002 marking a point at which the homelessness and housing allocation functions have been closely integrated. In this respect it signals a shift away from the Major Government's policy of somewhat restricting access to council housing by the homeless, lest what was perceived 'queue jumping' should become more pronounced. Even so it has to be admitted that the reforms of 2002 enshrine the Blair Government's policy of being tough on anti-social behaviour with authorities being free to reject applications for housing from those whose behaviour is 'unacceptable'. Furthermore a very considerable degree of discretion still surrounds allocations to those who fall into what are now the five reasonable preference categories – a discretion enhanced by authorities' *powers* (as opposed to *duties* under the 1996 Act) to give 'additional preference' to certain people within the reasonable preference categories, for example a homeless person who is also a victim of domestic violence or who has an urgent medical reason for rehousing. It can thus be argued that, despite apparent changes, housing allocation is still a highly discretionary procedure. The existence of that discretion has led many authorities to adopt points based systems of allocation as a means of allocating housing according to 'need'. However, questions may be asked as to what 'need' is. Is it the 'need' that the authority believes to exist rather than the need that is actually felt and expressed by those seeking housing? Questions such as that raised, inter alia, by Brown, T, Hunt, R, and Yates, N, in *A Question of Choice*, published by the Chartered Institute of Housing in 2000, have led to some authorities moving somewhat away from points-based systems to choice based systems – as was mentioned earlier – or 'sustainable community schemes'. Choice based schemes must, of course, have some banding of the various classes of applicants, but then grant priority to those within each band according to length of time spent on the waiting list, with applicants being free to balance their 'felt' need for accommodation against their preparedness to await the availability of a particular property or type of property. Sustainable Community Schemes on the other hand appear to have originated as alternatives to 'normal' lettings policies by allowing officers particular discretion in certain localities to encourage applicants for housing to take up offers of housing on

---

39 [2001] EWCA Civ 595, [2002] QB 48.
40 [2001] EWHC Admin 308, [2002] HLR 447.
41 [2001] EWHC Admin 672, [2001] All ER (D) 284 (Jul).

difficult-to-let estates. They have now progressed to the stage where those with lower priority for rehousing may be favoured in gaining rehousing in particular areas provided this will result in the creation of a more balanced or 'sustainable' community.

The provisions on 'choice' in the Homelessness Act 2002, together with the abolition of the requirement to maintain a housing register as the sole 'gateway' to obtaining accommodation, which was such a feature of the 1996 Act, mark a move away from a 'points based assessment of need' system, and allow authorities to pursue choice and sustainable community policies. Even so the changes made do not go all that far, and it must always be remembered that the prime mandatory obligation on authorities is to comply with the requirements of the statutory reasonable preference categories.

Recent research published by Shelter ('Local Authorities and the Homelessness Act 2002 – six months on' and 'Local Authorities and the Homelessness Act 2002 – the first year', February 2003 and July 2003 respectively) indicates some emerging trends under the new law.

- While a majority of a group of authorities surveyed (20 out of 26) had made changes to implement an element of choice in allocations systems, authorities in areas of high housing demand were sceptical about how much choice they could realistically allow, and overall most changes remained at a somewhat introductory stage. There was only a limited move away from making single offers only of available properties and from penalising applicants who refuse an offer considered reasonable by the authority.

- Most authorities surveyed proposed in any case to retain a housing register as the basis for allocation.

- Fifteen out of 23 other authorities surveyed in the first six months of the Act's life proposed to retain control over lettings by using their allocation scheme, with eight of those using a pointed based model, while four others had a system combining points and date order systems. It would thus appear that points based discretionary allocations remain central to local authority lettings policy.

- While the 2002 Act requires 'every application' for housing to be considered, irrespective of whether an applicant has a connection with the area of the authority applied to (a policy designed to encourage mobility) there may be resistance to this in practice. This may be achieved through the operation of a points system whereby additional points may be granted to those with local, employment or residential connections with an authority's area. This particular change in the law may be illusory in practice, especially in areas of high housing demand.

- With regard to use of the 'unacceptable behaviour' criteria most responding authorities indicated that they would utilise them, with the majority being prepared to do this at both the stage of determining initial eligibility and subsequently when determining whether any preference gained should be removed. Most authorities indicated a willingness to use these criteria with regard to both acts of nuisance and rent arrears. However, there was some diversity of view as to the evidence on which an authority should proceed. Some authorities indicated they would seek evidence of previous evictions, while others would look to the existence of an Anti Social Behaviour Order, yet others indicated they would consider complaints or serious allegations from neighbours or housing management staff. There was a similar diversity of view as to what level of rent arrears should trigger a finding of 'unacceptable behaviour', with a number of authorities indicating that quite low levels of arrears would be sufficient. That, as Shelter argues, is out of line with Government guidance given during the legislation's passage through Parliament when it was stated that modest arrears which arise through circumstances beyond a tenant's control should not act as a 'trigger' for a finding of unacceptable behaviour. Furthermore the government stated a person's circumstances such as the size of their family and the state of their health should be considered. There is a danger if low levels of arrears act as 'triggers' that over a period of time a sufficiently large number of people could be effectively automatically placed in the category of those whose behaviour is 'unacceptable'. That would mark a return to the blanket exclusion policies the 2002 Act was designed to outlaw.

The Shelter research also discovered a considerable diversity in the level of seniority at which decisions on unacceptable behaviour are taken, five authorities restricted such a power to senior managers only, while six allowed managers to take decisions and three allowed officers to take a decision.

There was also a considerable diversity of practice with regard to liaising with other social agencies when questions of unacceptable behaviour arose. Most authorities appear to favour only informal contact with, for example, the Health Service and social services in such circumstances.

There was also evidence that authorities do consider the behaviour of tenants generally with regard to lettings and re-lettings. One authority was prepared to consider evidence of a reformation in behaviour, while another was ready to defer consideration of applications where applicants had 'deliberately worsened their housing conditions after advice'. There were some differences of opinion about whether good behaviour by tenants should be positively rewarded. One authority was considering 'excellent tenancy' points for existing tenants while another considered this to be too subjective as a management practice.

It is hard to escape the conclusion that allocations and lettings policies remain – despite judicial and parliamentary intervention – diverse, highly localised, inherently discretionary and, to a considerable extent, judgmental.


## FURTHER READING

Credland, S, *Local Authorities and the Homelessness Act 2002 – six months on* (2003) Shelter.

Credland, S, *Local Authorities and the Homelessness Act 2002 – the first year* (2003) Shelter.

Povey, S, 'Top of the flops' (2004) Roof' March/April, p 31.

Laurie, E, 'The Homelessness Act 2002 and Housing Allocations: All Change or Business as Usual?' (2004) 67(1) MLR 48.

# CHAPTER 8

# Public Sector Tenants' Rights

## NO SECURITY OF TENURE BEFORE 1980

Local authority tenants had no legal security of tenure before the 1980 Housing Act was passed by the then newly elected Conservative Government. In practice few tenants were evicted from their homes before 1980 on any grounds other than rent arrears, but even model tenants could be evicted from their homes if the local authority thought the homes were under-occupied. This was only after the notice to quit requirements, which are now in s 3 and s 5 Protection from Eviction Act 1977, had been applied. Most tenants of private sector landlords, as we saw in Chapter 4, had had security since the Increase in Rent and Mortgage Interest (War Restrictions) Act 1915. In *Shelley v LCC*[1], the House of Lords dismissed Mrs Shelley's appeal against a possession order granted to the local authority landlords. Mrs Shelley had not broken any terms of her tenancy agreement, but was served with a notice to quit her flat in Barnaby Buildings solely because the council wanted to house someone else in the property. Lord Porter stated:

> 'If, then, the general management, regulation and control of houses includes the right to oust the tenant, the local authority, in giving notice to quit, were exercising their powers under [s 83(1) Housing Act 1936] … and the protection afforded to tenants of private owners does not apply … "management" must … include a right to terminate the tenancy so far as the general law allows, i.e., after due notice.'[2]

Lawton LJ followed *Shelley* in the case of *Cannock Chase District Council v Kelly*[3], holding that notice to quit might be given to tenants who had paid their rent and complied with the terms of their tenancy agreements, as there was a need to allocate scarce resources. The tenants in *Bristol District Council v Clark*[4] challenged the district council, arguing that the local authority should provide evidence to the court that they required possession for the purpose of housing people under the Housing Acts. The local authority deliberately refused to provide such evidence. Lord Denning MR:

[1]   [1948] 2 All ER 898.
[2]   At p 900.
[3]   [1978] 1 WLR 1.
[4]   [1975] 3 All ER 976.

' … the corporation … have the general management, regulation and control of houses provided by them. This means they can pick and choose their tenants at will; they can grant tenancies and determine them by notice to quit … They are not trammelled in any way by the Rent Acts.'

He then went on to qualify this by saying:

' … they must exercise [the powers] in good faith, taking into account relevant considerations … It applies, I think, to a decision whether to evict a tenant or not. The local authority shall not automatically evict a man when he falls into arrear with his rent.'[5]

It was assumed that democratically accountable public bodies would be model landlords who would treat their tenants fairly. In practice the security of council tenants may have been high, but the Report of the Committee on One-Parent Families[6] had argued that local authority and New Town tenants should have the basic protection of security of tenure which the Rent Acts gave to the tenants of private landlords[7]. It wished to interpose the court between the authority wanting possession and the tenant who was unwilling to go.

In addition to the lack of security, council tenants were faced with wholly one-sided tenancy agreements, or even no written agreements at all. Vast numbers of duties were often imposed on tenants – in 76 per cent of the agreements surveyed by the National Consumer Council in 1976 there was no mention of *any* obligations of the council as landlord[8]. Lord Wilberforce described the one-sided nature of the agreements in *Liverpool City Council v Irwin*:

'As is common with council lettings there is no formal demise or lease or tenancy agreement. There is a document headed "Liverpool Corporation, Liverpool City Housing Dept." and described as "Conditions of Tenancy". This contains a list of obligations on the tenant – he shall do this, he shall not do that or he shall not do that without the corporation's consent … . At the end there is form for signature by the tenant stating that he accepts the tenancy. On the landlord's side there is nothing, no signature, no demise, no covenant.'[9]

There were moves during the 1970s to put forward a 'Tenants' Charter' which would give statutory effect to a collection of rights for tenants including security of tenure. In June 1977 the Labour Government published a Green Paper, *Housing Policy*[10], which proposed such a charter which would be 'a code of principles and practices for local authority and new town tenancies, much of which will also be relevant to housing associations'[11]. A Bill was introduced the same year but failed to reach the statute book.

---

5   At p 980.
6   The Finer Report 1974 Cmnd 5629.
7   Finer Report 1974 Cmnd 5629 at para 6.90.
8   *Tenancy Agreements* National Consumer Council 1976.
9   [1976] 2 All ER 39 at 42.
10   Cmnd 6851.
11   *Housing Policy* Cmnd 6851 at para 11.06.

## WHO ARE SECURE TENANTS?

The question of tenants' rights was taken up by the incoming Conservative Government of 1979. It was given added impetus by the inclusion, in the Conservative manifesto, of the commitment to 'right to buy'. It was important to define precisely who could exercise this right, so the Housing Act 1980 (now the Housing Act 1985) defined the 'secure tenant' in s 1, and laid down that it was only secure tenants that had the right to buy. The security of tenure provisions are set out in ss 79–81 Housing Act 1985 (as amended).

### 79. **Secure tenancies**

(1) A tenancy under which a dwelling-house is let as a separate dwelling is a secure tenancy at any time when the conditions described in sections 80 and 81 as the landlord condition and the tenant condition are satisfied.

(2) Subsection (1) has effect subject to—

(a) the exceptions in Schedule 1 (tenancies which are not secure tenancies),

(b) sections 89(3) and (4) and 90(3) and (4) (tenancies ceasing to be secure after death of tenant), and

(c) sections 91(2) and 93(2) (tenancies ceasing to be secure in consequence of assignment or subletting).

(3) The provisions of this Part apply in relation to a licence to occupy a dwelling-house (whether or not granted for a consideration) as they apply in relation to a tenancy.

(4) Subsection (3) does not apply to a licence granted as a temporary expedient to a person who entered the dwelling-house or any other land as a trespasser (whether or not, before the grant of that licence, another licence to occupy that or another dwelling-house had been granted to him).

80. (1) The landlord condition is that the interest of the landlord belongs to one of the following authorities or bodies—

a local authority,

a new town corporation,

a housing action trust

an urban development corporation

…

81. The tenant condition is that the tenant is an individual and occupies the dwelling-house as his only or principal home; or, where the tenancy is a joint tenancy, that each of the joint tenants is an individual and at least one of them occupies the dwelling-house as his only or principal home.

## Let as a separate dwelling

The key concept is the secure tenancy. Provided the landlord and tenant conditions are fulfilled, it must be a tenancy under which a dwelling house is let as a separate dwelling. There are three components of this requirement: there must be 'a house', it must be a 'dwelling' and it must be 'separate'.

The term 'house' covers more than what would be called a house in everyday speech: by s 112 of the 1985 Act, it may be part of a house, such as a flat, and may include land let together with the house although physically separated from it. The definition clearly encompasses houses, flats (whether converted from houses or in a purpose-built block), maisonettes and bungalows.

A 'dwelling' is not defined in the Act, but Rent Act decisions define it as a place where the normal functions of life such as sleeping, eating and cooking are carried out. In *Central YMCA Housing Association Ltd v Goodman*[12], Goodman had been let a furnished room with en suite facilities in a hostel. He was not allowed to use any cooking apparatus in his room, to which he had his own key. He was given notice to quit after living in the hostel for 14 years as the YMCA wanted to sell the hostel to a hotel company. The Court of Appeal rejected his defence that he lived in a dwelling house and therefore had a secure tenancy under s 79. Dillon LJ stated that 'this room was no more a dwelling house than a hotel room is a dwelling house' and rejected the notion that, because the room had four walls, a ceiling and a floor and was lived in, it was a dwelling house.

However, a key recent decision, albeit on s 1 Housing Act 1988, has thrown the decision in *Goodman* into doubt. It is the House of Lords decision in *Uratemp Ventures Ltd v Collins*[13]. *Here, t*he claimants served a notice terminating Collins' long-term occupancy of a room in a hotel. The sparsely furnished room contained a shower and a wash-hand basin. It had no cooking facilities but did have a power point which Collins used for his pizza warmer, toasted sandwich maker and electric kettle. He was not prohibited from using this cooking equipment in his room. Collins did not share any accommodation with the other residents in the hotel. The Court of Appeal had decided that the room was not a dwelling house as it had no cooking facilities, so Collins was not an assured tenant under s 1 Housing Act 1988. Lord Millett:

> 'The words "dwell" and "dwelling" are not terms of art with a specialised legal meaning. They are ordinary English words, even if they are perhaps no longer in common use. They mean the same as "inhabit" and "habitation" or more precisely "abide" and "abode", and refer to the place where one lives and makes one's home. They suggest a greater degree of settled occupation than "reside" and "residence", connoting the place where the occupier habitually sleeps and usually eats, but the idea that he must also cook his meals there is found only in the law reports.

> … residential accommodation is "a dwelling" if it is the occupier's home (or one of his homes). It is the place where he lives and to which he returns and which forms the centre of his existence. Just what use he makes of it when living there, however, depends on his mode of life. No doubt he will sleep there and usually eat there; he will often prepare at least some of his meals there. But his home is not the less his home because he does not cook there but prefers to eat out or bring in ready-cooked meals. It has never been a legislative requirement that cooking facilities must be available for a premises to qualify as a dwelling. Nor is it at all evident what policy considerations dictate that a tenant who prepares his meals at home should enjoy security of tenure while a tenant who brings in all his meals ready-cooked should not …

> The legislative purpose of the Rent and Housing Acts is to protect people in the occupation of their homes, not to encourage them to cook their own meals …

12  (1991) 24 HLR 109.
13  [2002] 1 AC 301, [2002] 1 All ER 46, [2001] 3 WLR 806.

The first step is to identify the subject matter of the tenancy agreement. If this is a house or part of a house of which the tenant has exclusive possession with no element of sharing, the only question is whether, at the date when the proceedings were brought, it was the tenant's home. If so, it was his dwelling.'[14]

Before the decision in *Uratemp Ventures v Collins,* sharing a lavatory or a bathroom did not take the tenant outside the Act, whereas sharing a kitchen did. Decisions such as *Central YMCA Housing Association v Saunders*[15] might need to be reconsidered now. Saunders, who was another long-term resident of the YMCA hostel, had been given notice to quit because of his disruptive behaviour. He lived in a single bedroom and, unlike Goodman, shared the use of one of the kitchen and dining areas with 11 others. There were no cooking facilities in his room, although he did have an electric kettle in which he boiled eggs sometimes. It was held that it was not a separate dwelling as the kitchen was shared, his occupation was therefore not a secure tenancy, and possession was granted to the YMCA.

In the private sector, s 22 Rent Act 1977 and s 3 Housing Act 1988 specifically allow accommodation with shared facilities to be regarded as a separate dwelling. There is no equivalent section in the 1985 Act.

## The landlord condition

The landlord must be one of the public bodies listed in s 80. The Housing Act 1988 removed the Housing Corporation, housing associations and charitable trusts from the list and in effect transferred their tenancies into the private sector; however, secure tenancies granted by such bodies before 15 January 1989, are still governed by the 1985 Act.

The Law Commission Report, *Renting Homes*[16], has recommended that there should be a single occupation agreement for social housing in future. This would remove the current distinctions between local authority and housing association tenancies. Another recommendation is that there should be two agreement types: type 1 would have a high degree of security guaranteed by statute. Social landlords would be required to use type 1 agreements. Private landlords would use type 2 agreements which would have a limited degree of security which could be increased by agreement.

## The tenant condition

The tenant must be an individual. Limited companies are clearly outside the definition, and so too would be unincorporated associations such as a housing co-operative which had taken over and let out property that is soon to be demolished.

---

[14] [2002] 1 All ER 46 at 53.
[15] (1990) 23 HLR 212.
[16] Law Commission Report 284, November 2003.

## The tenant's only or principal home

The tenant must also occupy the property as their 'only or principal home'. The Court of Appeal considered the ambit of this definition in *Crawley Borough Council v Sawyer*[17]. Sawyer occupied a council house in Crawley from 1978 and was granted a tenancy in 1982. Early in 1985 he went to live with his girlfriend in Horsham and arranged for the electricity to be cut off in June 1985 and the gas some time the following year. While he lived in Horsham he continued to pay the rent and the rates on the Crawley house and visited it about once a month. In May 1986 the Borough Council became aware that the house was vacant. Sawyer told the authority that he was living with his girlfriend, he was intending to buy her home jointly with her and had been contributing to the mortgage. The authority served notice to quit at the end of August 1986 which expired four weeks later. In that period Sawyer split up with his girlfriend, ceased to make mortgage payments and two weeks later moved back to Crawley. The authority sued for possession alleging that Sawyer was not occupying the dwelling house as his only or principal home. The judge at first instance found that the premises had at all times been the defendant's principal home. The local authority appealed against that decision.

Parker LJ:

'The issue before the learned judge, on facts which to a very large extent were not disputed, was simply whether the tenant was or was not a secure tenant within the meaning of section 81 of the Housing Act, and I must now refer briefly to certain sections of that Act. Section 79(1) provides:

"A tenancy under which a dwelling-house is let as a separate dwelling is a secure tenancy at any time when the condition described in sections 80 and 81 as the landlord condition and the tenant condition are satisfied."

It would therefore appear that a tenancy can at one time be a secure tenancy, cease to be a secure tenancy and become a secure tenancy again if in the interim period it has not been determined ... Section 81 provides:

"The tenant condition is that the tenant is an individual and occupies the dwelling-house as his only or principal home."

The judge, therefore, had to determine, and only to determine, whether the defendant satisfied the provisions of section 81 ... It is quite plain that it is possible to occupy as a home two places at the same time, and indeed that is inherent in the wording of section 81. It is therefore plain that, if you can occupy two houses at the same time as a home, actual physical occupation cannot be necessary, because one cannot be physically in two places at the same time ...

Going through the whole thread of these matters is the common principle that in order to occupy premises as a home, first, there must be signs of occupation – that is to say, there must be furniture and so forth so that the house can be occupied as a home – and secondly, there must be an intention, if not physically present, to return to it. That is the situation envisaged in the

[17]   (1987) 20 HLR 98.

examples given by the Master of the Rolls [in *Herbert v Byrne* [1964] 1 All ER 882 at 886 (a Rent Act case)] of, for example, the sea captain who is away for a while. His house is left fully furnished, ready for occupation, no doubt the rent is paid in his absence, but he is not physically there and may not be for a very long period indeed.

In the present case the learned judge was, on the evidence, in my view, well entitled to hold that throughout the period the premises the subject of the action were occupied by the defendant as a home. The only question which really arose is whether it was occupied as a principal home. The learned judge considered the question. He came to the conclusion which he did on the basis that the defendant had left to live with his girlfriend but with no intention of giving up permanent residence of Cobnor Close [Crawley] ...

The position as at the time the notice to quit was served was that the girlfriend had already told him that he had to get out. He did not in fact move back into Cobnor Close until after the expiry of the notice to quit, but in my view it was well open to the learned judge to have come to the conclusion that, both when the notice to quit was served and when it expired and indeed throughout the whole period, Cobnor Close remained his principal home.'[18]

Although Cobnor Close was regarded as Sawyer's principal home throughout the period, Parker LJ noted that the phrase 'at any time' in s 79(1) appeared to mean that a tenancy could be a secure tenancy, cease to be a secure tenancy and then become a secure tenancy again. Despite that, it was decided that Sawyer never ceased to be a secure tenant of his home in Crawley. It might have been more consistent to have decided that while Sawyer lived in Horsham with his girlfriend her house was his principal home and that he became a secure tenant again when he returned to Crawley. This was the interpretation given to the phrase in *Hussey v Camden London Borough Council*[19] where the tenant lost security of tenure by not occupying his flat but moved back and was living in the flat when the notice to quit expired and was therefore able to revive the tenancy. If a tenant parts with possession or sub-lets the whole of the property, secure status is lost and cannot be revived (s 93(2)). In *Hussey* there was insufficient evidence that such a sub-letting had occurred as the county court judge decided that Hussey had lost security as he was not occupying the flat as his only or principal home. The Court of Appeal overturned this decision as at the date of expiry of the notice to quit Hussey was living in the property and had therefore regained security.

By way of contrast, the tenant in *Ujima Housing Association v Ansah*[20] said that it was his intention to return to live in the flat. He claimed he had only left because of the nuisance, caused by one of his neighbours, a problem which the Housing Association had ignored. He had left no clothing or personal items so the court held that objectively, such an intention to return was not shown. The test of intention to return is objective rather than subjective. The Court of Appeal, no doubt, was also swayed by the amount of profit made by the tenant in letting a flat, on which he paid a mere £31.50 a week rent, for the princely sum of £130 a week. The tenancy in this

[18]  (1987) 20 HLR 98 at 99.
[19]  (1994) 27 HLR 5.
[20]  (1997) 30 HLR 831.

case was a housing association assured tenancy, but the Housing Act 1988 lays down the same 'only or principal home' condition for assured tenancy status to be acquired[21].

The intention whether to leave the home permanently must not be some 'fleeting change of mind'. In *Hammersmith and Fulham London Borough Council v Clarke*[22] C had lived in her house for many years. After suffering a stroke her grandson and his wife moved in to look after her. She then went to live in a nursing home while her grandson continued to live in the house. While in the home, she signed a note, written by a social worker, that she had decided the move to the nursing home was permanent. The court applied the tests of signs of occupation (including relatives living in the house) and intention, deciding that the note that she had signed was but a fleeting change of mind while she was ill. The date for considering this intention is the date of the determination of the tenancy, ie when the notice to quit expired, although evidence from before or after that date could be put forward.

Prisoners are another group who will be away from their homes for a lengthy period. In *Amoah v London Borough of Barking and Dagenham*[23] the appellant was a secure tenant who was sentenced to 12 years' imprisonment for drug offences. Amoah successfully resisted the council's notice to quit by arguing that he intended to return and that his stepdaughter was living in the property and paying rent on his behalf while his furniture and possessions were there.

It is only a secure tenant who has the right to buy so if the house ceases to be the tenant's only or principal home, then the right to buy will be lost[24]. In *Jennings v Epping Forest District Council*[25] the Court of Appeal held that secure status had been lost where an elderly man, who had Alzheimer's disease, moved into a nursing home and his wife took a flat close to the home to be near him. Their house was sub-let in their absence so they lost the right to buy despite having started the process of buying the house. The secure status must exist right up until the time of completion.

It appears from s 79(2) that licensees gain the same rights as tenants (apart from the right to buy) but the House of Lords held in *Westminster City Council v Clarke*[26] that licensees must have exclusive possession to gain these rights[27].

[21]  See s 1 Housing Act 1988 and Chapter 4.
[22]  [2000] All ER (D) 1893, (2001) 33 HLR 881.
[23]  [2001] All ER (D) 138 (Jan), (2001) 82 P & CR D12.
[24]  S 139(2) Housing Act 1985.
[25]  (1992) 25 HLR 241.
[26]  [1992] 2 AC 288, [1992] 1 All ER 695, [1992] 2 WLR 229.
[27]  See Chapter 3.

TENANCIES WHICH ARE NOT SECURE

# HOUSING ACT 1985

# Schedule 1 [as amended]

*Long leases*

1. A tenancy is not a secure tenancy if it is a long tenancy.

*Introductory tenancies*

1A. A tenancy is not a secure tenancy if it is an introductory tenancy or a tenancy which has ceased to be an introductory tenancy—

(a) by virtue of section 133(3) of the Housing Act 1996 (disposal on death to non-qualifying person), or

(b) by virtue of the tenant, or in the case of a joint tenancy every tenant, ceasing to occupy the dwelling-house as his only or principal home.

*Premises occupied in connection with employment*

2.–(1) Subject to sub-paragraph (4B) a tenancy is not a secure tenancy if the tenant is an employee of the landlord or of—

a local authority,
a new town corporation,
a housing action trust,
an urban development corporation, or
the governors of an aided school,

and his contract of employment requires him to occupy the dwelling-house for the better performance of his duties.

(2) Subject to sub-paragraph (4B) A tenancy is not a secure tenancy if the tenant is a member of a police force and the dwelling-house is provided for him free of rent and rates in pursuance of regulations made under [section 50 of the Police Act 1996] (general regulations as to government, administration and conditions of service of police forces).

(3) Subject to sub-paragraph (4B) A tenancy is not a secure tenancy if the tenant is an employee of a fire authority (within the meaning of the Fire Services Acts 1947 to 1959) and—

(a) his contract of employment requires him to live in close proximity to a particular fire station, and

(b) the dwelling-house was let to him by the authority in consequence of that requirement.

(4) Subject to sub-paragraph (4A) and (4B) A tenancy is not a secure tenancy if—

(a) within the period of three years immediately preceding the grant the conditions mentioned in sub-paragraph (1), (2) or (3) have been satisfied with respect to a tenancy of the dwelling-house, and

(b) before the grant the landlord notified the tenant in writing of the circumstances in which this exception applies and that in its opinion the proposed tenancy would fall within this exception,

(4A) Except where the landlord is a local housing authority, a tenancy under sub-paragraph (4) shall become a secure tenancy when the periods during which the conditions mentioned in sub-paragraph (1), (2) or (3) are not satisfied with respect to the tenancy amount in aggregate to more than three years.

(4B) Where the landlord is a local housing authority, a tenancy under sub-paragraph (1), (2), (3) or (4) shall become a secure tenancy if the authority notify the tenant that the tenancy is to be regarded as a secure tenancy.

In this paragraph 'contract of employment' means a contract of service or apprenticeship, whether express or implied and (if express) whether oral or in writing.

### Land acquired for development

3.–(1) A tenancy is not a secure tenancy if the dwelling-house is on land which has been acquired for development and the dwelling-house is used by the landlord, pending development of the land, as temporary housing accommodation.

(2) In this paragraph 'development' has the meaning given by section 55 of the Town and Country Planning Act 1990 (general definition of development for purposes of that Act).

### Accommodation for homeless persons

4. A tenancy granted in pursuance of any function under Part VII of the Housing Act 1996 (homelessness) is not a secure tenancy unless the local housing authority concerned have notified the tenant that the tenancy is to be regarded as a secure tenancy.

### Accommodation for asylum seekers

4A.–(1) A tenancy is not a secure tenancy if it is granted in order to provide accommodation under Part VI of the Immigration and Asylum Act 1999.

(2) A tenancy mentioned in sub-paragraph (1) becomes a secure tenancy if the landlord notifies the tenant that it is to be regarded as a secure tenancy.

### Temporary accommodation for persons taking up employment

5.–(1) Subject to sub-paragraphs (1A) and (1B) a tenancy is not a secure tenancy if—

(a)  the person to whom the tenancy was granted was not, immediately before the grant, resident in the district in which the dwelling-house is situated,

(b)  before the grant of the tenancy, he obtained employment, or an offer of employment, in the district or its surrounding area,

(c)  the tenancy was granted to him for the purpose of meeting his need for temporary accommodation in the district or its surrounding area in order to work there, and of enabling him to find permanent accommodation there, and

(d)  the landlord notified him in writing of the circumstances in which this exception applies and that in its opinion the proposed tenancy would fall within this exception.

(1A) Except where the landlord is a local housing authority, a tenancy under sub-paragraph (1) shall become a secure tenancy on the expiry of one year from the grant or on earlier notification by the landlord to the tenant that the tenancy is to be regarded as a secure tenancy.

(1B) Where the landlord is local housing authority, a tenancy under sub-paragraph (1) shall become a secure tenancy if at any time the authority notify the tenant that the tenancy is to be regarded as secure tenancy.

(2) In this paragraph—

'district' means district of a local housing authority; and
'surrounding area', in relation to a district, means the area consisting of each district that adjoins it.

*Short-term arrangements*

6. A tenancy is not a secure tenancy if—

(a)   the dwelling-house has been leased to the landlord with vacant possession for use as temporary housing accommodation,

(b)   the terms on which it has been leased include provision for the lessor to obtain vacant possession from the landlord on the expiry of a specified period or when required by the lessor,

(c)   the lessor is not a body which is capable of granting secure tenancies, and

(d)   the landlord has no interest in the dwelling-house other than under the lease in question or as a mortgagee.

*Temporary accommodation during works*

7. A tenancy is not a secure tenancy if—

(a)   the dwelling-house has been made available for occupation by the tenant (or a predecessor in title of his) while works are carried out on the dwelling-house which he previously occupied as his home, and

(b)   the tenant or predecessor was not a secure tenant of that other dwelling-house at the time when he ceased to occupy it as his home.

*Agricultural holdings*

8.–(1) A tenancy is not a secure tenancy if—

(a)   the dwelling-house is comprised in an agricultural holding and is occupied by the person responsible for the control (whether as tenant or as servant or agent of the tenant) of the farming of the holdings, or

(b)   the dwelling-house is comprised in the holding held under a farm business tenancy and is occupied by the person responsible for the control (whether as tenant or as servant or agent of the tenant) of the management of the holding.

(2) In sub-paragraph (1) above—

(a)   'agricultural holding' means any agricultural holding within the meaning of Agricultural Holdings Act 1986 held under a tenancy in relation to which that Act applies, and

(b)   'farm business tenancy', and 'holding' in relation to such a tenancy, have the same meaning as in the Agricultural Tenancies Act 1995

*Licensed premises*

9. A tenancy is not a secure tenancy if the dwelling-house consists of or includes premises which, by virtue of a premises licence under the Licensing Act 2003, may be used for the supply of alcohol (within the meaning of section 14 of that Act) for consumption on the premises.

*Student lettings*

10.–(1) Subject to sub-paragraphs (2A) and (2B) a tenancy of a dwelling-house is not a secure tenancy if—

(a)   it is granted for the purpose of enabling the tenant to attend a designated course at an educational establishment, and

(b)   before the grant of the tenancy the landlord notified him in writing of the circumstances in which this exception applies and that in its opinion the proposed tenancy would fall within this exception;

...

(2) A landlord's notice under sub-paragraph (1)(b) shall specify the educational establishment which the person concerned proposes to attend.

(2A) Except where the landlord is a local housing authority, a tenancy under sub-paragraph (1) shall become a secure tenancy on the expiry of the period specified in sub-paragraph (3) or an earlier notification by the landlord to the tenant that the tenancy is to be regarded as a secure tenancy.

(2B) Where the landlord is a local housing authority, a tenancy under sub-paragraph (1) shall become a secure tenancy if at any time the authority notify the tenant that the tenancy is to be regarded as a secure tenancy.

(3) The period referred to in sub-paragraph (2A) is—

(a)   in a case where the tenant attends a designated course at the educational establishment specified in the landlord's notice, the period ending six months after the tenant ceases to attend that (or any other) designated course at that establishment;

(b)   in any other case, the period ending six months after the grant of the tenancy.

(4) In this paragraph—

'designated course' means a course of any kind designated by regulations made by the Secretary of State for the purposes of this paragraph;

'educational establishment' means a university or institution which provides higher education or further education (or both); and for the purposes of this definition 'higher education' and 'further education' have the same meaning as in the Education Act 1996.

(5) Regulations under sub-paragraph (4) shall be made by statutory instrument and may make different provision with respect to different cases or descriptions of case, including different provision for different areas.

*1954 Act tenancies*

11. A tenancy is not a secure tenancy if it is one to which Part II of the Landlord and Tenant Act 1954 applies (tenancies of premises occupied for business purposes).

*Almshouses*

12.–(1) A licence to occupy a dwelling-house is not a secure tenancy if—

(a)   the dwelling house is an almshouse, and

(b)   the licence was granted by or on behalf of a charity which—

(i)   is authorised under its trusts to maintain the dwelling house as an almshouse, and

(ii)   has no power under its trusts to grant a tenancy of the dwelling house;

and in this paragraph 'almshouse' means any premises maintained as an almshouse, whether they are called any almshouse or not; and 'trusts', in relation to a charity, means the provisions establishing it as a charity and regulating its purposes and administration, whether those provisions take effect by way of trust or not.

## Long Leases

'Long Leases' are defined in s 115 Housing Act 1985 as tenancies for a term of over 25 years, such leases are rare in the public sector.

## Introductory tenancies

Local authorities and housing action trusts can elect to run an introductory tenancy regime, a type of tenancy brought in by the Housing Act 1996 s 124. In 2002/2003, the latest year that the statistics collated by the Office of the Deputy Prime Minister are available, a third of the local housing authorities in England were operating schemes. In these areas all new tenancies are for a probationary period of 12 months and, other than security of tenure, the tenancies have many of the hallmarks of a secure tenancy. The introductory tenant has the right to succession of a spouse or family member, the right to repair, the right to be consulted on housing management issues but does not have the right to buy, the right to take lodgers, the right to sub-let, the right to improve, the right to exchange or the right to vote prior to a transfer to a new landlord[28].

The introductory tenancy regime is in Pt V of the Housing Act 1996 which is headed 'Conduct of tenants' and was designed to be one of the measures to deal with tenant 'anti-social behaviour'. The White Paper, *Our Future Homes*, put forward the purpose of this new type of tenancy:

> '[Introductory tenancies] would give a clear signal to new tenants that anti-social behaviour was unacceptable and that it would result in the loss of their home. It would also give reassurance to existing tenants that their authority would take prompt action to remove any new tenants acting in this way.'[29]

A survey[30] conducted two years after the start of introductory tenancies found that 30 per cent of the local housing authorities that responded had adopted introductory tenancies. The majority of introductory tenancy evictions in the survey, however, were for rent arrears (68 per cent) and only 19 per cent for anti-social behaviour.

Clause 156 Housing Bill 2003 inserts new ss 125A and 125B into the Housing Act 1996. These new sections give the conditions under which the normal 12-month period of an introductory tenancy can be increased by six months and the review procedure if the decision to extend the length of the introductory tenancy is challenged. The conditions are that the landlord has served a notice of extension on the tenant at least eight weeks before the original expiry date and that either the tenant has not requested a review under s 125B or if he has, the review has confirmed the landlord's decision to extend the trial period. The notice of extension must set out the reasons for the landlord's decision and inform the tenant of his right to request a review and that such a request must be made within 14 days of the notice being served. The extra six months gives local housing authorities some additional time to assess the suitability of an introductory tenant. The new provisions will only apply to introductory tenancies that are granted after the Housing Bill 2003 comes into force.

Sections 124 to 130 of the Housing Act 1996 are as follows.

### 124.  **Introductory tenacies**

(1) A local housing authority or a housing action trust may elect to operate an introductory tenancy regime.

(2) When such an election is in force, every periodic tenancy of a dwelling house entered into or adopted by the authority or trust shall, if it would otherwise be a secure tenancy, be an

---

[28]  Housing Act 1996, ss131–133.
[29]  Cm 2901 para 3.2.
[30]  Hunter, C, Nixon, J and Shayer, S, *Neighbour Nuisance, Social Landlords and the Law* (2000) Chartered Institute of Housing.

introductory tenancy, unless immediately before the tenancy was entered into or adopted the tenant or, in the case of joint tenants, one or more of them was—

(a)   a secure tenant of the same or another dwelling house or,

(b)   an assured tenant of a registered social landlord (otherwise than under an assured shorthold tenancy) in respect of the same or another dwelling house.

(3) Subsection (2) does not apply to a tenancy entered into or adopted in pursuance of a contract made before the election was made.

(4) For the purposes of this Chapter a periodic tenancy is adopted by a person if that person becomes the landlord under the tenancy, whether on a disposal or surrender of the interest of the former landlord.

(5)   An election under this section may be revoked at any time, without prejudice to the making of a further election.

### 125.   Duration of introductory tenancy

(1) A tenancy remains an introductory tenancy until the end of the trial period, unless one of the events mentioned in subsection (5) occurs before the end of that period.

(2) The 'trial period' is the period of one year beginning with—

(a)   in the case of a tenancy which was entered into by a local housing authority or housing action trust—

(i)   the date on which the tenancy was entered into, or

(ii)   if later, the date on which a tenant was first entitled to possession under the tenancy; or

(b)   in the case of a tenancy which was adopted by a local housing authority or housing action trust, the date of adoption;

subject as follows.

(3) Where the tenant under an introductory tenancy was formerly a tenant under another introductory tenancy, or held an assured shorthold tenancy from a registered social landlord, any period or periods during which he was such a tenant shall count towards the trial period, provided—

(a)   if there was one such period, it ended immediately before the date specified in subsection (2) and

(b)   if there was more than one such period, the most recent period ended immediately before that date and each period succeeded the other without interruption.

(4) Where there are joint tenants under an introductory tenancy, the reference in subsection (3) to the tenant shall be construed as referring to the joint tenant in whose case the application of that subsection produces the earliest starting date for the trial period.

(5) A tenancy ceases to be an introductory tenancy if, before the end of the trial period—

(a)   the circumstances are such that the tenancy would not otherwise be a secure tenancy,

(b)   a person or body other than a local housing authority or housing action trust becomes the landlord under the tenancy,

(c)   the election in force when the tenancy was entered into or adopted is revoked, or

(d)   the tenancy ceases to be an introductory tenancy by virtue of section 133(3) (succession).

(6) A tenancy does not come to an end merely because it ceases to be an introductory tenancy, but a tenancy which has once ceased to be an introductory tenancy cannot subsequently become an introductory tenancy.

(7) This section has effect subject to section 130 (effect of beginning proceedings for possession).

## 126.  **Licences**

(1) The provisions of this Chapter apply in relation to a licence to occupy a dwelling house (whether or not granted for a consideration) as they apply in relation to a tenancy.

(2) Subsection (1) does not apply to a licence granted as a temporary expedient to a person who entered the dwelling house or any other land as a trespasser (whether or not, before the grant of that licence, another licence to occupy that or another dwelling house had been granted to him).

*Proceedings for possession*

## 127.  **Proceedings for possession**

(1) The landlord may only bring an introductory tenancy to an end by obtaining an order of the court for the possession of the dwelling house.

(2) The court shall not make such an order unless the provisions of section 128 apply.

(3) Where the court makes such an order, the tenancy comes to an end on the date on which the tenant is to give up possession in pursuance of the order.

## 128.  **Notice of proceedings for possession**

(1) The court shall not entertain proceedings for the possession of a dwelling house let under an introductory tenancy unless the landlord has served on the tenant a notice of proceedings complying with this section.

(2) The notice shall state that the court will be asked to make an order for the possession of the dwelling house.

(3) The notice shall set out the reasons for the landlord's decision to apply for such an order.

(4) The notice shall specify a date after which proceedings for the possession of the dwelling house may be begun

The date so specified must not be earlier than the date on which the tenancy could, apart from this Chapter, be brought to an end by notice to quit given by the landlord on the same date as the notice of proceedings.

(5) The court shall not entertain any proceedings for possession of the dwelling house unless they are begun after the date specified in the notice of proceedings.

(6) The notice shall inform the tenant of his right to request a review of the landlord's decision to seek an order for possession and of the time within which such a request must be made.

(7) The notice shall also inform the tenant that if he needs help or advice about the notice, and what to do about it, he should take it immediately to a Citizens' Advice Bureau, a housing aid centre, a law centre or a solicitor.

## 129.  **Review of decision to seek possession**

(1) A request for review of the landlord's decision to seek an order for possession of a dwelling-house let under an introductory tenancy must be made before the end of the period of 14 days beginning with the day on which the notice of proceedings is served.

(2) On a request being duly made to it, the landlord shall review its decision.

(3) The Secretary of State may make provision by regulations as to the procedure to be followed in connection with a review under this section.

Nothing in the following provisions affects the generality of this power.

(4) Provision may be made by regulations—

(a) requiring the decision on review to be made by a person of appropriate seniority who was not involved in the original decision, and

(b) as to the circumstances in which the person concerned is entitled to an oral hearing, and whether and by whom he may be represented at such a hearing.

(5) The landlord shall notify the person concerned of the decision on the review.

If the decision is to confirm the original decision, the landlord shall also notify him of the reasons for the decision.

(6) The review shall be carried out and the tenant notified before the date specified in the notice of proceedings as the date after which proceedings for the possession of the dwelling-house may be begun.

### 130.　Effect of beginning proceedings for possession

(1) This section applies where the landlord has begun proceedings for the possession of a dwelling house let under an introductory tenancy and—

(a) the trial period ends, or

(b) any of the events specified in section 125(5) occurs (events on which a tenancy ceases to be an introductory tenancy).

(2) Subject to the following provisions, the tenancy remains an introductory tenancy until—

(a) the tenancy comes to an end in pursuance of section 127(3) (that is, on the date on which the tenant is to give up possession in pursuance of an order of the court), or

(b) the proceedings are otherwise finally determined.

(3) If any of the events specified in section 125(5)(b) to (d) occurs, the tenancy shall thereupon cease to be an introductory tenancy but—

(a) the landlord (or, as the case may be, the new landlord) may continue the proceedings, and

(b) if he does so, section 127(2) and (3) (termination by landlord) apply as if the tenancy had remained an introductory tenancy.

(4) Where in accordance with subsection (3) a tenancy ceases to be an introductory tenancy and becomes a secure tenancy, the tenant is not entitled to exercise the right to buy under Part V of the Housing Act 1985 unless and until the proceedings are finally determined on terms such that he is not required to give up possession of the dwelling-house.

(5) For the purposes of this section proceedings shall be treated as finally determined if they are withdrawn or any appeal is abandoned or the time for appealing expires without an appeal being brought.

# THE INTRODUCTORY TENANTS (REVIEW) REGULATIONS 1997

# SI 1997/72

...

*Right to a hearing*

2. The review under section 129 of the Housing Act 1996 of the decision to seek an order for possession of a dwelling-house let under an introductory tenancy shall not be by way of an oral hearing unless the tenant informs the landlord that he wishes to have such a hearing before the end of the time permitted under subsection (1) of that section to request a review of that decision.

*Who is to carry out the review*

3.—(1) The review shall be carried out by a person who was not involved in the decision to apply for an order for possession.

(2) Where the review of a decision made by an officer is also to be made by an officer, that officer shall be someone who is senior to the officer who made the original decision.

*Review without a hearing*

4. If there is not to be a hearing the tenant may make representations in writing in connection with the review and such representations shall be considered by the landlord who shall inform the tenant of the date by which such representations must be received, which shall not be earlier than five clear days after receipt of this information by the tenant.

*Review by way of a hearing*

5.—(1) Subject to the provisions of this regulation, the procedure in connection with a review by way of hearing shall be such as the person hearing the review shall determine.

(2) A tenant who has requested a hearing has the right to—

(a)   be heard and to be accompanied and may be represented by another person whether that person is professionally qualified or not, and for the purposes of the proceedings any representative shall have the rights and powers which the tenant has under these Regulations;

(b)   call persons to give evidence;

(c)   put questions to any person who gives evidence at the hearing; and

(d)   make representations in writing.

*Notice of the hearing*

6. The landlord shall give the tenant notice of the date, time and place of the hearing, which shall be not less than five days after receipt of the request for a hearing and if the tenant has not been given such notice, the hearing may only proceed with the consent of the tenant or his representative.

*Absence of tenant at hearing*

7. If any person shall fail to appear at the hearing, notice having been given to him in accordance with regulation 6, the person conducting the review may, having regard to all the circumstances including any explanation offered for the absence, proceed with the hearing notwithstanding his absence, or give such directions with a view to the conduct of the further review as that person may think proper.

*Postponement of hearing*

8. A tenant may apply to the landlord requesting a postponement of the hearing and the landlord may grant or refuse the application as they see fit.

*Adjournment of hearing*

9. A hearing may be adjourned by the person hearing the review at any time during the hearing on the application of the tenant, his representative, or at the motion of the person hearing the review and, if a hearing is adjourned part heard and after the adjournment the person or persons hearing the review differ from those at the first hearing, otherwise than through the operation of paragraph 7, proceedings shall be by way of a complete rehearing of the case.

*Absence of person hearing the review*

10. Where more than one person is conducting the review, any hearing may, with the consent of the tenant or his representative but not otherwise, be proceeded with in the absence of one of the persons who is to determine the review.

## Introductory tenancy reviews and human rights

The review process has been challenged as infringing Arts 6 and 8 of the European Convention on Human Rights in the case of *R (McLellan) v Bracknell Forest District Council*[31]. Two local authority introductory tenants facing eviction appealed to the Court of Appeal. It was decided that it was in the interests of tenants generally and local authorities to have a scheme where tenants were on probation for the first 12 months and could be evicted 'without long battles in the county court'. As far as Art 6 was concerned, although the review procedures did not have the independence necessary to comply with Art 6, the procedure had to be considered as a whole. The inclusion of the possibility of judicial review meant there were adequate safeguards for tenants to challenge the decision. Likewise, tenants were entitled to raise the question of whether their right to respect for family life and home under Art 8 was infringed but the same safeguards resulted in the overall procedure being fair. (For a fuller discussion of this case, see Chapter 14.)

There was a challenge to the legality of the introductory tenants' review hearing in *Manchester City Council v Cochrane*[32], where a local authority had granted a couple an introductory tenancy. That it was an introductory tenancy was made clear in the tenancy agreement, which also expressly stated the power of the landlord to dispossess the tenant for breaches of tenancy obligations, including acts of nuisance or annoyance to other people, or inflicting or threatening domestic violence. Using these powers the landlord served a notice in March 1998 to terminate the tenancy, and the validity of this notice was not disputed. The following month the tenants requested a review of the decision to seek possession. An oral hearing was held and the tenants alleged this was not carried out in accordance with the requirements of the Introductory Tenants (Review) Regulations[33]. After that oral hearing the landlord confirmed they would seek possession of the dwelling house.

The tenants sought to defend the possession action in the county court. They denied breaking their tenancy agreement and also argued they had been denied a fair review hearing. The question for the Court of Appeal was whether as a matter of law the tenants could raise such a defence.

Sir John Knox found:
- The terms of the statute (the Housing Act 1996) imposed a mandatory scheme which limited the tenants' rights – provided the council complied with the requirements of s 128 the court was bound to make a possession order under s 127(2).
- If the tenants wished to challenge the conduct of the review they had to apply to the High Court for judicial review, and, following *Avon County Council v*

---

[31] [2002] QB 1129, [2002] 1 All ER 899, [2002] 2 WLR 1448.
[32] [1999] 1 WLR 809, [1999] LGR 626, (1999) 31 HLR 810.
[33] SI 1997/72.

*Buscott*[34], in such circumstances the county court could adjourn the possession proceedings if satisfied the tenants would have a real chance of being
granted leave to apply for judicial review.

●   However, the county court could not entertain a defence to the possession
    proceedings based on a denial of breach of tenancy obligations, neither could
    it grant a stay of those proceedings based on the tenants' allegation that the
    landlord had failed to observe the rules of natural justice.

●   The county court may not review failures to exercise public duties unless
    Parliament has given it express authority to do so, see s 38(3) County Court
    Act 1983; such a jurisdiction had not been granted in relation to introductory
    tenancies.

●   If the county court had jurisdiction to entertain a defence based on the
    invalidity of the landlord's review procedures the result could be that the
    tenant might achieve secure status, an undesirable result and not what was
    clearly intended by Parliament.

## Premises occupied in connection with employment

If the tenant is an employee and the contract of employment requires occupation of
the dwelling house 'for the better performance of his duties' the tenancy will not be
secure. It would be extremely inconvenient if school caretakers living in houses on
site exercised the right to buy. The next caretaker in the post would not be readily on
hand to deal with emergencies. The Law Commission Report, *Renting Homes*, has
recommended that social landlords with employees occupying property 'for the
better performance of his duties' should be able to grant a 'Type 1 agreement' ie one
with fewer rights[35].

Difficulties have arisen where the contract of employment does not expressly lay
down that someone in the post *must* occupy the house, but it may be argued that
such a term could be implied. In *Hughes v Greenwich London Borough Council*[36],
Mr Hughes was the headmaster of a boarding school for children with special
educational needs. He received free board and lodging and lived in a purpose-built
house in the school grounds. When the school closed and he retired he claimed to be
a secure tenant thereby having the right to buy the freehold. The borough council
argued that, although it was not an express term of Mr Hughes' contract of
employment that he was obliged to live in the house for the better performance of
his duties, such a term could be implied. He would therefore come within the
employment exceptions in Sch 1 para 2 of the 1985 Act and his tenancy would not
be secure.

Lord Lowry stated:

'In order that a term may be implied, there has to be a compelling reason for
deeming that term to form part of the contract, and that compelling reason is
missing from this case, unless it was *essential* that Mr Hughes should live in
the house in order to do his job, but the facts contradict that proposition ... He

34   [1988] QB 656.
35   Law Commission, *Renting Homes*, 284 para 5.37, November 2003.
36   [1994] 1 AC 170, [1993] 4 All ER 577, [1993] 3 WLR 821.

was not required to occupy that house for the better performance of his duties. It is clear that the employer was providing a facility but not imposing an obligation.'[37]

Mr Hughes therefore was able to exercise the right to buy. One could pose the question of whether the result would have been the same if the school had not closed and there was a newly appointed head hoping (but not required) to move into the house.

In contrast, in *South Glamorgan County Council v Griffiths*[38] a school caretaker lived close to the school in a house owned by the local authority. In Mr Griffiths' conditions of service a term was included, 'It shall be a condition of employment that a caretaker must reside in school accommodation where such premises are available and a tenancy agreement must be entered into.' In fact there was no formal tenancy agreement and Mr Griffiths paid only £1 a week in rent. The school closed and Mr Griffiths retired from his post as school caretaker. He was given notice to quit as the house was required for a caretaker at the community centre which had been set up in the old school. Despite the fact that there was a short period when he was occupying the house after he had retired and so was not occupying it 'for the better performance of his duties', the notice to quit was upheld by the Court of Appeal.

This exception in Sch 1 para 2 is not a once and for all condition which must be satisfied at the start of the tenancy or, vice versa, if it was satisfied earlier, circumstances can change so that it no longer applies. In *Elvidge v Coventry City Council*[39], the employee, who lived in a cottage in a country park, first worked as a water bailiff and there was no express or implied term in his employment contract that he should occupy the cottage. When he was promoted to an assistant ranger post his terms of employment altered and he was required to live in the park. With his new job he came within the exclusion in Sch 1 para 2 and so he ceased to be a secure tenant.

The school caretaker in *Greenfield v Berkshire County Council*[40] came within the exclusion during the time he was employed. He was made redundant and remained in the house as the caretaker's house at his new school was still being occupied by the former caretaker. He could not cope with the travelling to his new post so he gave in his notice and therefore remained in the house for a period of months while he was not an employee of the County Council. He was given notice to quit which he resisted as he argued that as he was no longer a caretaker he had gained security of tenure. The Court of Appeal accepted this argument and held that the tenancy did not come within the exclusion and was therefore secure.

## Development land

Until the late 1960s certain areas of cities were declared to be clearance areas, all the properties compulsorily purchased and the owners given compensation. The housing was demolished and the local authority then built new estates of council

---

[37] [1994] 4 All ER 577 at 582.
[38] (1992) 24 HLR 334.
[39] [1993] QB 241, [1993] 4 All ER 903,(1994) 26 HLR 281.
[40] (1996) 28 HLR 691.

housing for rent. The powers were formerly contained in Housing Act 1957 Part III and are now in s 289 and s 290 Housing Act 1985. This process took many months, years in some cases, with boarded-up properties lying vacant. To utilise these properties until redevelopment took place, councils licensed them to housing associations and squatters' groups. If these groups acquired secure tenancies (although possession proceedings could still be brought under Ground 10, but then alternative accommodation would have to be found for the residents) the practice of using short-life housing would be put in jeopardy.

Local authority policy gradually changed after General Improvement Areas (GIAs) were introduced by the Housing Act 1969 and grants were available for private householders to improve their property by installing modern bathrooms, internal lavatories and central heating. Although compulsory purchase is rarely used nowadays to acquire whole areas of residential properties, individual houses may still be acquired for road schemes and for community buildings such as schools. Areas of derelict industrial or former railway land are still acquired for wholesale development. In the last few years these schemes have often included new housing.

Fox LJ held in *Hyde Housing Association Ltd v Harrison*[41] that the landlord did not have to be the person who has acquired the land for development. Paragraph 3(1) of Sch 1 imposes two distinct requirements. The first is that the dwelling house must be on land which has been acquired for development. The second is that the dwelling house is used by the landlord, pending development of the land, as temporary housing accommodation. If these two requirements are satisfied, the tenancy is not a secure tenancy.

In the *Harrison* case the Department of Transport had acquired a flat as part of land required for a road development scheme. Six months later the Department licensed the land to the housing association, who in turn granted a temporary licence to Harrison. When Mr Harrison was in arrears with his rent the housing association gave him a notice to bring his licence to an end. Mr Harrison argued that he had a secure tenancy because, to come within the exception in Sch 1, para 3 , the landlord must be the person who acquired the property for development. This was firmly rejected by the Court of Appeal.

Several other cases on this exception have reached the Court of Appeal. It was decided in *Attley v Cherwell District Council*[42] that even if the nature of the development planned altered, the exception still applied. In this case the property had been originally acquired in 1879 for a sewage works which were never built! If, however, no development at all is envisaged in the foreseeable future, the occupiers gain security (*Lillieshall Road Housing Co-operative Ltd v Brennan*[43]). In that case the question also arose of whether the 'land' referred to in para 3 was merely the land on which the house stood or whether it was all the land (in that case 29 houses) covered by the compulsory purchase order. The court decided it was the latter.

## Accommodation for homeless people

The Homelessness Act 2002 s 18 and Sch 2 removed the restrictions previously imposed on local housing authorities by s 207 Housing Act 1996. This section had

---

[41]  (1990) 23 HLR 57 at 58.
[42]  (1989) 21 HLR 613.
[43]  (1991) 24 HLR 195.

laid down that homeless people, owed a duty to be housed under Pt VII Housing Act 1996, could only be given accommodation for a maximum period of two years unless it was in a hostel or in private sector accommodation leased by the authority. Although the two-year time limit has disappeared the homeless person will not gain security of tenure. It is possible for the authority to notify the tenant at any time that the tenancy has become secure. Generally, however, the council give notice that the tenancy is secure when the homeless person is entitled to an allocation under the authority's housing allocation scheme[44].

## Accommodation for asylum-seekers

An asylum-seeker who is being housed by the National Asylum Support Service (NASS), set up under the Immigration and Asylum Act 1999 Part VI, does not have a secure tenancy unless the landlord notifies the tenant that it is secure[45].

## Temporary accommodation for persons taking up employment

Many local authorities keep a small stock of property for people taking up jobs with the authority who came from outside the area. Accommodation is needed until they have had time to make permanent arrangements. The amendments made by the 1996 Act[46] differentiate between local housing authorities and other public sector landlords. Local authority tenants remain insecure unless the authority inform them otherwise. For all other public sector tenants a tenancy automatically becomes secure after a year but the landlord can inform the tenant at any time that the tenancy has become secure.

## Short-term arrangements

Due to the shortage of council accommodation the practice has grown up in some areas of local authorities leasing properties from private landlords and then letting them in turn on a temporary basis to homeless people. This is clearly a cheaper option than housing homeless people in bed and breakfast accommodation in hotels. Some inner-London boroughs with large numbers of homeless people lease properties further away from the centre in the outer boroughs. Without such an exception private landlords would be unwilling to lease properties to local authorities, as they would not easily be able to regain possession.

The issue addressed in *Tower Hamlets London Borough Council v Miah*[47] was whether a licence came within Sch 1, para 6. The authority owed the defendant a duty to provide permanent accommodation with security of tenure. This duty could be fulfilled in stages: by providing temporary accommodation to start with, giving time to find suitable permanent accommodation later. As a temporary measure, the respondent was granted a licence of a property on which Tower Hamlets had taken a licence themselves. When served with a notice to quit Miah made two separate arguments: first, that under s 79(3) Housing Act 1985 the arrangement, despite being a licence, amounted to a secure tenancy; and, secondly, that the exception for

---

[44] See Chapter 7 for more details.
[45] Sch 1 para 4A.
[46] Housing Act 1996 ss 173, 127, Sch 16 paras 2 (5),(6), Sch 19 Pt VII.
[47] [1992] QB 622, [1992] 2 All ER 667, [1992] 2 WLR 761, (1992) 24 HLR 199.

short-term arrangements in Sch 1, para 6 only applied to leases and not to licences. The Court of Appeal held that para 6 was intended to apply to all arrangements by which a private owner granted rights which were less than a freehold to a local authority; therefore the term 'leases' in para 6 included licences.

## Remaining exceptions in Schedule 1

The remaining exceptions include agricultural holdings[48], public houses[49], business tenancies[50], almshouses[51] and lettings to students at designated courses and educational institutions[52].

# EVICTION PROCEDURES

## Court order necessary

Public sector tenants with security of tenure can only be evicted if the landlord obtains a court order for possession which is served on the tenant (s 82 Housing Act 1985). The tenancy ends on the date the court orders (s 82(2)). The landlord has to follow the correct procedure and one of the grounds listed in Sch 2 must exist. The procedure is in s 83 Housing Act 1985, which was completely replaced by a new s 83 substituted by s 147 Housing Act 1996[53].

The Law Commission Report, *Renting Homes*[54], has recommended that the notice of intention to take proceedings should be changed to a minimum of one, and a maximum of three months and if the proceedings are not started within six months of the expiry of the notice period, the notice should lapse.

Mohammed Sarwar MP introduced a Private Members' Bill, *The Prevention of Homelessness Bill*, which had its first reading on 16 March 2004. It would enable the courts to exercise discretion in every residential possession claim, enabling them to suspend the order for a short time so that the defendants could make other accommodation arrangements.

## Demoted tenancies

The Anti-Social Behaviour Act 2003 ss 13–15 introduced a new form of housing tenure, 'the demoted tenancy', by inserting the new s 82A into the Housing Act 1985. Local housing authorities, housing action trusts and registered social landlords can apply to court for the tenancy to be stripped of its secure status if the conditions in s 153A or s 153B Housing Act 1996 have been met (anti-social behaviour or using the premises for unlawful purposes). In addition it must be reasonable to make an order 'demoting' the tenancy. The orders listed in the new s 82(1A) inserted by the Anti-social Behaviour Act 2003 s 14(1)(b) include

---

[48]  Para 8.
[49]  Para 9.
[50]  Para 11.
[51]  Para 12.
[52]  Para 10; SI 1980/1407.
[53]  For more details about eviction procedures see Chapter 6.
[54]  Law Commission 284, November 2003.

possession orders and demotion orders. The effect of a demoted tenancy is discussed in more detail in Chapter 9. Sections 83 and 83A of the Housing Act 1985 relate to proceedings for possession:

### 83. Proceedings for possession or termination: notice requirements

(1) The court shall not entertain proceedings for an order mentioned in section 82(1A) unless—

(a) the landlord has served a notice on the tenant complying with the provisions of this section, or

(b) the court considers it just and equitable to dispense with the requirement of such a notice.

(2) A notice under this section shall—

(a) be in a form prescribed by regulations made by the Secretary of State,

(b) specify the ground on which the court will be asked to make the order, and

(c) give particulars of that ground.

(3) Where the tenancy is a periodic tenancy and the ground or one of the grounds specified in the notice is Ground 2 in Schedule 2 (nuisance or other anti-social behaviour), the notice—

(a) shall also—

(i) state that proceedings for the possession of the dwelling-house may be begun immediately, and

(ii) specify the date sought by the landlord as the date on which the tenant is to give up possession of the dwelling-house, and

(b) ceases to be in force twelve months after the date so specified.

(4) Where the tenancy is a periodic tenancy and Ground 2 in Schedule 2 is not specified in the notice, the notice—

(a) shall also specify the date after which proceedings for the possession of the dwelling-house may be begun, and

(b) ceases to be in force twelve months after the date so specified.

(4A) If the proceedings are for a demotion order under section 82A the notice

(a) must specify the date after which proceedings may be begun;

(b) ceases to be in force twelve months after the date so specified.

(5) The date specified in accordance with subsection (3) or (4) or (4A) must not be earlier than the date on which the tenancy could, apart from the Part, be brought to an end by notice to quit given by the landlord on the same date as the notice under this section.

(6) Where a notice under this section is served with respect to a secure tenancy for a term certain, it has effect also with respect to any periodic tenancy arising on the termination of that tenancy by virtue of section 86; and subsections (3) to (5) of this section do not apply to the notice.

(7) Regulations under this section shall be made by statutory instrument and may make different provision with respect to different cases or descriptions of case, including different provision for different areas.

### 83A. Additional requirements in relation to certain proceedings for possession

(1) Where a notice under section 83 has been served on a tenant containing the information mentioned in subsection (3)(a) of that section, the court shall not entertain proceedings for the possession of the dwelling-house unless they are begun at a time when the notice is still in force.

(2) Where—

(a)  a notice under section 83 has been served on a tenant, and

(b)  a date after which proceedings may be begun has been specified in the notice in accordance with subsection (4)(a) of that section,

the court shall not entertain proceedings for the possession of the dwelling-house unless they are begun after the date so specified and at a time when the notice is still in force.

(3) Where—

(a)  the ground or one of the grounds specified in a notice under section 83 is Ground 2A in Schedule 2 (domestic violence), and

(b)  the partner who has left the dwelling-house as mentioned in that ground is not a tenant of the dwelling-house,

the court shall not entertain proceedings for the possession of the dwelling house unless it is satisfied that the landlord has served a copy of the notice on the partner who has left or has taken all reasonable steps to serve a copy of the notice on that partner.

This subsection has effect subject to subsection (5).

(4) Where—

(a)  Ground 2A in Schedule 2 is added to a notice under section 83 with the leave of the court after proceedings for possession are begun, and

(b)  the partner who has left the dwelling-house as mentioned in that ground is not a party to the proceedings,

the court shall not continue to entertain the proceedings unless it is satisfied that the landlord has served a notice under subsection (6) on the partner who has left or has taken all reasonable steps to serve such a notice on that partner.

This subsection has effect subject to subsection (5).

(5) Where subsection (3) or (4) applies and Ground 2 in Schedule 2 (nuisance or other anti-social behaviour) is also specified in the notice under section 83, the court may dispense with the requirements as to service in relation to the partner who has left the dwelling-house if it considers it just and equitable to do so.

(6) A notice under this subsection shall—

(a)  state that proceedings for the possession of the dwelling-house have begun,

(b)  specify the ground or grounds on which possession is being sought, and

(c)  give particulars of the ground or grounds.

## Dispensing with the notice requirements if just and equitable to do so

The Housing Act 1996 amended s 83 of the Housing Act 1985 to enable the court to dispense with the notice requirements if it considers it just and equitable to do so[55]. The corresponding discretion for assured tenancies in s 8 Housing Act 1988 was considered in *Kelsey Housing Association v King*[56], where the tenant complained about the deficiencies in the notice of possession proceedings as it did not give sufficient details of the nuisance allegations made against the tenants and their children. The court exercised its discretion and allowed dispensation of the notice. Among the factors it took into account were the events occurring after the notice

[55]  S 83(1)(b).
[56]  (1995) 28 HLR 270.

had been given and the long delay: the tenant's complaint having been made six months after proceedings began. The Court of Appeal upheld the decision. Courts will probably not dispense with the need for *some* form of notice even in serious anti-social behaviour cases but as *Megarry on the Rent Acts* ( as approved by the court in *Kelsey*) states:

> 'This power [to dispense with the requirement of serving a possession notice] seems unlikely to be exercised unless the tenant has in some way become aware of the intended proceedings for possession, unless perhaps, his misconduct has been so grave as to invite proceedings for possession, in the sense of making such proceedings so likely that he may be taken to have expected them.'[57]

### Notice in anti-social behaviour cases

The possession proceedings can be started as soon as the notice has been served for cases based on Ground 2 (the anti-social behaviour ground). Also the notice must specify the date on which the tenant is to give up possession (s 83(3)). For all the other grounds the notice must give a date after which proceedings can begin and this date cannot be earlier than when a notice to quit would expire ie a minimum of four weeks.

### Notice in domestic violence cases

If the landlord is relying on Ground 2A (domestic violence), the court must be satisfied that the landlord has taken reasonable steps to serve a notice on the partner who has left (s 83A(3)). If the partner who has departed is a tenant a notice should have been served anyway.

### Inaccurate or incomplete notices

The requirements under the old law were strictly applied; if the notice was deficient in minor particulars this could lead to the notice being held to be invalid. In *Torridge District Council v Jones*[58] the notice was in the form prescribed by the regulations that were then in force but it stated that, 'The reasons for taking this action are non-payment of rent'. No details were given of the amount of rent owed. The Court of Appeal allowed the tenant's appeal holding the notice was invalid as the object of the notice was to enable the tenant to put matters right before the court hearing. This notice, by not specifying the precise amount of the rent owing, did not fulfil this requirement.

Imprecise information summarising the grounds given by local housing authorities in good faith where the tenant is not mislead, however, will not invalidate the notice. In *Swansea City Council v Hearn*[59] the notice to quit given to the licensee staying temporarily with her children in a hostel for the homeless was held to be valid

[57]   11th ed Volume 3 (Assured Tenancies) at p 140.
[58]   (1985) 18 HLR 107.
[59]   (1990) 23 HLR 284.

although it described her as a 'tenant' and the City Council as the 'landlord' (rather than the licensee and the licensor). Dillon LJ summed up by saying, that although the learned assistant recorder had held that certainty was necessary and that there was not sufficient certainty in this case, there was no suggestion that Miss Hearn herself was left in any doubt so the information for the tenant given in the notice to quit sufficiently complied with the requirements of the 1988 Regulations. Similarly, in *Dudley Metropolitan Borough Council v Bailey*[60] a notice seeking possession was served with minor deviation from the wording laid down in SI 1987/755, which was allowed as the notice had substantially the same effect. A figure of £145.96 for the rent arrears was given but it was accepted that the actual rent arrears were £72.88, with the remaining sum being made up of arrears of rates and water rates. The notice was not invalidated by this honest error by the council in its description of the arrears.

After the order for possession is granted to the landlord, a second order, a warrant for possession must be granted by the court before the tenant can be evicted. Paying off all the arrears once the warrant is granted is not sufficient to stop the eviction, as was seen in *Jephson Homes Housing Association v Moisejevs*[61]. The tenant must apply for a suspension of the order under s 85(2) Housing Act 1985 so it is vital that tenants receive legal advice if a possession order has been made against them[62].

## NOTICES TO QUIT

If a landlord wishes a tenant, who does not have a secure tenancy, to leave, a 'notice to quit' must be served. Tenants, for their part, it they wish to leave the property can bring any periodic tenancy, secure or insecure, to an end by serving a notice to quit. A landlord's notice to a tenant must contain certain information as laid down in the Notices to Quit (Prescribed Information) Regulations 1988[63]. The tenant's notice to a landlord has to be in writing but does not have to be in any particular form of words. Many tenants, however, think that merely handing in the keys is sufficient. Tenants owing large sums in rent arrears sometimes abandon properties and disappear, leaving no forwarding address. For all notices to quit a minimum period of four weeks' notice must be given, which is calculated so that it includes the first day and excludes the last day. Unless there is a special term, a notice to quit should be given so that it expires at the end of any complete period of the tenancy[64]. So, for example, for a weekly tenancy with rent payable on a Friday, the first day of the tenancy is normally a Friday and the last day of a complete period of tenancy is a Thursday. For a monthly tenancy the period of notice to quit must be one month expiring on the last day of a complete period of the tenancy. If the rent was payable on the fourth day each month, the last day of the period would be the third day of the month. Section 5 Protection from Eviction Act 1977 governs the validity of notices to quit.

[60]  (1990) 22 HLR 424.
[61]  [2001] 2 All ER 901, (2001) 33 HLR 594.
[62]  For a more detailed discussion see Chapter 6.
[63]  SI 1988/2201.
[64]  *Schnabel v Allard* [1967] 1 QB 627.

With a joint tenancy it is possible for one tenant, acting by themselves, to serve a notice to quit on the landlord bringing the tenancy to an end. There is no requirement for the other joint tenant to have consented or even that they should have been informed. This was decided in *Greenwich London Borough Council v McGrady*[65] which was confirmed by the House of Lords in *Hammersmith and Fulham London Borough Council v Monk*[66]. One of the recommendations in the Law Commission Report, *Renting Homes*, is that a joint occupier should be able to give notice and thereby terminate his interest in a tenancy without it bringing the whole agreement to an end[67]. For a more detailed discussion see Chapter 11.

## PROTECTION FROM EVICTION ACT 1977

### Validity of Notices to Quit

5. (1) Subject to subsection (1B) below no notice by a landlord or a tenant to quit any premises let (whether before or after the commencement of this Act) as a dwelling shall be valid unless—

(a) it is in writing and contains such information as may be prescribed, and
(b) it is given not less than 4 weeks before the date on which it is to take effect.

(1A) Subject to subsection (1B) below, no notice by a licensor or a licensee to determine a periodic licence to occupy premises as a dwelling (whether the licence was granted before or after the passing of this Act) shall be valid unless—

(a) it is in writing and contains such information as may be prescribed, and
(b) it is given not less than 4 weeks before the date on which it is to take effect.

(1B) Nothing in subsection (1) or subsection (1A) above applies to—

(a) premises let on an excluded tenancy which is entered into on or after the date on which the Housing Act 1988 came into force unless it is entered into pursuant to a contract made before that date, or
(b) premises occupied under an excluded licence.

(2) In this section 'prescribed' means prescribed by regulations made by the Secretary of State by statutory instrument, and a statutory instrument containing any such regulations shall be subject to annulment in pursuance of a resolution of either House of Parliament.

(3) Regulations under this section may make different provision in relation to different descriptions of lettings and different circumstances.

## GROUNDS FOR POSSESSION

To obtain a possession order the landlord must specify one of the 16 grounds in Sch 2 Housing Act 1985, some of which have been amended by the Housing Act 1996. For Grounds 1–8 the court will only make a possession order if it would, in addition, be reasonable to make an order (s 84(2)(a)). The Court of Appeal observed in *Manchester City Council v Green*[68] that in possession order cases it

---

[65]  (1982) 6 HLR 36.
[66]  [1992] 1 AC 478, [1992] 1 All ER 1, [1991] 3 WLR 1144.
[67]  Law Commission 284, para 3.63, November 2003.
[68]  [1999] January *Legal Action* 27.

would be helpful if trial judges expressly referred in their judgments to reasonableness. Grounds 1–8 in Sch 2 of the Housing Act 1985 for possession of dwelling-houses let under secure tenancies are as follows.

# Schedule 2

# Grounds for possession of dwelling-houses let under secure tenancies

## PART I

## GROUNDS ON WHICH COURT MAY ORDER POSSESSION IF IT CONSIDERS IT REASONABLE

### *Ground 1*

Rent lawfully due from the tenant has not been paid or an obligation of the tenancy has been broken or not performed.

### *Ground 2*

The tenant or a person residing in or visiting the dwelling-house—

(a)  has been guilty of conduct causing or likely to cause a nuisance or annoyance to a person residing, visiting or otherwise engaging in a lawful activity in the locality, or
(b)  has been convicted of—
  (i)   using the dwelling-house or allowing it to be used for immoral or illegal purposes, or
  (ii)  an arrestable offence committed in, or in the locality of, the dwelling-house.

### *Ground 2A*

The dwelling-house was occupied (whether alone or with others) by a married couple or a couple living together as husband and wife and—

(a)  one or both of the partners is a tenant of the dwelling-house,
(b)  one partner has left because of violence or threats of violence by the other towards—
  (i)   that partner, or
  (ii)  a member of the family of that partner who was residing with that partner immediately before the partner left, and

(c)  the court is satisfied that the partner who has left is unlikely to return.

### *Ground 3*

The condition of the dwelling-house or of any of the common parts has deteriorated owing to acts of waste by, or the neglect or default of, the tenant or a person residing in the dwelling-house and, in the case of an act of waste by, or the neglect or default of, a person lodging with the tenant or a sub-tenant of his, the tenant has not taken such steps as he ought reasonably to have taken for the removal of the lodger or sub-tenant.

*Ground 4*

The condition of furniture provided by the landlord for use under the tenancy, or in the common parts, has deteriorated owing to ill-treatment by the tenant or a person residing in the dwelling-house and, in the case of ill-treatment of a person lodging with the tenant or a sub-tenant of his, the tenant has not taken such steps as he ought reasonably to have taken for the removal of the lodger or sub-tenant.

*Ground 5*

The tenant is the person, or one of the persons, to whom the tenancy was granted and the landlord was induced to grant the tenancy by a false statement made knowingly or recklessly by (a) the tenant, or (b) a person acting at the tenant's instigation.

*Ground 6*

The tenancy was assigned to the tenant, or to a predecessor in title of his who is a member of his family and is residing in the dwelling-house, by an assignment made by virtue of section 92 (assignments by way of exchange) and a premium was paid either in connection with that assignment or the assignment which the tenant or predecessor himself made by virtue of that section.

In this paragraph 'premium' means any fine or other like sum and any other pecuniary consideration in addition to rent.

*Ground 7*

The dwelling-house forms part of, or is within the curtilage of, a building which, for so much of it as is held by the landlord, is held mainly for purposes other than housing purposes and consists mainly of accommodation other than housing accommodation, and—

(a)   the dwelling-house was let to the tenant or a predecessor in title of his in consequence of the tenant or predecessor being in the employment of the landlord, or of—
a local authority
a new town corporation
a housing action trust
an urban development corporation, or
the governors of an aided school, and

(b)   the tenant or a person residing in the dwelling-house has been guilty of conduct such that, having regard to the purpose for which the building is used, it would not be right for him to continue in occupation of the dwelling-house.

*Ground 8*

The dwelling-house was made available for occupation by the tenant (or a predecessor in title of his) while works were carried out on the dwelling-house which he previously occupied as his only or principal home and—

(a) the tenant (or predecessor) was a secure tenant of the other dwelling-house at the time when he ceased to occupy it as his home,
(b) the tenant (or predecessor) accepted the tenancy of the dwelling-house of which possession is sought on the understanding that he would give up occupation when, on completion of the works, the other dwelling-house was again available for occupation by him under a secure tenancy, and
(c) the works have been completed and the other dwelling-house is so available.

## Rent arrears

Rent arrears is by far the most common ground for possession orders[69]. Lord Woolf in *Access to Justice*[70] has suggested that there should be a two-stage procedure in possession cases based on rent arrears. The first stage would be limited to money claims and the second would be possession proceedings where the money judgment had not been complied with. There appear to be no government plans to implement these suggestions.

As the local authority's prime objective is the payment of the arrears rather than the eviction of the tenant, suspended possession orders are frequently made by the courts provided the tenant agrees to pay the current rent and the payment of the arrears by instalments. Difficulties often occur because of the slow processing of housing benefit claims by the same local authority as is taking the action – albeit by a separate department. The drawback to suspended possession orders is that any breach of the order, for example not paying off the arrears at the agreed rate, ends the secure tenancy and automatically triggers the possession order so the landlord may apply for a warrant to execute the order[71].

In deciding whether the order is reasonable the court will attempt to balance the interests of the community and those of the tenant. The previous rent record of the tenant together with reasons for non-payment such as illness or unemployment or housing benefit difficulties will be factors to be considered. In *Woodspring District Council v Taylor*[72]. a couple in their mid-fifties, who had lived in their council house for over 20 years with a good payment record, fell on hard times. The husband was made redundant and found it impossible to obtain employment and his wife became ill with diabetes and asthma. The rent arrears mounted when the husband received a tax bill for £500. Although the arrears were over £700 at the time of the trial and were only being paid off by a small weekly sum from the DHSS, the decision of the registrar to grant the authority a possession order was overturned on appeal.

If a possession order is granted and a warrant to execute the order is made the tenants may become homeless if they can find nowhere else to rent. Whether they are recognised as being owed duties under the homelessness legislation will depend in part on whether they are regarded as being intentionally homeless. The crucial question will be whether the rent arrears arose through misfortune or wilful refusal to pay; see Chapter 10.

Although the factors leading to the arrears will be considered when deciding whether it is reasonable for the court to make a possession order, many tenants do not defend the proceedings and fail to appear in court. In such cases, where the arrears are a result of misfortune, the authority may owe duties to a homeless person under Pt VII Housing Act 1996. A further question is if the likelihood of homelessness is one of the factors that the court should consider when they are deciding whether to grant a possession order (see below).

[69] Gary, B., Finch, H., Prescott-Clarke, T., Cameron, S., Gilroy, R., Kirby, K. and Mountford, J., *Rent Arrears in Local Authorities and Housing Associations in England* (1994) HMSO.
[70] Final Report to the Lord Chancellor on the Civil Justice System in England and Wales (1996)
[71] *Thompson v Elmbridge Borough Council* [1987] 1 WLR 1425, (1987) 19 HLR 526.
[72] (1982) 4 HLR 95.

If a tenant pays the full arrears before the commencement of the proceedings, in other words, between the service of the Notice of Possession Proceedings and the summons for possession, there will be no rent unpaid that is 'lawfully due' and so no possession order can be made. This point was decided under the Rent Acts, which have a similar wording to Ground 1[73]. In the Rent Act case of *Dellenty v Pellow* [74] the position of tenant who paid off the rent arrears after the commencement of the proceedings was considered. The court would have jurisdiction to make a possession order but prima facie it would not be reasonable to make one as the arrears had been paid. In the case, however, there was a long history of arrears and proceedings had been issued on a number of previous occasions so it was reasonable to make a possession order. The point was reconsidered and reconfirmed, more recently in *Lee-Steere v Jennings*[75].

Possession orders based on breach of tenancy conditions or on Ground 2 (antisocial behaviour) are discussed in Chapter 9.

## Ground 2A Domestic violence

This ground, introduced by the Housing Act 1996 s 145, is designed to address the problem of partners (usually women and their children) who leave accommodation because of violence or the threats of violence and the other partner remains alone in family-sized property with a secure tenancy. The partner who has left, if homeless, would be owed duties under the homelessness legislation as she would not be 'intentionally homeless'. If she had children with her the single-parent family would be classed as being in priority need. The end result is that the local authority provides two family-sized units for one family. If the departing partner had a joint tenancy they can serve a notice to quit and bring the tenancy to an end, *Newlon Housing Trust v Al-Sulaimen*[76], but the local authority cannot force the departing partner to do this (see Chapter 11). Local authorities are able to recover possession whether the tenant remaining in the property had a joint or a sole tenancy.

The violence or the threats of violence must be 'the real reason, effective reason, the immediate and causative reason' why the partner left[77]. It is not sufficient for the violence to be one amongst several factors. In Mrs Mallett's case the judge found as fact that she had left the flat to live with her then boyfriend and so Ground 2A was not made out. The decision was upheld by the Court of Appeal.

The Civil Partnership Bill 2004[78], if passed, would widen Ground 2A to include same-sex partners ('civil partners') and 'a couple living together as if they were civil partners'. Even with this amendment Ground 2A only applies if one member of a *couple* has left because of violence from the other member of the couple. It does not include violence where there is not 'a couple': violence by an adult child on a single parent for example.

---

[73]   Chapter 4; *Bird v Hildage* [1948] 1 KB 91.
[74]   [1951] 2 KB 858, [1951] 2 All ER 716.
[75]   (1986) 20 HLR 1.
[76]   [1999] 1 AC 313, [1998] 4 All ER 1, [1998] 3 WLR 451, (1998) 30 HLR 1132.
[77]   HHJ Cotran approved by the Court of Appeal in *Camden London Borough Council v Mallett* (2000) 33 HLR 204.
[78]   Sch 8 cl 33.

## Ground 5 False statements to obtain a tenancy

The Court of Appeal in *Bristol City Council v Mousah*[79] felt that too much weight was attached to the possibility of homelessness when considering the reasonableness of making a possession order[80]. Whether the judge had not taken enough account of the possibility of homelessness was the basis of an appeal against a possession order granted on Ground 5 (false statements made to obtain a tenancy) in *Rushcliffe Borough Council v Watson*[81]. The Court of Appeal agreed with the judge's finding that if the order was granted the tenant would be in difficulties as she may be regarded as being intentionally homeless. It was felt, however, that Miss Watson, a single mother, would be able to surmount the difficulties. There was no real likelihood that she would be separated from her children and there was no other real risk to them or to her. Rushcliffe Borough Council had granted a tenancy to Miss Watson and then discovered that she had an existing housing association tenancy. On her application form she had claimed to be staying with relatives, well aware that if she was a housing association tenant she had little chance of being granted a council tenancy. The court took into account that 'reasonableness' means having regard to the interests of the parties and those of the public at large[82]. On the issue in *Rushcliffe*, of balancing the public interest of keeping families together and the interest of local authorities allocating scarce housing resources fairly, Nourse LJ said that the judge in the county court had recognised the public interest in keeping a family together as a unit. But since he had thought that there was no real likelihood that this family would be split up, that was not something which affected his consideration of the public interest in this case. On the broader aspect of the public interest, the judge had been fully entitled to attach the importance which he evidently did to the policy of discouraging deceitful applications which result in the unjust relegation on the housing list of applicants who are honest. There are hundreds of families at the local authority's door in inadequate accommodation who are desperate – deprived by deceptions. If a deception of this kind succeeds, people will try to jump the queue, but the local authority cannot be expected to act as private detectives.

A stronger line against fraudulent applications was taken in *Shrewsbury and Atcham Borough Council v Evans*[83], where the appellant had tenancies of two local authority properties simultaneously. When Mrs Evans originally applied for a council tenancy she and her four children claimed to be living at her mother's house, which would have been grossly overcrowded with a total of 11 people there. At the time she was in fact living with her husband and children in an expensive country farmhouse which they were buying on mortgage. After she had been granted the council tenancy her husband left her and the mortgagees threatened possession proceedings. She then applied to a different local authority on the grounds that her home was being repossessed and was again granted a tenancy. At trial the judge found that it was reasonable to make a possession order. The defendant appealed on the grounds that insufficient weight had been given to the possibility of homelessness and that the family (by that time there were five

[79]  (1997) 30 HLR 32.
[80]  See Chapter 9.
[81]  (1991) 24 HLR 124.
[82]  *London Borough of Enfield v McKeon* (1986) 18 HLR 330.
[83]  (1997) 30 HLR 123.

children) might not be able to stay together. Beldam LJ said that where there has been a deliberate lying to obtain public housing, only in exceptional cases would the court consider the effect of the homelessness legislation. He went on to say that, in deciding questions of reasonableness in a case such as this, a court can in exceptional cases take into account the nature and degree of the untrue statements which have been made and the circumstances in which they are made and whether, for example, they are deliberate or reckless. The court could also reasonably, take into consideration the attitude of the appellant when the deception was discovered. Her attitude was to lie and lie again to deny completely that she had made the application to the District Council, suggesting that this had been made by someone using her name.

Deception does not always result in the tenant losing possession. In *Southwark London Borough Council v Erekin*[84], although Mrs Erekin was prosecuted for the untrue statements she made to obtain the tenancy and for other offences and sentenced to 18 months' imprisonment, a possession order was not granted. Mrs Erekin and her five children stayed in the house where they had lived for the previous five years as it would not be reasonable, in the circumstances, to grant the council a possession order.

### Grounds 9–16

For Grounds 9–11 the court will only make a possession order if it is satisfied that there is suitable alternative accommodation available (s 84(2)(b) Housing Act 1985).

For Grounds 12–16 the court will only make an order for possession if it considers it reasonable to do so *and* suitable alternative accommodation is available. Both conditions must be satisfied (s 84(2)(c) Housing Act 1985).

# Schedule 2

## PART II

## GROUNDS ON WHICH THE COURT MAY ORDER POSSESSION IF SUITABLE ALTERNATIVE ACCOMMODATION IS AVAILABLE

*Ground 9*

The dwelling-house is overcrowded, within the meaning of Part X, in such circumstances as to render the occupier guilty of an offence.

*Ground 10*

The landlord intends within a reasonable time of obtaining possession of the dwelling-house-

(a) to demolish or reconstruct the building or part of the building comprising the dwelling house, or

---

[84] [2003] EWHC 1765 (Ch), [2003] All ER (D) 303 (Jun).

(b)   to carry out work on that building or on land let together with, and thus treated as part of, the dwelling-house,

and cannot reasonably do so without obtaining possession of the dwelling-house.

Ground 10A (omitted)

### *Ground 11*

The landlord is a charity and the tenant's continued occupation of the dwelling-house could conflict with the objects of the charity.

## PART III

## GROUNDS ON WHICH THE COURT MAY ORDER POSSESSION IF IT CONSIDERS IT REASONABLE AND SUITABLE ALTERNATIVE ACCOMMODATION IS AVAILABLE

### *Ground 12*

The dwelling-house forms part of, or is within the curtilage of, a building which, or so much of it as is held by the landlord, is held mainly for purposes other than housing purposes and consists mainly of accommodation other than housing accommodation, or is situated in a cemetery, and—

(a)   the dwelling-house was let to the tenant or a predecessor in title of his in consequence of the tenant or predecessor being in the employment of the landlord or of—

> a local authority
> a new town corporation
> a housing action trust
> an urban development corporation or
> the governors of an aided school,
> and that employment has ceased, and

(b)   the landlord reasonably requires the dwelling-house for occupation as a residence for some person either engaged in the employment of the landlord, or of such a body, or with whom a contract for such employment has been entered into conditional on housing being provided.

### *Ground 13*

The dwelling-house has features which are substantially different from those of ordinary dwelling-houses and which are designed to make it suitable for occupation by a physically disabled person who requires accommodation of a kind provided by the dwelling-house and—

(a)   there is no longer such a person residing in the dwelling-house, and

(b)   the landlord requires it for occupation (whether alone or with members of his family) by such a person.

### *Ground 14*

Not applicable to local housing authority tenancies.

*Ground 15*

The dwelling-house is one of a group of dwelling-houses which it is the practice of the landlord to let for occupation by persons with special needs and—

(a)  a social service or special facility is provided in close proximity to the group of dwelling-houses in order to assist persons with those special needs

(b)  there is no longer a person with those special needs residing in the dwelling-house and—

the landlord requires the dwelling-house for occupation (whether alone or with members of his family) by a person who has those special needs.

*Ground 16*

The accommodation afforded by the dwelling-house is more extensive than is reasonably required by the tenant and—

(a)  the tenancy vested in the tenant by virtue of section 89 (succession to periodic tenancy), the tenant being qualified to succeed by virtue of section 87(b) (members of family other than spouse), and

(b)  notice of the proceedings for possession was served under section 83 or where no such notice was served, the proceedings for possession were begun more than six months but less than twelve months after the date of the previous tenant's death.

The matters to be taken into account by the court in determining whether it is reasonable to make an order on this ground include—

(a)  the age of the tenant

(b)  the period during which the tenant occupied the dwelling-house as his only or principal home, and

(c)  any financial or other support given by the tenant to the previous tenant.

## Overcrowding – Ground 9

Part X Housing Act 1985 defines overcrowding as when the number of persons sleeping in the dwelling-house is higher than 'the room standard' or 'the space standard'. The room standard is infringed when the number of living rooms and bedrooms available is insufficient for two people of opposite sexes over the age of ten not living together as husband and wife to sleep in separate rooms (s 325 Housing Act 1985). The space standard is calculated by precise mathematical formulae based on either the number of rooms or the floor area in square feet (s 326(3) Housing Act 1985). A government amendment to the Housing Bill 2003, cl 187, gives the power to make regulations to improve these statutory overcrowding standards. The Office of the Deputy Prime Minister published a report on the effect of overcrowding in May 2004[85].

The alternative accommodation offered by the landlord must be suitable for the tenant and his family, it does not have to be large enough to accommodate everyone from the overcrowded dwelling house (Pt IV para 3).

---

[85]  Office of the Deputy Prime Minister *The Impact of Overcrowding on Health and Education* ( a review of existing evidence on the impact of overcrowded housing on peoples' health and education) May 2004.

## Property needed for carrying out works – Ground 10

Some guidance on the interpretation of Ground 10(a) is given in *Wansbeck District Council v Marley*[86]. The tenant's husband had been the superintendent of Humford Mill Swimming Baths and they had lived for many years in the cottage next to the pool. The cottage was modernised a few years after the pool was closed in 1974, while they were tenants. The council wished to gain possession, not to carry out any work on the cottage, but because they had plans to redevelop the surrounding area, replacing the swimming pool with a paddling pool, a car park and a children's play area. The council intended that the whole area would become a country park. The cottage was needed to house a warden, as grants from the Countryside Commission were dependent on having a resident warden. The only construction planned was a doorway connecting the cottage to a new building which would provide facilities for the visitors to the country park. There was no evidence that this work could only be completed if Mrs Marley moved out.

The first question was whether Wansbeck District Council had the necessary intention. Purchas LJ said that the intention must be clearly defined and settled; he referred to Asquith LJ's judgment in *Cunliffe v Goodman*[87], although that case was considering the meaning of the word 'intention' in the context of s 18(1) Landlord and Tenant Act 1927. The principles in Asquith LJ's judgment were adopted by the House of Lords in *Betty's Cafes Ltd v Phillips Furnishing Stores Ltd*[88]. Asquith LJ said:

> 'An "intention" to my mind connotes a state of affairs which the party "intending" – I will call him X – does more than merely contemplate: it connotes a state of affairs which, on the contrary, he decides, so far as in him lies, to bring about, and which, in point of possibility, he has a reasonable prospect of being able to bring about, by his own act of volition ... This leads me to the second point bearing on the existence in this case of "intention" as opposed to mere contemplation. Not merely is the term "intention" unsatis-fied if the person professing it has too many hurdles to overcome, or too little control of events: it is equally inappropriate if at the material date that person is in effect not deciding to proceed but feeling his way and reserving his decision until he shall be in possession of financial data sufficient to enable him to determine whether the project will be commercially worthwhile. A purpose so qualified and suspended does not in my view amount to an "intention" or "decision" within the principle. It is mere contemplation until the materials necessary to a decision on the commercial merits are available and have resulted in such a decision.'[89]

The Humford Mill Development project was a 'rolling scheme' that would be altered and changed as work on the project progressed. There was no mention in the minutes of the District Council committee meetings of decisions affecting the cottage so no possession order was granted as the council had no settled and clearly

86  (1987) 20 HLR 247.
87  [1950] 2 KB 237, [1950] 1 All ER 720.
88  [1959] AC 20, [1958] 1 All ER 607, [1958] 2 WLR 513.
89  [1950] 1 All ER 720 at 723.

defined intention to carry out the work. Even if there was such an intention, the work planned was so minor that possession of the cottage was not required in order to do it.

If a tenant is moved out under Ground 10, 'home loss payments' under the Land Compensation Act 1973 s 29 can be claimed. The amount that can be claimed has recently been substantially increased[90].

## Charitable object – Ground 11

Ground 11 applies to pre-1988 Housing Act tenancies granted by housing associations which are registered as charities. The charity may house people of a recognised group, eg mothers with dependent children or people suffering from a mental illness. If the children grow up or the residents recover from their mental problems they will no longer fulfil the objects of the charity.

## Facilities for the disabled – Ground 13

The court in *Freeman v Wansbeck District Council*[91] considered, albeit in the context of the right to buy, which features make the dwelling-house 'substantially different from those of ordinary dwelling-houses and which are designed to make it suitable for occupation by a physically disabled person.' Mr and Mrs Freeman's daughter suffered from spina bifida. As she had difficulty climbing stairs the council converted the larder into an inside downstairs lavatory, under its powers in the Chronically Sick and Disabled Persons Act 1970. The local authority compared the house with other houses on the estate and argued that an inside lavatory downstairs was a 'special feature'.

The arguments of the local authority were rejected by Latey J sitting with Sir John Arnold P in the Court of Appeal in the following extract:

'The first question is whether the dwelling house concerned has features which are substantially different from those of ordinary dwelling houses; and the second question is whether, if such features exist, they are designed to make it suitable for occupation by physically disabled persons. The local authority contended before the judge that there were features in this house which fall within the ambit of para 3 as being substantially different from those of ordinary dwelling houses; and it says that the word "designed" means "intended" and that the downstairs lavatory, which it accepts is the only feature which could qualify under this paragraph, was intended to make the house suitable for occupation by physically disabled persons ...

I cannot find in para 3 of Pt 1 of Sch 1 anything to justify an approach of limiting the question whether or not a house has special features which are substantially different from those of ordinary dwelling houses, ... to draw comparisons merely with other houses locally. I do not believe that that is either the natural meaning of para 3 or was in any way intended by Parliament when one looks at the language which it has chosen.

---

90    The Home Loss Payments (England) Regulations 2003 SI 2003/1806 increase the amount of payments to tenants from £1,500 to £3,100.
91    [1984] 2 All ER 746.

If in fact there are no such features ... then of course that is the end of the case. But we have been asked to consider also the second limb, and that means what is meant by the word "designed"?

Of course the word "designed" is an ambiguous word ...but I think that light is thrown on its real meaning in this context when one looks at para 5(a) of Pt 1 of Sch1. Paragraph 5(a) reads as follows:

"... he shall so determine it satisfied – (a) that the dwelling-house is designed or specially adapted for occupation by persons of pensionable age ..."

I find it difficult to accept the contention of counsel for the local authority that "designed" means "intended" there when you read it in conjunction with the following words "or specially adapted". It seems to me that, using one's common sense, the meaning of that phrase [designed] is that the dwelling house was either built for occupation by persons of pensionable age or, if it was not so built, has been specially adapted, and that surely is talking in terms of structure.

... I think all becomes plain in this matter of interpretation if one exercises one's ordinary, everyday knowledge and regards the intention of the Act when it refers to features substantially different from those in ordinary dwelling houses as the sort of features we are all familiar with, such as ramps, specially widened doors, lifts, cooking surfaces at special heights for people who cannot stand up and do their cooking sitting down, and the like. At the end of it all one asks oneself this question: how (and I hope I do not put it too highly) in the name of common sense does the installation of one, small, rather cramped downstairs lavatory wholly incapable of accommodating a wheel-chair fit in with what the Act envisages? The answer, in my judgment, is that it does not by any stretch of the imagination.'[92]

# SUITABILITY OF THE ALTERNATIVE ACCOMMODATION

## HOUSING ACT 1985

## Schedule 2

## Grounds For Possession of Dwelling-Houses Let Under Secure Tenancies

### PART IV

### SUITABILITY OF ACCOMMODATION

1. For the purposes of section 84(2)(b) and (c) (cases in which court is not to make an order for possession unless satisfied that suitable accommodation will be available) accommodation is suitable if it consists of premises—

---

[92] At p 747.

(a)   Which are to be let as a separate dwelling under a secure tenancy, or

(b)   Which are to be let as a separate dwelling under a protected tenancy, not being a tenancy under which the landlord might recover possession under one of the Cases in Part II of Schedule 15 to the Rent Act 1977 (cases where court must order possession); or

(c)   which are to be let as a separate dwelling under an assured tenancy which is neither an assured shorthold tenancy, within the meaning of Part I, Housing Act 1988, nor a tenancy under which the landlord might recover possession under any of the Grounds 1–5 in Schedule 2 to that Act.

and, in the opinion of the court, the accommodation is reasonably suitable to the needs of the tenant and his family.

2. In determining whether the accommodation is reasonably suitable for the needs of the tenant and his family, regard shall be had to—

(a)   The nature of the accommodation which it is the practice of the landlord to allocate to persons with similar needs;

(b)   The distance of the accommodation available from the place of work or education of the tenant and of any members of his family;

(c)   Its distance from the home of any member of the tenant's family if proximity to it is essential to that member's or the tenant's well-being;

(d)   The needs (as regards extent of accommodation) and means of the tenant and his family;

(e)   The terms on which the accommodation is available and the terms of the secure tenancy;

(f)   If furniture was provided by the landlord for use under the secure tenancy, whether furniture is to be provided for use in the other accommodation, and if so the nature of the furniture to be provided.

## Private sector comparison

Unlike the private sector[93] the availability of suitable accommodation is not per se a ground for possession. Another difference between public and private housing is that the character of the proposed accommodation ie the age of the property, the social standing of the area is not one of the factors considered when deciding whether it is suitable.

## Suitable for the tenant and the rest of the family

The accommodation must be suitable for the tenant and the rest of the family as well. In *Wandsworth London Borough Council v Fadayomi*[94] a husband and wife who were in the throes of divorce proceedings were offered alternative accommodation. The council recognised their need for separate accommodation and several offers of accommodation on this basis were refused. When the application for a possession order on Ground 10 came to court, as the tenancy was in Mr Fadayomi's sole name, Mrs Fadayomi's views were not sought and she was not represented. Mr Fadayomi consented for the whole family to move to alternative accommodation together.

Parker LJ said:

---

93   Rent Act 1977 s 98(1)(a) and the Housing Act 1988 Sch 2 Pt II, Ground 9.
94   [1987] 3 All ER 474, [1987] 1 WLR 1473, (1988) 19 HLR 512.

'It is apparent from that, in my view, that every member of the tenant's family living in the premises is a person with a potential interest in any possession proceedings. He may not in many cases desire to advance any such interest, but it is abundantly apparent, in view of the terms of this provision, that any member of the family who considers that the accommodation is unsuitable because it is too far from his place of work or too far from some other member of the family to whom it is essential he should live in close proximity may be able to advance that if he so wishes. It might well be the case that the tenant himself does not wish to raise the matter, and this section can only work in the event that the tenant does not wish to raise it if the person who has the potential right, on the wording of these provisions, himself is allowed to be joined in order to raise it.'[95]

The possession order that had been granted in the lower court was set aside as Mrs Fadayomi's interests had not been considered.

## Meaning of 'suitable alternative accommodation'

A case which turned on the interpretation of 'suitable alternative accommodation' is *London Borough of Enfield v French*[96]. The tenant was under-occupying a flat that he had obtained by succession from his mother. The council sought possession on Ground 16 and had to show that suitable alternative accommodation was available and that it was reasonable for the court to grant a possession order. The council offered him alternative accommodation which he had refused because it lacked a garden. At his present flat he had turned a wilderness into a beautiful garden with a greenhouse, a pond and an aviary. The questions posed were, whether the list of factors in Pt IV, para 2 which must be taken into account when deciding whether the accommodation was suitable, was an indicative or an exhaustive one and the interpretation of the 'needs' of the tenant (Sch 2, para 2(d)).

Stephenson LJ[97]:

'The question of what is meant by "the needs of the tenant" is not, I think, an altogether easy one to decide. Mr Stephenson[98], for the landlords, has put his case in two ways. I think that the judge may also have been putting it in two ways which were different and inconsistent. The first is to regard the tenant's need for a garden in which to pursue his hobbies as not the kind of need which is referred to in the statute, and when the judge said in a passage which I should have read at the end of what he said when he was dealing with alternative accommodation, namely, "the alternative accommodation is reasonably suitable for the needs of the defendant – all his needs," that is the view he seems to have adopted. He is satisfied that all the needs of the tenant will be met, and I think that can only mean that he was regarding the need to pursue the tenant's hobbies in the garden as a need which was so insignificant as not to be the kind of need which was contemplated in the Act …

---

[95] [1981] 3 All ER 474 at 478.
[96] (1984) 17 HLR 211.
[97] At p 216.
[98] Rather confusingly counsel for the respondents was Mr G Stephenson and the case was heard before Stephenson LJ.

The other way of considering the matter is to suppose that the garden, and the tenant's use of it, are a need of the tenant. ... the standard and quality of a tenant's life has to be considered in the sense that the needs of the whole man have to be considered, and that it would be wrong to narrow them down simply from the considerations which I have put forward, or any other considerations, so as to exclude such a requirement, even if it is not an essential requirement, as this tenant's need to indulge his hobbies in his garden.

But, says Mr Stephenson, even if that view of the tenant's life in the garden, so to speak, is regarded as a need, what the court has to do is to consider whether the alternative accommodation – in this case, 14 Manisty Court – is reasonably suitable for his needs; and in considering that, the court is entitled to find that the alternative accommodation is reasonably suitable for those needs even if it does not meet every one of them; and the way in which Mr Stephenson asks us to uphold the judgment on this view of needs and of the evidence, is that this alternative accommodation was reasonably suitable for the tenant's needs as a whole, even though it did not meet this particular need, and indeed deprived him of the chance of satisfying at any rate most of it ...

If I had to choose between the two views, I think I would hold that it is right to regard the need for a garden and the pursuit of these hobbies in this case, as a need of the tenant; but taking that view, I am unable to say that the judge was wrong, or made any error of law or misdirected himself, in taking it into account, but in holding that it was outweighed by other considerations and by the fact, as the judge found, that all his other needs would be met by the alternative accommodation.'

Whether a possession order granted under Sch 2, Ground 16 can be challenged if, when considering the requirement of reasonableness, the judge did not specifically consider the tenant's Article 8 rights, (the right to respect for his home) was discussed in *Newham London Borough Council v Neal*[99]. The Court of Appeal refused permission for Mr Neal to bring a second appeal against a possession order granted to Newham forcing him to move from the four-bedroom property that he was occupying alone to a one-bedroom flat. The judge held the flat was suitable for Mr Neal's needs and had taken into account that the four-bedroom house had been his home.

## OTHER RIGHTS OF SECURE PUBLIC SECTOR TENANTS

So far in this chapter the major right of local housing authority tenants, that of security of tenure, has been discussed. The other rights in the 'Tenants' Charter' introduced in 1980 include the rights to take lodgers, to succeed to a tenancy, to be provided with information and to be consulted, with the major one being the right to buy. The National Consumer Council survey published in 1976, *Tenancy Agreements*, found that 93 per cent of the council tenancy agreements included in the survey prohibited lodgers and nearly all prohibited sub-letting. The prohibition on

---

[99] [2003] EWCA Civ 541, (2003) Legal Action Aug 30.

taking lodgers was lifted, although sub-letting is not forbidden it results in the tenancy ceasing to be secure, this is governed now by s 93 Housing Act 1985.

## Prohibition on assignment

In general council tenants do not have the freedom to assign (ie transfer) their tenancy. Section 91(1) Housing Act 1985 lays down that a secure tenancy is 'not capable of being assigned' apart from the three exceptions in s 91(3). If tenants had an unfettered right council tenancies could be assigned to those who were not in need. The right to buy has taken much former council property out of public ownership and complete freedom to assign would exacerbate the problem of the shortage of affordable publicly owned housing. Although the property would still be owned by the local housing authority it would not be available for people waiting to be rehoused.

Attempting to circumvent the bar on assignment by executing a 'deed of release' by one joint tenant thereby (it was hoped) leaving the tenancy in the hands of the remaining tenant was held to be ineffective in the House of Lords case of *Burton v Camden London Borough Council*[100]. Two women, B and H, shared a three-bedroom flat with H's young son for two years on a joint tenancy. H then bought another property and moved out leaving B alone in the flat. B applied to Camden for an increase in her housing benefit to cover the full rent. The council was not willing to grant her a sole tenancy of so large a flat as there were many families waiting in temporary accommodation. They, therefore, tried to persuade B to move to a one-bedroom flat but she refused. An assignment of the tenancy by H to B was prohibited by s 91(1) so B signed 'a deed of release' and then sought a declaration that she was the sole tenant. Lord Nicholls of Birkenhead said:

> 'Whatever precise form of words was chosen, this transaction would ordinarily be regarded as a transfer of Miss Hannawin's rights in the flat to Miss Burton. Miss Hannawin was passing over her interest to Miss Burton. As a matter of conveyancing this transfer could be achieved by one of two means: either by a deed of assignment (*"Miss Burton and Miss Hannawin hereby assign the tenancy to Miss Burton"*) or by a deed of release (*"Miss Hannawin hereby releases her estate and interest in the property to Miss Burton"*). Each would achieve the same result. In each case the legal estate in the tenancy, formerly held by the two of them, would become vested in one of them. It cannot be that s 91(1) bites or not according to which of these two conveyancing modes is used. That would make no sense.'[101]

Section 91(3) Housing Act 1985 lists the three exceptions. The first is an exchange with another local authority or housing association tenant which accords with s 92 of the Act. Both tenants must obtain written consent from their respective landlords and any rent arrears must be paid. Consent can only be withheld on one of the grounds listed in Sch 3. Clause 168 Housing Bill 2003 will insert a new Ground 2A into Sch 3 which would prohibit exchange if one of a range of court orders had been

---

[100] [2000] 2 AC 399, [2000] 1 All ER 943, [2000] 2 WLR 427, (2000) 32 HLR 625.
[101] [2000] 1 All ER 943 at 946.

made against the tenant for anti-social behaviour. The second exception is a transfer as a result of a property adjustment order after divorce or certain other family proceedings[102].

Lastly the tenant is allowed to assign to a person who would be qualified to succeed[103] if the tenant had died just before the assignment. An advantage of an assignment to a successor, rather than waiting for succession on the death of the tenant, is that Sch 2 Ground 16 does not apply to assignees. A successor can be deprived of a secure tenancy under Ground 16 and provided with alternative accommodation if the property is larger than reasonably required but an assignee in identical circumstances is safe from possession proceedings. To be legally binding the assignment must be by deed[104]. In *Camden London Borough Council v Goldenberg*[105] Mrs Goldenberg executed a deed of assignment of the flat where she lived transferring the tenancy to her grandson. She then moved into a nursing home. The majority of the Court of Appeal thought that the grandson showed that he fulfilled the residence requirements in s 87 Housing Act 1985 and so the assignment was valid.

The necessity for a deed when assigning a tenancy to a potential successor is shown by the harsh case of *London Borough of Croydon v Buston and Triance*[106]. Mr Triance's mother had a secure tenancy of a council house for seven years. She went to live with her new husband leaving her son in sole occupation. The tenancy ceased to be secure as the house was no longer Mrs Buston's 'only or principal home'; a contractual tenancy remained in existence. The son argued that as he had lived with his mother from time to time over the previous two years he was eligible to succeed to the tenancy. Although Mr Triance requested the council for an assignment, had consulted a solicitor about the matter and his mother wanted to assign the house to him, nothing was put in writing. The council were doubtful whether the house had been Mr Triance's only or principal home for the previous 12 months. The Court of Appeal held that no assignment took place; in order to assign the property a deed must be executed and as that did not happen a possession order was upheld. The Court did think, however, that if Mr Triance showed that he would have qualified this would be relevant when the council were fulfilling their duties to Mr Triance as a homeless person with a priority need.


# SUCCESSION


## HOUSING ACT 1985

*Succession on death of tenant*

### 87.  **Persons qualified to succeed secure tenant**

(1) A person is qualified to succeed the tenant under a secure tenancy if he occupies the dwelling-house as his only or principal home at the time of the tenant's death and either—

---

[102]  S 24 Matrimonial Causes Act 1973 and Sch 1 para1(2)(d)–(e) Children Act 1989.
[103]  S 87 Housing Act 1985.
[104]  S 52 Law of Property Act 1925.
[105]  (1996) 28 HLR 727.
[106]  (1991) 24 HLR 36.

(a)  he is the tenant's spouse, or

(b)  he is another member of the tenant's family and has resided with the tenant throughout the period of twelve months ending with the tenant's death;

unless, in either case, the tenant was himself a successor, as defined in section 88.

88.  (1) The tenant is himself a successor if—

(a)  the tenancy vested in him by virtue of section 89 (succession to a periodic tenancy), or

(b)  he was a joint tenant and has become the sole tenant, or

(c)  the tenancy arose by virtue of section 86 (periodic tenancy arising on ending of term certain) and the first tenancy there mentioned was granted to another person or jointly to him and another person, or

(d)  he became the tenant on the tenancy being assigned to him (but subject to subsections (2) and (3)), or

(e)  he became the tenant on the tenancy being vested in him on the death of the previous tenant.

(2) A tenant to whom the tenancy was assigned in pursuance of an order under section 24 of the Matrimonial Causes Act 1973 (property adjustment orders in connection with matrimonial proceedings) is a successor only if the other party to the marriage was a successor.

(3) A tenant to whom the tenancy was assigned by virtue of section 92 (assignments by way of exchange) is a successor only if he was a successor in relation to the tenancy which he himself assigned by virtue of that section.

(4) Where within six months of the coming to an end of a secure tenancy which is a periodic tenancy ('the former tenancy') the tenant becomes a tenant under another secure tenancy which is a periodic tenancy, and—

(a)  the tenant was a successor in relation to the former tenancy, and

(b)  under the other tenancy either the dwelling-house or the landlord, or both, are the same as under the former tenancy,

the tenant is also a successor in relation to the other tenancy unless the agreement creating that tenancy otherwise provides.

89.  (1) This section applies where a secure tenant dies and the tenancy is a periodic tenancy.

(2) Where there is a person qualified to succeed the tenant, the tenancy vests by virtue of this section in that person, or if there is more than one such person in the one to be preferred in accordance with the following rules—

(a)  the tenant's spouse is to be preferred to another member of the tenant's family;

(b)  of two or more other members of the tenant's family such of them is to be preferred as may be agreed between them or as may, where there is no such agreement, be selected by the landlord.

## Who is 'family'?

Section 113 Housing Act 1985 defines family quite widely to include a man and a woman living as husband and wife and a range of blood and step relations but does not extend to cousins. The Court of Appeal held in *Michalak v Wandsworth London Borough Council*[107] that the range of relatives in s 113 was an exhaustive list so

---

[107]  [2002] EWCA Civ 271, [2002] HLR 721.

more distant family members could not succeed to the tenancy. Mr Michalak also based his case on the Human Rights Act 1998 Art 8[108]. In another case, based on Art 8, a challenge was made by a family member who did not meet the conditions to succeed to a tenancy. Collins J in *R (on the application of Mays) v Brent London Borough Council*[109] dismissed the case stating that the requirements for succession that Parliament had enacted would be frustrated if individual circumstances had to be taken into account in all cases[110].

At the moment 'family' in s 113 does not include gay and lesbian relationships, neither are same sex couples regarded as spouses. This will be changed if the Civil Partnership Bill 2004 comes into effect. The Bill was preceded by a consultation paper, 'Civil Partnership: A Framework for the Legal Recognition of Same-Sex Couples', which was published in June 2003. The following November the report, *Responses to Civil Partnership* was published[111]. 'Family' in s 113 Housing Act 1985 will extend to civil partners and same sex couples who live together 'as if they were civil partners'[112] similarly after 'spouse' in s 87(a) Housing Act 1985 will be inserted 'or civil partner'. It is only same-sex partners that will be able to register as a civil partnership, unlike the earlier, unsuccessful Private Member's Bill[113], that would also have allowed registration of heterosexual partners who did not wish to go through the formalities of marriage. Gay rights campaigners are critical of the Civil Partnership Bill as it gives homosexual couples who register a civil partnership fewer rights than those of a married heterosexual couple. Their campaign has been bolstered by the House of Lords majority decision in *Ghaidan v Godin-Mendoza*[114], where the gay partner of a deceased Rent Act tenant was able to succeed to the tenancy as a 'spouse'. A same-sex relationship was covered by the words 'as his or her wife or husband'. By para 2(2) of Sch 1 to the Rent Act 1977 such a person was to be treated as the spouse of the original tenant. The earlier case of *Fitzpatrick v Sterling Housing Association*[115] was over-ruled on this point. In *Fitzpatrick* the survivor of a gay relationship was able to succeed on the basis of being a member of the tenant's family but not as being equivalent to the tenant's spouse[116].

The Law Commission Report, *Renting Homes*, has recommended that there should continue to be a statutory succession scheme. Spouses, 'broadly defined', other members of the family and *carers* would be able to succeed. Apart from 'spouses' the successor would be required to have lived in the property for a certain length of time[117]. Members of a person's family are defined in s 113 of the Housing Act 1985.

## Members of a person's family

113.   (1) A person is a member of another's family within the meaning of this Part if—

(a)   he is the spouse of that person, or he and that person live together as husband and wife, or

---

[108] See Chapter 14.
[109] [2003] All ER (D) 12 (Mar).
[110] See Chapter 14.
[111] Both the Consultation Paper and the Report were published by the Women and Equality Unit, www.womenandequalityunit.gov.uk.
[112] Civil Partnership Bill 2004 Sch 8 cl 27(2).
[113] Civil Partnership Bill 2001, a Private Member's Bill introduced by Lord Lester of Herne Hill, 2001.
[114] [2004] UKHL 30, [2004] 3 WLR 113.
[115] [2001] 1 AC 27, [1999] 4 All ER 705, [1999] 3 WLR 1113.
[116] For a more detailed discussion see Chapter 11 and Chapter 14.
[117] Law Commission Report, *Renting Homes*, 284 para 3.76, November 2003.

(b)   he is that person's parent, grandparent, child, grandchild, brother, sister, uncle, aunt, nephew or niece.

(2) For the purpose of subsection (1)(b)—

(a)   a relationship by marriage shall be treated as a relationship of blood,
(b)   a relationship of the half-blood shall be treated as a relationship of the whole blood
(c)   the stepchild of a person shall be treated as his child, and
(d)   an illegitimate child shall be treated as the legitimate child of his mother and reputed father.

## Can a minor succeed to a tenancy?

Whether a minor can succeed to a secure tenancy was addressed in *Kingston upon Thames Borough Council v Prince*[118]. When the tenant died his daughter, Wendy Prince, had lived with him for only six months, but her daughter Marie, aged 13, had lived with her grandfather for three years. Marie, it was asserted, fulfilled the succession conditions in s 87 of the Housing Act 1985. The local authority brought possession proceedings arguing that minors could not hold a legal estate in land and so could not succeed to a tenancy. The Court of Appeal rejected the local authority's argument and found that minors were capable of being 'persons' in housing law. Moreover, a minor could hold an equitable tenancy in any property, including a council house. Applying these principles to the case it upheld the county court judge who had decided that Wendy Price would hold the tenancy in trust for Marie until she was 18. The tenancy would be regarded as beginning on the date of Mr Prince's death. In the later case of *Newham London Borough Council v Ria*[119] the Court of Appeal upheld the county court judge's declaration that a child of 15 had succeeded in equity to the tenancy and her aunt would hold the legal estate until the child was 18.

## Residence

The 12-month residence requirement in s 87(b) Housing Act 1985 does not have to be met by the two family members having lived together in the *same* property throughout that period. In *Waltham Forest London Borough Council v Thomas*[120] the defendant had lived for two and half years with his brother. First they lived in one council house, and ten days before his brother's death they moved to another. The brother was the sole tenant of both houses. When the council sued for possession the defendant argued that he fulfilled the residence requirements of s 87. A unanimous House of Lords overruled *South Northamptonshire District Council v Power*[121] and held that it did not require the residence to have been in the same house for the whole 12-month period. The position is different in the private sector where the successor is required to reside with the deceased tenant 'in the dwelling house'[122].

---

[118]   [1999] 1 FLR 593, (1999) 31 HLR 794.
[119]   [2004] EWCA Civ 41.
[120]   [1992] 2 AC 198, [1992] 3 All ER 244, [1992] 3 WLR 131.
[121]   [1987] 3 All ER 831, [1987] 1 WLR 1433.
[122]   Rent Act 1977 s 2(1)(a).

Lord Templeman:

> 'My Lords, s 87 does not stipulate that the successor must have resided at a particular house for 12 months but only that he should have resided with the deceased tenant for that period. The effect of s 87 is to ensure that a qualified member of the tenant's family who has made his home with the tenant shall not lose his home when the tenant dies but shall succeed to that home and to the secure tenancy which protected both the tenant and the successor while the tenant was alive and which shall continue to protect the successor after the death of the tenant. In order to qualify, a successor must have resided with the tenant during the period of 12 months ending with the tenant's death ... .
>
> When a tenant and a potential successor move from one council house to another the tenant does not lose the protection of a secure tenancy and there is no good reason why the potential successor should lose the protection which he has obtained or is in the course of obtaining under s 87 ... . It frequently happens that a daughter lives with a widowed parent for 20 years or more; if the parent changes council houses or moves from the private sector to a council house within one year of the death of the parent then on the death of the parent the council house will be the home which contains all the furniture and other articles which form part of the home and have been fitted into the council house by the parent and the daughter. It would be cruel if the daughter could be evicted and left to find another home for herself and for her belongings simply because of the accident of the untimely death of the parent within one year. In the absence of express language, s 87 should not be construed in a manner which can only, as in the present case, produce unwelcome and unjustifiable distress and hardship in the event of an untimely death.'[123]

The effect of periods away interrupting the 12-month residence period was discussed in *Camden London Borough Council v Goldenberg*[124]. The Court of Appeal held that when deciding whether a period of absence breaks the continuity of the 12 months' residence the court must look at the nature and extent of the continuing connection with the premises and the quality of the intention to return. Mrs Goldenberg's grandson, Adam Bloom, lived with her when he arrived in Britain from Israel in 1985. He stayed four years, returning to Israel in 1989. In April 1991 he came back to London and lived with his grandmother again. He married in February 1992 but he and his wife could not afford their own accommodation in London. They 'house-sat' for a couple of months for some friends who were abroad and then lived apart as Adam moved back to his grandmother's flat. In November 1992 she executed a deed assigning the tenancy to him.

The question was whether the period of 'house-sitting' broke the 12 months' residence requirement. During the 'house-sitting' episode his grandmother's flat remained his postal address and most of his possessions were kept there so he was able to show a continuing connection with the premises. The main difficulty was his intention, after the 'house-sitting' was over, to move to a flat with his wife if a suitable one could be found. As his income was low, in reality he could scarcely

---

[123] [1992] 3 All ER 244 at 246 para d.
[124] (1996) 28 HLR 77.

afford any accommodation in London so it was held that he had the intention to return to his grandmother's flat unless something unexpected turned up. Nothing did, so he moved in with his grandmother again. The Court of Appeal, by a majority, allowed the grandson's appeal and held that he could succeed to his grandmother's tenancy.

## One succession only rule

Only one succession is allowed, so, if the deceased was himself a successor, no further succession is possible, s 87 Housing Act 1985. 'Successor' is defined in s 88 and includes surviving joint tenants. It does not include tenancies assigned by exchange with another council or housing association tenant, or those assigned under the provisions in the Matrimonial Causes Act 1973.

So, for example, whether a tenancy begins by being a sole tenancy in the name of the husband or a joint tenancy held by husband and wife, on the husband's death it can pass to the widow. On the widow's death it cannot pass to the children even if they fulfil the residence requirements. If, on the other hand, the tenancy passed to the wife under the Matrimonial Causes Act 1973 after a divorce, one of the children can succeed to the tenancy on the mother's death.

For the effects of intestacy on the succession rules an instructive case is *Epping Forest District Council v Pomphrett*[125]. Mr Pomphrett senior, who lived with his family in a council house, had the tenancy solely in his name. When he died in 1978, without leaving a will, no letters of administration were applied for, but his widow wrote to the council asking for the tenancy to be transferred to her name and the council agreed to 'formally transfer' the tenancy to her. On intestacy a tenancy vests in the President of the Family Division who, however, has no power to deal with it but can receive notices to quit. The family continued to live in the house until their mother's death in 1985. The two adult children who had lived there all their lives applied to succeed to the tenancy. The plaintiff council refused, arguing that this would constitute a second succession and therefore would be forbidden under s 87 Housing Act 1985. The council applied for a possession order but failed: when the mother became a tenant this was, in effect, a new tenancy because the father's legal estate in his periodic tenancy had vested in the President of the Family Division. As the mother had a 'new tenancy' and the children would be the first successors to this tenancy they would not be caught by the 'one succession only' rule.

## Introductory tenancies and succession

Members of the family can succeed to an introductory tenancy under s 133 Housing Act 1996. The conditions are identical to those for secure tenancies. If there is no-one qualified to succeed to the tenancy it ceases to be classed as 'introductory'.

[125]  (1990) 22 HLR 475.

## LODGERS AND SUB-LETTING

Before 1980, many public sector tenancy agreements forbade taking in lodgers even with the permission of the local authority. If lodgers were allowed there was frequently an extra item added to the rent, 'a lodger charge'. Lodgers are licensees who have permission to use the property but, as they do not have exclusive possession, they are not sub-tenants. If a tenant sub-lets the premises the security of tenure is lost and the landlord can serve a notice to quit. As was seen in the cases on the interpretation of 'only or principal home' in s 81 Housing Act 1985, there is a fine line between informally sub-letting premises and asking someone to act as a caretaker during a prolonged absence[126].

Whether a sub-tenancy has been created depends on whether the hallmarks of a tenancy are present rather than on the intentions of the tenant. In *Brent London Borough Council v Cronin*[127] the tenant was disabled and went to stay with his sister-in-law. He orally agreed with a young couple for them to occupy his flat while he was away. They paid him a deposit and £40 rent a week. The judge decided that as the tenant was confused and it was only a temporary arrangement, a sub-tenancy had not been created. The judgment was over-turned on appeal as all the elements of a sub-tenancy were present, the couple were unaware of the temporary nature of the arrangement. Sections 93 and 94 of the Housing Act 1985 deal with the issue:

93. **Lodgers and sub-letting**

(1) It is a term of every secure tenancy that the tenant—

(a)  may allow any persons to reside as lodgers in the dwelling-house, but
(b)  will not, without the written consent of the landlord, sublet or part with possession of part of the dwelling-house.

(2) If the tenant under a secure tenancy parts with the possession of the dwelling-house or sublets the whole of it (or sub-lets first part of it and then the remainder), the tenancy ceases to be a secure tenancy and cannot subsequently become a secure tenancy.

94. **Consent to sub-letting**

(1) This section applies to the consent required by virtue of section 93(1)(b) (landlord's consent to subletting of part of dwelling-house).

(2) Consent shall not be unreasonably withheld (and if unreasonably withheld shall be treated as given), and if a question arises whether the withholding of consent was unreasonable it is for the landlord to show that it was not.

(3) In determining that question the following matters, if shown by the landlord, are among those to be taken into account—

(a)  that the consent would lead to overcrowding of the dwelling-house within the meaning of Part X (overcrowding);
(b)  that the landlord proposes to carry out works on the dwelling-house, or on the building of which it forms part, and that the proposed works will affect the accommodation likely to be used by the sub-tenant who would reside in the dwelling-house as a result of the consent.

---

[126] *Hussey v Camden London Borough Council* (1994) 27 HLR 5; *Ujima Housing Association v Ansah* (1997) 30 HLR 831; *Amoah v Barking and Dagenham London Borough Council* [2001] All ER (D) 138.
[127] (1997) 30 HLR 43.

(4) Consent may be validly given notwithstanding that it follows, instead of preceding, the action requiring it.

(5) Consent cannot be given subject to a condition (and if purporting to be given subject to a condition shall be treated as given unconditionally).

(6) Where the tenant has applied in writing for consent, then—

(a)  if the landlord refuses to given consent, it shall give the tenant a written statement of the reasons why consent was refused, and

(b)  if the landlord neither gives nor refuses to give consent within a reasonable time, consent shall be taken to have been withheld.

## REPAIRS AND IMPROVEMENTS

### Repairs

Many council tenancy agreements were one-sided before 1980: they gave lists of the tenant's obligations but made no mention of the landlord's obligations, including those of repairing the property. *Liverpool City Council v Irwin*[128] is a graphic example of the former poor position of tenants – in this case tenants of a problematic estate in Liverpool where the corporation took on no obligations to repair in the tenancy agreement. The House of Lords implied terms governing repairs, as they felt that the test of necessity had been met.

The Housing Act 1985, s 96 originally allowed secure tenants to recover the costs of certain repairs from the local authority after the work had been done by the tenants themselves or by building contractors that they had employed. As few tenants exercised this right the scheme was abandoned and replaced by s 121 of the Leasehold Reform, Housing and Urban Development Act 1993 which substituted s 96 Housing Act 1985. This enables secure tenants to apply to have 'qualifying' repairs, such as faults in the electrical, gas or water systems, carried out. 'Qualifying repairs' are listed in the Secure Tenants of Local Housing Authorities (Right to Repair) Regulations 1994[129]. The landlord must then issue a notice giving the details of the repairs, the recommended contractor and the date the work must be completed. The tenant can claim compensation if the repairs are not finished on time.

### Improvements

Improvements, which are defined in s 97(2) of the 1985 Act, require the landlord's consent (ss 98 and 99). If the improvements have added to the value of the property or the rent the landlord could charge, the landlord may recognise this with an appropriate payment (s 100) at the end of the tenancy. For improvements begun after 1 April 1994, the compensation for improvements is governed by the Leasehold Reform, Housing and Urban Development Act 1993 s 122.

The Housing Act 1985 deals with these matters at ss 96–99.

96.  **Right to have repairs carried out**

---

[128]  [1977] AC 239, [1976] 2 WLR 562, [1976] 2 All ER 39.
[129]  SI 1994/133.

(1) The Secretary of State may make regulations for entitling secure tenants whose landlords are local housing authorities, subject to and in accordance with the regulations, to have qualifying repairs carried out, at their landlord's expense, to the dwelling-houses of which they are such tenants.

(2) The regulations may make all or any of the following provisions, namely—

(a) provisions that, where a secure tenant makes an application to his landlord for a qualifying repair to be carried out, the landlord shall issue a repair notice
   (i) specifying the nature of the repair, the listed contractor by whom the repair is to be carried out and the last day of any prescribed period, and
   (ii) containing such other particulars as may be prescribed;

(b) provision that, if the contractor specified in a repair notice fails to carry out the repair within a prescribed period, the landlord shall issue a further repair notice specifying such other listed contractor as the tenant may require; and

(c) provision that, if the contractor specified in the repair notice fails to carry out the repair within a prescribed period, the landlord shall pay the tenant such sum by way of compensation as may be determined by or under the regulations.

...

## 97.  Tenant's improvements require consent

(1) It is a term of every secure tenancy that the tenant will not make any improvement without the written consent of the landlord.

(2) In this Part 'improvement' means any alteration in, or addition to, a dwelling-house, and includes—

(a) any addition to or alteration in landlord's fixtures and fittings,
(b) any addition or alteration connected with the provision of services to the dwelling-house,
(c) the erection of a wireless or television aerial, and
(d) the carrying out of external decoration.

(3) The consent required by virtue of subsection (1) shall not be unreasonably withheld, and if unreasonably withheld shall be treated as given.

(4) The provisions of this section have effect, in relation to secure tenancies, in place of section 19(2) of the Landlord and Tenant Act 1927 (general provisions as to covenants, &c. not to make improvements without consent).

## 98.  Provisions as to consents required by section 97

(1) If a question arises whether the withholding of a consent required by virtue of section 97 (landlord's consent to improvements) was unreasonable, it is for the landlord to show that it was not.

(2) In determining that question the court shall, in particular, have regard to the extent to which the improvement would be likely—

(a) to make the dwelling-house, or any other premises, less safe for occupiers,
(b) to cause the landlord to incur expenditure which it would be unlikely to incur if the improvement were not made, or
(c) to reduce the price which the dwelling-house would fetch if sold on the open market or the rent which the landlord would be able to charge on letting the dwelling-house.

(3) A consent required by virtue of section 97 may be validly given notwithstanding that it follows, instead of preceding, the action requiring it.

(4) Where a tenant has applied in writing for a consent which is required by virtue of section 97—

(a)   the landlord shall if it refuses consent give the tenant a written statement of the reason why consent was refused, and

(b)   if the landlord neither gives nor refuses to give consent within a reasonable time, consent shall be taken to have been withheld.

## 99.   **Conditional consent to improvements**

(1) Consent required by virtue of section 97 (landlord's consent to improvements) may be given subject to conditions.

(2) If the tenant has applied in writing for consent and the landlord gives consent subject to an unreasonable condition, consent shall be taken to have been unreasonably withheld.

(3) If a question arises whether a condition was reasonable, it is for the landlord to show that it was.

(4) A failure by a secure tenant to satisfy a reasonable condition imposed by his landlord in giving consent to an improvement which the tenant proposes to make, or has made, shall be treated for the purposes of this Part as a breach of the tenant of an obligation of his tenancy.

## RIGHT TO BE CONSULTED

Local authorities have been under a limited duty, since 1980, to consult their secure tenants on 'housing management' matters. One of the most persistent criticisms of public housing authorities had been their paternalism on matters such as taking in lodgers and not allowing improvements to be made to the houses. This was especially acute in the lack of consultation with tenants over general environmental matters and area development plans. Section 105 gives authorities a fair amount of discretion over the matters about which they consult their tenants and the way that the consultation is organised. No detailed consultation mechanisms are laid down as s 105(1) merely states that the local authority 'shall maintain such arrangements as it considers appropriate'.

An early case which illustrates how limited the consultation duty is in practice is *Short v London Borough of Tower Hamlets*[130]. Ms Short, a secure tenant, was complaining about the lack of consultation with the tenants of the Waterlow Estate in Bethnal Green over the borough's plans to sell the estate to a private developer. It was agreed by the Court of Appeal that the tenants could have obtained an injunction if such a sale was taking place without consulting the tenants. However, the authority had decided to carry out a marketing exercise as a preliminary stage in looking for a buyer. It was argued by the authority and upheld by the court that that exercise would not substantially affect the tenants on the estate. The decision by the council's Development Committee to carry forward the sale of the whole estate and to abandon repair and rehabilitation of the properties was not regarded as a matter of housing management which was covered by s 105.

Ralph Gibson LJ, when he gave his reasons[131], said that three requirements had to satisfied, in the opinion of the local authority concerned, before a plan could be regarded as 'a matter of housing management' in s 105(2). First, it had to relate to the management, maintenance, improvement or demolition of the dwelling-houses

---

[130]   (1985) 18 HLR 171.
[131]   (1985) 18 HLR 171 at 184.

or to the provision of services or amenities in connection with them. The repair or redevelopment of the Waterlow Estate clearly fulfilled that requirement. Secondly, the 'matter' must be 'a new programme of maintenance, improvement or demolition or a *change* in the practice or policy of the authority'. Lastly he said that the matter must be, in the opinion of the local authority, 'likely substantially to affect its secure tenants as a whole or a group of them'. A decision in principle to sell did not come within the last two requirements. It was only when it was implemented that these requirements would have been met. The word 'implemented' was to be implied into s 105(3) and therefore judgment was given to the local authority. The addition of the word 'implemented' into s 105(3) gives a very restricted duty on local authorities to consult. It is hard for tenants to make their views known if the decisions have already been taken and it is only at the implementation stage that they are to be consulted.

The methods to be used to consult tenants are not laid down by statute, there is no requirement that a formal ballot should be conducted or if the local authority do organise a ballot that each estate should vote separately. In *R v Hackney London Borough Council, ex p Bourbour*[132] a tenant complained that there should have been a separate ballot for each estate when there was a plan to dispose of six estates. Buxton LJ held that the method of consultation was a matter for the authority.

When a local housing authority wishes to transfer their housing stock to a new owner the information given to their tenants should comply with the Code of Recommended Practice on local authority publicity[133]. It must be informative rather than persuasive and must not be issued close to a local election. Munby J held, in a case where two Camden tenants challenged, by way of judicial review, the authority's proposal to set up an 'Arm's-length Management Organisation' (ALMO) to raise money to improve the housing stock in the borough that it was for the Secretary of State and not the court to decide whether the information distributed by a local authority complied with the Code[134]. The authority sent its tenants information on the proposal including the arguments against it. The tenants thought that the information should be balanced and the counter arguments should have been given greater force. It was held that the obligation on local authorities in s 105(1) is to inform tenants of the proposals and there was no legal requirement that the case against the local authority should be included.

### 105. Consultation on matters of housing management

(1) A landlord authority shall maintain such arrangements as it considers appropriate to enable those of its secure tenants who are likely to be substantially affected by a matter of housing management to which this section applies—

(a)  to be informed of the authority's proposals in respect of the matter, and
(b)  to make their views known to the authority within a specified period;

and the authority shall, before making any decision on the matter, consider any representations made to it in accordance with those arrangements.

(2) For the purposes of this section, a matter is one of housing management if, in the opinion of the landlord authority, it relates to—

---

[132]  June 2000 *Legal Action* 24.
[133]  Available at www.odpm.gov.uk.
[134]  *R (Beale and Carty) v Camden London Borough Council* [2004] EWHC 6 (Admin).

(a) the management, maintenance, improvement or demolition of dwelling-houses let by the authority under secure tenancies, or

(b) the provision of services or amenities in connection with such dwelling-houses;

but not so far as it relates to the rent payable under a secure tenancy or to charges for services or facilities provided by the authority.

(3) This section applies to matters of housing management which, in the opinion of the landlord represent—

(a) a new programme of maintenance, improvement or demolition, or

(b) a change in the practice or policy of the authority,

and are likely substantially to affect either its secure tenants as a whole or a group of them who form a distinct social group or occupy dwelling-houses which constitute a distinct class (whether by reference to the kind of dwelling-house, or the housing estate or other larger area in which they are situated).

(4) In the case of a landlord authority which is a local housing authority, the reference in subsection (2) to the provision of services or amenities is a reference only to the provision of services or amenities by the authority acting in its capacity as landlord of the dwelling-houses concerned.

(5) A landlord authority shall publish details of arrangements which it makes under this section, and a copy of the documents published under this subsection shall—

(a) be made available at the authority's principal office for inspection at all reasonable hours, without charge, by members of the public, and

(b) be given, on payment of a reasonable fee, to any member of the public who asks for one.

…

# RIGHT TO BUY

## Who has the right to buy?

Only secure tenants have the right to buy[135] so the tenancies listed in Sch 1 Housing Act 1985 (tenancies taken by employees, students, almshouse residents etc) are outside the scheme. Tenancies of specially designed or adapted homes for the elderly or disabled also do not carry the right to buy[136]. The Office of the Deputy Prime Minister published a consultation paper in May 2004 suggesting a revision of the guidance on the exemption which is given in the Department of Environment Circular 13/93[137]. A secure tenant must have had a two-year qualifying period living in a public sector rented property as his only or principal home; it is, however, possible for the tenant to move from one secure tenancy to another and remain eligible[138]. Clause 157 Housing Bill 2003 increases the qualifying period from two years to five years to prevent exploitation of the rules by property developers and tenants. This change to the length of the qualifying period is based on research, published in January 2003, which was carried out on behalf of the Office of the Deputy Prime

[135] Housing Act 1985 s 118(1).
[136] Housing Act 1985 Sch 5 paras 6–10, see also *Freeman v Wansbeck District Council* [1984] 2 All ER 746, (1983) 10 HLR 54.
[137] Office of the Deputy Prime Minister, *Exemption from the Right to Buy of dwellings that are particularly suitable for occupation by elderly persons*, Consultation Paper, May 2004.
[138] Housing Act 1985 s 119 and Sch 4.

Minister by Heriot-Watt University[139]. It estimated that between 1998 and 2002, six per cent of the homes, sold under Right to Buy in inner London, had been bought by companies in conjunction with tenants, solely for speculative purposes.

Sections 118 and 119 of the Housing Act 1985 deal with the right to buy.

### 118. The right to buy

(1) A secure tenant has the right to buy, that is to say, the right, in the circumstances and subject to the conditions and exceptions stated in the following provisions of this Part—

    (a) if the dwelling-house is a house and the landlord owns the freehold, to acquire the freehold of the dwelling-house;

    (b) if the landlord does not own the freehold or if the dwelling-house is a flat (whether or not the landlord owns the freehold), to be granted a lease of the dwelling-house.

(2) Where a secure tenancy is a joint tenancy then, whether or not each of the joint tenants occupies the dwelling-house as his only or principal home, the right to buy belongs jointly to all of them or to such one or more of them as may be agreed between them; but such an agreement is not valid unless the person or at least one of the persons to whom the right to buy is to belong occupies the dwelling-house as his only or principal home.

### 119. Qualifying period for right to buy

(1) The right to buy does not arise unless the period which, in accordance with Schedule 4, is to be taken into account for the purposes of this section is at least two years.

(2) Where the secure tenancy is a joint tenancy the condition in subsection (1) need be satisfied with respect to one only of the joint tenants.

## Market value and discounts

The value is the price that the dwelling house would raise if it was sold on the open market on the date that the tenant serves a notice claiming the right to buy[140]. Any increase in value because of improvements made by the tenant is disregarded; equally any failure by the tenant to keep the property in good repair has no effect on the valuation[141]. The discount is on a sliding scale. For a house it currently runs from 32 per cent plus 1 per cent for each complete year by which the qualifying period exceeds two years, up to a maximum of 60 per cent. For a flat, it runs from 44 per cent plus 2 per cent for each additional qualifying year up to a maximum of 70 per cent. Since 1999 the discounts have been capped at a cash limit varying by region, from £22,000 in the North East to £38,000 in London and the South East. In addition, regulations[142] made under s 131(2) and (3) Housing Act 1985, which came into effect on 27 March 2003, set a lower maximum discount of £16,000 in 41 local authority areas (mainly in the south east) where there is acute housing pressure. The Housing Bill 2003 cl 157 lays down, that although the amount of the discount will be the same as the current entitlement, the discount will only apply after a five-year qualifying period. The new sliding scale, therefore, will run from 35 per cent for houses and from 50 per cent for flats and be subject to the same maximum percentages.

Tenants cannot make a quick profit by purchasing their homes at a discount and then selling for the full market price. The purchaser must repay the discount if the

---

[139] www.odpm.gov.uk.
[140] Housing Act 1985 s 126.
[141] Ibid s 127(1)(b).
[142] Housing (Right to Buy) (Limits on Discount) (Amendment) Order 2003 SI 2003/498.

property is sold[143]. Currently the time period is within three years, the amount of the claw-back reducing by one-third for each complete year since the conveyance[144]. By cl 162 Housing Bill 2003 the three-year period will be increased to five.

## Procedure for right to buy

In order to exercise the right to buy the tenant must first serve a written notice[145], in the prescribed form[146], on the landlord. The landlord must then serve a written notice, within four weeks, either admitting the right to buy or denying it and if denying it, stating the reasons for the denial[147]. It is possible for the tenant to challenge a denial of the right in the county court[148]. If the landlord agrees to the right to buy or the tenant mounts a successful challenge the landlord must serve a second notice which includes the purchase price and all the other contractual terms[149]. On receiving the landlord's second notice the tenant must then serve a written notice of intent within 12 weeks. Providing all is in order the landlord must complete within 12 months of the date of the landlord's second notice[150]. The Housing Bill 2003 cl 161 will reduce this 12-month period to three months.

## FURTHER READING

Cattermole, R, 'Introductory Tenancies and the Human Rights Act' [2002] Journal of Housing Law 7.

Cunningham, M and Moroney, L, 'Use it or lose it' [2003] Adviser Jan/Feb 10 (Residence conditions for secure and assured tenancies).

Cunningham, M, 'Pass it on', [2003] Adviser May/June 8 (succession rights).

Law Commission, *Renting Homes 1: Status and Security, CP 162,* Consultation Paper, April 2002.

Law Commission, *Renting Homes 2: Co-occupation, Transfer and Succession,* CP 168 , Consultation Paper, August 2002.

Law Commission, *Renting Homes*, Report 284, November 2003.

Office of the Deputy Prime Minister *Exemption from Right to Buy of dwellings that are particularly suitable for occupation by elderly persons*, Consultation Paper, May 2004.

Office of the Deputy Prime Minister *The Impact of Overcrowding on Health and Education* (a review of existing evidence on the impact of overcrowded housing on people's health and education) May 2004.

Smith, NJ and George, GA, 'Introductory Tenancies: a nuisance too far?' [1997] Journal of Social Welfare and Family Law 19(3) 307–320.

---

[143] Housing Act 1985 s 155.
[144] Ibid s 155(2).
[145] Ibid s 122(1).
[146] Housing (Right to Buy) (Prescribed Forms) Regulations 1986 SI 1986/2194 as amended.
[147] Housing Act 1985 s 124.
[148] Ibid s 181.
[149] Ibid s 125 as amended.
[150] Ibid s.140(2).

# CHAPTER 9

# Keeping the Peace on our Estates

'Bad' behaviour and 'bad relations' between neighbours affecting whole areas of housing are *not* confined to socially provided housing, although media attention and ministerial comment on the matter might well give that impression. Bad behaviour is, moreover, an issue that is bedevilled with problems such as what exactly is meant by the concept, and to what extent it is legitimate for landlords to intervene in the conduct of their tenants when such controls are not applicable to those who live in the owner-occupied sector. Even so, the issue is one that has attracted increasing attention from the 1980s onwards. To aid understanding, the following definitions are put forward.

- 'Bad neighbour relations' is a blanket term wide enough to cover a range of issues, from quite serious inter-neighbour disputes over boundaries and the control of property through to situations where people simply find aspects of their neighbours' behaviour unacceptable, such as thoughtlessly banging car doors late at night, or not keeping a garden tidy.

- 'Anti-social behaviour' is a rather more focused concept, and can be seen as deviant behaviour which may be criminal, or which at least leads to an unacceptable disruption of the enjoyment of a person's life or home. That concept has clearly informed the thinking of the framers of the Crime and Disorder Act 1998, who define anti-social behaviour in terms of 'harassment, alarm or distress' caused by a person to others. Thus in 1992 a long-running dispute between two teenagers on a council estate and a resident there led to the death of the latter – bad relations at its most extreme form. At the other end of the scale, work carried out in the early 1990s for the Institute of Housing discovered that 25 per cent of tenants' grievances generally concerned the behaviour of other tenants, covering issues as diverse as general household noise and loud music, pet nuisances, especially fouling by dogs, vandalism and graffiti, noise from children playing outside, parking disputes and disputes concerning the doing of car repairs. Most inter-neighbour grievances fall into this group, but there are others of a more worrying nature, such as property damage and intimidation, drink and drug abuse and racial disputes[1].

---

[1]    Karn, V, Lickiss, R, Hughes, D and Crawley, J, *Neighbour Disputes: Responses by Social Landlords* (1993) Institute of Housing.

The dividing line between the two concepts outlined above is not easy to draw. Very roughly, anti-social behaviour is that which departs from societally accepted norms, and it may well be defined in terms of moral disapproval and the allocation of blame and responsibility. Such a process may well be characterised by the use of words such as 'guilt' or 'guilty', 'responsibility', 'unacceptable' etc in descriptions of the behaviour in question, either by those experiencing it, or those who have to deal with it. One problem, however, is that what can start as a simple issue of bad relations between neighbours can develop into anti-social behaviour, as relationships between the parties deteriorate in a spiral of complaint, allegation, counter-allegation and vindictiveness.

While low level inter-neighbour disputes are best dealt with at an estate level by mediation schemes, more aggravated behaviour may require recourse to legal procedures such as eviction, injunctions and anti-social behaviour orders, and in this sense anti-social behaviour as a general concept has come to embrace a range of situations extending beyond the definition given by the 1998 legislation to behaviour which falls within the parameters of 'nuisance or annoyance' for the purposes of possession proceedings; see further below[2].

Initial attempts in the 1980s to confront the problem of unacceptable behaviour between neighbours arose in the context of racial disputes. Following the enactment of the Housing Act 1980 which gave, as has been discussed in the foregoing chapter, security of tenure to, inter alia, council tenants, it was no longer possible for local authorities simply to evict those who were guilty of unacceptable behaviour; their conduct had to be sufficiently severe to satisfy a court that it would be reasonable to grant a possession order either on grounds of breach of tenancy conditions or for acts of nuisance or annoyance against neighbours.

By the late 1980s a number of arguments could readily be cited as justification, or legitimisation, for intervention by an authority in a case of racially motivated bad behaviour by one tenant against another: evidence that victims of racial harassment frequently suffer repeat attacks; the fact that the home of the victim is frequently the focus of the attack; the severe psychological effects experienced by victims; the seriously worrying nature of the perpetrator's motivation which, even though expressed as a series of minor acts, nevertheless betokens a hate-inspired frame of mind, so that the bad behaviour is driven by a desire to make a person or family suffer solely on the basis of their race.

Nevertheless, initial attempts to deal with such behaviour by means of possession actions appear to have been somewhat less than successful. So, for example, of seven early possession actions in London taken on the basis that racially motivated misconduct breached either a condition of the tenancy or contravened the 'nuisance' ground of possession in Sch 2 to the Housing Act 1985, three resulted in 'immediate' orders for possession, two in suspended orders and two in refusals of orders[3]. The evidence, admittedly largely anecdotal, now shows it has become rather easier for local authorities to obtain possession in racially motivated tenant

---

[2]  Hughes, D, Karn, V and Lickiss, R, 'Neighbour Disputes, Social Landlords and the Law' [1994] JSWFL 201.
[3]  See, generally, Forbes, D, *Action on Racial Harassment* (1988) Legal Action Group.

harassment cases. Possession has been obtained, for instance, in cases in Birmingham and Leicester where tenants, or their families, engaged in overtly racist bad behaviour against their immediate neighbours. Many authorities also now include quite extensive clauses in their tenancy agreements specifically banning such behaviour.

The focus of attention then also widened so as to encompass racially motivated bad behaviour and other forms of disorder – noise, drug dealing, prostitution, breach of the peace, intimidation etc. To an extent this was prompted by media interest in the issue, particularly in the light of incidents on council estates, especially the death, alluded to earlier, of Edna Phillips in July 1992.

The media and politicians make much use of tendentious language such as 'neighbours from hell', which can have the effect of demonising whole sectors of society, for it obscures the fact that the vast majority of tenants are law-abiding (as are the vast majority of owner occupiers). There is, moreover, no nationwide empirical evidence in England and Wales as to the scale of the problem, or its nature. Media coverage and anecdotal evidence, expressions of concern from tenants' organisations and maladministration investigations by the Commission for Local Administration suggest there is a problem of bad behaviour, but what is its nature and how far is this confined to council estates, or to council tenants? The signal lack of hard investigative evidence did not, however, prevent the development of the law!

The pace of development with regard to anti-social behaviour issues quickened throughout the 1990s. In part this appears to have been attributable to media interest already referred to, in some part to ministerial involvement, in part to concern among officials of the Department of the Environment (DoE) (now the Office of the Deputy Prime Minister, ODPM), certainly at regional levels, and in part to concerns voiced by local government officers. Amongst those concerned, either as local or central government officers, with the administration of housing there grew a realisation that the increasing marginalisation of council estates, and the residualisation of the council tenancy as a form of tenure, was having the effect of creating areas where there could be concentrations of people variously vulnerable to the bad behaviour of others, and/or easy prey for drug dealers, and/or likely because of aspects of their personalities, family circumstances or particular needs to become the focus of complaints by others, for example families with children, those discharged from care under the care in the community policy, etc.

## THE CURRENT SITUATION UNDER THE HOUSING ACT 1996

By the mid-1990s there was a considerable body of opinion that the law should be recast so as to give local authorities in their capacity as landlords enhanced powers to deal with instances of tenant bad behaviour. Ministers took the opportunity to legislate on the issue in the Housing Act 1996, considerably widening the grounds on which possession can be sought, and providing a new legislative base for injunctive relief. Schedule 2 to the Housing Act 1985, as subsequently amended under the 1996 Act, provides as follows.

# Schedule 2

# Grounds for possession of dwelling-houses let under secure tenancies

## PART I

## GROUNDS ON WHICH COURT MAY ORDER POSSESSION IF IT CONSIDERS IT REASONABLE

*Ground 1*

Rent lawfully due from the tenant has not been paid *or an obligation of the tenancy has been broken or not performed.* [Emphasis provided.]

*Ground 2*

The tenant or a person residing in or visiting the dwelling-house—

(a) has been guilty of conduct causing or likely to cause a nuisance or annoyance to a person residing, visiting or otherwise engaging in a lawful activity in the locality, or
(b) has been convicted of—
    (i)   using the dwelling-house or allowing it to be used for immoral or illegal purposes, or
    (ii)  an arrestable offence committed in, or in the locality of, the dwelling-house.

## Comment

Tenancy agreements often contain clauses to control the activities and behaviour of the tenants in the property and the surrounding area. Clauses commonly found in local authority tenancy agreements cover matters such as the keeping of animals, the parking of trucks and caravans, the repair of cars and (in recent years) racist, sexist and homophobic harassment, as well as prohibitions on using property for criminal activities such as drug dealing and the handling of stolen goods. Loud music played regularly into the early hours and other noisy activities may also be caught by clauses in the agreements.

When asked by a landlord to make a possession order for the breach of a tenancy condition the court must, as has already been considered in the foregoing chapter, consider whether it is reasonable to make an order. It is for the landlord to prove the reasonableness of granting an order, but where there is an admitted breach of covenant and an intention to continue the breach a landlord is refused possession only in a very special case. In *Green v Sheffield City Council*[4] the court made a possession order on the ground of breach of the tenancy agreement which forbade the keeping of dogs. Mr Green had kept a dog for many years and wished to continue keeping a dog. In contrast, the tenant in *Wandsworth London Borough*

---

[4]   (1993) 26 HLR 349.

*Council v Hargreaves*[5] had allowed petrol bombs to be made in the flat by someone who was visiting. One was thrown out of the window, and a fire causing damage costing £14,000 started from some petrol spilt in the flat. The tenant had to move out for 15 months whilst the flat was repaired. The Court of Appeal refused to overturn the county court judge's decision not to grant a possession order as all the circumstances had been considered. The tenant had not taken an active part in the events leading to the fire and there had been no problems since he returned to the flat so it would not be reasonable to make an order.

Under the 1996 amendments to the 1985 Act, the 'nuisance' ground of possession was also altered to apply not just to tenants and those residing in a tenant's dwelling, but also to the conduct of those *visiting* the dwelling. Even more importantly, conduct capable of grounding a possession proceedings was redefined as that causing *or likely to cause* a nuisance or annoyance to *a person residing, visiting or otherwise engaging in a lawful activity in the locality of the dwelling*. In addition, the nuisance ground was further extended so that not only can a local authority landlord seek possession where the conduct in question consists of a conviction of using the dwelling or allowing it to be used for immoral or illegal purposes, but also where the conduct consist of conviction for an arrestable offence in or near *the locality* of the dwelling.

These were very considerable changes to the law, clearly indicating that the conduct in question was to be viewed objectively, so that protestations of 'I did not mean to be offensive', or 'I did not realise I was being offensive' should be set aside. They also put beyond doubt the practice of using 'professional witnesses' to give evidence in nuisance ground possession actions: for example, using housing officials as witnesses to overcome the problem of residents in affected areas being too fearful to come forward as witnesses. The amendments further enabled authorities to take action where it is their own staff who have been the victims of bad behaviour by tenants as those staff have sought to go about their lawful estate management functions. Though the 1996 amendments are not without their own problems of interpretation (for example, the meaning of 'locality' – an issue to both which the courts and central government have now given some attention, see below), overall they have certainly enhanced the powers of local authorities to deal with bad behaviour by tenants, their families and associates, and, in the present author's experience, they have been widely welcomed by authorities. However, an authority is not bound to take action against tenants who misbehave. In *Hussain v Lancaster City Council*[6] a shopkeeper who was racially abused was unsuccessful when he attempted to force Lancaster City Council to take action, as the court decided that the local authority was not liable to him in either nuisance or negligence.

It should further be noted that the 1996 amendments extended the geographical area within which action may be taken in respect of bad behaviour. In the original Bill the description was 'in the vicinity of a dwelling-house'. This was changed to the wider 'in the locality of' the dwelling-house.

---

[5]   (1994) 27 HLR 142.
[6]   (1998) 31 HLR 164.

The changes also enabled action to be taken in respect of those committing certain offences. Arrestable offences committed in, or in the locality of, the dwelling-house have been added to convictions of using the dwelling-house or allowing it to be used for immoral or illegal purposes. Arrestable offences, which are defined in s 24 of the Police and Criminal Evidence Act 1984, include offences with fixed penalties at law and those for which adults can be imprisoned for five years or more. So offences range from taking a vehicle without the owner's consent (TWOC) to criminal damage, theft, burglary, assaults occasioning bodily harm and drug dealing. This extension enables local authorities to take action against drug dealing taking place in the common parts of an estate, whereas they had previously been limited to taking action only if dealing was taking place inside a house or flat.

The notions of 'locality' and who may be 'neighbours' have also been addressed. Department of Environment, Transport and the Regions Circular 2/97 describes 'the locality' as the common parts of an estate. Some judicial guidance on the ambit of 'locality' can be gathered from *Manchester City Council v Lawler*[7]. In an action for possession under Grounds 1 and 2 of Sch 2 to the Housing Act 1985, the council applied for injunctions. The tenant gave six undertakings. The undertakings were breached; one specific breach was relied on. This occurred when Lawler threatened an 11-year-old child with a knife in the local shopping centre three streets from her home. The question was whether she was in contempt of court and should therefore be committed to prison. The undertakings forbade certain activities 'in the locality of …'. At first instance it was held that injunctions should be worded precisely and the terms of the undertakings were unclear. On appeal it was held that three streets from the tenant's home could constitute the 'locality'. The Court of Appeal held that the extent of the locality was a matter that the court could determine as a matter of fact.

In *Northampton Borough Council v Lovatt*[8] a tenant, his wife and family had been dispossessed after serious bad behaviour on the estate where they lived. Mrs Lovatt had a conviction for breaching the peace on the estate, Mr Lovatt used the house for the improper purpose of running a car maintenance and repair business, and they failed to control their sons who had 11 convictions for offences against persons or property on the estate. One tenant had been subject to harassing behaviour and had been forced to leave her home; there had also been incidents of racial abuse and threats to a local head teacher. There was clear evidence of 'bad behaviour' but the Lovatts sought to appeal against their dispossession on the basis that acts of nuisance or annoyance committed away from their home could not, *as the law stood before 1996*, be 'nuisance or annoyance' for the purposes of Ground 2 of Sch 2 to the Housing Act 1985 as the affected persons were not 'neighbours'.

The majority in the Court of Appeal (Henry and Chadwick LJJ) rejected that argument. Though quite clear that the obvious intention of Parliament to extend the ambit of tenant's liability under the proposals that became the 1996 Act could not of itself be a guide to what Parliament had intended under the 1985 Act, Henry LJ did

[7]   (1998) 31 HLR 119.
[8]   (1997) 30 HLR 875.

dwell at some length on the proposed changes. Furthermore, he was able to rely on, and develop, the pre-existing case law to come to a very extensive conception of who may be a tenant's 'neighbour'.

Henry LJ argued:

'All adjoining occupiers are neighbours, but not all neighbours are adjoining occupiers. Neighbours is a wider word, and was intended to be – I agree with the editors of *Woodfall on Landlord and Tenant* that the intention was to avoid "arid disputes as to proximity". It is clearly intended to cover all persons sufficiently close to the source of the conduct complained of to be adversely affected by that conduct. In these days of amplified music, there is force in G K Chesterton's observation:

"Your next-door neighbour ... is not a man; he is an environment."

Next [it was argued] that the conduct complained of must emanate from the demised premises. [It was argued] that most nuisances consist of unreasonable use by an occupier, and so such a limitation should be read into the Act ...There is no warrant for reading the first part of Ground 2 as if after the word "conduct" the qualifying words "at the dwelling-house" were read in. There would be no sense in a law which prevented you from playing your music at maximum volume in the middle of the night from your home but permitted you to walk round your neighbourhood with your "ghetto-blaster" at full pitch.

This example leads conveniently to the next submission. [It was contended] that Ground 2 is concerned with landlord and tenant "and the use to which the tenant puts the demised premises".

In my judgment, the restriction is not limited to his use of the premises, but his conduct in the neighbourhood, as the above example suggests ...

The trial judge found that the purpose of the relevant legislation affecting Ground 2 was to protect the local authority's interest in the Spencer Estate, and its efficient and economic management ...

With a public sector landlord, the case is a fortiori, as they are responsible for the quality of life of public sector tenants who will include many who are needy, vulnerable, isolated and probably without the ability to move from housing made a misery by the conduct of neighbours ...'

The result of that case was that while the test of who may be a neighbour requires some element of proximity in its formulation, that test is not based solely on questions of geographical proximity.

Indeed the 'test' is in reality a question of fact in each case, bearing in mind the ordinary usages and understanding of the word 'neighbour'. Chadwick LJ was also clearly swayed in his decision by the fact that the Lovatts' behaviour transgressed obligations in their tenancy agreement (which, of course, enabled their landlords to seek possession under Ground 1 of Sch 2 to the 1985 Act as well as under Ground 2). One of these obligations in particular forbade racial abuse and aggression 'within the neighbourhood'. Turning to the *Oxford English Dictionary,* Chadwick LJ discovered that 'neighbourhood' is defined in terms of people living near to or within a certain range of a place; people forming a community; a district or part of a town which is a relatively self-contained sector. On that basis he was additionally able to determine that the 'neighbourhood' in this case was the entire estate and its immediate surrounds. 'Neighbours' must thus be those people who live in that area.

The extent to which it is proper for a landlord to use housing powers to control behaviour also arose in *Lovatt.* Counsel for the tenants stressed that covenants in tenancy obligations are not intended to operate as instruments of social control entitling landlords (even local housing authorities) to evict tenants simply because they are in some way socially unacceptable. Both Henry and Chadwick LJJ dealt with this contention in a creative and novel way which does much to legitimise the use of a social landlord's powers in such circumstances.

Henry LJ, as we can see from the foregoing extract from his judgment, rejected arguments that a landlord is only concerned with a tenant's conduct insofar as it arises from the use to which the tenant puts the dwelling, largely on grounds of utility.

Nevertheless he stressed that there must be a link between a tenant's behaviour and the fact of residence in the area:

'That link is the legitimate interest the landlord has in requiring their tenants to respect the neighbourhood in which they live and the quiet enjoyment of their homes by those who live there ... [V]andalism ... racial abuse ... driving offences, and ... burglaries ... are all attacks on the neighbourhood and those who live there. All would damage the quality of life on the estate. All would increase the cost to the community of trying to keep the peace on the estate. All were legitimate concerns of the local authority as landlord ...'

Chadwick LJ adopted the same line of reasoning, laying much stress on the factual background which should have been clear to both landlord and tenant:

'The Council was the local housing authority ... the dwelling house was part of the Council's Spencer Estate ... there were, or were likely to be, many other Council tenants on the Spencer Estate ...the Council's tenants ... were likely to include many who were needy, vulnerable, isolated and probably without the ability to move from housing made a misery by the conduct of others ... it was likely to be in the interests of all tenants on the Estate that there should be some obligation, enforceable by the Council, as a safeguard against nuisance ...'

He subsequently continued:

'Ground 2 [of Sch 2 to the 1985 Act] has been included for the protection of the Council. The Council requires protection in this respect not because the conduct is a direct cause of nuisance or annoyance to it in its own enjoyment of neighbouring property or because the conduct damages its interest in the reversion of the demised premises; but because ...those who live or work on a Council Estate and are affected by the conduct of Council tenants on that estate will expect the Council to do something about it. The housing department will receive complaints which will have to be addressed. That will take management time and will cost money. Further, the Council will find it much the more difficult to relocate other applicants in need of housing into properties on an estate which is perceived to be out of control.'

Indeed, Chadwick LJ went on to opine that in respect of its estates, persons may fairly regard a local authority as being responsible for amenities, and quality of life issues such as freedom from harassment. He further added that while the provisions of the Housing Act 1985 are not intended for use as an instrument of social control outside the relationship of landlord and tenant, within that relationship they do provide such a means of control. To the thinking of Chadwick LJ the relevant provisions reflected a particular social policy: on the one hand they give tenants rights they could never enjoy at common law, but on the other social policy clearly indicates that landlords should be able to dispossess tenants in particular situations. Whether or not the landlord has included anti-nuisance requirements in the tenancy agreements as contractual obligations, where nuisances occur the landlord should be able to recover possession under the statute.

The Court of Appeal established not just the legitimacy of the use of housing powers in cases of bad behaviour by tenants and their families, but also that the behaviour which can fall within the concepts of 'nuisance' or 'annoyance' is not just confined to bad behaviour in the dwelling house in question, but will extend to bad behaviour throughout the neighbourhood in which the dwelling, possession of which is sought, is situated. The principal constraints on a landlord's powers are that they must still show that the conduct in question constituted nuisance or annoyance, or some other relevant criminal activity arising out of the use and occupation of the dwelling, and that it is reasonable for the court to grant possession.

Judicial guidance is also available at to the *type* of behaviour which may fall within the ambit of a social landlord's power of control.

Complaints of abusive and foul language were sufficient in *Woking Borough Council v Bystram*[9] for a suspended possession order to be granted to the local authority. The judge at first instance had thought that bad language was 'no doubt very much a common experience in certain areas' and refused a possession order; the decision was, however, reversed in the Court of Appeal.

In addition even before the extension and clarification of the law in 1996 the Court of Appeal had made it clear that tenants could be found liable for the bad behaviour of their children where that amounted to a breach of tenancy agreement or a nuisance towards neighbours.

A single parent tenant in *Kensington and Chelsea Royal London Borough Council v Simmonds*[10] contended that she had not breached the terms of her tenancy agreement because she could not be said to have 'allowed' her 13-year-old son to racially abuse her Pakistani neighbours. Clause 22 of her tenancy agreement with the council forbade 'The tenant ...allow[ing] members of his household to commit

9   [1993] EGCS 208.
10   (1996) 29 HLR 507.

any act ... cause offence to any other tenant ...by, reason of his race, colour, ethnic origin or nationality'. Simon Brown LJ said (at p 511):

> '[Clause 22] ... No doubt the tenant here could not properly have been found to have "allowed" Adam [her son], say, to racially abuse the Ahmeds had he merely done so once ... out of the blue. I am far from persuaded, however, that the judge's findings, which I have already quoted, even assuming (which I respectfully doubt) they are to be regarded as acquitting the appellant of all personal responsibility in this matter, preclude a finding that she allowed Adam to misconduct himself. The plain fact is that over a period of months she signally failed to prevent it.
>
> It seems to me wholly inappropriate and unnecessary for the court in a case such as this to embark upon a detailed analysis of the tenant's parenting skills or a day-to-day analysis of whether she could or could not more successfully have sought to discipline and control her son. In my judgment there was ample basis here for the judge's conclusions that ... clause 22 [was] breached. That of course founds statutory ground 1.'

Simon Brown LJ then turned to whether there was a case for possession under Ground 2.

> 'The essential submission in this regard is that, nevertheless, before any possession order could ever properly be made pursuant to this ground, the plaintiffs would have had to prove some particular degree of personal fault on the tenant's own individual part. In the case of nuisance and annoyance occasioned by an ill-disciplined and uncontrollable child in the age bracket of, say, 12 to 15 years (as in this case) namely, a case concerning a child too old to control but too young to put out of the house, that may well be impossible. The parents of such a child [it was argued], cannot in the result be dispossessed under this legislation.
>
> I would firmly reject this argument. To my mind, it finds no support in the authorities or in common sense or in justice ...
>
> As to the justice of the position, it must be remembered that not only are the interests of the tenant and her family here at stake; so too are the interests of their neighbours. It would in my judgment be quite intolerable if they were to be held necessarily deprived of all possibility of relief in these cases, merely because some ineffectual tenant next door was incapable of controlling his or her household ...
>
> Of course I accept that the extent, if any, of personal blame on the tenant's part is a relevant consideration in determining whether or not a possession order should reasonably be made and the terms of any such order. To assert, however, as a proposition of law that a lack of personal blame is necessarily decisive seems to me nothing short of absurd ...
>
> I would unhesitatingly dismiss this appeal.'

It should not be assumed, however, that bad behaviour on the part of a member of a tenant's family will *always* lead to possession being granted. In *Bryant v Portsmouth City Council*[11] the defendant was an elderly lady in ill health who was the tenant of the respondent local housing authority. She had been the tenant of a dwelling house on a council estate under a secure tenancy since 1970. In 1987 she became the guardian of her two grandsons. In the ensuing years the behaviour of her grandsons was such as to cause considerable nuisance and annoyance to her neighbours. There was, however, no suggestion that the defendant herself had acted in such a way, or that she had encouraged her grandsons' anti-social behaviour. In 1997 the local authority served a notice of possession upon the defendant under s 83 of the Housing Act 1985. The notice stated that the claimant sought possession of the property on, inter alia, the ground that the tenant or persons residing in or visiting the dwelling house had been guilty of conduct causing a nuisance or annoyance to persons residing, visiting or lawfully trading in the locality pursuant to Ground 2 of the Sch 2 to the Act. In 1999 (when the grandsons were aged 15 and 17 respectively) the authority commenced possession proceedings in respect of the property under s 84 of the Act. The district judge made an order for possession against the defendant, suspended in accordance with the terms and conditions of the tenancy agreement until April 2001. That order was upheld on appeal to a circuit judge. The circuit judge held that the terms of Ground 2 of Sch 2 to the Act were satisfied because the authority had proved that the grandsons had behaved in the way alleged regardless of the defendant's knowledge of the behaviour or what she could have done about it. The defendant appealed. On appeal it was argued, inter alia, that the circuit judge had erred in construing Ground 2 of Sch 2 to the Act as he had done and that the effect of such a construction was to create strict or absolute liability on the part of the defendant.

The Court of Appeal held that the condition for granting a possession order as specified in Ground 2 of Sch 2 to the Act was satisfied notwithstanding that a tenant had no personal knowledge of the nuisance caused by persons residing in or visiting the property in question or that there had been no personal fault on the part of the tenant for it. However, that did not create strict or absolute liability on the part of the tenant. It did not automatically follow that a possession order would be made if those residing at the tenant's property were found to have caused a nuisance because a judge had a discretion whether or not to make such an order under s 84 of the Act. When deciding whether an order should be made, the extent of the personal knowledge or blame on the part of the tenant was a relevant consideration. The court also had to balance the interests of the tenant (and their family) with those of the neighbours, because it would be intolerable if the neighbours were deprived of all relief due to an ineffectual tenant who was unable to control the actions of those residing or visiting their property. In the instant case, there being no dispute as to the behaviour complained of, given that the defendant had allowed her grandsons to act in that way and had closed her mind to the reality that her grandsons were out of control, the possession order had been rightly made pursuant to Ground 2 of Sch 2.

[11]    (2000) 32 HLR 906; see also *Darlington Borough Council v Sterling* (1996) 29 HLR 309, *West Kent Housing Association Ltd v Davies* (1998) 31 HLR 415 and *Newcastle upon Tyne City Council v Morrison* (2000) 32 HLR 891.

Another case where the application for a possession order was based partly on the acts of visitors to the property was *London Borough of Camden v Gilsenan*[12] where Camden relied on Ground 1 (rent arrears) and Ground 2 of Sch 2 to the Housing Act 1985. The tenant allegedly had frequently caused or permitted visitors to cause severe nuisance to her neighbours because of loud music, drunkenness, rubbish thrown from balconies and even wounding in a machete attack. Camden obtained an 'unless' order: that unless Gilsenan committed no further nuisance she would be prevented from defending in the possession order proceedings. Further nuisance occurred so she was unable to defend, but at the hearing her solicitors produced a letter requesting reasonableness and stating that she undertook to refrain from further nuisance; nevertheless the possession order was granted. On appeal the possession order was upheld.

The Court of Appeal has also signalled that, in cases of serious misbehaviour, it will not give great weight to an argument that making a possession order would be unreasonable as it would result in the tenant's homelessness. In *Bristol City Council v Mousah*[13] the local authority had let a house to Mousah in November 1993. Four months later they served a notice to quit after complaints of noise and nuisance. A few days earlier the police had searched the house as it was suspected that it was being used for drug dealing, and they arrested six people who were using cocaine. Another police search was carried out in June 1994 and a further six people were arrested for using crack cocaine. The authority served a notice of possession proceedings a few days later. Nevertheless, during a further police drugs raid in August crack cocaine was again found and two people were arrested. Mousah was not present during any of these police raids. Possession proceedings based on rent arrears and that the tenant or people living in the house had been guilty of conduct which was a nuisance to neighbours (Housing Act 1985, s 83 and Sch 2, Grounds 1 and 2) were started in November 1994.

By the time the case came to court in October 1995 Mousah argued that it would not be reasonable to make a possession order as he could not be held responsible for the acts of nuisance. He was not at the premises during any of the police searches as he spent time staying with his three dependent families. Also a considerable period of time had elapsed since the last incident and, lastly, he was schizophrenic and therefore vulnerable. At the trial the order was refused, on the grounds that if it was granted Mousah would become homeless, and with his medical condition might become dangerous. Mousah's psychiatrist gave evidence that eviction would have an adverse affect on his mental health.

In granting the appeal by Bristol City Council, Beldam LJ said:

> '... it is now well settled that this Court will only interfere with a discretion-
> ary decision on rare occasions, where, for example, a Judge has misdirected
> himself, where he has taken into account matters which he ought not to have
> taken into account, or where he has failed to take account of matters which he
> should have taken into account. In this case I am satisfied that the Assistant
> Recorder based his decision on matters which he ought not to have taken into

---

[12]   (1998) 31 HLR 81.
[13]   (1997) 30 HLR 32.

account. It seems to me that, whilst he was perfectly entitled to consider the effect which an order for possession would have, it was wrong for him to become so involved with the possible outcome of an application by the respondent under [homelessness legislation].

Evidence has been given by the appropriate housing officer that, if the respondent applied, his application would be dealt with on its merits. That, in my view, was all that the Judge could properly take into account. Equally it seems to me the Judge paid regard to the fact that, since August 1994, the respondent had not been found to have been in breach of covenant and, in particular, Condition 24, or to have committed any offence at these premises. He regarded that as a substantial time. But the truth of the matter was that a large portion of the time was attributed to the fact that the respondent was in breach of the Court's orders for delivery of his defence, and, in any event, this was not simply an isolated occasion on which someone had been found with a small quantity of a Class B drug in the premises …

This was a case in which there had been a most serious offence committed over a period of three or four months at these premises, and, as I have said, the lapse of time since the last occasion was largely due to the failure of the respondent (or those who were representing him) to comply with the requirements of the Court …

Where there is such a serious breach of a condition of the tenancy, it is only in exceptional cases that it could be said that it was not reasonable to make the order …

The public interest, in my view, is best served by making it abundantly clear to those who have the advantage of public housing benefits that, if they commit serious offences at the premises in breach of condition, save in exceptional cases, an order for possession will be made. The order will assist the housing authority who, under section 21 of the Act, have the duty to manage the housing stock and have the obligation to manage, regulate and control allocation of their houses, for the benefit of the public. In my view the public interest would best be served by [Bristol City Council] being able in a case such as this to relet the premises to someone who will not use them for peddling crack cocaine.'

See also *Barnet London Borough Council v Lincoln*[14], where the court considered that a neighbourhood disturbed for a considerable time by a tenant's anti-social activities was entitled to have that behaviour brought to an end. Note further that under s 85A of the Housing Act 1985, inserted by s 16 of the Anti-social Behaviour Act 2003, when a court is considering the reasonableness of making a possession order in a 'nuisance' case, the court must 'in particular' consider the effect that the conduct has had on other people, any continuing effect it is likely to have and any effect it would be likely to have if repeated. Similar provision is made in respect of assured tenancies by the insertion of s 9A into the Housing Act 1988.

---

[14]   [2001] EWCA Civ 823.

See also Chapter 14 below on the limited impact of the Human Rights Act 1998 in this area. It is apparent that where nothing less than a grant of possession will suffice to protect the victims of bad behaviour then the courts will regard it as proportionate to make such an order.

Note, however, the issues raised by *North Devon Homes Ltd v Brazier*[15]. Here a tenant had caused nuisance and annoyance to her neighbours by virtue of aggressive anti-social activity. The landlord sought possession under s 8 of the Housing Act 1988 alleging, inter alia, breach of tenancy condition. At first instance the landlord was successful, but the tenant appealed, relying on the Disability Discrimination Act 1995 on the basis that she was suffering from a psychotic illness which was the cause of her behaviour, and that it was because of her illness that she was subject to possession proceedings, which contravened s 22 of the 1995 Act. This provides that it is unlawful to treat a disabled person less favourably (for a reason related to the disability) than others to whom that reason did not apply, unless such treatment could be justified. The Court of Appeal found in favour of the tenant. The question, they stressed, in such cases is to ask whether the breach in question was caused by the tenant's disability. In this case it was, and that led to the conclusion that eviction was being sought because of the disability; that amounted to unlawful discrimination. In such cases, the Court of Appeal pointed out, s 24 of the 1995 Act may justify the seeking of possession but only where a landlord has carried out a full and proper review of the circumstances which leads to a reasonably formed conclusion that the behaviour of the tenant is, for example, prejudicing the health and safety of neighbours, as, for instance, where the tenant is causing a physical risk to other people. Contrast, however, *Servite Homes v Elaine Perry*[16], where a person falling within the 1995 Act was made subject to a possession. The tenant suffered from temporal lobe epilepsy which gave rise to seizures, for which medication was taken. However, the tenant had also caused nuisance and annoyance and had indulged in foul and abusive language in respect of other tenants and the landlord's staff. This continued, in breach of an undertaking not to act in such a way. The tenant also played music excessively loudly. The decision in *Brazier* was distinguished in that the bad behaviour in the present case was not caused by the tenant's disability and so no issue of discrimination arose. These restrictions on the ability of landlords to seek possession must carefully be borne in mind, particularly as under the Care in the Community policy a number of people who might at one time have been housed in institutions are now living in the community and must be accommodated there, in addition to others who may be vulnerable in other ways in consequence of disabilities, for example learning difficulties. See also Chapter 7 on the effect of the 1995 Act on allocations, and Foreword II on recent developments in this area in the *Romano* and *Samari* decisions.

## ALTERNATIVE REMEDIES TO SEEKING POSSESSION

Landlords may seek an injunction to restrain the behaviour of tenants, but it must be stressed that the grant of injunctive relief is always at the discretion of the court.

---

[15] [2003] HLR 905.
[16] (March 2004, unreported). See also *Manchester City Council v Romano, Manchester City Council v Samari* [2004] EWCA Civ 834, [2004] All ER (D) 349 (Jun).

## The contractual injunction

Landlords can seek an injunction (an order of the court ordering cessation of particular behaviour) where a breach of tenancy conditions is committed, even though the landlord has suffered no damage as a result of the breach, according to obiter dicta in *Doherty v Allman*[17].

It must, however, be noted that:
(1)   the only terms that can be enforced are those specifically in the contract – no 're-writing' is allowed in/by the court;
(2)   only a party to the contract can be injuncted, but it is possible to phrase a tenancy condition in such a way that a tenant is forbidden to allow third parties to behave in particular ways on the premises.

The advantages of injunctive proceedings are as follows:
1.   Injunctions are flexible:
   - they may be permanent/interlocutory (ie an interim order);
   - where the latter, they can be obtained ex parte (post the Woolf reforms 'without notice') (ie on the basis of the landlord's evidence);
   - where sought ex parte/without notice, they can be obtained on affidavit evidence;
   - if there is a need, however, for a serious issue to be shown before relief is granted.
2.   Injunctive relief can be combined with possession proceedings, which is useful where the possession action is defended – offensive conduct can be injuncted while possession proceedings continue – that can be enough in itself to end the problem.

Other advantages of injunctions are:
   - they can be rapidly obtained (within 24 hours);
   - their object is to change behaviour;
   - they can have the effect of protecting witnesses;
   - they can provide a 'breathing space' within which it can be seen whether the offender will amend his/her ways;
   - an undertaking to modify behaviour pending trial can be given;
   - a failure to respond to an injunction can make the court more likely to award a possession order.

The disadvantages of injunctive proceedings:
   - interlocutory injunctions are short-term remedies only;
   - where combined with possession proceedings the court may conclude only an injunction is needed;
   - punishment for breach of injunction *may* not be particularly condign;
   - contractual injunctions can only be used to enforce contractual terms, and are therefore, limited to what the terms say. Thus in *Lewisham London Borough v Simba-Tola*[18] there were tenancy terms not to commit nuisance 'against other people' on or around the tenant's home or its surrounding estate, or 'around

---

[17]   (1878) 3 App Cas 709.
[18]   (1991) 24 HLR 644.

any other housing property of the council'. It was held this did not extend to allow a nuisance committed by the tenant in the council's central offices to be restrained by an injunction.

## Section 222 Local Government Act 1972 Injunctions

Local housing authorities have a wider power enabling them to seek injunctions generally by virtue of their general ability to pursue legal action *for the benefit of their areas*. It is possible, and has been done, eg in Hackney, to seek an injunction against individuals who, for example, by criminal activity are disturbing the peace of a particular estate. Such injunctions are normally only encountered in situations where bad behaviour affecting an entire area is encountered[19].

## Injunctive powers under the Housing Act 1996

Section 152 of the 1996 Act provided that a local authority (note this restriction under the 1996 Act as enacted, which denied the power to registered landlords, but see further below) could apply to either the High Court or the county court for an injunction prohibiting any person from:

(i)   engaging in or threatening to engage in conduct causing or likely to cause a nuisance or annoyance to a person residing in, visiting or otherwise engaging in a lawful activity in residential premises (see below) or in their locality; *or*

(ii)   using or threatening to use such premises for immoral or illegal purposes; *or*

(iii)   entering such premises or being found in their locality.

The premises in question were dwellings held under secure tenancies, or used to provide accommodation in homelessness cases. But the injunctee did not need to be the actual tenant, a spouse/partner or a child, for example could be dealt with under these provisions.

The discretion to grant an injunction lay with the court which, however could *not* grant an injunction unless it considered:

(a)   that the respondent had used, or threatened to use violence to persons residing in a relevant dwelling or visiting or otherwise engaging in lawful activities in such a dwelling; *and*

(b)   there was a significant risk of harm to that person, or to a person of a similar description if the injunction was not granted. 'Harm' was defined as ill treatment or the impairment of health in the case of an adult and also extends to impairment of development in the case of a child.

Where an injunction was granted it could relate to particular acts or conduct or types of conduct or both, and could relate to particular premises or a particular locality. It could also be made for a specified period or until varied or discharged. A power of arrest could be attached to one or more of the provisions of such an

---

[19]   *Coventry City Council v Finnie* (1996) 29 HLR 658.

injunction. The court, provided it considered it just and convenient, could grant/vary an injunction even though the respondent had not been given the normally required notices.

The 1996 powers did not introduce a housing utopia for authorities wishing to seek injunctions. There was a considerable deal of proof of particular circumstances required before the court could grant an injunction. There could be situations where someone was engaging in menacing conduct which was short of violence or its threat – eg simply carrying an air gun around. Such a situation would not be caught by the law. Furthermore it appeared that as s 152 injunctions were civil in nature, not criminal, their breach was not a criminal matter and thus they could not be made against a minor[20], nor could a power of arrest be attached if the respondent gave an undertaking to honour the injunction[21].

Serious limitations on the use of s 152 flowed from the unsatisfactory Court of Appeal decision in *Enfield London Borough Council v B (a minor)*[22]. Here, a violent incident had occurred in a district housing office situated in a council owned shopping centre, within 300 metres of which were council properties let out on residential tenancies. It was clear the defendants had perpetrated violence, and a common law injunction prohibiting further tortious activity was granted by the county court, but no remedy was given under s 152 which would have carried with it an automatic power of arrest for any breach.

It was agreed in the Court of Appeal by Waller and Buxton LJJ that s 152 did not apply to protect persons who are engaging in a lawful activity in a place unconnected with residential premises. It would appear that the fact that the premises in question were used for housing management and were in the locality of residential premises was not enough to supply that connection, compare the *Simba-Tola* case above. There had to be a nexus between residential premises and the person it was sought to protect.

To overcome the problems outlined above the former provisions are repealed and replaced under the Anti-social Behaviour Act 2003, and under the Housing Act 1996 (as amended), the following now apply:

### 153A    Anti-social behaviour injunction

(1) This section applies to conduct—

(a)   which is capable of causing nuisance or annoyance to any person, and
(b)   which directly or indirectly relates to or affects the housing management functions of a relevant landlord.

(2) The court on the application of a relevant landlord may grant an injunction (an anti-social behaviour injunction) if each of the following two conditions is satisfied.

(3) The first condition is that the person against whom the injunction is sought is engaging, has engaged or threatens to engage in conduct to which this section applies.

(4) The second condition is that the conduct is capable of causing nuisance or annoyance to any of the following—

---

[20]  *Wookey v Wookey* [1991] 3 All ER 365 (and see further below).
[21]  *Carpenter v Carpenter* [1988] 1 FLR 121.
[22]  [2000] 1 All ER 255.

(a) a person with a right (of whatever description) to reside in or occupy housing accommodation owned or managed by the relevant landlord;

(b) a person with a right (of whatever description) to reside in or occupy housing accommodation in the neighbourhood of housing accommodation mentioned in paragraph (a);

(c) a person engaged in lawful activity in or in the neighbourhood of housing accommodation mentioned in paragraph (a);

(d) a person employed (whether or not by the relevant landlord) in connection with the exercise of the relevant landlord's housing management functions.

(5) It is immaterial where conduct to which this section applies occurs.

(6) An anti-social behaviour injunction prohibits the person in respect of whom it is granted from engaging in conduct to which this section applies.

### 153B   Injunction against immoral and unlawful use of premises

(1) This section applies to conduct which consists of or involves using or threatening to use housing accommodation owned or managed by a relevant landlord for an unlawful purpose.

(2) The court on the application of the relevant landlord may grant an injunction prohibiting the person in respect of whom the injunction is granted from engaging in conduct to which this section applies.

### 153C   Injunctions: exclusion order and power of arrest

(1) This section applies if the court grants an injunction under subsection (2) of section 153A or 153B and it thinks that either of the following paragraphs applies—

(a) the conduct consists of or includes the use or threatened use of violence;

(b) there is a significant risk of harm to a person mentioned in section 153A(4).

(2) The court may include in the injunction a provision prohibiting the person in respect of whom it is granted from entering or being in—

(a) any premises specified in the injunction;

(b) any area specified in the injunction.

(3)   The court may attach a power of arrest to any provision of the injunction.

### 153D   Injunction against breach of tenancy agreement

(1) This section applies if a relevant landlord applies for an injunction against a tenant in respect of the breach of anticipated breach of a tenancy agreement on the grounds that the tenant—

(a) is engaging or threatening to engage in conduct that is capable of causing nuisance or annoyance to any person, or

(b) is allowing, inciting or encouraging any other person to engage or threaten to engage in such conduct.

(2) The court may proceed under subsection (3) or (4) if it is satisfied—

(a) that the conduct includes the use or threatened use of violence, or

(b) that there is a significant risk of harm to any person.

(3) The court may include in the injunction a provision prohibiting the person in respect of whom it is granted from entering or being in—

(a) any premises specified in the injunction;

(b) any area specified in the injunction.

(4) The court may attach a power of arrest to any provision of the injunction.

(5) Tenancy agreement includes any agreement for the occupation of residential accommodation owned or managed by a relevant landlord.

Injunctions: supplementary

**153E**

(1) This section applies for the purposes of sections 153A to 153D.

(2) An injunction may—

(a)   be made for a specified period or until varied or discharged;

(b)   have the effect of excluding a person from his normal place of residence.

(3) An injunction may be varied or discharged by the court on an application by—

(a)   the person in respect of whom it is made;

(b)   the relevant landlord.

(4) If the court thinks it just and convenient it may grant or vary an injunction without the respondent having been given such notice as is otherwise required by rules of court.

(5) If the court acts under subsection (4) it must give the person against whom the injunction is made an opportunity to make representations in relation to the injunction as soon as it is practicable for him to do so.

(6) The court is the High Court or a county court.

(7) Each of the following is a relevant landlord—

(a)   a housing action trust;

(b)   a local authority (within the meaning of the Housing Act 1985);

(c)   a registered social landlord.

(8) A charitable housing trust which is not a registered social landlord is also a relevant landlord for the purposes of Section 153D.

(9) Housing accommodation includes—

(a)   flats, lodging-houses and hostels;

(b)   any yard, garden, outhouses and appurtenances belonging to the accommodation or usually enjoyed with it.

(c)   in relation to a neighbourhood, the whole of the housing accommodation owned or managed by a relevant landlord in the neighbourhood and any common areas used in connection with the accommodation.

(10) A landlord owns housing accommodation if either of the following paragraphs applies to him—

(a)   he is a person (other than a mortgagee not in possession) who is for the time being entitled to dispose of the fee simple in the premises, whether in possession or in reversion;

(b)   he is a person who holds or is entitled to the rents and profits of the premises under a lease of which the unexpired term exceeds three years.

(11) The housing management functions of a relevant landlord include—

(a)   functions conferred by or under any enactment;

(b)   the powers and duties of the landlords as the holder of an estate or interest in housing accommodation.

(12) Harm includes serious ill-treatment or abuse (whether physical or not).

The efficacy of these provisions with regard to badly behaving children must, however, be questioned in the light of the continued applicability of the decision in

*Wookey v Wookey* mentioned above. In *G v Harrow London Borough Council*[23] an injunction under the 'old' s 152 of the Housing Act 1996 was obtained against a 13-year-old boy preventing him from engaging in conduct likely to cause a nuisance in the locality of the council house which was his home. The injunction was granted on the basis that the decision in *Wookey's* case had been overtaken by the Crime and Disorder Act 1998 under which anti-social behaviour orders (see below) can be obtained against anyone over the age of 10. The Court of Appeal discharged the injunction on the basis that an injunction has to be enforced to be meaningful and there was no obvious means of enforcement in this case. The boy could not be imprisoned if he disobeyed the order, and he had no income or property which could be seized. Furthermore it was not appropriate to rely on threats or fear of indirect consequences. An injunction which cannot be properly or effectively enforced should not be granted. It may be asked whether there is anything in the new law considered above which weakens the conclusion of the Court of Appeal in this case. See also Foreword III on this issue.

## Commentary

Local authorities, housing action trusts and registered social landlords are enabled to seek injunctions prohibiting certain types of behaviour which relates to or affects the management of their housing stock. Indeed, such landlords are required by s 12 of the Anti-social Behaviour Act 2003 inserting s 218A into the Housing Act 1996 to prepare policies and procedures on, and for dealing with, instances of anti-social behaviour. These must be kept up to date and published and must reflect central guidance issued by either the Secretary of State in the case of authorities or the Housing Corporation in the case of other social landlords. The housing management function thus clearly extends to social control. See further below.

Relevant conduct includes that which is *capable* of causing nuisance or annoyance (no actual complaint need have been received) *and* which relates to or affects, either directly or indirectly, the management of housing stock. This is a very wide-ranging definition, but certain conditions have to be met for an order to be granted.

An order may be made against *any* person whose behaviour could cause *nuisance or annoyance* to those who are, for example, tenants of the landlord seeking the injunction, other local residents, or other people carrying out lawful activities in (or in the locality of) the landlord's housing accommodation (eg visitors to tenants or those who work in the locality) or who are staff employed in connection with managing the landlord's housing stock.

The conduct in question need not cause nuisance, etc to a specific person provided it is capable of having such an effect, though it is necessary to show *either* that the offender engaged in or is threatening to engage in relevant bad behaviour *or* that the bad behaviour in question is capable of causing nuisance or annoyance to anyone of a specified list of people which is so widely drawn as to be capable of including the employees of contractors working on the landlord's housing stock. That behaviour need not occur in the vicinity of the landlord's housing accommodation, but must

---

[23] [2004] EWHC 17 (QB), (2004) 11(2) Housing Law Monitor 6.

relate either directly or indirectly to the management of the landlord's housing stock. Thus, a landlord might seek an injunction to protect a tenant who has been subject to nuisance or annoyance committed by other tenants even where the behaviour in question has not happened on the estate where they are all resident. 'Housing management', according to government guidance issued at the Bill stage of the new legislation, should be broadly interpreted to cover activities such as regeneration, mediation, tenant training and participation, giving welfare advice to tenants etc.

The new law furthermore allows relevant landlords to seek an injunction where a person has used or has threatened to use his/her accommodation for an illegal purpose such as drug dealing.

A power of arrest may be attached by the court to the injunction, or the court may exclude persons from specified premises (including their homes), where there has been the use or the threat of violence or there is a significant risk of harm to residents, visitors, staff of the landlord, as previously considered above. Note that the powers are available where there is a significant risk of harm, even though there has been no actual or threatened violence – a considerable extension on the previous law. A 'significant risk of harm', furthermore, is defined widely so that it would include emotional or psychological harm such as depression or the effects of racial or sexual harassment.

New powers are granted to relevant landlords where there is a breach or an anticipated breach of a term of a tenancy agreement by a tenant. Provided the behaviour in question is prohibited by the agreement, the court may exclude a person from specified premises or areas, and attach a power of arrest to the order provided:

- the breach/anticipated breach relates to conduct by the tenant that amounts to *or* is capable of amounting to a nuisance or to any person;
- the behaviour of the tenant consists of allowing, inciting or encouraging such conduct by another person, for example a child of the tenant, *and* (in either case)
- the conduct must also include violence *or* a significant risk of harm to any person.

It may be seen that this new power is a wide-ranging alternative to granting possession against tenants who indulge in or permit bad behaviour in their homes etc, to affect other people. It is a power directed against specifically named persons which does not put the tenancy automatically at risk such as possession proceedings do.

Supplementary provisions confirm that the new injunctive powers may result in a person being excluded from his/her residence, while injunctions may be granted without the injunctee having been given prior notice, though in such cases that person must be given the chance to make subsequent representations.

## WIDER ISSUES IN ANTI-SOCIAL BEHAVIOUR

The involvement of the law in dealing with such behaviour is contentious. To some people, using legal means to deal with behaviour that is vaguely defined legally and generally classified as 'offensive' in general terms smacks of illiberality and heavy-handed authoritarianism, especially where there is a lack of consensus as to what the 'offensive' behaviour in question is. On 10 September 2003 *The Guardian* carried a news item on the issue in which it was reported the Home Office had drawn up a list of 60 types of anti-social behaviour, which could be summarised as: drug/substance misuse and dealing, including discarding needles; street drinking and begging; prostitution, kerb-crawling, sexual acts including discarding condoms, loitering and indecent exposure; abandoning vehicles; vehicle-related nuisances including illegal parking and repairing cars in the street; vehicle fires; joyriding; off-road motorcycling; cycling and skateboarding in pedestrian areas; noise, rowdy behaviour, including swearing and fighting; nuisance behaviour including urinating in public and lighting fires; hoax telephone calling; animal-related problems; Intimidation and bullying; criminal damage and vandalism; litter offences, including fly posting.

This is a very wide definition, and includes many types of behaviour already punishable under other legislation. The problem is that many types of behaviour might become subject to legal control which in the past might have been dealt with, if at all, in other less formal ways.

To some people, however, there are justifications for taking action based on arguments that as a whole, bodies of people, for example the tenants on an estate, have a collective moral right to live in peace and quiet and that right should 'trump' the ability of others to, for example, gather together on such estates and listen to loud music from car music systems. A further supporting argument is that publicly provided streets and open spaces are created on the democratic basis that their cost is borne by all for the benefit of all, and not for the use of those who may use them for purposes that are intimidating and may well be criminal, for example drug dealing and taking.

We have already seen how possession proceedings and injunctions can be used to control the behaviour of individual tenants, their families and visitors, and indeed it is clear from the development of the case law that the courts have been willing to develop the use of such measures of control. Even so there have been many who have argued for other remedies, though such developments have not been without controversy.

## The issue of legitimacy

Underlying the case law developments of the 1990s alluded to above was a current of unease. Three questions arose, the first being to what extent is it legitimate for a local authority to use its powers as a landlord to deal with questions that are in some ways questions of public order, crime prevention and enforcement? Secondly, was it not invidious for local authority tenants to be made subject to a particular regime of control that arose solely by virtue of their tenurial status, and which was not applicable to owner occupiers? Thirdly, was it not particularly unfair in an area of mixed tenures, for example, a council estate where some of the houses have been disposed of under the right-to-buy legislation, that some residents should be subject to a particular form of social control while their neighbours were not? Similar questions could be posed with regard to the tenants of registered social landlords, for it was a widely held, but utterly mistaken, view that such landlords only accommodated 'nice' people and had neither problem tenants nor difficult estates!

There were, nevertheless, both national/general and localised/ specific arguments why local authority landlords in particular should act as agents of social control.

There was a wide degree of consensus that authorities should act where this promotes racial harmony; indeed this falls within the general terms of their duties under s 71 of the Race Relations Act 1976.

Commentators generally agreed that tenants have clear expectations that their landlords will enforce tenancy conditions and byelaws and thus will undertake a disciplinary function[24]. While a landlord cannot be forced by one tenant to take legal action against another in respect of an alleged nuisance, landlords who neglect to act can find themselves subject to investigations for maladministration by the Commission for Local Administration.

Action by the local authority was consonant with the 'Citizen's Charter' approach to the delivery of public services advocated by John Major's Government, as an example of 'customer care'. It is also consonant with Tony Blair's Government's view of a civic society, and 'zero tolerance' of crime and disorder as evinced by the Prime Minister at the Labour Party's 1998 Blackpool Conference.

In some cases the nature of a landlord authority's stock justifies an interventionist stance, for example, where accommodation has been provided on a high-density basis with inadequate sound insulation and with layouts that juxtapose living rooms and bedrooms. Where a landlord has created a situation for potential conflict, that landlord should be involved in preventing conflict.

Intervention can be justified additionally where it serves to protect public investment in housing stock and prevents houses from standing empty and areas becoming 'hard to let'.

The nature of the landlord's client group may justify intervention. Those accommodated by social landlords rarely have any real choice as to where they are to be housed, and frequently find themselves placed in areas of high turnover with little social cohesion[25]. Such communities can rarely establish norms for behaviour, and have little social control by means of informal self-help processes such as negative public comment or even mild physical reprisals.

In some areas the local authority landlord is more acceptable than the police to local people as an agent of social control. This is particularly true in those areas, for example parts of Yorkshire, which experienced high levels of community anger

---

[24] Simpson, B and McCarthy, P, 'Conflict in the Community: Local Authorities in the Middle' (1990) 17 (No. 2, September) *Local Government Policy Making* 24.

[25] D Page, *Building for Communities: A Study of New Housing Association Estates* (1993) Joseph Rowntree Foundation.

against the police during the coal miners' strike of 1983–84. The police in some such areas remain objects of mistrust, even hatred, and so are less effective in acting as a bulwark to social cohesion.

The Social Landlords' Crime and Nuisance group was established in 1995 and argued strongly for new remedies to deal with both nuisance and anti-social behaviour. The 'anti-nuisance' outcome of this can be seen in the provisions of the Housing Act 1996 examined above. However, there was also an identified need for some form of community-based order, somewhat similar to an injunction. In due course this led to the emergence of the anti-social behaviour order which, because it is not tenure-specific nor necessarily tenancy related, is a means of social control which escapes the problems identified below.

Intervention by a landlord qua landlord into inter-tenant behavioural problems, though often necessary, can still be seen as biased in operation as between tenants and non-tenants, and harking back to old-fashioned styles of paternalist management in which the landlord decrees what constitutes socially acceptable behaviour. The emergence of new legislation after 1998 offers local authorities a new role *as authorities and not as landlords* – a role which, though not free of controversy in itself, being yet another stratum of public order provision, nevertheless avoids the implication of being partial vis-à-vis tenants. Even so, there are a number of problems in the wake of recent legislative changes.

## Crime and disorder: the strategic imperative

The Crime and Disorder Act 1998 (as amended) provides, inter alia, for a new strategic approach to preventing crime and public disorder which requires local authorities, registered social landlords, and police forces to act together in partnership within their areas to prevent and otherwise deal with crime and anti-social behaviour generally.

*Crime and disorder strategies*

5.   **Authorities responsible for strategies (as amended by the Police Reform Act 2002 and the Anti-social Behaviour Act 2003)**

(1) Subject to the provisions of this section, the functions conferred by section 6 below shall be exercisable in relation to each local government area by the responsible authorities, that is to say—

(a)   the council for the area and, where the area is a district and the council is not a unitary authority, the council for the county which includes the district; and
(b)   every chief officer of police any part of whose police area lies within the area;
[(c)   every police authority any part of whose police area so lies;
(d)   every fire authority any part of whose area so lies;
(e)   if the local government area is in England, every Primary Care Trust the whole or any part of whose area so lies; and
(f)   if the local government area is in Wales, every health authority the whole or any part of whose area so lies].

[(1A) The Secretary of State may by order provide in relation to any two or more local government areas in England—

(a) that the functions conferred by sections 6 to 7 below are to be carried out in relation to those areas taken together as if they constituted only one area; and

(b) that the persons who for the purposes of this Chapter are to be taken to be responsible authorities in relation to the combined area are the persons who comprise every person who (apart from the order) would be a responsible authority in relation to any one or more of the areas included in the combined area.

(1B) The Secretary of State shall not make an order under subsection (1A) above unless—

(a) an application for the order has been made jointly by all the persons who would be the responsible authorities in relation to the combined area or the Secretary of State has first consulted those persons; and

(b) he considers it would be in the interests of reducing crime and disorder, or of combating the misuse of drugs, to make the order.]

(2) In exercising those functions, the responsible authorities shall act in co-operation with the following persons and bodies, namely—

...

[(b) every local probation board any part of whose area lies within the area;]

(c) every person or body of a description which is for the time being prescribed by order of the Secretary of State under this subsection; [and

(d) where they are acting in relation to an area in Wales, every person or body which is of a description which is for the time being prescribed by an order under this subsection of the National Assembly for Wales;]

and it shall be the duty of those persons and bodies to co-operate in the exercise by the responsible authorities of those functions.

(3) The responsible authorities shall also invite the participation in their exercise of those functions of at least one person or body of each description which is for the time being prescribed by order of the Secretary of State under this subsection [and, in the case of the responsible authorities for an area in Wales, of any person or body of a description for the time being prescribed by an order unless this subsection of the National Assembly for Wales.]

(4) In this section and sections 6 and 7 below 'local government area' means—

(a) in relation to England, each district or London borough, the City of London, the Isle of Wight and the Isles of Scilly;

(b) in relation to Wales, each county or county borough.

[(5) In this section—

'fire authority' means—

(a) any fire authority constituted by a combination scheme under the Fire Services Act 1947;

(b) any metropolitan county fire and civil defence authority; or

(c) the London Fire and Emergency Planning Authority; and

'police authority' means—

(a) any police authority established under section 3 of the Police Act 1996; or

(b) the Metropolitan Police Authority.]

## 6. Formulation and implementation of strategies

(1) The responsible authorities for a local government area shall, in accordance with the provisions of section 5 above and this section, formulate and implement, for each relevant period, a strategy for the reduction of crime and disorder in the area—

[(a) in the case of an area in England—

(i) a strategy for the reduction of crime and disorder in the area; and

(ii) a strategy for combating the misuse of drugs in the area;

and

(b) in the case of an area in Wales—

 (i) a strategy for the reduction of crime and disorder in the area; and

 (ii) a strategy for combating substance misuse in the area].

[(1A) In determining what matters to include or not to include in their strategy for combating substance misuse, the responsible authorities for an area in Wales shall have regard to any guidance issued for the purposes of this section by the National Assembly for Wales].

(2) Before formulating a strategy, the responsible authorities shall—

[(a) carry out, taking due account of the knowledge and experience of persons in the area, a review—

 (i) in the case of an area in England, of the levels and patterns of crime and disorder in the area and of the level and patterns of the misuse of drugs in the area; and

 (ii) in the case of an area in Wales, of the levels and patterns of crime and disorder in the area and of the level and patterns of substance misuse in the area;]

(b) prepare an analysis of the results of that review;

(c) publish in the area a report of that analysis; and

(d) obtain the views on that report of persons or bodies in the area (including those of a description prescribed by order under section 5(3) above), whether by holding public meetings or otherwise.

(3) In formulating a strategy, the responsible authorities shall have regard to the analysis prepared under subsection (2)(b) above and the views obtained under subsection (2)(d) above.

(4) A strategy shall include—

(a) objectives to be pursued by the responsible authorities, by co-operating persons or bodies or, under agreements with the responsible authorities, by other persons or bodies; and

(b) long-term and short-term performance targets for measuring the extent to which such objectives are achieved.

(5) After formulating a strategy, the responsible authorities shall publish in the area a document which includes details of—

(a) co-operating persons and bodies;

(b) the review carried out under subsection (2)(a) above;

(c) the report published under subsection 2(c) above; and

(d) the strategy, including in particular—

 (i) the objectives mentioned in subsection (4)(a) above and, in each case, the authorities, persons or bodies by whom they are to be pursued; and

 (ii) the performance targets mentioned in subsection (4)(b) above.

(6) While implementing a strategy, the responsible authorities shall keep it under review with a view to monitoring its effectiveness and making any changes to it that appear necessary or expedient.

[(6A) Within one month of the end of each reporting period, the responsible authorities shall submit a report on the implementation of their strategies during that period—

(a) in the case of a report relating to the strategies for an area in England, to the Secretary of State; and

(b) in the case of a report relating to the strategies for an area in Wales, to the Secretary of State and to the National Assembly for Wales.]

(7) In this section—

'co-operating persons or bodies' means persons or bodies co-operating in the exercise of the responsible authorities' functions under this section;

'relevant period' means—

    (a)   the period of three years beginning with such day as the Secretary of State may by order appoint; and

    (b)   each subsequent period of three years.

['reporting period' means every period of one year which falls within a relevant period and which begins—

    (a)   in the case of the first reporting period in the relevant period, with the day on which the relevant period begins; and

    (b)   in any other case, with the day after the day on which the previous reporting period ends;

'substance misuse' includes the misuse of drugs or alcohol.]

## [6A    Powers of the Secretary of State and National Assembly for Wales

(1) The Secretary of State may, by order, require—

(a)   the responsible authorities for local government areas to formulate any section 6 strategy of theirs for the reduction of crime and disorder so as to include, in particular, provision for the reduction of—

    (i)   crime of a description specified in the order; or

    (ii)  disorder of a description so specified.

(b)   the responsible authorities for local government areas in England to prepare any section 6 strategy of theirs for combating the misuse of drugs so as to include in it a strategy for combating, in the area in question, such other forms of substance misuse as may be specified or described in the order.

(2) After formulating any section 6 strategy (whether in a case in which there has been an order under subsection or in any other case), the responsible authorities for a local government area shall send both—

(a)   a copy of the strategy, and

(b)   a copy of the document which they propose to publish under section 6(5),

to the Secretary of State.

(3) It shall be the duty of the responsible authorities, when preparing any document to be published under section 6(5), to have regard to any guidance issued by the Secretary of State as to the form and content of the documents to be so published.

(4) If the responsible authorities for a local government area propose to make any changes to a section 6 strategy of theirs, they shall send copies of the proposed changes to the Secretary of State.

(5) In subsections (2) to (4)—

(a)   references to the Secretary of State, in relation to responsible authorities for local government areas in Wales shall have effect as references to the Secretary of State and the National Assembly for Wales; and

(b)   accordingly, guidance issued for the purposes of subsection (3) in relation to local government areas in Wales must be issued by the Secretary of State and that Assembly acting jointly.

(6) In this section—

'responsible authorities' and 'local government area' have same meanings as in sections 5 and 6;

'section 6 strategy' means a strategy required to be formulated under section 6(1); and 'substance misuse' has the same meaning as in section 6.]

## 7.   Supplemental

(1) The responsible authorities for a local government area shall, whenever so required by the Secretary of State, submit to the Secretary of State a report on such matters connected with the exercise of their functions under section 6 above as may be specified in the requirement.

(2) A requirement under subsection (1) above may specify the form in which a report is to be given.

(3) The Secretary of State may arrange, or require the responsible authorities to arrange, for a report under subsection (1) above to be published in such manner as appears to him to be appropriate.

...

## 17.   Duty to consider crime and disorder implications

(1) Without prejudice to any other obligation imposed on it, it shall be the duty of each authority to which this section applies to exercise its various functions with due regard to the likely effect of the exercise of those functions on, and the need to do all that it reasonably can to prevent, crime and disorder in its area.

(2) This section applies to a local authority, a joint authority, [the London Fire and Emergency Planning Authority,] [a fire authority constituted by a combination scheme under the Fire Services Act 1947,] a police authority, a National Park authority and the Broads Authority.

(3) In this section—

'local authority' means a local authority within the meaning given by section 270(1) of the Local Government Act 1972 or the Common Council of the City of London;
'joint authority' has the same meaning as in the Local Government Act 1985;
'National Park authority' means an authority established under section 63 of the Environment Act 1995.

...

## 115.   Disclosure of information

(1) Any person who, apart from this subsection, would not have power to disclose information—

(a)   to a relevant authority; or
(b)   to a person acting on behalf of such an authority,

shall have power to do so in any case where the disclosure is necessary or expedient for the purposes of any provision of this Act.

(2) In subsection (1) above 'relevant authority' means—

(a)   the chief officer of police for a police area in England and Wales;
(b)   the chief constable of a police force maintained under the Police (Scotland) Act 1967;
(c)   a police authority within the meaning given by section 101(1) of the Police Act 1996;
(d)   a local authority, that is to say—
    (i)   in relation to England, a county council, a district council, a London borough council [, a parish council] or the Common Council of the City of London;
    (ii)   in relation to Wales, a county council [, a county borough council or a community council];
    (iii)   in relation to Scotland, a council constituted under section 2 of the Local Government etc (Scotland) Act 1994;
(e)   a [local probation board] in England and Wales;

[(ea) a Strategic Health Authority;]
(f)   a health authority;
[(g)  a Primary Care Trust].

Clause 167 of the Housing Bill 2003 further provides that, in future, *any* person may disclose 'relevant information' to a landlord under a secure tenancy provided the disclosure is for the purpose of, inter alia, enabling the landlord to decide whether to refuse a consent to a mutual exchange where an anti-social behaviour order is in force or an application is pending in connection with anti-social behaviour. The information in question is that relating to any relevant order or application. The purpose here is to ensure that those who are guilty of anti-social behaviour do not evade the consequences of their wrongdoing by exchanging properties and moving elsewhere.

Some of the amendments made to the 1998 Act by subsequent legislation were still in 2004 to be brought into effect; regular reference should be made to updating services such as Halsbury 'Is it in force?' to check on the exact state of the law.

Sections 5 and 6 lay down the broad framework for the formulation and implementation of crime and disorder strategies, and are based on the notion that local authorities are required to have such a strategy which they draw up in co-operation with the police for their area, and a number of other responsible bodies, such as the probation service. The strategy has to have as its objective the reduction of crime and disorder within the relevant authority's area and is based on a collaborative review of patterns of crime and disorder. The strategy has to be published, and kept under review. All of this was required within three years of a date to be appointed by the Secretary of State, and the commencement date of ss 5 to 9 of the Act was 30 September 1998.

In addition under s 17 of the 1998 Act each local authority, ie London boroughs, districts, counties etc, police authorities, joint authorities and National Park authorities, etc, is required to exercise its various functions with due regard to their likely effect on crime and disorder in its area, and the need to do all it reasonably can to prevent crime and disorder. In relation to housing, for example, this would appear to require, inter alia, allocation and homelessness functions to be carried out with a view, at least, to crime prevention.

Clearly a person's record has with regard to crime and anti-social behaviour may therefore be a pertinent issue with regard to the allocation of housing, see Chapter 7 above, though here it must be reiterated that there can be no blanket exclusions under the terms of the Homelessness Act 2002 of those who have records of past misbehaviour.

## SPECIFIC ASB POLICIES FOR SOCIAL LANDLORDS

While the 1998 placed local authorities generally under an obligation to create a strategic framework for dealing with anti-social behaviour, the Anti-social Behaviour Act 2003 amends the Housing Act 1985 to require social housing landlords to have ASB policies, and, with regard to registered social landlords, the Housing Corporation is empowered to issue guidance on the matter. The Housing Act 1985 (as amended) now provides as follows.

### 218A  Anti-social behaviour: landlords' policies and procedures

(1) This section applies to the following landlords—

(a) a local housing authority;
(b) a housing action trust;
(c) a registered social landlord.

(2) The landlord must prepare—

(a) a policy in relation to anti-social behaviour;
(b) procedures for dealing with occurrences of anti-social behaviour.

(3) The landlord must not later than 6 months after the commencement of section 12 of the Anti-social Behaviour Act 2003 publish a statement of the policy and procedures prepared under subsection (2).

(4) The landlord must from time to time keep the policy and procedures under review and, when it thinks appropriate, publish a revised statement.

(5) A copy of a statement published under subsection (3) or (4)—

(a) must be available for inspection at all reasonable hours at the landlord's principal office;
(b) must be provided on payment of a reasonable fee to any person who requests it.

(6) The landlord must also—

(a) prepare a summary of its current policy and procedures;
(b) provide without charge a copy of the summary to any person who requests it.

(7) In preparing and reviewing the policy and procedures the landlord must have regard to guidance issued—

(a) by the Secretary of State in the case of a local housing authority or a housing action trust;
(b) by the Relevant Authority under section 36 in the case of a registered social landlord.

(8) Anti-social behaviour is any conduct to which section 153A or 153B applies.

(9) Relevant Authority has the same meaning as in Part 2.

The foregoing is the new strategic framework. At the tactical level, a whole range of powers were created and made available to various types of authority, while others were entrusted to the courts. All in all this amounted to a quite bewildering array of new powers to be exercised by a variety of authorities and bodies. In the context of housing, however, it is 'anti-social behaviour' orders that are of most relevance. The Crime and Disorder Act 1998 (as amended) provides as follows.

### 1.  Anti-social behaviour orders

(1) An application for an order under this section may be made by a relevant authority if it appears to the authority that the following conditions are fulfilled with respect to any person aged 10 or over, namely—

(a) that the person has acted, since the commencement date, in an anti-social manner, that is to say, in a manner that caused or was likely to cause harassment, alarm or distress to one or more persons not of the same household as himself; and
[(b) that such an order is necessary to protect relevant persons from further anti-social acts by him.]

[(1A)  In this section and sections 1B and 1E 'relevant authority' means—

(a)  the council for a local government area;

(aa) in relation to England, a county council;

(b)  the chief officer of police of any police force maintained for a police area;

(c)  the chief constable of the British Transport Police Force;

(d)  any person registered under section 1 of the Housing Act 1996 as a social landlord who provides or manages any houses or hostel in a local government area; or

(e)  a housing action trust established by order in pursuance of section 62 of the Housing Act 1988.

(1B)   In this section 'relevant persons' means—

(a)  in relation to a relevant authority falling within paragraph (a) of subsection (1A), persons within the local government area of that council;

(aa) in relation to a relevant authority falling within paragraph (aa) of subsection (1A) persons within the county of the county council;

(b)  in relation to a relevant authority falling within paragraph (b) of that subsection, persons within the police area;

(c)  in relation to a relevant authority falling within paragraph (c) of that subsection—

   (i) persons who are on or likely to be on policed premises in a local government area; or

   (ii) persons who are in the vicinity of or likely to be in the vicinity of such premises;

(d)  in relation to a relevant authority falling within paragraph (d) or (e) of that subsection—

   (i) persons who are residing in or who are otherwise on or likely to be on premises provided or managed by that authority; or

   (ii) persons who are in the vicinity of or likely to be in the vicinity of such premises.]

(2)…

(3) Such an application shall be made by complaint to the magistrates' court whose commission area includes [the local government area or police area concerned].

(4) If, on such an application, it is proved that the conditions mentioned in subsection (1) above are fulfilled, the magistrates' court may make an order under this section (an 'anti-social behaviour order') which prohibits the defendant from doing anything described in the order.

(5) For the purposes of determining whether the condition mentioned in subsection (1)(a) above is fulfilled, the court shall disregard any act of the defendant which he shows was reasonable in the circumstances.

[(6) The prohibitions that may be imposed by an anti-social behaviour order are those necessary for the purpose of protecting persons (whether relevant persons or persons elsewhere in England and Wales) from further anti-social acts by the defendant.]

(7) An anti-social behaviour order shall have effect for a period (not less than two years) specified in the order or until further order.

(8) Subject to subsection (9) below, the applicant or the defendant may apply by complaint to the court which made an anti-social behaviour order for it to be varied or discharged by a further order.

(9) Except with the consent of both parties, no anti-social behaviour order shall be discharged before the end of the period of two years beginning with the date of service of the order.

(10)  If without reasonable excuse a person does anything which he is prohibited from doing by an anti-social behaviour order, he [is guilty of an offence and] liable—

(a)  on summary conviction, to imprisonment for a term not exceeding six months or to a fine not exceeding the statutory maximum, or to both; or

(b)  on conviction on indictment, to imprisonment for a term not exceeding five years or to a fine, or to both

(10A)  The following may bring proceedings for an offence under subsection (10).

(a)  a council which is a relevant authority;

(b)  the council for the local government area in which a person in respect of whom an anti-social behaviour order has been made resides or appears to reside.

(10B)  If proceedings for an offence under subsection (10) are brought in a youth court section 47(2) of the Children and Young Persons Act 1933 (c.12) has effect as if the persons entitled to be present at a sitting for the purposes of those proceedings include one person authorised to be present by a relevant authority.

(11)  Where a person is convicted of an offence under subsection (10) above, it shall not be open to the court by or before which he is so convicted to make an order under subsection (1)(b) (conditional discharge) of [section 12 of the Powers of Criminal Courts (Sentencing) Act 2000] in respect of the offence.

(12)  In this section—

['British Transport Police Force' means the force of constables appointed under section 53 of the British Transport Commission Act 1949;]
'the commencement date' means the date of the commencement of this section;
'local government area' means—
    (a)  in relation to England, a district or London borough, the City of London, the Isle of Wight and the Isles of Scilly;
    (b)  in relation to Wales, a county or county borough,
['policed premises' has the meaning given by section 53(3) of the British Transport Commission Act 1949].

## [1A.  Power of Secretary of State to add to relevant authorities

The Secretary of State may by order provide that the chief officer of a body of constables maintained otherwise than by a police authority is, in such cases and circumstances as may be prescribed by the order, to be a relevant authority for the purposes of section 1 above.]

## [1B.  Orders in county court proceedings

(1) This section applies to any proceedings in a county court ('the principal proceedings').

(2) If a relevant authority—

(a)  is a party to the principal proceedings, and

(b)  considers that a party to those proceedings is a person in relation to whom it would be reasonable for it to make an application under section 1,

it may make an application in those proceedings for an order under subsection (4).

(3) If a relevant authority—

(a)  is not a party to the principal proceedings, and

(b)  considers that a party to those proceedings is a person in relation to whom it would be reasonable for it to make an application under section 1, it may make an application to be joined to those proceedings to enable it to apply for an order under subsection (4) and, if it is so joined, may apply for such an order.

(3A)  Subsection (3B) applies if a relevant authority is a party to the principal proceedings and considers—

(a) that a person who is not a party to the proceedings has acted in an anti-social manner, and

(b) that the person's anti-social acts are material in relation to the principal proceedings.

(3B) The relevant authority may—

(a) make an application for the person mentioned in subsection (3A)(a) to be joined to the principal proceedings to enable an order under subsection (4) to be made in relation to that person;

(b) if that person is so joined, apply for an order under subsection (4).

(3C) But a person must not be joined to proceedings in pursuance of subsection (3B) unless his anti-social acts are material in relation to the principal proceedings.

(4) If, on an application for an order under this subsection, it is proved that the conditions mentioned in section 1(1) are fulfilled as respects that other party, the court may make an order which prohibits him from doing anything described in the order.

(5) Subject to subsection (6), the person against whom an order under this section has been made and the relevant authority on whose application that order was made may apply to the county court which made an order under this section for it to be varied or discharged by a further order.

(6) Except with the consent of the relevant authority and the person subject to the order, no order under this section shall be discharged before the end of the period of two years beginning with the date of service of the order.

(7) Subsections (5) to (7) and (10) to (12) of section 1 apply for the purposes of the making and effect of orders made under this section as they apply for the purposes of the making and effect of anti-social behaviour orders.]

[1C. **Orders on conviction in criminal proceedings**

(1) This section applies where a person (the 'offender') is convicted of a relevant offence.

(2) If the court considers—

(a) that the offender has acted, at any time since the commencement date, in an anti-social manner, that is to say in a manner that caused or was likely to cause harassment, alarm or distress to one or more persons not of the same household as himself, and

(b) that an order under this section is necessary to protect persons in any place in England and Wales from further anti-social acts by him,

it may make an order which prohibits the offender from doing anything described in the order.

(3) The court may make an order under this section

(a) if the prosecutor asks it to do so, or

(b) if the court thinks it is appropriate to do so.

(3A) For the purpose of deciding whether to make an order under this section the court may consider evidence led by the prosecution and the defence.

(3B) It is immaterial whether evidence led in pursuance of subsection (3A) would have been admissible in the proceedings in which the offender was convicted.

(4) An order under this section shall not be made except—

(a) in addition to a sentence imposed in respect of the relevant offence; or

(b) in addition to an order discharging him conditionally.

(5) An order under this section takes effect on the day on which it is made, but the court

may provide in any such order that such requirements
shall, during any period when the offender is detained
until his release from that custody.

(6) An offender subject to an order under this section may
it for it to be varied or discharged.

(7) In the case of an order under this section made by a m
subsection (6) to the court by which the order was r
magistrates' court acting for the same petty sessions

(8) No application may be made under subsection (6) for the discharge ᴜɪ ᴀɪɪ ᴠ.ᴇ
the end of the period of two years beginning with the day on which the order takes
effect.

(9) Subsections (7), (10) and (11) of section 1 apply for the purposes of the making and
effect of orders made by virtue of this section as they apply for the purposes of the
making and effect of anti-social behaviour orders.

(9A) The council for the local government area in which a person in respect of whom an
anti-social behaviour order has been made resides or appears to reside may bring
proceedings under section 1(10) (as applied by subsection (9) above) for breach of an
order under subsection (2) above.

(9B) Subjection (9C) applies in relation to proceedings in which an order under
subsection (2) is made against a child or young person who is convicted of an offence.

(9C) Insofar as the proceedings relate to the making of the order—

(a) section 49 of the Children and Young Persons Act 1933 (c.12) (restrictions on reports
of proceedings in which children and young persons are concerned) does not apply
in respect of the child or young person against whom the order is made;

(b) section 39 of that Act (power to prohibit publication of certain matter) does so apply.

(10) In this section—

'child' and 'young persons' have the same meaning as in the Children and Young Persons
Act 1933
'the commencement date' has the same meaning as in section 1 above;
'the court' in relation to an offender means—

(a) the court by or before which he is convicted of the relevant offence; or

(b) if he is committed to the Crown Court to be dealt with for that offence, the
Crown Court; and

'relevant offence' means an offence committed after the coming into force of section 64 of
the Police Reform Act 2002.]

[1D.    **Interim orders**

(1) The applications to which this section applies are—

(a) an application for an anti-social behaviour order; and

(b) an application for an order under section 1B.

(2) If, before determining an application to which this section applies, the court considers
that it is just to make an order under this section pending the determination of that
application ('the main application'), it may make such an order.

(3) An order under this section is an order which prohibits the defendant from doing
anything described in the order.

(4) An order under this section—

(a) shall be for a fixed period;

(b) may be varied, renewed or discharged;

l, if it has not previously ceased to have effect, cease to have effect on the etermination of the main application.

Subsections (6), (8) and (10) to (12) of section 1 apply for the purposes of the making and effect of orders under this section as they apply for the purposes of the making and effect of anti-social behaviour orders.]

[1E.  **Consultation requirements**

(1) This section applies to—

(a)   applications for an anti-social behaviour order; and

(b)   applications for an order under section 1B.

(2) Before making an application to which this section applies, the council for a local government area shall consult the chief officer of police of the police force maintained for the police area within which that local government area lies.

(3) Before making an application to which this section applies, a chief officer of police shall consult the council for the local government area in which the person in relation to whom the application is to be made resides or appears to reside.

(4) Before making an application to which this section applies, a relevant authority other than a council for a local government area or a chief officer of police shall consult—

(a)   the council for the local government area in which the person in relation to whom the application is to be made resides or appears to reside; and

(b)   the chief officer of police of the police force maintained for the police area within which that local government area lies.]

...

4.   **Appeals against orders**

(1) An appeal shall lie to the Crown Court against the making by a magistrates' court of an anti-social behaviour order [, an order under section 1D above,] [an order under section 2A above].

(2) On such an appeal the Crown Court—

(a)   may make such orders as may be necessary to give effect to its determination of the appeal; and

(b)   may also make such incidental or consequential orders as appear to it to be just.

Again, reference should be made to updating services to determine which of the amendments made by the Police Reform Act 2002 and the Anti-Social Behaviour Act 2003 are in force.

## ANTI-SOCIAL BEHAVIOUR ORDERS (ASBOS)

Section 1 of the 1998 Act (as amended) enables a 'relevant authority', eg a district council, London borough or a chief constable, to apply for an 'anti-social behaviour order' against any person aged 10 years or over where certain conditions are fulfilled:

- the person has acted – one 'act' might, initially, appear to be enough, but see further below on this issue – in an anti-social manner, ie a manner that caused or was likely to cause harassment, alarm or distress to one or more persons not of the same household as himself/herself; and

- such an order is necessary, ie there is a need to intervene, to protect relevant persons from further anti-social acts by the person in question. Such an order is, however, a last resort when other measures – such as mediation – have failed.

The persons protected by such an order can be those living within the area of the local authority in question or, in the case of a registered social landlord people who reside in or are otherwise likely to be on or in the vicinity of property managed by that body.

Currently, harassment, alarm or distress is not further defined, but it would appear to extend to verbal/racial abuse, harassment, assaults, 'adorning' premises with graffiti, making excessive noise, drunk and disorderly conduct, throwing missiles, indulging in vehicle crime and acts of prostitution. It should also be noted that the use of the phrase 'likely to cause' enables the employment of professional witnesses as the standard to be employed is objective and not a measurement of actual alarm, etc felt by any given individual.

From their inception, ASBOs have been somewhat controversial, partly because of the lack of definition of what constitutes anti-social behaviour, and who, because while an ASBO is civilly obtained its breach may result in criminal sanctions.

The provisions relating to Anti-Social Behaviour Orders of the Crime and Disorder Act 1998 came into force on 1 April 1999, and the Home Office then issued its Circular 9/99 on the matter and has continued since to update its website pages. It appears it was North Somerset District Council who were the first local authority in England and Wales to utilise the anti-social behaviour provisions when on 4 June 1999 they obtained an order against a young man who regularly attended an area housing office, threatened and abused staff, caused damage to the office and staff members' cars, and threatened staff as they went about their business on the housing estate in question. The authority chose this method of proceeding because previous injunctive relief obtained against the same individual had been granted for three months only, and because it was believed that, with a decentralised system of housing management, attacks on housing officers amounted to conduct that was likely to cause harassment, alarm or distress within the local community[26]. Controversy did, however, break forth in September 1999 when two Liverpool teenagers were made subject to ASBOs which banned them from walking in two named streets and from urinating and spitting in public. 'Liberty', the civil rights organisation, provided defence help for the two young men and has since continued its condemnation of the 1998 Act's provisions as being a 'mishmash' of civil and criminal procedures which mean that normal legal safeguards may be ignored. This provoked angry criticism from the Home Secretary himself, who condemned in public 'so-called civil liberties lawyers' and 'well-heeled and hypocritical' lawyers who 'represent the perpetrators of crime and then get back into their BMWs and drive to their homes in quiet and prosperous areas'[27].

---

[26] M Rowan, 'Crime and Disorder – ASBOs' (1999) 149 *New Law Journal* 1051.
[27] The Home Secretary speaking at the Annual Conference of the Police Superintendents' Association, see *The Times* and *The Independent* of 15 September 1999.

What is certain, leaving bluster and rhetoric on both sides to one side, is that ASBOs were not initially taken up rapidly by local authorities. This was hardly surprising given the need for policy decisions to be taken, training to be undergone, consultation with other relevant organisations to be set up and suitable cases identified. However, the apparent slowness of implementation led to seeming dismay at the Home Office, and shortly before his September 1999 speech, the Home Secretary wrote to all local authority chief executives urging them to make more use of the 1998 Act powers pointing out that the public would 'no doubt expect them to be used in appropriate cases'. The letter notes that at the time it was written, five ASBOs had been obtained and more were in the pipeline, but then continues: 'Nevertheless I am concerned that some authorities may have been put off from considering applying for orders in appropriate cases by some of the misconceptions which have gained ground as a result of comments by certain academics and civil libertarians.' This referred to claims that the 1998 Act's provisions were too sweeping and infringed the terms of the European Convention on Human Rights – a matter denied by the Home Secretary.

The Home Secretary's letter then went on to make two points of considerable importance, both of which he considered arose from misconceptions about ASBOs.

> 'First they are not a measure of last resort and there is no requirement for you or the police to have exhausted every other option before you decide to apply for an order. They should be sought where there is a need to intervene to protect the victim(s) from further anti-social acts by the perpetrator and other remedies are not considered to be as appropriate or effective.'

This merely supplements what is stated in the published guidance that a relevant authority is not required to demonstrate that every other remedy has been exhausted before applying for an order. What is, perhaps, more controversial is the following statement:

> 'Secondly ...I have been concerned by reports which suggest that the process of consultation [before an order is sought] may, in some cases, be being hampered by agencies taking a less than constructive approach. I do not need to remind you that any delay in taking early and, hopefully, effective action to deal with unacceptable and anti-social behaviour, is another day of misery for the victims of such behaviour. I hope therefore you will not allow the process of consultation to become too protracted.'

Then came the telling point:

> 'Ultimately, of course, although the Act requires consultation, agreement is not a requirement – the decision to apply for an order rests with you or the local police.'

This could well be interpreted as urging local authorities to 'go it alone', and does appear to add a gloss to the published guidance which states that differences of opinion should not prevent an application for an order being made: 'If it has been decided that an order is needed'. It also appeared to run counter to the published guidance then current that a failure to agree by relevant authorities before an application for an order is made might weaken the case in the courts.

However, were the fears of the 'certain academics and civil libertarians', to which the Home Secretary refers, borne out in practice? It was the basic structure of the ASBO provisions that were a cause of concern to some, a matter already alluded to above. The published guidance document itself alludes to this – the procedure for obtaining an order is civil, but breach of an order can lead to criminal sanctions. Thus an order obtained 'on the balance of probabilities', with the possible use of hearsay evidence according to civil evidence provisions, could be used to ground criminal charges based on its breach, though such a breach would have to be proved 'beyond reasonable doubt'.

Initially, however, it appeared local authorities were amassing sufficient evidence before applying for orders that would enable the criminal burden of proof to be discharged at the initial stage. They were aware of the criticisms that can be made of the 1998 Act's provisions and were anxious not only to avoid those criticisms but also wished to bring only those cases where they could be reasonably confident of a successful outcome. Hence the cautious approach taken to amassing evidence.

ASBOs are civil orders which prohibit specific types of behaviour, or bar individuals from particular areas, but they are not criminal punishments per se. The philosophy underlying them is that they are community based measures which should help and encourage particular localities to regulate themselves and to prevent bad behaviour. The test for obtaining an order is of two stages: the defendant must be shown to have behaved in an anti-social manner *and* an order must be shown to be necessary to protect people from further anti-social behaviour by the defendant. As will become clear from the discussion of case law below, the standard of proof with regard to showing past behaviour is the criminal one of 'beyond reasonable doubt', but that does not apply to the second stage test. ASBOs can be used to tackle collective bad behaviour, and often action taken against ringleaders can prevent bad behaviour by others, however, where there are multiple offenders a separate ASBO is needed against each one, though the cases may be heard together by the court. It is possible under the changes made in 2002 for an ASBO to be sought in proceedings before the County Court, for example where the offender in question is subject to possession proceedings by, inter alia, forbidding a person who is to be evicted from returning to an area or from further harassing his/her former neighbours. Again under changes made in 2002 an ASBO can extend to any defined area within England and Wales, and may even extend to the whole of England and Wales. This addresses the problem of those who are likely to 'export' their behaviour between areas. Particular note should also be taken of s 1D, under which an interim order can be made in advance of a full hearing. What, however, continued to disturb some commentators was the fact that breach of an ASBO is a criminal offence attracting criminal sanctions. A challenge to this under the Human Rights Act 1998 was not long delayed.

## THE HUMAN RIGHTS AND OTHER CHALLENGES

Despite the disquiet alluded to above there has not been a great deal of reported litigation under the 1998 Act but the House of Lords has pronounced in one major case. In *R (on the application of AB and SB) v Nottingham City Council*[28] it was held that the making of an ASBO can be challenged where it can be shown that other more appropriate measures should have been pursued. However, the principal decision is *R (on the application of McCann) v Crown Court at Manchester; Clingham v Kensington and Chelsea Royal Borough Council*[29] (and see also Chapter 14 below for further detail on Human Rights issues).

In the first of these two cases raising overlapping issues, the respondent chief constable, relying partly on hearsay evidence, applied to the magistrates by complaint pursuant to s 1(1) of the Crime and Disorder Act 1998 (the CAD), seeking the making of anti-social behaviour orders against three brothers under s 1(4) of the Act. Such an order could be made against a person if he had acted in a manner that had caused or was likely to cause harassment, alarm or distress to one or more persons not in the same household as himself (s 1(1)(b)). By virtue of s 1(10), the breach of such an order was a criminal offence with a maximum punishment of five years' imprisonment. The stipendiary magistrate made the orders sought by the chief constable. The Crown Court dismissed the brothers' appeals, and they applied unsuccessfully to the Divisional Court for judicial review of that decision. In dismissing the brothers' subsequent appeal, the Court of Appeal, like the courts below, held that proceedings under s 1(1) of the CAD were civil rather than criminal both as a matter of domestic law and for the purposes of the right to a fair hearing under Art 6(1) of the European Convention for the Protection of Human Rights and Fundamental Freedoms 1950 (as set out in Sch 1 to the Human Rights Act 1998). The Court further concluded, however, that, in view of the serious consequences of an anti-social behaviour order, it was likely to be appropriate to apply the criminal standard of proof in the majority of applications under s 1(1) of the CAD. The brothers appealed to the House of Lords against the Court of Appeal's view that such applications constituted civil proceedings. They contended, in particular, that the procedure leading to the making of an anti-social behaviour order under s 1(4) had to be considered together with the criminal proceedings for breach under s 1(10). The Secretary of State, as an interested party, challenged the Court of Appeal's ruling on the standard of proof, contending that it was preferable to apply a single fixed standard of a balance of probabilities.

In the second case, the respondent local authority applied for an anti-social behaviour order against the appellant, C. The application was based primarily on hearsay evidence. Following a preliminary ruling, the district judge stated a case for the decision of the Divisional Court that raised questions about the admissibility of hearsay evidence in proceedings under s 1(1) of the CAD. The Divisional Court concluded that such evidence was admissible since proceedings under s 1(1) were not criminal proceedings. C appealed to the House of Lords, relying on its jurisdiction to hear an appeal from a decision of the High Court in any criminal cause or matter.

The House of Lords held that proceedings under s 1(1) of the CAD for the imposition of an anti-social behaviour order were civil, not criminal, both as a matter of domestic law and for the purposes of Art 6 of the Convention. As regards

[28]   [2001] EWHC Admin 235, [2001] 3 FCR 350.
[29]   [2002] UKHL 39, [2003] IAC 787, [2002] 4 All ER 593.

domestic law, such proceedings involved no formal accusation of a breach of criminal law, and they were initiated by the civil process of a complaint. Section 1(1)(a) required an objective inquiry, and there was no need to prove mens rea of particular offences. It was unnecessary to establish criminal liability, the true purpose of the proceedings being preventative. That was clearly brought out by s 1(1)(b). It followed that the making of an anti-social behaviour order was not a conviction or condemnation that a person was guilty of an offence. It resulted in no penalty whatever. Moreover, the procedure leading to the making of an order under s 1(4) was separate and independent from the proceedings for breach under s 1(10). As for Art 6(1) of the Convention, the jurisdiction of the European Court of Human Rights recognised that proceedings to obtain an order designed to prevent future harmful conduct, but not to impose a penalty for past offences, did not constitute the bringing of a criminal charge. Indeed, there was no case in which that court had held proceedings to be criminal even though an adverse outcome for the defendant could not result in any penalty. Since proceedings under s 1(1) of the CAD were civil, hearsay evidence was admissible pursuant to the statutory machinery for the introduction of such evidence in civil proceedings. Accordingly, the appeal of the brothers in the first case would be dismissed, while the House had no jurisdiction to entertain C's appeal since it was not an appeal from a decision of the High Court in any criminal cause or matter.

Magistrates have to apply the criminal standard of proof in all cases under s 1 of the CAD. Although in principle the standard of proof ordinarily applicable in civil proceedings, namely the balance of probabilities, should apply to proceedings for anti-social behaviour orders, there were good reasons, in the interests of fairness, for applying the higher standard when allegations were made of criminal or quasi-criminal conduct which, if proved, would have serious consequences for the person against whom they were made. It followed that, when applying s 1(1)(a), magistrates have to be sure that a defendant has acted in the manner specified in that provision. The inquiry under s 1(1)(b) did not involve a standard of proof: it was an exercise of judgment or evaluation. Accordingly, the Secretary of State's challenge in the first case would be rejected.

Lord Steyn considered the background to the legislation.

### 'The social problem

Before the issues can be directly addressed it is necessary to sketch the social problem which led to the enactment of s 1(1) and the technique which underlies the first part of s 1. It is well known that in some urban areas, notably urban housing estates and deprived inner city areas, young persons, and groups of young persons, cause fear, distress and misery to law-abiding and innocent people by outrageous anti-social behaviour. It takes many forms. It includes behaviour which is criminal such as assaults and threats, particularly against old people and children, criminal damage to individual property and amenities of the community, burglary, theft, and so forth. Sometimes the conduct falls short of cognisable criminal offences. The culprits are mostly, but not exclusively, male. Usually they are relatively young, ranging particularly from about 10–18 years of age. Often people in the neighbourhood are in fear of such young culprits. In many cases, and probably in most, people will only report matters to the police anonymously or on the strict understanding that they will not directly or indirectly be identified. In recent years this phenomenon became a serious social problem. There appeared to be a gap in the law. The criminal law offered insufficient protection to communities. Public confidence in the rule of law was undermined by a not unreasonable view in some communities that the law failed them. This was the social problem which s 1 was designed to address.

## The legislative technique

The aim of the criminal law is not punishment for its own sake but to permit everyone to go about their daily lives without fear of harm to person or property. Unfortunately, by intimidating people the culprits, usually small in number, sometimes effectively silenced communities. Fear of the conse- quences of complaining to the police dominated the thoughts of people: reporting incidents to the police entailed a serious risk of reprisals. The criminal law by itself offered inadequate protection to them. There was a model available for remedial legislation. Before 1998 Parliament had, on a number of occasions, already used the technique of prohibiting by statutory injunction conduct deemed to be unacceptable and making a breach of the injunction punishable by penalties.

The Housing Act 1996 created the power to grant injunctions against anti-social behaviour (see ss 152 and 153 (breach)). This was, however, a power severely restricted in respect of locality. A broadly similar technique was adopted in the Protection from Harassment Act 1997 (see ss 3 and 3(6) (breach)). In all these cases the requirements for the granting of the statutory injunction depend on the criteria specified in the particular statute. The unifying element is, however, the use of the civil remedy of an injunction to prohibit conduct considered to be utterly unacceptable, with a remedy of criminal penalties in the event of disobedience.

There is no doubt that Parliament intended to adopt the model of a civil remedy of an injunction, backed up by criminal penalties, when it enacted s 1 of the [Crime and Disorder Act]. The view was taken that the proceedings for an anti-social behaviour order would be civil and would not attract the rigour of the inflexible and sometimes absurdly technical hearsay rule which applies in criminal cases. If this supposition was wrong, in the sense that Parliament did not objectively achieve its aim, it would inevitably follow that the procedure for obtaining anti-social behaviour orders is completely or virtually unworkable and useless. If that is what the law decrees, so be it. My starting point is, however, an initial scepticism of an outcome which would deprive communities of *their* fundamental rights.

Counsel for the defendants accepted that the purpose of Parliament was to cast proceedings under the first part of s 1, as opposed to proceedings for breach, in a civil mould. However, counsel submitted that objectively consid- ered, the objective was not achieved. They argued that in reality and in substance such proceedings are criminal in character. This is an important argument which must be carefully examined. The starting point is that in proceedings under the first part of s1 the Crown Prosecution Service is not involved at all. At that stage there is no formal accusation of a breach of criminal law. The proceedings are initiated by the civil process of a complaint. Under s 1(1)(a) all that has to be established is that the person has acted—

> "in an anti-social manner, that is to say, in a manner that caused or was likely to cause harassment, alarm or distress to one or more persons not of the same household as himself;"

This is an objective inquiry: mens rea as an ingredient of particular offences need not be proved. It is unnecessary to establish criminal liability. The true purpose of the proceedings is preventative. This appears from the heading of Pt 1. It is also clearly brought out by the requirement of s 1(1)(b)—

> "that such an order is necessary to protect persons in the local government area in which the harassment, alarm or distress was caused or was likely to be caused from further anti-social acts by him ..."

It follows that the making of an anti-social behaviour order is not a conviction or condemnation that the person is guilty of an offence. It results in no penalty whatever. It cannot be entered on a defendant's record as a conviction. It is also not a recordable offence for the purpose of taking fingerprints (see s 27 of the Police and Criminal Evidence Act 1984).

The view that proceedings for an anti-social behaviour order under s1 are civil in character is further supported by two important decisions. In *B v Chief Constable of the Avon and Somerset Constabulary* [2001] 1 All ER 562, [2001] 1 WLR 340 the question arose whether proceedings for a sex offender order under s 2 of the CDA are civil. Section 2 is different in conception from s 1 in as much as an order can only be made in respect of a person who has already been convicted as a sex offender. On the other hand, its purpose is preventative "to protect the public from serious harm from him". Lord Bingham of Cornhill CJ held ([2001] 1 All ER 562 at 571–572, [2001] 1 WLR 340 at 352 (para 25)):

> "The rationale of s 2 was, by means of an injunctive order, to seek to avoid the contingency of any further suffering by any further victim. It would also of course be to the advantage of a defendant if he were to be saved from further offending. As in the case of a civil injunction, a breach of the court's order may attract a sanction. But, also as in the case of a civil injunction, the order, although restraining the defendant from doing that which is prohibited, imposes no penalty or disability upon him. I am accordingly satisfied that, as a matter of English domestic law, the application is a civil proceeding, as Parliament undoubtedly intended it to be."

I conclude that proceedings to obtain an anti-social behaviour order are civil proceedings under domestic law.

### The classification under art 6

The question now arises whether, despite its domestic classification, an anti-social behaviour order nevertheless has a criminal character in accordance with the autonomous concepts of art 6. The fair trial guarantee under art 6(1) applies to both "the determination of [a person's] civil rights" and "the determination of ...any criminal charge". On the other hand, only the latter attract the additional protections under art 6(2) and 6(3). Insofar as the latter provisions apply to "everyone charged with a criminal offence" it is well established in the jurisprudence of the European Court of Human Rights that this concept is co-extensive with the concept of the determination of any criminal charge (see *Lutz v Germany* (1987) 10 EHRR 182). Germane to the present case is the minimum right under art 6(3)(d) of everyone charged with a criminal offence to examine or have examined witnesses against him or to obtain the attendance and examination of witnesses on his behalf under the same conditions as witnesses against him. If the proceedings under s 1 of the CDA are criminal within the meaning of art 6, this provision is applicable. If it is civil, art 6(3)(d) is inapplicable.

In *Engel v Netherlands* (1976) 1 EHRR 647 at 678–679 (para 82), the European court established three criteria for determining whether proceedings are "criminal" within the meaning of the convention, namely (a) the domestic classification, (b) the nature of the offence, and (c) the severity of the potential penalty which the defendant risks incurring. The character and attributes of the proceedings for an anti-social behaviour order have been outlined. Domestically, they are properly classified as civil. That is, however, only a starting point. Turning to factor (b), the position is that the order under the first part of s1 does not constitute a finding that an offence has been committed: contrast the community charge decision in *Benham v United Kingdom* (1996) 22 EHRR 293. It is right, however, to observe that the third factor is the most important. Here the position is that the order itself involves no penalty. The established criteria suggest that the proceedings were not in respect of a criminal charge.

The House has been taken on a tour d'horizon of the leading decisions of the European court: see the judgment of Potter LJ in *Han v Customs and Excise Comrs, Martins v Customs and Excise Comrs, Morris v Customs and Excise Comrs* [2001] EWCA Civ 1040, [2001] 4 All ER 687, [2001] 1 WLR 2253 for a recent review of the European case law. It will serve no purpose to review again decisions far removed from the present case. What does emerge, however, is that there is, as Lord Bingham of Cornhill CJ pointed out in *B v Chief Constable of the Avon and Somerset Constabulary* [2001] 1 All ER 562, [2001] 1 WLR 340, no case in which the European court has held proceedings to be criminal even though an adverse outcome for the defendant cannot result in any penalty. It could be said, of course, that there is scope for the law to be developed in this direction. On the other hand, an extensive interpretation of what is a criminal charge under art 6(1) would, by rendering the injunctive process ineffectual, prejudice the freedom of liberal democracies to maintain the rule of law by the use of civil injunctions.

The closest case in support of the defendants' submission is *Steel v UK* (1998) 5 BHRC 339 at 351 (paras 48–49) which is authority for the proposition that proceedings whereby in England and Wales a person may be bound over to keep the peace, involve the determination of a criminal charge for the purposes of art 6. This power goes back many centuries (see *Percy v DPP* [1995] 3 All ER 124 at 128–129, [1995] 1 WLR 1382 at 1389–1390). It is in a very real sense a judicial power sui generis. The European court found a punitive element in the fact that the magistrates may commit to prison any person who refuses to be bound over not to breach the peace where there is evidence beyond reasonable doubt that his or her conduct caused or was likely to cause a breach of the peace and that he would otherwise cause a breach of the peace (see (1998) 5 BHRC 339 at 351 (para 48)). There was an immediate and obvious penal consequence. Properly analysed this case does not assist the defendant's argument.

The conclusion I have reached is reinforced by a cogently reasoned judgment on the interpretation of art 6 by the Lord President (Rodger) in *S v Miller* 2001 SC 977. Section 52(2) of the Children (Scotland) Act 1995 provides that a child may have to be subjected to compulsory measures of supervision when he 'has committed an offence'. The question arose whether in such proceedings art 6 is applicable. The Lord President observed (2001 SC 977 at 989–990):

> "… at the stage when S was arrested and charged by the police on 31 October, he was indeed 'charged with a criminal offence' in terms of art 6, since he was liable to be brought before a criminal court in proceedings which could have resulted in the imposition of a penalty. He remained 'charged with a criminal offence' in terms of art 6 until the procurator fiscal decided the following day – in the language of sec 43(5) of the Criminal Procedure Act – 'not to proceed with the charge'. At that point the criminal proceedings came to an end and the reporter initiated the procedures under the 1995 Act by arranging a hearing in terms of sec 63(1). In my view, once the procurator fiscal has decided not to proceed with the charge against a child and so there is no longer any possibility of proceedings resulting in a penalty, any subsequent proceedings under the 1995 Act are not criminal for the purposes of art 6. Although the reporter does indeed intend to show that the child concerned committed an offence, this is not for the purpose of punishing him but in order to establish a basis for taking appropriate measures for his welfare. That being so, the child who is notified of grounds for referral setting out the offence in question is not thereby 'charged with a criminal offence' in terms of art 6.

> It is not now disputed, of course, that the children's hearing proceedings involve the determination of civil rights and obligations. Article 6 therefore applies. But, since the proceedings are not criminal, the specific guarantees in art 6(2) and (3) do not apply."

I am in complete agreement with this reasoning as correctly reflecting the purpose of art 6. And it applies a fortiori to proceedings under s 1. After all, s 1(1) does not require proof of a criminal offence.

In my view an application for an anti-social behaviour order does not involve the determination of a criminal charge.

It [was] submitted that, even if the relevant proceedings are civil, words must be implied into the Civil Evidence Act 1995 which give the court a wider power to exclude hearsay evidence. As the Divisional Court judgment makes clear this is unnecessary and unwarranted. Counsel in the *Clingham* case then argued that, even if the proceedings are civil, nevertheless the introduction of hearsay evidence infringes a defendant's right to a fair trial under art 6(1) "in the determination of his civil rights and obligations". This is a misconceived argument. The case has not been heard. Such a challenge is premature. Upon a due consideration of the evidence, direct or hearsay, it may turn out that the defendant has no answer to the case under s 1(1). For the sake of completeness, I need only add that the use of the Civil Evidence Act 1995 and the rules in cases under the first part of s 1 are not in any way incompatible with the HRA.

### The standard of proof

Having concluded that the relevant proceedings are civil, in principle if follows that the standard of proof ordinarily applicable in civil proceedings, namely the balance of probabilities, should apply. However, I agree that, given the seriousness of matters involved, at least some reference to the heightened civil standard would usually be necessary (see *Re H (minors) (sexual abuse: standard of proof)* [1996] 1 All ER 1 at 16–17, [1996] AC 563 at 586 per Lord Nicholls of Birkenhead). For essentially practical reasons, the Recorder of Manchester decided to apply the criminal standard. The Court of Appeal said that would usually be the right course to adopt. Lord Bingham of Cornhill has observed that the heightened civil standard and the criminal standard are virtually indistinguishable. I do not disagree with any of these views. But in my view pragmatism dictates that the task of magistrates should be made more straightforward by ruling that they must in all cases under s 1 apply the criminal standard. If the House takes this view it will be sufficient for the magistrates, when applying s 1(1)(a) *to be sure* that the defendant has acted in an anti-social manner, that is to say, in a manner that caused or was likely to cause harassment, alarm or distress to one or more persons not of the same household as himself. The inquiry under s 1(1)(b), namely that such an order is necessary to protect persons from further anti-social acts by him, does not involve a standard of proof: it is an exercise of judgment or evaluation. This approach should facilitate correct decision-making and should ensure consistency and predictability in this corner of the law. In coming to this conclusion I bear in mind that the use of hearsay evidence will often be of crucial importance. For my part, hearsay evidence depending on its logical probativeness is quite capable of satisfying the requirements of s 1(1).'

Thus it became established that proceedings for an ASBO are civil in nature which makes them subject to the civil *evidential* rules and the *possibility of the reception of hearsay evidence*. However, the applicant for an order must demonstrate that the defendant has acted in an anti-social fashion according to the criminal *standard* of proof, ie beyond reasonable doubt. However, that standard only applies to proving that anti-social behaviour has occurred; in deciding whether there is a need for an ASBO in consequence of that behaviour the court must exercise its judgment. There is no need to prove beyond reasonable doubt that an order is necessary. Furthermore such an order maybe justified once the bad behaviour in question has been proved even though the defendant subsequently behaves well, see *S v Poole Borough Council*[30].

The *McCann* decision has appeared to settle many of the issues relating to ASBOs and to have laid down guidelines according to which those who wish to utilise them can act while the critics of the ASBO appear to be, for the moment, reasonably satisfied. Briefly, the advantages of an ASBO as a remedy for dealing with bad behaviour are:
- The defendant does not need to be a tenant.
- It can apply anywhere and is not tied to specific localities or properties.
- It can be of long duration and can apply to a variety of behaviours.
- It does not put a tenancy automatically at risk as does a suspended possession order.
- It can apply to anyone over the age of 10.

The disadvantages are:
- Obtaining an ASBO is not necessarily cheap.
- Procedures can be slow and rely, as the extract from the statute shows, on co-operation between various statutory agencies, good consultative arrangements are essential.
- There remains some unease that it is wrong to impose a criminal penalty in respect of acts which in themselves may not be criminal.

It appears arguable, however, that ASBO proceedings enable early and focused action to be taken in respect of an individual's misconduct. Furthermore under the changes made in 2002 it is possible to obtain an interim ASBO which can be made where the court considers it just to do so pending the outcome of an application. The consultative requirements of the law have still to be satisfied – and the Home Office guidance referring to the revised procedures for consultation under s 1E of the 1998 Act, as amended, makes it clear now that such consultation *has* to take place, though it need *not* result in consensus as to whether an application is to be made. Interim ASBOs are thus useful measures where serious misconduct needs to be halted.

In *R (on the application of M) v Secretary of State for Constitutional Affairs, Lord Chancellor and Leeds City Council*[31] in consequence of disorder the local authority and the police applied for interim ASBOs without notice, and these were made under s 1D of the 1998 Act, as amended. M, who was the subject of one of the orders argued that such an order made without notice was both unfair and a breach of his right to have a proper hearing before being made subject to an order. The Court of Appeal considered there was no breach of M's human right to have a proper hearing (see further Chapter 14 below) as the orders were for a limited

---

[30]  [2002] EWHC 244 (Admin), [2002] All ER (D) 143 (Feb).
[31]  [2004] EWCA Civ 312, [2004] 2 All ER 531, [2004] 1 WLR 2298.

period only, there was a right to have a review, and the date for that had been fixed, and the order did not become effective until served. Thus there was no infringement of the right to a proper hearing.

A non-legal alternative to the ASBO has now emerged in the form of the 'Acceptable Behaviour Contract' (ABC). Such a contract may be made with anyone over the age of 10 and is an agreement between relevant agencies and a person. An ABC may contain, on a voluntary basis, the same terms which would have been sought in an ASBO, and if broken the ABC may be utilised in a subsequent ASBO application. Such a contract can be useful to nip bad behaviour in the bud.

An ABC is made in documentary form between the 'offender' and one or more of the responsible agencies. The contract specifies the bad behaviour in question and the offender agrees to refrain from such behaviour in future. As an incentive not to break the contract the legal sanction which may follow, for example seeking possession where the offender lives in social housing, may be written into the terms of the contract, and central guidance counsels that this should be done. ABCs have been most particularly used in respect of children, in which case their parents or guardians need to be involved in the discussion of the contract, and experience suggests that the terminology needs to be addressed to the individual, and should not be vague and generic with definite, but not over many, prohibitions. It is also policy that where a person is subject to an ABC other forms of appropriate social assistance should be afforded to him/her and their families. It is also necessary to ask at an early stage whether the individual is likely to respond well to the informal 'contractual' approach. Where there is a general problem of bad behaviour from children on particular estates – and there is good research evidence that bad behaviour levels are more likely in areas where the ratio of older people to children is low – the possibility of the use of ABCs may be publicised generally, and then those most likely to benefit from agreeing to modify their behaviour can be targeted and dealt with individually.

ABCs can last for any length of time though they are usually of no more than one year's duration and six months is not uncommon. They can be renewed if need be, though if there is a breach thought needs to be given to whether other legal action should be taken. For the purposes of renewal, etc., it is clear that ABCs need to be monitored and kept under review.

## ASBOs in practice and further developments in the law

Home Office figures show that between 1 April 1999 and 31 March 2003, 1,112 ASBOs were granted by courts in England and Wales, while only 31 were refused. This seems to indicate that the relevant authorities have not only worked together, as is required under the legislation, but also that orders have generally been sought only where a reasonable chance of success was anticipated. On the other hand other research in 2002 indicated that local authorities placed ASB in the 'top three' of their current 'public order' concerns, with most authorities already having a specific policy on the issue. The same research, however, pointed out that ASBOs can only *prohibit* bad behaviour and that other mechanisms are needed to ensure good behaviour and to give support to those who offend, many of whom may suffer from other problems including disabilities (physical or mental) and drug and alcohol abuse[32]. In such cases, can 'stop it' alone ever be an effective remedy? In this context ABCs seem to be a more appropriate response.

Other Home Office sponsored researched appeared, however, to give a more ambivalent picture of ASBOs in practice.

*Tackling Anti-social Behaviour: What really works*

A Home Office briefing[33] issued in September 2002 made the following key points:

- Young people and students were much more likely to state that they had experienced anti-social behaviour than older people.
- Between April 1999 and March 2002, a total of 583 Anti-social Behaviour Orders (ASBOs) were granted.
- Of the 466 ASBOs granted between April 1999 and September 2001, 84 per cent were on men, and 74 per cent were on those aged 21 years and under.
- A previous Home Office Review of ASBOs had found that 36 per cent of orders were breached within nine months of being granted (some up to five times).
- On average an ASBO costs more than £5,000 and takes over three months to obtain.
- In 2000, over half of those sentenced in court for a breach of an ASBO received a custodial sentence.

This report reinforced the finding that most local authorities have an active anti-social behaviour policy and pointed out that tackling ASB is high on the agenda of both national government and local agencies. It was also stressed that local partnerships of relevant authorities, together with their communities, need to identify local problems, develop strategies and action plans, and evaluate their interventions to inform future practice.

The report, however, concluded that:

> 'Evaluations of what works in reducing anti-social behaviour are scarce. Where they do exist, they are carried out locally with very little standardisation in methodology. For this reason, it is difficult to make informed judgements about what works and what does not work to reduce anti-social behaviour. Despite this, however, it is clear that a focus upon one element of intervention at the expense of others can only result in a quick fix at the expense of any long-term solutions. Partners need to address anti-social behaviour using a holistic approach that includes enforcement, prevention and education.'

*Implementing Anti-social Behaviour Orders: messages for practitioners*[34] found variations in policies and practices with ASBOs, indicating that, nationwide, there is inconsistency between agencies and areas, with some places finding them to be

---

[32] Lucas, R and Whitworth, J, 'Tackling Anti-Social Behaviour – information and case studies about local authority work' (2002) Local Government Association.
[33] Armitage, R, *Community Safety Practice Briefing* (2002) Home Office.
[34] Campbell, S, Home Office Research Findings 160 (2003) Home Office.

effective and efficient remedies, while exactly the opposite has been the experience in other places. The following key points were made, which stress the need for inter agency co-operation, particularly with regard to the release of information under protocols drawn up under s 115 of the 1998 Act.

> 'Areas should draw up simple, streamlined protocols created with their local area in mind. These should be designed to help practitioners on the ground deal with anti-social behaviour problems quickly, easily and successfully.
>
> - Some form of partnership working is desirable and can result in real benefits such as improved relationships, spreading costs and producing creative solutions. However, it should not be allowed to delay the process.
> - Strategic support and commitment from within the lead agency are essential for ASBOs to work successfully.
> - The work of agencies' solicitors is often crucial as they develop experience over time, and can give detailed advice on the process, evidence and legal matters.
> - Problem-solving can target the causes of anti-social behaviour and is often effective without the final step of applying for an ASBO being necessary.
> - Fostering a good working relationship with the courts, through consultation and training, can help mutual understanding.
> - After an order is granted, continued close working with partner agencies and the community is essential to sustain public confidence and ensure the problem behaviour does not escalate.
> - There is evidence of fear and intimidation amongst witnesses. To combat this, strategies must be developed to minimise intimidation and support witnesses.
> - Ultimately, the measure of success will be whether the anti-social behaviour stops. This focus should be maintained throughout the process.'

In 2003 the Home Office issued Cm 5778, *Respect and Responsibility – Taking a Stand Against Anti-social Behaviour*. This, inter alia, identified weak parenting as a major cause of anti-social behaviour, and pointed out that more than half of all ASBOs are made against 10–17 year olds. It looked forward to a new type of order which would require positive steps for those subject to ASBOs to accept help with regard to particular problems they may be suffering, eg drug abuse. Other measures were also outlined by the White Paper, including new powers to close down properties being used as 'crack houses' where Class A drugs are sold and used, and further powers for social landlords to obtain faster eviction in respect of tenants who are guilty of anti-social behaviour, and removing the Right to Buy from such offenders. It was envisaged that courts would be required to consider the impact of ASB on individual victims and the wider community in all housing possession cases, while a consultation exercise was promised on whether local authorities should have power to withhold housing benefit payments from those responsible for ASB. The Department of Work and Pensions subsequently undertook this exercise, but the proposal was later abandoned.

In March 2003 the government introduced its Anti-social Behaviour Bill into Parliament, and this subsequently became the Anti-social Behaviour Act 2003. Alongside the Bill in October 2003 the government launched a major new policy which stressed the responsibility of local authorities and police forces to deal with anti-social behaviour, which was said to include noise from neighbours, abandoning cars and gatherings of young people 'hanging around'. This policy was to be carried forward centrally by the Home Office Anti-social Behaviour Unit, established in January 2003, in the form of the Anti-social Behaviour Action Plan. The key strands of policy are: to improve responses by relevant agencies to complaints of anti-social behaviour; to create 10 'trailblazing' 'Together Action Areas' which will in particular target neighbour nuisances, begging and environmental crime such as litter, graffiti and abandoning cars; to set up 'Victims and Witnesses first' schemes to identify the best ways to support those who are victims of anti-social behaviour. A central 'actionline' was to be set up in 2004 to give advice and assistance to relevant professionals, backed up by a web-site, while a centre of excellence will be created to provide instruction and training for them also. Some £11m in 2003/2004 and 2004/2005 will be devoted to furthering the work of Crime and Disorder Reduction Partnerships, and a specialist team of Anti-social Behaviour Prosecutors will be formed in the Crown Prosecution Service, while magistrates were to be issued with new sentencing guidelines on the issue in January 2004. From the point of view of housing, of particular interest are the initiatives creating Nuisance Neighbour Panels to find solutions to the problems caused by the worst offending families, and further help for the parents of youngsters who engage in anti-social behaviour. Relevant authorities are expected under this policy initiative to use all their existing powers to tackle the problem of anti-social behaviour. Home Office figures in August 2004 indicated that the numbers of ASBOs are increasing, but implementation is patchy. Some London boroughs make no use of the remedy. The Government is to place officials in 'reluctant' authorities to improve their use of ASBO powers[35].

## BRINGING ISSUES TOGETHER

The decision of the Court of Appeal in *New Charter Housing v Ashcroft*[36] indicates how the various provisions considered above may interact. A registered social landlord sought possession of a property rented from them by A on the basis of the behaviour of A's son D, aged 17, who was himself the subject of an interim ASBO following harassment against neighbours. A final ASBO was made which D broke and he was given a period of detention. In the county court the judge in the possession proceedings suspended the possession order in order to give A the opportunity to show she could curb D's bad behaviour on his release. The landlord argued that too much weight had been given to A's claim that she could control D, while she had not explained how she would go about this, having previously failed to keep him under control. The Court of Appeal accepted the landlord's argument and pointed out that A herself had made threats to neighbours, while showing no remorse for her son's conduct. Furthermore the judge had failed to consider the

---

[35] The Times, 1 September 2004.
[36] [2004] EWCA Civ 310, (2004) Housing Law Monitor 11(3).

interests of the neighbours as is required following *Canterbury v Lowe*[37]. The decision to suspend the possession order was reversed. See also Foreword III.

## DEMOTED TENANCIES AND ASB – FULFILLING PROMISES MADE IN CM 5778

The following provisions create yet another new housing status, the 'demoted tenancy'. When the Introductory Tenancy regime (see Chapter 8) was introduced under the Housing Act 1996 as, effectively, a 'probationary' status it was objected that it was defective in that it could not apply to an existing secure tenant who indulged in anti-social behaviour and who could thus only be dispossessed where the behaviour in question also satisfied the grounds for a possession order under the Housing Act 1985. Similarly there was no similar provision made for housing owned by registered social landlords, though this gap in the law has been somewhat filled by advice from the Housing Corporation which allows such landlords to utilise the device of the time-limited assured shorthold tenancy as a means of giving a probationary period before the granting of a full assured tenancy.

Sections 15 to 17 of the Anti-social Behaviour Act 2003 make provision to implement proposals designed to overcome the above-mentioned defects, by amending the Housing Acts of 1985 and 1988, inserting ss 82A and 6A (of the Housing Acts 1985 and 1988 respectively), as follows.

82A.   **Demotion because of anti-social behaviour**

(1) This section applies to a secure tenancy if the landlord is—

(a)   a local housing authority;

(b)   a housing action trust;

(c)   a registered social landlord.

(2) The landlord may apply to a county court for a demotion order.

(3) A demotion order has the following effect—

(a)   the secure tenancy is terminated with effect from the date specified in the order;

(b)   if the tenant remains in occupation of the dwelling-house after that date a demoted tenancy is created with effect from that date;

(c)   it is a term of the demoted tenancy that any arrears of rent payable at the termination of the secure tenancy become payable under the demoted tenancy;

(d)   it is also a term of the demoted tenancy that any rent paid in advance or overpaid at the termination of the secure tenancy is credited to the tenant's liability to pay rent under the demoted tenancy.

(4) The court must not make a demotion order unless it is satisfied—

(a)   that the tenant or a person residing in or visiting the dwelling-house has engaged or has threatened to engage in conduct to which section 153A or 153B of the Housing Act 1996 (anti-social behaviour or use of premises for unlawful purposes) applies, and

(b)   that it is reasonable to make the order.

(5) Each of the following has effect in respect of a demoted tenancy at the time it is

---

[37]   (2001) 33 HLR 53.

created by virtue of an order under this section as it has effect in relation to the secure tenancy at the time it is terminated by virtue of the order—

(a)   the parties to the tenancy;

(b)   the period of the tenancy;

(c)   the amount of the rent;

(d)   the dates on which the rent is payable.

(6) Subsection (5)(b) does not apply if the secure tenancy was for a fixed term and in such a case the demoted tenancy is a weekly periodic tenancy.

(7) If the landlord of the demoted tenancy serves on the tenant a statement of any other express terms of the secure tenancy which are to apply to the demoted tenancy such terms are also terms of the demoted tenancy.

(8) For the purposes of this section a demoted tenancy is—

(a)   a tenancy to which section 143A of the Housing Act 1996 applies if the landlord of the secure tenancy is a local housing authority or a housing action trust;

(b)   a tenancy to which section 20B of the Housing Act 1988 applies if the landlord of the secure tenancy is a registered social landlord …

## 6A.   Demotion because of anti-social behaviour

(1) This section applies to an assured tenancy if the landlord is a registered social landlord.

(2) The landlord may apply to a county court for a demotion order.

(3) A demotion order has the following effect—

(a)   the assured tenancy is terminated with effect from the date specified in the order;

(b)   if the tenant remains in occupation of the dwelling-house after that date a demoted tenancy is created with effect from that date;

(c)   it is a term of the demoted tenancy that any arrears of rent payable at the termination of the assured tenancy become payable under the demoted tenancy;

(d)   it is also a term of the demoted tenancy that any rent paid in advance or overpaid at the termination of the assured tenancy is credited to the tenant's liability to pay rent under the demoted tenancy.

The court must not make a demotion order unless it is satisfied—

(a)   that the tenant or a person residing in or visiting the dwelling-house has engaged or has threatened to engage in conduct to which section 153A or 153B of the Housing Act 1996 (anti-social behaviour or use of premises for unlawful purposes) applies, and

(b)   that it is reasonable to make the order.

(5) The court must not entertain proceedings for a demotion order unless—

(a)   the landlord has served on the tenant a notice under subsection (6), or

(b)   the court thinks it is just and equitable to dispense with the requirement of the notice.

(6) The notice must—

(a)   give particulars of the conduct in respect of which the order is sought;

(b)   state that the proceedings will not begin before the date specified in the notice;

(c)   state that the proceedings will not begin after the end of the period of twelve months beginning with the date of service of the notice.

(7) The date specified for the purposes of subsection (6)(b) must not be before the end of the period of two weeks beginning with the date of service of the notice.

(8) Each of the following has effect in respect of a demoted tenancy at the time it is

created by virtue of an order under this section as it has effect in relation to the assured tenancy at the time it is terminated by virtue of the order—

(a) the parties to the tenancy;

(b) the period of the tenancy;

(c) the amount of the rent;

(d) the dates on which the rent is payable.

(9) Subsection (8)(b) does not apply if the assured tenancy was for a fixed term and in such a case the demoted tenancy is a weekly periodic tenancy.

(10) If the landlord of the demoted tenancy serves on the tenant a statement of any other express terms of the assured tenancy which are to apply to the demoted tenancy such terms are also terms of the demoted tenancy.

(11) For the purposes of this section a demoted tenancy is a tenancy to which section 20B of the Housing Act 1988 applies.

Further similar provision is made in respect of assured shorthold tenancies by inserting s 20B into the 1988 Act.

### 20B.    Demoted assured shorthold tenancies

(1) An assured tenancy is an assured shorthold tenancy to which this section applies (a demoted assured shorthold tenancy) if—

(a) the tenancy is created by virtue of an order of the court under section 82A of the Housing Act 1985 or section 6A of this Act (a demotion order), and

(b) the landlord is a registered social landlord.

(2) At the end of the period of one year starting with the day when the demotion order takes effect a demoted assured shorthold tenancy ceases to be an assured shorthold tenancy unless subsection (3) applies.

(3) This subsection applies if before the end of the period mentioned in subsection (2) the landlord gives notice of proceedings for possession of the dwelling house.

(4) If subsection (3) applies the tenancy continues to be a demoted assured shorthold tenancy until the end of the period mentioned in subsection (2) or (if later) until one of the following occurs—

(a) the notice of proceedings for possession is withdrawn;

(b) the proceedings are determined in favour of the tenant;

(c) the period of six months beginning with the date on which the notice is given ends and no proceedings for possession have been brought.

(5)    Registered social landlord has the same meaning as in Part 1 of the Housing Act 1996.

## Comment

It will be noted that in all cases the basic conditions for demotion to occur are that the tenant, or a person residing in or visiting his/her dwelling has engaged or threatened to engage in anti-social behaviour or unlawful use of the premises *and* that the court considers it is reasonable to make the order. The terms of such 'demoted tenancies' are then provided by s 143A et seq of the Housing Act 1996 inserted in 2003.

A demoted tenancy of a local authority or housing action trust dwelling will generally again become secure at the end of a 12-month 'demotion period', unless the demotion order is quashed, or the tenant dies without a successor, or the dwelling ceases to be owned by the local authority or housing action trust. The landlord may commence possession proceedings during the demotion period which has the effect of continuing the demoted status until the issue is settled. Even if there is a change of landlord the demoted status continues if the new landlord is another local authority or housing action trust. Where there is a transfer to, inter alia, a registered social landlord the tenancy becomes an assured shorthold tenancy.

Demoted tenancies may only be brought to an end by an order for possession which has to be granted unless the court concludes, under s 143D, that the mandatory procedure under ss 143E and F has not been followed. This procedure includes, inter alia, requirements for notice to be served on the tenant informing him/her of the situation and also stating the right to request a review of the decision to seek possession. The review is internal and is to be conducted according to regulations made centrally. Reviews will be carried out by a person of appropriate seniority not involved in the original decision to seek possession, and provision *may* be made for the tenant to have an oral hearing with representation.

There may, under s 143H, be a succession to a demoted tenancy. In general terms the scheme of succession is similar for that which applies to secure tenancies, etc, but any succession carries with it demoted status. Demoted tenancies may only be assigned in the limited circumstances of orders made in s 24 of the Matrimonial Causes Act 1973, s 17(1) of the Matrimonial and Family Proceedings Act 1984, and Sch 1 to the Children Act 1989, see s 143K. Under s 143M landlords are required to publish and supply information from time to time about demoted tenancies and their terms, including repairing obligations, and must supply demoted tenants with copies of such information. Demoted tenants are amongst those who have the right to be consulted on matters of housing management under s 105 of the Housing Act 1985, see s 143P, but of course they cannot enjoy any form of right to buy as they are not 'secure'. See also Foreword III.

## CONCLUSION

Bad and irresponsible behaviour wherever it occurs has consequences for individuals, communities and authorities, such as the police, the courts, local councils and registered social landlords. Not only are there the immediately obvious consequences such as vandalised facilities, and fear in the minds of those touched by the bad behaviour, but there are the longer-term economic costs, such as having to make good the damage, taking action against perpetrators, having to forgo income on housing that cannot be let because of, eg an area's reputation for bad behaviour. It must, however, be stressed that such behaviour is not confined to areas of social housing. It can occur on 'owner-occupied' suburban estates, or in areas of mixed tenures, for example places where a high proportion of the former council stock has been disposed of under the Right to Buy. Furthermore it is not only those who are 'tenants', in the popular sense of that word, who commit acts of ASB. We should also bear in mind that the current governmental concentration on ASB as an issue, and the succession of legislative attempts to deal with it in the form of the relevant provisions of the Housing Act 1996, the Crime and Disorder Act 1998, the Police Reform Act 2002 and now the Anti-Social Behaviour Act 2003, represents a continuing phenomenon in our public legal system. That phenomenon is an approach to dealing with perceived social problems by creating new legislative measures as responses rather than by asking whether existing legal measures could adequately serve to achieve the object. It is, for example, arguable that many instances of ASB could be dealt with under the existing common law of public nuisance. However, the 'new legislation syndrome' has been too well established as a feature of the governance of the UK for some two centuries or more for us to suppose that attachment to it by governments will wane.

We have seen in this chapter how the law has developed in response to acts of bad behaviour committed by tenants, particularly those of social landlords, their families and visitors. Many of the initial responses could be criticised on the basis that they were tenure specific, and in particular impacted on the tenants of local authorities and registered social landlords. The development of the ASBO was in many ways a more legitimate way of dealing with bad behaviour generally as it was directed at individuals, not their homes, and was not limited solely to those who rent their dwellings. We must now, however, ask whether the latest provisions are not moving back to a more tenure specific approach to the problem. In particular we should note the close connection in terms of definition between the concept of ASB and the ability of social landlords to seek injunctions. Similarly the proposals relating to demoted tenancies and a possible return to consider reductions in housing benefit support will clearly affect only certain sections of society.

The government's clearly articulated objective is the creation of an inclusive society in which rights and responsibilities are balanced, in which communities are to be healthily sustainable and encouraged to be as self regulating as possible, though with the assistance of outside agencies, and in which the 'price' of state help is the obligation to behave in a socially considerate fashion towards others. In this respect the government appears to be thinking along similar lines to those explored in Chapter 2 of this work, namely the need to ensure a correct balance between individual and collective rights. Certainly where, for example, an area is disfigured by graffiti, disrupted by noise and vandalism, and put in fear of aggressive behaviour, the collective interests of all who live there are adversely affected, and we may argue that publicly provided facilities should be protected for the benefit of all and not allowed to deteriorate at the hands of the few. What also must be borne in mind is, however, that social problems are not confined to one particular class of society, nor to particular areas and types of housing.

## FURTHER READING

Armitage, R, *Community Safety Practice Briefings* (2002) Home Office.

Campbell, S, *Home Office Research Findings 160* (2003) Home Office.

Card, P, 'Managing anti-social behaviour – inclusion or exclusion' in Cowan, D and Marsh, A (eds) *Two Steps Forward: Housing Policy into the New Millennium* (2001) Polity Press.

Cm 5778: *Respect and Responsibility – Taking a Stand Against Anti-social Behaviour* (2003) HMSO.

Hughes, D, Karn, V, and Lickiss, R, 'Neighbour Disputes, Social Landlords and the Law' [1994] JSWFL 201.

Hunter, C, 'Anti-social behaviour and housing – can law be the answer? in Cowan, D and Marsh, A (eds) *Two Steps Forward: Housing Policy into the New Millennium* (2001) Polity Press.

Hunter, C, *Tackling Anti-social Behaviour: Law and Practice in the management of Social Housing* (2nd ed) (2002) Lemos and Crane.

Karn, V, Lickiss, R, Hughes, D, Crawley, J, *Neighbour Disputes: Responses by Social Landlords* (1993) Institute of Housing.

Lucas, R, and Whitworth, J, *Tackling Anti-Social Behaviour: Information and Case Studies about Local Authority Work* (2002) Local Government Association.

Page, D, *Building for Communities: A Study of New Housing Association Estates* (1993) Joseph Rowntree Foundation.

Pema, A and Heels, S, *Anti-social Behaviour Orders* (2003) Jordans.

Rowan, M, 'Crime and Disorder – ASBOs' (1999) 149 New Law Journal 1051.

Simpson, B, and McCarthy, P, 'Conflict in the Community: Local Authorities in the Middle' (1990) 17(2) Local Government Policy Making 24.

## THE NATURE OF THE PROBLEM

Homelessness is not a new phenomenon. In the Middle Ages those lacking accommodation frequently looked to religious foundations to supply them with, albeit temporary, shelter. Following the abolition of the monasteries under Henry VIII this burden fell back on the civil authorities, though it was left to Henry's daughter Elizabeth I to pass a comprehensive 'poor law'. This made the destitute and indigent the responsibility of their home parishes, and harsh provision was made to ensure that 'sturdy beggars' could be forcibly returned to their places of origin if apprehended. Within parishes the better-off were taxed or 'rated' to pay something towards the cost of the poor, though this was an unpopular impost, and those responsible for collecting it did all they could in general to keep costs down[1].

It is not often appreciated that the Elizabethan Poor Law, though extensively modified, remained the essential basis of welfare provision down until the reforms of the National Assistance Act 1948. By then provision for accommodating homeless persons in workhouses owned by 'Poor Law Unions' of parishes had been made. The often harsh conditions in these establishments were graphically described by Charles Dickens in *Oliver Twist*, and by George R. Simms in his frequently parodied but nevertheless moving poem, 'It was Christmas Day in the Workhouse'.

In more recent times the problem of homelessness came to public attention in the mid-1960s with the television film 'Cathy, Come Home[2]. The then existing legal structure, which imposed an obligation on local social service authorities to deal with cases of emergency homelessness only – e.g. fire and flood – was unable to deal with chronic structural homelessness consequent on an increasing lack of affordable rented accommodation.

The Local Government Act 1972 gave local housing authorities powers to assist homeless persons, with a reserve power for the Secretary of State to reimpose a housing *duty* on social services authorities. The consequence was that no one was

---

[1]  The stigma which reliance on the Poor Law brought to recipients of assistance is demonstrated by the fact that as Cranston notes, '... it obliged all those receiving poor relief to wear the letter "P" on the right shoulder of their outermost garment' Cranston, R, *Legal Foundations of the Welfare State* (1985) Weidenfeld and Nicholson.

[2]  First screened by the BBC on 15 November, 1966.

certain where the responsibility for homelessness lay, and legal confusion was added to the social problem. In 1977, however, a private member's Bill, promoted by the Liberal MP Stephen Ross, drafted with the aid of Shelter and also in receipt of government assistance[3], was passed which imposed *duties* on local housing authorities in respect of those homeless persons who satisfied certain legal requirements.

In due course this legislation (with some minor amendments) was consolidated with other housing legislation and became Pt III of the Housing Act 1985. It was under this legislation that considerable efforts were made to deal with what appeared to be an inexorably rising tide of homelessness.

Over the period 1977–87, half a million people were accommodated under the law's homelessness provisions. In 1980, 8,660 persons were accepted as homeless in the first half-year in London, and 7,930 in the second half-year; in the rest of England the figures were 21,370 and 24,300 respectively. By 1985 the figures were 14,210 (second half – London) and 48,560 (second half) for the rest of England. These figures related to *acceptances*, not applications.

Increases in the number of acceptances of persons as 'homeless' led to a considerable expansion of the use of bed and breakfast ('B&B') and hostel accommodation. A further consequence of the increasing incidence of homelessness was the escalating cost of dealing with the problem. The Chartered Institute of Public Finance and Accounting calculated that the average cost of a case of homelessness in London dealt with by B&B accommodation was £7,670 in 1987, with hoteliers receiving a grand total of £78m.

The number of households homeless in Central London in the 1980s rose at 4 per cent pa, but in the outer boroughs the rate of increase was higher, e.g., 43 per cent in Kingston, 28 per cent in Bromley. In England in 1987, 250,000 persons were homeless according to Shelter.

Homelessness continued to rise into the 1990s, apparently faster in rural areas than in urban areas. The problem was compounded by rural poverty, inflation in rural house prices and the sale of council houses.

In 1989, the Government reviewed the law, but this was something of a legal damp squib. Far from suggesting any change in the law, the Government proposed to keep the existing law broadly as it was, considering, for example, the existing definitions of 'homeless' and 'priority need' to be 'adequate and appropriate'. Instead managerial change was urged to make better use of existing housing stock, closer liaison with housing associations, preventative advice and encouragement of those willing to provide lodgings. It was also recognised, however, that some areas needed greater assistance to provide new housing, and some mention of targeted resources was made and a newly revised Code of Guidance to ensure a greater degree of consistency between authorities' homelessness practices.

During the 1990s, according to official figures, homelessness *acceptances* declined, while the numbers of people in 'B&B' declined by two-thirds from 1992 levels (the peak year). Typically, acceptances declined around 10% year on year from the 1992

---

[3] This was the period of the 'Lib-Lab' pact and much of the Bill had its origins in work done by the Department of the Environment following the 1974 review of homelessness policy.

peak – so that despite a small rise in 1998, homelessness figures in that year were still 26% below the 1992 level. Since the mid-1990s there has been a steady process of legislative change and numerous 'tweaks' in official policy, all of which have (no doubt) had their effect on overall homelessness statistics. In any event, figures for 2002/2003 are that 296,416 households claimed homelessness assistance, of whom 46% were accepted (130,178). The number of households placed in B&B or other temporary accommodation showed an 11% increase in 2002/2003 or 2001/2002. Over 50% of total expenditure on the provision of temporary accommodation is incurred by the London boroughs.

The decline in acceptances during the 1990s was fuelled by many factors, but principal amongst them were:

- The decision of the House of Lords in *R v Brent London Borough Council, ex p Awua*[4] which indicated that the duty to accommodate homeless persons did not mean that authorities were always under a mandatory obligation to house homeless applicants in permanent accommodation.
- The general thrust of the 1996 Housing Act Part VII, and in particular s 193 which reduced the initial open-ended housing duty with a preliminary two-year duty.

Correspondingly the upturn in acceptances is also partly fuelled by legislative policy change – above all those contained in the Homelessness Act 2002.

## THE CURRENT LAW

In January 1994, hard-line proposals to change the law on homelessness which had been mooted during the 1989 review were again brought forward. The outcome was Part VII of the Housing Act 1996[5]. Conservative Ministers accepted the local authority argument alluded to above, that the homelessness route into council accommodation had become a 'fast track' whereby the normal waiting list procedures were being evaded. The new law which followed provided for a temporary entitlement only, although this has now been reversed under the 2002 Act.

Under the 1996 Act local housing authorities have both general and specific homelessness functions. In addition, under the 2002 Act, authorities have a vital strategic role in relation to both minimising the incidence of homelessness, and dealing with homelessness, as and when it arises.

### Strategic functions

By virtue of ss 1–3 of the 2002 Homelessness Act, local housing authorities have an obligation to carry out a homelessness review for their district and to formulate and publish a homelessness strategy based on this. The first strategy had to be in place within twelve months of the coming into force of the legislation (ie by 31 July 2003) and then a new one is required every five years. Section 2 of the Act defines 'homelessness review'. Section 3 defines 'homelessness strategy' – but does not provide for specific time scales over which it must be modified. The revised Code of Guidance (para 1.5)[6] states that 'it is unlikely that it would be possible for a

---

[4]   [1996] AC 551.
[5]   Which still provides the basic framework of the law.
[6]   *Homeless Code of Guidance*: ODPM November 2002.

housing authority to formulate an effective homelessness strategy without assistance from the social services authority'. It suggests (at para 1.15) that 'housing authorities may wish to develop a profile of those who have experienced homelessness', and that 'elements within a profile' might include:

- location of homelessness;
- reasons for homelessness;
- previous tenure;
- ethnic and other background;
- age;
- employment/benefits history;
- vulnerability;
- health.

At para 1.22 the Code lists in detail typical 'resources' available for securing accommodation for the homeless, ranging from nomination agreements with registered social landlords (RSLs) through private sector accreditation schemes to the provision of new owner occupied accommodation.

# HOMELESSNESS ACT 2002

## Duty of local housing authority to formulate a homelessness strategy

1. (1) A local housing authority ('the authority') may from time to time:

(a) carry out a homelessness review for their district; and

(b) formulate and publish a homelessness strategy based on the results of that review.

(2) The social services authority for the district of the authority (where that is a different local authority) shall give such assistance in connection with the exercise of the power under subsection (1) as the authority may reasonably require.

(3) The authority shall exercise that power so as to ensure that the first homelessness strategy for their district is published within the period of twelve months beginning with the day on which this section comes into force.

(4) The authority shall exercise that power so as to ensure that a new homelessness strategy for their district is published within the period of five years beginning with the day on which their last homelessness strategy was published.

(5) A local housing authority shall take their homelessness strategy into account in the exercise of their functions.

(6) A social services authority shall take the homelessness strategy for the district of a local housing authority into account in the exercise of their functions in relation to that district.

(7) Nothing in subsection (5) or (6) affects any duty or requirement arising apart from this section.

## Homelessness reviews

2. (1) For the purposes of this Act 'homelessness review' means a review by a local housing authority of:

(a) the levels, and likely future levels, of homelessness in their district;

(b) the activities which are carried out for any purpose mentioned in subsection (2) (or which contribute to their achievement); and

(c) the resources available to the authority, the social services authority for their district, other public authorities, voluntary organisations and other persons for such activities.

(2) Those purposes are:

(a)   preventing homelessness in the district of the authority;
(b)   securing that accommodation is or will be available for people in the district who are or may become homelessness;
(c)   providing support for people in the district-
    (i)   who are or may become homeless; or
    (ii)   who have been homeless and need support to prevent them becoming homeless again.

(3) A local housing authority shall, after completing a homelessness review—

(a)   arrange for the results of the review to be available at its principal office for inspection at all reasonable hours, without charge, by members of the public; and
(b)   provide (on payment if required by the authority of a reasonable charge) a copy of those results to any member of the public who asks for one.

## Homelessness strategies

3.   (1) For the purposes of this Act 'homelessness strategy' means a strategy formulated by a local housing authority for—

(a)   preventing homelessness in their district;
(b)   securing that sufficient accommodation is and will be available for people in their district who are or may become homeless;
(c)   securing the satisfactory provision of support for people in their district—
    (i)   who are or may become homelessness; or
    (ii)   who have been homelessness and need support to prevent them becoming homelessness again.

(2) A homelessness strategy may include specific objectives to be pursued, and specific action planned to be taken, in the course of the exercise of—

(a)   the functions of the authority as a local housing authority; or
(b)   the functions of the social services authority for the district.

(3) A homelessness strategy may also include provision relating to specific action which the authority expects to be taken—

(a)   by any public authority with functions (not being functions mentioned in subsection (2)) which are capable of contributing to the achievement of any of the objectives mentioned in subsection (1); or
(b)   by any voluntary organisation or other person whose activities are capable of contributing to the achievement of any of those objectives.

(4) The inclusion in a homelessness strategy of any provision relating to action mentioned in subsection (3) requires the approval of the body or person concerned.

(5) In formulating a homelessness strategy the authority shall consider (among other things) the extent to which any of the objectives mentioned in subsection (1) can be achieved through action involving two or more of the bodies or other persons mentioned in subsections (2) and (3).

It has been said that 'the requirement to carry out a review and formulate a strategy represents a cultural shift in the way that LHAs deliver services to homelessness households, from crisis management to proactive prevention'[7].

---

[7]   Agnew, J 'A strategy for success', *The Adviser* (98) July/August 2003, 11.

Certainly this 'culture shift' is regarded by government as a key component of its homelessness strategy, and a number of 'beacon'[8] councils have been identified who have demonstrated that they have effective partnerships in place to tackle homelessness, and a comprehensive housing advice service. Beacon councils are to spread best practice throughout the sector. Local housing authorities are, in particular being encouraged by the Office of the Deputy Prime Minister to reallocate resources from bed and breakfast budgets into homelessness prevention activities.

However, concerns have been expressed that some LHAs are not acting in the spirit of the legislation – using the new strategic approach to avoid some of their continuing substantive duties. Examples cited include 'persuading' potential applicants to continue to stay in clearly unsuitable private sector accommodation, and offering potentially vulnerable applicants lists of hostels and the option of finding their own accommodation with the help of a rent deposit scheme[9].

## General homelessness functions: advice services

Every local housing authority *must* under s 179 ensure that advice and assistance about homelessness and its prevention are freely available to all persons in their districts; and they *may* give assistance to any person by providing advice etc., or help by way of a grant/loan, and may permit that person to use their premises, along with the provision of furniture and goods and the services of authority staff.

Section 180 further empowers the giving of financial assistance to voluntary bodies (ie those who seek no profit) concerned with homelessness and related matters and a local housing authority may permit such bodies to use authority premises, furniture, goods and the services of authority staff.

Under s 181, the assistance given under ss 179 and 180 may be subject to conditions, and undertakings *must* be given by recipients that they will use money, premises, furniture, etc. for the specified purpose for which assistance is given. In all cases there must be conditions imposed as to keeping of books and auditing of accounts, keeping records as to how money has been spent, and provision for inspection of books, etc. by the aid donor. Where assistance etc. is abused, the donor must take steps to recover from the donee an amount equal to the assistance, but must first serve notice on the donee of that amount and how it has been calculated (s 181(5) and (6)).

## Central homelessness functions

The Secretary of State may also give financial assistance under s 180; however, his prime task is to issue guidance to authorities under s 182, to which *they must have regard*. Although authorities are not required to adhere slavishly to the Code of Guidance, which (having initially appeared in 1977) has been revised and reissued under s 182, they may not ignore it. It is a question of fact in each case whether or not the Code of Guidance has been considered, but where it is clear that the Code

---

[8]   Currently Bolton, Camden, Colchester, Harrow, Leicester, Rochdale and Trafford.
[9]   See Hawkey, E, 'Fobbed Off' *Roof*, May/June 2004, 20.

has been ignored in coming to a decision, that decision can be struck down (see *R v Newham London Borough Council, ex p Ojuri (No 3)*)[10].

## The specific homelessness function

Homeless persons can be assisted if they apply; thus there are two initial questions:

### (a) What is 'an application'?

In *R v Chiltern District Council, ex p. Roberts*[11], it was held that a letter from a third party may be enough provided it makes it clear what the issue is.

### (b) Who may be an applicant?

In *Garlick v Oldham Metropolitan Borough Council*[12], the House of Lords laid down that a child *may* be an applicant *provided* it is (i) independent of its parents, and (ii) has the capacity to appreciate the meaning of an offer of accommodation and to make a decision on it. Thus there is no 'cut-off' age such as 16. In the case of a disabled applicant, the rule is the person should either be able to make an application in person or be able to authorise another person to make it, and be able to comprehend and evaluate any offer of accommodation made.

In *Garlick* the applicant, who was four years old, applied through his mother to the local housing authority for accommodation under Pt III of the Housing Act 1985, stating that he was in priority need under s 59(1) of the Act. The authority refused to consider his application, on the ground that it was a device to circumvent the provisions of the legislation. The High Court dismissed the applicant's request for judicial review, and the Court of Appeal dismissed his appeal. The House of Lords unanimously dismissed his further appeal, but left the doors open for more realistic 'under age' applications.

As Lord Griffiths stated[13],

> 'Dependent children are not amongst those classified as in priority need. This is not surprising. Dependent children depend on their parents or those looking after them to decide where they are to live and the offer of accommodation can only sensibly be made to those in charge of them. There is no definition of a dependent child in the Act but the *Homelessness Code of Guidance for Local Authorities*, (3rd ed 1991), to which local authorities must have regard for guidance (see section 71) suggests in paragraph 6.3 that authorities should normally include as dependent all children under 16 and all children aged 16 to 18 who are in, or about to begin, full-time education or training or who for other reasons are unable to support themselves and who live at home. This seems to me to be sensible guidance and likely to result in families being housed together until the children are reasonably mature. There will obviously be the case from time to time when a child leaves home under the age of 16 and ceases to be dependent on the parents or those with who he or she was living and such a child may be vulnerable and in priority need by virtue of

---

[10] (1998) 31 HLR 631.
[11] (1990) 23 HLR 387.
[12] [1993] 2 All ER 65.
[13] At p 69.

section 59(1)(c): see *Kelly v Monklands District Council*, 1986 SLT 169. But however that may be, it cannot possibly be argued that a healthy four-year-old living with parents is other than a dependent child. Such a child is in my opinion owed no duty under this Act for it is the intention of the Act that the child's accommodation will be provided by the parents or those looking after him and it is to those people that the offer of accommodation must be made not to the dependent child.

I cannot accept the argument that extreme youth is a "special reason" making the child vulnerable and thus giving it a priority need under section 59(1)(c). "Old age" is mentioned as a cause of vulnerability but "young age" is not. The reason of course is that already stated, Parliament has provided for dependent children by giving priority right to accommodation to their parents or those looking after them. Nor can I accept the argument that if a dependent child suffers from some disability it thereby acquires an independent priority right to accommodation. A healthy four-year-old is just as vulnerable as a disabled four-year-old from a housing point of view; neither is capable of looking after himself let alone deciding whether to accept an offer of accommodation. I am satisfied that section 59(1)(c) was not intended to confer any rights upon dependent children.

It is also to be observed that the Act imposes a duty on the authority to give written advice to the applicant and makes it a criminal offence for an applicant not to notify an authority of a change in his circumstances: see section 64 and 74. This is all part of a pattern that supports the view that the intention of this Act was to create a duty to offer accommodation to those homeless persons in priority need who can decide whether or not to accept the offer and that this does not include dependent children.

If a family has lost its right to priority treatment through intentional homelessness the parent cannot achieve the same result through the back door by an application in the name of a dependent child; if he could it would mean that the disqualification of intentional homelessness had no application to families with dependent children. If this had been the intention of Parliament it would surely have said so.

For these reasons I would dismiss the first two appeals. I wish however to point out that there are other provisions of our social welfare legislation that provide for the accommodation and care of children and of the duty of cooperation between authorities in the discharge of their duties. Section 20(1) of the Children Act 1989 provides:

Every local authority shall provide accommodation for any child in need within their area who appears to them to require accommodation as a result of—(a) there being no person who has parental responsibility for him; (b) his being lost or having been abandoned; (c) the person who has been caring for him being prevented (whether or not permanently, and for whatever reason) from providing him with suitable accommodation or care. ...'

Once an application is made, the legal machinery provided under the following provisions of the 1996 Housing Act obligates the receiving authority to make inquiries to deal with it and to decide how most appropriately to act.

*Application for assistance in case of homelessness or threatened homelessness*

### 183. **Application for assistance**

(1) The following provisions of this Part apply where a person applies to a local housing authority for accommodation, or for assistance in obtaining accommodation, and the authority have reason to believe that he is or may be homeless or threatened with homelessness.

(2) In this Part—

'applicant' means a person making such an application,
'assistance under this Part' means the benefit of any function under the following provisions of this Part relating to accommodation or assistance in obtaining accommodation, and
'eligible for assistance' means not excluded from such assistance by section 185 (person from abroad not eligible for housing assistance) or section 186 (asylum seekers and their dependants).

(3) Nothing in this section or the following provisions of this Part affects a person's entitlement to advice and information under section 179 (duty to provide advisory services).

### 184. **Inquiry into cases of homelessness or threatened homelessness**

(1) If the local housing authority have reason to believe that an applicant may be homeless or threatened with homelessness, they shall make such inquiries as are necessary to satisfy themselves—

(a)  whether he is eligible for assistance, and
(b)  if so, whether any duty, and if so what duty, is owed to him under the following provisions of this Part.

(2) They may also make inquiries whether he has a local connection with the district of another local housing authority in England, Wales or Scotland.

(3) On completing their inquiries the authority shall notify the applicant of their decision and, so far as any issue is decided against his interests, inform him of the reasons for their decision.

(4) If the authority have notified or intend to notify another local housing authority under section 198 (referral of cases), they shall at the same time notify the applicant of that decision and inform him of the reasons for it.

(5) A notice under subsection (3) or (4) shall also inform the applicant of his right to request a review of the decision and of the time within which such a request must be made (see section 202).

(6) Notice required to be given to a person under this section shall be given in writing and, if not received by him, shall be treated as having been given to him if it is made available at the authority's office for a reasonable period for collection by him or on his behalf.


The onus of making inquiries is on the authority not on the applicant; once told that an applicant is homeless, and having been given the source of that information, an authority cannot then refuse to make further inquiries and insist that the applicant furnish further confirmation of the facts[14].

---

[14]  *R v Woodspring District Council, ex p Walters* (1984) 16 HLR 73.

Following *Lally v Kensington Royal Borough Council*[15] it is clear there is no need to make 'CID'-type inquiries, but there is a need to act fairly and sympathetically, and to enable applicants to make a case out. Thus there may be a need to supply an interpreter when an applicant's first language is not English[16].

The authority must elicit all relevant facts, though the applicant should ensure that they know all that they might not otherwise be able to find out[17]. Where an applicant's evidence is inconsistent, the inconsistency can be taken into account[18]. The authority are the judge of fact in inquiries and are entitled to decide which version of varying facts they wish to accept, provided it does not perversely fly in the fact of all logic[19].

A brief 10-minute interview is hardly likely to satisfy the law's requirements[20]. However, in conducting their inquiries, an authority may accept hearsay advice if it is reasonable to do so, eg, it is not obviously tittle-tattle. The authority are under no obligation to put any information received 'chapter-and-verse' to the applicant, though *they must give the applicant a fair chance to reply*, which means giving applicants the substance of allegations made against them[21].

Rubber stamping findings of another authority without giving an applicant a chance to explain his side is not a sufficient performance of the duty to make inquiries[22].

There is no clear obligation to the Act to operate a service 24 hours a day, seven days a week. However, attempts to withdraw 'out of hours' emergency cover have been blocked by court orders. In *R v Camden London Borough Council, ex p Gillan*[23], assistance from the authority's homeless persons unit was only available over a variable number of telephones, with no opportunity to meet an appropriate officer. The unit closed over weekends and was open on weekdays for half a day, so that only those who presented themselves first thing in the morning received a hearing. It was held that an authority are under a duty to take reasonable steps to hear and adjudicate upon homelessness applications. In a populous area, what is 'reasonable' may amount to 24-hour cover, but each case depends on its facts. The cover provided in the present instance was clearly not reasonable.

The legislation contains no timescales for decision taking, but the Code of Guidance indicates an initial assessment of the application should be made within 24 hours, and inquiries should be complete in 33 working days[24].

## THE LEGAL CONCEPT OF HOMELESSNESS

Homelessness may be actual or threatened, but in both cases the core concept is that the applicant has, or will have, 'no accommodation'.

---

[15] (1980) The Times, 27 March.
[16] *R v Surrey Health Borough Council, ex p Li* (1984) 16 HLR 79.
[17] *R v Harrow London Borough Council ex p Holland* (1982) 4 HLR 108 and *R v Wandsworth London Borough Council, ex p Henderson and Hayes* (1986) 18 HLR 522.
[18] *R v Hillingdon London Borough Council ex p Thomas* (1987) 19 HLR 196.
[19] *R v Dacorum Borough Council, ex p Taverner* (1988) 21 HLR 123.
[20] *R v Dacorum Borough Council, ex p Brown* (1989) 21 HLR 405.
[21] *R v Southampton City Council, ex p Ward* (1984) 14 HLR 114.
[22] *R v South Herefordshire District Council, ex p Miles* (1983) 17 HLR 82.
[23] (1988) 21 HLR 114.
[24] *Code of Guidance*, para 318.

# HOUSING ACT 1996

### 175.  **Homelessnss and threatened homelessness**

(1) A person is homeless if he has no accommodation available for his occupation, in the United Kingdom or elsewhere, which he—

(a)   is entitled to occupy by virtue of an interest in it or by virtue of an order of a court,

(b)   has an express or implied licence to occupy, or

(c)   occupies as a residence by virtue of any enactment or rule of law giving him the right to remain in occupation or restricting the right of another person to recover possession.

(2) A person is also homeless if he has accommodation but—

(a)   he cannot secure entry to it, or

(b)   it consists of a moveable structure, vehicle or vessel designed or adapted for human habitation and there is no place where he is entitled or permitted both to place it and to reside in it.

(3) A person shall not be treated as having accommodation unless it is accommodation which it would be reasonable for him to continue to occupy.

(4) A person is threatened with homelessness if it is likely that he will become homeless within 28 days.

### 176.  **Meaning of accommodation available for occupation**

Accommodation shall be regarded as available for a person's occupation only if it is available for occupation by him together with—

(a)   any other person who normally resides with him as a member of his family, or

(b)   any other person who might reasonably be expected to reside with him.

References to this Part to securing that accommodation is available for a person's occupation shall be construed accordingly.

### 177.  **Whether it is reasonable to continue to occupy accommodation**

(1) It is not reasonable for a person to continue to occupy accommodation if it is probable that this will lead to domestic violence, or other violence, against him, or against—

(a)   a person who normally resides with him as a member of his family, or

(b)   any other person who might reasonably be expected to reside with him.

(1A) For this purpose 'violence' means—

(a)   violence from another person; or

(b)   threats of violence from another person which are likely to be carried out;

and violence is 'domestic violence' if it is from a person who is associated with the victim.

(2) In determining whether it would be, or would have been, reasonable for a person to continue to occupy accommodation, regard may be had to the general circumstances prevailing in relation to housing in the district of the local housing authority to whom he has applied for accommodation or for assistance in obtaining accommodation.

(3) The Secretary of State may by order specify—

(a)   other circumstances in which it is to be regarded as reasonable or not reasonable for a person to continue to occupy accommodation, and

(b)   other matters to be taken into account or disregarded in determining whether it would be, or would have been, reasonable for a person to continue to occupy accommodation.

### 178. **Meaning of associated person**

(1) For the purposes of this Part, a person is associated with another person if—

(a)   they are or have been married to each other;

(b)   they are cohabitants or former cohabitants;

(c)   they live or lived in the same household;

(d)   they are relatives;

(e)   they have agreed to marry one another (whether or not that agreement has been terminated);

(f)   in relation to a child, each of them is a parent of the child or has, or has had, parental responsibility for the child.

(2) If a child has been adopted or has been freed for adoption by virtue of any of the enactments mentioned in section 16(1) of the Adoption Act 1976, two persons are also associated with each other for the purposes of this Part if—

(a)   one is a natural parent of the child or a parent of such a natural parent, and

(b)   the other is the child or a person—

> (i)   who has become a parent of the child by virtue of an adoption order or who has applied for an adoption order, or

> (ii)   with whom the child has at any time been placed for adoption.

(3) In this section—

'adoption order' has the meaning given by section 72(1) of the Adoption Act 1976;

'child' means a person under the age of 18 years;

'cohabitants' means a man and a woman who, although not married to each other, are living together as husband and wife, and 'former cohabitants' shall be construed accordingly;

'parental responsibility' has the same meaning as in the Children Act 1989; and

'relative', in relation to a person, means—

> (a)   the father, mother, stepfather, stepmother, son, daughter, stepson, stepdaughter, grandmother, grandfather, grandson or granddaughter of that person or of that person's spouse or former spouse, or

> (b)   the brother, sister, uncle, aunt, niece or nephew (whether of the full blood or of the half blood or by affinity) of that person or of that person's spouse or former spouse,

and includes, in relation to a person who is living or has lived with another person as husband and wife, a person who would fall within paragraph (a) or (b) if the parties were married to each other.

The issue of what it is to have 'no accommodation', while superficially straightforward, is, on reflection, potentially complex and has troubled the courts on many occasions since 1978. For example, although a mere licence can clearly count as 'accommodation' (see now s 175(1)(b)), a wholly transient and insecure temporary abode may not realistically qualify. Accommodation may exist, and yet be wholly inadequate. Some have argued that a person should (presumptively) be viewed as 'homeless' if the accommodation they occupy is inadequate. Given the state of much of the housing stock in the United Kingdom, it is not surprising that this position was never officially adopted; but subsequent to the decision in *R v Hillingdon London Borough Council, ex p Puhlhofer*[25] (see below) there were legislative amendments providing for the requirement that to be 'accommodation' for homelessness purposes, it must be 'reasonable' for the applicant to have

---

[25]   [1986] AC 484.

occupied the property in question. Of course, 'reasonableness' can entail not merely the condition of the property, but also the wider issue of whether the applicant can realistically be expected to carry on living in it. This may not be so, if the applicant is under threat of violence or harassment in the area (if the applicant is under such a threat in the property itself, which can be viewed as 'domestic violence', s 177(1) clearly indicates that it would not be reasonable to expect continued occupation).

Probably the first significant decision specifically on the 'accommodation' issue was *R v London Borough of Ealing, ex p Sidhu*[26] (although observations had been passed on the concept of earlier cases). In this case, Mrs Sidhu's marriage ran into difficulties in the late 1970s, largely because of her husband's violence towards her. Eventually in July 1981 she left her husband and (taking her two young children with her) went to live in a women's aid refuge. The refuge was small, consisting of eight bedrooms, and frequently more than one family had to share the same room. In August 1981, Mrs Sidhu applied as a homeless person to the London Borough of Ealing. Her application was rejected, in part, because the view was taken that the refuge constituted 'accommodation', precluding her and her family from being homeless. This approach was roundly rejected by the courts. Hodgson J stated[27]:

> 'In this court on behalf of the local authority some surprising, indeed in my judgment extremely bold, submissions have been made. The first is that the applicant and her two children are not homeless because they are being, as they have been for five months, accommodated by the charity of the Womens Aid organisation. It is suggested that Mrs Sidhu is not homeless because she cannot bring herself within the first sentence of Section 1(1) of the Act:
>
> > "A person is homeless for the purposes of this Act if he has no accommodation."
>
> In my judgment that is a totally unjustified submission to make.
>
> I am told that a County Court judge has made certain not very surprising remarks in this context. What I am told he said (and if he did not say it, it seems to me very good sense and I would be perfectly prepared to say it myself) was this.
>
> The judge said it was important that refuges be seen as temporary crisis accommodation, and that women living in refuges wee still homeless under the terms of the Act. If it was suggested that they were not homeless it would be necessary for voluntary organisations to issue immediate 28 days notice when women came in so that they would be under threat of homelessness. This would be totally undesirable and would simply add stress to stress. If living in crisis accommodation took women out of the "homeless" category then the Act was being watered down and its protections would be removed from a whole class of persons that it was set up to help and for whom it was extremely important.
>
> As I have said, I myself would be perfectly prepared to speak those words, and I adopt them without hesitation. Did I need further support for what I think is plain beyond a peradventure the correct construction of this Act, I find

[26]    (1983) 2 HLR 45.
[27]    Ibid, at p 53.

it in the speech of Lord Lowry in *Din v Wandsworth London Borough Council* (1981) 3 WLR 918. I think all I need read are two short sentences from Lord Lowry's speech at p. 933 F:

> "I consider that to be homeless and to have found some temporary accommodation are not mutually inconsistent concepts. Nor does a person cease to be homeless merely by having a roof over his head or a lodging, however precarious."
>
> …'

Subsequently, the issue of the meaning of 'accommodation', in the context of defining homelessness, has frequently come before the courts. Perhaps the easiest way to appreciate the issue is to think of it of a 'ladder' of questions.

(a) The first question is probably whether the premises can be seen as any kind of accommodation at all. This was, at root, the issue in *Sidhu* concerning the refuge, and this is also true in the cases of *R v Waveney District Council, ex p Bowers*[28] and *R v South Herefordshire District Council, ex p Miles*[29].

In *Bowers*, the 'premises' consisted of a place in a Salvation Army hostel to which the applicant had to reapply each day with no guarantee of a place. The High Court (applying *Sidhu*) had no difficulty in overturning a local authority finding that he was not homeless (the authority did not appeal this point). In *Miles*, the 'premises' consisted of a hop-pickers' hut, lacking all main services, Woolf J stated[30]:

> 'The accommodation in the hut in question was without any mains services and there were two rooms each measuring only 10 feet by 10 feet. According to the evidence, it was infested with rats. There was, however, a caravan nearby which did have services. The relevant committee of the respondent council were obviously concerned about the accommodation. I have little doubt that it was on the borderline of that which could be, in any circumstances, regarded as being capable of being suitable for human habitation. However, bearing in mind that that primary decision is for the Council, I have come to the conclusion that it would not be right for me to treat the accommodation as being of such a bad standard that any reasonable Council, having the information which was available to this Council, would have disregarded it for the purposes of the Act on March 10 1981. It followed, therefore, that the applicant is not entitled to have the second decision quashed. However, by April 8, 1981, the third child had been born and bearing in mind that there are now five members of the family to be housed in the hut, I have come to the conclusion, having regard to the evidence, that it was not reasonable of the Council to regard the hut as being any longer capable of being accommodation for that family now that it consisted of the mother and father, two children and he newly born baby. It was below the borderline for such a family. …'

(b) Assuming that the 'premises' occupied are not so transient or lacking in basic amenities as to render any claim that they represent 'accommodation' untenable, the

---

[28]  [1982] 3 All ER 727.
[29]  (1983) 17 HLR 82.
[30]  At p 92.

second question is probably the more general issue of the overall 'suitability' of the property for the applicant and (if relevant) his or her family. In *R v Westminster City Council, ex p Ali*[31], Mr Ali had applied to Westminster for housing for himself, his wife and their five youngest children (aged one to 13). He was accepted as homeless at the time of his application, but Westminster decided that he had made himself intentionally homeless in leaving overcrowded bed-sit accommodation some months earlier. In effect they decided that it had been reasonable for Mr Ali and his family to continue living in the room, despite its overcrowding. In most respects, however, this is the same issue as whether the 'premises' had represented true 'accommodation' for Mr Ali and his family in the first place. The authority's decision was overturned in the High Court. McCullough J stated[32]:

'The Westminster City Council was under a statutory duty to ask itself whether it was satisfied that the accommodation at 19 Sale Place was available for Mr Ali and his family immediately before he gave it up at the end of 1981. It seems to me that either Mr Bailey never considered the question at all or he simply assumed that, because the family had been able to stay there in 1976–77 and from 1979–80, that they would be able to do so again. What Mr Ali gave up at the end of December 1981 was, on the evidence, no more than the right to share one room with another man. There was no evidence at all before the Westminster City Council that accommodation was available for him, his wife and their five children at 19 Sale Place.

I find, therefore, that no reasonable authority could, upon the material before it, have reasonably reached the conclusion that there was, as at the end of December 1981, accommodation available for this whole family at 19 Sale Place.

I think that Mr Bailey did, on the authority's behalf, consider the question of whether it would have been reasonable for the family to stay at that address, on the assumption that accommodation was there available. His thinking on the matter seems to have been as follows. "They refused to go to the maisonette in 1977; therefore they preferred to stay in 19 Sale Place; therefore 19 Sale Place cannot have been unbearably bad to live in at that time; therefore it was reasonable for them to carry on living in 19 Sale Place in the year 1977". So far, perhaps, so good, but then comes the error. "Therefore it is reasonable from them to continue to live there now in 1981/82."

That last step overlooks the increase in the number and the ages of the children. When Mr Ali refused to go and look at the maisonette he and his wife had a boy of seven, a girl of two and a four month old baby. That was the position when he decided that he would rather carry on living at 19 Sale Place until the local authority, as he hoped, offered him a house in the area in which he preferred to live.

At the end of 1981 there were children of twelve, seven, four, one and four months. By the time he applied in August 1982 they were nearly thirteen, nearly eight, five, two and one. Even if one starts from the premise that it was reasonable for husband, wife, seven year old, two year old and baby to live in

---

[31]   (1983) 11 HLR 83.
[32]   At p 92.

one room, it does not follow that it was reasonable for husband, wife, twelve year old, seven year old, four year old, one year old and baby all to live in one room.

That anyone should regard it as reasonable that a family of that size should live in one room 10 ft x 12 ft in size, or thereabouts, is something which I find astonishing. However, the matter has to be seen in the light of s 17(4) [of the 1977 legislation] which requires that reasonableness must take account of the general circumstances prevailing in relation to housing in the area. No evidence has been placed before me that accommodation in the area of the Westminster City Council is so desperately short that it is reasonable to accept overcrowding of this degree. In the absence of such evidence I am driven to the conclusion that this question could not properly have been determined against the applicant.'

In 1983, the issue of 'accommodation' under (what was then) s 1 of the Housing (Homeless Persons) Act 1977 was not explicitly linked to the general housing conditions of the area (unlike the equivalent issue in s 17 concerning intentional homelessness). However, in practice the issue was always construed against the general background of area housing conditions, and the link is now explicitly made by s 177(2) of the Housing Act 1996.

Clearly, serious overcrowding, or the premises being seriously damp or otherwise unfit or a health hazard, raises fundamental questions about whether the premises constitute 'accommodation' at all. Unfortunately, until 1986 (amendments introduced by s 14(1), Housing and Planning Act 1986) there was no requirement that accommodation had to be 'reasonable'. In some cases, courts had fudged the issue by stating that accommodation had (at least) to be 'appropriate' (see, for example, *R v Preseli District Council, ex p Fisher* [33]). However, the issue was forced out into the open by the House of Lords judgment in *R v Hillingdon London Borough Council, ex p Puhlhofer*[34].

The Puhlhofers were at the date of the application in occupation of one room at a guesthouse containing a double and a single bed, a baby's cradle, dressing table, pram and steriliser unit. There were no cooking or washing facilities in the room. There were three bathrooms in the guesthouse, the total capacity of the guest housing being 36 people or thereabouts. The applicants were in consequence compelled to eat out and to use a launderette for washing their own and the children's clothing. This expense absorbed most of their state benefit of £78 a week. Were they homeless? Eventually, the courts concurred with the local authority that they were not. Lord Brightman stated[35]:

'It is the submission of the applicants that a person does not have "accommodation" within the meaning of the Act and is therefore "homeless" if he occupies premises which either are not large enough to accommodate the family unit or lack the basic amenities of family life; such basic amenities should include not only sleeping facilities, but also cooking, washing and eating facilities. If the premises are deficient in any of these respects, they are

---

[33]  (1984) 17 HLR 147 at p 157.
[34]  [1986] AC 484, [1986] 1 All ER 467.
[35]  At [1986] 1 All ER 470.

not accommodation. The local authority have to take into account the size of the family, and whether the premises occupied are capable of being regarded as a "home" for that family. Put shortly, 'accommodation' must provide the ordinary facilities of a residence. Therefore no local authority properly directing themselves could have formed the view that the room allotted to the applicants at the Rosslyn Guest House was "accommodation" within the meaning of section 1, at least after the child of the marriage was born in April 1984, because it was then overcrowded in the statutory sense, and lacked both exclusive and communal facilities for cooking and clothes washing. So ran the argument for the applicants. ...

There are several features of the Act which in my respectful opinion have to be borne in mind. First, although the Act bears the word "Housing" it its short title, it is not an Act which imposes any duty upon a local authority to house the homeless. As the long title indicates, its object is to make "further provision as to the functions of local authorities with respect to persons who are homeless or threatened with homelessness; ..." It is an Act to assist persons who are homeless, not an Act to provide them with homes. It is an Act which came into operation in England and Wales only four months, and in Scotland only seven months, after it was passed (section 21); not sufficient time to enable a local authority to achieve any dramatic increase in their available housing stock. It is intended to provide for the homeless a lifeline of last resort; not to enable them to make inroads into the local authority's waiting list of applicants for housing. Some inroads there probably are bound to be, but in the end the local authority will have to balance the priority needs of the homeless on the one hand, and the legitimate aspirations of those on their housing waiting list on the other hand.

In this situation, Parliament plainly, and wisely, placed no qualifying adjective before the word "accommodation" in section 1 or section 4 of the Act, and none is to be implied. The word "appropriate" or "reasonable" is not to be imported. Nor is accommodation not accommodation because it might in certain circumstances be unfit for habitation for the purposes of Part II of the Housing Act 1957 or might involve overcrowding within the meaning of Part IV. Those particular statutory criteria are not to be imported into the Homeless Persons Act for any purpose. What is properly to be regarded as accommodation is a question of fact to be decided by the local authority. There are no rules. Clearly some places in which a person might choose or be constrained to live could not properly be regarded as accommodation at all; it would be a misuse of language to describe Diogenes as having occupied accommodation within the meaning of the Act. What the local authority have to consider, in reaching a decision whether a person is homeless for the purposes of the Act, is whether he has what can properly be described as accommodation within the ordinary meaning of that word in the English language.

I do not, however, accept that overcrowding is a factor to be disregarded, as Glidewell LJ apparently thought. I agree that the statutory definition of overcrowding has no relevance. But accommodation must, by definition, be capable of accommodating. If, therefore, a place is properly capable of being regarded as accommodation from an objective standpoint, but is so small a space that it is incapable of accommodating the applicant together with other persons who normally reside with him as members of his family, then on the facts of such a case the applicant would be homeless because he would have no accommodation in any relevant sense.

In the instant case the bona fides of the borough is not in dispute. On the facts in evidence, it is in my opinion plain that the council were entitled to find that the applicants were not homeless for the purposes of the Homeless Persons Act because they had accommodation within the ordinary meaning of that expression.'

The legislative amendments introduced to draw some of the sting of *Puhlhofer* are now to be found in s 175(3) of the Housing Act 1996, providing that a person is only to be 'treated' as having accommodation of 'premises' which it would be 'reasonable' to expect him to continue to occupy. This reinforces the direction of cases like *Ali* (above), although, of course, it does not state, simply, that sub-standard accommodation does not count, and 'reasonableness' has to be judged in the light of all the circumstances, including family life, health issues, the ages of (any) children and local housing conditions in general[36].

(c) A third question has come into focus since the '*Puhlhofer*' amendments: to what extent does the 'reasonableness' of continued occupation in premises depend on factors other than the physical condition and size of the premises themselves? For example, to what extent is the issue of harassment and the risk of violence from current or ex-partners relevant? The 1977 Act provided that a person was to be regarded as homeless if any attempt to occupy accommodation to which he or she had access would be likely to lead to violence or threats of violence from some other person residing in it. However, the scope of the law was widened considerably by the incorporation of a specific 'reasonableness' test, as is demonstrated clearly by the Court of Appeal decision in *R v Kensington and Chelsea Royal London Borough Council, ex p Hammell*[37].

Although Mrs Hammell had a tenancy of a council house or flat in Alloa, Scotland, provided by the Clackmannan District Council, she had, in January 1988, been forced to flee due to violence and harassment on the part of her ex-husband and others instigated by him. He was living with a woman who had at least one child, only a matter of some 50 yards away. She arrived in London in January 1989 and stayed with her sister in a one-bedroomed flat in the council's area, however, her sister soon had enough of sharing a small flat with Mrs Hammell and her three children and required her to leave.

Mrs Hammell then applied to Kensington and Chelsea as a homeless person, but her application was rejected because she still had accommodation in Alloa and the violence had occurred outside the home. Judicial review of this decision was granted by the Court of Appeal. Parker LJ stated[38]:

'The notice itself can be attacked on a number of grounds. In the first place, the reason given was on its face bad in law. It would have been good in law

---

[36]  See *R v Medina Borough Council ex p Dee* (1992) 24 HLR 562 and *R v Kensington and Chelsea Royal London Borough Council, ex p Ben El Mabrouk* (1995) 27 HLR 564.
[37]  *R v Kensington and Chelsea Royal London Borough Council, ex p Hammill* (1988) 20 HLR 666.
[38]  At p 677.

until the enactment of section 58(2A) of the Act of 1985 by section 14 of the Act of 1986, but the result of that was that before the council could determine that the applicant was not homeless they had to reach a positive decision that it would be reasonable for her and her children to continue to occupy 24, Menteith Court.

Secondly, it can be attacked because there was material to show that the background reason was that the violence was outside the home and therefore did not matter. That, again, would no doubt have been a sufficient reason had it not been for the enactment of section 58(2A), because under section 58 there is provision that a person is homeless if he has accommodation but it is probable that occupation of it will lead to violence from some other person residing in it. Since, however, it is now the position that the test is reasonableness of occupation, it cannot be right in law to suggest, as the council appear to believe, that violence outside the home is not at least a very important factor going to the question of whether it is reasonable to occupy. There used to be – and, indeed, may still be – amongst the many complications of the criminal law an offence known as "watching and besetting", which is something quite sufficient to render life intolerable to somebody, albeit nothing takes place within the premises themselves.

Thirdly, the notice can be attacked on the ground that the real reason, albeit a bad one, was that the violence was outside the home, not the reason stated.'

The Court of Appeal decided that the applicant had made out a strong prima facie case for judicial review of the authority's decision because the authority appeared to have come to the erroneous conclusion that violence outside the home was irrelevant[39].

The Housing Act 1996 further clarifies matters by providing specifically (in s 177(1)) that it is *not* reasonable to expect continued occupation of accommodation if it is probable that this would lead to 'domestic violence'. This is further defined so as to encompass violence or threats of violence to the applicant or others residing with him or her (as members of his or her family or otherwise) by 'associated' persons. The important concept of 'associated person' (see further discussion in Chapter 11) extends (via s 178) to current or ex-partners (married or unmarried), to relatives and to anyone who lives, or has lived, with the applicant in the same household.

In the House of Lords debates on the Housing Bill[40], Earl Ferrers stated that:

'... the amendments to work together to deliver a commitment ... to broaden the definition of domestic violence so as to embrace violence from partners who are no longer living with the victim'.

The importance of the fact that s 177(3) *deems* that it is *not* reasonable for victims of violence to continue to occupy accommodation where they would be 'at risk' is demonstrated by *Bond v Leicester City Council*[41].

---

[39]  These issues are discussed further in *R v Broxbourne Borough Council ex p Willmoth* (1989) 22 HLR 118.

[40]  Hansard (House of Lords) 1674, para 70 (8 July 1996).

[41]  [2001] EWCA Civ 1544, [2002] 1 FCR 566, [2002] HLR 6.

Shinead Bond had two children, aged four and three. She was the tenant of a housing association, but following a number of illegal incidents of domestic violence involving the children's father she left that accommodation. She approached Leicester City Council claiming to be homeless, but her application was refused on the basis that it was reasonable for her to return to that accommodation (noting that, although she had a history of fleeing from harassment by her former partner, she had never taken any steps to secure an injunction against him, or taken any other 'preventative' measures). Although this decision was upheld on review and in the county court, it was overturned in the Court of Appeal. For the purposes of s 177(1) the test of 'reasonableness' was not 'at large' – the only test was the probability of violence recurring if the accommodation was reoccupied. Moreover, that test was a simple one of fact, devoid of value judgments about what an applicant might otherwise have done. Issues relating to preventative measures could have a bearing on the probability of renewed violence, but were otherwise irrelevant.

Hale LJ stated[42]:

'However, the difference between the old law and the new lies in the way in which the risk of domestic violence is related to the reasonableness test, and the effect this has upon the definition of intentional homelessness. Section 17(1) of the 1977 Act was for practical purposes identical to s 191 of the 1996 Act. In *R v London Borough of Wandsworth, ex p Nimako-Boateng* (1983) 11 HLR 95 at 103, Woolf J (as he then was) said:

"There are all sorts of protection that a woman can get if her husband misbehaves. The local authority could perfectly properly in many cases in this country take the view that it would be reasonable for the wife to continue to occupy accommodation and say to a wife, if she thinks it right: 'If you are having trouble with your husband, go to the appropriate authority, be it a magistrates' court or the Family Division, and get protection against your husband'. If the woman does not then take that course and chooses to leave, the authority could take the view that it was reasonable for the lady to remain".

That was not, however, a case of domestic violence. It was not argued that the lady was already homeless within the meaning of s 1(2)(b) of the 1977 Act. That argument was raised in *R v Purbeck District Council, ex p Cadney* [1986] 2 FLR 158, but the authority found as a fact that the applicant was not at risk and Nolan J (as he then was) did not feel able to interfere with that finding on judicial review.

These cases are of no help to us now in applying s 177(1). *Ex p Nimako-Boateng* was concerned with the test of reasonableness at large. Had that been applicable here, this court might well have agreed with the observations of Woolf J quoted above. But neither in deciding upon homelessness or upon intentionally is the test of reasonableness at large in domestic violence cases. The only test is what is probable.

This in my view is a pure question of fact, devoid of value judgments about what an applicant should or should not do. If there are measures which have

---

[42] Ibid at p 165.

been taken or probably will be taken which will probably prove effective in preventing actual or threatened violence, then that may reduce the level of risk below one of probability. But those are the questions which the authority must ask themselves, rather than assume that such measures will be taken or will be effective if taken.

For what it is worth, it appears that the Secretary of State shares this view of the law. A new code of guidance accompanied the 1996 Act.

Chapter 13 of that guidance is headed "HOMELESS OR THREATENED WITH HOMELESSNESS". A subheading above para 13.7 deals with "Is it reasonable for the applicant to continue to occupy the accommodation?".

This cover matters which may be taken into account when considering reasonableness at large, including at para 13.8(e) "violence or threats of violence from persons *not* associated with the applicant". This advises that—

> "In some instances, the authority may advise an applicant to pursue any available legal remedies. This should not be done as a matter of policy but on the merits of an individual case and will need to take account of the need to ensure the proper safety of the applicant."

Another subheading above para 13.9 deals with "Domestic Violence". Paragraph 13.10 includes the following:

> "The fact that violence has not yet occurred does not, on its own, suggest that it is not likely to occur. Authorities should not base their assessment of a likely threat of violence solely on whether there has been actual violence in the past. Injunctions ordering persons not to molest, or enter the home of, the applicant will not necessarily deter people and the applicant should not necessarily be asked to return to his/her home in this instance. Authorities may inform applicants of the option to take out an injunction, but should make it clear that there is no obligations to do so if s/he feels it would be ineffective."

Clearly, therefore, the Secretary of State considers that there should be no pressure to explore alternative remedies and the matter should be left to the applicant. A later consultation draft of the code went further and omitted the words "if s/he feels it would be ineffective" altogether, thus reinforcing the view that the mere availability of such remedies does not answer the probability question.

I do not find this conclusion at all surprising. Taken to the extreme, it could mean that a probable victim of domestic violence, who had been offered every assistance available for her protection, could reject it and seek re-housing even if there was good reason to think that it would be effective. But Mr Arden acknowledges that even cases like the present one, in which the applicant had twice before fled from domestic violence, are rare. It will be rare indeed for a parent of children (for this is what gives her the priority need) to uproot herself from a situation in which legal or practical measures are not only on offer but likely to be effective. But the issues are issues of fact in the particular case.

To hold otherwise would leave it open to local authorities to put pressures upon the victims of domestic violence which fail to take account of some of its well-known features. Once begun it is likely to be repeated, often with escalating severity. It induces a sense of shame and of powerlessness in the victims, who often blame themselves and find it impossible to escape. There are various legal and practical remedies available, but it is by no means easy for many victims to invoke these. However hard the family courts try, they are often ineffective. Escape may well be the only practicable answer. The victim is the one who knows the perpetrator best and is likely to be best able to judge this. It is not, after all, a decision to be lightly taken by a young mother of two young children.

The family courts also do their utmost to require parents with whom the children are living to arrange and encourage contact with the other parent. Only comparatively recently have we recognised that violence and threats towards the parent can have a damaging effect upon the children, such that it may constitute a good reason for refusing all contact. Even now, there is certainly no presumption to that effect. In those circumstances, it would be most unfair if one part of the system were to blame or penalise a mother for resuming contact with the father of her children, unless another part of the system has found that there should be no contact because it is harmful to them.

Whatever the facts of this particular case, therefore, I do not find it surprising that Parliament should have recognised a tendency in parts of the system to consider it reasonable to expect victims of domestic violence to do, or not to do, things which in reality place them in an almost impossible position; and that Parliament should therefore have enacted the clear rule in s 177(1) ...'

Moreover, the importance of s 177 has been extended by the amendments contained in the Homelessness Act 2002 which extend its ambit from domestic violence to violence per se. Therefore if it is probable that a return to accommodation still 'available' to an applicant will trigger renewal violence from anyone – inside or outside the home – it should be deemed not reasonable to occupy such accommodation.

(d) The final question is, probably, the most difficult. Can something be described as 'accommodation' if it is insecure, so that the applicant lives in permanent fear of being evicted from it? It is clear that once possession proceedings have begun (whether the applicant occupies as tenant or licensee), and it is clear that there is no defence to the claim for possession it is not reasonable to expect them to 'hang on to the bitter end'[43]. However, until 1996 the wider question – of whether the occupation of highly insecure, or 'unsettled', accommodation might allow the occupant to be treated as homeless – was unresolved. The issue was complicated by the fact that there was some judicial authority in support of the view that to amount to 'accommodation' breaking the chain of causation from an earlier instance of intentional homelessness, the later accommodation had to be sufficiently secure to be 'settled'[44]. Although this is a distinct point, it is sufficiently close to the core 'accommodation' issue to suggest that the same result could follow there also. Given that most private sector accommodation is, since the Housing Act 1988, highly insecure, guaranteeing at most short, fixed-term occupation rights (via an

---

[43] See *R v Portsmouth City Council, ex p Knight* (1984) 10 HLR 115.
[44] See *Lambert v Ealing London Borough Council* [1982] 1 WLR 550.

assured shorthold), and might therefore be seen as not representing a 'settled' home, the implication of any such result for local authorities would be serious.

However, in the House of Lords decision in *R v Brent London Borough Council, ex p Awua*[45] it was held that there was *no* absolute requirement that, to amount to 'accommodation', premises had to be occupied as a 'settled' home. In this case Lord Hoffmann stated[46]:

'A local authority is entitled to regard a person as having accommodation (and therefore as not being homeless) if he has accommodation which, having regard to the matters mentioned in subsection (2B), it can reasonably consider that it would be reasonable for him to continue to occupy. This produces symmetry between the key concept of homelessness in section 58(1) and intentional homelessness in section 60(1). If the accommodation is so bad that leaving for that reason would not make one intentionally homeless, then one is in law already homeless. But there is nothing in the Act to say that a local authority cannot take the view that a person can reasonably be expected to continue to occupy accommodation which is temporary. If, notwithstanding that the accommodation is physically suitable, the occupier's tenure is so precarious that he is likely to have to leave within 28 days, then he will be "threatened with homelessness" within section 58(4). But I find it hard to imagine circumstances in which a person who is not threatened with home-lessness cannot reasonably be expected to continue to occupy his accommo-dation simply because it is temporary.

On the other hand, the extent to which the accommodation is physically suitable, so that it would be reasonable for a person to continue to occupy it, must be related to the time for which he has been there and is expected to stay. A local housing authority could take the view that a family like the Puhlhofers, put into a single cramped and squalid bedroom, can be expected to make do for a temporary period. On the other hand, there will come a time at which it is no longer reasonable to expect them to continue to occupy such accommodation. At this point they come back within the definition of homeless in section 58(1).

I would therefore reject the submission of Mr Roger Henderson that "accom-modation" in section 58 and section 60 must be construed as "a settled home". There is absolutely no warrant in the language of the statute or the decision of this House in *Puhlhofer* for implying such a concept. Yet Sir Louis Blom-Cooper and the Court of Appeal thought that the authorities required it. Where did such an idea come from?

The answer is that it comes from an altogether different context. In *Dyson v Kerrier District Council* [1980] 3 All ER 313 1 WLR 1205 Miss Fiona Dyson gave up her flat in Huntingdon and went to live in Cornwall. But the only accommodation which she had arranged for herself was a three-month winter let of a cottage in Helston. She knew that the tenancy was not protected and that she would have to leave. When she was finally evicted, she applied to the local council for accommodation on the ground that she was now homeless. The council said that she was intentionally homeless because she had given

---

[45] [1996] AC 55, [1995] 3 All ER 493.
[46] [1995] 3 All ER at p 497.

up the Huntingdon flat knowing that after the expiry of the winter let she would have nowhere to live. Miss Dyson's argument was that in applying the predecessor of section 60(1) (section 17(1) of the Act of 1977) one was concerned only with the accommodation one had been occupying at the time when one became homeless. This was the cottage in Cornwall and it was not reasonable to expect her to continue to occupy that accommodation because the court had ordered her to leave it. Brightman LJ, at p 1214, described this as a formidable argument on the literal wording of the statute. But the Court of Appeal held that such a construction would enable people to jump the housing queues by making themselves intentionally homeless at one remove. They would only have to move into temporary accommodation and wait until evicted. The court therefore held that one was not confined to asking whether it would have been reasonable to continue to occupy the cottage in Cornwall. If it would have been reasonable to continue to occupy the flat in Huntingdon and there was a causal link between deliberately leaving that flat and her subsequent homelessness in Cornwall, then she was intentionally homeless.

What constitutes such a causal link? In *Din v Wandsworth London Borough Council* [1983] 1 AC 657 Lord Wilberforce referred with approval to the analysis of Ackner LJ in the Court of Appeal. He summarised it by saying that a disqualification on the grounds of having made oneself intentionally homeless (such as attached to Miss Dyson when she left Huntingdon) was not displaced by obtaining temporary accommodation, Ackner LJ had said (in a passage later cited by the Court of Appeal in *Lambert v Ealing Borough Council* [1982] 2 All ER 394 at 398 1 WLR 550 at 557):

> "To remove his self-imposed disqualification, he must therefore have achieved what can be loosely described as a 'settled residence,' as opposed to what from the outset is known (as in *Dyson's* case [1980] 1 WLR 1205) to be only temporary accommodation. What amounts to 'a settled residence' is a question of fact and degree depending upon the circumstances of each individual case."

The distinction between a settled residence and temporary accommodation is thus being used to identify what will break the causal link between departure from accommodation which it would have been reasonable to continue to occupy and homelessness separated from that departure by a period or periods of accommodation elsewhere. This jurisprudence is well-established (it was approved by this House in *Din v Wandsworth London BC*) and nothing I have said is intended to cast any doubt upon it, although I would wish to reserve the question of whether the occupation of a settled residence is the sole and exclusive method by which the causal link can be broken. It is the importation of the distinction between settled and temporary accommodation into other questions arising under Part III of the Act which seems to me unwarranted.

Thus there has occasionally been a tendency to treat *Dyson* as entailing that Miss Dyson became homeless when she left Huntingdon and remained homeless while living in her winter let in Cornwall. By this means, the notion of settled accommodation is introduced into the concept of homelessness. I cannot however accept that a lady spending Christmas in a cottage in Cornwall which she has the right to occupy for another three months (and therefore not threatened with homelessness within the meaning of section 58(4)) should somehow be deemed to be homeless. And of course *Dyson* implies no such thing. It decides only that her homelessness after eviction from the cottage in Cornwall is intentional because it was caused by her decision to leave the flat in Huntingdon. Some support for a contrary view can be found in the speech of Lord Lowry in *Din's* case but this opinion was not shared by the other members of the House, who analysed the case solely in terms of causation. What persists until the causal link is broken is the intentionality, not the homelessness.

I would therefore hold that "accommodation" in section 58(1) and section 60(1) means a place which can fairly be described as accommodation (*Puhlhofer*) and which it would be reasonable, having regard to the general housing conditions in the local housing authority's district, for the person in question to continue to occupy (section 58(2A) and (2B)). There is no additional requirement that it should be settled or permanent.'

## ELIGIBILITY FOR ASSISTANCE

It is not enough to be 'homeless'; the applicant must also be 'eligible'. This was a qualification introduced into the law in 1996 as part of the Government's intention to exclude from housing assistance asylum seekers and certain categories of persons subject to immigration control. Similar exclusions, of course, also apply to such persons with regard to 'qualifying person' status in relation to the allocation of council housing (see Chapter 7).

# HOUSING ACT 1996

*Eligibility for assistance*

### 185.  **Persons from abroad not eligible for housing assistance**

(1) A person is not eligible for assistance under this Part if he is a person from abroad who is ineligible for housing assistance.

(2) A person who is subject to immigration control within the meaning of the Asylum and Immigration Act 1996 is not eligible for housing assistance unless he is of a class prescribed by regulations made by the Secretary of State.

(2A) No person who is excluded from entitlement to housing benefit by section 115 of the Immigration and Asylum Act 1999 (exclusion from benefits) shall be included in any class prescribed under subsection (2).

(3) The Secretary of State may make provision by regulations as to other descriptions of persons who are to be treated for the purposes of this Part as persons from abroad who are ineligible for housing assistance.

(4) A person from abroad who is not eligible for housing assistance shall be disregarded in determining for the purposes of this Part whether another person—

(a)   is homeless or threatened with homelessness, or
(b)   has a priority need for accommodation.

# HOMELESSNESS (ENGLAND) REGULATIONS 2000

SI 2000/701

## Citation, commencement and extent

1.   (1) These Regulations may be cited as the Homelessness (England) Regulations 2000 and shall come into force on 3rd April 2000.

(2) These Regulations extend to England only.

## Interpretation

2.   (1) In these Regulations—

'the 1971 Act' means the Immigration Act 1971;

'the 1995 Act' means the Jobseekers Act 1995;

'the 1996 Act' means the Housing Act 1996;

'asylum-seeker' means a person who is not under 18 and who made a claim for asylum which is recorded by the Secretary of State as having been made before 3rd April 2000 but which has not been determined;

'claim for asylum' means a claim that it would be contrary to the United Kingdom's obligations under the Refugee Convention for the claimant to be removed from, or required to leave, the United Kingdom.

'the Common Travel Area' means the United Kingdom, the Channel Islands.

'the immigration rules' means the rules laid down as mentioned in section 3(2) of the 1971 Act (general provisions for regulation and control);

'limited leave' means leave under the 1971 Act to enter or remain in the United Kingdom which is limited as to duration; and

'the Refugee Convention' means the Convention relating to the Status of Refugees done at Geneva on 28th July 1951, as extended by Article 1(2) of the Protocol relating to the Status of Refugees done at New York on 31st January 1967.

(2) For the purposes of the definition of "asylum-seeker", a claim for asylum is determined at the end of such period beginning—

(a)   on the day on which the Secretary of State notifies the claimant of his decision on the claim; or

(b)   if the claimant has appealed against the Secretary of State's decision, on the day on which the appeal is disposed of,

as may be prescribed under section 94(3) of the Immigration and Asylum Act 1999.

## Classes of persons subject to immigration control who are eligible for housing assistance

3.   (1) The following are classes of persons prescribed for the purposes of section 185(2) of the 1996 Act (persons subject to immigration control who are eligible for housing assistance)—

(a)   Class A – a person recorded by the Secretary of State as a refugee within the definition in Article 1 of the Refugee Convention;

(b)   Class B – a person—

(i)   who has been granted by the Secretary of State exceptional leave to enter or remain in the United Kingdom outside the provisions of the immigration rules; and

(ii)   whose leave is not subject to a condition requiring him to maintain and accommodate himself, and any person who is dependent on him, without recourse to public funds;

(c)   Class C – a person who has current leave to enter or remains in the United Kingdom which is not subject to any limitation or condition and who is habitually resident in the Common Travel Area other than a person—

(i)   who has been given leave to enter or remain in the United Kingdom upon an undertaking given by another person (his 'sponsor') in writing in pursuance of the immigration rules to be responsible for

(ii)   who has been resident in the United Kingdom for less than five years beginning on the date of entry or the date on which the undertaking was given in respect of him, whichever date is the later; and

(iii)   whose sponsor or, where there is more than one sponsor, at least one of whose sponsors, is still alive;

(d)   Class D – a person who left the territory of Montserrat after 1st November 1995 because of the effect on that territory of a volcanic eruption;

(e)   Class E – a person who is habitually resident in the Common Travel Area and who—

(i)   is a national of a state which has ratified the European Convention on Social and Medical Assistance done at Paris on 11th December 1953 or a state which has ratified the European Social Charter done at Turin on 18th October 1961 and is lawfully present in the United Kingdom; or

(ii)   before 3rd April 2000 was owed a duty by a housing authority under Part III of the Housing Act 1985 (housing the homeless) or Part VII of the 1996 Act (homelessness) which is extant, and who is a national of a state which is a signatory to the European Convention on Social and Medical Assistance done at Paris on 11th December 1953 or a state which is a signatory to the European Social Charter done at Turin on 18th October 1961;

(f)   Class F – a person who is an asylum-seeker and who made a claim for asylum—

(i)   which is recorded by the Secretary of State as having been made on his arrival (other than on his re-entry) in the United Kingdom from a country outside the Common Travel Area; and

(ii)   which has not been recorded by the Secretary of State as having been either decided (other than on appeal) or abandoned;

(g)   Class G – a person who is an asylum-seeker and—

(i)   who was in Great Britain when the Secretary of State made a declaration to the effect that the country of which that person is a national is subject to such a fundamental change in circumstances that he would not normally order the return of a person to that country;

(ii)   who made a claim for asylum which is recorded by the Secretary of State as having been made within a period of three months from the day on which that declaration was made; and

(iii)   whose claim for asylum has not been recorded by the Secretary of State as having been either decided (other than on appeal) or abandoned;

(h)   Class H – a person who is an asylum-seeker and—

(i)   who made a relevant claim for asylum on or before 4th February 1996; and

(ii)   who was, on 4th February 1996, entitled to benefit under regulation 7A of the Housing Benefit (General) Regulations 1987 (persons from abroad); and

(i)   Class I – a person who is on an income-based jobseeker's allowance or in receipt of income support and is eligible for that benefit other than because—

(i)   he has limited leave to enter or remain in the United Kingdom which was given in accordance with the relevant immigration rules; and

(ii)   he is temporarily without funds because remittances to him from abroad have been disrupted.

**Description of persons who are to be treated as persons from abroad ineligible for housing assistance**

4.   (1) The following are descriptions of persons, other than persons who are subject to immigration control, who are to be treated for the purposes of Part 7 of the 1996 Act (homelessness) as persons from abroad who are ineligible for housing assistance—

(a)   subject to paragraphs (2) and (3), a person who is not habitually resident in the United Kingdom, the Channel Islands, the Isle of Man or the Republic of Ireland;

(b)   a person whose right to reside in the United Kingdom, the Channel Islands, the Isle of Man or the Republic of Ireland is derived solely from Council Directive No. 90/364/EEC or Council Directive No. 90/365/EEC.

(2) The following persons shall not, however, be treated as persons from abroad who are ineligible pursuant to paragraph (1)(a)—

(a)   a person who is a worker for the purposes of Council Regulation (EEC) No. 1612/68 or (EEC) No. 1251/70;

(b)   a person who is an accession state worker requiring registration who is treated as a worker for the purpose of the definition of 'qualified person' in regulation 5(1) of the Immigration (European Economic Area) Regulations 2000 pursuant to regulation 5 of the Accession (Immigration and Worker Registration) Regulations 2004;

(c)   a person with a right to reside pursuant to the Immigration (European Economic Area) Regulations 2000, which is derived from Council Directive No. 68/360/EEC, No. 73/148/EEC or No. 75/34/EEC;

(d)   a person who left the territory of Montserrat after 1st November 1995 because of the effect on that territory of a volcanic eruption.

(3) A person shall not be treated as habitually resident in the United Kingdom, the Channel Islands, the Isle of Man or the Republic of Ireland for the purposes of paragraph (1)(a) if he does not have a right to reside in the United Kingdom, the Channel Islands, the Isle of Man or the Republic of Ireland.

# PERSONS SUBJECT TO IMMIGRATION CONTROL (HOUSING AUTHORITY ACCOMMODATION AND HOMELESSNESS) ORDER 2000

SI 2000/706

. . .

**Housing authority accommodation – England, Scotland and Northern Ireland**

5.   The following are classes of persons specified for the purposes of section 118(1) of the 1999 Act (housing authority accommodation) in respect of England, Scotland and Northern Ireland—

(a)   Class A – a person recorded by the Secretary of State as a refugee within the definition in Article 1 of the Refugee Convention;

(b)   Class B – a person—

(i)   who has been granted by the Secretary of State exceptional leave to enter or remain in the United Kingdom outside the provisions of the immigration rules; and

(ii)   whose leave is not subject to a condition requiring him to maintain and accommodate himself, and any person who is dependent on him, without recourse to public funds;

(c)   Class C – a person who has current leave to enter or remain in the United Kingdom which is not subject to any limitation or condition and who is habitually resident in the Common Travel Area other than a person—

(i)   who has been given leave to enter or remain in the United Kingdom upon an undertaking given by another person (his 'sponsor') in writing in pursuance of the immigration rules to be responsible for his maintenance and accommodation;

(ii)   who has been resident in the United Kingdom for less than five years beginning on the date of entry or the date on which the undertaking was given in respect of him, whichever date is the later; and

(iii)   whose sponsor or, where there is more than one sponsor, at least one of whose sponsors, is still alive.

(d)   Class D – a person who left the territory of Montserrat after 1st November 1995 because of the effect on that territory of a volcanic eruption;

(e)   Class E – a person who is—

(i)   a national of a state which has ratified the European Convention on Social and Medical Assistance done at Paris on 11th December 1953 or a state which has ratified the European Social Charter done at Turin on 18th October 1961;

(ii)   lawfully present in the United Kingdom; and

(iii)   habitually resident in the Common Travel Area;

(f)   Class F – a person who is attending a full-time course at a specified education institution in a case where the housing accommodation which is or may be provided to him—

(i)   is let by a housing authority to that specified education institution for the purposes of enabling that institution to provide accommodation for students attending a full-time course at that institution; and

(ii)   would otherwise be difficult for that housing authority to let on terms which, in the opinion of the housing authority, are satisfactory.

## Housing authority accommodation – England

**6.**   (1) The following are classes of persons specified for the purposes of section 118(1) of the 1999 Act in respect of England—

(a)   Class G – a person who is owed a duty under section 21 of the National Assistance Act 1948 (duty of local authorities to provide accommodation);

(b)   Class H – a person who is either a child in need or a member of the family of a child in need;

(c)   Class I – a person—

(i)   who is owed a duty under section 63(1) (interim duty to accommodate in case of apparent priority need), 65(2) or (3) (duties to persons found to be homeless) or 68(1) or (2) (duties to persons whose applications are referred) of the 1985 Act;

(ii)   who is owed a duty under section 188(1) (interim duty to accommodate in case of apparent priority need, 190(2) duties to persons becoming homeless intentionally), 193(2) (duty to persons with priority need who are not homeless intentionally), 195(2) (duties in case of threatened homelessness) or 200(1), (3) or (4) (duties to applicant whose case is considered for referral or referred) of the Housing Act 1996; or

(iii)   in respect of whom a local housing authority are exercising their power under section 194(1) (power exercisable after minimum period of duty under section 193) of the Housing Act 1996;

(d)   Class J – an asylum-seeker to whom, or a dependant of an asylum-seeker to whom, a local authority is required to provide support in accordance with regulations made under Schedule 9 to the 1999 Act (asylum support: interim provision);

(e)   Class K – a person who is attending a designated course, which is a full-time course, at an educational establishment in a case where the housing accommodation which is or may be provided to him by a local housing authority—

(i)   is not and will not be let to him as a secure tenancy by virtue of paragraph 10 of Schedule 1 to the 1985 Act (student lettings which are not secure tenancies); and

(ii)   would otherwise be difficult for that local housing authority to let on terms which, in the opinion of the local housing authority, are satisfactory;

(f)   Class L – a person who has a secure tenancy within the meaning of section 79 of the 1985 Act (secure tenancies).

Ineligibility is similar to lack of qualification to be allocated housing under the normal allocation principles (see Chapter 7). The ineligible are basically those from abroad subject to immigration control under the Asylum and Immigration Act 1996, *unless* a member of a class of persons specified by the Secretary of State, (England) ie the *exceptions* created by the Homelessness Regulations 2000 (SI 2000/701). A number of people are re-qualified by the Regulations, even though initially from abroad. There then follow a number of *specifically excluded* persons. These persons are ineligible for assistance as 'persons from abroad':

(a)   Those persons not falling within classes A to I who are also not *habitually resident* in the Common Travel Area (CTA). Thus a person not habitually resident in the CTA will be ineligible. However, this exclusion does *not* apply to migrant workers from EC countries, so they *can* be assisted.

(b)   Persons who are EEA nationals required by the Secretary of State to leave the UK, ie nationals of EC Member States plus Norway, Iceland and Liechtenstein. So even if a person is an EC migrant workers, he or she can be 'ineligible' if required to leave the UK by the Secretary of State.

Asylum-seekers or their dependants not otherwise falling within s 185, ie not excluded by that section from eligibility, are however, still *not eligible*, where they have *any* accommodation – *however temporary* – available for occupation in the UK. That accommodation must still, however, be 'accommodation' for the purposes of the Act.

In *Lismane v Hammersmith and Fulham London Borough Council*[47], Lismane – a Latvian – arrived in the UK in 1997 claiming to flee from persecution. She was allowed to enter and brought her son. They settled with her husband, in a single room. L was at that time pregnant. Was the room 'accommodation'? The Court of Appeal held not – the room could not count as accommodation, available for L's occupation. It was not reasonable that L should continue to occupy the accommodation, and so it was not 'accommodation' and thus L did not have any accommodation falling within s 186 and accordingly was not excluded from eligibility by that section.

In *R v City of Westminster, ex p Castelli*[48], the Court of Appeal decided that an EC national who ceases to be a qualified person in fact, but who has not been given (and overstayed) a limited leave to remain in the United Kingdom and has not been informed that the Secretary of State had decided that he should be removed, does not belong to a category of persons 'not lawfully here'; there is no obligation on such a person to apply for leave to remain, and he or she cannot properly be regarded as being in breach of the immigration laws by his or her failure to do so. (This does not, of course, prevent such a person from falling foul of the requirement

[47]   (1998) 31 HLR 427.
[48]   (1996) 28 HLR 616.

under s 185(3) of the Housing Act 1996 and the Homelessness Regulations 2000 to be 'habitually resident in the Common Travel Area', effectively the United Kingdom, Eire, the Isle of Man and the Channel Islands).

Very recently the accession of ten new states[49] into the European Union has triggered yet further regulations to restrict the access of nationals of these states to local authority accommodation. In relation to homelessness eligibility the amending regulations (the Allocation of Housing and Homelessness (Amendment) (England) Regulation SI 2004/1235) substitute a new reg 4 into the Homelessness (England) Regulations (this has already been incorporated in the text of the 2000 Regulations outlined above). Aside from nationals of Malta and Cyprus, nationals of the 'new' EU states will have to overcome further eligibility hurdles to gain access to local authority housing, for example:

- workers from these states will only be eligible in their first 12 months in the country if they are registered and actually working for a registered employer;
- work-seekers from these states will not be eligible if, despite having a habitual residence here, they are required to register for work under the Home Officer Worker Registration scheme.

## INTERIM DUTY TO ACCOMMODATE

## HOUSING ACT 1996

### 188.    Interim duty to accommodate in case of apparent priority need

(1) If the local housing authority have reason to believe that an applicant may be homeless, eligible for assistance and have a priority need, they shall secure that accommodation is available for his occupation pending a decision as to the duty (if any) owed to him under the following provisions of this Part.

(2) The duty under this section arises irrespective of any possibility of the referral of the applicant's case to another local housing authority (see sections 198 to 200).

(3) The duty ceases when the authority's decision is notified to the applicant, even if the applicant requests a review of the decision (see section 202).

The authority may continue to secure that accommodation is available for the applicant's occupation pending a decision on a review.

Where an authority have reason to believe that an applicant may be (i) homeless, (ii) eligible for assistance, and (iii) have a priority need they must secure accommodation for that person pending a decision as to the duty (if any) owed. This duty arises irrespective of any referral to another authority, but continues *only until* the authority's decision is notified to the applicant *even if the applicant requests a review of the decision*, though the authority *may* continue to secure accommodation pending a decision on a review.

There could be room for conflict here, ie the *duty* is limited in point of time and the *power* will have to be exercised according to the requirements of the *Wednesbury* principles, eg, on the basis of relevant considerations and reasonably, etc.

---

[49]    Cyprus, Malta, Poland, Lithuania, Estonia, Latvia, Slovenia, Slovakia, Hungary and the Czech Republic. Accession occurred on 1 May 2004.

Note that by virtue of ss 205 and 206 of the 1996 Act, the accommodation provided under this interim duty to accommodate must be 'suitable', ie there is a need to avoid unfit, overcrowded or multiply-occupied premises.[50]

## PRIORITY NEED FOR ACCOMMODATION

## HOUSING ACT 1996

### 189.   **Priority need for accommodation**

(1) The following have a priority need for accommodation—

(a)   a pregnant woman or a person with whom she resides or might reasonably be expected to reside;
(b)   a person with whom dependent children reside or might reasonably be expected to reside;
(c)   a person who is vulnerable as a result of old age, mental illness or handicap or physical disability or other special reason, or with whom such a person resides or might reasonably be expected to reside;
(d)   a person who is homeless or threatened with homelessness as a result of an emergency such as flood, fire or other disaster.

(2) The Secretary of State may by order—

(a)   specify further descriptions of persons as having a priority need for accommodation, and
(b)   amend or repeal any part of subsection (1).

(3) Before making such an order the Secretary of State shall consult such associations representing relevant authorities, and such other persons, as he considers appropriate.

(4) No such order shall be made unless a draft of it has been approved by resolution of each House of Parliament.

No order was made under s 189(2) – or its predecessors – until 2001 (Wales) and 2002 (England). The relevant orders for England and Wales differ significantly and, for that reason, both are included here. The implications of the new orders and new priority need categories are discussed later in this section.

## THE HOMELESSNESS (PRIORITY NEED FOR ACCOMMODATION) (ENGLAND) ORDER 2002

SI 2002/2051

### Citation, commencement and interpretation

1.   (1) This Order may be cited as the Homelessness (Priority Need for Accommodation) (England) Order 2002 and shall come into force on the day after the day on which it is made.

(2) This Order extends to England only.

(3) In this Order—

'looked after, accommodated or fostered' has the meaning given by section 24(2) of the Children Act 1989[2]; and
'relevant student' means a person to whom section 24B(3) of that Act applies—

---

[50]   And see now specifically, the Homelessness (Suitability of Accommodation) (England) Order 2003 SI 2003/3326.

(a)   who is in full-time further or higher education; and

(b)   whose term-time accommodation is not available to him during a vacation.

## Priority need for accommodation

2.   The descriptions of person specified in the following articles have a priority need for accommodation for the purposes of Part 7 of the Housing Act 1996.

## Children aged 16 or 17

3.   (1) A person (other than a person to whom paragraph (2) below applies) aged sixteen or seventeen who is not a relevant child for the purposes of section 23A of the Children Act 1989.

(2) This paragraph applies to a person to whom a local authority owe a duty to provide accommodation under section 20 of that Act (provision of accommodation for children in need).

## Young people under 21

4.   (1) A person (other than a relevant student) who—

(a)   is under twenty-one; and

(b)   at any time after reaching the age of sixteen, but while still under eighteen, was, but is no longer, looked after, accommodated or fostered.

## Vulnerability: institutional backgrounds

5.   (1) A person (other than a relevant student) who has reached the age of twenty-one and who is vulnerable as a result of having been looked after, accommodated or fostered.

(2) A person who is vulnerable as a result of having been a member of Her Majesty's regular naval, military or air forces.

(3) A person who is vulnerable as a result of:

(a)   having served a custodial sentence (within the meaning of section 76 of the Powers of Criminal Courts (Sentencing) Act 2000)[3];

(b)   having been committed for contempt of court or any other kindred offence;

(c)   having been remanded in custody (within the meaning of paragraph (b), (c), or (d) of section 88(1) of that Act).

## Vulnerability: fleeing violence or threats of violence

6.   A person who is vulnerable as a result of ceasing to occupy accommodation by reason of violence from another person or threats of violence from another person which are likely to be carried out.

# THE HOMELESS PERSONS (PRIORITY NEED) (WALES) ORDER 2001

SI 2001/607

## Name, commencement and application

1.   (1) The name of this Order is the Homeless Persons (Priority Need) (Wales) Order 2001 and it shall come into force on St David's Day, 1st March 2001.

(2) This Order applies to Wales only.

## Persons with priority need for accommodation

2.   The descriptions of person specified in articles 3 to 7 have priority need for accommodation under section 189 of the Housing Act 1996.

**A Care leaver or person at particular risk of sexual or financial exploitation, 18 years or over but under the age of 21**

3.    (1) A Person Who

(a)   is 18 years old or older but under the age of 21; and

(b)   at anytime while still a child was, but is no longer, looked after, accommodated or fostered; or

(c)   is at particular risk of sexual or financial exploitation.

(2) In paragraph (1)(b) above 'looked after, accommodated or fostered' means:

(a)   looked after by a local authority;

(b)   accommodated by or on behalf of a voluntary organisation;

(c)   accommodated in a private children's home;

(d)   accommodated for a consecutive period of at least three months—

    (i)   by any health authority, special health authority or local education authority, or

    (ii)   in any residential care home, nursing home or mental nursing home or in any accommodation provided by a National Health Service Trust; or

(e)   privately fostered.

**A 16 or 17 year old**

4.    A person who is 16 or 17 years old.

**A person fleeing domestic violence or threatened domestic violence**

5.    A person without dependant children who has been subject to domestic violence or is at risk of such violence, or if he or she returns home is at risk of domestic violence.

**A person homeless after leaving the armed forces**

6.    (1) A person formerly serving in the regular armed forces of the crown who has been homeless since leaving those forces.

(2) A 'prisoner' means any person for the time being detained in lawful custody as the result of a requirement imposed by a court that he or she be detained.

Most of the litigation on this provision has concerned the meaning of the word 'vulnerable'. Over the years the courts have developed an understanding of the concept of vulnerability. The basic test is whether the applicant is less able to fend for himself so that he will suffer injury in circumstances where a less vulnerable person would be able to cope.

What makes a person 'vulnerable' is thus a question of fact and degree in all cases for the local authority to decide. They should consider the frequency of affliction, however[51].

An authority should consider all the facts of the case, and should consult relevant experts in housing and social welfare; and should not rely on the opinion of a single doctor who has neither seen nor examined the homeless person, and certainly should not 'rubber stamp' his assessment[52].

Where priority need depends on the presence of dependent children, the child(ren) in question need not live exclusively with the applicant; but much depends on the facts of each case and it is for the authority to decide with whom children 'normally

---

[51]   *R v Wandsworth London Borough Council, ex p Banbury* (1986) 19 HLR 76.

[52]   *R v Lambeth London Borough Council, ex p Carroll* (1987) 20 HLR 142.

reside'[53]. There is no definition of 'dependent' in the Act. Normally a child in employment or in a YTS place is not dependent[54].

A closer examination of two cases, *R v Lambeth London Borough Council, ex p Carroll*[55] and *Ortiz v City of Westminster*[56], can serve to demonstrate the working out of the law and practice, in relation to the key 'vulnerability' issue. In *Carroll*, Dr Dellaportas (a Lambeth medical officer) reported that he had seen and examined the applicant, who was 49 years old, on 14 February 1986. He reported that the applicant told him, amongst other things, that he drank six or seven pints of beer daily, but no spirits, that his past history included a fracture of the skull when he was nine years old, when he fell off a bank into a concrete yard. He told Dr Dellaportas that in 1983 he was involved in a road traffic accident, in which he sustained a fracture of his skull affecting mostly the frontal bone, which had been substantially depressed on the right.

In expressing his opinion, Dr Dellaportas wrote:

'There is no doubt that as a result of the accident he sustained in 1983 he has had severe damage of the bony structure of his right orbit. This has caused him double vision which will be present indefinitely. Whether relevant orthopaedic or plastic surgery could improve his current double vision is debatable but obviously the opinion of an orthopaedic surgeon, a plastic surgeon and an ophthalmologist should be sought.'

Finally, a social report written by a Mr D S Gibson of the 'Vauxhall Action for Homeless in the Community' stated that Mr Carroll was a friendly man inclined to play down and avoid the difficulties he faced. He would have liked to live in a flat of his own, but he had been unsuccessful in achieving this. He had spent almost all of the last two years sleeping on a friend's floor. However, in December 1986 his friend left to return to Ireland. Since then Mr Carroll had no fixed abode. He suffered from blurred vision and had a drink problem.

Webster J stated[57]:

'In my view, therefore, the respondent's decision of June 18, 1986 was bad in law because they failed properly to inquire into or consider the question of whether, notwithstanding the medical opinion of Dr Siva, the applicant was vulnerable for some other special reason or for a combination of one or more of the reasons set out in 59(1)(c), in that they never asked themselves the question whether in this case the obtaining of Dr Siva's opinion constituted sufficient inquiries necessary to enable them to be satisfied about the applicant's vulnerability. Moreover I think it likely, although I do not unequivocally decide, that the decision was invalid because the respondents never themselves considered the question of the applicant's priority need by or with the assistance of someone experienced in housing and social welfare matters.

Mr Watkinson's second submission is that in acting on Dr Siva's recommendation the respondents' decision was bad because that recommendation, and

---

[53]    *R v Lambeth London Borough Council, ex p Vagliviello* (1990) 22 HLR 392.
[54]    *R v Kensington and Chelsea London Borough Council, ex p Amarfio* (1995) 27 HLR 543.
[55]    (1987) 20 HLR 142.
[56]    (1993) 27 HLR 364.
[57]    (1987) 20 HLR 142, at p 151.

therefore their own decision, did not properly take into account – and the emphasis is on "properly" – the report of Dr Dellaportas. Mr Watkinson submits that far from that report being of little value, it was the best material available because, whereas neither Dr Simon nor Dr Siva had seen the applicant and whereas the applicant's general practitioner (to whom I will assume one or both of them had spoken) had not seen the applicant since early 1985, Dr Dellaportas had seen and examined him on February 14, 1986. Although in my view this aspect of the case is most unsatisfactory, it does amount in my judgment to a contention only that the respondents and Dr Siva gave insufficient weight to Dr Dellaportas' report, and that is not a point of law. I am only just able to conclude that in this respect Dr Siva or the respondents failed to take Dr Dellaportas' report into account, although if they had failed to do so that would have been a reason for invalidating this decision. In my view, however, as I have said, the decision was invalid in any event for the reasons I have given in considering Mr Watkinson's first submission.

It is reassuring to note that the respondents have apparently, at least tentatively, themselves come to the same conclusion. In the notes before the court someone on behalf of the respondents has noted that all parties agreed that the current procedure – referral to Dr Simon – is open to question on vulnerability assessment and that the best course would be referral to the Vulnerability Panel as soon as it is convened. I am told that that Panel has not yet been convened because of the unavailability of funds, but if, as I assume, the Panel will include one or more persons experienced in housing and social welfare problems, referral to it on the question of vulnerability seems to me a most sensible course.'

In *Ortiz v City of Westminster*[58], the applicant was a 24 year old woman who had had problems with drugs and drink. She had lost her previous accommodation when she was admitted to the detoxification unit at Ealing Hospital in August 1993. She made the application to be rehoused when she was on the point of being released from that treatment. She had two medical certificates from those concerned in her treatment, both stressing the problems that she would suffer were she not, on discharge, to acquire suitable accommodation. The authority decided that her drug/alcohol problem made life difficult for her, but that she was not 'vulnerable' in legal terms.

Simon Brown LJ stated[59]:

'The basis upon which leave to appeal is sought in this case is that the authority, and indeed the learned deputy judge, were wrong to have regard at all to the question as to whether or not the applicant would have difficulty in securing accommodation. The essence of her case is that once she established that she had a particular need for suitable accommodation, and would suffer more than most if she failed to acquire it then that of itself was sufficient to establish that she was vulnerable within the meaning of the legislation so as to give her a priority need.

In his helpful submissions before us Mr Critchley recognises the difficulty of such an argument and very properly draws our attention to the decision of

---

[58] (1993) 27 HLR 364.
[59] At p 366.

Mann J, as he then was, in *R v Reigate and Banstead BC, ex parte Di Dominico* (1988) 20 HLR 15 where he said this:

> "Vulnerable, in my judgment, means vulnerable in the housing market. There is no indication here of difficulty in finding accommodation or of maintaining the need for special accommodation. There is not one word of evidence upon those matters. There were the reports from the consultants, from the general practitioner and the observations of the medical officer. Those were before the local authority. The decision is one for them. I am quite unable to say, on the basis of the material before me, that their decision was either absurd or perverse."

He then continued by expressing the sympathy which anyone would have for such applicants, just as we have for the applicant before us.

In my judgment that approach is plainly right. In order to satisfy the test of vulnerability, as explained in the decision in *Ex parte Bowers*, an applicant must in my judgment surmount two hurdles. First, he (or she) must show that to some material extent he or she is less able to obtain suitable accommodation than the ordinary person and secondly, that if he fails to obtain it, then he will suffer more than most. It is in my judgment the first of those hurdles which the applicant so conspicuously fails to surmount in the present case. The position is strikingly different from that in *Ex parte Bowers* itself where, as the judgment recorded: "Since the accident nobody will give him lodging ..."

Here, for the reasons already indicated, there is no factual basis upon which the authority could conclude, let alone were bound to conclude, that this applicant would suffer peculiar difficulty in obtaining suitable accommodation. For those reasons, the learned deputy judge was undoubtedly in my judgment correct in the approach he adopted and in the conclusions he arrived at. I for my part do not think there is any worthwhile argument to pursue on appeal. I would accordingly refuse leave.'

Before the new priority need categories were introduced in 2001 (Wales) and 2002 (England), there had been an extensive consultation process. Concerns were expressed by many authorities as to the width of the originally proposed categories, particularly concerning 16/17-year-olds. In the event, the Welsh regulations were amended very little, whereas the English Order links a number of the new categories to the a priori issue of 'vulnerability', so curbing the significance of the provisions. Vulnerability is, of course, a concept with a long legislative pedigree, as already discussed. It seems likely that for most authorities the most important new priority need category is that of 16/17-year-olds – particularly as the categories of those leaving custody and the armed forces will only seriously impact on a minority of authorities and most authorities already treat those at risk of domestic violence as de facto vulnerable.

The revised Code of Guidance[60] (in Chapter 8) gives extensive guidance to authorities on the application of the new priority need categories. For example, as regards 16/17-year-olds, it states[61]:

---

[60]   ODPM 2002.
[61]   Ibid para 8.38.

'In all cases involving applicants who are 16 or 17 years of age (except those for whom social services have responsibility), housing authorities will firstly need to establish whether there is genuine homelessness, and if so, should then consider the possibility of family reconciliation. Some 16 and 17 year olds may have left home because of a temporary breakdown in their relationship with their family. In such cases, the housing authority may be able to effect a reconciliation with the family. Wherever appropriate, this should be the hosing authority's first response in cases involving this client group. In some cases, however, relationships may have broken down irretrievably, and in others it may not be safe or desirable for the applicant to return to the family home, for example, in cases involving violence or abuse. Therefore, any medication or reconciliation will need careful brokering and it is recommended that the assistance of social services is sought in all such cases. The process of reconciliation may take time and housing authorities may need to provide interim accommodation under s188 in the meantime. If so, the normal 33 working day target for completing inquiries may not be appropriate, and may need to be extended.'

It seems likely that housing and social services departments/authorities will work together on this rather than instantly accept that a full rehousing duty is owed by any 16/17-year-old who applies to them.

As regards the 'leaving custody' and 'leaving the armed forces' categories there is specific guidance on the issue of 'vulnerability'[62]:

'In considering whether former members of the armed forces are vulnerable (as set out in paragraph 8.13, above) as a result of their time spent in the forces, a housing authority may wish to take into account the following factors:
 (i) the length of time the applicant spent in the armed forces;
 (ii) the type of service the applicant was engaged in (those on active service may find it more difficult to cope with civilian life);
 (iii) whether the applicant spent any time in a military hospital (this could be an indicator of a serious health problem or of post-traumatic stress);
 (iv) the length of time since the applicant left the armed forces, and whether he or she had been able to obtain and/or maintain accommodation during that time;
 (v) whether the applicant has any existing support networks, particularly by way of family or friends.

Applicants have a priority need for accommodation only if they are vulnerable (see paragraph 8.13, above) as a result of having served a period in prison or custody. It is envisaged that only a minority of those falling within the categories in paragraph 8.23 are likely to be vulnerable as a result of their period in prison or custody. Those who have served a sentence of more than one year will have probation supervision on release, and the probation service have primary responsibility for ensuring that their accommodation needs are

---

[62] Ibid paras 8.22 and 8.24.

met. In determining whether applicants who fall within one of the descriptions in paragraph 8.23 are vulnerable as a result of their period in prison or custody, a housing authority may wish to take into account the following factors:

(i)   the length of time the applicant served in prison or custody;

(ii)  whether the applicant is receiving probation service supervision;

(iii) the length of time since the applicant was released from prison or custody, and whether the applicant had been able to obtain and/or maintain accommodation during that time;

(iv)  whether the applicant has any existing support networks, particularly by way of family or friends.'

# INTENTIONAL HOMELESSNESS

# HOUSING ACT 1996

*Duties to persons found to be homeless or threatened with homelessness*

190.   (1) This section applies where the local housing authority are satisfied that an applicant is homeless and is eligible for assistance but are also satisfied that he became homeless intentionally.

(2) If the authority are satisfied that the applicant has a priority need, they shall—

(a)   secure that accommodation is available for his occupation for such period as they consider will give him a reasonable opportunity of securing accommodation for his occupation, and

(b)   provide him with advice and such assistance as they consider appropriate in the circumstances in any attempts he may make to secure that accommodation becomes available for his occupation.

(3) If they are not satisfied that he has a priority need, they shall provide him with advice and such assistance as they consider appropriate to the circumstances in any attempts he may make to secure that accommodation becomes available for his occupation.

## 191.   Becoming homeless intentionally

(1) A person becomes homeless intentionally if he deliberately does or fails to do anything in consequence of which he ceases to occupy accommodation which is available for his occupation and which it would have been reasonable for him to continue to occupy.

(2) For the purposes of subsection (1) an act or omission in good faith on the part of a person who was unaware of any relevant fact shall not be treated as deliberate.

(3) A person shall be treated as becoming homeless intentionally if—

(a)   he enters into an arrangement under which he is required to cease to occupy accommodation which it would have been reasonable for him to continue to occupy, and

(b)   the purpose of the arrangement is to enable him to become entitled to assistance under this Part,

and there is no other good reason why he is homeless.

(4) A person who is given advice or assistance under section 197 (duty where other suitable alternative accommodation available), but fails to secure suitable accommodation in

circumstances in which it was reasonably to be expected that he would do so, shall, if he makes a further application under this Part, be treated as having become homeless intentionally.

...

### 196.   **Becoming threatened with homelessness intentionally**

(1) A person becomes threatened with homelessness intentionally if he deliberately does or fails to do anything the likely result of which is that he will be forced to leave accommodation which is available for his occupation and which it would have been reasonable for him to continue to occupy.

(2) For the purposes of subsection (1) an act or omission in good faith on the part of a person who was unaware of any relevant fact shall not be treated as deliberate.

(3) A person shall be treated as becoming threatened with homelessness intentionally if—

(a)   he enters into an arrangement under which he is required to cease to occupy accommodation which it would have been reasonable for him to continue to occupy, and
(b)   the purpose of the arrangement is to enable him to become entitled to assistance under this Part,
and there is no other good reason why he is threatened with homelessness.

(4) A person who is given advice or assistance under section 197 (duty where other suitable alternative accommodation available), but fails to secure suitable accommodation in circumstances in which it was reasonably to be expected that he would do so, shall, if he makes a further application under this Part, be treated as having become threatened with homelessness intentionally.

## The concept of intentional homelessness

The concept of intentional homelessness dates from the Housing (Homeless Persons) Act 1977, where it was inserted at a late stage in the progress of the legislation through the House of Lords. Local authorities wanted a provision to enable them to exclude obvious 'queue jumpers'. However, few pieces of legislation can have given rise to more litigation – litigation costly in terms of expense and local authority officer time.

The definition was modified in 1996 by the insertion of s 191(3). Thus, a person *must* also be treated as becoming homeless intentionally where:

(a)   he or she enters into an arrangement under which he or she is *required* to cease to occupy accommodation which it would have been reasonable for him or her to continue to occupy; *and*
(b)   the purpose of the arrangement was to enable him or her to be entitled to assistance as homeless; *and*
(c)   there is no other 'good reason' why he or she is homeless, in other words the homelessness must arise as a result of the arrangement and for no other reason such as, say, the accommodation burning down before the arrangement 'bites'.

The object of the provision is to strike at deliberate 'doomed from the outset' schemes, whereby an insecure short letting or licence is accepted simply to obtain the protection of the homelessness legislation.

Note also that under s 191(4), where a person is given advice or assistance in the circumstance of suitable alternative accommodation being available (see further below), and then fails to secure suitable accommodation in circumstances in which it was reasonably to be expected that he or she would, that person, if he or she makes a further application, is to be treated as having become homeless intentionally. This is an instance of 'deemed' intention which will affect a subsequent application, and because of the use of the word 'reasonable' it needs to be applied carefully.

The burden clearly lies on the authority to satisfy themselves that the homelessness was intentional: if there is any doubt, the applicant is entitled to the benefit of that doubt.

At the very heart of the concept of 'intentional homelessness' lies uncertainty. Should its application be confined to cases of deliberate homelessness (particularly in the light of the perceived need to ward off 'queue jumpers'), or can it be extended to any situation where the initial act or omission of the applicant is deliberate and there is an inexorable consequence of subsequent homelessness, even if that consequence was not specifically intended? An obvious example is the tenant who fails persistently to pay rent; he or she may not intend to be the subject of possession proceedings and certainly does not necessarily intend to be evicted! However, there is a close and intimate relationship between the failure to pay the rent and the subsequent homelessness.

After some initial doubt, the courts soon decided that the wider view of 'deliberateness' should apply. The decisive decision was that of the Court of Appeal in *Devenport v Salford City Council*[63].

Mr and Mrs Devenport were tenants of one of the council's properties. They were joint tenants. The council received complaints from people living near the Devenports about the conduct of their children. As a result, on 12 September 1980 they sent the Devenports a letter, which stated:

> 'Numerous complaints have been received about the conduct of your children thereby contravening [the council's] conditions of tenancy.
>
> I would ask your co-operation to ensure that your family maintains an accepted standard of behaviour so alleviating the necessity for me to consider any further action.
>
> Should this appeal be ignored and no marked improvement be reported then I shall have no alternative but to recommend that legal proceedings be commenced to obtain the vacant possession of your present dwelling.'

Things did not improve. In March 1981 the council received a petition signed by 237 of its tenants. The petition was expressed to be directed against Mr and Mrs Devenport and two of their children, Joanne and Shirley, and also against another family. The petition asked for the removal of the two families and appended a lengthy list of complaints of vandalism, assaults and violent misconduct.

On 13 April 1981 the Corporation gave to Mr and Mrs Devenport notice of intention to seek possession of 77 Rowan Close in accordance with the requirements of the Housing Act 1980. In particular the Council relied (inter alia) upon the following:

● Acts of vandalism by the children.
● The threats and actual use of physical violence by Mr and Mrs Devenport against persons living in the neighbourhood.

---

[63]   (1983) 8 HLR 54.

- Mr Devenport threatened to knife Mrs Mona James and members of her family.
- Shirley Devenport physically attacked Mrs James's son.
- Mrs Devenport and two of her children physically attacked Mrs Mona James and her daughter.
- Mr and Mrs Devenport and their children repeatedly shouted abuse at neighbours.
- Despite requests, Mr and Mrs Devenport had failed to control their children.

The judge found that the plaintiff's case was established and he made an order for possession in 28 days. Mr and Mrs Devenport gave up possession of the premises in accordance with the order.

On 25 September the Council resolved that the Devenports be deemed to be intentionally homeless for the purposes of the Housing (Homeless Persons) Act 1977.

Fox LJ stated[64]:

'In my opinion, the words "homeless intentionally" are merely a formula which is given a specific meaning by the definition which follows. It is the definition which one has to construe and not the words "homeless intentionally". The sub-section, in my view, provides that a person becomes homeless intentionally if:
  (i)   he ceases to occupy accommodation.
  (ii)  That accommodation was available for his occupation.
  (iii) It would have been reasonable for him to continue to occupy it.
  (iv)  The person deliberately did or failed to do something in consequence of which he ceased to occupy.
which he ceased to occupy.

The section does not, in my opinion, require that the person should have intended to become homeless and should have done or failed to do something with the intention of becoming homeless.
We were referred to some observations of Lord Denning MR in *R v Slough BC* [1981] 1 QB 801 at p 809 as follows:

"… The Slough Council found that she was homeless intentionally. It was, I should have thought, a debatable point. Many people would have thought that Miss Jack's conduct however deplorable was not 'deliberate' in the sense required by s 17(1) of the 1977 Act. She did not deliberately do anything to get herself turned out."

In my view it is not necessary to show that the tenant deliberately did something intending to get himself turned out. That seems to me to be contrary to the language of s 17(1). The word "deliberately" in my opinion, governs only the act or omission. There is no requirement that the person deliberately became homeless. Only that he deliberately did, or omitted to do something in consequence of which he ceased to occupy etc. That is quite a different concept. I agree with the conclusion reached on the matter by Judge

---

[64] At p 62.

Goodall in *Robinson v Torbay BC* [1982] 1 All ER 726. Accordingly, in my judgment, the first question in the present case is whether the Corporation could reasonably conclude that Mr and Mrs Devenport deliberately did or failed to do something in consequence of which they became homeless. The immediate cause of Mr and Mrs Devenport's ceasing to occupy 77 Rowan Close was the order of the county court in August 1981. That order could only be made if one or both of the grounds 1 and 2 set forth in Schedule 4 to the Housing Act 1980 was established to the satisfaction of the county court. The county court judge plainly concluded that the case did come within one or both of the grounds. He specifically refers in one copy of the Note of his judgment before us to s 34 of the 1980 Act (which directs one to Schedule 4) and in the other note to Schedule 4 itself.

...

But could the Corporation conclude that Mr and Mrs Devenport had deliberately done or failed to do something in consequence of which they cease to occupy?

So far as any acts of their own are concerned, I think they had. It is no doubt true that the warning letter in September 1980 related only to the conduct of the children, but it would have been obvious to Mr and Mrs Devenport that misconduct by either of them would be regarded even more seriously; many of the particularised complaints are after the warning letter.

As regards the children, Mr and Mrs Devenport were warned in the clearest terms in September 1980. So far from producing any effect it was followed by the first petition in March 1981 and, on the basis of the county court decision, continued misconduct. In my opinion there was ample evidence upon which the Corporation could conclude that Mr and Mrs Devenport deliberately failed to take any steps to control their children. In the face of the facts to which I have referred I cannot regard the bare assertion by Mrs Devenport in para 9 of her affidavit, that she and Mr Devenport have at all times used their best endeavours to control their children as sufficient evidence to the contrary. It is quite unsupported by any detailed explanation of the position at all. Whatever the position as to the acts of Mr and Mrs Devenport themselves, their omissions in relation to the children would, in my view, be quite sufficient to justify the Corporation's resolution.

I should add comments on three matters. First, I see no reason to suppose that the Corporation misdirected itself in law. The Housing Manager's analysis of the position in his report was, in my view, adequate. Secondly, Mr Hytner made a formal submission that an occupier cannot deliberately have done anything in consequence of which he ceases to occupy, if he is evicted by a court order which he opposes. But in my opinion the question is whether he deliberately did or failed to do something in consequence of which he ceases to occupy.

Thirdly, in my view the Corporation are not limited to the finding in the county court. The matter which they have to decide is not the same as that before the county court. The Corporation's task was to review all the facts as they knew them (including the decision of the county court) and reach a conclusion accordingly.

Looking at the whole matter I reach the conclusion that the facts known to the Corporation would justify it in concluding that Mr and Mrs Devenport deliberately did or failed to do acts the consequence of which was that they ceased to occupy the accommodation.'

Acts or omissions in good faith on the part of a person who is unaware of any relevant fact are not deliberate, but this does not cover mistakes of law, eg, bad legal advice. It can, however, be difficult to distinguish bad advice from a genuine misapprehension of fact. On this point see *R v Mole Valley District Council, ex p Burton*[65].

In *Burton*, a husband resigned from a job with tied accommodation. This was a deliberate act, and he was intentionally homeless. His wife then applied for rehousing. She alleged that her husband had assured her that the family would be rehoused under an agreement between his trade union and the local authorities to rehouse those employed with tied accommodation for seven years. The authority refused to consider the wife's application on this basis. It was held that they should have considered her misapprehension because it meant that she was not guilty of acquiescence.

In *Wincentzen v Monklands District Council*[66] Ms W was a single, homeless, epileptic teenager who until the age of 16 lived with her father but then decided to stay temporarily with her mother (who was separated from her father) while at college. Her father warned her that if she left he would not have her back. She did not believe him, but he refused to let her return. The local authority considered her intentionally homeless, but the court found that she had acted in genuine ignorance of her father's true intention and so her acts could not be regarded as 'deliberate'. Simple lack of realisation of facts is not enough if a reasonable person would have understood them, but in this case there was a bona fide belief that the threat was not real.

What about criminal activities leading to a custodial sentence? In *R v Hounslow London Borough Council, ex p R*[67], R was sentenced to seven years' imprisonment for paedophile offences, and had to terminate his tenancy as he could no longer pay the rent. On his release he applied as a homeless person and was found intentionally homeless on the basis that his situation was the result of the offences, which were deliberate acts in consequence of which he had ceased to occupy accommodation, etc. It was held that, objectively, R's cessation of occupation of accommodation could have been regarded as a likely consequence of his deliberate actions. The issue came before the Court of Appeal again recently in *Stewart v Lambeth London Borough Council*[68]. Delroy Stewart had been a secure tenant of Lambeth since 1983. He fell into rent arrears and in August 1997 the authority obtained a suspended possession order against him, conditional on the payment off of the arrears. In 1998 Stewart was sentenced to five years' imprisonment for supplying heroin. He made an arrangement with his sister to maintain the tenancy and pay the rent. No rent was, in fact, paid and in February 1999 the authority executed a warrant for possession. In December 2000 Stewart was released from

---

[65]  (1988) 20 HLR 479.
[66]  (1988) SLT 847.
[67]  (1997) 29 HLR 939.
[68]  [2002] EWCA Civ 753, [2002] HLR 747.

prison and applied to Lambeth as a homeless person. The authority decided he had made himself intentionally homeless by deliberately committing a serious criminal offence likely to result in a prison sentence. Longmore LJ stated[69]:

'The question whether a prisoner is or may be intentionally homeless is not virgin territory. In *R v Hounslow London Borough Council ex parte R* [1997] 29 HLR 939, R had been convicted of a number of indecent assaults and sentenced to seven years' imprisonment. Under the then current arrangements, housing benefit ceased after a year in prison and, realising he would not be able to pay the rent for his dwelling, he surrendered his tenancy. He then applied for accommodation as a homeless person on his release. The local authority decided that his offences were deliberate acts leading to his imprisonment and that the surrender of his tenancy was the "direct and reasonable" result of his criminal offences. R applied for judicial review on the basis that the local authority were not entitled to find that he was intentionally homeless merely because there was an unbroken chain of events leading from his deliberate act of committing the offences, because the rest of causation for intentional homelessness was limited by concepts of remoteness, or reasonable likelihood, or public policy. Despite Mr Luba's advocacy for the applicant in the case, Mr Stephen Richards, sitting as a Judge of the Queen's Bench Division, held that in considering whether a person had ceased to occupy the accommodation in consequence of his deliberate conduct, the right question to be asked was whether his ceasing to occupy the accommodation would reasonably have been regarded at the time as a likely consequence of the applicant's deliberate conduct. The test was objective and not subjective. The use of the word "likely" in that formulation thus brought the test for intentional homelessness in what is now s 191 of the 1996 Act and the test for threatened intentional homelessness in what is now s 196 of the 1996 Act into line with one another. The Deputy Judge accepted Mr Luba's submission that some limitation had to be implied into the statutory wording in respect of causation in s 191, and he also accepted Mr Luba's second suggestion as to what that limitation should be. He said at p 947 of the report:

"The second alternative put forward by Mr Luba is a test of 'reasonable likelihood'. Within that formulation he encompasses the various expressions used in *Robinson v Torbay* [1982] 1 All ER 726: 'the reasonable result' of the deliberate conduct (as applied to actual homelessness) 'the likely result' of such conduct (as applied to threatened homelessness) and the fair-minded bystander saying to himself 'he asked for it' (as applied to both contexts). In my view that is a helpful distillation of the approach adopted in *Robinson* and applied in *R v Westminster City Council ex parte Reid* (1994) 26 HLR 690, Lexis UK Property 677, and represents the right test. It ensures a coherent approach as between section 60(1) and section 60(2), meets many of the concerns expressed about findings of intentional homelessness in circumstances where the consequences of the deliberate conduct were unforeseeable, unpredictable or otherwise very remote, and is a workable test for councils to apply. Thus, in considering

[69]  [2002] HLR 747, at p 752.

whether a person ceased to occupy accommodation 'in consequence of' his deliberate conduct, the question to be asked is whether his ceasing to occupy the accommodation would reasonably have been regarded at the time as a likely consequence of the deliberate conduct. It is an objective, not a subjective test. It might be imputed to the fair-minded bystander in possession of all the relevant facts. I do not think it necessary, however, to express the test by reference to the fair-minded bystander and I doubt whether his assistance will often be needed in applying it."

As to the arguments of public policy in relation to the resettlement and rehabilitation of offenders, the learned Deputy Judge said this at p 948:

"In my judgment the arguments based on public policy do not carry the matter further forward. Considerations of policy may assist in the construction of the statute. Once the statutory provisions have been construed, however, they fall to be applied by local authorities and the courts alike. They cannot be disapplied by reference to the broad concept of public policy. In the present case the policy considerations advanced by Mr Luba do not cause me to doubt the construction of section 60(1) above. The statute lays down no special regime for ex-prisoners and cannot be construed in such a way as to create one. Whether such as those that occurred in the present case – deliberate criminal conduct leading to a prison sentence and loss of accommodation – can justify a finding of intentional homelessness must be determined on the basis of the general test to which I have referred".

Mr Luba said that for the purposes of his argument before us today he did not need to challenge anything said by Mr Richards in *ex parte R* [1997] 29 HLR 939. For my part, I would approve, adopt and gratefully follow Mr Richards' decision in that case.

Mr Luba, of course, submits that the present case is wholly different because Mr Stewart made the intervening arrangement with his sister which I have described. The failure of that arrangement, he says, was not deliberate, or at least has not been determined by the local authority to have been deliberate, and the matter should be remitted to them for that determination to be made. I cannot accept that argument for two main reasons:

(1) On any sensible view of the matter, the chain of events that ultimately led to Mr Stewart's eviction began with the supply of heroin in respect of which he was in due course convicted. The statute by s 191 requires the local authority to determine whether Mr Stewart deliberately did "anything" in consequence of which he ceased to occupy the accommodation available for his occupation. One thing he deliberately did do was to supply heroin. The consequence of that was (as the local authority have decided) reasonably likely to have been his imprisonment and the loss of his flat by eviction for non-payment of rent. The mere fact that arrangements could have been or were made to avoid or avert the consequences of that eviction, does not mean that the local authority has to address its mind to those subsequent possibilities and decide, if they fail, whether that failure was deliberate or not. On such a view, it might have to make any number of further inquiries of a possibly difficult or delicate nature. An inquiry into

whether an applicant such as Mr Stewart might have reason to believe that an arrangement made with a member of his family might or might not be expected to work goes much further than the statute requires.

(2) In this case, moreover, the arrangement was in fact ineffectual. Mrs Bourke says in terms in her letter of 20 July 2001 that local authority records show that no rent was paid during the imprisonment. That has not been challenged. It seems to me that an ineffectual arrangement cannot in any way break the natural chain of causation starting with the supply of heroin and ending with Mr Stewart's eviction from his flat for non-payment of rent when he was in prison. If an initially effective arrangement had been made and then later broke down, different considerations might arise. But I do not consider the local authority was in this case under any obligation to consider the arrangement which Mr Stewart said he had made but which never resulted in fact in any payment of rent as being any more than part of the narrative in relation to the events on which they relied to conclude that the loss of Mr Stewart's accommodation was the direct result of his deliberate act.'

## The chain of causation

The deliberate act or omission must be one in *consequence* of which the applicant ceased to occupy available accommodation: there must be a continuing causal connection between the deliberate act in consequence of which homelessness resulted and the homelessness existing at the date of the inquiry; but in looking at the cause of the homelessness it is necessary to have primary regard to the position at the time when the homelessness arose, and not to the position at the time of the application or inquiry. Sometimes it is necessary to look beyond the most immediate cause of the homelessness, and go back to the cessation of occupation of 'available' accommodation. The key decisions were again made relatively early in the interpretative sequence of homelessness provisions. They are, respectively, the Court of Appeal decision in *Dyson v Kerrier District Council*[70] and the subsequent House of Lords decision in *Din v Wandsworth Borough Council*[71]. In *Dyson*, in September 1978 the plaintiff, who was expecting a baby, went to live with her sister in a council flat in Huntingdon, where the child was born. Shortly afterwards her sister moved to Helston, but the plaintiff remained in occupation of the flat and on 2 October 1978, the council transferred the tenancy into her name. On 10 November the plaintiff signed a tenancy agreement for a 'winter let' of a flat in Helston which expired on 31 March 1979. The tenancy was not protected by the Rent Act 1977. She then surrendered the tenancy of the flat in Huntingdon. Early in 1979 she applied to the defendant council, as housing authority, for accommodation representing to them that she was homeless because her sister had left the Huntingdon flat. The council having ascertained the true position in relation to that flat, informed her through their housing officer by a letter dated 19 March, after a further application by her for accommodation, that her homelessness was going to be treated as 'self-induced'. The plaintiff failed to leave the flat at the end of the tenancy and the landlord obtained an order for possession on 18 May to take effect on 25 May. Four days before the order took effect the council informed the plaintiff

[70] [1980] 3 All ER 313.
[71] [1983] 1 AC 657.

that since this was a case of self-induced homelessness they would provide her with accommodation for one month from 25 May. In fact they allowed her to remain in hotel accommodation until 6 July. On 3 July they advised her formally of the decision of the housing committee on 2 July that she was homeless with a priority need but that she had become homeless intentionally.

The plaintiff brought proceedings against the council in the county court seeking declarations that she had not become homeless intentionally, that the council were in breach of their duty under s 4(4) of the Housing (Homeless Persons) Act 1977 in failing to ensure that accommodation was available for her from 6 July 1979, an order that the council secure such accommodation was available, and damages. The Court of Appeal rejected her claim.

Brightman LJ stated[72]:

'Two issues arise. First, did the district council correctly construe and apply section 17 in deciding that she became threatened with homelessness, and became homeless, "intentionally"? If so, did they secure that accommodation was made available for her occupation for a period which could properly be considered as giving her a reasonable opportunity of herself securing accommodation for her occupation? The first question is the important one. If the plaintiff's homelessness could not properly be treated as "intentional", then there is no doubt that the district council became and are liable to secure accommodation for her occupation indefinitely. The second question arises under section 4(3). It depends on whether the district council had completed their statutory inquiries under section 3 and made their decision at the time when they wrote their letter of May 21, and whether such letter was a sufficient notification to the plaintiff of their decision, or whether such decision was not made until July 2, and notified on July 3. In the latter case the period of two or three days allowed to her for making her own arrangements to secure accommodation was admittedly inadequate.

The argument on behalf of the plaintiff before the judge in the county court was that the district council were not entitled under section 17 to look at what had happened at Huntingdon. The council were only entitled to look at what the plaintiff had done or omitted to do in relation to the accommodation she was occupying immediately before she became homeless or threatened with homelessness. By taking into account what happened at Huntingdon, the district council considered matters which they were not entitled to consider on a proper interpretation of section 17. The judge came to the conclusion that section 17(1) included an act or omission deliberately contrived in respect of accommodation other than that last occupied by the applicant. Section 17(2) was to be construed in parallel manner. The district council were therefore entitled to find on March 19, 1979, that she had become threatened with homelessness intentionally; and that, when she became actually homeless, that also was "intentional". He also held that, as she was notified on March 19, 1979, that she was being treated as a case of intentional homelessness, she was allowed sufficient time pursuant to section 4(3) for securing her own accommodation.

---

[72]   Ibid at p 318.

...

As we have already indicated, counsel for the plaintiff submits that, as both subsections (1) and (2) are couched in the present tense, they relate only to the existing home, if one exists, or to the last home if none exists. That is to say, subsection (1) is directed to the case of a homeless person who loses his last home because he has done or failed to do something in consequence of which he ceases to occupy that accommodation which is available for his occupation. Subsection (2) is directed to the case of a person who is threatened with the loss of his existing home because he does or fails to do something the likely result of which is that he will be forced to leave that accommodation which is available for his occupation.

Neither subsection, it was submitted, can apply to this case. The argument is formidable. On March 19, 1979, when the district council made their decision, the plaintiff was threatened with homelessness. Therefore, the relevant subsection is subsection (2). Subsection (2) says that a person becomes threatened with homelessness "intentionally" if he deliberately does or fails to do anything the likely result of which is that he will be forced to leave accommodation which is available for his occupation. The Huntingdon flat cannot be treated as that accommodation, because it was not accommodation which, on March 19, the plaintiff "will be forced to leave". She had already left it. Nor could it be said on March 19 that it was accommodation "which is available" for the plaintiff's occupation, because it was not so available. Nor can the Helston flat be treated as accommodation within the subsection. It was not available for her after March 31, 1979. In the result, it was submitted, neither the Huntingdon flat nor the Helston flat was accommodation within subsection (2). Nor does subsection (1) apply. She did not become finally homeless until May 25, 1979. The accommodation which she then ceased to occupy was not accommodation "which is available" for her occupation.

Although subsections (1) and (2) of section 17 are drafted in the present and future tenses, they are in fact also referring to past events. Subsection (1) reads:

> "... a person becomes homeless intentionally if he deliberately does or fails to do anything in consequence of which he ceases to occupy accommodation which is available for his occupation and which it would have been reasonable for him to continue to occupy."

This subsection is dealing with cause and effect. The subsection states the effect first. The specified effect is the state of being homeless. The subsection specifies that effect and then describes a particular cause which, if it exists, requires the effect to be treated as intentional. The subsection therefore means

> "a person becomes homeless intentionally if he deliberately has done or failed to do anything in consequence of which he has ceased to occupy accommodation which was available for his occupation and which it would have been reasonable for him to continue to occupy."

Does that formulation apply to the Huntingdon flat? In our judgment it does. The district council were entitled to reach the conclusion that the plaintiff became homeless on May 25, 1979, intentionally because she deliberately had done something (surrendered the Huntingdon tenancy) in consequence of which she ceased to occupy accommodation (the Huntingdon flat) which was available for her occupation and which it would have been reasonable for her to continue to occupy; and that, therefore, if she had not done that deliberate act she would not have become homeless on May 25.

In the result, when the plaintiff became homeless on May 25, the district council had no duty under section 4(5) to house her permanently.

We must now consider whether a similar result flows from subsection (2). By parity of reasoning this subsection means that a person becomes threatened with homelessness intentionally if he deliberately has done or failed to do anything the likely result of which is that he will be forced to leave accommodation which is available for his occupation and which it would have been reasonable for him to continue to occupy. On March 19, 1979, it could properly be said of the plaintiff that she had previously done something (surrendered the Huntingdon tenancy) the likely and indeed the inevitable result of which was that she would be forced to leave accommodation (the Huntingdon flat) which was available for her occupation and which it would have been reasonable for her to continue to occupy; as a result of which she was, on March 19, 1979, threatened with homelessness on March 31, intentionally. Therefore, the district council could properly take the view, which they did take, on March 19 that subsection (2) was satisfied.

In the result the only duty of the district council on March 19, 1979, when the plaintiff was threatened with homelessness, was to furnish advice and appropriate assistance under section 4(2), and their only duty on May 25, 1979, when she became homeless, was to secure short-term accommodation for her under section 4(3).'

In *Din v Wandsworth Borough Council*[73], in 1977, Mr Din and his wife, the appellants, and their four children were occupying suitable accommodation in Wandsworth. By the middle of 1979 Mr Din was in financial difficulties and arrears of rent were mounting, but because the landlord had not begun legal proceedings against him, officials of the housing authority (at a housing aid centre) advised Mr Din to stay. Nevertheless he and his family left the premises in August 1979 when a distress warrant for non-payment of rates was served on him, moving into unsuitable accommodation in Upminster (unsuitable largely because it was over-crowded). It was accepted that by December the landlord would probably have evicted him. On 20 December the appellants applied to the housing authority for accommodation as homeless persons under the Act of 1977. That was refused on the ground that their homelessness was 'intentional' within the Act.

The appellants brought an action against the housing authority claiming damages and a mandatory injunction to house them. The judge in the county court having found in their favour, the Court of Appeal reversed his decision.

The House of Lords by a majority of 3:2 (Lords Russell and Bridge dissenting) upheld the decision of the Court of Appeal.

[73] [1983] 1 AC 657, [1981] 3 All ER 881.

Lord Wilberforce stated[74]:

> 'So how does the matter stand? If one takes the words of the statute, the council has to be satisfied that the applicants became homeless intentionally (section 17). Under section 4(2)(b) their duty is limited to advice and assistance if "they are satisfied ... that they became homeless ... intentionally." The time factors here are clearly indicated: at the time of decision (the present), the local authority must look at the time (the past) when the applicants became homeless, and consider whether their action then was intentional in the statutory sense. If this was the right approach there could only be one answer: when the Dins left 56, Trinity Road their action was intentional within section 17, and the council was entitled to find that it would have been reasonable for them to continue to occupy 56, Trinity Road.
>
> The appellants' argument against this is as follows: whatever the position may have been in July 1979 when they left 56, Trinity Road, at the time of the decision in December 1979 they would have been homeless in any event: the original cause of homelessness (even if intentional) had ceased to operate. For section 17 to apply there must be a causal nexus between the intentional action and the homelessness subsisting at the time of the decision. On the facts of the case there was not, so that the decision was wrong in law. I am unable to accept this argument.
>
> 1. It cannot be reconciled with the wording of the Act. this is completely and repeatedly clear in concentrating attention on when the appellants became homeless and requiring the question of intention to be ascertained as at that time. To achieve the result desired by the appellants it is either necessary to distort the meaning of "in consequence of which he ceases to occupy" (section 17(1)) or to read in a number of words. These are difficult to devise. Donaldson LJ suggests adding at the end of section 17(1) "and still to occupy": the appellants, as an alternative "to the date of his application." Both are radical – and awkward – reconstructions of the section.
>
> 2. Such an interpretation, or reconstruction, of the Act is not called for by any purposive approach. As I have pointed out, the Act reflects a complex interplay of interests. It confers great benefits upon one category of persons in need of housing, to the detriment of others. This being so, it does not seem unreasonable that, in order to benefit from the priority provisions, persons in the first category should bring themselves within the plain words. Failure to do so involves, as Mr Bruneau pointed out, greater expense for a hard pressed authority, and greater pressure on the housing stock.
>
> 3. The appellants' interpretation adds greatly to the difficulties of the local authority's task in administering this Act. It requires the authority, as well as investigating the original and actual cause of homelessness, to inquire into hypotheses – what would have happened if the appellants had not moved, hypotheses involving uncertain attitudes of landlords, rating authorities, the applicants themselves, and even intervening physical events. The difficulty of this is well shown by the singularly imprecise and speculative evidence given as to what was likely to have happened in December 1979 – see above. This

[74] [1981] 3 All ER 881 at p 886.

approach almost invites challenge to the courts – all the more if it is open to applicants to litigate the whole state of facts with witnesses, de novo, in the county court, but still significantly if the applicants are limited to judicial review. On the other hand the respondents' contention involves a straightforward inquiry into the circumstances in which the applicants became homeless.

4. The appellants' argument is not assisted by the case of *Dyson v Kerrier District Council* [1980] 3 All ER 313, [1980] 1 WLR 1205. There (as here) the applicant intentionally surrendered available accommodation in order to go to precarious accommodation (a "winter letting") from which she was ejected and so became homeless. It was held (in my opinion, rightly) that she had become homeless in consequence of her intentional surrender. This does not in any way support an argument that a subsequent hypothetical cause should be considered to supersede an earlier actual cause. It merely decides that a disqualification for priority by reason of an intentional surrender is not displaced by obtaining temporary accommodation. As pointed out by Ackner LJ in the Court of Appeal, it can be displaced by obtaining "settled" accommodation.

5. It does not follow from accepting the respondents' argument that occupants who move before a notice to quit takes effect will be held to be intentionally homeless. Such cases are likely to be covered by section 1(3), referred to above.

I agree therefore with the majority of the Court of Appeal in holding that the present case falls squarely within the provisions of the Act as to intentional homelessness and that there is no justification for reading these provisions otherwise than in their natural sense.

In the result the local authority was entitled to decide, on the facts, and in law, that the appellants became intentionally homeless. I would dismiss this appeal.'

Lord Fraser, and Lowry delivered concurring judgments.

Their Lordships clearly found the issue difficult, and the dissents of Lords Bridge and Russell are clear and powerful. For example, Lord Bridge stated[75]:

'But if a housing authority are minded to rely against an applicant on the fact that he voluntarily left accommodation on some date in the past as the cause of his present homelessness and to make that the basis of their conclusion that he became homeless intentionally, I do not see how the question how long the accommodation would otherwise have continued to be available for his occupation, hypothetical though it may be, can in all cases be avoided. In a sense perhaps it is a matter of degree. At one end of the spectrum, as already indicated, is the case (as in *Dyson*) where there was no reason to anticipate eviction from the vacated accommodation and the housing authority can properly assume that it would have remained available indefinitely. At the other end is the case where a court order for possession has already been made but the applicant, for some reason, leaves voluntarily more than 28 days before the date names in the order when, in the authority's view, it would have

---

[75] At p 898.

been reasonable for him to remain. But between these two extremes there may be an almost infinite variety of circumstances in which an occupier of residential accommodation will find himself in more or less obvious and more or less imminent danger of eviction on grounds which cannot be attributed to any earlier deliberate act or omission on his part and where he may choose to leave voluntarily rather than wait for a court order for possession to be made against him. In any such case, the housing authority, on considering a later application for accommodation under the Act, assuming they find that he left the previous accommodation prematurely, having ascertained the relevant facts, must ask themselves the question: if the applicant had not left his previous accommodation, is it likely that he would now be homeless? If they answer that question in the negative, and that conclusion is one which a reasonable authority could reasonably reach on the facts, their conclusion that the applicant became homeless intentionally will, of course, be beyond challenge in the courts. But if they simply ignore the question, they fail to take account of the relevant issue which arises as to the cause of his present homelessness, and thus proceed upon an erroneous construction of the Act.

. . .

I am not at all sorry to reach this conclusion. It would seem to me a great injustice if a homeless person in priority need having once left accommodation prematurely, no matter how short the period for which the accommodation would have remained available and in which it would have been reasonable for him to continue to occupy it, may thereafter be treated as intentionally homeless for an indefinite period and thus disqualified from claiming the major benefit which the Act confers.'

Nevertheless, the majority view clearly represents the law, enabling the authority to relate back current homelessness to past intentionality unless, of course, the 'chain of causation' is too flimsy or extended, or something occurs to break it. Perhaps the most obvious way to 'break the chain' is via the acquisition of a 'settled residence'[76].

It is, however, not completely clear how secure, or prospectively longstanding, accommodation must be to count as 'settled' for this purpose, a point of some importance given that the majority of premises available in the private sector are now let on short-term assured shorthold tenancies[77].It *is* certainly clear that the causal link can, in principle, be broken by matters other than the acquisition of a 'settled' residence. In *R v Brent London Borough Council, ex p Awua*[78], Lord Hoffmann stated:

'The distinction between a settled residence and temporary accommodation is thus being used to identify what will break the causal link between departure from accommodation which it would have been reasonable to continue to occupy and homelessness separated from that departure by a period or periods of accommodation elsewhere. This jurisprudence if well-established ... and nothing I have said is intended to cast any doubt upon it, although I would

---

[76] See, for example, *Lambert v Ealing Borough Council* [1982] 2 All ER 394, at p 348 (per Lord Denning MR).
[77] On which see now *Knight v Vale Royal Borough Council* [2003] EWCA Civ 1258, [2004] HLR 106.
[78] [1995] 3 All ER 493, at p 499.

wish to reserve the question of whether the occupation of a settled residence is the sole and exclusive method by which the causal link can be broken.'

Further comment on the concept of breaks in the chain of causation can be found in *Stewart v Lambeth London Borough Council*[79] – discussed above. Stewart had further argued that his time in prison had broken the causal chain (even assuming his original 'intentionality'). The Court of Appeal dismissed this argument. Longmore LJ stated[80]:

### 'The untainted homelessness point

This is a more general point and arises on the hypothesis that it is (as I consider it is) open to this court to proceed on the basis that other matters beside the obtaining of settled accommodation can break the chain between an original intentional homelessness and a subsequent application to be accommodated. The broad point is that a term of imprisonment should be treated as a factor which supersedes the original homelessness in rather the same way as giving up one's home to go and serve in the Armed Forces or a closed religious order would be. Ingenious as this argument is, I cannot accept it. In the two examples given, the operative cause of the applicant's homelessness would be the decision to leave the Armed Forces or the monastic order at a particular time. In the present case, it was not up to Mr Stewart to decide when or where he would leave prison. As a result of his previous activities, he only came back into society when he was permitted to do so. There is, of course, much to be said for making resettlement of offenders into society easier than it often is, and Mr Luba said some of it in the course of his submissions. But that seems to me a matter of general public policy which this court cannot take into account on an individual application of the present kind for the reasons given by Mr Stephen Richards in his judgment *ex parte R* [1997] 29 HLR 939 which I have recited.

### The settled accommodation point

Mr Luba is correct to submit that the local authority did not consider whether Mr Stewart's term in prison constituted settled accommodation, so as to break the chain of causation between (1) eviction from his flat as a result of his deliberate act and (2) his release from custody and looking for accommodation anew. The question is whether, if they had considered the matter, there would have been any prospect of a different conclusion. In my view there would not. Prison is, to my mind, the opposite of settled accommodation. The prisoner hopes that it will be as temporary as possible. Any such hope on the part of Mr Stewart was triumphantly justified in this case since, although he was sentenced as a long-term prisoner, he appears to have been released only two days after he would have been released if he had been a short-term prisoner. The learned judge, Judge Cox, gave this argument short shrift. He said:

---

"The position of Mr Stewart upon his incarceration was first of all I suspect, though I do not know, that, in common with many other prisoners, he would have taken every legitimate means that he considered available to him to curtail the period of his incarceration. I know not whether he appealed or appealed against sentence, but it is to be expected that he might have done. He would have taken steps likewise to obtain release as quickly as he possibly could. He was in fact released after two and a half years of a five year sentence, albeit on licence. During the period that he was incarcerated he was perforce moved from one prison to another. He did not have in any sense a settled home in any one prison, and I have to say that my mind recoils from the idea that a cell in any one prison, for example Brixton, could be regarded as one's home and, as has been pointed out to me by Mr Redpath-Stevens in the skeleton which has placed before me, the concept of accommodation as it is defined in the Oxford English Dictionary involved at least the consideration of having one's habitual residence, house or home. It seems to me that incarceration in one of Her Majesty's prisons is the antithesis of having a home. It is just that. It is incarceration. It is detention against one's will and it seems to me that in those circumstances it cannot be said that that amounts to any sort of accommodation within the expressions used in the Act."

I need only say that I entirely agree.'

## Accommodation available for occupation

The vacated property must be 'accommodation' (see earlier notes) and must have been *available for occupation* by the applicant's family unit. Note that accommodation is 'available' for a person's occupation only if it is available for occupation both 'by him [*and* by] any other person who might reasonably be expected to reside with him' (Housing Act 1996, s 176).

In *R v Peterborough City Council, ex p Carr*[81] Ms Carr, who was pregnant, left her sister's house after her sister had refused to let her boyfriend (the putative father of her child) move in. The local authority found her intentionally homeless. This was quashed. The accommodation she left was not available for her occupation because it was not also reasonably available to her boyfriend, with whom she could reasonably be expected to reside.

## Reasonableness of continued occupation

The question is whether it would have been *reasonable to stay*, not whether it was reasonable to go. It may not be reasonable to continue to occupy overcrowded or poor quality accommodation. With regard to domestic disputes, the case law seems to draw a distinction between violent and non-violent disputes: as regards the former, it may not be reasonable to continue to occupy; as regards the latter, it may nevertheless be reasonable to stay.

In *R v London Borough of Wandsworth, ex p Nimako Boateng*[82] the applicant was living with her husband and child in Ghana. In March 1982, when she was pregnant

[81]   (1990) 22 HLR 206.
[82]   (1983) 11 HLR 95.

with her second child, she left the matrimonial home, and went to stay with her grandparents. In June 1982, she left Ghana and came to the United Kingdom, of which she was a citizen. For a period, during which her second child was born, she was housed by relatives, and in due course applied to the local authority as homeless.

During interviews with the authority, the applicant stated that she had left her husband because he had been treating her badly, although not with violence, and that she had left him voluntarily. It appeared that her accommodation with her grandparents was not settled or secure, nor was the accommodation with relatives in this country more than of limited benefit. The applicant stated that she had wanted her second child to be born in this country, where medical facilities would be available which would have been too expensive for her in Ghana.

The authority concluded that she had become homeless intentionally in that it would have been reasonable for her to remain in occupation of the marital home, rather than to leave Ghana to come to England without settled or secure accommodation available to her here. The applicant sought judicial review of this decision.

Woolf LJ stated[83]:

'The first interview that was held with the applicant on behalf of the authority was carried out by a Mrs Grzybek on 16 February 1983. The applicant explained to Mrs Grzybek why the accommodation with her sister was of limited benefit. When asked about the reasons why she left Ghana, she replied that it was because her marriage had broken down three months beforehand and she wanted to give birth to her second child in England. She was asked why this was so, and she replied that the medical facilities in Ghana would have been inadequate for her needs. On further questioning it was established that there were hospital facilities available to her, but the type of treatment that she required would have been too expensive. The applicant also dealt with the accommodation that she had shared with the grandmother.

A further interview was held with the applicant on 22 February 1983. On that occasion the accommodation which had been the matrimonial home in Ghana was discussed and she was asked to explain the circumstances leading up to her quitting that accommodation. The answer that the applicant gave was that her husband had been treating her badly. When she was asked in what form that treatment had been, she said that he had been staying away from home, sometimes several days at a time, without giving her any explanation. She was asked if her husband had ever been violent towards her. She said that she had left the accommodation voluntarily and that when she left her husband was still in occupation of it. She added that she had not been in touch with her husband since.

That account of the matter was passed to the Principal Housing Aid Officer, Mr Bruneau, who was responsible for making the decision in this case. Mr Bruneau dealt with the reasons for coming to the decision that he did in paragraph 5 of his affidavit. He said:

"In reaching a decision, my decision to find the applicant intentionally homeless I considered her previous addresses both in England and Ghana.

---

[83] At p 100.

I was satisfied that there were no extraordinary reasons which had forced the applicant to flee from Ghana to England despite the obvious lack of settled, secure accommodation available on arrival in England. I did not consider her stay at her grandmother's in Ghana as settled or secure but concluded that the cause of homelessness, therefore her present state of homelessness was as a result of abandoning her marital home in Ghana. Despite incertitude towards her relationship with her husband, the applicant did not indicate any violence or fear of violence from the husband or anyone else within the marital home. That being the case, I concluded that it would have, on evidence obtained from the applicant, been reasonable for her to remain in occupation of her marital home. I therefore decided after taking account of all the facts known to the Council, that it was unreasonable for the applicant to leave Ghana to come to England."

Mr Bruneau then went on to consider the problems with regard to accommodation in the Wandsworth area, which I do not need to go into, but they were clearly relevant having regard to subs (4) of s 17 of the 1977 Act.

The first point which is taken on that reasoning of Mr Bruneau, which, if I may say so with respect, I find very comprehensive, is that he dealt with an irrelevant consideration and had clearly taken it into account, namely, the reason why the applicant left Ghana. It is submitted that what was relevant was why the applicant left the former matrimonial home.

I am afraid I do not agree with that submission. Here, one of the matters that was put to the officer who interviewed the applicant on the two occasions was that the applicant had been coming to this country apparently in order to obtain medical assistance in relation to the child which she was expecting. Of course, that could have given rise to a situation where, apart from the matrimonial difficulties, she could not reasonably have been expected to continue to occupy the matrimonial home. If there was a good reason, quite apart from the matrimonial reasons, for her leaving Ghana, that was clearly something which could cause the authority to take the view that she was not intentionally homeless. If I may take a situation where, for some political reason, perfectly satisfactory accommodation in Ghana becomes accommodation which a particular person cannot reasonably be expected to continue to occupy, that is something which, in my view, the housing authority would be entitled to take into account when considering the obligations and the duties it owes when exercising its functions under s 17 of the Act. So it seems to me that here it was reasonable, having regard to the matters put forward by the applicant, for the local authority to look at the position in relation to why the applicant left Ghana to come to England.

Having come to the conclusion that there was nothing which justified the applicant leaving Ghana to come to England, which the authority thought would affect their position under s 17, what they then did, if I may say so perfectly sensibly, was first of all to decide which of the accommodations in Ghana it was proper to look at: Was it the grandmother's accommodation, which was the accommodation the applicant occupied immediately before leaving Ghana, or was it the accommodation she had occupied with her husband? The authority came to a conclusion, in favour of the applicant in some ways, that it was the accommodation which was the matrimonial home because they took the view that the grandmother's accommodation was not sufficiently settled and secure to be relevant.

In considering the matrimonial accommodation, what was relevant was the marital conduct to which the applicant was subjected by her husband whilst she was living there. Of course, there could be conduct on the part of a husband, who could not be prevented from entering the home, which could make it quite impossible to say that it would reasonable for the wife to continue to occupy that accommodation. Having regard to the paragraph of the affidavit which I have read, that is quite clearly something that has been accepted by the deponent on behalf of the authority because he is assessing the quality of this particular conduct. The conclusion that he came to was that there was no fear of any violence and, on that basis, he formed the opinion that it would be reasonable for the applicant to remain in the accommodation provided by the matrimonial home, having regard to the fact that she had no secure accommodation elsewhere: the grandmother's accommodation was unsatisfactory and she had no accommodation when she came back to this country, which ultimately she decided to do.

In my opinion, that is a conclusion to which the authority was fully entitled to come. I am afraid that I fundamentally disagree with Mr Allfrey's approach to the problem because he admits as part of his third submission that here no local authority could reasonably come to the conclusion that this authority did and, what is more, as a second submission, they misdirected themselves in law in taking the view that they could come to that conclusion. As I understand Mr Allfrey's submissions – and I may be doing them an injustice (although I hope not) in dealing with them in this way – it is fundamental to his approach that you start off with the premise that it is for a wife and not a local authority to decide whether or not she can go on living with her husband. As long as she is acting in good faith when she decides to leave the matrimonial home because of her husband, that is something which the local authority must accept.

That is not the situation as I understand it. It is certainly, in my view, not the situation when it comes to somebody who is leaving a home in this country. There are all sorts of protection that a woman can get if her husband misbehaves. The local authority could perfectly properly in many cases in this country take the view that it would be reasonable for the wife to continue to occupy accommodation and to say to a wife, if she thinks it right:

> "If you are having trouble with your husband, go the appropriate authority, be it a magistrates' court or the Family Division, and get protection against your husband."

If the woman does not then take that course and chooses to leave, the authority could then take the view that it was reasonable for the lady to remain.

Section 17 of the Act could have been drawn on the basis that as long as the person was reasonable in leaving the matrimonial home, then they should not be regarded as intentionally homeless. However, that is not how s 17 is worded. It deals with a different situation, namely, whether or not the person concerned could reasonably have continued to occupy the accommodation.

That results in a different test and in a different situation. It is understandable that Parliament should have approached the matter in that restricted way because it must be borne in mind that, as in Wandsworth, there is a great scarcity of accommodation which would be appropriate for the occupation of a person who is not regarded as intentionally homeless. Housing authorities have demands made upon their accommodation not only from persons making applications under this Act, but from ordinary members of the public who are on housing lists. One result of the Act is to promote persons falling within the provisions of the Act over the heads of those who are on housing lists. Parliament clearly recognised that there were cases where that should happen. But if a person is to have the benefit of that assistance, they have got to be put before the housing authority a situation which, on investigation by the authority, indicates that the person seeking assistance is not intentionally homeless. If the housing authority, on the material they have before them, find that as a result of their investigations properly carried out, they can regard the person as intentionally homeless, then it is their duty not only to ratepayers, but to those on their housing list, to say fairly and squarely to the applicant:

"This is a case where you have rendered yourself intentionally homeless."

It follows from all that I have said in this judgment that this is an application, now that I have the evidence of the housing authority before me, which is bound to fail. Accordingly, I dismiss the application.'

Further discussion of domestic violence and the reasonableness (or otherwise) of continued occupation can be found in *R v Kensington and Chelsea Royal Borough Council, ex p Hammell*[84]. In the case of violence or threats of violence outside the domestic sphere, there is some suggestion in *R v Croydon London Borough Council, ex p Toth*[85] that there will be cases where the applicant may be expected to remain and seek police protection but this will depend entirely on the circumstances of each case (as would be expected from an issue of 'reasonableness'), as is demonstrated well by the rather extreme case of *R v Hillingdon London Borough Council, ex p H*[86], where the applicant (an ex-soldier) has been threatened and harassed by the IRA.

Further important issues are, first, the economic circumstances of the applicant had he or she remained in his or her previous accommodation, and (secondly) the general housing circumstances in the area to which the person has applied for accommodation (see now s 177(2), Housing Act 1996, which links this issue both to intentional homelessness and homelessness *per se*).

As to the first issue, in *R v Royal Borough of Kensington and Chelsea, ex p Bayani*[87], Nicholls LJ (concerning departure from accommodation in the Philippines) stated:

'Mrs Bayani's contribution was one aspect of the financial picture. The other aspect was the family's financial position in the Philippines. On that the housing officer knew, from his inquiries, that Mr Bayani had employment in

---

[84] [1989] QB 518.
[85] (1987) 20 HLR 576, at p 583 per Connor LJ.
[86] (1988) 20 HLR 554.
[87] *R v Royal Borough of Kensington and Chelsea, ex p Bayani* (1990) 22 HLR 406, at p 417.

the Philippines, since at least 1985. The housing officer also knew that Mr Bayani's income was supplemented from Mrs Bayani's earnings. In my view, given the question to which the housing authority's inquiries were directed, it was not incumbent on the housing authority to probe further in this case. The question, it will be recalled was not whether it was reasonable for Mrs Bayani to leave her home in Manilla and come to the United Kingdom temporarily for work. It may very well be that Mrs Bayani acted reasonably, and with considerable selflessness and devotion to her family, in doing so. The question facing the housing authority was a different one. The question was whether it would have been reasonable for Mrs Bayani to have remained with her family in Manilla. Only if it would have been unreasonable for her to have stayed there would she be outside the statutory definition of intentionally homeless. I suppose there might be a case in which a decision by a wife, coping with a difficult pregnancy, to remain with her husband and older child in adequate, available accommodation in her home country, where her husband was employed, rather than to leave them and travel to the United Kingdom by herself, with no secure accommodation arrangements here, in order to preserve her immigration status and her ability to supplement the family income from temporary earnings, could be castigated as unreasonable, but it would need to be an altogether remarkable and exceptional set of circumstances for that to be so. In the present case, the housing officer would know, as we all do, that comparatively modest sums of sterling sent from this country to some, less developed, countries can have a value to recipients there out of all proportion to the value such sums have here. He knew that Mrs Bayani had been coming to this country every year for some years in order to boost the family income in just that way. I consider that, given that knowledge, and given what he knew about the accommodation in Manilla, the housing officer knew enough to form a view, fairly, on the question he had to answer. He was entitled, without making further inquiries, to conclude, as he did, that the financial situation did not render it unreasonable for Mrs Bayani to live in the Philippines.'

As to the second issue, in *R v Leeds City Council, ex p Adamiec and Adamiec*[88], Webster J cited, with approval, the following affidavit from the respondent's director of housing services:

'The stock of council housing within the area administered by Leeds City Council comprises approximately 83,244 properties. The council has sold approximately 14,000 houses to tenants under the provisions of the Housing Act 1980 – about 16% of the original stock. Controls on capital financing have resulted in virtually no new council house building. The number of council houses administered by my Department are therefore steadily decreasing.

At the present time there are over 21,000 applicants on the waiting list for council accommodation. These include about 500 families who, although accorded homeless persons priority, are as yet without permanent accommodation.

---

[88]  (1991) 24 HLR 138, at p 153.

The lettable voids level within this authority is no more than 0.7%

About 12,000 housing applications are received each year of which 5,000 are from applicants claiming homelessness. There are many demands for housing which the Council endeavour to satisfy. As well as discharging its duties to the homeless under the provisions of the Housing Act 1985, my Department seeks to satisfy the demands of other groups which are considered to have urgent need for housing. These include those with urgent medical need; in clearance areas; persons requiring housing under the provisions of the National Mobility Scheme; those with a confirmed social need or confirmed urgent sheltered need, and a very small number of key workers.

As well as housing unintentionally homeless persons accorded priority, the Council aims to house others with an urgent need. My Department have housed about 4,000 families since April 1990, and by March 31, 1991 it is anticipated that this figure will have risen to 5,000. Of these approximately 1,500 will be those families to whom the Council have accorded homeless persons status and have thus been housed pursuant to the provisions relating to homeless persons. The remainder are largely from those groups referred to earlier in this affidavit who also have a pressing need.

My Department works within a framework of an increasing number of applications for housing from a decreasing housing stock. It is of vital importance that only those persons or families who are genuinely unintentionally homeless are given priority for rehousing, otherwise other groups would suffer. It can be seen that for several thousand families on the waiting list there is little or no prospect of housing being offered to them for many years.'

## Can a person found to be intentionally homeless make a subsequent application?

An applicant may not make a second application based on exactly the same facts (see *Delahaye v Oswestry Borough Council*[89]. What, however, if the facts of the applicant's circumstances change?

In *R v Harrow London Borough Council, ex p Fahia*[90], F was evicted in 1994 from her home following a possession order. She applied to Harrow who found her intentionally homeless. They accordingly owed her only a time limited duty to accommodation (see now s 190 of the 1996 Act) and placed her in a guesthouse. That accommodation was due to end on 17 February 1994, but F did not then leave, and Harrow continued to pay her rent for a further year while she stayed there. In July 1995 Harrow decided it should no longer meet the cost of F's stay in the guesthouse, and in consequence the owner of the guesthouse told F she would have to leave. A charity asked Harrow to find F accommodation, but they argued that they were under no duty at all to assist her as there had been no change in her circumstances from the first finding of intentional homelessness. They carried out an informal investigation but concluded that the stay in the guesthouse did not break the chain of causation from her original act of intentional homelessness because she had had no settled accommodation. It was held at first instance and in the Court of Appeal that the chain of causation can be broken otherwise than by obtaining a

[89]  (1980) Times 29 July.
[90]  [1998] 4 All ER 137.

period of settled accommodation. Harrow conceded that point in the House of Lords. Harrow, however, then argued that they were not bound to consider a second application from F unless she could show a change in circumstances which might lead to the second application being successful. The House of Lords rejected that argument. There is a *duty* to make a proper statutory inquiry once an authority have reason to believe a person may be homeless or threatened with it and may have a priority need. In the instant case F was clearly threatened with homelessness, and her application was not the same as her initial one – she had had the intervening year in the guesthouse and that changed her circumstances.

## REFERRAL TO ANOTHER HOUSING AUTHORITY

### HOUSING ACT 1996

**198. Referral of case to another local housing authority**

(1) If the local housing authority would be subject to the duty under section 193 (accommodation for those with priority need who are not homeless intentionally) but consider that the conditions are met for referral of the case to another local housing authority, they may notify that other authority of their opinion.

The authority need not consider under section 197 whether other suitable accommodation is available before proceeding under this section.

(2) The conditions for referral of the case to another authority are met if—

(a) neither the applicant nor any person who might reasonably be expected to reside with him has a local connection with the district of the authority to whom his application was made,

(b) the applicant or a person who might reasonably be expected to reside with him has a local connection with the district of that other authority, and

(c) neither the applicant nor any person who might reasonably be expected to reside with him will run the risk of domestic violence in that other district.

(3) For this purpose a person runs the risk of domestic violence—

(a) if he runs the risk of violence from a person with whom he is associated, or

(b) if he runs the risk of threats of violence from such a person which are likely to be carried out.

(4) The conditions for referral of the case to another authority are also met if—

(a) the applicant was on a previous application made to that other authority placed (in pursuance of their functions under this Part) in accommodation in the district of the authority to whom his application is now made, and

(b) the previous application was within such period as may be prescribed of the present application.

(5) The question whether the conditions for referral of a case are satisfied shall be decided by agreement between the notifying authority and the notified authority or, in default of agreement, in accordance with such arrangements as the Secretary of State may direct by order.

(6) An order may direct that the arrangements shall be—

(a) those agreed by any relevant authorities or associations of relevant authorities, or

(b) in default of such agreement, such arrangements as appear to the Secretary of State to be suitable, after consultation with such associations representing relevant authorities, and such other persons, as he thinks appropriate.

(7) No such order shall be made unless a draft of the order has been approved by a resolution of each House of Parliament.

## 199. Local Connection

(1) A person has a local connection with the district of a local housing authority if he has a connection with it—

(a) because he is, or in the past was, normally resident there, and that residence is or was of his own choice,

(b) because he is employed there,

(c) because of family associations, or

(d) because of special circumstances.

(2) A person is not employed in a district if he is serving in the regular armed forces of the Crown.

(3) Residence in a district is not of a person's own choice, if—

(a) he becomes resident there because he, or a person who might reasonably be expected to reside with him, is serving in the regular armed forces of the Crown, or

(b) he, or a person who might reasonably be expected to reside with him, becomes resident there because he is detained under the authority of an Act of Parliament.

(4) In subsections (2) and (3) 'regular armed forces of the Crown' means the Royal Navy, the regular forces as defined by section 225 of the Army Act 1955, the regular air force as defined by section 223 of the Air Force Act 1955 and Queen Alexandra's Royal Naval Nursing Service.

(5) The Secretary of State may by order specify other circumstances in which—

(a) a person is not to be treated as employed in a district, or

(b) residence in a district is not to be treated as of a person's own choice.

## 200. Duties to applicant whose case is considered for referral or referred

(1) Where a local housing authority notify an applicant that they intend to notify or have notified another local housing authority of their opinion that the conditions are met for the referral of his case to that other authority—

(a) they cease to be subject to any duty under section 188 (interim duty to accommodate in case of apparent priority need), and

(b) they are not subject to any duty under section 193 (the main housing duty), but they shall secure that accommodation is available for occupation by the applicant until he is notified of the decision whether the conditions for referral of his case are met.

(2) When it has been decided whether the conditions for referral are met, the notifying authority shall notify the applicant of the decision and inform him of the reasons for it.

The notice shall also inform the applicant of his right to request a review of the decision and of the time within which such a request must be made.

(3) If it is decided that the conditions for referral are not met, the notifying authority shall secure that accommodation is available for occupation by the applicant until they have considered whether other suitable accommodation is available for his occupation in their district.

If they are satisfied that other suitable accommodation is available for his occupation in their district, section 197(2) applies; and if they are not so satisfied, they are subject to the duty under section 193 (the main housing duty).

(4) If it is decided that the conditions for referral are met, the notified authority shall secure that accommodation is available for occupation by the applicant until they have considered whether other suitable accommodation is available for his occupation in their district.

If they are satisfied that other suitable accommodation is available for his occupation in their district, section 197(2) applies; and if they are not so satisfied, they are subject to the duty under section 193 (the main housing duty).

(5) The duty under subsection (1), (3) or (4) ceases as provided in that subsection even if the applicant requests a review of the authority's decision (see section 202).

The authority may continue to secure that accommodation is available for the applicant's occupation pending the decision on a review.

(6) Notice required to be given to an applicant under this section shall be given in writing and, if not received by him, shall be treated as having been given to him if it is made available at the authority's office for a reasonable period for collection by him or on his behalf.

The 'local connection' or 'referral' provisions should be only used once all the prior issues (save that under s 197) have been determined. The basic requirements are:
(a)  the applicant has no local connection with area of the authority applied to (notifying authority);
(b)  there is a local connection with another local housing authority's area (notified authority) (NB: not a *greater* connection);
(c)  there is no risk of domestic violence to the applicant, etc. in the area of the notified authority.

In addition, a further ground for referral is:
(d)  the applicant was placed in the area of the notifying authority by the notified authority in pursuance of the notified authority's homelessness functions within the previous period of five years (see s 198(4) and SI 1996/2754, reg 6).

Note that ground (d) is free-standing and can be relied on even if the other conditions outlined above are not met.

Section 199 defines basic factors for determining the existence of a 'local connection':
(a)  normal residence of choice in an area;
(b)  employment in an area;
(c)  family associations with an area;
(d)  any other special circumstances.

However, in each case whether such a connection exists is a matter of fact and (a)–(d) above must be reasonably applied to the facts in coming to a decision.

Section 200 lays down the duties to referred applicants. There is no interim duty to accommodate under s 188 (see above), nor a 'main housing duty' under s 193 (see below), but only a duty to make accommodation available for occupation by the applicant until notified of the decision whether the conditions for referral are met. If conditions are met the applicant must be informed. The applicant can request a review (see further below), but otherwise the applicant is the responsibility of the notified authority, and they must accommodate him until they decide whether or not there is other suitable accommodation for the applicant in there area; and if there is not, they come under the main housing duty. If the conditions for referral are not met, the notifying authority comes under these obligations.

## Local connection: meaning of 'normal residence'

'Normal residence' is, of course, a concept the meaning of which is open to wide variations in interpretation. The concept was authoritatively discussed in *Eastleigh Borough Council v Betts*[91].

In 1978 Mr Betts secured a job in Leicester and went to live in a council house in the Blaby area with his wife and two daughters (aged 9 and 4). In August 1980 Mr Betts left his family temporarily in order to take up employment with Southern Television in Southampton. In October he secured rented accommodation in the Eastleigh area, and Mrs Betts and their daughters joined him there. He gave up his Blaby council house, without giving the council any notice and with arrears of rent outstanding. Unfortunately Southern Television lost their franchise shortly afterwards and as a result Mr Betts lost his employment. He again fell into arrears with his rent. On 3 February 1981, an order for possession was made against him, to take effect on 3 March. On 6 February he was given an interview with Mr Renouf, a senior assistant in the Estates Management Department of Eastleigh, and he applied under the Act for accommodation.

The immediate result of that application was that Eastleigh became under a statutory duty to make inquiries to satisfy themselves that Mr and Mrs Betts were in fact homeless, and to ascertain whether they had a 'priority need' for accommodation by reason of dependent children and whether they had become homeless 'intentionally' within the meaning of the Act: Furthermore Eastleigh became entitled, if they thought fit, to make inquiries as to whether the applicants had 'a local connection with the area of another housing authority'. Eastleigh also became under a duty to secure that temporary accommodation was made available for occupation by Mr and Mrs Betts pending any decision which Eastleigh might make as a result of their inquiries.

As a result of inquiries, Eastleigh, satisfied themselves that Mr and Mrs Betts were homeless, had a priority need for accommodation, and were not homeless intentionally. Eastleigh thereby became under a duty to secure that (permanent) accommodation became available for Mr and Mrs Betts, subject however to the linked issues of local connection and consequent referral. In the event Eastleigh referred the Betts to Blaby, on the basis that Mr Betts had no local connection with Eastleigh (having lived in the area for less than six months), but did have a local connection with Blaby. Mr Betts sought judicial review of this decision. Eventually the case reached the House of Lords, where the council's decision was upheld (overturning the Court of Appeal).

Lord Brightman stated:

> 'My Lords, the fundamental question is the existence of a "local connection". In construing section 5 it is only to be expected that the emphasis falls on "local connection," and not on past or present residence or current employment, etc. The Act is one which enables a homeless person in certain circumstances to jump over the heads of all other persons on a housing authority's waiting list, to jump the queue. One would not expect any just legislation to permit this to be done unless the applicant has in a real sense a

---

[91]    [1983] 2 AC 613, [1983] 2 All ER 1111.

local connection with the area in question. I accept that "residence" may be changed in a day, and that in appropriate circumstances a single day's residence may be enough to enable a person to say that he was normally resident in the area in which he arrived only yesterday. But "local connection" means far more than that. It must be built up and established; by a period of residence; or by a period of employment; or by family associations which have endured in the area; or by other special circumstances which spell out a local connection in real terms.

I return to the Agreement on Procedures. Faced with section 5 of the Act, a housing authority is involved, not with the question whether the applicant is or was normally resident etc. in the area in question, but whether the applicant has a local connection with that area. Has the normal residence of the applicant in the area been of such a duration as to establish for him a local connection with the area? To answer that question speedily it is sensible for local authorities to have agreed guidelines. I see nothing in the least unreasonable with a norm of six months' residence during the previous twelve months, or three years' residence during the previous five years. Seeing that the section is concerned with a subsisting and not with a past local connection, it is also reasonable to work on the basis that, after five years have gone by, no local connection based on residence is likely to have any relevance.

So I start my conclusions on this appeal by expressing the view that paragraph 2.5 of the Agreement on Procedures is eminently sensible and proper to have been included in the agreement. Although "an opinion" formed by a housing authority under section 5(1) must be concluded by reference to the facts of each individual case, there is no objection to the authority operating a policy or establishing guidelines, for reasons which the authority may legitimately entertain, and then applying such policy or guidelines generally to all the applications which come before them, provided that the authority do not close their mind to the particular facts of the individual case. There is ample authority that a body which is charged with exercising an administrative discretion is entitled to promulgate a policy or guidelines as an indication of a norm which is intended to be followed: see, for example, the speech of Lord Reid in *British Oxygen Co. Ltd v Board of Trade* [1970] 3 All ER 165, [1971] AC 610.

As regards the meaning of "normally resident" in the context of section 18(1)(a), this will take its colour from the fact that residence of any sort will be irrelevant unless and until it has been such as to establish a local connection with the area in which such residence subsists or has subsisted. I doubt whether in these circumstances any elaborate attempt at definition of "normally resident" will be profitable. They are ordinary English words, which in many contexts will mean what this House said "ordinary resident" meant in *Shah v Barnet London BC*. But they are only a subsidiary component of the formula which a housing authority will be applying under section 5 of the Act. If the residence of an applicant has been of a sufficient duration to create a local connection, no difficulty is likely to arise in deciding whether such residence was normal. But if it were necessary to decide such a point in a particular case, I do not think that the housing authority would be wrong if they applied to the words "normally resident" the meaning which in

*Shah* was attached to the words "ordinarily resident", remembering that the real exercise will be to decide whether the normal residence has been such as to establish a subsisting local connection.

That leaves me with a single question, which is the ultimate one in this appeal; whether Eastleigh misdirected themselves in reaching the opinion that the applicants did not have a local connection with the Eastleigh area. The onus of establishing this is upon the applicants. They rely principally on the wording of the letter of February 25, 1981, which says that Blaby have been notified "because you have lived in this borough for less than six months". The question before Eastleigh being whether the applicants had a local connection with the Eastleigh area as a result of residence, I see nothing whatever wrong with the decision by Eastleigh that as the applicants had lived in the area for less than six months, it was considered that they did not have a local connection with that area. It is true that the letter does not expressly refer to the absence of a local connection, only to the briefness of the residence, but it is to be observed that in his affidavit of June 21, 1982, which I have quoted, Mr Renouf attributes the decision under section 5 to lack of a local connection, which is the correct approach.

In my opinion the applicants have not made out any ground for attacking the validity of the opinion formed by Eastleigh under section 5(1). Eastleigh therefore are not under a duty under section 4(5) of the Act to house the applicants. I would allow this appeal.'

## 'Domestic violence': section 198(2) and (3)

As regards the issue of potential domestic violence in the area of the notified authority, a controversial conclusion was reached in *R v Bristol City Council, ex p Browne*[92].

Mrs Browne arrived in the UK from Limerick in Eire on 12 March 1979. She was accompanied by her seven children. She was married in 1967 and lived with her husband at Tralee in County Kerry. As a result of domestic violence, she as advised by her doctor to leave the matrimonial home and go to the Women's Aid hostel in Limerick, where she remained with her children for some four and a half months. She left that hostel in March 1979, and she says she did so because her husband had discovered her whereabouts, the people who run the hostel in Limerick made arrangements for her to come to Bristol, where they put her in touch with the Bristol Women's Aid office. She arrived in Bristol on 12 March. She was met by a representative of the Bristol Women's Aid at the airport, and she spent her first night in England at their hostel.

The next day she visited the Bristol council's housing aid centre, accompanied by two representatives of Bristol Women's Aid. On the next day, 14 March the authority telephoned a Mr Burke, the community welfare officer in Tralee responsible for homeless families in that part of Ireland. Mr Burke said that if the applicant were to return to Tralee with her children he would make provision for her and her children. He also assured the council that the accommodation provided would take account of the risk of reviewed violence. In the light of this, the council, resolved

---

[92]   [1979] 3 All ER 344.

that it could perform its duty under the legislation by assisting Mrs Browne to return to Ireland with her children to access the accommodation in Tralee. Mrs Browne sought judicial review of this decision, but the High Court upheld it.

Lloyd J stated[93]:

> 'The sole question for our consideration is whether the council has complied with its statutory duty under the Act. That turns on the language of section 6(1) of the Act, which I have already read in full and need not read again. It provides in effect, that the council can perform its duty either by providing accommodation itself or by securing that the homeless person obtains accommodation from some other person or by giving such advice and assistance as will secure that the homeless person obtains accommodation from some other person.
>
> In the present case, on the facts which I have recited, it is clear beyond any doubt that the council has given such advice and offered such assistance (although it has not been accepted) as would enable the applicant to obtain accommodation from Mr Burke, the community welfare officer in Tralee. It is true that there is no affidavit from Mr Burke himself, but there is no reason why we should not accept what is said by Mr Ball and Mr Hodgkinson in that respect.
>
> Thus the question comes down to this very narrow point: is Mr Burke a "person" within the meaning of section 6(1)(c) of the Act? In my judgment, he is. Indeed, Mr Denyer, who has appeared on behalf of the applicant, did not suggest the contrary, or at any rate did not suggest it very strenuously. Putting the question of violence on one side, Mr Denyer accepted that the council could fulfil its duty under the Act by assisting the applicant and her children to go back to Tralee, even though Tralee is outside the jurisdiction. It may well be that in most cases the person referred to in section 6(1)(c) of the Act will be a person within the area of the housing authority in question. But there is nothing in the Act which expressly so confines it; and, as I say, Mr Denyer did not strenuously argue that it should be so confined.
>
> The real point which Mr Denyer makes is that the applicant should not, on the special facts of this case, be asked to go back to Tralee, because that is the place where she has suffered the domestic violence in the past. In that connection Mr Denyer referred us to section 5(3) and (4) of the Act, which I should now read in full:
>
> > "(3) It shall be the duty of the notified authority to secure that accommodation becomes available for occupation by the person to whom the notification relates if neither he nor any person who might reasonably be expected to reside with him has a local connection with the area of the notifying authority but the conditions specified in subsection (4) below are satisfied.
> >
> > (4) The conditions mentioned in subsection (3) above are (a) that the person to whom the notification relates or some person who might reasonably be expected to reside with him has a local connection with the

area of the notified authority, and ' – and this is the important condition' (b) that neither he nor any such person will run the risk of domestic violence in that area."

It is not of course argued that Tralee is itself a housing authority within the meaning of the Act of 1977; nobody suggests that the conditions set out in section 5(4) apply as such. But what is suggested is that section 5(4) can and should be applied, as it were, by analogy.

There is, I think, a short answer to that submission. The fact that Tralee is the place from which the applicant has come and the place where she has suffered violence in the past does not mean that she would necessarily suffer any risk of violence if she goes back. Obviously she will not go back to the same house; but there is other accommodation in the same area. The risk involved in her going back was, in my judgment, a matter for the council to consider together with the community welfare officer in Tralee. The passages from the affidavits which I have read show that that risk was considered very carefully by the council. The view which they have formed is quite clear, namely, that accommodation can be provided in Tralee without risk to the applicant or her children. There is no material on which this court can possibly interfere with that conclusion or say that it was not justified. Mr Denyer's main point, therefore fails.'

Although strictly this is not a 'local connection' case (Tralee not being a notifiable authority), the analogies are clear enough, and indeed are specifically alluded to in Lloyd J's judgment. The decision might be thought to be overly sanguine as to the lack of likelihood of violence, but the subsequent decision in *R v London Borough of Islington, ex p Adigun*[94] again illustrates judicial unwillingness to interfere too far with local authority judgment in this area.

The applicant was the joint tenant with her husband of a house owned by the City of Liverpool District Council. The applicant left her husband because of his violence towards her and came to London in June 1984 to stay with a friend, who lived in the area of the respondent authority. On 18 June 1984 the applicant presented as homeless to the authority. On the interview form the authority noted that there was no local connection with their area, and that responsibility lay with Liverpool City Council.

The respondent authority contacted the Liverpool City Council and established that the applicant's husband had moved out of the property, taking his furniture with him. The property had been re-let in May 1984 and it was believed that the applicant's husband had returned to Nigeria. The respondent authority referred the application to the Liverpool City Council under the local connection provisions and so notified the applicant in August 1984. The applicant, who did not wish to return to Liverpool's area, sought judicial review of this decision.

Mann J stated[95]:

'The officer of the respondent who took the decision is Mrs Brown who has deposed as follows:

---

[94] (1986) 20 HLR 600.
[95] Ibid at p 604.

"The reasons for my decision were that Mrs Adigun had left a joint tenancy in Liverpool in April 1984 as the result of a marital dispute. I did address my mind as to whether, if Mrs Adigun returned to Liverpool, she would run the risk of domestic violence in that area. I relied on the information supplied to us by Liverpool Council that the applicant's husband had moved out of the previous matrimonial home and returned to Nigeria. Liverpool Council had also stated that they had taken possession of the previous matrimonial home and it had been re-let in May 1984. I therefore believe that I was entitled to rely on this information as being correct. Although there is no reference to violence in the form completed by Mrs E. Edwards, she told me that the marital dispute involved violence. I am fully aware of the provisions of section 5 of the 1977 Act and in considering the application and the obvious local connection with Liverpool I also considered quite specifically the allegation of domestic violence. Though there was no independent evidence of this violence I accepted for the purpose of my decision that Mrs Adigun was correct in her assertions. Had there been no other information I should not have referred the matter to Liverpool because of the requirement in section 5(1)(a). However, the inquiries made of the Liverpool District Housing Office showed that Mr Adigun had given up possession of the former home, that someone else had moved in, and that he was believed to have returned to Nigeria with his furniture. Since the authority had re-let the property on May 7, 1984 this was credible information and I believed it to be accurate; nothing that has happened since indicates it was not accurate. On that basis I concluded that there was no risk of violence if the applicant returned to Liverpool. I therefore instructed that a notice under section 8 of the Housing (Homeless Persons) Act 1977 should be served which is in the form of a letter referred to in the applicant's affidavit and is in fact dated August 2, 1984."

The applicant is and has been unwilling to return to Liverpool and is still resident in Islington. The reason for her reluctance is her fear of her husband. On her behalf three points are taken. The first is this. The decision of August 2, is flawed because the respondent did not as a matter of law have sufficient information which could have led them to be satisfied that there was no risk of domestic violence in Liverpool. The available material is that to which I have referred, that is to say the re-letting of the flat by the City of Liverpool District Council and the observation that the husband was believed to have gone to Nigeria with his furniture, and it is said that material was insufficient in point of law to negative a risk. The task of determining risk or not is the task of the local authority. (See the opening words of paragraph 5 of section 5(1).)

In considering the submission I have in mind the words of Lord Brightman in *Puhlhofer (A.P.) and Another (A.P.) v London Borough of Hillingdon* (February 6, 1986) where his Lordships [sic] said:

"My Lords, I am troubled at the prolific use of judicial review for the purpose of challenging the performance by local authorities of their functions under the Act. Parliament intended the local authority to be the judge of fact. The Act abounds with the formula when, or if, the housing authority are satisfied as to this, or that, or have reason to believe this, or that. Although the action or inaction of a local authority is clearly susceptible to judicial review where they have misconstrued the Act, or abused their powers or otherwise acted perversely, I think that great restraint should be exercised in giving leave to proceed by judicial review. The plight of the homeless is a desperate one, and the plight of the applicants in the present case commands the deepest sympathy. But it is not, in my opinion, appropriate that the remedy of judicial review, which is a discretionary remedy, should be made use of to monitor the actions of local authorities under the Act save in the exceptional case. The ground upon which the courts will review the exercise of an administrative discretion is abuse of power – e.g. bad faith, a mistake in construing the limits of the power, a procedural irregularity, or unreasonableness in the *Wednesbury* sense – unreasonableness verging on an absurdity: see the speech of Lord Scarman in *R v Secretary of State for the Environment, ex parte Nottinghamshire County Council* [1986] 2 WLR 1 at p. 5. Where the existence or non-existence of a fact is left to the judgment and discretion of a public body and that fact involves a broad spectrum ranging from the obvious to the debatable to the just conceivable, it is the duty of the court to leave the decision of that fact to the public body to whom Parliament has entrusted the decision-making power save in a case where it is obvious, that the public body, consciously or unconsciously, are acting perversely."

There is material upon which the respondent could have decided as it did. No doubt criticisms could be made of the quality of that material and criticisms have been made of the quality of that material. However, in practical terms I see no other sensible course that the local authority could have adopted other than that of contacting the City of Liverpool District Council. Material was, as a result of that contact, put before Islington and I find it impossible to say that they acted perversely. The first ground, therefore fails.'

## Residence of his own choice

It has already been noted that in *Eastleigh Borough Council v Betts*[96] the House of Lords decided that the 'overarching concept' of local connection could legitimately involve a view of 'normal residence' wider than where an applicant lived at the time of the application and (in particular) a normative approach of six months' residence in an area 'qualifying' an applicant was appropriate, so long as account could be taken of the circumstances of individual cases. Recently, the House of Lords has twice returned to the question of 'normal residence' – in this case examining the question of when/where a 'residence' is/is not of a person's 'own choice'. The issue has been thrown into sharp relief by the 'dispersal' policy of the National Asylum Support Service (NASS) under asylum and immigration legislation. Do such 'dispersees' reside in the area to which they are sent of their choice? If so, they may acquire a local connection with that authority.

---

[96]  [1983] 2 AC 613, [1983] 2 All ER 1111.

The first case is not, as such, a 'dispersal' case but does lead on to the same underlying issue. In *Mohammed v Hammersmith and Fulham LBC*[97] the appellant, his wife and two sons fled from Somalia during the civil war and went to live in Kenya. In 1994, the appellant's wife came to the United Kingdom. She lived in various properties in Ealing until January 1998, when she moved to an address within the respondent authority's district. On 31 January 1998 the appellant arrived in the United Kingdom and went to live with a friend who lived in the authority's district.

On 16 April 1998, the appellant and his wife applied to the authority as homeless persons and were secured interim accommodation in the authority's district. In July 1998, the authority, disregarding the period in interim accommodation, decided that the appellant did not have a local connection with their district and referred the application to Ealing London Borough Council.

The appellant requested a review of the decision. On 23 September 1998, the authority confirmed their decision. After dealing with the facts, the review decision concluded that the applicant did not have 'an essential compassionate, social or support need' sufficient to give rise to a local connection. An appeal to the county court was dismissed.

The appellant's appeal to the Court of Appeal was allowed. The Court held that the date for determining whether an applicant has a local connection with a local authority's district is the date of their decision under s 184(3) and, if that decision is reviewed, the date of the review. It was also held that the occupation of interim accommodation could constitute normal residence for the purposes of establishing a local connection. It was further held that the reference to 'an essential compassionate, social or support need' was a misdirection in law.

The authority appealed to the House of Lords, which dismissed the appeal, holding that 'interim' accommodation provided under s 188 of the Housing Act 1996 can 'count' for the purpose of deciding whether a local connection exists, such accommodation was (inter alia) occupied 'of a person's own choice'. Lord Slynn[98] stated:

> 'It is clear that words like ordinary residence and normal residence may take their precise meaning from the context of the legislation in which they appear but it seems to me that the prima facie meaning of normal residence is a place where at the relevant time the person in fact resides. That therefore is the question to be asked and it is not appropriate to consider whether in a general or abstract sense such a place would be considered an ordinary or normal residence. So long as that place where he eats and sleeps is voluntarily accepted by him, the reason why he is there rather than somewhere else does not prevent that place from being his normal residence. He may not like it, he may prefer some other place, but that place is for the relevant time the place where he normally resides. If a person, having no other accommodation, takes his few belongings and moves into a barn for a period to work on a farm that is where during that period he is normally residence, however much he might prefer some more permanent or better accommodation. In a sense it is

97  [2001] UKHL 57, [2002] 1 All ER 176 at p 182.
98  [2002] 1 All ER 176, at p 182.

"shelter" but it is also where he resides. Where he is given interim accommodation by a local housing authority even more clearly is that the place where for the time being he is normally residence. The fact that it is provided subject to statutory duty does not, contrary to the appellant authority's argument, prevent it from being such.

Although the point is not conclusive counsel for the respondent are entitled as they do to point to the fact that Parliament has specifically provided in section 199 that residence due to service in the armed forces or through detention under statutory powers is not "of choice" and the Secretary of State may specify other circumstances in which residence in a district is not to be treated as of a person's own choice, but nothing has been done to exclude residence under the homelessness provisions with which this appeal is concerned as not being of a person's own choice. If it had been intended to exclude such accommodation it would have been easy to have done so in the section or by the exercise of powers by the Secretary of State under section 119(5).

The appellant authority contends that interim accommodation cannot lead to the creation of a local connection attributable to normal residence even "if a person is in interim accommodation for an extensive period, e.g. years" though it recognises that local connection through other factors specified (e.g. special circumstances) can arise during the occupation of interim accommodation. The authority says that to allow such interim accommodation to count as normal residence defeats the purpose.

I agree with Henry LJ [2002] 2 All ER 597 at 606 [2001] QB 97 at 109 (para 45) that although there is a re-distributive purpose to the Act, it has to be read with the other statutory purpose of providing for people to stay in a borough with which they have established a local connection and that there is no overriding reason or principle why interim accommodation should not count as normal residence for that purpose.

In *Eastleigh Borough Council v Betts* [1983] 2 AC 613 at 628 Lord Brightman stressed that "the real exercise will be to decide whether the normal residence has been such as to establish a subsisting local connection". In my opinion the occupation of interim accommodation can be taken into account in deciding whether such a local connection exists.

A second question which has been raised is whether the correct date to decide whether a person has a local connection is the date of the making of his application or the date of the decision or, if there is a review, the date of the review. It seems to me plain that since the question for the local housing authority is whether the applicant "has a local connection" that must mean such a connection at the date of decision or review, whether in the meantime the applicant has acquired or lost (by moving away) his local connection'.

However, important though the *Mohammed* decision is, the crucial decision is that involving two asylum seekers, Al Ameri (from Iraq) and Osmani (from Afghanistan), both 'dispersed' to Glasgow by NASS.

In *Al Ameri v Kensington and Chelsea Royal London Borough Council*[99], in May 2001, Al Ameri and his family, who were Iraqi nationals, arrived in the United

---

[99]   [2004] UKHL 4, [2004] 1 All ER 1104.

Kingdom and claimed asylum. Later that month they were accommodated in Glasgow. In June, the claimant was granted exceptional leave to remain in the United Kingdom. He remained in Glasgow until March 2002, when he applied to the Kensington and Chelsea Council for housing assistance.

In December 2000 Osmani, who was an Afghani national, arrived in the United Kingdom. In February 2001, she was accommodated in Glasgow. In May 2001, she was granted indefinite leave to remain in the United Kingdom and was required to leave her accommodation. She remained in Glasgow until September 2001, when she applied to Harrow for housing assistance.

The two London boroughs referred the cases to Glasgow on the ground that the applicants had no local connection with them, but did have a local connection with Glasgow. These decisions were confirmed on review, but were overturned (Buxton LJ dissenting) by the Court of Appeal on the basis that residence in Glasgow had not been 'of their own choice'. The House of Lords unanimously upheld the Court of Appeal. Lord Bingham stated[100]:

'It was common ground in argument before the House that the respondents had been "normally resident" in the district of the Glasgow City Council as local housing authority during their residence in Glasgow as asylum seekers. Thus the first condition of establishing a local connection under s 199(1)(a) of the 1996 Act was satisfied. The crucial issue dividing the parties was whether such residence had been of the respondents' own choice, an issue turning on the construction of these words in the context of this Act. For the appellant local authorities it was argued that the residence had been of the respondents' own choice. They had had the choice of accepting the offer of accommodation (and living needs support) in Glasgow or not accepting it. That was not the less a choice because the alternative to accepting it was continuing destitution, subject to any possible provision for the children under s 122. The respondents lived in Glasgow as the result of a conscious and intentional decision to do so.

The respondents (supported by the intervener) contended that the relevant choice for the purpose of s 199(1)(a), read as a whole and in context, was the choice a person has made or not made to reside in a particular area. Thus the relevant enquiry of each respondent was "Did you choose to live in Glasgow?", to which the answer could only be "No".

This issue of construction, like many such issues, bears little elaboration. Section 199(1) describes a number of ways in which a local connection may be established between a person and the district of a local housing authority. Under subs (1)(a) a period of normal residence is necessary. But such residence must be of the resident's own choice. So the question to be asked of each respondent is "Did you reside in Glasgow of your own choice?" To that question there can be, in the case of each respondent, only one possible answer: "No. I was given no choice about where I resided. I resided in Glasgow because, and only because, that was the only place where I was offered accommodation and the means to meet the most basic of human needs". To the extent that historical or fictional analogies assist, the same result follows. If a customer of Hobson had been asked whether he was riding a horse of his own choice, he would have been bound to reply that he had had no choice, it was that horse or none, he took what he was given.

...

If there were room for doubt about the correctness of this construction, consideration of the wider context would resolve it. The object of the NASS scheme introduced under the 1999 Act was to relieve pressure on local housing authorities in London and the South East of England by dispersing asylum seekers, while awaiting determination of their asylum claims, in other parts of the United Kingdom, particularly those parts where accommodation was more readily available. It was always seen as a cardinal feature of the scheme that asylum seekers in need of accommodation should go where they were sent. Thus the White Paper "Fairer, Faster and Firmer – A Modern Approach to Immigration and Asylum" (July 1998) (Cm 4018) stated (p.39 (para 8.22):

> "Asylum seekers would be expected to take what was available, and would not be able to pick and choose where they were accommodated, but where possible placements would take account of the value of linking to existing communities and the support of voluntary and community groups."

Thus the asylum seeker was to have no choice, and s 97(2)(a) of the 1999 Act expressly enjoined the Secretary of State to have no regard to any preference that the asylum seeker or his dependants might have as to the locality in which accommodation was to be provided.

...

The subject matter of *Mohamed v Hammersmith and Fulham LBC* [2001] UKHL 57: [2002] 1 All ER 176 [2002] 1 AC 547 was closer, although neither the applicant (Mr Mohamed) nor his wife were asylum seekers. The wife came to England in 1994 and lived for most of the time in flats in Ealing until in January 1998 she moved to live with a friend in Hammersmith. The husband came to England in January 1998 and lived with a (different) friend in Hammersmith. In April 1998 they jointly asked the London Borough of Hammersmith and Fulham for accommodation, and were given temporary accommodation in the authority's district, first in a hotel and then in a flat, presumably under s 188 of the 1996 Act. They then applied for accommodation under s 193. In July 1998 the authority told the wife that they accepted a duty to arrange accommodation for her but that, although she had a local connection with Ealing where she had lived, she had no connection with Hammersmith, so the applications of both husband and wife were referred to Ealing on the basis that the husband's residence in Hammersmith was not such as could amount to normal residence for the purpose of s 199(1)(a) of the 1996 Act. Hammersmith argued that the occupation of interim accommodation pending a decision on the husband's application under s 193 could not amount to normal residence. This argument was rejected by the Court of Appeal and the House. In the course of his opinion (with which the other members of the Committee agreed) Lord Slynn of Hadley referred to the notion of voluntariness, held in *Shah's* case to be an ingredient of ordinary residence, and pointed out that the Secretary of State had not exercised his power under s 199(5) to provide that residence in interim accommodation.'

## Dispute resolution procedures

Disputes over referrals between authorities are to be referred to resolution procedures. These are provided, pursuant to s 198(5) of the 1996 Act, by a Local Authority Agreement procedure originally made in 1979. In addition there is now an Order regulating the procedure and processes for referral[101].

## HOMELESSNESS (DECISIONS ON REFERRALS) ORDER 1998

SI 1998/1578

### Citation and commencement

1.   This Order may be cited as the Homelessness (Decisions on Referrals) Order 1998 and shall come into force on the twenty-eighth day after the day on which it is approved by resolution of each House of Parliament.

### Arrangements for deciding whether conditions for referral are satisfied

2.   The arrangements set out in the Schedule to this Schedule to this Order are those agreed by the Local Government Association, the Welsh Local Government Association, the Association of London Government and the Convention of Scottish Local Authorities, and shall be the arrangements for the purposes of section 198(5) and (6)(a) of the Housing Act 1996.

### Revocation of order

3.   (1) Subject to paragraph (2), the Housing (Homeless Persons) (Appropriate Arrangements) Order 1978 ('the 1978 Order') is hereby revoked.

(2) The 1978 Order shall remain in force for any case where a notified authority has received a notification under section 67(1) of the Housing Act 1985 or section 198(1) of the Housing Act 1996 (referral to another local housing authority) prior to the date on which this Order comes into force. [20th July 1998]

# SCHEDULE

## THE ARRANGEMENTS

*Appointment of person by agreement between notifying authority and notified authority*

1. Where the question whether the conditions for referral of a case are satisfied has not been decided by agreement between the notifying authority and the notified authority, the question shall be decided by a person appointed by those authorities.

*Appointment of person other than by agreement between notifying authority and notified authority*

2. If within a period of 21 days commencing on the day on which the notified authority receives a notification under section 198(1) of the Housing Act 1996 a person has not been appointed in accordance with paragraph 1, the question shall be decided by a person—

(a)   from the panel constituted in accordance with paragraph 3, and

(b)   appointed in accordance with paragraph 4.

---

[101]  For a stark illustration of the conflict which can arise between authorities, see *R v Slough Borough Council, ex p Ealing London Borough Council* [1981] 1 All ER 601.

3.—(1) Subject to sub-paragraph (2), the Local Government Association shall establish and maintain a panel of persons from which a person may be appointed to decide the question whether the conditions for referral of a case are satisfied.

(2) The Local Government Association shall consult such other associations of relevant authorities as they think appropriate before—

(a) establishing the panel,

(b) inviting a person to join the panel after it has been established, and

(c) removing a person from the panel.

4.—(1) The notifying authority and the notified authority shall jointly request the Chairman of the Local Government Association or his nominee ('the proper officer') to appoint a person from the panel.

(2) If within a period of six weeks commencing on the day on which the notified authority receives a notification under section 198(1) of the Housing Act 1996 a person has not been appointed, the notifying authority shall request the proper officer to appoint a person from the panel.

# DUTIES TO VARIOUS CLASSES OF HOMELESS PERSONS

# HOUSING ACT 1996

## 192. **Duty to persons not in priority need who are not homeless intentionally**

(1) This section applies where the local housing authority—

(a) are satisfied that an applicant is homeless and eligible for assistance, and

(b) are not satisfied that he became homeless intentionally,

but are not satisfied that he has a priority need.

(2) The authority shall provide the applicant with advice and such assistance as they consider appropriate in the circumstances in any attempts he may make to secure that accommodation becomes available for his occupation.

(3 The authority may secure that accommodation is available for occupation by the applicant.

## 193. **Duty to persons with priority need who are not homeless intentionally**

(1) This section applies where the local housing authority are satisfied that an applicant is homeless, eligible for assistance and has a priority need, and are not satisfied that he became homeless intentionally.

This section has effect subject to section 197 (duty where other suitable accommodation available).

(2) Unless the authority refer the application to another local housing authority (see section 198), they shall secure that accommodation is available for occupation by the applicant.

(3) The authority are subject to the duty under this section until it ceases by virtue of any of the following provisions of this section.

...

(5) The local housing authority shall cease to be subject to the duty under this section if the applicant, having been informed by the authority of the possible consequence of refusal and of his right to request a review of the suitability of the accommodation, refuses an offer of accommodation which the authority are satisfied is suitable for him and the authority notify him that they regard themselves as having discharged their duty under this section.

(6) The local housing authority shall cease to be subject to the duty under this section if the applicant—

(a) ceases to be eligible for assistance,

(b) becomes homeless intentionally from the accommodation made available for his occupation,

(c) accepts an offer of accommodation under Part VI (allocation of housing) or,

(cc) accepts an offer of an assured tenancy (other than a assured short hold tenancy) from a private landlord,

(d) otherwise voluntarily ceases to occupy as his only or principal home the accommodation made available for his occupation.

(7) The local housing authority shall also cease to be subject to the duty under this section if the applicant, having been informed of the possible consequence of refusal and of his right to request a review of the suitability of the accommodation, refuses a final offer of accommodation under Part 6.

(7A) An offer of accommodation under Part 6 is a final offer for the purposes of subsection (7) if it is made in writing and states that it is a final offer for the purposes of subsection (7).

(7B) The authority shall also cease to be subject to the duty under this section if the applicant accepts a qualifying offer of an assured short hold tenancy which is made by a private landlord in relation to any accommodation which is, or may become, available for the applicant's occupation.

(7C) The applicant is free to reject a qualifying offer without affecting the duty owed to him under this section by the authority.

(7D) For the purposes of subsection (7B) an offer of an assured short hold tenancy is a qualifying offer if—

(a) it is made, with the approval of the authority, in pursuance of arrangements made by the authority with the landlord with a view to bringing the authority's duty under this section to an end;

(b) the tenancy being offered is a fixed term tenancy (within the meaning of Part 1 of the Housing Act 1988 (c 50)); and

(c) it is accompanied by a statement in writing which states the term of the tenancy being offered and explains in ordinary language that—

(i) there is no obligation to accept the offer, but

(ii) if the offer is accepted the local housing authority will cease to be subject to the duty under this section in relation to the applicant.

(7E) An acceptance of a qualifying offer is only effective for the purposes of subsection (6B) if the applicant signs a statement acknowledging that he has understood the statement mentioned in subsection (7D).

(7F) The local housing authority shall not—

(a) make a final offer of accommodation under Part 6 for the purposes of subsection (7); or

(b) approve an offer of an assured shorthold tenancy for the purposes of subsection (7B),

unless they are satisfied that the accommodation is suitable for the applicant and that it is reasonable for him to accept the offer.

(8) For the purposes of subsection (7F) an applicant may reasonably be expected to accept an offer of accommodation under Part VI even though he is under contractual or other obligations in respect of his existing accommodation, provided he is able to bring those obligations to an end before he is required to take up the offer.

(9)   A person who ceases to be owed the duty under this section may make a fresh application to the authority for accommodation or assistance in obtaining accommodation.

...

### 195.   **Duties in cases of threatened homelessness**

(1) This section applies where the local housing authority are satisfied that an applicant is threatened with homelessness and is eligible for assistance.

(2) If the authority—

(a)   are satisfied that he has apriority need, and

(b)   are not satisfied that he became threatened with homelessness intentionally, they shall take reasonable steps to secure that accommodation does not cease to be available for his occupation.

This subsection has effect subject to section 197 (duty where other suitable accommodation available).

(3) Subsection (2) does not affect any right of the authority, whether by virtue of a contract, enactment or rule of law, to secure vacant possession of any accommodation.

(4) Where in pursuance of the duty under subsection (2) the authority secure that accommodation other than that occupied by the applicant when he made his application is available for occupation by him, the provisions of section 193(3) to (9) (period for which duty owed) and section 194 (power exercisable after minimum period of duty) apply, with any necessary modifications, in relation to the duty under this section as they apply in relation to the duty under section 193.

(5) If the authority

(a)   are not satisfied that the applicant has a priority need, or

(b)   are satisfied that he has a priority need but are also satisfied that he became threatened with homelessness intentionally,

they shall furnish him with advice and such assistance as they consider appropriate in the circumstances in any attempts he may make to secure that accommodation does not cease to be available for his occupation.

...

(9) If the authority—

(a)   are not satisfied that the applicant has a priority need; and

(b)   are not satisfied that he became threatened with homelessness intentionally the authority may take reasonable steps to secure that accommodation does not cease to be available for the applicant's occupation.

## The 'full' or 'main housing duty'

Under the Housing Act 1996, s 193, where an authority are satisfied that a person is homeless, eligible, in priority need and unintentionally homeless (subject to s 197) they shall secure that accommodation is available to the applicant unless there is a referral to another authority. However, this does not necessarily mean that the authority will have to provide the accommodation itself. As the amendments to s 193 contained in the Homelessness Act 2002 make entirely clear, offer of assured or even (in limited circumstances) assured shorthold tenancy may discharge the authority's duty. However, crucially the 2002 Act restores the duty as a potentially 'open-ended; one – in stark contrast to the two-year limited duty introduced by the Housing Act 1996. The offer of an assured shorthold must be a 'qualifying' one – as to which see the (new) s 193 (6D) and (6E). Applicants need to be clearly informed in writing of the implications of accepting an AST, and that losing an AST may not amount to 'intentional' homelessness so that the short-term benefits to a authority of using the AST route to discharge their s 193 duty may not get the applicant 'off the books' permanently.

The authority will in any case be freed of their duty if the applicant, having been informed by the authority of the consequences of a refusal and (since the 2002 Act of their request for a review of the authority's decision), refuses accommodation the authority are satisfied is 'suitable' for him or her *and* the authority notify the applicant that they regard themselves as having discharged their duty (s 193(5)). (For 'suitability' see s 210 of the 1996 Act and SI 1996/3204 below.)

An authority will, also cease to be under the 'full duty' where an applicant:

(a) ceases to be 'eligible' (s 193(6)(b);

(b) becomes homeless intentionally from that accommodation made available for his or her occupation (eg, gets thrown out of a homelessness hostel for bad behaviour) (s 193(6)(b);

(c) accepts an offer of ordinary housing under the general allocation (Part VI) procedure (s 193(6)(c);

(d) otherwise voluntarily ceases to occupy as his or her only or principal home accommodation made available (s 193(6)(d)).

For the purposes of s 193, an applicant may reasonably be expected to receive an offer of accommodation under general allocation powers even though under contractual or other obligations with regard to existing accommodation, provided that he or she is able to bring those obligations to an end before being required to take up the offer (s 193(8)).

Where the main housing duty is terminated, or where an authority cease to be subject to it the person to whom the duty was owed may make a fresh application (s 193(9)).

## 'Reasonable' discharge of duties

The foregoing duties are to be *reasonably* discharged[102] ie there must be no oppression of, or vindictiveness towards the applicant in relation to the accommodation offered. Any property provided to be 'accommodation' must be habitable bearing in mind the applicants' health.

In *R v Ryedale District Council, ex p Smith*[103], Mr and Mrs Smith and their son lived in a caravan. They were visited by a local authority housing officer who recorded no details about Mr Smith, who was 67 and suffered from chronic fibrosis of the lungs and emphysema. The Smiths claimed that in the circumstances they were homeless, and pending determination of their case a further caravan was offered to them. This they refused. The local authority said that having refused this second caravan they were intentionally homeless. That assertion failed because the Smiths had not ceased to occupy the accommodation in question, they had never occupied it at all. However, the local authority then argued that by offering that second caravan they had discharged their duty, as it was all the accommodation available at the time. It was held that offers of accommodation under the Act must

---

[102] *R v Wyre Borough Council, ex p Parr* (1982) 2 HLR 7.
[103] (1983) 16 HLR 66.

be considered in the light of appropriate inquiries – inquiries the local authority had failed to make. The caravan was probably not a suitable home for an old and sick man. The court, however, would not order the local authority to provide a council house, but ordered them to reconsider the matter in the light of proper inquiries.

Decisions on the issue of the 'suitability' of accommodation offered continue to mount up. For example in *R (Yumsak) v Enfield London Borough Council*[104] it was held by the High Court that offering a single mother, with three small children, who was epileptic and did not speak English, accommodation 100 miles away in Birmingham where she had no friends and family was *not* an offer of suitable accommodation.

Perhaps the most extensive discussion is to be found in the Court of Appeal decision in *R v Newham London Borough Council, ex p Sacupima*[105]. *Sacupima* indicates that the location of accommodation is relevant as regards its suitability, as also are the circumstances of the applicant and her/his family. Latham LJ stated[106]:

'There is no doubt that the question of whether or not the accommodation is suitable requires an assessment of all the qualities of the accommodation in the light of the needs and requirements of the homeless person and his or her family. This was recognised as long as 1991 by Henry J as he then was, in ... *Ex p Omar* ... As far as I am aware, this approach has not been doubted in any subsequent case. It seems to me that, if it be right that the relevant question is whether the relevant accommodation is suitable for the particular homeless person and his or her family, it is inevitable that the location of that accommodation may be relevant to an assessment of its suitability.'

In particular, bed and breakfast accommodation outside an authority's area *may* be suitable but the issue needs closely relating to the individual needs of the applicant and her/his family – as to work, education and health.

Legislation has further delineated the issue of suitability. The general provisions are contained in the Homelessness (Suitability of Accommodation) Order 1996 and s 210 of the Housing Act 1996.

## HOMELESSNESS (SUITABILITY OF ACCOMMODATION) ORDER 1996

SI 1996/3204

### Matters to be taken into account

2.   In determining whether it would be, or would have been, reasonable for a person to continue to occupy accommodation and in determining whether accommodation is suitable for a person there shall be taken into account whether or not the accommodation is affordable for that person and, in particular, the following matters—

   (a)   the financial resources available to that person, including, but not limited to—
   
      (i)   salary, fees and other remuneration;
      (ii)   social security benefits;

---

[104] [2002] EWHC 280 (Admin), [2003] HLR 1.
[105] (2000) 33 HLR 2.
[106] At p 28.

(iii) payments due under a court order for the making of periodical payments to a spouse or a former spouse, or to, or for the benefit of, a child;

(iv) payments of child support maintenance due under the Child Support Act 1991;

(v) pensions;

(vi) contributions to the costs in respect of the accommodation which are or were made or which might reasonably be expected to be, or have been, made by other members of his household;

(vii) financial assistance towards the costs in respect of the accommodation, including loans, provided by a local authority, voluntary organisation or other body;

(viii) benefits derived from a policy of insurance;

(ix) savings and other capital sums;

(b) the costs in respect of the accommodation, including, but not limited to,—

(i) payments of, or by way of, rent;

(ii) payments in respect of a licence or permission to occupy the accommodation;

(iii) mortgage costs;

(iv) payments of, or by way of, service charges;

(v) mooring charges payable for a houseboat;

(vi) where the accommodation is a caravan or a mobile home, payments in respect of the site on which it stands;

(vii) the amount of council tax payable in respect of the accommodation;

(viii) payments by way of deposit or security in respect of the accommodation;

(ix) payments required by an accommodation agency;

(c) payments which that person is required to make under a court order for the making of periodical payments to a souse or a former spouse, or to, or for the benefit of, a child and payments of child support maintenance required to be made under the Child Support Act 1991;

(d) that person's other reasonable living expenses.

Section 210 HA 1996 provides that in determining the issue of 'suitability', the authority should have regard to Parts IX, X and XI HA 1985 (slum clearance, overcrowding, houses in multiple occupation).

Recently, the Homelessness (Suitability of Accommodation) (England) Order 2003 (SI 2003/3326) has been introduced, curtailing the use of bed and breakfast accommodation where children are involved.

### Citation, commencement and application

1. (1) This Order may be cited as the Homelessness (Suitability of Accommodation) (England) Order 2003 and shall come into force on 1 April 2004.

(2) This Order applies in relation to the duties of local housing authorities in England to make accommodation available for occupation by applicants under Part 7 of the Housing Act 1996.

### Interpretation

2. In this Order—

'applicant with family commitments' means an applicant—

(a) who is pregnant

(b) with whom a pregnant woman resides or might reasonably be expected to reside; or

(c) with whom dependent children reside or might reasonably be expected to reside;

'B & B accommodation' means accommodation (whether or not breakfast is included).

(a)   which is not separate and self-contained premises; and

(b)   in which any one of the following amenities is shared by more than one household—

    (i)   a toilet;

    (ii)   personal washing facilities

    (iii)   cooking facilities

### Accommodation unsuitable where there is a family commitment

3.   Subject to the exceptions contained in article 4, B & B accommodation is not to be regarded as suitable for an applicant with family commitments where accommodation is made available for occupation—

(a)   under section 188(1), 190(2), 193(2) or 200(1); or

(b)   under section 195(2), where the accommodation is other than that occupied by the applicant t the time of making his application.

### Exceptions

4.   (1) Article 3 does not apply—

(a)   where no accommodation other than B & B accommodation is available for occupation by an applicant with family commitments; and

(b)   the applicant occupies B & B accommodation for a period, or a total of periods, which does not exceed 6 weeks.

(2) In calculating the period, or total period, of an applicant's occupation of B & B accommodation for the purposes of paragraph (1)(b), there shall be disregarded—

(a)   any period before 1 April 2004; and

(b)   where a local housing authority is subject to the duty under section 193 by virtue of section 200(4), any period before that authority became subject to that duty.

## RIGHT TO REQUEST REVIEW OF DECISION

## HOUSING ACT 1996

### 202.   Right to request review of decision

(1) An applicant has the right to request a review of—

(a)   any decision of a local housing authority as to his eligibility for assistance,

(b)   any decision of a local housing authority as to what duty (if any) is owed to him under sections 190 to 193 and 195 and 197 (duties to persons found to be homeless or threatened with homelessness),

(c)   any decision of a local housing authority to notify another authority under section 198(1) (referral of cases),

(d)   any decision under section 198(5) whether the conditions are met for the referral of his case,

(e)   any decision under section 200 (3) or (4) (decision as to duty owed to applicant whose case is considered for referral or referred), or

(f)   any decision of a local housing authority as to the suitability of accommodation offered to him in discharge of their duty under any of the provisions mentioned in paragraph (b) or (e).

(2) There is no right to request a review of the decision reached on an earlier review.

(3) A request for review must be made before the end of the period of 21 days beginning with the day on which he is notified of the authority's decision or such longer period as the authority may in writing allow.

(4) On a request being duly made to them, the authority or authorities concerned shall review their decision.

## 203. **Procedure on a review**

(1) The Secretary of State may make provision by regulations as to the procedure to be followed in connection with a review under section 202.

Nothing in the following provisions affects the generality of this power.

(2) Provision may be made by regulations—

(a) requiring the decision on review to be made by a person of appropriate seniority who was not involved in the original decision, and

(b) as to the circumstances in which the applicant is entitled to an oral hearing, and whether and by whom he may be represented at such a hearing.

(3) The authority, or as the case may be either of the authorities, concerned shall notify the applicant of the decision on the review.

(4) If the decision is—

(a) to confirm the original decision on any issue against the interests of the applicant, or

(b) to confirm a previous decision—

   (i) to notify another authority under section 198 (referral of cases), or

   (ii) that the conditions are met for the referral of his case,

they shall also notify him for the reasons of the decision.

(5) In any case they shall inform the applicant of his right to appeal to a county court on a point of law, and of the period within which such an appeal must be made (see section 204).

(6) Notice of the decision shall not be treated as given unless and until subsection (5), and where applicable subsection (4), is complied with.

(7) Provision may be made by regulations as to the period within which the review must be carried out and notice given of the decision.

(8) Notice required to be given to a person under this section shall be given in writing and, if not received by him, shall be treated as having been given if it is made available at the authority's office for a reasonable period for collection by him or on his behalf.

## 204. **Right of appeal to county court on point of law**

(1) If an applicant who has requested a review under section 202—

(a) is dissatisfied with the decision on the review, or

(b) is not notified of the decision on the review within the time prescribed under section 203,

he may appeal to the county court on any point of law arising from the decision or, as the case may be, the original decision.

(2) An appeal must be brought within 21 days of his being notified of the decision or, as the case may be, of the date on which he should have been notified of a decision on review.

(3) On appeal the court may make such order confirming, quashing or varying the decision as it thinks fit.

(4) Where the authority wee under a duty under section 199, 190 or 200 to secure that accommodation is available for the applicant's occupation, they may continue to secure that accommodation is so available—

(a) during the period for appealing under this section against the authority's decision, and

(b) if an appeal is brought, until the appeal (and any further appeal) is finally determined.

### 204A.   Section 204: appeals

(1) This section applies where an applicant has the right to appeal to the county court against a local housing authority's decision on a review.

(2) If the applicant is dissatisfied with a decision by the authority—

(a)   not to exercise their power under section 204(4) ('the section 204(4) power') in his case;

(b)   to exercise that power for a limited period ending before the final determination by the county court of his appeal under section 204(1) ('the main appeal'); or

(c)   to cease exercising that power before that time,

he may appeal to the county court against the decision.

(3) An appeal under this section may not be brought after the final determination by the county court of the main appeal.

(4) On an appeal under this section the court—

(a)   may order the authority to secure that accommodation is available for the applicant's occupation until the determination of the appeal (or such earlier time as the court may specify); and

(b)   shall confirm or quash the decision appealed against,

and in considering whether to confirm or quash the decision the court shall apply the principles applied by the High Court on an application for judicial review.

(5) If the court quashes the decision it may order the authority to exercise the section 204(4) power in the applicant's case for such period as may be specified in the order.

(6) An order under subsection (5)—

(a)   may only be made if the court is satisfied that failure to exercise the section 204(4) power in accordance with the order would substantially prejudice the applicant's ability to pursue the main appeal;

(b)   may not specify any period ending after the final determination by the county court of the main appeal.

For further discussion of review (appeal procedures see Chapter 6. For further discussion of homelessness and human rights issues see Chapter 14.

## SUPPLEMENTARY PROVISIONS OF THE HOUSING ACT 1996

### 205.   Discharge of functions: introductory

(1) The following sections have effect in relation to the discharge by a local housing authority of their functions under this Part to secure that accommodation is available for the occupation of a person—

section 206 (general provisions)
section 207 (provision of accommodation by authority)
section 208 (out-of-area placements)
section 209 (arrangements with private landlord).

### 206.   Discharge of functions by local housing authorities

(1) A local housing authority may discharge their housing functions under this Part only in the following ways—

(a)   by securing that suitable accommodation provided by them is available,

(b)   by securing that he obtains suitable accommodation from some other person, or

(c)   by giving him such advice and assistance as will secure that suitable accommodation is available from some other person.

(2) A local housing authority may require a person in relation to whom they are discharging such functions—

(a) to pay such reasonable charges as they may determine in respect of accommodation which they secure for his occupation (either by making it available themselves or otherwise), or

(b) to pay such reasonable amount as they may determine in respect of sums payable by them for accommodation made available by another person.

### 207. Discharge of functions: provision of accommodation by the authority

(1) A local housing authority shall not under section 206(1)(a) discharge their housing functions under this Part by providing accommodation other than—

(a) accommodation in a hostel within the meaning of section 622 of the Housing Act 1985, or

(b) accommodation leased to the authority as mentioned in subsection (2) below,

for more than two years (continuously or in aggregate) in any period of three years.

This applies irrespective of the number of applications for accommodation or assistance in obtaining accommodation made by the person concerned.

(2) The accommodation referred to in subsection (1)(b) is accommodation—

(a) leased to the authority with vacant possession for use as temporary housing accommodation on terms which include provision for the lessor to obtain vacant possession from the authority on the expiry of a specified period or when required by the lessor,

(b) the lessor of which is not an authority or body within section 80(1) of the Housing Act 1985 (the landlord condition for secure tenancies), and

(c) in which the authority have no interest other than under the lease in question or as a mortgagee.

(3) The authority shall not discharge such functions in relation to a person who—

(a) normally resides with another person as a member of his family, or

(b) might reasonably be expected to reside with another person,

in such a way that subsection (1) would be contravened if the functions were discharged in relation to that other person.

(4) The Secretary of State may, on the application of a local housing authority, by direction exclude or modify the operation of subsection (1) in relation to that authority if it appears to him that the authority will not otherwise be able reasonably to discharge their housing functions under this Part.

(5) Any such direction shall have effect only—

(a) with respect to applicants of a description specified in the direction, and

(b) for a period specified in the direction, which shall not exceed one year,

and may be expressed to have effect subject to any conditions specified in the direction.

(6) Where the Secretary of State gives or has given a direction under subsection (4), he may give the authority such directions as he considers appropriate as to the discharge of their housing functions under this Part in cases affected by the direction having or ceasing to have effect.

### 208. Discharge of functions: out-of-area placements

(1) So far as reasonably practicable a local housing authority shall in discharging their housing functions under this Part secure that accommodation is available for the occupation of the applicant in their district.

(2) If they secure that accommodation is available for the occupation of the applicant outside their district, they shall give notice to the local housing authority in whose district the accommodation is situated.

(3) The notice shall state—

(a)   the name of the applicant,
(b)   the number and description of other persons who normally reside with him as a member of his family or might reasonably be expected to reside with him,
(c)   the address of the accommodation,
(d)   the date on which the accommodation was made available to him, and
(e)   which function under this Part the authority was discharging in securing that the accommodation is available for his occupation.

(4) The notice must be in writing, and must be given before the end of the period of 14 days beginning with the day on which the accommodation was made available to the applicant.

### 209.   Discharge of functions: arrangements with private landlord

(1) This section applies where in pursuance of any of their housing functions under this Part a local housing authority make arrangements with a private landlord to provide accommodation.

For this purpose a 'private landlord' means a landlord who is not within section 80(1) of the Housing Act 1985 (the landlord condition for secure tenancies).

(2) If the housing function arises under section 188, 190, 200 or 204(4) (interim duties), a tenancy granted in pursuance of the arrangements to a person specified by the authority cannot be an assured tenancy before the end of the period of twelve months beginning with—

(a)   the date on which the applicant was notified of the authority's decision under section 184(3) or 198(5), or
(b)   if there is a review of that decision under section 202 or an appeal to the court under section 204, the date on which he is notified of the decision on review or the appeal is finally determined,

unless, before or during that period, the tenant is notified by the landlord (or, in the cases of joint landlords, at least one of them) that the tenancy is to be regarded as an assured shorthold tenancy or an assured tenancy other than an assured shorthold tenancy.

A registered social landlord cannot serve such a notice making such a tenancy an assured tenancy other than an assured shorthold tenancy.

(3) Where in any other case a tenancy is granted in pursuance of the arrangements by a registered social landlord to a person specified by the authority—#

(a)   the tenancy cannot be an assured tenancy unless it is an assured shorthold tenancy, and
(b)   the landlord cannot convert the tenancy to an assured tenancy unless the accommodation is allocated to the tenant under Part VI.

## FURTHER READING

Arden, A and Hunter, C, *Homelessness and Allocations* (6th ed, 2002) Legal Action Group.

Cowan, D, *Housing Law and Policy* (1999) Macmillan, Chapter 7.

Hughes, D and Lowe, S, *Public Sector Housing Law* (3rd ed, 2000) Butterworths, Chapter 6.

Robson, P and Poustie, M, *Homeless People and the Law* (3rd ed, 1996) Planning Exchange (Butterworths).

# Chapter 11

# HOUSING AND THE FAMILY

## INTRODUCTION

The interface between housing law and family law, with which this chapter is concerned, is complex and uncertain. Not least amongst the uncertainties is that involved in deciding on the exact focus of coverage. The death of a partner to a relationship, or another family member, or the breakdown of a relationship have many serious consequences that are far from the sole preserve of housing law, or, indeed, of the law at all. Most of the key issues concerning (for example) property transfers between partners, or the interests of (any) children of the relationship, are clearly the concern of family law and are wholly outside the scope of this book. However, in other areas, for example the future of a tenanted family home, a housing law perspective may well be distinctive and valuable, even if there is inevitable overlap with family law issues. Moreover, there are other areas which are clearly of chief concern to housing law rather than family law, such as statutory rights of succession to tenanted property (see also Chapter 4 and Chapter 8) and the difficulties raised by joint tenancies. (See Chapter 3).

A key issue which threads through this chapter is the shifting and relative concept of the 'family' itself. Judicial and legislative attitudes towards the scope of the idea of what can constitute a 'family' have changed enormously over the last 50 years. For example, in *Gammans v Ekins*[1] a cohabiting heterosexual couple were adjudged by the Court of Appeal not to be members of the same family, for the purposes of succession to a tenancy. Asquith LJ[2] summed up the view of the court: 'To say of two people masquerading ... as husband and wife ... that they were members of the same family, seems to be an abuse of the English language.' By 1999 in *Fitzpatrick v Sterling Housing Association Ltd*[3], the House of Lords decided that a longstanding homosexual relationship could be seen as putting the 'partners' to it in a 'family' relationship for succession purposes. Moreover, in the Court of Appeal one of the lord justices, Ward LJ, had gone so far as to decide that same-sex partners should be (in all respects) equated with married and unmarried heterosexual couples. He stated[4]: 'In my judgment, our society has shown itself to be tolerant enough to free

---

[1]  [1950] 2 KB 328.
[2]  At p 331.
[3]  [2001] 1 AC 27.
[4]  [1997] 4 All ER 991, at p 1023.

itself from the burdens of stereotype and prejudice … the common man … would recognise that [this] relationship was to all intents and purposes a marriage'.

The House of Lords felt unable to go this far, but judicial thinking has clearly shifted considerably from a view of the 'family' as solely a function of biology or marriage, and is certainly moving in the direction of viewing any relatively long-term and stable relationship as conferring 'family' status. Nevertheless, serious issues remain concerning the consistency of the approach of the courts and of inconsistency between differing legislative provisions. These inconsistencies have been thrown into sharp relief by decisions since 1999 invoking the Human Rights Act 1998[5], which are discussed in depth in Chapter 14 and again below.

The following material is divided into three sections: an initial section on the meaning of 'family', as seen by the courts and by legislation; a section concerned with the housing law consequences of relationship breakdown, at common law and under legislation; and, the distinct problems raised by the existence of joint tenancies between family members.

## Note

Though it is confusing, in 1996, following the Family Law Act of that year, the law changed from speaking of 'cohabitees' to 'cohabitants'. This should be remembered in reading what follows.

## THE FAMILY: A PROBLEM OF DEFINITION

Most of the relevant judicial discussion of the definition of 'family' has taken place in the context of the succession provisions in the Rent Act 1977, the Housing Act 1988 and the Housing Act 1985. The detailed rules as to what types of tenancy can pass on death were considered in Chapters 4 and 8, but running through all the detailed, and often highly technical, law on the subject is the general notion that succession should be available to spouses and other 'family' members and not more widely. This, in its turn, has forced the courts to return on many occasions to consider how widely 'family' should be construed for this purpose. From time to time legislative amendments have refocused the discussion, as, for example, in the Housing Act 1988 amendments to the definition of 'family' in Sch 1 to the Rent Act 1977 (set out in Chapter 4) which clarified the legal position of cohabitees. Equally, legislation is not always consistent in its approach, as a comparison of the amended Sch 1 to the Rent Act 1977 with s 113 of the Housing Act 1985 will demonstrate. Although the most recent case law indicates a desire in the courts to achieve a greater degree of consistency across the various statutory provisions (see *Fitzpatrick v Sterling Housing Association Ltd* [1997] 4 All ER[6]), for ease of exposition the law is considered respectively under the Rent Act 1977, the Housing Act 1988, and the Housing Act 1985.

---

[5]   For example, [2002] 4 All ER 1162 and [2002] 4 All ER 1136.
[6]   [2001] 1 AC 27.

## Rent Act 1977

The relevant provisions are contained in Sch 1 to the Rent Act 1977, as amended by Sch 4 to the Housing Act 1988. They are set out in detail in Chapter 4.

The crucial amendments introduced by the 1988 Act were that 'family' members other than spouses could succeed only to an assured tenancy, that to do so such a person must have resided with the deceased tenant for at least two years (previously six months had been sufficient to 'trigger' potential succession to a statutory tenancy) and that those living together 'as wife or husband' were henceforward to be treated as spouses. The last amendment is of particular importance to the question of defining 'family'. Prior to *Dyson Holdings Ltd v Fox*[7], the courts had taken a narrow approach to the definition, refusing to extend it beyond close and clearly established biological relationships. Following *Dyson*, a cohabitee of long standing qualified, provided there had been a sexual relationship, but doubts remained about the position of short-term cohabitees, even though there had been a sexual relationship (see *Helby v Rafferty*[8]), and a purely platonic relationship, however longstanding, certainly did not qualify (see *Carega Properties SA v Sharratt*)[9]. The 1988 Act amendments remove any uncertainty concerning heterosexual couples who have been sharing a common household long enough for them to be seen to be living together 'as ... wife or husband'. Indeed such couples now have superior status to other 'family' members, such as sons and daughters, in that, like spouses, they can succeed to a statutory tenancy and need have served no 'qualification' period prior to the death to gain such rights.

What was left uncertain by the 1988 amendments was the extent to which 'family' covered non-heterosexual relationships, in particular whether it could be extended to friends who have shared a common household for a significant period, and homosexual relationships. *Carega Properties SA v Sharratt*[10] indicated that such relationships did *not* generally convert those involved into members of a 'family'.

In 1957, when he was aged 24, Sharratt had formed a friendship with a widow of 75. From 1958, he lived with her in a flat of which she was the contractual tenant. Initially, he paid for the use of a room in the flat, but later the widow paid the whole rent, although other expenses were shared. Neither party was dependent on the other, but a close 'platonic' relationship developed, akin to aunt and nephew. On the expiry of the contractual tenancy, in 1973, the widow became a statutory tenant. In 1976 she died, but Sharratt continued to reside in the flat.

In an action for possession by the landlords, Sharratt claimed that he had succeeded to the widow's statutory tenancy, in that he had been a member of her 'family' resident with her for the requisite six-month period (now Rent Act 1977 Sch 3, para 3). However, although this claim was upheld by the High Court, the Court of Appeal allowed the landlord's appeal, finding that no 'familial nexus' had come into being. The House of Lords unanimously agreed with the Court of Appeal.

---

[7]   [1976] QB 503.
[8]   [1979] 1 WLR 13.
[9]   [1979] 2 All ER 1084.
[10]  [1979] 1 WLR 13.

Lord Diplock stated[11]:

'…

My Lords, the only question in this appeal is one of construction of the Rent Act 1968. It is whether a person between whom and the deceased statutory tenant of a dwelling house there is no connection by way of consanguinity, of affinity, of adoption (de jure or de facto) during minority or of regular sexual intercourse (past or present) can be a member of the tenant's family within the meaning of Schedule 1, paragraph 3 to the Act, so as to entitle him to become the statutory tenant of the dwelling house by succession to the deceased.

…

The deceased statutory tenant of the flat 48, Coleherne Court, London, SW5, of which the respondents claim possession, was Lady Salter, the widow of a High Court judge, who had died as long ago as 1929. In 1957, when she was aged 75, she first met the appellant, Mr Sharratt, who was then aged 24. They shared a mutual interest in politics and the theatre and a close friendship grew up between them. In the following year, Lady Salter suggested that Mr Sharratt should come to live in her flat at Coleherne Court. He fell in with this suggestion and for the first three years that he resided there he paid her £4 a week for bed and breakfast. After that the payments ceased. Lady Salter at all times paid the rent of the flat, but the other expenses were shared between them. This continued until her death at the age of 94 in April 1976.

The relationship between them throughout was platonic and filial. He behaved towards her as a dutiful and affectionate son and looked after her during her declining years. She would have liked to speak of him as her son, but this was not acceptable to Mr Sharratt, whose mother was still alive; so they decided that he would call her Aunt Nora and she addressed him by an affectionate nickname. There was throughout no question of his being financially dependent on her. All that he did for her over the 18 years that he resided with her in the flat had no other motive than kindness and affection.

My Lords, the bare recital of these facts makes one desirous, if one can, to gratify Mr Sharratt's wish to continue to reside in the flat where he had lived for so long before Lady Salter's death. Judge Solomon in the West London County Court, where the action by the landlords for possession of the flat was brought, felt himself able to do so.

"I have come to the conclusion, he said, that Lady Salter and this defendant achieved through their relationship what must surely be regarded in a popular sense, and in common sense, as a familial nexus. That is to say, a nexus such as one would find only within a family. I am sure Shakespeare's man would say: 'Yes, it is stranger than fiction, but they established a familial tie. Everyone linked to her through the blood was remote by comparison with the defendant'."

[11] Ibid, at p 1085.

The reference to Shakespeare's man is an allusion to the description 'base, common and popular' which in *Langdon v Horton* [1951] Sir Raymond Evershed MR borrowed from Henry V, Act IV, scene 1, to describe the ordinary man mentioned by Cohen LJ in *Brock v Wollams* [1949] where he said:

> "The question the county court judge should have asked himself was this: Would an ordinary man, addressing his mind to the question whether Mrs Wollams was a member of the family or not, have answered 'yes' or 'no'?"

This test, which does no more than say that "family" where it is used in the Rent Acts is not a term of art but is used in its ordinary popular meaning, has been repeatedly referred to and applied in subsequent cases.

The Court of Appeal (Megaw, Lawton and Browne LJJ) unanimously reversed the judgment of Judge Solmon. Megaw LJ after quoting the "Cohen question" went on to say, in my view quite correctly:

> "... it is for this court to decide, where such an issue arises, whether, assuming all the facts found by the judge to be correct, the question may, as a matter of law, within the permissible limits of the meaning of the phrase 'a member of the tenant's family,' be answered 'Yes'."

Megaw LJ and Lawton LJ both answered the question with a confident 'No'; and so would I. Browne LJ agreed, but rather more hesitantly. However, he also thought that the Court of Appeal was bound to allow the appeal because of two previous decisions of its own, *Gammans v Ekins* and *Ross v Collins*.

*Gammans v Ekins* was a case of co-habitation by an unmarried couple, a relationship which raises questions upon which I find it unnecessary and inappropriate to enter for the purpose of disposing of the instant appeal. *Ross v Collins*, on the other hand, was much like the instant case, save that the sexes of the older party, who was devotedly cared for, and the younger party who did the caring, were reversed. As my reason for dismissing the instant appeal, I would not seek to improve upon what was said there by my noble and learned friend (then Russell LJ):

> "Granted that 'family' is not limited to cases of a strict legal familial nexus, I cannot agree that it extends to a case such as this. It still requires, it seems to me, at least a broadly recognisable de facto familial nexus. This may be capable of being found and recognised as such by the ordinary man – where the link would be strictly familial had there been a marriage, or where the link is through adoption of a minor, de jure or de facto, or where the link is 'step-', or where the link is 'in-law' or by marriage. But two strangers cannot, it seems to me, ever establish artificially for the purposes of this section a familial nexus by acting as brothers or as sisters, even if they call each other such and consider their relationship to be tantamount to that. Nor, in my view, can an adult man and woman who establish a platonic relationship establish a familial nexus by acting as a devoted brother and sister or father and daughter would act, even if they address

each other as such and even if they refer to each other as such and regard their association as tantamount to such. Nor, in my view, would they indeed be recognised as familial links by the ordinary man."

I would accordingly dismiss this appeal.'

The judgments in *Carega v Sharratt* are brief and narrowly focused, not attempting any extensive examination of the concept of 'family'[12]. However, more recently in *Fitzpatrick v Sterling Housing Association*[13] the House of Lords ranges very widely indeed, considering the approach of foreign jurisdictions, legislative provisions in other fields (for example, social security) and some of the academic material on the subject.

In 1976, Martin Fitzpatrick moved into a flat of which John Thompson was the statutory tenant. From that date onwards Fitzpatrick and Thompson maintained a close and faithful homosexual relationship together, and shared the flat on this basis. In 1986 Thompson suffered head injuries in a fall, and a subsequent stroke, which left him tetraplegic. From then on, Fitzpatrick nursed Thompson and provided him with 24-hour care (giving up his own job to do so). Thompson died in 1994, and Fitzpatrick applied to take over the statutory tenancy. The landlords, who wished to re-house Fitzpatrick in smaller accommodation, refused to agree. Fitzpatrick then applied to the courts for a declaration that he was entitled to succeed to the statutory tenancy. His application was dismissed, somewhat reluctantly, by the county court. By a 2:1 majority (Ward LJ dissenting) the Court of Appeal upheld the county court judgment. However, the House of Lords held (by a 3:2 majority) that Fitzpatrick could succeed to an assured tenancy under Rent Act 1977 Sch 1, para 3 as a member of Thompson's 'family'.

Lord Slynn stated[14]:

'It has been suggested that for your Lordships to decide this appeal in favour of the plaintiff would be to usurp the function of Parliament. It is trite that that is something the courts must not do. When considering social issues in particular judges must not substitute their own views to fill gaps. They must consider whether the new facts "fall within the Parliamentary intention": *Royal College of Nursing of the United Kingdom v Department of Health and Social Security* [1981] AC 800, 822 per Lord Wilberforce. Thus in the present context if, for example, it was explicit or clear that Parliament intended the word "family" to have a narrow meaning for all time, it would be a court's duty to give effect to it whatever changes in social attitudes a court might think ought to be reflected in the legislation. Similarly if it were explicit or clear that the word must be given a very wide meaning so as to cover relationships for which a court, conscious of the traditional views of society might disapprove, the court's duty would be to give effect to it. It is, however, for the court in the first place to interpret each phrase in its statutory context. To do so is not to usurp Parliament's function; not to do so would be to

---

[12]  Although they are on all fours with the approach taken by the Court of Appeal in relation to a carer – see *Ross v Collins* [1964] 1 All ER 861, referred to by Lord Diplock in the above extract.

[13]  [2001] 1 AC 27, [1999] 4 All ER 705.

[14]  Ibid at p 33 in the AC report, p 710 in All ER.

abdicate the judicial function. If Parliament takes the view that the result is not what is wanted it will change the legislation.

The question is, therefore, was the plaintiff the spouse of or a member of the family of Mr Thompson within the meaning of this Act? I stress "within the meaning of this Act" since it is all that your Lordships are concerned with. In other statutes, in other contexts, the words may have a wider or a narrower meaning than here.

...

It is, however, obvious that the word "family" is used in a number of different senses, some wider, some narrower. "Do you have any family?" usually means "Do you have children?" "We're having a family gathering" may include often distant relatives and even very close friends. "The family of nations", "the Christian family" are very wide. This is no new phenomenon. Roman law, as I understand it, included in the familiar all members of the social unit though other rights might be limited to spouses or heirs.

It is not an answer to the problem to assume (as I accept may be correct) that if in 1920 people had been asked whether one person was a member of another same-sex person's family the answer would have been "No". That is not the right question. The first question is what were the characteristics of a family in the 1920 Act and the second whether two same-sex partners can satisfy those characteristics so as today to fall within the word "family". An alternative question is whether the word "family" in the 1920 Act has to be updated so as to be capable of including persons who today would be regarded as being of each other's family, whatever might have been said in 1920: see *R v Ireland* [1998] AC 147, 158, per Lord Steyn; *Bennion, Statutory Interpretation,* 3rd ed (1997), p 686 and *Halsbury's Laws of England*, 4th ed reissue, vol 44(I) (1995), p 904, para 1473.

If "family" could only mean a legal relationship (of blood or by legal ceremony of marriage or by legal adoption) then the plaintiff must obviously fail. Over the years, however, the courts have held that this is not so.

In the first place it has been said that the ordinary meaning of the word is to be taken; "family" where it is used in the Rent Acts is not a term of art: *Joram Developments Ltd v Sharratt* [1979] 1 WLR 928, 931 per Lord Diplock, though the meaning for Viscount Dilhorne, at p 932, is a question of law and "family" is not the same as "household".

In the second place it has been accepted that de facto relationships can be recognised as constituting a family. Thus in *Brock v Wollams* [1949] 2 KB 388, a child adopted in fact who lived with the tenant for many years, but who was not adopted under the Adoption of Children Act 1926, was held to be a member of his family living with him at his death within the meaning of the Act 1920. Bucknill LJ, at p 393, cited with apparent approval the judgment of Wright J in *Price v Gould* (1930) 46 TLR 411 where he said in relation to wills and settlements that the legislature had used the word "family" "to introduce a flexible and wide term" so that brothers and sisters of the tenant were family for the purposes of the Act. Bucknill L J had not doubt that both de facto adopted and illegitimate children were included as family. Denning LJ added, at p 396:

> "It seems to me that 'members of the tenant's family' within section 12(1)(g) of the 1920 Act, include not only legitimate children but also step-children, illegitimate children and adopted children, whether adopted in due form of law or not."

...

In the application of this "ordinary meaning", "de facto" approach there are not surprisingly decisions on both sides of the line. In *Helby v Rafferty* [1979] 1 WLR 13, the court refused to hold that a mean who had lived with a woman tenant for five years before her death, but they had deliberately opted to retain their formal independence and they had not been recognised as being married, were part of the same family. In *Watson v Lucas* [1980] 1 WLR 1493, on the other hand, the Court of Appeal by a majority held that a woman who had lived with a man, although he remained married to his wife, was a member of his family for the purpose of Schedule 1 to the 1977 Act because of the lasting relationship between them. In *Hawes v Evenden* [1953] 1 WLR 1169, the claimant was an unmarried woman who had lived with the deceased tenant for 12 years and had had two children with him. The court held that there was evidence that the claimant and the tenant and the children had lived together as a family and she was therefore a member of his family for the purposes of the 1920 Act. In *Chios Property Investment Co Ltd v Lopez* (1987) 20 HLR 120 the court stressed the importance of a "sufficient state of permanence and stability" having been reached in the relationship so as to constitute family. In *Jones v Whitehill* [1950] 2 KB 204, a woman who out of love and kindness went to live with her aunt and uncle, was held on the uncle's death to be a member of his family.

The high water mark one way is *Gammans v Ekins* [1950] 2 KB 328. There the claimant had lived with a woman tenant and they were regarded in he neighbourhood as man and wife. It was held that he could not be a member of her family for the 1920 Act. Asquith LJ, at p 331, said that if their relationship was sexual "it seems to me anomalous that a person can acquire a 'status of irremovability' by living or having lived in sin, even if the liaison has not been a mere casual encounter but protracted in time and conclusive in character". Lord Evershed MR saw considerable force in the claimant's argument but finally agreed in the result. He added, at p 334:

> "It may not be a bad thing that by this decision it is shown that, in the Christian society in which we live, one, at any rate, of the privileges which may be derived from marriage is not equally enjoyed by those living together as man and wife but who are not married."

The high water mark the other way is *Dyson Holdings Ltd v Fox* [1976] QB 503. This decision has however been confined to its own facts or doubted by Roskill LJ in *Helby v Rafferty* [1979] 1 WLR 13, 23–24 and by Oliver LJ in *Watson v Lucas* [1980] 1 WLR 1493, 1503–1504. In the *Dyson* case the defendant had lived with the tenant for 21 years until his death. They were unmarried and had no children. Reversing the county court judge, the Court of Appeal ruled that she was a member of his family.

…

Given, on the basis of these earlier decisions that the word is to be applied, flexibly, and does not cover only legally binding relationships, it is necessary to ask what are its characteristics in this legislation and to answer that question to ask further what was Parliament's purpose. It seems to me that the intention in 1920 was that not just the legal wife but also the other members of the family unit occupying the property on the death of the tenant with him should qualify for the succession. The former did not need to prove a qualifying period; as a member of the tenant's family a two-year residence had to be shown. If more than one person qualified then if no agreement could be reached between them the court decided who should succeed.

The hallmarks of the relationship were essentially that there should be a degree of mutual interdependence, of the sharing of lives, of caring and love, of commitment and support. In respect of legal relationships these are presumed, though evidently are not always present as the family law and criminal courts now only too well. In de facto relationships these are capable, if proved, of creating membership of the tenant's family. If, as I consider, this was the purpose of the legislation, the question is then who in 1994 or today (I draw no distinction between them) are capable in law of being members of the tenant's family. It is not who would have been so considered in 1920. In considering this question it is necessary to have regard to changes in attitude. The point cannot have been better put than it was by Sir Thomas Bingham MR in *R v Ministry of Defence, ex p Smith* [1996] QB 517, 552–554 when, although dealing with the validity of an administrative decision rather than the meaning of a few words in a statute, he said, after referring to changes of attitude in society towards same-sex relationships:

> "I regard the progressive development and refinement of public and professional opinion at home and abroad, here very briefly described, as an important feature of this case. A belief which represented unquestioned orthodoxy in year X may have become questionable by year Y and unsustainable by Year Z Public and professional opinion are a continuum."

If "meaning" is substituted for "opinion" the words are no less appropriate. In *Barclays Bank plc v O'Brien* [1994] 1 AC 180, 198 Lord Browne-Wilkinson (with whom other members of the House agreed) said that in relation to the equity arising from undue influence in a loan transaction:

> "But in my judgment the same principles are applicable to all other cases where there is an emotional relationship between cohabitees. The 'tenderness' shown by the law to married women is not based on the marriage ceremony but reflects the underlying risk of one cohabite exploiting the emotional involvement and trust of the other. Now that unmarried cohabitation, whether heterosexual or homosexual, is widespread in our society, the law should recognise this."

...

If, as I think, in the light of all the authorities this is the proper interpretation of the Act of 1920 I hold that as a matter of law a same-sex partner of a deceased tenant can establish the necessary familial link. They are capable of being in Russell LJ's words in *Ross v Collins* [1964] 1 WLR 425, 432: "A broadly recognisable de facto familial nexus". It is then a question of fact as to whether he or she does establish the necessary link.

It is accordingly not necessary to consider the alternative question as to whether by 1999 the meaning of the word in the 1920 Act needs to be updated. I prefer to say that it is not the meaning which has changed but that those who are capable of falling within the words have changed.

We have been referred to a number of authorities in other jurisdictions. I wish to mention only two. Your Lordships' attention has been drawn to *Braschi v Stahl Associates Co* (1989) 544 NYS'sd 784. There the issue was as to the meaning of the New York City Rent and Eviction Regulations which provided that a landlord might not dispossess "either the surviving spouse of the deceased tenant or some other member of the deceased's tenant's family who has been living with the tenant". The majority of the New York Court of Appeals held, at pp 788–789:

> "The intended protection against sudden eviction should not rest on fictitious legal distinctions or genetic history, but instead should find its foundation in the reality of family life. In the context of eviction, a more realistic, and certainly equally valid, view of a family includes two adult lifetime partners whose relationship is long term and characterised by an emotional and financial commitment and interdependence."

In law therefore, a same-sex partner of the deceased tenant was, it was held, able to qualify if he could produce the necessary evidence.

The second case to which I refer is *El-Al, The Israeli Airlines Ltd v Danilowitz* (unreported) 4 May 1994; National Journal of Sexual Orientation Law, vol I, pp 307–308. That was a case involving the provision of airline tickets for a married spouse and an unmarried cohabitant of a different sex. It was not provided to same-sex partners. Vice-Chief Justice Barak, sitting in the Supreme Court of Israel, said:

> "The benefit is thus provided to a lasting 'living-together' partnership which displays a strongly tied up social relationship. It is therefore obvious, in my view, that to take this benefit away from homosexual spouses constitutes a discriminatory violation of the equality principle. The differentiating reason sanding behind this decision has to do with sexual orientation. But this latter fact was both immaterial and unfair ... Does a homosexual cohabitation differ from a heterosexual one, as far as partner-ship, unity and a social-cell relationship are concerned?"

European Convention for the Protection of Human Rights and Fundament al Freedoms (1953) (Cmd 8969) refers to family and family lie in articles 8 and 12 and the Court of Human Rights has not so far accepted claims by same-sex partners to family rights. Leaving aside the fact that these cases are still in an early stage of development of the law and that attitudes may change as to what is acceptable throughout Europe, I do not consider that these decisions impinge on the decision which your Lordships have to take on a specific statutory provision.

In this regard I refer to *Attorney-General of Canada v Mossop* (1993) 100 DLR (4th) 658 where the High Court of Canada held by a majority of four to three that the term "family status" in the Canadian Human Rights Act does not include a homosexual relationship between two individuals. Lamer CJC (of the majority), however, concluded, at p 674:

> "Nor should this decision be interpreted as meaning that homosexual couples cannot constitute a 'family' for the purposes of legislation other than the CHRA. In this regard, each statute must be interpreted in its own context."

Sopinka and Iacobucci JJ agreed with Lamer CJC.

It seems to be suggested that the result which I have so far indicated would be cataclysmic. In relation to this Act it is plainly not so. The onus on one person claiming that he or she was a member of the same-sex original tenant's family will involve that person establishing rather than merely asserting the necessary indicia of the relationship. A transient superficial relationship will not do even if it is intimate. Mere cohabitation by friends as a matter of convenience will not do. There is, in any event, a minimum residence qualification; the succession is limited to that of the original tenant. Far from being cataclysmic it is, as both the judge in the county court and the Court of Appeal appear to recognise, and as I consider, in accordance with contemporary notions of social justice. In other statutes, in other contexts, the same meaning may or not be the right one. If a narrower meaning is required, so be it. It seems also to be suggested that such a result in this statute undermines the traditional (whether religious or social) concept of marriage and the family. It does nothing of the sort. It merely recognises that, for the purposes of this Act, two people of the same sex can be regarded as having established membership of a family, one of the most significant of human relationships which both gives benefits and imposes obligations.

It is plain on the findings of the judge in the county court that in this case, on the view of the law which I have accepted, on the facts the plaintiff succeeds as a member of Mr Thompson's family living with him at his death.

On that ground I would allow the appeal.'

Lords Nicholls and Clyde agreed with Lord Slynn. Lords Hutton and Hobhouse dissented, in effect because the legislation involved the assessment of conflicting social priorities, the resolutions of which were more properly the province of Parliament than the courts. Parliament had had ample opportunity to extend the statutory definitions to include same-sex couples (for example in the Housing Act 1988) and had failed to do so. It was, however, inappropriate for the courts to usurp Parliament's function[15]. They also pointed out that the decision of the majority, whilst removing one anomaly, opened up others, in that carers, friends and all others in relationships lacking a sexual element (heterosexual or homosexual) remained outside the scheme of statutory protection.

It needs to be remembered that whilst the decision of the majority in *Fitzpatrick* recognised Fitzpatrick's right as a member of Thompson's family the House unanimously emphasised that his position could not be equated with that of a heterosexual cohabitant able under the Rent Act 1977 Sch 1 para 2(2) to succeed to a statutory tenancy (and without a further two year residential qualification). To qualify under para 2(2) and so be 'treated as [a] spouse' it was necessary to have been 'living with the original tenant as his or her wife or husband'. As a matter of legislative construction, the House found that a same-sex relationship could not be brought within these words. As Lord Slynn put it[16]:

> 'The first question then is whether the plaintiff was the "spouse" of Mr Thompson within the meaning of paragraph 2 of Schedule 1 to the 1977 Act, as amended. I recognise that if the non-gender specific noun "spouse" stood alone the matter might be more debatable as Mr Blake contends, though the ordinary meaning is plainly "husband" or "wife". In the context of this Act, however, a "spouse" means in my view legally a husband or wife. The 1988 amendment extended the meaning to include as a "spouse" a person living with the original tenant "as his or her wife or husband". This was obviously intended to include persons not legally husband and wife who lived as such without being married. That prima facie means a man and a woman, and the man must show that the woman was living with him as "his" wife; the woman that he was living with her as "her" husband. I do not think that Parliament as recently as 1988 intended that these words should be read as meaning "my same sex partner" rather than specifically "my husband" or "my wife"; if that had been the intention it would have been spelled out. The words cannot in my view be read as the plaintiff contends. I thus agree as to the result with the decision in *Harrogate Borough Council v Simpson* (1984) 17 HLR 205. The plaintiff accordingly fails in the first way he puts his appeal. Whether that result is discriminatory against same-sex couples in the light of the fact that non-married different sex couples living together are t be treated as spouses so as to allow one to succeed to the tenancy of the other ma have to be considered when the Human Rights Act 1998 is in force. Whether the result is socially desirable in 1999 is a matter for Parliament'.

Lord Slynn acknowledged that this result could be seen as discriminatory, and might have to be reconsidered when the (then pending) Human Rights Act 1998 came into force[17]. His words have proved prophetic, in that the Law Commission have proposed major changes in this area of the law[18] and there are pending legislative reforms contained in the Civil Partnerships Bill 2004. Moreover, in

---

[15]  See also S Cretney and F Reynolds, 'Limits of the Judicial Function' (2000) LQR Vol 116, p 181 who agree with the dissentients.
[16]  [2001] 1 AC 27, at p 34, [1999] 4 All ER 705, at p 710.
[17]  See Chapter 14.
[18]  Law Commission, *Renting Homes*, Cm 6018 Part XIV.

*Ghaidan v Godin-Mendoza*[19] a human rights challenge finally reached the courts. The wider issues raised by the case are discussed Chapter 14. However, in the immediate context it should be noted that, having established that discrimination incompatible with human rights legislation did exist in relation to the pre-existing state of the law, the Court of Appeal chose to remedy this not by a declaration of incompatibility but by using its wide interpretive powers under s 3 of the Human Rights Act 1998. Specifically, the court read the words 'as his or her wife or husband' to mean 'as if they were his or her wife or husband', thereby enabling Juan Godin-Mendoza to succeed to a statutory tenancy, and not merely an assured tenancy. The House of Lords has now confirmed this decision.

*Godin-Mendoza* has been welcomed by many as injecting an anti-discriminatory impulse into the law of housing under the influence of human rights thinking[20]. It has also been criticised as 'usurping Parliament' and creating 'a new category of de facto marriage'[21]. Certainly the courts use of its powers under s 3 to (in effect) re-write the relevant Rent Act succession provisions is contentious. However, legislative amendments have now been brought forward which, if they become law, will provide for the equivalence of same-sex and heterosexual relationships, in this as in many other fields (see below). In the interim *Godin-Mendoza* itself represents a major step in the same.

## Housing Act 1988

The relevant provisions are contained in s 17 of the Housing Act 1988, which is set out in detail in Chapter 4. As noted there, rights of succession under the 1988 Act are far more limited than under the Rent Act 1977. Only 'spouses' (inclusive of heterosexual relationships under s 17(4)) can succeed to the tenancy, and not any other 'family' member. The definition of putative spouse in s 17(4) clearly excludes homosexual relationships. The legislative amendments contained in the Civil Partnerships Bill 2004 extend to the Housing Act 1988 in equivalent fashion to the Rent Act 1977.

## Housing Act 1985

Secure tenancies (as discussed in Chapter 8) devolve by law to spouses and family members (see s 87 and s 89, Housing Act 1985). Further, there is an absolute right to assign the tenancy to anyone who would have been qualified to succeed to the secure tenancy on death (s 91(3)(c), Housing Act 1985). This is in clear contrast with the private sector position (for example, under s 15 of the Housing Act 1988 it is an implied term of every assured tenancy that no assignment of the tenancy is permissible without the landlord's consent). In addition, s 113 of the Housing Act 1985 appears to adopt a helpfully wide definition of 'family':

---

[19]  [2002] EWCA Civ 1533, [2002] 4 All ER 1162; confirmed (HL) [2004] UKHL 30, [2004] 3 All ER 411.
[20]  A Grear, 'A tale of the land, the insider, the outsider and human rights' (2003) 23(1) Legal Studies 33.
[21]  B Hewson, 'Usurping Parliament?' (2002) (146) SJ 1127.

113. **Member of a person's family**

(1) A person is a member of another's family within the meaning of this Part if—

(a) he is the spouse of that person, or he and that person live together as husband and wife, or

(b) he is that person's parent, grandparent, child, grandchild, brother, sister, uncle, aunt, nephew or niece.

(2) For the purpose of subsection (1)(b)—

(a) a relationship by marriage shall be treated as a relationship by blood,

(b) a relationship of the half-blood shall be treated as a relationship of the whole blood,

(c) the stepchild of a person shall be treated as his child, and

(d) an illegitimate child shall be treated as the legitimate child of his mother and reputed father.

There is little doubt that this explicitness is, in general, helpful in removing much of the uncertainty encountered in the private sector. Moreover, the definition, in general, adopts a wide ('extended'?) view of the 'family', encompassing both blood and marriage relationships and clearly including heterosexual cohabitants. However, there is a clear anomaly in that such cohabitants do not acquire the same status as married couples, but rather are treated in the same way as all other 'family' members in that 12 months' residence with the deceased tenant prior to the death is required before succession rights arise.

More generally, could it be that the very explicitness of s 113 is a barrier to any judicial desire to reflect changing views as to the meaning of 'family'? The *Dyson v Fox* approach, applied in the private sector (with varying degrees of enthusiasm) since 1975, allows the courts to reflect changing 'popular' attitudes as to the meaning of 'family', the concept being statutorily undefined. Section 113, on the other hand, appears to provide a definitive and all-inclusive list of those relationships which can be treated as 'family' ones for Housing Act 1985 purposes. Specifically, since homosexual relationships are not mentioned, *must* they be seen as implicitly *excluded*, particularly since heterosexual cohabitation is specifically included? This was certainly the view of the Court of Appeal in *Harrogate Borough Council v Simpson*[22]. In particular, at p 210, Watkins LJ stated: 'Mrs Davies who appears for the plaintiffs, contends that, if Parliament had wished homosexual relationships to be brought into the realm of the lawfully recognised state of a living together of man and wife for the purpose of the relevant legislation, it would plainly have so stated in that legislation, and it had not done so. I am bound to day that I entirely agree with that.'

*Harrogate Borough Council v Simpson* was approved by the House of Lords in *Fitzpatrick*, and an early attempt to involve the European Convention on Human Rights in the case also failed therefore before the ECHR in *S v United Kingdom*[23]. It has, however, been argued[24] that in the light of *Godin-Mendoza* the results, in a similar case, would be different today. This view is highly controversial in that, as stated above, on a strict matter of statutory interpretation the list of qualifying

---

[22]   (1984) 17 HLR 205.
[23]   *S v United Kingdom* (1986) 47 DR 274.
[24]   A Redpath-Stevens, 'Succession Rights 2: *Mendoza*' [2003] Journal of Housing Law 41.

persons in s 113 Housing Act 1985 is a 'closed' one. However, all this may soon become irrelevant in the light of changes to the 1985 Act provisions contained in the Civil Partnership Bill 2004.

What is entirely clear, and what will remain unaltered by the proposed legislation is that non-sexual relationships, however 'close and intimate', will not receive similar protection. An attempt to involve the Human Rights Act 1998 in this context failed in *Wandsworth London Borough Council v Michalak*[25]. Again, *Michalak* is discussed in detail in Chapter 14.

When the Housing Act 1996 was before Parliament, Glenda Jackson MP proposed amendments to both s 113 of the Housing Act 1985 and s 17(4) of the Housing Act 1988 expressly to include homosexual relationships. Initially these were accepted by the Standing Committee considering the Bill, but they were later withdrawn after the Minister (David Curry) agreed to issue guidance to local authorities that they should normally grant a tenancy to the surviving partner of a relationship (whether homosexual or heterosexual) either in the same home, or in suitable alternative accommodation. The Minister further took the view that a preferable solution would be for a joint tenancy to have been granted in the first place (see later in this chapter), but that he understood that this would not always have occurred (276 HC Official Report coll. 985–986)[26]. The guidance referred to by the Minister was subsequently issued as Annex C to the Code of Guidance on Parts VI and VII of the Housing Act 1996[27] (for the remainder of the Code, see Chapters 7 and 10).

The decision in *Fitzpatrick* specifically only referred to the position under the Rent Act 1977, and was facilitated by the lack of a definition of 'family' under that Act. It is hard to see how, the Courts could easily get round the highly preclusive wording of s 113 of the 1985 Act. On the traditional construction basis of 'expressio unius alterius' only persons falling within the literal wording of s 113 can be regarded as 'family'. This is most unfortunate because a yawning void, in legal terms at least, is thereby opened up between those parts of the private rented sector still enjoying Rent Act protection and the public sector, and the rights of same sex couples will thus vary according to the nature of their landlord and the date of commencement of the tenancy. This can hardly be logically defended, and it is of little comfort to anyone that administrative practice *may* supply the law's omissions. Current legislative proposals (below) would close this void.

### 'Code of Guidance for Local Housing Authorities Allocation of Accommodation (November 2002)

*Chapter 3*
*Joint Tenants*

3.7 The Secretary of State considers joint tenancies can play an important role in the effective use and equitable allocation of housing. Where household

---

[25] *Wandsworth London Borough Council v Michalak* [2002] EWCA 271, [2002] 4 All ER 1136.
[26] Indeed the same dispensation was recommended in relation to close long-standing friends and unpaid live-in carers as well.
[27] Now contained in Code of Guidance for Local Housing Authorities on Allocation of Accommodation (ODPM, November 2002).

members have long term commitments to the home, for example, when adults accommodation as partners (including same sex partners), friends or unpaid live-in carers, housing authorities should normally grant a joint tenancy. In this way the ability of other adult household members to remain in the accommodation on the death of the tenant would not be prejudiced. Housing authorities should ensure that there are no adverse implications from the joint tenancy for the good use of their housing stock and for their ability to continue to provide for housing need.

3.8 Housing authorities should ensure that applicants, including where they are existing tenants, are made aware of the option of joint tenancies. When doing so, the legal and financial implications and obligations of joint tenancies must be made clear, including the implications for succession rights of partners and children. Where housing authorities refuse an application for a joint tenancy, clear, written reasons for the refusal should be given.

3.9 Where a joint tenant serves notice to quit, housing authorities have a discretion to grant a sole tenancy to the remaining tenant. In exercising this discretion, they should ensure that there are no adverse implications for the good use of their housing stock and their ability to continue to provide for housing need. Where housing authorities decide that they may wish to exercise their discretion in this respect, they must reflect this in their allocation scheme.

3.10 Where a tenant dies and another household member (who does not have succession rights to the tenancy) has:
(a)   been living with the tenant for the year prior to the tenant's death; or
(b)   been providing care for the tenant; or
(c)   accepted responsibility for the tenant's dependants and needs to live
        with them in order to do so,
housing authorities should consider granting a tenancy to the remaining person or persons, either in the same home or in suitable alternative accommodation, provided the allocation has no adverse implications for the good use of the housing stock and has sufficient priority under the allocation scheme. In the case of (a) and (b), the accommodation in question must be the principal or only residence of the survivor at the time the tenant dies.'

Empirical evidence is awaited as to how far local authority practice is now in line with this guidance. Prior to the guidance there was an admitted 'lack of uniformity ... in how they respond to such situations' (see David Curry in the HC Official Report, above). It is particularly worrying that the guidance applies only where the authority consider it a priority to offer accommodation. There is also inevitable doubt over the exact interpretation to be given to 'member of a household' in para 6.

## Current reform proposals

### The Law Commission

Recently the Law Commission has made recommendations in relation both to succession to tenancies, and the granting of joint tenancies[28]. It should first be appreciated that this is set in the context of the Commission's general recommendation that in place of the current plethora of tenancy types there should, in future, be only two main forms of tenancy – the short-term Type II agreement conferring little legal security and the longer-term Type I agreement conferring a high degree of security[29]. The material concerning joint tenancies is discussed in Chapter 3 and later in this chapter.

As regards succession on death, the Commission make a number of specific proposals[30], generally aimed in policy terms at 'remedy[ing] ... injustices which have emerged as more fluid family formations here evolved'[31]. The proposals include:

- Extending the definition of 'spouse' in the Housing Act 1985 to relationships 'that have the characteristics of husband and wife', whether heterosexual or same-sex, a proposal clearly taken up by the Civil Partnerships Bill 2004.
- Recognising the 'reality of the sacrifices that [carers] make in order to provide care' ... particularly 'to protect the position of unpaid carers who give up their own home to provide care for another in that another person's home'.
- Modifying succession rules (particularly in relation to the Housing Act 1985) to allow for some succession rights to other family members even after a first succession to the spouse of the deceased.

1.   Equally, the Commission are at pains to ensure that, overall, succession would take place 'within the sensible constraints of estate management'. In particular, there is a perceived need to ensure that social landlords are able to use their housing stock efficiently, and for the social purposes for which it was provided. The Commission therefore recommends that social landlords should have available to them a ground for seeking possession based on under-occupation of the home, following the death of the occupier[32]. The ground would not apply to spouse successors.

The scheme proposed by the Commission in outline is that[33]:

- those who should be within the statutory succession rules are partners of deceased occupiers, members of the family of the occupier and/or the occupier's partner;
- partners should be given priority over other potential 'successors';
- two successions may be possible if the first succession is to a surviving partner;

---

[28]   Law Commission, *Renting Homes* Cm 6018 (2003) Pts XI and XIV.
[29]   See further Chapter 2.
[30]   Law Commission, *Renting Homes* Pt XIV.
[31]   Ibid para 14.4.
[32]   Based on ground 16 of Sch 2 Housing Act 1985 (see Chapter 8).
[33]   Law Commission, *Renting Homes* paras 14.25–14.57.

- a 'spouse or partner' should include both heterosexual and same-sex relationships and 'should embrace couples where either partner has undergone gender re-assignment';
- protection as a 'standard successor' would only apply to carers who had a previous 'only or principal home' which was given up;
- all 'standard successors' would need to fulfil a 12-month residence requirement in the premises.

Taken together, if implemented, the Law Commission's proposals would provide for a significantly clearer and more coherent and fair legal framework. However, some anomalies and oddities would remain. For example, all the discussion on succession on death centres on the Housing Act 1985 and (therefore) predominantly on local authority tenancies. It can probably be assumed that (at the very least) the Law Commission intends its proposals to apply to all Type I tenancies and therefore to what would currently be housing association assured tenancies, but it would have been helpful if this had been made explicit. Secondly, it seems more than a little odd that no succession rights are even tentatively proposed for close and socially 'intimate' long-term companions – save where they fulfil the definition of a 'carer'. Perhaps it is assumed that such co-occupants will be added to the tenancy under the proposed joint-occupation scheme (below) but this, of course, assumes (at the very least) an awareness in the tenant of the importance of applying for this.

### Civil Partnership Bill

In the Queen's speech of 26 November 2003, it was announced that 'my government will maintain their commitment to increased equality and social justice by bringing forward legislation on the registration of civil partnerships between same-sex couples'. These proposals are now to be found in draft legislative form in the Civil Partnership Bill, presented to the House of Lords in May 2004. The proposed changes to the law on succession to rented property is to be found in Sch 8 of the Bill[34] (as regards the law for England and Wales).

## CIVIL PARTNERSHIP BILL

# Schedule 8

*Paragraph 13*

(1) In Part 1 of Schedule 1 (statutory tenants by succession), amend paragraph 2 (succession by surviving spouse) as follows.

(2) In sub-paragraph (1), after 'surviving spouse' insert ', or surviving civil partner,'.

(3) For sub-paragraph (2) substitute—

'(2) For the purposes of this paragraph—
    (a) a persons who was living with the original tenant as his or her wife or husband shall be treated as the spouse of the original tenant, and

---

[34] They were originally to be found in the Housing Bill 2003.

(b) a person who was living with the original tenant as if they were civil partners shall be treated as the civil partner of the original tenant.'

In similar vein, see:

*Paragraph 41*

(1) Amend section 17 (succession to assured periodic tenancy by spouse) as follows.

(2) In subsection (1), after 'spouse' (in each place) insert 'or civil partner'.

(3) For subsection (4) substitute—

'(4) For the purposes of this section—
  (a) a person who was living with the tenant as his or her wife or husband shall be treated as the tenant's spouse, and
  (b) a person who was living with the tenant as if they were civil partners shall be treated as the tenant's civil partner'.

The changes to the Housing Act 1985 are slightly more convoluted but, broadly, s 113 of the Act is amended so that after 'spouse' is inserted 'or civil partner'; after 'live together as husband and wife' is inserted 'or as if they were civil partners', and after 'a relationship by marriage' is inserted 'or civil partnership'.

If passed as drafted the proposed legislation would in all respects equate the legal position concerning succession of heterosexual and same-sex couples – a registered 'civil partner' is to be seen as the same as a 'spouse' and a person living with another 'as if they were civil partners' is to be seen as the same as a heterosexual cohabitant.

However, it can be asked whether these changes will effectively preclude the further implementation of the Law Commission's proposals, at least for the reasonably foreseeable future. Furthermore, both the Law Commission proposals and the changes proposed in the Civil Partnership Bill 2003 proceed on the assumption that 'partners' in a sexual relationship (heterosexual or same-sex) should always take priority over other successors.

## HOUSING AND RELATIONSHIP BREAKDOWN

The sharing of accommodation by couples, married or unmarried, homosexual or heterosexual, raises important questions as to the housing rights thereby acquired by the partners to the relationship. During the subsistence of the relationship such questions remain largely academic, but once the relationship comes under strain, or finally breaks down, the distribution and allocation of housing rights between the (ex) partners is a matter of crucial importance. Family law has tended to concentrate on owner-occupied property, whereas the focus here (as elsewhere in this book) is on the rented sector. As will be seen, however, many 'domestic' provisions are, in this area, much the same whether the 'home' involved is rented or owner-occupied. A factor of key significance is the existence (or otherwise) of a joint tenancy between the partners. This is discussed separately this chapter, and it should be assumed, in general, in this part that no joint tenancy exists.

For clarity of exposition the following discussion is divided between 'short-term' remedies, where the partners may still be living together despite their difficulties, and 'long-term' remedies, where the partners appear to have finally separated. In practice significant overlaps exist between the two areas.

## Short-term remedies

At common law the sole responsibilities and rights concerning the tenancy reside in the tenant. There appears to be no legal way that the non-tenant partner can protect his or her interests by (say) forcing the tenant spouse to pay the rent or take remedial action concerning repairs. Of course, in practice, in the still all too common situation of the non-tenant partner being a woman with children, it is highly likely that a local authority or registered social landlord would in practice accept rent from her, while seeking to deal with the male tenant's recalcitrance themselves. The Housing Benefit (General) Regulations 1987 (SI 1987/1971 as amended), reg 6, deems as 'liable' to pay rent a partner of tenant who is not paying, so that the partner can personally make a housing benefit claim.

A non-tenant spouse does at least have the common law right to occupy and use the matrimonial home during the subsistence of the marriage. This right is significantly reinforced by legislation (previously s 1 of the Matrimonial Homes Act 1983, now (with minor modifications) s 30 of the Family Law Act 1996):

30.    **Rights concerning matrimonial home where one spouse has no estate, etc.**

(1) This section applies if—

(a) one spouse is entitled to occupy a dwelling-house by virtue of—
  (i) a beneficial estate or interest or contract; or
  (ii)any enactment giving that spouse the right to remain in occupation; and

(b) the other spouse is not so entitled.

(2) Subject to the provisions of this Part, the spouse not so entitled has the following rights ('matrimonial home rights')—

(a) if in occupation, a right not to be evicted or excluded from the dwelling-house or any part of it by the other spouse except with the leave of the court given by an order under section 33;

(b) if not in occupation, a right with the leave of the court so given to enter into and occupy the dwelling-house.

(3) If a spouse is entitled under this section to occupy a dwelling-house or any part of a dwelling-house, any payment or tender made or other thing done by that spouse in or towards satisfaction of any liability of the other spouse in respect of rent, mortgage payments or other outgoings affecting the dwelling-house is, whether or not it is made or done in pursuance of an order under section 40, as good as if made or done by the other spouse.

(4) A spouse's occupation by virtue of this section—

(a) is to be treated, for the purposes of the Rent (Agriculture) Act 1976 and the Rent Act 1977 (other than Part V and sections 103 to 106 of that Act), as occupation by the other spouse as the other spouse's residence, and

(b) if the spouse occupies the dwelling-house as that spouse's only or principal home, is to be treated, for the purposes of the Housing Act 1985 and Part I of the Housing Act 1988, as occupation by the other spouse as the other spouse's only or principal home.

(5) If a spouse ('the first spouse')—

(a) is entitled under this section to occupy a dwelling-house or any part of a dwelling-house, and

(b) makes any payment in or towards satisfaction of any liability of the other spouse ('the second spouse') in respect of mortgage payments affecting the dwelling-house, the person to whom the payment is made may treat it as having been made by the second spouse, but the fact that that person has treated any such payment as having been so made does not affect any claim of the first spouse against the second spouse to an interest in the dwelling-house by virtue of the payment.

(6) If a spouse is entitled under this section to occupy a dwelling-house or part of a dwelling-house by reason of an interest of the other spouse under a trust, all the provisions of subsections (3) to (5) apply in relation to the trustees as they apply in relation to the other spouse.

(7) This section does not apply to a dwelling-house which has at no time been, and which was at no time intended by the spouses to be, a matrimonial home of theirs.

The rights conferred by s 30 on a non-tenant spouse ('matrimonial home rights' – formerly known as 'statutory rights of occupation') are considerable. They include:
(a) a right not to be evicted or excluded from the dwelling (owner-occupied or tenanted) by the other spouse except with leave of the court;
(b) a right to tender rent or other payment for occupation of the dwelling;
(c) a right, with leave of the court, to re-enter the dwelling, if not in occupation.

Occupation by the non-tenant spouse is sufficient to satisfy the 'residence' test for a Rent Act statutory tenancy and the 'only or principal home' test for a Housing Act 1985 secure tenancy and a Housing Act 1988 assured tenancy (see s 30(4)).

Section 30, like its predecessors, significantly strengthens the position of a non-tenant spouse. In itself, it does nothing to assist the position of co-habitees, heterosexual or homosexual. The Law Commission in *Renting Homes*[35] recommends some amendments to s 30 which would explicitly make reference to 'occupiers' under the new scheme. The Commission states[36]:

> 'We recommend that section 30 of the Family Law Act 1996 should be amended to refer to occupiers under the new scheme. Where the occupier obtains an adjournment, stay, suspension or postponement of a possession order, the rights of other parties to occupy and tender rent should be preserved until the possession order is enforced. The holders of these statutory rights should be given the right to be joined to possession proceedings and the same rights as the occupier to defend themselves against the making of a possession order and to apply after a possession order for any adjournment, stay, suspension or postponement.'

Further reinforcement of the rights of non-tenant spouses is provided for by s 33 of the Family Law Act 1996:

33.   **Occupational orders where applicant has estate or interest etc. or has matrimonial home rights**

(1) If—

(a) a person ('the person entitled')—
   (i) is entitled to occupy a dwelling-house by virtue of a beneficial estate or interest or contract or by virtue of any enactment giving him the right to remain in occupation, or
   (ii) has matrimonial home rights in relation to a dwelling-house, and

---

[35]   Law Commission, *Renting Homes* Cm 6018 (2003) paras 11.40 to 11.43.
[36]   Ibid para 11.43.

(b) the dwelling-house—

(i) is or at any time has been the home of the person entitled and of another person with whom he is associated, or

(ii)was at any time intended by the person entitled and any such other person to be their home,

the person entitled may apply to the court for an order containing any of the provisions specified in subsections (3), (4) and (5).

(2) If an agreement to marry is terminated, no application under this section may be made by virtue of section 62(3)(e) by reference to that agreement after the end of the period of three years beginning with the day on which it is terminated.

(3) An order under this section may—

(a) enforce the applicant's entitlement to remain in occupation as against the other person ('the respondent');

(b) require the respondent to permit the applicant to enter and remain in the dwelling-house or part of the dwelling-house;

(c) regulate the occupation of the dwelling-house by either or both parties;

(d) if the respondent is entitled as mentioned in subsection (1)(a)(i), prohibit, suspend or restrict the exercise by him of his right to occupy the dwelling-house;

(e) if the respondent has matrimonial home rights in relation to the dwelling-house and the applicant is the other spouse, restrict or terminate those rights;

(f) require the respondent to leave the dwelling-house or part of the dwelling-house; or

(g) exclude the respondent from a defined area in which the dwelling-house is included.

(4) An order under this section may declare that the applicant is entitled as mentioned in subsection (1)(a)(i) or has matrimonial home rights.

(5) If the applicant has matrimonial home rights and the respondent is the other spouse, an order under this section made during the marriage may provide that those rights are not brought to an end by—

(a) the death of the other spouse; or

(b) the termination (otherwise than by death) of the marriage.

(6) In deciding whether to exercise its powers under subsection (3) and (if so) in what manner, the court shall have regard to all the circumstances including—

(a) the housing needs and housing resources of each of the parties and of any relevant child;

(b) the financial resources of each of the parties;

(c) the likely effect of any order, or of any decision by the court not to exercise its powers under subsection (3), on the health, safety or well-being of the parties and of any relevant child; and

(d) the conduct of the parties in relation to each other and otherwise.

(7) If it appears to the court that the applicant or any relevant child is likely to suffer significant harm attributable to conduct of the respondent if an order under this section containing one or more of the provisions mentioned in subsection (3) is not made, the court shall make the order unless it appears to it that—

(a) the respondent or any relevant child is likely to suffer significant harm if the order is made; and

(b) the harm likely to be suffered by the respondent or child in that event is as great as, or greater than, the harm attributable to conduct of the respondent which is likely to be suffered by the applicant or child if the order is not made.

(8) The court may exercise its powers under subsection (5) in any case where it considers that in all the circumstances it is just and reasonable to do so.

...

Unlike s 30, s 33 significantly expands the scope of its predecessor, s 1(2) and (3) of the Matrimonial Homes Act 1983, above all by having at its foundation not only 'matrimonial homes rights', arising under s 30 and applicable only to spouses, but also rights arising by virtue of 'a beneficial estate or interest or contract' (s 33(1)(a)(i)). The most obvious way for such rights to arise in relation to a non-spouse partner is via a joint tenancy.

The orders which a court can make under s 33 are diverse, and its discretion is wide (s 33(6)), although specific attention is directed to the needs of (any) children of the relationship and the conduct of the parties, and an order *shall* be made if 'significant harm' would otherwise be likely to result to the applicant or any 'relevant child' (s 33(7)). The main orders (under s 33(3)) are to:
(a) enforce the applicant's right to remain in occupation;
(b) suspend or restrict the other partner's right to occupy the dwelling;
(c) require the other partner to leave the dwelling.

As applied to tenanted property, this means that a non-tenant spouse with 'matrimonial homes rights', or (for example) a joint tenant cohabitant can apply for an order excluding the tenant from the dwelling (s 33(3)) or some part of it.

Although such 'occupation' orders do not settle the long-term disposition of the tenancy (or other matrimonial home) they remain highly controversial, both in their existence (overturning, even if only temporarily, entrenched property rights) and in their application. A detailed discussion of the relevant case law is outside the scope of this book, being properly the preserve of family law, but it is now clear that, although a major factor, the welfare of children is not of overriding significance (see s 33(6)). The Law Commission in its report *Domestic Violence and the Occupation of the Family Home*[37] rejected suggestions that regulatory orders should be governed by a 'welfare paramountcy' test, and this is reflected in s 33. What is clear is that the 'balance of harm' test in s 33(7) will often be decisive. Of particular interest from a housing law perspective is s 33(6)(a), referring to the 'housing needs and housing resources ... of the parties'. Under the previous law it had been held[38] that the prospect of the parties being re-housed by a local authority was a relevant factor, so that an application by a wife might be refused if the local authority had a statutory obligation to re-house[39]. This of course increases the risk that the courts are being used as levers to 'prise open' the doors of public housing. Correspondingly, a court will not make an order merely to aid an authority in obtaining possession of a dwelling where it is clear that the applicant partner will not return if the tenant is excluded[40]. For the most authoritative discussion of the predecessor provisions to s 33, see *Richards v Richards*[41].

All the above presupposes that the applicant partner has 'matrimonial home' or other 'occupational' rights, which will not be the case for all spouses and will only be the case for those partners in non-marital relationships who do have joint

[37] No 207 (7 May 1992) (HC1).
[38] [1984] FLR 87.
[39] See Chapter 10.
[40] (1982) 1 HLR 139.
[41] [1984] AC 174.

tenancies. Prior to the Family Law Act 1996, the main legislative protection for non-marital partners lay in the well-known Domestic Violence and Matrimonial Proceedings Act 1976, which applied (s 1(2)) equally to marriages and heterosexual cohabitation. The law is now contained in s 36 of the Family Law Act 1996:

### 36. One cohabitant or former cohabitant with no existing right to occupy

(1) This section applies if—

(a) one cohabitant or former cohabitant is entitled to occupy a dwelling-house by virtue of a beneficial estate or interest or contract or by virtue of any enactment giving him the right to remain in occupation;
(b) the other cohabitant or former cohabitant is not so entitled; and
(c) that dwelling-house is the home in which they live together as husband and wife or a home in which they at any time so lived together or intended so to live together.

(2) The cohabitant or former cohabitant not so entitled may apply to the court for an order under this section against the other cohabitant or former cohabitant ('the respondent').

(3) If the applicant is in occupation, an order under this section must contain provision—

(a) giving the applicant the right not to be evicted or excluded from the dwelling-house or any part of it by the respondent for the period specified in the order; and
(b) prohibiting the respondent from evicting or excluding the applicant during that period.

(4) If the applicant is not in occupation, an order under this section must contain provision—

(a) giving the applicant the right to enter into and occupy the dwelling-house for the period specified in the order; and
(b) requiring the respondent to permit the exercise of that right.

(5) An order under this section may also—

(a) regulate the occupation of the dwelling-house by either or both of the parties;
(b) prohibit, suspend or restrict the exercise by the respondent of his right to occupy the dwelling-house;
(c) require the respondent to leave the dwelling-house or part of the dwelling-house; or
(d) exclude the respondent from a defined area in which the dwelling-house is included.

(6) In deciding whether to make an order under this section containing provision of the kind mentioned in subsection (3) or (4) and (if so) in what manner, the court shall have regard to all the circumstances including—

(a) the housing needs and housing resources of each of the parties and of any relevant child;
(b) the financial resources of each of the parties;
(c) the likely effect of any order, or of any decision by the court not to exercise its powers under subsection (3) or (4), on the health, safety or well-being of the parties and of any relevant child;
(d) the conduct of the parties in relation to each other and otherwise;
(e) the nature of the parties' relationship;
(f) the length of time during which they have lived together as husband and wife;
(g) whether there are or have been any children who are children of both parties or for whom both parties have or have had parental responsibility;
(h) the length of time that has elapsed since the parties ceased to live together; and
(i) the existence of any pending proceedings between the parties—
(i) for an order under paragraph 1(2)(d) or (e) of Schedule 1 to the Children Act 1989 (orders for financial relief against parents);
(ii) relating to the legal or beneficial ownership of the dwelling-house.

(7) In deciding whether to exercise its powers to include one or more of the provisions referred to in subsection (5) ('a subsection (5) provision') and (if so) in what manner, the court shall have regard to all the circumstances including—

(a) the matter mentioned in subsection (6)(a) to (d); and
(b) the questions mentioned in subsection (8).

(8) The questions are—

(a) whether the applicant or any relevant child is likely to suffer significant harm attributable to conduct of the respondent if the subsection (5) provision is not included in the order; and
(b) whether the harm likely to be suffered by the respondent or child if the provision is included is as great as or greater than the harm attributable to conduct of the respondent which is likely to be suffered by the applicant or child if the provision is not included.

(9) An order under this section—

(a) may not be made after the death of either of the parties; and
(b) ceases to have effect on the death of either of them.

(10) an order under this section must be limited so as to have effect for a specified period not exceeding six months, but may be extended on one occasion for a further specified period not exceeding six months.

...

In part, s 36, like the remainder of Pt IV of the Family Law Act 1996, can be seen as a further legislative response to the problem of 'domestic violence', and as a successor to the abortive Family Homes and Domestic Violence Bill 1995. It is largely based on the Law Commission recommendations in its 1992 Report *Domestic Violence and the Occupation of the Family Home*. The *overall* aim of Pt IV is to replace the former 'hotchpotch' of provisions with a more coherent and structured code, and this is demonstrated very well by s 36. Under the previous law lacking joint tenant status had to rely on the 'domestic violence' provisions of the Domestic Violence and Matrimonial Proceedings Act 1976 to obtain 'non-molestation' orders and 'ouster' orders and had not access to the more clear-cut orders generally available to spouses. Now the provisions in s 36 for occupation orders are, at least, comparable with those available under s 30 and s 33 to those with 'matrimonial home' rights. However, complete consistency has not been achieved, in that in deciding whether to make an order courts should consider (amongst other things):
(a) the nature of the parties' relationship (s 36(6)(e)), limited (via s 41(2)) by the fact that they 'have not given each other the commitment involved in marriage';
(b) the length of time they have lived together (s 36(6)(f)); and
(c) whether there are any children of the relationship (s 36(6)(g)).

Moreover, whereas under s 33(10) orders can be for any period, under s 36(10) they are limited to a maximum of sic months (although they can be extended, once, for a further six months).

Although s 36 provides for a much clearer and less 'stop gap' approach than the previous law[42] there is still obvious reluctance wholly to equate the position of

---

[42]   On which see *Wooton v Wooton* [1984] FLR 871.

cohabitants and spouses, and non-heterosexual relationships are still not encompassed. However, the provisions in Pt IV of the 1996 Act dealing specifically with domestic violence, for example s 42 (non-molestation orders), do extend more widely to cover anyone 'associated' with the respondent. 'Associated person' is defined by s 62 of the Act in terms identical to those in s 178 of the Housing Act 1996 (see Chapter 10) and includes (s 62(3)) anyone who 'live[s] or [has] lived in the same household', as the respondent 'otherwise than merely by reason of one of them being the other's employee, tenant, lodger or boarder'. This appears to cover homosexual relationships, and also friends sharing a dwelling as joint tenants.

Section 30 of the Family Law Act 1996 protects the 'matrimonial home' rights of spouses and joint tenant partners. Section 30(4) buttresses these rights by providing that, if the tenant spouse leaves, continued occupation by the non-tenant spouse satisfies the 'residence' and 'only or principal home' conditions under the Rent Act 1977 and the Housing Acts 1985 and 1988. The position of a non-tenant cohabitant remains considerably weaker. In the typical case, such a person probably possesses only a licence, lacking the necessary 'exclusive possession' to claim even sub-tenant status (see Chapter 3 and *Monmouth Borough Council v Marlog*[43]). Moreover, even in the unlikely event of a sub-tenancy existing it would seem to lack protected tenant status (s 12, Rent Act 1977) or assured tenant status (Sch 1, para 10, Housing Act 1988) because the tenant partner would be a 'resident landlord' (see generally on this Chapter 4). It is even doubtful whether the Protection from Eviction Act 1977 applies in the majority of cases since there will be a sharing of 'accommodation' with the landlord/licensor (s 3A of the Protection from Eviction Act 1977). Therefore, if no protection can be found under the Family Law Act 1996, the non-tenant partner can be removed from the property simply by being served with 'reasonable' notice, and without even the protection of a court order being required.

If the tenant partner departs leaving the other in occupation, although in practice the position of the non-tenant partner may be treated sympathetically, in theory his or her position is weak. It is even doubtful whether any new tenancy will arise, where the landlord accepts 'rent' from the 'deserted' partner, unless a clear new agreement can be inferred. This might depend on the terms on which the 'rent' is accepted (purely 'concessionary' or otherwise) and over how long a period it is accepted. The issues are discussed in *Marcroft Wagons v Smith*[44], where a landlord accepted rent from a daughter on the death of her mother, the statutory tenant of the dwelling, for a period of approximately five months. The Court of Appeal upheld a county court ruling that she remained a mere licensee and that no new tenancy had come into being. Evershed MR stated[45]: '... I should be extremely sorry ... [if] ... A landlord could never grant to a person in the position of the defendant any kind of indulgence, particularly in circumstances such as existed in March 1950, when the defendant lost her mother'. Subsequently, in *Westminster City Council v Basson*[46], a similar approach was adopted specifically in relation to a 'deserted' cohabitee. Westminster had granted a joint secure tenancy to a Mr and Mrs Simpson in 1977.

43   (1994) 27 HLR 30.
44   [1951] 2 KB 496.
45   At p 501.
46   (1990) 23 HLR 225.

In 1984, Mrs Simpson moved out, and (subsequently) Basson moved in, living with Mr Simpson as 'husband and wife'. The relationship broke down and Mr Simpson moved out in February 1985. The authority continued to accept money from Basson for her occupation and use of the property, but as early as September 1985 had stated that they regarded her occupation as 'unlawful' and that they did not intend to create 'a tenancy or a licence akin to a tenancy'. Possession proceedings were commenced only in November 1986, but despite the long delay the Court of Appeal upheld a county court ruling that no tenancy had come into being.

Spouses *with* 'matrimonial home' rights also have rights in possession proceedings, so long as they remain in occupation, to apply for adjournments, stays, suspensions or postponements of the proceedings even if the tenancy would otherwise be terminated as a result of the proceedings (see s 85(5) Housing Act 1985 and s 9(5), Housing Act 1988).

Section 35 of the Family Law Act 1996 gives the court powers to make occupation orders where the applicant is divorced from the respondent, and the latter is the one who retains a right to occupy the dwelling-house. The structure of s 35 is very similar to ss 30 and 33 concerning current spouses, but further factors are introduced (for example, the length of time that has elapsed since the parties last lived together and since the divorce) and (as with s 36) orders are limited to a maximum of six months.

Section 36 of the Family Law Act 1996 was discussed extensively in *Gay v Sheeran*[47]. In the case Enfield LBC had granted Sheeran and his partner Gunn a joint secure tenancy of a flat. Gunn left and Gay moved in, where she lived as Sheeran's cohabitant. Sheeran later moved out of the flat himself. Eighteen months later Enfield discovered that both the original joint tenants were no longer in occupation. They sought to recover possession of the flat. Gay then sought an order under s 53 of and para 7(1) of Sch 7 of the 1996 Act (see below) transferring Sheeran's interest in the flat to her. The district judge refused a transfer order under s 53/Sch 7 (this point in the case is discussed below), but allowed Gay's further application for an occupation order under s 36 protecting her from eviction by Sheeran and treating her occupation of the flat as occupation by him. The Court of Appeal upheld the district judge on both the s 53/Sch 7 and s 36 points. Peter Gibson LJ stated[48]:

> '[Was] the judge entitled to make an occupation order under s 36? Mr Arden submits that the purpose of an occupation order is to regulate occupation of a home as distinct from determining proprietorship of it. He says that it is essentially a holding order, pending the long-term disposition of the property. He argues that no such orders can be granted where there is no real possibility of the entitled cohabitant returning; in support he points to the mandatory words of s 36(3) and (4). He submits that the purpose of the application was to enable Miss Gay to apply for a transfer order and that it was not open to the judge to make an order to that end.

[47]  [1999] 3 All ER 795.
[48]  At p 807.

Mr Arden in my opinion is right to characterise the occupation order as a short-term holding order. That is obvious from the limited term of the order. He may well be right that where there is no possibility of the provisions to be inserted in that order by reason of s 36(3) or (4) serving any purpose, such a case would fall outside to the ambit of the section. But in the present case the judge found, and in my view was entitled to find, that there was a possibility that Mr Sheeran might return and that the regulation of the occupation of the flat served a practical purpose. I accept that an order under s 36 is not intended to determine property rights, though plainly it does confer and was intended to confer temporary rights on the non-entitled cohabitant with consequences for the landlord as to the tenancy as to the tenancy under which those rights are enjoyed, as can be seen from s 36(13). But for my part I can see no objection to the utilisation by a non-entitled cohabitant who obtains an occupation order of those rights for the purpose of seeking a transfer order. There is nothing in the section or elsewhere in the 1996 Act to suggest that that is improper. I have already pointed out that the Law Commission's report and s 36(6)(i) itself contemplate that the obtaining of an occupation order might be made with a view to obtaining a quite different order, and while nothing in the report or the Act expressly indicates that to obtain a transfer order is a legitimate further purpose in obtaining an occupation order, there is to my mind no objection in principle that there should be such further purpose in an applicant seeking or the court granting an occupation order, provided that the conditions of s 36 are satisfied. In the present case, however, the judge did not say that that was the purpose of the occupation order. In my judgment, the judge was plainly entitled to make an occupation order.'

## Long-term rights and remedies

Here, the concern of the law is less intervention to deal with the immediate crises inherent in the breakdown of a relationship, and more to settle the long-term consequences of the final breakdown of the relationship. The resolution of the property interests of the parties is, then, one aspect of the overall financial position which they are to be left in. Unsurprisingly the law has always been much clearer concerning spouses than other relationships. The key legislative provision has for many years been s 24 of the Matrimonial Causes Act 1973, which grants the court extensive jurisdiction to adjust the property rights of parties on the breakdown of a marriage, and to order one party to transfer property to the other. Since amendments introduced by Sch 2 to the Family Law Act 1996, s 24 of the 1973 Act contains the basic powers to adjust property rights, and the orders themselves are contained in s 21(2) of the 1973 Act. For this purpose a secure tenancy is as much 'property' as an owner-occupied dwelling, since s 91(3)(b) of the Housing Act 1985 specifically allows assignments of secure tenancies by courts using their s 24 powers. In the case of private sector tenancies it is much more doubtful whether the courts have 'property transfer' powers since, generally, assignments are permissible only with the consent of the landlord (see, for example, s 15 of the Housing Act 1988). However, the courts have wider and more 'tailored' powers to transfer tenancies under s 53 of and Sch 7 of the Family Law Act 1996:

## 53.   **Transfer of certain tenancies**

Schedule 7 makes provision in relation to the transfer of certain tenancies on divorce etc. or on separation of cohabitants.

# Schedule 7
# Transfer of certain tenancies on divorce etc. or on separation of cohabitants

## PART I
## GENERAL

*Interpretation*

1. In this Schedule—

'cohabitant', except in paragraph 3, includes (where the context requires) former cohabitant; and

'the court' does not include a magistrates' court,

'landlord' includes—

(a) any person from time to time deriving title under the original landlord; and

(b) in relation to any dwelling-house any person other than the tenant who is, or (but for Part VII of the Rent Act 1977 or Part II of the Rent (Agriculture) Act 1976) would be, entitled to possession of the dwelling-house;

'a relevant tenancy' means—

(a) a protected tenancy or statutory tenancy within the meaning of the Rent Act 1977;

(b) a statutory tenancy within the meaning the Rent (Agriculture) Act 1976;

(c) a secure tenancy within the meaning of section 79 of the Housing Act 1985; or

(d) an assured tenancy or assured agricultural occupancy within the meaning of Part I of the Housing Act 1988;

'spouse', except in paragraph 2, includes (where the context requires) former spouse; and

'tenancy' includes sub-tenancy.

*Cases in which the court may make an order*

2.—(1) This paragraph applies if one spouse is entitled, either in his own right or jointly with the other spouse, to occupy a dwelling-house by virtue of a relevant tenancy.

(2) At any time when it has power to make a property adjustment order under section 23A (divorce or separation) or 24 (nullity) of the Matrimonial Causes Act 1973 with respect to the marriage, the court may make a Part II order.

3.—(1) This paragraph applies if one cohabitant is entitled, either in his own right or jointly with the other cohabitant, to occupy a dwelling-house by virtue of a relevant tenancy.

(2) If the cohabitants cease to live together as husband and wife, the court may make a Part II order.

4. The court shall not make a Part II order unless the dwelling-house is or was—

(a) in the case of spouses, a matrimonial home; or

(b) in the case of cohabitants, a home in which they lived together as husband and wife.

*Matters to which the court must have regard*

5. In determining whether to exercise its powers under Part II of this Schedule and, if so, in what manner, the court shall have regard to all the circumstances of the case including—

(a) the circumstances in which the tenancy was granted to either or both of the spouses or cohabitants or, as the case requires, the circumstances in which either or both of them became tenant under the tenancy;

(b) the matters mentioned in section 33(6)(a), (b) and (c) and, where the parties are cohabitants and only one of them is entitled to occupy the dwelling-house by virtue of the relevant tenancy, the further matters mentioned in section 36(6)(e), (f), (g), and (h); and

(c) the suitability of the parties as tenants.

# PART II
# ORDERS THAT MAY BE MADE

*References to entitlement to occupy*

6. References in this Part of this Schedule to a spouse or a cohabitant being entitled to occupy a dwelling-house by virtue of a relevant tenancy apply whether that entitlement is in his own right or jointly with the other spouse or cohabitant.

*Protected, secure or assured tenancy or assured agricultural occupancy*

7.—(1) If a spouse or cohabitant is entitled to occupy the dwelling-house by virtue of a protected tenancy within the meaning of the Rent Act 1977, a secure tenancy within the meaning of the Housing Act 1985 or an assured tenancy or assured agricultural occupancy within the meaning of Part I of the Housing Act 1988, the court may by order direct that, as from such date as may be specified in the order, there shall, by virtue of the order and without further assurance, be transferred to, and vested in, the other spouse or cohabitant—

(a) the estate or interest which the spouse or cohabitant so entitled had in the dwelling-house immediately before that date by virtue of the lease or agreement creating the tenancy and any assignment of that lease or agreement, with all rights, privileges and appurtenances attaching to that estate or interest but subject to all covenants, obligations, liabilities and encumbrances to which it is subject; and

(b) where the spouse or cohabitant so entitled is an assignee of such lease or agreement, the liability of that spouse or cohabitant under any covenant of indemnity by the assignee express or implied in the assignment of the lease or agreement to that spouse or cohabitant.

(2) If an order is made under this paragraph, any liability or obligation to which the spouse or cohabitant so entitled is subject under any covenant having reference to the dwelling-house in the lease or agreement, being a liability or obligation falling due to be discharged or performed on or after the date so specified, shall not be enforceable against that spouse or cohabitant.

(3) If the spouse so entitled is a successor within the meaning of Part IV of the Housing Act 1985, his former spouse or former cohabitant (or, if a separation order is in force, his spouse) shall be deemed also to be a successor within the meaning of that Part.

(4) If the spouse or cohabitant so entitled is for the purpose of section 17 of the Housing Act 1988 a successor in relation to the tenancy or occupancy, his former spouse or former cohabitant (or, if a separation order is in force, his spouse) is to be deemed to be a successor in relation to the tenancy or occupancy for the purposes of that section.

(5) …

(6) In this paragraph, references to a separation order being in force include references to their being a judicial separation in force.

*Statutory tenancy within the meaning of the Rent Act 1977*

8.—(1) This paragraph applies if the spouse or cohabitant is entitled to occupy the dwelling-house by virtue of a statutory tenancy within the meaning of the Rent Act 1977.

(2) The court may by order direct that, as from the date specified in the order—

(a) that spouse or cohabitant is to cease to be entitled to occupy the dwelling-house; and
(b) the other spouse or cohabitant is to be deemed to be the tenant or, as the case may be, the sole tenant under that statutory tenancy.

(3) The question whether the provision of paragraphs 1 to 3, or (as the case may be) paragraphs 5 to 7 of Schedule 1 to the Rent Act 1977, as to the succession by the surviving spouse of a deceased tenant, or by a member of the deceased tenant's family, to the right to retain possession are capable of having effect in the event of the death of the person deemed by an order under this paragraph to be the tenant or sole tenant under the statutory tenancy is to be determined according as those provisions have or have not already had effect in relation to the statutory tenancy.

Section 53 and Sch 7 repeal and replace s 7 and Sch 1 to the Matrimonial Homes Act 1983. The crucial difference between the old and new law is that the new law extends to cohabitants, indeed (except in para 3) to former cohabitants, as the context requires. It expressly applies to Rent Act tenancies, secure tenancies and assured tenancies. In all such cases, the court may (as regards the matrimonial home, or dwelling in which the cohabitants lived together as husband and wife) order a transfer of the appropriate tenancy held by the respondent partner to the applicant partner. The court may also direct that some compensation be paid by the transferee partner to the transferor partner (taking account of the overall financial position of the parties): Sch 7, para 10). In deciding whether to make an order, the court is specifically directed to consider s 33(6)(a) to (c) and s 36(6)(e), (f) and (g). These have already been discussed. In addition (Sch 7, para 5(c)) the court is directed to have regard to the suitability of the parties as tenants.

Where the court makes a transfer under Sch 7, there is no assignment and therefore the consent of the landlord is not required. Paragraph 14, however, provides that rules of court shall be made requiring the court, before it makes an order, to give the landlord an opportunity of being heard. A particular issue on which the landlord may well wish to be 'heard' is that of rent arrears. Where a joint tenancy becomes a sole tenancy, after a relationship breakdown, most landlords will look to the 'survivor' for the arrears[49] and all have the power to do so. However, in the case of a sole tenant the tenant alone is responsible for rent arrears (like any other debt), and a 'successor' tenant, whether a 'successor' because of death, assignment, or under Sch 7, has no responsibility for arrears. It is not uncommon for local authority landlords, in particular, still to look to the incoming tenant to discharge arrears[50], but it is very doubtful whether such a 'requirement' is legally enforceable. Moreover, Sch 7, para 7(2) clearly states that any 'obligation' of the former tenant is not enforceable against the transferee (implicitly precluding any arrears liability in the transferee) and specific powers are given to *the court* under Sch 7, para 11, to direct that the transferor and transferee are to be jointly and severally liable for

---

[49] In the survey by Kay, A, Legg, C, and Foot, J, *The 1980 Tenants Rights in Practice*, 83% of local authorities did so.
[50] 22% of local authorities surveyed by Key, Legg and Foot.

obligations concerning the dwelling. Arguably, in the light of all this, a local authority pressing a transferee tenant to discharge arrears is guilty of maladministration.

The extension of these 'tailored' tenancy transfer powers to cohabitants applies irrespective of whether there are children of the relationship or not. In addition, the Children Act 1989, s 15 and Sch 1 give the courts powers to order the transfer of property between partners (married or unmarried) for the benefit of children of the relationship. In *K v K*[51], this was held to include tenants or owner-occupied property.

Schedule 7 was discussed extensively by the Court of Appeal in *Gay v Sheeran*[52], the facts of which have already been outlined. The Court ruled that a transfer of Sheeran's interest to Gay could not be made because:

● A transfer could only be made where one cohabitant was 'entitled ... to occupy the property' (see Sch 7 Pt I para 2(1)). In the immediate context that meant an entitlement to occupy under a *current* secure tenancy. Sheeran's tenancy was not 'secure' as he had ceased to occupy the flat as his only or principal dwelling. The court left open the issue as to whether the 'entitlement' condition had to be satisfied at the time the application for a transfer order was made, or at the later time when the order actually was made (their inclination was towards the latter).

● In any case a transfer could not be made to Gay of a tenancy held by Sheeran and Gunn; the legislation did not allow such an order where the property in question is that of a cohabitant who is a joint tenant with a person other than the intended transferee. To hold otherwise would 'foist' Gay as a joint tenant on the long-departed Gunn. A transfer could only take place where either *both* cohabitants were jointly entitled to the property or else one of them was solely entitled.

Although concurring in the decision Ward LJ was 'troubled' by some of its implications – both in relation to the construction the court was placing on Sch 7 and on the interrelationship between Sch 7 and s 36. He stated[53]:

'Could it really be the intention of the legislature to require a cohabitant (Miss Gay), who wished to apply for a transfer of her partner's tenancy to her, first to apply for an occupation order even when the two applications can, as it seems to me, be issued simultaneously, heard together but the orders pronounced one before the other. I see nothing improper in the two applications being dealt with in this way because nothing in the scheme of the Family Law Act 1996, or in the Law Commission report *Family Law, Domestic Violence and Occupation of the Family Home* (Law Com No 207) (1992) which precedes it suggests it would be an improper procedure. Paragraph 15(2) of Sch 7 to the 1996 Act provides that the court's powers to make a transfer of tenancy order are additional to the powers to make an occupation order. Why, therefore, I have asked myself rhetorically, is the occupation order a necessary

---

[51]  [1992] 1 WLR 530.
[52]  [1999] 3 All ER 795.
[53]  At p 808.

pre-requisite? The answer seems to me to be that it is only the occupation order which can by operation of s 36(13) equate the position of a cohabitant with that of a spouse and thereby, pursuant to s 30(4), treat her occupation of the dwelling house as occupation by her partner, the tenant, so as to fulfil the tenant condition necessary to establish a secure tenancy. It must be the deliberate policy of the 1996 Act to underline the social fact that there is a difference between spouses and cohabitants and that for the cohabitant to enjoy the rights of occupation which the spouse has as 'matrimonial home rights' under s 30(2) and enjoys as of right as spouse, the cohabitant must, in effect, prove his or her worth by satisfying the court that he or she is entitled to be given similar recognition having regard to all the circumstances of the case and particularly to those set out in s 36(6).

...

The occupation order is an order of limited duration: the transfer of tenancy is an enhancement of the cohabitant's right to remain in the property and enjoy the benefits so long as the tenancy endures. it seems to me, therefore, the legislative purpose is to require the cohabitant first to show a right to occupy before this additional benefit is conferred upon her.

For those reasons and the reasons given by Peter Gibson LJ, I agree that Miss Gay could not proceed straight to her transfer application: she had first to cross the occupation threshold. Without that occupation order Mr Sheeran was not at material times entitled to occupy the dwelling house by virtue of secure tenancy.

(2) The second aspect which troubles me is whether it is right to restrict the interpretation of the words 'either in his own right or jointly with the other spouse/cohabitant to occupy a dwelling house by virtue of a relevant tenancy' restrictively. The phrase has been used since the Matrimonial Homes Act 1967 and I know of no authority on the point. On facts like those before us, a proper exercise of discretion can, it seems to me, meet the justice of the case, protect an unwilling co-tenant having an unwelcome invitee foist upon him or her and always take account of the local authority's objections. There are other cases which one can easily envisage, eg where a number of young people share a flat as joint secure tenants; one begins to cohabit and later moves out; but all are happy to accept the incomer as their co-tenant. One can also imagine an aged parent and his adult child as the joint tenants; the son begins to cohabit; the father is taken into permanent residential geriatric care; then the son moves out leaving his cohabitant and his family in occupation. I struggle to see why it cannot be said in each of those cases that the cohabitant is entitled in his own right to occupy the dwelling house by virtue of a relevant tenancy, in his own right meaning no more than not as a nominee. But the problem remains with the words 'jointly with the other spouse/cohabitant' and I have faithfully to construe them, not supplement any defects I may perceive in the legislative purpose ...'

## JOINT TENANCIES

As has been noted at several points already in this chapter, joint tenant status confers significant advantages on non-spouse partners in particular[54]. All landlords, public or private, have the power to grant joint tenancies, whether the tenancies in question are protected, assured or secure. Private sector landlords seem increasingly to favour joint tenancies, not least because of the control it gives them over rent in particular. In the public sector, as note earlier in this chapter, Chapter 3 of the Code of Guidance for Local Housing Authorities as Allocation on Accommodation (2002) advises local authorities 'normally' to grant a joint tenancy where the members of a household have a long-term commitment to the home, whether as married couples, as friends, in other relationships or even as live-in carers. Moreover, the authority should inform applicants in writing of their reasons if they refuse to grant a joint tenancy.

Generally joint tenants have collective responsibilities, and normally they must act together. Therefore, if joint tenants wish to surrender a fixed-term lease they must all act together to do so. As Somervell LJ stated in *Leek and Moorlands Building Society v Clark*[55]: 'They all have the right to the full term, and all must concur if this right is to be abandoned'. However, it now seems that is *not* the case concerning the service of notices to quit, and in the context of local authority tenancies in particular, this has proved to be a point of considerable importance in recent years.

### Joint tenants and notices to quit: the issues

Prior to the Housing Act 1980, it was common for local authority landlords to issue a notice to quit against a deserted joint tenant before granting a new sole tenancy. Since the 1980 Act, however, the authority must show grounds for possession before the joint tenancy can be brought to an end, and possession can be obtained by the landlord only via a court order (s 82, Housing Act 1985 and generally Chapter 8). What if the authority try a different approach and come to an understanding with the deserted joint tenant that *he or she* will serve a notice to quit on the authority, following the expiry of which the authority will re-grant a sole tenancy to the tenant?

The issues came to a head in *Greenwich London Borough Council v McGrady*[56]. On October 25, 1976, the local authority let a house to Mr and Mrs McGrady on a joint weekly tenancy. In 1980 there were divorce proceedings and the parties separated. On May 11, 1981, Mrs McGrady gave the authority a notice to quit taking effect on June 15. Mr McGrady refused to leave, and proceedings were brought in the county court. The registrar found in favour of Mr McGrady, but on appeal the judge found for the local authority and the Court of Appeal agreed with the judge. Sir John Donaldson MR stated[57]:

> 'The law can for practical purposes be taken from the decision of this court in *Leek and Moorlands Building Society v Clark.*

---

[54]  For a general discussion of joint tenancies, see Chapter 3.
[55]  [1952] 2 QB 788, at p 794.
[56]  (1982) 46 P & CR 223.
[57]  At p 223.

In that case, the husband had bought a long leasehold interest jointly held by himself and his wife. He then purported to sell with vacant possession, and the court was concerned with whether the sale constituted an effective surrender of that long leasehold interest. It was held that it did not. Somervell LJ, however, in a reserved judgment delivered as the judgment of the court, reviewed the general position of joint tenants, relying in particular on *Doe d. Aslin v Summersett* [(1830) 1 B & Ad 135, 109 ER 738], in which Lord Tenterden CJ had adverted to the position of joint tenants on a periodic tenancy. It is quite clear that this court was approving the earlier case. Somervell LJ quoted the *ratio* of the earlier decision in the following passage:

> "'Upon a joint demise by joint tenants' that is, the lessors in that case 'upon a tenancy from year to year, the true character of the tenancy is this, not that the tenant holds of each the share of each so long as he and each shall please, but that he holds the whole of all so long as he and all shall please, and as soon as any one of the joint tenants … gives a notice to quit, he effectively puts an end to that tenancy'."

Later, he adverted again to *Doe d. Aslim v Summersett* and said:

> "That case, for reasons which we have given, is not in our view an exception to the rule we have just stated. It is an illustration, in a highly technical field, of the general principle that if a joint enterprise is due to terminate on a particular day, all concerned must agree if it is to be renewed or continued beyond that day. To use Lord Tenterden's phrase, it will only be continued if 'all shall please.'"

> In my judgment, it is clear that, if there is to be a surrender of a joint tenancy – that is, a surrender before its natural termination – then all must agree to the surrender. If there is to be a renewal, which is the position at the end of each period of a periodic tenancy, then again all must concur. In this case, Mrs McGrady made it quite clear by her notice to quit that she was not content to renew the joint tenancy on and after June 15, 1981. That left Mr McGrady without any tenancy at all, although it was faintly argued by Mr Osman that on, as he put it, the severance of a joint tenancy the joint tenant who did not concur was left with a sole tenancy. That cannot be the law, and no authority has been cited in support of it.'

The reasoning in *McGrady* (that a periodic joint tenancy requires the continued desire of all the joint tenants that it should continue, so that a notice to quit by one of them effectively brings the joint tenancy to an end) was approved by the House of Lords in *Hammersmith and Fulham London Borough Council v Monk*[58]. Mr Monk and Mrs Powell were granted by Hammersmith council a weekly tenancy of a flat, where they cohabited. The tenancy was terminable by four weeks' notice. In 1998 Mr Monk and Mrs Powell fell out and Mrs Powell left the flat. She consulted the council, who agreed to rehouse her if she would terminate the tenancy of the flat by giving an appropriate notice, which she did,. The notice was given without Mr Monk's knowledge or consent, but the council immediately notified him

---

[58]  [1992] 1 All ER 1.

that the tenancy had been determined and in due course brought proceedings to recover possession. The judge held that Mrs Powell's notice to quit was ineffective to determine the tenancy and dismissed the claim. The Court of Appeal allowed the respondent's appeal and made an order for possession. The House of Lords upheld the Court of Appeal. Lord Bridge stated[59]:

'Your Lordships are not technically bound by any previous decision and before examining the relevant authorities I think it helpful to consider whether the application of first principles suggests the answer to the question at issue. For a large part of this century there have been many categories of tenancy of property occupied for agricultural, residential and commercial-purposes where the legislature has intervened to confer upon tenants extra-contractual rights entitling them to continue in occupation without the consent of the landlord, either after the expiry of a contractual lease for a fixed term or after notice to quit given by the landlord to determine a contractual periodic tenancy. It is primarily in relation to joint tenancies in these categories that the question whether or not notice to quit given by one of the joint tenants can determine the tenancy is of practical importance, particularly where, as in the instant case, the effect of the determination will be to deprive the other joint tenant of statutory protection. This may appear an untoward result and may consequently provoke a certain reluctance to hold that the law can permit one of two joint tenants unilaterally to deprive his co-tenant of "rights" which both are equally entitled to enjoy. But the statutory consequences are in truth of no relevance to the question which your Lordships have to decide. That question is whether, at common law, a contractual periodic tenancy granted to two or more joint tenants is incapable of termination by a tenant's notice to quit unless it is served with the concurrence of all the joint tenants. That is the proposition which the appellant must establish in order to succeed.

As a matter of principle I see no reason why this question should receive any different answer in the context of the contractual relationship of landlord and tenant than that which it would receive in any other contractual context. If A and B contract with C on terms which are to continue in operation for one year in the first place and thereafter from year to year unless determined by notice at the end of the first or any subsequent year, neither A nor B has bound himself contractually for longer than one year. To hold that A could not determine the contract at the end of any year without the concurrence of B and vice versa would presuppose that each had assumed a potentially irrevocable contractual obligation for the direction of their joint lives, which, whatever the nature of the contractual obligations undertaken, would be such an improbable intention to impute to the parties that nothing less than the clearest express contractual language would suffice to manifest it. Hence, in an ordinary agreement for an initial term which is to continue for successive terms unless determined by notice, the obvious inference is that the agreement is intended to continue beyond the initial term only if and so long as all parties to the agreement are willing that it should do so. In a common law

---

[59]   At p 2.

situation, where parties are free to contract as they wish and are bound only so far as they have agreed to be bound, this leads to the only sensible result.

Thus the application of ordinary contractual principles leads me to expect that a periodic tenancy granted to two or more joint tenants must be terminable at common law by an appropriate notice to quit given by any one of them whether or not the others are prepared to concur.

… Thus the fact that the law regards a tenancy from year to year which has continued for a number of years, considered retrospectively, as a single term in no way affects the principle that continuation beyond the end of each year depends on the will of the parties that it should continue or that, considered prospectively, the tenancy continues no further than the parties have already impliedly agreed upon by their omission to serve notice to quit.

Finally, it is said that all positive dealings with a joint tenancy require the concurrence of all joint tenants if they are to be effective. Thus, a single joint tenant cannot exercise a break clause in a lease, surrender the term, make a disclaimer, exercise an option to renew the term or apply for relief from forfeiture. All these positive acts which joint tenants must concur in performing are said to afford analogies with the service of notice to determine a periodic tenancy which is likewise a positive act. But this is to confuse the form with the substance. The action of giving notice to determine a periodic tenancy is in form positive; but both on authority and on the principle so aptly summed up in the pithy Scottish phrase "tacit relocation" the substance of the matter is that it is by his omission to give notice of termination that each party signifies the necessary positive assent to the extension of the term for a further period.

For all these reasons I agree with the Court of Appeal that, unless the terms of the tenancy agreement otherwise provide, notice to quit given by one joint tenant without the concurrence of any other joint tenant is effective to determine a periodic tenancy.'

From this is it clear that a secure tenancy can be effectively terminated by the service of a notice to quit by one of the former joint tenants. However, other decisions of the courts have emphasised difficulties hidden within the apparent simplicity of this, and, in particular, the formalities which need to be satisfied before the procedure can operate effectively.

## Joint tenants and notices to quit: the difficulties

As soon as *Greenwich v McGrady* was reported, the general academic view was that extreme care needed to be taken both by local authorities and by the deserted (partner) joint tenant, most typically a woman. The first issue to arise judicially came in *Parsons v Parsons*[60], in which Donald Rattee QC, then sitting as a deputy High Court judge, stated[61] that while the general *McGrady* principle seemed to be a sound one:

---

[60]  [1983] 1 WLR 1390.
[61]  At p 1400.

'... it may be that if in a particular case the service of notice to quit by one joint tenant of the reversion to a periodic tenancy involved the joint tenants or some of them in a liability greater than the resultant increase in value of the reversion, those injured would have a claim in breach of trust against the joint tenant serving the notice: compare *Megarry and Wade, the Law of Real Property*, 4th ed. (1975), pp 394–5, though I do not understand why the authors say in that passage that service of a notice to quit by one joint tenant will *usually* be a breach of trust.'

This difficulty stems from the fact that all jointly held land (including assured and secure tenancies) is subject to an implied trust, and the joint tenants are trustees for themselves. If one of the joint tenants, therefore, acts detrimentally to the interests of the other(s) under the trust, it can be argued that he or she can be liable for any financial loss thereby incurred. Moreover, under s 26(3) of the Law of Property Act 1925, one trustee was obliged to consult with and, as consistent with the general interests of the trust, give effect to the wishes of the other(s). It could obviously be argued that a failure by one joint tenant to consult with the other joint tenant(s) before serving a notice to quit could amount to a breach of s 26(3).

The issues came to a head in *Crawley Borough Council v Ure*[62]. In 1986 Mr and Mrs Ure were granted a joint tenancy by the council of the flat on a weekly tenancy, subject to the statutory requirement that the tenancy could only be terminated on not less than four weeks' notice. In August 1991 Mrs Ure and her daughter left the matrimonial home. At some time after that, Mrs Ure started divorce proceedings. She and her daughter moved into 'emergency accommodation'. In September 1991 Mr Ure's son moved into the flat to live with him. As joint tenant Mrs Ure was entitled to continue to occupy the property. She did not apply for an order to oust her husband from the matrimonial home. At some stage she applied to the council for assistance or accommodation as a homeless person under the (then) Part III of the Housing Act 1985. It was suggested to Mrs Ure by the council that she could give a notice which should have the effect of terminating her tenancy of the flat. She therefore did so. On 6 April 1992 she gave a notice to the council in a form provided to her by them.

The council submitted that the wife's notice had the effect of terminating the tenancy. Mr Ure refused to leave the property. The council therefore brought proceedings against him in the county court. The Court of Appeal agreed with the Judge. Glidewell LJ stated[63]:

'...

Mr Berry QC, for Mr Ure, accepts of course that *Monk's case* [1992] 1 AC 478 is binding authority for the proposition that in principle a notice to quit given by one of two joint tenants without the consent of the other is nevertheless effective to terminate the tenancy. He takes up, however, the suggestion made by Lord Browne-Wilkinson and, earlier, by Slade LJ that in some circumstances the joint tenant who serves the notice may be doing so in breach of trust. Mr Berry's argument can be summarised as follows. (1) By

[62]  [1996] QB 13, [1996] 1 All ER 724, [1995] 3 WLR 95.
[63]  At p 731 of the All England Report.

section 36 of the Law of Property Act 1925 a joint tenancy is held on trust for sale. The joint tenants in the present circumstances are both trustees and beneficiaries. (2) Although he now accepts (or at least does not argue to the contrary) that the service of the notice to quit itself was not a breach of trust, section 26(3) of the Law of Property Act 1925 required a joint tenant who wished to terminate the joint tenancy first to consult the other joint tenant, that is to say consult Mr Ure. (3) Mrs Ure did not consult her husband and thus acted in breach of trust. (4) If she had consulted, Mr Ure could have (a) objected to her terminating the tenancy and (b) sought a property adjustment order under section 24 of the Matrimonial Cases Act 1973 which, if it were granted, would have had the effect of vesting the joint tenancy in him alone. (5) The council, who advised and indeed encouraged Mrs Ure to serve the notice to quit, were thus parties to her breach of trust. It follows, submits Mr Berry, that the council, despite what was said by Slade LJ in *Metall and Rohstoff AG v Donaldson Lufkin & Jenrette Inc* [1990] 1 QB 391 in this court, were guilty of the tort of procuring a breach of trust, and, since it is a basic principle that equity will not allow a wrongdoer to take advantage of his own wrong, that is precisely what the council, in suing Mr Ure for possession and indeed in accepting the notice to quit served by Mrs Ure, were doing. Thus they should not have been allowed to succeed in their action for possession.

The passage in the judgment of Slade LJ in the *Metall and Rohstoff* case to which I have just referred is at p 481, where, delivering the judgment of the court, he said in relation to an argument that there was a tort of procuring a breach of trust:

> "The principles of the law of trusts, in particular those expounded by Lord Selbourne LC in *Barnes v Addy* (1874) LR 9 Ch App 244, are quite sufficient to deal with those persons who incite a breach of trust or wrongfully meddle with trust assets or interfere with the relationship of trustee and beneficiary. We know of no authority supporting the existence of the alleged tort and can see no sufficient justification for the introduction of a new tort of this nature."

In reply to Mr Berry's submissions Mr Arden QC, for the council, submits, firstly, that the joint tenancy in this case was not held on trust for sale. The parties' interest in the property had no capital value. Therefore in practice it was not capable of being sold. Therefore there could not be a trust for sale. The last stage of this attractively simple argument is, in my view, wrong. It disregards the clear words of section 36(1) of the Law or Property Act 1925, and I do not find it necessary to say any more about it, with all due respect to Mr Arden.

However, his second argument demands more detailed consideration. This relates to the effect of section 26(3) of the Law of Property Act 1925. Section 26(1) of that Act provides:

> "If the consent of more than two persons is by the disposition made requisite to the execution of a trust for sale of land, then, in favour of a purchaser, the consent of any two of such persons to the execution of the

trust or to the exercise of any statutory or other powers vested in the trustees for sale shall be deemed sufficient."

I need not refer to subsection (2).

Subsection (3) (as substituted by section 7 of, and the Schedule to, the Law of Property (Amendment) Act 1926), which is the critical subsection, provides:

"Trustees for sale shall so far as practicable consult the persons of full age for the time being beneficially interested in possession in the rents and profits of the land until sale, and shall, so far as consistent with the general interest of the trust, give effect to the wishes of such persons ..."

If that subsection applied to the circumstances of this case Mrs Ure, in her capacity as a trustee for sale, was required to consult Mr Ure as a person beneficially interested in possession and, so far as consistent with the general interests of the trust, to give effect to his wishes; that did not require necessarily that she should follow his wishes, but at least she was required to consider them.

To whom and to what types of transaction, therefore, does section 26(3) apply? Mr Arden submits that what it requires is consultation by the trustees, or a trustee, with the beneficiaries or another beneficiary before either the execution of the trust for sale or "the exercise of any statutory or other powers vested in the trustees for sale" – that last phrase coming from subsection (1). In this respect Mr Arden accepts, as I do, the correctness of the decision of Bennett J in *In re Jones*; *Jones v Cusack-Smith* [1931] 1 Ch 375. Bennett J summed up his judgment (which was a commendably short judgment in total) firstly by posing at the beginning the question he was seeking to answer, which was, at p 377:

"Must trustees for sale consult the persons of full age for the time being entitled in possession to the rents and profits of the land on the occasion of the exercise of any of their statutory trusts and powers, or is their duty limited to consulting the beneficiaries when they propose to exercise the trust for sale?"

He answered that question, at p 378:

"It seems that, there being nothing expressed to limit subsection (3) or to indicate that subsection (3) is to have a different meaning from subsections (1) and (2), I ought to adopt an interpretation which would make the whole section hang together, and the result is that the answer to the question is that the trustees must consult the beneficiaries, not only in the exe4rcise of the trust for sale, but also in the exercise of all other trusts and powers arising under the Settled Land Act 1925 and the Law of Property Acts, and the additional or larger powers conferred by the settlement upon the trustees or otherwise."

However, Mr Arden submits that what that subsection requires is consultation before a trustee does what Lord Bridge in the passage I have already read from *Monk's* case [1992] 1 AC 478, 490–491 described as a "positive act". It is clear, says Mr Arden, from the decision in *Monk's* case that a notice by a joint tenant that she was not willing for the tenancy to continue beyond the end of the current four-week period was not, in substance, a "positive act". Thus, section 26(3) did not apply so as to require prior consultation to the giving of such a notice. Mr Berry, in reply, said that, though Lord Bridge said that in substance it was not a "positive Act", he accepted that in form the giving of a notice was such an act, and that that was sufficient to bring it within the ambit of section 26(3).

In my judgment Mr Arden's argument is correct. I can see that a regime which required that, where a council dwelling is occupied on a joint tenancy either joint tenant must consult with the other before taking any action which would have the effect of terminating the tenancy, might well be thought to have merit. But as Nicholls LJ said in the passage I quote from his judgment in *Monk's* case, 89 LGR 357, 382–382, the point her at issue applies to all periodic tenancies. We cannot carve out an exception from the general law which is to apply only to tenants of residential property let by local authorities or similar authorities. In my judgment, therefore, Mr Berry's argument fails at this critical point. We need not therefore express any opinion about his further detailed argument, that in the short passage from the judgment of the court in the *Metall and Rohstoff AG* case [1990] 1 QB 391, 481, where Slade LJ said he knew of no authority supporting the existence of the alleged tort, he was speaking per incuriam. I specifically make no comment about Mr Berry's submissions to that effect.

Despite Mr Berry's persuasive argument, I would therefore dismiss this appeal.'

Hobhouse and Aldous LJJ concurred with this approach, which seems to be decisive. In effect, the obligation to consult only arises where one trustee wishes to do something positive about the property; a desire to not proceed with a tenancy is negative and so is not subject to consultation. The 'breach of trust' argument seemed generally to founder on the same point. The only continuing doubt on the matter is provided by the fact that, on 1 January 1997, s 26(3) was replaced by s 11 of the Trusts of Land and Appointment of Trustees Act 1996. However, it seems doubtful whether there is sufficient difference in the content of s 11 compared with s 26(3) to lead to a different result.

Even if the interests of the other joint tenant(s) do not appear to be protected by the 'breach of trust' argument, the courts have proved sensitive, in general, to the injustices which an inflexible application of the *McGrady* principle can cause. In particular, the House of Lords' acceptance of the *McGrady* principle in *Monk* leaves a cohabiting joint tenant highly vulnerable to vindictive action by a disaffected partner (acting either wholly independently, or in collusion with the landlord authority). The origins of *McGrady* lie, as indicated above, in the understandable desire of many local authorities to rationalise housing tenure and the realities of how a property may be currently occupied. The inability of an authority simply to 'switch' the tenancy from the absentee tenant partner to the partner in occupation must be highly frustrating. However, the principle applies in non-meritorious cases, as much as in meritorious ones. It does not even preclude the partner in *desertion* attempting to remove the tenancy rights of the other, by the service of a notice to quit.

The issues came to a head in *Hounslow LBC v Pilling*[64]. In 1991, the plaintiffs granted the defendant and a Miss Doubtfire(!) a secure joint tenancy of a flat. The recitals to the agreement stated that: 'If the tenancy granted is a joint tenancy the rights and liabilities of the tenant apply both jointly and individually.' By clause 14 of the agreement the tenant was obliged: 'to give the Council four weeks' written notice or such lesser period as the Council may accept when the tenant wishes to end the tenancy and give possession of the premises.'

In September 1991, following incidents of domestic violence, Miss Doubtfire left the premises permanently. The plaintiffs had a domestic violence policy whereby they undertook to rehouse any tenant who was proved to have been a victim of violence, provided that the victim surrendered his or her tenancy. On 6 December 1991, Miss Doubtfire wrote to the plaintiffs with respect to the flat stating 'I wish to terminate my tenancy ... with immediate effect.'

On 11 December 1991, the plaintiffs wrote to the defendant stating:

'The Council has received a letter ending the tenancy of 107 Highfield. It is now accepted, and from December 9, 1991, you are no longer a council tenant and should find somewhere else to live. You have no right to remain at 107 Highfield and have become an illegal occupier.'

The defendant refused to give up possession and possession proceedings were taken against him. In March 1992, the district judge made an order for possession which was affirmed on appeal by the judge. The defendant appealed to the Court of Appeal which allowed the appeal.

Nourse LJ stated[65]:

'In this case Mr Luba, for the defendant, has raised several points on the notice by which he seeks to show that it was not an appropriate notice for the purposes of the decision in *Monk*. He has argued, for example, that it is ambiguous in its terms; that it is not clear that it was intended to take effect immediately; and that, if it was, it was not a valid notice within clause 14, because there was no "period" between the giving of the notice and the date or time when it was expressed to take effect. So far as those and other arguments in the same vein are concerned, I would reject them. I think that the terms of Miss Doubtfire's letter of December 6, 1991 were such that it was capable of taking effect as an immediate notice to quite.

Whether it did take effect as a notice to quit is quite a different matter. It was expressed to take effect immediately and it was accepted as taking effect on Monday, December 9; that is to say, on a day on which the tenancy could not have been determined by a notice to quit given on Friday, December 6. Accordingly, argues Mr Luba, it was not a notice to quit properly so called. It

[64]   [1994] 1 All ER 432.
[65]   At p 436.

was a notice purporting to be given in exercise of a break clause contained in the lease, namely that contained in clause 14.

In my judgment that argument is correct and the decision of the House of Lords in *Monk* is distinguishable on that ground. All that that case decided was that the continuation of a periodic joint tenancy beyond the end of each period of it depends on the joint will of the tenants, so that if one of them gives notice determining it at the end of a period it does not continue. Here the notice purported to determine the tenancy not at the end of a period but in the middle of one. On the assumption, which I certainly make, that clause 14 permitted notice to be given for an immediate determination, the effect of Miss Doubtfire's letter of December 6, and the council's acceptance of it was to determine the tenancy on December 9, and not on December 16. I therefore agree with Mr Lubna that the notice was not a notice to quit, but one operating a break clause in the tenancy agreement. Such a notice could not be given by one only of the joint tenants, see *Re Viola's Indenture of Lease* (1909) 1 Ch 244.

That is indeed the case and that *Monk* should be distinguished on that ground appears clearly from the speech of Lord Bridge. At p 490G, he said:

"Finally, it is said that all positive dealings with a joint tenancy require the concurrence of all joint tenants if they are to be effective. Thus, a single joint tenant cannot exercise a break clause in a lease, surrender the term, make a disclaimer, exercise an option to renew the term or apply for relief from forfeiture. All these positive acts which joint tenants must concur in performing are said to afford analogies with the service of notice to determine a periodic tenancy which is likewise a positive act. But this is to confuse the form with the substance. The action of giving notice to determine a periodic tenancy is in form positive; but both on authority and on the principle so aptly summed up in the pithy Scottish phrase 'tacit relocation' the substance of the matter is that it is by his omission to give notice of termination that each party signifies the necessary positive assent to the extension of the term for a further period."

The invalidity of the notice is in itself a sufficient basis for deciding this case in favour of the defendant. However, Mr Luba submits that, even if it had been valid at common law, it would have been rendered invalid by section 5(1) of the Protection from Eviction Act 1977, which, as amended by section 32 of the Housing Act 1988, is in these terms:

"5—(1). Subject to subsection (1B) below, no notice by a landlord or a tenant to quit any premises let (whether before or after the commencement of this Act) as a dwelling shall be valid unless—

(a) it is in writing and contains such information as may be prescribed, and

(b) it is given not less than 4 weeks before the date on which it is to take effect."

No other part of the section is material. It is to be observed that section 5(1) applies as much to a notice to quit given by a tenant as to one given by a landlord. Accordingly, on the assumption that Miss Doubtfire's notice to quit was otherwise valid, it would nevertheless appear to have been invalidated by this provision....

Here clause 14 contains an agreement that the tenancy may be determined by notice to quit given by the tenant if the period of notice is (a) four weeks or (b) such lesser period as the council may accept. The parties therefore agreed under (b) that the tenancy should in certain circumstances be determined by less than the four weeks' notice required by section 5(1). Notwithstanding Mr Cottle's arguments to the contrary, that is clearly an agreement to contract out of the provisions of section 5(1). ...

Here the council are asking us to hold that the protection afforded by section 5(1) can be brought to an end by an agreement made between them and only one of two joint tenants. It is obvious that such an agreement cannot deprive the other joint tenant of the protection to which he is entitled under the Act. That is not a point which can be elaborated.

For these reasons I would also decide the second point in favour of the defendant. I would allow the appeal and discharge the district judge's order for possession.'

Superficially this decision is a technical one, on the question as to whether a clause in a tenancy agreement can override the provisions of the Protection from Eviction Act 1977, and whether the notice given in the instant case was a notice to quit, or one operating a 'break' clause in the tenancy agreement (in which case *McGrady/Monk* had no application). However, the reasoning of Nourse LJ is 'result orientated' and he is clearly influenced by the perceived injustice of a unilateral destruction of the 'domestic' rights of the remaining joint tenant (there are echoes here of Lord Browne-Wilkinson's view in *Monk* that a 'property based' perspective of the landlord and tenant relationship in this sort of case led to a 'revulsion against [one joint tenant] being able unilaterally to terminate [the other joint tenant's] rights in his home'[66]. Following *Pilling*, parties intending to use the *McGrady/Monk* approach must be very wary of the difference between a 'break' clause and a notice to quit. To be 'on the safe side', the notice should clearly be of a minimum four weeks' duration, be not shorter than the periodic length of the tenancy, and should be given so as to expire on the anniversary date of the tenancy. Indeed, a local authority who, under the mistaken belief that a joint tenancy had been validly terminated by one joint tenant, refuse the other joint tenant admission to the premises will be liable in damages under s 27 of the Housing Act 1988 for unlawful eviction and cannot rely on the 'reasonable cause' defence under s 27(8).[67] This is demonstrated by *Wandsworth London Borough Council v Osei-Bonsu*.[68]

A joint secure tenancy had been granted by Wandsworth to the plaintiff and his wife in March 1989. The parties separated in January 1990, the wife and five children moving into bed and breakfast accommodation, following complaints against her husband of domestic violence. The wife subsequently obtained a non-molestation

---

[66] [1992] 1 All ER 1, at p 10.
[67] See further Chapter 5.
[68] [1999] 1 All ER 265.

order and an 'ouster' injunction, and in February the plaintiff vacated the property. On 30 April, as part of an arrangement with the authority to transfer her to alternative accommodation, the wife served a notice to quit on the council. However, this notice was set to expire on 14 May, less than the 28 days required under s 5 of the Protection from Eviction Act 1977. At the time (this being before the decision in *Pilling*) the authority took the view that the notice had been valid and had effectively terminated the joint tenancy. The plaintiff was refused re-admission to the property, which was subsequently re-let, and the wife was rehoused elsewhere. Following *Pilling* the notice was seen to be invalid and the eviction unlawful. The Court of Appeal confirmed an award of substantial damages to the plaintiff (whilst reducing the amount from £30,000 to £10,000). It appears that the only sensible course for an authority unsure of their legal ground, is not to attempt eviction without being completely sure that the Protection from Eviction Act 1977 has been complied with.

The final difficulty in applying *McGrady/Monk* is the uneasy relationship between the (apparently) conclusive effect of a valid notice to quit served by one joint tenant, and any injunction which might already exist under 'domestic' legislation guaranteeing (at least in the short term) the rights of the *other* joint tenant in the property.

Given that it is most often a woman (with children) who serves the notice to quit as part of a rehousing agreement with the authority landlord, and that it is most often that (any) injunctions would also favour such a female partner, the point may not arise frequently, but it did surface in the case of *Harrow London Borough Council v Johnstone*[69]. Here, the defendant and his wife were joint tenants of a house owned by the plaintiff council. The wife commenced divorce proceedings in 1992. They both continued to live in the house. In February 1994 the wife left, taking the children of the marriage with her. On an *ex parte* application by the defendant pursuant to the Domestic Violence and Matrimonial Proceedings Act 1976 the judge made an order restraining the wife from using or threatening violence against the defendant or harassing or interfering with him, and from excluding or attempting to exclude him from the house. The wife applied to the council for rehousing. The council, pursuant to their policy of not providing accommodation to someone who already had a council tenancy, suggested that she should serve notice to quit on them. They were then unaware of the injunction granted to the defendant. The wife gave notice to quit, and the defendant, having received a copy, told the council about the injunction. He remained in occupation of the house, and the council brought proceedings against him for possession.

The judge dismissed the claim, holding that by giving the notice to quit the wife had acted in breach of the injunction and was in contempt of court; and that by bringing the proceedings for possession when they were aware of the injunction the council had aided and abetted the wife in that breach and were also in contempt of court, and that the proceedings were an abuse of the process of the court. The Court of Appeal by a majority dismissed the council's appeal. However, the House of Lords unanimously allowed the council's further appeal holding that the injunction had been directed at preventing the wife from molesting the defendant and at excluding

---

[69] [1997] 1 All ER 929.

him from the exercise of occupation rights under the joint tenancy *while it existed*. It had not been intended to prohibit the wife from serving a notice to quit. Therefore, the wife and the council had not acted in breach of the injunction and so had not been in contempt of court. As a consequence, the wife's notice to quit had been effective to terminate the joint tenancy, and the defendant had not defence to the claim for possession.

Lord Mustill stated[70]:

'My Lords in the light of the principles it seems to me quite beyond doubt that, absent the special procedural background, the wife's notice to the council of 22 March 1994 was effective to allow the joint tenancy to terminate on the expiry of the notice. I am unable to see how clause 19 of the tenancy agreement could lead to any other result, nor has anything in the Act of 1985 been identified which could alter the position. The husband's right to remain in occupation, and the security of tenure which he had hitherto enjoyed, came to an end on the due date for renewal. Other things being equal, the husband remained in the house without legal warrant, and the council was entitled to take steps to remove him.

The question is whether, in the particular circumstances, other things were indeed equal. The husband maintains that they were not, for two quite distinct reasons. The first depends on the injunction of 3 February 1994. It is said that, by giving the notice of 22 March 1994, the wife was in breach of the injunction of 3 February 1994. It is said that, by giving the notice of 22 March 1994, the wife was in breach of the injunction and that all the subsequent acts of the wife and council are either inherently flawed or were abusive and hence unenforceable.

An examination of this argument must begin with the terms of the injunction. Did the requirement that the wife should not "exclude or attempt to exclude" the husband from the house prohibit her from notifying the council that the tenancy would not be renewed?

...

The husband's application was led by an affidavit alleging that the wife had assaulted him and locked him out of the house. The application was typed on a printed form reciting the Act of 1976. It invited the court to make orders:

"That [the wife] be forbidden ... from: (1) To use or threaten to use violence upon the applicant. (2) To harass threaten pester or otherwise interfere with the applicant. (3) To leave and not return to the former matrimonial home situated and known as 5 Waghorn Road, Kenton, Harrow, Middlesex. (4) To remove or attempt to remove the children of the family from the day to day care of the applicant or attempt to remove from the jurisdiction."

and concluded with the words: "and that the respondent not prevent the applicant from returning to 5, Waghorn Road ..."

---

[70]    At p 935.

Regrettably, even on this second appeal neither side is able to provide any information about what happened when this application came before the judge. It is not even known whether the ex parte application was followed, as it should have been, by inter partes proceedings; and if so, with what result. What we do know, however, is that an injunction was made in the terms already recited: an injunction which so far as is known the wife has never sought to discharge or vary.

My Lords, reading this application together with the statute which it invoked and with the terms of the order as made it is in my view absolutely plain that the prohibition against excluding the husband was not intended to be a mandatory order requiring the wife to co-operate in maintaining in force the rights created by the joint tenancy pending the adjustment of those rights on a future date in proceedings not yet started. The application was made at a time of crisis when the husband had been locked out of the house and wanted to get back in. His concern was that his wife had excluded him from the exercise of the rights of occupation which he undoubtedly possessed under the joint tenancy. There is no sign in the documents of an apprehension on his part that the rights themselves were under threat and would require protection by an order requiring the wife to keep the tenancy in being. If the court was to grant something on the lines of a mandatory *Mareva*-like injunction the first step was to ask for one. This the husband did not do. Instead he invited the court to make an order designed to ensure that the molestation of which she was accused did not happen again. The Act of 1976 was the right vehicle for such an order, and although the injunction actually issued did not follow precisely the wording of the Act I have no doubt that this was the foundation of the order which Judge Krikler intended to make and did make. As such it was concerned with the exercise of rights under the tenancy and not with the continued existence of the rights themselves.

On this view the husband's first line of argument fails at the outset.

…

Counsel for the husband [then argued] to this effect. Faced with a spouse who showed real signs of desiring a permanent end to the marriage the council should have foreseen that there already were, or in the future might be, proceedings in which the court would be called on to address the proprietary rights of the spouses, including the valuable (if vulnerable) security of tenure of the house; it should also have foreseen that the destruction of the tenure would cause irreparable damage to the husband, since the loss of his tenancy coupled with the rehousing of the wife might critically determine the question of where the young children lived; even if it was not at first in possession of enough information to form a judgment the council should have informed itself by making inquiries; and having done so should have abstained from joining with the wife in any course of action which might put out of the husband's reach the possibility of obtaining some kind of relief in any proceedings which he or the wife might, in the parlous state of the marriage, ultimately come to begin.

My Lords, I acknowledge the appeal of this argument in human terms. We know insufficient of the marital discord to say that the wife was in the wrong, but at least there was sufficient merit on the husband's side for him (rather unusually, given the reversal of gender) to obtain an anti-molestation order which the wife has never tried to displace. Nevertheless, I see no ground to treat the notice by the wife as ineffectual, and still less to convict the council of a wrongful intention to frustrate the ends of justice. Exactly what passed between the council and the wife has never been investigated, as it should have been if they were to be held in contempt. One may, however, test the matter by envisaging a situation where the wife came to the council and simply asked to be rehoused; where the official explained that this could not be done because she was already a tenant; where she told the official that she no longer wanted to keep the joint tenancy in being and asked what to do; where the official recommended that she should take legal advice; and where her lawyer, familiar with the principle of *Hammersmith and Fulham London Borough Council v Monk* [1992] 1 AC 478, prepared the notice which was in fact served. Would it be possible to say that anyone involved had acted in contempt of court? Surely not. All one needs, then, to reach the present case is to telescope the course of events. The contrast between this case and *A-G v Times Newspapers Ltd* [1992] 1 AC 191 is obvious. There the newspaper defiantly acted in detriment to the obvious interests of justice. Here, the council simply carried through the logic of its housing policy, that one person could not have two council tenancies at the same time. I find it impossible to hold that by putting its statutory duty as housing authority before the interests of a matrimonial relationship of which it was not the guardian the council contemptuously subverted the authority of the court or intentionally nullified the aims of any legal proceedings. This being so I can see no ground upon which it could be held that the dealings of the council with the wife and the husband were completely ineffectual, leaving the parties in the same position as if the notice had never been given. The conclusion is to my mind inescapable that by the time the matter reached Judge Hunter the interest of the husband under the tenancy had come to an end by effluxion of time, so that there was no longer any ground on which he could deny the council the right to resume possession of the house.

These conclusions are sufficient to dispose of the appeal ...'

*Johnstone* was specifically concerned with an injunction under s 1 of the Domestic Violence and Matrimonial Proceedings Act 1976, focusing on the immediate difficulties produced by violence or potential violence in a 'domestic' context (see now s 33(3), s 35(5), s 36(5) and s 42, Family Law Act 1996). Nothing in the injunction purported to resolve the longer-term 'disposition' of the tenancy, a fact which 'opened the door' for the service of the notice to quit by the wife. Equally, once a court order is made providing for such 'disposition' the resultant transfer of the tenancy rules out any scope for the (ex) joint tenant subsequently to serve a notice to quit (see s 24, Matrimonial Causes Act 1973 (as amended) and Sch 7, Family Law Act 1996).

What of a tenant spouse who intends to apply for an 'occupation' order transferring the tenancy into his or her sole name? Is it a defence to a landlord's claim for possession, subsequent to the service of a notice to quit by the other joint tenant, for a joint tenant to argue that he or she intended to apply for an order transferring the tenancy? The most recent authority indicates that the answer is 'no'.

In *Newlon Housing Trust v Alsulaimen*[71] husband and wife held a joint assured weekly tenancy of a property, where they lived until the wife left and commenced divorce proceedings. On 1 November 1995 the wife served on the landlords a notice to quite the premises. The notice expired on 4 December 1995 but the husband continued to live there. In March 1996 the landlords commenced proceedings for possession of the premises. At the hearing the husband sought an adjournment on the ground that he proposed to make an application under (what was then) s 24 of the Matrimonial Causes Act 1973 for a property adjustment order transferring the joint tenancy into his sole name. The judge refused the adjournment, on the ground that the application was too late. The Court of Appeal reversed the judge's decision and ruled that the husband had a good prospect of obtaining a transfer of the tenancy and that justice required that he be given an opportunity to pursue his application. However, the House of Lords unanimously allowed the landlord's appeal, holding that a notice to quit simply caused the tenancy to terminate 'by effluxion of time' and did not involve any 'disposition' of property. Therefore, the courts had no powers to set aside the notice to quit for the purpose of making a property adjustment order.

Lord Mustill states[72]:

'The concession before the Court of Appeal was that the court could make an order setting aside the termination of the tenancy on the ground that it was a "disposition" of property by the wife made with the intention of defeating the husband's claim for a property adjustment order. Your Lordships gave Mr Andrew Arden, who appeared for the trust, leave to withdraw this concession and he submitted that the termination of a tenancy by the effluxion of a notice to quit was not a disposition of property at all. It followed that the court had no power to resurrect the joint tenancy and accordingly there was no property in respect of which an adjustment order could be made. In those circumstances, there could be no defence to the claim for possession.

The question is therefore whether the termination of a tenancy can be a disposition of property. "Disposition" is a familiar enough word in the law of property and ordinarily means an act by which someone ceases to be the owner of that property in law or in equity: see the formulation of Mr R. O. Wilberforce QC in *Grey v IRC* [1960] AC 1, at 18. In some contexts it may include the case in which the property ceases to exist. It is unnecessary to decide whether it has such an extended meaning in this case. There are contrary indications, namely that section 37 contemplates, first, that the disposition will be capable of being set aside and secondly, that the benefici-ary of the disposition may be able to show that he took in good faith and without notice. On the other hand, I feel sure that "disposition" was intended to include the surrender of a subsisting proprietary interest, such as a tenancy

---

[71]  [1998] 4 All ER 1.
[72]  At p 4.

for years or for life, so as to merge in the reversion or remainder: see *IRC v Buchanan* [1957] 2 All ER 400 at 402, [1958] Ch 289, at 296, per Lord Goddard CJ. But, be that all as it may, I think it is essential to the notion of a disposition of property in this context that there is property of which the disponor disposes, whether to someone else or not. It is this property which the court can restore to his estate by setting aside the disposition.

One asks, the, whether the effect of the termination of the tenancy by notice was to dispose of any property belonging to the wife. What property did she hold at the time she gave the notice? The answer is: a joint interest in a weekly tenancy of the flat. In considering the nature of that interest, it is important to bear in mind that, in English law, rights of property in land are four-dimensional. They are defined not only by reference to the physical boundaries of the property but also by reference to the time for which the interest will endure. Thus a life interest in a property is an item of property with a temporal dimension, ceasing to exist on the death of the tenant for life. When that event happens, no property passes from the tenant for life to the remainderman. The latter's interest falls into possession but he becomes entitled to possession by virtue of his own interest and not by having acquired that of the tenant for life. The same is true when a lease for a term of years terminates by effluxion of time. The tenant does not dispose of his interest. At the moment when it expires, he has no property of which he can dispose. It ceases to exist and the landlord's reversion falls into possession.

The analysis of a periodic tenancy by Lord Bridge of Harwich in *Hammersmith and Fulham London Borough Council v Monk* [1992] 1 All ER 1, [1992] 1 AC 478 demonstrates that what I have said of a tenancy for a term of years is equally true of a periodic tenancy. It also comes to an end by effluxion of time, namely the expiry of the last period for which the tenant or tenants have been willing for it to continue. The respondents invite your Lordships to treat the notice to quit as an act which is dispositive, or at any rate destructive, of the tenant. But this, as Lord Bridge said, at p 490, is to "confuse the form with the substance". The notice merely signifies that the tenant is not willing to consent to the continuation of the tenancy beyond the date at which it could otherwise expire. In the absence of such consent, it terminates by effluxion of time in the same way as a tenancy for a term of years.

Mr Buckhaven, who appeared for the respondents, invited your Lordships to give a purposive construction to section 37. It was, he said, intended to give the court power to undo any disposition of assets by one of the parties to the marriage. In many cases, a periodic tenancy would be one of the most important assets. Although in legal theory the tenancy might be said to have ceased to exist, the flat was still there. There was no physical problem about ordering a reinstatement of the tenancy and the courts should not let mere conceptual difficulties stand in their way.

I would certainly not wish to give section 37(2) a construction which defeats its evident purpose, but I am far from confident that the legislation was meant to have the broad effect for which Mr Buckhaven contents. The difference in section 37(2) between the language of paragraph (a), which confers the power to grant restraining orders in advance, and paragraph (b), which deals with past transactions, is very striking. The restraining power applies not only when a party is about to make 'any disposition' but also to transfer out of the jurisdiction or "otherwise deal with" any property. Paragraph (b), on the other hand, deals only with dispositions.

… if the periodic tenancy had still been in existence, the court would have had power to order its transfer to the husband … But since it has duly expired, I do not think that it can be revived and the husband therefore has no answer to the claim for possession.'

In part, Lord Hoffmann's reasoning is of general application, focusing as it does on the consequences for property rights of the valid service of a notice to quit. It also turns on his analysis of the precise wording of s 37 of the Matrimonial Causes Act 1973, in particular the meaning of 'reviewable disposition' in s 37(2)(b). The Matrimonial Causes Act provisions survive (with some amendments) the implementation of the Family Law Act 1996. Moreover, the point seems to be even clearer under the 'tailored' tenancy transfer provisions, now contained in Sch 7 of the Family Law Act 1996, which apply only if 'one spouse [or cohabitant] is entitled, either in his own right or jointly with the other spouse, to occupy a dwelling-house by virtue of a relevant tenancy' (Sch 7, para 2). Once the notice to quit has expired, it seems that no 'relevant tenancy' continues to exist (see the analogy with *Thompson v Elmbridge Borough Council*[73].

The *McGrady/Monk* principle applies as much to assured tenancies under the Housing Act 1988, as it does to secure tenancies subsist until (amongst other things) the notice to quit served by one of the joint tenants expires. However, the principle does not apply to Rent Act tenancies. A notice to quit will have the effect of bringing the contractual protected joint tenancy to an end, but this, in its turn, gives rise to a statutory joint tenancy under s 2 of the Rent Act 1977. Statutory tenancies, having no contractual basis, cannot be brought to an end by notices to quit, but only by a court possession order pursuant to s 98 of and Sch 15 to the Rent Act 1977. Indeed notices to quit are wholly inapplicable to statutory tenancies (s 3(4), Rent Act 1977). Even if only one of the (former) joint tenants remains in the property, his or her rights as a statutory tenant continue (*Lloyd v Sadler*[74]).

In *Hammersmith London Borough Council v Monk*, although Lord Browne-Wilkinson concurred in the decision of the House of Lords, he did so with some misgivings. As he puts it[75]:

'… there are two instinctive reactions to this case which lead to diametrically opposite conclusions. The first is that the flat in question was the joint home of the appellant and Mrs Powell: it therefore cannot be right that one them unilaterally can join with the landlords to put an end to the other's rights in the home. The second is that the appellant and Mrs Powell undertook joint liabilities on tenants for the purpose of providing themselves with a joint

[73]  (1987) 19 HLR 526.
[74]  [1978] QB 777.
[75]  [1992] 1 All ER 1, at p 10.

home and that once the desire to live together has ended, it is impossible to require that the one who quits the home should continue indefinitely to be liable for the discharge of the obligations to the landlord under the tenancy agreement'.

Putting the 'instinctive reaction' in a theoretical context, he later states that

'the revulsion against Mrs Powell being able unilaterally to terminate the appellant's rights in his home is property based ... the other reaction is contract based: Mrs Powell cannot be held to a tenancy contract which is dependent for its continuance on the will of the tenant.'

In the end, he was sufficiently satisfied that the 'contract' approach was the correct one.

One uncertainty left by *Newlon Housing Trust v Alsulaimen*[76]: is the legal position in the (far from unlikely) scenario of one of the joint tenants becoming aware that the other was *about* to serve a notice to quit, thereby ending their property rights. Clearly if the application for a tenancy transfer is heard by the courts before (any) notice to quit expires there is no difficulty, since there is still a tenancy in existence to be transferred. However, is the giving of a notice to quit a 'dealing' with the property, which, in any event, can be 'restrained' by the courts (under s 37(2)(a), Matrimonial Causes Act 1973) so as to 'protect' the right to apply for a judicial tenancy transfer? Unfortunately, Lord Hoffmann expressly states no view on this point,[77] so leaving the matter to be resolved in the future by the courts.

Subsequently in *Bater v Greenwich London Borough Council, Bater v Bater*[78], the Court of Appeal followed the *Alsulaimen* decision and held the Court had no jurisdiction under s 37(2)(b) of the Matrimonial Causes Act 1973 to set aside a unilateral notice to terminate a joint tenancy by one of two joint tenants in a matrimonial dispute. This is because such a notice is not a disposition of property within the terms of the subsection. However, Thorp LJ went on, though alone on the point, to argue that under s 37(2)(a) there was jurisdiction to intervene where a unilateral notice is about to be served as that is a situation where the server of the notice is attempting 'otherwise [to] deal with any property'. He also argued that the court had an inherent jurisdiction to deal with acts or omissions by either side in a divorce either before or after the issue of divorce proceedings if such acts or omissions are able to harass or molest the other side or could affect adversely the welfare of any child. Equally such a power existed to prevent acts whose conse-quence would be to diminish the power of the court to distribute or redistribute assets in order to promote the welfare of any child or to secure the financial future of any financially dependent applicant. He then went on to argue that a similar jurisdiction existed in relation to unmarried joint tenants provided they have children under the wordships powers of the court and the powers of the Children Act 1989. The powers of the court could be activated by practitioners in family proceedings seeking undertakings from the other side where a joint tenancy is involved not to deal with it in any way detrimental to the interest of their client until

---

[76]  [1998] 4 All ER 1.
[77]  [1999] 1 AC at p 319.
[78]  [1999] 4 All ER 944.

the future of the property is decided by the court. Such an undertaking could then be brought to the notice of the landlord, and, if necessary, could be reinforced or superseded by an injunction from the court which could be served on the landlord preventing service or a unilateral notice.

If Thorpe LJ's arguments are correct, and Roch and Lloyd LJJ expressed no opinion on the point, then a 'race' could begin in disputes between joint tenants as to who can get which procedure under way first; either that of a unilateral notice to quit, or that under s 37(2)(a) restraining, or seeking an undertaking not to serve, such a notice.

## Postscript

Since *McGrady* the law on joint tenancies and notices to quit has become increasingly complex. Since 1992 the area has been considered three times by the House of Lords and on numerous occasions by the Court of Appeal, and yet uncertainties still remain. In many ways the current law is something of a blunt instrument, facilitating a sensible regularising of housing arrangements where spouses with children have been deserted, or have fled the home because of domestic violence, yet also providing an opportunity for vindictive action by disaffected partners.[79] Moreover, the *McGrady/Monk* principle operates only when there is a joint tenancy and does nothing to assist a non-tenant partner. It is likely that most local authority and social landlords *do* grant joint tenancies to partners of all descriptions today (particularly in the light of Annex C, Code of Guidance to Parts VI and VII, Housing Act 1996), but the practice is still not universal. Another approach has often been thought to be the creation of a new ground for possession against a secure tenant who is guilty of violence; and to some extent this is now provided for by the Housing Act 1996 which, via s 145 and s 149, creates a new Ground 2A in Sch 2 to the housing Act 1985 and a new Ground 14A in Sch 2 to the Housing Act 1988. Both new grounds apply to married couples and heterosexual cohabitants, but not to homosexual relationships. They apply equally to sole and joint tenancies. It must be demonstrated that one partner has left the property in question because of violence (or threats of violence) to themselves or a member of their family in residence at the relevant time, *and* that the partner who has left is unlikely to return. The grounds are discretionary, thus requiring the landlord to demonstrate that it is reasonably to grant possession. No doubt the existence of appropriate arrangements for rehousing the partner who has left because of violence will often be a relevant factor. In the case of the Housing Act 1988, the new Ground 14A applies only to social landlords (for example, housing associations).

A further important question is the extent to which the Human Rights Act 1998 can be deployed to assist an occupant liable to eviction and of thereby losing secure/ assured tenancy rights by what might be termed the joint tenancy 'route'. As explained in Chapter 14, the initial signs – in particular in the Court of Appeal decision in *Qazi*[80] – were that the impact would be considerable. However, the

---

[79] See generally in Davis, M and Hughes, D, 'An end of the affair – Social Housing Relationship Breakdown and the Human Rights Act 1998' [2004] 68 Conv Jan/Feb 19.
[80] *London Borough of Harrow v Qazi* [2001] EWCA Civ 1834, [2002] HLR 276.

House of Lords' decision in *Qazi*, while controversial, has, for the time being at least, closed off much of the scope for change in the pre-existing law. As *Qazi* is currently on appeal to the European Court of Human Rights it would be premature to assume that the House of Lords' decision[81] is the last word (particularly as the case demonstrated deep divisions in the house). Whatever the final outcome in the case, the law in this area is, as already stated, hardly in a satisfactory state. Another way forward might be to adopt the Law Commission proposal[82] that:

> '... a joint occupier shall be able to terminate his or her interest in a joint agreement by means of a notice, without bringing the whole of the agreement to an end.'

In such a case a landlord would be able to seek possession against the remaining occupier, on the basis that the property is too large for them alone, or contains special features which they do not need, or (concerning social landlords) that they 'do not ... have the requisite degree of housing need'.[83] However, this would only be a discretionary ground for possession and, in any event, aside from the court having the capacity to make a final judgment based on the overall 'reasonableness' of the case, the possession issue would at least have the capacity to be fought out like other possession cases in 'the social' sector rather than following inevitably from an accident of property law!

## FURTHER READING

Law Commission, *Domestic Violence and the Occupation of the Family Home*, No 207 (7 May 1992) (HCI).

Law Commission, *Renting Homes*, Cm 6018 (2003)

Cowan D, *Housing Law and Policy* (1999) Macmillan, Chapter 16.

Hughes, D and Lowe, S, *Public Sector Housing Law* (3rd ed, 2000), Chapter 5.

---

[81]  [2003] UKHL 43, [2003] 3 WLR 792.
[82]  Law Commission, *Renting Homes*. Law Com No 284 Cm 6018 (2003), para 11.27.
[83]  Ibid paras 11.33 to 11.35.

# CHAPTER 12

# Housing Standards and Repair

## HISTORICAL CONTEXT

The issue of housing standards and the renewal of the housing stock became important issues during the nineteenth century due to the public health consequences of rapid urbanisation. Appallingly high mortality and morbidity was endemic in Victorian slum housing. As described in Chapter 1 the insanitary condition of urban housing was one of the principal reasons for state intervention in the housing market. As early as 1868, in the Artizans' and Labourers' Dwellings Act (the Torrens Act), local authorities with populations over 10,000 were granted considerable powers to enforce compulsory unfitness notices against landlords, and so provided for the closure and demolition of dwellings unfit for human habitation. There was, of course, at this time no financial assistance for repair and improvement grants did not become available in urban areas until after World War Two. The Housing (Rural Workers) Act 1926 gave authorities in rural locations discretion to award grants and make loans for improvements but these powers were rarely used.

In the Artizans' and Labourers' Dwellings Improvement Act 1875 (the Cross Act) authorities were given powers to clear and redevelop areas of unfit housing but they had very limited possibilities to rebuild even after the Housing of the Working Classes Act 1890 and, in the absence of any significant central government funding until the conclusion of the 1914–18 war, far more slums were cleared than were rebuilt. Individual closures and the redevelopment of whole areas of housing have been enshrined in the issue of housing standards ever since.

For most of the twentieth century renovation and improvement of existing housing stock was subsumed under both the slum clearance programme and the drive for new building. It was not until the end of the 1960s that investment in the renovation of existing property became more cost effective than demolition and rebuilding due to the decline in the absolute shortage of housing stock. Renovation of existing property is, of course, one way in which new supply can be achieved – by giving existing dwellings a longer life expectancy than they would have otherwise[1]. Under the different circumstances of the 1920s the renovation and reconditioning of existing housing was promoted as an alternative to local authority building by the opponents of municipal housing. Bowley estimates that between 1919 and 1930

---

[1]  Needleman, L 'The comparative economics of improvement and new building' (1969) Urban Studies, Vol 6 No 2, pp 196–209.

some 300,000 houses per annum were rehabilitated by forcing private landlords to recondition and improve their property by statutory orders against them[2]. Renovation of housing in the private rented sector thus made a considerable contribution to the inter-war drive to increase housing supply but the standard of improvement was frequently poor and many rehabilitated houses were later demolished as slums. Improvement of this stock up to the very basic standard inherited from late-Victorian housing legislation was not, therefore, an adequate response to the problem of slum housing. Accordingly a specific subsidy for slum clearance and their replacement by new houses was adopted in the Labour Government's second Housing Act 1930. This legislation was not as some commentators argue a major break in policy but, seen in the light of the reconditioning of housing in the 1920s, can be viewed as an extension of existing concern about the state of the private rented sector.

This is not the place for a detailed evaluation of the slum clearance programme and readers are referred to Chapter 2 of Gibson and Langstaff's *An Introduction to Urban Renewal* [3] for a full account. The clearances were of massive dimensions and some two million dwellings have been demolished since the Housing Act 1930 (Greenwood Act) with the built environment of almost every major town and city changed as a result. Clearances were halted during the Second World War and only started again in the mid-1950s when the economy had recovered from the catastrophic consequences of the war. In the five years between 1955 and 1959 213,000 houses were demolished or closed affecting nearly 670,000 people. The clearance programme reached its post-war peak in the second half of the 1960s when between 1964 and 1969 339,000 house were demolished. The rate of clearance fell, in the mid-1970s, to about 50,000 per annum and declined sharply thereafter; by 1989 it was down to only 6,000 and has stayed below that level subsequently.

It has long been accepted that the worst of the housing stock is concentrated in the private rented sector. However, a simplistic analysis should be avoided, and much depends on factors as diverse as the age of the property, the identity of the landlord and the time at which the property entered the rented sector. Generally speaking, pre-1919 housing owned by landlords operating a few properties is in the worst condition. However, the 2001 English House Condition Survey (published in 2003) indicated an improvement overall in private rented housing with the percentage of those not meeting 'decent' standards (ie the fitness standard plus an assessment of the state of repair, the presence of a modern bathroom and kitchen, together with adequate levels of insulation and heating) falling from 63.2 per cent in 1996 to 49.4 per cent in 2001.

## The current law

The rest of this chapter describes the current law and unless where expressly stated the remedies referred to apply to both public and private sector tenancies, and begins by considering the common law remedies available to tenants and others injured by the substandard condition of rented property.

---

[2] Bowley, M *Housing and the State* (Allen and Unwin, 1945).
[3] Hutchinson, 1982.

Historically neither contract nor tort gave protection to tenants. The attitude of the law was encapsulated in the maxim caveat emptor, or as Erle CJ said in *Robbins v Jones*[4]: '... fraud apart, there is no law against letting a tumbledown house: and the tenant's remedy is upon his contract, if any'[5]. There was no liability in tort whether the damage arose from the landlord's mere neglect or from the careless doing of works of maintenance or installation. In *Travers v Gloucester Corpn*[6] a local authority let a house with the vent pipe of a gas geyser terminating under the eaves of the house. This dangerous installation led to a build-up of toxic exhaust fumes and as a consequence the tenant's lodger was gassed in the bathroom. The corporation was held not liable in tort.

A growing body of opinion viewed the exemption of lessors from liability in negligence with growing distaste and various attempts were made to end it. For example it was said in *Ball v LCC*[7] that landlords could be liable in contract to tenants for negligent installation work carried out after the start of the lease, though non-contracting parties could not sue under this rule. Great changes have now, however, been made in the law.

## LANDLORDS' OBLIGATIONS IN TORT

### At common law

Following the decisions in *Cunard v Antifyre Ltd* [8] and *Taylor v Liverpool Corpn*[9] there is no difficulty in holding landlords liable in negligence for damage caused *by buildings retained in their occupation* to persons or to buildings let to a tenant. In *AC Billings & Sons Ltd v Riden*[10] the House of Lords stated that, irrespective of the lack of a contractual relationship, persons who execute work on premises are under a general duty to use reasonable care for the safety of those whom they know, or ought reasonably to know, may be affected by or lawfully in the vicinity of the work. Thus landlords can be liable in tort for dangers created *after* the commencement of the tenancy. Even so the claimant must still show that the landlord was under a duty of care in respect of a particular hazard. If a landlord can show that their policy with regard to any such hazard has been properly arrived at, and that no exceptional risk arises with regard to the claimant it is unlikely a duty of care will exist.[11]

In *Rimmer v Liverpool City Council* [12], the claimant was the tenant of a flat owned, designed and built by the local authority. One internal passageway contained an unprotected thin glass panel. The tenant tripped in the passageway, put out his hand to save himself, and his hand went through the panel, as a result of which he

---

4   (1863) 15 CBNS 221 at 239.
5   See *Gordon and Teixeira v Selico and Select Management Ltd* (1986) 18 HLR 219 for an application of this principle; see also *Southwark London Borough Council v Mills, Baxter v Camden London Borough Council* [1999] 4 All ER 449, [1999] 3 WLR 939, HL, on the point that a lack of sound insulation is no breach of covenant of quiet enjoyment.
6   [1947] KB 71, [1946] 2 All ER 506.
7   [1949] 2 KB 159, [1949] 1 All ER 1056.
8   [1933] 1 KB 551.
9   [1939] 3 All ER 329.
10  [1958] AC 240, [1957] 3 All ER 1.
11  *Stevens v Blaenau Gwent Borough Council* [2004] EWCA Civ 715, [2004] All ER (D) 116 (Jun).
12  [1985] QB 1, [1984] 1 All ER 930.

suffered injury. The Court of Appeal repeated that the 'bare' landlord of unfurnished premises, who has done no work on them , owes no duty of care to a tenant in respect of the state of the premises when they were let, but held that a landlord may owe a duty of care in respect of being the designer or builder of premises. This duty is owed to all persons who may reasonably be expected to be affected by the design or construction of the premises, and is a duty to take reasonable care to ensure such persons do not suffer injury from design or construction defects (which may extend to defects in work of modernisation or conversion etc). The authority was in breach of that duty on this occasion. Liability here arose from the fact of negligent design and/or construction. Where, however, there is no evidence of negligent design or construction, the old rule survives[13]. In *Targett v Torfaen Borough Council*[14] it was held that the fact that a claimant knows of the landlord's bad design or construction work will not automatically negative the landlord's duty of care. The question in such cases is whether the claimant can reasonably be expected to remove or avoid the danger. It is not normally reasonable to expect a tenant to avoid a danger by giving up the property, though knowledge of a defect may point to a need for a tenant to take greater heed for personal safety, and failure to do that may result in the tenant being contributorily negligent in respect of harm suffered. See also *Sharpe v Manchester Metropolitan District Council*[15] where the plaintiff took a tenancy of a flat in 1972 and found it infested with cockroaches. The authority tried to eliminate the insects for two years by using emulsified DDT, but failed in their attempts. They were found negligent in that they had failed to treat the service ducts and other spaces in the walls and floor and had used a discredited insecticide. However, this decision should not be over much relied on following *Habinteg Housing Association v James*[16], where there was held to be no liability on a landlord where a flat was infested but there was no part of the property in the landlord's possession from which an invasion of the tenant's home could be shown to have proceeded.

It also appears liability cannot arise where a landlord can show its repairing policies and equipment ordering practices comply with the practices of other reasonably skilled and competent people engaged in property maintenance[17].

## Under statute

Civil liability may arise under the Defective Premises Act 1972. Section 1 provides (inter alia):

> '(1) A person taking on work for or in connection with the provision of a dwelling (whether the dwelling is provided by the erection or by the conversion or enlargement of a building) owes a duty:
> (a)   if the building is provided to the order of any person to that person; and
> (b)   without prejudice to paragraph (a) above to every person who acquires

[13]   *McNerney v Lambeth London Borough Council* (1988) 21 HLR 188, and *Boldack v East Lindsey District Council* (1998) 31 HLR 41, CA.
[14]   [1992] 3 All ER 27.
[15]   (1977) 5 HLR 71.
[16]   (1994) 27 HLR 299.
[17]   *Adams v Rhymney Valley District Council* [2000] 3 EGLR 25.

an interest (whether legal or equitable) in the dwelling; to see that the work which he takes on is done in a workmanlike or, as the case may be, professional manner, with proper materials and so that as regard that work the dwelling will be fit for habitation when completed …

(4) A person who:
(a) in the course of a business which consists of or includes providing or arranging for the provision of dwellings or installation in dwellings; or
(b) in the exercise of a power of making such provision or arrangements conferred by or by virtue of any enactment; arranges for another to take on work for or in connection with the provision of a dwelling shall be treated for the purposes of this section as included among the persons who have taken on the work.'

This provision imposes liability on authorities and associations, their builders, sub-contractors and architects if they fail to build in a professional or workmanlike manner (as the case may be) with proper materials, or fail to ensure the dwelling is fit for human habitation, a phrase which may be capable of covering such matters as defective design or lay-out. It extends to necessary work not done as well as that badly done so that a dwelling lacks after the work is done some essential attribute making it unfit[18]. The duty, which is strict, is owed to, inter alia, those persons having legal interests in the dwelling, for example tenants, but not their children or visitors. Moreover, the duty only arises in connection with the provision, whether by new construction, conversion or enlargement, of a dwelling. The provision only applies to dwellings constructed after 1 January 1974, by virtue of s 7(2) of the Act. This provision seems to have been strangely ignored by public sector tenants affected by design or construction defects[19].

Section 3(1) of the Defective Premises Act 1972 provides:

'Where work of construction, repair, maintenance or demolition or any other work is done on or in relation to premises, any duty of care owed, because of the doing of the work, to persons who might reasonably be expected to be affected by the defects in the state of the premises created by the doing of the work shall not be abated by the subsequent disposal of the premises by the person who owed the duty'.

This statutory displacement of a landlord's immunity in negligence only applies, by virtue of s 3(2)(a), to those lettings of premises entered into after the commencement of the Act, 1 January 1974. Liability can only arise where there has been a defect created by a positive act classifiable as 'work of construction, repair, maintenance or demolition or any other work done on or in relation to premises'. It seems not *all* 'work' can give rise to liability but only that of specified kinds, or other 'work' which can be said to be 'done on or in relation to premises' such as, for example, installation of central heating. Nor does this section impose any liability for negligent omissions to do repairs.

---

[18] *Andrews v Schooling* [1991] 3 All ER 723, [1991] 1 WLR 783 – a house converted into flats did not have work done to prevent the progress of damp into the bottom flat from the cellar.
[19] See further *Mirza v Bhandal* (1999) Housing Law Monitor (June) 4 where a person who arranged for a house to be substantially rebuilt was found liable under s 1(4) when the house was given inadequate foundations and subsided.

Liability for an omission may arise under s 4 of the 1972 Act. Section 4(1) provides:

> 'Where premises are let under a tenancy which puts on the landlord an obligation to the tenant for the maintenance or repair of the premises, the landlord owes to all persons who might reasonably be expected to be affected by defects in the state of the premises a duty to take such care as is reasonable in all the circumstances to see that they are reasonably safe from personal injury or from damage to their property caused by a relevant defect.'

This imposes tortious liability on landlords towards tenants, their families and those other persons foreseeably likely to be in the premises, and, by s 6(3) of the Act landlords cannot exclude or restrict this duty.

This section also poses problems of interpretation. Liability can only arise in respect of a 'relevant defect'. Such is defined by subs (3) as

> ' ... a defect in the state of the premises existing at or after the material time and arising from, or continuing because of, an act or omission by the landlord which constitutes or would if he had notice of the defect, have constituted a failure by him to carry out his obligation to the tenant for the maintenance or repair of the premises ...'.

Such defects must arise 'at or after the material time', which is further defined by the subs as being, in general terms, for tenancies commencing before the Act, the commencement date of the Act (1 January 1974), and in other cases the earliest date on which the tenancy commenced or the tenancy agreement was entered into. Liability arises out of those defects which constitute a breach of the landlord's obligations to repair and maintain. These obligations will include any express covenant to repair given by the landlord and, by virtue of subs (5), those implied by statute, such as s 11 of the Landlord and Tenant Act 1985. An even more extended meaning is given to 'obligation' by subs (4) which deems for the purposes of the section any power a landlord has to repair actually to be an obligation to repair. Such powers can arise in many situations. A landlord may have power to enter and do repairs simply because the tenant has defaulted on the tenant's repairing covenants. In such circumstances the Act provides that the landlord, while remaining liable to third parties, shall not be liable to the tenant. The effect of dicta in *Mint v Good*[20] should also be remembered. Somervell LJ said: '... in the case of a weekly tenancy, business efficacy will not be effected if the house is allowed to fall into disrepair and no one keeps it in reasonable condition; and it seems to be, therefore, necessary ... that the ... landlord should at any rate have the power to keep the place in proper repair ...'.

An implied power to enter and do repairs may arise in relation to any weekly tenancy of a dwelling-house and will be deemed to be an obligation to repair under subs (4).

In *Smith v Bradford Metropolitan Council*[21], a tenancy agreement provided the tenant should give the authority and its officers and workmen reasonable facilities for inspecting the premises let, their state of repair, and to carry out repairs, and the 'premises' in question were defined as the dwelling, and, where the context

---

[20]   [1951] 1 KB 517 at 522, [1950] 2 All ER 1159.
[21]   (1982) 44 P & CR 171.

required, its garage, outbuildings, yards and gardens. The tenant of the dwelling was injured by the defective condition of a rear concrete patio constructed between the house and its garden by a previous tenant. The Court of Appeal found the power to enter the premises fell within s 4(4) of the 1972 Act, and was a deemed obligation to repair. The context required that the patio be regarded as part of the premises in relation to which the power, and deemed obligation, to repair existed. In *McAuley v Bristol City Council*[22], however, there was merely a clause that the tenant should give the authority 'all reasonable facilities for entering upon the premises ... for any purpose which may from time to time be required by the council'. It was, nevertheless, held that this clause gave the council power to enter the premises, and that the tenancy agreement contemplated that the council would keep the premises in a reasonable and habitable condition. To give business efficacy to that understanding there had to be implied a term that the council would carry out repairs wherever there were defects in the premises – in this case including the garden – which would expose a tenant or visitor to a serious risk of injury. Thus because the council had the right to enter the premises they could be liable under s 4. However, the removal of a paving slab which was then stacked against a wall and subsequently fell on and injured the son of the tenant was not considered work of repair or maintenance for the purposes of s 4 in *Boldack v East Lindsey District Council*[23]. The claimant must show that the harm has arisen as a result of a relevant defect.

There are a number of subsidiary points to note about s 4. Sub-s (2) provides:

> 'The said duty is owed if the landlord knows (whether as the result of being notified by the tenant or otherwise) or if he ought in all the circumstances to have known of the relevant defect'.

There is no need to give notice of defects provided they would be patent on reasonable inspection. Indeed there are dicta that a local authority landlord should carry out pre-lettings checks of houses to detect defects[24].

In *Clarke v Taff Ely Borough Council*[25], Mrs Clarke visited her sister's council house and was injured when the rotten floorboards gave way beneath a table on which she was standing. The house was one of a number of pre-war council houses known to have a potentially dangerous floor construction. The authority's chief housing surveyor agreed that in view of the age of the house, its type and the presence of damp it was foreseeable that rot would occur. Damages of £5,100 were awarded.

A very extended meaning is given to 'tenancy' by s 6 of the 1972 Act. The term includes leases and underleases, tenancies at will and sufferance and statutory tenancies, and rights of occupation given by contract, see also s 4(6).

## LIABILITY UNDER THE OCCUPIERS' LIABILITY ACT 1957

The common law imposes liability on landlords for defects on their premises, eg the common parts of blocks of flats, which cause injury to their tenants. The Occupiers'

---

[22]  [1992] QB 134, [1992] 1 All ER 749, CA.
[23]  (1998) 30 HLR 41.
[24]  *Morley v Knowsley Borough Council* (1998) Legal Action (May) 22.
[25]  (1980) 10 HLR 44.

Liability Act 1957, s 2, also imposes liability in such circumstances, and the 1957 Act adds to the landlord's obligation by stating in s 3(1):

> 'Where an occupier of premises is bound by contract to permit persons who are strangers to the contract to enter or use the premises, the duty of care which he owes to them as his visitors cannot be restricted or excluded by that contract, but (subject to any provision of the contract to the contrary) shall include the duty to perform his obligations under the contract, whether undertaken for their protection or not, in so far as those obligations go beyond the obligations otherwise involved in that duty.'

The effect is that landlords cannot by virtue of their contracts with tenants reduce obligations to tenants' visitors below the standard required by the Act, the 'common duty of care'. Furthermore tenants' visitors are enabled to claim the benefit of any more onerous obligations inserted in the lease, unless the lease itself specifically excludes this.

## LANDLORDS' OBLIGATIONS IN CONTRACT

### At common law

Contractual remedies generally only apply as between contracting parties. Any third party injured by the defective state of a dwelling-house must find a remedy in tort. That said, landlords may be liable to tenants for a breach of express covenants to repair and maintain a dwelling-house. In such a case the extent of the liability will depend upon the wording of the covenant. Such express covenants are rare, particularly as many leases of ordinary dwelling-houses in the past have been created orally on a weekly basis under s 54(2) of the Law of Property Act 1925. Where authorities and registered social landlords use express terms in their tenancy agreement these frequently do no more than replicate the statutorily implied terms considered below. However, such terms may go further and relate not just to the dwelling-house but to the whole of the premises let. They may also impose specific burdens such as promises that particular items of repair will be carried out within particular periods of time. Express covenants are construed taking into account the state of the dwelling at the time it was let, its age and locality[26], thus a simple covenant to repair is not to be interpreted to require a landlord to renew a decayed hovel by turning it into an up-to-date home. However, a covenant to keep a building in 'good and tenantable' condition may require a landlord to put it into that state even where it has not previously attained it, *Crédit Suisse v Beegas Nominees Ltd*[27]. A covenant to keep premises in 'good condition' may extend, in the context of housing, to requiring work in respect of severe condensation problems[28].

The common law has also been unwilling to imply terms into leases. In *Smith v Marrable*[29], Parke B implied a term into a letting of furnished premises that, at the start of the lease, they would be in a habitable condition. According to *Sarson v*

---

[26]    *Anstruther-Gough-Calthorpe v McOscar* [1924] 1 KB 716.
[27]    [1994] 4 All ER 803; see also *Smedley v Chumley & Hawkes Ltd* (1981) 44 P & CR 50.
[28]    *Welsh v Greenwich London Borough Council* (2000) 33 HLR 40.
[29]    (1843) 11 M & W 5.

*Roberts*[30], the obligation will not arise if the premises become uninhabitable during the course of the lease. What is likely to make a house unfit for habitation in this context are matters likely to affect the health of incoming tenants such as infestation by bugs, or defects in drains, or recent occupation by a person suffering from an easily communicable disease. The meaning given by the common law to 'unfit for human habitation' is therefore different from the meaning the phrase has under the unfitness provisions of the Housing Act 1985. If furnished premises are 'unfit' at common law the tenant is entitled to quit them by repudiating the tenancy, and may also sue for any loss suffered, see *Wilson v Finch Hatton*[31], and *Charsley v Jones*[32]. This implied condition is limited to lettings of furnished dwellings. In *Sleafer v Lambeth Borough Council*[33] it was said that where a landlord lets unfurnished dwellings there will generally be no implied term that they are free of defects. Thus the courts will not imply conditions to keep dwellings in 'good condition'[34]. But a covenant to 'maintain and keep in good and substantial repair and condition' can impose extensive express liabilities[35].

However, in *Liverpool City Council v Irwin*[36] the House of Lords implied a term into a letting of a flat in a high rise block. The authority owned a tower block of flats, access to which was provided by a common staircase and electrically operated lifts. The tenants also had the use of internal chutes into which to discharge rubbish. The condition of the block deteriorated, partly as a result of vandalism, and defects included: failed lifts; a lack of lighting on the staircases, and blocked rubbish chutes. The tenants refused to pay rent and the landlord applied for possession orders on the flats, to which the tenants replied with a counterclaim that (inter alia) the landlord was in breach of covenant of quiet enjoyment. The House of Lords said this was a contract in which the parties had not themselves fully expressed the terms and the court could imply certain terms solely to prevent the contract of letting from becoming inefficacious and absurdly futile. The House of Lords then went on to state:

(1)    the tenants had in their leases an implied right or easement to use the stairs, lifts and rubbish chutes as these were necessarily incidental to their occupation of high-rise flats;

(2)    the landlord was therefore under an implied obligation to take reasonable care to maintain those common areas and facilities;

(3)    such an obligation is not, however, absolute because tenants of high-rise blocks must themselves resist vandalism and co-operate in maintaining the common areas in reasonable condition, and

(4)    the courts have no power to imply such terms in tenancy agreements as they think 'reasonable'. They may only supply such terms as are truly necessary for the functioning of the contract.

Thus in *King v South Northamptonshire District Council*[37] where a wheelchair bound tenant was forced to use a rear access path, over which she had only a right

---

[30]   [1895] 2 QB 395.
[31]   (1877) 2 Ex D 336.
[32]   (1889) 53 JP 280.
[33]   [1960] 1 QB 43, [1959] 3 All ER 378.
[34]   *Lee v Leeds City Council, Ratcliffe v Sandwell Metropolitan Borough Council* [2002] HLR 367.
[35]   *Hallisey v Petmoor Developments Ltd* [2000] All ER (D) 1632.
[36]   [1977] AC 239, [1976] 2 All ER 39.
[37]   (1991) 24 HLR 284.

of way, as the way into her home, and it was clear the dwelling could not be enjoyed without that access way, an obligation on the part of the landlord was upheld to keep the path in repair. However, even where there is a breach of an implied term the landlord will only be liable for the foreseeable consequences of the breach, and not, for example, in respect of a stumble on a flight of stairs in a flat block where the lift is unavailable[38].

There are dicta supporting an argument that where a landlord has let out flats on long leases in a block (for example by virtue of the Right to Buy) the landlord is under an implied obligation to take reasonable care to see that those parts of the block that the landlord retains do not damage the flats that have been let[39].

## Under statute

Parliament has on a number of occasions attempted to remedy the omission of the common law, but, sadly, the courts have adopted a somewhat restrictive interpretation of the legislation, while Parliament itself has been remiss in not keeping some of the remedies up-to-date. This is particularly true of the provision which began life as s 12 of the Housing of the Working Classes Act 1885, and which is now s 8 of the Landlord and Tenant Act 1985. This states that in a letting to which it applies there is an implied term of fitness for human habitation at the commencement of the tenancy and that the landlord will keep it so fit throughout its currency.

The problem is that s 8(3) limits its applicability to contracts of letting where the rent was not originally, on or after 1 April 1965, more than £80 in relation to Inner London Boroughs or £52 elsewhere in the country, and thus hardly any properties are now covered. The courts have 'discovered' other difficulties in the wording of the provision, and these have hardened into rules of interpretation which apply not only to s 8 but also to s 11 of the Landlord and Tenant Act 1985. Thus *Middleton v Hall*[40] and *Ryall v Kidwell & Son*[41] state that only the tenant can sue. While these decisions have been effectively overruled in tort by s 4 of the Defective Premises Act 1972 (see above) the technical rule remains that privity of contract limits the possibility of suing on the implied covenant only to the contracting parties. Next it should be noted that landlords cannot be liable under the implied covenant unless tenants have previously given notice of the defect. This was decided, in the case of patent defects, by *McCarrick v Liverpool Corpn*[42], and was applied to latent defects by *O'Brien v Robinson*[43]: again remember the tortious remedy under s 4 of the Defective Premises Act 1972 is not made so dependent upon the giving of actual notice. In the case of authority dwellings, it was held in *Sheldon v West Bromwich Corpn*[44] that where an appropriately qualified authority employee knows that

---

[38]   *Berryman v Hounslow London Borough Council* (1996) 30 HLR 567.
[39]   *Gordon and Teixeira v Selico Ltd and Select Managements Ltd* (1986) 18 HLR 219, though the unwillingness of the courts generally to imply obligations to repair the structure of blocks of flats was reiterated in *Adami v Lincoln Grange Management Ltd* [1998] 1 EGLR 58; but see also *Loria v Hammer* [1989] 2 EGLR 249.
[40]   (1913) 108 LT 804.
[41]   [1914] 3 KB 135.
[42]   [1947] AC 219, [1946] 2 All ER 646.
[43]   [1973] AC 912, [1973] 1 All ER 583.
[44]   (1973) 25 P & CR 360; see also *Griffin v Pillet* [1926] 1 KB 17.

premises are defective that knowledge will be treated as giving the authority notice, and notice does not have to be given personally by the tenant.

In *McGreal v Wake*[45] though it was stressed that tenants should inform landlords of works necessary to meet breaches of repairing obligations, it can be enough to 'trigger' a landlord's responsibilities if the tenant complains to the local authority and they then serve notice requiring works under their Housing Act 1985 powers. Similarly in *Dinefwr Borough Council v Jones*[46] a district valuer's 'right to buy' report to an authority which specified defects was held to constitute notice, even though it was not submitted as a disrepair complaint.

A solicitor's letter complaining about a lack of repair can be sufficient to put a landlord 'on notice' and need not specify the exact nature or degree of the disrepair, provided it makes clear to the landlord that the tenant is giving notice the work should be done[47].

The most serious limitation on s 8 was imposed by the Court of Appeal in *Buswell v Goodwin*[48]. Here a cottage was statutorily unfit and, as the local authority had made a closing order on it, the landlord had commenced possession proceedings against the tenant. He argued the house was only unfit because the landlord was in breach of implied contractual obligations under s 8. The Court of Appeal, however, restricted the ambit of operation of the implied covenant to cases where houses are capable of being made fit at reasonable expense. The obligation is not absolute. Where a house has fallen into an extreme state of disrepair the tenant can no longer rely on the implied covenant. The paradox thus emerges of tenants of the worst housing receiving the lowest level of legal protection. Furthermore where statutorily unfit houses are retained by authorities under their Housing Act 1985 powers, s 8 will not apply to letting such houses, see s 302(c) of the Housing Act 1985.

## Section 11 of the Landlord and Tenant Act 1985

A similar process of judicial reasoning has emptied much of the meaning from the other statutorily implied covenant: s 11 of the Landlord and Tenant Act 1985. This applies, under s 13 of the Act, to leases of dwelling-houses granted on or after 24 October 1961 for terms of less than seven years, so a lease for a term of seven years is not caught[49]. Note, however, that the obligation is not implied in a licence to occupy, neither does it apply where a former tenant is allowed to remain as a 'tolerated trespasser' in a dwelling in respect of which his/her tenancy has been brought to an end by a court order[50]. The obligation is to keep in repair the structure and exterior of the dwelling, including its drains, gutters and external pipes, *and* to keep in repair *and* proper working order the mains services installations, including basins, sinks, baths and sanitary conveniences, but excluding appliances etc, for making use of a mains service, eg a refrigerator, *and* to keep in repair and working

---

[45] (1984) 269 Estates Gazette 1254.
[46] (1987) 19 HLR 445, see also *Hall v Howard* (1988) 20 HLR 566.
[47] *Al Hassani v Merrigan* (1987) 20 HLR 238.
[48] [1971] 1 All ER 418, [1971] 1 WLR 92.
[49] *Brikom Investments Ltd v Seaford* [1981] 2 All ER 783, [1981] 1 WLR 863 and *Demetriou v Poolaction Ltd* [1991] 1 EGLR 100, CA.
[50] *Rogers v Lambeth London Borough Council* (2000) 32 HLR 361 and *Pemberton v Southwark London Borough Council* (2000) 32 HLR 784.

order space and water heating installations. The standard of repair required is determined by having regard to the age, character, prospective life and locality of the dwelling. It is not possible to contract out of this obligation, see s 12 of the Act, save with the consent of the county court.

The provision now requires, with regard to tenancies granted on or after 15 January 1989, that a landlord is to keep in repair the structure and exterior of any part of a building he/she owns of which the tenant's dwelling forms part, see s 11(1A) of the 1985 Act. A similar extension of the original s 11 covers mains services installations which serve a dwelling-house directly or indirectly and which either form part of any part of the building in which the landlord has an interest or are owned by the landlord or are under the landlord's control. However, the landlord's obligations can only be relied on where the disrepair, etc, is such as to affect the tenant's enjoyment of the dwelling or of the common parts of the property in which it is, see s 11(1B). Nevertheless this provision may be relied upon by, for example, tenants of flats adversely affected by disrepair of stairways and access paths. It appears liability in respect of defects in retained common parts is absolute, and that a landlord here can be liable, even in the absence of knowledge: see *Passley v Wandsworth London Borough Council*[51] where water pipes in a block of flats burst in freezing weather and flooded a tenant's flat. The obligation 'to repair' implied an obligation to 'keep in good order'.

The policy of Parliament in creating the implied covenant was to prevent unscrupulous landlords from imposing unreasonable repairing obligations on tenants. It cannot be said, however, that the law has been successful in preventing disrepair and bad housing conditions. Tenants are generally ignorant of their rights, and often do not complain about disrepair until it becomes exceptional and intolerable. Alongside this there exists the same restrictive judicial attitude already seen in relation to the s 8 covenant.

This can be seen in decisions as to which matters fall within the scope of the implied covenant. In *Brown v Liverpool Corpn*[52], paving flagstones and shallow steps leading to a house were held to be part of its 'exterior'. They were necessary for the purpose of gaining access to the house and fell within the scope of the implied covenant. In *Hopwood v Cannock Chase District Council*[53] slabs in a back yard were held not to fall within the scope of the covenant as the back yard was not the essential means of access to the house. In *Irvine v Moran*[54] it was considered 'structure' is that which gives a property its 'essential stability and shape', not the ways and means in which a house is fitted out, eg garages, gates, wall plaster, door locks, internal decoration, though external doors, windows, window glass and painting are part of the 'exterior'. So far as flats are concerned, dicta in *Campden Hill Towers Ltd v Gardner*[55] are most important. Where the structure is concerned the landlord's obligation extends to anything which can ordinarily be regarded as part of the structure or exterior of the dwelling in question. Thus s 11(1)(a) applies, irrespective of the words of the lease, to the outside walls of a flat (even though they

---

[51]   (1996) 30 HLR 165; see also *Stockley v Knowsley Metropolitan Borough Council* [1986] 2 EGLR 141 a case where the tenant had warned the landlord of a problem of frozen pipes in an adjacent flat.
[52]   [1969] 3 All ER 1345.
[53]   [1975] 1 All ER 796, [1975] 1 WLR 373.
[54]   [1991] 1 EGLR 261.
[55]   [1977] QB 823, [1977] 1 All ER 739.

may have been excluded from the lease), the outer sides of horizontal divisions between flats, the outside of the inner party walls of the flat and the structural framework and beams directly supporting the floors, ceilings and walls of a flat. The test to be used in determining the scope of the implied covenant is whether the particular item of disrepair affects the stability or usability of the particular flat in question.

In *Douglas-Scott v Scorgie*[56] the Court of Appeal held that the roof of a building above a top floor flat may be part of the structure and exterior of that flat, irrespective of whether or not it forms part of the demised premises. The content of the obligations of public and private sector landlords are the same under this implied covenant[57].

The covenant is one to repair, so what is the meaning of the word 'repair'? In *Ravenseft Properties Ltd v Davstone (Holdings) Ltd*[58] a distinction was made between the process of repair and a completely different process which is replacement. Replacement is a process of reconstruction so drastic that at the end of the lease the landlord receives back a wholly different property from that which he/she demised. 'Repair' on the other hand, according to the decision in *Greg v Planque*[59], simply means making good defects, including renewal where necessary. In other words, simply keeping the property in a condition suitable for the purpose for which it was let. The distinction between these two processes is the scale and degree of the work involved. The fact that work, because of modern statutory requirements or building practices, has to be done to a higher standard than that of the original does not necessarily mean that it cannot be classed as 'repair'. Work will not be classifiable as 'repair' if it results in a reconstruction of the whole, or substantially the whole, of a building.

In *McDougall v Easington District Council*[60] Mustill LJ put forward three tests which may be applied 'separately or concurrently' to decide whether a matter is one of repair or renewal/replacement:
(1)  do any alterations go to the whole, or substantially the whole of the structure;
(2)  is the effect of the work to produce a building of a wholly different character from that which was let;
(3)  what is the cost of works in relation to the building's previous value, and what is their effect on its value and life expectancy?

Thus if the landlord can show that the work required on any given house is so drastic that it would amount to his/her getting back, at the end of the term, a substantially different house from that which was let, then that work is outside the obligation to repair. In *Pembery v Lamdin*[61] a landlord let certain old premises not constructed with a damp-course or with waterproofing for the external walls, and covenanted to keep the external part of the let premises in good repair and condition. The tenant claimed this put the landlord under an obligation to waterproof the outside walls and render the premises dry. It was held the obligation was

---

[56]  [1984] 1 All ER 1086, [1984] 1 WLR 716.
[57]  *Wainwright v Leeds City Council* (1984) 270 Estates Gazette 1289.
[58]  [1980] QB 12, [1979] 1 All ER 929.
[59]  [1936] 1 KB 669.
[60]  (1989) 21 HLR 310. This test was reitterated by the Court of Appeal in *Eyre v McCracken* (2000) 33 HLR 16.
[61]  [1940] 2 All ER 434.

only to keep the premises in repair in the condition in which they were let. In this case the landlord would be required only to point the external brickwork. However, contrast *Elmcroft Developments Ltd v Tankersley-Sawyer*[62]. The court found that replacing an incorrectly laid and existing damp proof course in a block of flats was an act of 'repair'. Similarly, contrast *Mullaney v Maybourne Grange (Croydon) Management Co Ltd*[63] and *Reston Ltd v Hudson*[64]. In the former the replacement of wooden framed windows with double glazed ones was considered an improvement, in the latter the comprehensive replacement of all windows at one time when only some were rotted was considered a 'repair'.

The burden of proving a particular repair is needed is, moreover, on the person alleging its need and as a landlord may normally repair on a piecemeal 'make good as we go' basis,[65] should the tenant wish to argue for a major replacement evidence will have to be adduced showing why a piece meal job is no longer enough[66].

It is also necessary to show disrepair as opposed to a lack of amenity or inefficiency, see *Quick v Taff-Ely Borough Council*[67]. Here a council house built in the early 1970s was thermally inefficient with uninsulated concrete window lintels giving rise to condensation that produced intolerable living conditions. The Court of Appeal accepted that the eradication of a design defect, such as affected the dwelling, may fall within the ambit of the implied covenant, provided the work required does not amount to substantial reconstruction or improvement, *and* provided the work is necessary to remedy disrepair. To repair is to make good some damage: eradicating a design defect that simply makes a dwelling inefficient or ineffective as a habitation is not automatically therefore repair. In *Quick* the court found the condensation simply made the house function badly or inefficiently, there was no damage or deterioration as such to any components of the structure of the dwelling. The obligation to repair only arises where there is damage or deterioration, though where this can be shown to exist, discharging the obligation may require eradicating a design defect giving rise to the damage so that to some extent the dwelling is 'improved'. Note also *Stent v Monmouth District Council*[68] where there was actual deterioration damage of a badly designed and installed entrance door which could be characterised as 'disrepair'.

The content of the obligation to repair has also been the subject of judicial attention. In *Newham London Borough v Patel*[69] the Court of Appeal considered the forerunner of s 11(3) of the Landlord and Tenant Act 1985. This states that the standard of repair is to be determined by having regard to the 'age, character and prospective life of the dwelling-house and the locality in which it is situated'. Mr Patel's house was a poor, old dwelling in bad condition shortly destined for redevelopment. The court concluded the prospective life of the dwelling affected the content of the s 11 duty. The authority could not be required to carry out repairs which the court categorised as 'wholly useless'.

---

[62] [1984] 1 EGLR 47, CA.
[63] [1986] 1 EGLR 70.
[64] [1990] 2 EGLR 51.
[65] *Dame Margaret Hungerford Charity Trustees v Beazeley* (1993) 26 HLR 269.
[66] *Murray v Birmingham City Council* (1987) 20 HLR 39.
[67] [1986] QB 809, [1985] 3 All ER 321.
[68] (1987) 19 HLR 269.
[69] [1979] JPL 303.

On the other hand a landlord cannot always justify a poor standard of repair simply on the basis of a low rent being charged for an old house, see *McClean v Liverpool City Council*[70] and *Sturolson & Co v Mauroux*[71]. To succeed on this basis a landlord would need to show that the rent is truly 'nominal' or very low, while any repairs needed would be wholly useless, or that the dwelling has no prospective life.

Once the landlord has notice of disrepair the work should be carried out within a reasonable time – this will depend upon the nature of the work needed, any problems associated with obtaining the necessary materials, the landlord's work load, etc – and the burden of proving unreasonable delay in doing work lies on the tenant[72].

Even where a landlord is in breach of an express or implied repairing covenant, liability will only extend to those matters which are foreseeable consequences of the breach[73].

Tenants are not, however, entitled to treat their homes in a cavalier fashion. It was made clear in *Warren v Keen*[74] that tenants are always under some sort of obligation to look after their homes. In the case of a long lease, say 99 years, the tenant is usually made subject to full repairing covenants.

On the other hand weekly tenants are usually bound to use the premises in a tenant-like manner. This means taking proper care of the premises, for example cleaning chimneys and windows, replacing electric light bulbs, mending fuses, and unstopping blocked sinks. In *Wycombe Health Authority v Barnett*[75] it was stated that in very cold climatic conditions a tenant *may* have to lag water pipes, or use additional heat, or turn off the water supply according to the circumstances, such as the severity of the cold, the duration of contemplated absence from home and the internal condition of the house, in order to behave in a tenant-like manner. See also *Mickel v M'Coard*[76] where a tenant left a house for a month, without telling the landlord, in very cold weather and was held liable for burst pipes.

## REMEDIES FOR BREACHES OF COVENANT

### Specific performance

Though there appear to be few reported cases on the issue, s 17 of the Landlord and Tenant Act 1985 permits orders of specific performance to be made in cases where tenants allege breach of their landlords' repairing covenants. The remedy is available whether or not the breach relates to a part of the premises let to the tenant, and notwithstanding any equitable rule which would otherwise restrict the scope of the remedy, eg that the tenant does not have 'clean hands' because of arrears of rent.

---

[70]   [1987] 2 EGLR 56, CA.
[71]   (1988) 20 HLR 332.
[72]   *Morris v Liverpool City Council* [1988] 1 EGLR 47, CA.
[73]   Stumbling on stairs which the tenant has to use because lifts are out of action (in breach of covenant) is not foreseeable, while being burgled via a front door which is clearly in a state of disrepair is; contrast *Berryman v Hounslow London Borough Council* (1996) 30 HLR 567 with *Marshall v Rubypoint Ltd* (1997) 29 HLR 850.
[74]   [1954] 1 QB 15, [1953] 2 All ER 1118.
[75]   [1982] 2 EGLR 35, CA.
[76]   1913 SC 896.

Specific performance is, however, a discretionary remedy and the court will not order a landlord to do unnecessary or extravagant work. Though the remedy is available as a final[77] or an interim order[78] it is arguable an interim order would only be made before a decision on liability for repairs where the situation was extreme and some immediate danger needs to be removed.

Landlords may give undertakings to do works or consent to mandatory orders made in repairs proceedings: neglect to honour these may result in contempt proceedings[79].

## Appointing a receiver

Where a landlord is neglectful, and in breach which is likely to continue, of repairing obligations, so that serious deterioration of the dwelling(s) in question is likely, and it can be shown that the landlord is taking no real interest in the property, either to collect rent or to perform obligations, it may be possible to apply for the appointment of a receiver by the High Court if it appears just and convenient. The receiver will then manage the property in accordance with the lease until further order, see *Hart v Emelkirk Ltd*[80]. However, this remedy may not be sought by *local authority* tenants, see *Parker v Camden London Borough Council*[81]. Though even against a local authority landlord a mandatory order commanding performance of repairing obligations may be made if there is a clear breach of a covenant which gives rise to major discomfort and annoyance *and* a real risk of damage to health consequent on the breach.

Where the premises consist of two or more flats in a block, s 21 of the Landlord and Tenant Act 1987 permits a tenant to apply for the appointment of a manager of the premises, though a preliminary warning notice has to be given to the landlord under s 22 specifying the grounds on which the court will be asked to appoint a manager. A manager may be appointed where the landlord is in breach of obligation, where that breach is likely to continue and where it is just and convenient to make the appointment. See s 24 of the 1987 Act as amended in 1996. This power, does not, however, apply to any premises where the landlord is 'exempt' (eg a district or London borough council, an urban development corporation, a housing action trust, the Housing Corporation, a housing trust or a registered housing association) or where the premises are on the functional land of any charity. The power to appoint a manager has been vested in Leasehold Valuation Tribunals under s 86 of the Housing Act 1996.

## Self-help

In *Lee-Parker v Izzet*[82] it was held that, irrespective of the common law rules as to set off, occupiers of property had a right to recoup themselves out of *future* rent for

---

[77] *Francis v Cowcliffe* (1976) 33 P & CR 368; see also *Rainbow Estates Ltd v Tokenhold Ltd* [1999] Ch 64, [1998] 2 All ER 860.
[78] *Kotecha v Manchester City Council* (4 October 1982, unreported, County Court).
[79] *Mullen v Hackney London Borough Council* [1997] 2 All ER 906, [1997] 1 WLR 1103 and *R v Wandsworth County Court, ex p Munn* (1994) 26 HLR 697.
[80] [1983] 3 All ER 15, [1983] 1 WLR 1289, and see *Daiches v Bluelake Investments Ltd* (1985) 17 HLR 543.
[81] [1986] Ch 162, [1985] 2 All ER 141.
[82] [1971] 3 All ER 1099, [1971] 1 WLR 1688.

the cost of repairs to the property, in so far as the repairs fell within the landlord's express or implied covenants, provided the landlord was in fact in breach, and only after due notice had been given. Tenants have no rights to *withhold* payment of rent to compel landlords to carry out repairs, and if they do they will be in breach of their own obligations under the lease. The rule only authorises the deducting of the *proper* costs of repairs from future rent: a tenant is not entitled to expend vast sums and then present the landlord with the bill. The following steps should be taken before reliance is placed on the rule:

(1)   the tenant *must* notify the landlord of the disrepair which itself must arise from a breach of the landlord's covenants;

(2)   the tenant should obtain at least two builders' estimates as to the likely costs of the repairs and send them to the landlord, warning that if repairs are not affected the tenant will carry out the work and will deduct the cost from future rent;

(3)   to be absolutely safe, a county court declaration should be obtained authorising this course of action, and

(4)   having given his landlord time to execute the repairs, the tenant may then proceed to do them.

Some authorities phrase their tenancy agreements in such a way as to attempt to exclude the operation of the *Lee-Parker* principle. Such a clause, provided it specifically denies the right to 'set-off' and is not merely a clause denying a right to make deductions from rent may be sufficient to exclude the *Lee-Parker* principle[83].

In *Asco Developments Ltd v Lowes*[84] a landlord sought summary judgment for arrears of rent under RSC Ord 14 alleging that there was no defence to the action. The tenants sought to defend on the grounds that the landlord was in breach of repairing obligations. Megarry V-C held that in certain special circumstances the *Lee-Parker* principle could be applied to monies accrued in rent arrears, and the tenants could defend the action. However, the court stated that nothing in the decision should be taken to encourage rent strikes as a means of forcing action on the part of a landlord. It was made clear in *Camden Nominees v Forcey*[85] that it is no answer to a claim for rent by a landlord for the tenant to say that the landlord has failed to perform his obligations. If tenants are to use the *Lee-Parker* principle in respect of rent arrears, they must specify to the court the sums and costs in question, and must particularise the issues. A judge faced with such issues should act with considerable discretion before allowing the tenant to defend the claim for rent.

In *British Anzani (Felixstowe) Ltd v International Marine Management (UK) Ltd*[86], Forbes J indicated that in equity, as a set-off raised by way of defence, unliquidated damages, for example claims for inconvenience and loss of enjoyment, might be recoverable against rent under a tenancy agreement. The tenant must be able to show it would be inequitable in view of the condition of the dwelling to allow the landlord to recover the whole amount of rent claimed. The tenant's contention should be raised as a defence to the landlord's action, and the tenant should make a counter-claim which particularises the nature of the landlord's breach of obligation

83   *Electricity Supply Nominees Ltd v IAF Group plc* [1993] 3 All ER 372, [1993] 1 WLR 1059.
84   (1978) 248 Estates Gazette 683.
85   [1940] Ch 352, [1940] 2 All ER 1.
86   [1980] QB 137, [1979] 2 All ER 1063.

and the consequent damage. Though it is not absolutely necessary that a claim and counterclaim should arise from the same contract, both must stem from very closely connected transactions so that equity can recognise that the tenant's counterclaim goes to the very root of the landlord's claim.

A set-off of unliquidated damages is a defence to as much of the plaintiff's claim as is represented by the eventual amount of the award made. If defendants limit damages to a sum less than that claimed from them then they must pay the balance over and above the counterclaim. But where the defendants' damages are claimed at large, finally to be decided by the court, and where it is bona fide claimed they top the claimant's claim, even though they are not yet quantified, then the defendant's set-off amounts to a complete defence to the whole of the claimant's claim.

However, this equitable relief is discretionary, and as 'he who comes to equity must come with clean hands', it is unlikely to be available to a tenant who has been guilty of wrongdoing in relation to the transaction in question.

## Damages

What damages can be recovered for breach of a covenant to repair? The law was extensively reviewed in *Calabar Properties Ltd v Stitcher*[87]. The object of damages is to restore the tenant to the position he/she would have been in had there been no breach. In relation to periodic lettings the measure of damages will, in general, be as stated in *Hewitt v Rowlands*[88], ie the difference in value to the tenant of the premises, from the date of notice of want of repair down to the time of the assessment of damages, between the house in the condition in which it currently is and the condition in which it would be had the landlord, on receipt of notice, fulfilled the obligation; in other words the difference in value to the tenant of the premises in their current condition and the condition in which they should be, bearing in mind age, character and locality. This sum is likely to be what the tenant would have to spend in performing the landlord's obligations for him, though it may be a sum computed by reference to a proportion of the periodic rent, plus a sum in respect of inconvenience and discomfort.

Where the dwelling is occupied under a 'long' lease the appropriate measure of damages will be either, where the tenant wishes to sell the dwelling, the difference in the price he/she received for the dwelling as damaged and the price it would have fetched on the open market had it been repaired, or, where the tenant wishes to remain in the dwelling, the cost of taking reasonable alternative accommodation, the cost of redecorating plus some compensation for inconvenience in addition to the cost of repairs[89].

It is not enough simply to claim 'damages', the issues must be particularised. 'Special damage' ie the precise amount of pecuniary loss suffered by the tenant flowing from the facts must be specifically pleaded. This means that claims for, inter alia, damaged personal property, money spent discharging a landlord's

---

[87]  [1983] 3 All ER 759, [1984] 1 WLR 287, see also *Wallace v Manchester City Council* (1998) 30 HLR 1111.

[88]  (1924) 93 LJKB 1080.

[89]  *Bradley v Chorley Borough Council* (1985) 17 HLR 305.

obligations, or remedying damage consequent on a landlord's failure to act, costs of redecorating, the cost of taking alternative accommodation, should this be reasonable, have to be specified. Some general damage, compensation for which will be computed by the court according to the nature of the tenant's interest in the property, must also be generally pleaded, and this includes matters such as inconvenience and discomfort, as mentioned above[90].

Awards of damages historically varied, but the trend is for awards to be increasing following *Calabar Properties*. It will be of no avail to a landlord to plead a low rent has been paid where a tenant has had to endure extremely poor living conditions for a long period of time, and where a tenant is clearly a victim of a landlord's default a substantial award of damages is acceptable, see *Chiodi's Personal Representatives v De Marney*[91], and *Davies v Peterson*[92].

It should be remembered that the onus of proof in relation to these matters is on the tenant, see *Foster v Day*[93], and tenants should act in good time and ensure relevant defects are brought to their landlord's attention, otherwise general damages may be reduced[94].

The existence of a 'tariff of damages' for discomfort and inconvenience, has been judicially noted with a range of £1,000 to £2,750 per annum. Such damages are payable in appropriate cases, and it is irrelevant that the tenant is otherwise on state benefits which go towards paying the rent: tenants are not to be doubly penalised for poverty and poor living conditions[95].

## The right to repair

Section 96 of the Housing Act 1985 and SI 1985/1493 established a 'right to repair' under which *secure* tenants were entitled to carry out certain repairs for which their landlords were responsible and to recover the costs from their landlords. In practice this right was little used.

A new s 96 was substituted by s 121 of the Leasehold Reform, Housing and Urban Development Act 1993. This empowers the Secretary of State to make regulations to allow local authority secure (and introductory) tenants to have certain repairs carried out at their landlord's expense. (Housing association tenants were excluded from the scope of the statutory scheme, but a scheme appropriate to associations was drawn up by the Housing Corporation: see Housing Corporation Circular 33/94.) The basic notion of the scheme is that landlords should inform tenants of the existence of the right to repair and should maintain lists of approved contractors (which may include the landlord's own workforce) prepared to carry out qualifying repairs.

---

[90]  See *Ezekiel v McDade* [1995] 2 EGLR 107 where a sum of £4,000 was awarded for the inconvenience of living in a substandard home, and *Lubren v Lambeth London Borough Council* (1987) 20 HLR 165 where the offer of alternative accommodation made to the tenant was held *not* to affect the question of damages.
[91]  [1988] 2 EGLR 64, CA.
[92]  (1988) 21 HLR 63; see also *Brent London Borough Council v Carmel (Sued as Murphy)* (1995) 28 HLR 203 where the £50,000 was awarded on a counterclaim for lack of repair raised as a defence to a possession action for non-payment of rent – the disrepair was characterised as 'appalling and intolerable'.
[93]  (1968) 208 Estates Gazette 495.
[94]  *Minchburn Ltd v Peck* [1988] 1 EGLR 53, CA.
[95]  *Wallace v Manchester City Council* [1998] 3 EGLR 38, CA.

The matters as specified in SI 1994/133 (Schedule) (as amended by SI 1994/844, and SI 1997/73) include: electrical power/lighting faults; faults in or loss of gas supply; faults in or loss of water supply; loss of heating (November to April); burst pipes, blocked or leaking foul drains and WCs, leaking central heating pipes and cisterns; water penetration of roofs; non-flushing WC; loss of heating (May–October); loose handrails; weeping pipes; seized stopcocks; defective WCs and unusable or insanitary sanitary ware; blocked flues; solid fuel heating defects; entryphone defects; non-securable doors and windows; rotten timber flooring; failed extractor fans. Most such defects should be repaired in one working day, though some may take three and others up to seven. For a repair to qualify, a financial limit of £250 is also imposed, while a landlord must also have at least 100 houses let on secure tenancies to fall within the scheme.

Tenants may apply for qualifying repairs to be carried out. Landlords must then inspect, if this is felt necessary, and if satisfied the disrepair in question in 'qualifying' must issue a notice specifying the nature of the repair, the listed contractor by whom it is to be carried out and the target time by which any work is to be done. Where such a notice is issued the tenant must be provided with a copy. If the initially specified contractor fails to carry out the work in the prescribed time, the landlord must (if the tenant states he/she requires another contractor to do the work) issue a further notice specifying a new target time for the work. The landlord may be liable to pay some compensation to reflect the inconvenience of delay to the tenant determined in accordance with the regulations if a repair remains incomplete after the second target time has passed.

## The right to information

Section 104 of the Housing Act 1985 (as amended) requires landlords who grant secure tenancies to publish within two years of the commencement of the Act (and thereafter to revise and republish) information, in simple terms, about their secure tenancies. This information must explain, inter alia, the effect of the implied covenant to repair under s 11 et seq of the Landlord and Tenant Act 1985. All secure tenants must be supplied at least yearly with a copy of this information.

## PUBLIC LAW REMEDIES FOR DEALING WITH SUB-STANDARD HOUSING

Grudging Parliamentary interference with the contractual relations of landlords and tenants has never been enough by itself to deal with bad housing conditions. In many – maybe most – cases tenants have lacked the financial and other resources to enable them to vindicate their rights via breach of covenant actions, while, historically, some dwellings have been in such poor conditions as to be beyond the help of 'repair' within the meaning outlined above. The existence of *areas* of substandard housing also made it unrealistic to expect action to depend solely on individual initiative. The Artizans' and Labourers' Dwellings (or Torrens) Act 1868 first made provision for clearance, while the subsequent Artizans' and Labourers' Dwellings Improvement (or Cross) Act 1875 coupled clearance with area redevelopment procedures. However, little use was made of this or subsequent legislation until after the First World War when the Acquisition of Land (Assessment of Compensation) Act 1919 – coupled with Exchequer subsidies for new council house building – helped to lay an effective legal basis for authorities to acquire sub-standard dwellings and rehouse their occupants. Even so many of the acquisition procedures remained cumbersome until the Housing Act 1930 was passed which streamlined the process and led to a demolition rate of some 90,000 houses per annum by 1939.

Area action was then interrupted by the Second World War and it was not until 1955 that area clearance of poor housing recommenced and continued into the 1970s. Housing improvement was not a new policy in the 1970s. The Moyne (1933), Ridley (1945) and Hobhouse (1947) Reports had all drawn attention to the need to prevent housing decline and to take action on improveable property. Some limited powers in this connection were given by the Housing Act 1935, but it was the Housing Act 1949 which introduced grant aid for housing improvement.

Powers to bring about area improvement were introduced by the Housing Act 1964, and an area based rehabilitation policy to deal with sub-standard housing was promoted by the Housing Acts of 1969 and 1974. This policy remains the basis of dealing with poor quality housing conditions although it has been of limited success in reaching the poorest households in the very worst housing. Legislative changes introduced in the Local Government and Housing Act 1989 were an attempt to deal with this and put into formal order policy changes heralded in 1983 by the Green Paper *Home Improvements: A New Approach*, Cmnd 9153 which promised the introduction of means testing for grant aid to target grants at those in most financial hardship while at the same time reducing public expenditure.

Further massive changes were wrought by the housing legislation of 1996 to which attention will be paid below.

The 1989 legislation also provided an opportunity for revision of the definition of unfit housing which had by then become hopelessly outmoded, the version on the statute book being traceable back to 1909.

## The 1989 fitness requirements: the current law

Section 605 of the Housing Act 1985, inserted in 1989, imposes a *yearly* obligation on district and London borough councils to inspect their areas to consider action in relation to:
(1)    repair notices;
(2)    slum clearance;
(3)    houses in multiple occupation;
(4)    housing renewal areas;
(5)    grant aid for housing.

DoE Circular 6/90 indicated this meant there should be a yearly planning exercise to:
(a)    identify types and numbers of unfit housing, and the best ways of dealing with problems;
(b)    monitor action in progress;
(c)    initiate regular physical surveys;

(d) develop comprehensive renewal strategies to direct funding more effectively;
(e) consider data available from other sources.

These powers apply to dwellings generally, ie houses, houses in multiple occupation, flats, 'bedsitters' and indeed any property used as a dwelling[96]. Under the Housing Bill 2003 the obligation to carry out a periodical review of housing needs will exist under what is proposed to be s 3 of the Housing Act 2004, see further below.

Sub-standard housing may also be brought to the attention of authorities by individuals. Authorities must take account of reports of unfit housing made by their 'proper officers' while local magistrates and parish and community councils may also complain in writing to such an officer that a dwelling is 'unfit', and that imposes a duty on the officer to inspect and report on the dwelling, see s 606 of the 1985 Act. The consideration of information received activates the specific duties to take action.

Authorities must in the discharge of functions pay attention to the new unfitness standard of s 604 of the 1985 Act (as substituted). This is stricter and more up to date than previous law, and lists criteria which must be positively met if a dwelling is to be classed as 'fit'.

The criteria for houses (including HMOs) are is the house:
(1) structurally stable;
(2) free from serious disrepair[97];
(3) free from dampness prejudicial to health of occupants;
(4) adequately provided with lighting, heating, and ventilation;
(5) adequately provided with wholesome water;
(6) adequately provided with facilities for cooking/preparing food, including a sink with hot and cold water;
(7) provided with a suitably located water closet for occupants' exclusive use[98];
(8) provided with a suitably located bath/shower and basin with hot and cold water for occupants' exclusive use;
(9) provided with a system for water drainage?
Thus:
(a) a house is unfit if, in the opinion of the authority taking into account the effect of the defect on the dwelling as a whole, it fails to meet one or more of the above criteria, *and*
(b) by reason of that failure it is not reasonably suitable for occupation.[99]

The criteria for flats are as for houses, but a flat may also be unfit if the building of which it is part is affected by structural instability/disrepair/dampness/inadequate ventilation/an ineffective drainage system, and by reason of that the flat is not reasonably suitable for occupation.

Though there is considerable room for subjective evaluation in a decision as to whether a property is/is not 'fit', the 1989 standard encourages a 'check list' approach to decision making which prevents authorities considering the effect of an

---

[96] *Ashbridge Investments Ltd v Minister of Housing and Local Government* [1965] 3 All ER 371, [1965] 1 WLR 1320.
[97] A fall of ceiling plaster can be such a disrepair: *Porter v Jones* [1942] 2 All ER 570, 112 LJKB 173.
[98] Defective lavatories and guttering can make dwellings 'unfit': *Horrex v Pidwell* [1958] CLY 1461.
[99] *Hall v Manchester Corpn* (1915) 84 LJ Ch 732.

accumulation of minor defects, which was the position under the previous law, and some authorities now consider a property which might previously have been considered unfit because of its cumulative defects may now evade control: it does not fail to meet any one of the stated criteria, see further DoE, *Monitoring the New Housing Fitness Standard*, HMSO, 1993, pp 45–47. See also further below on the relationship between ss 189 and 190.

Further guidance on the new fitness standard was to be found in Annex A of DoE Circular 17/96: *Private Sector Renewal: A Strategic Approach*. This stressed that the various matters listed in the statute were to be considered separately to determine whether there was a complete failure under any of them. Where 'serious disrepair' is concerned, however, it may be the result of a single item or a combination of a number each of which in itself would not be 'serious', provided the cumulative effect is. In *Dover District Council v Sherred and Tarling*[100] the Court of Appeal stated that, inter alia, the absence of imminent danger to the occupants in relation to an item of disrepair is a factor to consider in relation to whether disrepair is 'serious', for the test remains as posited in *Morgan v Liverpool Corpn*[101] – whether or not the state of repair is such that by ordinary use damage may naturally be caused to the occupants. The Court of Appeal further added that while local authorities must apply the unfitness test in an objective fashion the experience and wishes of the occupants can be taken into account as not irrelevant in determining the standard of 'ordinary use', and this could extend to the standards accepted by neighbours living in identical housing. Circular 17/96 counsels authorities to base their decisions on socio-environmental considerations, and the courts are unwilling to upset their findings on this basis unless a decision is *Wednesbury* 'unreasonable'[102]. However, the court may intervene where an authority departs significantly from the guidance, or where an authority acts on the basis of a report containing significant omissions so that a balanced judgment cannot be reached[103].

## General guidance on the fitness standard

The courts have held that the test of 'serious disrepair' is whether by ordinary use of the property personal injury or injury to health by damage may naturally be caused to the occupier[104], irrespective of whether an individual item of disrepair is one that can be quickly and easily repaired. In coming to a decision on such matters authorities must act in a judicial spirit[105].

Certain matters are not listed as statutory criteria for fitness, for example infestation by bugs or vermin, a lack of gas or electricity or modern wiring or insulation, though, under case law, it appears such matters may be considered, provided a dwelling also falls in some way to satisfy the statutory criteria, and, of course, they

---

[100] (1997) 29 HLR 864.
[101] [1927] 2 KB 131.
[102] *R v London Borough of Southwark, ex p Cordwell* (1994) 27 HLR 594.
[103] *Zaman and Bibi v Secretary of State* (1999) 32 HLR 734 and *Taggart v Leeds City Council* (1998) 31 HLR 693.
[104] *Morgan v Liverpool Corpn*, above, and *Summers v Salford Corpn* [1943] AC 283, [1943] 1 All ER 68.
[105] *Hall v Manchester Corpn* (1915) 84 LJ Ch 732.

may be evidence of serious disrepair, see *Steele v Minister of Housing and Local Government*[106].

Once an unfit dwelling is discovered a duty to take action arises, and under the 1989 amendments action is primarily to take place according to an integrated area based policy. Section 604A of the 1985 Act provides that authorities must consider with regard to sub-standard housing the most satisfactory course of action, whether it be repair, closing, demolition, etc. This is to ensure a flexible area based response to the eradication of bad housing, which allows for an approach that is appropriate to the problems and needs of the area ranging from renovation to demolition and rebuilding, in conjunction with the private sector according to central policy.

But what is the most satisfactory course of action? Using powers under s 604A the Secretary of State initially issued a code of guidance which formed Annex F to DoE Circular 6/90. The current guidance is now to be found in Annex B of DoE Circular 17/96 while Annex A gives detailed guidance on the Housing Fitness Standard.

## The Code

This is a 'factor to be taken into account' but it is so detailed that it will be hard for authorities to adopt alternative modes of proceeding, see the case law outlined above. It lays down the following principles.

First, identify the need for action either by means of survey, or complaints from tenants or applications for grant aid. Where a survey is required, the recommended means is the Neighbourhood Renewal Assessment (NRA) which has the following components: (a) stated purposes, (b) defined aims and objectives, (c) a defined area, (d) a physical survey, (e) a survey of residents' socio-economic characteristics, and their views and preferences, (f) a survey of the non-residential characteristics of the area, (g) a socio-environmental assessment, (h) consideration of scope for private investment, (i) creation of a broad range of options for dwelling(s) in the area and (j) development of options into workable categories for option appraisal on economic and socio-environmental bases, and (k) reporting the reasoned preferred option for the dwelling(s).

Socio-environmental factors should have equal weight with economic issues, though costs are also to be considered over a period of years using a formula which is to include all action costs, including administrative costs, not just those attributable to publicly aided/required works. This enables authorities to consider the overall economics of various forms of action over a 30-year period. It may be necessary to work the formula more than once in relation to any given property to consider both its individual fate and that of a group of dwellings in which it is situated. While the formula is expressed in the circular in algebraic form, there is considerable room for subjectivity in its application. In all circumstances the object is effectively to allow authorities to take decisions following a series of sequential steps designed to enable the costs and socio-environmental implications of decisions to be explored, with a systematic appraisal of alternative courses of action, so as to identify the option likely to produce the greatest community benefit on a long term basis.

---

[106] (1956) 168 Estates Gazette 37; see also *Stanton v Southwick* [1920] 2 KB 642 (infestation by rats) and *Thompson v Arkell* (1949) 99 LJ 597 (infestation by fleas).

Second, consider most satisfactory course of action by taking into account a wide range of issues such as: (a) costs, (b) social implications of any action taken, (c) alternative courses and their implications, (d) impact of the various forms of action on other nearby dwellings, (e) area strategy factors, (f) the local character and life of the community, (g) the views of those affected by the work/action, (h) the effect of any action in relation to the total needs of an area, and (i) the size of the area against which the effect of the work is measured.

The 1996 Guidance in addition stresses the need for authorities to deal with unfit housing as part of the strategy for an entire area, and thus the effect of any action which could be taken – eg a repair notice under s 189 of the 1985 Act – must be considered according to the context of the property within its area. This, of course, means that authorities have to determine what the appropriate area for this contextual determination is, and that depends on the geographical location and type of the dwelling. The object of the NRA in such circumstance, it is reiterated, is to ensure that economic, social and environmental issues are considered when determining the most appropriate course of action, together with the long-term consequences of the action, and the effect of the action on any neighbouring properties. Following completion of the NRA an authority should consider:

- each option within the context of the overall private sector renewal strategy and the resources available for its implementation;
- the practicability of any given option, bearing in mind the physical condition of the premises and others on which they abut;
- the potential life of the property if repaired;
- the relationship of the premises with neighbouring properties and their condition;
- proposals for the future of the area as a whole – eg whether it is to be a conservation area;
- the nature and circumstances of the owner/occupier of the dwelling and their wishes and proposals for the future of the property;
- the management record of the landlord (if any);
- the effect of each option on the local community;
- the way in which an option will affect the local environment and its appearance.

The courts, as has been stated above, have been unwilling to interfere overmuch in this exercise which, it is recognised, must inevitably be somewhat subjective and imprecise. Thus it is not appropriate for a court to attempt to review the balance between socio-environmental and economic factors struck by an authority, and a decision should only be upset if it can be shown to be clearly wrong in law, or *Wednesbury* unreasonable[107].

A similar judicial line was taken in *Taggart v Leeds City Council*[108] where it was alleged no socio-environmental assessment of the kind envisaged by the Code had been carried out, and that the socio-environmental issues should have been placed before the relevant committee of the local authority instead of being merely considered by council officers. It was further alleged that the economic issues had

---

[107] *R v London Borough of Southwark, ex p Cordwell* (1994) 27 HLR 594.
[108] (1998) 31 HLR 693.

been incorrectly considered so that the recommendation of the officers was weighted against renovation of the property in question and in favour of its closure. The court pointed out that the provisions of the Code are not mandatory, nevertheless there should have been more socio-environmental material in the report to the committee, so that these could be weighed against the economic issues, for the ultimate responsibility lay with the committee not the officers. However, even if all the issues had been presented to the committee, there was no possibility that their decision would have been different, as it was clear the socio-environmental factors themselves weighed in favour of closure. Neither could it be said that the methodology adopted by the officers was irrational.

Thus while socio-environmental and economic factors are to be given equal weight in the generation of options for the future of a property, and while the decision taking bodies need to have before them the material needed to enable them to reach a decision, the courts are unwilling to interfere with the exercise of 'housing' judgement in this area – which may be contrasted with their increasing willingness to intervene with regard to selection and allocation issues. The courts are only likely to interfere where an obviously important issue is completely ignored, or where weight is given to a clearly irrelevant one.

### The courses of action available

After the evaluation process described above authorities should be in a position to make a choice as to which course of action to take in relation to the area/property in question. (However, see further below on the possibility of 'deferred action'.)

### Individual houses (including flats)

A number of choices are currently available, the 'most satisfactory' should be chosen from: serving notice under s 189(1) or 189(1A) of the 1985 Act (repairs procedure), or under s 264 (1) or 264(2) (closure of whole premises or parts), or under s 265 (1) or 265(2) (demolition). (For action under s 289 clearance procedure for areas, or group repair action, see further below.) Section 604A(2) provides that the Secretary of State may issue guidance in relation to the choice of action. That guidance is contained in DoE Circular 17/96. This provides that general considerations in relation to *all* choices include: an area based approach; the encouragement of private sector investment, and the use of enabling strategies by authorities.

The overall object of the various unfitness provisions is to ensure flexibility of action in respect of unfit dwellings. It appears judicial review of an authority's decision is available should irrelevant factors be taken into account, for example a general desire to protect the environment when it was alleged a cottage was unfit because it discharged sewage directly into a stream, see *R v Forest of Dean District Council, ex p Trigg*[109], and this remedy is available to tenants as well as landlords.

---

[109]  (1989) 22 HLR 167.

## THE LEGAL PROCEDURES: THE EXISTING LAW[110]

### Action under section 189 etc (repair notices)

Where an authority is satisfied this is the most satisfactory course of action in respect of a dwelling house or flat or house or flat in multiple occupation (HMO) they *must* serve a repair notice on the person having control, or, in the case of a HMO, on its manager. With regard to unfit flats, whether or not in multiple occupation, where the cause of unfitness is the condition of another part of the overall building notice is served on the person having control of the relevant part. 'The person having control' is defined by s 207 of the 1985 Act as the person who receives the rack rent of the premises, ie a rent of not less than two thirds of their full net annual (or 'rateable') value, or who would receive it if the premises were let. Thus the 'person having control' is that person who is in a position to let the premises out, *and* to receive, a rack rent of them.[111] Where only part of a building is made subject to a notice the person to be served is the fee simple owner in relation to that part of the building and who in the opinion of the serving authority ought to have executed the works[112].

A repair notice requires the execution of specified works of repair or improvement which are to be begun by a reasonable date, not earlier than 28 days after the notice is served, and are to be completed within a specified reasonable time. The notice must state that in the authority's opinion the works will make the property fit for human habitation. Copies of the notice must also be served on the freeholder, mortgagee or lessee of the property. The notice becomes operative if there is no appeal at the expiry of 21 days from its date of service, and is then a local land charge. The notice must specify works, though over much technical precision is not required, and it may be enough simply to require a roof to be overhauled[113].

An authority is not, however, under a duty to serve a repair notice if, though satisfied the property in question is unfit, they determine that the premises form part of a building which would be a 'qualifying building' in a group repair scheme, and that they expect to prepare such a scheme for the building within a period of 12 months, see s 190A of the 1985 Act. See further below on group repair schemes.

### Action under section 190

A repair notice *may* also be served under s 190 where an authority is satisfied a dwelling house or HMO is in such a state of disrepair that though it is *not* unfit either *substantial repairs* are necessary to bring it to a reasonable standard considering its age, character and locality, *or* though not unfit that the state of disrepair is such as to interfere materially with the personal comfort of the occupying tenant, or persons occupying the HMO as the case may be. These powers extend to buildings containing a flat under s 190(1A), whether singly or multiply occupied, where though the flat is not fit, *either* substantial repairs are required to

---

[110] See below on the proposed new law under the Housing Bill 2003.
[111] *Truman, Hanbury, Buxton & Co Ltd v Kerslake* [1894] 2 QB 774.
[112] Section 207 of the 1985 Act as amended – this specifically provides that it covers flats, and common parts in blocks of flats.
[113] *Church of Our Lady of Hal v Camden London Borough Council* (1980) 255 Estates Gazette 991.

parts of the building outside the flat to bring it to a reasonable standard in view of its age, character and locality, *or* where the condition of part of the building is such as to interfere with the personal comfort of occupying tenants. But under s 190(1B) such a notice may *not* be served, unless there is an occupying tenant of the dwelling house or flat in question, *or* the property is within a renewal area within Part VII of the Local Government and Housing Act 1989 (see further below). An 'occupying tenant' is a person *other than* an owner occupier, who occupies the dwelling as a lessee, while an 'owner occupier' is a freeholder or 'long' leaseholder, ie one for more than 21 years. The person served with the notice will normally be the 'person having control', ie generally the landlord or owner of the premises, see s 207 of the 1985 Act as amended, but in the case of a HMO notice may be served on the manager, see s 190 (1C). Copies must also be served on any other person having an interest in the property as freeholder, mortgagee or tenant, see s 190(3).

The notice may not require the doing of works of internal decorative repair, s 190(2), and must be clear on its face as to what works are required, see *Our Lady of Hal Church v Camden London Borough Council*[114]. Once a repair notice has become operative it is a local land charge, see s 190(5), and a deliberate failure to comply with a notice is a criminal offence under s 198A.

Section 190 contemplates action against two kinds of property, houses in need of substantial repair and fit houses in disrepair where conditions interfere with the personal comfort of occupying tenants, and though there is evidence to suggest authorities make less use of these powers than they could, the powers have been recognised as permitting action to prevent properties becoming unfit, and as allowing the consideration of wider policy issues in the taking of decisions on houses falling into disrepair[115]. It appears the financial position of the owner of the property can also be considered, as can the cost of repairs, the value of the house as it would be if repaired, as well as its unrepaired value assessed on a realistic basis, ie with a sitting tenant, if any, the likely fate of the house if it is not repaired, and the safety of the property in its present condition, together with any deliberate acts of neglect by the owner. However, what is this provision's relationship with s 189? Section 189 deals with properties that are unfit, s 190 with those that are fit. Yet a property may be unfit and also affected by other defects which fall only within s 190. It appears practice is to serve notices under both sections each requiring specific works to commence on the same date, yet it would be preferable if s 189 was amended to allow the requiring of works to make a dwelling fit and to bring it up to a reasonable standard considering its age, character and locality[116].

## Appeals and challenges

A person aggrieved (a phrase undefined by the statutes, though here it may extend to include tenants) by the service of a repair notice may, under s 191, within 21 days of service appeal to the county court. There are particular grounds of appeal, without prejudice to the general right to appeal, allowing the appellant to argue that some other person who is an owner of the property ought to execute required works

---

[114] (1980) 255 Estates Gazette 991.
[115] *Kenny v Kingston upon Thames Royal London Borough Council* (1985) 17 HLR 344.
[116] *Monitoring the New Housing Fitness Standard*, p 78.

or pay their cost in whole or full, see s 190(1A), and, in the case of a notice under s 189, that some other action, such as closure or demolition would have been the most satisfactory course of action, see s 190(1B). On an appeal the court has discretion to confirm, quash or vary the repair notice, and all relevant factors can be taken into account such as the expense of the works required, the value of the property, the financial position of the owner[117], though where an appeal is brought under s 190(1B), see above, the court *must* have regard to the guidance issued under s 604A. Where an appeal against a s 189 notice is allowed and the reason is that making a closing or demolition order would be the most satisfactory answer the judge shall, if requested by the appellant or the authority, include a finding to that effect in his judgment. A notice incorrectly served, for example where the person does not have control, may be ignored as invalid[118], it has been argued that a notice illegally served could also be challenged by way of judicial review[119]. However, the more recent view of the court is that the existence of a right of appeal makes it undesirable for a challenge to be made by way of judicial review[120].

## Enforcement of repair notices

Authorities have power under s 191A to execute required works by agreement with the person having control of the property, at that person's expense. Otherwise, if a repair notice is not complied with authorities have power under s 193 to do required work, and may recover their costs under Sch 10 of the 1985 Act. 'Compliance' in this context means that the works specified in the notice must be begun and completed within the due time allowed, see s 193(2), while s 193(2A) also allows authorities to do required works where it appears that reasonable progress is not being made towards compliance before the end of the appropriate period for doing the works. Written notice of intention to exercise the s 193 powers *must* be given to the person having control of the property, and may be given to any owner of them, see s 194, while s 195, inter alia, empowers a magistrates' court to order a person who has received notice of intended action (and who prevents the officers, servants or agents of an authority from carrying into effect any of the relevant statutory provisions) to permit all things requisite to be done, on pain of committing an offence. Powers of entry for survey and examination purposes before or after a repair notice has been served are given by s 197 which enables authorities to authorise their officers in writing to enter premises for a specified purpose(s), and thereafter such an officer may enter the premises by giving seven days' notice to the occupier and owner, and it is an offence under s 198 to obstruct such an authorised officer. It is a further offence under s 198A for a person having control of premises subject to a repair notice to fail intentionally to comply with that notice *either* by not starting the works by their due commencement date *or* by not completing works on time, and the obligation to complete required works continues notwithstanding that the period for their completion has expired.

---

[117] *Hillbank Properties Ltd v Hackney London Borough Council* [1978] QB 998, [1978] 3 All ER 343.
[118] *Graddage v London Borough of Haringey* [1975] 1 All ER 224, [1975] 1 WLR 241.
[119] *R v London Borough of Southwark, ex p Lewis Levy Ltd* (1983) 8 HLR 1.
[120] *R v Mansfield District Council, ex p Ashfield Nominees Ltd* (1998) 31 HLR 805.

It should be noted that under s 203(3) no action taken under, inter alia, s 189 and 190 etc, prejudices or affects any remedy available at common law or under statute to the tenant of any premises against the landlord. Under the 2003 proposals ss 189 to 208 of the Housing Act 1985 will be repealed and the procedures outlined above will cease to be available and will be replaced by the new Housing Hazards system considered below.

## Action under section 264 etc (closure/demolition)

Section 264 (as substituted in 1989) provides that where an authority is satisfied, having considered the Secretary of State's guidance, that a dwelling house or HMO or one or more of the flats in a building is unfit and that the most satisfactory course of action is closure of the relevant premises it shall make a closing order. This is an order under s 267(2) which prohibits the use of the premises in question for any purpose not approved by the authority, though such approval is not to be unreasonably withheld, and a person aggrieved by its withholding may appeal to the county court.

Section 265(1) (as substituted in 1989) provides that where an authority is satisfied that a dwelling house (but not a flat) or an HMO (but not a flat multiply occupied) is unfit and that demolition is the most satisfactory course of action it must make a demolition order. Where a building contains one or more flats and some or all are unfit and the authority considers demolition is the most satisfactory course of action it must make a demolition order under s 265(2). Such an order requires premises to be vacated within a specified period (of at least 28 days) from the time it becomes operative and to be demolished within six weeks after the end of that period, or if not vacated before the end of that period to be demolished within six weeks of when it is vacated, though the authority may specify such longer period as they consider reasonable, see s 267(1). The provision that the premises are to be required to be vacated is mandatory, even where they are vacant when the order is made[121]. It should further be noted that where a closing order has been made the authority may at any time revoke it – save where the building in question is listed, or the dwelling is a flat – and substitute a demolition order, see s 279. Under the 2003 proposals a further substituted s 265 will enable the making of a demolition order in respect of a dwelling house or house in multiple occupation (HMO) where a 'category 1' hazard exists (see further below on such hazards), though this power will not be generally available where an interim or final management order is in force in relation to the premises (see further chapter 13 on such orders). In the case of buildings containing one or more flats one or more of which is affected by a category 1 hazard (or where such a hazard affects the common parts of the building) the power to make a demolition order will also exist, provided no interim or final management order is in force in respect of the property. Demolition orders will also be capable of being made in respect of dwelling houses and HMOs (provided these are not flats) affected by Category 2 hazards (see further below) provided no interim or final management order is in force, and provided the circumstances fall within

---

[121] *Pocklington v Melksham UDC* [1964] 2 QB 673, [1964] 2 All ER 862 and *R v Epsom and Ewell Corpn, ex p RB Property Investments (Eastern) Ltd* [1964] 2 All ER 832, [1964] 1 WLR 1060.

the terms of an order to be made by the Secretary of State. A similar power will exist in relation to buildings containing flats which are affected by Category 2 hazards.

Note that no demolition order may be made in respect of a building that is 'listed', ie it is of historical or architectural significance.

Where a demolition or closing order is made copies must, under s 268, be served on any person who is an owner of the premises and on any reasonably ascertainable mortgagee. Where the premises in question is a building containing flats notice must in addition be served on those who are the owners of the flats, see s 268(1A). An order against which no appeal is brought becomes operative at the end of 21 days from its date of service, see s 268(2). A person aggrieved by such an order thus has 21 days under s 269 to appeal to the county court, though this right does not extend to any person who is in occupation under a lease with an unexpired term of three years or less, however, such a person may be able to challenge by way of judicial review where there is clear illegality[122]. Under the changes to be made by the Housing Bill 2003 a substituted s 268 will require notice of a demolition order to be served on every owner or occupier of the premises in question, on every person entitled or authorised to permit person to occupy the premises, and on all mortgagees.

The grounds of appeal include, under s 269 (2A) that another course of action, eg a repair notice, was the most satisfactory course of action rather than demolition/ closure as the case may be, and in such cases the court must consider the Secretary of State's guidance in coming to a decision. Otherwise the court has considerable discretion in deciding appeals. Under the 2003 proposals the jurisdiction of the court will be transferred to a residential property tribunal, see below.

### Residential property tribunals: procedure

Under the 2003 Bill proposals provision is made for the procedure of Residential Property Tribunals. This is to be contained in regulations made in England by the Secretary of State and in Wales by the National Assembly. One important point to note is that where in any proceedings before a court an issue arises which falls within the jurisdiction of a tribunal the court may transfer the relevant issues to a tribunal, and may then dispose of the proceedings or adjourn them pending the tribunal's decision as it thinks fit. The procedure before a tribunal may be quite 'court-like' and provision is made for a tribunal to require parties to disputes to provide the tribunal with information, and for the holding of pre-trial reviews. Tribunals are also to be empowered to make orders on a final or interim basis, and to charge fees in respect of their activities. Powers to award the costs of one party against another party are also provided, and enforcement of Tribunal decisions will be via the powers of the county court.

Under the 2003 proposals a new s 269A will enable new grounds of appeal to exist in respect of demolition orders. Where a person is served with such a notice on the basis that a particular hazard affects the property, he/she will be able to argue that some other course of action would be more appropriate, ie

---

[122]  *R v Woking Borough Council, ex p Adams* (1995) 28 HLR 513.

- serving an improvement notice;
- making a prohibition order;
- serving a hazard awareness notice;
- declaring the area in which the property is situated to be a clearance area.

See further below for details of these various orders.

Under the proposals, appeals against demolition orders will, in line with the 2003 scheme of appeals, be heard by Residential Property Tribunals. In dealing with such appeals tribunals will be required to take into account any central guidance which has been issued to authorities in relation to their housing functions. See further below.

Once a demolition order has become operative in respect of any premises the authority must serve on any occupier of them, or any part of them, a notice which states the order's effect, the date by which the premises are to be vacated and requiring the surrender of possession before the vacation date. Possession may thereafter be obtained by order in the county court, irrespective of any security of tenure existing under the Rent Act 1977 or the Housing Act 1988, see s 270. But a property owner may not recover damages for loss as a result of an authority's failure to serve a s 270 notice on a sitting tenant[123]. It is an offence under s 270(5) to enter into occupation of premises, or to permit someone to enter into occupation, after the date by which an order requires it to be vacated, provided it is known that the order has become operative and applies to the premises. Similar provisions apply in respect of closing orders under ss 276 and 277.

Section 271 and 272 grant powers to authorities to demolish relevant premises in default of action by their owners and to recover their expenses. They may also secure, under s 273, the cleansing of premises subject to demolition orders of vermin.

Once a demolition order has become operative the owner of the premises, or any other person in a position in the opinion of the authority to put his/her proposals into effect, may propose the reconstruction of the premises, including their enlargement or improvement. If satisfied this work will lead to the creation of one or more fit dwelling houses or houses in multiple occupation, as the case may be, they may afford the person an opportunity to do the work by extending the period within which demolition is required, and further extensions of this time may be granted provided satisfactory progress with no unreasonable delays is being made on the work. If this is then completed to the authority's satisfaction they may revoke the demolition order, see s 274. Under the 2003 proposals s 273 will be substantially modified so that the power of authorities to permit reconstruction of houses condemned for demolition will enable them to allow persons submitting reconstruction proposals to have time to carry out those works. The proposals must, however, have the effect of bringing about the cessation of Category 1 hazards (see further below) where these affect the property, or otherwise ensuring that a 'prescribed state of affairs exists', this being such a state of affairs as is prescribed by order made by the Secretary of State. A period of time allowed under this provision may be extended in cases where despite non completion satisfactory progress is being

---

[123]  *R v Lambeth London Borough Council, ex p Sarkbrook Ltd* (1994) 27 HLR 380.

made, or, where works have not been started the delay has not been unreasonable. On satisfactory completion of works the demolition order is to be revoked. Note also that under the proposed s 274A where a demolition order has been made in respect of residential premises, it will cease to have effect if an interim or final management order comes into force in respect of them. (For such orders see Chapter 13 below). The existing law (s 275 of the Housing Act 1985) permits the substitution of a closing order for a demolition order by an authority where proposals are submitted by the owner of the premises (or any other person interested in them) for their use other than as housing accommodation. The 2003 proposals substitute a new s 275 which will allow owners and others interested in the premises to continue to be able to submit proposals for their use other than as housing accommodation. In such cases the authority may determine the demolition order and instead make a prohibition order (see further below) in respect of the hazard which affects the property.

Where either a closing or a demolition order is made under ss 264 or 265, compensation must be paid to affected owners under s 584A. The basis of compensation is the diminution in the compulsory purchase value of the property determined in accordance with the Land Compensation Act 1961. But where such an order is brought to an end, any compensation received must be repaid, see s 584B.

## OBSTRUCTIVE BUILDINGS

A building which is 'obstructive', ie dangerous or injurious to health simply because of its contact with or proximity to other buildings, may be made subject to an obstructive building notice which gives the owner notice of a time and place when the building's demolition will be considered by the local authority, see ss 283 and 284 of the 1985 Act. After giving the owner a hearing on this matter the authority may determine, by an obstructive buildings order, to demolish the building or part of it, and to require its vacation. If no appeal is then made the order will then become operative on the expiration of 21 days from the date of service of the order on the building's owner(s). A person aggrieved by such an order may, however, within that time appeal to the county court under s 285, though this right does not extend to occupiers who hold the building under leases or agreements whose unexpired term is three years or less. The court has wide discretion to confirm, quash or vary the order on an appeal, the making of which suspends the order until the final determination of the appeal. Once such an order has become effective the authority may serve notice on the occupier stating the effect of the order and requiring vacation of the premises; thereafter possession may be obtained by court order, irrespective of any security of tenure under the Rent Act 1977 or the Housing Act 1988, see s 286. The prime responsibility for executing an order lies on the relevant building owner(s), under s 287(2) but such owners may, before the end of the period within which an obstructive building is required to be vacated, sell their interests to the authority for the compulsory purchase value of the premises, and the authority is then under a duty to carry out demolition, see s 287(1). Where there is a failure by owners to carry out demolition the authority is under a duty under s 287(3) to do the necessary work and they may recover their expenses from owners under s 288.

Note that buildings other than houses can be dealt with under these provisions[124], while they are specifically excluded from applying to buildings owned by local authorities, and statutory undertakers unless in this case they are used as dwellings, showrooms or offices, see s 283(2). Under the 2003 proposals the provisions of ss 283 to 288 of the 1985 Act on the demolition of obstructive buildings will be repealed as no longer needed under the new legislative scheme.

Where an authority would otherwise be required under ss 264 or 265 to make a demolition or closing order in respect of a dwelling house, HMO or the whole of a building, they may, under s 300, where it appears to them that the premises can be made to provide accommodation of a standard 'adequate for the time being' purchase the property instead. Notice of determination to purchase the property must be served on those persons who would otherwise have been served with copies of a demolition/closing order. Thereafter the property may be acquired by agreement or compulsorily. This provision only allows authorities to acquire property on a temporary basis, it may not be used to add to an authority's permanent housing stock[125].

The power to acquire substandard accommodation is continued under the 2003 proposals in a slightly modified form. A substituted s 300 will allow authorities to purchase dwellings, houses in multiple occupation and buildings containing one or more flats where a demolition order would otherwise be required, provided it appears to them that the property in question is, or can be rendered, capable of providing accommodation of a standard which is adequate for the time being. A similar power exists in relation to situations where an authority would be required to make a prohibition order under what is proposed as s 5 of the new Act (see further below). Where a determination to make a notice to purchase has been made it must be served on relevant owners, etc, and the usual right of appeal against such a determination exists, ie to a residential property tribunal. Once the notice has become operative the authority may proceed to purchase the property by agreement or compulsorily if authorised by the Secretary of State. Note that this power of purchase does not exist in respect of listed buildings, ie those of historic or architectural importance.

## THE NEW APPEAL STRUCTURE

As mentioned above s 269 of the Housing Act 1985 (a right of appeal against a demolition order) will be modified under the 2003 proposals to transfer the right of appeal to a 'Residential Property Tribunal'. This is part of a general overhaul of the structure of housing standards appeals whereby the county court will lose its historic jurisdiction in such matters. The change also applies to s 272 (further provision on demolition orders), and s 318 (power to authorise execution of works on unfit premises). Residential Property Tribunals will exist under Part 7 of the proposed legislation, and are the Rent Assessment Committees constituted under

---

[124] *Jackson v Knutsford Urban Council* [1914] 2 Ch 686.
[125] *Victoria Square Property Co Ltd v London Borough of Southwark* [1978] 2 All ER 281, [1978] 1 WLR 463 – 'temporary' use may, however, continue for quite a while; 24 years in *R v City of Birmingham Corpn, ex p Sale* (1983) 9 HLR 33.

Sch 10 to the Rent Act 1977. Appeals from the decisions of such a tribunal will lie to the Lands Tribunal, and thence, on a point of law, to the Court of Appeal.


## DEFERRED ACTION: THE CURRENT POSITION

Important changes in the law on unfitness were made by the Housing Grants, Construction and Regeneration Act 1996 to give authorities a little more leeway with regard to taking action.

Under s 81 of this Act where an authority are satisfied a dwelling house or HMO is unfit but are also satisfied that serving a deferred action notice (DAN) is the most satisfactory course of action they are to serve such a notice. See further DoE Circular 17/96 especially Annex B for detailed guidance on this issue. A DAN states:

(i)   that the premises are 'unfit',

(ii)  the works required in the authority's opinion to make them 'fit',

(iii) the other courses of action available to the authority if the premises remain unfit.

Such a DAN becomes operative, where no appeal is brought, on the expiry of 21 days from its date of service and thereafter is final, and while it remains operative it is a local land charge. However, the existence of a DAN does not prevent the authority from taking other action with regard to the premises.

DANs are served under s 82 of the 1996 Act on the person 'having control' of a dwelling house or HMO as the case may be (see ss 207 and 398 of the Housing Act 1985). Such a notice may also be served in respect of a flat or flat in multiple occupation, but in the case of an HMO the notice may be served on the manager rather than the person having control. Other appropriate freeholders, mortgages and lessees of the property are also to be served.

A person aggrieved by the service of a DAN under s 83 may appeal to the county court, and may in particular argue that a more satisfactory course of action would be to require repairs, closure or demolition. In such a case the court is required to take account of the guidance issued by the Secretary of State: see further above. The court has a wide discretion on appeal but where it allows an appeal and the reasons include that another course of action would have been more satisfactory the court must, if the appellant requests, include a finding as to the satisfactory course of action. Bringing an appeal defers the operation of the DAN.

Authorities may at any time under s 84 of the 1996 Act review any DAN and must do so at two yearly intervals having carried out an inspection for this purpose. The DAN must be renewed if the authority conclude this is the most satisfactory course of action, but again an appeal against such a finding is possible on the same terms as outlined above. In deciding on the most satisfactory course of action authorities must, of course have regard to guidance issued by the Secretary of State: see s 85 of the 1996 Act.

The ability to serve a DAN, inter alia, enables authorities to hold back from taking action in relation to technically unfit properties (bearing in mind that the number and range of these were increased where the criteria for unfitness were revised in 1989) where, eg, the conditions are not too bad and where the occupant is, say, an elderly person who would be seriously upset or affected by requirements for extensive works. On the occupant's death or removal to more suitable premises the authority may then take other action to bring the property up to standard.

## POWER TO 'IMPROVE' ENFORCEMENT PROCEDURES

Under s 86 of the 1996 Act the Secretary of State may, by order, require authorities to act in a specified way before taking any of the following types of action:
  (i)   serving or renewing a DAN;
 (ii)   serving a repair notice;
(iii)   serving repair notice on house not yet unfit;
 (iv)   making a closing order;
  (v)   making a demolition order.

Such an order may provide that authorities must, as soon as practicable, give the person against whom action is intended an 'appropriate notice' and must not take any further action before the end of a specified period. Such a notice is one which:
  (i)   states the nature of remedial action the authority thinks should be taken;
 (ii)   explains the grounds on which it appears to the authority a statutory notice of any of the specified varieties might be served;
(iii)   states the nature of the action which might be taken and whether there is either a right to make representations before, or a right of appeal against, taking such action.

The order may further provide that before an authority takes any action against a person they must give that person a written notice stating they are considering taking the action and the reasons why, and that that person may make written representations or oral representations before some other person to be determined according to the Secretary of State's order. Any representations made must be considered. This is known as the 'minded to' procedure. It was introduced under the government's deregulation policy, the object being to avoid unnecessary formal action.

The section goes on to provide, however, that nothing is to preclude an authority from taking immediate action against a person, or requiring immediate remedial action where such appears 'necessary'. This is clearly designed to deal with emergency cases where it is imperative that immediate action is taken. Notices are thus not to be served 'out of the blue' on 'persons having control'. Indeed provision is made for a preparatory process – an initial notice stating the authority is considering taking action, and why, and allowing for representations to be made and considered and/or stating that there is a right of appeal. The object is to ensure that some premises will be dealt with informally without the need to resort to the full legal procedure.

'Meat' was placed on the bones of the statue by the Housing (Fitness Enforcement Procedures) Order 1996, SI 1996/2885. This provides that before an authority takes enforcement action of the types specified above, save in cases of emergency, they must
(a)   give to the proposed subject of their action a written notice stating:
        (i) that they are considering taking the specified action and the reasons therefor – that is the 'minded to' notice;

(ii) that the recipient may, within a specified period (not less than 14 days) make *either* written representations to the authority, or (where the recipient so requests) oral representations to the authority in the presence of an officer appointed by them – a request to make oral representations must be made not later than seven days beginning with the day the 'minded to' notice is given;

(b)    consider any representations duty made and not withdrawn.

Failure to comply with this procedure will be an additional ground of appeal against any enforcement action taken in addition to those already existing under the statute: see reg. 3.

## CHARGING FOR ENFORCEMENT ACTION

Under s 87 of the 1996 Act authorities are given power to make *reasonable* charges to recover their administrative costs and certain other specified costs where:

(i)   they have served/renewed a DAN;
(ii)  they have served a notice under s 189 (1985 Act);
(iii) they have served a notice under s 190 (1985 Act);
(iv)  they have made a closing order under s 264 (1985 Act);
(v)   they have made a demolition order under s 265 (1985 Act).

Specified costs include expenses incurred in deciding whether to service a notice, identifying works to be specified (where appropriate) therein and actually serving the notice. However, a ceiling may be set on such costs by an order made by the Secretary of State, and if the court allows an appeal against a notice it may further order a reduction or cancellation of any charge made. Charges may be recovered, under s 88 of the 1996 Act from persons on whom notices are served, and are recovered by serving a 'demand for payment' on the person from whom recovery is sought, whereafter the demand becomes effective on the expiry of 21 days unless an appeal is brought. The sum recoverable will then be a charge on the property which the authority may recover by selling or leasing the property or by appointing a receiver as if the authority were a mortgagee acting under the Law of Property Act 1925.

The maximum charge is fixed by the Housing (Maximum Charge for Enforcement Action) Order 1996, SI 1996/2886. Regulation 2 fixed the maximum charge at £300.

NB Under the proposals contained in the Housing Bill 2003 ss 81 to 91 of the 1996 Act will be repealed as no longer needed within the new housing standards and enforcement regime. See further below for those standards.

### New powers to charge

In place of the existing powers to charge the 2003 proposals will enable authorities to make 'such reasonable changes as they consider appropriate' as a means of recovering their administrative costs in respect of serving notices, making orders, or taking emergency remedial action, as the case may be, in respect of improvement notices, prohibition orders, hazard awareness orders, remedial action and demolition orders, see further below for a general discussion of these terms. Charges will, in general, be recoverable from the person served with the notice or order etc as the case may be, and the sum recoverable by an authority will be fixed as a charge on the property until it is recovered. This will give authorities the powers of mortgagees, eg to sell or to appoint a receiver in respect of the property in question.

## CLEARANCE AREA PROCEDURE UNDER SECTION 289 ET SEQ OF THE 1985 ACT

Clearance area procedure remains available where, after survey procedures (see above) an authority is satisfied this is the most satisfactory way of dealing with the condition in the area. Authorities must therefore consider alternative options, the views of residents, rehousing provision, after use of the area, and the ability to attract private sector investment. They must then be satisfied that the residential buildings in the area (ie houses, HMOs or buildings containing flats) are unfit, or are by reason of their poor arrangement, or by virtue of the narrowness and poor arrangement of streets, dangerous or injurious to the health of inhabitants, and that other buildings in the area are similarly dangerous or injurious to health, see s 289(2)(a) and (b). 'Houses' has been interpreted as covering a wide range of premises eg shops and garages with living rooms over them , see *Re Bainbridge, South Shields (D'Arcy Street) Compulsory Purchase Order 1937*[126], and *Re Butler, Camberwell (Wingfield Mews) No 2 Clearance Order 1936*[127], and also tenement houses, *Quiltotex Co Ltd v Minister of Housing and Local Government*[128].

Clearance area procedure was modified in 1989 so that s 289 (2B)–(2F) of the 1985 Act now provide that consultation with those persons directly affected (ie freeholders, lessees and mortgagees of affected buildings) must be undertaken before a clearance area is declared, with notice served on every person having an interest in any building in the area, while other occupants of residential property should be informed of the authority's proposals. Local press advertisement must take place and representations invited and considered. As a matter of good practice consideration should be given to ensuring the provision of the above information in languages other than English where appropriate. At least 28 days shall be allowed for the making of representations. The consideration of representations procedure necessitates that those who are asked for their views should be given full information as to the proposals so that they may make a properly informed response; there is, however, no obligation to consult before the initial resolution to proceed by way of clearance area procedure[129]. Before deciding to declare a clearance area an authority should also consider the relative proportions of fit and unfit dwellings in the proposed area.

As a result of considering representations the authority may decide to declare/not declare a clearance area, or declare it subject to the exemption of certain unfit residential buildings, see s 289(2F)(a), (b) and (c). Where they decide to declare a

---

[126] [1939] 1 KB 500.
[127] [1939] 1 KB 570.
[128] [1966] 1 QB 704, [1965] 2 All ER 913.
[129] *Fredman v Minister of Health* (1935) 154 LT 240.

clearance area, the authority must pass a resolution to that effect and have the area defined by a map, but excluding any residential building which is not unfit, or dangerous or injurious to health, any residential buildings which though unfit have been exempted, and any other buildings which are not dangerous or injurious to health. A clearance area should, generally, be a contiguous area of land, with no outlying separated parcels of land, see s 289(5B), though the authority may also include land in a clearance area which belongs to them, provided they could have included it had it not belonged to them, see s 293(1). Furthermore before the resolution is passed the authority must be satisfied that, in so far as suitable accommodation does not exist for those who will be displaced by clearance, they will be able to secure such accommodation as it becomes necessary and that they have the necessary resources to carry their resolution into effect, s 289(4). 'Suitable accommodation' in this context means suitable dwelling accommodation[130], while the need for an authority to be satisfied as to its resources does not require the placing before the authority of specific figures[131]. Upon making the resolution the authority must 'forthwith' send a copy to the Secretary of State together with a statement of the number of occupants of buildings in the clearance area on a specified day.

Where a residential building which is unfit is not included in a clearance area, for example because of exemption under s 289(2F)(b), the authority is under a duty to take action in respect of it under whichever of ss 189, 264 or 265 it considers the most appropriate course of action.

In addition before declaring a clearance area the authority must also consider whether they have the resources to pay relocation grants under ss 131 to 140 of the Housing Grants, Construction and Regeneration Act 1996. Such grants allow owner occupiers (freehold or leasehold where their term is for more than a year) to relocate to designated areas on the acquisition of their homes within the clearance area. Grants are discretionary, including their amount, which is also means tested and subject to a limit: see s 134 of the 1996 Act. Grants made are conditional on the grantee remaining an owner-occupier of the dwelling purchased, and are repayable if the grant conditions are broken: see ss 135, 136 and 138. Under the 2003 proposals s 289 will be amended to enable authorities to declare clearance areas in respect of areas where they are satisfied that each of the residential buildings in the area contains a Category 1 hazard and that the other buildings in the area (if any) are harmful to the health and safety of the inhabitants of the area. Thus declaring a clearance area becomes a 'course of action available to the authority' for the purpose of their enforcement functions under s 5 of the proposed new legislation. In addition an authority may make a clearance order declaration if they are satisfied that:

- the residential buildings in the area are dangerous to the health or safety of the area's inhabitants as a result of their bad arrangement or the narrowness or bad arrangement of streets *and*
- that the other buildings (if any) in the area are dangerous or harmful to the health and safety of the area's inhabitants.

---

[130] *Re Gateshead County Borough (Barn Close) Clearance Order 1931* [1933] 1 KB 429.
[131] *Goddard v Minister of Housing and Local Government* [1958] 3 All ER 482, [1958] 1 WLR 1151.

Authorities *may* also declare clearance areas where:

- each of the residential buildings in the area contains a Category 2 hazard, and
- The other buildings (if any) are dangerous or harmful to the health of the area's inhabitants, and
- the circumstances fall within the parameters of an order to be made by the Secretary of State.

'Residential buildings' in the present context are in general those that are dwelling or HMOs or contain one or more flats.

As soon as the authority have declared land to be a clearance area they must, under s 290, proceed to secure its clearance by purchasing the land and undertaking clearance themselves, or by otherwise securing demolition of buildings. The power to acquire the land (which may be exercised by agreement, or under compulsory powers if authorised by the Secretary of State) extends to land surrounded by the clearance area acquisition of which is reasonably necessary for securing a cleared area of convenient shape and dimensions, and adjoining land whose acquisition is reasonably necessary for the satisfactory development or use of the cleared area. Such adjoining land must be shown by the authority, should they wish to acquire it compulsorily, to be reasonably necessary as a question of fact. The land must be partly contiguous with land in the clearance area[132].

Detailed treatment of compulsory purchase procedure is beyond the scope of this work, but it should be noted that since 1 April 1990 under ss 578 and 578A of the 1985 Act, the appropriate procedure has been that under the Acquisition of Land Act 1981, Part II, under which the authority makes a compulsory purchase order on the land in prescribed form, which is then given publicity in local newspapers, while notice of the effect of the order is also served on all owners, lessees and occupiers of relevant land, except tenants for a month or less. The order is then submitted for ministerial confirmation which may not be given until after any objections to the order have been heard and considered. Once the order is confirmed the acquiring authority must publicise that fact locally, and serve notice of that fact on the affected landholders. Compensation for compulsorily acquired unfit property is paid on the same basis as acquisitions of fit property assessed under the Land Compensation Acts 1961 and 1973, which is, effectively, market valuation. Under the 2003 proposals the compensation provisions of the 1985 Act are amended so that, by virtue of a new s 584A where a prohibition order (see further below) or a demolition order is made in respect of premises compensation is to be paid to every owner on the basis of the diminution of the compulsory purchase value of that person's interest consequent on the making of the order in question. Where such a payment has been made, a new s 584B will provide for the repayment of the compensation on the revocation of the demolition or prohibition order as the case may be.

Where a person is displaced from a dwelling in consequence, inter alia, of its compulsory acquisition, and he/she occupied that dwelling as an only or main residence for a period of one year ending with the displacement, by virtue of an interest in it or as a statutory tenant under the Rent Act 1977, etc; a home loss

---

[132] *Coleen Properties Ltd v Minister of Housing and Local Government* [1971] 1 All ER 1049, [1971] 1 WLR 433 and *Gosling v Secretary of State for the Environment* [1975] JPL 406 and see *Bass Charrington (North) Ltd v Minster of Housing and Local Government* (1970) 22 P & CR 31.

payment may be claimed under s 29 of the Land Compensation Act 1973, and the position is similar where a tenant is displaced by the acquisition of the landlord's interest in a property by agreement by an authority possessing compulsory purchase powers, see s 29(6). Where the conditions relating to entitlement to claim a home loss payment are not met a discretionary payment may still be made to a displaced occupier, see s 29(2) of the 1973 Act as amended. Note that a person is not 'displaced' if he/she gives up occupation before the date on which the acquiring authority was authorised to acquire under s 29(3). Claims must be made in writing, with particulars as required by the authority, within six years of displacement, s 32. The amount of a home loss payment for a periodic tenant is fixed at £1,500 by s 30 of the 1973 Act. Similar payments may be payable to local authority tenants who are required to move because their homes are being redeveloped. In such cases it appears alleged rent arrears due from the tenant can be deducted by way of set-off by the landlord from the statutory sum[133].

A disturbance payment may additionally be payable to a tenant displaced by compulsory acquisition under s 32 of the 1973 Act and this will cover, inter alia, reasonable removal expenses, see s 38. To qualify for a disturbance payment a person must be in lawful possession of the land in question, and must have no entitlement to compensation under another statute.

It has been policy that clearance and compulsory purchase procedure should only be used where there is a compelling case for their use on grounds of public interest, with the burden of justification falling on the acquiring authority. An authority must be satisfied that clearance is the most satisfactory way of dealing with the area, and must have considered alternative uses for the area, the views of residents, arrangements for rehousing and after use of the land. More than one survey may be needed to satisfy an authority on these issues. Compulsory purchase orders have depended on the Secretary of State being satisfied that the economic and other interests of an area are best served by clearance. Authorities have had to argue their case for being granted compulsory purchase powers in a written document, including statements of the reasons for concluding relevant buildings are unfit, the proposals for rehousing residents and relocating any commercial or industrial uses, evidence as to the proposed after use of the site, evidence that the economic aspect of clearance has been considered.

Once an authority has acquired land under s 290, s 291 requires them to ensure that buildings on the land are vacated and are then demolished, though they may, under s 301 postpone the demolition of residential buildings on land they acquire if they consider those buildings are capable of providing accommodation of a standard 'adequate for the time being'. Such property will almost certainly be of a standard lower than that of 'fitness', but it must not be of such a poor quality that it is prejudicial to health or a nuisance, otherwise its occupants will be in a position to take statutory nuisance proceedings against the authority, see further below *Nottingham Friendship Housing Association v Newton*[134] and *Salford City Council v McNally*[135]. The period of postponement of demolition can be quite long – 24 years was considered not unreasonable on the facts in *R v Birmingham City Council,*

---

[133] *Khan v Islington London Borough Council* [1999] EGCS 87, CA.
[134] [1974] 2 All ER 760, [1974] 1 WLR 923.
[135] [1976] AC 379, [1975] 2 All ER 860, HL.

*ex p Sale*[136]. However, in that case Forbes J argued that exercise of the power to postpone requires more than that the housing is 'capable of providing accommodation adequate for the time being'. There must be some exceptional reason why demolition is postponed over and above 'need' for houses and the fact that the houses in question can be maintained to the standard of adequacy. The scheme of the Act is that once demolition is decided on, demolition should proceed unless proper and exceptional reasons justify postponement of demolition. Section 583 of the 1985 Act further permits authorities to permit continuation of tenancies of houses compulsorily acquired and to continue in use as housing accommodation. In such cases they may serve notice on the occupants authorising continued occupation on specified terms.

Those who are displaced from residential accommodation as a result of compulsory purchase action, and who have no suitable alternative accommodation available to them on reasonable terms, are entitled to look to the acquiring authority for housing, see further below on s 39 of the Land Compensation Act 1973.

## TOWARDS REFORM OF THE FITNESS STANDARD

In 1993 the Department of the Environment published research undertaken by the Legal Research Institute of the University of Warwick, *Monitoring the New Housing Fitness Standard,* following local authority concern at possible variation in interpreting the 1989 fitness standard.

It was found that the phrase 'not reasonably suitable for occupation' allowed divergent findings as to fitness because of the element of subjective evaluation, and officials indicated they would welcome clarification on a number of issues, for example the requirements as to stability, heating, cooking facilities and locations of water closets. Similarly there was often local confusion as to what is meant by a 'building' for the purposes of the legislation. When it came to taking action in respect of properties found to be unfit, in 54 per cent of instances local officials were likely to recommend action by way of grant aid (see further below) with repair notices being served in 23 per cent of instances, and clearance, demolition or closure is an option in 3 per cent of cases. Some authorities, however, had an informal 'do-nothing' option where an occupier was unwilling to undergo disruption consequent on works needed to make a dwelling fit.

In February 1998 the DETR issued a consultation paper on the housing fitness standard. This was followed by a further consultation paper in March 2001, 'Health and Safety in Housing: Replacement of the Housing Fitness Standard by the Housing Health and Safety Rating System'. This argued that there was broad agreement that the standard enshrined in the 1985 Act, even as amended, did not reflect modern understandings of the risks and hazards posed by dwellings and proposed its replacement by a Housing Health and Safety Rating System (HHSRS). The proposals, in outline, were that:

- Environmental Health Officers (EHOs) should measure the severity of risks associated with health and safety hazards in a dwelling;

---

[136] (1983) 9 HLR 33.

- there would be (as initially proposed) twenty-four broad categories of 'risk' subsuming the 1985 'heads' of unfitness, but with new ones added;
- assessment of a property should depend first on the likelihood of its condition resulting in an incident and then on the range of 'harm outcomes' that could eventuate;
- this should result in a 'hazard score' directly related to the equivalent annual risk of death, leading to the banding of properties;
- assessment should be based on the risk to a potential occupant most vulnerable to a particular risk, eg rickety internal stairs pose particular risks to elderly persons;
- the 'hazard score' could thus take account of the characteristics of current occupants;
- each hazard in a dwelling should be separately scored, though decisions on what to do with regard to a particular hazard could be influenced by the existence and 'score' of other hazards;
- HHSRS should also consider the needs of neighbours, visitors and passers-by, and thus the risk to a visitor from a hazard could be considered in determining appropriate actions to secure a particular outcome.

The basis of the new system would be a requirement on authorities, after a risk assessment, to take 'the most appropriate action', though a mandatory duty to take action should exist in respect of any unacceptable health and safety risk. Otherwise authorities would be guided by centrally issued enforcement guidance. Thus it was proposed that a *duty* would be imposed to deal with serious hazards (ie those where a hazard score of 1,000 or more is calculated – property bands A–C) with a *power* to take action in respect of lesser hazards. Even so the requirement to take 'the most appropriate action' could still be influenced by an authority's judgment on whether, taking all considerations into account, a dwelling gives risk to unacceptable hazards. This would enable authorities to adopt deferred action in respect of properties where, though risks exist, they would be unlikely to affect occupants because, for example, they are young and fit.

The HHSRS system, it was proposed, would generate 'hazard scores' for each category of occupant most vulnerable to a particular hazard, whether or not such a person is actually in occupation of a particular dwelling. This would enable authorities to make an assessment of a property on a long term basis so that they would be in a position to take action should a person of the 'most vulnerable' group move into the property at some future time. This would enable the service in respect of the property of a Suspended Improvement Notice informing the owner or landlord of requisite action before a vulnerable new occupant moved in. In carrying out HHSRS assessments authorities would, in general, be concerned with harm of sufficient severity to require medical attention. However, in all cases the procedure to follow would be the same:

- Authorities would be required to take 'the most appropriate action' to remove or minimise hazards;
- In assessing a hazard and in deciding on the appropriate action, authorities would take account of central guidance and the range of enforcement powers available;

- Once a hazard had been assessed this would be followed by the service of reasoned notice on the owner, though in some cases the notice could require no more than suspended action.

How have these proposals been carried forward by the Housing Bill 2003?

## THE HOUSING FITNESS STANDARD

The Government's 2003 Housing Bill[137] proposed to implement the new Housing Health and Safety Rating System (HHSRS), devised at Warwick University. This new system as we have seen was designed to replace the 1989 fitness requirements imposed by the Housing Act 1985 (inserted in 1989)[138]. What does the new system involve and how does it differ from the 1989 fitness standard that it was designed to replace?

According to the Office of the Deputy Prime Minister, '1.6 million dwellings have one or more health and safety hazards that would exceed the threshold triggering mandatory intervention by LHAs'[139]. This would extend the scope of the law from the 880,000 homes estimated to be unfit for human habitation under the 1989 fitness standard[140]. We will remind ourselves first of the 1989 fitness standard and then consider the new system proposed by the 2003 Housing Bill.

## THE 1989 'FITNESS FOR HUMAN HABITATION' REQUIREMENTS

District councils and London borough councils were under an annual duty to inspect their areas and consider measures such as repair notices that would require remedial action[141]. Government guidance indicated that local authorities should undertake a planning exercise every year to determine how many unfit properties existed, the types of unfit properties and the best solutions[142]. This exercise should, according to the guidance, monitor the progress of action and regularly carry out physical surveys.

The 1989 standard required houses (including HMOs) to meet all of nine standards. Houses were required to be:
(1)    structurally stable;
(2)    free from serious disrepair;
(3)    free from dampness prejudicial to the health of the occupants;
(4)    adequately provided with lighting, heat and ventilation;
(5)    adequately provided with wholesome water;

---

[137] By June 2004, the Housing Bill had completed all of its stages in the House of Commons but was not yet enacted. The material that follows is based on the expectation that the Bill will be enacted and that the relevant sections will be brought into force. If that does not happen, the 1989 fitness for human habitation requirements will continue to apply.

[138] For more on the 1989 fitness requirements, see Hughes, David and Stuart Lowe (2000) 'Public Sector Housing Law' London: Butterworths pp 362–390. What follows draws substantially on the work of Hughes and Lowe.

[139] Office of the Deputy Prime Minister 'Housing Bill Part 1 – Housing Health and Safety Rating System'. Figures were based on the 2001 English House Condition Survey.

[140] Office of the Deputy Prime Minister 'Housing Bill Part 1 – Housing Health and Safety Rating System'. Figures were based on the 2001 English House Condition Survey.

[141] s 605 of the Housing Act 1985.

[142] DoE Circular 17/96.

(6) adequately provided with facilities for cooking/preparing food, including a sink with hot and cold water;

(7) provided with a suitably located water closet for occupants' exclusive use;

(8) provided with a suitably located bath/shower and basic with hot and cold water for occupants' exclusive use;

(9) provided with a system for water drainage.

A house was regarded as unfit for human habitation if, considering the effects of the defects on the whole property, it fell short of any one of the nine criteria, and if by reason for that failure it was not reasonably suitable for occupation[143].

A number of criticisms could be made of the 1989 requirements. For example the standard prevented authorities from taking into account the effect of an accumulation of minor defects, in a property which met the nine criteria[144]. David Ormandy noted that a number of potentially serious conditions fall outside the nine criteria, including inadequate provision for fire safety, dangerous design features, insufficient energy efficiency and radon gas[145]. Ormandy also commented on the need for professional judgement, the vagueness of the official guidance on the meaning of 'not reasonably suitable for occupation', that the standard is set in primary legislation making updating difficult and that the 1989 standard was a pass/fail model. So there was no indication of degrees of unfitness.

Will the new system meet these objections? Consultation by the DETR[146] in 1998 considered adapting the existing standard to fill gaps, for example to include properties with poor energy ratings. However a more ambitious option was selected following the 2001 consultations outlined above.

## THE HOUSING HEALTH AND SAFETY RATING SYSTEM

Under the new scheme[147], each local housing authority would continue to be under an annual duty to inspect the housing conditions in their district[148]. They would also have a duty to investigate when official complaints[149] indicate that a hazard may exist or that an area should be treated as a clearance area[150].

The basis of the system is the principle that '[a]ny residential premises should provide a safe and healthy environment for any potential occupier or visitor.'[151] Rather than providing for pass/fail assessment against criteria, the system provides for the measurement of risk using the concept of a hazard.

---

[143] *Hall v Manchester Corpn* (1915) 84 LJ Ch 732.

[144] Hughes, David and Stuart Lowe (2000) 'Public Section Housing Law' London: Butterworths p 363.

[145] Ormandy, David 'Towards Safe and Healthy Housing' [2002] Journal of Housing Law pp 50–54 at 50.

[146] Department for the Environment, Transport and the Regions, then the department responsible for housing policy. Currently the responsible department is the Office of the Deputy Prime Minister (ODPM).

[147] At the time of writing, the Housing Bill had been passed by the House of Commons and had received its First Reading in the House of Lords. The following material was prepared in the expectation that the Bill will be enacted and brought into force.

[148] Cl 3(1) of the Housing Bill 2003.

[149] Official complaints are defined in cl 4(2) of the Housing Bill 2004 as written complaints made by a justice of the peace or a parish or community council.

[150] Cl 4(1) of the Housing Bill 2003.

[151] This and much of the material that follows comes from: Office of the Deputy Prime Minister 'Housing Health and Safety Rating Systems Guidance, Version 2' (Draft version released in December 2003 on the ODPM website).

As Caroline Hunter has observed, these changes deserve to be welcomed and their effectiveness will depend on the commitment and financial resources of local authorities[152]. For category 2 hazards, where local authorities have discretion to intervene, financial constraints may prevent them from using their new powers. Lack of financial resources was identified as one reason for the limited effectiveness of the previous regulatory system based on 'fitness for human habitation.' [153] Local authorities would, of course, owe a duty in public law to treat category 2 hazards on an individual basis. Any local authority that adopted a blanket policy of never using their powers in relation to category 2 hazards could be exposed to a claim for judicial review[154].

One of the issues faced by Parliament in establishing the system was the need to balance the need for protection of tenants at risk with the rights of property owners. A system of appeals aims to protect owners' property rights and prevent any abuse by local authorities of their powers. The proper balance between regulation and respect for property rights has been a contentious issue since at least the Victorian era[155].

It remains to be seen whether the system of appeals will allow wealthier and less scrupulous landlords to delay essential remedial work. For improvement notices, for example, there is scope for an initial appeal to a residential property tribunal and a further appeal to the Lands Tribunal. We shall also find that, when a prohibition order has been served, the owner could nevertheless request permission to use the property. If permission was refused, the owner could appeal against that refusal of permission as well as the prohibition order itself. Does the system of appeals endanger the effectiveness of the system?

In defence of the Housing Bill, it would provide for emergency measures to protect residents in danger, such as emergency prohibition orders. Emergency measures could be used when there is an 'imminent risk of serious harm'[156]. While the owner of a property could appeal, the Explanatory Note issued while the Bill was in Parliament commented that the appeal would not stop the emergency action or prohibition from being put into effect. The Note added that '[a]ctions may begin and be completed before a notice is served.' Provided that these measures are properly used, these provisions appear to reduce the danger that the appeals process could leave tenants at risk.

It appears that there will be, in effect, a hierarchy of hazards in Housing Health and Safety Rating System. Hazards posing an 'imminent risk of serious harm' would be the most serious, justifying emergency action. Below them would be category 1

---

[152] Hunter, Caroline 'A Farewell to Unfitness: New Housing Legislation' [2003] Journal of Housing Law 51.

[153] Blandy, Sarah 'Housing standards in the private rented sector and the three Rs: regulation, responsibility and rights' in '(eds) David Cowan and Alex Marsh (2001) 'Two steps forward: housing policy into the new millennium' Bristol: Policy Press pp 73–92 at 81–83.

[154] Parpworth, Neil 'Constitutional and Administrative Law' Butterworths Lexis Nexis: 2000 (2nd edition; the third edition is expected in September 2004) pp 295–297; Wade, H.W.R. and C.F. Forsyth 'Administrative Law' Oxford University Press: 2000 (8th edition; the ninth edition is expected in August 2004) pp 328–329.

[155] Stebbings, Chantal 'State intervention and private property rights in Victorian England' in (ed) Alastair Hudson (2004) 'New Perspectives on Property Law, Human Rights and the Home' London: Cavendish pp 217–237.

[156] Explanatory Note for the Housing Bill (Guidance which does not form part of the Bill itself), para 128.

hazards, for which local authorities would have a duty to take action. Any resources left over from emergency action and non-emergency category 1 hazards could be used to deal with category 2 hazards. While the system would appear to enable effective action for the most urgent risks, whether it can cope with less serious, but ongoing, problems remains open to question.

## THE CONCEPT OF A HAZARD

A hazard is defined as:

> 'any risk of harm to the health and safety of an actual or potential occupier of a dwelling or HMO which arises from a deficiency in the dwelling or HMO[157] or in any building or land in the vicinity (whether the deficiency arises as a result of the construction of any building, an absence of maintenance or repair, or otherwise.' [158]

How would the existence of hazards be determined? The Housing Bill provides for regulations to prescribe for the measurement of risks[159]. The new system is more comprehensive than the old standard. It is based on 29 types of potential hazard[160] rather than the nine criteria of the 1989 standard. The system is also more dynamic, being based on the impact of defects on residents rather than static defects in themselves.

The following 29 types of potential housing hazards were identified for Version 2 of the Housing Health and Safety Rating System[161]. They are broken down into four hazard groups: physiological requirements, psychological requirements, protection against infection and protection against accidents. These groups are further broken down into sub-groups and individual hazards:

## The 29 types of hazard according to ODPM Guidance

*Physiological Requirements*

HYGROTHERMAL CONDITIONS
1. Damp and mould growth
2. Excessive cold
3. Excessive heat

POLLUTANTS (NON-MICROBIAL)
4. Asbestos (and MMFs[162])

---

[157] HMOs are Houses in Multiple Occupation, defined for the purposes of this Bill in cll 217–222.
[158] Cl 2(1) Housing Bill 2003.
[159] Cll 2(1), (2) and (3) and see the Explanatory Notes published with the Bill.
[160] Draft Version 2 of the HHSRS includes 29 categories, replacing the 24 categories of Version 1. For the 24 categories, see Ormandy, David 'Towards Safe and Healthy Housing' [2002] Journal of Housing Law 50–54.
[161] Office of the Deputy Prime Minister 'Housing Health and Safety Rating System, Guidance (Version 2)'. (Draft version released in December 2003 on the ODPM website.)
[162] MMFs are skin, eye and respiratory irritants such as loft and cavity wall insulation.

5.    Biocides[163]
6.    Carbon monoxide and fuel combustion products
7.    Lead
8.    Radiation
9.    Uncombusted fuel gas
10.   Volatile organic Compounds

## Psychological Requirements

### SPACE, SECURITY, LIGHT AND NOISE
11.   Crowding and space
12.   Entry by intruders
13.   Lighting
14.   Noise

## Protection against Infection

### HYGIENE, SANITATION AND WATER SUPPLY
15.   Domestic hygiene, pets and refuse
16.   Food safety
17.   Personal hygiene, sanitation and drainage
18.   Water supply

## Protection against Accidents

### FALLS
19.   Falls associated with baths etc
20.   Falls on the level
21.   Falls associated with stairs and steps
22.   Falls between levels

### ELECTRIC SHOCKS, FIRES, BURNS AND SCALDS
23.   Electrical hazards
24.   Fire
25.   Hot surfaces and materials

### COLLISIONS, CUTS AND STRAINS
26.   Collisions and entrapment
27.   Explosions
28.   Ergonomics
29.   Structural collapse and falling elements

---

[163] Biocides are chemicals used for treating timber and mould growth and to kill pest infections including insects and rodents: Office of the Deputy Prime Minister 'Housing Health and Safety Rating System, Guidance (Version 2)'. See para 5.05 of Version 2 for a list of the relevant regulations.

According to the draft Guidance issued in December 2003, the new system would require local authorities to take into account the local environment, including noise, air pollution, ground conditions and local weather[164]. Whether the property is situated in a rural or urban area will be a relevant factor, which may extend the application of the famous dictum in the law of nuisance of Thesiger LJ that 'what would be a nuisance in Belgrave Square would not necessarily be so in Bermondsey'[165].

A surveyor would assess properties for the 29 types of hazard to produce a numerical hazard score. That numerical score would be converted into a Hazard Band. Each Hazard Band would be identified by a letter, ranging from A (most dangerous, for hazard scores of 5,000 or above) to J (least dangerous, for scores of 9 or below). According to the Explanatory Note issued with the Housing Bill (which does not form part of the legislation) the Government intends that hazards within bands A to C are to be described as category 1 hazards[166]. Hazards within bands D to J are to be category 2 hazards. What, then, is the legal significance of fitting hazards into categories 1 and 2?

## Category 1 and 2 hazards and the duty to take action

The Bill further defines 'harm' as including temporary harm and 'health' as including mental health[167]. Two categories of hazard are identified. The more serious are 'category 1' hazards and the less serious 'category 2'. Clause 2 of the Bill offers a general description, but not a complete definition, of category 1 and 2 hazards:

2.    **Meaning of 'category 1 hazard' and 'category 2 hazard'**

(1) In this Act—

'category 1 hazard' means a hazard of a prescribed description which falls within a prescribed band as a result of achieving, under a prescribed method for calculating the seriousness of hazards of that description, a numerical score of or above a prescribed amount;

'category 2 hazard' means a hazard of a prescribed description which falls within a prescribed band as a result of achieving, under a prescribed method for calculating the seriousness of hazards of that description, a numerical score below the minimum amount prescribed for a category 1 hazard of that description.

What, then, is the significance of the difference between the two categories of hazard? Clause 5 of the Housing Bill would impose a duty on local authorities to take 'appropriate enforcement action' in relation to category 1 hazards. The local authority would then have to consider a list of enforcement actions provided for in the Bill:

(a) serving an improvement notice under s 10;

(b) making a prohibition order under s 19;

(c) serving a hazard awareness notice under s 27;

---

[164]  Office of the Deputy Prime Minister 'Housing Health and Safety Rating System Guidance, Version 2' (Draft version released in December 2003 on the ODPM website) para 1.11.
[165]  *Sturges v Bridgman* (1879) 11 Ch D 852 at 865.
[166]  See para 47 of the Explanatory Note for the Housing Bill 2003.
[167]  Cll 2(4) and 2(5) of the Housing Bill 2003, respectively.

(d) taking emergency remedial action under s 39;

(e) making an emergency prohibition order under s 42;

(f) making a demolition order under subs (1) or (2) of s 265 of the Housing Act 1985 (c.68);

(g) declaring the area in which the premises concerned are situated to be a clearance area by virtue of s 289(2) of that Act[168]

If only one course of action is available, the local authority would have a duty to pursue that action[169]. If more than one course of action is available, the local authority would have a duty to take action and discretion to select the course of action that they consider to be most appropriate[170]. In exercising that discretion, a local authority would have a duty to have regard to relevant Government guidance[171].

Local authorities would acquire the power to make reasonable charges for relevant administrative costs in enforcement[172]. For example, for improvement and prohibition notices, local authorities would be able to charge for the administrative work involved in determining whether to serve the notice, identifying any action to be specified in the notice and serving the notice[173].

If the administrative costs are significant, some may be concerned that smaller private landlords could withdraw from the housing market. Research has shown that two-thirds of private landlords own a small number (between one and four) of properties and only one in seven landlords regard being a landlord as a full-time job[174]. Experts have found that residential letting performs poorly compared with other forms of investment[175]. However, it could be argued that landlords can (generally) afford to make their properties safe since rising real incomes provide landlords with resources to spend about £16 billion per year in aggregate on repair and renovation[176]. Also, David Cowan has argued that previous forms of regulation (rent control and security of tenure) were not the sole reason for the decline of the private rented sector during the twentieth century and that other reasons can be found in general housing policy and the promotion of alternative tenures[177].

Will the new system do enough to deter landlords from allowing residents of their properties to be exposed to risks? Arguably, the sort of minor offences established by the Bill would not be proportionate or effective. Gavin Dingwall has argued that:

---

[168]  Cl 5(2) of the Housing Bill 2003.
[169]  Cl 5(3) of the Housing Bill 2003.
[170]  Cl 5(4) of the Housing Bill 2003.
[171]  Cl 8 of the Housing Bill 2003.
[172]  Cl 48 of the Housing Bill 2003.
[173]  Cl 48(2) of the Housing Bill 2003.
[174]  Crook, ADH and PA Kemp *Private Landlords in England* (1996) HMSO; see also research cited by Hughes, D and Lowe, S, (eds) 'The new private rented sector' in *The Private Rented Sector in a New Century: revival or false dawn?* (2002) The Polity Press, pp 1–18 at 8–9.
[175]  Cowan, D, *Housing Law and Policy* (1999) Macmillan, p 58; Crook, ADH, 'Private renting in the 21st century: lessons from the last decade of the twentieth century', in S Lowe and D Hughes (eds), *The Private Rented Sector in a New Century: revival or false dawn?* (2002) Polity Press, pp 19–29 at 27–28.
[176]  Leather, P, 'Housing standards in the private sector' in D Cowan and A Marsh (eds), *Two Steps Forward: Housing policy into the new millennium* (2001) Polity Press, pp 93–110 at 94; see also Rhodes, D and Kemp, P, 'Rents and returns in the residential lettings market' in S Lowe and D Hughes (eds) *The Private Rented Sector in a New Century: revival or false dawn?* (2002) Polity Press, pp 43–64, Satsangi, M, 'Rental housing supply in rural Scotland: the role of private landlords' in (eds) Lowe and Hughes (2002), pp 79–94 and Crook, ADH 'Housing conditions in the private rented sector within a market framework' in Lowe and Hughes (2002) pp 153–176.
[177]  Cowan, D, *Housing Law and Policy* (1999) Macmillan, pp 57–83.

'Recent case law has highlighted the need for adequate inter-agency liaison to ensure that the most appropriate [criminal] charges are brought, as a failure to do so can result in individuals being convicted only of minor offences and, consequently, nor receiving a punishment commensurate with the harm that their neglect could cause.' [178]

Sarah Blandy has pointed out the tension between deregulation (to encourage landlords to enter or remain in the market) and the need to ensure that the worst landlords make improvements to their properties[179]. There is a risk that the cost of the system could drive those who Crook calls 'cottage industry' landlords out of the market[180], while not doing enough to deter the worst landlords from allowing their tenants to be at risk of serious harm. Whether these twin threats will be realised depends on a number of factors, including the Government guidance, the costs of landlords, the policies and funding of local authorities, the approach of the tribunals to appeals and whether there is sufficient inter-agency liaison to ensure that appropriate criminal charges are brought in the more serious cases.

## IMPROVEMENT NOTICES

An improvement notice is defined by the Housing Bill as 'a notice requiring the person on whom it is served to take such remedial action in respect of the hazard concerned as is specified in the notice'[181]. When a local authority detects a category 1 hazard on residential premises, this appears to be a mandatory response unless an interim or final management order is in force under Part 4 of the Bill[182]. When local authorities respond to category 1 hazards, the Bill would empower them to require greater action than the minimum required to remove the category 1 hazard[183].

Clause 12(2) of the Bill would require improvement notices to specify certain information:

(a) whether the notice is served under s 10 [category 1 hazards] or 11 [category 2 hazards],

(b) the nature of the hazards and the residential premises on which it exists,

(c) the deficiency giving rise to the hazard,

(d) the premises in relation to which remedial action is to be taken in respect of the hazard and the nature of that remedial action,

(e) the date when the remedial action is to be started (see subs (3)), and

(f) the period within which the remedial work is to be completed or the periods within which each part of it is to be completed.

---

[178] Dingwall, G 'Why it is necessary to prioritise responses to landlords who let dangerous properties' [2000] Journal of Housing Law pp 25–29 at 25.

[179] Blandy, Sarah 'Housing standards in the private rented sector and the three Rs: regulation, responsibility and rights' in D Cowan and A Marsh (eds), *Two Steps Forward: Housing policy into the new millennium* (2001) Polity Press, pp 73–92 at 75.

[180] Crook, ADH 'Private renting in the 21st century': lessons from the last decade of the twentieth century; in S Lowe and D Hughes (eds) *The Private Rented Sector in a New Century: revival or false dawn?* (2002) Polity Press, pp 19–29 at 29.

[181] Cl 10(2) of the Housing Bill 2003.

[182] Cl 10(1)(b) of the Housing Bill 2003.

[183] Cl 10(5)(b) of the Housing Bill 2003.

The date on which remedial action would have to be started would have to be no earlier than the 28th day after the day on which the notice was served[184]. The notice would have to notify the recipient of their right to appeal against the decision and the period allowed for an appeal[185]. Provision was made in the Bill for suspended operation of notices[186]. If the local authority were satisfied that they requirements of an improvement notice were complied with, they would have a duty to revoke the notice[187]. On whom should the notice be served?

- For properties licensed under the Bill: on the licence holder[188] (for licensing of properties see further Chapter 13).

- For dwelling houses that are not licensed under the Bill: on the person having control of the dwelling or, if the property is an HMO, either on the person having control or the person managing the property[189].

- For flats that are not licensed under the Bill, whether HMOs or not, and for the common parts a building containing one or more flats, the local authority must serve the notice on the owner and the person who, in the opinion of the authority, ought to take the specified action[190] (for HMOs etc see further Chapter 13).

Copies of the notice must be served on every other person who, to the authority's knowledge, ahs a 'relevant interest' (freeholder, mortgagee or lessee) or is an 'occupier'[191].

Appeals are provided for in cll 10–20 of Sch 1. A person on whom an improvement notice was served could appeal to a residential property tribunal on two possible grounds[192]. The first ground for appeal is that one or more other person(s) should, as owner of the premises, either take the action required or pay for it. The second ground for appeal is that, considering the hazard, one of the following courses of action would be the best course of action:

(a) making a prohibition order under s 19 or 20 of this Act;

(b) serving a hazard awareness notice under s 27 or 28 of this Act, and

(c) making a demolition order under s 265 of the Housing Act 1985[193].

An appeal would stop the notice from becoming operative until the notice was confirmed on appeal, the period for further appeal expired or suspension ended. If the appellant is not satisfied with the decision of the residential property tribunal, they may have a further opportunity to appeal to the Lands Tribunal[194]. Whether this two-stage appeal process will be vulnerable to abuse by landlords who can afford to take maximum advantage of it remains to be seen.

---

[184] Cl 12(3) of the Housing Bill 2003.
[185] Cl 12(4) of the Housing Bill 2003.
[186] Cl 13 of the Housing Bill 2003.
[187] Cl 14 of the Housing Bill 2003.
[188] Sch 1, Part 1, para 1 of the Housing Bill 2003.
[189] Sch 1, Part 1, para 2 of the Housing Bill 2003.
[190] Sch 1, Part 1, para 3 and 4 of the Housing Bill 2003.
[191] Sch 1, Part 1, para 5 of the Housing Bill 2003.
[192] The jurisdiction conferred on a residential property tribunal will, in practice, be exercised by a rent assessment committee. When exercising this jurisdiction, the rent assessment committee would be known as a residential property tribunal: cl 194 of the Housing Bill 2004.
[193] Cl 12(2) of the Housing Bill 2003.
[194] Further appeal to the Lands Tribunal may only be made with permission of the residential property tribunal or the Lands Tribunal, within a time limit: cl 195 of the Housing Bill 2003.

What would happen if an improvement notice was ignored? The penalty for non-compliance with an improvement notice, on summary conviction, would be a fine[195]. Anyone charged under this section could escape a fine by showing either compliance or reasonable excuse for non-compliance[196]. If the notice was not being complied with, or reasonable progress was not being made, the local authority would acquire a power to do the work[197]. This power would include a right of entry for persons with written permission from the local authority, to enter and carry out the necessary work at any reasonable time. Obstruction of such work would be an offence[198]. It is important to note that specific notice requirements for any local authority wishing to use this power of entry:

4. (1) The local housing authority must serve a notice under this paragraph before they enter any premises under paragraph 3 of the purpose of taking action in relation to a hazard.

(2) The notice must identify the improvement notice to which it relates and state—

(a) the premises and hazard concerned;
(b) that the authority intend to enter the premises;
(c) the action which the authority intend to take on the premises; and
(d) the power under which the authority intend to enter the premises and take the action.

(3) The notice must be served on the person on whom the improvement notice was served, and a copy of the notice must be served on any other person who is an occupier of the premises.

(4) The notice and any such copy must be served sufficiently in advance of the time when the authority intend to enter the premises as to give the recipients reasonable notice of the intended entry[199].

(5) A copy of the notice may also be served on any owner of the premises.

If the remedial action required was not being done because the owner refused to grant access to the property, a magistrates' court would be able to order the owner to permit access and to allow work that is 'necessary or expedient' to be done[200]. Suppose the person on whom the improvement notice has been served was unwilling or unable to do the work but was willing to give the local authority permission to do so. Under those circumstances the local authority would be able to do the necessary work[201]. If that happens, the person who received the improvement notice would be responsible for paying for the work.

## PROHIBITION ORDERS

The effect of a prohibition order would be to stop the use of the premises. This type of order need not be used to impose blanket bans on using properties. Local authorities would acquire powers to make prohibition orders to stop use of properties by 'more than a particular number of households or persons; or ...

---

[195] Cl 29(3) of the Housing Bill 2003.
[196] Cll 29(2) and 29(4) respectively, of the Housing Bill 2003.
[197] Sch 3, Part 2 of the Housing Bill 2003.
[198] See Sch 3, Part 2, para 5(1)(b) and cl 205(1) of the Housing Bill 2003. The penalty would be a fine not exceeding level 4 on the standard scale.
[199] Sch 3, Part 2, para 4 of the Housing Bill 2003.
[200] Cl 34(2) of the Housing Bill 2003.
[201] Sch 3, Part 1, para 1 of the Housing Bill 2003.

occupation ... by particular descriptions of persons.' [202] Where there was 'an imminent risk of serious harm to the health or safety of any of the occupiers of those or any other residential premises,' local authorities could use emergency measures, including the power to issue emergency prohibition orders[203].

Local authorities' powers would also include stopping use of the common parts of a building, subject to conditions:

> The notice may not ... prohibit use of any part of the building or its external common parts that is not included in any residential premises on which the hazard exists, unless the authority are satisfied—
>
> (a)  that the deficiency from which the hazard arises is situated there, and
> (b)  that it is necessary for such use to be prohibited in order to protect the health or safety of any actual or potential occupiers of one or more of the flats[204].

The Bill also prescribes certain contents for prohibition orders:

### 21.  Contents of prohibition orders

> (1) A prohibition order under s 19 or 20 must comply with the following provisions of this section.
>
> (2) The order must specify, in relation to the hazard (or each of the hazards) to which it relates—
>
> (a)  whether the order is made under s 19 or 20,
> (b)  the nature of the hazard concerned and the residential premises on which it exists,
> (c)  the deficiency giving rise to the hazard,
> (d)  the premises in relation to which prohibitions are imposed by the order (see subss (3) and (4)), and
> (e)  any remedial action which the authority consider would, if taken in relation to the hazard, result in their revoking the order under s 24[205].
>
> (6) The order must also contain information about—
>
> (a)  the right under part 3 of Sch 2 to appeal against the order, and
> (b)  the period within which an appeal may be made, and specify the date on which the order is made'[206].

Those subject to prohibition orders would be able to appeal[207]. They would also be able to apply to the local authority to use the property, despite the prohibition order. If permission was refused, a specific appeal against this refusal would also be available[208].

When the prohibition order has been made, those affected may ask the local authority for approval to use the property, despite the prohibition order. The local authority would have the power to permit use of the property (or any part of it) for all or any purposes and such permission must not be unreasonably withheld[209].

---

[202]  Cl 21(5) of the Housing Bill 2003.
[203]  See the section of this chapter on Emergency Measures.
[204]  Cl 19(4) of the Housing Bill 2003.
[205]  Cl 21(2) of the Housing Bill 2003.
[206]  Cl 21(6) of the Housing Bill 2003.
[207]  Sch 3, Part 2 of the Housing Bill 2003.
[208]  Cl 21(9) of the Housing Bill 2003.
[209]  Cls 21(4) and 21(7), respectively, of the Housing Bill 2003.

Any refusal to grant permission could also be the subject of an appeal[210]. Prohibition orders would have to be reviewed by the local authority at least once a year[211]. They could also be suspended, revoked and varied[212].

Non-compliance with a prohibition order would become an offence, punishable by a fine[213]. Owners would be able to recover possession against tenants of premises subject to prohibition orders by a notice to quit, despite the protection of tenancies created by the Housing Act 1988, the Rent (Agriculture) Act 1976 or the Rent Act 1977[214].

## EMERGENCY MEASURES UNDER THE HOUSING BILL

Emergency measures would be available when there is an 'imminent risk of serious harm to the health and safety' of occupiers:

39.   **Emergency remedial action**

(1) If—

(a)   the local housing authority are satisfied that a Category 1 hazard exists on any residential premises, and

(b)   they are further satisfied that the hazard involves an imminent risk of serious harm to the health or safety of any of the occupiers of those or any other residential premises, and

(c)   no interim or final management order is in force under Part 4 in relation to the premises mentioned in paragraph (a),

the taking by the authority of emergency remedial action under this section in respect of the hazard is a course of action available to the authority in relation to the hazard for the purposes of s 5 (category 1 hazards: general duty to take enforcement action[215].

Any appeal should not stop the emergency action or prohibition from being put into effect. The Notes to the Bill added that '[a]ctions may begin and be completed before a notice is served.' Provided that these measures are properly used, these provisions appear to reduce the danger that the appeals process could leave tenants at risk.

Emergency Prohibition Orders would be available, subject to conditions, as follows:

42.   **Emergency prohibition orders**

(1) If—

(a)   the local housing authority are satisfied that a Category 1 hazard exists on any residential premises, and

(b)   they are further satisfied that the hazard involves an imminent risk of serious harm to the health or safety of any of the occupiers of those or any other residential premises, and

(c)   no interim or final management order is in force under Part 4 in relation to the premises mentioned in paragraph (a),

---

[210]   Cl 21(9) of the Housing Bill 2003.
[211]   Cl 25 of the Housing Bill 2003.
[212]   See cll 22 (suspension) and 24 (revocation and variation) of the Housing Bill 2003.
[213]   The fine would be level 5 on the standard scale: cl 31 of the Housing Bill 2003.
[214]   Tenancies protected by the Rent Act 1977 were generally created before the relevant provisions of the Housing Act 1988 came into force on 15 January 1989.
[215]   Cl 39 of the Housing Bill 2003.

making an emergency prohibition order under this section in respect of the hazard is a course of action available to the authority in relation to the hazard for the purposes of s 5 (category 1 hazards: general duty to take enforcement action)[216].

## HAZARD AWARENESS NOTICES

A hazard awareness notice, according to the Housing Bill, would be 'a notice advising the person on whom it is served of the existence of a ... hazard on the residential premises concerned which arises as a result of a deficiency on the premises in respect of which the notice is served'[217].

The minimum contents of a hazard awareness notice would be as follows:

A notice under this section must specify, in relation to the hazard (or each of the hazards) to which it relates—

(a)  the nature of the hazard and the residential premises on which it exists,
(b)  the deficiency giving rise to the hazard,
(c)  the premises on which the deficiency exists,
(d)  the authority's reasons for deciding to serve the notice, including their reasons for deciding that serving the notice is the most appropriate course of action, and
(e)  details of the remedial action (if any) which the authority consider that it would be practicable and appropriate to take in relation to the hazard[218].

The Bill is silent on enforcement measures for hazard awareness notices. This might prompt speculation about why the power to issue hazard awareness notices was included in the Bill. Perhaps hazard awareness notices are meant to local authorities to be seen to be taking action with regard to less serious hazards when resources do not permit tougher action. The formality of the notices may itself encourage those responsible to take action. Hazard awareness notices may be designed to promote a 'light touch' form of regulation and a cooperative relationship between local authorities and landlords. They may also be a first step, to be used as a warning before measures that can be enforced are deployed. If property owners make vigorous use of the appeals process to delay enforcement, perhaps local authorities could reinforce their argument about the need for serious action by showing that hazard awareness notices were issued and ignored.

## HOUSING RENEWAL AND IMPROVEMENT

### Renewal areas

Improvement of poor housing conditions on an area basis has been a policy option available to authorities for many years. The Housing Act 1969 introduced the notion of the General Improvement Area (GIA). Housing Action Areas (HAA) were introduced under the Housing Act 1974 to deal with more run-down areas. These types of action continued to be available under the Housing Act 1985, but the law was subject to criticism in that it did not provide one single, comprehensive mode of dealing with poor housing and also because it tended to separate consideration of

---

[216]  Cl 42 of the Housing Bill 2003.
[217]  Cll 27(2) for category 1 and 28(2) for category 2 hazards.
[218]  Cll 27(6) for category 1 and 28(5) for category 2 hazards.

housing conditions from other important issues such as employment, education facilities etc. Though changes have been made to the law it is by no means certain that these have come about as a result of desires to answer the foregoing criticisms as opposed to wishes to foster individual effort to target resources and to reduce overall public expenditure. Under the changes made by the Local Government and Housing Act 1989, HAAs and GIAs can no longer be declared, see s 98 of the 1989 Act.

In place of GIAs and HAAs the 1989 Act introduced the concept of the Renewal Area (RA) and Annex C of DoE Circular 6/90 made it clear that land within a GIA or HAA could be instead designated as, or as part of, a RA.

The new law is part of the overall 'flexible approach' to a renewal and improvement strategy introduced by the 1989 Act. Renewal action is to be undertaken after careful appraisal of the options available for an area. Where declared, RAs will be larger than GIAs and HAAs were, and will normally last for ten years, during which time comprehensive action is to be undertaken to renew housing and tackle social and environmental problems. The basis is akin to partnership between the authority, residents, associations, and the private sector, including financial institutions, for the object of using local authority powers is to give others 'market confidence' in the area, so helping to reverse processes of decline and to encourage spin offs for the local economy in the form of employment and training opportunities. The overall trend of the legislation has also been to erode the link between renewal on the one hand and unfitness and disrepair on the other, with authorities being given increased discretion, subject to central guidance, to finance projects. This trend is likely to continue under future legislation.

Authorities are required by s 605 of the Housing Act 1985 to consider declaring RAs. This will involve selecting appropriate areas for action. DoE 6/90 made it clear the worst will not necessarily be the first; in some cases preventive action in respect of areas in danger of decline may be more appropriate.

Major changes were brought about by the Regulatory Reform (Housing Assistance) (England and Wales) Order SI 2002/1860, enabling authorities to provide assistance with housing renewal where they have an adopted and published policy on the issue. The declaration and operation of RAs is streamlined under these procedures and concentrates on an area based strategy with aims and objectives linking housing renewal to other community services, in connection with which note earlier criticism of the historic failure to make this link. Section 89 of the 1989 Act was extensively amended to enable the new policy to take effect. Authorities may now proceed on the basis of a published and publicised report from their own staff or other suitably qualified persons. That report must, inter alia, address the living conditions in the area in question, the ways in which they may be improved, the powers available to the authority, the detailed proposals for the exercise of those powers, the cost of proposals, the financial resources available, any representations received. If the report indicates that the living conditions in the area in question (which must consist primarily of housing accommodation) are unsatisfactory and can be most effectively dealt with by declaring a RA, and after carrying out an assessment of the area sufficient to satisfy themselves that a declaration is the most effective way to bring about improvement, the authority may declare the area. The

RA will continue for such period as the declaration indicates. Further guidance may be found in *Housing Renewal Guidance* published by the Office of the Deputy Prime Minister in 2002.

Under s 91 of the 1989 Act (as substituted) once a RA is declared its existence must be publicised to those who reside or own property in the area, and must thereafter, under s 92, continue to inform such persons of the action they propose to take in relation to the area and the assistance that is available for carrying out works.

Provided an authority has a publicly adopted policy of providing assistance, for the purpose of improving housing conditions they may give assistance to a person directly or indirectly to enable that individual to: acquire living accommodation where his/her own is otherwise being acquired; or to adopt or improve living accommodation, eg by alteration, conversion or enlargement or by carrying out repairs; or to demolish and replace living accommodation. Such assistance may be given subject to conditions, eg as to the payment of contributions towards costs by individuals.

It is central government policy that authorities should take HHSRS into account in taking decisions under the foregoing general discretionary housing renewal assistance powers, as surveys will indicate the existence of health and safety risks within the private sector housing stock (owner occupied and rented) which will feed into stock condition surveys and neighbourhood renewal assessments.

Under s 93 of the 1989 Act extensive powers are conferred on authorities to implement RA strategy. They may, under s 93(2), acquire land by agreement or compulsorily, and provide housing thereon. Such activity must serve one or more of the following objectives, ie the improvement or repair of relevant premises, the proper and effective management of housing accommodation, or the well being of residents. Land may also be similarly acquired for the purposes of effecting or assisting the improvement of the amenities of the area, s 93(4). Authorities may carry out works on land they own and may assist in respect of works on other land by making grants, loans and providing guarantees and materials, etc.

The compulsory purchase procedure to be used is that under Part XVIII of the 1985 Act and the Acquisition of Land Act 1981. Land may be acquired to secure the improvement or repair of housing either by the authority or another body to whom they wish to transfer the land, eg a registered social landlord, *or* bring about the proper and effective use of housing in the area, *or* to secure the well being of the residents of the area.

Section 96 of the 1989 Act empowers the Secretary of State to grant subsidies to authorities in respect of RAs, though this is effectively entirely at the discretion of central government. Circular 17/96, Annex C1, para 8, details the expenditure towards which contributions will be paid, these include street works, traffic management schemes, landscaping, improving the exteriors of buildings, converting buildings to provide community facilities and other environmental works, but exclude, inter alia, works on the interior of houses, works on commercial or industrial premises, works to improve or provide facilities which are intended primarily to produce revenue for the authority, and works of routine maintenance. The rate of contribution is 50 per cent of costs per annum up to a limit of 'aggregate eligible expenditure' of £1,000 multiplied by the number of dwellings in the area. See also DoE Circular 17/96 Annex C1, para 10.

## Grant aid

Improvement of dwellings, either by their owners or tenants, and on either an individual or group basis, under the aegis of Grant Aid given by authorities has been a feature of housing improvement for many years, and there have been many forms of grant aiding scheme, see inter alia the House Purchase and Housing Act 1959 and the Housing Act 1974. Between 1989 and 1996 the relevant law was to be found in Part VIII of the Local Government and Housing Act. This has now been repealed and replaced by the Housing Grants, Construction and Regeneration Act 1996, the chief object of which was to reduce the amount of central funding for housing improvement by moving away from a mixed pattern of mandatory and discretionary grants to one in which nearly all grants are discretionary. [References to section numbers following are to the Housing Grants, Construction and Regeneration Act (HGCRA) 1996 unless otherwise specified]. (see also DETR Circular 06/99 on Part I of the 1996 Act.) Further considerable changes were introduced by the Regulatory Reform (Housing Assistance) (England and Wales) Order SI 2002/1860 made under the Regulatory Reform Act 2001, see further above, which introduced local schemes for area based renewal assistance.

### The types of grant available

#### DISABLED FACILITIES GRANTS (DFG)

Section 1 of the 1996 Act as amended by the 2002 Order lists the only grant that is now available.

The disabled facilities grant is available in respect of the provision of facilities for disabled persons in dwellings, qualifying house boats and qualifying park ('mobile') homes and in the common parts of buildings containing one or more flats.

Grant applications must be made in due form under s 2 of the Act, and must in particular give details of the works in respect of which a grant is sought, and, normally, must be accompanied by at least two contractors' estimates of the costs of carrying out those works.

Applicants must be 'eligible' under s 3 ie they must be aged 18 or more, and public bodies such as authorities are specifically excluded from eligibility, while the Secretary of State has further powers to prescribe further classes of ineligible persons.

Section 19 lays down initial application requirements, ie that the applicant has or proposes to acquire an owner's interest in the relevant property *or* that the applicant is a tenant of the relevant dwelling. Furthermore 'tenant' in this context *includes* secure and introductory tenants amongst those who may apply. In addition the occupiers of qualifying house boats and qualifying park homes may apply. The applicant need not be the 'disabled occupant' for whose benefit the work is intended, but such a person there must be: see generally s 20. Where an owner's application is received there must be a certificate of intended residence by the disabled occupant in the dwelling (see s 21) and a similar certificate is required in respect of a tenant's application under s 22, while, once again, the authority must also require an owner's certificate from the tenant's landlord unless they consider it unreasonable in the circumstances to do so. Under s 22A of the 1996 Act inserted by the 2002 Order, where the applicant is the occupier of a qualifying house boat or park home, there must be a certificate that the boat/park home will be the intended residence of the disabled person. Generally the consent of the person entitled to possession of the place where the boat is moored or the park home is stationed will also be required.

DFGs are mandatory – an exception to the generally discretionary nature of grant aid – and the purposes for which an application must be approved are:

- facilitating access to the dwelling, the house boat or park home or the building in which it is situated;
- making the dwelling/building, house boat or park home safe for the disabled occupant and others residing with him/her;
- facilitating access by the disabled occupant to the principal family room;
- facilitating access by the disabled occupant to, or providing for that person, a sleeping room;
- facilitating access by the disabled occupant to, or providing for that person, a lavatory;
- facilitating access etc to a bath or shower room;
- facilitating access etc to a room with a wash hand basin;
- facilitating the preparation and cooking of food by the disabled occupant;
- improving the heating system to meet the disabled occupant's needs, or providing a suitable system;
- facilitating use by the disabled occupant of sources of power, light and heat – eg by repositioning switches;
- facilitating access around the dwelling by the disabled occupant in order for him/her to care for someone else normally resident there;
- other purposes as specified by the Secretary of State.

See also s 24 on the mandatory nature of DFGs, but note that an application for such a grant may not be approved unless the authority are satisfied that:

- where the application is from an intending owner of the property that he/she has acquired an owner's interest;
- the relevant works are necessary and appropriate to meet the needs of the disabled occupant and that it is reasonable and practicable to carry them out having regard to the age and condition of the property (and in relation to this issue the opinion of the Social Services Authority must be sought). Authorities historically had to consider whether the dwelling was fit. This requirement will be removed under the 2003 proposals.

It should be noted generally that in relation to determining DFG issues an authority are not entitled to have regard to their resources, and that taking such an issue into account is taking account of an irrelevant consideration open to judicial review[219].

---

[219] *R v Birmingham City Council, ex p Mohammed* [1998] 3 All ER 788, [1999] 1 WLR 33.

Section 58 defines 'qualifying house boat' and 'qualifying park home'. The former is a boat adopted as a place of permanent habitation which is moored with the area of a single housing authority in pursuance of a right to moor and in a dwelling for council tax purposes. The latter is a caravan or mobile home stationed on land and occupied under an agreement falling under the Mobile Homes Act 1983, and is a dwelling for council tax purposes.

Section 58 defines 'qualifying house boat' and 'qualifying park home'. The former is a boat adapted as a place of permanent habitation which is moored within the area of a single housing authority in pursuance of a right to moor and is a dwelling for council tax purposes. The latter is a caravan or mobile home stationed on land and occupied under an agreement falling under the Mobile Homes Act 1983, and is a dwelling for council tax purposes.

## General restrictions on grant aid

Where works subject to a grant application are *commenced* before approval under s 29 the general rule is that the authority *may* still approve the application (and that applies to otherwise mandatory grants) provided they are satisfied there were good reasons for commencing work without approval. This discretion is *not* available in respect of *completed* works.

## Means testing

Not only are grants now generally given only on a discretionary basis, they are also under s 30 means tested in the case of applications from those seeking DFG. The means testing formula is contained in regulations made under s 30(5) but proceeds on the well tried basis of comparing the applicant's financial resources (income, assets, needs and outgoings – including those of spouses, persons living with the applicant and dependants) against the 'applicable amount', ie an amount fixed by regulations in relation to grants, so that where 'resources' exceed 'applicable amount' the amount of any grant otherwise payable is proportionally reduced.

In the case of landlord's applications the amount of grant to be paid is broadly at the discretion of the authority under s 31. Authorities must, however, have regard to:

- the extent to which a landlord will be able to charge an increased rent because of the grant aided works and
- such other matters as may be directed by the Secretary of State.

In addition authorities may seek and act upon the advice of rent officers in relation to any matter.

The Secretary of State has power under s 33 of the 1996 Act to fix a maximum level of grant, though authorities have a limited discretion to exceed this on the case of DFG: see, inter alia, the Disabled Facilities Grants and Home Repair Assistance (Maximum Amounts) Order 1996, SI 1996/2888, and also SI 2001/4036 (England) and SI 2002/387 (Wales).

## Decisions, notification and payment

Section 34 requires authorities to notify applicants as soon as reasonably practicable, and in any case not later than six months from the date of application, of the outcome. Authorities approving an application must also inter alia determine those relevant works which are eligible for assistance according to the formulae for the various grants, the amount of the expenses which in their opinion are properly to be incurred in carrying out eligible works, and the amount of grant they have decided to pay. They must inform the applicant of approved eligible works and the amounts they have determined. Where a grant is refused reasons must be given.

An approved grant may be redetermined under s 34(5) if circumstances beyond the applicant's control lead to increases in costs. Section 35 requires an authority to pay approved grants either in whole after the completion of eligible works or by instalments as the works progress with the balance paid on completion. While the grant determining function is essentially a matter of public law only open to challenge by way of judicial review so that, for example, a refusal to approve a grant application would give rise to no cause of action for damages, where an application has been approved, and payment is withheld because of disputes over fulfilment of grant conditions, it appears an ordinary action may be brought to enforce payment of the grant[220]. However, conditions may only be imposed on approved grants if allowed for under the Housing Grants, Construction and Renovation Act 1996, or consented by the Secretary of State: see s 34(6) of the 1996 Act.

Payment of mandatory DFG may be delayed under s 36 but only up to a period of 12 months from the date specified in the notification of the decision on the application.

## Grant payment conditions

Under s 37 there is an implied condition in *all* grants that, as a general rule, eligible works are carried out within 12 months of the approval date. Authorities *may* also require that works are carried out according to their specification. Payment is in any case, however, conditional upon works being carried out to the authority's satisfaction, and their being provided with appropriate invoices and receipts for the work – ie proof of expenditure.

Section 38 imposes a condition that, in general, the works may only be carried out by a contractor whose estimate accompanied the application, while under s 39 grants may be paid in whole or part to the contractor, provided the work has been done to the applicant's satisfaction, and provided the applicant was told before approval that this method of payment might be adopted.

Section 40 of the 1996 Act applies a general principle that where an application is approved and the applicant ceases to be a person entitled to a grant before the 'certified date' ie the date certified by the authority as the date on which the execution of eligible works was completed according to their satisfaction (see s 44(3)(b)) no grant is to be paid, or no further instalment, as the case may be.

---

[220] *Dennis Rye Pension Fund Trustees v Sheffield City Council* [1997] 4 All ER 747, 30 HLR 645, CA.

Where a change of circumstance, however, affects a disabled occupant between the date of approval of a DFG application and the 'certified date', as, for example where the works are no longer appropriate for that person's needs, or where that person ceases to occupy the dwelling in question, s 41 enables the authority to take such action as they consider appropriate, including determining that no grant should be paid, taking into account all the circumstances of the case.

Authorities may under s 42 recalculate, withhold or demand repayment of grants in a number of circumstances including cases where they discover that the amount of a grant was decided on the basis of inaccurate or incomplete information so that it exceeds the applicant's entitlements, or where eligible works were begun before approval or were not completed within the due time, or were carried out by the incorrect contractor. As the provision is discretionary, before making a decision, authorities must consider all the circumstances of the case, though their discretion is wide and enables them to take into account delay in the completion of works[221]. Where after completion it appears that an applicant was not entitled to a grant s 45 provides no grant, or further instalment of a grant, as the case may be, is to be paid, and the authority may demand repayment.

## General grant conditions

Section 44 provides for a number of general grant conditions, in particular s 44(3)(a) provides that the 'grant condition period' shall be five years from the certified date which, has already been said, is the date the authority certify as that on which the execution of eligible works is completed to their satisfaction.

Section 51 empowers authorities, subject to the consent of the Secretary of State, to impose a condition requiring the applicant to take reasonable steps to pursue 'any relevant claim' and then to repay the grant out of the proceeds. Relevant claims include insurance claims and those for damages in respect of the property. Non-compliance with the condition entails a liability to repay the grant. Other conditions may be imposed with the consent of the Secretary of State under s 52, while under s 55 grant conditions cease to have effect on the voluntary repayment of a grant.

## Supplementary provision

Section 57 empowers authorities to make agreements with the owners of dwellings to enable an authority to carry out at the owner's expense, any grant aided or grant aidable works, and any additional works, and any additional works the authority consider necessary or desirable. In the case of qualifying home boats and qualifying park homes this power exists in respect of the owner of the moorings or place where the park home is stationed (as the case may be) or the person entitled to dispose of the boat or park home.

---

[221] *R v Newham London Borough Council, ex p Watts* (1998) 32 HLR 255 and *R v Newham London Borough Council, ex p Trendgrove Properties Ltd* (1999) 32 HLR 424.

## REMEDIES UNDER THE ENVIRONMENTAL PROTECTION ACT 1990

So far as housing is concerned the general object of this Act is the protection of public health, the measures being derived from the Public Health Act 1936 which in turn followed on from the 'great' Public Health Act 1875. The law is therefore here not so much designed to lay down housing standards as to protect the health of individuals. The existence of separate housing and public health 'codes' of legislation has undoubtedly caused confusion over the years, though the ability of, for example, a tenant to initiate criminal sanctions against a neglectful landlord under public health law has undoubtedly enabled individuals to bring about improvements in their housing conditions. One thing is clear: compliance by a landlord with standards under housing legislation will not automatically mean there is compliance with public health standards under the 1990 Act, see *Salford City Council v McNally*[222]. Likewise the fact that a tenant is seeking a parallel civil remedy in respect of a housing defect is no reason for refusing a remedy under the 1990 Act[223].

It is the duty, under s 79 of the 1990 Act, of district councils and London boroughs, and in Wales county and county borough councils, to inspect their areas from time to time, and also to investigate complaints from the inhabitants of their areas, in respect of 'statutory nuisances'. These include: premises; accumulations or deposits; animals; noise emitted from premises, or from vehicles, machinery or equipment in a street, though not from general traffic noise[224]; any other matter declared by statute to be a statutory nuisance, provided in each case the matter is prejudicial to health, ie actually injurious, or likely to cause injury, to health, or a nuisance, see s 79(7). Health seems to mean physical as opposed to mental health, see *Coventry City Council v Cartwright*[225]. This case arose out of an alleged nuisance caused by dumping of rubbish, the Divisional Court gave some consideration to whether mental health could be within the protection of the law but reached no concluded opinion on this point. It can be argued that a breakdown in mental health can be caused as a result of a person having to live in a sub-standard house. However, judicial opinion seems to disagree, and to hold that conditions that are 'prejudicial to health' are those which are likely to cause physical illness or disease or to result in an infestation by vermin.

If premises are to be shown to be a statutory nuisance their condition *as a whole* must be so serious that in consequence they are a real risk to health or are a nuisance; a mere lack of internal decorative repair is not enough: see *Springett v Harold*[226]. Nor is any matter which merely affects the comfort of the occupants, even if it amounts to an act of harrassment. However, it is unnecessary to prove that a dwelling is both prejudicial to health, and a nuisance. It may be enough for conditions to be 'prejudicial to health' if they are such as to cause a person who is

---

[222] [1976] AC 379, [1975] 2 All ER 860.
[223] *R v Highbury Corner Magistrates' Court, ex p Edwards* (1994) 26 HLR 682.
[224] *Haringey London Borough Council v Jowett* [1999] EGCS 64, and s 79(1)(ga) and (6A) of the 1990 Act.
[225] [1975] 2 All ER 99, [1975] 1 WLR 845.
[226] [1954] 1 All ER 568, [1954] 1 WLR 521.

already ill to become worse: see Kelly CB in *Malton Board of Health v Malton Manure Co*[227].

In *Bennett v Preston District Council*[228] it was held that defective wiring in a dwelling may be prejudicial to health. This may now be open to question following the decision in *R v Bristol City Council, ex p Everett*[229] that poor internal arrangements in a house leading to a risk of physical *injury* – in this case a steep staircase – are not capable of being statutory nuisances. In *Southwark London Borough Council v Ince and Williams*[230] it was held that noise penetrating a dwelling made it prejudicial to health. This case may be limited to its own particular facts as it concerned both road and rail noise, and was decided before amendments made to the 1990 Act excluding street traffic noise from the definition of statutory nuisances, see n 224.

Furthermore condensation may amount to a statutory nuisance, even where the structure is unaffected, see *Dover District Council v Farrar*[231] and *Greater London Council v Tower Hamlets London Borough Council*[232], especially where it gives rise to extensive growths of mould and dampness, and results from a condition arising from the failure of the responsible person (in this case the landlord) to take remedial or preventative action, such as the installation of ventilation, insulation and heating systems[233]. The cases appear to support the propositions that a landlord may be liable for a statutory nuisance arising from condensation caused by an unsuitable or defective heating system, lack of a reasonable system of heating and ventilation, design and construction defects and disrepair. Once, however, a proper system of heating, insulation and ventilation is provided it is for the tenant to use that system sensibly so as to avoid condensation. It remains a moot point as to whether questions of the expense of running a heating system can be considered in determining whether the system is reasonable and proper. In Scotland it appears that where an adequate heating system is provided the failure of the occupier to use it properly can negate liability on the part of the landlord of premises[234]. Certainly a refusal by a tenant to allow a landlord to install a heating system will act as a defence in statutory nuisance proceedings[235].

Premises may also come within the statutory definition if they are 'a nuisance'. Does this mean that any common law nuisance is also ipso facto a statutory nuisance? The answer is partly 'yes'. For a person to prove an allegation based on the 'or a nuisance' limb of the definition he/she must show that the act or default complained of is either a public or private nuisance, ie something causing deleterious affectation to a class of Her Majesty's subjects, or a substantial interference with land (or the use and enjoyment thereof) arising outside that land and then

---

[227] (1879) 4 Ex D 302 at 305.
[228] (1983) Environmental Health (April).
[229] [1998] 3 All ER 603, [1999] 1 WLR 92; affd [1999] 2 All ER 193, [1999] 1 WLR 1170, CA.
[230] (1989) 21 HLR 504. This case is unlikely to be followed in the light of comments in the House of Lords in *Southwark London Borough Council v Mills* [1999] 4 All ER 449, [1999] 3 WLR 939, HL, that a lack of sound insulation gives a tenant no civil claim for breach of covenant for quiet enjoyment.
[231] (1980) 2 HLR 32.
[232] (1983) 15 HLR 54.
[233] See further *Birmingham District Council v Kelly* (1985) 17 HLR 572.
[234] *Anderson v Dundee City Council* [1999] 11 ELM 24 and *Robb v Dundee City Council* [1999] 11 ELM 84.
[235] *Carr v Hackney London Borough Council* (1995) 28 HLR 749.

proceeding to affect it. So much is clear from *National Coal Board v Neath Borough Council*[236]. However, there is a judicial tradition stretching back to *Malton Board of Health v Malton Manure Co*[237], *Great Western Rly Co v Bishop*[238], and *Bishop Auckland Local Board v Bishop Auckland Iron and Steel Co*[239], that situations contemplated as falling within the 'or a nuisance' limb of the definition must have some relation to health.

Furthermore whether something is either prejudiced to health, or a nuisance has to be objectively determined, and not according to the subjective news of the occupant of premises[240]. The legislation is, however, designed to protect public health, hence the mere arrangement of rooms in a home is unlikely to make it 'prejudicial to health' simply because a person has to traverse a kitchen in order to wash hands after using a lavatory. The mere existence of a risk of infection is not enough to fall within the legislation[241].

Where it is alleged that premises are 'prejudicial to health' it will not matter that only the occupier is affected by the acts, defaults or state of affairs complained of. Where on the other hand it is alleged that the premises are 'a nuisance' the act or default, etc, must affect persons other than the occupier of the premises. Furthermore in this latter situation the person must, it appears, be able to prove that the nuisance is one that in some way affects, or has relevance, to health. It must also be remembered that *R v Newham Justices, ex p Hunt* and *R v Oxted Justices, ex p Franklin*[242] established that proceedings brought in respect of a statutory nuisance are criminal in nature and thus the burden of proof on any informant will be correspondingly high. In *Patel v Mehtab*[243] the court pointed out that the question whether premises are prejudicial to health will turn upon expert evidence, and that the magistrates must pay due heed to the expert testimonies given by one or both sides, and not advance their own lay assessments of the facts over those of expert witnesses. Similarly magistrates are not entitled to ignore expert evidence from Environmental Health Officers that premises are 'prejudicial to health' and to demand medical proof[244].

## The procedure for taking action in respect of a statutory nuisance

Local authorities and private citizens may take action in respect of statutory nuisances: it is convenient to consider authorities first.

Section 80 of the 1990 Act provides that where an authority is satisfied a statutory nuisance exists, or is likely to occur or recur, they *must* (see further, however, below) serve an abatement notice which will require the nuisance's abatement or

---

[236] [1976] 2 All ER 478, [1976] 1 WLR 543.
[237] (1879) 4 Ex D 302.
[238] (1872) LR 7 QB 550.
[239] (1882) 10 QBD 138.
[240] *Cunningham v Birmingham City Council* (1997) 30 HLR 158.
[241] *Birmingham City Council v Oakley* [2001] 1 AC 617, [2001] 33 HLR 30.
[242] [1976] 1 All ER 839, [1976] 1 WLR 420; see also *Botross v Hammersmith and Fulham London Borough Council* (1994) 27 HLR 179 and *R v Inner London Crown Court, ex p Bentham* [1989] 1 WLR 408.
[243] (1980) 5 HLR 78 and see also *Westminster City Council v McDonald* [2003] EWHC 2698 (Admin).
[244] *R v Knowsley Metropolitan Borough Council, ex p O'Toole* [1999] 22 LS Gaz R 36.

prohibit or restrict its occurrence or recurrence, and may require the execution of works or taking of steps for such purposes, specifying the time within which compliance is required[245]. Where works are required they must be specified for notices must be clear and certain both as to the works and the time within which they are to be done, for the recipient must be able to know what is required[246]. It is not necessary for the notice to specify whether the nuisance is 'prejudicial to health' or 'a nuisance'[247]. Where a nuisance affecting a dwelling consists of excessive noise there is no need to specify particular works, nor even an acceptable level of noise, but the requirement to prevent recurrences of nuisances must be expressly or clearly impliedly stated[248]. This notice is to be served on the person responsible for the nuisance, save in cases of nuisances arising from structural defects, or where the person responsible cannot be found, in which case the owner is to be served. This is apparently so in relation to structural defects even where the tenant is responsible[249]. The 'owner' is the person who receives the rack rent, ie the economic rent, of the property, or who would receive it if it was let, whether in his/her own right, or as an agent[250]. Failure to comply with a notice without reasonable excuse is an offence. However, it should be noted that authorities are not statutorily bound to prosecute offences (see further below) even though they may have taken default action themselves under s 81(3), which enables them, under s 81(4) to recover their expenses. Section 81(5) further empowers authorities to commence High Court proceedings where they are of the opinion that statutory nuisance proceedings before the justices would provide an inadequate remedy. Authorities undertaking works under s 81(3) may recover their reasonable expenses under s 81(4), and these may be recovered as a charge on the premises under s 81A, even though payment may be made by instalments under s 81B.

A person served with an abatement notice may, under s 80(3) of the 1990 Act, appeal to the justices within a period of 21 days beginning with the date of service of the notice. Schedule 3 to the Act enables regulations to be made concerning such appeals. The Statutory Nuisance (Appeals) Regulations SI 1995/2644, provide in reg 2 as grounds of appeal that: the abatement notice was not justified; there has been an informality, defect or error in, or in connection with the notice; the authority has unreasonably refused compliance with alternative requirements, or the notice's requirements are otherwise unreasonable in character or extent or unnecessary; a reasonable amount of time has not been specified for compliance; that specific statutory defences applicable under s 80(7) or (9), but these are not relevant to premises cases; the notice should have been served on some other person (eg the owner where a nuisance arises from a defect of a structural character) or it might lawfully have been served on someone else, or on someone else in addition to the appellant. On hearing proceedings on appeal the magistrates have a wide

---

[245] See also *Bristol Corpn v Sinnott* [1918] 1 Ch 62.
[246] *R v Wheatley, ex p Cowburn* (1885) 16 QBD 34; *R v Fenny Stafford Justices, ex p Watney Mann (Midlands) Ltd* [1976] 2 All ER 888, [1976] 1 WLR 1101; *Kirklees Metropolitan Borough Council v Field* (1997) 30 HLR 869; and *Network Housing Association v Westminster City Council* (1994) 27 HLR 189.
[247] *Lowe v South Somerset District Council* (1997) 96 LGR 487.
[248] *Budd v Colchester Borough Council* [1999] LGR 601 and *Stanley v Ealing London Borough Council* (1999) 32 HLR 745.
[249] *Warner v Lambeth London Borough Council* (1984) 15 HLR 42.
[250] *Pollway Nominees Ltd v Havering London Borough Council* (1989) 21 HLR 462 and *Camden London Borough Council v Gunby* [1999] 4 All ER 602.

discretion to dismiss the appeal, quash the abatement notice or vary it. However, they must consider whether the notice was justified as at the date of service, not the date of the hearing[251]. Making an appeal leads to the abatement notice being suspended, but an authority may prevent this by making a non-suspension statement in the notice.

Certain general requirements from decisions on the previous law relating to statutory nuisances would also seem to apply under the 1990 Act. Thus the legislation lays down a procedure which an authority has to follow in the abatement of statutory nuisances, and it would seem from *Cocker v Cardwell*[252] that this procedure is mandatory once an authority decide to act. Where an authority are satisfied of the existence of a statutory nuisance the Act says they 'shall serve' an abatement notice on the person responsible requiring the abatement of the nuisance. However, it was said in *Nottingham Friendship Housing Association v Newton*[253], the first case where an authority was successfully prosecuted in respect of unfit property also constituting a statutory nuisance, by Lord Widgery CJ that 'shall' is not mandatory. Where an authority has a choice of remedies between the 1985 and 1990 Acts the courts may not order them to use the latter in preference to the former. The Encyclopaedia of Housing Law and Practice, however, argues the 'requirement to serve an abatement notice is mandatory ... the local authority have no discretion'. The point is not therefore entirely clear or decided.

It is a defence to a prosecution under s 79 to show that there was a 'reasonable excuse', see s 79(4). If evidence of such an excuse is put forward by the defence, it is for the prosecution to disprove it according to the criminal burden of proof[254].

### Taking action in respect of statutory nuisances by private citizens

The majority of statutory nuisances are dealt with by authorities but an individual wishing to proceed may rely on s 82 of the 1990 Act. This provides that the magistrates may act on a complaint made by a 'person aggrieved', and where they are convinced the alleged nuisance exists, or although abated is likely to recur, they must make an order to require the defendant to abate the nuisance, and execute any necessary works, and/or may prohibit a recurrence of the nuisance. Where a recurrence is forbidden there is no need to state a specific compliance date[255]. The magistrates may also fine the defendant. In addition the magistrates have powers to direct the local authority to take abatement measures in respect of a nuisance where neither the person responsible or the owner/occupier of the premises can be found, and to prohibit the use of premises for human habitation where a nuisance renders them unfit for that purpose, see s 82(1) and (3). As with local authority proceedings it is the person responsible for the nuisance who is generally to be proceeded against, though where the nuisance is of a structural character, or where the 'person responsible' cannot be found, it is the owner of the premises who will be liable. Before complaining to the magistrates, however, the person aggrieved must give the

---

[251] *Surrey Free Inns v Gosport Borough Council* (1998) 96 LGR 369.
[252] (1869) LR 5 QB 15.
[253] [1974] 2 All ER 760, [1974] 1 WLR 923.
[254] *Polychronakis v Richards and Jerrom Ltd* [1998] Env LR 347.
[255] *R v Tunbridge Wells Justices, ex p Tunbridge Wells Borough Council* (1995) 160 JP 574.

potential defendant written notice of intention to commence proceedings, specifying the matter complained of. In the case of alleged noise nuisances three days' notice must be given, in all other cases not less than 21 days' notice is required, see s 82(6) and (7).

A notice served under s 82(6) is not, however, the equivalent of an abatement notice, and therefore does not have to specify works needed, nor to identify the capacity in which the defendant is to be proceeded against ie as 'owner' or 'person responsible'. There is no prescribed form for a s 82(6) notice, all that is needed is a specification of the matters complained of, so that the recipient has a chance to remedy the situation. While it is desirable that the notice should give as much information as is reasonably possible, the courts accept that s 82 exists to give remedy to citizens and are unwilling to see it bogged down in unnecessary technicalities[256]. Similarly attempts by landlords to require formalities by stipulating that notices may only be served at their principal offices have been judicially disapproved[257].

## Who is a 'person aggrieved'?

It was held in *R v Epping (Waltham Abbey) Justices, ex p Burlinson*[258] that a private citizen can proceed against a defaulting local authority under this provision, and in *Salford City Council v McNally* (above) it was further held that the fact that the nuisance arose as a result of an authority's exercise of Housing Act powers was no defence to an action taken by one of their tenants deleteriously affected in consequence. In order to use the provision an individual must be a 'person aggrieved'. In the present context this includes anyone whose health has actually been injured by the nuisance, or any occupant of the premises or indeed anyone with a legal interest in a house which is permanently affected by the nuisance. In *Gould v Times Square Estates Ltd*[259], even a squatter in an empty former shop and dwelling accommodation was held able to use this procedure, but the applicability of this provision to trespassers was expressly left undecided in *Coventry City Council v Cartwright* (above). Where, however, a person is a tenant in a block of flats and only some of the flats are in sub-standard order, it is not possible for that person to be 'aggrieved' in relation to the whole block[260].

## The consequences of action taken

Once the court is satisfied under s 82(2) that a statutory nuisance exists, or though abated is likely to recur on the same premises, they *must* make an order as outlined above[261]. Similarly, evidence of the existence of a statutory nuisance will normally require the court to issue the necessary summons against the defendant[262].

---

[256] *East Staffordshire Borough Council v Fairless* (1998) 31 HLR 677, and *Pearshouse v Birmingham City Council* (1998) 31 HLR 756.
[257] *Hall v Kingston-Upon-Hull City Council* [1999] 2 All ER 609; overruling *Leeds v Islington London Borough Council* (1998) 31 HLR 545.
[258] [1948] 1 KB 79, [1947] 2 All ER 537.
[259] [1975] LAG Bulletin 147, Camberwell Magistrates Court.
[260] *Birmingham District Council v McMahon* (1987) 19 HLR 452.
[261] *Coventry City Council v Doyle* [1981] 2 All ER 184, [1981] 1 WLR 1325.
[262] *R v Highbury Corner Magistrates' Court, ex p Edwards* (1994) 26 HLR 682.

In this context the *Newton* case states clearly that the justices must issue a nuisance order if the existence or future recurrence of the nuisance is proved. But they have a very considerable discretion as to the terms of the order. When deciding the terms of the order justices should consider all the circumstances of the case including the possible gravity of the danger to the health of the occupants and the imminence of demolition. They may properly require work to be done in phases, allowing for absolutely necessary jobs to be done first, while other tasks can be left till later, perhaps to be rendered unnecessary by demolition, thus saving expense.

A decision illustrates the ambit of the justices' discretion. In *Lambeth London Borough Council v Stubbs*[263], an authority owned an old house the tenants of which were Mr and Mrs Stubbs. The condition of the house constituted a statutory nuisance, which was admitted by the council before the justices in proceedings commenced by the tenants. The justices refused to adjourn the hearing so that the authority could obtain vacant possession, and instead made a nuisance order requiring the remedying of the most serious defects within 21 days of the vacation of the premises and of the others in 42 days. Shortly thereafter Mr and Mrs Stubbs were rehoused and the house was simply left vacant until it was demolished. The question for the court was whether the action of the council in securing vacant possession was sufficient abatement to comply with the nuisance order. It was held that it was not. Where a house is prejudicial to health simply to move the present occupiers out does not cure the problem, for if other occupiers should move in at a future date their health will then be imperilled. Where justices make a nuisance order requiring the doing of remedial work, that work must be done; moving the sitting tenant is not enough. See also *Coventry City Council v Doyle* (above), where it was, however, pointed out that different considerations might apply in a case where the premises have been effectively rendered incapable of occupation. Of course where the authority intend to demolish the property within a very short time the court should take that into account when drawing up the order. In such circumstances the authority should ask the justices to exercise their discretion to order that the house shall not be used for human habitation. Such an order will remove the need for great expenditure. Any order made, however, must be clear and certain.

Where on the hearing of proceedings in respect of an alleged nuisance it is shown that the nuisance did exist when the initial complaint was made, then, irrespective of whether it still exists or is likely to recur at the date of the hearing, the court is to order the defendant to compensate the complainant for expenses incurred in bringing the proceedings: see s 82(12). The court may also direct the relevant local authority to perform any requirements of an order to abate a nuisance where the defendant is in default, see s 82(11). Section 82(12) is mandatory and requires the justices to award costs once they are satisfied that the nuisance existed at the time the complaint was made. They may not refuse to award costs where they believe proceedings should not have been brought, for their only discretion is in relation to deciding the sum believed 'reasonably sufficient' to compensate the complainant for any expenses properly incurred in taking action[264]. Properly incurred costs may be

[263] (1980) 78 LGR 650.
[264] *Hollis v Dudley Borough Council* [1998] 1 All ER 759, [1999] 1 WLR 642.

awarded even where a claim for a compensation order (see further below) fails[265], and indeed magistrates have a very wide discretion on how to assess costs, there being no formal assessment procedures[266]. It has, however, been argued that, as a matter of course, a complainant should give advance notice of cost claims, so that the respondent may indicate whether the claim is accepted or challenged. Furthermore the magistrates should take proper steps to investigate how a claim for a substantial amount has been arrived at, and on what basis it is challenged[267].

Where a tenant commences and then withdraws proceedings the award of costs against him/her is limited by ss 16 to 19 of the Prosecution of Offences Act 1985, which limits costs in cases where there has been no unnecessary or improper conduct by the tenant[268].

## Compensation orders

As proceedings under s 82 are criminal in nature, compensation may be awarded to the complainant under s 35 of the Powers of Criminal Courts Act 1973[269]. This power exists to ensure compensation is paid in cases where a civil remedy might not otherwise be available. It is inappropriate to use it to award substantial sums for what may generally be classified as personal injuries. Furthermore the absence of a civil remedy does not mean that a compensation order should be made[270], and the fact that a complainant might not succeed in a civil claim should be taken into account by the magistrates. Furthermore a compensation order can only be made in respect of the period of the offence as alleged in the information. Thus compensation may be awarded only for that injury, loss or damage as is proved to have been caused by the continuation of the nuisance after the expiry of the period stated in the notice under s 82(6) until the date of the hearing. Section 35 does not give to magistrates' courts a power to take account of the whole period for which a nuisance is alleged to exist. For while such courts may be able to award sums up to £5,000, they should be wary of involving themselves in what are effectively civil claims, though a compensation order if sufficiently large to be punitive may be imposed instead of as well as in addition to a fine[271]. Any fine imposed should, however, reflect a guilty plea (if one has been entered) and any work done by the defendant to abate the statutory nuisance[272].

## The relationship between the Housing and Environmental Protection Acts

It cannot be sufficiently stressed that the requirements of the two 'codes' are separate and equal. Remedial action taken under one will not necessarily satisfy the

---

[265] *Davenport v Walsall Metropolitan Borough Council* (1995) 28 HLR 754.
[266] *R v Southend Stipendiary Magistrate, ex p Rochford District Council* [1994] Env LR D15.
[267] *Taylor v Walsall and District Property and Investment Co* (1998) 30 HLR 1062.
[268] *R v Enfield Justices, ex p Whittle* (1993) Legal Action (June) p 15.
[269] *Herbert v Lambeth London Borough Council* (1991) 24 HLR 299 and *R v Inner London Crown Court, ex p Bentham* [1989] 1 WLR 408.
[270] *Davenport v Walsall Metropolitan Borough Council (above)*.
[271] *R v Liverpool Crown Court, ex p Cooke* [1996] 4 All ER 589, [1997] 1 WLR 700, and *R v Knightsbridge Crown Court, ex p Hobin Abdillahi* (1998) Legal Action (May) p 24.
[272] *R (on the application of Islington London Borough Council) v Inner London Crown Court* [2003] All ER (D) 197 (Oct).

requirements of the other. Of course action taken to eliminate unfitness in a house will nearly always ensure that it will not be prejudicial to health because in general the fitness standards are higher than those under the 1990 Act. This can be illustrated by a simple example: if a house is unfit through dampness caused by the lack of a damp-proof course then the fitness standard would require the insertion of such a course to make the house fit and free from damp; if the same house is prejudicial to health because of damp, then the 1990 Act will only require it to be made reasonably free from damp on a periodic basis, which may be achieved by lining the walls with damp-proof paper.

There are times when the two codes do appear to be in conflict: thus in the *Newton* case the court said local authorities have a discretion as to how best to deal with sub-standard housing; in *R v Kerrier District Council, ex p Guppy's (Bridport) Ltd*[273] the unfitness provisions were said to be mandatory, while in the *Salford* case action taken under the Housing Act was said to be no defence to subsequent prosecution under the public health legislation. In fact there is no real conflict between the codes and the cases can be reconciled. The question always to bear in mind in these situations is: who is seeking to do what to whom by which procedures? This question can receive different answers in different circumstances as the following instances will show.

### The individual sub-standard house in private or housing association ownership

This situation can be illustrated by the facts of the *Kerrier* case. The landlords owned two unfit dwelling-houses, both tenanted. The owners were prepared to make one good house of the two but could not do so without obtaining vacant possession, and had no accommodation for the displaced tenants. The local authority said it had no accommodation either and decided to commence proceedings against the landlords under the Public Health Act 1936 (predecessor of the 1990 Act) to require remedial action on the roofs of the houses. The landlords countered by alleging the houses were statutorily unfit and that the authority were in breach of mandatory duties under the unfitness provisions if they failed to proceed under them. The court accepted the landlords' contention. Thus where a *local authority* commence proceedings under the 1990 Act in respect of any house which is a statutory nuisance, the *owner* of the house may allege that they are in dereliction of duties under the fitness standard and may apply for mandamus to compel the performance of relevant duties. Even here it must be remembered that mandamus is a discretionary remedy and so landlords are not guaranteed success if they adopt the counter argument developed in the *Kerrier* case. Where the proceedings are between the *tenant* and the *landlord* the authority's duties have no relevance save insofar as the landlord, having begun separate proceedings against an authority to compel performances of their duties, might argue that the justices should consider the possible outcome of those proceedings when deciding the content of any order issued under s 82 of the 1990 Act.

### The sub-standard house in local authority ownership

The unfitness provisions do not apply to a local authority's own houses *within its own area*, save in the cases where another person also has a relevant interest in the

---

[273] (1975) 30 P & CR 194.

property, for an authority cannot serve a housing order on themselves, see *R v Cardiff City Council, ex p Cross*[274]. However, in such circumstances provided the existence of a statutory nuisance can be proved, the 1990 Act can be used and any prior action taken under the 1985 Act will be no defence to the local authority.

This was the situation in the *Salford* case. In 1967 Salford Corporation declared certain areas to be clearance areas, and at the same time made compulsory purchase orders on the houses within the areas. However, the Corporation realising it could not rehouse all the residents quickly, deferred demolition of the houses for a minimum period of seven years. By 1974 Mrs McNally's house suffered from an accumulation of refuse, dampness, defective sanitary fittings, unsealed drains, rats, defective windows and/or doors, a leaking roof, defective drainage, and defective plaster work. She commenced proceedings in respect of the statutory nuisance comprised by her house and succeeded. The House of Lords held that the resolution to defer demolition was no defence to statutory nuisance proceedings. It must be remembered, however, that where an old sub-standard house is made the subject of a nuisance order the justice's discretion should be so used as to prevent expenditure of unnecessary sums. The best that can be hoped for is a 'make and mend' operation designed to make the house reasonably bearable as a dwelling, though following *Saddleworth UDC v Aggregate and Sand Ltd*[275], a lack of finance does not seem to be a reasonable excuse for not complying with a nuisance order. Landlords cannot plead poverty in the hope of entirely escaping from the requirements of nuisance orders!

### The sub-standard modern council-built house

Evidence is not lacking that bad construction, poor design, unproved building techniques and misguided planning policies have led to the erection of many council houses and flats whose inhabitants frequently have to endure extremely unpleasant living conditions. In some modern council properties there are severe problems of damp and condensation which can lead to ruined furniture and clothes and illness in the occupants.

The decision in *R v Cardiff City Council, ex p Cross* (above) of course applies to council built as well as council acquired housing. But statutory nuisance proceedings can bring some relief to tenants. In *Birmingham District Council v Kelly*[276] the proceedings concerned council built dwellings comprising low rise flats. The dwellings had defective windows, and were also extensively affected by mould which was found to be prejudicial to health. The mould was found to be the result of the act, default or sufferance of the local authority because of, inter alia, the poor thermal quality of the flats, the absence of heating provision in the hallways, a gap under the front door of one flat, the poor quality of ventilation in bathrooms and kitchens. In some, but not all cases, mould could be attributable, in part to disrepair, though the court found that there was no breach of any obligation laid on the authority as a landlord qua landlord. But that was not enough to prevent inquiry into whether there was liability for the existence of a statutory nuisance. The court

---

[274] (1982) 6 HLR 1.
[275] (1970) 69 LGR 103.
[276] (1985) 17 HLR 572.

pointed out that three questions arise: is there a statutory nuisance, is it due to the act, default or sufferance of the local authority, and what steps are necessary to abate it? The court concluded that the answer to the first two questions was 'yes': the mould was a consequence of condensation attributable to design defects in the flats. But the court pointed out that magistrates should use discretion as to the terms of a nuisance order, and that statutory nuisance proceedings should not be used as a means of obtaining for tenants benefits which they were aware did not exist when they took their tenancies, and which would over generously favour them in relation to other tenants of the authority. An authority may be required to do works of improvement, but the need for such works must be justified by the evidence and the circumstances. Magistrates should behave reasonably in imposing orders on local authorities, bearing in mind the heavy duties already laid upon them. Even so it appears that use of the statutory nuisance provisions, while enabling individuals to secure improvements of their conditions, can also have the effect of disrupting planned maintenance and improvement programmes devised by authorities as they are forced to switch resources from the programme into reactive responses to individual problem premises whose existence and needs have been made inescapable following actual or threatened statutory nuisance proceedings.

### Statutory nuisances – an uncertain future?

Statutory nuisance proceedings are particularly unpopular with some local authority landlords who allege their misuse by lawyers and community workers, pointing out that where an individual tenant secures an individual remedy under the 1990 Act, this does not necessarily lead to an upgrading of the circumstances of neighbours who may be suffering equally bad conditions, while resources to comply with a court order may have to be diverted from elsewhere disrupting planned maintenance and improvement programmes. Following DoE sponsored research in 1996 it was recommended that s 82 of the 1990 Act should be amended to:

- define clearly the initial offence;
- allow for a 'reasonable response' to be made to the person aggrieved's notice, *either* that the landlord is doing or what is needed to abate the nuisance, *or* to enable service of a counter notice which specifies works to be done and gives a timetable for doing them;
- allow for action other than works to be ordered as a means of abatement;
- allow enhanced discretion to the courts over questions of costs.

Action to translate these proposals into law is still to be taken.

It is permitted for solicitors to pursue proceedings under s 82 on a conditional fee basis, see s 27(1) of the Access to Justice Act 1999.

## REHOUSING DISPLACED RESIDENTS

Section 39 of the Land Compensation Act 1973, as amended, provides:

(1) Where a person is displaced from residential accommodation on any land in consequence of

(a)   the acquisition of the land by an authority possessing compulsory purchase powers;

(b) the making ... or acceptance of a housing order ... or undertaking in respect of a house or building on the land;

(c) where the land has been previously acquired by an authority possessing compulsory purchase powers or appropriated by a local authority and is for the time being held by the authority for the purposes for which it was acquired or appropriated, the carrying out of any improvement to a house or building on the land or of redevelopment on the land; ...

and suitable alternative accommodation is not otherwise available to that person, then, subject to the provisions of this section, it shall be the duty of the relevant authority to secure that he will be provided with such other accommodation.

Within the context of action on unfit properties, this means that authorities have an obligation to rehouse persons displaced as a result of the making of demolition, closing or clearance orders or the accepting of undertakings under s 264 of the Housing Act 1985. Some authorities adopt a wider obligation as a matter of administrative practice, and the strictly limited nature of the s 39 obligation should be noted. It does not apply to squatters, nor to persons permitted to reside in a house pending its demolition or improvement. The duty only applies, in general terms, to persons resident in the dwelling on the date when the order, or undertaking, etc, was made or accepted or when notice of its making was published, as the case may be. Moreover, in the case of displacements arising out of the doing of works of improvement, the obligation is only owed to persons who are *permanently* displaced.

The greatest restriction on the obligation is that it confers no right on persons displaced to have priority over other persons on the housing waiting list. In *R v Bristol Corpn, ex p Hendy*[277] the applicant lived in a basement flat where he enjoyed Rent Act security of tenure but which was also statutorily unfit. Mr Hendy had a history of rent arrears with another local authority and Bristol Corporation offered him only temporary accommodation, pending an offer of suitable residential accommodation, on the terms usually offered to prospective municipal tenants. He applied for an order of mandamus to compel the authority to fulfil their rehousing duty, contending this was to provide him with permanent accommodation on terms that gave him a security of tenure equivalent to that which he had enjoyed under his former tenancy. The Court of Appeal refused the order. They concluded that the duty is only to act reasonably and to do the best practicable job in providing a displaced person with other accommodation.

NB Where a dwelling is closed for human habitation by order of the justices under s 82(3) of the Environmental Protection Act 1990, there is no obligation to rehouse on the local authority under s 39 of the 1973 Act.

## FURTHER READING

Burridge, R, Ormandy, D, Battersby, S, *Monitoring the New Housing Fitness Standard* (1993) DoE/HMSO.

---

[277] [1974] 1 All ER 1047, [1974] 1 WLR 498; see also *R v East Hertfordshire District Council, ex p Smith* (1990) 23 HLR 26.

Crook, ADH, 'Housing conditions in the private rented sector within a market framework', in Lowe, S and Hughes, D, *The Private Rented Sector in a New Century* (2002) Policy Press.

DoE *English House Condition Survey 2001* (2003) HMSO.

DoE *The Use of Section 82 of the Environmental Protection Act 1990 against Local Authorities and Housing Associations* (1996) HMSO.

Ellison, M, 'Room for improvement the impact of the local authority grant system', in Lowe, S and Hughes, D *The Private Rented Sector in a New Century* (2002) Policy Press.

Hadden, TB, *Compulsory Repair and Improvement* (1978) Centre for Socio Legal Studies, Wolfson College, Oxford University.

Hadden, TB, 'Public Health and Housing Legislation' (1976) 27 NILQ 245.

Hawke, JN and Taylor, GA, 'The Compulsory Repair of Individual Physically Substandard Housing: The Law in Practice' [1984] JSWL 129.

Hughes, D, 'Public Health Legislation and the Improvement of Housing Conditions' (1976) 27 NILQ 1.

Hughes, D, 'What is a Nuisance? The Public Health Act Revisited' (1976) 27 NILQ 131.

Hughes, D, 'Housing and Public Health – A Continuing Saga' (1977) 28 NILQ 233.

Hughes, D, 'Housing Repairs: A Suitable Case for Reform' [1984] JSWL 137.

Luba, J, *Repairs: Tenants' Rights* (3rd ed, 1999) Legal Action Group.

Reynolds, JI, 'Statutory Covenants of Fitness and Repair' (1974) 37 MLR 377.

Watkinson, D, 'Legal Remedies for Condensation Damp in the Home' Legal Action November 1985, p 153 and April 1986, p 49.

# CHAPTER 13

# Multi-occupancy and Selective Licensing of Rented Housing

## INTRODUCTION

The Government's decision to reform the law of multi-occupation via the provisions of the Housing Bill 2003 will result in the total replacement of the former provisions of the Housing Act 1985, which in their turn derived from a number of previous Acts of Parliament, and which had been subsequently greatly amended. At the time of writing, spring 2004, the Housing Bill was not yet enacted. This work is based on the Bill as it stood at the end of May 2004, having returned from the Lords to the Commons. Hence it has been thought necessary to retain an outline textual treatment of the 1985 provisions, which will be followed by further text stating the general principles of the new law which themselves may yet undergo detailed amendment following the publication of this work. Until the 'new' law is finalised and is commenced, readers requiring a fuller statement of the 'old' law are referred to Hughes and Lowe, *Public Sector Housing Law*, 3rd ed., Chapter 8.

## THE SUPERVISION OF MULTI-OCCUPATION UNDER PREVIOUS HOUSING ACTS

Section 345 of the Housing Act 1985, and Pt XI was the principal legislation, as amended in 1989.

### The definition of multi-occupation: House in Multiple Occupation (HMO)

Section 345 of the Housing Act 1985, as amended, provided that multi-occupancy arose when a house 'is occupied by persons who do not form a single household'. 'House' was not defined by the legislation, though it included any part of a building which would not, apart from the requirements of the statutory provision, be regarded as a house, and which was *originally constructed* or *subsequently adapted* for occupation by a single household. Similarly a unit of accommodation which was a flat could be in multiple occupation.

A great deal of artful device was employed by devious landlords trying to ensure their premises were not 'houses', so as to escape regulation. Property was described as 'hostels' or 'hotels', and was deconstructed and reconstructed. The judges responded by giving an extended meaning to the word 'house'. Whether or not any given property is a 'house' was a question of mixed fact and law – 'fact' in that the first question was to determine all relevant facts about a building, and 'law' in that the application of the word 'house' was a matter for judicial interpretation of relevant statutory provisions. Essentially a house was a building used for ordinary dwelling purposes, see *Reed v Hastings Corpn[1]* or one constructed or adapted for use as a dwelling. A shop with living accommodation attached could be a house, as might premises consisting of a workshop with dwelling rooms over it. A building used partly for residential and non-residential purposes might be a house; even an unfinished house might be a house. Hostels and lodging houses might be houses, and properties subdivided into flats might remain houses, see *Pollway Nominees v Croydon London Borough Council[2]*. A large holiday home might be a house, and only a totally drastic process of rebuilding would take a property built as a house outside that classification, see *R v Kerrier District Council, ex p Guppys (Bridport) Ltd[3]*. The basic principle was that 'house' covered any place fitted and used and adapted for human habitation[4], see *Living Waters Christian Centres Ltd v Conwy Borough Council and Fetherstonhaugh[5]*, where two old houses used for religious retreats were held to be HMOs: they provided sleeping accommodation and communal dining facilities.

On the question of whether premises are an HMO or a house in which individuals merely board, see *R v Mabbott[6]*. There, the Court of Appeal held the distinction to be a matter of fact and degree; where persons were transient occupiers, that was a factor to take into account. However, the Court also considered it would be wrong to conclude that in *all* cases premises that are boarding houses could not also be HMOs. The important point is that the 'label' placed on a property by its owner was not conclusive of its status; see *Thrasyvoulou v Hackney London Borough[7]*.

'Household' was also undefined. In *Wolkind v Ali[8]*. Mr Ali occupied certain premises which he used as a lodging house. Subsequently Mr Ali was joined by his large family from abroad. Thereafter the premises were occupied solely by the family. The Divisional Court held multi-occupancy powers did not apply to this house as it was being used by a single household.

In *Okereke v Brent London Borough Council[9]*. it was held that once a property was divided between separate households, it made no difference whether multiple occupation arose from physical division of the building or not. Where there was a clear division of control over a house between two or more households, the

---

[1]　(1964) 62 LGR 588.
[2]　[1987] AC 79, [1986] 2 All ER 849.
[3]　(1985) 17 HLR 426.
[4]　*R v Southwark London Borough, ex p Lewis Levy Ltd* (1983) 8 HLR 1 and *R v Hackney London Borough, ex p Evenbray Ltd* (1987) 19 HLR 557.
[5]　(1998) 77 P & CR 54, CA.
[6]　[1988] RVR 131.
[7]　(1986) 18 HLR 370.
[8]　[1975] 1 All ER 193, [1975] 1 WLR 170.
[9]　[1967] 1 QB 42, [1966] 1 All ER 150.

multi-occupancy powers applied. Likewise, where a person lived in or occupied a house and shared control with others living there, as a commercial enterprise, a multiple occupation arose.

But what about the situation where persons lived together freely and communally in a house? In *Simmons v Pizzey*[10] Mrs Pizzey occupied a property in a London suburb as a refuge for 'battered women'. The local authority fixed a maximum number of persons who might lawfully occupy the house. Mrs Pizzey was subsequently charged with a failure to comply with this. Her defence was that the house was not multi-occupied, as all residents lived there communally as one household. The House of Lords rejected this and laid down tests to be applied in deciding whether a group of persons do/do not form a single household.

1. The number of persons occupying the property, and the place of its location had to be considered: 30 or more persons occupying a suburban house could hardly be regarded as forming a single household.
2. The length of time for which each person occupied the property had to be considered. A fluctuating and constantly altering population is a clear indication that the property was multi-occupied.
3. The intention of the owner of the property had to be taken into account.

This approach was also applied in *Silbers v Southwark London Borough Council*[11] where it was held that a large fluctuating group of persons could not be regarded as forming a single household. It seemed from dicta in *Milford Properties v London Borough of Hammersmith*[12] that a multi-occupancy could arise even where some occupiers were in the premises unlawfully, for example as unlawful sub-tenants. In *Hackney London Borough v Ezedinma*[13] the court stressed that what constitutes a household is a question of fact and degree. Students each of whom had a separate tenancy of a room in a house might nevertheless together form a 'household'. In *Barnes v Sheffield City Council*[14] it was indicated the sort of issues to be considered included:

- whether the occupants originally came to the house as a group or were individually recruited;
- what facilities were shared;
- whether the occupants were responsible for the whole house or merely individual parts;
- whether occupants were able to lock other occupants out of their rooms;
- when an occupant left, whose responsibility it was to replace him/her;
- who allocated rooms to occupants;
- what size was the property;
- how stable a group were the occupants?

In all cases, however, the question whether there was an HMO would be a matter of fact and degree, and could not be decided in advance by the application of predetermined local policies or professional guidelines: this in itself was a problem.

---

[10] [1979] AC 37, [1977] 2 All ER 432.
[11] (1977) 76 LGR 421, CA.
[12] [1978] JPL 766.
[13] [1981] 3 All ER 438.
[14] (1995) 27 HLR 719, see also *R v Kensington and Chelsea Royal Borough Council, ex p Westwoods Ltd* (1995) 28 HLR 291.

The problem was the clash between legal and administrative ways of thinking. The lawyer's approach to the HMO problem was to consider the definition given by the law and then to determine on a case-by-case basis whether any given property is an HMO. Housing Management and Environmental Health officials on the other hand needed clear-cut categorisation to assist them in their work – and they might have wished to include within their concept of HMO properties which did not fit into the parameters allowed by s 345.

The Chartered Institute of Environmental Health (CIEH) classified HMOs into six groups, while the former Department of the Environment Transport and the Regions (DETR) had six classifications of its own. In both cases shared houses and houses containing lodgers were classified as HMOs, when it was by no means certain that a court would find any such property to be multiply occupied.

In *Rogers v Islington Borough Council[15]*, Mr Rogers had a three-storey, ten-bedroomed house let out to up to nine single, young professional adults on individual verbal agreements. Each had the right to a room and the right to share communal facilities, and each lived there for about two years. Mr Rogers lived in France but kept a room for himself, and he called the premises a private residential club because though new occupants were recruited via newspaper advertisements, current occupants decided whether or not a person should be admitted. Was this house an HMO?

Nourse LJ concluded a good working test of multiple occupation was needed, and found a way forward by clarifying what constitutes a 'household'. A 'household' existed where a number of people lived together in some form of relationship, and that could include a house where an occupier has a few paying guests living with the family. Students could form such relationships where they clubbed together to rent a property, even though they were unknown to each other before coming to university and paid rent individually. They had a reason to live together and form a community. In such cases where four or five people came together and took a house as a preformed group for a predetermined length of time, they would form a 'household'. In the instant case there was no such relationship. The label placed on the house by Mr Rogers did not change its status; it was an HMO.

## LOCAL AUTHORITY HOUSING AND FIRE PRECAUTION POWERS

### Registration

Section 346 of the 1985 Act (as inserted in 1996) empowered, but did *not* require authorities to make various registration schemes for HMOs for the whole or part of their area, these did not have to apply to all types of HMO.

Registration schemes could contain 'control' or 'special' conditions. Under s 346A, inserted in 1996, once a scheme was in force it was the duty of those persons

---

[15] [1999] 37 EG 178, CA.

specified in it to register their HMOs. In general, registration was for a period of five years and was renewable, 'reasonable' registration fees being payable on registration.

Section 346B enabled the Secretary of State to prepare model schemes and any local scheme confirming to a model required no central confirmation. Schemes not conforming to a model still required central confirmation and the Secretary of State could modify such a scheme before confirmation. Under s 347, as substituted in 1996, limits could be set on the number of persons occupying an HMO, and preventing multiple occupation of a house unless registered. Under s 348G it was a criminal offence to break or otherwise fail to comply with the requirements of a registration scheme once it was in force.

Section 348, as substituted, enabled local authorities on an application for the first registration of house, or on the renewal or variation of a registration, to:
- refuse the application on the basis that the property was unsuitable for multiple occupation and was incapable of being made suitable;
- refuse the application on the basis that the person having control was not a 'fit and proper person';
- require the carrying out of works on the property;
- impose conditions as to the management of the property.

Section 348A further enabled authorities who had control schemes at any time during a period of registration to alter the number of persons or households permitted in the house, or to revoke registration altogether, on the basis that the house was unsuitable for such occupation as was permitted by the registration and was incapable of being made suitable, or to alter the number of permitted persons or households until specified works were executed within a set time to make the house 'suitable'. Registration could also be revoked where an authority concluded the person having control of the house, or the person managing the HMO (ie the person who owned the premises and who received the rents from them either directly or via an agent, *or* who would have received those rents but for the existence of an arrangement with a third party: see s 398) was not fit and proper, or where there was a breach of the conditions of management relation to the HMO.

## Special control provisions

Sections 348B to 348F inserted special controls in respect of hotels/hostels which, it was alleged by ministers, were sometimes the scene of drug abuse and other forms of anti-social behaviour. Under these powers authorities could insert additional control conditions in a registration scheme, also to control occupancy levels. Once an authority had determined to have a registration scheme with control provisions, additional specific controls could be included to prevent an HMO or the behaviour of its residents from 'adversely affecting the amenity or character of the area'. Authorisation could be given for registration to be refused, the number of occupants reduced, and for conditions to be imposed on registration. In particular authorisation could be given for the revocation of registration where a house was occupied by more households than was permitted or where a breach of conditions had occurred and this was due to a 'relevant management failure'. Such a failure was 'relevant' (under s 348F) where the person having control of or managing the HMO failed to take reasonable steps to prevent the HMO or the behaviour of residents from adversely affecting the amenity or character of the area in which it is situated, or to reduce such an effect. In a case where special control provisions applied, when considering an application for registration of an HMO authorities could also take account of existing HMOs in the vicinity of the proposed HMO.

Special control provisions were draconian in effect. The debates leading up to the passing of the Housing Act 1996 indicated that they were to be targeted at situations where, inter alia, large numbers of people on state benefits were drawn to particular areas by the availability of cheap accommodation.

Where special control provisions were included in a scheme, provision was made under s 348C for notification of decisions and for appeals. Where an application was refused or the conditions or registration varied or there was a revocation the authority had to given written reasoned notice of its decision. There was a 21-day right of appeal to the county court. The court had power to vary or reverse the authority's decision if some material informality, defect or error was found, or where the authority had behaved unreasonably. The court could direct the authority to grant applications either as made or as varied. Conditions imposed could also be varied.

Under s 348D special control provisions in a scheme could allow an authority to direct that where registration should be revoked, they could also direct that the level of occupation was to be reduced to such a level where the registration scheme no longer applied.

Where such an occupancy direction was given, those who had control or management of the HMO had to take all reasonably practicable steps to comply with it, and security of tenure for assured tenants and assured shorthold tenants in the property was effectively removed for this purpose. Again, written reasoned notice had to be given and there was a right of appeal to the county court: see s 348E.

Under s 349 authorities proposing to make registration schemes conforming with the central model had to publish notice of their intention one month before the scheme was made and had to give local notice of the actual making. Similar requirements applied to local schemes needing the Secretary of State's confirmation. The scheme had to be available for public inspection, and the local press utilised to give publicity to schemes.

## Management regulations

By virtue of s 369 of the Housing Act 1985 (as amended) the Secretary of State had power to make a code to ensure proper standards of management in HMOs. By virtue of Sch 9 to the Local Government and Housing Act 1989, the code automatically applied to HMOs, and its breach could lead to immediate prosecution under s 369(5), and service of a notice under s 372 of the principal Act requiring rectification of specified relevant defects of management. Under s 369(5) it was an offence either knowingly to contravene management regulations, or to fail without reasonable excuse to comply with the regulations (an offence of strict liability).

Regulations made generally required managers of HMOs to ensure that:

1. all means of water supply and drainage were maintained in repair, clean condition, good and proper working order with water fittings being protected against frost damage;

2. supplies of water, gas and electricity to any resident were not unreasonably interrupted;

3. common parts were maintained in repair, clean condition and good order, reasonably free from obstruction;

4 specified installations in common use, or serving parts of premises in common use, were maintained in repair, clean condition and good working order, including installations for supplying gas and electricity for lighting and heat, sanitary provision, sinks, installations for cooking/storing food;

5. internal structures of any part of a house occupied as living accommodation were in clean condition at the start of a period of residence, and were maintained in repair, with mains installations being kept in repair and working order, though managers were absolved from carrying out repairs needed in consequence of failures by residents to use accommodation in a tenant-like manner;

6. windows and means of ventilation were to be maintained in repair and proper working order;

7. means of escape from fire and associated fire precautions and apparatus were in good order and repair and were unobstructed, with suitably displayed signs indicating all means of escape from fire;

8. outbuildings, yards, areas, forecourts, gardens in common use were to be kept in repair, clean condition and good order;

9. refuse and litter were not to accumulate;

10. reasonably requisite precautions were taken to ensure residents were pro-tected against injury having regard to the design and structural conditions of any given HMO;

11. the name, address and telephone number of the manager were to be visibly and suitably displayed;

12. information was given to the authority as to numbers of individuals and households accommodated in response to specific written requests by that authority.

## Powers to require the doing of further works

If in the opinion of a local authority an HMO was defective because of neglect in complying with the management regulations, they could serve notice under s 372 of the 1985 Act on the manager specifying and requiring execution of works necessary to make good the defects. The notice had to allow at least 21 days for doing the works, though this could be extended from time to time with the written permission of the authority. Information of service of the notice had also to be served on all other persons known to the authority to be owners, lessees or mortgagees of the house. Following service the person served had, under s 373, a period of 21 days (or such longer period as the authority might allow) to appeal to the county court. The grounds on which an appeal could be made were that:

1.    the condition of the house did not justify the authority in requiring execution of the specified works;
2.    there had been some material error, defect or informality in, or in connection with the notice;
3.    the authority had refused unreasonably to approve execution of alternative works, or that works required were otherwise unreasonable in character or extent, or were unnecessary;
4.    the time allowed for doing the works was not reasonably sufficient, or the date specified for doing the works was unreasonable, or
5.    some person other than the appellant was wholly or partly responsible for the state of affairs, or would benefit from the doing of the works, and therefore ought to bear the whole or part of their costs.

## POWER TO REQUIRE EXECUTION OF WORKS TO RENDER PREMISES FIT FOR NUMBER OF OCCUPANTS

Section 352 of the 1985 Act, as amended in 1989 and 1996, empowered authorities to require execution of works to render premises fit for the number of their inhabitants. An authority could, subject to s 365 which related to means of escape from fire, serve a notice, on the person 'having control' where (a) it considered an HMO failed to meet one or more of a number of stated criteria, and (b) having regard to the number of individuals or households (or both) accommodated in the premises, by reason of that failure the premises were not reasonably suitable for occupation by the individuals or households in question. The listed criteria were, under s 352(1A):

1.    Were there satisfactory facilities for storage, preparation and cooking of food including adequate numbers of sinks with hot and cold water?
2.    Was there an adequate number of suitably located WCs for exclusive use by by occupants?
3.    Similarly were there fixed baths/showers and wash hand basins with hot and cold water for occupants?
4.    Subject to s 365, were there adequate means of escape from fire?
5.    Were there other adequate fire precautions?

Note that there was no power to fix an occupation level for an HMO under this section: that fell to be done under s 354.

Authorities had a general discretion under s 352(2) to serve notice requiring works to be done to make a property fit for the number of occupants for the time being accommodated or for a smaller number the house would reasonably accommodate if the works were carried out. Subsection (2A) provided that where an authority had exercised or proposed to exercise powers under s 368 to secure closure of part of a house, they could in their s 352 notice specify such work as were necessary to make the house fit bearing in mind that a part had been closed. Where a s 352 notice was served the authority was under a duty, under subs (3), as amended, to inform the occupiers of the property, as well as the person having control and the house's manager.

Where notice was served s 352(4) provided that the person served had to begin required work not later than a specified reasonable date – which had to be not earlier than 21 days after the date of service of the notice, and had further to complete them within a specified reasonable period. Where notice was served in respect of s 352 requirements and the specified works were carried out a further notice could not be served within a period of five years, unless the authority considered there had been a change of circumstances, see s 352(7) and (8).

## SUPPLEMENTAL PROVISIONS

Section 352A (inserted in 1996) enabled authorities to levy reasonable charges in respect of their administrative expenses on persons served with s 352 notices. These were limited to expenses incurred in determining whether a notice should be served, identifying the works and actually serving the notice – and there was a statutory limit of £300 per notice.

Appeals against s 352 notices were available under s 353. It was a ground of appeal that, inter alia, the condition of the premises in respect of means of escape from fire and fire precautions did not justify requiring the specified works, and further that the date specified for beginning these works was not reasonable. It could alternatively be argued that an authority had no power to serve the notice because the property was not an HMO.

### Further supplemental provisions to section 352

The power of authorities under s 354 to limit the number of occupants of a house so as to prevent the occurrence of, or to remedy, a state of affairs otherwise calling for service of notice under s 352 was modified in 1989, and further amended in 1996. They could limit by direction the number of occupants allowed for an HMO based on consideration, inter alia, of whether the property had adequate means of escape from fire and other adequate fire precautions in addition to consideration of whether it had adequate cooking and sanitary facilities. This power also extended to parts of houses, see s 354(2). The direction once given made it the duty under s 355, of 'the occupier', which included any person entitled or authorised to permit individuals to take up residence in the house, to keep the number of persons within the permitted number. Copies of the direction had to be served, within seven days of its making, on the owner and known lessees of the house and also posted within the house in some place where the occupants could have access to it. It was an offence under s 355(2) knowingly to fail to comply with a direction.

A s 354 direction could only be issued when the house to which it applied was multi-occupied, and multiple occupation of the premises at the time of an alleged offence was an essential requirement for liability. There was no right to appeal against a s 354 direction as such. However, authorities had power under s 357 to revoke or vary directions, following changes of circumstances affecting the house, or the execution of works there, on the application of anyone having an estate or interest in the house. A s 354 direction could be served in addition to, or instead of, one under s 352. The latter was designed to ensure that facilities in an HMO were adequate for the number of occupants, while the former was used to specify a maximum number who could occupy the house with existing facilities.

## Special provisions with regard to fire

Section 365 of the 1985 Act (as amended in 1989 and further in 1996) gave authorities wide power of choice in cases where an HMO presented fire risks. Where an authority considered an HMO failed to meet the requirements of s 352, and one reason, or the reason, why they were of this opinion was because there were *no* adequate means of escape from fire *or* no other adequate fire precautions, they might, as an alternative to requiring works, accept an undertaking *or* make a closing order under s 368.

Section 365(2) (as amended) provided that where the foregoing powers were available, the authority's discretion was total. However, they were under a duty to make some appropriate order where the house was of such a description, or was occupied in such a way, as might be specified by the Secretary of State in an order. The Secretary of State was also given power by s 365(2A) to specify houses of a particular description or occupied in a particular way in respect of which the range of powers was not to be exercised. Properties subject to the duty to take action were those comprising at least three storeys. The *excluded* properties were:

- houses used as children's homes;
- houses registered under the Registered Homes Act 1984;
- houses occupied by health service bodies;
- houses for which the responsible person was a university or further education body;
- houses approved centrally for the purposes of the probation service;
- houses in which the local housing authority had a freehold or leasehold interest;
- houses subject to control orders (see further below);
- houses occupied by persons forming only two households;
- houses occupied by no more than four persons, or by three persons in addition to a responsible person and any other member of that person's household;
- houses consisting of self-contained flats where at least one-third were *either* let on leases of more than 21 years to their occupiers, *or* were wholly occupied by any freeholder of the house, *or* when the flats were created they complied with building regulations requirements;
- houses in respect of which the responsible person was a registered social landlord.

Apart from those cases specified by the Secretary of State, the 'fire powers' were discretionary: there was no general duty to take action in respect of HMOs save that under s 605 of the Housing Act 1985 (as amended) whereunder authorities had at least once every year, to consider the housing conditions of their district to decide what action to take in pursuance of, inter alia, their HMO powers.

However, before action could be taken under s 352 in respect of remedying want of adequate means of escape from fire, the housing authority had under s 365(3) to consult the relevant fire authority.

Where (subject to s 365) it appeared that means of escape from fire would be adequate if part of a house ceased to be used for human habitation, the authority could under s 368 secure that. They could also secure closure of part of a house while serving notice under s 365 specifying works necessary to supply the rest with adequate fire escapes. In the execution of these powers they could, after consultation with owners or mortgagees, accept undertakings from such persons that part or parts of houses would not be used for human habitation without the consent of the authority. It was an offence to use, or to permit use of, any part of a house subject to a closure undertaking. Where such an undertaking was not accepted, or if one accepted was found to be broken, the authority could make a closing order on the relevant part of the house.

If a notice under s 352 or 372 was not complied with, or if persons on whom they had been served informed the authority in writing they were unable to do the works, s 375 of the 1985 Act allowed the authority to do the work. They could recover reasonable expenses under Sch 10 to the Act from the person on whom notice was served, or where an agent or trustee was served, in whole or part from the person on whose behalf the agent or trustee was acting.

A wilful failure to comply with notices issued under ss 352 or 372 of the 1985 Act was, by virtue of s 376(1), an offence punishable by a fine. It appeared the only allowable reasons for acting were force majeure, accident or impossibility.

Section 377 of the 1985 Act applied where any person, being an occupier, or owner of premises, and having received notice of intended action under ss 352 or 372 of the Act prevented the carrying into effect of proposals. A magistrates' court would order that person to allow doing what is necessary. Failure to comply with a court order was an offence.

## Further powers to prevent overcrowding in multi-occupied houses

Section 358 of the Housing Act 1985 applied where it appeared to an authority that an excessive number of persons, having regard to the number of rooms available, was being, or was likely to be, accommodated in an HMO. They might serve on the occupier, or on the person exercising management of the house, or on both, an 'overcrowding notice'. This had to state, under s 359, in relation to every room what the authority considered to be the maximum number of persons who could suitably sleep therein, if any. An authority could require a number of courses of action from persons on whom such notice was served. The first, under s 360, was to refrain from:

1.  knowingly permitting any room to be occupied as sleeping accommodation otherwise than in accordance with the notice, or
2.  knowingly permitting persons to occupy the premises as sleeping accommodation in such numbers that it was not possible to avoid persons of opposite sexes, not living together as husband and wife, and over the age of 12, sleeping in the same room.

The alternative course of action, under s 361, was that the person on whom notice was served had to refrain from:

1. knowingly permitting any *new* resident (ie a person not living in the premises immediately before the notice was served) to occupy a room as sleeping accommodation otherwise than in accordance with the notice, or

2. knowingly permitting a new resident to occupy part of the premises for sleeping if that was not possible without persons of opposite sexes, and not living as man and wife, sleeping in the same room.

Not less than seven days before serving notice, under s 358(2), the authority had to:

1. inform the occupier of the premises, and any person appearing to exercise management, in writing of their intention to serve the notice, and

2. ensure, so far as reasonably possible, that every other person living in the house was informed of their intention.

Those informed had to be given an opportunity of making representations regarding this proposal. A person aggrieved by such an 'overcrowding notice' could, under section 362, appeal to the county court within 21 days of service. The court could confirm, quash or vary the order. Once an order was in force it was an offence to contravene it.

A notice could, under s 363, be revoked or varied at any time by the authority on the application of any person having an estate or interest in the housed.

## CONTROL ORDERS

To deal with HMOs in the worst condition, authorities could make 'control orders' allowing them to take over management for up to five years and act as if they were the owners. An order allowed an authority to take the necessary steps (other than sale) to bring a property up to a satisfactory standard.

Under s 379 of the 1985 Act an order could be made if:

1. a notice had been served under ss 352 or 372 (execution of works) or if a direction had been given under s 354 (limits on numbers of occupants); *or*

2. it appeared to the authority that the state and condition of the house was such as to call for taking any such action, *and*

3. it also appeared that the state of the house was such that it is necessary to make a control order to protect the safety, welfare or health of persons living therein.

An order came into force when made (s 379(2)) and as soon as practicable thereafter the authority had to enter the premises and take such immediate steps as were necessary to protect residents' health, welfare and safety.

### The effects of a control order

A control order transferred full possession and control of the house to the authority (see generally s 381) and cancelled orders, notices or directions already made under the management provisions, but without prejudice to criminal liabilities incurred.

The authority could grant, under s 381(2), weekly or monthly tenancies within the property, but rights and obligations of existing residents were protected by s 382.

Section 385 laid a double duty on the authority:
1.  to maintain proper standards of management and take any action necessary under the management provision of the Act, and
2.  to keep the house insured against fire.

Thereafter s 386 required them to prepare a scheme and to serve a copy on the dispossessed proprietor and on all other owners, lessees and mortgagees, not later than eight weeks from the making of the control order. The object of such an order was to ensure the property was in a proper condition to accommodate its occupants.

During the currency of a control order s 389 of the 1985 Act required the authority to pay the dispossessed proprietor (ie the person otherwise entitled to rents from the property) compensation at an annual rate of one half of the rental value of the house, ie the amount the house might reasonably be expected to fetch if let.

## APPEALS AND COMPULSORY PURCHASE OF HMOS

Any person having an estate or interest in the house, or otherwise prejudiced by a control order, could appeal to the county court under s 384.

Control orders expired after five years, unless revoked earlier by the authority; Housing Act 1985, s 392. A person could apply, with reasons, for early revocation. If this application was rejected, or ignored for six weeks, he/she could appeal to the county court for revocation of the order.

An authority had power under s 17 and Sch 13 Pt IV of the 1985 Act to make a compulsory purchase order (CPO) on a property subject to a control order. Provision was made for satisfaction of the financial obligations of both authority and owner. A CPO was a last resort measure, generally only authorised where an authority proposed to transfer the property on or after improvement to an acceptable manager such as registered social landlord.

## THE PROPOSED LAW OF MULTIPLE OCCUPATION

### Initial definitions

For the purposes of the new law outlined below certain definitions are needed at the outset:
*   **Authority**: the local housing authority, ie (in England) a unitary authority, a district council or a London Borough Council.
*   **Regulations centrally made** – 'Appropriate national authorities' may make regulations, these are in England, the Secretary of State, and, in Wales, the National Assembly.
*   **'Health':** this includes mental health.
*   **'Lease':** includes tenancy.

- **Occupants/occupiers**: those who occupy the property as a residence, whether as lessees/tenants or licensees.
- **'Licence'**: includes those granted freely, but does not extend to licensed squatting.
- **'Person having control'**: the person who receives the rack rent (ie not less than two thirds of the full net anual value of the property) or who would receive it if it was let at such a rent.
- **'Person managing'**: a person who, being an owner or lessee of the premises receives payments (either directly or via an agent) from tenants/licensees of the property or who would receive them but for the existence of some arrangement (eg a court order) and includes the agent through whom rent is received.

Part 2 of the Housing Bill 2003 introduces a new code for dealing with multiple occupation. cl 217 et seq. define 'house in multiple occupation'. Initially there are cumulative defining conditions. The property must meet one of a number of conditions, which are as follows:
- the 'standard test', ie it is one or more units of living accommodation which are not self contained flats *and* this is occupied by persons not forming a single household who occupy it as their only or main residence, *and* that occupation is the only use of the accommodation, *and* rent is payable in respect of the occupation, *and* two or more of the occupying households share one or more basic amenities *or* the accommodation is lacking in one or more basic amenities;
- the self-contained flat test, ie it is a flat which meets the criteria outlined above;
- the converted building test, ie it is a building which has been converted from its original purpose and meets the criteria outlined above.

Basic amenities are toilets, personal washing facilities and cooking facilities.

Certain buildings are excluded from the definition if they fall within Sch 11. These are:
- buildings managed or controlled by local housing authorities;
- or where the manager is a registered social landlord or Police Authority, or Fire Authority or health service body;
- or where control is regulated under other legislation;
- or where the building is occupied solely or principally by further or higher education students at a specified educational establishment and where the person having control is the establishment in question or is otherwise of a specified description;
- or where the building is occupied under long leases (ie more than 21 years) – this largely applies to conversions of houses into flats;
- any building occupied by only two people forming two households.

In some cases it may not be clear what a building's status is. For example, is it a hotel which is being used for short-term guests only, or is it a hostel with long-term residents? Clause 218 permits a local housing authority, where they are satisfied that though a property is not exclusively occupied by people as their only home, it is nevertheless occupied to a significant degree in this way, *and* the building otherwise satisfies one of the 'tests' outlined above, to declare the property to be an HMO. Notice of intention to make such a declaration must be given to those having control of the building and they may appeal to the Residential Property Tribunal (and thence to the Lands Tribunal) against the notice. The basic structure of appeals as examined in foregoing chapter applies to such proceedings. Authorities may, if they feel the conditions for an HMO declaration no longer apply, revoke such a declaration under cl 219.

Under cl 220 certain buildings converted into self contained flats will still nevertheless be considered as HMOs where the conversion work did not and still does not comply with appropriate building standards *and* less than two-thirds of the flats are owner-occupied.

The concept of forming a single household is expanded by cl 221 so that people are not to be regarded as a single household unless they are all members of the same family or they fall within classes specified in regulations. 'Family' is given quite a wide meaning to include spouses, cohabitants, same sex partners, parents, grandparents, children, siblings, aunts, uncles, nephews and nieces, treating relationships by marriage as if by blood, half blood as whole blood and stepchildren as children. Under cl 222, people are to be treated as occupying premises as their only or main residence where they do so in order to undertake a full-time further or higher education course, or where they are in a refuge, or where they fall within specified classes under regulations. Thus students living away from home will be treated as occupying their term-time addresses.

It will be noted that the old issue of the definition of 'single household' has been sidestepped. Those who are all of one family will be a 'household', while others may fall into that classification by virtue of regulations. It may thus be, for example, that houses rented by students from private landlords may be classified as HMOs on the basis that the regulations, once made, do not classify the occupants as a 'single household'.

## Licensing of HMOs by local authorities

Clauses 54 et seq provide for licensing of HMOs, which will be mandatory in some cases. Certain centrally designated types of HMO will be subject to mandatory licensing, while authorities may extend licensing to other specified types of HMO which are within areas designated as subject to 'additional licensing'. Authorities are under a duty to ensure the effective implementation of licensing, and they may designate either the whole or a part(s) of their area as subject to 'additional licensing', though only where they consider a significant proportion of HMOs in the area are being managed so ineffectively that they are giving rise to, or are likely to give rise to, particular problems for residents of the HMOs or for the general public. Designations may only be made after consultation with those likely to be affected by them and consideration of whether persons managing HMOs have complied with management codes of practice, and can only take place if this is consistent with the authority's overall housing strategy. In addition designation should be keyed in to other policies dealing with homelessness, empty properties and anti-social behaviour affecting the private rented sector, and it may *not* take place unless the authority have considered whether there are other courses of action – eg use of Anti-Social Behaviour Orders – which might provide an effective means of dealing with the problem in question *and* they have considered that making the designation will significantly assist in dealing with the particular problem. 'Anti-social behaviour' is defined to mean conduct on the part of occupiers or visitors to HMOs which causes or is likely to cause nuisance or annoyance to neighbours and others otherwise engaged in lawful activities in the locality *or* which involves or is likely to involve the use of the premises for illegal purposes, eg drug dealing. Designations, furthermore, have to be centrally confirmed before coming into force. In England the confirming authority will be the Secretary of State who may give approval on a case-by-case basis or by general approval given in relation to the designations of a specified authority or of an authority belonging to a particular class, or to designations relating to specified types of HMOs. Designations have to be publicised, for example, in relation to the date in which they are to come into force, and copies of designations must be publicly available. A designation once made must come to an end not later than five years after the date it comes into effect, and must be kept under periodic review by the authority which made it with a view to its revocation where this is appropriate, an act which also requires publicity.

Under cl 60, where an HMO is subject to licensing (unless it is subject to a temporary exemption notice or an interim or final management order – see further below) the licence will fix the maximum number of households or persons authorised to occupy the property. It s furthermore the duty of the local authority to take all reasonable steps to secure that HMO licence applications are made. A temporary exemption from these requirements *may* be made under cl 61 where the controller or manager of an unlicensed HMO notifies the authority of an intention to take particular steps to ensure the property no longer requires licensing. Such an exemption in general lasts for three months, though that period may, exceptionally, be extended, but only once. Where an exemption application is refused there is a right of appeal to a residential property tribunal which may rehear the issue and may take into account matters of which the authority were unaware.

Licence applications have, under cl 62, to be made in specified form, and this may entail payment of a fee to be fixed locally. Fees are, inter alia, to reflect the administrative costs of licensing and the general costs of HMO supervision. A licence may under cl 63 either be granted (either to the applicant or to some other person if both that person and the applicant agree) or refused. This provision would enable a registered social landlord to be the licence holder in respect of an HMO owned by another body. Before granting a licence the authority must be satisfied:

- The HMO is reasonably suitable for occupation by not more than the maximum number of persons/households permitted, *or* that it can be made suitable by the imposition of conditions.
- The proposed licence holder is a 'fit and proper person' *and*, out of all those reasonably available to be the holder, is the most appropriate person.
- The proposed manager is either the person who controls the HMO, or is that person's agent or employee, *and* is also a fit and proper person *and* that the proposed management arrangements are satisfactory.

There are particular requirements of suitability for multiple occupation under cl 64 as to which the authority must be satisfied before a licence can be granted. These requirements relate to national standards to be centrally laid down in relation to bathrooms, toilets, wash basins, showers, food storage (including preparation and cooking) and laundry facilities. In addition the new law will, under cl 65, lay down tests for who is a 'fit and proper person'. The authority will have to have regard to any evidence of:

- offences involving fraud, dishonesty, violence or drugs;
- acts of unlawful discrimination on grounds of sex, race, colour, ethnic or national origins or disability in the course of or in connection with carrying on a business;
- contravention of any provision of landlord and tenant law;
- acts not in accordance with applicable codes of practice approved under cl 197 (see below).

Such evidence is to be considered where it appears relevant to the question of 'fit and proper' status. It is generally to be assumed that the person having control of a property is more appropriate to be the licence holder than others.

The authority must in addition take into account in deciding whether proposed management arrangements are satisfactory:

- whether proposed managers are sufficiently competent;
- whether persons other than the proposed manager who will nevertheless be involved in management are 'fit and proper' to be involved;
- whether proposed management structures and funding arrangements are suitable.

Clause 66 enables authorities to impose conditions on the management, use or occupation of an HMO, its conditions and contents with regard to, inter alia:

- the use or occupation of particular parts of the HMO;
- the behaviour of persons occupying or visiting the HMO;
- requiring the provision of facilities and equipment to meet prescribed amenity standards;
- requiring facilities and equipment to be kept in repair and proper working order and that any works of, eg maintenance on such facilities, etc are carried out within specified periods;
- requiring licence holders and managers to attend prescribed training courses with regard to approved codes of practice issued under cl 197. These codes will be centrally approved and will lay down standards of conduct and practice with regard to the management of HMOs.

Licences *must* include those conditions specified by Sch 4 to the Housing Bill 2003, ie

- a requirement for an annual gas safety certificate;
- requirements that the licence holder will keep furniture and electrical appliances made available by him in safe condition;
- requirements to keep smoke alarms in the HMO in proper working order;
- requirements as to the supply to occupiers of the HMO of written statements of the terms on which they occupy the property.

It should be noted that where Category 1 or 2 hazards in a property exist (see foregoing chapter) they should be in general dealt with by the powers contained in Pt I of the Housing Bill 2003.

Conditions may not impose restrictions or obligations on persons other than the licence holder without their consent, and neither may they bring about an alteration in tenancy or licence to occupy terms. Licences, where granted, are for to individual HMOs and last for not more than five years. They are not transferable and will terminate within their five-year life span should the licence-holder die; see cl 67.

## Variation and revocation

Clause 68 et seq provide for the variation and revocation of licences. An authority may vary a licence either with the consent of the licence holder or if they consider there has been a change of circumstances (including new information coming to light) since the licence was granted. Where an authority propose to vary, on their initiative, the number of permitted households/persons, or the standards applicable to that level of occupations, they *must* apply the same standards as were applicable at the times of the grant of the licence, *unless* the standards were prescribed under cl 64 and have subsequently been revised, in which case the new standards *may* be applied. Where a variation takes place by agreement it will come into force at the agreed time, otherwise it will become operative after the time for any appeal has elapsed. Persons other than the licence holder may request an authority to vary a licence, for example a manager of the HMO, or the freeholder or leaseholder with an unexpired term of three years or more who is not otherwise the licence holder.

Licences may under cl 69 be revoked:
- with the consent of the licence holder;
- where the licence holder or any other person has failed to comply with licence conditions;
- where the licence holder is no longer 'fit and proper';
- where the management of the HMO is no longer being carried on by a 'fit and proper' person;
- where the property ceases to be an HMO falling within the legislation;
- where at any time the granting authority consider that, if the licence were to expire, they would refuse to grant a new licence;
- in any other case specified under centrally made regulations.

Where revocation is under consideration on the basis of the lack of reasonable suitability of an HMO to accommodate the number of licensed households/persons, the authority must generally apply the standards applicable at the time of the grant, save that where those standards were made under cl 64 and have subsequently been revised the new standards may be applied.

The procedures for revocation, for example with regard to commencement and appeal times, are similar to those for variation; see cl 70 and Sch 5.

## Enforcement

Various offences which can be committed by licence holders or managers are created by cl 71:

- failure to have a licence where one is required;
- allowing a person to occupy an HMO with the consequence that the licensed number of occupants is exceeded;
- failure to comply with licence conditions.

Various defences are also available, including:

- that a licence application had been made and was still effective;
- that there was a reasonable excuse for permitting occupation in excess of the licensed number;
- that there was a reasonable excuse for failure to comply with licence conditions.

Clause 72 further provides that in respect of any period for which a licence is required but is not in existence, no rent or licence fee that would be payable by an occupant of the HMO is to be payable, and no other compensation otherwise payable for use or occupation of the HMO is to be payable. The validity of tenancies or licences is not affected by this provision, neither is any other statutory protection enjoyed by their holders reduced.

## SELECTIVE LICENSING OF OTHER RESIDENTIAL ACCOMMODATION

Whilst licensing applies generally to HMOs, it will under Pt 3 of the Housing Bill 2003 apply selectively to other houses. Such premises are under cl 76 those which:

- are in areas designated under cl 77 for licensing and are occupied under a single tenancy or licence that is not otherwise 'exempt' or under two or more tenancies or licences in respect of different dwellings in the house which are not 'exempt', and
- are required to be licensed; see further below.

Tenancies or licenses granted by registered social landlords are 'exempt' and other lettings may be excluded under centrally made orders.

## Designation

Authorities may under cl 77 designate the whole or part of their areas where they are satisfied that:

- the area is, or is likely to become, one of 'low housing demand' *and* making the designation will, in combination with other measures pursued by the authority acting alone or in conjunction with others, contribute to the social or economic conditions of the area, *or*
- the area is experiencing a significant and persistent problem of anti-social behaviour which some/all of the private landlords (but not registered social landlords) in the area are failing to take appropriate steps to combat, and that

making the order will, in conjunction with other measures to be pursued alone (or in concert with others) by the authority, lead to an elimination or reduction of the problem.

In either of the above cases further conditions may be additionally centrally specified. Before any such designation is made the authority must consult with those likely to be affected by it and must take their views into account.

'Low housing demand' is a matter to be determined by the authority, taking into account, inter alia:

- the value of residential premises in the areas compared with values of other areas comparable in terms of types of housing, local amenities and transport, etc;
- the turnover of occupancies;
- the number of premises available to buy or rent and the length of time for which they are void.

Before making any designations, under cl 78 the authority must be satisfied it is consistent with their overall housing strategy, and they must adopt a coordinated approach with regard to dealing with empty properties, homelessness and anti social behaviour with regard to the use of their licensing powers and the measures which they may pursue along with other people. They must also first of all consider whether other measures under other powers might achieve the same objective as designation and must be satisfied that designation will, either alone or in part, assist them to achieve their objectives.

Designations will have to be centrally approved before coming into effect; see cl 79. Such approval may be specific or may be generic in that it relates to designations made by a specified authority, or by an authority falling within a particular class, or to houses of a specified description. Where a designation is confirmed it will in general come into effect three months later, and its effect must be published in due form by the authority; see cl 80.

Once made, designations will last for the period specified in the designation documents, and in general that will be a period of five years. However, designations must be periodically reviewed and this may lead to the designation being revoked; see cl 81.

## Which houses will be licensed?

Under cl 82 *every* non-exempt rented house in a designated area will have to be licensed *unless* it is otherwise licensed as an HMO, *or* it is temporarily exempted, *or* it is subject to an interim or final management order (see further below). Temporary exemption may, under cl 83, be granted where the person having control of a property or otherwise managing it notifies the authority of an intention to take particular steps to ensure it no longer requires licensing. They may if they think fit then serve on that person a 'temporary exemption notice' which will confer such exemption for, in general, a period of three months, which may, exceptionally, be extended for one further three-month period. If such an exemption is refused there is a right of appeal a residential property tribunal, where the whole matter will be reheard, even in relation to issues of which the authority were unaware.

For the purpose of Pt 3, 'house' is defined by cl 94 as a building or part of a building which consists of one or more dwellings, and a 'dwelling' is a building or part of a building occupied or intended to be occupied as a separate dwelling.

Licence applications, under cl 84, have to be made to the local housing authority, and a fee reflecting their costs may be charged, while any centrally made regulations must be complied with in relation to the form and content of notices and fees to be charged. Licences may, under cl 85, be refused or granted (either to the applicant or to some other person where both that person and the applicant agree). The proposed licence holder must be 'fit and proper' and the most appropriate person to be the licence holder, and the proposed manager must be either the person having control or an agent or employee of that person. The manager must also be 'fit and proper' and the proposed management arrangements must be satisfactory. The tests for 'fitness' are laid down in cl 86 and are very similar to those relating to HMO licence holders considered above – eg conviction of an offence involving fraud, dishonesty, violence or drugs will be evidence that a person is not 'fit and proper'. Management competence will have to be considered in relation to whether proposed management arrangements are satisfactory.

As with HMOs, conditions may, under cl 87, be imposed on licences, for example with regard to the management, use or occupation of the house, its condition or contents. In particular conditions may impose restrictions or prohibitions on the use or occupation of particular parts of the house, or for controlling the behaviour of residents or visitors, or in order to meet requirements imposed by centrally made regulations, or for ensuring that facilities and equipment required to be provided by centrally made regulations are kept in repair and proper working order, and that such work is done within prescribed periods.

Further conditions *must* be imposed under Sch 4, and these, of course, relate to the licensing of *both* HMOs and other properties. In particular it should be remembered that there will be a requirement, where gas is supplied to a property, for an annual gas safety certificate, that electrical appliances and furniture will be kept in safe condition, that smoke alarms will be kept in proper working order. In respect of houses licensed under Pt 3 there will also be a requirement for the licence holder to demand references from would-be occupants.

Licences will be granted, under cl 88, on an individual house basis and will last for a maximum period of five years, though a lesser period may be specified. Licences will not be transferable.

## Variation and revocation

As with HMOs, licences may under cl 89 be varied with the consent of the licence holder, or by the authority where they are satisfied a change of circumstances has occurred, and the procedures are similar to those descried above in respect of

HMOs. Similarly under cl 90 licences can be revoked, for example where the licence holder is longer considered to be 'fit and proper', in a manner once again similar to that applying to HMOs.

## Enforcement

By virtue of cl 92 it is an offence to have control of or to manage a house which is required to be licensed but in respect of which there is no licence, or to fail to comply with licence conditions. Once again, the provisions here are similar to those in respect of HMOs, as also are the provisions of cl 93 which lay down that during any period during which a requisite licence is not held, no rent or other occupation fee is payable by occupants of the house in questions.

## ADDITIONAL CONTROL PROVISIONS IN RELATION TO RESIDENTIAL ACCOMMODATION

Part 4 of the Bill consists of cll 96 to 128 which relate to powers for authorities to make Interim (IMO) and Final (FMO) management orders in respect of HMOs and houses requiring to be licensed under Pt 3.

An IMO is an order lasting for up to 12 months made to ensure that any immediate steps considered necessary by the authority to protect the health, safety or welfare of occupants of a relevant property, or of persons occupying or having an estate or interest in any premises in its vicinity, and any other steps considered appropriate with a view to proper management of the property pending the grant of a Pt 2 or Pt 3 licence (or pending the making of an FMO) are taken. An FMO is an order lasting for up to five years which is made to secure the proper management of a property on a long-term basis in accordance with a management scheme.

## IMOs

Authorities *must* under cl 97 make IMOs in respect of HMOs or Pt 3 houses which require licences but do not have them where they consider there is no reasonable prospect of a licence being obtained in the near future, *or* where, under cl 99, this is needed to protect the health, safety or welfare of occupants or of those having estates or interests in any premises in the vicinity of the property, and it is particularly provided that a threat to evict occupants in order to avoid the need for a licence is a threat to their welfare. (This is known as the 'health and safety condition'.) Similarly IMOs *must* be made in respect of any HMO or Pt 3 house which is licensed and the licence has been revoked, though the revocation is yet to come into force, and they consider that once the revocation comes into force there is no reasonable prospect of relicensing in the near future, *or* that on revocation the health and safety condition outlined above will apply.

Authorities may also make IMOs in respect of a house if it is an HMO which does not require licensing *and* they gain authorisation for such a move from a residential property tribunal, which may only authorise the making of the IMO if the health and safety condition is satisfied. In making its decision the Tribunal must consider whether any cl 197 Code of Practice applicable to the property has been complied with in the past. Similarly an authority may make an IMO in respect of a house subject to a Special Interim Management Order (SIMO), see below, where, once again, they obtain authorisation from a residential property tribunal. Nothing requires or authorises the making of an IMO where one has previously been made in respect of a property and the authority have not then exercised any 'relevant function ', ie granting a licence, making a temporary exemption notice or making an FMO.

Under cl 98, SIMOs can be made where a whole house is occupied under a tenancy or licence which is not granted by a registered social landlord or when it is occupied under two or more tenancies or licences in respect of different dwellings in it, none of which has been granted by a registered social landlord. A residential property tribunal may authorise a SIMO where the property falls with regulations to be centrally made and the order is needed to protect the health, safety or welfare of occupants, or other people otherwise engaging in lawful activities in the locality of the house.

In general, an IMO will come into effect under cl 100, when made and will normally come to an end 12 months later. Once the IMO is in force the authority's duties under cl 101 are:
- to take those immediate steps considered necessary to protect the health, safety or welfare of occupants or those having an estate or interest in any premises in the locality;
- to take such other steps as they consider appropriate with a view to the proper management of the property pending further action, such as making an FMO;
- where a house is one requiring to be licensed the authority must consider all the circumstances of the case and proceed either to license it or to make an FMO;
- where a property is an HMO *not* falling within Pt 2 of the Housing Bill 2003 the authority must consider all the circumstances and proceed either to make an FMO or revoke the IMO.

It is specifically provided that the authority's obligations include a duty to make reasonable provision for fire insurance.

Once an IMO is in force the authority have particular rights by virtue of cl 102, namely:
- the right to possession – subject to the interests of existing occupants;
- the right to do, or to authorise the doing of, anything a person having an estate or interest in the house would be able to do;
- the right to create leasehold interests and licences to occupy the house, though here they will require the written consent of the person who, but for the IMO, would have power to create leases or licences.

The authority do not by virtue of the IMO acquire an estate or interest in the house and so cannot sell or mortgage it, neither does the house become part of their housing stock for the purpose of statutes, etc, relating to local authority accommodation. An authority may be liable to persons having estates or interests in the house if they do, or omit to do, anything in the performance of their duties with regard to the house negligently.

Clause 103 provides that where an IMO is in force the immediate landlord of the property is not entitled to receive rents from the house, may not exercise management rights and powers over it, and may not create leasehold interests in it or licences to occupy it. Rent or other payments in respect of the house are to be collected by the authority, and, under cl 104, may be used to meet the reasonably incurred costs of performing their duties in respect of the house. They must also keep copies of their income and expenditure in respect of the house and must also make these available to the landlords of the house and others who have an estate or interest in it. Landlords may challenge these accounts in a residential property tribunal on the basis that items of expenditure have not been reasonably incurred.

## Variation and revocation

Authorities may, by virtue of cl 105, vary IMOs where they consider this appropriate, either on their own initiative or on the application of a 'relevant person', eg a person who would, but for the IMO, be the person managing the house or having control of it. IMOs may be revoked under cl 106 in particular circumstances:

- where the house ceases to be an HMO falling within Pt 2 of the Housing Bill 2003 or a house within Pt 3;
- where the IMO was made under cl 87 and a licence made under either Pt 2 or Pt 3 is due to come into force;
- where they have made an FMO to replace the IMO;
- in any other circumstances where they consider revocation is appropriate.

## Final Management Orders (FMOs)

Where an IMO is in force, cl 107 *requires* an authority to make an FMO where, on the expiry date of the IMO, the property would require a licence under either Pt 2 or Pt 3 and the authority consider they are unable to grant such a licence. Authorities may make FMOs to replace IMOs in respect of houses that will be, on an IMO's expiry date, an HMO falling outside Pt 2 *and* consider an FMO is necessary for the long-term protection of the health, safety or welfare of the occupants of the house, or of people having estates or interests in any premises in the vicinity. As FMOs have a finite life of a maximum of five years (see cl 108), provision is also made for new FMOs to be made to replace existing ones. These will be mandatory where a licence under Pt 2 or Pt 3 would be required and it still appears that one could not be given.

Where an FMO is in force, cl 109 requires the authority to take appropriate steps to secure the proper management of the property in accordance with the scheme contained in the order. The FMO must also be kept under review to determine whether it should be kept in force, with or without variations. They may also review an FMO with a view to determining whether licensing under Pts 2 or 3 is appropriate, or whether revocation should take place and must take appropriate action as a result of their review.

The FMO will, under cl 110, transfer rights of possession and management to the authority in a manner similar to that considered above with regard to IMOs, though they have no power to create leasehold interests or licences to occupy for fixed terms expiring after the date of expiry of the FMO itself, nor may they create interests terminable by notice to quit of more than four weeks' duration, ie 'long' periodic lettings such as two-monthly terms, unless these are agreed to in writing by the person who, but for the FMO, would otherwise have power to create the lease or licence in question. They may, however, create assured shorthold tenancies without such consent, provided they are created before the beginning of the period of six months ending with the date on which the FMO is due to expire. As with an IMO, an FMO confers no estate or interest in a property on the authority making it and hence they may not sell or mortgage it, etc. Also, as with IMOs authorities will only be liable for anything done or omitted to be done to the property where negligence can be shown.

Under cl 111 an FMO prevents the immediate landlord of the property in question from receiving rents or other payments from occupants which instead go to the authority. Furthermore such a person is barred from exercising any management powers over the property and may not create leasehold interests in it, nor licences to occupy it, though, inter alia, such a person may if, for example, entitled to the freehold, dispose of that. The validity of mortgages on the property is not affected by this provision.

Clause 112 provides for 'management schemes' to be a mandatory feature of FMOs. Such schemes set out how an authority propose to carry out their duties in respect of the property. Part 1 of such a scheme must contain a plan of management relating in particular to details of works to be done, estimates of capital and other expenditure, the amounts of rents and other payments the authority will seek having regard to the condition of the property, the amount to be paid to the landlord of the property after the authority have deducted their expenditure, and payment to the landlord of any sums due on the termination of the FMO. It may also, inter alia, contain details of how the authority intend to use rent, etc to meet their expenditure. Part 2 of the scheme is to describe in general terms how the authority intend to deal with the issues which caused them to make the FMO, including for example, taking steps to ensure that occupants comply with their obligations under their leases/ licences and the general law, and describing and explaining any repairs needed to the property. Authorities will be required to keep accounts of their income and expenditure with regard to FMOs and to make these available to landlords and others having interests in the property.

Clauses 113 and 114 make provision for the variation and revocation of FMOs, and these are very similar to the provisions in respect of IMOs described above.

Clauses 116 to 119 deal with the consequential effects of management orders. So far as existing occupiers, ie those in occupation at the making of the IMO or FMO, are concerned their rights continue unaffected. 'New occupiers', ie those who take up occupation after the order is made, will have the authority in place of the landlord of the property, but this will not make them secure tenants of the authority. In effect occupants will be dealt with under either the Rent Act 1977 or the Housing Act 1988 (as amended in both cases) according to the time at which their tenancies/licences commenced. Any agreements, instruments or legal proceedings in respect of the property in effect on the commencement date of the order take effect with the substitution of the authority for the landlord. Any furniture in the property at the commencement date which occupants have the right to use in return for a payment to the landlord will pass into the possession of the authority, subject to the rights of the occupants, and the authority will have power during the period of the order to supply such other furniture as they consider is required.

On the termination of a management order under cl 120 where no further order is made the balance, if any, of any rent and other payments collected by the authority must be paid over to the landlord of the property where this balance exceeds the authority's expenditure on the property. This provision may, however, be excluded by the management scheme in an FMO. In the case of an IMO where the total amount of rent, etc, collected is less than the authority's expenditure, they may recover the balance from the landlord, and where any amount is so recoverable until it is paid it stands as a charge on the house.

Clause 121 provides for the continuation of leases and licences granted by the authority after the end of a management order, and similarly in respect of other agreements entered into by the authority in the performance of their duties in respect of the property, though this will be dependent on the authority serving notice on all affected parties. The general effect of the provision is to transfer the authority's rights and obligations (subject in the latter case to an indemnity where any damages are payable) from them to the landlord of the property.

Clause 122 grants power of entry to authorities to enter, at all reasonable times, any part of a house, subject to a management order for the purposes of carrying out works. This power can be enforced by an order from the magistrates' court with which it is an offence not to comply.

## OVERCROWDING NOTICES IN HMOS

HMOs where no management order is in force and which are not required to be licensed under Pt 2 may be subject to overcrowding notices served on 'relevant persons' by the authority where, having regard to the number of rooms available, they consider an excessive number of people are, or are likely to be, accommodated in the property; see cl 123. At least seven days' notice of an intention to serve such an order must be given to all relevant persons and to occupants, and an opportunity must be given for them to make representations. If no appeal is then made the notice becomes effective 21 days after service and becomes final and conclusive. It is then an offence to contravene the notice, though a defence of reasonable excuse is available. 'Relevant persons' for the purposes of this provision are those who have estates or interests in the house and those who manage and control it.

A notice must, under cl 124, state in relation to each room the maximum number of persons for which in the opinion of the authority it is suitable sleeping accommodation, *or* that any given room is unsuitable for this purpose. Special maxima may apply in the case of rooms occupied by persons below a specified age. A notice must also contain either a requirement under cl 125 that the recipient of the notice must refrain from permitting a room to be occupied as sleeping accommodation otherwise than as is permitted by the notice, or from permitting people to occupy the HMO as sleeping accommodation in such numbers that it is not possible to avoid persons of opposite sexes (who are not living together as husband and wife) from sleeping in the same room (disregarding children under the age of 12) *or*, under cl 126, the recipient of the notice must refrain from permitting a new resident to occupy a room as sleeping accommodation otherwise than as permitted by the notice, or from permitting a new resident to occupy so that it is not possible to prevent persons of opposite sexes (who are not living together as husband and wife) from sleeping in the same room.

Clause 127 permits appeals against overcrowding notices to be made to a residential property tribunal, and are to be determined by way of a rehearing. The tribunal may confirm, quash, or vary the notice. Clause 128 permits the authority to revoke or vary and overcrowding notice. This may be done on the application of a 'relevant person' (see above) and, if refused, there is a right of appeal to a residential property tribunal. Note also cl 187 which enables central authorities to make extensive orders in connection with overcrowding of dwellings. Note also cll 194 and 195 on the creation of residential property tribunals and the provision of an appeal from them to the Lands Tribunal. For further details of this see the foregoing chapter.

## GENERAL SUPPLEMENTARY AND APPEAL PROVISIONS

Clause 196 requires authorities to keep a register of all Pt 2 or Pt 3 licences in force, all management orders in force and any temporary exemption notices. This register must be publicly available at an authority's chief office. Particular provision with regard to registration may exist under centrally made regulations.

Central authorities may also approve (or withdraw approval from) codes of practice laying down standards of conduct and practice with regard to the management of HMOs; see cl 197. Approval of such codes is subject to prior consultation with the groups who manage/occupy HMOs, and furthermore is subject to adequate publicity being given to the proposed code so that those affected by it are made aware of it. Failure to comply with a code does not, however, make a person liable to any civil or criminal proceedings.

The power of central bodies to make HMO regulations is specifically conferred by cl 198. These regulations are to ensure that satisfactory management arrangements are in place and that satisfactory standards of management are maintained. The regulations may imposed duties on occupants to enable managers to effectively discharge their duties, and breaches of the regulations are offences, though a defence of 'reasonable excuse' exists. The power to make regulations is exercisable by statutory instrument; see cl 187.

Clause 199 empowers authorities to require the production of documents from, inter alia, managers, licence holders and occupants of houses with regard to, inter alia, their functions in respect of Pt 2 or Pt 3 of the Housing Bill 2003, and also for the purpose of investigating whether offences have been committed in respect of those functions, and it is an offence under cl 200 to fail to comply with a notice seeking production of documents. It is similarly an offence under cl 202 to supply false or misleading information. Powers of entry (if necessary by warrant) for the purposes of enforcement are granted to authorities by cll 203 and 204 to enable them to carry out surveys and examination of premises in respect of their function. cl 205 provides for penalties where these powers of an authority are obstructed by any person without reasonable excuse. (These powers also exist with regard to the new hazard standards under Pt 1 of the Bill; see Chapter 12.)

The detailed procedures for granting/refusing licences under Pts 2 and 3 are to be found in Sch 5 of the Housing Bill 2003, while Sch 6 contains the detailed provisions relating to the making of management orders.

## COMMENT

Overall the new provisions relating to HMOs and the selective licensing of certain rented properties are to be welcomed. Some might argue that *all* rented property should be subject to licensing, but this might have the effect of diminishing the amount of property available for renting, as landlords might decide to get out of renting rather than face regulation, for example on grounds of cost. Even so, the introduction of a defined notion of a 'fit and proper' person to be the landlord/ manager of rented properties – even in relation to a limited range of dwellings – is a clear step forward in ensuring the proper management and maintenance of such dwellings and the protection of their occupants. Where, however, the provisions of the Housing Bill 2003 may be criticised is in relation to their skeletal nature. The real 'meat' of the licensing system will not be known until regulations are centrally made. Until then a considerable number of questions will remain unanswered, for example the relationship of the powers of housing authorities with those of planning authorities under the Town and Country Planning Act 1990 and those of Fire Authorities under the Fire Precautions Act 1971; see below. Indeed it remains to be seen whether those issues will even be addressed at all.

## SUPERVISION OF MULTI-OCCUPATION BY PLANNING CONTROL

Under planning law 'development' may not generally be carried out without planning permission from the local planning authority. Can authorities use planning powers to prevent the inception of undesirable multi-occupation developments?

Section 55(1) of the Town and Country Planning Act 1990 defines development as:

'the carrying out of building, engineering, mining or other operations in, on, over or under land, or the making of any material change in the use of any buildings or other land'.

Section 55(2)(a) excludes from this definition:

'the carrying out for the maintenance, improvement or other alteration of any building of works which (i) affect only the interior of the building or (ii) do not materially affect the external appearance of the building ...'

But s 55(3)(a) goes on to provide:

'For the avoidable of doubt it is hereby declared for the purposes of this section – the use as two or more separate dwelling-houses of any building previously used as a single dwelling-house involves a material change in the use of the building and of each part thereof which is so used.'

Unfortunately doubt has not been avoided. It is uncertain whether any change from single residential to multi-occupied use inevitably constitutes an act of development by falling within s 55(3)(a) above, and so requiring planning permission. In *Ealing Corpn v Ryan*[16] a planning authority alleged unauthorised development had taken place in that the use of a house had changed from being a single dwelling to use as two or more separate dwellings. The house contained several families who all shared a common kitchen, and presumably the lavatory and bathroom also. It was held the house had not been divided into *separate* dwellings. A house may be occupied by two or more persons living separately under one roof, without their occupying 'separate dwellings', provided they are sharing certain common living accommodation, which, following *Goodrich v Paisner*[17], includes kitchens. Multiple occupation of itself *may* be insufficient to bring s 55(3)(a) of the Town and Country Planning Act 1990 into operation. This is designed to deal with situations where new dwellings can be regarded as truly separate, self-contained and independent; here the existence of physical reconstruction will be a factor of great importance.

But multi-occupation may still constitute development where conversion amounts to a material change of use under s 55(1) of the 1990 Act. In *Birmingham Corpn v Minister of Housing and Local Government and Habib Ullah*[18] three former singly-occupied houses were let in parts to a number of occupants each paying a weekly rent. The Divisional Court pointed out there had been a change of use. The houses, which had previously been used as single family accommodation, were being used for gain by their owner letting them out as rooms. The material change of use is constituted by alteration from family/residential to commercial/residential use.

It has been argued, following *Duffy v Pilling*[19], that where a single person owns or rents a house and lives there with lodgers, generally providing meals for them but sometimes allowing them to provide for themselves, there is no change of use unless there is some physical division between the parts each person occupies. This decision is most unsatisfactory. The better view of the law is that a material change of use occurs as soon as predominantly single family use alters into a predominantly non-family use. Once the lodgers predominate then a change of use has taken place.

---

[16]   [1965] 2 QB 486, [1965] 1 All ER 137.
[17]   [1957] AC 65, [1956] 2 All ER 176.
[18]   [1964]1 QB 178, [1963] 3 All ER 668.
[19]   (1977) 33 P & CR 85.

In *Lipson v Secretary of State for the Environment*[20] a change of use of premises from self-contained flats to individual bed-sitters was found to be a material change of use. The test is to ask a simple question of fact in each case: 'who has control over the property?' If control is in the hands of one person who has a small number of others living with him/her there is no material change of use, but if effective control has been 'parcelled out' amongst individuals, the best evidence of which is physical partitioning of the premises, then multi-occupancy will have arisen and a material change of use. See also *Panayi v Secretary of State for the Environment*[21], where use of four self-contained flats as a hostel to house homeless families was held to constitute a material change of use.

Central guidance points out that housing and planning policies on HMOs should complement each other. But there can be conflicts between housing and planning functions in an authority – particularly where one department wishes to improve a property which another wishes to eradicate. Use of corporate strategy should help to minimise conflict, while placing policies on HMOs in development plans is another way of ensuring harmonious relationships.

It is questionable how far an authority may go in using planning powers to prevent the spread of undesirable multi-occupation. An outright policy of always refusing any application for planning permission to convert premises to multi-occupation would be an illegal fetter on discretion. Nor would it appear generally proper for an authority to take into account the character of the person applying for planning permission. Past housing misdeeds are matters relevant to other areas of law and do not raise planning issues as such. Neither could an authority impose restrictive conditions designed to regulate future behaviour on a grant of permission; the whole thrust of the cases is that planning conditions must always relate fairly to physical development, and not subsequent use by developers of powers of letting and management.

On the basis of ministerial decisions on planning appeals the proper factors to be taken into account by planning authority in deciding applications to convert houses to multiple use include: density of housing; possibility of overcrowding; amenities of the neighbourhood; any locally prevailing shortage of accommodation; suitability of premises for conversion; architectural considerations and, occasionally, problems that might arise from an increase in numbers of cars that incoming residents might wish to park. All these are proper land use considerations.

The HMO Management Guide issued by the former Department of the Environment in 1992 and the same Department's Planning Circular 12/93 reminded authorities that, under s 171B of the Town and Country Planning Act 1990, any unauthorised change of use to multiple occupation acquires immunity from planning enforcement action, and becomes a lawful use of land, once 10 years have elapsed from the time the change was made. They also pointed out that enforcement action does not have to be taken, and where planning considerations indicate that no action would be appropriate then an unauthorised change of use may be allowed to continue, though permission may be retrospectively granted and subject to conditions. Where,

---

[20]  (1976) 33 P & CR 95.
[21]  [1985] JPL 783.

however, it is desired to take enforcement action a number of considerations should be borne in mind before it is taken, eg effects on residents and on any housing action that has been, or may be, taken to improve the state of the property.

One issue worthy of special mention is whether taking housing action may undermine subsequent planning action. The 1992 Guide made it clear that safeguarding the occupants of HMOs is the first and most important consideration. Where dangerous housing conditions exist they should not be left unremedied simply because planning enforcement action is pending. Where the situation is not one of danger, it should be remembered the Housing and Planning Acts are separate codes. Use of one does not preclude use of the other provided what is required is reasonable, and provided one is not used as a covert way of achieving the objects of the other. In practical terms this means where an unauthorised HMO is discovered and planning enforcement is a possibility, housing action should be limited to requiring what is reasonable in the circumstances, bearing in mind the overriding duty to protect health and safety, and the need to minimise wasteful expenditure.

Clearly, new guidance, at the very least, will be needed for planning authorities under the new HMO legislation.

## MULTI-OCCUPATION AND THE POWERS OF FIRE AUTHORITIES

Section 10(1) of the Fire Precautions Act 1971 (as substituted) applies, inter alia, to any premises which are being, or are proposed to be, put to use to provide sleeping accommodation other than single private dwellings. With regard to such premises where the fire authority consider use of the premises involves, or will involve, a risk to persons so serious that their use ought to be restricted or prohibited, they may serve on the occupier a prohibition notice stating and specifying the issues, and giving directions as to the use of the premises until remedial measures are taken. In the case of imminent risk of serious personal injury a prohibition may take immediate effect. It is an offence under s 10B of the 1971 Act to contravene a prohibition notice, though s 10A allows an appeal to the magistrates' court within 21 days of service of the notice. The court may cancel, affirm or modify the notice. This statutory mode of appeal, it appears, is a preclusive mode of challenge, even where it is alleged the premises do not fall within the fire authority's jurisdiction, see *R v Chesterfield Justices, ex p Kovacs*[22].

The powers of fire authorities with regard to multi-occupied premises are extensive. It should be a matter of good practice for housing and fire authorities to work together in an integrated and coordinated way to ensure premises are not made subject to conflicting sets of requirements. Over-zealous use of fire control powers may result in premises being closed and their occupants, only some of whom may qualify as 'homeless', displaced to the streets. Much depends upon the attitude of individual fire prevention officers and the nature and quality of relationships between authorities and their officers.

---

[22] [1992] 2 All ER 325.

For landlords' duties in respect of gas appliances see the Gas Safety (Installation and Use) Regulations 1998 SI 1998/2451. Note also that a landlord who fails to maintain gas appliances as a result of his gross negligence may additionally run the risk of a conviction for manslaughter should a tenant die of carbon monoxide poisoning.[23]

## FURTHER READING

Blake, J, 'Safe as Houses?' *Roof* January/February 1995, pp 34–35.

Department of the Environment, *The HMO Management Guide* DoE (1992).

Department of the Environment, Transport and the Regions, *English House Condition Survey 1996: Houses in Multiple Occupation in the Private Rented Sector* (1999) HMSO.

Department of the Environment, Transport and the Regions, *Fire Risk in Houses in Multiple Occupation: Research Report* (1998) HMSO.

Grosskurth, A, 'Lives on the line' *Roof* November/December 1984, pp 11–14.

Kirby, K, and Sopp, L, *Houses in Multiple Occupation in England and Wales* (1986) HMSO.

National Consumer Council, *Deathtrap Housing* (1991) NCC.

Randall, G, Brown, S and Pipe, J, *Houses in Multiple Occupation, Policy and Practice in the 1990s* (1993) The Campaign for Bed Sit Rights.

Thomas, A D and Hedges, A, *The 1985 Physical and Social Survey of Houses in Multiple Occupation in England and Wales* (1986) HMSO.

---

[23] *R v Singh (Gurpal)* [1999] Crim LR 582, CA.

# CHAPTER 14

# Housing and Human Rights

## HOW DID WE GET HERE?

At the end of the Second World War Europe lay in ruins, and the world had a legacy of atrocities committed on behalf of states and their interests. In particular this affected territories that had been occupied by the Nazis, but we should remember that the Nazis were not the only people to commit atrocities. Against this backdrop of oppression and contempt for human dignity there arose a general determination to give human rights a greater degree of importance and legal protection. Thus in 1948 the UN adopted the Universal Declaration of Human Rights – much wider than the European Convention – but only morally binding. Some might argue rightly so, as it could never be legally binding for it is utopian in its aspirations: eg 'Everyone has the right to rest and leisure, including reasonable limitation of working hours and periodic holidays with pay' – many a case could be brought over that if it were to be law!

In 1949 the Council of Europe was established, and this drew up the European Convention on Human Rights in 1950. This was largely drafted by UK lawyers, an important point to remember for it has implications for the form and content of the rights it enshrines. This is particularly apparent in the balancing exercise that has to be carried out in determining whether an infringement of a Convention Right has taken place, in many, though not all, cases.

The Convention came into effect in 1953, and has since been amended by what are called 'protocols', though not all the states that are parties to the Convention have ratified all of the protocols.

The UK was a signatory state, but did not incorporate the Convention into UK law. This had a number of consequences:

- the Convention was not a source of legal rights for UK citizens;
- our judges would try to find a meaning for UK Acts of Parliament which was consistent with the Convention wherever possible, as the UK was under an international obligation to conform with the Convention by virtue of having signed up to it;
- in cases where there was a clear and inescapable conflict between the Convention and UK law, our courts had to apply UK law;

- anyone wishing to challenge the UK government on a Human Rights issue had to go to Strasbourg to do so. If the point of law there was decided against the UK, our government would, as a matter of practice, amend UK domestic law to come into line with the declarations of the European Court of Human Rights (ECtHR) (situated at Strasbourg and *not* to be confused with the European Court of Justice (ECJ), which is in Luxembourg and which deals with EC law).

## WHAT DOES THE CONVENTION SAY?

The Convention is quite a short document, but it contains a number of different kinds of rights. Some are absolute, ie, they cannot be modified by a signatory state – in lawyer's language there can be 'no derogation' from them. Some are qualified, ie there can be exceptions. Thus according to Art 2, 'Everyone's right to life shall be protected by law'; however, under the Convention itself (as opposed to subsequent protocols) the death penalty was allowed, so this right is not absolute, and there is no breach of Art 2 where someone is killed as a result of the 'use of force which is no more than absolutely necessary', in the following situations:

- defending a person against unlawful violence (eg, self-defence);
- during the course of a lawful arrest, or in preventing the escape of a lawfully detained person;
- during the course of lawful action taken to put down a riot.

It also has to be remembered that the ECtHR interpreted and applied the Convention in certain ways which were sympathetic to the interests of states. This gave rise to the following notion.

## 'MARGIN OF APPRECIATION' OR DEFERENCE TO A DEMOCRATIC LEGISLATURE?

Because some of the rights in the Convention are not absolute – a number allow for departures from rights where this is 'necessary in a democratic society', for example on the basis of national security, public safety, protection of public order, health, morality, or the protection of the rights and freedoms of other people – the ECtHR developed the idea that states should have a degree of discretion – some freedom of manoeuvre – in complying with and applying the Convention. Thus arose 'the margin of appreciation'. The ECtHR accepted that state authorities were in day-to-day contact with events in their own countries and were thus equipped to decide on issues of morality within these countries, and so could be allowed some freedom of action. However, this has never given states total freedom of action – rather they have limits within which they, and subordinate public bodies such as local authorities, must act. The exact limits of the 'margin of appreciation' have also been decided on a case-by-case basis, and the prime obligation remains on the state to ensure that Convention rights are applied and protected. Nothing must take place under the margin of appreciation which goes beyond what can be demonstrated to be strictly required.

Strictly speaking, the notion of the margin of appreciation relates properly to the supervisory role of the ECtHR with regard to its task of overseeing the performance of signatory states' obligations. Alongside it lies a further notion that courts in general have to observe a degree of deference to the wishes of a democratically elected legislature when it comes to the interpretation and application of the provisions of the Convention.

There is already good evidence to suggest that our own courts have adopted and will apply the 'deference' notion where Parliament has addressed a pressing social problem by means of legislation. The courts may be inclined to find that where a balance has to be struck between the rights of an individual and those of the wider community, it is not improper to decide the issue in favour of restricting individual rights, as a democratically elected legislature has passed the legislation. Thus in *Sheffield City Council v Emma Smart; Central Southerland Housing Co Ltd v Janet Wilson*[1], Laws LJ accepted that our Parliament could enact legal provisions, indeed entire legislative schemes, which would run contrary to the Convention, and if that were to happen UK courts would have to make declarations of incompatibility, though (see further below) they could do no more than that. He accepted further, however, that such situations would be very rare, but went on to state:

> 'distribution of Convention rights goes hand in hand with deference to the democratic legislature. A democratic system of government is a premise of all the Convention's philosophy, underlined in the multiple references to what is "necessary in a democratic society", a phrase which not only invokes the claims of proportionality, but also calls for respect for the elected arm of State.'

Even so it must be remembered that in any case where an infringement of a 'Convention Right' is alleged to have occurred, any restriction on such a right has to be shown to be justifiable. Nothing less than an important competing public interest will be sufficient to justify such a restriction, though, as we shall, our courts have largely accepted, in the context of housing, that the balance which has to be struck in cases where Convention rights are engaged is provided by schemes made by the legislature with little room to argue balance issues on the facts of individual cases.

## BRINGING RIGHTS HOME

Following the White Paper 'Bringing Rights Home', the Government introduced legislation which became the Human Rights Act 1998. This now imposes positive duties on courts and public bodies to ensure that rights under the Convention are neither breached nor otherwise interfered with.

Thus it is unlawful for any public body – including any court – to act in any way incompatible with 'Convention rights'. Courts and tribunals also in effect have a power of review over both new and existing legislation – even if a point arises in a case concerning only two private parties.

---

[1]   [2002] EWCA Civ 4, [2002] HLR 639; see also *R v Lambert* [2000] 1 All ER 1014 in the context of drugs legislation. See also *Porter v South Bucks District Council* [2001] EWCA Civ 1549, [2002] 1 All ER 425 in the context of the enforcement of planning law.

These principles apply to what are called 'The Convention rights' which are to be found in Sch 1 to the 1998 Act – these are Arts 2–12 and 14 of the Convention and certain provisions which have been included in subsequent amendments or protocols to the Convention.

## THE SCHEME OF THE 1998 ACT

The task of applying the law falls to the courts – in doing this they may take into account all the existing decisions on the Convention, but they will also be free to develop further interpretations and application of the law.

So far as possible, all UK legislation (ie statutes, 'rules and regulations' etc) is to be interpreted and applied in a way that is compatible with Convention rights under s 3 of the 1998 Act.

### What if a court cannot achieve compatibility?

Under s 4 the court can only make a 'declaration of incompatibility'. Note, a court cannot declare the legislation invalid. Note also that only the High Court, Court of Appeal or House of Lords can make such a declaration, in other words magistrates' and the county and Crown Courts cannot. If the issue arises in such a court there will have to be either an appeal or a 'case stated' to get the issue into the appropriate superior court.

### Who can do anything about such an incompatibility?

Under s 10(2) it is up to Ministers to take action where there are 'compelling' reasons to act, and then they may make amendments to the incompatible legislation. The procedure for doing this is found in Sch 2 to the 1998 Act, and as a general rule the approval of Parliament is required for any remedial order made by a minister, though in 'urgent cases' Ministers may act without Parliamentary approval, in which case an explanation has to be given to Parliament, and the subsequent approval of Parliament sought.

It must be remembered, however, that Ministers may decide not to take remedial action. Furthermore, while under s 19 of the 1998 Act before new legislation is passed by Parliament the sponsors of that legislation are generally required to make declarations of the compatibility of their proposals with the Convention, provision is made for express and deliberate derogations from the Convention to be enacted by Parliament.

### Duties of Public Authorities – including Local Authorities

Unless a public authority has to act in a particular way because of the requirements of incompatible legislation, it must otherwise act in ways which are compatible with Convention rights; see s 6.

## What if such an authority breaks that rule?

'A person' may proceed against such an authority which has acted or proposes to act in an incompatible fashion, but only if he/she is or would be the victim of the unlawful act. We shall return later to the question of who are public authorities for this purpose.

## How can action be taken?

Either by initiating proceedings against the authority, or by relying on Convention rights in any other relevant legal proceedings, ie the rights can be used as a sword and as a shield.

Section 7 of the 1998 Act lays down the procedures for challenging public authorities who have acted or who propose to act unlawfully. So, for example, where a local authority takes possession proceedings the issue of Convention rights may be raised in them, or in any subsequent appeal, by way of an allegation that the authority has behaved illegally. Under s 8 a court may grant such relief or remedy as it considers just and appropriate in respect of unlawful acts. This may include an award of damages where that is necessary to afford 'just satisfaction'[2].

## WHICH CONVENTION RIGHTS ARE MOST APPLICABLE TO HOUSING?

These are Arts 8 and 6 and Art 1 of the First Protocol. They provide as follows:

Article 8
    Everyone has the right to respect for his private and family life, his home and his correspondence.

    There shall be no interference by a public authority with the exercise of this right except such as in accordance with the law and is necessary in a democratic society in the interests of national security, public safety or the economic well-being of the country, for the prevention of disorder or crime, for the protection of health or morals, or for the protection of the rights and freedoms of others.

It will be noted that this right is not absolute and that there is room for justifiable derogations.

*THE FIRST PROTOCOL*

Article 1

### Protection of Property

    Every natural or legal person is entitled to the peaceful enjoyment of his possessions. No one shall be deprived of his possessions except in the public interest and subject to the conditions provided for by the law and by the general principles of international law.

---

[2]   *Marcic v Thames Water Utilities Ltd* [2002] EWCA Civ 64, [2002] QB 929.

The preceding provisions shall not, however, in any way impair the right of a State to enforce such laws as it deems necessary to control the use of property in accordance with the general interest or to secure the payment of taxes or other contributions or penalties.

Again it will be noted that this right is not absolute.

It may be asked what the distinction between these two provisions is. In brief the answer is that Art 8 is designed to protect people from invasions of their 'home', while Art 1 of the First Protocol is designed to protect property interests to which a person is legally entitled. This important distinction has to be borne in mind and has had repercussions as a consideration of the case law below will demonstrate.

Article 6

1. In the determination of his civil rights and obligations or of any criminal charge against him, everyone is entitled to a fair and public hearing within a reasonable time by an independent and impartial tribunal established by law. Judgment shall be pronounced publicly but the press and the public may be excluded from all or part of the trial in the interest of morals, public order or national security in a democratic society, where the interests of juveniles or the protection of the private life of the parties so require, or to the extent strictly necessary in the opinion of the court in special circumstances where publicity would prejudice the interests of justice.

2. Everyone charged with a criminal offence shall be presumed innocent until proved guilty according to law.

3. Everyone charged with a *criminal offence* [emphasis supplied] has the following minimum rights:

(a) to be informed promptly, in a language which he understands and in detail, of the nature and cause of the accusation against him;

(b) to have adequate time and facilities for the preparation of his defence;

(c) to defend himself in person or through legal assistance of his own choosing or, if he has not sufficient means to pay for legal assistance, to be given it free when the interests of justice so require;

(d) to examine or have examined witnesses against him and to obtain the attendance and examination of witnesses on his behalf under the same conditions as witnesses against him;

(e) to have the free assistance of an interpreter if he cannot understand or speak the language used in court.

It will be noted that this right is highly procedural and not entirely absolute. However, it does raise important issues relating to the need for all procedures to be shown to be fair – which, of course, raises implications for the amount of information to be given to people who are made subject to, for example, possession proceedings or proceedings in respect of Anti-Social Behaviour Orders.

## ARTICLE 8

Many decisions may fall within the band of what may be controlled under Art 8, for example questions of landlord/tenant relationships, security of tenure, maintenance and repairs/rent levels, homelessness, environmental health issues/etc. However, two matters are clear:

1.   There is no general right to housing under the Convention;

2.    There is no direct Convention requirement that housing should be of a particular standard.

In *X v Germany*[3] it was held inadmissible to argue that a government had breached Art 8 by failing to provide a refugee with a home. Similarly in *Buxton v United Kingdom*[4] it was said there was no breach where the applicant, who was suffering from cancer, complained the local authority had failed to provide her with a caravan in which to live out her days according to her Romany upbringing – there is no positive obligation to provide alternative accommodation of an applicant's choosing.

In general, arguments on Art 8 will usually arise where it is the landlord seeking to take action against the tenant, but in some cases a tenant may be able to argue the landlord is in breach of a positive duty to take steps to ensure that the tenant's Art 8 rights are respected. See *Whiteside v United Kingdom*[5], where there was said to be a positive duty on the state to provide anti-harassment remedies for a woman against her former cohabitee.

## What is protected by Art 8?

The home is a place where a person lives on a settled basis, and where the everyday functions of life are carried out – thus a mere postal address cannot be a home. However, in the opinion of the ECtHR, the word will cover a property in which a person is not resident, but to which he/she intends to return and in which he/she intends to return and in which he/she has furniture, see *Gillow v United Kingdom*[6]. 'Home' can also cover mixed residential and business premises, see *Niemitz v Germany*[7]. It can cover a house which a person owns but has currently no legal right to occupy, as in *Wiggins v United Kingdom*[8] but not a property which the person has no right at all of any sort to occupy or own, or inherit, see *S v United Kingdom*[9]. However, the fact that a person is living in a unit of accommodation he/she owns despite not having planning permission for it will not prevent that unit being a 'home' as in *Buckley v United Kingdom*[10], though that may not extend to a camper van parked on a public highway![11]

## What is required by Art 8?

It is 'respect' for the 'home', and overall the ECtHR took a narrow view of this requirement. In any case we must remember the right is not an absolute one. A right to access and accommodation must not be unjustifiably interfered with, ie any interference must be:

3    (1956) 1 YB 292.
4    (1996) 22 EHRR CD 135.
5    (1994) 76 ADR 80.
6    (1986) Series A, No 109, 11 EHRR 335.
7    (1992) Series A, No 251-B, 16 EHRR 97.
8    (1978) 13 DR 40.
9    (1986) 47 DR 274, and see further below the House of Lords decision in *London Borough of Harrow v Qazi* [2003] UKHL 43, [2004] 1 AC 983.
10   (1996) 23 EHRR 101.
11   *Kanthak v Germany* (1988) 58 DR 94.

- in accordance with clear law and according to legal procedures;
- as a result of pursuit of a legitimate aim, eg to protect health and/or the rights of other people;

only such as is necessary and proportionate, ie there must be relevant and sufficient reasons for the action taken, the rights of all interested parties must have been considered and the advantages and disadvantages of the course of action considered and balanced, and there must be adequate safeguards to check or prevent any abuse of power.

The eviction of a tenant for non-payment of rent, for example, is most unlikely to result in a successful human rights challenge under Art 8, provided all due processes have been observed. But what about cases of only modest arrears, or a minor breach of a tenancy, or a case where overcrowding has occurred because a tenant has taken in a homeless relative? On the basis of the authorities surveyed later, even cases such as these would be unlikely to succeed on a human rights basis because of the position taken by our courts to the effect that the statutory scheme provides general justification for taking action, while in any case a court would have ample discretion for refuse to grant possession on the basis that granting it would not be reasonable. Indeed, that was the line taken in *Gallagher v Castle Vale Action Trust Ltd*[12]. Here the appellant had been a secure tenant of a dwelling for 15 years. A 28-day possession order had been made against her in consequence of anti-social behaviour by her daughter and that daughter's boyfriend which had resulted in nuisance to neighbours. The appellant argued in the county court that the alternatives to granting a possession order had not been considered and that there had been a breach of her rights under Art 8. The Court of Appeal held the judge had failed to consider suspending the possession order, which would have been appropriate as the actual troublemakers had moved out and there was no complaint against the appellant personally. The court stated that Art 8 added nothing to the normal requirement for reasonableness to be shown. There may be issues surrounding obtaining possession where the only evidence against the tenant is of an anonymous or hearsay variety, but such matters could, if they arose, have more relevance to Art 6; see further below.

The concept of respect for the home is somewhat nebulous, encapsulating both an absence of degrading invasions of a person's home and family life, and some obligation on the part of public authorities to facilitate persons' lifestyles, particularly where these are based on well-established ethnic customs. However, it stops short of obliging authorities to realise such a lifestyle choice for any given individual. This should be borne in mind when the UK case law on this issue is considered below.

However, 'respect', as a concept also extends to ensuring the protection of peaceful enjoyment of a home, and there are many powers available to local and other public authorities to enable them to ensure that private citizens have that peaceful enjoyment – eg under noise nuisance and other environmental health powers. In this context a possible argument on a Convention rights issue might arise.

---

[12]    [2001] EWCA Civ 944, (2001) 33 HLR 810.

What of the situation where an authority stands by and allows victimisation of one of its tenants on an estate by others? Currently our law states there is no obligation on a landlord to protect one tenant against nuisances committed by another, see *O'Leary v Islington London Borough Council*[13], *Smith v Scott*[14], *Hussain v Lancaster City Council*[15], but will that stand in future?

Commentators have raised the following as a possible breach, namely a failure to take action in respect of a tenanted house which is in poor structural condition because of damp. It is possible to envisage other situations where, arguably, a claim under Art 8 could arise. For example, where a disrepair claim by a tenant is confined to the small claims track in the county court and legal aid is not available – would the inability to pursue that claim amount to a breach of Art 8? Similarly the rule that there is no liability in negligence on a landlord simply by virtue of the fact of being a landlord for a defect in a dwelling existing at the start of a tenancy may breach Art 8.

## ARTICLE 1 OF THE FIRST PROTOCOL

Housing issues may arise under Art 1 of the First Protocol. This has three limbs: the entitlement to peaceful enjoyments of one's possessions; restrictions on deprivation of possessions; and the reservation of a power to authorities to control the use of property by individuals.

'Possessions' includes all forms of legal interest in land and even mere contractual rights of occupation – *Mellacher v Austria*[16] and *AB and Company AS v Germany*[17].

A breach of this right can occur where the state deprives a person of rights of occupation, or reduces those rights with regard to other persons. Clearly there is an overlap between Art 8 and Art 1 of the First Protocol, and the ECtHR has reconciled them by arguing that in determining whether a deprivation is justified in the public interest a similar approach must be taken to that adopted in determining questions of justification under Art 8 – ie a fair balance has to be pursued between the rights of the individual and the rights of the community as a whole.

### A possible argument

What about the practice, found in some local authorities, of changing the locks in houses apparently abandoned by tenants? It can already amount to an illegal eviction in English law, see *Akinbolu v Hackney London Borough Council*[18], but this would also appear to be a breach of Art 1 First Protocol.

---

13 (1983) 9 HLR 81.
14 [1973] Ch 314.
15 [2000] QB 1.
16 (1989) 12 EHRR 391.
17 (1978) 14 DR 146.
18 (1996) 29 HLR 259.

## ARTICLE 6 – THE PROCEDURAL RIGHTS

1. In the determination of his civil rights and obligations or of any criminal charge against him, everyone is entitled to a fair and public hearing within a reasonable time by an independent and impartial tribunal established by law.

Article 6 protects commercial as well as private interests while the concept of 'civil rights and obligations' is wide enough to extend to matters such as planning control, compulsory purchase and licensing; see further below.

There is a three-fold test as to the application of Art 6:
- 'civil rights and obligations' must be shown to be at issue;
- there must be a dispute which is genuine and justiciable; and
- the proceedings under attack must be determinative of the rights at issue.

However, a further issue then arises, namely what is a 'civil right or obligation'?
- Rights of property, including tenancies, are.
- Refusals of planning permission are as they affect rights of property.
- Compulsory purchase orders are.

However, the dispute in question must be serious and genuine. Furthermore Art 6 grants only procedural rights, it does not guarantee any particular content of any given right. Even so what is required under Art 6 will be:
- a right of access to a court;
- a fair hearing procedure;
- a right to a public hearing and a judgment;
- a right to a prompt adjudication;
- a right to an impartial and independent tribunal established by law.

## ARTICLE 14 – DISCRIMINATION

We should also note the foregoing because, as will be discussed below, it has been raised in housing cases.

The enjoyment of the rights and freedoms set forth in the Convention shall be secured without discrimination on any ground such as sex, colour, language, religion, political or other opinion, national or social origin, association with a national minority, property, birth or other status.

This, it should be noted, does not outlaw all forms of discrimination, rather it applies only where another Convention right is engaged.

## THE IMPLICATIONS OF THE 1998 ACT FOR HOUSING

Commentators raised various issues as possible implications for the Law of Housing once the 1998 Act was passed.
- Decisions on homelessness applications are subject to internal review and appeal to the county court, and were thought to be generally not open to challenges – but questions could arise about any decision not open to review, for example decisions about taking care of a homeless person's possessions.

- Decisions on the suitability of property offered to homeless persons: disputes here are subject to internal review procedures which UK courts traditionally regard as not being matters of 'private rights'. This issue has, however, been largely dealt with by changes to the law relating to challenges on the issue of 'suitability' made under the Homelessness Act 2002.

- Introductory tenancy reviews are similarly internal and do concern property rights, and the county court has only a limited jurisdiction on appeal. Judicial review is available of an authority's decision to end an introductory tenancy so it again seems the procedural requirements of Art 6 are satisfied.

## How did the law initially develop?

The principal decision on the impact of Art 6 has been *R v Secretary of State for the Environment, Transport and the Regions, ex p Holding and Barnes plc* (the popularly named '*Alconbury*' case)[19], which arose in the context of planning law. The House of Lords stressed that where an administrative body, such as a local authority, makes a decision the requirements of Art 6 are met if that body is subject to control by a judicial body that has full jurisdiction which meets the requirements of the Article.

Lord Hoffmann in particular argued that while all administrative decisions should be subject to some form of judicial review, the extent of that review may be limited. Where a case involves a decision made in relation to applying public policy in a particular context, the law's requirements are met if judicial review is generally available on the issue of the legality of the decision, though not on its merits. A similar line of argument has been followed in subsequent cases. In *R (on the application of Kathro) v Rhondda Cynon Taff County Borough Council*[20], another planning case, Richards J considered that the existence of the supervisory jurisdiction of the court, ie the jurisdiction to determine whether a decision has been taken legally, is sufficient to ensure that administrative decisions do not automatically fall foul of Art 6. However, it then has to be asked on a case-by-case basis whether that jurisdiction is sufficient to prevent an actual breach. The test to apply is whether the decision-making procedure must inevitably lead to a breach of Convention rights. It is for those who oppose the decision to prove this, and they thus face a tough uphill struggle. A similar decision was reached by Forbes J in *R (on the application of Friends Provident Life and Pensions Ltd) v Secretary of State for Transport, Local Government and the Regions*[21].

In the context of housing a similar decision was reached, once again by Richards J, in *R v Harlow District Council, ex p Bono*[22]. This arose out of a dispute over Housing Benefit. Before July 2001 the appeal mechanism in such cases was to an internal panel of members of the decision-making authority. Since July 2001 appeals have gone to an independent tribunal which satisfies the requirements of Art 6, but what of the former procedure? On the question of the actual legality of

19   [2001] UKHL 23, [2001] 2 All ER 929.
20   [2001] EWHC Admin 527, [2001] All ER (D) 130 (Jul).
21   [2001] EWHC Admin 820, [2002] 1 WLR 1450.
22   [2002] EWHC 423 (Admin), [2002] 1 WLR 2475.

the decision in the case Richards J found that the internal review board had failed to exercise its statutory discretion and thus judicial review was available to quash the decision. That in the present case was enough to satisfy the demands of Art 6.

However, it is arguable that judicial review may not satisfy Art 6 requirements where what was in contention between parties is a disputed question of primary fact, for judicial review is not available in such circumstances[23]. In this context certain statements made by the Court of Appeal in *Adan v Newham London Borough Council* are of interest[24]. The issue here arose in connection with a request for a review of a homelessness decision. It was accepted by all the parties that any internal review procedure would not satisfy the requirements of Art 6. However, as there is a further right of appeal to the county court following an authority's internal review does that satisfy Art 6? Once again it was common ground between the parties 'that the county court's powers on an appeal ... are akin to those of judicial review exercisable in the High Court'. In most cases this will be sufficient to satisfy Art 6 as the majority of appeals to the county court relate to questions of law and the Court of Appeal concluded:

> 'the appellate jurisdiction of the county court on points of law will usually be sufficient to ensure that the proceedings, taken as a whole, are Article 6 compliant ... It is only where housing officers have to resolve a dispute of fact which is material to the decision, and the appeal against their finding cannot properly be categorised as an appeal on a point of law, however elastic that expression may be taken to be, that difficulties are likely to arise over ECtHR compliance.'

The Court of Appeal cited as an instance of such a dispute of fact the question of why a homeless applicant left his/her last home.

Brooke LJ, with whom David Steel J agreed, argued that where such a dispute arises authorities should utilise their powers under Art 3 of the Local Authorities (Contracting Out of Allocation of Housing and Homelessness Functions) Order SI 1996/3205, to utilise the services of an independent third party.

> 'It follows that if a case arises on a ... review where there is a dispute about the primary facts of a kind which has to be resolved because it is material to the decision-making process, then the danger will arise that the proceedings, taken as a whole, will not be ECtHR compliant. The reviewing officer will lack the independent status of the planning inspector in the *Alconbury* case and the county court does not have full jurisdiction to decide questions of disputed fact (except in a *Wednesbury*, or super-*Wednesbury*, sense). If such a case arises before the law is changed in order to correct the deficiencies identified in this judgment, then it appears to me that the local authority will have to exercise its contracting-out powers so as to ensure that any such dispute is determined by a tribunal with the appropriate attributes of independence and impartiality.

---

[23]  *R (Bewry) v Norwich City Council* [2001] EWHC Admin 657.
[24]  [2001] EWCA Civ 1916, [2002] 1 All ER 931.

It was suggested in argument that this escape route would not be open because s 202(4) of the Act prescribes that on a review "the authority or authorities concerned shall review their decision", so that the review power would still be being exercised, even if it was contracted out, by an authority which lacked independence and impartiality. I do not consider that this argument is soundly based. Article 3 of the Local Authorities (Contracting Out of Allocation of Housing and Homelessness Functions) Order 1996 above) makes it clear that the performance of the authority's function (in this case the function of reviewing the earlier decision) is transferred to the third party to whom the function has been contracted out. It would be inappropriate in this judgment to discuss on a hypothetical basis any of the practical difficulties that may arise when trying to ensure that the third party has the requisite independence.'

The views of the Court in *Adan* were, however, only *obiter dicta* and thus did not constitute a binding precedent and hence did not have to be followed in the Court of Appeal in *Runa Begum v London Borough of Tower Hamlets*[25] and certainly not by the House of Lords, where, in any case, they were strongly doubted by Lord Bingham when the case reached that level. The case concerned an internal review of a decision on the suitability of a property offered to a homeless person. This had been rejected on the basis, inter alia, that it lay in a 'drug addicted' area which was also 'racist'. The review concluded these allegations could not be substantiated.

Three issues had to be determined:
- Was the internal review a determination of 'civil rights' within Art 6?
- Was the internal review an 'independent tribunal'?
- Did the county court have 'full jurisdiction' to provide compliance with Art 6?

So far as the second question was concerned, a summary answer could be given. An internal reviewer is not an independent tribunal, no matter how conscientious or competent they are. That led the House of Lords to concentrate on the first and third issues.

The principal judgment was given by Lord Hoffmann, but it is important to note points made by other members of the House of Lords.

Lord Bingham dealt at some length with the question whether the applicant's 'civil rights' were engaged for the purposes of Art 6. He stated:

'The importance of this case is that it exposes, more clearly than any earlier case has done, the interrelation between the Art 6(1) concept of "civil rights" on the one hand and the Art 6(1) requirement of "an independent and impartial tribunal" on the other. The narrower the interpretation given to "civil rights", the greater the need to insist on review by a judicial tribunal exercising full powers. Conversely, the more elastic the interpretation given to "civil rights", the more flexible must be the approach to the requirement of independent and impartial review if the emasculation (by over-judicialisation)

25 [2002] EWCA Civ 239, [2002] 2 All ER 668, [2002] 1 WLR 249, [2002] HLR 29; affd [2003] UKHL 5, [2003] 2 AC 430. For further comment see 'Does Homelessness Decision-making Engage Article 6(1) of the European Convention on Human Rights?', Loveland, I, [2003] EHRLR 176.

of administrative welfare schemes is to be avoided. Once it is accepted that "full jurisdiction" means "full jurisdiction to deal with the case as the nature of the decision requires" (per Lord Hoffmann, *R (Alconbury Developments Ltd) v Secretary of State for the Environment, Transport and the Regions* [2001] 2 WLR 1389 at 1416, [2001] UKHL 23, paragraph 97), it must also be accepted that the decisions whether a right recognised in domestic law is also a "civil right" and whether the procedure provided to determine that right meets the requirements of Art 6 are very closely bound up with each other. It is not entirely easy, in a case such as the present, to apply clear rules derived from the Strasbourg case law since, in a way that any common lawyer would recognise and respect, the case law has developed and evolved as new cases have fallen for decision, testing the bounds set by those already decided.'

Without deciding the issue Lord Bingham assumed that the applicant's rights under the homelessness legislation constituted a 'civil right'. He then turned to the question of whether the jurisdiction of the county court on appeals following a homelessness review is sufficient to meet the requirements of Art 6, bearing in mind that, contrary to what was said in the Court of Appeal by Laws LJ in the instant case, a county court judge is not required to carry out a closer or more rigorous examination of the issues than that which a careful and competent judge would carry out on an application for judicial review.

In reaching a decision on this issue, Lord Bingham was clearly swayed by the argument that homelessness decisions are rarely simple factual matters, rather they involve the application of judgment. On considering the decisions of the Strasbourg court, Lord Bingham concluded:

'they provide compelling support for the conclusion that, in a context such as this, the absence of a full-fact finding jurisdiction in the tribunal to which appeal lies from an administrative decision-making body does not disqualify that tribunal for the purposes of Art 6(1).'

Lord Millett was rather more satisfied that Art 6 was engaged in the present instant case.

'Article 6(1) was originally intended to have a more limited application than a common lawyer would suppose. It is confined to the determination of civil rights and criminal charges, and in civilian systems these do not cover the whole field. There are three systems of justice in Europe, civil, criminal, and administrative, the last-named covering all actions against the state … Art 6(1) was intended to be supplemented by further measures in relation to the making of administrative decisions. These would, no doubt, have included guarantees of fairness, impartiality and a hearing within a reasonable time; but any requirement that the hearing should be in public before an independent tribunal would have serious consequences for efficient administration …

No such measures have been introduced, and in their absence the Strasbourg court has found it necessary to extend the scope of Art 6(1) to cover some, but not all, administrative decisions. The process has been a gradual one, and may not yet be complete. Underlying the process there must, I think, have been a desire not to restrict the guarantees of a fair hearing within a reasonable time by an impartial tribunal. But the Strasbourg court has not proceeded by reference to principle or on policy grounds; instead it has adopted an incremental and to English eyes disappointingly formalistic approach, making it difficult to know where the line will finally come to be drawn.'

Having considered the relevant decisions of the Strasbourg court, Lord Millett concluded that they were not on 'all fours' with the instant case:

'The present case ... has four features which take it beyond the existing case law:
  (i)   it is concerned with a benefit in kind;
  (ii)  it therefore involves priority between competing claimants. There is only a finite amount of housing stock, whether it belongs to the local housing authority or is bought in; and if one applicant is allowed to remain on the unintentionally homeless register it will be to the detriment of other homeless persons;
  (iii) the housing authority has a discretion as to the manner in which it will discharge its duties; and
  (iv)  ultimately the question for determination calls for an exercise of judgment: whether the applicant has behaved reasonably in refusing an offer of accommodation, having regard to all the circumstances, and in particular housing conditions in the area ...

It is not difficult to conclude that the nature of the dispute in her case makes it inappropriate for determination by the ordinary judicial process. But it is more difficult, at least in principle, to justify withdrawing it from the protection of Art 6(1). Most European States possess limited judicial control of administrative decisions; and if such decisions are outside the scope of Art 6(1) then judicial control could be dispensed with altogether. The individual could be left without any right to a tribunal which was impartial or to a hearing within a reasonable time. This would be incompatible with the fundamental human right which Art 6(1) was designed to secure.'

However, having said this, Lord Millett then went on to agree with Lord Bingham and Lord Hoffmann that the decision should proceed only on the assumption that the applicant's case involved a determination of her civil rights within the meaning of Art 6.

Lord Walker of Gestingthorpe came closest of all their Lordships to expressing a concluded view on this issue, but even he did not make a definite statement on the issue, simply stating:

'If the local housing authority's duty does create a civil right within the autonomous Convention meaning, it must in my view lie close to the boundary of that aggregation of rights.'

This brings us to principal decision, that of Lord Hoffmann. On his way to reaching a view on the issue he too appeared to doubt the accuracy of the decision of the majority of the Court of Appeal in *Adan* as to the contracting out of decisions on purely factual issues in homelessness reviews. He turned first, however, to the notion of 'civil rights and obligations' for the purposes of Art 6, a concept which is said to be 'autonomous'. He pointed out that the Strasbourg court:

'has been concerned to ensure that state parties do not exploit the gap left in Art 6 by changing their law so as to convert a question which would ordinarily be regarded as appropriate for civil adjudication into an administrative decision outside the reach of the Art. It has done this by treating "civil rights and obligations" as an autonomous concept, not dependent upon the domestic law classification of the right or obligation, which a citizen should have access to a court to determine. Otherwise, as the court said in *Golder v United Kingdom* (1975) 1 EHRR 524, 536, para 35:

"A Contracting State could, without acting in breach of [Art 6], do away with its courts, or take away their jurisdiction to determine certain classes of civil actions and entrust it to organs dependent on the Government. Such assumptions, indissociable from a danger of arbitrary power, would have serious consequences which are repugnant to [the rule of law] and which the Court cannot overlook."

The second development has been the doctrine, starting with *Ringeisen v Austria* (1971) 1 EHRR 455, by which the Strasbourg court has extended Art 6 to cover a wide range of administrative decision-making on the ground that the decision determines or decisively affects rights or obligations in private law. I traced some of the history of this doctrine in my speech in *Alconbury*, at pp 1413–1416, paras 77–88, and need not cover the same ground. More recently the scope of Art 6 has also been extended to public law rights, such as entitlement to social security or welfare benefits under publicly funded statutory schemes, on the ground that they closely resemble rights in private law: *Salesi v Italy* (1993) 26 EHRR 187.'

Lord Hoffmann then stressed that these developments do not result in Art 6 affording a right to full appeal on the merits of every administrative decision affecting private rights.

'The Strasbourg court has said, first, that an administrative decision within the extended scope of Art 6 is a determination of civil rights and obligations and therefore prima facie has to be made by an independent tribunal. But, secondly, if the administrator is not independent (as will virtually by definition be the case) it is permissible to consider whether the composite procedure of administrative decision together with a right of appeal to a court is sufficient. Thirdly, it will be sufficient if the appellate (or reviewing) court has "full jurisdiction" over the administrative decision. And fourthly, as established in the landmark case of *Bryan v United Kingdom* (1995) 21 EHRR 342, "full jurisdiction" does not necessarily mean jurisdiction to re-examine the merits of the case but, as I said in *Alconbury*, at p 1416, para 87, "jurisdiction to deal with the case as the nature of the decision requires ..."

In this way the first and third issues [in this case] are connected with each other. An English lawyer can view with equanimity the extension of the scope of Art 6 because the English conception of the rule of law requires the legality of virtually all governmental decisions affecting the individual to be subject to the scrutiny of the ordinary courts. As Laws LJ pointed out in the Court of Appeal [2002] 1 WLR, 2491, 2500, para 14, all that matters is that the applicant should have a sufficient interest. But this breadth of scope is accompanied by an approach to the grounds of review which requires that regard be had to democratic accountability, efficient administration and the sovereignty of Parliament. As will appear, I think that the Strasbourg jurisprudence gives adequate recognition to all three of these factors.'

Lord Hoffmann then proceeded to deal with the third issue, ie did the county court have 'full jurisdiction' to provide compliance with Art 6? He drew a distinction between differing types of fact finding exercise. Where a question arises as to whether the criminal law has been broken, or where what are clearly private rights have to be the subject of adjudication the decision has to be entrusted to the judicial branch of government.

'But utilitarian considerations have their place when it comes to setting up, for example, schemes of regulation or social welfare. I said earlier that in determining the appropriate scope of judicial review of administrative action, regard must be had to democratic accountability, efficient administration and the sovereignty of Parliament. This case raises no question of democratic accountability. As Hale LJ said in *Adan's* case [2002] 1 WLR 2120, 2138, para 57:

"The policy decisions were taken by Parliament when it enacted the 1996 Act. Individual eligibility decisions are taken in the first instance by local housing authorities but policy questions of the availability of resources or equity between the homeless and those on the waiting list for social housing are irrelevant to individual eligibility."

On the other hand, efficient administration and the sovereignty of Parliament are very relevant. Parliament is entitled to take the view that it is not in the public interest that an excessive proportion of the funds available for a welfare scheme should be consumed in administration and legal disputes …

It therefore seems to me that it would be inappropriate to require that findings of fact for the purposes of administering the homelessness scheme in Part VII should be made by a person or body independent of the authority which has been entrusted with its administration. I certainly see nothing to recommend the recourse to contracting out which was suggested by the majority in *Adan's* case. Some of the arguments against it are well made by Hale LJ at p2144, paras 77–78 of her judgment. Four points seem to me important. First, if contracting out is not adopted across the board, it would be bound to generate disputes about whether the factual questions which had to be decided by the housing officer were sufficiently material to require contracting out. Secondly, if it were adopted in every case, it would add significantly to the cost and delay. Thirdly, it would mean that the housing officer, instead of being able to exercise his discretionary powers, such as whether he considered accommodation suitable for the applicant, on a first-hand assessment of the situation, would be bound by a written report from the independent fact finder. Fourthly, I am by no means confident that Strasbourg would regard a contracted fact finder, whose services could be dispensed with, as more independent than an established local government employee …

Although I do not think that the exercise of administrative functions requires a mechanism for independent findings of fact or a full appeal, it does need to be lawful and fair. It is at this point that the arguments which Mr Underwood urged about the impartiality of Mrs Hayes and the regulations for the conduct of reviews become relevant. To these safeguards one adds the supervisory powers of the judge on an appeal under s 204 to quash the decision for procedural impropriety or irrationality. In any case, the gap between judicial review and a full right of appeal is seldom in practice very wide. Even with a full right of appeal it is not easy for an appellate tribunal which has not itself seen the witnesses to differ from the decision-maker on questions of primary fact and more especially relevant to this case, on questions of credibility.'

Lord Hoffmann stressed that a case-by-case approach has to be taken in determining whether the jurisdiction of a court is sufficient to satisfy the requirements of Art 6 and, if it is, the degree of intensity with which the court must then approach the issue of whether a decision should be overturned. Where none of the substantive Convention rights is engaged, this is a particularly pertinent issue. The court in such a case will have to determine the intensity of review by asking what degree of intensity is most consistent with the statutory scheme of decision making in question. Lord Hoffmann appeared to argue that in homelessness cases the degree of intensity need not be great and should be restricted to traditional 'judicial' issues such as whether an authority has abused its powers or has misconstrued legislation. However, where a substantive Convention Right is involved in a case the intensity of review must inevitably reflect the need to determine whether the interference with that right is justifiable. This will involve the court in looking beyond 'traditional' judicial review issues such as 'was the decision one within the range open to a reasonable decision taker?' The particular interference in question will have to be justified, though the existence of a statutory scheme for determining rights and entitlements may well, if complied with, normally convince the court on this issue. Where no substantive Convention Right is involved and the issue is one where only Art 6 is engaged Lord Hoffmann's suggestion appears to be that the degree of intensity of review will not be great, and should be determined according to the nature of the statutory provision in question.

'All that we are concerned with in this appeal is the requirements of Art 6, which I do not think mandates a more intensive approach to judicial review of questions of fact. These nuances are well within the margin of appreciation which the Convention allows to contracting states and which, in a case like this, the courts should concede to Parliament. So I do not propose to say anything about whether a review of fact going beyond conventional principles of judicial review would be either permissible or appropriate. It seems to me sufficient to say that in the case of the normal Part VII decision, engaging no human rights other than Art 6, conventional judicial review such as the Strasbourg court considered in the *Bryan* case (1995) 21 EHRR 342 is sufficient …

In this case the subject matter of the decision was the suitability of accommodation for occupation by Runa Begum; the kind of decision which the Strasbourg court has on several occasions called a "classic exercise of an administrative discretion". The manner in which the decision was arrived at was by the review process, at a senior level in the authority's administration and subject to rules designed to promote fair decision-making. The content of the dispute is that the authority made its decision on the basis of findings of fact which Runa Begum says were mistaken.

In my opinion the Strasbourg court has accepted, on the basis of general state practice and for the reasons of good administration which I have discussed, that in such cases a limited right of review on questions of fact is sufficient.

For these reasons I agree with the Court of Appeal that the right of appeal to the court was sufficient to satisfy Art 6. I should however say that I do not agree with the view of Laws LJ that the test for whether it is necessary to have an independent fact finder depends upon the extent to which the administrative scheme is likely to involve the resolution of disputes of fact. I think that a spectrum of the relative degree of factual and discretionary content is too uncertain. I rather think that Laws LJ himself, nine months later, in *R (Beeson's Personal Representatives) v Secretary of State for Health* [2002] EWCA Civ 1812 (unreported) 18 December 2002, had come to the same conclusion. He said, at para 15:

> "There is some danger, we think, of undermining the imperative of legal certainty by excessive debates over how many angels can stand on the head of the Art 6 pin."

Amen to that, I say. In my opinion the question is whether, consistently with the rule of law and constitutional propriety, the relevant decision-making powers may be entrusted to administrators. If so, it does not matter that there are many or few occasions on which they need to make findings of fact. The schemes for the provision of accommodation under Part III of the National Assistance Act 1948, considered in *Beeson's case;* for introductory tenancies under Part V of the Housing Act 1996, considered in *R (McLellan) v Bracknell Forest Borough Council* [2002] 2 WLR 1448; and for granting planning permission, considered in *R (Adlard) v Secretary of State for the Environment, Transport and the Regions* [2002] 1 WLR 2515 all fall within recognised categories of administrative decision-making. Finally, I entirely endorse what Laws LJ said in *Beeson's* case, at paras 21–23, about the courts being slow to conclude that Parliament has produced an administrative scheme which does not comply with constitutional principles.'

Having come to this particular conclusion on the third issue Lord Hoffmann stated it was strictly unnecessary for him to consider whether the applicant's case did involve an issue of 'civil rights'. He was, however, clearly unwilling to conclude that the facts clearly fell within the 'autonomous' concept of civil rights under Art 6, largely because the 'benefits' provided under the homelessness legislation are so highly discretionary in nature. To characterise those as 'rights' seemed to Lord Hoffmann to go beyond the bounds currently allowed by the Strasbourg court. At that point, however, Lord Hoffmann left the issue open.

Thus in *Begum, Adan* was doubted, and the preferred approach was that it is the statutory scheme as a whole which has to be judged to determine whether there is compliance with Art 6. For the moment we appear to be moving in the direction of saying that where there is a dispute of fact, the interpretation put on allegations received and the response made to them by a public authority is a question of law which is open to appeal in the particular context of homelessness, thus satisfying Art 6.

The issue remains, perhaps, slightly open in the light of the decision in *R (on the application of Hetoja) v Secretary of State for the Home Department*[26]. Here the claimant was an asylum seeker who had been living with her sons in local authority accommodation. Her eldest son and his fiancée had two children and were dependent on the claimant for support and childcare. In due course responsibility for accommodating the claimant passed to the Home Office under the National Asylum Support Service (NASS). NASS offered the claimant accommodation in a hostel, along with her husband and sons, but the fiancée and her children could not be accommodated there. The eldest son and the fiancée and their children were, however, due to move into local authority accommodation some two miles away. The claimant sought judicial review arguing that the proposals would damage her family and that the Immigration and Asylum Act 1999 and regulations made under it prevented proper consideration of factors necessary to determine her case in accordance with her Convention rights. Thus she claimed a failure had taken place in respect of Art 6.

The claim here failed as Lightman J held there was no dispute over a question of fact, rather there was an allegation of an error of law over which, of course, the court had full jurisdiction, thus satisfying the requirements of Art 6. The core of the claimant's case turned on the locality and quality of the accommodation offered. In making a decision on that NASS was acting in a discretionary fashion, which is subject to judicial review, as opposed to making a determination of primary fact. That was enough to deal with the case on this point so far as Lightman J was concerned. He did not deal with the question raised in *Begum* as to whether there was a question about whether the claimant's 'civil rights' had been engaged. It is only in such a case that Art 6 applies and so if a court determines in an individual case there is no issue of civil rights then Art 6 cannot apply. It will also not apply if the matter is one in which the court concludes that even though an issue of civil rights arises the nature of the decision taken is such that there is adequate judicial oversight by way of judicial review.

The problems which arise from this line of decisions are as follows:
- The emerging notion that, with regard to the sort of administrative processes which characterises so many decisions with regard to housing, there are really no disputed questions of fact, only disputed questions of judgment, and that these are in reality questions of law for which an adequate system of oversight for the purposes of Art 6 exists either in the form of judicial review or by means of statutory appeal. This appears to be the view of Lords Bingham and Hoffmann in *Begum*.

---

[26]  [2002] EWHC 2146 (Admin).

- There could, however, surely be issues which do not neatly fit into the foregoing categorisation. Let us say a person claimed he/she had been rendered homeless as a result of statutory overcrowding, and in response to this the local authority had carried out a fact-finding exercise which was wholly incapable of determining the extent of overcrowding. Presumably, following Lords Bingham and Hoffmann, the 'wrong' there is not the disputed question of fact but the ultra vires nature of the authority's investigative procedure, and that is a question of law.

- At a more general level of criticism, however, there is the issue that both Lords Bingham and Hoffman appear to display more than a little reluctance to involve themselves in 'judicialisation' of housing disputes. It is quite true that the issues concern scarce social assets in whose allocation and management judges are not trained. It is equally arguable that we live in a society where basic issues such as entitlements to shelter, warmth and income are decided by bureaucratic processes for considerable numbers of people. These matters do not sit easily within the framework of Convention rights whose concepts, language and origins have to be traced back to the events leading up to and during the Second World War. What is particularly worrying is that the tenor of the statements made by Lords Bingham and Hoffmann is antipathetic towards attempts to try to mould the language and concepts of the Convention rights into something capable of more effective application to what one may call people's administrative and social welfare rights. There is a degree of judicial formalism at work which tends too easily to categorise issues as matters of administrative concern only, and therefore easily addressable solely within the highly procedural context of traditional judicial review.

## BODIES SUBJECT TO THE HUMAN RIGHTS ACT 1998

We saw above that the 1998 Act imposes duties on 'public authorities'. This expression would surely include local authorities when exercising their public housing functions. Section 6 of the 1998 Act applies, inter alia, to courts and tribunals, and also to 'any persons certain of whose functions are of a public nature', but in relation to any given action by such a 'person' it has to be remembered that 'a person is not a public authority … if the nature of the act is private'.

It appears that this, far from clear and exhaustive definition, gives rise to a threefold classification of 'public authorities', namely courts and tribunals, 'mainstream' or 'core' public authorities and 'hybrid' authorities who are 'public' only in respect of functions which are not of a private nature. Whilst a local housing authority will nearly always be classified as a 'mainstream' body under this classification because it is, in the broad sense of the word, 'governmental', it is less clear how a registered social landlord is to be classified; at best such bodies will be 'hybrid' and 'public' only in respect of some of their functions. As a 'core' public authority appears incapable of enjoying Convention rights, whether any given body is capable of enjoying such rights may be a pointer to its 'hybrid' status.

In *Poplar Housing & Regeneration Community Association Ltd v Donoghue*[27] the landlord was a registered social landlord which had been purposely created to take over part of the housing stock of Tower Hamlets London Borough Council under the Government's Estate Renewal Challenge Fund. The tenant had been referred to the landlord by the local authority in pursuance of homelessness functions and, in line with guidance issued by the Housing Corporation, the landlord had granted the tenant an assured shorthold tenancy only. The question of the status of the landlord arose in connection with possession proceedings brought in respect of that tenancy. Lord Woolf CJ expressed himself as follows on this issue:

> 'The importance of whether Poplar was at the material times a public body or performing public functions is this: the Human Rights Act 1998 will only apply to Poplar if it is deemed to be a public body or performing public functions. Section 6(1) of the Human Rights Act 1998 makes it unlawful for a public authority to act in a way which is incompatible with a Convention right. Section 6(3) states that a "public authority" includes "(b) any person certain of whose functions are functions of a public nature". Section 6(5) provides: "In relation to a particular act, a person is not a public authority by virtue only of subs (3)(b) if the nature of the act is private …"
>
> We agree … that the definition of who is a public authority, and what is a public function for the purposes of section 6, should be given a generous interpretation …The fact that a body performs an activity which otherwise a public body would be under a duty to perform cannot mean that such performance is necessarily a public function. A public body in order to perform its public duties can use the services of a private body. Section 6 should not be applied so that if a private body provides such services, the nature of the functions are inevitably public. If this were to be the position, then when a small hotel provides bed and breakfast accommodation as a temporary measure, at the request of a housing authority that is under a duty to provide that accommodation, the small hotel would be performing public functions and required to comply with the Human Rights Act 1998. This is not what the Human Rights Act 1998 intended. The consequence would be the same where a hospital uses a private company to carry out specialist services, such as analysing blood samples. The position under the Human Rights Act 1998 is necessarily more complex. Section 6(3) means that hybrid bodies, who have functions of a public and private nature are public authorities, but not in relation to acts which are of a private nature. The renting out of accommodation can certainly be of a private nature. The fact that through the act of renting by a private body a public authority may be fulfilling its public duty, does not automatically change into a public act what would otherwise be a private act …
>
> The purpose of s 6(3)(b) is to deal with hybrid bodies which have both public and private functions. It is not to make a body, which does not have responsibilities to the public, a public body merely because it performs acts on behalf of a public body which would constitute public functions were such

[27] [2001] EWCA Civ 595, [2001] 4 All ER 604, and see also *Aston Cantlow and Wilmcote with Billesley Parochial Church Council v Wallbanks* [2003] HRLR 28.

acts to be performed by the public body itself. An act can remain of a private nature even though it is performed because another body is under a public duty to ensure that that act is performed.

A useful illustration is provided by the decision of the European Court of Human Rights in *Costello-Roberts v United Kingdom* (1993) 19 EHRR 112. The case concerned a seven-year-old boy receiving corporal punishment from the headmaster of an independent school. The Court of Human Rights made it clear that the state cannot absolve itself of its Convention obligations by delegating the fulfilment of such obligations to private bodies or individuals, including the headmaster of an independent school. However, if a local authority, in order to fulfil its duties, sent a child to a private school, the fact that it did this would not mean that the private school was performing public functions. The school would not be a hybrid body. It would remain a private body. The local authority would, however, not escape its duties by delegating the performance to the private school. If there were a breach of the Convention, then the responsibility would be that of the local authority and not that of the school …

In coming to our conclusion as to whether Poplar is a public authority within the Human Rights Act 1998 meaning of that term, we regard it of particular importance in this case that:

(i) While s 6 of the Human Rights Act 1998 requires a generous interpretation of who is a public authority, it is clearly inspired by the approach developed by the courts in identifying the bodies and activities subject to judicial review. The emphasis on public functions reflects the approach adopted in judicial review by the courts and textbooks since the decision of the Court of Appeal (the judgment of Lloyd LJ) in *R v Panel on Take-overs and Mergers, ex p Datafin plc* [1987] QB 815.

(ii) Tower Hamlets, in transferring its housing stock to Poplar, does not transfer its primary public duties to Poplar. Poplar is no more than the means by which it seeks to perform those duties.

(iii) The act of providing accommodation to rent is not, without more, a public function for the purposes of s 6 of the Human Rights Act 1998. Furthermore, that is true irrespective of the section of society for whom the accommodation is provided.

(iv) The fact that a body is a charity or is conducted not for profit means that it is likely to be motivated in performing its activities by what it perceives to be the public interest. However, this does not point to the body being a public authority. In addition, even if such a body performs functions, that would be considered to be of a public nature if performed by a public body, nevertheless such acts may remain of a private nature for the purpose of ss 6(3)(b) and 6(5).

(v) What can make an act, which would otherwise be private, public is a feature or a combination of features which impose a public character or stamp on the act. Statutory authority for what is done can at least help to mark the act as being public; so can the extent of control over the function exercised by another body which is a public authority. The more closely the acts that could be of a private nature are enmeshed in the activities of a public body, the more likely they are to be public. However, the fact that the acts are supervised by a public regulatory body may be deemed public but the activities of the body which is regulated may be categorised private.

(vi) The closeness of the relationship which exists between Tower Hamlets and Poplar. Poplar was created by Tower Hamlets to take a transfer of local authority housing stock; five of its board members are also members of Tower Hamlets; Poplar is subject to the guidance of Tower Hamlets as to the manner in which it acts towards the defendant.

(vii) The defendant, at the time of transfer, was a sitting tenant ... and it was intended that she would be treated no better and no worse that if she remained a tenant of Tower Hamlets. While she remained a tenant, Poplar therefore stood in relation to her in very much the position previously occupied by Tower Hamlets.

While these are the most important factors in coming to our conclusion, it is desirable to step back and look at the situation as a whole. As is the position on applications for judicial review, there is no clear demarcation line which can be drawn between public and private bodies and functions. In a borderline case, such as this, the decision is very much one of fact and degree. Taking into account all the circumstances, we have come to the conclusion that while activities of housing associations need not involve the performance of public functions, in this case, in providing accommodation for the defendant and then seeking possession, the role of Poplar is so closely assimilated to that of Tower Hamlets that it was performing public and not private functions. Poplar therefore is a functional public authority, at least to that extent. We emphasise that this does not mean that all Poplar's functions are public. We do not even decide that the position would be the same if the defendant was a secure tenant. The activities of housing associations can be ambiguous. For example, their activities in raising private or public finance could be very different from those that are under consideration here. The raising of finance by Poplar could well be a private function.'

The approach adopted by the Court of Appeal in effect applies the test developed with regard to whether a body's actions are susceptible to judicial review, as the reference to the *Datafin* decision indicates. This test is itself complex and depends on a consideration of various factors, primarily whether the function in question is essentially part of a system of governmental control and public regulation. In this context the courts will also consider whether the power in question is underpinned by the state, and whether the body exercising the power is closely proximate to some other public body. The court in this case appeared more concerned with a body's type and form than with the character and impact of its acts.

However, in the *Aston Cantlow* case referred to in note 27, the House of Lords departed somewhat from what Lord Woolf had said in the *Poplar* case, and preferred the view that the division into 'core', and 'hybrid' authorities is a question to be decided by reference to the Strasbourg Court's jurisprudence. A 'non-governmental organisation' on this basis can be regarded as one established for public administration purposes if its establishment was with a view to public administration as part of the process of government. Whether any such body is such an organisation has to depend on a case-by-case analysis of its functions having regard to the Strasbourg jurisprudence. The tests applicable may therefore include whether its functioning is part of the processes of either central or local government, whether it is accountable to the public for its activities, and whether it receives public funding for its activities. In the case of an, apparently 'hybrid' body therefore there has to be first of all an assessment of the functions of the body overall to determine whether it is 'hybrid' and then an analysis of the particular function in question to determine whether that is 'public' or 'private'. the nature of the functions overall must not be confused with the issue of the particular function in question.

On this basis the body in the *Poplar* case would still have been considered at least 'hybrid' because of the nature of it functioning as, in effect, a provider of publicly funded social housing within a particular local authority area, and the accountability of the body to Parliament and public via the oversight of the Housing Corporation.

Thus in certain circumstances and situations a registered social landlord may be a public authority for the purposes of the 1998 Act when, as Lord Woolf CJ pointed out, its role is closely 'assimilated' to that of a local authority. However, this will only be in the case in certain limited circumstances as Lord Woolf CJ himself made clear in *R v Leonard Cheshire Foundation (Heather)*[28].

Here two residents of a residential home sought judicial review of a decision to close that home by the charity (LCF) which owned it. It was argued that the charity was exercising functions of a public nature within s 6 of the Human Rights Act 1998 and so was a public authority bound by that Act.

> 'In our judgment the role that LCF was performing manifestly did not involve the performance of public functions. The fact that LCF is a large and flourishing organisation does not change the nature of its activities from private to public.
>
> (i)  it is not in issue that it is possible for LCF to perform some public functions and some private functions. In this case it is contended that this was what has been happening in regard to those residents who are privately funded and those residents who are publicly funded. But in this case except for the resources needed to fund the residents of the different occupants of Le Court, there is no material distinction between the nature of the services LCF has provided for residents funded by a local authority and those provided to residents funded privately. While the degree of public funding of the activities of an otherwise private body is certainly relevant as to the nature of the functions performed, by itself it is not determinative of whether the functions are public or private …
>
> (ii)  There is no other evidence of there being a public flavour to the functions of LCF or LCF itself. LCF is not standing in the shoes of the

---

[28]  [2002] EWCA Civ 366, [2002] 2 All ER 936, though see also *Boyle v Castlemilk East Housing Cooperative Ltd* 1998 SLT 56 where a registered social landlord exercising statutory powers was held to be subject to judicial review.

local authorities. Section 26 of the [National Assistance Act] provides
statutory authority for the actions of the local authorities but it provides
LCF with no powers. LCF is not exercising statutory powers in
performing functions for the appellants.

(iii)   In truth, all that Mr Gordon can rely upon is the fact that if LCF is not
performing a public function the appellants would not be able to rely
upon Article 8 as against LCF. However, this is a circular argument. If
LCF was performing a public function, that would mean that the
appellants could rely in relation to that function on Article 8, but, if the
situation is otherwise Article 8 cannot change the appropriate classification of the function. On the approach adopted in *Donoghue*, it can be
said that LCF is clearly not performing any public function.'

(These two cases arose, it should be noted, from the need of individuals to rely on
an argument that particular bodies fall within the terms of Art 6 and so are bound to
observe its procedural requirements. Where, however, it is clear that a body or
person has infringed one of the substantive rights granted under the Convention, for
example Art 8, then the court itself is a public authority which must give effect to
that right.)

The distinctions made by the Court of Appeal seem eminently acceptable in the
context of the facts of each case. But is there not an element of somewhat ad hoc
decision-making here? Our courts have traditionally been wary of investing housing
associations with the same mantle as bodies who discharge public functions, at least
not in relation to the performance of their normal and essential functions as
landlords.[29] However, the position may be different where such a body has been
exclusively formed to take over all the housing authority stock in an area.[30]

Clearly the position of the Leonard Cheshire Foundation lay a considerable distance
from that of any such body, but in relation to such creations Lord Woolf CJ's
judgments seem to point to the need for both the purpose of taking over an
authority's stock and then a 'close assimilation' to the position of the authority in
relation to particular housing functions before 'public authority' status can be
recognised for Art 6 purposes.

But how is 'close assimilation' to be recognised? The case law hardly gives much
guidance here. Does it depend on the nature and quality of the function in question?
It would appear not. In the *Poplar Housing* case the function was accommodating
the homeless – a group who have particular needs. However, the residents in the
*Leonard Cheshire Foundation* case also had very clear needs. Is it the case that
'close assimilation' is a judicial formula designed to ensure that there is only a very
narrow range of possibilities in which a registered social landlord is made subject to
Art 6 requirements? In other words, despite its apparent blandness, it is in reality an
exclusionary and negative statement.

---

[29]   *Peabody Housing Association Ltd v Green* (1978) 38 P & CR 644 and *R v Servite Houses, ex p Goldsmith* [2001] LGR 55.
[30]   *R v West Kent Housing Association, ex p Sevenoaks District Council* (1994) 'Inside Housing' 28 October p 3.

For the future what may have to be looked for in similar cases is an assimilation of housing management functions, together with the organisation in question having the outward form of a registered social landlord as a result of the decision of the local authority to pursue a policy of divesting itself of its housing stock to such a body. In such cases the registered social landlord is likely to be seen as the *alter ego* of the local authority and its actions as those of the authority. However, could the same be said of a pre-existing registered social landlord simply appointed as an agent to discharge housing management functions on behalf of a local authority? Furthermore what is the position of a registered social landlord with regard to taking action in respect of anti-social behaviour? Section 61 of the Police Reform Act 2002 provides that such bodies are 'relevant authorities' for the purposes of applying for Anti-Social Behaviour Orders under the Crime and Disorder Act 1998. This provision came into force by virtue of The Police Reform Act 2002 (Commencement No 3) Order SI 2002/2750 on 2 December 2002. It is surely now arguable that a registered social landlord seeking such an order should be considered to be acting as a public authority. What appears inescapable is that for 'close assimilation' to exist there must be statutory authority for the action or activity in question, a considerable degree of control over the activities of the subsidiary 'private' body by another body which is 'public', and a notable degree of 'enmeshing' between the activities of the private and public bodies involved. There is also a question as to the relationship between the 'close assimilation' notion and the case by case analysis approach favoured by the House of Lords in the *Aston Cantlow* case.

It will not be enough, however, to argue in any given case that a public authority has entrusted the performance of one of its tasks to a private body thus rendering that body 'public'. Indeed the presumption is likely to be that the act in question has become 'private' unless a degree of oversight and control over the private body by the public body can be shown, together with a degree of interweaving of their functions.

The reluctance on the part of the Court of Appeal in the *Poplar* and *Leonard Cheshire* cases to develop a bolder notion of 'public authority' which, arguably, fails to take a functional, as opposed to a formal, view of what a public act is, may have consequences wherever public services are privatised. It is arguable that in such circumstances public authorities should ensure adequate protection for those utilising the services by means of contractual provisions. Where such contractual arrangements are elaborate and clearly made in contemplation of the 1998 Act it is then further arguable that the body exercising the function may be for relevant purposes a 'hybrid' public authority. This issue was at least recognised by Lord Nicholls in the *Aston Cantlow* case. He seemed to indicate that where in the interests of, inter alia, efficiency and economy functions of a governmental nature are discharged by non-governmental bodies, such as the running of prisons by commercial organisations, such bodies fall into the class of 'hybrid' organisations. The arguments of one commentator need also to be considered.

'The better response would surely be to adopt a wide function driven test of what constitutes a public authority ... based on an assumption that where a particular act is performed by a private entity on behalf of a public body which would otherwise be directly responsible for performing that act, that act should be considered a public act, and the body performing it a public authority ...'[31]

Such arguments (which are generally supported by strong academic opinion and argument) may have a better chance of prevailing over the judicial formalism which was apparent in the *Poplar* and *Begum* cases and to which allusion has already been made, given the approach taken by the House of Lords in the *Aston Cantlow* case, especially by Lord Nicholls.

## THE SUBSEQUENT APPLICATION OF THE 1998 ACT

Those who were enthusiasts for the 1998 Act might well have thought that it could, would, and indeed should, make a very considerable impact on the law of housing. If so they have been disappointed. There has been case law but in most cases existing laws and understandings have been upheld. For those who are more agnostic, which includes the present writer, this was perhaps unsurprising, and is not only attributable to judicial conservatism. The legal and political traditions of this nation see rights as the end of a process not its inception. That process is one of argument, either legal or political in court or Parliament as the case may be. At first sight, the existence of the 1998 Act may seem to indicate that certain 'inherent' rights are given which have a primary or constitutive significance. On reflection the situation is not so clear, for the wording of the Convention rights in nearly all cases implies the existence of such a process of argument. Those rights most applicable to housing issues are not absolute and are designed to accommodate flexibility and provision for the legitimate concerns of administrative bodies. Thus the courts have been less than willing to find incompatibility between existing laws and the 1998 Act.

In *R (on the application of McLellan) v Bracknell Forest Borough Council.*[32] An issue already alluded to in the context of Art 6 arose, namely review processes conducted internally. Longmore J held that the review process was not inherently unfair as the availability of judicial review was sufficient to ensure compatibility with Art 6. In addition, however, it was alleged that the Introductory Tenancy regime under the Housing Act 1996 was incompatible with Art 8 as it enables the tenants' interest to be brought to an end without due process of law (as in the case with a secure tenancy) and thus contravened the right to respect for a person's family home. This too was rejected on the basis that though there was an

---

[31]   Burton, J, 'Mind the Gap' (2002) 152 New Law Journal No 7061 p 1922, to which indebtedness is acknowledged. See also Craig, P, 'Contracting out, the Human Rights Act and the Scope of Judicial Review' (2002) 118 LQR 551–568, and Carrs-Frisk, M, 'Public Authorities: The Developing Definition' [2002] EHLR 319, MacDermott, M, 'The Elusive Nature of the 'Public Function': *Poplar Housing and Regeneration Community Association v Donoghue'* (2003) 66 MLR 113, and Oliver, D, 'The Frontiers of the State: Public Authorities and Public Functions under the Human Rights Act' [2002] Public Law 477.

[32]   (2001) 33 HLR 989, (and also *Reigate and Banstead Borough Council v Benfield, Forrest v Reigate and Banstead Borough Council* and *R (on the application of Johns) v Bracknell Forest District Council),* and see also in the context of Housing Benefit Review Boards (which have now been replaced by independent appeal bodies) *R v Harlow District Council, ex p Bono* [2002] EWHC 423 (Admin) where a mistake of law was held to be judicially reviewable and hence on the facts of the case there was compliance with Art 6.

interference with that right inherent in the legislative scheme it existed because of pressing social needs and was in no way disproportionate. The Art 6 findings in *McLellan* were subsequently applied in *R (on the application of McDonagh) v Salisbury District Council*.[33] We also have the cases already examined above in the context of Art 6, namely *Bono, Bewry* and *Adan*. In the Court of Appeal, the decision in *McLellan* was affirmed.[34]

So far as Art 6 is concerned Waller LJ made the following points:

'Is Article 6 engaged? Article 6 is concerned with the "determination of civil rights", ie with the resolution of a dispute between persons as to their civil rights. The initial decision by the council's Housing Section to serve notice of proceedings is said not to be such a determination … If that decision were simply characterised as a decision by one party to seek termination of a contract or tenancy that might no doubt be right. That was how it was characterised before Longmore J and on that basis it was so accepted by Longmore J … Indeed it is right to emphasise … that no decision by one party to terminate a contract will be a determination within the meaning of that term in Article 6.

But it also is right to emphasise that Article 6 may be engaged where the decision is of an administrative nature which affects the civil rights of individuals. Lord Clyde in Alconbury … said this:

"It is thus clear that Article 6(1) is engaged where the decision which is to be given is of an administrative character, that is to say one given in an exercise of a discretionary power, as well as a dispute in a court of law regarding the private rights of the citizen, provided that it directly affects civil rights and obligations and is of a genuine and serious nature …"

It is accepted that the review panel itself could not have the degree of independence to comply with Article 6. But it is also accepted that it is necessary to consider the decision making process as a whole in determining whether the requirements of Article 6 are met. *Albert and Le Compte v Belgium* (1983) 5 EHRR 533 … puts it this way:

"The Convention calls for at least one of the two following systems: either the jurisdictional organs themselves comply with the requirements of Article 6(1), or they do not so comply but are subject to subsequent control by a judicial body that has full jurisdiction and does provide the guarantees of Article 6(1) …"

Judicial control over the legality of a decision does not require a complete rehearing of the merits. But it seems to me that in considering whether a section of a statute is compatible or not, this court should be inclined to assume that the administrative court will at least be likely to ensure that its procedures will enable it to test the legality of a decision, and in particular whether that decision infringes the human rights of a tenant such as the

---

[33] [2001] EWHC Admin 567.
[34] [2001] EWCA Civ 1510, [2002] 1 All ER 899.

tenants in the appeals before us. Support for this view appears from paragraph 89 of Halsburys Laws Vol. 1(1) (4th ed.) reissue 2001, where it says "Where the exercise of a discretionary power is liable to interfere with fundamental human rights, the courts will examine the decision maker's actions more rigorously than where such interests are not directly affected by the action taken ..." citing Lord Hope in *R v DPP ex p Kebeline* [1999] 3 WLR 972 at 993–94.

With the above in mind I return to the relevant considerations. Are material facts likely to be an issue? That seems to me to depend on the circumstances of individual cases. In relation to rent arrears, for example, the facts can be established with certainty, and the question in issue as between the council and an individual tenant is likely to be whether in the circumstances it was reasonable for the council to proceed with terminating the introductory tenancy. That question, if it is to be reviewed by a court, seems to me to be clearly suitable for judicial review even of the traditional variety.

There may however be circumstances of a more difficult nature. If the council in providing reasons alleges acts constituting nuisance, and if the allegations themselves are disputed that at first sight seems to raise issues of fact. But under the introductory tenancy scheme it is not a requirement that the council should be satisfied that breaches of the tenancy agreement have in fact taken place. The right question under the scheme will be whether in the context of allegation and counter-allegation it was reasonable for the council to take a decision to proceed with termination of the introductory tenancy. That is again a matter which can be dealt with under judicial review either of the traditional kind or if it is necessary so to do intensified so as to ensure that the tenant's rights are protected.'

The reference by Waller LJ to 'intensification' appears to refer back to comments by Lord Slynn in the *Alconbury* decision where he pointed out that where a Convention Right is involved in a case it is not enough to ask whether an impugned decision is reasonable or not in the traditional *Wednesbury* sense. The question must be taken slightly further and the issue of whether it is proportionate also arises. In other words has more been done than is needed, or is the decision disproportionate to the object to be achieved? Waller LJ then continued:

'What about the quality of the tribunal carrying out the review and what about the important point taken by Mr Pleming that if the administrative court formed the view that the decision of a review panel ought to be quashed then its only power would be to remit the matter to the landlord? This was a point of significance in *Kingsley v United Kingdom*, November 7, 2000, ECtHR ...

It is in my view legitimate to take into account in this context that the review panel is a body chosen by Parliament. If, of course, it was simply impossible for such a tribunal to reach a fair decision, that would lead inevitably to the conclusion that the scheme could not work without infringement of Article 6. Would it be impossible for there to be a fair decision from any person who would be appointed to review matters under the introductory tenancy scheme. Would a court inevitably come to the conclusion that any officer, however senior, could not constitute a fair tribunal for hearing the matter? Is the position such that judicial review could not provide the check as to whether a decision had been reached fairly and lawfully?

One has to remember that the council are in reality making decisions which are not simply decisions as to whether it has a right to terminate. The council is not anxious to terminate unless other considerations prevail. The council is having to have regard to competing interests of other tenants and the competing interest of others who need the housing that they can supply. In my view there is no reason to think that such a decision cannot be taken fairly at a senior level of the council reviewing the decisions already reached by less senior people. Furthermore it seems to me that judicial review will be able to check the fairness and legality of decisions taken.

Thus, it is my view (i) that there is no reason to hold that the review procedure cannot be operated fairly, and (ii) that there is no reason to hold that the remedy of judicial review will not provide an adequate safeguard to tenants enabling them to challenge any unfairness and/or any infringement of their Convention rights particularly under Article 8.

Thus, as it seems to me, it cannot be said that s 127 or the scheme at the macro level is incompatible with Article 6.

What I would stress is that where a review has taken place, in a case in which the council is seeking to take possession, it should be the norm for the council to spell out in affidavits before the county court judge, how the procedure was operated in the individual case dealing with the degree of independence of the tribunal from persons who took the original decision, the way the hearing was conducted and the reason for taking the decision to continue with the proceedings. In that way the judge will have the information on which he can take an informed view as to whether the matter should be adjourned to allow for an application to be made for judicial review. In this way also s 7 of the HRA can be complied with so that the question whether it is arguable that any breach of human rights occurred can be considered at the county court stage.'

With regard to issues under Art 8 the Court of Appeal in *McLellan* had to take into account statements made by Lord Woolf CJ in the *Poplar* case. Here he considers the impact of the qualification contained in Art 8(2) on the basic right to respect for home life.

'However, in considering whether Poplar can rely on Art 8(2), the court has to pay considerable attention to the fact that Parliament intended when enacting s 21(4) of the 1988 Act to give preference to the needs of those dependent on social housing as a whole over those in the position of the defendant. The economic and other implications of any policy in this area are extremely complex and far-reaching. This is an area where, in our judgment, the courts must treat the decisions of Parliament as to what is in the public interest with particular deference. The limited role given to the court under s 21(4) is a legislative policy decision. The correctness of this decision is more appropriate for Parliament than the courts and the Human Rights Act 1998 does not require the courts to disregard the decisions of Parliament in relation to situations of this sort when deciding whether there has been a breach of the Convention.

The defendant's lack of security is due to her low priority under the legislation because she was found to be intentionally homeless. She was and must be taken to be aware that she was never more than a tenant as a temporary measure. In the case of someone in her position, even if she is a mother of young children, it is perfectly understandable that Parliament should have provided a procedure which ensured possession could be obtained expeditiously and that Poplar should have availed itself of that procedure.

Tenants in the position of the defendant have remedies other than under s 21(4) which are relevant when considering Art 8. There are provisions for appeal against the decision that a person is intentionally homeless. There is the regulatory role of the [Housing] Corporation and there is the ombudsman. There is also the fact that [Registered Social Landlords] are subject to considerable guidance as to how they use their powers.

We are satisfied that, notwithstanding its mandatory terms, s 21(4) of the 1988 Act does not conflict with the defendant's right to family life. Section 21(4) is certainly necessary in a democratic society insofar as there must be a procedure for recovering possession of property at the end of a tenancy. The question is whether the restricted power of the court is legitimate and proportionate. This is the area of policy where the court should defer to the decision of Parliament. We have come to the conclusion that there was no contravention of Art 8 or of Art 6.'

Those comments were made, of course, in the context of homelessness provision. Waller LJ, however, came to broadly similar conclusions in the context of introductory tenancies, while, of course, making due allowance for the fact that there is a particular procedure to be followed with regard to dispossession. The question of eviction in such cases has to be decided, under Art 8(1), by reference to whether it is in accordance with the law, ie whether it is supported by relevant and sufficient reasons to justify the interference, whether it is necessary for the protection of the rights and freedom of others, ie it corresponds to a pressing social need, and whether it is proportionate to the aim being pursued.

'It seems to me that a tenant under an introductory tenancy must have the right to raise the question whether it is reasonable in his or her particular case to insist on eviction, ie the question whether Article 8(2) justifies the eviction. That much has in reality to be conceded because under the relevant section reasons must be given and there is then an entitlement to review, ie an opportunity to argue, that it is not reasonable in the particular case.

The tenant must then have the right to rely on his or her Convention rights in any proceedings ...

[In] the context of the introductory tenancy scheme Parliament decided that it was necessary in the interest of tenants generally and the local authorities to have a scheme whereby during the first 12 months tenants were on probation and could be evicted without long battles in the county court. The scheme does not require the local authorities to be satisfied that breaches of the tenancy agreements have taken place, although alleged behaviour that would constitute a breach will be relevant. There is in place a review procedure and that procedure is quasi-judicial in the sense that it is required to be fair. It contains a number of important safeguards. First, the local authority has a statutory obligation to set out a full statement of reasons for terminating the introductory tenancy in the notice for possession. Second, an attempt is made to remove any bias that there may be by requiring the review to be conducted by an officer senior to the officer who took the decision to issue the notice for possession, and someone who was not involved in that previous decision. Third, the tenant has an opportunity to make representations at an oral hearing or to make written representations … Fourth, the tenant has the right to representation including legal representation … Fifth, the tenant has the right to call witnesses to give evidence … Sixth, the tenant has the right to put questions to any person who gives evidence at the hearing …

If following the review the council decide to continue with the possession proceedings, they again must give their reasons. The application for possession then comes before the county court. If there is a challenge to the reasons given and/or if the tenant asserts that the exceptions in Article 8 (2) do not apply in the particular case, and the judge thinks that arguable, the judge will adjourn to allow an application to be made for judicial review. Should the decision of the review panel be found to have been reached without proper evidential basis or upon a view of the facts which could not reasonably be entertained or on the basis of a material error of fact, then that would be a ground for a review in the High Court … In addition, if the judge thought that although the decision to evict was not in breach of Article 8 the pace of the eviction which was taking place was out of proportion and an infringement of the tenant's human rights, he could use s 89 [of the 1996 Act] and grant an extension of time, albeit for a limited period.

What then if the tenant has not sought to review the decision to seek possession under the section as in the Reigate appeal? This will be relevant but it would not deprive the county court of the power to consider whether the particular decision might arguably be a breach of the Convention. If the judge concludes that the point is arguable then he can adjourn to allow an application to be made for judicial review.

In relation to arguability the county court will in any event bear in mind that the scope of judicial review is not necessarily set in stone …

In my view therefore the introductory tenancy scheme is not as such incompatible with Article 8, and there is no reason to think that individuals' rights will be infringed without remedy from the courts.'

Similar views were expressed by the Court of Appeal in *Sheffield City Council v Smart*[35] in the context of possession proceedings of a non-secure tenancy granted in pursuance of homelessness functions under s 193 of the Housing Act 1996. The Court considered that Parliament has made a clear distinction legally between the various tenancy regimes whereby some have a degree of institutional insecurity built into them. In line with 'deference' notions referred to above our courts defer to a democratically elected legislature on such issues, and decline to find such schemes incompatible with Convention rights or generally subject to exceptions in individual cases whereby judges may inquire into the rightfulness of granting possession as opposed to its lawfulness. Laws LJ stated:

> 'In truth as it seems to me, *Donoghue* and *McLellan* march together. They offer strong support for the view that where Parliament has established in the context of a particular sector in the public housing field, a scheme for the creation and distribution of housing authorities' duties such that the authority is entitled (on certain conditions being met) to demand possession of let property from a tenant, Article 8(2) exonerates the authority from any liability under Article 8(1) arising from the tenant's eviction if it has acted fairly and reasonably in conformity with the scheme.'

*McLellan* was followed in *Merton London Borough Council v Williams*[36]. An introductory tenancy was due to start in April 2000, but the tenant did not move in and the local authority sought possession on grounds of failure to take occupation and rent arrears. The tenant requested an internal oral review but then failed to attend and the authority proceeded to gain possession. The tenant had made certain housing benefit applications and appealed arguing the authority should have given greater attention to the benefits issues, and he further argued that considerations of necessity and proportionality had been ignored, which raised matters of Convention rights.

Mance LJ pointed out that, following *McLellan* where possession proceedings commence in respect of an introductory tenancy the judge must take steps enabling the tenant to seek judicial review of the decision to seek possession if there are clear legal defects in that decision. Had there been such defects here? He argued that an authority does not have to spell out necessity and proportionality arguments in full in its statements of why it is seeking possession where there is a clear good reason otherwise – in this case the significant rent arrears, and the fact that the tenant had never moved into the dwelling. It might, however, be different if the authority had unjustifiably failed to meet a request for housing benefit. In the instant case the tenant had failed to attend the internal review hearings and so had not given the authority any chance to consider his arguments about a lack of proportionality.

There were some slight defects in the review procedure, such as the failure to deal with the tenant's arguments relating to outstanding requests for housing benefit, and the relationship between that issue and the stated reason for seeking possession based on the tenant's failure to take up occupation. So it could be argued that there

---

[35]  [2002] EWCA Civ 4, (2002) 9(2) Housing Law Monitor p1, [2002] HLR 639 and see also *Bromley London Borough Council v Smith* [2003] EWHC 1166 (QB), [2003] All ER (D) 361 (May).
[36]  [2002] EWCA Civ 980, [2003] HLR 257.

had been a failure to give full reasons for the review decision and that this should have entitled the tenant to seek judicial review. However, in the present case any ambiguity in the review reasoning process could easily be corrected at the possession order stage. Moreover, on the facts of the case it could not be said that the nature of the defect was such that the decision could have been different had the defect not been present. This case continues the restrictive line laid down in *McLellan.*

## OTHER CONSERVATIVE DECISIONS

Generally restrictive attitudes have carried across into other cognate areas of housing law. Thus for many years, since the *O'Rourke* decision, it has been established that there could be no civil action for damages in respect of a failure to perform homelessness functions[37]. However, in *R (on the application of Morris) v Newham London Borough Council*[38] the question arose whether that rule survived the enactment of the 1998 Act and Art 8. Jackson J pointed out that Mr O'Rourke had unsuccessfully taken his case to Strasbourg following the House of Lords' decision. The ECtHR pointed out that Art 8 confers no right to be provided with a home, though matters may be different where assistance is refused to an individual suffering from a serious disease because of the impact of the refusal on the life of that person[39]. Jackson J applied that reasoning and considered there is no obligation on a public authority to provide a homeless person with a home under Art 8. Similarly such a person has no right to claim damages against a local authority for failures to provide accommodation under their homelessness functions, nor, in general, does any such claim arise by virtue of Art 8 though special circumstances might give rise to a different outcome.

In *Lee v Leeds City Council, Ratcliffe v Sandwell Metropolitan Borough Council*[40], Convention rights arose in the context of housing repairs, namely the rule in *Quick v Taff Ely Borough Council*[41] that where condensation and damp problems affecting a house are attributable to a design defect as opposed to disrepair no remedy is available under s 11 of the Landlord and Tenant Act 1985. Did that rule survive the enactment of the 1998 Act? One distinction between the instant case and the foregoing ones is that secure tenancies were involved, hence the Court itself in addition to the local authority was under the 'public authority' obligation to give effect to the tenants' convention rights – if they had been infringed. As a matter of fact the Court of Appeal agreed with the finding of the trial judge in *Lee* that the problems affecting the property were not so serious as to give rise to an infringement of Art 8. This was not a case of a major environmental health hazard as in *Lopez Ostra v Spain*[42]. Chadwick LJ then asked whether on the facts of the cases before him the condition of the houses was such that the tenants' convention rights had been infringed. In answering that question, he argued, regard had to be had to

[37]  *O'Rourke v London Borough of Camden* [1998] AC 188.
[38]  [2002] EWHC 1262, (2002) 9(7) Housing Law Monitor p 1.
[39]  *Marzari v Italy* 28 EHRR CD 175.
[40]  [2002] 1 WLR 1488.
[41]  [1986] QB 809.
[42]  (1994) 20 EHRR 277.

striking a fair balance between the competing interests of the individual and the community as a whole. What constitutes giving effect to 'respect for family life' will vary from case to case, and the process must take into account the needs and resources of the community and individuals. With regard to social housing the allocation of resources for remediation work has to take place according to democratically determined priorities. In addition it was clear that there is no 'general and unqualified obligation on local authorities in relation to the condition of their housing stock' under the Convention and the 1998 Act. Chadwick LJ repeated observations of Lord Hoffmann in *Southwark London Borough Council v Tanner*[43] on 'the need 'to show a proper sensitivity to the limits of judicial creativity' in the field of social housing responsibilities, a field which is 'so very much a matter for the allocation of resources in accordance with democratically determined priorities ...'.

A similar position was reached in *P (on the application of Price) v Carmarthenshire County Council*[44]. Here the claimant was an Irish traveller who lived with her family in caravans stati..ed in an area of public open space in Llanelli. The defendant local authority owned the site. The claimant's occupation of the site arose out of a compromise which she and the authority entered into when settling proceedings taken by the authority under the Criminal Justice and Public Order Act 1994 to secure her removal from another site on which she was trespassing. It was agreed as part of the compromise that both parties would seek to identify a suitable, more permanent caravan site for the claimant and her family. In spite of endeavouring to find such accommodation the authority failed to do so. In April 2002 the claimant by her solicitors applied to the authority for accommodation pursuant to Pt VII of the Housing Act 1996. The authority accepted a duty under the 1996 Act to secure accommodation for the claimant and her family and, in July 2002, offered the claimant a three-bedroom house and gave her notice that she could no longer occupy the caravan site. The authority's decision letter stated that the claimant's desire not to live in a house did not, in the circumstances, amount to a 'cultural aversion', since her mother lived in a house and her sister had done so until recently. It also referred to the fact that she had evinced a preparedness to live in conventional housing in 2001. The claimant applied for judicial review of the authority's decision. She submitted, inter alia, that if a claimant had an aversion to accommodation in bricks and mortar then the offer of such accommodation could not amount to the offer of suitable alternative accommodation. She further contended that the authority's decision did not accord respect to her rights under Art 8 of the European Convention on Human Rights.

Newman J argued that there was no authority to support the proposition that an offer of bricks and mortar was incapable of constituting an offer of alternative accommodation. On the facts, however, the authority had erred in regarding the fact that she had evinced a preparedness to live in conventional housing in 2001 was sufficient to disregard her gypsy way of life. It was plain that there could be degrees of aversion to conventional housing. The fact that members of the family of an applicant, other than the applicant herself, had given up the traditional way of life was not a

---

[43] [2001] 1 AC 1.
[44] [2003] EWHC 42 (Admin), [2003] All ER (D) 272 (Jan) (2003) 10 (2) Housing Law Monitor p 2.

particularly strong factor, although it could be relevant. Thus, in the instant case, the authority had reached a decision without a proper evidential basis. It had thereby failed to accord respect to the claimant's rights under Art 8, and the matter should be reconsidered by the authority. Article 8 requires authorities to do more than simply taking a person's way of life into account. That way of life should be facilitated, though the obligation does not amount to a positive requirement that there will always be a guarantee that a person will be able to continue with their lifestyle unchanged.

## THE LIMITED IMPACT OF THE 1998 ACT

In some cases the courts have looked favourably on Convention rights based arguments. *London Borough of Harrow v Qazi*[45] concerned the position of a former joint secure tenant whose legal interest in his home had been brought to an end by duly given notice to quit by his estranged wife. Mr Qazi had no subsisting legal interest in the property when the local authority sought to repossess it, though he had never left the dwelling and had in fact remarried and had his new wife and her child living with him. The Court of Appeal found that it was clear from Convention jurisprudence that a 'home', for the purposes of Art 8(1), was not limited to a property that was lawfully occupied or a home that was lawfully established. Rather, 'home', is an autonomous concept that does not depend on the introduction of domestic legal concepts. Whilst, in the view of the Court of Appeal, it was clearly inherent in the definition of 'home' that an individual must be in actual residence, whether that individual has a legitimate proprietary or contractual interest in the property forms no part of the test. Whether habitation of a property by an individual means that property was an individual's home depends on the existence of sufficient and continuous links between the individual and that property. The fact that, in the instant case, the defendant had ceased lawfully to occupy the property on the termination of the tenancy did not mean that the defendant had ceased to inhabit the property as his home. The defendant's home was at the property and the Court of Appeal remitted the case back to the county court. The House of Lords, however, reversed that decision, a matter we shall return to below.

*R v Enfield London Borough Council, ex p Bernard*[46] concerned a severely disabled, wheelchair-bound, claimant who also suffered from incontinence and diabetes and was cared for by her husband who also parented their six children. Following the loss of their original home the family had been accommodated in a council property which had not been adapted to meet the claimant's needs. The family were then further re-housed but that property was also unsuitable for the needs of the claimant. The Local Authority's Social Services Department then created a care plan for the claimant, acknowledging her need to move to a suitably adapted property. That was in September 2000, but no further action was taken, despite a letter from the claimant's solicitor to the Authority in August 2001 reminding them of the assessment. In February 2002 the Authority sought to evict the claimant, but

---

[45] [2002] EWCA Civ 1834, (2002) 9(1) Housing Law Monitor p 1, [2002] L & TR 23, [2002] HLR 276; revsd [2003] UKHL 43.

[46] [2002] EWHC 2282 (Admin), [2003] HLR 354, (2002) 9 (12) Housing Law Monitor p 5.

withdrew that threat when the claimant sought leave to apply for judicial review of the Authority's action. The Authority then accepted it was under a duty to provide suitably adapted accommodation under s 21(1)(a) of the National Assistance Act 1948, but no explanation was given as to why no action under that provision had been taken. Judicial review of the Authority's action was obtained and they were ordered to re-house the claimant in appropriate housing within six months, whilst at the same time the claimant's action for damages against the Authority was adjourned. The court's order was not complied with until 14 October 2002 when the claimant threatened to seek an order in respect of alleged contempt of court in respect of the failure to act.

The claimant additionally sought damages based on alleged breaches of her human rights, in particular Arts 3 and 8, ie a claim that she had been subject to degrading treatment and that there had been failure to respect her 'home rights'. The first argument was rejected by Sullivan J on the basis that, while the claimant had been badly treated, the level of severity demanded by the notion of 'degrading treatment' had not been crossed, especially bearing in mind that the Authority had not intended to humiliate or degrade the claimant. However, the claim under Art 8 succeeded. The Authority had been under an obligation to enable the claimant and her family to lead as normal a family life as possible, and that included a duty to support the claimant's dignity as a human being. This the Authority had failed to do, and so they were required to make 'just satisfaction' for their breach under s 8 of the 1998 Act and Art 41 of the Convention.

However, what should constitute 'just satisfaction'? In an important decision Sullivan J argued first of all that the award of damages should be broadly comparable to a tortious claim – though in the instant case there was no easily comparable tort. He drew an analogy with awards of compensation made by the Commission for Local Administration in respect of maladministration claims; he then drew attention to the humiliating conditions which the claimant had endured for 20 months and argued that the award of damages should not be minimal as that might diminish respect for the scheme of rights enshrined in the 1998 Act. He concluded there was no justification for reducing damages in this case below those generally obtainable in tort actions, and then took as a starting point maladministration award levels, which are generally between £5,000 and £10,000. In the instant case the claimant's problems had been compounded by the Authority's inaction and an award of £10,000 was justified.

*Bernard* was quite an important decision. It seemed to confirm that the courts might be willing to regard some breaches of Convention rights as a new type of breach of statutory duty. Where a public body has been guilty of gross misconduct, as was the case here, there may also be justification for including a punitive element in any damages awarded[47]. This decision suggests that our courts are somewhat more willing to develop and apply Human Rights arguments in the context of Art 8 than under Art 6.

---

[47]  See also the Law Commission 'Report on Damages under the Human Rights Act' Report Law Com No 266/Scottish Law Com No 180, London, Law Commission, no date and *Kuddus v Chief Constable of Leicestershire Constabulary* [2001] UKHL 29, [2002] 2 AC 122.

The applicability of Art 8 was further relevant in the *Hetoja* case already mentioned above. It was considered there that the decision taker had complied with the need to respect the claimant's home rights by arranging for her to live rent-free in a hostel which was an improvement on her previous condition. This decision once again underlines the point that Art 8 gives no right to a home, nor to express preferences for a dwelling of a particular sort. Article 8 is most applicable where a claimant has a home that has been invaded or treated in some grossly disrespectful way, etc, by an authority.

This latter point was strongly reinforced by *Anufrijeva (as personal representative of the estate of Kazjeva) v Southwark London Borough Council.*[48] Here an asylum seeker claimed a breach of Art 8 had occurred following the provision to her and her family of a local authority two-floor maisonette which contained a steep flight of stairs. From the outset the claimant complained of the unsuitability of this accommodation. The claimant's mother was aged and in deteriorating health before she died. The claimant alleged her quality of life was adversely affected by the quality of the accommodation, and furthermore that the way in which the local authority had exercised its powers had violated the right to respect for private and family home life.

In particular it was alleged that the authority had acted in such a way as to affect adversely the health and safety of the claimant and her family, that they had committed themselves to providing a particular type of home for the family and had failed to do that without justification, and that they had failed to provide assistance knowing that the claimant's mother was suffering from severe disability and illness.

The authority had reassessed the family's needs after complaints had been made about their initial temporary accommodation, and solicitors acting for the family further made requests for the family to be re-housed in 'secure and suitable accommodation' on the basis that the accommodation they had was unsuitable to the needs of the claimant's mother who by that time had been hospitalised. The local authority then offered the family a ground floor flat, on one level, with four bedrooms, but this was rejected on the basis that the bathroom was too small to enable the claimant's mother to use it as at such times she had to be accompanied by a carer, though the evidence did indicate that this particular need had been brought to the authority's attention. The authority, through one of its officers who had carried out an assessment of the claimant's mother's condition, argued that though the dwelling they had was not ideal, nevertheless the claimant's mother was warm, housed properly, cared for and had provision for her personal needs; many others in the same borough were not so fortunate. Subsequently, however, they conceded further that the dwelling was not suitable for the claimant's needs. In separate proceedings under the provisions relating to housing, homelessness and asylum seekers the authority had been ordered to find suitable accommodation, and a further offer of another property was made. This too was rejected on the basis that as it contained steps it would be unsuitable for the claimant's mother on the basis that she would shortly have to undergo surgery which would result in confinement

---

[48] [2002] All ER (D) 37 (Dec); on appeal [2003] EWCA Civ 1406, [2004] 1 All ER 833, and see also *Morris v London Borough of Newham* [2002] EWHC 1262 (Admin).

to a wheelchair. Various other legal proceedings then followed in which assessments of the claimant's mother were required, and the suitability of proffered accommodation was considered.

In the High Court Newman J considered the jurisprudence of the Strasbourg Court and referred to the well established understanding that Art 8 confers no right on a person to be provided with a home. In particular he stated:

> 'the Convention can and will serve to fashion and control the exercise of legislative powers even though there is no legislative inadequacy, but where there is tension between the aims of the legislation and the rights protected by the Convention. It is of little assistance in determining how the sphere of Article 8 can extend to legislation or conduct pursuant to legislation which is entirely compatible with Convention rights and gives rise to no tension between the aims of the legislation and Convention rights.'

He pointed out that the Strasbourg jurisprudence makes it clear that an obligation to respect Art 8 rights does not mean there is an obligation to provide accommodation of the applicant's choosing. Furthermore attempts by public authorities to offer alternatives have to be considered by courts. Newman J reiterated that under the Strasbourg jurisprudence Art 8 gives no right to any person to be provided with a home. However, there may be situations where a home is provided and then circumstances are alleged to have impacted on family and private life by reason of some failure to act in connection with what has been provided. Such situations have arisen in the past where particular people or groups of people have been found to be particularly vulnerable, for example by virtue of severe disease, and yet authorities have refused to assist them. That, he found was not the position in the case before him. Furthermore, he considered it would be rare for an error of judgment, inefficiency or maladministration arising in connection with the performance of statutory functions to give rise to a breach of Art 8. He argued that for such a breach to occur the acts of the authority would have to depart so far from the performance of a function as to amount to a denial or contradiction of any duty to act, in other words cases of flagrant and deliberate failures to act in the face of obvious and gross circumstances affecting a person's Art 8 rights. That also was not, he concluded, the case here.

Quite clearly in *Anufrijeva* Newman J wished to draw a clear distinction between the facts of the case before him, and those of *Bernard*. However, though points of distinction can be seen between these cases, the impression must nevertheless arise that the distinctions are somewhat nice ones and are indicative of judicial reluctance to be bold in developing the law of housing by reference to human rights concepts. Indeed one major factor of importance to Newman J was the argument that 'the Strasbourg jurisprudence is premised upon the basis that legislation in the sphere of housing and social welfare is in the "political sphere" and further that it is primarily the responsibility of national authorities to interpret and apply domestic law, [hence] caution is called for on the part of this Court ...'.

In the Court of Appeal, where the case was heard along with two others concerning claims by asylum seekers, Lord Woolf CJ identified a common issue, namely the claim in each case that a failure to perform a statutorily imposed public law duty gave rise to an entitlement to damages in consequence of the maladministration involved in the failure. The essence of the claim was that positive action should have been taken to protect rights under Art 8, and it was the failure to do this which gave rise to the entitlement to compensation. Lord Woolf accordingly identified six issues: what is the nature of rights under Art 8, when does a duty arise under Art 8 to take positive action, when will maladministration constitute a breach of Art 8, when should damages be awarded, on what basis should they be assessed, and what procedures should be followed to ensure that the costs of obtaining relief are proportionate to that relief?

Addressing the first question, Lord Woolf, basing his judgment on the decision of the House of Lords in *Qazi* (see below), argued that the essence of Art 8 is 'the right to live one's personal life without unjustified interference; the right to one's personal integrity'. This, he argued, may also extend to enable members of a family to share life together where they are prevented from doing so. However, that led Lord Woolf to consider the second question, when does a duty arise under Art 8 to take positive action. Reviewing the jurisprudence of the Strasbourg court, he concluded that this is an issue where requirements can vary greatly from case to case, and where states enjoy a wide margin of appreciation in determining what had to be done, bearing in mind the needs and resources of the community. However, where a right under Art 8 arises to ensure respect for home and family life, that right has to be competently protected, and hence maladministration in that respect may lead to a breach of Art 8. Positive duties can arise where there is a need to protect the quality of life a person enjoys in his/her existing home, but that is not the same thing as saying that there is a positive duty to provide a home or financial support. The question in the instant case was whether there was such a positive duty in respect of asylum seekers to ensure they may enjoy a particular (minimum) standard of private and family life, an issue on which the Strasbourg jurisprudence gave little assistance, save to point out that there may be a positive duty where a direct and immediate link exists between what a person seeks under a scheme of welfare benefits and that person's private life, though any such duty is likely to be limited in extent and content. Lord Woolf argued:

> 'while Strasbourg has recognised the possibility that Article 8 may oblige a State to provide positive welfare support, such as housing, in special circumstances, it has equally made it plain that neither Article 3 nor Article 8 imposes such a requirement as a matter of course. It is not possible to deduce from the Strasbourg jurisprudence any specific criteria for the imposition of such a positive duty.'

In the instant appeal Lord Woolf turned to the statutory scheme of provision for asylum seekers in the UK to determine whether any assistance could be found there as to the content of any positive obligation under Art 8. He concluded:

> 'There is a stage at which the dictates of humanity require the State to intervene to prevent any person within its territory suffering dire consequences as a result of the deprivation of sustenance.'

That duty arises in the context of Art 3, however, and it is hard, Lord Woolf concluded, to see how it may also arise under Art 8, for Art 3 is concerned with the prevention of degradation, if necessary by welfare support:

'it is much more difficult to identify some other basic standard of private and
family life which Article 8 requires the State to maintain by the provision of
support.'

Lord Woolf considered the previous High Court decisions in this area, including
*Bernard* supra which was a case where human dignity had been invaded, but
indicated that the trend of authority is that in the absence of such special
circumstances it is hard to find support for an argument that having to live in grossly
overcrowded and unsatisfactory accommodation for a period of time will give rise
to a claim for damages under Art 8. Lord Woolf rehearsed the arguments put
forward by Newman J in *Anufrijeva* at first instance and concluded:

'Article 8 is capable of imposing on a state an obligation to provide support.
We find it hard to conceive, however, of a situation in which the predicament
of an individual will be such that Article 8 requires him to be provided with
welfare support, where his predicament is not sufficiently severe to engage
Article 3. Article 8 may more readily be engaged where a family unit is
involved. Where the welfare of children is at stake, Article 8 may require the
provision of welfare support in a manner which enables family life to
continue.'

In other words Art 8 may come into play where parent and child are separated or
where particularly hideous housing conditions exist, as was the case in *Bernard*.

Turning next to the issue of whether and when maladministration may constitute a
breach of Art 8, Lord Woolf argued that mere inaction alone is not enough, 'there
must be some ground for criticising the failure to act. There must be an element of
culpability. At the very least there must be knowledge that the claimant's private and
family life were at risk'. Maladministration in general will not therefore normally
amount to a breach of Art 8 unless a person has been caused substantial prejudice,
for instance as a result of excessive delay, and where the consequences of that are
serious. Departing from Newman J's reasoning at first instance, Lord Woolf
considered that the test in such cases has to take into account both the extent of the
culpability of any failure to act and the severity of consequences. Glaring deficiencies on the part of public authorities may be good evidence of a lack of respect for
Art 8 rights, but 'isolated acts of even significant carelessness are unlikely to
suffice'.

Lord Woolf then turned to the question of what damages should be awarded in a
case where a breach of Art 8 is found. He considered the relevant provisions of the
Human Rights Act 1998, ss 6 and 7, and also the requirement under the Convention
itself for people to have effective remedies for their wrongs, and just satisfaction of
their claims. Lord Woolf argued that the principal need where an infringement of a
Convention Right has occurred is for it to be brought to an end, thus the principal
remedies will be those usually obtained on judicial review. Damages may be a
remedy, but only on a discretionary basis, where it is 'just and appropriate', and
where they are necessary to achieve 'just satisfaction' in the case. There is no
entitlement to damages as of right, and no entitlement to exemplary damages. In all
cases where damages are awarded a proper balance has to be struck between rights
of the individual and the public interest. The Strasbourg jurisprudence, however,

gives little coherent guidance on the principles governing the award of damages, but some principles can be deduced. One such is 'restitutio in integrum', ie that an applicant should, so far as is possible, be placed in the position he/she would have been in but for the breach of Convention rights. One other 'clear' strand of judgment is a general disinclination to award damages in cases of mere procedural error. UK case law on the issue, Lord Woolf considered, has had to find its own way, and he favoured a 'broad brush approach', taking into account, in cases where there is no pecuniary loss, issues such as the ability of other remedies to satisfy the claim, the complainant's own responsibility for what has happened, and the seriousness of the infringement, including the scale and manner of the violation, and the way in which it occurred. Any loss suffered must also be sufficient to render an award of damages necessary before any such award is made.

Lord Woolf proceeded to argue that awards of damages for breaches of Art 8 should take as guidelines levels of damages awarded in tort, awards made by the Criminal Injuries Compensation Board, and those made by the Parliamentary and Local Government ombudsmen. Even so, he accepted, appropriate comparators may be rare. He went on, however, to warn that 'where the breach arises from maladministration ... the scale of such damages should be modest. The cost of supporting those in need falls on society as a whole. Resources are limited and payments of substantial damages will deplete the resources available for other needs of the public including primary care'. He furthermore endorsed the approach taken by Sullivan J in *Bernard*, above.

Lord Woolf finally turned to the issue of proportionality between any award of damages made and the costs incurred in obtaining such an award. He pointed out that costs are likely to exceed any award made where the basis of the claim is alleged maladministration such as administrative delay. Courts should therefore look critically at any attempt to recover such damages other than by way of judicial review, ie as part of a judicial review application.

The findings and decision of Newman J at first instance were affirmed. The family in this case had had to live in accommodation which was not ideal, but that was a long way from saying that their conditions were such that the local authority came under a positive obligation to upgrade that accommodation. Moreover the local authority had acted throughout in good faith and had tried to accommodate the family adequately. As one learned commentator on the decision states[49]:

> 'Most prospective applicants will now be aware that there is no realistic chance of their commanding compensation absent the deplorable conditions in which, say, the Bernard family were forced to live. The possibility of a positive obligation to upgrade accommodation remains but only in the most dire circumstances where the threshold of Art 3 is in danger of being crossed as well ... If, as in *Bernard* the threshold can be crossed and damages made available for maladministration, the level awarded must be modest.'

[49]  (2003) 10(11) Housing Law Monitor.

## THE CONVENTION RIGHTS AND SURVIVORSHIP ISSUES

Of interest here, and as evidence of a rather bolder approach than that encountered above is the Court of Appeal decision in *Ghaidan v Godin-Mendoza*.[50] (See also the House of Lords' decision in this case, considered at Foreword I.)

Here, two homosexual males had lived together in a property subject to a Rent Act 1977 protected tenancy. On the death of the one who was the tenant the survivor, following the House of Lords decision in *Fitzpatrick v Sterling Housing Association*[51], had certain succession rights. These, however, were limited to his being an assured tenant only under Sch 1 para 3 of the 1977 Act (as amended) because he had been living as a member of his deceased partner's 'family' but not in the relationship of husband and wife. The survivor challenged this under Art 14 of the Convention arguing that he had been discriminated against in that the survivor in a heterosexual relationship would have been entitled to a more beneficial statutory tenancy, complete with fair rent provision under Sch 1 para 2 of the 1977 Act. Article 14 lays down that those rights and freedoms which are protected under the Convention are also to be secured without any discrimination on grounds of sex, race, colour, language, religion, political or other opinion, national or social origin, association with a national minority, property, birth or other status. It will be noted that sexual orientation is not explicitly mentioned as such.

Two issues in effect arose: was there an engagement of the survivor's Convention rights, ie could it be said that any right had been infringed, and, if so, was that infringement justifiable. It was accepted, on the basis of *Petrovic v Austria*[52] even 'the most tenuous link with another provision in the Convention' would attract the operation of Art 14. The Court considered the state is under a positive obligation to promote the values protected by Art 8, and that means that legislation affecting the home, which falls generally within Art 8, falls also within Art 14, see also *Marckx v Belgium*.[53] It could thus be said that the survivor's convention rights had been infringed. However, could the landlord then argue the infringement was justifiable, ie that there was a sound basis for treating homosexual and heterosexual relationships differently?

The landlord sought to rely on 'deference' arguments, and that this was an area where Parliament had laid down a policy which rendered the matter non-justiciable. Such an approach had, of course, been adopted in the public sector housing cases examined above. That argument was, however, rejected here. Buxton LJ could not find that Parliament had laid down a clear policy to which deference should be paid:

> 'If it is accepted for the moment that Parliament seeks by the Schedule to promote the interests of landlords; flexibility in the housing market; and the protection of the family, how is any of that significantly forwarded by depriving the survivors of same-sex partnerships of statutory but not of assured tenancies? ... The fundamental weakness of this whole argument is two-fold. First, as to the interests of landlords and flexibility in the housing

---

[50]  [2002] EWCA Civ 1533 Y (2002) 9(12) Housing Law Monitor p1; [2002] 3 FCR 591, [2003] HLR 505. The House of Lords' decision is reported at [2004] UKHL 30, [2004] 3 All ER 411.

[51]  [2001] 1 AC 27.

[52]  (1998) 33 EHRR 14.

[53]  (1979–80) 2 EHRR 330.

market, Parliament has, by paragraph 2(2) of the Schedule already extended full Rent Act protection to survivors of heterosexual unmarried relationships, a class that one would instinctively think to be more numerous, and thus whose recognition was much more threatening to flexibility, than would be the category of same-sex partnerships. And so far as the protection of the family is concerned, it is quite unclear how heterosexual family life (which includes unmarried partnerships) is promoted by handicapping persons who are constitutionally unable, or strongly unwilling, to enter into family relationships so defined. Secondly, if deference is really the objective, the means used to that end are singularly unimpressive ... [hardly] any effective social policy could be achieved through the award of an assured rather than a statutory tenancy.'

Having thus rejected the argument that the statutory provisions laid down a clear social policy statement from Parliament to which deference was required, the Court was able to deal with the case on the basis of discrimination in respect of a Convention Right. In such cases the onus of proof lies on the discriminator to show that there is an objective and reasonable justification for the discrimination. The Court further relied on Lord Hope's statement in *R v DPP, ex p Kebilene*[54] that a discretionary area of judgment to which a Court may defer is more easily recognised 'where the issues involve questions of social or economic policy, much less so where the rights are of high constitutional importance or are of a kind where the courts are especially well placed to assess the need for protection'. Freedom from discrimination is, the Court argued, an issue of the latter kind.

The Court concluded that discrimination had taken place. Following *Fitzpatrick* stable monogamous homosexual relationships gave rise to succession rights under the Rent Act 1977, and there would be no rational reason thereafter for discriminating further between homosexual and heterosexual relationships when the question arose of which type of tenancy a person should succeed to.

The question then arose of how the discrimination should be remedied. Rather than make a declaration of incompatibility in respect of the provisions of the 1977 Act, the Court relied on its powers under s 3 of the Human Rights Act 1998 and interpreted the wording of the 1977 Act 'as his or her wife or husband' to mean 'as if they were his or her wife or husband'. Thus the survivor of this homosexual partnership was able to succeed to a statutory tenancy.

It is possible to regard this decision as an example of the injection of an anti-discriminatory impulse into the law of housing under the influence of human rights thinking[55]. However, it must be remembered that the real issue in the case was not whether there was a right to be enjoyed (which there was) but rather the way in which that right was to be enjoyed. The impact of Art 14 is much more limited in cases where the other Convention Right with which it is connected is less clearly established.

---

54  [2000] 2 AC 326 at 381.
55  See Grear, A, 'A tale of the land, the insider, the outsider and human rights (an exploration of some problems and possibilities in the relationship between the English common law property concept, human rights law and discourses of exclusion and inclusion'. (2003) 23(1) Legal Studies 33 at 57.

The foregoing case should thus be compared with *Michalak v Wandsworth London Borough Council*.[56] Here a succession dispute arose over a public sector property. This had been let to an elderly man originally from Poland, with whom a distant, and rather tenuously related, younger man, also from Poland, had come to live in 1981. It appeared that though there had been some arrangement whereby the younger man would contribute towards the rent of the dwelling this in fact rarely occurred, and for most of the time he lived off the benevolence of the older man whom he affectionately addressed as 'uncle'. As the older man declined in health the younger provided some care for him, but was not a full-time carer and the two lived essentially separate lives. When the older man died the local authority sought possession of the dwelling.

Mr Michalak sought to defend the action arguing that he fell within the definition of a 'member of the family' for the purposes of succession under the Housing Act 1985, and also by relying on the Human Rights Act 1998. The first argument failed on the basis that definition of 'family' in the Housing Act 1985 is exclusive and preclusive and is clearly intended to be different from the vaguer and more expandable notion of 'family' under the Rent Act 1977. On that basis Mr Michalak clearly had no statutory right to succeed.

What, however, of arguments based on Act 8 of the Convention? Brooke LJ argued that Art 8 can only be relied on in so far as it accords a person a right to respect for his/her home, and pointed out, following *Qazi* that the right to respect for a home can be asserted by a person who has no legal right or entitlement to live in the premises, as was the case with Mr Michalak. It had been argued for Mr Michalak that as Art 8 was engaged, Art 14 should also apply to ensure that he was not treated in a discriminatory way by suffering eviction when people in analogous situations would not be evicted. The Court responded to that argument by saying that four tests have to be passed before Art 14 can apply:

1.    Do the facts fall within the ambit of one or more of the substantive Convention provisions;
2.    If so, was there different treatment as respects that right as between the complainant on the one hand and other persons put forward for comparison;
3.    Were those other persons in an analogous situation to that of the complainant;
4.    If so did the different treatment have an objective and reasonable justification?

Brooke LJ applied those tests in order and found that Mr Michalak satisfied the first; the property in question was his home and Art 8 was therefore engaged. Turning to the second question Brooke LJ found this too to be affirmatively answered. Turning then to the third question Brooke LJ had to deal with the argument that by way of comparison with potential successors to Rent Act 1977 tenancies Mr Michalak had been differently treated. There were two issues here, the first whether Mr Michalak could truly be described as a member of the deceased's family so as to enable a factual comparison to be made, and the second being the legal question of whether a meaningful comparison could be made between the succession regime under the 1977 Act and that under the Housing Act 1985. With

---

[56]    [2002] EWCA Civ 271, [2002] 4 All ER 1136.

regard to the first question Brooke LJ agreed with the findings of fact in the county court and concluded that the notion of 'family' even though it has expanded over the years, could not extend to apply to Mr Michalak. Even if, however, it could so extend Brooke LJ argued that there were too many differences between the two tenancy regimes for there to be a meaningful comparison made between Mr Michalak and someone claiming to succeed under the 1977 Act.

However, Brooke LJ did accept that a comparison could be made between Mr Michalak and persons more closely related to a deceased tenant who could satisfy the succession requirements of the 1985 Act. He then turned to the fourth question, did the difference in treatment have an objective and reasonable justification? At this point he concluded the Court had to show deference to what was a clearly long historically established policy on the part of Parliament, namely that local housing authorities have to be regarded as in a special position with regard to their dwellings:

'Parliament ... has determined the manner in which public resources should be allocated for local authority housing on preferential terms.'

In addition he pointed out that in 1985 Parliament had introduced

'a measure of legal certainty, a concept prized by Strasbourg, when explaining with precision the type of close relative who should be entitled to be the first (and only) successor to a secure tenancy.'

On that basis he concluded that the distinction made between Mr Michalak and other closer relatives was acceptable and that no incompatibility arose between the succession provisions of the 1985 Act and those of Art 14.

Counsel for Mr Michalak raised another argument, namely that as the Court was not under the same sort of statutory duty to grant possession, as for example in relation to introductory tenancies, it was therefore obliged, as a public authority, to act in a way which was compatible with s 6(1) of the Human Rights Act 1998, ie evidence was needed that the making of an order was necessary for one of the reasons set out in Art 8(2). Both Brooke LJ and Mance LJ dealt with this issue, but the latter did so in greater detail. He stated:

'The starting point to the submission, is that the flat ... was (and is) the appellant's home, so that Article 8(1) of the Convention is potentially engaged, irrespective of the appellant's status or entitlement in law to remain there ... Home ... is an autonomous concept and does not depend on any legal status as owner ... Accordingly ... it was unlawful to interfere with the Appellant's right to respect for his home except under conditions specified in Article 8 (2).'

It was accepted by Mr Michalak's counsel that of those conditions the interference was 'in accordance with the law' because Mr Michalak was a trespasser, furthermore the possession order was made 'for the protection of the rights' of the landlord. However, it was argued for Mr Michalak that the order was not 'necessary in a democratic society' and was not a proportionate response to the issue. In such circumstances, it was argued, no order should be made unless the landlord puts forward evidence as to why possession is needed. After reviewing the Strasbourg jurisprudence on this issue, Mance LJ concluded there was no authority for saying 'that a court before ordering possession must undertake any wide-ranging excuse of balancing the comparative needs of a landlord … against those of a home occupier'. To hold otherwise, Mance LJ indicated, would mean that housing authorities would have

> 'in every case to justify a particular need to recover possession. [Their] general social and housing policy would be open for examination … in every case and the court would have to undertake the exercise of balancing the general needs of the community and other actual or potential residents against the specific need or desire of the resident … to remain.'

If that were to be so, it may be commented, the position of the court would move from the situation in which possession orders may be made if they are, overall, 'reasonable' to one in which the court would be determining the merits of individual housing situations.

The argument here for Mr Michalak in effect raises the 'macro' and 'micro' issue alluded to in the discussion of cases such as *McLellan*. Mance LJ accepted that in that case Waller LJ had laid down that these two levels exist in cases where Convention rights are engaged. In some cases a legislative scheme may determine that, at a macro level, a person's Convention rights may be limited because the legislation itself complies with the requirements of relevant Convention Arts. In other cases, micro level ones, an individual may be able to rely on Convention rights in relation to the determination of his/her entitlements under a legislative scheme. These are the cases where a court is required by statute to determine the merits of actions on an individual basis. This, however, according to Mance LJ, did not mean that those rights 'had to be available in every context by way of a defence'. Furthermore Mance LJ alluded to the decision of Laws LJ in the decision in *Smart* considered above in which he made it clear that attacks on the 'macro' aspect of a legislative scheme should not be mounted under the guise of 'micro' arguments that in the instant case such contentions are justified on the basis of particular applications of Convention rights. Mance LJ accordingly argued:

> 'The scheme of the Housing Act … deliberately excludes a person in the appellant's position from having security. The natural consequence … is to entitle the local authority to recover possession … That scheme would be undermined if, following the death of a tenant, other residents of the [dwelling] could insist on arguing, as a defence in the possession proceedings, the general or particular merits of possession being retaken, when compared with the hardship to a particular remaining resident whose home was involved.'

*Michalak* was applied in *R (on the application of Mays) v Brent London Borough Council*[57]. Here Ms Mays' mother had been a local authority secure tenant who had lost her tenancy in consequence of breaching a suspended possession order granted in respect of rent arrears. That occurred in 1996 but the authority apparently allowed the former tenant and her family to live on in the house as 'tolerated trespassers'.

---

[57]   [2003] All ER (D) 12 (Mar).

The mother died in 2002 and Ms Mays claimed to succeed on the basis that she was a member of the deceased tenant's family who had lived in the house during the entire course of the tenancy. This, of course, was a difficult argument to sustain as Ms Mays's mother's tenancy had come to an end and so, technically, there was nothing from a purely legal point of view, to which she could succeed. Succession to a secure tenancy is only possible, inter alia, where the would be successor resided with someone who was a tenant, not someone who was a tolerated trespasser. However, in addition the deceased woman's ex-husband had also been living there, while the deceased had also been receiving housing benefit. It was uncertain when and how Ms Mays had informed the authority of these facts. The authority refused to allow Ms Mays to succeed and she sought judicial review arguing their ruling and the subsequent decision to seek possession were incompatible with her right to respect for her family life under Art 8(1).

Collins J dismissed the application, arguing that Parliament's scheme of succession would be frustrated if in every case where a person who was not in the category of successor (and so could be evicted) could argue for consideration of their individual circumstances. That clearly harks back to what has been argued above about the macro/micro issue. The judge went on to argue that the authority had properly considered the issues and had been entitled under statute to apply for possession, particularly as the property would be under-occupied if Ms Mays was allowed to live there, see ground 16 of Sch 2 of the Housing Act 1985. Furthermore, the authority's decision to seek possession was not disproportionate. A further succession case was *Kensington and Chelsea Royal London Borough v O'Sullivan*[58]. Here a local authority had granted a tenancy of a council house to the appellant's husband in 1970. The appellant resided in the house as her husband's licensee, though she left him twice and in 1981 or 1982 was offered her own tenancy of a flat, which she did not take up. She moved back in with her husband but they lived separately, and she knew she was not a tenant of the house, while her husband was opposed also to her becoming a joint tenant. In 2001 the husband brought the tenancy to an end by notice to quit, and the local authority considered that the appellant had not been resident for some time. The husband was granted, by way of 'transfer', a tenancy of a new, smaller, flat. It was found as a fact that he had misled the authority into thinking he was living alone at the time of the notice to quit.

It was accepted that the original dwelling was the appellant's 'home' for the purposes of Art 8. The local authority was prepared to offer her a tenancy of a small flat, but she wanted something larger. The local authority sought possession.

In the Court of Appeal Arden LJ referred to the judgment in the county court in which the judge had applied 'micro' arguments to test the facts of the instant case against the requirements of Art 8 ('macro' arguments being reserved for asking whether a particular legislative scheme complies with Art 8). The judge asked whether there was anything on the special facts of the appellant's case which made it unnecessary or disproportionate to grant the possession order sought. In weighing

[58]   [2003] EWCA Civ 371, [2003] HLR 877.

the interests of the appellant against those of the authority, which included the protection of other people on the housing waiting list, the judge concluded the balance lay in favour of the landlord.

There was an appeal on the basis that the decision contravened Arts 8 and 14, ie that the appellant's home rights had been unjustifiably interfered with, and furthermore that had arisen in a way that was clearly discriminatory in view of her sex.

Arden LJ pointed out that though Art 8 became engaged at the possession stage, it did not apply at the time the tenancy was originally offered to the husband for at that point the property was not the appellant's home, and Art 8 gives no right to a home, it only protects the home a person already has. Furthermore, she held that Art 14 applies only within the ambit of the application of another Convention Right, it does not protect access to such a right. Accordingly there had been no discrimination in 1970 when the dwelling house was offered in the sole name of the husband. However, she accepted that the possession order subsequently sought violated Art 8, though on the basis of *Michalak* the legislative scheme of the Housing Act 1985 then satisfied the justifiability requirements of Art 8. Thus to overcome that,

> 'The appellant has to show a violation of Art 14 in conjunction with Art 8, and that by reason of such violation she is now subject to a possession order to which she would not have been subject if that violation had not occurred.'

Arden LJ accepted that in granting the tenancy to the husband alone there had been a discriminatory act, and added that 'there can be discrimination not only where some legislation requires an unjustified distinction to be made between the sexes but also where public authorities make such distinctions without legislative compulsion'. However, had that discrimination resulted in a violation of 'Art 8 taken with Art 14'?

Arden LJ argued that the combined effect of the Arts could not produce a situation where an unjustifiable violation could be found to have taken place. Could it be said, first of all, that the authority was under an obligation ever to take the positive step of seeking to convert all sole tenancies into joint ones. Arden LJ concluded that this would be making the notion of positive steps needed to ensure 'respect' under Art 8 quite excessive.

Furthermore, she continued, the local authority 'had no positive obligation, for Art 8 or Art 14 purposes, to treat the appellant as a remaining joint tenant under its Housing Allocation Scheme policy unless it at least knew that the appellant was in occupation before it transferred the tenancy ... the respondent had no obligation to ensure that the appellant was treated in the same way as a remaining joint tenant ... before it was made aware that the property was also her home. It only acquired the necessary knowledge after the tenancy for the property had been transferred to the husband's new home'. In this respect, of course, this case is easily distinguished from *Qazi* where the tenancy had been joint.

Having determined the content of the local authority's obligation – at a comparatively modest level it should be pointed out – Arden LJ was able to deal with the issue of whether any breach of Art 14 had occurred by asking whether discrimination could be shown by reference to an appropriate comparator. The appropriate comparator was a joint tenant remaining in a property after the joint interest has been brought to an end by the other joint tenant who had secured a transfer to another dwelling. The appellant was certainly in no worse position than such a joint tenant. In addition Arden LJ went on to hold, on the basis of *Sheffield City Council v Smart* and *Wandsworth London Borough Council v Michalak* that the authority's action in seeking possession was justifiable with regard to Art 8 simply on the basis that they were acting in accordance with the statutory scheme. She stressed the position that, while there may be wholly exceptional cases where particular events might justify a finding that a court should interfere with the normal workings of possession procedures, the normal position is that Parliament has laid down a legislative scheme which, for the purposes of Art 8, strikes a justifiable balance between the interests of all parties. Arden LJ stated:

> 'the court must, save in exceptional circumstances, proceed on the basis that the balance required to be struck by Art 8(2) is struck by the scheme which the legislature has provided … Laws LJ in the *Smart* case recognised that in rare cases the county court judge might have to consider an argument under Art 8(2) … I would accept that one such rare case would be where the defendant shows that there is a real prospect of success in his or her argument that to grant possession would violate his or her right under Art 8 taken in conjunction with Art 14.'

It is clear, however, that Arden LJ considered that only rarely could such cases arise, a view strengthened by he House of Lords' decision in *Qazi* to be considered below. In the present case the county court judge had listened to arguments but had correctly decided that there was no violation of rights under either Art 8 in conjunction with Art 14 or under Art 8 alone.

Waller LJ added the following arguments:

> 'The courts have recognised that a tenant and even a trespasser may establish that particular premises constitute a home within Art 8(1). On that there is no dispute and it is now accepted on the facts as they now turn out to be that this was [Mrs O'Sullivan's] home within Art 8(1), and that the taking of possession of the same would prima facie infringe Art 8(1).
>
> The question, as the authorities demonstrate, is whether Art 8(2) justifies the action of the claimants. When the courts have come to consider Art 8(2), they of course have been concerned to see whether the enforcement is in accordance with the law. That is the most obvious protection against interference with a person's home. But arguments have also been addressed on behalf of tenants or former tenants seeking a ruling that although the landlord in seeking possession is acting in accordance with the law, the granting of possession is not "necessary in a democratic society in the interest of or for the protection of the rights and freedoms of others". The scope for some free standing argument, insofar as it would result in some form of security of tenure, based simply on those words of the Art is now, in the light of such authorities as *Smart* and *Michalak,* and *Qazi* practically impossible. The

judgment of Mance LJ in *Michalak* puts the matter with particular clarity. The landlord and owner of property has rights, other persons in need of social housing have at the very least expectations, there is extensive legislation dealing with housing needs and extensive learning in the common law as to the rights to possession on which the legislation has placed such curbs as it thinks appropriate. The court has time and again refused to get drawn into the arguments at what has been termed the macro level, and will not allow policy considerations to come back in at what has been termed the micro level. It is not open in my view to [Mrs O'Sullivan] to argue that there is some defence to the possession proceedings based on an assertion that although the claimants have acted in accordance with the law, and are otherwise entitled to an order for possession, it is unnecessary for the protection of the rights and freedom of others for possession to be granted.'

So far as the discrimination issue was concerned, Waller LJ argued:

'Mr Short in his argument wished to concentrate on the possibility of there having been discrimination in the granting of the tenancy in 1970 a time when it was the custom to make the husband the tenant and not the husband and wife joint tenants. He wishes to argue that this "discriminatory practice" continued into the policy adopted by the claimants in relation to the situation where spouses separated. He would suggest that the male spouse who was left in the home would be treated differently from the female spouse left in the home, because the female spouse was likely not to have been a joint tenant, whereas the male would have been. But this is not a fair reflection of the policy which the claimants were applying in the decision being taken in this case. The policy they were applying ... related to situations in which a joint tenancy had been brought to an end and the remaining "tenant" was eligible for rehousing. The remaining "tenant" would of course actually not be a tenant but a trespasser. But more importantly, it was an important aspect of the policy ... only to grant one tenancy that being either of the property in which the former tenant remained, or if that property was not of the right size by transfer to another property. It was contrary to the policy to grant two tenancies because that would enable one of the previous occupiers to jump the housing queue.

If the council had known the full facts when [Mr O'Sullivan] terminated the tenancy, and in considering whether to grant the one tenancy of the property or to transfer to a smaller property, had decided not to grant that tenancy to [Mrs O'Sullivan] because she was a female that would clearly have been a breach of Art 14 in combination with Art 8. If there had been a breach of the Convention ... that might have affected the position. Furthermore, if knowing the full facts as they are now accepted, they had refused to grant [Mrs O'Sullivan] the tenancy simply on the grounds that she was never a joint tenant, it would have been arguable that a breach of Art 14 together with Art 8 was taking place. It could have been said that it was a policy which could now be seen to have had the effect of discriminating against wives, that placed [her] in the position of not being a joint tenant, and that in dealing with the question as to whom a tenancy should be granted it would not be right to place her in a disadvantageous position as a trespasser, as compared with a male former tenant who was also a trespasser.

But the policy that the claimants pursued in this instance of transferring the tenancy to [Mr O'Sullivan] was pursued in total ignorance of [Mrs O'Sullivan's] position. The policy thus pursued in relation to [Mrs O'Sullivan] was simply the policy of not granting more than one tenancy. Once the claimants cannot be criticised for getting themselves into the position of having transferred the tenancy to [Mr O'Sullivan] (and no such criticism is levelled at them), there is no question of discrimination, they simply could not grant a further tenancy.'

It appears that Waller LJ is arguing that discrimination might have occurred if either the landlord had refused a tenancy to Mrs O'Sullivan on the basis that she was female, or on the basis that she had never been a joint tenant. However, in either situation for there to be discrimination there would also have to be knowledge on the part of the landlord of the presence of the female non-tenant in the property at the relevant time. As this latter condition was not satisfied no claim of discrimination could arise.

*Michalak* and *O'Sullivan* were followed in *R (on the application of Gangera) v Hounslow London Borough Council*[59]. Here the applicant for judicial review of a decision to seek possession of a dwelling was a person subject to immigration control and therefore ineligible for assistance as a homeless person under the Housing Act 1996. He had lived with his parents on coming to this country from Tanzania. The parents had been joint secure tenants. The applicant's father had died and the applicant's mother had then succeeded by virtue of the principle of survivorship, and hence was deemed to be a successor tenant under the scheme of Pt IV of the Housing Act 1985. On her death no further succession was possible and the local authority as landlord sought possession from the applicant who was himself in poor health. The possession proceedings were postponed in order for an assessment of the applicant to be made under the National Health Service and Community Care Act 1990. There was some disagreement as to the basis on which the adjournment was made pending the outcome of a determination of the applicant's immigration status, and that matter was to arise later in the context of an argument that the pursuit of the possession proceedings was disproportionate and irrational before an assessment was made of the applicant under the 1990 Act to determine whether assistance should be provided to him under s 21 of the National Assistant Act 1948. That assessment took place on 28 June 2002, but the hearing for possession went ahead on 20 June 2002, though it was subsequently further adjourned. The matter was then transferred from the county court to the Administrative Court where it was directed that the issue should be dealt with by way of judicial review proceedings.

Moses J stated that the applicant's case rested on two arguments: that the rules of succession under the Housing Act 1985 infringe Art 14 of the European Convention read with Art 8, and that the decision to seek possession was disproportionate and irrational at a time when his needs had not been assessed under the National

---

[59]  [2003] EWHC 794 (Admin), [2003] HLR 1028.

Assistance Act 1948 and when he was threatened with eviction. Moses J also identified a question as to whether these issues could in any case be raised as a defence in possession proceedings.

After reviewing the statutory provisions relating to obtaining possession of dwellings let subject to secure tenancies, and the succession provisions of the Housing Act 1985, Moses J pointed out that where a secure tenant dies without a qualified successor the tenancy ceases to be secure and so can be brought to an end by notice to quit. However, if there is someone still living in the dwelling the right to possession has to be enforced by a court order. The power to make an order in the county court is found in s 2(1) of the County Courts Act 1984, and that jurisdiction is subject only to a very limited power of adjournment under s 89 of the Housing Act 1980. The applicant was a person who could not succeed to a secure tenancy and hence he was subject to the landlord's right to seek possession by virtue of notice to quit. This served as the background to the applicant's first argument, namely that the statutory succession provisions infringed Arts 14 and 8 of the Convention, ie that he had been made the victim of discrimination. It was not argued that there was a free standing breach of Art 8 by the succession provisions, and Moses J made it clear he would have had little time for any such contention.

'Parliament had to strike a balance between security of tenure and the wider need for systematic allocation of ... housing resources in circumstances where those housing resources are not unlimited. The striking of such a balance is pre-eminently a matter of policy for the legislature ... There is no basis for contending that the statutory scheme, which seeks to allocate public resources ... to those most in need amounts to a disproportionate interference with a person's right to respect for his home.'

That, however, left the discrimination issue. Three questions, following the decision in *Michalak*, had to be asked:
1.   Did the facts fall within the ambit of a substantive Convention Right? The answer here was yes as Art 8 was engaged, the dwelling was the applicant's home.
2.   Was there a difference in treatment in respect of Art 8 rights between the complainant and appropriate comparators?
3.   Were those comparators in an analogous situation to that of the applicant?

It was argued that the comparators should be a son who would have been able to succeed a deceased mother who had been a sole tenant from the commencement of the tenancy, and a nephew who would have been able to succeed an uncle or aunt who again had been a sole tenant from commencement, provided that nephew had resided with the deceased for the required amount of time. Moses J, however, rejected the comparators as not appropriate. In the instant case the applicant's mother had not been a sole tenant. Furthermore, on the basis of decisions of the Strasbourg Court, Moses J took the notion of discrimination as having its basis in the less favourable treatment of a person on the basis of some personal characteristic by which that person, or a group of persons, is distinguishable from others. That element was clearly present in *Ghaidan* on the basis of the claimant's sexuality, but it was not present in the instant case. Moses J argued that Art 14 applies in cases where discrimination takes place on the basis of status, that was not the case here.

The applicant's predicament arose simply because his mother had been a deemed successor tenant and hence no further succession was possible.

Moses J then adverted to a fourth question identified in *Michalak* but which did not need to be addressed in the instant case because no question of discrimination by reference to an appropriate comparator had to be determined. That fourth question was whether there was an objective and reasonable justification for the discriminatory treatment. Moses J indicated that if he had had to address that question he would have followed *Michalak* in arguing that the justification is to be found in the statutory scheme of succession. Parliament has determined that only a single succession to a secure tenancy should exist and that is a decision to which courts should defer. The argument on discrimination therefore fell.

Attention then turned to the issue of whether the decision to seek possession was disproportionate and irrational. Proportionality arose as an issue here for though the applicant was a trespasser from a strictly legal point of view it is now established beyond doubt that the concept of 'home' in Art 8 is autonomous and the property in question was the applicant's home. The core argument was that there had been disagreement about the initial adjournment of the possession proceedings to allow for an assessment of the applicant because he then laboured under a misapprehension that he would be housed until his immigration status was settled. It was argued it was disproportionate or irrational to seek to obtain possession without further assessing whether, in the absence of a determination of the immigration status issue, the local authority would meet the applicant's needs under s 21 of the National Assistance Act 1948 whereby authorities may make residential accommodation available to those needing it on a basis of age, illness or disability where accommodation is not otherwise available to them. The applicant claimed to fall within the ambit of this provision by virtue of his illness. Moses J accepted that in carrying out an assessment an authority has to consider not only a person's actual situation, but also imminent events which might point to a deterioration in that person's condition which might arise in the absence of assistance given under s 21 of the 1948 Act. However, Moses J then argued that this did not extend to an obligation to consider future hypothetical needs. At the point of time in question the applicant was not actually homeless, and so was not in need of accommodation.

> 'He is not homeless at the moment and there is, accordingly, no warrant for anticipating any re-assessment of his needs or the result of any such re-assessment until such time as the court makes an order for possession and determines the [limited] period pursuant to s 89(1) of the Housing Act 1980 for postponement of the giving up of possession.'

On that basis the decision to seek possession could not be considered disproportionate or irrational.

The question then arose whether the issue of proportionality could have been maintained in the possession proceedings with which the present case had commenced. This further raised the issue of whether a public law matter appropriate to judicial review proceedings can be utilised in the essentially private law forum of a possession action.

Moses J began by pointing out that eviction may be justified as necessary in a democratic society in order to protect the sights of others, and under the Convention the process of justification may not need consideration of the particular circumstances of the parties who are directly involved. Thus it is clear that an issue concerning proportionality may be determined at the 'macro' or collective level. In other words the justification for a particular action may be supplied by a general scheme which is in itself compliant with the Convention. That applied in the present instance and Moses J stated:

> 'The fact that the court is required to intervene when the landlord seeks to enforce rights of possession does not lead to the conclusion that the court is bound, in each case, to consider whether an order for possession would, in the circumstances of the individual case, be disproportionate and contrary to Article 8.'

Provided the domestic system of law under which the court gives judgment is itself proportionate there is no general requirement for the court to consider proportionality issues on an individual case by case basis,

> 'so long as the system as a whole is compatible with the Convention, it is not for the court to arrogate to itself a discretion in other cases. Nor does it make any difference in principle that the landlord seeking to enforce its civil right is a public authority.'

Here it should be noted Moses J is impliedly stating that the nature of the relationship between a local authority as a landlord and its tenants is essentially a private law matter and that is its most important characteristic. It may be asked whether that sits entirely comfortably with other passages in this case, and others, where the scarce nature of the public resource available, ie council housing, has been alluded to.

Moses J continued by basing his arguments on the *Michalak* decision where it had been held that there is no need for evidence to be placed before the court tending to show that making a possession order is necessary for one of the particular reasons or justifications set out in Art 8(2). The appropriate justification derives from the statutory scheme itself. There is no need for a demonstration of justification on a case-by-case basis. He further relied on the *O'Sullivan* decision, and argued:

> 'These authorities demonstrate that the statutory scheme in relation to the termination of secure tenancies complies with Art 8(2). But they also establish the further point that it is not open to an individual such as the claimant to resurrect arguments as to necessity and proportionality in an individual case.'

The general position thus has to be that a court is not required to consider the necessity and proportionality of a possession action on a case-by-case basis.

Might there be, however, instances where the actual decision to seek possession could be challenged on a disproportionality basis. This had been suggested as a remote and rare possibility by Laws LJ in *Sheffield City Council v Smart*. Such cases, he suggested, would openly arise in wholly exceptional circumstances where something had happened after the service of notice to quit which would fundamentally alter the rights and wrongs of the proposed eviction. Such an exceptional situation might be apt for judicial review, and Laws LJ in *Smart* also considered that such an issue could arise at the trial stage of the possession proceedings, in which case it would have to be dealt with by the trial judge.

Moses J pointed out that what Laws LJ was referring to was a wholly exceptional circumstance, and, furthermore, that the remarks in question were obiter. Moses J was firmly of the opinion that what Laws LJ had suggested could not in any case be extended into a general argument that all possession actions have to be fought on the basis that the court must be convinced it is (a) justifiable to seek possession, and (b) proportionate to make an order.

That then left the actual question whether the public law argument concerning proportionality might be raised a defence in particular possession proceedings. It is clear that in certain private proceedings it is possible to raise a defence that some public law decision underlying these proceedings is invalid[60]. Where a private right exists it may be permissible to raise public law issues where that right is under attack. It is otherwise where a person seeks to utilise private law proceedings to attack a public law decision. Relying on *Michalak* Moses J cast doubts on the obiter opinion of Laws LJ in *Smart* and concluded that the applicant in the instant case had no private rights at all to defend.

> 'He seems to me to fall within the same category as *Michalak* and can, accordingly, only rely upon his rights entwined in Article 8 and arguments as to rationality by challenging the Council's decision in judicial review proceedings following notice to quit.'

It thus appears that it is exceptionally unlikely that the courts will countenance a proportionality argument being utilised as a defence to possession proceedings save in some highly exceptional circumstances – assuming what Laws LJ opined in *Smart* still survives – or in those cases where there is an extant private right under attack.

There was, however, some question as to whether these decisions could easily be reconciled with the Court of Appeal decision in *Qazi* considered earlier. In all cases the person concerned had factual occupation of the property which grounded a claim under Art 8(1). Mr Quazi, however, had only lost his legal entitlement under the Housing Act 1985 because of the operation of the rule that all joint tenants must agree to the continuation of a joint tenancy if it is to survive for the benefit of any of them. On the other hand Mr Michalak had never been a tenant of the property he lived in, while Ms Mays was, at best, a tolerated trespasser. Furthermore, the existence of a clear legislative system for determining succession rights following the death of a council tenant seems sufficient to have convinced the court that the interference with their Art 8(1) rights was justified and proportionate. Mrs O'Sullivan also had never been a tenant of the property in question, and her status at the time possession was sought was also that of a trespasser, while Mr Gangera was present only in the capacity of someone who could not statutorily succeed to the property. On the other hand it appears Mrs O'Sullivan's situation could have been different had the authority known of her presence in the property at

---

[60] *Wandsworth London Borough Council v Winder* [1985] AC 461 and *Wandsworth London Borough Council v A* [2000] 1 WLR 1246.

the time her husband was negotiating his transfer. She might have been able to rely on Art 14 had the authority then refused to effect a transfer to her on the basis that she was female. The position thus seemed to be that where a joint tenancy has been brought to an end by the unilateral act of one tenant, the other, if having the property as his/her 'home' is entitled (no more than that) to put forward arguments under Art 8(2) as to the justifiability of the particular possession order sought. A non-tenant spouse whose presence in the dwelling is known appeared similarly entitled on the basis of the need to avoid discrimination under Art 14. Other persons have no such entitlement. The distinctions made are nice ones.

The problems outlined above, however, are less following the decision of the House of Lords in *Qazi,* and the outcome of that decision appears to be that the room for raising 'micro' arguments is even more limited than might have been supposed. The majority decision in the House of Lords is conservative. The facts of *Qazi* are well known. There was a joint tenancy of a council house which was brought to an end by Mr Qazi giving notice to quite in due form. This ended Mr Qazi's legal entitlement to stay in the dwelling. The House of Lords were unanimous, however, that the dwelling remained his 'home' by virtue of his long and continuing factual occupation of it. Whether a property is someone's home thus depends on a factual question of whether they have a sufficient continuing link with it. What divided the House of Lords was the question of whether there had been an invasion of Mr Qazi's right to 'respect' for his home and how to deal with the consequences of that. (See n 45 for the House of Lords reference.)

## The minority view

Lord Bingham and Lord Steyn favoured a view put forward by Laws LJ in *Sheffield Council v Smart.* Where someone's 'home' is 'invaded', for example by possession proceedings, an interference with the right of respect for that home arises; possible eviction is thus a prima facie violation of the right. Can that be simply dealt with under Art 8(1) by saying there is not a problem for there is no lack of 'respect' as the statutory scheme under which possession is sought provides that element? Or does the court have to go further and say that a prima facie violation demands that the court should then apply the rigorous standards of Art 8(2) to determine whether the possession proceedings are proportionate. Laws LJ had argued that the Convention is more 'remotely engaged' in domestic law if the first view as opposed to the second is taken. Lord Bingham in particular endorsed the argument that favouring the second view is a justified purposive approach which ensures full protection for rights, even though he argued that it would only be very rarely that a court would decline to make a possession order at the stage of hearing arguments under Art 8(2).

## The majority view

Lord Hope argued that the 'core' issue was whether under Art 8(1)

> 'it is unlawful for a public authority to recover possession from a former tenant by a procedure which leads to possession being granted automatically,

or whether the court must always be given an opportunity to consider whether the making of an order for possession would be proportionate.'

Lord Hope pointed out that in none of the challenges to the substantive provisions of housing law made under the 1998 Act has the applicant so far been successful in that no declarations of incompatibility have been made. However, as we have already seen there have been questions raised about the procedure to be followed where Art 8 is relied on, and the extent to which the courts must go in considering issues such as justifiability and proportionality.

Lord Hope reviewed the history of the Strasbourg jurisprudence and relied heavily on the dissenting judgment of Sir Gerald Fitzmaurice in *Marckx v Belgium*[61] with regard to what Art 8 is designed to achieve. The argument here is that Art 8 is concerned with 'domiciliary protection', ie protection against 'domestic intrusions, searches and questionings; to examinations, delayings and confiscation of correspondence; to the planting of listening devices (bugging); to restrictions on the use of radio and television; to telephone tapping or disconnection; to measures of coercion such as cutting off the electricity or water supply; to such abominations as children being required to report upon the activities of their parents, and even sometimes the same for one spouse against another – in short, the whole gamut of fascist and communist inquisitorial practices'. In other words Art 8 is rather more concerned with protecting a person's private life within his/her home than with protecting property interests. Lord Hope argued:

'Article 8(1) does not concern itself with the person's right to the peaceful enjoyment of his home as a possession or as a property right. Rights of that sort are protected by Art 1 of the First Protocol.'

Thus in *Stretch v United Kingdom*[62] a person could rely on Art 1 of the First Protocol where a local authority had refused to renew a lease they had granted to him. Article 8 on the other hand, Lord Hope argued, is concerned with protecting the right to privacy, not the right to own or occupy property. Though agreeing with Lords Bingham and Steyn that 'home' under the Convention is an autonomous concept whose applicability is to be determined on a factual basis, Lord Hope stressed, following *Khatun v United Kingdom*[63] that for Art 8 purpose no distinction is to be made between those who have a proprietory interest in land and those who do not. The real distinction then arises when it is asked what the purposes of Art 8 are, ie when it is 'engaged' or when it is 'applicable', and here Lord Hope was clear that 'the object of Art 8 is to protect the individual against arbitrary invasion by the public authorities of his/her privacy; it is not concerned with creating a right to a home, for no such right exists'. While, on the basis of *Lambeth London Borough Council v Howard*[64] any attempt at eviction from or to gain possession of a home is prima facie a derogation from the right of respect for a home, it does not follow, according to Lord Hope, that this necessarily means that the rigorous requirements of Art 8(2) have to be applied. Furthermore, he pointed out, in many cases questions

---

[61] (1979) 2 EHRR 330.
[62] Application No 44277/98, [2004] LGR 401.
[63] (1998) 26 EHRR CD 212 at 215.
[64] [2001] EWCA Civ 468, (2001) 33 HLR 636

of reasonableness and proportionality have to be considered in possession proceedings because statute already requires this, so that renders attempts to create further rights and entitlements under Art 8(2) unnecessary. Lord Hope pointed here to the 'subsidiary role' of the Convention which gives 'special weight to the role of the domestic policy maker'.

In the instant case Mr Qazi's rights had been brought to an end by a rule of domestic law that due notice to quit by one joint tenant automatically ends the rights of all. In such circumstances the court does not have a discretion to consider whether granting a possession order to the landlord is justifiable, the process is automatic and there was no argument that this rule of law was in itself incompatible with the Convention, see *Ure v United Kingdom*[65]. Neither had it been alleged that the landlord had acted improperly in relying on that rule of domestic law, and in any case any such allegation would surely have to be made by way of a judicial review application, not by way of defence to possession proceedings, for example by way of challenge to a decision not to consider a dispossessed former joint tenant for rehousing following acceptance of the notice to quit. Lord Hope argued:

> 'My understanding of the European jurisprudence leads me to the conclusion that Art 8(2) is met where the law affords an unqualified right to possession on proof that the tenancy has been terminated.'

In other words the rules relating to the termination of joint tenancies provide by their very existence a sufficient answer to any question which might arise under the justifiability provisions of Art 8(2) – an unqualified right to possession is not questionable by means of justifiability and proportionality arguments. He concluded:

> 'the Strasbourg jurisprudence has shown that contractual and proprietory rights to possession cannot be defeated by a defence based on Art 8. It follows that the question whether any interference is permitted by Art 8(2) does not require, in this case, to be considered by the county court.'

Lord Millett echoed Lord Hope's arguments. Article 8 was 'applicable' in the instant case because the dwelling was Mr Qazi's 'home', but 'it does not follow that it was even arguably infringed'. Article 8 'is not ordinarily infringed by enforcing the terms on which the applicant occupies premises in his home'. Article 8(2) does not grant further rights in such a situation, it in fact limits the scope of Art 8(1) by laying down particular requirements such as that the interference with the Art 8(1) right must not be arbitrary and must be in accordance with law: that was the case here. The Art 8(2) requirement for justifiability in the context of the present case was met by the need to protect the 'rights and freedoms of others' which in the instant case referred to the rights of the landlord. Lord Millett was at some pains to point out that there are numerous instances where our law already requires balancing of the rights of one landholder against those of another and in such cases there is no need to resort further to any exercise under Art 8. In the instant case, however, there was no such need as the outcome was a foregone conclusion.

---

[65]   Application No. 28027/95, 27 November 1996.

'In the present case ... the local authority had an immediate right to posses-sion. The premises were Mr Qazi's home, and evicting him would obviously amount to an interference with his enjoyment of the premises as his home. But his right to occupy them as such was circumscribed by the terms of his tenancy and had come to an end. Eviction was plainly necessary to protect the rights of the local authority as landowner. Its obligation to "respect" Mr Qa-zi's home was not infringed by its requirement that he vacate the premises at the expiry of the period during which it had agreed he might occupy them. There was simply no balance to be struck.'

The fact that the landlord was also a local authority and therefore a 'public authority' was also irrelevant, for in this case the landlord was not relying on its public powers but on powers it shared with other landlords. Lord Millett continued:

'It follows that I do not accept without qualification the suggestion of Laws LJ in *Sheffield City Council v Smart* ... that, once it is established that the premises in question are the applicant's home, an order for possession amounts to an interference with (and prima facie an infringement of) his Art 8 right of respect for his home. The qualification, which is built into the provisions of Art 8 itself, is that save in wholly exceptional circumstances ... there is no lack of respect, and no infringement of Art 8, where the order is made in favour of the person entitled to possession by national law.'

Lord Millett also went on to argue that the court need not (as a public authority) consider whether the order is justified under Art 8(2) before making it. The fact that a court order is needed for an eviction does not mean the court must in all cases consider its proportionality and whether making it would infringe Art 8.

'The court is merely the forum for the determination of the civil right in dispute between the parties ... Its task is to resolve the dispute according to law. In doing so it would, of course, have to consider whether the landlord was entitled to possession as a matter of our ordinary domestic law ... once it concludes that the landlord is entitled to an order for possession, there is nothing further to investigate.'

Lord Millett endorsed the arguments of Moses J in *Gangera* (see above) and stated:

'In most cases the statutory scheme established by Parliament will provide the objective justification for [a local authority's] decision to seek possession, which need not be demonstrated on a case by case basis ... In the exceptional cases where the applicant believes that the local authority is acting unfairly or from improper or ulterior motives he can apply to the High Court for judicial review.'

Lord Millett concluded that right coupled with the fact that possession cannot be obtained without a court order is enough to satisfy the Art 8 requirement for 'respect' for a person's home in the present context.

Lord Scott similarly denied that Art 8 can give rights to stay in a property over and above those otherwise granted by domestic law. He considered the structure of Art 8 and pointed out that Art 8(1) is a general principle, not a specific legal rule. The specific issues arise in Art 8(2) where there are 'gateways' through which one has to pass in order to interfere justifiably with a person's house. However, these gateways do not have to be considered unless the interference in question is capable of amounting to an interference with the right to respect for home life. As with the rest of the majority Lord Scott considered this right to be limited; it is concerned with privacy, it is not designed to override the property rights of others, including landlords. Article 8 was never intended, he argued, to diminish the property rights of landlords, rather it is designed to prevent arbitrary intrusions into a citizen's life by the state. Where legislation diminishes a landlord's property rights and grants protection to tenants any infringement of the tenant's rights should thus be dealt with by an application under Art 1 of the First Protocol.

> 'Article 8 … was not intended to operate as an amendment or improvement of whatever social housing legislation [a] signatory state [has] chosen to enact.'

Lord Scott further doubted the approach in the *Poplar* case that it might in certain circumstances be arguable whether justifiability for a possession order would be needed under Art 8(2). He argued that Art 8 in itself neither vests in a home-occupier any contractual or proprietary rights that he/she does not otherwise have, neither does it diminish or detract from the contractual or proprietary rights of an owner who is seeking possession. 'The fate of every possession application will be determined by the respective contractual and proprietary rights of the parties'. The termination of a tenancy in a manner consistent with its contractual and proprietary incidents is not an infringement of 'respect' for the tenant's home. Thus while cases such as *Poplar*, *McLellan* and *Smart* were, in their outcomes, correctly decided, Lord Scott argued that insofar as they suggested Art 8 confers protection for tenants as tenants over and above that granted by ordinary law, they were incorrect.

## After Qazi

The House of Lords decision seems to draw a line under a series of cases and to take us back to the position declared in *Gallagher* in 2001, see above. Article 8 seems to add very little now to the Law of Housing. Certainly in any case where there is an absolute rule entitling a landlord to possession the existence of that rule appears to preclude any discussion of whether reliance on it in some way contravenes a tenant's right to 'respect' for his/her home. Similarly in cases where a court has a discretion whether or not to dispossess there seems to be little room for a consideration of issues other than those set out in the statutory scheme.

Though the decision in *Qazi* appears to mark an attempt to downplay the significance of Human Rights concepts in relation to housing issues, it may be objected by 'rights sceptics' that this was to be expected, as the overall effect of the 1998 Act has not been greatly marked in what may be termed the 'social' area of the law, where so much depends on the allocation of scarce public assets, an area into which issues judges feel unwilling to venture. In addition it may be asked why we should expect the very generally phrased measures of the European Convention on Human Rights to be utilisable to deal with perceived defects consequent on complex technical issues of housing law which have become a feature of our legal system over so many years. Against this it may be asked whether our judges are still being over formalistic and unwilling to adopt purposive interpretations to give rights of new sorts within the area of resource allocation. It also appears that the *Qazi* decision is an abdication of any form of control over housing matters utilising the justifiability yardstick of Art 8(2). There was little room for utilising that even before *Qazi*, but now that 'longstop' itself appears to have been abandoned. The line of argument established in *Qazi* can be traced in *Oregjudos v Kensington and Chelsea Royal London Borough Council*[66]. Here a homeless person was accommodated in bed and breakfast accommodation on terms requiring him to register at and stay in a particular hotel each night. If he failed to do so, or failed to give an adequate reason for his failure, the booking would be cancelled. The claimant did fail to stay for a number of nights and the local authority then considered it had discharged its duties under the homelessness provisions (see Chapter 10). The claimant challenged this, inter alia, on the basis that the registration requirements infringed his rights under Art 8. The local authority contended that they had acted reasonably in monitoring the use of what they were paying for, and that if there had been an interference with Art 8 rights it was necessary for the economic wellbeing and the rights and freedoms of other homeless persons. The Court of Appeal considered that the concept of private life under Art 8 is a broad one and can extend to cover the freedom of a person to choose how he/she lives. However, restrictions may be imposed on such a choice, particularly where there is an interface between a person's private space and the public sphere, as there was here because the accommodation was provided at a cost to the public purse. In such circumstances Art 8 is not even engaged. Even if it had been the terms of the agreement made with the claimant would have satisfied Art 8(2) as being necessary to protect the wellbeing and freedoms of others.

A similarly restrictive attitude was displayed in *R (on the application of Erskine) v Lambeth Borough Council*[67]. Here it was argued that the housing conditions provisions of Part VI of the Housing Act 1985 (see Chapter 12) are designed to promote and protect public health and to raise the condition of the housing stock, but are not intended to promote the advancement of an individual's rights under Art 8. Accordingly as Art 8 was not engaged Art 14 could not be engaged when it was argued that there was a degree of discrimination between the enforcement regimes applicable to bad housing conditions endured by local authority tenants as opposed to tenants of private landlords. Legislation does not have to be specifically enacted to protect Convention rights for those rights to be engaged, but before they can be engaged it has to be clear that the legislation does apply to a right falling within their ambit. The same line of argument was followed in *Birmingham City Council v Bradney, Birmingham City Council v McCann*[68]. Here defendants had remained in occupation of dwellings owned by the local authority after the termination of their tenancies and had no rights of occupation at all. In possession proceedings each defendant attempted to rely on Art 8. The Court of Appeal held that Art 8 could not be relied on as defence where an authority was attempting to enforce its ordinary property rights after having lawfully terminated tenancies. There was nothing exceptional in either case to require the authority to have to justify its actions further under Art 8. The Court applied *Newham London Borough*

---

[66] [2003] All ER (D) 369 (Oct).
[67] [2003] All ER (D) 227 (Oct).
[68] [2003] EWCA Civ 1783, [2003] All ER (D) 163 (Dec).

*Council v Kibata*[69] where a local authority sought possession against a man who continued to live in a council property after his wife (the tenant) had given notice to quit in due form. In the county court the judge refused to make an order for possession on the basis that the authority had not justified under Art 8(2) the interference with Art 8(1) rights. The Court of Appeal, applying *Qazi* argued Art 8 was simply not available as a defence. The defendant had no right to the dwelling and the authority was entitled to immediate possession. In such a case Art 8 was not infringed at all and there was no reason to enter into a detailed consideration of the merits of the case under Art 8(2). A similar argument was followed in *Hounslow London Borough Council v Adjei*[70]. Here, as in *Qazi* a joint secure tenancy was ended by notice to quit from the wife. The husband continued to occupy the dwelling and the authority sought possession against him as a trespasser, which he sought to defend on the basis of Art 8. Pumfrey J argued that, save in exceptional circumstances, where Art 8(1) rights are infringed and the question of whether this is 'justifiable', the balance which has to be struck under Art 8(2) will be struck by the very scheme itself which the legislature has provided to enable possession to be sought – in the present case against a trespasser.

## WHICH WAY IS THE LAW GOING?

Overall, the impact of Convention rights on case law has to be said to be very limited. This may reflect the innate unwillingness of the judiciary to become involved in questions of resource allocation in an area where there are so many conflicting calls on the available resources. It may also indicate a willingness to apply and develop 'deference' notions. In most cases the courts appear to accept that a legislative scheme made by a democratically elected legislative is sufficient at a 'macro' level to ensure compliance with Convention requirements. In others there has appeared some room to argue that individual determinations may have to take place at a 'micro' level to determine whether in the circumstances a person's Convention rights may be engaged. These, however, have never been common and after *Qazi* they appear to be even less so. Indeed as has been argued above attempts to raise the 'micro' issue may meet with judicial resistance on the basis that they are attempts to reopen or circumvent the 'macro' question[71].

It would be unwise, however, to argue that a distinction appears to be growing up between the handling of cases in the public and private sectors of housing. Successful actions to vindicate Convention rights have been mounted in respect of public housing, as witness *Bernard*. It is more arguable that there is something of a distinction between cases where Arts 8 and 14 are engaged and those where only Art 6 is engaged. Our courts seem willing to develop traditional notions of protecting people against unfair and unjustifiable discrimination, similarly arguments relating to a person's established home rights. What they appear much less willing to do is to use the procedural Art 6 to ground the development of substantive housing rights. They are certainly apparently unwilling to undermine legislative

---

[69]   [2003] EWCA Civ 1785, [2003] 3 FCR 724.
[70]   [2004] EWHC 207 (Ch), [2004] All ER (D) 402 (Feb).
[71]   See generally Findlay, J and Bird S, 'Alconbury a year on: Article 6 challenges face in stiff uphill struggle after Court of Appeal. *Begum* and *Allard* adopts a schematic approach' [2002] JPEL 1945.

schemes made by the democratically elected legislature. This may change, however, as at the time of writing it is believed the decision in *Qazi* may be appealed to the Strasbourg Court.


## THE REGULATION OF INVESTIGATORY POWERS

Where local authority tenants do enjoy Convention rights, for example in consequence of holding secure tenancies, any infringement of those rights has to be justifiable. The need to ensure that justifiability can be shown may well have an effect on local authority practice. In one respect at least these requirements have been translated into law. We thus turn to consider the Regulation of Investigatory Powers Act 2000 (RIPA 2000).

This creates a system of authorisations for a number of different types of surveillance. There is no obligation on a relevant 'public authority' to obtain an authorisation where one could be available (RIPA 2000, s 80) but one consequence of not obtaining an authorisation could be that there is an infringement of Art 8 rights and an unjustifiable, and hence unlawful, interference with those rights. A number of bodies are prescribed as 'public authorities' under RIPA 2000, ss 28 and 29. These include local authorities.

There are two basic types of surveillance – 'Directed' and 'Intrusive'. The former is, under RIPA 2000, s 26, a covert process taken in relation to a specific investigation or operation, where the result is likely to be that private information is gathered about a person, otherwise than by way of immediate response to events whose nature is such that it would not be reasonably practicable to seek an authorisation. 'Covert' processes are those carried out in ways calculated to ensure the person subject to surveillance is unaware of what is happening. 'Intrusive' surveillance is similarly 'covert' but relates to activities taking place on residential premises or in private vehicles, and involves the employment of persons or devices located within such premises or vehicles, or devices outside which consistently provide data of equivalent quality to internal devices. This latter type of surveillance is what is popularly known as 'bugging'.

Surveillance is, under RIPA 2000, s 27, lawful where it is carried out in accordance with a relevant authorisation. Authorisations under RIPA 2000, ss 28, 29 and 30 have to be granted by designated persons within the relevant authority: see SI 2000/2417. Before, however, an authorisation is granted, the person granting it must believe, under RIPA 2000, ss 28 and 29, that it is needed on specified grounds (ie inter alia, that it is necessary in the interests of national security, or to prevent or detect crime or prevent disorder, or to protect public health) *and* that the authorised activity is proportionate to what it is sought to achieve by the surveillance. The clear parallel here between the language of RIPA 2000 and that of the Convention and the cases decided under it should be noted. These provisions apply to directed surveillance; a more restrictive regime under RIPA 2000, ss 32 to 39 of the Act applies to intrusive surveillance, as this is largely an activity likely to involve the police or customs officers.

RIPA 2000, s 43 lays down certain procedural requirements in respect of authorisations. Normally an authorisation must be in writing, though one may be granted or renewed orally in urgent cases. Authorisations are generally time-limited, and will usually in the case of local authorities last for three months, subject to renewal. Where a renewal is sought (which must take place before the initial authorisation runs out) the criteria to be applied are those for the initial grant (see above). Authorisations may be cancelled by those who grant them under RIPA 2000, s 45 where they are satisfied the criteria leading to the initial grant are no longer satisfied.

It should finally be noted that under RIPA 2000, s 71 the Secretary of State must issue Codes of Practice in relation to the provisions of RIPA 2000, and these will explain in detail the Act's provisions.

RIPA 2000 could clearly have relevance to the activities of an authority seeing to gather evidence against, for example, a tenant in respect of proposed possession proceedings arising from an allegation of neighbour nuisance, or in respect of obtaining an Anti-Social Behaviour Order.

The provisions of the Act of 2000 are, however, generally procedural. Such provisions in themselves do not answer the concerns of those who hoped to see under the Human Rights Act 1998 a considerable increase in the legal entitlements of tenants, especially those whose tenancies are purposely lacking in security and, consequentially, any real protection in domestic law. Those concerns can only be heightened by the case law decided so far.

## FURTHER READING

Alston, P (ed) *The EU and Human Rights* (1999) OUP.

Baker, C, *Human Rights Act 1998: A Practitioner's Guide* (1998) Sweet & Maxwell.

Burton, J, 'Mind the gap' (2002) vol 152 New Law Journal No 7061 p 1933.

Carrs-Frisk, M, 'Public Authorities: The Developing Definition' [2002] EHLR 319.

Clayton, R, and Tomlinson, H, *The Law of Human Rights* (2002) OUP.

Coppel, J, *Human Rights Act 1998: Enforcing the European Convention in the Domestic Courts* (1999) Wiley.

Craig, P, 'Contracting Out, The Human Rights Act and the scope of judicial review' (2002) 118 LQR 551.

Drabble, R, Maurici, J, and Buley, T, (Eds) *Local Authorities and Human Rights* (2004) OUP, Chapters 7, 8 and 9.

Findlay, J, and Bird, S, 'Alconbury a year on: Article 6 challenges face a stiff uphill struggle after Court of Appeal *Begum* and *Allard* adopts a schematic approach' [2002] JPEL 1045.

Grear, A, 'A tale of the land, the insider, the outsider and human rights (an exploration of some problems and possibilities in the relationship between the English common law property concept, human rights law, and discourses of exclusion and inclusion' (2003) 23(1) Legal Studies 33.

Lester, A and Pannick, D, *Human Rights Law and Practice* (1999) Butterworths.

Loveland, I, 'Does Homelessness in Decision-making engage Article 6(1) of the European Convention on Human Rights?' [2003] EHRLR 176.

McDermont, M, 'The Elusive Nature of the Public Function: *Poplar Housing and Regeneration Community Association v Donoghue*' (2003) 66 MLR 113.

Morgan, J, 'The Alchemists' search for the Philosophers' Stone: The Status of Registered Social Landlords under the Human Rights Act' (2003) 66(5) MLR 700.

Oliver, D, 'The Frontiers of the State: Public Authorities and Public Functions under the Human Rights Act' [2002] PL 477.

Reid, K, *A Practitioner's Guide to the European Convention of Human Rights* (1998) Sweet & Maxwell.

Starmer, K, *European Human Rights Law* (1999) LAG.

Supperstone, M, and Coppel, J, 'Judicial Review after the Human Rights Act' [1999] EHLR 301.

# Index